Berlitz®

Complete Guide to
CRUISING
& CRUISE SHIPS

2009

BY DOUGLAS WARD
President
The Maritime Evaluations Group

Editorial

Written by
Douglas Ward

Managing Editor
Brian Bell

Editorial address
Berlitz Publishing
PO Box 7910, London SE1 1WE
United Kingdom
Fax: (44) 20-7403 0290
berlitz@apaguide.co.uk

Distribution

North America
Langenscheidt Publishers, Inc.
36–36 33rd Street, 4th Floor
Long Island City, NY 11106
Fax: (718) 784 0640

UK & Ireland
GeoCenter International Ltd
Meridian House, Churchill Way West
Basingstoke, Hampshire RG21 6YR
Fax: (44) 1256 817988

Worldwide
**Apa Publications GmbH & Co.
Verlag KG (Singapore branch)**
38 Joo Koon Road, Singapore 628990
Tel: (65) 6865 1600. Fax: (65) 6861 6438

Printing

Insight Print Services (Pte) Ltd
38 Joo Koon Road, Singapore 628990
Tel: (65) 6865-1600. Fax: (65) 6861-6438

©2008 **Apa Publications GmbH & Co.
Verlag KG (Singapore branch)**
All Rights Reserved

*Berlitz Trademark Reg. U.S. Patent Office
and other countries. Marca Registrada.
Used under licence from the Berlitz
Investment Corporation*

*First Edition 1985
Eighteenth Edition 2009*

CONTACTING THE AUTHOR
Although every effort is made to
provide accurate information, we live
in a fast-changing world and would
appreciate it if readers would call our
attention to any outdated information by
writing to Douglas Ward at:
**The Maritime Evaluations Group
Canada House, 1 Carrick Way
New Milton, Hants BH25 6UD
United Kingdom**
dw@berlitzcruising.com
www.berlitzcruising.com

www.berlitzpublishing.com

THE RIGHT CHOICE FOR YOU

Douglas Ward introduces the "bible" of the cruising world

The cruise industry's marketing men are quick to advertise the fact that they have won this award or that award (Readers' Choice Poll is a favorite) from travel magazines, as the "Best Ship in the World," or "Best Cruise Line in the World," or "Best Large Cruise Ship" and so on.

In truth, these polls are only as good as the number of people who vote in them, the criteria established, its regulation and tabulation, and the number of ships included. For example, if a magazine in the United States initiates a readers' poll and no readers have cruised aboard a British or Japanese or German or Spanish-speaking cruise ship, that ship will get no votes. It stands to reason that the votes will go to the most traveled ships. The magazines never state the criteria for their decisions.

At Berlitz, we do. That's why *Berlitz Complete Guide to Cruising and Cruise Ships 2009* is the most authoritative guide you can buy. What's more, it is totally independent and in no way subsidized by advertising or sponsorship.

Value for money
The international cruise industry consists of more than 75
ocean-going cruise ship opera-

tors carrying more than 16 million passengers a year. It can provide extremely safe and hassle-free vaca-tions but offers an almost over-whelming choice. What this book will do is help you choose the right ship, for the right reasons, and will leave you as well-informed as most specialists in the industry.

An uncertain economic outlook has led to much innovative market-ing activity in the industry. Although standards suffered from cost-cutting as the major cruise lines tried to counter the industry's deep discount-ing (mostly in North America), the lines have since been adding new items to woo passengers. Examples

The trend is to ever larger cruise ships.

WHAT THIS BOOK GIVES YOU

This book is divided into two main parts, followed by a short section of practical information and useful addresses. The first part helps you define what you are looking for in a cruise vacation and advises you on how to find it. It provides a wealth of information, including a look at life aboard ship and how to get the best from it. Specialist cruises are discussed, too, culminating with that ultimate travel experience: the around-the-world cruise.

The book's main section pro-files 272 ocean-going cruise ves-sels. From large to small, from unabashed luxury and exclusivity to ships for the budget-minded, new and old, they are all here.

The ratings and evaluations are a painstaking documentation of the author's personal work. He travels constantly throughout the world, and is at sea for up to 200 days each year. All evaluations have been made objectively, without bias, partiality, or preju-

Douglas Ward cuts the ribbon to declare open the Kaito Japanese Restaurant aboard the new *MSC Poesia*.

include premium mattresses and bed linen, and wi-fi access. Whatever the compromises, it remains true that cruise companies can provide vacation experiences seldom matched in product delivery, cleanliness and friendliness by land-based resorts.

Some things that used to be included in the price of a cruise now cost extra, the resulting "onboard revenue" helping to compensate the industry for the fact that basic prices are as low now as in 1980 – though fuel surcharges may widen the gap. Discounted pricing has done one thing, however, and that is to open up cruising to a much wider range of customers, including younger people and more families with children.

The above changes have in-evitably affected the ratings of some cruise ships; these changes are reflected in this book.

My 5,500 days at sea

In welcoming new readers to this edition, I should mention my qualifi-cations for assessing cruise ships on your behalf. Ships and the sea have always captivated me. My first job at sea was as leader of a small jazz and dance band aboard Cunard Line's 83,673-ton ocean liner *RMS Queen Elizabeth* – then the largest passenger ship in the world. Over 17 years, I worked for eight cruise com-panies, lastly as cruise director.

To date, I have completed over 5,500 days at sea, participating in more than 970 cruises, 153 trans-atlantic crossings, and countless Panama Canal transits, shipyard vis-its, ship naming ceremonies, maiden voyages and overnight stays.

The first edition of this book, re-viewing 120 ships, appeared in 1985, when cruising seemed to most peo-ple a rarefied experience. Today, the book is the most highly regarded source of comparative information not only for cruise purchasers, but also for cruise industry executives, crew members, and travel agents.

This book is a tribute to everyone who has made my seafaring experi-ences possible, and I would like to thank the cruise lines for their cooper-ation and assistance during the com-plex scheduling, sailing, inspection, evaluation and rating processes.

dice. In almost all instances, the ships have been visited recently by the author or one of his team in order to assess current status. Passenger comments are taken into account in the final evalua-tions *(see form on page 688)*.

Please note that, although price indicators are supplied for such things as alternative restau-rants, spa treatments and other items, prices may have changed since this book went to press.

Most of the statistical informa-tion contained in the ship profiles was supplied and checked by the cruise lines and ship owners. Any errors or updated information should be sent to the author at the address shown on the facing page.

Please note that the author's constant ship inspection schedule means he is seldom on land, and is no longer able to answer letters. However, every comment received will be studied and will help main-tain the authority of the next edi-tion for the benefit of all.

CONTENTS

WHAT'S NEW FOR 2009

The world's largest cruise ship, *Oasis of the Seas*, 16 decks high, debuts in 2009 as large resort ships continue to dominate the industry. But what most concerns passengers is the effect that harsher economic conditions will have on prices

In 2009 more than 30 ships over 100,000 tons are in service *(see list on page 144)*. And the introduction of new ships continues, with more than 40 new ships scheduled for delivery between January 2009 and December 2012, fueled by the continuing increase in demand for high-value cruise vacations, and ever larger ships with more facilities and options. But orders may slow down because most cruise lines earn their money in US dollars, and ships are built in Europe, where the weak dollar buys far fewer euros than it once did.

So, is cruising still good value?

Yes. If you want to cruise in Europe, for example, book early, particularly if the ship operates in US dollars, because the cruise lines have to fix their brochure prices at least a year in advance. Going by cruise ship, therefore, makes economic sense since the price of your vacation is protected by advance pricing. A fuel surcharge is the only additional cost that may change at the last minute.

How do I get the best price?

Read the newspapers and check on the internet. But, to get the best deals, go to an agency that specializes in cruises – they will have access to deals and upgrades not available anywhere else.

The latest trends

● More large resort ships, charging for "extras" at every turn.
● More multi-generational cruising aboard the large resort ships.
● An increase in single-parent cruising.
● More child-free ships for those who have matured beyond noise and games.
● Small ship cruising (for those seeking to avoid large resort ships and crowds).
● More themed dining venues.
● More sophisticated spas and well-being treatment options.

PRECEDING PAGES: a seagull's-eye view of a large resort ship, *Carnival Pride*.
LEFT: the shopping promenade aboard the 154,407-ton *Freedom of the Seas*.
RIGHT: Hurtigruten's expedition ship *Nordnorge* explores the Antarctic.

● More "healthy eating" and "spa" menu choices.
● Widest ever variety of adventures ashore.
● Greater demand for smoking-free ships.
● More demand for longer cruises.
● More demand for short "getaway" cruises.
● Advertisements will appear on those big movie screens on deck.
● Traditional ballroom dancing will make a comeback aboard more ships.

Bigger – but better?

The latest "largest ever" cruise ship arrives in 2009. At 220,000 tons, 1,181 ft (360 meters) long and carrying up to 6,400 passengers, Royal Caribbean International's *Oasis of the Seas* is innovative and exciting – as opposed to quiet and relaxing.

Being aboard such a floating playground can be like being in a large shopping mall (still, lots of people love

A shore excursion on an Australian beach.

shopping malls). But waiting for an elevator can be frustrating. What if 5,000 people all want an omelet or room service at the same time? Or if they all go to the same beach? Disembarkation could also be like getting out of a sports stadium at the end of a big game. And then there's the matter of locating your luggage.

Mid-size ships will benefit from the introduction of so many large resort ships because more and more experienced cruisegoers will choose smaller ships in order to avoid the big ships' sanitized cruise experience and long lines. Indeed, customization and personalization will grow markedly.

Better air, less smoke

After a fire aboard *Star Princess* in 2006, much thinking went into dealing with the possibility of serious fires and the mass evacuation and repatriation of passengers. So, expect more cruise lines to ban smoking in all cabins and on balconies.

More exclusivity

Pay more, get more. The large resort ships include more spaces for "privacy" – exclusive areas that cost extra. Now you can book a specially designed spa suite with all its extra perks (*Costa Concordia, Costa Luminosa, Costa Pacifica, Costa Serena, Europa*); or a villa with private garden (*Norwegian Dawn, Norwegian Star*); or a cabin in the exclusive "Yacht Club" area aboard *MSC Fantasia*. Such "one-upmanship" is rife.

So two-class cruising (in some cases, three-class cruising) is back. What's to come: private alcove sunbathing space, tailor-made excursions, and more. But you'll still have to mingle with the masses when you go through security. While the ships have grown larger, the facilities available to all have shrunk, as has the open deck space that has become a "private" sanctuary area.

Sleep well

Most cruise lines have now upgraded to "premium" or "better sleep" mattresses and finer quality bed linen so you can sleep better after long and tiring days ashore.

The growth of shopping malls

Onboard "enhancement" items – such as luggage and tote bags, bed linen, personal amenities, wooden deck lounge (steamer) chairs, coffee tables and chairs, ship posters, cruise line memorabilia and collectibles, wine glasses, chocolate, flowers, and even mattresses – can now be purchased online from the major cruise lines (examples: www.carnivalcomfortbed.com; www.shop-hollandamerica.com). But such online shopping only works if you have a US address and credit card.

Celebrity Millennium's extra-cost Olympic Restaurant.

The long and short of it

There's growth at both ends. More cruise lines offer short "getaway" cruises for those with little time – good for those who want just a "taste" of cruising. And more cruise lines are offering around-the-world cruises and other grand voyages for those with time; around 20 ships offer complete world cruises in 2009, and more ships offer long voyages – a convenient way to escape those winter blues.

More people are choosing to live permanently aboard ship after retirement – it saves having to deal with all those troublesome family members, while being looked after in style by people who understand hospitality.

Active shore adventures

Can-do, must-do adventurous excursions ashore are hot, as more "active" types and thrill seekers want to vacation on the edge. Depending on ship, region, and itinerary, you can go crocodile hunting by Zodiac (Amazon, Australia's Kimberley Region); go diving in the best places (Maldives, Sharm-el-Sheik); go dog sledding on a glacier (Alaska, Greenland); go horseback riding (Jamaica); mountain biking (Alaska, Caribbean, Europe); go drive a race-car (Monaco); go floatplane riding (Alaska, Australia); go heli-hiking (Maui); go jungle canopy "ziplining" (Belize, Costa Rica, Hawaii); go cave tubing and jungle hiking (Belize); go hiking (Juneau icefield, Alaska, or the prehistoric Larsbreen Glacier (Norway); go canoeing amid the icebergs (Alaska), or kayaking (Alaska, Hamburg, Vietnam); go swimming with sharks (Melbourne, Australia); go white-water rafting (Kota Kinabalu); go elephant riding (Phuket, Thailand); go on a MIG jet flight over Moscow (a mere $28,000 for a long day out – but great if you like flying fast); go on an off-road 4x4 adventure (Antigua, Provence); go bicycling (British/ European itineraries), or go for a dip in the Lake of the Pregnant Maidens (Langkawi).

Fencing lessons aboard Cunard Line's *Queen Victoria.*

In addition, cruise lines are beginning to offer other shore excursions for small groups, as well as the traditional "big bus-sightsee-look at churches and museums" city tours.

The sporting life

Cruise lines are creatively sporting. Cunard Line's *Queen Victoria* offers fencing lessons; Norwegian Cruise Line has bowling alleys *(Norwegian Gem, Norwegian Pearl)*; Royal Caribbean International has boxing, ice-skating and surfing on a "flowrider" pool (Freedom- and Oasis-class ships). Costa Cruises has a Formula 1 simulator *(Costa Concordia, Costa Luminosa, Costa Pacifica, Costa Serena).* Expect Carnival Cruise Lines to get Daytona simulators. What's next? Probably a go-kart track.

Propulsion powers ahead

While the cruise industry has recently flirted with environmentally-friendly gas turbines, the fuel is far too expensive. The favored drivers are now eco-friendly diesel-electric or diesel-mechanical propulsion systems that propel ships at speeds of up to 28 knots (32mph) Only Cunard Line's *QM2*, with a top speed of more than 30 knots, is faster.

Dining and service

"Alternative" restaurants are fashionable, particularly aboard the large resort ships, and are ideal for escaping from huge dining halls full of noise and singing, table-dancing waiters. These are typically à la carte restaurants where you must make a reservation, and pay to dine in small, intimate places with superior food cooked à la minute, good wines and service, and a less frenetic ambiance.

Cruise lines stuck with traditional two-seating dining are looking for ways to be more flexible (without placing an extra burden on the staff). More ships offer flexible dining and 24-hour casual (get-your-own food) eateries, so you can eat or snack when you want. Although the concept is good, the delivery often is not; it is typically self-service eating, and not the dining and service experience most passengers envisage. ❑

BEST AND WORST HOMELAND PORTS

FACILITIES RATED OUT OF 100	
Port	Total
Baltimore	63
Boston	44
Cape Liberty, Bayonne, New Jersey	57
Charleston	53
Fort Lauderdale (Port Everglades)	45
Galveston	45
Gulfport	44
Honolulu	54
Houston	52
Jacksonville	44
Los Angeles (Long Beach)	48
Los Angeles (San Pedro)	52
Miami	42
Montreal	53
New Orleans	50
New York (Brooklyn)	77
New York (Manhattan)	55
Norfolk	52
Philadelphia	49
Port Canaveral	54
St. Thomas	51
San Diego	55
San Francisco	49
San Juan	46
Seattle	59
Tampa	53
Vancouver	72

After the terrorist attacks of September 11, 2001, many American passengers simply didn't want to fly overseas, and so the main US-based cruise lines decided to start sending more ships cruising from US and Canadian ports. This resulted in "Homeland Cruising ports." The half a dozen ports that ships regularly sailed from grew almost overnight to around 25.

One of the unfortunate results of the "fear of terror" mentality was that overnight the welcoming by personnel in embarkation ports – called the "hospitality factor" – decreased dramatically, as all passengers were treated as potential terrorists. Sadly, the "hospitality factor" has turned into the "hostility factor," with many overenthusiastic security personnel at ports having undergone a hospitality by-pass. After so many complaints, the Maritime Evaluations Group has built a picture of ports based on their user-friendliness and sense of hospitality.

As a benchmark, the terminal facilities, luggage handling, user-friendliness and hospitality factor of personnel at the Port of Yokohama (Japan) score an excellent 94 out of a possible 100. The comparisons are telling.

Coping with the giants

Much work is going on at two of the (US) South Florida ports, particularly at Port Everglades (Fort Lauderdale) and Miami, where the port authorities are

ABOVE: *Queen Mary 2* berthed at Brooklyn, New York.
BELOW: *Carnival Spirit* cruises out of Miami, Florida.

to build terminals for the new large resort ships coming in 2009 and beyond, such as Royal Caribbean International's *Oasis*-class ships (Fort Lauderdale) and Norwegian Cruise Lines' F3-class ships (Miami).

Some other, smaller ports, such as Baltimore, have been busy upgrading their facilities in order to attract more cruise ship business – hence an increased score for the current edition of this book.

New York's Brooklyn Cruise Terminal has recently been brightened up by the addition of a 24ft by 9ft mural. It originally graced the Longshoremen's Medical Center in Cobble Hill, Brooklyn, and was saved when the building was demolished and was reinstalled in the cruise terminal due largely to the efforts of members of ILA Local 1814.

What the berth marks mean

In allocating points, we took account of the following factors: terminals and appearance and cleanliness, security personnel, attitude, check-in, security control, luggage handling by porters (often seeking tips), ease of disembarkation, immigration and customs, security personnel, luggage storage and identification system, porters, and ease of access to transportation and car parks. ❏

GIVING NEW SHIPS A GOOD NAME

Once, ships were christened with water, sacrificial animals, or blood, and blessed by a priest. Today the liquid of choice is champagne, the bubbles representing the frothy seas, and the christening is usually performed by a royal personage – Britain's Queen Elizabeth II has named five ships – a politician's wife such as Barbara Bush or Roslyn Carter, or a celebrity.

Celebrities, chosen for their ability to attract the media to the ceremony, can range from tennis stars (Chris Evert, Steffi Graff) and singers (Diana Ross, Dame Kiri Te Kanawa) to astronauts (Dr Sally Ride, Dr Tamara Jernigan) – and even the entire Harlem Boys Choir, who named *Crystal Symphony*.

But it's film stars who most reliably attract publicity. Ali MacGraw and Ryan O'Neal together named *Ocean Princess*, and the unlikely pairing of Liv Ullman and Whoopi Goldberg jointly named *Viking Serenade* (now *Island Escape*). Audrey Hepburn, Ingrid Bergman, Claudia Cardinale, Judi Dench and Kim Cattrall have all let loose the champagne. As befits its more serious intent, the luxury expedition ship *Orion* was named by five American godmothers from Harvard University and the Smithsonian Institute.

What's in a name?

Ideally, a ship name has to fit in with a succession of similar names in an existing fleet. Louis Cruise Lines adopted a gemstone theme: *Aegean Pearl, Coral, Cristal, Sapphire*. Celebrity Cruises plundered the universe for *Celebrity Galaxy, Celebrity Constellation, Celebrity Infinity, Celebrity Mercury*. MSC Cruises said it with music, as in *MSC Lirica,* *MSC Melody, MSC Musica, MSC Opera, MSC Orchestra, MSC Rhapsody, MSC Sinfonia*, etc.

Alternatively, the name has to be easy to remember for marketing purposes. Examples include Fred Olsen Cruise Lines' *Balmoral*; Hapag-Lloyd Cruises' *Bremen*; Disney Cruise Lines' *Disney Magic*; Cunard Line's *Queen Mary 2* and *Queen Victoria*.

An old nautical tradition was to maintain a name from one generation to another, so that six *Rotterdams* spanned more than a century of Holland America's maritime history. The modern trend is to brand the ship by incorporating the cruise line's name (*Carnival Ecstasy, Celebrity Solstice, Costa Fortuna, Ruby Princess*).

Some ship names just don't fit the image (for example, *Ocean Majesty* is a small ship), some don't sound quite right (*easyCruise Life*), and some are far too long (*National Geographic Endeavour*). And some are unlikely to be revived; in 1946, for instance, United States Lines had a ship called *Marine Flasher*. ❏

ABOVE: actress Helen Mirren christens P&O's *Ventura* in 2008.
BELOW: Sophia Loren names the French-built *MSC Opera* in 2007.

WHAT THE BROCHURES DON'T ALWAYS TELL YOU

We answer frankly the questions about ocean cruising most frequently asked both by those new to this type of vacation and by experienced passengers

GENERAL DEFINITIONS

What exactly *is* a cruise?

A cruise is a vacation – an escape from the stress and strain of life ashore. It offers you a chance to relax and unwind in comfortable surroundings, with attentive service, good food, and a ship that changes the scenery for you. It is virtually a hassle-free, and, more importantly, a crime-free vacation. Everything's close to hand, and there are always polite people to help you. A cruise provides great value for money, variety (in ship size, destinations, facilities, cuisine, entertainment, activities and shore excursions), a chance to explore new places, meet new people, make friends, and, above all, provides the ingredients for a wonderful vacation.

More than 350 ocean-going cruise ships carrying from 50 to more than 6,000 passengers visit almost 2,000 destinations throughout the world, and new ships are being constantly introduced. They range from under 200 ft (60 meters) to over 1,000 ft (300 meters) in length, and their shapes vary enormously. Facilities, food, and service vary from company to company, and according to the size of the ship.

Ambiance ranges from ultra-casual to very formal (starchy and reserved). Entertainment ranges from amateur dramatics to full-fledged high-tech production shows and circus-like theatrics, from the corner cabaret to a world-famous headliner.

How long does a cruise last?

The popular standard length is seven days, although cruises can vary from two-day party cruises to a slow exotic voyage around the world of up to 180 days (there are even passengers who stay aboard some ships all year round, and disembark only when the ship has to go into dry dock for refits). If you are new to cruising and want to "get your feet wet," try a short cruise first. Its length will depend on the time and money at your disposal and the degree of comfort you are seeking, but more leisurely cruises can last 14 days or more. To operate long, low-density voyages, cruise lines must charge high rates to cover the extensive preparations, high food and transportation costs, port operations, fuel, and so on.

WHO GOES CRUISING

Isn't cruising just for old people?

The average age of passengers gets younger each year, with the average age of first-timers now well under 40. But retirees find cruising a safe and comfortable way to travel and many have plenty of get-up-and-go.

On a typical cruise you'll meet singles, couples, families with children of all ages (including single parents and grandparents), honeymooners (some second- or third-time around), groups of friends, and college buddies. You may even meet your next-door neighbors.

Visiting the bridge of the boutique ship *Celebrity Xpedition*.

P&O Cruises' *Artemis* visits Stockholm, Sweden.

Won't I get bored?

Usually, it's the men who ask this question, but get them aboard and often there's not enough time in the day to try all the things they want to do – as long as you choose the right ship, for the right reasons. There are more things to do aboard today's ships than there is on almost any Caribbean island. So, whether you want to lie back and be pampered, or be active nonstop, you can do it on a cruise holiday, and you will only have to pack and unpack once.

Just being at sea provides an intoxicating sense of freedom that few places on dry land can offer. And, in case you think you may feel cut off without contact, almost all large resort ships (those carrying over 1,600 passengers) offer internet access, pay-per-view movies, digital music libraries, and ship-wide wi-fi access.

Isn't it all very regimented?

Some cruises simply aren't relaxing despite cruise brochure claims that "you can do as much or as little as you want to." For example, the large resort ships carrying more than 1,600 passengers, and particularly those with 5,000-plus, cram lots of people into small cabins and provide nonstop activities that insult the intelligence and assault the wallet. The purpose of this book is to help you identify the cruise that's right for you.

Disney Cruise Line creates that theme park feel.

Are there facilities for singles?

Yes. A cruise holiday is good for those traveling alone (over 25 percent of all passengers are solo travelers – worldwide, that's over 4 million a year), because it is easy to meet other people in a non-competitive environment. Many ships have dedicated cabins for singles and special add-on rates for single occupancy of double cabins. Some cruise lines will even find a cabin mate for you to share with, if you so desire.

However, in cabins with three or four berths (two beds plus upper berths), personal privacy doesn't exist. Also, some companies sell two-bed cabins at a special single rate, forgetting that many people who cruise solo do so because their spouse or partner has died, and the last thing they want is to be in a cabin with two beds.

Why is it so expensive for singles?

Because it's a couples world. Almost all cruise lines base their rates on double occupancy, as do hotels. Thus, when you travel alone, the cabin portion of your fare reflects an additional supplement. While almost all new ships are built with cabins for double occupancy, older ships have more single occupancy cabins.

Is there enough to keep children busy?

A cruise provides families with more quality time than any other type of vacation, and family cruising is the industry's largest growth segment. Activities are tailored to various age groups – even Disney has cruise ships for families. A cruise is also educational, allows children to interact in a crime-free environment, and takes them to destinations in comfortable, familiar surroundings. In fact, children have such a good time aboard ship and ashore, you may have difficulty getting them home after the cruise – as long as you have chosen the right ship.

If you cruise aboard one of the major cruise lines, you may find gratuities for your children automatically added to your onboard account. NCL, for example, requests $5 per day from each child of 3–12 years, while those over 13 pay the adult rate of $10 per day.

Are there child-free ships?

If you don't like crowds, noise, and long lines, try a small ship – a sail-cruise vessel or a river or barge cruise could also provide the right escape. Companies that operate child-free ships include P&O Cruises (*Arcadia, Artemis*), Saga Cruises (*Spirit of Adventure, Saga Rose, Saga Ruby*) and Thomson Cruises (*The Calypso*).

DO CRUISES SUIT HONEYMOONERS?

Absolutely. A cruise is the ideal setting for romance, for shipboard weddings aboard ships with the right registry (they can also be arranged in some ports, depending on local regulations), receptions, and honeymoons. Most decisions are already made for you, so all you have to do is show up. Many ships have double, queen- or king-sized beds, too. And for those on a second honeymoon, many ships can perform a "renewal of vows" ceremony; some will make a charge for this service.

HEALTH ISSUES

Will I get seasick?

Today's ships have stabilizers – large underwater "fins" on each side of the hull – to counteract any rolling motion, and most cruises are in warm, calm waters. As a result, fewer than 3 percent of passengers become seasick. Yet it's possible to develop some symptoms – anything from slight nausea to vomiting.

Both old-time sailors and modern physicians have their own remedies, and you can take your choice or try them all (but not at the same time):

● When you notice the first movement of a ship, walk back and forth on the deck. You will find that your knees, which are our own form of stabilizer, will start getting their feel of balance and counteraction. This is known as "getting your sea legs."

● Get the fresh sea breeze into your face (arguably the best antidote of all), and if nauseated, suck an orange or a lemon.

● Eat lightly. Do not make the mistake of thinking a heavy meal will keep your stomach anchored. It won't.

● When on deck, focus on a steady point, such as the horizon.

Drugs: Dramamine (dimenhydrinate, an anti-histamine and sedative introduced just after World War II) will be available aboard in tablet (chewable) form.
Ciba-Geigy's Scopoderm (or Transderm Scop), known as "The Patch," contains scopolamine and has proven effective. Possible side effects are dry mouth, blurred vision, drowsiness and problems with urinating.

If you are really distressed, the ship's doctor can give you an injection to alleviate discomfort. It may make you drowsy, but the last thing on your mind will be staying awake during the movie.

A natural preventive is ginger in powder form. Mix half a teaspoon in a glass of warm water or milk, and drink it before sailing. This is said to settle any stomach for up to eight hours.

"Sea Bands" (or "Aquastraps") are a drug-free method of controlling motion sickness. These are slim bands (in varying colors) that are wrapped around the wrist, with a circular "button" that presses against the acupressure point Pericardium 6 (nei kuan) on the lower arm. Attach them a few minutes before you step aboard and wear on both wrists throughout the cruise.

Another drug-free remedy can be found in ReliefBand, a watch-like device worn on the wrist. It is said to "emit gentle electrical signals that interfere with nerves that cause nausea."

Can I go cruising if pregnant?

Yes, but most cruise lines will not allow a mother-to-be to cruise past her 28th week of pregnancy, and some set the limit at the 24th week. You may need to produce a doctor's certificate.

Is having hay fever a problem?

Actually, people who suffer from hay fever and pollen allergies benefit greatly from a cruise. Most sufferers I have talked to say that their problems simply disappear on a cruise – particularly when the ship is at sea.

Are hygiene standards high enough?

News reports often focus on hygiene and sanitation aboard cruise ships. In the 1980s, the North American cruise industry agreed with the Centers for Disease Control (CDC) that hygiene and sanitation inspections should be carried out once or twice yearly aboard all cruise ships carrying American passengers, and the Vessel Sanitation Program (VSP) was born. The original intention of the VSP was to achieve and maintain a level of sanitation that would lower the risk of gastro-intestinal disease outbreaks and assist the cruise industry to provide a healthy environment for passengers and crew.

It is a voluntary inspection, and cruise lines pay handsomely for each inspection. However, the 42 inspection points are judged to be a good system that all should adhere to. The inspections cover two main areas:

● Water sanitation, including free chlorine residuals in the potable water system, swimming pool and hot tub filters.

● Food sanitation: food storage, preparation and serving areas, including bars and passenger service pantries.

The ships score extremely well – the ones that undergo inspections, that is. Some ships that don't call on US ports would possibly not pass the inspections every time. Older ships with outdated galley equipment and poor food storage facilities would have a harder time complying with the USPH inspection standards. Some other countries also have strict health inspection standards. However, if the same USPH inspection standards were applied to restaurants and hotels ashore, it is estimated that at least 90 percent or more would fail, consistently.

Holland America Line runs cookery classes for children.

Evening entertainment aboard *MSC Musica*.

Anyone concerned about personal hygiene should note that some ships have fixed shower heads. A removable shower and hose are better for reaching those parts that fixed head showers can't. Check with your cruise provider *before* you book.

What about the Norwalk virus?

This temporary but highly contagious condition occurs worldwide. Humans are the only known hosts, and only the common cold is reported more frequently than viral gastroenteritis as a cause of illness in the USA. About 23 million Americans each year are diagnosed with the effects of the Norwalk-like virus (NLV gastroenteritis, sometimes known as winter vomiting virus). It is more prevalent in adults and older children than in the very young.

Norwalk is part of the "calicivirus" family. The name derives from the chalice or calyx, meaning cuplike; this refers to the indentations of the surface of the virus. The disease itself is self-limiting, is mild, and is characterized by nausea, vomiting, diarrhoea, and abdominal pain. Although it can be transmitted by person-to-person contact, it is more likely to arrive via contaminated foods and water, so make sure you wash your hands thoroughly after using the toilet.

Shellfish (most notably clams and oysters), salad ingredients (particular salad dressings) and fruits are the foods most often implicated in Norwalk outbreaks.

Water can also be a common source of outbreaks – water aboard cruise ships stored in tanks, etc. A mild and brief illness typically occurs 24 to 48 hours after contaminated food or water has been consumed, and lasts for 24 to 72 hours. The virus can also be brought on board when passengers are ashore in foreign ports with poor hygiene standards.

Note that only cruise ships are required to report every incidence of gastrointestinal illness. Nowhere else in the health system of the US are such viruses a reportable illness.

Where is smoking allowed?

Some cruise lines allow smoking in cabins, while some permit it only in cabins with balconies. Almost all cruise lines prohibit smoking in restaurants and food service areas; very few ships have smoking sections in dining rooms. If you are concerned, check with the cruise line or your travel agent before booking.

Non-smokers will be pleased to know that most ships now have totally non-smoking dining rooms and show lounges, and many ships now allow smoking only on the open decks. However, you could be sunbathing on an open deck and the person next to you can light up – not a healthy situation.

Cigar smoking is still in vogue, and several ships have cigar bars and lounges. Examples: *Adventure of the Seas, Amadea, Asuka II, Bleu de France, Brilliance of the Seas, Crystal Serenity, Crystal Symphony, Europa, Explorer of the Seas, Freedom of the Seas, Grand Mistral, Independence of the Seas, Liberty of the Seas, Mariner of the Seas, MSC Armonia, MSC Fantasia, MSC Lirica, MSC Musica, MSC Opera, MSC Orchestra, MSC Poesia, MSC Sinfonia, Navigator of the Seas, Norwegian Dawn, Norwegian Gem, Norwegian Jewel, Norwegian Pearl, Norwegian Star, Norwegian*

Sun, *Queen Mary 2, Queen Victoria, Radiance of the Seas, Serenade of the Seas, Seven Seas Mariner, Seven Seas Voyager, Silver Shadow, Silver Whisper, SuperStar Virgo,* and *Voyager of the Seas.* Note, however, that ships starting or ending their cruises in a US port are not permitted to carry genuine Cuban cigars. Instead, most cigars will be made in the Dominican Republic.

Have there been murders during a cruise?

Violent crime is much less common on a cruise than during land-based vacations, but there have been a few suspicious deaths, and a number of passengers have gone missing, mainly in the Caribbean and on Mexican Riviera cruises. A small number have been thrown over a balcony by another passenger, typically after an alcohol-fueled argument.

Murder is hard to prove if no body is found (did he jump or was he pushed?). Another headache is that, if the alleged crime happens at sea, the jurisdiction responsible for investigating it will depend on the ship's registry, perhaps in Panama, Liberia or Malta.

CAN I BRING MY PETS?

Pet animals are not allowed aboard cruise ships, with one exception: the regular transatlantic crossings aboard Cunard Line's ocean liner *Queen Mary 2.* It provides air-conditioned kennels, plus a genuine British lamppost and New York fire hydrant for dogs' convenience, and cat containers.

be for a four-berth cabin adjacent to the ship's laundry or above the disco, but in any event, not in a desirable location – just like a dirt-cheap hotel room in London or New York.

Should I pay the price given in the brochure?

Not without checking around. A cruise's brochure price is set by the sales and marketing departments of cruise lines, rather like the "recommended retail price" of a new car is set by the manufacturer. It's the price they would like to achieve to cover themselves against currency fluctuations, international bonding schemes and the like. But, in the real world, discounts attract business, and so there is always some leeway. Also, travel agents receive a commission (typically 10–15%, plus special overrides for volume bookings). So, as a consumer, always ask for the "best price" and watch for special offers in newspapers and magazines.

European cruises cost more than in the Caribbean. Why?

There are several reasons. Almost all aspects of operations, including fuel costs, port charges, air transportation, supplying food to the ships, are higher.

WHAT CRUISING COSTS

Isn't cruising expensive?

Compare what it would cost on land to have all your meals and entertainment provided, as well as transportation, fitness and sports facilities, social activities, educational talks, parties, and other functions, and you can see the remarkable value of a cruise.

Cost provides a useful guideline to a ship's ambience, type of passengers, and degree of luxury, food, and service. The amount you pay determines the size, location, and style of accommodation you get. Be wary of huge discounts – it either means that the product was unrealistically priced at source or that quality will be reduced somewhere. Ships are as individual as fingerprints: each can change its "personality" from cruise to cruise, depending on the mix of passengers (and crew). The choice ranges from basic to luxury, so give yourself a budget, and ask your professional travel supplier how to make the best use of it.

A seven-day cruise is advertised at a very cheap price. Is there a catch?

As a rule, yes. If the price is a fraction of what you might pay for a decent hotel room in London or New York without meals or entertainment, something is not quite as it seems. Before booking, read the fine print. Look at all the extra costs such as tips to cabin and dining room stewards, shore excursions, drinks, plus getting to and from the ship. The price per person advertised could well

Cruising's classic image: Half Moon Cay, the Bahamas.

Aboard some ships, all cabins have balconies.

European-sourced food has more taste – eggs with real yellow yolks, and food free from chemical additives, coloring and flavoring – than is found in the processed foods that cruise lines often purchase from US-based suppliers.

Companies can make more money than in the cut-price Caribbean, where sun, sea, and sand are the main attractions, whereas sightseeing, architecture, culture, and other things are part of a more enriching cruise experience. The price of shore excursions in Europe is high. Admission prices to some historic sites and museums have more than doubled recently.

How inclusive is "all-inclusive"?

That's like asking how much sand is on the beach. It usually means that transportation (often including flights), accommodation, food, and entertainment are wrapped up in one neat package. Today on land, however, "super clubs" offer everything "all-in" including drinks, although mostly low-quality brands are provided, with a much smaller selection than aboard most cruise ships.

While that concept works better aboard small ships (those carrying fewer than 500 passengers), large cruise ships (those carrying more than 1,600 passengers) provide more facilities and more reasons for you to spend money on board. So "mostly inclusive" might be a better term to use, particularly as spa treatments and medical services are definitely *not* included.

Do ships have different classes?

Yes and no. Gone are the class distinctions and the pretensions of formality of the past. Differences are now found mainly in the type of accommodation chosen, in the price you pay for a larger cabin (or suite), the loca-tion of your cabin (or suite), and whether or not you have butler service.

Some cruise lines, including Holland America Line and Royal Caribbean International (*Freedom*-class ships only), provide a "concierge lounge" which can be used only by occupants of accommodation designated as suites (thus re-creating a two-class system). Private areas have been created by MSC Cruises (Yacht Club) and Norwegian Cruise Line (The Courtyard) for occupants of the top suites, in an effort to provide exclusivity – and insulation from the masses. In effect, this is like devising a "ship within a ship."

Celebrity Cruises has, in essence, created three classes: 1) Suites; 2) Concierge Class (middle-level) mini-suites/cabins; 3) Standard (exterior view and interior – no view) cabins. Perhaps it's easier to think in terms of "Balcony Class" and "Non-Balcony Class."

Cabins advertised in newspapers aren't always available. Why not?

Newspaper advertisements are written way ahead of publication. Meanwhile, some cabin price grades may have sold out. Often, the cheapest "lead-in" price is for a cabin that is small, or has obstructed views, or is in an "inconvenient" or "noisy" location.

What is a category guarantee?

It means you have purchased a specific grade of accommodation (just as in a hotel), although the actual cabin may not have been assigned to your booking yet. Your cabin may be assigned before you go, or when you arrive for embarkation.

What are port charges?

These are levied by the various ports visited by cruise ships, rather like city taxes imposed on hotel guests.

They help pay for the infrastructure required to provide facilities including docks, linesmen, security and operations personnel, and porters at embarkation and disembarkation ports.

FACILITIES ABOARD

Can I eat when I want to?

Yes, you can – well, almost. Several major cruise lines offer "flexible dining" which allows you to choose (with some limitations) when you want to eat, and with whom you dine. Just like going out to restaurants ashore, reservations may be required, you may also have to wait in line at busy periods, and occupants of the most expensive suites get priority.

Aboard large resort ships (1,600-plus passengers) the big evening entertainment shows typically are staged twice each evening, so you end up with the equivalent of two-seating dining anyway.

What is "alternative" dining?

Some ships now have alternative dining spots other than the main restaurant. These usually cost extra – typically between $15 and $50 a person, but the food quality, preparation and presentation are decidedly better, as is service and ambience. Most alternative dining spots are also typically more intimate, and much quieter than the main dining rooms.

What's the difference between an "outside" and an "interior" cabin?

An "outside" (or "exterior") cabin doesn't mean it's outside the ship; it simply means that it has a window (or porthole) with a view of the outside, or there is a private balcony for you to physically be (or look) outside. An "interior" cabin means that it does not have a view of the outside, but it will have artwork or curtains on one wall instead of a window or patio-like (balcony) door. Naturally, an outside cabin costs more than an interior cabin of the same size.

Should I tip for room service?

No. It's part of the normal onboard duties that the hotel staff are paid to carry out. For more on tipping other staff, see page 51.

Is it hard to find one's way around large resort ships?

Well, it can take at least a few hours, so wear good walking shoes. However, in general, remember that decks are horizontal, while stairs are vertical. The rest comes naturally, with practice. If you're arranging to meet someone, you need to be very specific indeed about the place.

Isn't it very noisy aboard these huge ships?

They can be, because of the constant activities and music, and many announcements. Anyone who is allergic to noise should consider taking earplugs, just in case.

Can I visit the bridge?

Not any more. For insurance and security reasons, almost all cruise ships prohibit bridge visits. However, a Behind the Scenes video on how the ship is run may be shown on the cabin television system.

Are there any ships with walk-in pools (instead of ladders)?

Not many, due to space considerations, although they are useful for older passengers. Examples: *Aurora, Crystal Serenity, Crystal Symphony, Ocean Village, Oriana.*

The bigger the ship, the greater the variety of sports.

Can I bring my golf clubs?

Yes, you can. However, although cruise lines do not charge for carrying them, some airlines do – worth checking if you have to fly to join your cruise. Some ships cater for golfers with mini-golf courses on deck and electronically monitored practice areas.

What about my bicycle?

Most cruise lines will let you take your bike (preferably the folding variety due to lack of storage space). If you use a flight case, however, it may not be easy to find storage space for it. Airlines will also charge you to transport your bike. Ask your travel provider to contact the cruise line for its rules. Note that very few ships provide bicycles for free. Those that do include Hapag-Lloyd's *Europa* and *Hanseatic*.

Do cellular phones work on board?

Cruise passengers use cellular phones on open decks, in cabins, and, sadly, even in restaurants. Most cruise lines have contracts with land-based phone service companies – rates for usage vary, but you will typically pay international roaming rates. Mobile phone signals piggyback off systems that transmit internet data via satellite. When your ship is in port, the ship's network may be switched off and you will pay the going local (country-specific) rate for mobile calls.

Keeping in touch with children's whereabouts on a big resort ship can be expensive using mobile phones.

Personal service is best aboard smaller, luxury ships.

It's permissible to use two-way radio transceivers (walkie-talkies) for this purpose; at sea they won't interfere with any public-service radio frequency.

Can I send and receive emails?

Aboard most ships, email facilities have now been added to some degree or other. Many ships have wi-fi, for a fee, allowing you to connect your own laptop. Several ships have an internet café, or internet-connect center, where you can log on for about 50¢ per minute. Note that connections and downloads are often slow compared to land-based services (shipboard emails link through satellite systems, and are therefore more expensive than land-based connections). For many cruise companies, email has now become an important revenue generator.

Where can you see movies?

Some – but not many – ships have a dedicated movie theater. The movies are provided by a licensed film distribution/leasing service. Many newer ships have replaced or supplemented the movie theater with TV sets and DVD players in cabins, or with giant poolside screens for after-dark viewing.

DESTINATIONS

Where can I go on a cruise?

As the saying goes: The world is your oyster! There are over 30,000 different cruises to choose from each year, and about 2,000 cruise destinations in the world. A cruise can also take you to places inaccessible by almost any other means, such as Antarctica, the North Cape, the South Sea islands, and so on. In fact, if you close your eyes and think of almost anywhere in the world where there's water, there's probably a cruise ship or river vessel to take you there. To get an idea of the choice available, see pages 24–7 and 78–99.

What is "homeland" cruising?

The term stems from cruise ships sailing out of an increased number of ports in the United States (more than 20 at last count, with over 4,000 cruises a year). While some, like Miami and Fort Lauderdale, have good facilities for checking in, many do not, and long lines are the result, particularly when 50 motorcoaches arrive at virtually the same time *(see page 10 for rating of ports)*.

"Homeland" cruising has great appeal for people who can drive themselves to a local (regional) port of embarkation. The result, however, is that one ship sailing out of, say, Baltimore, will attract many other people from the surrounding area, and that could mean you'll bump into any of your neighbors who've had the same idea as you. It also makes for particularly strong regional dialects aboard any given ship, and can even change the ways that cruise consumers act and dress.

What is expedition cruising?

Expedition cruises are operated by small ships that have ice-strengthened hulls or with specially constructed ice-breakers that enable them to reach areas totally inaccessible to "normal" cruise ships. The ships are typically converted to carry passengers in some degree of basic comfort, with comfortable accommodation and a relaxed, informal atmosphere, with expert lecturers and expedition leaders accompanying every cruise.

These cruises really are for small groups, and much care and attention is placed on minimizing the impact on the environment. For more information, see pages 78–81.

What is a Panamax ship?

This is one that conforms to the maximum dimensions possible for passage through the Panama Canal – useful particularly for around-the-world voyages. These dimensions are: 294 meters (964.56 ft) long, with a beam of 32.3 meters (105.97 ft); or below approximately 90,000 gross tons. Because of the locks, the 50-mile (80-km) journey takes from eight to nine hours.

Is there a cruise that skips ports?

Yes, but it isn't really a cruise. It's a transatlantic crossing, from New York to Southampton, England (or vice versa), aboard Cunard Line's *Queen Mary 2*. See page 90.

Can I shop in ports of call?

Yes, you can. Many passengers embrace retail therapy when visiting ports of call such as Dubai, Hong Kong, Singapore, St. Maarten, and St. Thomas, among many others. However, it's prudent to exercise self-control. Remember that you'll have to carry all those purchases home at the end of your cruise; duty-free liquor – a favourite, for example – is heavy.

Do I have to go ashore in each port?

Absolutely not. In fact, many repeat passengers enjoy being aboard "their" ships when there are virtually no other passengers aboard. Also, if you have a spa treatment, it could be less expensive during this period than when the ship is at sea; some ships, such as *Queen Mary 2*, have price differentials for sea days/port days.

MAKING BOOKINGS

Can I fly in the day before or stay an extra day after the cruise?

Cruise lines often offer pre- and post-cruise stay packages at an additional cost. The advantage is that you don't have to do anything else. All will be taken care of, as they say. If you book a hotel on your own, however, you may have to pay an "air deviation" fee, payable if you do not take the cruise line's air arrangements or you want to change them.

Safety is a top priority for the highly trained crews.

The McKinley Explorer is a tempting excursion during cruises to Alaska – but it's a significant extra cost.

Can I pre-book seats on flights?

With packaged holidays such as cruises, it is normally not possible to reserve airline seats prior to check-in, and, although the cruise line will typically forward your requests for preferred seating, these may not be guaranteed. However, some airlines allow you to check-in online, access the seating plan and select a seat.

Should I book early?

The further you book ahead, the greater will be any discount applied by the cruise line. You'll also get the cabin you want, in the location you want, and you may even be upgraded. When you book late (close to the sailing date), you may get a low price, but you typically won't get the cabin or location you might like, or – worse still – in ships with two seatings for dinner, you won't be able to choose early or late seating.

AND FINALLY...

What are cruising's downsides?

Much anticipated ports of call can be aborted or changed due to poor weather or other conditions. Some popular ports (particularly in the Caribbean) can become extremely crowded – there can be up to 12 ships in St. Thomas, or six in St. Maarten at the same time, disgorging 20,000 people. Fellow passengers, and those lacking social manners can be irritating, notably in the dining room where you may have to share a table with strangers.

Many frequent irritations could be fixed if the cruise lines really tried. See the list on the opposite page.

Where did all the money go?

Apart from the cruise fare itself, there could be other incidentals such as government taxes, port charges, air ticket tax, and fuel surcharges. On board, extra costs may include drinks, mini-bar items, cappuccino and espresso coffees, shore excursions (especially those involving flightseeing tours), internet access, sending or receiving email, beauty treatments, casino gaming, photographs, laundry and dry-cleaning, babysitting services, wine tasting, bottled water placed in your cabin, and medical services.

A cruise aboard a ship belonging to a major cruise line could be compared to buying a car, whereby motor manufacturers offer a basic model at a set price, and then tempt you with optional extras to inflate the price.

Cruise lines say income generated on board helps to keep the basic cost of a cruise reasonable. In the end, it's up to your self-restraint to stop those little extras mounting up to an unacceptably large sum.

What rights do passengers have?

Very few. After reading a cruise line's Passenger Ticket Contract, you'll see why. A 189-word sentence in one contract begins "The Carrier shall not be liable for…" and goes on to cover the legal waterfront.

Where do old cruise ships go when they're scrapped?

They go to the beach. Actually, they are driven at speed onto a not very nice beach at Alang in India, or to Chittagong in Bangladesh, or to Pan Yo in China – the principal shipbreaking places. Greenpeace has claimed that workers, including children, at some of these sites have to work under primitive conditions without adequate protective equipment. ❏

What could be improved?

It's not all perfect. Here are some aspects of cruising in 2009 that the brochures certainly won't mention

● Large resort ships travel by night and are in port during the day, but provide little connection to nature and the sea, the ship being the destination (small town takes to water). Increasingly, the idea is to keep you inside the ship, spending money.

● Entertainment, whether production shows or cabaret acts, are much the same aboard nearly every large resort ship and lack originality.

● Aggressive, young, so-called "cruise directors" who insist on interposing themselves into every part of your cruise, day and night, military-style through the public address system. Some of these cruise directors may make good cheerleaders, but seem unable to communicate with anyone over 25.

● As identically sized standard cabins are the same shape and layout (good for incentive planners and groups, not for individual passengers), they are also the same colors: eggshell white, off-white, or computer-colored beige. While these are welcome soft colors after days in the sun, they are boring on voyages over long stretches of water. Only bold bedspreads or the occasional color prints that adorn a spare wall bring relief. Plain ceilings are also tedious. Close to useless are wall-mounted hairdryers in modular bathrooms; they should, instead, be located in the vanity desk or dressing area.

● Calling passengers "guests" is now widespread. But ships are different from hotels, and should remain so. They provide a nautical experience and move through water; passengers have cabins and suites, and decks, not floors. However, many cruise lines think they are in the hotel business – that's because hoteliers, ex-airline people, accountants and equity investors run them, not shipping people.

● The use of "hotel-speak" is invading the industry. One example: Royal Caribbean International calls its in-cabin refrigerators "Automatic Refreshment Centers.""

● The meet and greet staff at airports in general are a weak link in the chain.

● Two things that have almost disappeared: streamers and free champagne, formerly provided at bon voyage parties on deck on sailing day (exception: world cruises and Japanese-registered cruise ships). Instead, waiters hustle you to buy a "bon voyage" cocktail, or some "Bahamaramamaslammer" in a plastic or polystyrene sports cup. The little goodies, such as travel bags, and extensive personal amenity kits, have been taken away by the bean counters, believing that passengers won't notice. Believe me, they do.

● As for food, note that ships that offer seven-day cruises repeat menu cycles each week. You can take two, back-to-back 7-day Eastern and Western Caribbean cruises, but the menu may be repeated for the second week. The same goes for the whole entertainment program and the cruise director's robotic spiel.

● Cruise ship food and service standards have suffered as a result of deep discounting. Most large resort ships don't consistently live up to the brochure descriptions.

● One thing that *should* go into deep waters is the intrusive "Baked Alaska Parade." Popular with first-time passengers, it is old hat for many. The industry should also find a better way to sing "Happy Birthday" than a waiter-induced chant that usually sounds like a funeral dirge.

● In the standard seven-day cruise market, particularly from US ports, disembarkation is mostly an untidy and hostile process. Passengers are unceremoniously dumped ashore, with little help after the trying procedures of locating their luggage and going through customs inspection. The same procedure applies to all passengers, even if they've paid for the finest penthouse suite. ❑

ABOVE: much entertainment is quite old-fashioned.
BELOW: very large ships mean there's a lot of luggage.

WHERE TO?

Cruise lines currently visit around 2,000 destinations, so there is almost certainly a ship to take you where you've always wanted to go

Because itineraries vary widely, it is wise to make as many comparisons as you can by reading the cruise brochures for descriptions of the ports of call. Several ships may offer the same or similar itineraries simply because these have been tried and tested. Narrow the choice further by noting the time spent at each port, and whether the ship actually docks in port or lies at anchor. Then, compare the size of each vessel and its facilities.

Caribbean cruises

There are over 7,000 islands in the Caribbean Sea, although many are small or uninhabited. Caribbean cruises are usually destination-intensive, cramming between four and eight ports into one week, depending on whether you sail from a Florida port or from a port already in the Caribbean, such as Barbados or San Juan. This means you could be visiting at least one port a day, with little time at sea for relaxation. This kind of island-hopping leaves little time to explore a destination (but you'd probably get bored after a few days on one island). Although you see a

RCI organizes watersports off Labadee, Haiti.

lot of places in a week, by the end of the cruise you may need another week to unwind. *Note*: June 10 to November 10 is the official hurricane season in the Caribbean (including the Bahamas and Florida).

● **Eastern Caribbean** cruises include ports such as Antigua, Barbados, Dominica, Martinique, Puerto Rico, St. Croix, St. Kitts, St. Maarten, St. Lucia and St. Thomas.

● **Western Caribbean** cruises typically include ports such as Calica, Cozumel, Grand Cayman, Grand Turk, Playa del Carmen, Ocho Rios, and Roatan Island.

● **Southern Caribbean** cruises typically include ports such as Antigua, Aruba, Barbados, La Guaira (Venezuela), Tortola, San Juan.

Private islands

Several cruise lines with Bahamas/Caribbean itineraries feature a "private island" (also called an "out-island"). This is a small island close to Nassau in the Bahamas outfitted with all the ingredients to make an all-day beach party a "nice day out." Also available are water sports, scuba, snorkeling, crystal-clear waters, warm sands, even a hammock or two, and,

Inspecting Dubai's modernity from a Costa ship.

possibly, massage in a beach cabana. There are no reservations to make, no tickets to buy, and no hassles with taxis. But you may be sharing your private island with more than 5,000 others from a single large resort ship anchored for a "beach barbecue."

One bonus is that a "private island" will not be cluttered with hawkers and hustlers, as are so many Caribbean beaches. And, because they *are* private, there is security, and no fear of passengers being mugged, as occurs in some islands.

Private island beach days are not all-inclusive, however, and attract premium prices for snorkel gear (and mandatory swim vest), rental pleasure craft, and "banana" boat fun rides; it has become yet another way for cruise lines to increase revenue. But then it does cost a lot of money to develop a private island. Examples: Disney Cruise Line spent $25 million developing and outfitting Castaway Cay (formerly Gorda Cay), while Holland America Line spent $16 million developing Half Moon Cay.

Although private islands sound attractive, remember that many items are at extra cost. Examples: Sunfish sailboat rental, $40 per hour; snorkel gear rental, $10 per hour; floating foam mattress, $6; bottle of water, $2.50–$4; ice cream, $1.50–$3; water bicycle, $5–$10 per 15 minutes; use of hammock, $2.50–$5.

European and Mediterranean cruises

Traveling within Europe (including the Aegean, Baltic, Black Sea, Mediterranean, and Norwegian fjord areas) by cruise ship makes economic sense. Although no single cruise covers every port, cruise ships do offer a comfortable way of exploring the area's rich mix of destinations, cultures, history, architecture, lifestyles and cuisines – and without having to pack and unpack each day. For some, the appeal is mainly to have a safe, crime-free holiday.

These cruises are increasingly popular because:
● So many of Europe's major cosmopolitan cities – Amsterdam, Athens, Barcelona, Copenhagen, Genoa, Helsinki, Lisbon, London, Monte Carlo, Nice, Oslo, St. Petersburg, Stockholm, and Venice – are on the water. It is far less expensive to take a cruise than to fly and stay in decent hotels (and then

THE CRUISE LINES THAT OWN PRIVATE ISLANDS

Cruise Line	Name of Island	Location	First Used	Berlitz Rating (out of 10)
Celebrity Cruises	Catalina Island	Dominican Republic	1995	5.7
Costa Cruises	Serena Cay	Dominican Republic	1996	5.7
Disney Cruise Line	Castaway Cay	Bahamas	1998	8.5
Holland America Line	Half Moon Cay	Bahamas	1997	8.6
MSC Cruises	Cayo Levantado	Dominican Republic	2005	4.7
Norwegian Cruise Line	Great Stirrup Cay	Bahamas	1977	7.5
Princess Cruises	Princess Bay	Mayreau, Genadines	1986	7.3
Princess Cruises	Princess Cays	Eleuthera, Bahamas	1992	7.5
Royal Caribbean International	Coco Cay	Bahamas	1990	6.4
Royal Caribbean International	Labadee	Haiti	1986	7.2

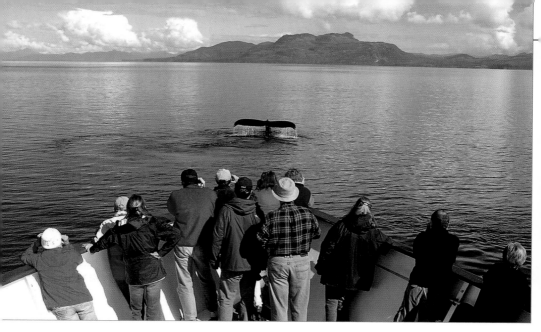

A whalewatching trip along Alaska's Inside Passage.

have to pay for food and transport in addition).
● You will not have to try to speak or understand different languages when you are aboard ship as you would ashore (if you choose the right ship).
● Aboard ship you use a single currency (typically US dollars, British pounds, or euros).
● A wide variety of shore excursions are offered.
● Lecture programs provide insights before you step ashore. Small ships are arguably better than large resort ships, as they can obtain berthing space (the large resort ships may have to anchor in more of the smaller ports, so it can take time to get to and from shore, and you'll probably have to wait for shore tender tickets). Many Greek islands are accessible only by shore tender. Some companies allow more time ashore than others, so compare itineraries in the brochures; it's probably best to choose a regional cruise line (such as Louis Hellenic Cruises) for these destination-intensive cruises, for example.

Alaska cruises

These are especially popular because:
● They offer the best way to see the state's magnificent shoreline and glaciers.
● Alaska is a vast, relatively unexplored region.
● There are a wide range of shore excursions, including many floatplane and helicopter tours.
● There are many excursions, including "dome car" rail journeys to Denali National Park to see North America's highest peak, Mt. McKinley.
● Pre- and post-cruise journeys to Banff and Jasper National Parks can be made from Vancouver.
    There are two popular cruise routes:
The Inside Passage Route, a 1,000-mile (1,600-km)

stretch of protected waterways carved a million years ago by Ice Age glaciers. This usually includes visits to tidewater glaciers, such as those in Glacier Bay's Hubbard Glacier or Tracy Arm (just two of the 15 active glaciers along the 60-mile/100-km Glacier Bay coastline). Typical ports of call might include Juneau, Ketchikan, Skagway, and Haines.
The Glacier Route, which usually includes the Gulf of Alaska during a one-way cruise between Vancouver and Anchorage. Typical ports of call might include Seward, Sitka, and Valdez.
    Holland America Line and Princess Cruises own many facilities in Alaska (hotels, tour buses, even trains), and between them have invested more than $300 million in the state. Indeed, Holland America Line-Westours is Alaska's largest private employer. Both companies take in excess of 250,000 passengers to Alaska each year. Other lines depend on what's left of the local transportation for their land tours.
    In ports where docking space is limited, some ships anchor rather than dock. Many cruise

---

DID YOU KNOW?

● that Alaska has two time zones? Most of Alaska is one hour behind Pacific Standard Time, whereas the Aleutian Islands are two hours behind Pacific Standard Time.
● that the Pacific Ocean has a tide of 22 feet (6.7 meters) and the Atlantic Ocean has a tide of only 8 inches (20.3 centimeters)?
● that the Wallace Line is not a new cruise company, but the scientific demarcation separating Asia and Oceania?
● that the average time for a ship to pass through the Panama Canal is eight hours? The fastest transit time was set by the *USS Manley* at 4 hours and 38 minutes.

brochures unfortunately do not indicate which ports are known to be anchor (tender) ports.

With almost 1 million cruise passengers a year visiting Alaska and several large resort ships likely to be in port on any given day, there's so much congestion in many of the small ports that avoiding crowded streets can be difficult. Even nature is retreating; with more people around, wildlife is harder to spot. And many of the same shops are now found in Alaska as well as in the Caribbean.

The more adventurous might consider one of the more unusual Alaska cruises to the far north, around the Pribilof Islands (superb for bird watching) and into the Bering Sea.

Finally, remember that Alaska isn't always good weather cruising – it can be very wet and windy and excursions may be canceled or changed.

Mexican Riviera cruises

These typically sail from Los Angeles or San Diego, along Mexico's west coast, calling at ports such as Cabo San Lucas, Mazatlan, Puerto Vallarta, Manzanillo, Ixtapa/Zihuatanejo, and Acapulco.

Route Canal (Transcanal cruises)

These take you through the Panama Canal, constructed by the United States after the failure of a French effort which began in 1882 with a labor force of over 10,000 but was plagued by disease and financial problems (over 22,000 people died). The US took over the building effort in 1904 and the waterway opened on August 15, 1914, shaving over 7,900 nautical miles off the distance between New York and San Francisco. The Panama Canal runs from *north-west* to *southeast* (not west to east), covering 51 miles (82 km) of locks and gates and dams.

Control of the canal passed from the US to Panama in 2000. The $6.0 billion widening of the canal and new locks, to be built by 2010, will double its capacity, enabling the latest large resort ships to use it.

Between the Caribbean and the Pacific, a ship is lifted 85 ft (26 meters) in a continuous flight of three steps at Gatun Locks to Gatun Lake through which it travels to Gaillard Cut where the Canal slices through the Continental Divide. It is lowered at Pedro Miguel Locks 31 ft (9.4 meters) in one step to Miraflores Lake, then the remaining two steps to sea level at Miraflores Locks before passing into the Pacific. Ships move through the locks under their own power, guided by towing locomotives. The 50-mile (80-km) trip takes 8–9 hours.

Panama Canal cruises typically depart from Fort Lauderdale or San Juan, calling at islands such as Aruba or Curacao before entering the canal and ending in Acapulco, Los Angeles, or San Francisco.

Australasia and Orient cruises

If you live in Europe or North America, be aware that the flight to your port of embarkation will be long. It's advisable to arrive at least two days before the cruise, as time changes and jet lag can be severe. The region has so much to offer that it's worth taking a cruise of at least 14 days. Australia, New Zealand, the islands of the South Pacific, Hong Kong, China, Japan, Indonesia, Malaysia, Singapore, Thailand, and Vietnam are all fascinating. ❏

Legend of the Seas passes along the Panama Canal.

Caribbean

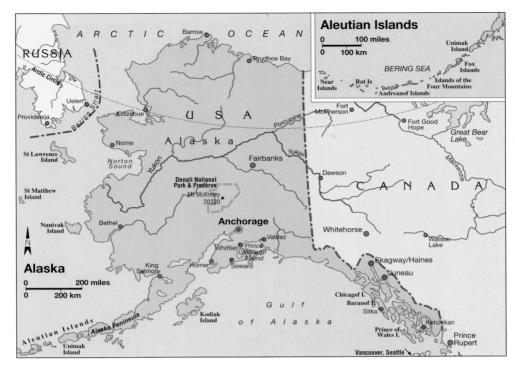

Aleutian Islands

Alaska

The Arctic

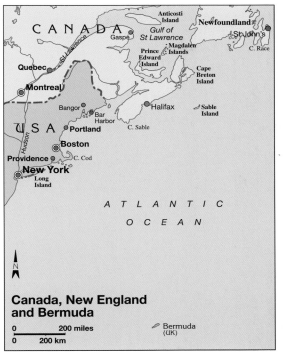

Canada, New England and Bermuda

0	200 miles
0	200 km

United Kingdom

0	200 km
0	200 miles

Australasia

0	500 km
0	500 miles

Western Mediterranean

Eastern Mediterranean

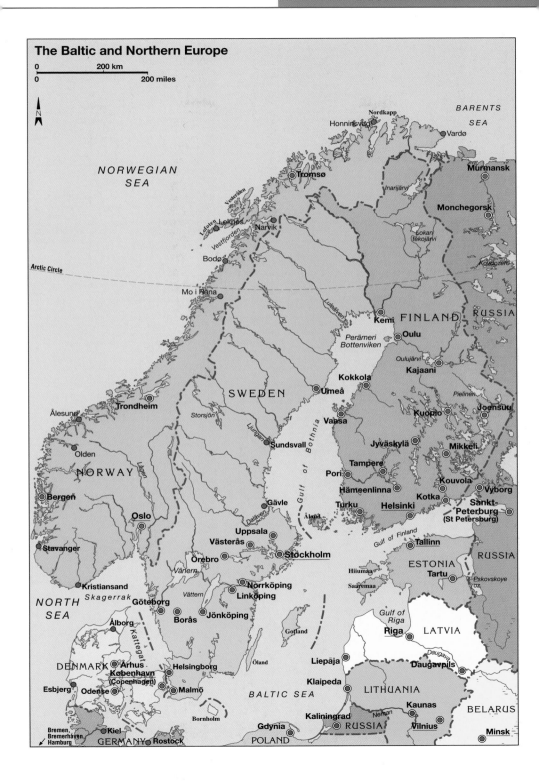

The Baltic and Northern Europe

0   200 km
0   200 miles

N

BARENTS SEA

Nordkapp

Honningsvåg

Vardø

NORWEGIAN SEA

Tromsø

Inarijärvi

Murmansk

Monchegorsk

Vesterålen

Lofoten Leknes

Narvik

Lokan (tekojärvi)

Vestfjorden

Bodø

Koudozero

Arctic Circle

Mo i Rana

Kemi **FINLAND** **RUSSIA**

Perämeri Bottenviken

Oulu

Luleälven

Oulujärvi

Kajaani

Kokkola

Pielinen

SWEDEN Umeå

Ålesund

Trondheim

Kuopio

Joensuu

Storsjön

Vaasa

Mikkeli

Ljungan

Jyväskylä

Olden

Sundsvall

Tampere

NORWAY

Lagen

Gulf of Bothnia

Pori

Hämeenlinna

Kouvola

Vyborg

Bergen

Gävle

Åland

Turku

Kotka

Helsinki

Sankt-Peterburg (St Petersburg)

Dalälven

Oslo

Uppsala

Väster ås

Gulf of Finland

Stavanger

Örebro

Stockholm

Tallinn

RUSSIA

Vänern

Hiiumaa

ESTONIA

Tartu

Kristiansand

Skagerrak

Göteborg

Vättern

Norrköping

Linköping

Saaremaa

Pskovskoye oz.

NORTH SEA

Ålborg

Borås

Jönköping

Gotland

Gulf of Riga

Riga

LATVIA

Öland

Liepāja

Daugava

Daugavpils

DENMARK Århus

København (Copenhagen)

Helsingborg

Klaipeda

LITHUANIA

Esbjerg Odense

Malmö

BALTIC SEA

Kaunas

BELARUS

Bornholm

Kaliningrad

Neman

Vilnius

Bremen, Bremerhaven, Hamburg

Kiel

GERMANY Rostock

Gdynia

RUSSIA

POLAND

Minsk

Africa

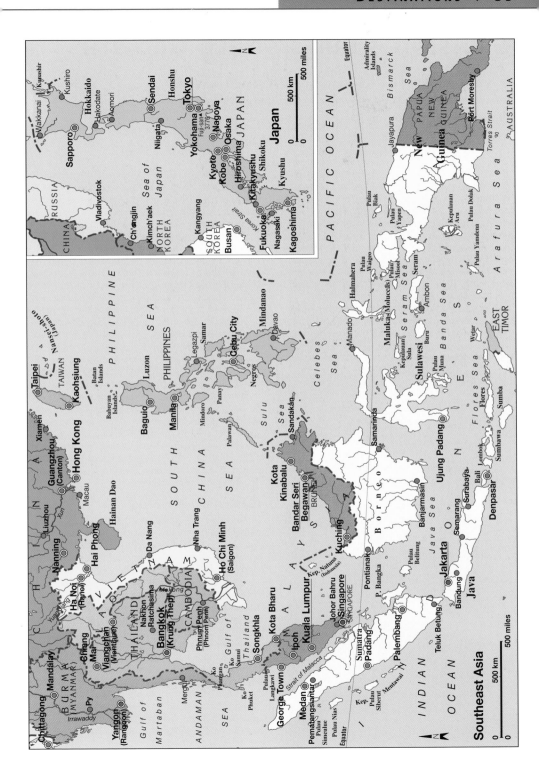

Southeast Asia

CRUISING'S IRRESISTIBLE GROWTH

Outpaced by jet aircraft, passenger liners semed destined for the scrapyard. Then they began transforming themselves into floating resorts

I n 1835, a curious advertisement appeared in the first issue of the *Shetland Journal*. Headed "To Tourists," it proposed an imaginary cruise from Stromness in Scotland, round Iceland and the Faroe Islands, and hinted at the pleasures of cruising under the Spanish sun in winter. Thus, it is said, the journal's founder, Arthur Anderson, invented the concept of cruising. Just two years later, Anderson, along with his partner Brodie Wilcox, founded the great Peninsular Steam Navigation Company (later to become P&O).

Soon after, Samuel Cunard started his transatlantic sailings, from Liverpool to Halifax, across the most dangerous ocean in the world, the North Atlantic,

BELOW AND RIGHT: classic Holland America Line posters.

with a steam-powered sailing vessel, *Britannia*, on July 4, 1840. Every year since then, except for the winter of 1970–1, a Cunard Line ship has operated scheduled transatlantic liner service between the old and new worlds.

Sailing for leisure soon caught on. Even writers such as William Makepeace Thackeray and Charles Dickens boarded ships for the excitement of the voyage, not just to reach a destination. The Victorians, having discovered tourism, promoted the idea widely. Indeed, Thackeray's account of his legendary voyage in 1844, from Cornhill to Grand Cairo by means of the P&O ships of the day, makes fascinating reading, as does the account by Dickens of his transatlantic crossing aboard a Cunard ship in 1842. The subject of Mark Twain's *The Innocents Abroad*, published in 1869, was Vanderbilt's *Quaker City*, which journeyed from New York to the Holy Land in 1867.

In the 1920s, cruising became the thing to do for the world's well-to-do. Being pampered in such grand style was fashionable – and is still the underlying concept of cruising. The ship took you and your belongings anywhere, and fed you, accommodated you, relaxed you, and entertained you. At the same time, it even catered for your servants – who, of course, accompanied you.

The first booze cruises

Cruising for Americans was helped greatly by Prohibition in the 1930s. After all, just a few miles out at sea, you were free to consume as much liquor as you wished. And cheap three- and four-day weekend "booze cruises" out of New York were preferable to "bathtub gin." Then came short "getaway" cruises, with destinations as well as alcohol. In time, the short cruise was to become one of the principal sources of profit for the steamship companies of the day.

In the 1930s a battle raged between the giant cruising companies of the world, as Britain, France, Germany, and the United States built liners of unprecedented luxury, elegance, glamour, and comfort. Each country was competing to produce the biggest and best afloat. For a time, quality was somehow related to smokestacks: the more a ship had the better. Although speed had always been a factor, particularly on the transatlantic run, it now became a matter of national pride and ambition.

The first ship designed specifically for cruising from the US after World War II was *Ocean Monarch* (Furness Withy & Company Ltd), which was awarded a gold medal by the US Academy of Designing for "outstanding beauty and unusual design features of a cruise ship." Its maiden voyage was from New York to Bermuda in 1951. I worked aboard the ship for a short time.

The birth of modern cruising

In June 1958, the first commercial jet aircraft flew across the Atlantic and altered the economics of transatlantic travel forever. It was the last year in which more passengers crossed the North Atlantic by sea than by air.

In the early 1960s, passenger-shipping directories listed over 100 passenger lines. Until the mid-1960s, it was cheaper to cross the Atlantic by ship than by plane, but the appearance of the jet aircraft changed that rapidly, particularly with the introduction of the Boeing 747 in the early 1970s. In 1962, more than 1 million people crossed the North Atlantic by ship; in 1970, that number was down to 250,000.

The success of the jumbo jets created a fleet of unprofitable and out-of-work passenger liners that appeared doomed for the scrap heap. Even the famous big "Queens," noted for their regular weekly transatlantic service, were at risk. Cunard White Star Line's *Queen Mary* (80,774 tons) was withdrawn in September 1967.

Cunard Line's sister ship *Queen Elizabeth*, at 83,673 tons the largest-ever passenger liner (until 1996), made its final crossing in November 1968.

Ships were sold for a fraction of their value. Many lines went out of business and ships were scrapped. Those that survived attempted to mix transatlantic crossings with voyages south to the sun. The Caribbean (including the Bahamas) became appealing, cruising became an alternative, and an entire new industry was born, with new lines being formed exclusively for cruising.

Then smaller, more specialized ships arrived, capable of getting into the tiny ports of developing Caribbean islands; there were no commercial airlines taking vacationers to the Caribbean then, and few hotels. Instead of cruising long distances south from more northerly ports such as New York, companies established their headquarters in Florida. This avoided the cold weather, choppy seas, and expense of the northern ports and saved fuel costs with shorter runs to the Caribbean.

Cruising was reborn. California became the base for cruises to the Mexican Riviera, and Vancouver on Canada's west coast became the focus for summer cruises to Alaska.

Flying passengers to embarkation ports was the next logical step, and soon a working relationship emerged between the cruise lines and the airlines. Air/sea and "sail and stay" packages thrived – joint cruise and hotel vacations with inclusive pricing. Some of the old liners came out of mothballs, purchased by emerging cruise lines and refurbished for warm-weather cruising operations, often with their interiors redesigned and refitted. During the late 1970s, the modern cruise industry grew at a rapid rate.

Cruising today

Today's cruise concept hasn't changed much from that of earlier days, although it has been improved, refined, expanded, and packaged for ease of consumption. No longer the domain of affluent, retired people, cruising today is vibrant and alive with passengers of *every* age and socio-economic background. It's no longer the shipping business, but the hospitality industry (although it has to be said that some cruise ship personnel appear to be in the hostility industry).

New ships are generally larger than their predecessors, yet cabin size is "standardized" to provide more space for entertainment and other public facilities. Today's ships boast air conditioning to keep out heat and humidity; stabilizers to keep the ship on an even keel; a high level of maintenance, safety, and hygiene; and more emphasis on health and fitness facilities.

Cruise ship design has moved from the traditional, classic, rounded profiles of the past (example: *Queen Elizabeth 2*) to boxy shapes with squared-off sterns and towering superstructures today (examples: *Celebrity Constellation, Celebrity Infinity, Celebrity Millennium, Celebrity Summit*).

While ship lovers lament these design changes, they have resulted from the need to squeeze as much as possible in the space provided (you can squeeze more in a square box than you can in a round one, though it may be less aesthetically appealing). But form followed function as ships changed from ocean transportation to floating vacation resorts.

Although ships have long been devoted to eating and relaxation in comfort, ships today offer more activities, and more learning and life-enriching

ABOVE AND RIGHT: classic cruising posters.

experiences than before. And there are many more places you can visit on a cruise: from Antarctica to Acapulco, Bermuda to Bergen, Dakar to Dominica, Shanghai to St. Thomas, or if you prefer, perhaps nowhere at all.

The cruise industry is a $60 billion business worldwide and still growing. It employs a growing number, both directly (there are over 100,000 shipboard officers, staff and crew, as well as about 20,000 employees in cruise company offices), and indirectly (suppliers of foodstuffs and mechanical and electrical parts, port agents, transport companies, destinations, airlines, railways, hotels, car rental companies). In 2006, more than 16 million people worldwide took a cruise, packaged and sold by cruise lines through tour operators and travel agents, or by direct bookings.

Cruising tomorrow

Current thinking in ship design follows two quite distinct paths: large resort ships or smaller ships.
● Large "resort" ships, where "economy of scale" helps the operator to keep the cost per passengers down. Six companies (Carnival Cruise Lines, Celebrity Cruises, Costa Cruises, Cunard Line, MSC Cruises, Princess Cruises, and Royal Caribbean International) have ships measuring over 100,000 tons, accommodating more than 5,000 passengers,

---

DID YOU KNOW?

● that the first vessel built exclusively for cruising was Hamburg-Amerika Line's two-funnel yacht, the 4,409-ton *Princessin Victoria Luise*? This luxury ship even included a private suite for the German kaiser.

● that the first ship to be fitted with real stabilizers (not an autogyro device) was the Peninsular & Oriental Steam Navigation Company's 1949-built 24,215-ton *Chusan*?

● that the first consecrated oceangoing Roman Catholic chapel aboard a passenger ship was in Compagnie Generale Transatlantique's *Ile de France* of 1928?

● that the latest life rafts called Hydrostatic Release Units (HRU), designed in Britain and approved by the Royal Navy, are now compulsory on all British-registered ships? Briefly, an HRU is capable of automatically releasing a life raft from its mountings when a ship sinks (even after it sinks) but can also be operated manually at the installation point, saving precious time in an emergency.

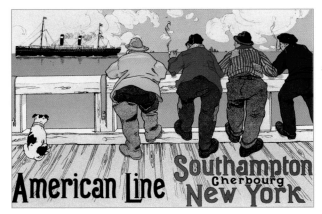

American Line   Southampton   Cherbourg   New York

with the "bigger is better" principle being pursued for all it's worth. Many of these ships are, however, too wide to transit the Panama Canal and so are designated non-Panamax.

● Small ships, where the "small is beautiful" concept has taken hold, particularly in the exclusive and luxury categories. Cruise lines offer high-quality ships of low capacity, which can provide a highly personalized range of quality services. This means better trained, more experienced staff (and more of them to serve fewer passengers), higher-quality food and more meals cooked to order. Small ships can also visit the less overcrowded ports.

Chop and stretch

Other cruise lines have expanded by "stretching" their ships. This is accomplished literally by cutting a ship in half, and inserting a newly constructed midsection, thus instantly adding more accommodation and public rooms, while maintaining the same draft.

Ships that have been "stretched" (with year and length of "stretch") include: *Albatros* (1983; 27.7meters), *Arielle* (1980; 26 meters), *Balmoral* (2007, 30 meters), *Black Watch* (1981, 27.7 meters), *Boudicca* (1982, 27.7 meters), *Braemar* (2008, 31.2 meters), *Costa Europa* (1990; 40 meters), *Enchantment of the Seas* (2005; 22.2 meters), *Norwegian Dream* (1998; 40 meters), *Norwegian Majesty* (1999; 30 meters), *Spirit of Adventure* (1986/20 meters), and *SuperStar Aquarius* (1998; 40 meters).

Whatever direction the design of cruise vessels takes in the future, ships are becoming increasingly environmentally friendly. With growing concern, particularly in eco-sensitive areas such as Alaska and the South Pacific, better safeguards against environmental pollution and damage are being built into the vessels. The cruise industry is fast approaching "zero discharge," which means that nothing is discharged into the world's oceans at any time. ❏

HOW A MODERN CRUISE SHIP IS BUILT

It is the job of the shipyard, its marine architects, consultants, interior designers, and a mass of specialist suppliers to turn those dreams and concepts into a ship without unduly straining the laws of naval architecture and safety regulations, not to mention budgets. Computers have simplified this complex process, although shipboard management and operations personnel often become frustrated with designers who are more idealistic than they are practical.

Ships represent a compromise between ideals and restrictions of space (particularly storage space) and finance, the solution being to design ships for specific areas and conditions of service.

Ships used to be constructed from the keel (backbone) up. Today they are built in huge sections, and joined together in an assembly area – typically as many as 100 sections for a resort ship such as *Carnival Freedom*, each

Holland America's *Maasdam* under construction.

section weighing up to 450 tons, most of which are extensively pre-outfitted. The sections may not even be constructed in the shipyard – simply assembled there. The design of today's ships is completely computer-based.

Formerly, passenger spaces were slotted in wherever there was space within a given hull. Today, computers provide targeted ship design, enabling a new ship to be built within two years instead of within the four or five years it would take in the 1950s.

Maximum noise and vibration levels

allowable in the accommodation spaces and recreation areas are stipulated in any owner's contract with the shipyard. Vibration tests are carried out once a ship is built and launched, using a finite method element of evaluation; this embraces analyses of prime sources of noise and excitation, namely the ship's propellers and main engines.

Prefabricated cabin modules, including in situ bathrooms complete with toilets and plumbing, are used today. When the steel structure of the relevant deck is ready, with main lines and insulation installed, cabin modules are then affixed to the deck, and power lines and sanitary plumbing are swiftly connected. All waste and power connections, together with hot/cold water mixing valves, are arranged in the service area of the bathroom and can be reached from the passageway outside the cabin for maintenance.

At the helm of the *Queen Mary*, withdrawn in 1967.

A Chronology of Modern Cruising

1960 Passenger shipping directories listed more than 30 companies operating transatlantic voyages. Many ships were laid up from 1960 to 1970, and most sold for a fraction of their value. *Britannic,* the last White Star Line ship, went out of service.
1962 Compagnie Générale Transatlantique's 1,035-ft liner *France*, (then the longest passenger ship ever built, entered service from Le Havre to New York. It was scrapped in 2007.
1963 Cunard Line's RMS *Queen Elizabeth* made an experimental cruise from New York to the West Indies. As a result, full air conditioning was fitted in 1965–66 to facilitate more extensive cruising.
1965 The Orient Steam Navigation Company was absorbed into the P&O Group. The new company became known as the Peninsular & Oriental Steam Navigation Company. Stanley B. McDonald founded Princess Cruises.
1966 The Norwegian company Klosters Reederei joined Miami businessman Ted Arison in marketing Caribbean cruises from Miami. Sanford Chobol founded Commodore Cruise Line.
1967 Cunard Line withdrew the transatlantic liner *Queen Mary* from service.
1968 Cunard Line's *Queen Elizabeth* withdrawn. Cunard delayed taking delivery of *Queen Elizabeth*

2 from its builder, John Brown, in December, because of unacceptable turbine vibration.
1969 Lars-Eric Lindblad's *Lindblad Explorer*, designed for close-in expedition cruising, made its debut. Royal Caribbean Cruise Line was created by a consortium of Norwegian shipping companies. The loss-making *United States* was laid up.
1970 Royal Viking Line was founded. Germany's Norddeutscher Lloyd and Hapag (Hamburg American Line) merged as Hapag-Lloyd.
1971 Cunard Line was sold to Trafalgar House Investments. Royal Cruise Line was founded.
1972 Ted Arison split with Knut Kloster and founded Carnival Cruise Lines. It began with just one ship, *Mardi Gras* (ex-*Empress of Canada*), which ran aground on its first voyage from Miami.
1974 P&O bought Princess Cruises. Compagnie Générale Transatlantique laid up the loss-making *France*. The Port Authority of New York and New Jersey opened its Passenger Ship Terminal. Royal Cruise Lines introduced *Golden Odyssey*, built to accommodate the 425 passengers of a Boeing 747 aircraft (425 passengers).
1975 *Island Princess* and *Pacific Princess* (Princess Cruises) became "stars" in the American television show *The Love Boat*.
1976 The Italian Line and Lloyd Triestino ceased transatlantic passenger operations.
1977 World Explorer Cruises was founded with

one ship, *Universe*. Holland America Line absorbed Monarch Cruise Lines.

1978 Royal Caribbean's *Song of Norway* was the first cruise ship to be given a "chop and stretch" operation to add a mid-section.

1979 American Hawaii Cruises was formed. In June, SS *France* was purchased by Lauritz Kloster, rebuilt for Caribbean cruises, renamed *Norway* and transferred to Norwegian Caribbean Lines. Peter Deilmann ordered his first new cruise ship, *Berlin*.

1980 Sea Goddess Cruises was founded by Helge Naarstad.

1981 Transatlantic service provided by Soviet-registered ships discontinued after a US embargo.

1982 The British government chartered Cunard's *Queen Elizabeth 2* and P&O Cruises' *Canberra* for use as troop carriers during the Falklands War between Argentina and Britain.

1983 P&O appointed Jeffrey Sterling as chairman in order to fend off an unwanted takeover bid by Cunard Line's owners, Trafalgar House, which purchased Norwegian America Cruises (NAC), together with *Sagafjord* and *Vistafjord*. Salen-Lindblad Cruising's *Lindblad Explorer* became the first passenger ship to navigate the Northwest Passage, sailing 4,790 miles (7,700 km) from Saint John's, Newfoundland, to Point Barrow, Alaska.

1984 Dolphin Cruise Line, Premier Cruise Lines, Regency Cruises, and Sundance Cruises were created. Windstar Sail Cruises re-launched commercial sail. Network TV advertising was used in the US for the first time, by Carnival Cruise Lines.

1985 The Chandris Group of Companies acquired Fantasy Cruises from GoGo Tours, renaming it Chandris Fantasy Cruises in the US and Chandris Cruises in the UK.

1986 Direct-dial satellite calls were introduced.

Signet Cruise Line was founded in Norway. Owing to a lawsuit brought by an American who claimed the right to the name Signet, the company became Seabourn Cruise Line in 1988. Eastern Cruise Lines, Western Cruise Lines, and Sundance Cruises merged to become Admiral Cruises. Cunard acquired Sea Goddess Cruises.

1987 Carnival Cruise Lines made its first public stock offering. *QE2* was converted from steam turbine to diesel-electric power. Princess Cruises replaced almost 500 unionized British hotel and catering staff aboard its five ships.

1988 Commodore Cruise Lines sold its *Bohème* (now *Freewinds*) to the Church of Scientology. Crystal Cruises was formed as a wholly-owned division of Japan's Nippon Yusen Kaisha (NYK). Princess Cruises merged with Sitmar Cruises. Royal Caribbean Cruise Line merged with Admiral Cruises to form Royal Admiral Cruises (later Royal Caribbean Cruises). Carnival Cruise Lines acquired Holland America Line, including its land-based hotel/transport operations and Windstar Cruises. Seabourn Cruise Line's first ship, *Seabourn Pride*, entered service.

1989 American Cruise Lines, which operated small vessels for intracoastal cruising, ceased operations. The Chandris Group of Companies created Celebrity Cruises. Renaissance Cruises was created by Fearnley & Eger, a 120-year-old Oslo-based shipping concern, to build eight small premium ships. The Panama Canal celebrated its 75th birthday. Lindblad Travel went bankrupt.

1990 At the start of the Gulf War, the US government chartered *Cunard Princess* for six months as

Goodbye to SS *France* as it is laid up in 1974. It was later renamed *Norway* and was broken up in 2007–8.

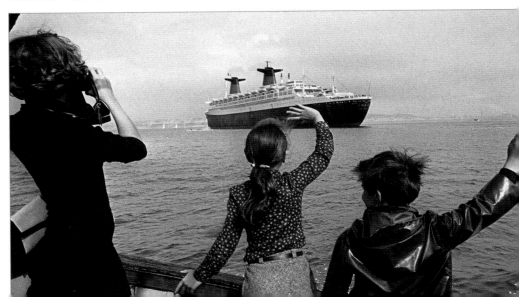

a rest and relaxation center for US service personnel in the Bahrain.

1991 Carnival Cruise Lines acquired a 25 percent stake in Seabourn Cruise Line. Renaissance Cruises was sold to an international group of investors. Effjohn International purchased Crown Cruise Line. Seawind Cruise Line commenced cruise operations. Nippon Yusen Kaisha (NYK) purchased Salen Lindblad Cruising.

1992 Admiral Cruises (two ships) ceased operations. Carnival Cruise Lines deployed *Mardi Gras* to accommodate 600 staff members made homeless by the Hurricane Andrew. The Chandris Group and Overseas Shipholding Group (OSG) agreed to form a joint venture company, Celebrity Cruise Lines, Inc. Chargeurs and Accor, the French property and leisure industries group, bought 23% of Costa Crociere, parent of Costa Cruises.

1993 Carnival Cruise Lines formed Fiesta Marina Cruises for the Spanish-speaking Latin American market; it failed. George Poulides founded Festival Cruises. *Frontier Spirit* was returned to its Japanese owners and then chartered as *Bremen* to Germany's Hanseatic Tours. Star Cruises was founded.

1994 Trafalgar House, Cunard Line's parent, agreed to buy the rights to the name Royal Viking Line, together with *Royal Viking Sun. Royal Viking Queen* went to Royal Cruise Line, becoming *Queen Odyssey* and later *Seabourn Legend*. Radisson Diamond Cruises and Seven Seas Cruise Line merged to become Radisson Seven Seas Cruises. Star Cruises was founded by Genting Group.

1995 British company Airtours purchased *Southward* from Norwegian Cruise Line and *Nordic Prince* from Royal Caribbean Cruises.

1996 Kloster Cruise (parent of Norwegian Cruise Line and Royal Cruise Line) closed its Royal Cruise Line division. Cunard (and parent company Trafal-

gar House) were bought by Kvaerner.

1997 Hapag-Lloyd acquired Hanseatic Tours, together with its expedition ship, *Hanseatic*. Carnival Corporation, jointly with Airtours, purchased Costa Cruises. Royal Caribbean International bought Celebrity Cruises for $1.3 billion. P&O Cruises' *Canberra* was sent to Pakistan for scrap.

1998 Australia repealed its cabotage laws, allowing international cruise ships to dock and operate from Australian ports without restrictions. Kvaerner sold Cunard for $500 million to a consortium that included Carnival Corporation.

1999 Crown Cruise Line was reintroduced as an upscale part of Commodore Cruise Line. It chartered *Crown Dynasty* and later purchased the ship for $86.2 million.

2000 Star Cruises took full control of Norwegian Cruise Line (including Orient Lines) after buying the outstanding shares held by Carnival Corporation. P&O Group separated its cruising activities from the rest of the group. Costa Cruises became 100% owned by Carnival Corporation. Canaveral Cruise Lines (one ship), Commodore Cruise Lines (two ships), Crown Cruise Line (one ship), Delfin Cruises (two ships), and Norwegian Capricorn Line (one ship), Premier Cruise Line (7 ships) and Sun Cruises (three ships) ceased operations.

2001 Spain's Pullmantur bought *Oceanic* and *Seawind Crown* for the Spanish-speaking market. Carnival Corporation sold its 25.1% shareholding in Airtours. Renaissance Cruises (10 ships) ceased operations after the September 11 terrorist attacks on the US. So did American Hawaii Cruises, United States Lines, Delta Queen Coastal Cruises, Hyundai Asan, and Leisure Cruises.

2002 Empress Cruise Lines (one ship) and Valtur Tourism (one ship) ceased operations. SeaDream Yacht Club began with *SeaDream I* and *SeaDream II*. Golden Sun Cruises became Golden Star Cruises with

Micky Arison, boss of the Carnival Corporation congomerate. His father, Ted Arison, founded the company in 1972.

Queen Elizabeth 2, Queen Mary 2 and *Queen Victoria* together in Southampton for the last time in 2008 before *QE2* retired to become a floating hotel in Dubai.

one ship, *Aegean I*. P&O Cruises created *Ocean Village* for a younger market.

2003 Oceania Cruises was founded by Frank del Rio and Joe Watters, with two ships, *Insignia* and *Regatta*. Regal Cruises (one ship) and Sun Bay Cruises (two ships) ceased operations. Mauritius Island Cruises was founded with two ships, *Island Sky* and *Island Sun*. NCL America launched its US-flag operation.

2004 Carnival Corporation and P&O Princess plc merged to become the world's largest cruise company, with more than 60 ships and 13 brands. Festival Cruises ceased operations; its six ships were impounded and auctioned. Royal Olympia Cruises also suffered the same fate (but recovered, albeit with a smaller fleet), a victim of high ship and operating costs. Australian tour operator Around the World Cruises (one ship) and Mare Nostrum Cruises (one ship) ceased operations.

2005 Orion Expedition Cruises launchedwith one ship, *Orion*. Royal Olympia Cruises (two ships), Siam Cruise (one ship), Spanish Cruise Line (one ship), My Travel/Sun Cruises (four ships) and Mauritius Island Cruises (two ships) ceased operations.

2006 Radisson Seven Seas Cruises became Regent Seven Seas Cruises. Royal Caribbean International bought Pullmantur. Abou Merhi Cruises ceased operations; its ship, *Orient Queen*, was acquired by Louis Cruise Lines. Glacier Bay Cruiseline ceased operations (two ships). Holiday Kreutzfahrten (Holiday Cruises) ceased operations. Pearl Seas Cruises was founded by Charles Robertson (American Cruise Lines) for international cruises, with two ships on order. CLIA (Cruise Lines International Organization) and ICCL (International Council of Cruise Lines) merged into CLIA, and moved to Miami.

2007 Carnival Corporation sold Swan Hellenic Cruises to the UK's Lord Sterling. Carnival Corpora-

tion acquired 75% of Spain-based Iberostar Cruises (now Iberocruceros), sold Windstar Cruises to Ambassadors International for $100 million, and entered into a joint venture with Germany's TUI. Caspi Cruises (one ship) ceased operations. Louis Cruise Lines' *Sea Diamond* ran aground and sank off Santorini. Oceania Cruises was bought for $850 million by equity group Apollo Management. Celebrity Cruises created a sub-brand, Azamara Cruises. *Queen Elizabeth 2* was sold for £50 million ($100 million) to a state investment company in Dubai, to become a floating hotel and museum. Royal Caribbean created CDF Croisières de France. Quark Expeditions and its fleet of ships (both owned and chartered), was acquired by First Choice, co-owners (with RCCL) of Island Cruises. Regent Seven Seas Cruises was acquired by Apollo Management for around $1 billion. Windjammer Barefoot Cruises ceased operations in October; its four ships (*Legacy, Mandalay, Polynesia* and *Yankee Clipper*) left passengers and crew stranded in the Caribbean and South America. Clipper Cruise Line, Travelscope Cruises and Globalia's Travelplan Cruceros ceased operations.

2008 Van Gogh Cruises (Club Cruise) was formed to take over the former Travelscope Cruises, but soon ceased operations. CDF Croisières de France started operations with one ship *(Bleu de France)*. Fred Olsen Cruise Lines "stretched" its Braemar by 102ft (31.2 meters). Carnival Cruise Lines' *Celebration* became *Grand Celebration* for Spain's Iberocruceros. Almost all cruise lines added or increased their fuel surcharges to future cruises in the face of rising oil prices. ❏

WHO GOES CRUISING

The Maritime Evaluations Group has analyzed by nationality the breakdown of passengers choosing to take an oceangoing cruise vacation:

United States	11,350,000
UK	1,337,000
Germany	763,000
Asia (not including Japan)	600,000
Italy	640,000
Spain	518,000
Australia/New Zealand	292,750
Canada	300,000
France	252,000
Greece	104,000
Rest of Europe/Scandinavia	250,000
Japan	180,000
Cyprus *	75,000
Freighter Passengers	3,000
Total	**16,661,750**

* Local Cyprus market only.

Note: The above numbers do not include the approximately 1 million passengers who took a river/inland waterway cruise, nor the 300,000 passengers who took a coastal sailing aboard the the the Hurtigruten (Norwegian Coastal Voyages) ships. All figures are for 2007.

LIFE ABOARD

This A to Z survey covers the astonishing range of facilities that modern cruise ships offer and tells you how to make the most of them

Air-conditioning

Cabin temperature can be regulated by an individually controlled thermostat, so you can adjust it to suit yourself. Public room temperatures are controlled automatically. Air temperatures are often kept cooler than you may be used to. Note that in some ships, the air-conditioning cannot be turned off.

Art auctions

Beware of these. Aboard most large resort ships, intrusive art auctions form part of the "entertainment" program, with flyers, brochures, and forceful announcements that almost demand that you attend. They may be fun participation events – though the "free champagne" given to entice you is mostly sparkling wine and *not* champagne – but don't expect to purchase an heirloom, as most of the art pieces (lithographs and seriographs) are rubbish. It's funny how so many identical pieces can be found aboard so many ships.

Note that art "appraisal prices" are done in-house by the art provider, a company that *pays* a cruise line to be onboard. Watch out for the words: "retail replacement value". Also, listen for phrases such as "signed in the stone" – it means that the artists did not sign the work – or "pochoire" (a stencil print less valuable than an original etching or lithograph). If you do buy something, do so because it will look good hanging on your wall, not as an investment. But read the fine print, and buy only with caution.

Baby-sitting

In some ships, stewards, stewardesses, and other staff may be available as babysitters for an hourly fee. Make arrangements at the reception desk. Aboard some ships, evening baby-sitting services may not start until late; check times and availability before you book a cruise.

Beauty salon/Barber shop

Make appointments as soon after boarding as possible, particularly on short cruises. Appointment times fill up rapidly, especially before social events such as a captain's cocktail party. Charges are comparable to those

ashore. Typical services: haircut for men and women, styling, permanent waving, coloring, manicure, pedicure, leg waxing. *See Shipboard Spas, page 60–65.*

Cashless cruising

It is now the norm to settle your account with one payment (by cash or credit card) before disembarking on the last day. An imprint of your credit card is taken at embarkation or when you register online, permitting you to sign for everything. Before the end of the cruise, a detailed statement is delivered to your cabin. Some cruise lines, irritatingly, may discontinue their "cashless" system for the last day of the cruise. Some may add a "currency conversion service charge" to your credit card account if it is not in the currency of the cruise line.

Ships visiting a "private island" on a Bahamas or general Caribbean itinerary will probably ask you to pay cash for beverages, water sports and scuba diving gear, and other items that you purchase ashore.

Casino gaming

Many cruise ships have casinos, where the range of table games includes blackjack or 21, Caribbean stud poker, roulette, craps, and baccarat. Under-18s are not allowed in casinos, and photography is usually banned inside them. Customs regulations mean that casinos generally don't open when the ship is in port. Gaming casino oper-

LEFT: dining aboard *Voyager of the Seas*.
RIGHT: an art auction aboard *Noordam*.

Roulette tables in *Queen Mary 2*'s Empire Casino.

ations aboard cruise ships are unregulated. However, some companies, such as Celebrity Cruises and Royal Caribbean International, abide by Nevada Gaming Control Board regulations. Most table games have a $5 minimum and $200 maximum – but, for serious players, Carnival Cruise Lines' casinos have blackjack tables with a $25 minimum and $500 maximum.

Some cruise lines have "private gaming club" memberships, with regular newsletters, rebates and special offers (example: Star Cruises). Slot machines are also in evidence and make more than half a casino's profits.

Note that, for American citizens and resident aliens in the US, slot machine winnings may be subject to WG-2 tax withholding.

Comment cards

On the last day of the cruise you will be asked to fill out a company "comment card." Some lines offer "incentives" such as a bottle of champagne. Be truthful, as the form serves as a means of communication between you and the cruise line. Pressure from staff to write "excellent" for everything is rampant but, unless you highlight problems you have encountered, things are less likely to improve.

Daily program

This contains a useful list of the day's activities, entertainment, and social events. It is normally delivered to your cabin the evening before the day that it covers.

Departure Tax

If you are disembarking in a foreign port and flying home, there could be a departure tax to pay, in local currency, at the airport.

Disembarkation

This can be the most trying part of any cruise. The cruise director will already have given an informal talk on customs, immigration, and disembarkation procedures. The night before the ship reaches its destination, you will be given a customs form. Include any duty-free items, whether purchased aboard or ashore. Save the receipts in case a customs officer asks for them.

The night before arrival, place your main baggage outside your cabin on retiring, or before 2am. It will be collected and off-loaded on arrival. Leave out fragile items, liquor, and the clothes you intend to wear for disembarkation and onward travel – it is amazing just how many people pack absolutely everything. Anything left in your cabin will be considered hand luggage to be hand-carried off when you leave.

On disembarkation day, breakfast will probably be early. It might be better to miss breakfast and sleep later, providing announcements on the ship's public address system do not wake you (it may be possible to turn off such announcements). Even worse than early breakfast

Disembarkation is seldom a delightful experience.

is the fact that aboard many ships you will be commanded – requested, if you are lucky – to leave your cabin early, only to wait in crowded public rooms, sometimes for hours. To add insult to injury, your cabin steward – after he has received his tip, of course – will knock on the door to take the sheets off the bed so the cabin can be made up for the incoming passengers. This will not happen aboard the smaller "upscale" ships.

Some companies now offer a slightly more relaxed system that allows you to stay in your cabin as long as they wish, or until your tag color is called, instead of waiting in public areas, where it's difficult to avoid the mass of wheeled luggage waiting to trip you up.

Before leaving the ship, remember to claim any items you have placed in your in-cabin personal safe. Passengers cannot go ashore until all baggage has been offloaded, and customs and/or immigration inspections or pre-inspections have been carried out. In most ports, this takes two to three hours after arrival. It is wise to leave at least three hours from the time of arrival to catch a connecting flight or other transportation. Once off the ship, you identify your baggage on the pier before going through customs inspection. Porters may be there to assist you.

Duty-free liquor purchases

If you buy a box of "duty-free" liquor in the Caribbean, it will be taken from you at the gangway as you reboard and given back to you the day before you disembark. Also, be aware that if you fly home from a US airport after your cruise, you are not permitted to take any liquid items larger than 100ml in your hand luggage. Unless you place the liquor in your checked baggage, there's no point purchasing it – it will be confiscated.

Engine room

For insurance and security reasons, visits to the engine room are seldom allowed. Some ships may have a technical information leaflet. Aboard others, a Behind the Scenes video may be shown on cabin TV system.

Gift shops

The gift shop/boutique/drugstore offers souvenirs, gifts, toiletries, logo and duty-free items, as well as a basic stock of essential items. Opening hours are posted at the store and in the Daily Program.

Internet access and email

Most large resort ships have internet access, for a fee. This can be slow, due to uplink/downlink to satellites, and the fact that ships often move out of the satellite's "footprint." Charges are typically 50–75 cents per minute, although bulk packages of 30, 60, or 100 minutes may be available. If you can wait, an internet café ashore will be faster and cheaper. Almost all large resort ships have wi-fi for your computer or cell phone. You can send and receive emails – but at a price, because all internet connection is via satellite.

Launch (shore tender) services

Enclosed or open motor launches ("tenders") are used when your cruise ship is unable to berth at a port or island. In such cases, a regular launch service is operated between ship and shore for the duration of the port call.

When stepping on or off a tender, extend "forearm to forearm" to the person who is assisting you. Do not grip their hands because this has the unintentional effect of immobilizing the helper.

Laundry and dry cleaning

Most ships offer a full laundry and pressing service. Some ships may in addition offer dry cleaning facilities. A detailed list of services, and prices, can be found in your cabin. Your steward will collect and deliver your clothes.

Some ships have self-service launderettes, well equipped with washers, dryers, and ironing facilities. There may be a charge for washing powder and for the use of the machines.

The cyber café aboard *MSC Poesia*.

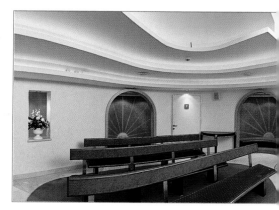

LEFT: the library aboard Cunard Line's *Queen Victoria*.
ABOVE: the Skylight Chapel, *Mariner of the Seas*.

Books. Aboard most other ships a member of the cruise staff or entertainment staff – with little knowledge of books – staffs the library. The library may also have board games such as Scrabble, backgammon and chess.

Lido

This is a deck devoted to swimming pools, hot tubs, showers, and recreation. Aboard most cruise ships, it has a self-serve buffet.

Library

Most cruise ships have a library offering a good selection of books, reference material, and periodicals. A small, refundable deposit may be required when you borrow a book. Aboard small luxury ships, the library is open 24 hours a day, and no deposit is required. Aboard the large resort ships, the library may be open only a couple of hours a day. *Aurora, Oriana, QM2* and *Queen Victoria* are examples of ships with full-time, qualified librarians sourced by the specialist company Ocean

Lost property

Contact the reception desk immediately if you lose or find something on the ship. Notices regarding lost and found property may be posted on the bulletin boards.

Mail

You can buy stamps and mail letters aboard most ships, at the reception desk. Some ships use the postal

P IS FOR PET PEEVES – AND HERE ARE 30 OF THE MOST COMMON

❶ Long lines and waiting periods for disembarkation.
❷ The appalling number of merchandising flyers that come under the cabin door.
❸ Tiny tub chairs (for size-challenged passengers).
❹ Aboard most ships, 15 percent is automatically added to wine bills. Thus, a wine waiter makes much more money on a more expensive bottle of wine, whether he knows anything about that wine (or how to decant and serve it) or not. For doing the same job for a wine costing $125 as for one costing $15 he makes a lot more. Insist on adding your own gratuity, and politely refuse to be told how much you have to tip.
❺ Cruise brochures that use models, and provide the anticipation of an onboard product that a ship cannot deliver; the result is disappointment for passengers.
❻ Cruise brochures that state that their ship has a "small ship feel, big ship choice" when it really caters to more than 2,000 passengers (often more than 3,000).

❼ Aboard large resort ships, getting Cabin Services, or the "Guest Relations Desk," or an Operator to answer the telephone can be an exercise in frustration, patience, and gross irritation.
❽ Constant, irritating, and repetitive announcements for bingo, horse racing, art auctions, and the latest gizmos for sale in the shops.
❾ "Elevator" music playing continuously in passageways and on open decks (even worse: rock and rap music).
❿ Any announcement that is repeated. Any announcement that is repeated.
⓫ In-cabin announcements at any time, except for emergencies; they are completely unnecessary for programmed events and shore excursions.
⓬ Flowers in one's cabin that are not watered or refreshed by the steward(ess).
⓭ Bathrobes provided but never changed during the cruise.

privileges and stamps of their flag of registration, while others buy local stamps at ports of call. Mail is usually taken ashore by the ship's port agent just before the ship sails. You will receive a list of port agents and mailing addresses with your tickets and documents, so you can advise friends and family how they can send mail to you.

News and sports bulletins

The world's news and sports results are reported in the ship's newspaper or placed on a bulletin board near the reception desk or in the library. For sports results not listed, inquire at the reception desk.

Photographs

Professional photographers take digital pictures of passengers during embarkation and throughout the cruise. They cover all the main events and social functions, such as the captain's cocktail party. The pictures can be viewed without any obligation to purchase, but the prices may surprise. The cost is likely to exceed $10

for a postcard-sized photograph, and a 10 x 8-inch embarkation photo aboard *Queen Mary 2* will set you back a whopping $27.50.

Postcards and writing paper

These are available from the writing room, the library, or the purser's office/reception desk. Some cruise lines charge for them.

Reception desk

This is also known as the Purser's Office, guest relations, or information desk. Centrally located, it is the nerve center of the ship for general passenger information and problems. Opening hours – in some ships, 24 hours a day – are posted outside the office and given in the Daily Program.

Religious services

Interdenominational services are conducted on board, usually by the captain or staff captain. A few older ships and Costa Cruises' ships have a small private chapel.

❹ Mini-bar/refrigerators that do not provide limes and lemons for drink mixes.

❺ Skimpy towels.

❻ Garnishes, when "parsley with everything" seems to be the rule of the seagoing entrée experience.

❼ Baked Alaska parades.

❽ Paper, plastic, or polystyrene plastic cups for drinks of any kind.

❾ Paper napkins for meals or informal buffets; they should be linen or cotton.

⓴ Plastic plates, often too small, for buffets.

㉑ Buffets where only cold plates are available, even for hot food items.

㉒ Repetitious breakfast and luncheon buffets and uncreative displays.

㉓ Shopping lecturers, shopping videos, art auctions, and carpet auctions.

㉔ Artwork placed aboard ships, but with the cruise line

not caring or knowing enough about it to place the name of the artist and the year of creation alongside, whether it is a painting or a sculpture.

㉕ Shore-side porters who take your bags when you get off the bus, or out of your car, then stand there until you tip them before they move your bags or drop them (worst ports: Ft. Lauderdale and Miami).

㉖ Cabin stewards/stewardesses who place small folded pieces of paper in cabin door frames to show when their passengers have left their cabins.

㉗ Audiovisual technicians who think that the volume level of the show should equal that for a major rock concert.

㉘ Private island days, when the tender ride to get to the island is longer than the flight to get to the ship.

㉙ Ships that ask you to settle your shipboard account before the morning of disembarkation.

㉚ The use of cellphones in ships' public rooms.

Denominational services may be taken by clergy traveling as passengers.

Room service

Beverages and snacks are available at most times. Liquor is normally limited to the opening hours of the ship's bars. Some ships may charge for room service.

Sailing time

In each port of call, sailing and all-aboard times are posted at the gangway. The all-aboard time is usually half an hour before sailing. If you miss the ship, it's entirely your responsibility to get to the next port of call to re-join the vessel.

Shipboard etiquette

Here are a few points that are sometimes overlooked:
● In public rooms, smoking and nonsmoking sections are available. In the dining room, cigar and pipe smoking are banned.
● If you take a video camera with you, be aware that international copyright laws will prohibit you from recording any of the professional entertainment shows.
● It is all right to be casual but not to enter a ship's dining room in just a bathing suit, or with bare feet.
● If you are uncomfortable eating with the typical 10-piece dining room cutlery setting, some cruise lines have introduced etiquette classes to help you.

Shopping

Many cruise lines operating in Alaska, the Bahamas, the Caribbean, and the Mexican Riviera engage an outside company that provides the services of a "shopping lecturer." This person promotes "selected" shops, goods, and services heavily, fully authorized by the cruise line (which receives a commission). This relieves the cruise director of responsibility, together with any questions concerning his involvement, credibility, and financial remuneration. Shopping maps, with "selected" stores highlighted, are placed in your cabin, and sometimes include a guarantee of satisfaction valid for 30 days.

During shore excursions, be wary of stores recommended by tour guides – they may be receiving commissions from the merchants. Shop around before you buy. Good hints and recommendations are often given in the port lecture at the start of your cruise. When buying local handicrafts, make sure they have indeed been made locally. Be wary of "bargain-priced" name brands, as they may be counterfeit. For watches, check the guarantee.

The ship's shops are also duty-free and, for the most part, competitive in price. The shops on board are closed while in port, however, due to international customs regulations. Worthwhile discounts are often offered on the last day of the cruise.

Swimming pools

Most ships have outdoor or indoor swimming pools, or both. They may be closed in port owing to local health regulations or cleaning requirements. Diving is not allowed – pools are shallow.

Parents should note that most pools are unsupervised. Some ships use excessive chlorine or bleaching agent; these could cause bathing suit colors to run.

Telephone calls

Most ships have a direct-dial satellite telephone system, so you can call from your cabin to anywhere in the world. All ships have an internationally recognized call sign, a combination of letters and digits. Satellite calls can also be made when the ship is in port. Satellite telephone calls cost between US$5 and $15 a minute, depending on the type of equipment the ship carries, and are charged to your onboard account.

To reach any ship dial the International Direct Dial (IDD) code for the country you are calling from, followed by the ship's telephone number.

Anyone without a direct-dial telephone should call the High Seas Operator (in the United States, dial 1-800-SEA-CALL). The operator will need the name of the ship, together with the ocean code (Atlantic East is 871; Pacific is 872; Indian Ocean is 873; Atlantic West/ Caribbean/US is 874).

Television

Programming is obtained from a mixture of satellite feeds and onboard videos. Some ships lock on to live international news programs such as CNN or BBC World, or to text-only news services. Satellite TV recep-

Shopping on a shore excursion on RCI's Labadee Island, Haiti.

tion can be poor because ships constantly move out of the narrow beam transmitted from the satellite.

Tipping

Gratuities, at about $10 per person, per day, are added automatically to onboard accounts by almost all the major cruise lines. Gratuities are included in the cruise fare aboard a small number of ships, principally those in the luxury end of the market, where no extra tipping is permitted – at least in theory.

In some ships, subtle suggestions are made regarding tips; in others, cruise directors get carried away and dictate rules. Although some cruise brochures state "tipping is not required," it will be expected by the staff.

Here are the accepted industry guidelines: dining room waiter, $3–$4 per person per day; busboy (assistant waiter), $1.50–$2 per day; cabin steward or stewardess, $3–$3.50 per person per day; Butler: $5–$6 per person per day. Tips are normally given on the last evening of a cruise of up to 14 days' duration. For longer cruises, you would hand over half of the tip halfway through and the rest on your last evening. Aboard many ships, a gratuity of 10 or 15 percent is automatically added to your bar check, whether you get good service or not, and to spa treatments.

Valuables

Most ships have a small personal safe in each cabin, but items of special value should be kept in a safety deposit box in the purser's office. This is accessible during the cruise.

Water sports

Some small ships have a water sports platform that is lowered from the ship's stern or side. These ships carry windsurfers, water-ski boats, jet skis, water skis, and scuba and snorkel equipment, usually at no extra charge. Some may have an enclosed swimming "cage" if local fish are unwelcoming.

Such facilities look good in brochures, but

Some small ships provide free scuba diving equipment.

ships are often reluctant to use them. This is because many itineraries have too few useful anchor ports. Also, the sea must be in an almost flat calm condition – seldom the case. Insurance regulations can be restrictive too.

Wine and liquor

The cost of drinks on board is generally lower than on land, since ships have access to duty-free liquor. Drinks may be ordered in the dining room, at any of the ship's bars, or from room service. Dining rooms have extensive and reasonably priced wine lists.

Some ships sell duty-free wine and liquor to drink in your cabin. You can not normally bring these into the dining room or public rooms, nor any duty-free wine or liquor bought in port. These rules protect bar sales, a substantial source of onboard revenue. ❏

Service staff on most cruise ships rely on receiving tips.

CUISINE

Anyone wanting to eat 24 hours a day could do so aboard many ships, and the variety of food would keep boredom at bay

Rubberized duck, rock-hard lobster, brittle pizza, elasticized croissants, grenade-quality fruit, coffee that tastes like army surplus paint… you can find all this and more in the cruise industry's global cafeteria. On the other hand, you can enjoy the finest caviar and vintage champagne. The message to remember is this: generally speaking, as in most restaurants on land, you get what you pay for.

High-quality food ingredients cost money, so it's pointless expecting low-cost cruises to offer anything other than low-cost food. It's not that the cruise lines don't try. They know that you will spend more time eating on board than doing anything else, so their intention is to cater as well as they can to your palate while keeping the cruise price competitive. They even boast about their food, but the reality is that meals aboard most ships are not gourmet affairs. How could they be when a kitchen has to turn out hundreds of meals at the same time? Most of the cuisine compares favorably with "banquet" food in a family restaurant – in other words, often

tasteless. What you will find, therefore, is a good selection of palatable, pleasing, and complete meals served in comfortable surroundings. Maybe you will even dine by candlelight, which at least creates some atmosphere.

Fresh versus frozen

Aboard low-priced cruises, you will typically be served portion-controlled frozen food that has been reheated. Fresh fish and the best cuts of meats cost the cruise lines more, and that cost is reflected in the cruise price. Aboard some ships, the "fresh" fish – often described as "Catch of the Day" (but *which* day?) – has clearly had no contact with the sea for quite some time.

Sushi bars are the latest fad but, in 90% of cases, fish used in sushi (with rice) is cooked, and raw (sashimi-style, without rice) fish is not available, as storage and preparation facilities are inadequate. The only ships with authentic sushi bars and authentic sushi/ sashimi are *Asuka II*, *Crystal Serenity*, *MSC Musica* and *MSC Poesia*.

Note also that many items of "fresh" fruit may have been treated with 1-MCP (methylcyclopropene) to make them last longer – apples, for example, may be up to a year old.

A typical day

From morning till night, food is offered to the point of overkill, even aboard the most modest cruise ship. Aboard the large resort ships, pizzas, hamburgers, hot dogs, ice-cream and frozen yoghurt are almost always available. And if you're still hungry, there's 24-hour room service. Some ships also have extra-charge cafés and patisseries.

If you prefer to eat at set times rather than graze, these are the options:
● **6am:** hot coffee and tea on deck for early risers (or late-to-bed types).
● **Full breakfast:** typically with as many as 60 different items, in the main dining room. For a more casual meal, you can serve yourself buffet-style at an indoor/outdoor deck café, although the choice may be more restricted.
● **Lunchtime:** with service in the dining room, buffet-style at a casual café, or at a separate grill for hot dogs and hamburgers, and a pizzeria, where you can watch the cooking.
● **4pm:** Afternoon tea, in the British tradition, complete with finger sandwiches and cakes. This may be served in a main lounge to the accompa-

Some ship restaurants try to match fine dining ashore.

Dining as theater aboard RCI's *Explorer of the Seas*.

niment of live music (it may even be a "tea-dance") or recorded classical music.

● **Dinner:** the main event of the evening, and apart from the casualness of the first and last nights, it is generally formal in style.

● **Light Bites:** sometimes served in public rooms late at night. These have mostly replaced the traditional midnight buffet.

● **Gala Midnight Buffet:** It's almost extinct, but if there is one, it is usually held on the penultimate evening of a cruise when the chefs pull out all the stops. It features a grand, colorful spread, with much intricate decoration that can take up to 48 hours to prepare.

Seating arrangments

On ships with open seating, you can sit at any available table, with whomever you wish, at any time within dining room opening hours – just like going out to a restaurant ashore. On ships without open seating, unless you are with your own family or group of friends, you will be seated next to strangers. It is the responsibility of the restaurant manager – who is also known as the maître d'hôtel – to seat you with compatible fellow passengers. If a reservation has been arranged prior to boarding, you will find a table assignment/seating card in your cabin when you embark. If not, make your reservation with the restaurant manager or one of his assistants as soon as you embark.

Tables for two are a rarity; most tables seat four, six, or eight. It is a good idea to ask in advance to be seated at a larger table, because if you are a couple seated at a table for four and you don't get along with your table partners, there is no one else to talk to. And remember, if the ship is full, it may be difficult to change tables once the cruise has started.

Depending on the size of the ship, it may have one, two or four seatings:

● **Single Seating:** you can choose when you wish to eat (within dining room hours) but have the same table assigned for the cruise.

● **Two Seatings:** you are assigned (or choose) one of two seatings, early or late. Typical meal times for two-seating ships are: Breakfast: 6.30am–8.30am; Lunch: 12 noon–1.30pm; Dinner: 6.30pm–8.30pm.

Some ships operate two seatings for all meals and some just for dinner. Dinner hours may vary when the ship is in port to allow for the timing of shore excursions. Ships that operate in Europe and the Mediterranean or in South America may have later meal times.

● **Four Seatings:** Only Carnival Cruise Lines operates four seatings – with dinner, for example,

THE RISE OF CELEBRITY CHEFS

Several cruise lines have signed up well-known chefs to devise menus for their alternative dining venues. Celebrity Cruises, for example, worked with three-star Michelin chef Michel Roux from 1989 until 2007. The partnership worked because Roux insisted that the cruise line buy high-quality ingredients and make everything from scratch, avoiding pre-made sauces, soup mixes and the like.

Other celebrated chefs have included Georges Blanc (Carnival Cruise Lines), Elizabeth Blau (Celebrity Cruises), Nobu Matsuhisa (Crystal Cruises), Todd English (Cunard Line), Gary Rhodes and Marco Pierre White (P&O Cruises), Charlie Palmer (Seabourn Cruise Line), Aldo Zilli (Thomson Cruises), and Joachim Splichal (Windstar Cruises.

P&O's Marco Pierre White.

at 5.30pm, 6.45pm, 7.30pm or 8.45pm (except *Carnival Legend, Carnival Miracle, Carnival Pride* and *Carnival Spirit*, each with two seatings). You choose a time, and cannot change it later.

The captain's table

The captain usually occupies a large table in or near the center of the dining room on "formal" nights. The table seats eight or more people picked from the passenger or "commend" list by the hotel manager. If you are invited to the captain's table, it is gracious to accept, and you will have the chance to ask all the questions you like about shipboard life.

Alternative Dining

"Alternative" restaurants are trendy, particularly aboard the large resort ships, and are ideal for escaping from huge, noisy dining halls and singing, table-dancing waiters. These are typically smaller, à la carte venues where you must make a reservation, and pay an extra charge of between $6 and $30 a person. In return, you get better food, wines, service and ambiance. The costs can soon add up, just as when you dine out ashore. As an example, take David's Supper Club aboard *Carnival Pride*. The food is very good, and the ambiance is refined. But a couple having two glasses of decent wine each can, with the cover charge, easily end up paying $100 for dinner.

Special needs

Cruise lines tend to cater to general tastes. If you are allergic to any kind of ingredients (such as nuts or shellfish), do let the cruise line know in writing well ahead of time and, once on board, check with the restaurant

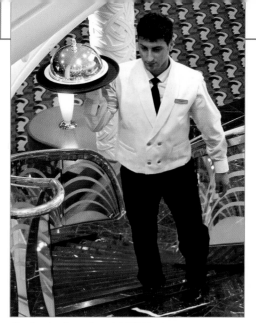

The food arrives aboard *MSC Musica*.

manager. Vegetarians should make sure that soups are not made with a chicken stock, as many so-called "vegetarian" soups are.

Menus are typically displayed outside the dining room each day so that you can preview each meal. Menus are delivered to suites.

Plate service versus silver service

PLATE SERVICE: When the food is presented as a complete dish, it is as the chef wants it to look. In most cruise ships, "plate service" is now the norm. It works well and means that most people seated at a table will be served

In the Arctic, the *Hanseatic* lays on a shoreside buffet.

at the same time and can eat together, rather than let their food become cold.

SILVER SERVICE: When the component parts are brought to the table separately, so that the diner, not the chef, can choose what goes on the plate and in what proportion. Silver service is best when there is plenty of time, and is rare aboard today's ships. What some cruise lines class as silver service is actually silver service of vegetables only, with the main item, whether it is fish, fowl, or meat, already on the plate.

Self-serve buffets

Most ships have self-serve buffets for breakfast and luncheon (some also for dinner), one of the effects of discounted fares and dumbing down – and fewer staff are needed. Strangely, passengers don't seem to mind lining up for self-service food (reminiscent of school lunches and army canteens). But while buffets look fine when they are fresh, they don't after a few minutes of passengers helping themselves. And, one soon learns, otherwise sweet little old ladies can become ruthlessly competitive at opening time.

Passengers should not have to play guessing games when it comes to food, but many cruise lines forget to put labels on food items; this slows down any buffet line. Labels on salad dressings, sauces, and cheeses would be particularly useful.

What's not good is that if you ask anyone behind the self-serve buffet counters what kind of apples are in the fruit bowl they haven't a clue, "red" or "green" being the usual answer (red apples, for example, could be Braeburn, Egremont Russet, Gala, Pink Lady, Starking Delicious, or Worcester Pearmain). Staff should know – but seldom do – the most basic details about food on display.

10 RECOMMENDED ALTERNATIVE RESTAURANTS

L'Enoteca *MSC Orchestra*
Le Champagne *Silver Shadow*
Le Cordon Bleu *Seven Seas Voyager*
Nobu's Sushi Bar *Crystal Serenity*
(pictured below)
Olympic Restaurant *Celebrity Millennium*
Oriental Restaurant *Europa*
Palo's *Disney Wonder*
Queens Grill *Queen Victoria*
Teppanyaki Grill *Norwegian Pearl*
Umihiko *Asuka II*

Healthy eating

It's easy to gain weight when cruising – but not inevitable. First, weight-conscious passengers should exercise self-restraint, particularly at the self-service buffets. Second, most ships have "heart-healthy" or "lean and light" options on the menu, or "spa" menus, with calorie-filled sauces replaced by spa cuisine. Third, there are plenty of opportunities for exercise, either in the spa or gym, on the jogging track often found above the main swimming pool deck, or by signing up for active shore excursions involving biking, hiking or river-rafting.

If you are vegetarian, vegan, macrobiotic, counting calories, want a salt-free, sugar-restricted, low-fat, low-cholesterol, or any other diet, advise your travel agent when you book, and get the cruise line to confirm that the ship can meet your needs. Cruise ship food tends to be liberally sprinkled with salt, and vegetables are often cooked with sauces containing dairy products, salt, and sugar.

An outdoor snack aboard *MSC Rhapsody*.

Seabourn Pride takes pride in its cuisine.

Most cruise ships don't cope well with those on vegan or macrobiotic diets who regularly need fresh-squeezed juices; most large resort ships use commercial canned or bottled juices containing preservatives and can't provide really fresh juices in their bars.

National differences

Most cruise lines feature mainly American-style cuisine, or cuisine that is often described as international, while more European-style cuisine is typically provided aboard the ships of European cruise lines (examples: Cunard Line, Fred Olsen Cruise Lines, Hebridean International Cruises, and P&O Cruises).

Note that beef, lamb and pork cuts are different on both sides of the Atlantic, so what you ordered may not be quite the cut, shape or size you thought it was going to be. For example, there are 15 British cuts of beef, 17 American cuts, and 24 French cuts. There are 6 American cuts of lamb, 8 British cuts, and 9 French cuts. There are 8 American cuts of pork, 10 British cuts, and 17 French cuts.

While American passengers typically like iced water, or a jug of iced tea at lunch, most European passengers don't like ice in their water, and few drink iced tea.

If you care about cutlery, note that only a few cruise lines with large resort ships provide the correct, specially shaped fish knives, or the correct soup spoons (oval for thin bouillon-style soups and round for creamy soups).

Dining room and kitchen staff

Celebrity chefs *(see box on page 53)* make the headlines, but it's the executive chef who plans the menus, orders the food, organizes his staff, and arranges all the meals on the menus. He makes sure that menus are not repeated, even on long cruises. On some cruises, he works with guest chefs from restaurants ashore to offer tastes of regional cuisine. He may also purchase fish, seafood, fruit, and various other local produce in "wayside" ports and incorporate them into the menu with a "special of the day" announcement.

The Restaurant Manager – also known as the Maître d'Hôtel and not to be confused with the ship's Hotel

---

DID YOU KNOW?

● that an unwritten rule called "Ward's Third Law of Gluttony," states that passengers will take precisely twice as much food as they need from breakfast and luncheon buffets, then add a lettuce leaf or two at dinner in order to justify the guilt complex brought about by over-consumption?

● that Cunard Line is reputed to be the world's largest single buyer of caviar – spending about $500,000 a year – after the Russian and Ukrainian governments?

● that most of the major cruise lines have replaced champagne with sparkling wine for the captain's welcome aboard cocktail party?

● that the liner *Amerika* in 1938 was the first ship to have an alternative restaurant open separately from the dining saloons? It was named the Ritz Carlton.

● that the first à la carte restaurant aboard a passenger ship was in the German ship *Amerika* of 1905?

● that the longest bar aboard any current cruise ship can be found aboard *AIDAcara*? It is 195 feet (59.5 meters) long.

● that a whole county in Iowa raises all its beef cattle for sale to Carnival Cruise Lines?

● that *Legend of the Seas* was christened in 1995 with the world's largest bottle of champagne? It had to be specially made, and was a "Sovereign-size" bottle (the equivalent of 34 bottles) of Moët & Chandon champagne.

● that the United States Line's *Manhattan* in 1931 was the first ship to have a cocktail named after it – perhaps the only ship that can claim such a distinction?

● that 2,000 Methuselah-sized bottles (the equivalent of 12 bottles) of Cristal champagne were made specially for Crystal Cruises' passengers to purchase for the millennium celebrations on the eve of the year 2000? The cost: $2,000 each.

Going to dinner in style, *Norwegian Pearl*.

Manager – is an experienced host, with shrewd perceptions about compatibility. It is his responsibility to seat you with compatible fellow passengers. If a reservation has been arranged prior to boarding, you will find a table assignment or seating card in your cabin when you embark. If not, make your reservation with the restaurant manager or one of his assistants immediately after you embark.

If you are unhappy with any aspect of the dining room operation, the sooner you tell someone the better. Don't wait until the cruise is over to send a scathing letter to the cruise line – it's too late then to do anything positive.

The best waiters are those trained in European hotels or catering schools. They provide fine service and quickly learn your likes and dislikes. They normally work aboard the best ships, where dignified professionalism is expected and living conditions are good.

Many lines contract the running and staffing of dining rooms to a specialist maritime catering organization. Ships that cruise far from their home country find that professional catering companies do a good job. However, ships that control their own catering staff and food often try very hard for good quality.

Hygiene standards

Galley equipment is in almost constant use, and regular inspections and maintenance help detect potential problems. There is continual cleaning of equipment, utensils, bulkheads, floors, and hands.

Cruise ships sailing from or visiting US ports are subject to in-port sanitation inspections. These are voluntary, not mandatory inspections, based on 42 inspection items, undertaken by the United States Public Health (USPH) Department of Health and Human Services, under the auspices of the Centers for Disease Control. The cruise line pays for each ship inspection. A similar process takes place in Britain under the Port Health Authority, which has even more stringent guidelines and requirements.

A tour of the galley proves to be a highlight for some passengers, when a ship's insurance company permits. A video of Behind the Scenes, for use on in-cabin television, may be provided instead.

In accordance with international standards, all potable water brought on board, or produced by distillation aboard cruise ships, should contain a free chlorine or bromine residual equal to or greater than 0.2 ppm (parts per million). This is why drinking water served in dining rooms often tastes of chlorine.

Smoking/nonsmoking areas

Most ships now have totally nonsmoking dining rooms, while some still provide smoking (cigarettes only, not cigars or pipes) and nonsmoking sections. Those wishing to sit in a no-smoking area should tell the restaurant manager when reserving a table.

At open seating breakfasts and luncheons in the dining room or at a casual self-serve buffet venue, it is sometimes possible that smokers and nonsmokers may be seated close together. ❑

THAT'S ENTERTAINMENT?

After food, the most subjective part of any mainstream cruise is the entertainment, which has to be diversified and innovative but never controversial

Many passengers, despite having paid so little for their cruise, expect to see top-notch entertainment, "headline" marquee-name cabaret artists, the world's most "popular" singers, and the most dazzling shows with slick special effects, just as one would find in the best venues in Las Vegas, London, or Paris. There are many reasons why it is not exactly so. International star acts invariably have an entourage that accompanies them to any venue: their personal manager, their musical director (often a pianist or conductor), a rhythm section (with bass player and drummer), even their hairdresser.

On land, one-night shows are possible, but with a ship, an artist cannot always disembark after just one night, especially when it involves moving equipment, costumes, and baggage. This makes the whole matter logistically and financially unattractive for all but the very largest ships on fixed itineraries, where a marquee-name act might be a marketing plus.

When you are at home you can bring the world's top talent into your home via television. Cruise ships are a different matter. Most entertainers don't like to be away from their "home base" for long periods, as they rely on telephone contact. They don't like the long contracts that most ships must offer in order to amortize the cost.

A certain sameness

So many acts working aboard cruise ships are interchangeable with so many other acts also working aboard cruise ships. Ever wonder why? Entertainers aboard ship must also *live* with their audiences for several days (sometimes weeks) – something unheard-of on land – as well as work on stages aboard older ships that weren't designed for live performances. However, there is no question that cruise ships are the new location for vaudeville acts, where a guaranteed audience is a bonus for many former club-date acts, as well as fresh acts trying to break in to the big time on land.

Entertainment in today's large resort ships is market-driven. In other words, it is directed toward that segment of the industry that marketing departments are specifically targeting. This is predominantly a family audience, so the fare must appeal to a broad age range.

A cruise line with several ships will normally employ an entertainment director and several assistants, and most cruise lines use entertainment agencies that specialize in entertainment for cruise ships. Regular passengers will notice that they seem to see the same acts time after time on various ships.

Mistakes do happen. It is no use, for example, booking a juggler who needs a floor-to-ceiling height of 12 feet but finds that the ship has a show lounge with a height of just 7 feet (although I did overhear one cruise director ask if the act "couldn't juggle sideways"); or an acrobatic knife-throwing act (in a moving ship?); or a concert pianist when the ship only has an upright honky-tonk piano; or a singer who sings only in English when the passengers are German-speaking.

Trying to please everyone

The toughest audience is one of mixed nationalities (each of whom will expect entertainers to cater exclusively to their particular linguistic group). Given that cruise lines are now marketing to more international audiences in order to fill ever-larger ships, the problem of finding the right entertainment is far more acute.

The "luxury" cruise lines (typically those operating small ships) offer more classical music, even some light opera, more guest lecturers and top authors than the seven-day package cruises heading for the sun.

Carnival Cruise Lines lays on razzle-dazzle shows.

These performers and ship entertainers generally, need to enjoy socializing. Successful shipboard acts tend to be good mixers, are presentable when in public, do not do drugs or take excess alcohol, are not late for rehearsals, and must cooperate with the cruise director.

Part of the entertainment experience aboard large resort ships is the glamorous "production show," the kind of show you would expect to see in any good Las Vegas show palace, with male and female lead singers and Marilyn Monroe look-alike dancers, a production manager, lavish backdrops, extravagant sets, grand lighting, special effects, and stunning custom-designed costumes. Unfortunately, most cruise line executives, who know little or nothing about entertainment, still favor plumes and huge feather boas paraded by show-girls who *step*, but don't *dance*. Some cruise ships have coarse shows that are not becoming to either dancer or passenger (topless shows can be found aboard the ships of Star Cruises, for example).

Book back-to-back seven-day cruises (on alternating eastern and western Caribbean itineraries, for example), and you will probably find the same two or three production shows and the same acts on the second week of your cruise. The way to avoid seeing everything twice is to pace yourself. Go to some shows during the first week and save the rest for the second week.

Sadly, entertainment has of late been a major target for some companies (particularly the smaller operators) who have targeted entertainment as a major area for cost-cutting. This translates to bringing on,

for example, lower-cost singers (who often turn out to be vocally challenged) and bands that cannot read charts (musician-speak for musical arrangements).

Other entertainment

Most cruise ships organize acts that, while perhaps not nationally recognized "names," can provide two or three different shows during a seven-day cruise. These will be male/female singers, illusionists, puppeteers, hypnotists, and even circus acts, with wide age-range appeal.

Many comedians who perform "clean" material and who may find employment year-round on the "cruise ship circuit." These popular comics enjoy good accommodation, are stars while on board, and often go from ship to ship on a standard rotation every few days. There are raunchy, late-night "adults only" comedy acts in some of the ships with younger, "hip" audiences, but few have enough material for several shows. The larger a ship, the broader the entertainment program.

Playing the game

TV game shows could be the next audience participation event aboard the big resort ships with their large showlounges. These professionally produced game shows, licensed from TV companies, involve all passengers seated in the show lounge with interactive buttons wired into every seat. While they are expensive to mount, they provide something different from the expensive costumed production extravaganzas. ❑

THE COST OF STAGING A SHOW

In today's high-tech world, staging a lavish 50-minute production show can easily cost between $500,000 and $1 million, plus performers' pay, costume cleaning and repair, royalties, and so on. To justify that cost, shows have to stay aboard a ship for 18 to 24 months.

Some smaller operators have targeted entertainment as an area for cost-cutting, so you could find yourself entertained by cheaper singers (who sound cheaper) and bands that can't read musical arrangements.

SPAS AND WELLNESS FACILITIES

The "feelgood factor" is alive and well aboard the latest cruise ships, which offer a growing array of body-pampering treatments to renew your sense of well-being

As we constantly move in "fast-forward" mode we create stress, our energy becomes impaired. Muscles become taut and knotted. So, taking time out to pamper ourselves is a good way to combine "me" vacation time with moments of indulgence.

Land-based health spas have long provided a range of body treatments and services for those who wanted to hide away at a venue (health farm) in the countryside. With the increase in awareness of the body beautiful and the importance of well-being has come a whole new array of shipboard spas to rival those on land, particularly in the range of body-pampering treatments available. Today's cruise ships have elaborate spas where, for an extra fee, whole days of almost continuous treatments are on offer. Once the domain of adult women, spas now cater almost as equally to men.

A visit to the ship's spa will help you to relax and feel pampered. Many people not used to spas may find some of the terminology daunting: aromatherapy, hydrotherapy, ionithermie, rasul, thalassotherapy. But don't worry, spa staff are used to first-time users, and will help you choose the massage or other treatment that best suits you and your needs. It's a good idea to visit the spa on embarkation day, when staff will be on hand to show you round, and answer your questions.

Spa facilities aboard *SuperStar Virgo*.

Facilities

Large resort ships will have a large gymnasium with ocean views, saunas, steam rooms, rasul chamber, several body treatment rooms, thalassotherapy pool, relaxation area, changing/locker rooms, and a beauty salon. Some ships even have acupuncture treatment clinics, and some have a built-in juice bar.

Thermal suites

Thermal Suites (no, they're not specially insulated cabins) are private areas that provide a combination of various warm scented rain showers, saunas, steam rooms, thalassotherapy (saltwater) pools and relaxation zones offer the promise of ultimate relaxation. While most ships do not charge for use of the sauna or steam room, some make a per-day charge (examples: *MSC Musica* $30; *Norwegian Gem* $20; *Queen Mary 2*, $25).

Spa suites

Some ships have "spa suites," which include spa access and even a treatment or two (whereas regular cabin occupants pay extra to use the sauna/steam room/relaxation rooms), and special spa amenities (examples: *Costa Concordia, Costa Luminosa, Costa Pacifica, Costa Serena, Europa*), and even a special spa-food-menu-only restaurant (examples: *Celebrity Solstice, Costa Concordia, Costa Serena*).

Spa design

The latest sea-going spas have Asian-themed decor as an aid to relaxation, with warm woods and gently flowing water to provide a natural aesthetic environment aimed to caress and soothe, with therapy staff dressed in Balinese attire. But interior designers often forget to include dimmers and mood lighting, particularly in reception areas, where lighting is often too bright.

Pampering treatments

Stress reducing and relaxation treatments are featured, combined with the use of seawater, which contains minerals, micronutrients, and vitamins. Massages might include Swedish remedial massage, shiatsu, and aromatherapy oils. You can even get a massage on your private balcony aboard some ships.

Having body-pampering treatments aboard a cruise ship can be wonderful, as the ship can provide a serene environment in itself; so, when enhanced by something like a massage or facial, the benefits can be more therapeutic. Ship interior designers do, however, need to pay more attention to soundproofing so that facilities can be used at all hours (lighting dimmers are also essential – it's surprising how often this simple, but essential, item is overlooked). Examples of poor soundproofing include the treatment rooms aboard *Golden Princess*, *Grand Princess*, where they are located directly underneath a sports court. So, before you actually book your relaxing massage, find out if the treatment rooms are quiet enough.

Unfortunately, treatments are usually available only until about 8pm, whereas some passengers would welcome being able to have a massage late at night before retiring to bed (the problem is that most shipboard spas are run by concessions, with well-being treated as a daytime-only event). Also, be aware that the latest 'con' in the revenue game is to charge more for treatments on days at sea, and lower on port days. Check the daily program for "port day specials" and packages that make prices more palatable.

Some of the smaller, more upscale ships now offer "Spa Days" with a whole day of body-pampering treatments (often termed "wellness packages"). Expect to pay up to $500 a day in addition to the basic cruise cost.

Fitness centers

A typical large resort ship spa will include a gymnasium, probably with ocean-view windows. Virtual-reality exercise machines and weapons of mass reduction are found in the techno-gyms aboard most large resort ships, with state-of-the-art equipment muscle-pumping

Keeping fit aboard HAL's *Zuiderdam*.

and body-strengthening equipment, universal stations, treadmills, bicycles, rowing machines, and free weights.

Most fitness centers are open only until early evening (one exception: NCL ships, whose gyms are open 24 hours a day). And if you've forgotten your workout clothes, you can probably purchase new items on board.

Typical exercise classes

These include aerobics (for beginners, intermediate, and advanced), high intensity/low impact aerobics, step aerobics, interval training, stretch and relax, super body sculpting, fab abdominals, sit and be fit, and walk-a-mile.

Group exercycling, kick-boxing, pilates and yoga classes, body composition analysis, and sessions with a personal trainer, will cost extra.

Massage

Having a massage aboard ship is a treat that more people are discovering. Today, many ships have suites and cabins with a "private" balcony, although you'll need a balcony with plenty of space in order to set up a proper portable massage table and allow the masseur/masseuse room to walk around it and work from all sides. It can be a real stress-busting experience, but if it's not right it can prove frustrating, and expensive.

Here are some of my favourite massages (always taken in the late afternoon or early evening, preferably just before sundown):

● Aboard *Celebrity Constella-*

---

10 GREAT SHIPBOARD SPAS

AIDAbella
Asuka II
Celebrity Solstice
Crystal Serenity
Emerald Princess
Europa
MSC Fantasia
Ocean Village Two
Queen Mary 2
Silver Shadow

tion, *Celebrity Infinity, Celebrity Millennium, Celebrity Summit* (on the balcony of a Sky Suite).
● Aboard *Royal Clipper* (in a private massage hut on an outside deck).
● Aboard *SuperStar Virgo* (on the floor of a junior suite bedroom).
● Inside a beach cabana ashore on Castaway Cay or Half Moon Cay in the Bahamas, or as part of the beach, caviar and champagne experience of ships such as *SeaDream I* and *II* in the British Virgin Islands.

Make appointments for a massage as soon after embarkation as possible, so you can obtain the time and day of your choice. Large resort ships have more staff and offer more flexibility in appointment times, although cruises tend to be shorter than those aboard smaller, more upscale ships. The cost averages $2 a minute. In some ships, a massage service may be available in your cabin (or on your private balcony), if it is large enough to accommodate a portable massage table.

While it's easy to telephone and make an appointment for a massage or facial or two (some cruise lines let you do this online), do watch the cost. When you charge treatments to your onboard account, remember that gratuities are often added automatically (typically 10–15%). Elixirs of youth, lotions and potions, creams and scrubs – all are sold by therapists, typically at the end of your treatment, for you to use when you get home. But be warned, these are expensive items; beware of falling for sales talk.

A whole range of treatments and styles has evolved from the standard Swedish Remedial Massage. The most popular are:

Entrance to the Aloha Beauty Farm, *MSC Musica*.

Hot stones massage as provided by AIDA Cruises

Swedish Massage: There are two main effects of massage – a reflex effect and a mechanical effect. There are four basic movements in this general massage: effleurage (the stroking movements that benefit the circulation of lymphatic fluids and drainage), petrissage (the picking, kneading, rolling and wringing movements), friction (the application of circular pressure) and tapotement (percussive tapping, flicking and hacking movements that stimulate circulation).

Well-being Massage: This is really another term for general Swedish Massage but with more emphasis on effleurage movements, the use of complementary, warmed aromatic (aromatherapy) oils and four-hand massage (two therapists working rhythmically in unison).

Shiatsu Massage: This literally means "finger pressure" and in Japan for thousands of years has been applied to the pressure points of the body as a preventative measure. It typically promotes a peaceful awareness of both body and mind, and is administered in a calm, relaxed environment, without oil.

Hot Stones Massage: The therapist places 24 to 36 smooth basalt volcanic stones of varying sizes in a special oven. These are then applied to various key energy points of the body, using the stones to gently massage specific areas and muscles. The heated volcanic stones are then left in place while the therapist works on other parts of the body. The heat from the stones helps the body to achieve a sense of deep relaxation.

Ayurvedic Head Massage: Using a selection of warmed herbal oils, the therapist will apply the oil to the scalp, neck and shoulders to stimulate circulation and nourish the hair (you'll need to wash your hair afterwards, as it will be extremely oily). Shirodhara is the form of Ayurvedic medicine that involves gently pouring warm oil (made from tulsi, or holy basil) over the forehead (including the "third eye"). Ayurveda is a compound word meaning life and knowledge.

Underwater Massage: You soak in a large tub of warm water, possibly with rose petals floating around you, while the therapist massages joints and muscles.

Sports Massage: Typically provided by a male therapist, sports massage is a deep-tissue massage designed to unlock the kinks and knots.

Lomi-Lomi Massage: This is a more rhythmic massage inspired by Hawaiian healing traditions that restore the free flow of "mana" or life force; it is typically given using warm aromatherapy oils, and may be a two-hand or four-hand massage.

Lymphatic Massage: This massage is designed to improve circulation by releasing body toxins and nodes that build up in key lymphatic points. This massage is usually recommended for those who have poor circulation or suffer from exhaustion.

Thai Massage: Uses pressure points and stretching techniques to stretch and relax muscles, improve circulation, and reduce stress.

Chinese Tuina: This is a therapeutic massage based on a diagnostic evaluation, manipulation of the joints and muscle fibers, and identification and prevention of wrong body postures, habits and degenerative conditions.

Couples Massage: Sometimes known as a "duet massage," this is typically a 90-minute session for a couple that includes a hands-on lesson from a massage specialist on the art of massaging each other.

Ultimate Massage: Two therapists provide a synchronized full body massage, using Swedish massage movements to provide the ultimate in stress-busting relief. But it can be less than good if the two therapists are even slightly out of sync.

OTHER TREATMENTS
While massage is the most popular shipboard spa treatment, some ships offer a whole range of body-pampering treatments, such as facials, manicures, pedicures, teeth whitening – even acupuncture. Most treatments are based on holistic Asian therapies. Some examples:

THE 10 RULES OF SPA ETIQUETTE

❶ It is important to wear proper attire (including shoes) in the gym.

❷ Wipe the equipment off with a clean towel (or sanitized cloth) after you have used it.

❸ Limit your time on the equipment or in the hot tub to a maximum of 30 minutes when others are waiting.

❹ Most ships allow jogging on a designated deck or area at selected times which will be posted. Adhere to the times posted because cabins are usually located directly below the designated deck and you may disturb fellow passengers who are sleeping.

❺ If there's a mixed sauna, men should not shave in it – it's unclean, and uncool.

❻ Arrive at least 10 minutes before your appointment.

❼ Take a shower or wash off all suntan lotions or oils.

❽ It's better not to talk during a massage – simply close your eyes, relax and enjoy.

❾ Shipboard spas are no-smoking zones – so no quick drag in the sauna.

❿ You can cancel an appointment up to 24 hours before your treatment time without charge. If you cancel within the 24 hours before your appointment time, you will be charged for the treatment you booked.

Bali or Java, Indonesia (*ural* and *pijat* massage; *mandi lulur*, a scrub made from herbs, essential oils and rice to soften the skin; Balinese *boreh* (a warm herb, rice, spice, galangal water and oil body wrap for detoxification); China (*acupuncture*); Japan (shiatsu massage; enzyme baths made from warmed finely shaved cedar chips, rice bran and vegetable enzymes to improve the metabolic system); Malaysia (Malay massage, which focuses on the body's 600,666 nerves); Philippines (*Hilot* massage, using virgin coconut oil and banana leaves); Thailand (Thai massage, or *nuad boran*).

Typically, the spa will provide items such as towels, robes and slippers, but it's best to store valuables safely in your cabin prior to your appointment.

Don't worry about having to get naked; you'll typically change into a robe and slippers in the men's or women's changing rooms. You then go to the treatment room, and the therapist will leave while you disrobe and lie down, placing a towel over your body, ready for massage. Some spas offer disposable panties for body treatments such as a Body Salt Glow or Seaweed Wrap. They may be optional, or mandatory.

Acupuncture

This can be used to prevent and remedy many maladies. Moxibustion is the treatment which involves hair-thin needles and heat transfer based on a special plant, the Artemisa Capillaris, placed into one of the more than 1,100 acupuncture points located along the meridians of the body.

Inspiring statuary in a Celebrity Cruises AquaSpa.

Body scrub

The aim of this treatment is to cleanse and soften the skin, and to draw out impurities from within, using aromatic oils, creams, lotions, and perhaps sea salt, together with exfoliation (removal of dead skin cells) using skin brushing techniques.

Body wrap

Often called a body mask, this treatment typically includes the use of algae and seaweeds applied to the whole body. The body is then covered in aluminium foil and blankets. There are many variations on this theme, using mud from the Dead Sea or Mediterranean Sea, or sea salt and ginger, or cooling cucumber and aloe, or combinations of herbs and oils that leave you with a warm glow. The aim of this treatment is to detoxify, firm and tone the skin, and reduce cellulite.

Dry flotation

This hydrobath gives you the sensation of floating without getting wet; you lie on a plush warm blanket between your body and the water. A therapist then gently massages your head and neck while you drift to somewhere beyond.

Facials

Aromatherapy facial: This treatment typically uses aromatic oils such as lavender, sandalwood and geranium, plus a rejuvenating mask and accompanying creams and essences to "lift" the skin and facial muscles.

Rejuvenation facial: Typically a classic French facial which utilizes the latest skin care products that may include essential plant and vitamin-rich oils. This facial aims to reduce lines and wrinkles.

Rasul chamber

This is a steam chamber (also known as Hammam) that is typically fully tiled, featuring a domed roof and Moorish decor. When you enter, you paste yourself or your partner (it's a much better experience with a partner) with three types of mud, and sit down while gentle steam surrounds you. The various types of mud become heated and then you're in a mud bath, after which you rub yourself (and each other) with large crystals of rock salt. Then shower, sit, and relax, all in the privacy of the chamber. Your skin will visibly glow.

Reflexology

The body's energy meridians exist as reflex points on the soles of the feet. The therapist uses thumb pressure to stimulate these points to improve circulation and restore energy flow throughout the body.

Some RCI cruise ships have a full-size boxing ring.

Thalassotherapy

The use of seawater to promote well-being and healing dates back to ancient Greece. Today, shipboard spas have whole bath rituals involving water and flower petals, herbs or mineral salts.

Sample prices

Prices of body-pampering treatments have escalated recently, and are now equal to the prices you would find at land-based spas in the United States. You can expect to pay up to:
$195 for a 75-minute Hot Stones Massage
$120 for a 50 minute Well-Being Massage
$190 for a 75-minute Seaweed Wrap
$120 for a 50-minute Reflexology Session

Spa cuisine

Originally designed as low-fat, low-calorie (almost tasteless) meals for weight loss using grains, greens, and sprouts, spa cuisine now includes whole grains, seasonal fruits and vegetables, and lean proteins – ingredients that are low in saturated fats and cholesterol, low-fat dairy products, and reduced salt. These ingredients provide the basis for balanced nutrition and portion sizes while maintaining a degree of flavor, texture and taste. Spa cuisine should be about using natural, not artificial, ingredients, flavor enhancers, coloring mediums, preservatives, or foods laden with sodium.

To eat healthier meals, choose steamed or grilled items rather than baked or fried items.

Sports facilities

Sports facilities might include basketball and paddle tennis (a sort of downsized tennis court), and electronic golf simulators. Aboard some of the boutique/small "luxury" ships, facilities include kayaking, water-skiing, jet skiing, wake boarding are all included in the cruise fare. In reality, however, the watersports equipment is typically only used on one or two days (or part days) during a 7-day cruise. ❑

WHO RUNS THE SPAS

Aboard most ships, the spa and fitness areas are operated by a specialist concession, although each cruise line may have a separate name for the spa, such as AquaSpa (Celebrity Cruises), The Greenhouse Spa (Holland America Line), Lotus Spas (Princess Cruises), etc.

Aboard the large resort ships, spa staff tend to be young and enthusiastic, and will try hard to sell you own-brand beauty products, for a commission. Steiner Leisure is by far the largest concession, operating spas aboard more than 100 ships.

This company, founded in London in 1901 by Henry Steiner, began its ambitious growth in 1926 when Herman Steiner got involved in the family beauty salon on his father's death. He opened salons throughout England, became official cosmetician to Queen Elizabeth the Queen Mother, and won his first cruise ship contract in 1956.

The company closed its land-based salons in the 1990s as its cruise ship business burgeoned. It bought Elemis, a lifestyle range of plant-based beauty products, and acquired Mandara Spas, which it has developed in the US alongside its Elemis Spas. It runs 14 training schools. Steiner's corporate headquarters is now in the Bahamas.

Other shipboard concessions include Blue Ocean, Canyon Ranch At Sea, Espace Elegance, Futuresse, and Harding Brothers.

Different Kinds of Cruising

CRUISING FOR FAMILIES

Many cruise lines, recognizing the needs of parents, have added a whole variety of children's programs to their daily activities

There are few better vacations for families than a ship cruise, especially during school breaks. Active parents can have the best of all worlds: family togetherness, social contact, and privacy. Cruise ships provide a safe, crime-free, encapsulated environment, and give junior passengers a lot of freedom without parents having to be concerned about where their children are at all times. Because the days aboard are long, youngsters will be able to spend time with their parents or grandparents, as well as with their peers. They can also meet senior officers and learn about the navigation, radar, and communications equipment. They will be exposed to different environments, and experience many types of food. They will discover different cultures during shore excursions.

Although children may not like organized school-like clubs, they will probably make new friends quickly in the surroundings of a cruise ship. Whether you share a cabin with them or book an adjoining cabin, there will be plenty to keep them occupied.

Some cruise lines have token family programs, with limited activities and only a couple of general staff allocated to look after children, even though their brochures might claim otherwise. Other lines dedicate teams of counselors who run special programs off-limits to adults. They also have provide practical facilities such as high chairs in the dining room, cots, and real playrooms.

Small children who are not toilet-trained will not be allowed in the swimming pool, and it may be difficult to bathe small children in cabins with no bathtub but only a shower enclosure with a fixed-head shower.

Children's entertainment

Most entertainment for children is designed to run simultaneously with adult programs; few ships have dedicated children's entertainers. For those cruising with very young children, baby-sitting services may be available. For example, *QM2* has children's nurses and even fully qualified English nannies. *Aurora, Oceana* and *Oriana* have a "night nursery" for two- to five-year-olds. Some ships have children's pools and play areas, as well as junior discos, video rooms, and teen "chill-out" centers.

LEFT: resort ships appeal to the gregarious.
RIGHT: Celebrity Cruises can teach kids to cook.

In some ships, stewards, stewardesses, and other staff may be available as private babysitters for an hourly charge; otherwise, group babysitting may be offered. Make arrangements at the reception desk. Aboard some ships, evening baby-sitting services may not start until late – check details before booking.

Cruise lines serious about children typically divide them into distinct age groups: Toddlers (ages 2–4); Juniors (ages 5–7); Intermediate (ages 8–10); Tweens (ages 11–13); and Teens (ages 14–17). It often seems to be children under 12 who get the most from a cruise.

Safety tips

● In case children get lost or separated from their parents, most cruise lines provide them with colored wristbands, which must be worn at all times.
● Young children love to climb, so don't ever leave them on a balcony alone. On the open decks, ships have railings – these are either horizontal bars through which children cannot get their heads, or they are covered in glass/plexiglass under a thick wooden top rail.
● While children find their way around easily, walk

Disney Cruise Line stages family entertainment.

with them to and from the playroom/activity from and to your cabin, so that you both know the way.
● Discuss safety issues with them, and warn them not to walk into "Crew Only" areas at any time.

The right food

Selected baby foods, along with cribs and high chairs, are stocked by ships that cater to children, but ask your travel agent to check first. If you need a special brand of baby food, or a high chair in the restaurant, a crib, baby bathtub, baby stroller (few ships have them to rent), or monitoring service, let your travel agent know well in advance, and obtain confirmation in writing that the facilities will be available.

Parents using organic baby foods, such as those obtained from health food stores, should be aware that cruise lines buy their supplies from major general food suppliers and not the smaller specialized food houses.

Activities for children

Although many ships have full programs for children during days at sea, these may be limited when the ship is in port. Ships expect you to take your children with you on organized excursions, which sometimes have lower prices for children. If the ship has a playroom, find out if it is open and supervised on all days of the cruise.

When going ashore, remember that if you want to

take your children swimming or to the beach, it is wise to telephone ahead to a local hotel with a beach or pool. Many hotels will be happy to show off their property to you, hoping to gain your future business.

Some cruise ships in the Caribbean have the use of a "private" island for a day, including waterpark areas for children and adults. A lifeguard will be on duty, and there will be water sports and snorkeling equipment you can rent. But remember that the beaches on some "private" islands are fine for 200 passengers, but with 2,000 they quickly become crowded, forcing you to stand in line for beach barbecues and toilet facilities.

Although the sun and warm sea might attract juniors to the Caribbean, many older children will find a Baltic, Black Sea, or Mediterranean cruise fascinating as they are exposed to different cultures.

Activities for teens

Many large resort ships have dedicated "no adults allowed" zones. Teen-only activities include deck parties, pool parties, games, karaoke, discos, dances, computer gaming consoles and talent shows. Some Royal Caribbean International ships provide musical instruments for jam sessions. Sports include rock-climbing and basketball. There's usually almost unlimited food, too, although some of it may not be very nutritious.

Disney goes cruising

In 1998, Disney Cruise Line entered the family cruise market with a splash. The giant entertainment and theme park company introduced the first of two large resort ships to cater to families with children, with cruises of 3, 4 and 7 days. *Disney Magic* and *Disney Wonder* cater to 1,750 adults and up to 1,000 children (sometimes more), and have ambitious entertainment programs.

Disney has its own art-deco passenger terminal and facilities at Port Canaveral, Florida, as well as a fleet of motorcoaches. One ship also sails in the Mediterranean in summer, from Barcelona. Disney has two more ships on order, for delivery in 2010 and 2011.

DID YOU KNOW?

● that the French liner *Ile de France* was the first, and only, ship to have a real carousel in the children's playroom? This was also the ship used in the 1960 movie *The Last Voyage*, with Robert Stack and Dorothy Malone.
● that a 15-ft-high model of Goofy hangs upside down over the stern of *Disney Magic*? He's painting the ship.
● that Carnival Cruise Lines and Mattel teamed up to produce a nautical-themed Barbie Doll? She can be found in the gift shops aboard all the company's ships.

Children's rates

Children under two travel free on most cruise lines and airlines. If they're older, however, you have to pay. Most cruise lines offer special rates for children sharing their parents' cabin. The cost is often lower than third and fourth person share rates. To get the best rates, it's wise to book early. If you don't anticipate spending much time in your cabin, consider a cheaper interior (no-view) cabin.

Although many adult cruise rates include airfare, most children's rates don't. Also, although some lines say children sail "free," they must pay port taxes as well as airfare. The cruise line will get the airfare at the best rate, so there is no need to shop around. If you have very young children and can get to your ship without having to fly, you'll save yourself the hassles of airports.

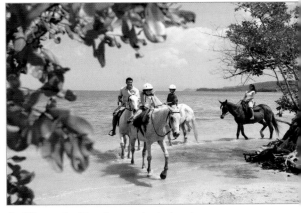

An RCI-organized beach excursion in Jamaica,

Single parents

Only a few cruise lines have introduced their versions of the "Single Parent Plan." This offers an economical way for single parents to take their children on a cruise, with parent and child sharing a two-berth cabin, or parent and children sharing a three-berth cabin.

Single parents will pay about one-third the normal single-person rate for their children.

Family reunions

A cruise can provide the ideal place for a family get-together, with or without children. Let your travel agent make the arrangements and ask for a group discount there are more than 15 of you.

Take care to choose a cruise line with a suitable ambience. Book 12 months in advance if possible so that you can arrange cabins close to each other. If the ship operates two dinner seatings, you may also wish to arrange for everyone to be at the same one.

Birthday specials

If anyone in the group has a birthday or anniversary, tell your travel agent to arrange a special cake – most cruise lines don't charge extra for this. Special private parties can also be arranged, at a price. If the group isn't too large, you may be able to request to dine at the captain's table. Shore excursions, too, can be booked in advance for a group.

Finally, get everything in writing, particularly cabin assignments and locations. ❑

THE SHIPS THAT CATER BEST FOR CHILDREN

These cruise lines and ships have been selected by Berlitz for the quality of their children's programs and care:

Aida Cruises: *AIDAaura, AIDAbella, AIDAcara, AIDAdiva, AIDAluna, AIDAvita*

Carnival has strong children's programs.

Carnival Cruise Lines: *Carnival Conquest, Carnival Destiny, Carnival Freedom, Carnival Glory, Carnival Legend, Carnival Liberty, Carnival Pride, Carnival Spirit, Carnival Splendor, Carnival Triumph, Carnival Valor, Carnival Victory, Carnival Ecstasy, Carnival Elation, Carnival Fantasy, Carnival Fascination, Carnival Imagination, Carnival Inspiration, Carnival Paradise, Carnival Sensation*

Celebrity Cruises: *Celebrity Century, Celebrity Constellation, Celebrity Eclipse, Celebrity Galaxy, Celebrity Infinity, Celebrity Mercury, Celebrity Millennium, Celebrity Solstice, Celebrity Summit*

Cunard Line: *Queen Mary 2, Queen Victoria*

Disney Cruise Line: *Disney Magic, Disney Wonder*

Norwegian Cruise Line: *Norwegian Dawn, Norwegian Gem, Norwegian Jade, Norwegian Jewel, Norwegian Pearl, Norwegian Spirit, Norwegian Star, Norwegian Sun*

P&O Cruises: *Aurora, Oceana, Oriana, Ventura*

Princess Cruises: *Crown Princess, Diamond Princess, Emerald Princess, Golden Princess, Grand Princess, Ruby Princess, Sapphire Princess, Star Princess*

Royal Caribbean International: *Adventure of the Seas, Explorer of the Seas, Freedom of the Seas, Independence of the Seas, Liberty of the Seas, Mariner of the Seas, Navigator of the Seas, Voyager of the Seas*

Star Cruises: *Star Pisces, SuperStar Aquarius, SuperStar Libra, SuperStar Virgo*

Thomson Cruises: *Thomson Celebration, Thomson Destiny, Thomson Spirit*

CRUISING FOR ROMANTICS

No need to worry about getting to the church
on time – you can be married at sea, or
get engaged, or have a second honeymoon

Two famous TV shows, *The Love Boat* (US) and *Traumschiff* (Germany), boosted the concept of cruising as a romantic vacation, though the plots didn't always match reality. The real captain of one ship, when asked the difference between his job and that of the captain of *The Love Boat*, remarked: "On TV they can do a retake if things aren't right the first time around, whereas I have to get it right the first time."

Getting engaged aboard ship

Princess Cruises has a special "Engagement Under the Stars" package that allows you to propose to your loved one in a personal video that is then screened just before an evening movie at a large outdoor screen aboard some of the company's ships. Current cost: $695.

Getting married at sea

Instead of the hassle of arranging flights, hotels, transportation and packages, you can let a specialist wedding planner do it all for you. As in all those old romantic black-and-white movies, a ship's captain can indeed marry you when at sea if properly certified – unless the ship's country of registry prohibits or does not recognize such marriages.

You first need to inquire in your country of domicile whether such a marriage is legal, and ascertain what paperwork and blood tests are required. The onus is on you to prove the validity of such a marriage. The captain could be held legally responsible if he married a couple not entitled to be wed.

It's relatively easy to get married aboard almost any cruise ship when it is alongside in port. Carnival Cruise Lines, Holland America Line, and Princess Cruises, among others, offer special wedding packages. These include the services of a minister to marry you, wedding cake, champagne, bridal bouquet and matching boutonnière for the bridal party, a band to perform at the ceremony, and an album of wedding photos. Note that US citizens and "green card" residents may need to pay sales tax on wedding packages.

Several cruise lines can arrange a marriage ceremony on a Caribbean beach – a dream for many. For example, Princess Cruises offers weddings on a beach in St. Thomas (prices range from $525 to $1,175 per package). Or how about a romantic wedding Disney-style on its private island, Castaway Cay?

Azamara Cruises, Celebrity Cruises and Princess Cruises offer weddings aboard many of their ship. The ceremonies can be performed by the captain, who is certified as a notary, when the ships' registry – Bermuda or Malta, for example – recognizes such unions.

Expect to pay about $2,500, plus about $500 for licensing fees. Harborside or shore-side packages vary according to the port. A wedding coordinator at the line handles all the details, enabling you to be married aboard ship and honeymoon aboard, too.

Even if you don't get married aboard ship, you could have your wedding reception aboard one. Many cruise lines offer good facilities and provide complete services to help you plan your reception. Contact the director of hotel services at the cruise line of your choice. The cruise line should go out of its way to help, especially if you follow the reception with a honeymoon cruise – and a cruise, of course, also makes a fine, no-worry honeymoon *(see below)*.

Carnival Cruise Lines pus its heart into romance.

Honeymooners might prefer a small, intimate ship.

UK-based passengers should know that P&O Cruises hosts a series of cruises called the "Red-Letter Anniversary Collection" for those celebrating 10, 15, 20, 25, 30, 35, 40, 45, 50, 55, or 60 years of marriage; the cruise comes with a complimentary gift, such as a brass carriage clock, leather photograph album, or free car parking at Southampton.

Renewal of vows

Many cruise lines now perform "renewal of vows" ceremonies. A cruise is a wonderful setting for reaffirming to one's partner the strength of commitment. A handful of ships have a small chapel where this ceremony can take place; otherwise it can be anywhere aboard ship – a most romantic time is at sunrise or sunset on the open deck. The renewal of vows ceremony is conducted by the ship's captain, using a non-denominational text.

PRACTICAL TIPS FOR HONEYMOONERS

Remember to take a copy of your marriage license or certificate, for immigration (or marriage) purposes, as your passports will not yet have been amended. Also, allow extra in your budget for things like drinks, shipboard gratuities, shore excursions, and spending money while ashore.

Since you will probably wish to share a large bed with your partner, check with your travel agent and cruise line to make sure the cabin you have booked has such a bed. Better still, book a suite if you can afford to. It's important to check and double-check to avoid disappointment.

If you plan to combine your honeymoon with getting married along the way – in Hawaii or Bermuda, for example – and need to take your wedding gown aboard, there is usually space to hang it in the dressing room next to the stage in the main showlounge, especially aboard the large resort ships.

Although some companies, such as Carnival Cruise Lines, Celebrity Cruises, Holland America Line, P&O Cruises and Princess Cruises, have complete packages for purchase, which include music, champagne, hors d'oeuvres, certificate, corsages for the women, and so on, most other companies do not charge – yet.

Cruising for honeymooners

Cruising is the new hot honeymoon. The advantages are appealing: you pack and unpack only once; it is a hassle-free and crime-free environment; and you get special attention, if you want it. It is also easy to budget in advance, as one price often includes airfare, cruise, food, entertainment, several destinations, shore excursions, and pre- and post-cruise hotel stays.

Once you are married, some cruise lines make a point of offering discounts to entice you to book a future cruise to celebrate an anniversary. Just think: no cooking meals, everything will be done for you.

Although no ship as yet provides bridal suites, many ships have suites with king- or queen-sized beds. Some also provide tables for two in the dining room should you wish to dine together without having to make friends with others. A variety of honeymoon packages is available; these might include champagne and caviar for breakfast, flowers in the suite or cabin, a complementary cake, and a private captain's cocktail party.

Some cruise ships feature Sunday departures, so couples can plan a Saturday wedding and reception before traveling to their ship. Pre- and post-cruise hotel accommodation can also be arranged.

Most large resort ships accommodate honeymoon couples well. However, those preferring to honeymoon without the crowds might try one of the smaller, yacht-like cruise vessels such as those of Seabourn Cruise Line, Regent Seven Seas Cruises, Silversea Cruises, or Windstar Cruises.

And for quiet moments? The deck to the forward part of a ship, near the bridge, is the most dimly lit part and the quietest (except perhaps for some wind noise). ❑

CRUISING FOR SOLO PASSENGERS

Cruise prices are geared towards couples.
Yet more than one in four cruise passengers
travels alone or as a single parent

Many solo passengers are prejudiced against cruising because most lines charge them a single occupancy supplement. The reason is that the most precious commodity aboard any ship is space. Since a solo-occupancy cabin is often as large as a double and is just as expensive to build, cruise lines feel the premium price is justified, What's more, because solo-occupancy cabins are at a premium, they are unlikely to be discounted.

Single supplements

If you are not sharing a cabin, you'll be asked to pay either a flat rate or a single "supplement" if you occupy a double cabin. Some lines charge a fixed amount – $250, for instance – as a supplement, no matter what the cabin category, ship, itinerary, or length of cruise. Such rates vary between lines, and sometimes between a line's ships. Because there are so few single-occu-

pancy cabins, it's best to book as far ahead as you can.

Lines that charge low single supplements include Crystal Cruises, Peter Deilmann Ocean Cruises, and Voyages of Discovery. Only a few of the smaller cruise lines, such as Saga Cruises and Voyages of Discovery, have no additional supplements for singles.

Guaranteed singles rates

Some lines offer singles a set price for a double cabin but reserve the right to choose the cabin. So you could end up with a rotten cabin in a poor location or a wonderful stateroom that happened to be unallocated.

Guaranteed share programs

These allow you to pay what it would cost each half of a couple for a double-occupancy cabin, but the cruise line will find another passenger of the same sex (and preferences such as smoking or non-smoking) to share it with you. If the line does not find a cabin-mate, the single passenger may get the cabin to himself or herself at no extra charge. Some cruise lines do not advertise a guaranteed-share program in their brochures but will often try to accommodate such bookings when demand for space is light.

Solo dining

A common complaint concerns dining arrangements. Before you take your cruise, make sure that you request a table assignment based on your personal preferences; table sizes are typically for 2, 4, 6, or 8 people. Do you want to sit with other singles? Or do you like to sit with couples? Or perhaps with a mixture of both? Or with passengers who may not speak your language?

When you are on board, make sure that you are comfortable with the dining arrangements, particularly in ships with fixed table assignments, or ask the maître d' to move you to a different table. Aboard ships with open seating or with several different dining venues, you can choose which venue you want to eat in, and when; Norwegian Cruise Line (NCL) is an excellent example of this arrangement, with its Freestyle Dining.

Cruising for single women

A cruise ship is at least as safe for single women as any major vacation destination, but of course that doesn't mean it is entirely hassle-free.

It's easy to strike up conversations with other

Afternoon tea on Carnival with a view of the ocean.

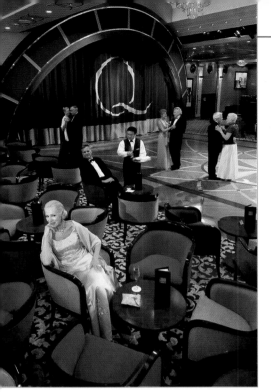

Awaiting a gentleman host aboard *Queen Mary 2*.

passengers, and cruising is not a "meat market" that keeps you under constant observation. The easiest way to meet other singles, however, is to participate in scheduled activities. Single black women may find there is often a dearth of single black men for dancing or socializing with.

Beware of embarking on an easy affair with a ship's officer or crew member. They meet new people on every cruise and could consequently transmit sexual diseases.

Gentlemen cruise hosts

The female-to-male passenger ratio is typically high, especially among older people, so some cruise lines provide male social hosts. They may host a table in the dining room, appear as dance partners at cocktail parties and dance classes, join bridge games, and accompany women on shore excursions.

These men, usually over 55 and retired, are outgoing, mingle easily, and are well groomed. First introduced aboard Cunard Line's *QE2* in the mid-1970s, gentlemen hosts are now employed by a number of cruise lines, including Crystal Cruises, Cunard Line, Holland America Line, Regent Seven Seas Cruises, and Silversea Cruises.

If you think you'd like such a job, do remember that you'll have to dance for several hours most nights, and be proficient in just about every kind of dance. ❏

THE BEST OPTIONS FOR GAYS AND LESBIANS

Several US companies specialize in ship charters or large group bookings for gay and lesbian passengers. These include the California-based Atlantis (tel: 310-859 8800; www.atlantis events.com), San Francisco's lesbian specialist Olivia (www. olivia.com) or New York's Pied Piper Travel (tel: 212-239 2412; http:// home.att.net/~gaygroupcruises).

One drawback of gay charters is that they're as much as 20% more expensive than the equivalent general cruise. Another is that they have been greeted with hostility by church groups on some Caribbean islands such as Grand Cayman, Jamaica and Bermuda. One Atlantis cruise was even denied the right to dock. But their great advantage is that they provide an accepting environment and gay-geared entertainment, with some big-name comedians and singers.

Another idea is to join a gay affinity group on a regular cruise at normal prices; these groups may be offered amenities such as private dining

Rosie O'Donnell promotes a gay family cruise.

rooms and separate shore excursions.

Many gays, of course, have no wish to travel exclusively with other gays but may worry that, on a mainstream cruise, they might be seated for dinner with unsympathetic companions. They would prefer to sit where they want, when they want, and such open seating is offered by Norwegian Cruise Line

and Princess Cruises, and by more upscale lines such as Crystal, Silversea and Seabourn. Open seating is not offered by Carnival, Celebrity or Royal Caribbean International.

That doesn't mean that any of the major cruise companies are not gay-friendly – many hold regular "Friends of Dorothy" gatherings, sometimes scheduled and sometimes on request – though it would be prudent to realize that Disney Cruise Line, for example, will not offer the ideal entertainment and ambience. Among the smaller companies, Windstar's sail-powered cruise yachts have a reputation for being gay-friendly.

Gay familes are catered for by R Family Vacations (tel: 866-732 6822; www.rfamilyvacations.com), although it's not essential to bring children. Events may include seminars on adoption and discussion groups for teenagers in gay families. One of the company's founders was the former TV talk show host Rosie O'Donnell, herself a lesbian mother.

CRUISES TO SUIT SPECIAL NEEDS

Cruising for the physically challenged offers one of the most hassle-free vacations possible. But it's important to choose the right ship and to prepare in advance

Cruise ships have become much more accessible for people with most types of disabilities. Many new ships also have text telephones, listening device kits for the hearing-impaired (including show lounges aboard some ships). Special dietary needs can often be accommodated, and many cabins have refrigerators (useful for those with diabetes who need to keep supplies of insulin cool). Special cruises cater for dialysis patients and for those who need oxygen regularly.

If you use a wheelchair, take it with you, as ships carry only a limited number for emergency hospital use only. An alternative is to rent an electric wheelchair, which can be delivered to the ship on your sailing date.

Six problems to consider

It is as well to begin with the disadvantages of a cruise for the physically challenged:

❶ Unless cabins and bathrooms are specifically designed, problem areas include the entrance, furniture configuration, closet hanging rails, beds, grab bars, height of toiletries cabinet, and wheel-in shower stall.

❷ Elevators: the width of the door is important; in older ships, controls often can't be reached from a wheelchair.

❸ Few ships have access-help lifts installed at swimming pools (exception: P&O Cruises) or angled steps with handrail, or thalassotherapy pools or shore tenders (exception: Holland America Line).

❹ It can be hard to access areas like self-serve buffets.

❺ Some insurance companies may prohibit smaller ships from accepting passengers with severe disabilities.

❻ Only five cruise ships have direct access ramps to lifeboats: *Amadea, Asuka II, Crystal Serenity, Crystal Symphony* and *Europa*.

12 tips to avoid pitfalls

❶ Start by planning an itinerary and date, and find a travel agent who knows your needs. But follow up on all aspects of the booking yourself to avoid slip-ups; many cruise lines have a department or person to handle requests from disabled passengers.

❷ Choose a cruise line that permits you to select a specific cabin, not just a price category.

If the ship does not have any specially equipped cabins, book the best outside cabin in your price range, or choose another ship.

❸ Check whether your wheelchair will fit through your cabin's bathroom door, or into the shower area whether there is a "lip" at the door. Don't accept "I think so" as an answer. Get specific measurements.

❹ Choose a cabin close to an elevator. Not all elevators go to all decks, so check the deck plan carefully. Smaller and older vessels may not even have elevators, making access to even the dining room difficult.

❺ Avoid, at all costs, a cabin down a little alleyway shared by several other cabins, even if the price is attractive. It's hard to access a cabin in a wheelchair from such an alleyway.

❻ Cabins located amidships are less affected by vessel motion, so choose something in the middle of the ship if you are concerned about possible rough seas. The larger – and therefore more expensive – the cabin, the more room you will have to maneuver in. And a tub provides more space than a shower.

❼ Hanging rails in the closets on most ships are positioned too high for someone in a wheelchair to reach – even the latest ships seem to repeat this basic error. Many cruise ships, however, have cabins specially fitted out to suit the mobility-limited. They are typically

If you need a wheelchair, you should take one with you.

fitted with roll-in closets and have a pull-down facility to bring your clothes down to any height you want.

❽ Meals in some ships may be served in your cabin, on special request – an advantage should you wish to avoid dressing for every meal. But few ships have enough space in the cabin for dining tables. If you opt for a dining room with two fixed-time seatings for meals, choose the second – it's more leisurely. Alert the restaurant manager in advance that you would like a table that leaves plenty of room for your wheelchair.

❾ Hand-carry medical records. Once on board, tell the reception desk help may be needed in an emergency.
❿ Make sure that the contract specifically states that if, for any reason, the cabin is not available, that you will get a full refund and transportation back home as well as a refund on any hotel bills incurred.
⓫ Advise the cruise line of the need for proper transfer facilities such as buses or vans with wheelchair ramps or hydraulic lifts.
⓬ If you live near the port of embarkation, arrange to visit the ship to check its suitability (most cruise lines will be accommodating).

Coping with embarkation

The boarding process can pose problems. If you embark at ground level, the gangway may be level or inclined. It will depend on the embarkation deck of the ship and/or the tide in the port.

Alternatively, you may be required to embark from an upper level of a terminal, in which case the gangway could well be of the floating loading-bridge type, like those used at major airports. Some have flat floors; others may have raised lips at regular intervals. The lips can be awkward to negotiate in a wheelchair, especially if the gangway is made steeper by a rising tide.

Ship-to-shore launches

Cruise lines should – but don't always – provide an anchor emblem in brochures for those ports of call where a ship will be at anchor instead of alongside. If the ship is at anchor, the crew will lower you and your wheelchair into a waiting tender and then, after a short boat-ride, lift you out again onto a rigged gangway or integral platform. If the sea is calm, this maneuver proceeds uneventfully; if the sea is choppy, it could vary from exciting to somewhat harrowing.

WHY DOORS CAN PRESENT A PROBLEM FOR WHEELCHAIR USERS

The design of ships has traditionally worked against the mobility-limited. To keep water out or to prevent water escaping from a flooded area, raised edges ("lips") – unfriendly to wheelchairs – are often placed in doorways and across exit pathways. Also, cabin doorways, at a standard 24 inches (60cm) wide, are often not wide enough for wheelchairs – about 30 inches (76 cm) is needed.

Bathroom doors, whether they open outward or inward, similarly hinder maneuverability. An electrically operated sliding door would be better.

Bathrooms in many older ships are small and full of plumbing fixtures, often at odd angles, awkward when moving about in a wheelchair. Those aboard

The author tests accessibility.

new ships are more accessible, but the plumbing may be located beneath the complete prefabricated module, making the floor higher than that in the cabin, which means a ramp is needed.

Some cruise lines will, if given advance notice, remove a bathroom door and hang a fabric curtain in its place. Many lines will provide ramps for the bathroom doorway if needed.

Access to outside decks is usually through doors that must be opened manually rather than via automatic electric-eye doors.

It's not cheap to provide facilities for wheelchair-bound passengers. Trained crew members are needed to assist them, which translates to two crew members per eight-hour shift. Thus, six crew members would be required according to the latest safety and evacuation regulations solely to provide support for one wheelchair-bound passenger – a big drain on labor resources.

This type of embarkation is rare except in a busy port with several ships sailing the same day. Holland America Line is one of the few companies to make shore tenders accessible to the disabled, with a special boarding ramp and scissor lift so that wheelchair passengers can see out of the shore tender's windows.

Help for the hearing impaired

Difficulties for such passengers include hearing announcements on the public address system; using the telephone; and poor acoustics in key areas such as boarding shore tenders.

Take a spare hearing aid battery. More new ships have cabins specially fitted with colored signs to help those who are hearing impaired. Crystal Cruises' *Crystal Serenity* and *Crystal Symphony*, and Celebrity

Cruises' *Celebrity Century, Celebrity Galaxy*, and *Celebrity Mercury* have movie theaters fitted with special headsets for those with hearing difficulties.

Finally, when going ashore, particularly on organized excursions, be aware that most destinations, particularly in Europe and Southeast Asia, are simply not equipped to handle people with hearing impairment.

The latest improvements

Things are getting better. For example, the large resort ships *Norwegian Gem, Norwegian Jewel* and *Norwegian Pearl* provide:
● 11 wheelchair-accessible public toilets throughout each ship (including the spa).
● 27 wheelchair-accessible cabins, including suites. All have collapsible shower stools mounted on shower

WHICH SHIPS BEST CATER FOR THE PHYSICALLY CHALLENGED

Adventure of the Seas	A	Carnival Fascination	C	Costa Marina	D	Insignia	B
Aegean Pearl	D	Carnival Freedom	B	Costa Mediterranea	B	Island Escape	D
AIDAaura	B	Carnival Glory	B	Costa Pacifica	B	Island Princess	B
AIDAbella	B	Carnival Imagination	C	Costa Romantica	B	Island Sky	D
AIDAcara	B	Carnival Inspiration	C	Costa Serena	B	Island Star	B
AIDAdiva	B	Carnival Legend	B	Costa Victoria	B	Ivory	D
AIDAluna	B	Carnival Liberty	B	Crown Princess	A	Jewel of the Seas	B
AIDAvita	B	Carnival Miracle	B	Crystal Serenity	A	Kapitan Dranitsyn	D
Albatros	C	Carnival Paradise	C	Crystal Symphony	A	Kapitan Khlebnikov	D
Alexander von Humboldt	D	Carnival Pride	B	Dawn Princess	B	Kristina Regina	D
Amadea	C	Carnival Sensation	C	Delphin	D	Le Diamant	D
American Eagle	D	Carnival Spirit	B	Delphin Voyager	C	Le Levant	D
American Glory	D	Carnival Splendor	B	Deutschland	C	Le Ponant	D
American Spirit	D	Carnival Triumph	B	Diamond Princess	B	Legend of the Seas	B
American Star	D	Carnival Valor	B	Discovery	C	Liberty of the Seas	A
Amsterdam	B	Carnival Victory	B	Disney Magic	B	Maasdam	B
Andrea	D	Celebrity Century	B	Disney Wonder	B	Majesty of the Seas	C
Aquamarine	D	Celebrity Constellation	A	Emerald Princess	B	Marco Polo	C
Arcadia	B	Celebrity Galaxy	B	Empress	C	Mariner of the Seas	A
Arion	D	Celebrity Infinity	A	Enchantment of		Minerva	C
Artemis	B	Celebrity Mercury	B	the Seas	B	Monarch of the Seas	C
Astor	C	Celebrity Millennium	A	Eurodam	B	Monet	D
Asuka II	A	Celebrity Solstice	A	Europa	B	MSC Armonia	B
Aurora	B	Celebrity Summit	A	Explorer of the Seas	A	MSC Fantasia	A
Azamara Journey	C	Celebrity Xpedition	D	Freedom of the Seas	A	MSC Lirica	B
Azamara Quest	C	Clelia II	D	Fuji Maru	D	MSC Melody	C
Balmoral	B	Clipper Adventurer	D	Funchal	D	MSC Musica	B
Black Prince	D	Clipper Odyssey	C	Galapagos Explorer II	D	MSC Opera	B
Black Watch	C	Club Med 2	D	Golden Princess	A	MSC Orchestra	B
Bleu de France	B	C. Columbus	D	Grand Mistral	C	MSC Poesia	B
Blue Monarch	D	Coral	D	Grand Princess	A	MSC Rhapsody	D
Boudicca	C	Coral Princess	B	Grand Voyager	B	MSC Sinfonia	B
Braemar	B	Corinthian II	D	Grande Caribe	D	MSC Splendida	B
Bremen	D	Costa Allegra	D	Grande Mariner	D	National Geographic	
Brilliance of the Seas	B	Costa Atlantica	B	Grandeur of the Seas	B	Endeavour	D
Caribbean Princess	B	Costa Classica	B	Hanseatic	D	Nautica	B
Carnival Conquest	B	Costa Concordia	B	Hebridean Princess	D	Navigator of the Seas	A
Carnival Destiny	B	Costa Europa	C	Hebridean Spirit	D	Nippon Maru	C
Carnival Ecstacy	C	Costa Fortuna	B	Holiday	D	Noordam	B
Carnival Elation	C	Costa Luminosa	B	Independence of		Norwegian Dawn	A
Carnival Fantasy	C	Costa Magica	B	the Seas	B	Norwegian Gem	B

Carnival's colorful elevators, good for wheelchair users.

walls; all bathroom toilets have collapsible arm guards and lower washbasin. Other cabin equipment includes a vibrating alarm clock, door beacon (light flashes when someone knock on the door), television with closed caption decoders, and a flashing light as fire alarm.
● Hearing-impaired kits on request.
● Dedicated wheelchair positions in the showlounge (including induction systems).
● Electrical hoist to access pool and hot tubs.
● All elevators and cabins have Braille text.

Check the ratings

During a comprehensive inspection for this book, the author or one of his inspectors wheel around each ship to check wheelchair accessibility. Their ratings are shown in the chart below.   ❑

Norwegian Jade	B	Royal Princess	B	Silver Cloud	C	SuperStar Libra	C
Norwegian Jewel	B	Royal Star	D	Silver Shadow	B	SuperStar Virgo	B
Norwegian Majesty	D	Ruby Princess	B	Silver Whisper	B	The Calypso	D
Norwegian Pearl	B	Ryndam	C	Silver Wind	C	The Emerald	D
Norwegian Sky	B	Saga Rose	C	Sky Wonder	C	The Iris	D
Norwegian Spirit	B	Saga Ruby	C	Sovereign	C	Thomson Celebration	C
Norwegian Star	A	Sapphire	D	Spirit of '98	D	Thomson Destiny	C
Norwegian Sun	B	Sapphire Princess	B	Spirit of Adventure	D	Thomson Spirit	C
Ocean Dream	C	Seabourn Legend	D	Spirit of Alaska	D	Veendam	C
Ocean Majesty	D	Seabourn Odyssey	B	Spirit of Columbia	D	Ventura	B
Ocean Princess	B	Seabourn Pride	D	Spirit of Discovery	D	Vision of the Seas	B
Ocean Village	B	Seabourn Spirit	D	Spirit of Endeavour	D	Vistamar	D
Ocean Village Two	B	SeaDream I	D	Spirit of Glacier Bay	D	Volendam	B
Oceana	B	SeaDream II	D	Spirit of Oceanus	D	Voyager of the Seas	A
Oceanic	C	Sea Bird	D	Spirit of Yorktown	D	Westerdam	B
Oosterdam	B	Sea Cloud	D	Splendour of the Seas	B	Wind Spirit	D
Opera	C	Sea Cloud II	D	Star Clipper	D	Wind Star	D
Oriana	B	Sea Lion	D	Star Flyer	D	Wind Surf	D
Orient Queen	D	Sea Princess	B	Star Pisces	D	Yamal	D
Orion	D	Serenade of the Seas	A	Star Princess	A	Zaandam	B
Pacific	C	Seven Seas Mariner	A	Statendam	B	Zenith	B
Pacific Dawn	C	Seven Seas Navigator	B	Sun Princess	B	Zuiderdam	B
Pacific Princess	B	Seven Seas Voyager	A	SuperStar Aquarius	C		
Pacific Venus	C						
Paul Gauguin	C						
Polaris	D						
Pride of America	B						
Prince Albert II	D						
Princess Danae	D						
Prinsendam	A						
Professor Molchanov	D						
Professor Multanovskiy	D						
Queen Mary 2	A						
Queen Victoria	B						
Radiance of the Seas	B						
Regal Empress	D						
Regatta	B						
Rhapsody of the Seas	B						
Rotterdam	A						
Royal Clipper	D						
Royal Iris	D						

KEY A) Recommended as most suitable for wheelchair passengers
B) Reasonably accessible for wheelchair passengers
C) Moderately accessible for wheelchair passengers
D) Not suitable for wheelchair passengers

● The following ships of Carnival Cruise Lines have double-width entertainment deck promenades that are good for wheelchair passengers, but the public restrooms are not accessible. In addition, although the cabin bathrooms are equipped with shower stalls and grab rails, the bathrooms have a steel "lip" and are therefore neither suitable nor accessible when stepping out of a wheelchair: *Carnival Ecstasy, Carnival Elation, Carnival Fantasy, Carnival Fascination, Carnival Imagination, Carnival Inspiration, Carnival Paradise, Carnival Sensation, Holiday.*

● *Asuka II* (NYK Cruises), *Crystal Symphony* (Crystal Cruises) and *Europa* (Hapag-Lloyd Cruises) are the only ships presently in operation that provide special access ramps from an accommodation deck directly to the ship's lifeboats.

EXPEDITIONS AND NATURE CRUISES

**There are still some less explored areas to be
visited by the more adventurous, who want
to experience them before they are spoiled**

Passengers joining expeditions tend to be more self-reliant and more interested in doing or learning than in being entertained. They become "participants" and take an active role in almost every aspect of the voyage, which is destination-, exploration- and nature-intensive.

Naturalists, historians, and lecturers (rather than entertainers) are aboard each ship to provide background information and observations about wildlife. Each participant receives a personal logbook, illustrated and written by the wildlife artists and writers who accompany each cruise – a fine souvenir.

You can walk on pack ice in the islands and land masses in the Arctic Ocean and Arctic Circle, explore a huge penguin rookery on an island in the Antarctic Peninsula, the Falkland Islands or South Georgia, or search for "lost" peoples in Melanesia. Or you can cruise close to the source of the Amazon, gaze at species of flora and fauna in the Galápagos Islands (Darwin's laboratory), or watch a genuine dragon on the island of Komodo – from a comfortable distance, of course.

Briefings and lectures bring cultural and intellectual elements to expedition cruise vessels. There is no formal entertainment as such; passengers enjoy this type of cruise more for the camaraderie and learning experience, and being close to nature. The ships are designed and equipped to sail in ice-laden waters, yet they have a shallow enough draft to glide over coral reefs.

Travel in comfort

Despite being rugged, expedition cruise vessels can provide comfortable and even elegant surroundings for up to 200 passengers, and offer first-class food and service. Without traditional cruise ports at which to stop, a ship must be self-sufficient, be capable of long-range cruising, and be totally environmentally friendly.

Lars-Eric Lindblad pioneered expedition cruising in the late 1960s. A Swedish American, he turned travel into adventure by going to parts of the world tourists had not visited. After chartering several vessels for voyages to Antarctica, he organized the design and construction of a small ship capable of going almost anywhere in comfort and safety. In 1969, *Lindblad Explorer* was launched; it soon earned an enviable reputation in adventure travel. Others followed.

To put together cruise expeditions, companies turn to knowledgeable sources and advisors. Scientific institutions are consulted; experienced world explorers and naturalists provide up-to-date reports on wildlife sightings, migrations, and other natural phenomena. Although some days are scheduled for relaxation, participants are kept physically and mentally active. Thus it is unwise to consider such an adventure cruise if you are not completely ambulatory.

Adventure cruise companies provide expedition parkas and waterproof boots, but you will need to take waterproof trousers for Antarctica and the Arctic.

Antarctica

This is perhaps the ultimate place to chill out. It was first sighted only in 1820 by the American sealer Nathaniel Palmer, British naval officer Edward Bransfield, and Russian captain Fabian Bellingshausen.

For most, it is just a windswept frozen wasteland – it has been calculated that the ice mass contains almost 90 percent of the world's snow and ice, while its land mass is twice the size of Australia. For others, it represents the last pristine place on earth, empty of people,

A group from *Hanseatic* explores the Amazon.

A Hurtigruten expedition explores the Antarctic.

commerce, and pollution, yet offering awesome icescape scenery and a truly wonderful abundance of marine and bird life. There are no germs, and not a single tree.

As many as 35,000 people a year visit the continent – the only smoke-free continent on earth – yet the first human to come here did so within a generation of man landing on the moon. There is not a single permanent inhabitant of the continent, whose ice is as much as 2 miles (3km) thick. Its total land mass equals more than all the rivers and lakes on earth and exceeds that of China and India combined. Icebergs can easily be the size of Belgium. The continent has a raw beauty and an ever-changing landscape.

This region is, perhaps, the closest thing on earth to another planet, and it has an incredibly fragile ecosystem that needs international protection. It contains two-thirds of all the fresh water on Earth (covered by ice, in September there are 8.5 million square miles of sea ice, but only 1.2 million in March). Antarctica lies in the southern ocean, whose global reach is a crucial link in the chain that is the Earth's heat engine; the southern Ocean absorbs heat from the atmosphere, which in turn can cause sea levels to rise through thermal expansion and ocean currents.

Although visited by "soft" expedition cruise ships and even "normal"-sized cruise ships with ice-hardened hulls, the more remote "far side" – the

Oates and Scott Coasts, McMurdo Sound, and the famous Ross Ice Shelf – can be visited only by genuine icebreakers such as the 114-passenger *Kapitan Khlebnikov*, the first vessel to circumnavigate Antarctica with passengers, as the katabatic winds can easily reach more than 100 mph (160 km/h).

Only 100 passengers per ship are allowed ashore at any given time, so if you choose to sail aboard one of the larger ships that claim to include Antarctica on their itineraries, it will probably be to view it – but only from the ship. For real expedition cruising, choose a ship that includes a flotilla of Zodiac rubber inflatable landing craft, proper boot washing stations, and expedition equipment. Cruise ships that carry more than 500 passengers should not be allowed to sail in Antarctic waters, as the chances of rescue in the event of pack ice crushing a normal cruise ship hull, are virtually nil.

There are no docks in Antarctica – venturing "ashore" is done by Zodiacs, which is an integral part of the experience. So avoid the large resort ships in this region – they don't carry Zodiacs, cannot dock anywhere, and you will almost certainly be disappointed.

Be aware that you can get stuck even aboard these specialized expedition ships, as did *Nordkapp*, which ran aground near Deception Island in 2007, and *Clipper Adventurer* in February

10 TOP EXPEDITIONS

Aleutian-Pribiloff Islands
Amazon (Manaus-Iquitos)
Antarctic Peninsula
Galapagos Islands
Islands of Micronesia
Northwest Passage
Northeast Passage
Papua New Guinea
Ross Ice Shelf in Antarctica
Solomon Islands

2000, in an ice field – it had to be rescued by an Argentine Navy icebreaker. And, in November 2007, Canadian company GAP Expeditions' *Explorer* hit an iceberg in Bransfield Strait off King George Island and sank; all 91 passengers, nine expedition staff and 54 crew members were rescued thanks to the coordination efforts of the British Coast Guard and the Hurtigruten cruise ship *Nordnorge*.

Tip: Passengers would be advised to wear an identification bracelet or belt at all times while on an Antarctic expedition cruise.

Wildlife you may see or come into contact with include orcas, dolphins, the six species of Antarctic seals, penguins, birds, and various species of lichen and flora, depending on the area visited.

Note to photographers: take plastic bags to cover your camera, so that condensation forms inside the bag and not on your camera when changing from the cold of the outside Antarctic air to the warmth of your expedition cruise vessel. Make sure you know how to operate your camera with gloves on – frostbite is a real danger.

The Arctic

Want some Northern Exposure? Try the Arctic. The Arctic is an ocean surrounded by continents, whereas

An iguana basks in the sun in the Galápagos Islands.

Antarctica is an ice-covered continent surrounded by ocean. The Arctic Circle is located at 66 degrees, 33 minutes, and 3 seconds north, although this really designates where 24-hour days and nights begin.

THE LEADING EXPEDITION CRUISE VESSELS: HOW THEY RATE

Research Vessels/ True Expedition Vessels	Rating (Facilities max: 100)	Company/ Operator [1]	Built	Pass. Cabins	Max No. Passengers	Tonnage	Registry	Length (m)
Akademik Ioffe	48	Quark Expeditions	1988	55	110	6,460	Russia	117.10
Akademik Sergey Vavilov	50	Quark Expeditions	1988	40	110	6,231	Russia	117.80
Akademik Sholaskiy	44	Quark Expeditions	1982	22	44	2,140	Russia	71.56
Aleksey Maryshev	46	Oceanwide Expeditions	1990	22	44	2,000	Russia	70.00
Antarctic Dream	41	Antarctic Shipping	1959	39	78	2,180	Chile	83.00
Grigoriy Mikheev	46	Oceanwide Expeditions	1990	22	44	2,000	Russia	70.00
Kapitan Dranitsyn	50	Poseidon Arctic Voyages	1980	53	113	10,471	Russia	131.00
Kapitan Khlebnikov	51	Quark Expeditions	1981	54	114	12,288	Russia	132.49
Marina Svetaeva	45	Aurora Expeditions	1989	45	100	4,575	Russia	90.00
Polar Pioneer	47	Aurora Expeditions	1985	26	54	2,140	Russia	71.60
Professor Molchanov	44	Oceanwide Expeditions	1983	29	52	1,753	Russia	71.60
Professor Multanovskiy	44	Quark Expeditions	1983	29	49	1,753	Russia	71.60
Ocean Nova	48	Quark Expeditions/Albatros	1992	45	96	1,753	Greenland	73.00
Spirit of Enderby	44	Heritage Expeditions	1984	22	48	6,231	Russia	72.00
Yamal [2]	76	Quark Expeditions	1992	50	100	23,445	Russia	150.00
Other Expedition Cruise Ships								
Andrea	41	Various Tour Operators	1960	57	112	2,568	Norway	87.40
Bremen	76	Hapag-Lloyd Cruises	1990	82	184	6,752	Bahamas	111.51
Clipper Adventurer	56	Quark Expeditions	1976	61	122	5,750	Bahamas	100.01
Hanseatic	84	Hapag-Lloyd Cruises	1993	92	194	8,378	Bahamas	122.80
Lyubov Orlova	63	Quark Expeditions	1976	61	129	4,251	Malta	100.02
Marco Polo	55	Orient Lines	1965	425	915	22,080	Bahamas	176.28
Minerva	66	Swan Hellenic Cruises/ Voyages of Discovery	1996	178	474	12,500	Bahamas	133.00
National Geographic Endeavour	51	Lindblad Expeditions	1966	62	110	3,132	Bahamas	89.20
National Geographic Explorer	45	Lindblad Expeditions	1982	81	148	6,200	Bahamas	108.6
Orion	82	Orion Expedition Cruises	2003	53	139	4,050	Bahamas	102.70
Polar Star	56	Karlsen Shipping/ Polar Star Expeditions	1969	45	105	4,998	Barbados	86.50

NOTES: (1) = most expedition ships are sold by multiple expedition companies, or under full charter to one operator
(2) = nuclear powered

The Arctic is best defined as that region north of which no trees grow, and where water is the primary feature of the landscape. It is technically a desert (receiving less than 10 inches of rainfall a year) but actually teems with wildlife, including polar bears, walruses, seals, and Arctic birds.

It has short, cool summers; long, cold winters; and frequent high winds. Canada's Northwest Territories, which cover 1.3 million square miles, is part of the Arctic region, as are some of Russia's northernmost islands such as Franz Josef Land.

Passenger ships that have navigated the Northwest Passage linking the Atlantic and Pacific Oceans include *Lindblad Explorer* (1984), *World Discoverer* (1985), *Society Explorer* (1988), *Frontier Spirit* (1992), *Kapitan Khlebnikov* (1994, 1995, 1998, 2006, 2007, 2008), and *Hanseatic* (1995, 1996, 1997, 1999, 2007).

Greenland

The world's largest island, the inappropriately named Greenland, in the Arctic Circle, is 82 percent covered with ice – actually compressed snow – up to 11,000 feet thick (3,350 meters). Its rocks are among the world's oldest (the 3.8 billion-year-old Isukasia formations), and its ecosystem is one of the newest.

The glacier at Jacobshavn, also known as Ilulissat, is the world's fastest moving and creates a new iceberg every five minutes. Greenland, which was granted home rule by Denmark in 1978, makes its living from fishing. It is said to have more dogs than people – its population is 68,400 – and dogs are an important means of transport.

The Galápagos Islands

The Galápagos Islands, 600 miles (960km) off the coast of Ecuador in the Pacific Ocean, are a microcosm of our planet. More than 100 islands, mineral-rich outcroppings and lava outcroppings make up the Galápagos, which are fed by the nutrient-rich Cromwell and Humboldt currents. The fertile waters can be cold, even on the equator.

The Ecuadorians jealously guard their islands and prohibit the movement of almost all non-Ecuadorian-registered cruise vessels within its boundaries. The best way to follow in the footsteps of Charles Darwin, who visited the islands in 1835 aboard the *Beagle*, is to fly to Quito and cruise aboard an Ecuadorian-registered vessel.

The government of Ecuador set aside most of the islands as a wildlife sanctuary in 1934, while uninhabited areas were declared national parks in 1959. The national park includes approximately 97 per cent of the islands' landmass, together with 20,000 sq miles (50,000 sq km) of ocean. The Charles Darwin Research Station was established in 1964, and the government created the Galápagos Marine Resources Reserve in 1986.

The Galápagos National Park tax is about $100 per person. Smoking is prohibited on the islands, and no more than 50,000 visitors a year are admitted. ❑

HOW TO PROTECT SENSITIVE ENVIRONMENTS

Polar bears are under threat.

In the future, only ships capable of meeting new "zero discharge" standards, such as those introduced in the Arctic by the Canadian Coast Guard will be allowed to proceed through environmentally sensitive areas. Expedition cruise companies are concerned about the environment, and they spend much time and money in educating their crews and passengers about safe environmental procedures.

The "Antarctic Traveler's Code" (whose rules are enforced by all expedition cruise companies) is based on the Antarctic Conservation Act of 1978, designed to protect the region's ecosystem, flora, and fauna.

The Antarctic Treaty Meeting in Kyoto in 1994 made it unlawful, unless authorized by permit, to take native animals or birds, to collect any special native plant or introduce species, to enter certain special protected areas (SPAs), or to discharge or dispose of any pollutants.

To "take" means to remove, harass, molest, harm, pursue, hunt, shoot, kill, trap, capture, restrain, or tag any native mammal or bird, or to attempt to do so. Violators face civil penalties, including a fine of up to $10,000 and one-year imprisonment for each violation. A copy of the Act can be found in the library of each adventure or expedition ship that visits the continent.

Will large resort ships ever cruise in Antarctica? I hope not. Ships are limited to a maximum of 400 passengers, so the likelihood of a mega-ship zooming in on the penguins with 2,000-plus passengers is unlikely. Nor would it be possible to rescue so many passengers and crew in the event of an emergency.

COASTAL CRUISES

**Being all at sea doesn't appeal? You can stay close
to dry land by journeying round the coasts of
Australia, Europe, and North and South America**

AUSTRALIA

The marine wonderland of the Great Barrier Reef, a
World Heritage site off the northeast coast of Australia,
is the earth's largest living coral reef – it actually consists
of more than 2,800 individual coral reefs. It is visited by
around 70 local Australian boutique ship operators, who
mostly offer 1- to 4-night cruises to the reefs and Whit-
sunday Islands. The area is excellent for scuba diving
and snorkelers.

June through September is humpback whale-watching
season; the Reef shelters the young whales while the
adults nurture them in the shallow waters. Note that the
Australian government levies an environmental charge of
A$5 on everyone over four years of age visiting the Great
Barrier Reef and its environs.

NORWAY

There is year-round coastal cruising along the shores
of Norway to the Land of the Midnight Sun aboard the
ships of the Hurtigruten Group, formerly known as Norwegian Coastal Voyages. The fleet consists of small,
comfortable, working express coastal packet steamers
and contemporary cruise vessels that deliver mail, small
packaged goods, and foodstuffs, and take passengers, to
the communities spread on the shoreline.

Invariably dubbed "the world's most beautiful voyage." this is a 1,250-mile (2,000-km) journey from
Bergen in Norway to Kirkenes, close to the Russian border (half of which is north of the Arctic Circle) and takes
12 days. The service started in 1893, and the name Hurtigruten – meaning "fast route" – reflects the fact that
this coastal express was once the most reliable communication link between southern Norway and its remote
north. Today the company carries more than 300,000
passengers a year. It's a good way to meet Norwegians,
who treat the service like a bus.

You can join it at any of the 34 ports of call and stay

HURTIGRUTEN SHIPS			
Ship	**Tonnage**	**Built**	**Berths**
Finnmarken	15,000	2002	638
Fram	12,700	2007	328
Kong Harald	11,200	1993	490
Lofoten	2,621	1964	147
Lyngen	16,053	2003	652
Nordkapp	11,386	1996	464
Nordlys	11,200	1994	482
Nordnorge	11,386	1997	455
Nordstjernen *	2,621	1956	114
Polar Star *	4,998	1969	100
Polarlys	12,000	1996	479
Richard With	11,205	1993	483
Trollfjord	15,000	2002	648
Vesteralen	6,261	1983	316
* for expedition voyages only			

LEFT: sailing along Gieranger Fjord in Norway.

as long as you wish because the vessels, being working ships, sail every day of the year. At the height of summer, north of the Arctic Circle, there are 24 hours of daylight, and between November and February the northern lights create spectacular arcs across the sky. Some specialist voyages are aimed at birdwatchers and others include onboard concerts and lectures celebrating the work of Norwegian composer Edvard Grieg.

The ships can accommodate between 144 and 652 passengers. The newest ships have an elevator that can accommodate a wheelchair passenger, but otherwise, they are fairly plain and basic, practical vessels, with food that is more bistro than restaurant. Note that alcohol prices are extremely high, as they are throughout Norway, and that the currency is the Norwegian krone.

Archipelago hopping can be done along Sweden's eastern coast, too, by sailing in the daytime and staying overnight in one of the many small hotels. One vessel sails from Norrtalje, north of Stockholm, to Oskarshamn, near the Baltic island of Öland, right through the spectacular Swedish archipelago. You can also cruise from the Finnish city of Lappeenranta to the Estonian city of Viborg without a visa, thanks to perestroika. Point-to-point coastal transportation between neighboring countries, major cities, and commercial centers is big business in Northern Europe.

The Hurtigruten Group also operates utilitarian ships for expedition-style cruising in the Arctic, Antarctic, and Greenland.

SCOTLAND

The fishing town of Oban, two hours west of Glasgow by road, perhaps seems an unlikely point to start a cruise, but it is the base for one of the world's finest cruise experiences. *Hebridean Princess* is a little gem, with Laura Ashley-style interiors – elegant enough to have been chartered by Queen Elizabeth II for a family-only celebration of her 80th birthday in 2006. The food is great, and includes Scottish beef, local seafood and seasonal vegetables. There's fine personal service.

This ship, owned by Hebridean International Cruises, carries up to 49 passengers around some of Scotland's most magnificent coastline and islands. If you cruise from Oban, you can be met at Glasgow airport or rail station and taken to the ship by motor coach. Take lots of warm clothing, however (layers are best), as the weather can be flexible and often unkind.

As an alternative, there's *Lord of the Glens*, operated by Magna Carta Steamship Company and accommodating 54 passengers. It's another treat for small ship lovers, cruising in style through Scotland's lakes and canals.

NORTH AMERICA

Coastal cruise ships flying the American flag offer a complete change of style from the large resort cruise ships. They are American-owned and American-crewed, and informality is the order of the day. Because of their US registry, they can start from and return to a US port without being required by the Passenger Vessel Services Act to call at a foreign port along the way – which a foreign-flagged cruise ship must do.

Accommodating up to 150 passengers, the ships are more like private family affairs, and are rarely out of sight of land. These cruises are low-key, low pace, and not for active, adventurous types. Their operators seek out lesser-known areas, offering in-depth visits to destinations inaccessible to larger ships, both along the eastern and western seaboards of the USA, including Alaska.

Most passengers are over 60, and many over 70. They may prefer not to fly, and wherever possible drive or take a train to join their ship. During the summer, you might see a couple of children on board, but in general small kids are not allowed. There are no facilities for them, and no staff to look after them.

Destinations: Eastern US and Canadian seaboard cruises include the St. Lawrence River, Atlantic Coastal Waterways, New England (good for fall cruises), Cape Cod and the Islands (and Cape Cod Canal), the Great Lakes (and Welland Canal), the Colonial Deep South, and Florida waterways.

Western seaboard cruises cover Alaska, the Pacific Northwest, California Wine Country. and Baja California/Sea of Cortés. Cruises focus on historically-relevant destinations, nature and wildlife spotting, and coastal viewing. On some cruises, these boutique ships can dock adjacent to a town, allowing easy access on foot.

Getting close to the whales in Baja California.

SMALL COASTAL CRUISE VESSELS (more than 10 cabins)

Ship	Cruise Line	Cabins	Region	Built
American Eagle	American Cruise Lines	27	USA Coastal Cruises	2000
American Glory	American Cruise Lines	27	USA Coastal Cruises	2002
American Spirit	American Cruise Lines	50	USA Coastal Cruises	2005
American Star	American Cruise Lines	52	USA Coastal Cruises	2007
Andrea	Elegant Cruises & Tours	56	Antarctica/Patagonia	1960
Aranui 3	Campagnie Polynesienne de Transport Maritime	63	Tahiti/Marquesas	2003
Callisto	Travel Dynamics International	17	Greek Isles	1963
Celebrity Xpedition	Celebrity Cruises	47	Galápagos Islands	2001
CoCo Explorer	CoCo Explorer Cruises	56	Philippines	1967
Contessa	Majestic America Line	25	Alaska	1986
Coral Princess	Coral Princess Cruises	27	Australia (Great Barrier Reef)	1988
Corinthian	Ecoventura/Galápagos Network	45	Galápagos Islands	1967
Discovery	EPanama Marine Adventures	12	Panama	2004
Disko II	Arctic Umiaq Line	26	Greenland	1992
Emeraude	Emeraude Classic Cruises	38	Halong Bay (Vietnam)	2003
Evolution	various	17	Galápagos Islands	2004
Fantasea Ammari	Fantasea Adventure Cruising	32	Whitsunday Islands	2007
Galápagos Legend	GlobalQuest	57	Galápagos Islands	1963
Grande Caribe	American Canadian Caribbean Line	48	USA Coastal Cruises	1997
Grande Mariner	American Canadian Caribbean Line	50	USA Coastal Cruises	1999
Halcyon	various operators	24	Greek Islands, Mediterranean	1990
Haumana	Bora Bora Cruises	19	Tahiti and Islands	1997
Independence	American Cruise Lines	52	USA Coastal Cruises	2009
Isabela II	Metropolitan Touring	21	Galápagos Islands	1989
La Pinta	South American Experience	24	Galápagos Islands	2008
Lord of the Glens	Magna Carta Cruises	27	Scotland	1985
Lycianda	Blue Lagoon Cruises	21	Yasawa Islands (Fiji)	1984
Marco Polo	CroisiEurope	100	European Coast	2006
Mare Australis	Cruceros Australis	63	Patagonia	2002
Megastar Aries	Star Cruises	33	Southeast Asia	2000
Megastar Taurus	Star Cruises	33	Southeast Asia	2000
Monet	Elegant Cruises & Tours	30	Croatian Coast	1970
Mystique Princess	Blue Lagoon Cruises	36	Yasawa Islands (Fiji)	1996
Nanuya Princess	Blue Lagoon Cruises	25	Yasawa Islands (Fiji)	1987
National Geographic Islander	Lindblad Expeditions	24	Galápagos Islands	1995
Oceanic Discoverer	Coral Princess Cruises	38	Australia (Great Barrier Reef)	2005
Pacific Aurora	British Columbia Discovery Voyages	34	British Columbia (Canada)	1962
Pacific Explorer	Cruise West	50	Central America	1970
Pearl	Pearl Seas Cruises	108	USA Coastal Cruises	2008
Pegasus	Classical Cruises	23	Greek Islands, Mediterranean	1992
Quest	Noble Caledonia	26	Scotland, Norway, Greenland	1992
Reef Escape	Captain Cook Cruises	60	Australia	1987
Safari Explorer	American Safari Cruises	18	Alaska/Mexico Coast	1998
Safari Quest	American Safari Cruises	11	Alaska/Mexico Coast	1992
Santa Cruz	Metropolitan Touring	43	Galápagos Islands	1979
Sea Bird	Lindblad Expeditions	35	Alaska, Baja	1981
Sea Lion	Lindblad Expeditions	35	Alaska, Baja	1982
Sea Voyager	Lindblad Expeditions	33	Central America	1982
Shearwater	various operators	40	Worldwide	1962
Skorpios III	GlobalQuest	50	Chilean Fjords	1988
Spirit of '98	Cruise West	48	Alaska	1984
Spirit of Alaska	Cruise West	39	Alaska	1980
Spirit of Columbia	Cruise West	39	Alaska	1979
Spirit of Discovery	Cruise West	25	Alaska	1982
Spirit of Endeavor	Cruise West	51	Alaska	1983
Spirit of Glacier Bay	Cruise West	51	Alaska	1984
Spirit of Oceanus	Cruise West	50	Alaska/South Pacific	1991
Spirit of Yorktown	Cruise West	69	Alaska	1988
Tia Moana	Bora Bora Cruises	37	Tahitian Islands	2003
Tu Moana	Bora Bora Cruises	37	Tahitian Islands	2003
Tropic Sun	Aquanaut Cruise Lines	24	Galápagos Islands	1967
True North	North Star Cruises	18	Australia (west coast)	2005

LEFT: cruising the inland waterways near Lake Erie.

The ships: These "D-class" vessels are less than 2,500 tons, and are subject neither to bureaucratic regulations nor to union rules. They are restricted to cruising no more than 20 miles (32 km) offshore, at a comfortable 12 knots (13.8mph). Public room facilities are limited. Because the vessels are American-registered, there is no casino. They really are ultra-casual, no-frills ships with the most basic of facilities, no swimming pools, little artwork, and no glitz in interior decor. They usually have three or four decks and, except for the ships of American Cruise Lines, no elevator. Stairs can be steep and are not recommended for people with walking difficulties. Because of this, some ships have an electric chair-lift on indoor or outdoor stairways.

Cabins: Accommodation is in outside-view cabins, some of which open directly onto a walking deck – inconvenient when it rains. Each has a picture window and small bathroom. They are small and basic, with very limited closet space – perhaps just a curtain across a space with a hanging rod for clothes. Many do not have a television or telephone. There's no room service, and you may have to turn your own bed down. Cabins are closer to the engines and generators than aboard the large resort ships, so generator humming noises can be disturbing at night. The quietest cabins are at the ship's bows – although there could be noise if the ship is equipped with a bow thruster – and most cruising is done in the early morning so that passengers can sleep better at night.

Tall passengers should note that the overall length of beds rarely exceeds 6 ft (1.82 meters). While soap is provided, it's best to bring your own shampoo, conditioner, and other personal toiletries. American Canadian Caribbean Line's ships do not have cabin keys, and most passengers don't feel they need to lock their doors at night anyway.

Although some of the older ships are really basic, the latest ones, particularly those of American Cruise Lines, are very comfortable. Because they are not classified for open-water cruising, though, they don't have to conform to the same rigorous shipbuilding standards that larger ocean-going cruise ships do. You may find that hot and cold water lines run close to each other in your bathroom, thus delivering neither really hot nor really cold water. Sound insulation could be almost non-existent.

Activities: The principal evening event is dinner in the dining room, which accommodates all passengers at once. This can be a family-style affair, with passengers at long tables, and the food passed around.

The cuisine is decidedly American, with fresh local specialties featured. However, menus aboard the ships of American Canadian Caribbean Cruise Line and Cruise West are very limited, while those aboard the ships of American Cruise Lines offer slightly more variety, including seasonal items. You'll probably be asked in the morning to choose which of two main courses you would like for dinner.

Evening entertainment consists mainly of after-dinner conversation. Most vessels are in port during the time, so you can easily go ashore for the local nightlife, although most passengers simply go to bed early.

If you have taken a cruise aboard one of the large resort ships, you'll know that standing in long lines waiting to get back on board and go through the security check can be a painful experience – in every port. However, passengers aboard the small coastal ships sometimes aren't asked to show their ID cards when rejoining a ship, because gangway staff recognize them. Another advantage is that you won't get seasick because these ships sail mostly in sheltered waters and inshore bays, inlets and rivers.

The cost: This kind of cruising is expensive, with an average daily rate of around $400–$800 a person. Suggested gratuities are high – typically about $125 per person, per 7-day cruise – but they are at least shared by all the personnel on board. ❑

COASTAL CRUISE LINES IN NORTH AMERICA

There are five cruise companies: American Canadian Caribbean Line, American Cruise Lines, American Safari Cruises, Cruise West, and Lindblad Expeditions.

What differentiates them? American Cruise Lines and American Safari Cruises provide better food and service than the others. American Cruise Lines' ships have larger cabins, and more public rooms. Drinks are included aboard the ships of American Cruise Lines only. American Canadian Caribbean Line and American Cruise Lines operate on the USA's east coast; American Safari Cruises and Lindblad Expeditions operate on the USA's west coast and Alaska.

Pearl Seas Cruises, a new company under the same ownership as American Cruise Lines, introduced its first new ship in 2009. Considerably larger than those of the other lines, they accommodate 210 passengers, have an all-American registry and crew, are certified for oceangoing voyages, have more lounges and facilities and much larger cabins, and aspire to the standards set by international boutique ships. Itineraries include cruises around Newfoundland, the Caribbean and Central America.

SAILING SHIPS

Want to be free as the wind? Think about cruising under sail, with towering masts, the creak of taut ropes and gleaming white sails to power you along

There is simply nothing that beats the thrill of being aboard a multi-mast tall ship, sailing under thousands of square feet of canvas through waters that mariners have sailed for centuries. This is cruising in the traditional manner, aboard authentic sailing ships, contemporary copies of clipper ships, or aboard high-tech cruise-sail ships.

There are no rigid schedules, and life aboard equates to an unstructured lifestyle, apart from meal times. Weather conditions may often dictate whether a scheduled port visit will be made or not, but passengers sailing on these vessels are usually unconcerned. They would rather savor the thrill of being one with nature, albeit in a comfortable, civilized setting, and without having to do the work themselves. The more luxurious sailing ships are the closest most people will get to owning their own mega-yacht.

Sailing ships allow lots of time for relaxation.

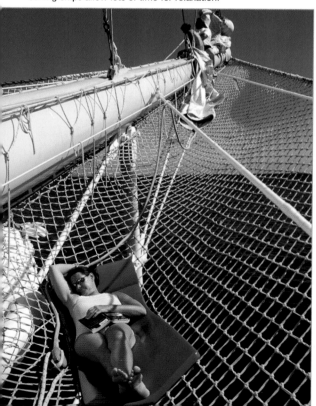

Real tall ships

While we have all been dreaming of adventure, a pocketful of designers and yachtsmen committed pen to paper, hand in pocket and rigging to mast, and came up with a potpourri of stunning vessels to delight the eye and refresh the spirit. Examples are *Royal Clipper, Sea Cloud, Sea Cloud II, Star Clipper,* and *Star Flyer.*

Of these, *Sea Cloud*, built in 1931 and restored in 1979, is the most romantic sailing ship afloat. It operates under charter for much of the year, and sails in both the Caribbean and the Mediterranean. A kind of stately home afloat, *Sea Cloud* remains one of the finest and most exhilarating travel experiences in the world.

The activities are few, and so relaxation is the key, in a stylish but unpretentious setting. The food and service are good, as is the interaction between the 69 passengers and 60 crew, many of whom have worked aboard the ship for many years. One bonus is the fact that the doctor on board is available at no charge for emergencies or seasickness medication.

Although passengers may be able to participate occasionally in the furling and unfurling of the sails, they are not permitted to climb the rigging, as may be possible aboard some of the other, more modern tall ships.

Both Sea Cloud Cruises and Star Clippers are building new, real tall ships.

Contemporary sail-cruise ships

To combine sailing with push-button automation, try *Club Med 2* (Club Méditerranée) or *Wind Surf* (Windstar Cruises) – with five tall aluminum masts, they are the world's largest sail-cruise ships – and *Wind Spirit* and *Wind Star* (Windstar Cruises), with four masts. Not a hand touches the sails; they are computer-controlled from the navigation bridge.

There's little sense of sailing in these oceangoing robots because the computer keeps the ship on an even keel. Also, some people find it hard to get used to the whine of the vessels' generators, which run the lighting and air-conditioning systems 24 hours a day.

From a yachtsman's viewpoint, the sail-to-power ratio is poor. That's why these cruise ships with sails have engine power to get them into and out of port. The Star Clipper ships, by contrast, do it by sail alone, except when there is no wind, which doesn't happen often.

Star Clippers' superb *Royal Clipper* under full sail.

On some itineraries, when there is little wind, you could be motor-powered for most of the cruise, with only a few hours under sail. The three Windstar Cruises vessels and one Club Med ship are typically under sail for about 40 percent of the time.

The Windstar ships carry mainly North Americans and the Club Med vessel mainly French-speakers.

Another slightly smaller but chic vessel is *Le Ponant*. This three-mast ship caters to just 64 French-speaking passengers in elegant, yet casual, high-tech surroundings, developing the original Windstar concept to an advanced state of contemporary technology. The ship made news in 2008 when its crew were held to ransom by pirates off the Somali coast; no passengers were on board at the time.

When the engine cuts in

So, do you get to cruise under sail most of the time? The answer is – not really. Aboard the ships of Sea Cloud Cruises and Star Clippers, because they are real tall ships, you could be under sail for most of the night when the ships are under way, as long as there is wind, of course, and on the days or part days at sea. The ship's small engine is used for maneuvering in and out of port. In the Caribbean, for example, the trade winds are good for most of the year, while in the Med iterranean, the winds are not so potent. But the thrill for many passengers is getting involved and helping to furl and unfurl the sails, and being able to climb the rigging, and to lie in the netting under the bows – it's a memorable experience.

Aboard the ships of Windstar Cruises, however, the itineraries are so port-intensive that the computer-controlled sails are hardly ever used today – so the experience can be disappointing. ❏

HOW TO MEASURE WIND SPEEDS

Understanding wind patterns is important to sailing ships, but it's easy to be confused by the numbering system for wind velocity. There are 12 velocities, known as "force" on the Beaufort scale, devised in 1805 by Commodore Francis Beaufort and adopted internationally in 1874 as the official means of recording wind velocity. They are as follows, with descriptions of the ocean surface:

Force 0 (0–1mph): Calm; glassy (like a mirror).
Force 1 (1–3mph): Light wind; rippled surface.
Force 2 (4–7mph): Light breeze; small wavelets.
Force 3 (8–12mph): Gentle breeze; large wavelets, scattered whitecaps.
Force 4 (13–18mph): Moderate breeze; small waves, frequent whitecaps.
Force 5 (19–24mph): Fresh breeze; moderate waves, numerous whitecaps.
Force 6 (25–31mph): Strong breeze; large waves, white foam crests.
Force 7 (32–38mph): Moderate gale; streaky white foam.
Force 8 (39–46mph): Fresh gale; moderately high waves.
Force 9 (47–54mph): Strong gale; high waves.
Force 10 (55–63mph): Whole gale; very high waves, curling crests.
Force 11 (64–73mph): Violent storm; extremely high waves, froth and foam, poor visibility.
Force 12 (73+mph): Hurricane; huge waves, thundering white spray, visibility nil.

FREIGHTER TRAVEL

These slow voyages appeal to independent
types who don't require constant entertainment,
and the accommodation can be surprisingly comfortable

More than 3,000 passengers travel by freighter each year, and the number is growing as passengers become further disenchanted with the large resort ships that dominate the cruise industry. Traveling by freighter is also the ultimate way to travel for those seeking a totally unstructured voyage without entertainment or other diversions. The experience has particular appeal for retirees, relocating executives, those with far-flung family connections, graduates returning home from an overseas college, or professors on sabbatical leave.

There are about 250 cargo ships (freighters and container vessels) offering berths, with German operators accounting for more than half of them. True freighters – the general breakbulk carrier ships and feeder container vessels – carry up to 12 passengers; the only exception is the Royal Mail Ship *RMS St. Helena*, which carries up

Double cabin on *Hansa Flensburg* (USA to Australia).

to 128 passengers, animals such as goats and sheep, and goods from the UK to the island of Ascension, While *RMS St. Helena* carries a doctor, freighters do not, and remember that they are working vessels, not cruise ships.

Freighter schedules change constantly, depending on the whim of the owner and the cargo to be carried, whereas container ships travel on regular schedules. For the sake of simplicity, they are all termed freighters. But freighters have changed dramatically as cost management and efficiency have become vital. Container ships are operated as passenger liners used to be: running line voyages on set schedules.

Most freighter companies do not allow children or pregnant women to travel. Because there are no medical facilities, anyone over 65 is usually required to produce a medical certificate of good health.

Freighter facilities

What do you get when you book a freighter voyage? You get a cabin with double or twin beds, a small writing table, and a private bathroom. You also get good company, cocktails with conversation, hearty food (you'll eat in one seating with the ship's officers), an interesting voyage, a lot of water, and the allure of days at sea. What don't you get? Organized entertainment. You will certainly have time to relax and read books (some freighters have a small library).

The accommodation will consist of a spacious, well-equipped outside-view cabin high above the water line, with a large window rather than a porthole, comfortable lounge/sitting area, and private facilities – far larger than

---

most standard cruise ship cabins are.

While freighter travel can be less expensive than regular cruise ship travel on a per day basis ($75–$150), remember that voyages last much longer – typically 30 days or more – so the cost can be considerable. Most are sold out far in advance (often more than a year ahead), so plan ahead, and purchase trip cancellation insurance.

What to bring

What to take with you? Casual clothing (check with the freighter line, as some require a jacket and tie for dinner), all medications, cosmetics, and toiletry items, hairdryer, multi-voltage converter plug, washing powder, and other sundry items such as soap, sun protection, insect repellent, and small flashlight. There may be a small "shop" on board (for the crew) carrying bare essentials like toothpaste.

Bring along your medical certificate, travel insurance details, money in cash, and some extra photos of yourself in case the ship makes unannounced port stops and visas are required. The only gratuities needed are for the waiter and cabin steward, which are generally set at about $1–$2 per day, per person.

New international security regulations mean that if you book a one-way voyage, you must have all onward travel documents with you. Check with embassies and consulates of the countries you will visit. Note that freighters visit cargo ports, so private transportation such as taxis will need to be arranged in advance.

Freighters sometimes have to cancel port calls for various commercial reasons at short notice. Bear this in mind if you are attracted by a particular itinerary or a certain port. ❏

ABOVE: the *Hatsu Crystal* carries five passengers.
BELOW: *Ital Contessa* plies between Europe and Asia.

Queen Mary 2

1. Minnows Pool
2. Terrace Pool
3. Grand Duplex & Duplex Apartments
4. Kennels
5. Boardwalk Café
6. Fairways – Golf Simulators
7. The Pavilion
8. Splash Pool
9. Sports Centre
10. The Lookout – Observation Deck
11. Atlantic Room
12. Commodore Club Lounge
13. Library & Bookshop
14. Royal Suites with private lift access
15. Illuminations – Theatre & Auditorium
16. Canyon Ranch SpaClub

NORTH ATLANTIC CROSSINGS

You're facing the world's most unpredictable
weather, but there's still something romantic
about this classic ocean voyage

C rossing the 3,000 miles (4,800km) of the North Atlantic by passenger vessel can be considered an art. I have done it 153 times and always enjoy it immensely. I consider crossings as rests in musical parlance, for both are described as "passages." Indeed, musicians do often "hear" rests in between notes. So if ports of call are the musical notes of a voyage, then the rests are the days at sea – temporary interludes, when physical and mental indulgence become ends in themselves.

Experienced mariners will tell you that a ship behaves like a ship only when it is doing a crossing, for that's what a real ship is built for. Yet the days when ships were built specifically for crossings are almost gone. The only one offering a regularly scheduled transatlantic service (a "crossing") is Cunard Line's *Queen Mary 2*, a 148,151-ton ship, built with a thick hull designed to

hold well against the worst weather the North Atlantic has to offer. The most unpredictable weather in the world, together with fog off the Grand Banks of Newfoundland, can mean that the captain will spend torturous hours on the bridge, with little time for socializing.

When it is foggy, the crew of *Queen Mary 2* is often pestered by passengers wanting to know if the ship has yet approached latitude 41°46' north, longitude 50°14' west – where White Star Line's 43,326-ton *Titanic* struck an Arctic iceberg on that fateful April night in 1912.

A great tradition

There is something magical in "doing a crossing." It takes you back to the days when hordes of passengers turned up at the piers of the ports of New York, Southampton, Cherbourg, or Hamburg, accompanied by

QUEEN MARY 2

An anatomy of the world's premier ocean liner

- ⑰ Cunard ConneXions
- ⑱ Royal Court Theatre
- ⑲ Winter Garden Lounge
- ⑳ Grand Lobby
- ㉑ Empire Casino
- ㉒ King's Court Alternative Dining Venues
- ㉓ Champagne Bar
- ㉔ Golden Lion Pub
- ㉕ Chart Room Bar and Lounge
- ㉖ Britannia Restaurant
- ㉗ Queen's Grill Lounge
- ㉘ Todd English Restaurant
- ㉙ Queen's Room – Ballroom
- ㉚ Queen's Grill
- ㉛ Children's Facilities
- ㉜ G32 Nightclub

chauffeurs and steamer trunks, jewels and finery. Even today, excitement and anticipation usually precede a crossing. First there is the hubbub and bustle of check-in, then the crossing of the threshold on the gangway before being welcomed into the calmness aboard, and finally escorted to one's accommodation.

Once the umbilical cord of the gangway is severed, bow and stern mooring lines are cast off, and with three long blasts on the ship's deep whistle, the *QM2* is pried gently from its berth. The ship sails silently down the waterway, away from the world, as serene as a Rolls-Royce. Passengers on deck often observe motorboats trying to keep up with the giant liner as it edges away from Brooklyn's Red Hook Pier 12 towards the Statue of Liberty, the restored Ellis Island, then under the Verrazano-Narrows Bridge, and out to the open sea. Coming westbound, arriving in New York by ship is one of the world's thrilling travel experiences.

The *QM2* has year-round scheduled cross-ings, whereas other cruise ships crossing the Atlantic are little more than repositioning cruises – a way of moving ships that cruise the Mediterranean in summer to the Caribbean in winter, and vice versa – they offer more chances to experience the romance and adventure of a crossing, usually in spring and fall. These satisfy those wanting uninterrupted days at sea and lots of leisure time.

Most cruise ships operating repositioning crossings cross the Atlantic using the "sunny southern route" – departing from southern ports such as Ft. Lauderdale, San Juan, or Barbados, and ending the journey in Lis-bon, Genoa, or Copenhagen via the Azores or the Canary Islands off the coast of northern Africa. In this way, they avoid the more difficult weather often encountered in the North Atlantic. Such crossings take longer, however: between eight and 12 days. ❑

Queen Mary 2 sails out of New York.

WORLD CRUISES

They sound like a great way to see the world without having to pack and unpack constantly. But choose carefully: some cruises spend very little time in ports

The ultimate classic voyage for any experienced traveler is a round-the-world cruise, defined as the complete circumnavigation of the earth in a continuous one-way voyage. Ports of call are carefully planned for their interest and diversity, and the entire voyage can last six months or longer. Galas, themed balls, special social events, top entertainers, and, typically, well-known lecturers are all part of the package. It's a great way of exchanging the northern winter for the southern sun.

A world cruise aboard a modern ship means experiencing stabilized, air-conditioned comfort in luxury cabins, and extraordinary sight-seeing and excursions on shore and overland. In some ships, every passenger will get to dine with the captain at least once.

Check brochures and itineraries carefully. Some ships spend surprisingly little time in port. On the 2003 world cruise of *Aurora*, for example, there were no overnight stays at all, even in some of the planet's most desirable port cities such as San Francisco, Sydney, Hong Kong, Tokyo, or Singapore.

World cruise segments

If you haven't the time or the funds for a full world cruise, it's possible to book a specific segment, flying to join the ship at one of its ports of call and disembarking at another port. In this way you can visit exotic destinations such as China, the South Pacific, the Indian Ocean, or South America while enjoying the elegance, comfort, splendid food, and good company that are associated with world cruises.

Bear in mind that you tend to get what you pay for.

AROUND THE WORLD CRUISES 2009–10

Ship	Company	Days	Date	From (Start)	Date (Finish)
Albatros	Phoenix Reisen	140	December 12, 2009	Monte Carlo	May 5, 2010
Amadea	Phoenix Reisen	148	December 20, 2009	Hamburg	May 17, 2010
Arcadia	P&O Cruises	102	January 5, 2009	Southampton	April 16, 2009
Astoria	Transocean Tours	124	November 11, 2008	Nice	April 4, 2009
Asuka II	NYK Cruises	104	April 12, 2009	Yokohama	July 25, 2009
Aurora	P&O Cruises	94	January 11, 2009	Southampton	April 1, 2009
Balmoral	Fred Olsen Cruise Lines	105	February 14, 2009	Dover	May 29, 2009
Black Watch	Fred Olsen Cruise Lines	98	January 6, 2009	Southampton	April 13, 2009
Columbus	Hapag-Lloyd Cruises	167	November 28, 2008	Genoa	May 13, 2009
Crystal Serenity *	Crystal Cruises	105	January 21, 2009	Los Angeles	May 7, 2009
Europa	Hapag-Lloyd Cruises	165	November 6, 2008	Dubai	April 22, 2009
Ocean Princess	Princess Cruises	118	January 14, 2009	Fort Lauderdale	May 1, 2009
Oriana	P&O Cruises	83	January 8, 2009	Southampton	March 13, 2009
Pacific Princess	Princess Cruises	103	April 1, 2009	Yokohama	July 13, 2009
Pacific Venus	Venus Cruise	101	April 1, 2009	Yokohama	July 13, 2009
Rotterdam	Holland America Line	131	January 5, 2009	Fort Lauderdale	May 15, 2009
Royal Princess	Princess Cruises	107	January 20, 2009	Fort Lauderdale	May 8, 2009
Queen Mary 2	Cunard Line	85	January 20, 2009	Fort Lauderdale	April 8, 2009
Queen Victoria	Cunard Line	108	January 2, 2009	Southampton	April 20, 2009
Saga Rose	Saga Cruises	105	January 5, 2009	Southampton	April 20, 2009
Seabourn Odyssey	Seabourn Cruise Line	108	January 5, 2010	Fort Lauderdale	April 24, 2010
Seven Seas Mariner	Regent Seven Seas Cruises	122	January 26, 2009	Fort Lauderdale	May 27, 2009
Seven Seas Voyager	Regent Seven Seas Cruises	117	January 13, 2009	Los Angeles	May 8, 2009
Silver Shadow *	Silversea Cruises	92	March 7, 2009	Los Angeles	June 7, 2009

* Grand Circle Pacific Cruise

ABOVE: *Crystal Serenity* in Sorrento, Italy.
BELOW: P&O's *Oriana* in Sydney's stunning harbor.

Ships rated at four stars or more, for example, will probably include shuttle buses from your ship to town centers, but ships rated three stars or less will not lay on such transport.

Ships that roam worldwide during the year offer the most experienced world cruises or segments. Most operate at about 75 percent capacity, providing much more space per person than they could normally expect.

Planning and preparation

For the operator, planning a world cruise involves daunting organization. For example, more than 700,000 main meals will be prepared in the galleys during a typical world cruise aboard the *Queen Mary 2*. A ship of its size needs two major crew changes during a three-month-long voyage. Hundreds of professional entertainers, lecturers, bands, and musicians must be booked a year in advance.

Because a modern world cruise ship has to be totally self-contained, a warehouse-full of spare parts – such as electrical, plumbing, and engineering supplies – must be ordered, loaded, and stored aboard ship prior to sailing. Once at sea, it will be impossible to pick up a replacement projector bulb, air-conditioning belt, table tennis ball, saxophone reed, or anything else the ship might run out of.

A cruise line must give advance notice of the date and time that pilots will be needed, together with requirements for tugs, docking services, and customs and immigration staff. Dockside labor and stevedoring services must be organized at each port of call, plus fuel supplies and transportation for shore excursions. It's an invigorating business for the cruise line as well as for the passengers. ❑

To	Direction	Number of Ports
Genoa	Westbound	75
Nice	Westbound	76
Southampton	Westbound	35
Venice	Westbound	59
Yokohama	Westbound	26
Southampton	Eastbound	31
Dover	Eastbound	33
Southampton	Westbound	29
Nice	Eastbound	82
Los Angeles	Westbound	46
Dubai	Westbound	82
Stockholm	Westbound	50
Southampton	Westbound	28
Kobe	Westbound	29
Yokohama	Westbound	29
New York	Westbound	39
Dover	Westbound	39
Southampton	Westbound	24
Southampton	Westbound	35
Southampton	Westbound	38
Athens (Piraeus)	Westbound	40
Vancouver	Westbound	57
Fort Lauderdale	Westbound	53
Vancouver	Westbound	43

RIVER CRUISING

**More than 1 million people a year take a river
or inland waterway cruise, making this one
of the industry's fastest growing sectors**

Whether you want to cruise down the Nile, along the mighty Amazon or the lesser Orinoco, the stately Volga or the primal Sepik, the magnificent Rhine or the "blue" Danube, along the mystical Ayeyarwady (formerly the Irrawaddy) or the "yellow" Yangtze – to say nothing of the Don and the Dnieper, the Elbe, or Australia's Murray – there are more than 1,000 river cruise vessels to choose from.

What sort of person enjoys cruising aboard these vessels? Well, anyone who survives well without formal dinners, bingo, casinos, discos, or lavish entertainment, and those who want a totally unstructured lifestyle.

The plus points

● Rivercruise vessels are built to enable you to enjoy the ever-changing scenery (the "riverscape"), all at eye level.

● You'll wake up in a different place each day, often in the very heart of a city or town.

● You never have to take a tender ashore – you simply step off the vessel when it ties up.

● The atmosphere on board is friendly and informal, never stuffy or pretentious.

The waterfront of Cologne, Germany, by night.

● Cruising along one of the world's rivers is a delightful way to unwind at a slow pace.

● The ride is typically silky smooth – there's no rolling like aboard many of the ocean-going cruise ships, so you won't suffer from seasickness.

● Good food and service are essential elements of a successful river cruise operation.

● All meals are provided, typically in a self-serve buffet arrangement for breakfast and lunch, with sit-down service for dinner. Additionally, basic table wines may also be included for lunch and dinner (included wines are typical of the German river cruise operators or cruise/tour packagers).

● Almost all cabins have outside views; there are virtually no interior (no view) cabins, as aboard most of the ocean-going cruise ships.

● A whole range of optional, extra-cost excursions is available, while some excursions may be included.

● You will typically sail by day, and dock at night (exceptions: Danube and Russian river cruises, where most vessels sail at night), so you can get a restful sleep without engine noise. However, bear in mind that, if your cabin is towards the aft, there may well be the soft humming of a generator, which supplies power for air-conditioning, heating, water supply, lighting and cooking.

● You can, if you wish, leave the vessel in the evening to go out to dinner, or to the cinema, theater or a concert (exceptions: Danube and Russian river cruises).

● Rivers provide a sense of continuity – difficult to achieve from a coach tour, where you may change lodgings each night, and encounter border crossings. Also, while on board, you deal in a single currency.

● The dress code is completely casual.

● There are no cars to drive, or park.

● There are no intrusive art auctions, bingo, wet T-shirt contests and the like.

The negative points

● The flow of water in almost all rivers cannot always be controlled, so there will be times when the water level is so low that even a specially constructed rivercruise vessel, with its shallow draft, cannot travel.

● If you are tall, note that the beds aboard most rivercruise vessels are less than 6 ft (1.8 meters) long.

● Don't wear white. Rivercruise vessels are long and low, which means that their funnels are also low. Soot, created by the emissions from diesel engines and generators, can be a problem, particularly at the stern of the vessel, and on the upper (open) deck.

A Seabourn cruise on the Seine near Rouen, France.

● Aboard some of the vessels that have an aft, open but sheltered deck area, or an open upper deck – almost all rivercruise vessels have one – smokers may be seated next to you. Few vessels distinguish between smoking and non-smoking areas outdoors, and staff rarely enforce no-smoking areas anyway.

● Depending on the vessel, river, the operating company, and tour operators that send passengers to the vessels, there could be passengers of several nationalities. While this can make for interesting social interaction, communication could be a problem if you don't speak the same language.

European river cruising

Cruising down one of Europe's great waterways is a soothing experience – different from sailing on an open sea, where wave motion is a factor. These cruises provide a constant change of scenery, often passing through several countries, each with its own history and architecture, in a week-long journey.

River vessels are always close to land and provide a chance to visit cities and areas inaccessible to the large resort ships. A cruise along the Danube, for example, will take you through nine countries and from Germany's Black Forest to the Black Sea (Germany, Austria, Slovakia, Hungary, Croatia, Serbia, Romania, Bulgaria, Ukraine).

The Rhine–Main–Danube waterway, at 2,175 miles (3,500 km), is the longest waterway in Europe. It connects 14 countries, from Rotterdam on the North Sea to Sulina and Izmail on the Black Sea, and offers river travelers some of the most varied and fascinating sights to be seen anywhere.

River vessels are long and low in the water, and their masts fold down in order to negotiate low bridges. Although small when compared to ocean-going cruise ships, they have a unique and friendly international atmosphere. The most modern are air-conditioned and offer the discreet luxury of a small floating hotel, with several public rooms including a dining room, observation lounge, bar, heated swimming "dip" pool (some even have a heated indoor pool), sauna, solarium, whirlpool, gymnasium, massage, hairdresser, and shop kiosk.

Although the cabins may be small, with limited closet space (take casual clothing, as informality is the

WHAT GENDER IS A RIVER?

Whether a river is known as a he or a she depends on its behaviour. Take the River Rhône, for example – almost always referred to in the masculine because the waters can be turbulent, bothersome and rough at times. The Saône, on the other hand, is a gentler kind of river – more beautiful, more tranquil – and is thus referred to as "she", as is the "beautiful" Blue Danube (although Napoleon described the Danube as the "king of the rivers of Europe"). The Rhine is male, always referred to as "Father Rhine". The Nile is also deemed a masculine river. The River Volga is always referred to as the "dear little mother" (even though it is the mightiest river in Europe).

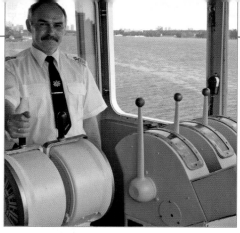

order of the day), they are functional. Almost all have an outside view (facing the river), with a private bathroom, and will prove very comfortable for a one-week journey. Romantics may lament the fact that twin beds are the norm – and they can seldom be pushed together. Many cabins in the latest vessels have a personal safe, a mini-bar, a TV set, and an alarm clock/radio. The ceilings are rather low, and the beds are short.

River cruising in Europe has reached quite a sophisticated level, and you can be assured of good service and meals of a consistently good local standard. Dining is a pleasant although not a gourmet experience. The best food is that catered by Austrian, German or Swiss companies. While lunch is generally a buffet affair, dinners feature a set menu consisting of three or four courses.

Typical fares for river cruises are from $800 to over $3,000 per person for a one-week cruise, including meals, cabin with private facilities, side trips, and airport/railway transfers. If you are already in Europe, many cruises can be purchased "cruise-only."

Tip: To ensure a degree of peace and quiet, it is best to go for a cabin on a deck that does not have a promenade deck walkway outside it. Normally, cabins on the lowest deck have a four-berth configuration. It does not matter which side of the vessel you are on, as you will see a riverbank and scenery on both sides of the vessel.

Russia's rivers

Often referred to as the "Waterways of the Tsars," the country benefits from a well-developed network of rivers, lakes, and canals. Geographically, river routes for tourists are divided into three main areas: Central European Russia, Northwestern European Russia, and Asian Russia. There are more than 80 river cruise vessels carrying international tourists.

In the Central Basin, Moscow is the hub of river tourism, and the newly opened waterways between Moscow and St. Petersburg allow a 7-day cruise link between the present and former capitals. The best-

At the helm of *Volga Dream* in Russia.

known Russian rivers are the Don, Moskva, Neva, and Volga, but the lesser known Belaya, Dvina (and North Dvina) Irtysh, Kama, Ob (longest river in Siberia), Oka, Svir, Tura, and Vyatka connect the great system of rivers and lakes in the vast Russian hinterland.

Many Russian vessels are chartered for foreign cruise wholesalers and tour packagers, and dedicated to a specific onboard language. The vessels do vary quite a lot in quality and facilities. Some are air-conditioned and most are clean. Cruises include the services of a cruise manager and lecturers. Recommended vessels: *Volga Dream* and *Viking Surkov*.

The Nile

A journey along the Nile is a journey through history, to more than 4,000 years before the birth of Christ, when one of the greatest civilizations in history lived along the river's banks. The scenery has changed remarkably little in more than 2,000 years. The best way to see it, of course, is from a river vessel.

In all, there are over 7,000 departures every year aboard 300 or so Nile cruise vessels, which offer standards of comfort, food, and service that vary between

---

THE BEST TIME TO CRUISE IN EUROPE AND ON THE NILE

There are advantages and disadvantages to every season in Europe. Early spring and late summer will be less crowded and can have beautiful weather. In July and August the weather is often at its most reliable, though it can be too hot for some and there will be more crowds.

It's possible to time a river cruise to coincide with certain events, such as the Rhine in Flames festival in high summer, or the paprika harvest in Hungary, or the beautiful autumn colors along the Danube's Wachau Valley. Special winter cruises operate on the Rhine and Danube to take in the Christmas markets – if you're lucky you'll get crisp, cool weather and snow on the ground, but

rain and slush are just as likely.

Russia tends to be hot and humid in summer, so spring and autumn are to be

preferred. Take insect repellent for travel in August and September, when midges can be a problem, and something warm to wear in the evening in spring and fall.

In Egypt the seasons are different. Nile cruises operate year-round, the peak months being January to March when it's cooler. August is really too hot for anybody except the most dedicated sun-worshipper. September is tolerable if you take things slowly, with the added advantage that there'll be hardly any crowds at the temples. Wearing shorts and a tank top might keep you cool, but they'll indicate a lack of respect if you wear them when visiting tombs and you may be hassled.

A Nile cruise is the perfect way to see Egypt.

very good and extremely poor. Most have a small, shallow "plunge" pool, lounge, piano bar, and disco. A specialist lecturer in ancient Egyptian history accompanies almost all sailings, which cruise the 140 miles (220 km) between Aswân and Luxor in four or five days. Extended cruises, typically of seven or eight days, cover about 295 miles (475 km) and visit Dendera and Abydos. The longest cruises, of 10 to 12 days, cover 590 miles (950 km) and may include visits to Sohâg, El Amarna, Tuna El Gabal, and Ashmuneim, ending in Cairo.

Most Nile cruises include sightseeing excursions, accompanied by experienced guides who may reside on board, or who may meet the vessel at each call. Security in Egypt has been much improved in recent years, but the terrorist threat remains, and it's wise to be vigilant.

It's also prudent to subtract two stars from any rating provided in brochures or on cruise company and tour operator websites.

China's rivers

More than 80 vessels cruise along the Yangtze, the world's third-longest river, particularly through the area known as the Three Yangtze River Gorges, a 100-mile (160-km) stretch between Nanjin Pass in the east and White King City in the west.

The Yangtze stretches 3,900 miles (6,300 km) from Shanghai through the very heartland of China. The Three Gorges include the 47-mile-long (76-km) Xiling Gorge, the 25-mile-long (40-km) Wu Gorge, and the 28-mile-long (45-km) Qutang Gorge, known locally as

Exploring the Yangtze, the world's third longest river.

Above: tranquillity on the Burgundy Canal, France.
Below: paddling along Australia's Murray River.

"Wind Box Gorge." The Lesser Three Gorges (or Three Small Gorges) are also an impressive sight, often part of the main cruise but also reached by small vessels from Wushan. If possible, take a cabin with a balcony. It is worth the extra money, and the view is better.

Standards of hygiene are generally far lower than you may be used to at home. In China, rats and rivers often go together, and rat poison may well be found under your bed. Some vessels, such as those of Viking River Cruises, have Chinese- and western-style restaurants, a beauty salon, a small health club with sauna,

and private mahjong and karaoke rooms. Fine Asian hospitality and service prevail, and cabins are kept supplied with fresh towels and hot tea.

There are several operators, but do check on the facilities, meet-and-greet service, and the newness of the vessels before booking. The best time of the year to go is May–June, and late August–October (July and early August are extremely hot and humid).

River Murray, Australia

The fifth-largest river in the world, the Murray, was the lifeblood of the pioneers who lived on the driest continent on earth. Today, the river flows for more than 1,250 miles (2,760 km) across a third of Australia, its banks forming protected lagoons for an astonishing variety of bird and animal life. Paddlewheel boats such as *Murray Princess* offer most of the amenities found aboard America's *Mississippi Queen*. There are even six cabins for the physically disabled.

Barge cruising in Europe

Smaller and more intimate than river vessels and more accurately called boats, "cruise barges" ply the inland waterways and canals of Europe from spring to fall, when the weather is best. Barge cruises (usually of 3 to 13 days' duration) offer a completely informal atmosphere, and a slow pace of life, for up to a dozen passengers. They chug along slowly in the daytime, and moor early each evening, giving you time to pay a visit to a local village and get a restful night's sleep.

Most cruise barges are comfortable and beautifully fitted out with rich wood paneling, full carpeting, custom-built furniture and tastefully chosen fabrics. Each has a dining room or lounge-bar.

Captains take pride in their vessel, often displaying some rare memorabilia.

Locally grown fresh foods are usually purchased and prepared each day, allowing you to live well and feel like a houseguest. Most cruise barges can be chartered exclusively so you can just take your family and friends.

The waterways of France especially offer beauty, tranquility, and a diversity of interests, and barge cruising is an excellent way of exploring an unfamiliar area. Most cruises include a visit to a famous vineyard and wine cellar, as well as side trips to places of historic, architectural, or scenic interest. Shopping opportunities are limited, evening entertainment is impromptu.

You will be accompanied by a crew member familiar with the surrounding countryside. You can even go hot-air ballooning over the local countryside – an expensive but memorable extra – and land to a glass of champagne and your flight certificate.

How you dine on board a barge will depend on the barge and area; dining ranges from home-style cooking to some outstanding nouvelle cuisine, with all the trimmings. Often, the barge's owner, or spouse, cooks.

Barging on the canals often means going through a constant succession of locks. Nowhere is this more enjoyable and entertaining than in the Burgundy region of France where, between Dijon and Mâcon, for example, a barge can negotiate as many as 54 locks during a 6-day cruise. Interestingly, all lockkeepers in France are women.

Rates range from $600 to more than $3,000 per person for a 6-day cruise. I do not recommend taking children. Rates include a cabin with private facilities, all meals, good wine with lunch and dinner, all other beverages, use of bicycles, side trips, and airport or railway transfers.

Some operators provide a hotel the night before or after the cruise. Clothing is totally casual – but, at the beginning and end of the season, it's a good idea to take sweaters and rain gear.

Steamboating in the United States

The most famous of all American river cruises are those aboard the steamboats of the mighty Mississippi River. Mark Twain, a fan of such travel, said: "When man can go 700 miles an hour, he'll want to go seven again."

The grand traditions of the steamboat era are maintained by the *American Queen*, and by the smaller *Mississippi Queen* (Majestic America Line), powered by steam engines that drive huge wooden paddlewheels at the stern. The $27-million, 400-passenger Mississippi Queen was constructed in Jefferson, Indiana, where nearly 5,000 steamboats were built during the 19th century, and was refurbished in 2008.

Steamboats have a charm and old-world graciousness as well as delightful woods (real or faux), brass, and flowing staircases. Steamboat cruises, up and down the Mississippi and Ohio rivers, last from 2 to 12 days, and include theme cruises, with big bands and lively entertainment. The food is American fare, which means steak, and shrimp, Creole sauces, and fried foods. ❑

Cruising the traditional way on the Mississippi.

CHOOSING THE RIGHT SHIP

What's the difference between large and small ships? Are new ships better than older ones? Should you consider a maiden voyage? Is corporate cruising good value? Are theme cruises fun?

Which ship? There's something to suit virtually all tastes, so take into account your own personality and tastes. Ships are measured (not weighed) in gross tons (gt) and come in four principal size categories:

● **Large Resort Ships**: for over 1,600 passengers (typically measure 50,000–220,000 tons)
● **Mid-Size Ships**: for 600–1,600 passengers (typically measure 25,000–50,000 tons)
● **Small Ships**: for 200–600 passengers (typically measure 5,000–25,000 tons)
● **Boutique Ships**: for up to 200 passengers (typically measure 1,000–5,000 tons)

Whatever the physical dimensions, all cruise ships provide the same basic ingredients: accommodation, activities, entertainment, plenty of food, good service, and ports of call, although some do it much better than others (and charge more).

Space

For an idea of the amount of the space around you, check the Passenger Space Ratio given for each ship in the listings section (gross tonnage divided by number of passengers). A Passenger Space Ratio of **50 and above** is the ultimate; **30 to 50** is very spacious; **20 to 30** is reasonably spacious; **10 to 20** is high density; and **10 or below** is extremely cramped.

LARGE RESORT SHIPS
(1,600–6,000+ passengers)

Choose a large resort ship if you enjoy being with lots of other people, in a bustling big-city environment, you enjoy being sociable, and like to experience plenty of entertainment and dining (no, make that eating) options. These ships provide a well packaged standard or premium cruise vacation experience, usually in a seven-day cruise. It is the interaction between passengers and crew that determines the quality of the onboard experience.

Large resort ships have extensive facilities and programs for families with children of all ages. But if you meet someone on the first day and want to meet them again, make sure you appoint a place and time, or you may not see them again (apart from the size of the ship,

they may be at a different meal seating). These ships have a highly structured array of activities and passenger participation events each day, together with large entertainment venues, and the most lavish production shows at sea.

It is in the standard of service, entertainment, lecture programs, level of communication, and finesse in dining services that really can move these ships into high rating categories, but they must be exceptional to do so. Choose higher-priced suite accommodation and the service improves. In other words: pay more, get more.

Large resort ships are highly programmed. It is difficult, for example, to go swimming in the late evening, or after dinner (decks are cleaned and pools are often netted over by 6pm). Having champagne delivered to outdoor hot tubs late at night is virtually impossible. They have

Large resort ships create a big-city ambiance and environment.

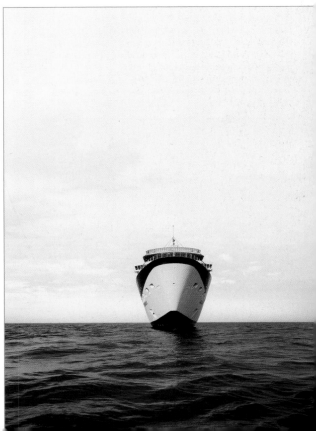

lost the flexibility for which cruise ships were once known, and have become victims of company "policy" legislation and insurance regulations. There can be a feeling of "conveyor-belt" cruising.

LARGE RESORT SHIPS: Advantages

● Have the widest range of public rooms and facilities, often a walk-around promenade deck outdoors, and more space (but more passengers).

● Generally have more dining options.

● The newest ships have state-of-the-art electronic interactive entertainment facilities (good if you like computers and high-tech gadgetry).

● Generally sail well in open seas in bad weather.

● There are more facilities and activities for people of all ages, particularly for families with children.

LARGE RESORT SHIPS: Disadvantages

● Trying to find your way around the ship can prove frustrating.

● Lines to wait in: for embarkation, the information desk, elevators, informal buffet meals, fast food grills, shore tenders, shore excursions, security checkpoint (when returning to the ship), immigration, and disembarkation.

● They resemble floating hotels (but with constant announcements), and so many items cost extra. They are like retail parks surrounded by cabins.

● No matter how big your suite is, or how many public rooms the ship has, you can't help feeling like just one of the crowd, and the individual attention or recognition is missing. You also have to mingle with all the other (lesser paying) passengers in the public rooms.

● The itineraries may be limited by ship size, and there

Artemis, a mid-size ship, visits Valletta, Malta.

are typically too many tender ports wher you need to take a number, and sit in a lounge and wait, and wait.

● Signage is often confusing; there will be a lack of elevators at peak times.

● The larger the ship, the more impersonal the service (except for "butler" service in penthouse suites).

● You will probably have to use a sign-up sheet to use gym equipment such as treadmills or exercise bicycles.

●There are too many announcements (they could be in several languages).

● Dining room staff is so trained to provide fast service, it is almost impossible to sit and dine in leisurely fashion.

● Food may well be bland (cooking for 4,000 is not quite the same as cooking for a dinner party of 8).

● Telephoning room service can be frustrating, particularly in ships with automatic telephone answering systems that state "your call will be answered by room service personnel in the order it was received."

● Room service breakfast is not generally available on the day of disembarkation.

● In early evening, the deck chairs are taken away, or strapped up so they can't be used.

● The in-cabin music aboard the latest ships is supplied through the television set, and it may be impossible to turn off the picture (so much for quiet, romantic late-night music, and darkened cabins).

● Some of the large resort ships have only two main passenger staircases. In an emergency, the evacuation of more than 4,000 passengers could be difficult.

MID-SIZE SHIPS (600–1,600 passengers)

These are well suited to the smaller ports of the Aegean and Mediterranean, and are more maneuverable than larger ships. Several operate around-the-world cruises and other long-distance itineraries to exotic destinations not really feasible aboard many of the ships in the small or large resort ship categories.

There is a big difference in the amount of space available. Accommodation varies from large "penthouse suites" complete with butler service to tiny interior (no-view) cabins. These ships will generally be more stable at sea than "small ships", due to their increased size and draft. They provide more facilities, more entertainment, and more dining options. There is some entertainment, and more structured activities than aboard small ships, but less than aboard the large resort ships.

MID-SIZE SHIPS: Advantages

● They are neither too large, nor too small; their size and facilities often strike a happy balance.
● It is easy to find one's way around.
● They generally sail well in areas of bad weather, being neither high-sided like the large resort ships, nor of too shallow draft like some of the small ships.
● Lines seldom form (except for ships approaching 1,600 passengers), but if they do, they are likely to be short.
● They appear more like traditional ships than most of the larger vessels, which tend to be more "boxy" in shape and profile.

MID-SIZE SHIPS: Disadvantages

● They do not offer as wide a range of public rooms and facilities as do the large resort ships.
● Few have large show lounges for large-scale production shows; hence entertainment tends to be more of the cabaret variety.

BOUTIQUE SHIPS (50–200 passengers) and SMALL SHIPS (200–600 passengers)

Choose a boutique or small ship for an intimate cruise experience and a small number of passengers. Some of the

Privacy is at a premium on the large resort ships.

most exclusive cruise ships in the world belong in this group (but so do most of the coastal vessels with basic, unpretentious amenities, sail-cruise ships, and the expedition-style cruise vessels that take passengers to see nature). Choose this size ship if you do not need much entertainment, large resort ship facilities, gambling casinos, several restaurants, and if you don't like to wait in lines for anything. If you want to swim in the late evening, or have champagne in the hot tub at midnight, it is easier aboard boutique or small ships than aboard larger ships, where more rigid programs lead to inflexible, passenger-unfriendly thinking.

BOUTIQUE/SMALL SHIPS: Advantages

● More like small inns than mega-resorts.
● Easy to find your way around, and signage is usually clear and concise.
● At their best in warm weather areas.
● Capable of true culinary excellence, with fresh foods cooked individually to order.
● Most provide an "open seating" in the dining room; this means that you can sit with whomever you wish, whenever you wish, for all meals.
● Provide a totally unstructured lifestyle, offering a level of service not found aboard most of the larger ships, and no or almost no announcements.
● Provide an "open bridge" policy, allowing passengers to go to the navigational bridge when safe to do so.
● Some small ships have a hydraulic marina water sports platform located at the stern and carry equipment such as jet skis, windsurfers, a water ski powerboat, and scuba and snorkeling gear.
● Go to the more off-beat ports of call that larger ships can't get into.

Breakfast on deck aboard *Hanseatic*, a boutique ship.

- When the ship is at anchor, going ashore is easy and speedy, with a continuous tender service and no lines.
- Less crowded ports mean more exclusivity.

BOUTIQUE/SMALL SHIPS: Disadvantages

- Do not have the bulk, length, or beam to sail well in open seas in inclement weather conditions.
- Do not have the range of public rooms or open spaces that the large resort ships can provide. Options for entertainment, therefore, are limited.

What about age?

A ship built before 1980 is considered old. However, this really depends on the level of maintenance it has received, and whether it has operated on short or longer cruises (short cruises get more passenger throughput, and so more wear and tear). Yet many passengers like older ships, as they tend to have fewer synthetic materials in their interior decor. Although it is inevitable that some older tonnage cannot match the latest in high-tech, ships today are not constructed with the same loving care as in the past.

Most cruise advertising you'll see revolves around the newer, larger ships, there are many older ships that have much to offer if you don't want the latest trendy facilities and city high street feel. Indeed, some of the older, smaller ships have adequate facilities, tend to have more character, and provide a more relaxing vacation experience than the go-go-go contemporary ships, where you're just one of a crowd.

Newer ships (post-1990): Advantages

- Incorporate the latest in high-tech electronic equipment and in advanced ship design and construction.
- Meet the latest safety and operating standards.

- Typically have "pod" propulsion system, which replaces conventional propeller shafts, propellers and rudders, with the result that there is little or no vibration (*details: page 175*).
- Have more interior public rooms, and maybe no exterior promenade deck.
- More standardized cabin layouts, fewer categories.
- Are more fuel-efficient.
- Have a shallower draft, which makes it easier for them to enter and leave ports.
- Have bow and stern thrusters, so they seldom require tug assistance in many ports, reducing operating costs.
- Have good plumbing and air-conditioning systems.
- Usually have the latest submersible lifeboats.

New ships: Disadvantages

- Do not "take the weather" as well as older ships (sailing across the North Atlantic in November on one of the new large resort ships can be unforgettable). Because of their shallow draft, these ships roll, even when there's the slightest puff of wind.
- Tend to have smaller standard cabins, which can mean narrow, short beds.
- Have thin hulls and do not withstand the bangs and dents as well as older, more heavily plated vessels.
- Have decor made mostly from synthetic materials (due to stringent regulations) and could cause problems for passengers sensitive to such materials.
- Have toilets of the powerful vacuum suction "barking dog" type.
- Are powered mainly by diesel (or diesel-electric) engines, which inevitably cause some vibration; although on the latest vessels, the engines are mounted on pliable, floating rubber cushions and are, therefore, virtually vibration-free.
- Have cabin windows that are completely sealed instead of portholes that can be opened.

Pre-1990 ships: Advantages

● Have strong, plated hulls (often riveted) that can withstand tremendously hard wear and tear; they "take the weather" well.

● Have large cabins with long, wide beds/berths, because passengers needed more space in the days when voyages were much longer.

● Have a wide range of cabin sizes, shapes, and grades more suited to families with children.

● Have toilets that are of the "gentle flush" variety instead of today's "barking dog" vacuum toilets.

● Are mostly powered by steam turbines, which are virtually free of vibration or noise and are considerably quieter and smoother than modern vessels.

● Have portholes that sometimes actually open.

● Have interiors built from traditional materials such as wood and brass, with less use of synthetic fibers (less likely to affect anyone allergic to synthetics).

● Have deep drafts that help them to achieve a smooth ride in the open seas.

Pre-1980 ships: Disadvantages

● They are not so fuel-efficient and, therefore, are more expensive to operate than the new ships.

● Need a larger crew, because of the more awkward, labor-intensive layouts of the ships.

● Have a deep draft (necessary for a smooth ride) but need tugs to negotiate ports and tight berths.

● Have a tougher job complying with the current international fire, safety, and environmental regulations.

● Are usually fitted with older-type open lifeboats.

● If 10 years or older, plumbing and air-conditioning problems in cabins and public areas are commoner.

The crew

You can estimate the standard of service by looking at the crew-to-passenger ratio (provided in the ship profiles in this book). The best service levels are aboard ships that have a ratio of one crew member to every two passengers, or higher. The best ships in the world, from the point of view of crew living and working conditions, also tend to be the most expensive ones (the adage "you get what you pay for" tends to be true).

Most ships now have multinational crews, with one or two exceptions. The crew mixture can resemble a miniature United Nations. If the crew is happy, the ship will be happy, too, and passengers will sense it.

Corporate cruising

Corporate, incentive organizations and seagoing conferences provide a growing market for cruise companies. Ships of all sizes, types and styles can provide an exciting venue for between 50 and 3,000 participants. Corporate organizers like having such things as accommodation, food or entertainment for their delegates organized as one contract.

Cruise companies have specialized departments and personnel to deal with all the details. Corporate organizers don't even have to think about car rentals either. Many larger ships have almost identical cabin sizes and configurations, a bonus for incentive houses.

Once you have signed the contract and paid the deposit for a charter, no refund is possible (thus insurance is essential). Although you may need only 70% of the capacity of a ship for your purposes, you will have to pay for the whole ship if you want an *exclusive* charter.

If you want to charter a whole ship (popular among corporations and associations), where you have complete control over the utilization of public areas, do the following:

● Decide which part of the world you want to be in.

● Decide how long you want to cruise for.

● Estimate how many will be in your group.

● Make arrangements as early as possible (at least one year ahead, preferably more).

● Although you can contact cruise lines directly, I would recommend contacting the experienced Miami-based cruise charter specialist organizer Landry & Kling (www.landryandkling.com).

Maiden and inaugural voyages

It can be fun to take part in the maiden voyage of a new cruise ship, or in joining the inaugural voyage of a

Resort ships vie with each other in futuristic design.

refurbished, reconstructed, or stretched vessel, if you have a degree of tolerance and don't mind some inconvenience, slow or nonexistent service in the dining room. Otherwise, wait until the ship has been in service for at least three months. Then again, if you book a cruise on the third or fourth voyage, and the ship's introduction is delayed, you could find yourself on the maiden voyage.

One thing is certain: any maiden voyage is a collector's item, but Murphy's Law – "If anything can go wrong, it will" – can prevail. For example:

● Service aboard new or recently refurbished ships (or a new cruise line) is likely to be uncertain and could be a disaster. An existing cruise line may use experienced crew from its other vessels to help "bring out" a new ship, but they may be unfamiliar with the ship's layout and may have problems training other staff.

● Plumbing and electrical items tend to cause the most problems, particularly aboard reconstructed and refurbished vessels. Examples: toilets that don't flush or don't stop flushing; faucets incorrectly marked, where "hot" really means "cold"; and "automatic" telephones that refuse to function.

● The galley (kitchen) of a new ship if the right supplies don't turn up on time.

● Items such as menus, postcards, writing paper, or TV remote control units, door keys, towels, pillowcases, glassware, and even toilet paper may be lost in the bowels of the ship, or simply not ordered.

Chess aboard Fred Olsen Cruise Line's *Black Prince*.

● In the entertainment department, items such as spare spotlight bulbs may not be in stock. Or what if the pianos arrive damaged, or "flip" charts for the lecturers didn't show up? Manuals for high-tech sound and lighting equipment may be in a foreign language.

Theme cruises

A wide variety of theme cruises is available, with a focus on many cultural, ecological, and educational subjects. Typical topics range from antiques to wine tasting; from archaeology to holistic health; from sports stars to music festivals. There are also specially chartered voyages for nudists, as well as gay and lesbian cruises.

Signs you've chosen the wrong ship

● When, as you embark, a waiter hands you a drink in a tall plastic glass from a tray of drinks of identical color and froth, then gives you a bill to sign without even saying "Welcome Aboard."

● When your "luxury" cabin has walls so thin you can hear your neighbors combing their hair.

● When the brochure's "full bathtub" turns out to be "a large washbasin" located at floor level.

● When you wanted a quiet, restful cruise, but your travel agent booked you aboard a ship with 300 baseball fans and provided them all with signed baseball bats and boom boxes for their use on deck.

● When you packed your tuxedo, but other passengers take "formal" attire to mean clean cut-off jeans and a less stained T-shirt.

● When the "medical facility" is located in the purser's

Big-ship shows can be spectacular – but very loud.

office and consists of a box of adhesive bandages with instructions in a foreign language.

● When the gymnasium equipment is kept in the restaurant manager's office.

● When you have a cabin with an "obstructed view" (usually there is a lifeboat hanging outside it), and it is next to or below the disco. Or the laundry. Or the garbage disposal facility. Or the anchor.

● When "fresh selected greens" means a sprig of parsley on the entrée plate, at every lunch and dinner seating (boring even on a three-day cruise).

● When the cruise director tries to sell passengers a watch, or an artwork, over the public address system.

● When front-row seats at a rock concert would be quieter than a poolside deck chair at midday.

● When you hear the same rap tracks 10 times during the first morning.

● When you need shin pads to prevent injury caused by 600 children chasing through passageways.

● When the cruise brochure shows your cabin with flowers and champagne, but you get neither.

● When the bottled water on your dining room table incurs a bill as soon as you open the bottle.

● When the brochure says "Butler Service," but you have to clean your own shoes, get your own ice, and still tip twice the amount you would for an "ordinary" cabin steward.

● When the Beer Drinking or Hog Calling Contest, Knobby Knees Contest, and Pajama Bingo are listed as "enrichment lectures."

● When the "fresh-squeezed orange juice" you just ordered means fresh-squeezed, but last week, on land,

and poured into industrial-size containers, before transfer to your polystyrene plastic cup on deck.

● When the brochure says tipping is not required, but your waiter and cabin steward insist otherwise.

● When the cruise director thoughtfully telephones you at 2.30am to let you know that the bingo jackpot is up to $1,000 and that an exciting art auction is about to start.

● When, on the final day, the words "early breakfast" means 5am, and "vacate your cabin by 7.30am" means you must spend about three hours sitting in the show lounge waiting for disembarkation, with 500 available seats, your hand luggage, and up to 5,000 other passengers, probably playing bingo.

● When on deck, you notice a large hole in the bottom of one or more of the ship's lifeboats.

● When the cabin steward tries to sell you a cut-price time-share in his uncle's coal mine.

● When the proclaimed "five-course gourmet meal" in the dining room turns out to be four courses of salty chicken soup and a potato.

● When the "Deck Buffet" means that there are no tables and chairs, only the deck, to eat off.

● When the brochure shows photos of smiling young couples, but you and your spouse/partner are the only passengers under 80.

● When the library is located in the engine room.

● When the captain tells you he is really a concert pianist and his professional diploma is really for the piano, not navigation.　　　　　❏

Choosing the Right Cabin

Does cabin size count? Are suites sweeter than cabins?
Is a balcony desirable? What about location?

Ideally, you should feel at home when at sea, so it is important to choose the right accommodation, even if most of your time in it is spent with your eyes shut. Accommodation sizes range from a whopping 5,350 sq.ft. (497 sq. meters) to a minuscule 60 sq.ft. (5.5 sq. meters). Like houses ashore, all cabins have good and bad points. Choose wisely, for if you find your cabin (incorrectly called a "stateroom" by some companies) is too small when you get to the ship, it may be impossible to change it or to upgrade, as the ship could be full.

Cruise lines designate cabins only when deposits have been received (they may, however, guarantee the grade and rate requested). If this is not done, or if you find a disclaimer such as "All cabin assignments are confirmed upon embarkation of the vessel", get a guarantee in writing that your cabin will *not* be changed on embarkation.

There are three main types of accommodation, but many variations on each theme:

● **Suites**: (the largest living spaces, typically with a private balcony); and "junior" suites (with or without private balcony).

● **Outside-view cabins**: a large picture window or one or more portholes (with or without private balcony).

● **Interior (no-view) cabins**: so called because there is no window or porthole.

Private Balconies

Continuing the trend that Romeo and Juliet started a few Shakespearean years ago, balconies are all the rage today – in hotels, apartments, and aboard cruise ships. Once you've had one, you won't be able to do without one on your next cruise. Balconies add another dimen-

ABOVE: Zodiac Suite bedroom, *Norwegian Spirit.*

sion to your home away from home. A private balcony (or "veranda," or "terrace") is just that. It is a balcony (or mini-terrace) adjoining your cabin where you can sit, enjoy the view, dine, or even have a massage. The value of a private balcony, for which you pay a premium, comes into its own in warm weather areas. It also allows floor-to-ceiling light to flood the interior space.

Some private balconies are not so private, however. Balconies not separated by full floor-to-ceiling partitions (examples: *Carnival Destiny, Carnival Triumph, Carnival Victory, Maasdam, Oriana, Queen Mary 2, Ryndam, Seven Seas Mariner, Seven Seas Voyager, Statendam,* and *Veendam*) don't quite cut it. You could get noise or smoke from your neighbor. Some ships have balconies with full floor-to-ceiling privacy partitions *and* an outside light (examples: *Celebrity Century, Celebrity Galaxy, Celebrity Mercury*). Some partitions in *Celebrity Century, Celebrity Galaxy,* and *Celebrity Mercury* are of the full type, while some are partial. Another downside of private balconies is that you can't escape the loud music being played on the open swimming pool deck atop the ship – annoying when "island night" goes on until the early hours. Note that many of the large resort ships have balconies too small to accommodate even two reclining chairs.

Some suites with forward-facing private balconies may not be so good, as the wind speed can make them all but unusable. And when the ship drops anchor in ports of call, the noise pollution can be deafening (examples, *Silver Cloud, Silver Wind*).

All private balconies (except French balconies – *see*

below) have railings to lean on, but the balconies in some ships have solid steel plates between railing and deck, so you can't look out to sea when seated (examples: *Costa Classica, Costa Romantica, Dawn Princess, Oceana, Sea Princess,* and *Sun Princess*). Better are ships whose balconies have clear glass (examples: *Aurora, Brilliance of the Seas, Celebrity Century, Celebrity Galaxy, Celebrity Mercury, Empress, Radiance of the Seas,* and *Serenade of the Seas*) or horizontal bars.

A "French balcony" is one where the doors open to fresh air, but there's no balcony for you to step onto unless your feet are less than six inches long.

How Much?

The amount you pay for accommodation is directly related to the size of the cabin, its location, and the facilities and services provided.

● Each line implements its own system according to ship size, age, construction, and profit potential.

● Many cruise lines still do not give accurate cabin sizes in their brochures, but you will find the size range in the ship profiles in this book.

● If this is your first cruise, choose the most expensive cabin you can afford.

● It may be better to book a low-grade cabin on a good ship than a high-grade cabin on a poor ship.

● If you are in a party of three or more and do not mind sharing a cabin, you'll save a lot per person, so you may be able to afford a higher-grade cabin.

Cabin Sizes

Cabins provide more or less the same facilities as hotel rooms, except space. Viewed by most owners as little more than a convenient place for passengers to sleep, shower, and change, cabin space is often compromised in favor of large public rooms. In some smaller interior (no-view) and outside cabins, changing clothes is a major challenge.

The latest ships have more standardized cabin sizes, because they are made in modular form (I consider 180 sq. ft/16.7sq. meters to be the *minimum* acceptable size for a "standard" cruise ship cabin today). They all have integrated bathrooms (mostly made from non-combustible phenolic-glass-reinforced plastics) fitted during the ships' construction. Ask your travel agent for the dimensions of the cabin you have selected.

Cabin Location

● An "outside-view" cabin is recommended for first-time passengers: an "interior (no-view)" cabin has no portholes or windows, making it more difficult to orient you or to gauge the weather or time.

● Cabins in the center of a ship are more stable and tend to be noise and vibration-free. Ships powered by diesel engines (i.e. most modern vessels) create and transmit some vibration, especially at the stern.

● Take into account personal habits when choosing the cabin location. If you like to go to bed early, avoid a cabin close to the disco. If you have trouble walking, choose a cabin close to the elevator.

● Generally, the higher the deck, the higher the cabin price, and the better the service. This is an inheritance from transoceanic times, when upper-deck cabins and suites were sunnier and warmer.

● Cabins at the front of a ship are slightly crescent-shaped, given that the outer wall follows the curvature of the ship's hull. But they can be exposed to early-morning noises, such as the anchor being dropped at ports where the ship is too big to dock.

● Cabins with interconnecting doors are fine for families or close friends, but the dividing wall is usually so thin you can hear the conversation next door.

● Many brochures indicate cabins with "obstructed-views." Cabins on lower decks are closer to engine noise and heat, especially at the aft of the vessel and around the engine casing. In many older ships, elevators may not operate to the lowermost decks.

Facilities

Cabins provide some, or all, of the following:

● Private bathroom (generally small) with shower, washbasin, and toilet. Higher-grade cabins and suites may have full-size bathtubs. Some have a whirlpool bath and/or bidet, a hairdryer, and more space.

● Electrical outlets for personal appliances, usually 110 and/or 220 volts.

● Multi-channel radio, TV (regular satellite channels or closed circuit), and VCR or DVD player.

● Two beds or a lower and upper berth (possibly, another one or two upper berths) or a double-, queen- or king-size bed. In some ships, twin beds can be pushed together to form a double.

● Telephone, for inter-cabin or ship-to-shore calls.

● Depending on cabin size, a chair, or chair and table, or sofa and table, or even a separate lounge/ sitting area (higher accommodation grades).

DID YOU KNOW...

● that the first "en suite" rooms (with private bathroom) were on board Cunard Line's *Campania* of 1893?

● that the first single-berth cabins built as such were also aboard the *Campania*?

● that the first liner to offer private terraces with their first-class suites was *Normandie* in 1935 (the Trouville Suite had four bedrooms as well as a private terrace)?

● that the first ships to feature private balconies were the *Saturnia* and *Vulcania* in the early 1900s?

● that the first ship to be fitted with interior plumbing was the 6,283-ton *Normandie* of 1883?

● that the first ship fitted with an internal electric lighting system was the Inman liner *City of Berlin* in 1879?

● that Carnival Cruise Lines places more than 10 million chocolates on passenger pillows each year?

● that orders enforced on all entertainment-free ships sailing from Great Britain in 1849 instructed all passengers to be in their beds by 10pm?

Typical Cabin Layouts

The following rates are typical of those you can expect to pay for ❶ a seven-day and ❷ a 10-day Caribbean cruise aboard a modern cruise ship. The rates are per person and include free roundtrip airfare or low-cost air add-ons from principal North American gateways

Luxury outside-view suite with private verandah, separate lounge area, vanity area, extra-large double or queen-sized bed, bathroom with tub, shower, and extensive closet and storage space.

Ⓐ **$2,000** Ⓑ **$3,500**

Deluxe outside-view cabin with lounge area, double or queen-size beds, bathroom with tub, shower, and ample closet and storage space.

Ⓐ **$1,750** Ⓑ **$2,500**

■ **Note that in some ships, third- and fourth-person upper berths are available for families or friends wishing to share. The upper Pullman berths, not shown on these cabin layouts, are recessed into the wall or ceiling above the lower beds.**

Large outside-view double with bed and convertible daytime sofabed, bathroom with shower, and good closet and drawer space.

Ⓐ **$1,500** Ⓑ **$2,250**

Junior suite with twin beds, lounge area, bathroom with shower, large walk-in closet, and private balcony.

Ⓐ **$1,750** Ⓑ **$2,500**

Interior no-view cabin with two lower beds convertible to queen-size bed (plus a possible upper third/fourth berth), bathroom with shower, and some closet space.

Ⓐ **$800** Ⓑ **1,000**

- Refrigerator/wet bar (higher grades).
- Vanity/desk unit with chair or stool.
- Personal safe.
- Closet space, some drawer space, plus storage room under beds for suitcases.
- Bedside night stand/table unit.
- Towels, soap, shampoo, and conditioner. (Upscale ships provide a greater selection.)

Many first-time passengers are surprised to find their cabin has twin beds. Double beds are a comparative rarity except in the higher-priced suites. Aboard some ships you will find upper and lower berths. A "berth" is a nautical term for a bed held in a wooden or metal frame. A "Pullman berth" tucks away out of sight during the day, usually into the bulkhead or ceiling. You climb up a short ladder at night to get into an upper berth.

A suite aboard the 2,450-passenger *Celebrity Constellation*.

The suite life

Suites are the most luxurious and spacious of all shipboard accommodation, and typically come with butler service. A suite (which means a "suite of rooms") should measure a *minimum* 400 sq. ft. (37 sq. meters), and comprise a lounge or sitting room separated from a bedroom by a solid door (not just a curtain); a bedroom with a large bed; one or more bathrooms, and an abundance of closet, drawer, and other storage space. The best suites have the most desirable position, and both privacy and good views should be standard.

Many cruise lines inaccurately describe some accommodation as suites, when they are nothing more than a large cabin with a curtain that divides sitting and sleeping areas.

Suites are best on long voyages with several days at sea. Be aware that in the large resort ships (those carrying more than 1,600 passengers), there may be a whole deck or two devoted to penthouses and suites, but you will have to share the rest of the ship with those in lower-priced accommodation.

That means there is no preferential seating in the showroom, the dining rooms, or on sunbathing decks. You may, however, get separate check-in facilities and preferential treatment upon disembarkation, but your luggage will be lumped together with everyone else's. ❏

Ship	Cruise Line	Total (sq. ft)	Total (sq. m)
THE 20 LARGEST SUITES AFLOAT			
Norwegian Dawn	Norwegian Cruise Line	4,390.0	407.8
Norwegian Gem	Norwegian Cruise Line	4,390.0	407.8
Norwegian Jade	Norwegian Cruise Line	4,390.0	407.8
Norwegian Jewel	Norwegian Cruise Line	4,390.0	407.8
Norwegian Pearl	Norwegian Cruise Line	4,390.0	407.8
Norwegian Star	Norwegian Cruise Line	4,390.0	407.8
Celebrity Constellation	Celebrity Cruises	2,530.0	235.0
Celebrity Infinity	Celebrity Cruises	2,530.0	235.0
Celebrity Millennium	Celebrity Cruises	2,530.0	235.0
Celebrity Summit	Celebrity Cruises	2,530.0	235.0
Queen Mary 2	Cunard Line	2,249.7	209.0
Freedom of the Seas	Royal Caribbean International	2,025.0	188.0
Independence of the Seas	Royal Caribbean International	2,025.0	188.0
Liberty of the Seas	Royal Caribbean International	2,025.0	188.0
Seven Seas Mariner	Regent Seven Seas Cruises	2,002.0	186.0
Celebrity Century	Celebrity Cruises	1,514.5	140.7
Celebrity Galaxy	Celebrity Cruises	1,514.5	140.7
Celebrity Mercury	Celebrity Cruises	1,514.5	140.7
Silver Shadow	Silversea Cruises	1,435.0	133.3
Silver Whisper	Silversea Cruises	1,435.0	133.3

Note: The sizes shown include balconies.

(This list does not include the suites aboard ships such as The World, which is for residents and not normal cruise passengers)

Suites aboard *Silver Shadow*, (top), *Norwegian Dawn* (above), and *Freedom of the Seas* (below).

THE MAJOR CRUISE LINES

Is big necessarily better? We compare what the
world's largest cruise companies have to offer
when it comes to cuisine, service and ambiance

The mainstream cruise industry may appear diverse, but it is dominated by a few major players: Carnival Cruise Lines, Celebrity Cruises, Costa Cruises, Cunard Line, Holland America Line, MSC Cruises, Norwegian Cruise Line, P&O Cruises, Princess Cruises, Royal Caribbean International, and Star Cruises. In fact, the consolidation of power is even greater: eight of these 11 lines are owned by just three corporations:

● *Carnival Corporation* (head office: Miami, Florida) owns major brands such as Carnival Cruise Lines, Costa Cruises, Cunard Line, Holland America, and Princess Cruises. It also owns Aida Cruises, Ocean Village, P&O Cruises, P&O Cruises (Australia), and Seabourn Cruise Line, as well as 75 percent of Spain-based Iberocruceros.

● *Royal Caribbean Cruises* (head office: Miami, Florida) owns Azamara Cruises, CDF Croisières de France, Celebrity Cruises, Pullmantur Cruises, and Royal Caribbean International.

● *Star Cruises Group* (head office: Kuala Lumpur, Malaysia) owns Star Cruises, Norwegian Cruise Line and NCL America.

Between them, Holland America Line and Princess Cruises virtually control large resort ship cruising in Alaska, and own hotels, lodges, tour companies and much land-based transportation (other operators have to buy their services). This virtual monopoly came about in 2002–3 when Princess Cruises' parent company, P&O Group, sold its cruising division to the Carnival Corporation.

It sounds monopolistic, but it is not really more so than some tour operators in Europe that own travel agency chains, hotels, an airline, and cruise ships.

What makes them different

So how does one choose between the companies? The marketing tags they use in television advertising provide a clue: Carnival Cruise Lines (*Ain't We Got Fun*); Celebrity Cruises (*Starring You*); Costa Cruises (*Cruising Italian Style*); Holland America Line (*Signature of Excellence*); Norwegian Cruise Line (*Freestyle Cruising*); P&O Cruises *(Freedom)*; Princess Cruises (*Escape Completely*); and Royal Caribbean International (*Way More than a Cruise*). Cunard Line, MSC Cruises and Star Cruises do not advertise on television.

What they have in common

All offer one thing: a well-packaged cruise vacation (generally of seven days), typically with a mix of days at sea and days in port, plenty of food, reasonable service, large-scale production shows and trendy cabaret acts, plus large casinos, shopping malls, and extensive spa and fitness facilities. Nine offer a variety of "drive to" embarkation ports within the US ("homeland cruising").

THE MAJORS UNDER THE MICROSCOPE: WHO DOES WHAT BEST

● **Carnival Cruise Lines** is known for all-round fun, activities and casinos for the lively, no-sleep-needed youth market (although many passengers are over 45).

● **Celebrity Cruises** has the best food, the most elegant ships and spas, and its cruises are really underpriced.

● **Costa Cruises** has the edge on European style and lively ambiance, with multi-nationality passengers, but the swimming pools are full of noisy children in peak holiday periods.

● **Cunard Line** has one real ocean liner that provides a regularly scheduled transatlantic service, while its other ship is more about regular cruising. Both ships carry over some fine British traditions.

● **Holland America Line** has all the right touches for seniors and retirees: smiling service staff, lots of flowers, traditions of the past, good cooking demonstrations and alternative grill rooms.

● **MSC Cruises** tailors its onboard product to pan-European passengers of all ages, and displays fine Italian flair, with a high level of service and hospitality.

● **Norwegian Cruise Line** is good for a first cruise for families with children, with a great choice of eating places, good entertainment, and friendly service staff.

● **P&O Cruises** operates ex-UK cruises for its predominantly UK-based passengers, with good facilities for families with children, as well as child-free ships, and a liking for Indian curries and cuisine.

● **Princess Cruises** has consistent product delivery, although the ships have decor that is rather bland, and passengers tend to be older.

● **Royal Caribbean International** is good for the Caribbean (naturally), for first-time cruisers and families, with a good variety of entertainment, and interesting programs designed to engage families with children.

● **Star Cruises** has ships that are based in Southeast Asia and specializes in cruises for Asians, Australians, and British passengers, with a good choice of restaurants and ethnic cuisine.

Carnival ships can dominate a destination.

The major lines' ships have a lot in common, too. They all have art auctions (except MSC Cruises and Star Cruises), bingo, horse racing, shopping talks for ports of call (pushing "recommended" stores), programs for children and teens, wedding vows renewal programs, and wi-fi or internet connect centers (costing, typically, about 50 cents per minute). All (except MSC Cruises) still feature the "Peppermill Routine" (the waiter brings a huge peppermill to your table before you've even tasted the food), but none offer tableside carving or flambée items.

Extra costs include port taxes, insurance, gratuities to staff, and use of washer/dryers in self-serve launderettes. Some lines offer their own credit cards, with points useable for upgrades, discounts, and "free" cruises.

Standing in line for embarkation, disembarkation, shore tenders and for self-serve buffet meals is inevitable aboard all large resort ships. The ships do, however, differ in their characters, facilities, maintenance, space, crew-to-passenger ratio, food and service, crew training, and other aspects.

CARNIVAL CRUISE LINES

Ships

Fantasy-class ships: *Carnival Ecstasy* (1991), *Carnival Elation* (1998), *Carnival Fantasy* (1990), *Carnival Fascination* (1994), *Carnival Imagination* (1995), *Carnival Inspiration* (1996), *Carnival Paradise* (1998), *Carnival Sensation* (1993)

Destiny-class ships: *Carnival Conquest* (2002), *Carnival Destiny* (1996), *Carnival Dream* (2009), *Carnival*
Freedom (2007), *Carnival Glory* (2003), *Carnival Liberty* (2005), *Carnival Splendor* (2008), *Carnival Triumph* (1999), *Carnival Valor* (2004), *Carnival Victory* (2000)

Spirit-class ships: *Carnival Legend* (2002), *Carnival Miracle* (2004), *Carnival Pride* (2002), *Carnival Spirit* (2001)

Odd ship out: *Holiday* (1985)

About the company

Israel-born Ted Arison founded Carnival Cruise Lines, now the world's largest and most successful single cruise line, in 1972 with one ship, *Mardi Gras* (formerly *Empress of Canada*). Carnival wanted to be different, youthful, and fun, and so the company developed the "Fun Ship" concept. It worked, appealing to people of all ages and backgrounds. The company's first new ship, *Tropicale*, debuted in 1982. In 1984 Carnival started advertising on television, introducing a wider public to the idea of cruising. It introduced the first cruise ship measuring over 100,000 tons, *Carnival Destiny*.

Today, the Carnival Corporation, parent company of Carnival Cruise Lines, is run by Ted Arison's son, Micky Arison, who is chairman of the board – as well owning the NBA's Miami Heat basketball team. Carnival owns several cruise brands: AIDA Cruises, Carnival Cruise Lines, Costa Cruises, Cunard Line, Holland America Line, Ocean Village, P&O Cruises, P&O Cruises (Australia), Princess Cruises, Seabourn Cruise Line, and 75% of Iberocruceros. More than 20 new ships have been introduced since the line was founded in 1972.

Self-dubbed the "fun ship" cruise line, the brilliantly organized company attracts passengers of all ages, although the majority are between 30 and 55. Carnival does not sell itself as a "luxury" or "premium" cruise line. It consistently delivers exactly the well-packaged cruise vacation its brochures promise, for which there is a huge and growing first-time cruise market. Its smart ships have the latest high-tech entertainment facilities and features, and some include extra-cost alternative dining spots.

The line has upgraded some aspects of its operation and product (it needed to). The *Carnival Fantasy*-class ships are receiving an overdue multi-million dollar make-over, including an adults-only sunbathing area, pool decks (a thatched roof over one of two hot tubs and the addition of palm trees and new mid-deck stairways), the creation of a new lobby bar, expanded children's and teens areas, and more inter-connecting cabins.

✪ **Frequent passengers' club:** Carnival Concierge Club.

So what's it really like?

It's an all-American experience: cruising for those with a low boredom threshold – exciting, noisy, challenging, but blood pressure-raising, organized fun, slickly packaged with about 60 different itineraries. So forget relaxation – save that for when you get home.

Carnival's "fun" cruising really is for families with children and teens (anyone under 21 must be accompanied by a parent, relative or guardian) and youthful adults. Carnival ships are also good for whole-ship charters and incentive groups, for multi-generational passengers and for family reunions. Typically, about half of Carnival's passengers are taking their first cruise. About 30 percent are under the age of 35, 30 percent are over 55, the other 40 percent are between 35 and 55.

One of Carnival's action-packed shore excursions.

Carnival projects an image of "funship" cruising.

The dress code is decidedly casual – indeed, most waiters are better dressed than most passengers – particularly during youth-heavy holiday seasons and spring breaks, when clothes appear almost optional. Although Carnival is all about "happy," it's an impersonal cruise experience, overseen by young cruise directors who deliver the same jokes and banter on every trip. Perhaps it doesn't matter so much because this will be the first cruise for most passengers. Repeat customers, however, have a distinct sense of déjà vu, but carry a Gold Card for better recognition from hotel staff (Platinum for those who have cruised with Carnival more than 10 times).

The ships are clean and well maintained – if you don't peer too closely. Open deck space may look adequate when you board, but on days at sea you can expect your plastic deck chair, if you can find one that's free, to be kissing its neighbor – it's probably tied to it. There are no cushioned pads for the deck lounge chairs, which are hard to sit on (if you use just a towel) for any length of time.

You may well encounter lots of smokers, and masses of fellow passengers walking around in unharmonious clothing – passengers dress better on longer cruises such as Panama Canal sailings – clutching plastic sport drinks bottles at any time of the day or night. The decibel level is high: it is difficult to escape from noise and loud music, and "background" music is played even in cabin hallways and elevators 24 hours a day. Huge poolside movie screens are being fitted aboard Carnival's ships.

Expect to be subjected to a stream of flyers advertising daily art auctions, "designer" watches, "inch of gold/silver" and other promotions, while "artworks" for auction are strewn throughout the ships. Also, expect intrusive announcements (particularly for activities that bring revenue), and waiters hustling you to have drinks. *Carnival Capers*, the ship's daily program, is among the industry's poorest information sheets, in terms of layout and print quality, and most of it is devoted to persuading you to spend money.

There are libraries but few or no books, and bookshelves are always locked by 6pm, because you are expected to be out in the (revenue-earning) public areas each evening. If you enjoy casino gaming at sea, you could join Carnival's Ocean Players Club, which brings benefits to frequent players, depending on your level of skill.

● **Accommodation:** The balconies in many of the cabins with "private" balconies aren't so private – most can be overlooked from other cabins located on the deck above and from various public locations. You may have to carry a credit card to operate the personal safes – inconvenient. New mattresses and bed linen, also available for sale, have been fitted to all beds.

● **Passenger niggles:** The most consistent complaints include the fact that most activities are geared around trying to sell you something. Free-to-enter onboard games have pint-sized "prizes," while the cost of playing bingo keeps rising. Many people object to the heavy sales pitches for products in spas. The intrusive photographers are almost impossible to escape. The recorded poolside music is repetitious. And then there's disembarkation…

● **Embarkation and disembarkation:** This can be a bothersome procedure, depending on the port. When you do finally walk across the gangway after check-in, the few staff members on duty will merely point you in the direction of your deck or to the ship's elevators instead of escorting you to your cabin. There is little finesse and not enough attention to individuals.

Carnival operates from many "drive to" embarkation ports within the United States, and the company promotes a "vacation guarantee program" that is almost useless (check the Carnival brochure for details).

Decor

The decor is stunningly creative, although you probably wouldn't want to let the ships' interior designer loose in your home. But there's no denying that Joe Farcus, the "neon-lithic" genius behind the decor, creates a dramatic impact, from the carpets to the ceiling, mixing more col-

Carnival Triumph in the Caribbean.

ors than a rainbow could aspire to. Strangely, the sensory overload works. It's pure magic, whimsical, and very entertaining.

So, if you love color, you'll be fine. If you prefer monochrome, take sunglasses. Excepted from the dazzle are the clinical public toilets, which could do with a litle bit of cheering up – the designer clearly hasn't been in one lately.

Gratuities

Added to your onboard account will be $9.75 per person per day (the amount charged when this book went to press). You can have this amount adjusted, although this will mean visiting the information desk. Additionally, 15% is added to your account for all bar, wine and spa charges. The onboard currency is the US dollar – and this applies even when the ship is operating in European waters.

Cuisine/Dining

All Carnival ships have one or two main dining rooms, and dinner has four seating times (except aboard *Carnival Legend, Carnival Miracle, Carnival Pride* and *Carnival Spirit*, which have two main restaurants, each with two seating times). Menus are standardized across

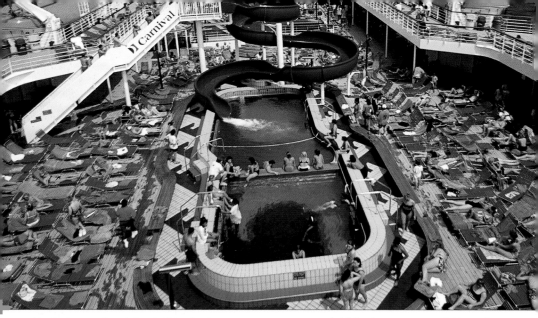

Fun in the sun aboard *Carnival Fascination*.

the fleet, and all the dining venues are non-smoking.

Don't even think about a quiet table for two, or a candlelight dinner on deck – it's not Carnival's style (unless you pay extra to go to an "alternative" restaurant). Dining aboard a Carnival ship is all about table mates, social chat, lively meals, and fast eating. Tables are, however, nicely set with white tablecloths, plenty of silverware, and iced water/iced tea whenever you want it. Oh, and the tired old peppermill routine (where the waiter brings a huge peppermill to your table before you've even tasted the food) is all part of the show – delivered with friendly service that lacks polish but invites extra gratuities.

The main dining rooms marry food and show business. Waiters sing and dance, and there are constant waiter parades with flashing lights in an attempt to create some excitement.

Taste-filled food is not the company's strong point, but quantity, not quality, is – although consultant chef Georges Blanc has created daily "Georges Blanc Signature" menu items. The company does strive to improve its cuisine and the menu choices look good, but the actual food delivered is simply banquet-style catering, with its attendant standardization and production cooking.

While meats are of a decent quality, poultry, fish, seafood and desserts are disappointing. Sauces and gravies are used well as disguises, and there are few garnishes. The selection of fresh green vegetables, breads, rolls, cheese and ripe fruit is limited, and there is much use of canned fruit and jellied desserts, not to mention packets of jam, marmalade, butter, sugar – the same stuff you'd find in the average family eatery in the USA.

It is virtually impossible to obtain anything remotely unusual or off-menu, and the "always available" items appear to have disappeared from the menus. Vegetarian menus and children's menus are available at all meals, although they wouldn't get a generous score for their nutritional content. Spa Carnival Fare has been introduced to provide healthy dining options.

The wine list, however, is good and quite varied – it even includes some fine Bordeaux reds of good vintage – but there are no wine waiters or decent-sized wine glasses. Carnival has also initiated a really good "wines by the glass" program, with state-of-the-art storage and presentation facilities that enable wines to be served properly in several locations and not just in the restaurants aboard each ship.

● **Alternative Dining Spots**

Carnival Conquest, Carnival Destiny, Carnival Freedom, Carnival Glory, Carnival Liberty, Carnival Miracle, Carnival Splendor, Carnival Triumph, Carnival Valor

These extra-cost restaurants feature fine table settings, china and silverware, and leather-bound menus. Menu favorites include prime American steaks such as filet mignon (9 ounces), porterhouse steak (24 ounces) and New York strip loin (be prepared for huge cuts of meat – shown to you at your table before you order), and broiled lobster tail, as well as stone crab claws from Joe's Stone Crabs of South Miami Beach.

Reservations are necessary, and a cover charge of $30 per person for service and gratuity is payable.

A connoisseur's wine list is impressive – it includes such names as Opus One and Château Lafite-Rothschild. The food is very good, and the ambience is reasonably quiet. But if you are a couple and you have just two glasses of wine each (Grgich Hills Chardonnay or Merlot, for example, at $12.50 a glass), and pay the cover charge, that's over $100 for dinner. Caviar would cost an extra $29 for a 1-ounce serving.

Are alternative dining spots worth the extra money? Yes, I believe they are.

● Casual Eateries

All ships also have large food court-style spaces for casual food, fast-food items, grilled meats, pizzas (each ship serves over 800 pizzas in a typical day), stir fry, deli and salad items. There are self-help beverage stands, coffee that looks like rusty water, and tea provided in paper cups with a teabag (tea dust, as far as I'm concerned), plastic or wooden stirrers (no teaspoons and no saucers), and packets of chemical "milk" or "creamer."

But some people are happy to have it that way, and it's actually better than what's offered aboard the ships of its competitor, Royal Caribbean International.

● The Coffee/Tea Factor

Regular coffee is weak and poor, scoring 1 out of 10 (paper/foam cups in buffet areas). Espresso and cappuccino coffees score 2 out of 10 (paper/foam cups, in buffet areas).

For Children:

Carnival is a fine family-friendly cruise line, carrying more than 575,000 children a year, and "Camp Carnival," the line's extensive child/youth program, is well organized and extensive. There are five age groups: Toddlers (ages 2–5); Juniors (6–8); Intermediate (9–11); Tweens (12–14, Circle C) and late Teens (15–17, with Club 02). Even the under-twos are now being catered to, with special programs aboard each ship. Meanwhile, Family Fun Nights are all about reconnecting parents to their children – something many can do only on vacation.

Soft-drinks packages can be bought for children (adults, too). Note that a babysitting service is not available after 10pm.

Best ships for children: *Carnival Conquest, Carnival Destiny, Carnival Freedom, Carnival Glory, Carnival Legend, Carnival Liberty, Carnival Miracle, Carnival Pride, Carnival Spirit, Carnival Splendor, Carnival Triumph, Carnival Valor, Carnival Victory.* **Ships with fewer facilities:** *Carnival Ecstasy, Carnival Elation, Carnival Fantasy, Carnival Fascination, Carnival Imagination, Carnival Inspiration, Carnival Paradise, Carnival Sensation* (note: *Holiday* has almost no facilities).

Entertainment

The ships have big showlounges, all non-smoking, and large-scale flesh-and-feather production shows. On a typical cruise, there will be one or two large-scale shows, with male and female lead singers and a clutch of dancers backed by a 10-piece live orchestra and supported by pre-recorded backing tracks.

These are loud, ritzy-glitzy, razzle-dazzle, Las Vegas-style revues with little or no story line or flow – lots of running around on stage and stepping in place, but little real dancing. The skimpy costumes are very colorful, as is the lighting, with extensive use of "color mover" lights. Stage "smoke" is much overused – to the irritation of anyone seated in the front few rows.

Carnival rotates entertainers aboard its ships, so that passengers see different acts each night, and specialty acts take center stage on nights when there is no production show. There's also live music in just about every bar and lounge – although there appears to be a trend to replace live music with more DJs – and smutty late-night adults-only comedy.

Cabaret acts include vocalists, magic acts, ventriloquists, and comedy jugglers. Each cruise has karaoke nights, a passenger talent show, and a discotheque with ear-splitting volumes and megaphones to enable you to converse with your partner.

Spa/Fitness Facilities

Spa/Fitness facilities are operated by Steiner Leisure, a specialist concession, whose young, revenue-conscious staff will try to sell you Steiner's own-brand beauty products. Some fitness classes are free; others, such as yoga and kick-boxing, cost extra (typically $10 per class), and you'll need to sign up to join.

Examples of treatments: Swedish Massage ($116 for 50 minutes); Aroma Stone Massage ($175 for 75 minutes); Couples Massage ($242 for 50 minutes); Facial ($109 for 50 minutes); Seaweed Body Wrap, with half-body massage ($176 for 90 minutes). It's prudent to book appointments early.

The Spa Carnival layout spaces and facilities are identical to other ships in the same "class," as follows:

● *Carnival Legend, Carnival Miracle, Carnival Pride, Carnival Spirit*

SpaCarnival spans two decks, is located directly above the navigation bridge in the forward part of the ship and has 13,700 sq ft (1,272 sq meters) of space. Facilities on

The deck can double as an outdoor gym.

the lower level include a solarium, eight treatment rooms, lecture rooms, sauna and steam rooms for men and women, and a beauty parlor; the upper level consists of a large gymnasium with floor-to-ceiling windows on three sides, including forward-facing ocean views (with a large array of the latest in muscle-pumping electronic machines), and an aerobics room with instructor-led classes (the aerobics room and gymnasium together measure almost 6,000 sq ft/560 sq meters).

● *Carnival Conquest, Carnival Destiny, Carnival Freedom, Carnival Glory, Carnival Miracle, Carnival Splendor, Carnival Triumph, Carnival Valor*
SpaCarnival spans two decks (with a total area of 13,700 sq ft/1,272 sq meters), and is located directly above the navigation bridge in the forward part of the ship (accessible from the forward stairway). Facilities on the lower level include a solarium, eight treatment rooms, lecture rooms, sauna and steam rooms for men and women, and a beauty parlor; the upper level consists of a large gymnasium with floor-to-ceiling windows on three sides, including forward-facing ocean views. It has the latest in muscle-pumping electronic machines, and an aerobics room with instructor-led classes, some costing extra.

● *Carnival Ecstasy, Carnival Elation, Carnival Fantasy, Carnival Fascination, Carnival Imagination, Carnival Inspiration, Carnival Paradise, Carnival Sensation*
SpaCarnival is located on Sports Deck, forward of the ship's mast, and accessed from the forward stairway. It consists of a gymnasium with ocean-view windows that look out over the ship's bow – you could "cycle" your way to the next port of call if you so wish – complete with a good array of the latest in muscle-pumping electronic machines, an aerobics exercise room, men's and women's changing rooms (towels are provided), sauna and steam rooms, and beauty salon.

A Celebrity shore excursion on the Galápagos.

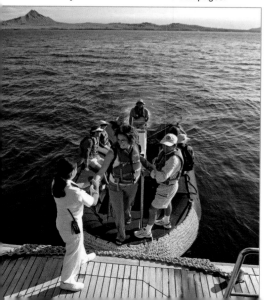

CELEBRITY CRUISES

Ships

Century-class ships: *Celebrity Century* (1995), *Celebrity Galaxy* (1996), *Celebrity Mercury* (1997)
Millennium-class ships: *Celebrity Constellation* (2002), *Celebrity Infinity* (2001), *Celebrity Millennium* (2000), *Celebrity Summit* (2001)
Solstice-class ships: *Celebrity Equinox* (2009), *Celebrity Solstice* (2008)
Other ships: *Celebrity Xpedition* (2001)

About the company

Celebrity Cruises was the brainchild of Harry H. Haralambopoulos and brothers John and Michael Chandris, Greek cargo ship owners and operators of Chandris Lines and Chandris Cruises. In 1989, as the cruise industry was gaining momentum, they determined to create a newer, better cruise line, with new ships, larger, more standard cabins, and focusing more on food and service in the European tradition.

In its formative years, Celebrity Cruises forged an alliance, since dissolved, with three-star Michelin chef Michel Roux, who insisted on using only fresh ingredients. The company established an outstanding reputation for its cuisine, particularly in the main dining rooms, with a formal presentation and service.

Today it advertises itself as a premium line with a taste of luxury. That sums it up nicely because the product delivery on board is superior to that of its parent company, Royal Caribbean International, which bought it in 1997 for $1.3 billion. The ships are instantly recognizable, thanks to the "X" on the funnel denoting the third letter of the Greek alphabet, the Greek "chi" or "C" in English, for Chandris, the founding family.

In 2007 Celebrity Cruises created a new company, **Azamara Cruises**, with mid-size ships, including *Azamara Journey* (2000) and *Azamara Quest* (2000). The idea is to focus on lesser-visited destinations around the world, and offer in-depth shore experiences. All hotel services and cruise operations are, however, operated by Celebrity Cruises.
✪ **Frequent passengers' club:** Captain's Club.

So what's it really like?

The ships are spotlessly clean and extremely well maintained. There are always lots of flowers and flower displays – some ships have flower shops, where you can buy fresh blooms for special occasions.

There is a lot of fine artwork aboard Celebrity's ships; it may not be to everybody's taste, but it is probably the most remarkable collection of contemporary art in the cruise industry. The company provides a lot of the niceties that other lines have long forgotten, although some are now playing "catch up": being escorted to your cabin on arrival by a steward; waiters who carry your trays when you obtain food from buffets or casual eater-

A busy deck – but topless sunbathers have a space too.

ies; water spritzes on the pool deck. On days at sea in warm weather areas, if you are sunbathing on deck, someone will bring you a cold towel, and a sorbet, ice water or iced tea.

Regardless of the accommodation grade, Celebrity Cruises delivers a well-defined North American cruise experience at a modest price. Book a suite-category cabin for the extra benefits it brings – it's worth it. Strong points include the many European staff and the high level of service, fine spas with a good range of facilities and treatments, taste-filled food served in fine European dining tradition, a "zero announcement policy," cloth towels in public restrooms instead of the paper towels found aboard most major companies. Such touches differentiate Celebrity Cruises from its competitors.

Its ships have significantly more staff than other ships of comparable size and capacity. This is especially noticeable in the housekeeping and food and beverage departments, and results in a superior product.

Celebrity's ships are best suited to well-educated, more sophisticated adult couples, families with older children and teenagers, and singles who like to mingle in a large ship setting with stylish surroundings, reasonably decent entertainment, and food and service that are extremely good, for a fare that's excellent value.

Even so, such things as topless sunbathing spaces are now available aboard all ships (except *Azamara Journey, Azamara Quest, Celebrity Xpedition*). Meanwhile, what were formerly cigar smoking lounges have been turned into cozy jazz/piano lounges. Some cruises aboard some ships are designated as child-free.

Sadly, background music is now played almost everywhere, and any lounge designated as "music-free" is typically full of activities and participation events, so it's hard to find a quiet corner to sit and read.

Embarkation: When you first embark, a member of staff, dressed in a crisp white uniform (or black butler's uniform if you are in one of the more expensive suites) will escort you and carry your hand luggage to your cabin, with white glove service and a smile.

So, what's the difference between Celebrity Cruises and its parent, Royal Caribbean International? Here are a few examples relating to food items:

● **RCI** (*Brilliance of the Seas*)
Café: Seattle Coffee Company coffee served in paper cups.
Dining Room Food: overcooked, poor quality (think leather briefcase) meat.
Dining Room: no tables for two.
In the Windjammer Café, waiters do not help passengers to tables with trays; plastic plates are used, cutlery is wrapped in paper napkins, melamine mugs for coffee/tea, tea selection disappointing, and poor-quality (Lipton) teas.
Public restrooms have paper towels.

● **Celebrity Cruises** (*Celebrity Century*):
Cova Café: Coffees/teas served in china cups/ saucers, with doily and chocolate.
Dining Room Food: Good quality and presentation.
Dining Room: Tables for two are available.
Lido Cafe: Waiters line up to help passengers with trays

CELEBRITY'S CLASS CONSCIOUSNESS

There really are three different "classes" aboard Celebrity ships: those in accommodation designated as suites; those in standard exterior-view and interior (no view) cabins; and a third that comes between the two, known as "Concierge Class."

Concierge Class adds another dimension and items that bring added value to passengers. Enhanced facilities include priority embarkation, disembarkation, tender tickets, alternative dining and spa reservations; European duvet; double bed overlay (no more falling "between the cracks" for couples); choice of four pillows (goose down pillow, isotonic pillow, body pillow, conformance pillow); eight-vial flower vase on vanity desk; throw pillows on sofa; fruit basket; binoculars; golf umbrella; leather telephone notepad; larger beach towels; hand-held hairdryer. Balconies get better furniture. In the bathrooms: plusher Frette bathrobe; larger towels in sea green and pink (alternating days); flower in silver vase in bathroom.

to tables. Real china, white cloth napkins, polished cutlery, and a decent selection of teas are provided.
The public restrooms have cloth towels.

Decor

The decor is elegant – Greek, classical, minimalist, although a little antiseptic and cool in places. Celebrity Cruises has some of the most eclectic sculptures and original artwork, from Picasso to Warhol, found at sea. The colors don't jar the senses, and cannot be said to be glitzy – except for the casinos, which are mostly vulgar.

The ships absorb people well, and the flow is, for the most part, good, except for entrances to showlounges and in photo galleries. Each public room subtly invites you to move on to the next.

Gratuities

US$10 per person per day is added to your onboard account. You can have this amount adjusted if you visit the guest relations desk before the end of the cruise. Additionally, 15% is added for all bar, wine purchases, and 10% for spa treatments. The onboard currency is the US dollar.

For Children

Junior passengers are divided into Shipmates (3–6 years), Cadets (7–9), Ensigns (10–12), Teens (13–17).
● **Best ships for children:** *Celebrity Constellation, Celebrity Infinity, Celebrity Millennium, Celebrity Solstice, Celebrity Summit.* Almost as good: *Celebrity Century, Celebrity Galaxy, Celebrity Mercury.*

Cuisine/Dining

The dining rooms aboard all ships are non-smoking areas. There are two seatings for dinner, and open seating for breakfast and lunch. Table settings are excellent, with fine quality linen, china and glassware. Tables for

two are available – far more than by most other major lines. What sets Celebrity apart is the superior training and supervision of dining room waiters, and the service.

The food represents a wide range of culinary influences; it is based on classical French cuisine, modified to appeal to North Americans and European alike. Menus are standardized across the fleet. The variety of cuisine in the main dining rooms is good, the food has taste, and it is very attractively presented and served. Full service in-cabin dining is also available for all meals, including dinner.

The food is made fresh from high-quality ingredients – no pre-made sauces and soups here. Take croissants, for example. Those found aboard Celebrity ships are made fresh each morning, while aboard most competitors' ships they are purchased ashore. There's a big difference in their taste and consistency, depending on what kind of dough and butter are used.

Celebrity Cruises also has well-trained sommeliers and wine waiters who know their subject. The four largest ships (*Celebrity Constellation, Celebrity Infinity, Celebrity Millennium, Celebrity Summit*) have special wine rooms in their "alternative" restaurants that you can dine in, and fine wines that can cost more than $10,000 a bottle – but also wines that start at about $20.

● **Casual Eateries**

There are casual self-serve buffets aboard all Celebrity Cruises' ships. Most are laid out in continuous lines, which causes lines to form at peak times. However, Celebrity is trying to be more creative with these buffets, and, like other cruise lines, has stations for pasta, sushi, salads, grilled and rotisserie items, and hot food items. A waiter will take your tray to a table. A bar trolley service for drinks and wines is provided at lunchtime, and wine waiters are always on hand to discuss and take wine orders for dinner. All the ships make great martinis.

● **The Coffee/Tea Factor**

Regular Coffee: Weak and poor. Score: 2 out of 10. Espresso/Cappuccino coffees: Score: 3 out of 10. If you order espresso/ cappuccino coffees in the dining room, there is a charge; they are treated like a bar item.

Cova Café: All ships have a Cova Café, a seagoing version of the original Café di Milano that was located next to La Scala Opera House in Milan. The shipboard cafés are in prominent locations, and display cases show off the extensive range of Cova coffee, chocolates and alcoholic digestives for sale. Cova Cafés provide an agreeable setting for those who like fine Italian coffees, pastries and cakes. Breakfast pastries are superb. Cova coffee comes in a proper china cup, with a Cova chocolate on the side, and the tables have tablecloths.

The casino aboard *Azamara Journey.*

Entertainment

The company has little cohesive policy regarding big production shows, and can't seem to get them right. Shows aboard some ships are quite decent, with good costuming and lighting, but others look dated and lack story line, flow or connectivity. Each ship carries its own resident troupe of singers/dancers and audio-visual support staff. Bar service, available throughout shows, disrupts concentration. While some cabaret acts are good, they are the same ones seen aboard many ships. All showlounges are non-smoking venues.

Celebrity vessels have a variety of bands and small musical units, although there is very little music for social dancing, other than disco and pop music.

Then there are the summer camp-style audience participation events, games and talent shows that don't sit well with Celebrity's quality of food and service. It's time for some new ones. There are also the inevitable country line dances and playschool routines.

On days at sea the program is crammed with things to do, though the emphasis is on revenue-enhancing activities such as art auctions, giant jackpot bingo, and horse racing.

Spa/Fitness Facilities

Celebrity Cruises, acknowledging the popularity of spas and fitness facilities, has been improving its offerings. Spa/fitness programs are staffed and operated by Steiner Leisure, a specialist concession, whose staff, who have sales targets as well as enthusiasm, will try to sell you Steiner's own-brand beauty products. Some fitness classes are free; others, such as yoga, and kickboxing, cost $10 per class. Being aboard will give you an opportunity to try some of the more exotic massages.

Celebrity's large-scale shows get mixed reviews.

Massage (including exotic massages such as Aroma Stone massage, Chakra Balancing massage and other well-being massages), facials, pedicures, and beauty salon treatments cost extra. Examples: massage at $120 (50 minutes), facial at $120, seaweed wrap (75 minutes) $190 – to which you need to add a gratuity of 10 percent. Personal training sessions in the gymnasium cost $83 for one hour.

COSTA CRUISES

Ships

Atlantica-**class ships:** *Costa Atlantica* (2000), *Costa Mediterranea* (2003)
Fortuna-**class ships:** *Costa Concordia* (2006), *Costa Fortuna* (2003), *Costa Luminosa* (2009), *Costa Magica* (2004), *Costa Pacifica* (2009), *Costa Serena* (2007)
Classica-**class ships:** *Costa Classica* (1992), *Costa Romantica* (1993)
Other ships: *Costa Allegra* (1992), *Costa Europa* (1986), *Costa Marina* (1990), *Costa Victoria* (1996)

About the company

Costa Crociere (Italian for Costa Cruises) traces its history back to 1860 when Giacomo Costa started an olive oil business. The first ship, in 1924, transported that oil. After he died in 1924, his sons, Federico, Eugenio and Enrico, inherited the business. In 1924 they bought *Ravenna*, a freighter to cut transport costs for their olive oil empire. In 1948 Costa's first passenger ship, the *Anna "C"*, carried passengers in style from Genoa to South

One of the pools aboard *Costa Magica*.

America. In 1997, Costa Cruises was bought by the USA's Carnival Corporation and UK's Airtours plc. Three years later Carnival took full control.

Costa specializes in cruises for Europeans or passengers with European tastes, and particularly Italians, during the summer. Costa has initiated an aggressive newbuild policy in recent years, in order to modernize the company's previously aging fleet of different sized ships. The ships operate in three main markets: the Mediterranean, the Caribbean, and South America.

Most ships are well maintained, although there are inconsistencies throughout the fleet. The same is true of cleanliness – some ships are very clean, while others are a little dusty around the edges, as are its shore tenders. The ships have a laid-back European "feel" to their decor and manner of product delivery.

○ **Frequent passengers' club:** Costa Club.

So what's it really like?

Costa is noted for its "Italian" ambiance. There are few Italian crew members, however, although many officers are Italian. Nevertheless, Costa's lifestyle is perceived to be Italian – lively, very noisy, yet easygoing. The dress code is casual, even on formal nights.

Costa does a good job of providing first-time cruise passengers with a packaged holiday that is a mix of sophistication and basic fare, albeit accompanied by loud music. Most passengers are Italian, with a generous sprinkling of other Europeans. One night at the end of each cruise is reserved for a "Roman Bacchanal," when passengers dress up toga-style for dinner and beyond. This is a cruise line for those who like to party. If you want quiet, take earplugs – good ones.

On European and Mediterranean cruises, English will be the language least spoken, as most passengers will be Italian, Spanish, French and German. On Caribbean itineraries, a high percentage of passengers will speak Spanish, as the ships carry passengers from Latin American countries in addition to passengers from North America.

Expect to cruise with a lot of children of all ages if you book for peak holiday cruises – and remember that in Europe schoolchildren at certain times such as Easter have longer vacations. On some European itineraries, passengers embark and disembark in almost every port along the way, which makes for a disjointed cruise experience since there's almost no start or end to the cruise. There is almost no information for passengers who want to be independent in ports of call, and not take the ship's organized general excursions.

There is extensive smoking on board. No-smoking zones and signs are often ignored to the frustration of non-smoking passengers, and ashtrays are moved at whim; many of the officers and crew also smoke, even when moving through public rooms, so they don't bother to enforce the no-smoking zones.

The cabins tend to be on the mean side in size, but the decor is fresh and upbeat, and the bathrooms are very practical units. Some ships have cabin bathrooms with sliding doors – an excellent alternative to inward-openers that use up space.

COSTA CRUISES: BEST SUITED TO...

Costa ships are best suited to young couples, singles and families with children who enjoy big-city life, outdoor cafés, constant and noisy activity, eating late, loud entertainment, and food more notable for quantity than quality.

All printed materials (room service folio, menus, etc.) are in six languages (Italian, English, French, German, Portuguese, and Spanish). Announcements are made in at least two languages in the Caribbean and at least four in Europe and the Mediterranean.

At embarkation, few staff members are on duty at the gangway, and they will merely point you in the direction of your deck, if you're lucky, or to the ship's elevators instead of escorting you to your cabin. Depending on the port, disembarkation is very much a do-it-yourself procedure, with no staff outside the terminals to help you find the right buses.

Decor

Older Ships: *Costa Allegra, Costa Classica, Costa Europa, Costa Marina, Costa Romantica, Costa Victoria* have a distinctively European feel. They are lively without being brash, or pastel-toned without being boring, depending on the ship you choose.

Newer, larger ships – *Costa Atlantica, Costa Concordia, Costa Fortuna, Costa Luminosa, Costa Magica, Costa Mediterranea, Costa Pacifica, Costa Serena* – have an "in-your-face" brashness similar to Carnival's ships, with grainy and unflattering digital artwork on walls and panels, and even inside elevators.

The "entertainment architecture," as designer Joe Farcus calls it, can't be ignored. There is an abundance of jazzy colors, fine or grotesque sculptures (depending on your taste) and huge murals that are both impressive and mind-numbing.

Gratuities

The onboard currency is the euro (Europe/ Mediterranean cruises), or US dollar (Caribbean cruises). On the former, €32 per 7-day cruise per person is charged to your onboard account, plus 10% to all bar and wine orders. On Caribbean cruises, the figures are $53 per 7-day cruise per person and 15% for bar and wine orders. Many non-Italians would prefer to choose when to tip and how much. To have these amounts adjusted, you need to visit the information desk.

Cuisine/Dining

If you expect to be served by jovial Italian waiters, you'll be disappointed – although the restaurant managers might be Italian. All ships have two seatings for dinner; dining times on Europe/Mediterranean and South America cruises are usually later than those in the Caribbean because Europeans and Latin passengers eat much later than North Americans. Few tables for two are available, most being for four, six, or eight. All dining rooms are smoke-free – in theory.

The cuisine is best described as continental, with many regional Italian dishes and much emphasis on pasta: 50 pasta dishes per cruise. Except for pasta dishes (made fresh on board) and cream sauces, presentation and food quality are not memorable, and are the subject of many negative comments from passengers. While the quality of meat is adequate, it is

often disguised with gravies and rich sauces. Fish and seafood tend to lack taste, and are often overcooked. Green vegetables are hard to come by. Breads and bread rolls are usually good, but the desserts are of supermarket quality and lack taste.

There is a wine list but no wine waiters; table waiters are expected to serve both food and wine, which doesn't work well. Almost all wines are young – very young.

● Alternative Dining

If you opt for one of the "alternative" restaurants aboard the larger ships, note that a cover charge applies: €20 per person plus 10% service charge (Europe/Mediterranean cruises), or $20 per person plus 15% service charge (Caribbean cruises).

● Casual Eateries

All ships have self-serve lido buffets. In most, you have to move along with your tray, but the latest ships have more active stations and individual islands. The items available are quite basic. All ships except *Costa Europa* also have a pizzeria.

● The Coffee/Tea Factor

Regular Coffee: Decent and quite strong. Score: 5 out of 10.

Espresso/Cappuccino coffees (Lavazza) are among the best served by the major cruise lines: the main competition is from Celebrity Cruises' Cova Café; Star Cruises also serves Lavazza. All Costa ships have coffee machines in most lounges/bars. Score: 8 out of 10.

For children

Junior passengers are in four groups: Kids Club is for 3–6; Junior Club is for 7–12; Teen Club is for 13–17. The program varies by ship, itinerary and season. Group

The statuesque atrium aboard *Costa Allegra*.

A sculpture enlivens the deck of a Costa ship.

babysitting is available 6.30–11pm. During port days, babysitting is available generally 8.30am–12.30pm and 2.30–6.30pm.

● **Best ships for children:** *Costa Atlantica, Costa Concordia, Costa Fortuna, Costa Luminosa, Costa Magica, Costa Mediterranea, Costa Pacifica, Costa Serena.* But not: *Costa Allegra, Costa Classica, Costa Europa, Costa Marina, Costa Romantica, Costa Victoria.*

Entertainment

Each ship carries its own resident troupe of singers/dancers and audio-visual support staff, but Costa Cruises is not known for the quality of its entertainment. What it does present tends to be of the "no finesse" variety, with revue-style shows that have little story line, poor choreography and execution, but plenty of fast-moving action – more stepping in place than dancing – and lots of volume. It's entertainment to pass the time rather than remember.

Cabaret acts (typically singers, magicians, comedy jugglers, ventriloquists, and so on) are entertaining but rather ho-hum. Most passenger participation activities include poolside games such as a "Belly Flop" competition, election of the "Ideal Couple," and other juvenile games – but some families love them. There are also dance classes, and the inevitable "Fine Art Auction."

Spa/Fitness Facilities

These vary according to ship and size. The newest and largest ships (*Costa Atlantica, Costa Concordia, Costa Fortuna, Costa Magica, Costa Mediterranea* and *Costa Serena*) have more space and better facilities, while the others (*Costa Allegra, Costa Europa, Costa Marina*) have only basic facilities.

Spa/fitness facilities are staffed and operated by Steiner Leisure, a specialist concession, whose young staff will try to sell you Steiner's own-brand beauty products. Some fitness classes are free, while some, such as yoga, and kick-boxing, cost $10 per class.

However, being aboard will give you an opportunity to try some of the more exotic treatments, particularly some of the massages available. Massage (including exotic massages such as Aroma Stone massage, Chakra Balancing massage and other well-being massages), facials, pedicures, and beauty salon treatments cost extra – massage, for example, costs about $2 per minute, plus gratuity.

Aboard *Costa Concordia* and *Costa Serena*, Samsara Spa accommodation grades benefit from Oriental-themed decor and Samsara bathroom amenities, and 12 Samsara Suites have direct access to the Samsara Spa facilities and special packages and concessions. To use the sauna/steam and relaxation areas aboard some of the ships, you'll need to buy a day pass, for €35 per person.

CUNARD LINE

Ships:
Queen Mary 2 (2004), *Queen Victoria* (2007).

About the company

Cunard Line was established in 1839, as the British and North American Steam Packet Company, to carry the Royal Mail and passengers from the Old World to the New. Its first ship, *Britannia*, sailed on its maiden voyage on American Independence Day in 1840. The author Charles Dickens crossed the Atlantic aboard the ship in 1842 together with 62 other passengers, 93 crew members, one cow, and, most important, Her Majesty's mails and despatches.

Since 1840, Cunard Line has always had ships built to sail across the North Atlantic. From 1850 until the arrival of *QE2* in 1969, all of the line's ships and those of White Star Line (with which Cunard merged in 1934) had several classes. Your luggage label, therefore, declared not only your name but also what you could afford. Today, there's no class distinction, other than by the grade of accommodation you choose. In other words, you get what you pay for, as on any cruise ship.

But one is still reminded of the company's illustrious history. For example, Cunard Line:
● was the first company to take passengers on regularly scheduled transatlantic crossings.
● introduced the first passenger ship to be lit by electricity (*Servia*, 1881).
● introduced the first steam turbine engines in an ocean liner (*Carmania*, 1905).
● introduced the first indoor swimming pool aboard a ship (*Aquitania*, 1914).
● pioneered an around-the-world cruise (*Laconia*, 1922).
● held the record for the largest passenger ship ever built (*Queen Elizabeth*, between 1940 and 1996).
● is presently the only company to sail regularly scheduled year-round transatlantic crossings (*Queen Mary 2*).
✪ **Frequent passengers' club:** Cunard World Club

So what's it really like?

Sailing aboard a Cunard Line ship is quite different to being aboard a standard cruise ship. The vessels incorporate a lot of maritime history and the grand traditions of ocean liners – as opposed to the average cruise ship, with its tendency to tacky high-street trappings. Assuming your sea legs can cope with sometimes less than calm waters, a transatlantic crossing is supremely civilized, particularly if you are able to enjoy being cosseted in accommodation that allows you to dine in the "grill"-class restaurants with their fine cuisine and presentation.

Cunard Line ships are best suited to a wide range of seasoned and well-traveled couples and single passengers who enjoy the cosmopolitan setting of an ocean liner, with their extensive array of facilities, public rooms, dining rooms, and lecture programs. Male social hosts – typically 10 on an around-the-world cruise – serve as dancing partners for women traveling alone.

Cunard Line is the only cruise line that allows you to take your dog or cat with you (*Queen Mary 2* transatlantic crossings only).

Cuisine/Dining

Cunard Line provides good-quality ingredients (sourced in Europe and the USA). The cuisine is still of a mass market standard – you'll find butter in packets in some venues. However, at the self-serve buffets, salt and pepper are usually provided on each table. Espressos and cappuccinos are available in the dining rooms, and at extra cost in many bars. Cunard uses Colombian coffee.

Both ships have "grill rooms" as well as traditional large restaurants, and casual self-service dining venues. Grill rooms are more exclusive and some have à la carte menus, while the main restaurants have fixed menus. The grill rooms have seating dining at assigned tables, when you wish, while the main Britannia Restaurants (in both ships) have two seatings.

The cuisine includes many traditional British favorites, together with extensive French dishes as well as regional specialties from around the world, nicely presented on Wedgwood china.

For Children

Children's facilities are quite good aboard both *Queen Mary 2* and *Queen Victoria,* though they aren't as extensive as aboard the former *Queen Elizabeth 2.* Youngsters are supervised by real English nannies.

Gratuities

The onboard currencies are the British pound and the US dollar, depending on the operating area. Gratuities are automatically charged to your onboard account – you will need to visit the information desk to change them. The amount is $13 per person per day (Grill Class accommodation, including children) or $11 per person per day (other accommodation). In addition, 15% is added to all bar and wine, and health spa/salon bills.

Entertainment

Production shows are colourful and visual, with pre-recorded backing tracks supplementing the showband. Other shows consist of cabaret acts – typically singers, magicians, mime artistes, comedy jugglers, and, occasionally, comedians – doing the cruise ship circuit. A number of bands and small musical units provide live music for dancing and listening.

Spa/Fitness Facilities

The spa/fitness centers are operated by Canyon Ranch (*QM2*) and Harding Brothers/Multitrax Maritime under the brand name The Onboard Spa Company (*Queen Victoria*), with prices that generally match those of land-based health resorts.

Queen Victoria includes a traditional London theater.

HOLLAND AMERICA LINE

Ships

Amsterdam (2000), *Eurodam* (2008), *Maasdam* (1993), *Noordam* (2006), *Oosterdam* (2003), *Prinsendam* (1988), *Rotterdam* (1997), *Ryndam* (1994), *Statendam* (1993), *Veendam* (1996), *Volendam* (1999), *Westerdam* (2004), *Zaandam* (2000), *Zuiderdam* (2002).

About the company

Holland America Line was founded in 1873 as the Netherlands-America Steamship Company, shipping immigrants to the New World. In 1989, it was acquired by Carnival Cruise Lines, but retained its Seattle-based headquarters. It bought into Alaskan hotels and transportation when it acquired Westours in 1971, and is now one of the state's biggest employers.

HAL has grown fast, and carries both traditional cruise passengers (senior citizens, alumni groups) and multi-generational families. It tries hard to keep its Dutch connections, with antique artefacts and traditional decor, as well as Indonesian stewards. It has a private island, Half Moon Cay, in the Bahamas.
○ **Frequent passengers' club:** Mariner Society

So what's it really like?

Fresh management with updated ideas, the line's "Signature of Excellence" program, the food variety and creativity have all improved the HAL experience. The ships

The atrium aboard Holland America's *Zuiderdam*.

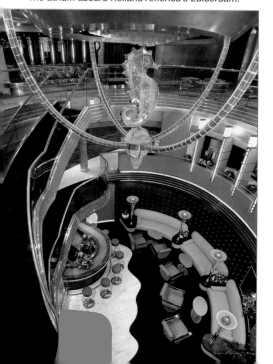

benefit from lots of fresh flowers, museum-quality art pieces, and more attention to detail than all the other major lines with the exception of Celebrity Cruises.

The brand encompasses basically two types of ship. Younger families with children and grandchildren are best suited to the new, larger vessels such as *Eurodam, Noordam, Oosterdam, Westerdam*, and *Zuiderdam*, whereas those of senior years – HAL's traditional audience of repeat passengers from alumni groups – are best suited to ships that are smaller and less glitzy (*Amsterdam, Maasdam, Prinsendam, Rotterdam, Ryndam, Statendam, Veendam*, and *Zaandam*). All the ships are well maintained, and cleaning takes place constantly. All ships have teakwood outdoors promenade decks, whereas most rivals have artificial grass or some other form of indoor-outdoor carpeting.

Holland America Line has its own training school in Jakarta, Indonesia, and so is able to "pre-train" crew members who have never been to sea before. Many crew members have been promoted to supervisory positions due to a host of new ships introduced, but few of those promoted have the formal training, professional or management skills, or experience to do the job well. Internal promotion is fine, but decreased professionalism is not the price that passengers should pay. However, HAL's mainly Indonesian crew members are willing, polite, and smile a lot – particularly if extra tips are forthcoming – which is more than can be said for service staff on land today, particularly in western countries.

HAL is one of only three of the 11 major cruise lines with proper cinemas built into all its ships. It also operates many theme-related cruises, and has an extensive "University at Sea" program of life-enrichment lecturers. The cinemas also have superb full demonstration kitchens built in for a new "Culinary Arts" program that includes celebrity chefs, and interactive cooking demos.

HAL has established smoking and no-smoking areas throughout its ships, but there are many more smokers than you might expect, depending on ship and itinerary.

The ships are best suited to older couples and singles (and their grandchildren), who like to mingle in a large ship, in an unhurried setting with fine-quality surroundings, with plenty of eclectic antique artwork, decent – though not gourmet – food and service from a smiling Indonesian/Filipino crew who don't have the finesse many passengers expect from a "premium" product.

Decor

Aboard *Amsterdam, Maasdam, Prinsendam, Rotterdam, Ryndam, Statendam, Veendam, Volendam, Zaandam*, the decor is rather bland (restful), with eclectic artwork that is focused on Dutch artefacts, mainly from the 16th and 17th centuries.

Aboard the newest ships (*Eurodam, Oosterdam, Westerdam, Zuiderdam*) the decor is more lively and glitzy – acceptable for families with children who like bright things such as large wall panels with digital "in-your-face" artwork that present an *Alice in Wonderland* look.

Aft pool and hot tubs, Holland America style.

You wouldn't go for it in your living room, but aboard these large resort ships it works. It is important, therefore, to choose the right ship for your personality type, and for the facilities that appeal.

Gratuities

$10 per person per day (the amount charged when this book went to press) is added to your onboard account. You can have this amount adjusted at the information desk to do so. Additionally, 15% is added to bar and wine accounts. The onboard currency is the US dollar.

Cuisine/Dining

For dinner, Holland America Line features both open seating (on one level) or assigned tables (at fixed times, on the other level) in its dining rooms; it's called "As You Wish" dining. For breakfast and lunch in the main dining room, an open seating policy applies. All dining venues are non-smoking.

Some tables for two are available, but most are for four, six, eight or 10. The larger tables are ideal for multi-generational families. Fine Rosenthal china and cutlery are used. Live music is provided for dinner. "Lighter option" meals are always available for the nutrition-conscious and the weight-conscious.

Holland America Line food was greatly upgraded when master chef Rudi Sodamin arrived in 2005 as a consultant; he introduced his "Wild About Salmon" and other creative ideas, and the "Culinary Arts Center" (with its own dedicated live interactive demonstration kitchen and guest chef program) has been a success story. In 2008 menus were revamped to include more regional cuisine and more local ingredients.

However, while the USDA beef is very good, poul-

try and most fish tend to be overcooked (except when the ships are in Alaska, where halibut and salmon are excellent). What are not "premium" are the packets of sugar, and packets (instead of glass jars) of supermarket-brand breakfast jams, marmalade and honey, sugar, and butter. Also, coffee and teas are poor-quality, except in the extra-charge Explorations Café. While packets may be suitable for a family diner, they do not belong aboard ships that claim "award-winning cuisine."

Dessert and pastry items are good, suited to American tastes, but canned fruit and jellied desserts are much in evidence. Most of the "international" cheeses are highly colored, processed cheese (cruises in Europe have better access to European cheeses).

HAL also offers complimentary ice cream during certain hours of the day, as well as hot hors d'oeuvres in all bars – something other major lines seem to have dropped, or charge extra for. Cabin service breakfasts

HAL's SIGNATURE OF EXCELLENCE

Between 2004 and 2006, "Signature of Excellence" improvements were introduced, at a cost of $225 million. These cover dining, service, accommodation, and activities, and include "Premium-Plus" Euro-Top mattresses, 100 percent cotton bed linens or duvets (top suites only), massage showerheads, fruit baskets, and DVD players. Elemis personal bathroom amenities are pro-

vided for all passengers (these are better than Celebrity's present bathroom amenities, for example). Suite occupants also have access to the exclusive Neptune Lounge (with concierge services), thus in effect creating a two-class system that suite occupants like. Bathrobes and a range of personal toiletries are provided for all passengers, and hot hors d'oeuvres and canapés are always part of the pre-dinner cocktail scene.

are very basic, with only Continental breakfast available and few hot food items.

HAL can provide kosher meals. As the ships do not have kosher kitchens, these are prepared ashore, frozen, and brought to your table sealed in containers.

The wine list relies heavily on wines from California and Washington State, with few decent French or German wines, other than those found in a typical supermarket ashore. A Connoisseur List is available in the Pinnacle Grill.

● **Alternative Dining**

All HAL ships have "alternative dining" spots called "Pinnacle Grill" (or "Pinnacle Grill at the Odyssey Restaurant"), specializing in "Pacific Northwest Cuisine." Items include sesame-crusted halibut with ginger-miso; and an array of premium quality steaks, presented tableside prior to cooking. These are more intimate restaurants with tablecloths, linen napkins and decently sized wine glasses. The food is better than in the main dining rooms. There is a cover charge, and reservations are required. Bulgari china, Frette linens, and Reidel glasses are part of this enhanced dining experience.

● **Casual Eateries**

All ships feature a Lido Deck self-serve buffet. Most are lines you move along with your tray, although the latest ships have more "active" stations (examples: omelets and pasta cooked to order) and individual islands. There are decent salad bars, dessert bars, regional specialties, and grilled fast-food items such as hamburgers, salmon burgers, hot dogs and French fries.

● **The Coffee/Tea Factor**

Regular Coffee: Half decent, but weak (Score: 3 out of 10). Espresso/cappuccino coffees (Dutch) are adequate, served in proper china, but not quite up to the standard of Celebrity or Costa. Score: 6 out of 10.

Costumes and lighting hide the weak spots.

For Children

Club HAL: Junior passengers are divided into three age-appropriate groups: 3–8, 9–12, and teens. Programming is based on the number of children booked on any given sailing, and children's counsellors are provided accordingly. HAL's children's programs are not as extensive as those of Carnival Cruise Lines, for example, although they are improving with the latest ships.

● **Best ships for children:** *Eurodam, Noordam, Oosterdam, Westerdam, Zaandam, Zuiderdam,* but not: *Amsterdam, Maasdam, Prinsendam, Rotterdam, Ryndam, Statendam, Veendam.*

Entertainment

Holland America Line is not known for lavish entertainment (the budgets aren't high enough). The production shows, while a good attempt, fall short on story line, choreography and performance, while colorful costuming and lighting hide the weak spots. Each ship carries its own resident troupe of singers and dancers and audio-visual support staff. HAL also offers a consistently good, tried and tested array of cabaret acts that constantly pop up on the cruise ship circuit. All showlounges are non-smoking venues.

A number of bands, a string ensemble and solo musicians present live music for dancing and listening in many of the lounges and bars. Each ship has a Crow's Nest Lounge (by day an observation lounge) for social dancing, and there is always serenading string music in the Explorer's Lounge and dining room. Each cruise includes a Crew Show; these vary from poor to very entertaining, depending on your taste. Passengers always seem enthusiastic, because they like connecting staff that they know and have seen during their cruise.

Spa/Fitness Facilities

The Greenhouse Spa, beauty and fitness amenities named

after the Texas-based facility, aboard all HAL ships are staffed and operated by Steiner Leisure, a specialist concession, whose young staff will try to sell you Steiner's own-brand Elemis beauty products. Some fitness classes are free; others, such as yoga, kickboxing or Pilates essentials, cost $11 per class (a special price is offered for unlimited classes).

Massages (including exotic massages such as Aroma Stone massage, Chakra Balancing massage and other well-being massages), facials, pedicures, and beauty treatments cost extra. Examples: well-being massage $109 for 50 minutes; hot stone therapy massage $175 for 75 minutes; reflexology $109 for 50 minutes; Japanese Silk Booster facial 129 for 75 minutes; personal fitness instruction $75 for 60 minutes (course of three for $191).

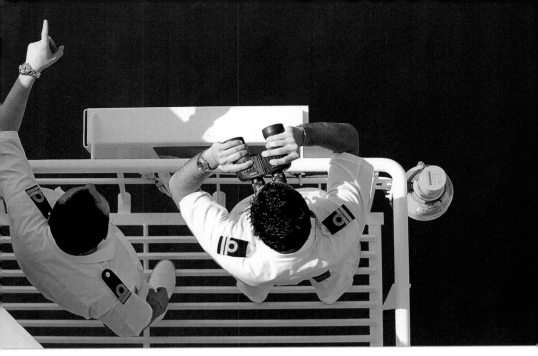

MSC crews typically operate in five languages.

MSC CRUISES

Ships

Fantasia-class ships: *MSC Fantasia* (2008)
Armonia-class ships: *MSC Armonia* (2001), *MSC Lirica* (2003), *MSC Musica* (2006), *MSC Opera* (2004), *MSC Orchestra* (2007), *MSC Poesia* (2008), *MSC Splendida* (2002)
Other ships: *MSC Melody* (1982), *MSC Rhapsody* (1977)

About the company

The headquarters of Europe's largest privately-owned cruise line are in Geneva, Switzerland, home of parent company Mediterranean Shipping Company, the world's second largest container shipping company. Operations are based in Naples, Italy. It started in the passenger shipping business by acquiring the Italian company Star Lauro in 1995, together with two older ships, *Monterey* and *Rhapsody*. It expanded with the purchase of *Melody*, followed by almost new ships bought from the bankrupt Festival Cruises.

MSC Cruises has grown extremely fast in a few years, and has a number of large resort ships on order. It aims to have the world's youngest fleet by 2010.
✪ **Frequent passengers' club:** MSC Club

So what's it really like?

MSC Cruises' ships are best suited to adult couples and singles, and families with children. They are good for those who enjoy big city life, outdoor cafés, constant activity accompanied by plenty of music, late nights, and food ranging from adequate to very good.

The company has evolved quickly as the "new kid on the block." Of all the major cruise lines, it's also the cleanest. It changes bed linen and towels the most; typically, bed linen is changed every second day, towels daily, and bathrobes in suites daily.

The ships typically operate in five languages, with embarkation-day announcements in English, French, German, Italian, and Spanish. Mercifully, during the cruise, there are almost no announcements. Given this multilingual emphasis, production shows and other major entertainment displays are more visual than verbal. For the same reason, the ships do not generally carry lecturers. By culling news from 600 major newspapers around the world, in up to 36 languages, Newspapers Direct can supply you with a daily newspaper on board to your liking.

The roving band of photographers, taking your picture at every opportunity, can irritate. Particularly intrusive are the tacky photographs taken during dinner, when "pirates" and other costumed staff appear behind the smartly dressed diners.
● **Embarkation:** When you first embark, a member of staff in a crisp white uniform – or black butler's uniform if you are in one of the more expensive suites – will escort you and carry your hand luggage to your suite or cabin, with white-glove service and a smile.

Decor

Except for the two oldest ships, *MSC Melody* and *MSC Rhapsody*, the decor aboard the newer ships is decidedly European, with much understated elegance and high-

MSC Opera on home territory, visiting Venice.

quality soft furnishings and other materials – although the latest ships have become brighter.

Gratuities

These are charged to your onboard cabin at €6 per person, per day. Drinks prices, however, already include a service charge.

Cuisine/Dining

MSC Cruises provides better-quality ingredients, almost all sourced in Europe, than some other major cruise lines. The cuisine is still mainstream – you'll find butter in packets. However, at the self-serve buffets, salt and pepper are typically provided on each table, not in packets as on most rival cruise lines.

Espresso and cappuccino (Segafredo brand Italian coffee) are available in the dining rooms, at extra cost, and in almost all bars.

Aboard the newest ships, MSC Cruises has introduced the Italian "slow food" concept. Always available items include spaghetti, chicken breast, salmon fillet, and vegetables of the day. Refreshingly, the company spotlights regional Italian cuisine and wine, so daily dining room menus feature food from regions such as Calabria, Piedmont, Lazio, Puglia, and Sicily.

All pizza dough is made on board, not brought from ashore, while risotto (featured daily) has become a signature item for MSC Cruises and something the ships make really well. Spaghetti is always available, with a tomato sauce freshly made each day. Many varieties of Italian breads such as bruschetta, focaccia, and panettone, are provided.

● **Alternative dining:** The newest ships have an alternative specialty restaurant. Aboard *MSC Opera* and *MSC Poesia*, it is Kaito – an authentic Japanese restaurant with an extensive, outstanding menu. Aboard *MSC Orchestra* it is Shanghai, a Chinese restaurant with real wok cooking and dim sum. The quality is high, and it really is worth having at least one meal in these venues.

● **Room service:** Continental breakfast is complimentary from 7.30 to 10am, while room service snacks can be bought at any other time. A basket of fruit is provided to all cabins at embarkation, and replenished daily for suite-grade accommodation.

For Children

Children are divided into three age groups, with facilities to match: Mini Club for 3 to 9-year-olds; Junior Club for 10–13s; Teenagers Club for those over 14. While the facilities and play areas are not as extensive as those aboard most major cruise lines, a "baby parking" service is useful when parents want to go ashore on excursions. MSC Cruises' mascot is Do-Re-Mi – the von Trapp family of *Sound of Music* fame would no doubt be delighted.

Entertainment

The main production shows are colorful and visual, particularly aboard the newest ships. Other shows consist of unknown cabaret acts (typically singers, magicians, mime artistes, comedy jugglers, and others) doing the cruise ship circuit. The ship carries a number of bands and small musical units that provide live music for dancing or listening, but there is no show band, and all production shows are done to pre-recorded backing tracks.

Spa/Fitness Facilities

The spas are operated as a concession by Blue Ocean – except *MSC Musica*, which is operated by Steiner Leisure. Treatments include acupuncture (not aboard *MSC Rhapsody*).

NORWEGIAN CRUISE LINE / NCL AMERICA

Ships

NCL: *Norwegian Dawn* (2002), *Norwegian Dream* (1992), *Norwegian Gem* (2007), *Norwegian Jade* (2006), *Norwegian Jewel* (2005), *Norwegian Majesty* (1992), *Norwegian Pearl* (2006), *Norwegian Spirit* (1998), *Norwegian Star* (2002), *Norwegian Sun* (2001), *as yet unnamed ship* (2009)

NCL America: *Pride of America* (2005)

About the company

Norwegian Cruise Line, the originator of contemporary cruising, was founded in 1966 by three Norwegian shipping companies as Norwegian Caribbean Line. The line was bought by Star Cruises in 2000, and has been replacing its older, smaller ships with brand new, larger vessels. NCL also operates NCL America, with mostly American crews and a base in Hawaii. Most comments in this section apply to both brands.

Freestyle Cruising is how NCL describes its operation. Its fleet is diverse, so the cruise experience can vary, although this makes for interesting character variation between the various ship categories. There is more standardization aboard the larger, newer ships. The senior officers are the only thing that's Norwegian – except aboard NCL America vessels, where they are mostly American.

Choose this line for a good all-round family cruise with a sporty feel, interesting itineraries, many from "Homeland USA" ports, and lots of dining choices, particularly aboard the newest ships.

Most standard cabins are small, though they have reasonably attractive decor and are functional. Closet and drawer space is limited aboard the newest ships.

✪ **Frequent passengers' club:** Latitudes

So what's it really like?

If this is your first cruise, you should enjoy a good overall vacation in an upbeat setting. The onboard lifestyle is contemporary, fresh, creative and sporty, with a casualness typical of youthful city dwellers, and with its "eat when you want" philosophy, the shipboard ambiance is casual. So is the dress code – indeed, the waiters may be better dressed than many passengers. The staff is congenial, and you'll find a high percentage of females in cabin and restaurant service departments – more than most major cruise lines. However, revenue centers are everywhere, including "inch of gold," tee shirts, and sunscreen lotion, all sold at tables on the open decks adjacent to swimming pools.

All ships can provide an almost full-size newspaper from a wide choice of US and European titles on the Multicast satellite delivery system (the cost: $3.95 per newspaper, per day). You can also make a special request for your favorite newspaper that's not in the list, although it may cost more.

NCL ships are best suited to first-time young and young-at-heart couples, single passengers, children and teenagers who want upbeat, color-rich surroundings, plenty of entertainment lounges and bars, and high-tech sophistication – all in one programmed but well packaged cruise vacation. There's plenty of lively music, constant activity, entertainment, and food that's mainstream and acceptable but nothing more – unless you pay extra to eat in the "alternative" dining spots. All this is delivered by a smiling, very friendly service staff who lacks polish but are willing.

● **Embarkation:** Few staff members are on duty at the gangway when you first arrive, and they merely point you in the direction of your deck, or to the ship's elevators instead of escorting you to your cabin.

● **NCL's Private Island (Great Stirrup Cay):** Only coffee and ice-water are free (there's no iced tea), and all other drinks are charged.

Decor

The newest ships have colorful, eye-catching designs on their hulls, differentiating them from the competition.

Gratuities

A fixed $10 per person per day service charge is added to your onboard account. Children over 13 pay the full adult rate; those aged 3–12 pay $5 per day, and under-3s pay nothing. A 15% gratuity is added to bar, wine and spa charges. Onboard currency: the US dollar.

NCL's evocation of Hawaii's charms.

Cuisine/Dining

NCL has recognized the increasing trend away from formal restaurants (for dining) toward bistros (for eating faster). For cruising, NCL has championed more choices in dining than any other cruise line, except parent company Star Cruises, with its "Freestyle Dining." This allows you to try different types of cuisine, in different settings, when you want. In practice, however, it means that you have to make reservations, which can prove frustrating at times, and getting it just right takes a little planning and, sometimes, waiting.

Freestyle Dining works best aboard the newest ships, which have been specially designed for it: *Norwegian Dawn, Norwegian Gem, Norwegian Jade, Norwegian Jewel, Norwegian Pearl, Norwegian Spirit, Norwegian Star, Norwegian Sun, Pride of America*. The others (*Norwegian Dream, Norwegian Majesty*) have been modified to accommodate the concept, but you end up with food outlets, not restaurants.

On Formal Nights production show presentation nights, most people want to eat at the same time in order to see the shows, and this causes prime-time congestion, fast service and frustration. However, the ships now have plasma screens in various locations so you can make reservations when you want, and see at a glance the waiting times for a table.

After-dinner espresso/cappuccino coffees are available in the dining rooms without extra charge – a nice feature. Once each cruise, NCL features a Chocoholics Buffet with paper plates and plastic cutlery. The wine list is quite good, with many excellent wines in the $20–$30 range. But the wine is typically served by table waiters, whose knowledge of wines is minimal.

Cabin service breakfasts are very basic, with only Continental breakfast available and no hot food items – for those, you'll need to go to a restaurants or buffet. The non-breakfast Room Service menu has only two hot items available throughout the day: Oriental soup and pizza – the rest is cold (salads and sandwiches).

● **The Coffee/Tea Factor:** Regular Coffee: Weak and poor. Score: 2 out of 10.

Espresso/Cappuccino coffees: Score: 4 out of 10. Some bars have espresso/cappuccino machines, which are extra-charge items.

For Children

NCL's Junior Cruisers (Kids Crew) program divides children into three groups, according to age: Junior sailors (ages 2–5); First Mates and Navigators (6–12); Teens (13–17). Babysitting services are available (group only, not individual) at an extra change. Special packages are available for soft drinks.

● **Best ships for children:** *Norwegian Dawn, Norwegian Gem, Norwegian Jade, Norwegian Jewel, Norwegian Pearl, Norwegian Spirit, Norwegian Star, Norwegian Sun*. But not: *Norwegian Dream* or *Norwegian Majesty*.

Entertainment

NCL has always had good production shows that provide lots of color and spectacle in a predictable – though a little dated – format. Each ship has a resident troupe of singers/dancers. There are two or three production shows in a typical 7-day cruise.

They are all very colorful, high-energy, razzle-dazzle shows, with much use of laser and color-mover lights. They're not memorable but, it must be said, they're very entertaining. All showlounges are non-smoking.

Most activities and passenger participation events range from poor to extremely poor. Nintendo Wii interactive games are available on large screens.

Spa/Fitness Facilities

The spas are staffed and operated by the Hawaii-based Mandara Spa, owned by Steiner Leisure. Many of the staff are young, and will try to sell you Steiner's own-brand Elemis beauty products. Some fitness classes are free, while others, such as yoga and kick-boxing, cost $10 per class.

However, being aboard will give you an opportunity to try some of the more exotic treatments, particularly the various massages. Massage (including Aroma Stone massage, Chakra Balancing massage and other well-being massages), facials, pedicures, and beauty salon treatments cost

Norwegian Pearl has a ten-pin bowling alley.

P&O's latest ship, *Ventura*, sails out of Southampton.

extra. Examples: Lomi Lomi Massage ($99 for 50 minutes/$140 for 80 minutes); Mandara Four Hands Massage ($180 for 50 minutes; $280 for 80 minutes).

Aboard some ships, a "Thermal Suite" (sauna, steam room, aroma-showers and relaxation area) costs $20 per day, or $75 for a 7-day pass.

NCL America

This "all-American" division of NCL operates *Pride of America,* dedicated to cruising the Hawaiian islands with a year-round base in Honolulu. Having a mostly American crew means that the niceties of food service do not match the standard of some international cruise lines. In general, there's too much of a casual attitude among the unionized staff to guarantee consistent product delivery. However, the ship provides a great way to see the islands of Hawaii in a comfortable, family-oriented way.

P&O CRUISES

Ships

Child-free ships: *Arcadia* (2005); *Artemis* (1984)
Family-friendly ships: *Aurora* (2000); *Oceana* (2000); *Oriana* (1995); *Ventura* (2008)

About the company

Its full name is the Peninsular and Oriental Steam Navigation Company, though none of its ships is still operated by steam turbines. Based in Southampton, England, it was founded in 1837, just before Samuel Cunard established his company, and was awarded a UK government contract in 1840 to carry the mails from Gibraltar to Alexandria.

P&O Cruises acquired Princess Cruises in 1974, Swan Hellenic in 1982, and Sitmar Cruises in 1988. In 2000 it demerged from its parent to establish itself as P&O Princess plc. It was bought by Carnival Corporation in 2003.

So what's it really like?

P&O Cruises has always been a traditional cruise company, never quite keeping up with the better quality cruise experience provided aboard the Cunard Line ships. However, it has been reinventing itself, and the result is a contemporary onboard cruise product well aimed at the high-street traveler. It specializes in providing all the little things that British passengers have come to expect, including tea/coffee making sets in all cabins, and a wide choice of Indian-cuisine themed food.

Traditionally, P&O Cruises was known for British families who wanted to sail from a UK port – except for winter Caribbean cruises from Barbados. But now it's also known for having child-free ships, and so the two products differ widely in their communal spaces. It also makes an effort to provide theme cruises – antiques, art appreciation, classical music, comedy, cricket, gardening, jazz, Scottish dance, etc. The ships typically carry ballroom dance instructors. Bed linen is not changed as often as on some lines, like MSC Cruises.

Decor

A mix of British "traditional" (think: comfy, dated armchairs, wood paneling, bistro-style food, non-glitzy). British artists are featured aboard all ship – *Ventura,* for example, displays works from more than 40 of them.

Gratuities

For gratuities, you should typically allow £3.50 ($6.80) per person, per day.

Cuisine/Dining

The cuisine is straightforward, no-nonsense British food, reasonably well presented well on nice Wedgwood china. But it tends to be rather bland and uninspiring. It is typical of mass banquet catering with standard fare comparable to that found in a family hotel in an English seaside town like Scarborough.

The ingredients of many meals are disguised by gravies and sauces, as in Indian curries – well liked, of course, by most British passengers. Bread, desserts and cakes are made well, and there is a wide variety. P&O Cruises always carries a decent selection of British, and some French, cheeses.

Most of the dining room staff are from India, and provide service with a warmth that many other nationals find hard to equal. Wine service is amateurish and the lack of knowledge is lamentable.

● **Alternative Dining**

Extra-cost restaurants with menus designed by some of Britain's well-known television celebrity chefs, such as Gary Rhodes and Marco Pierre-White, have been introduced aboard the ships (exception: *Artemis*). They are a mix of trendy bistro-style venues, and restaurants with an Asia-Pacific theme.

● **Casual Eateries**

Self-serve buffets have become popular. However, most of the ships have small, cramped facilities, and passengers complain of having to share them with the countless concession staff who take over tables and congregate in groups. In other words, the buffets are too small to accommodate the needs of most passengers today.

● **The Coffee/Tea Factor:** Regular Coffee: Weak, and poor. Score: 3 out of 10. Tea and coffee-making machines are provided in all cabins. Self-serve beverage stations are provided at the buffets, but it's often difficult to find proper teaspoons – often only wooden stirrers are available. Espresso/cappuccino coffees in the extra-charge venues are slightly better, but not as good as aboard the ships of Costa Cruises or MSC Cruises, for example.

For Children

P&O Cruises really excels in looking after children. The ships – apart from the child-free ones, of course – have very good facilities and children's counsellors, with lots of activities and participation events that make it a pleasure to take to take the kids on your cruise.

Entertainment

P&O Cruises has always been known for its traditional, "end of pier" entertainment, with lots of pub-like singalong sessions for the masses. These have been augmented with production shows that provide lots of color and costume changes. All ships carry their own resident troupe of singers and dancers.

P&O Cruises does a good job in providing guest lec-

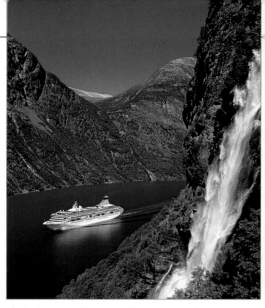

P&O's *Artemis* sailing in the Norwegian fjords.

turers with varying themes, as well as occasional after-dinner speakers such as well-known television personalities and book authors.

Spa/Fitness Facilities

The spa/fitness facilities are operated by the UK concession Harding Brothers, which also provides a wide range of beauty products. Examples of prices: a full body massage is £60 for 50 minutes; an Indian head massage is £42 for 45 minutes; a holistic facial is £45 for 75 minutes. A manicure is £24 for 45 minutes, while a pedicure is £35 for 45 minutes.

PRINCESS CRUISES

Ships

Grand-class ships (over 100,000 tons): *Caribbean Princess* (2004), *Diamond Princess* (2004), *Emerald Princess* (2007), *Golden Princess* (2001), *Grand Princess* (1998), *Ruby Princess* (2008), *Sapphire Princess* (2005), *Star Princess* (2002)

Pacific-class ships: *Ocean Princess* (1999), *Pacific Princess* (1999), *Royal Princess* (2001)

Coral-class ships: *Coral Princess* (2002), *Island Princess* (2003)

Other ships: *Sea Princess* (1998), *Sun Princess* (1995)

About the company

Princess Cruises was founded by Stanley McDonald in 1965 with one ship, the former passenger ferry *Princess Patricia*, for cruises along the Mexican Rivera. In 1974, the company was bought by the UK's Peninsular and Oriental Steam Navigation Company (P&O), and in 1988 P&O/Princess Cruises merged with the Italian line Sitmar Cruises. In 2000, Carnival Corporation and

Royal Caribbean Cruises fought a protracted battle to buy Princess Cruises. Carnival won.

Princess Cruises benefited hugely from its involvement in the American television series *The Love Boat*, and its brand became known as "The Love Boat Cruise Line." Today it provides comfortable mainstream cruising aboard a fleet of mainly large resort ships (plus three mid-sized ships), and covers the world. The ships have a higher-than-average Passenger Space Ratio than competitors Carnival or RCI, and the service is friendly without being showy.

❂ **Frequent passengers' club:** Captain's Circle.

So what's it really like?

Ships in both the mid-size and large categories operated by Princess Cruises are clean and always well maintained, and the promenade decks of some ships have teak deck lounge chairs – others are plastic. Princess Cruises also has a nice balance of officers, staff and crew members, and the line's British connections help it to achieve the feeling of calmness aboard its ships that some other lines lack.

Choose Princess Cruises if you enjoy being with families and fellow passengers of mid-50s and upwards, who want a well-organized cruise experience with unpretentious middle-of-the-road cuisine, a good range of entertainment, and an excellent shore excursion program – arguably the best run of any of the major cruise lines. There are proper cinemas aboard most ships as well as outdoor poolside mega-screens for showing "movies under the skies" in the evening.

Lines can form at peak times for elevators, the purser's (information) office, and for open-seating breakfast and lunch in the main dining rooms. Lines for shore excursions and shore tenders are also a fact of life aboard large resort ships.

All passengers receive turndown service and chocolates on pillows each night, as well as bathrobes (on request) and toiletry amenity kits – larger, naturally, for suite/mini-suite occupants – that typically include soap, shampoo, conditioner, and hand/body lotion. A hairdryer is provided in all cabins, sensibly located at a lounge area vanity desk unit.

If you want to keep up with the world, BBC World, CNN, CNBC, ESPN and TNT can be found on the in-cabin color TV system (when available).

Countless pieces of questionable "art" are encountered in almost every foyer and public room – an annoying reminder that cruising aboard large resort ships is like living in a bazaar of paintings surrounded by a ship.

The dress code is either formal – usually one formal night per 7-day cruise – or smart casual. The latter is interpreted by many as jeans or tracksuits and trainers.

The newest ships – *Crown Princess, Emerald Princess, Ruby Princess* – include an adult-only area called The Sanctuary, an extra-cost retreat at the top of the ship, forward of the mast. This provides a "private" place to relax and unwind and includes attendants to provide chilled face towels and deliver light bites. It has thick padded sunloungers both in the sun and in the shade, a swim-against-the-current pool, and there are also two outdoor cabanas for massages. I particularly recommend The Sanctuary in hot weather during Caribbean cruises. It's worth the extra $15 a head per half-day.

Princess's onboard product, especially the food and entertainment, is totally geared to the North American market. But British and other European nationalities should feel at home, as long as they realize that this is all about highly organized, packaged cruising, food and service, with an increasing emphasis on onboard revenue.

Expect to be subjected to a stream of flyers advertising daily art auctions, "designer" watches, specialized classes (Princess Cruises' "ScholarShip@Sea" programs), and the like.

You'll also have to live with many extra-charge items such as ice cream, non-standard coffees and pastry item taken in venues other than the restaurants, $4 per hour for group babysitting services, and $40 for an

---

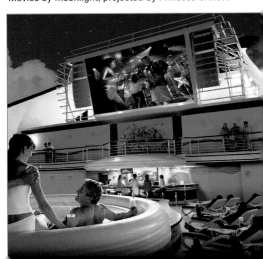

Movies by moonlight, projected by Princess Cruises.

HOW TO GET HITCHED AT SEA

Princess Cruises has the most extensive wedding program of any of the major lines, with its "Tie the Knot" wedding packages. The ship's captain can legally marry American couples at sea aboard its ships registered in Bermuda. This is by special dispensation, and should be verified when in the planning stage, and may vary according to where you reside. The basic wedding at sea package costs $1,800, plus $400 for licensing fees. Live music, champagne, a bridal bouquet, a photographer and a wedding cake can all be laid on. Tuxedo rental is available. Harborside or shore-side packages vary according to the port. For the latest rates, see the Princess Cruises website or your travel agent.

Passengers on a Princess cruise learn the elements of sailing.

"introduction to pottery" class. There's a charge for using washers and dryers in self-service launderettes.

Princess Cruises' ships are best suited to couples, families with children and teenagers, and older singles who like to mingle in a large ship setting with pleasing, sophisticated surroundings and lifestyle, reasonably good entertainment and fairly decent food and service, all packaged affordably.

The few staff members on duty at the gangway when you first arrive will merely point you in the direction of your deck, or to the ship's elevators instead of escorting you to your cabin. An "express check-in" option is available by completing certain documentation 40 days in advance of your cruise.

Decor

If Carnival's ships have the brightest decor imaginable, the decor aboard Princess Cruises' ships is almost the opposite – perhaps a little bland in places, with much use of neutral tones, calm colors and pastels. This really does suit the passengers who cruise with Princess.

Gratuities

Gratuities to staff are added to your account, at $10 per person, per day (gratuities for children are charged at the same rate). If you want to pay less, you'll need to go to the reception desk to have these charges adjusted (that could mean lining up with many other passengers wanting to do the same). Additionally, 15% is added to bar and wine bills. The onboard currency is the US dollar.

Cuisine/Dining

Although portions are generous, the food and its presentation are disappointing. Fish is often disguised by crumb or batter coating, the selection of fresh green vegetables is limited, and few garnishes are used. However, do remember that this is big-ship banquet catering, with all its attendant standardization and production cooking. Meats are of a decent quality, although often disguised by gravy-based sauces, and pasta dishes are acceptable (though voluminous), and are typically served by section headwaiters who may also make "something special just for you" – in search of favorable comments and gratuities.

If you like desserts, order a sundae at dinner, as most other desserts are just so-so. Ice cream, when ordered in the dining room, is included, but costs extra elsewhere (Häagen Dazs can be found at poolside).

Specially designed dinnerware and good quality linens and silverware are used, such as Dudson of England dinnerware, Frette Egyptian cotton table linens, and silverware by Hepp of Germany. All dining rooms and eateries are smoke-free.

Themed dinners are a feature. On a 7-day cruise, a typical menu cycle will include a Sailaway Dinner, Captain's Welcome Dinner, Captain's Gala Dinner, and Landfall Dinner. An extra-cost "Chef's Table Dinner" is an indulgent, three-hour "foodertainment" event (at $75 per person, maximum 10 persons) in which the executive chef interacts with diners; appetizers and cocktails in the galley are followed by a multi-course tasting dinner with wines paired to the meal.

The wine list is reasonable, but not good, and there are no wine waiters – table waiters or section head waiters serve the wine.

Passengers occupying balcony-grade accommodation can enjoy a full-service "Balcony Dinner" for two at $50 per person extra, plus wine, and a truly indulgent Balcony Breakfast – superb value at $25 per person.

● **Casual Eateries:** For casual eating, each ship has a Horizon Buffet (open almost round the clock), and, at night, provides an informal dinner setting with sit-down waiter service. A small, limited bistro menu is also available. The buffet displays are mostly repetitious, but far better than in past years. There is no finesse in presentation, however, as plastic plates are provided, instead of trays. The cabin service menu is quite limited, and the presentation of food items featured is poor.

● **The Coffee/Tea Factor:** Regular Coffee: Weak and poor. Score: 2 out of 10. Espresso/ Cappuccino coffees: Score: 3 out of 10. Except for beverage station at the serve-yourself buffets, coffees/teas in bars cost extra.

For Children

Children are divided into three age groups: Princess Pelicans (ages 2–5), Shockwaves (ages 8–12), and Off-Limits or Remix (13–17). The groups are split into age-related activities, and Princess Cruises has good children's counselors and supervised activities.

● **Best ships for children:** *Caribbean Princess, Coral Princess, Crown Princess, Dawn Princess, Diamond Princess, Emerald Princess, Golden Princess, Grand Princess, Island Princess, Ruby Princess, Sapphire Princess, Sea Princess, Star Princess, Sun Princess.* But not: *Ocean Princess, Pacific Princess, Royal Princess*

Entertainment

Princess Cruises' production shows have always been aimed at its slightly older, more elegant passengers. The company prides itself on its glamorous all-American shows, and they should not disappoint. There are typically two or three shows during each 7-day cruise. Each ship has a resident troupe of singers and dancers.

Passenger participation events are put on by members of the cruise staff, who would be well advised to hang on to their day jobs. Most lounges and bars have live music. Musical units range from solo pianists to string quartets, from a cappella singers to bands that can provide music for ballroom dancing. Princess Cruises also provides a number of male hosts as dance partners for women traveling alone. Show lounges are non-smoking.

Spa/Fitness Facilities

All Lotus Spa/beauty treatments and fitness facilities are operated and staffed by the Steiner Leisure concession, whose offerings are similar to those already described for Celebrity Cruises and Costa Cruises. You can now make online reservations for spa treatments before your cruise. But be careful not to clash with shore excursions and other diversions. Days at sea are easiest to book online, and hardest to obtain on board.

ROYAL CARIBBEAN INTERNATIONAL

Ships

Oasis-class ships: *Oasis of the Seas* (2009)
Freedom-class ships: *Freedom of the Seas* (2006), *Independence of the Seas* (2008), *Liberty of the Seas* (2007)
Voyager-class ships: *Adventure of the Seas* (2001), *Explorer of the Seas (2000)*, *Mariner of the Seas* (2004), *Navigator of the Seas* (2003), *Voyager of the Seas* (1999)
Radiance-class ships: *Brilliance of the Seas* (2002), *Jewel of the Seas* (2004), *Radiance of the Seas* (2001), *Serenade of the Seas* (2003)
Vision-class ships: *Enchantment of the Seas (1997)*, *Grandeur of the Seas* (1996), *Legend of the Seas*(1995), *Rhapsody of the Seas* (1997), *Splendour of the Seas* (1996), *Vision of the Seas* (1998)
Sovereign-class ships: *Majesty of the Seas* (1992), *Monarch of the Seas* (1991)

About the company

Royal Caribbean Cruise Line (RCCL) was set up by three Norwegian shipping company dynasties in 1969: Arne Wilhelmsen, and I.M. Skaugen, and Gotaas-Larsen (who was more of a sleeping partner). Its first ship, *Song of Norway*, debuted in 1970, followed by *Nordic Prince* and *Sun Viking*. Royal Caribbean was different to Carnival and NCL in that it launched its cruise operations with brand new ships, whereas the others had only older, pre-owned tonnage. In 1978 the cruise industry's first

Dolphins greet RCI's *Adventure of the Seas*.

- FLOWRIDER® (DECK 13)
- GOLF COURSE (DECK 13)
- ROCK-CLIMBING WALL (DECK 13)
- JOHNNY ROCKETS® (DECK 12)
- ADVENTURE OCEAN® (DECK 12)
- SPORTS COURT (DECK 13)
- CHOPS (DECK 10)
- VIKING CROWN LOUNGE® (DECK 14)
- POOLS (DECK 11)
- CHAMPAGNE BAR (DECK 5)
- H2O ZONE (DECK 11)
- BULL & BEAR PUB (DECK 5)
- CAFE POMENADE BOOK NOOK (DECK 5)
- JOGGING TRACK (DECK)
- FREEDOM OF T WHIRPOOL (D
- PRESIDENTIAL FAMILY SUITE (DECK 6)
- WINDJAMMER (DECK 11)
- DINING ROOM (DECKS 3,4,5)
- PORTOFINO (DECK 11)
- BOLEROS (DECK 4)
- ON AIR CLUB STUDIO B (DECK 3)
- VINTAGES WINE BAR (DECK 5)
- BEN&JERRY'S ICE CREAM (DECK 5)
- ROYAL PROMENADE (DECK 5)
- ICE SKATING (DECK 2)
- CASINO ROYALE™ (DECK 4)

"chop-and-stretch" operation took place aboard *Song of Norway*, and 1988 saw the debut of the first really large cruise ship, *Sovereign of the Seas*.

In 1997 Royal Caribbean International bought Celebrity Cruises for $1.3 billion and in 2006 acquired Pullmantur Cruises for $889.9 million. In 2007 its Celebrity Cruises division created a new cruise line, Azamara Cruises, with two ships. In 2007 Royal Caribbean established CDF Croisières de France with one ship, diverted from the Pullmantur Cruises fleet.

At first the operation was excellent. But there are now shareholders to please, and the onboard product has slipped to equal that of Carnival Cruise Lines (whose ships, in general, have larger standard cabins). RCI's ships are shapely, with well-rounded sterns, and interesting design profiles that make them instantly recognizable. Large, brightly lit casinos are provided, as are shopping galleries that passengers have to walk through to get almost anywhere else. All are cleverly designed to extract maximum revenue.

✪ **Frequent passengers club:** Crown and Anchor Society.

So what's it really like?

RCI provides a well-integrated, fine-tuned, and comfortable cruise experience, but there's nothing royal about it except the name. The product is consistent but homogenous. This is cruising for mainstream America. The ships are all quite pleasing, and some have really comfortable public rooms, lounges, bars, and innovative gimmicks such as ice-skating rinks.

The company competes directly with Carnival Cruise Lines, Norwegian Cruise Lines and Princess Cruises in terms of what's offered on board, as well as the hard sell for onboard revenue (the result of highly discounted pricing in the marketplace). But RCI ships have more glass area and connection with the outdoors and the sea than Carnival's ships, and are a better bet for families with children.

RCI's largest ships are termed Freedom-class (*Free-*

Anatomy of a large resort ship

Freedom of the Seas can accommodate 4,375 vacationers and 1,397 crew members. Its facilities include a full-size boxing ring, a wave simulator for surfers, and an ice rink.

PHARAOH PALACE (SECONDARY LOUNGE) (DECK 5)

RIUM (DECK 11)

FREEDOM OF THE SEAS DAY SPA (DECK 12)

FREEDOM OF THE SEAS FITNESS CENTER (DECK 11)

PEEK-A-BOO BRIDGE (DECK 10)

FREEDOM OF THE SEAS

RRENTO'S (DECK 5)

ER BAR (DECK 4)

DISCO (DECK 4)

ARCADIA THEATRE (DECKS 2,3 & 4)

THE SEAS CENTER (DECK 2)

dom of the Seas, Independence of the Seas, Liberty of the Seas) and *Voyager*-class (*Adventure of the Seas, Explorer of the Seas, Mariner of the Seas, Navigator of the Seas, Voyager of the Seas*). They differ from other ships in the fleet – mainly in the internal layout – by having a large mall-like high street – the focal point for most passengers. Many public rooms, lounges and bars are located as adjuncts to the mall. It's rather like a mall with a ship built around it. Unfortunately, in placing so much emphasis on "active" outdoors areas, space has been taken away from the pool areas, leaving little room left just to sit and relax or sunbathe.

The next group of ships (*Brilliance of the Seas, Jewel of the Seas, Radiance of the Seas, Serenade of the Seas*) have lots of balcony cabins, and large expanses of glass, which help to provide more of a connection with the sea. *Enchantment of the Seas, Grandeur of the Seas, Legend of the Seas, Rhapsody of the Seas, Splendour of the Seas,* and *Vision of the Seas* also have large expanses of glass in the public areas, but not so many balcony cabins.

The oldest ships (*Majesty of the Seas, Monarch of the Seas*), innovative in the late 1980s, now look dated. They have very small, barely adequate cabins, and tiny tub chairs in public rooms, for example, although the average passenger has become larger.

With the introduction of *Freedom of the Seas*, a concierge lounge (available only to suite occupants) was introduced, thus creating a two-class system.

The onboard product is dedicated to those with an active, contemporary lifestyle. All ships have a 30-ft (9-meter) high rock-climbing wall, with five separate climbing tracks. You'll need to plan what you want to take part in wisely as almost everything requires you to sign up in advance.

There are few quiet places to sit and read – almost everywhere has intrusive background music, played even in elevators and all passenger hallways. Bars also have very loud music. There are many, many intrusive announcements for activities that bring revenue, such as art auctions and bingo. Standing in line for embarkation, the reception desk, disembarkation, for port visits, shore tenders and for the self-serve buffet stations in the Windjammer Café is an inevitable aspect of cruising aboard large resort ships. It's often hard to escape the ship's photographers – they're everywhere. Take lots of extra pennies – you'll need them to pay for all the additional-cost items. Expect to be subjected to a stream of flyers advertising promotions, while "artworks" for auction are strewn throughout the ship, and frosted drinks in "souvenir" glasses are pushed to the hilt. There are no cushioned pads for the deck lounge chairs (they have plastic webbing and, even with a towel placed on them, soon become uncomfortable).

These niggles apart, RCI ships are liked by active, young-minded couples and singles of all ages, families with toddlers, children, and teenagers who enjoy mingling in a large ship setting with plenty of life and high-energy entertainment. The food is more notable for quantity than quality – unless you pay extra for dining in the "alternative" restaurant (not all ships have them). Smoking is not allowed in cabins without a balcony.

Service personnel are friendly, but not many offer a greeting when passing you in the corridors, so the hospitality factor could be improved. However, the elevators talk to you – "going up/going down" is informative but monotonous, of course, but the illuminated picture displays of decks are good.

● **Embarkation**: There are few staff members on duty at the gangway when you first arrive, and they will merely point you in the direction of your deck, or to the ship's elevators, instead of escorting you to your cabin. Lines for check-in, embarkation and disembarkation are a bit daunting, but the company does well in making it all flow as smoothly as possible. If you are a non-US resident and stay at an RCI-booked hotel, formalities can be completed there, allowing you simply to walk on board to your cabin (after the usual security checks).

Decor

The interior decor of all the ships is bright and contemporary, but not as neon-intensive and glitzy as Carnival's ships. There is much Scandinavian design influence, with some eclectic sculpture and artwork. The "you are here" signage and deck plans are excellent. The furniture in public lounges tends to include small "tub" chairs that are often broken by large passengers.

Gratuities

Gratuities can be paid in cash or added to your onboard account daily at the suggested rate of $9 per person. Also, 15% is added to all bar, wine and spa charges. The onboard currency is the US dollar, except for ships operating out of the United Kingdom.

Cuisine/Dining

Most ships have large dining halls that are two or three decks high, giving a sense of space and grandeur. Few tables for two are available, most being for four, six, or eight persons. All dining rooms and eateries are non-smoking. The efficient dining operation emphasizes

The billiards table is gyroscopically controlled.

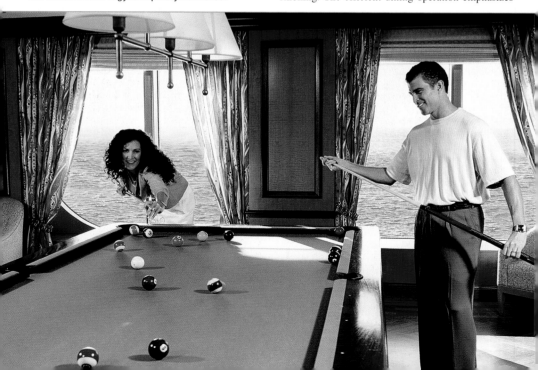

highly programmed, extremely hurried service that many find insensitive. There are no fish knives.

The cuisine in the main dining rooms is typical of mass banquet catering with standard fare comparable to that found in American family-style restaurants ashore. The food costs per passenger are well below those for sister company Celebrity Cruises, so you should not expect the same food quality. Dinner menus typically include a Welcome-Aboard Dinner, French Dinner, Italian Dinner, International Dinner, and Captain's Gala Dinner, and all offer plenty of choice. Menu descriptions sound tempting, but the food, although well enough prepared, is unmemorable. A decent selection of light meals is provided, and there is a vegetarian menu.

An ice-skating rink is an attraction aboard *Voyager of the Seas*.

While the USDA prime beef supplied is good, other meats are often disguised with gravies or heavy sauces. Most fish (except salmon) and seafood items tend to be overcooked and lack taste. Green vegetables are scarce, although salad items are plentiful. Rice is often used as a source of carbohydrates, potatoes being more expensive. Breads and pastry items are generally good, although some items, such as croissants, may not be made on board. Dessert items are standardized and lack flavor, and the cheese selection and crackers are poor. The selection of breads, rolls, and fruit could be better. Caviar – once a standard menu item – incurs a hefty extra charge.

Although prices are moderate, the wine list is not extensive, and almost all wines are very young. Only small glasses are provided. The waiters tend to be overly friendly for some tastes – particularly on the last night of the cruise, when tips are expected.

● **Alternative Dining Venues:** All Freedom, Radiance and Voyager-class ships have two additional dining venues: Chops Grill Steakhouse (for premium veal chops and steaks, cover charge $30 per person), and Portofino (for Italian-American cuisine; cover charge $25 per person). Both venues serve food of a much higher quality than that in the main dining room. Reservations are required in both venues. Vision-class ships have one extra-charge alternative dining venue, Portofino. Be prepared to eat Texas-sized portions, presented on large plates. Note that menus do not change throughout the cruise. The dress code is smart casual.

● **Casual Eateries:** All RCI ships have casual eateries called Windjammer Café for fast-food items, salads, and other casual meals. Some are of the single line type (move along with your tray), while the newest ships have individual islands for more variety and fewer lines. However, the actual quality of cooked food items is nutritionally poor, as are the rather tacky salad dressings.

Breakfast buffet items are virtually the same each day, monotonous and even below the standards of diner food. The same is true of lunchtime salad items, which have little taste. The beverage stations have only the most basic items. Hamburgers and hot dogs in self-serve buffet locations are generally left in steam tables. They are steamed rather than grilled, although you can ask for one to be grilled in front of you.

Freedom and Voyager-class ships also have Johnny Rockets diners ($3.95 extra charge, per person, whether you eat in or take out). These serve hamburgers, hot dogs and sodas, although the typical waiting time is about 30 minutes – pagers are provided, in case you want to wander off while waiting for a table.

Drinks packages are available in bars, in the form of cards or stickers so that you can pre-pay for a selection of soft drinks and alcoholic drinks. However, the rules for using the pre-paid packages are a bit cumbersome.

● **The Coffee/Tea Factor:** Regular Coffee: Weak, poor quality. Score: 1 out of 10. Espresso/Cappuccino coffees (Seattle's Best): Score: 4 out of 10 – it comes in paper cups.

For Children

Adventure Ocean is RCI's "edutainment" area. Junior passengers are divided into four age-appropriate groups: Aquanaut Center (ages 3–5); Explorer Center (6–8); Voyager Center (9–12); and Optix Teen Center (13–17). An unlimited soda and juice package for under-17s costs $4 a day. There are lots of activities, and a host of children's counsellors, so they will never be bored.

● **Best ships for children:** *Adventure of the Seas, Explorer of the Seas, Freedom of the Seas, Independence of the Seas, Liberty of the Seas, Mariner of the Seas, Navigator of the Seas, Voyager of the Seas.* **Ships that are acceptable, but with fewer facilities:** *Brilliance of the Seas, Enchantment of the Seas, Grandeur of the Seas, Jewel of the Seas, Legend of the Seas, Radi-*

The Windjammer Café is RCI's casual eatery.

ance of the Seas, Rhapsody of the Seas, Serenade of the Seas, Splendour of the Seas, Vision of the Seas. **Ships with few facilities for children:** Majesty of the Seas, Monarch of the Seas.

Entertainment

The entertainment is upbeat (in fact, it's hard to get away from music and noise) – what you would find in a resort hotel in Las Vegas. Production shows are colorful, fast-paced, high volume razzle-dazzle spectaculars, but with little or no storyline, poor linkage between themes and scenes, and basic choreography. The live band is augmented by prerecorded backing tracks to make it sound like a big, professional orchestra. Each ship has its resident troupe of singers and dancers.

Then there are silly audience participation (summer camp-style, but often funny) events and activities – something that RCI has always done well.

All showlounges are non-smoking venues.

Spa/Fitness Facilities

The Spa facilities in RCI ships are operated by the Steiner Leisure concession, whose offerings are similar to those already described for Celebrity Cruises and Costa Cruises.

For the more sporting, all RCI ships have a rock-climbing wall, with several separate climbing tracks. There is a 30-minute instruction period before anyone is allowed to climb, and this is done in pairs. It's free, and all safety gear is included, but you'll need to sign up. It's worth remembering that it's quieter on port days, but the hours of operation are limited – typically two hours each in the morning and afternoon. Playing a round of golf in the golf simulator costs $25 per hour (for up to four persons).

STAR CRUISES

Ships
MegaStar Aries (1991); MegaStar Taurus (1991); Star Pisces (1990); SuperStar Aquarius (1993); SuperStar Gemini (1992); SuperStar Libra (1988); SuperStar Virgo (1999)

About the company

Star Cruises, the world's third largest cruise operator, was set up in 1993 as a subsidiary of the Genting Group, founded in 1965. The company operates ships dedicated to specific markets, and its brands include Star Cruises, Norwegian Cruise Line (NCL), NCL America, and Cruise Ferries.

Star Cruises is the only cruise line to have its own ship simulators – useful training tools when a captain these days may be in charge of a speeding vessel measuring more than 150,000 tons. It also owns and operates the cruise terminal at its base in Port Klang, Malaysia, and the pier facility in Langkawi.
○ **Frequent passengers' club:** Star VIP Club

So what's it really like?

Star Cruises' ships are best suited to adult couples and singles, and families with children. They are good for those who enjoy big city life, constant activity accompanied by plenty of music, late nights, and abundant food. Star Cruises was the originator of the "Freestyle Cruising" concept, which offered more flexibility and was later adopted by NCL. A strictly casual dress code prevails aboard all the ships.

Star Pisces, SuperStar Libra and SuperStar Aquarius are based in Hong Kong, mainly for the local gaming market, and specialize in short cruises. SuperStar Virgo, based in Hong Kong and Singapore, operates 2-, 3-, and

5-night cruises for the local market. Singapore-based *MegaStar Aries* and *MegaStar Taurus* are boutique ships available only for charter or private parties. All ships have gaming casinos, including members-only private gaming rooms for serious players – a major attraction for Asian passengers.

● **Embarkation:** There are basically two distinct passenger segments – those that book "balcony-class" cabins, and those that don't. "Balcony Class" passengers and members of the Star VIP Club check-in in a separate area to "non-balcony" class passengers.

The 2,156-passenger *SuperStar Aquarius* is based in Hong Kong.

Decor

The ships have stunning Asian interior decor, with bright, fresh, happy, warm colors, and carpets with rich patterns. Many cabins have rich lacquered wood furniture and highly polished wood accents, with colorful soft furnishings as accompaniments. Some ships have original artwork costing millions.

Gratuities

Gratuities are included aboard all Star Cruises ships, and drink prices already include a service charge.

Cuisine/Dining

Star Cruises provides a wide variety of food to suit both Asian and Western tastes. However, the cuisine is still of a mainstream market standard – you'll find butter in packets. At self-serve buffets, salt and pepper are typically provided on each table, not in packets as aboard many other cruise lines. Espresso and cappuccino (Lavazza brand Italian coffee) are available fleet-wide, at extra cost. Service aboard the ships is usually by Asian staff, many from China and the Philippines.

Some ships have up to 10 restaurants and eateries; some are included in the fare, while others cost extra and serve à la carte items.

● **Room service:** Continental breakfast typically costs extra, and room service snacks are also available at extra cost throughout the day. A basket of fruit is provided to all cabins at embarkation, and is replenished daily for suite-grade accommodation.

HOW THE MAJOR CRUISE LINES SCORE ON CUISINE AND SERVICE

Scores out of maximum 10. Note that these ratings do not reflect extra-cost "alternative" restaurants

	Carnival Cruise Lines	Celebrity Cruises	Costa Cruises	Cunard Line	Holland America Line	MSC Cruises	Norwegian Cruise Line	P&O Cruises	Princess Cruises	Royal Caribbean Int.	Star Cruises
Food											
Dining Room/Cuisine	6.1	7.6	6.4	8.1	7.4	7.8	6.2	7.1	7.3	6.0	6.5
Buffets/Informal Dining	5.9	7.1	5.8	7.4	6.5	6.8	6.3	6.0	6.7	6.1	6.1
Quality of Ingredients	6.0	8.0	6.2	8.0	6.9	7.5	6.3	7.1	6.7	6.3	7.7
Afternoon Tea/Snacks	4.2	6.9	5.1	7.8	5.7	6.8	4.8	6.6	5.9	4.0	6.4
Wine List	5.8	8.2	5.6	8.0	6.2	7.3	6.5	7.2	6.5	5.5	6.0
Overall Food Score	**5.60**	**7.56**	**5.82**	**7.86**	**6.54**	**7.24**	**6.02**	**6.80**	**6.62**	**5.58**	**6.54**
Service											
Dining Rooms	6.2	8.2	6.2	8.0	7.4	7.6	6.8	7.0	7.3	6.1	7.3
Bars	6.3	7.7	6.5	7.8	7.1	7.5	6.9	7.1	7.4	6.3	6.7
Cabins	6.4	7.7	6.8	7.9	7.5	7.6	6.5	7.6	7.2	6.2	6.6
Open Decks	6.0	7.5	5.8	7.6	6.6	7.5	6.2	6.4	6.8	6.1	6.4
Wines	5.0	7.7	5.3	8.0	6.1	7.6	6.4	6.0	6.2	5.2	6.0
Overall Service Score	**5.98**	**7.76**	**6.12**	**7.86**	**6.94**	**7.56**	**6.56**	**6.82**	**6.98**	**5.98**	**6.60**
Combined food/service	**5.79**	**7.66**	**5.97**	**7.86**	**6.74**	**7.40**	**6.29**	**6.81**	**6.80**	**5.78**	**6.57**

A game of mahjong aboard *SuperStar Aquarius*.

SuperStar Virgo. The facilities and play areas are extensive aboard *SuperStar Virgo*, and less so aboard the other ships.

Entertainment

The main production shows are colorful, visual shows, particularly aboard the largest ships. Brazilian dancers, Chinese acrobats, and many top Asian entertainers are featured.

Small units provide live music for dancing or listening, but there is no real show band. Production shows are performed to pre-recorded backing tracks. Each ship has karaoke rooms for rent.

For Children

Children are divided into three age groups, with facilities, activities and entertainment to match: for children from 6 to 9 years; for children 10–13; for teens 14–17. There's also a StarKids Club (for Singapore residents only), created for children below 12 who sail aboard

Spa/Fitness Facilities

The spas are an in-house operation, with Asian staff. Thai massage is the house specialty. Examples of prices: Thai Massage, S$60 (60 minutes); Hot Stones Massage, S$80 (75 minutes). A Singapore dollar is worth roughly 66 cents (US) or 33p (UK). ❏

THE BIGGEST OF THE BIG: CRUISE SHIPS OVER 100,000 TONS

Ship Name	Cruise Line	Tonnage	Built
Oasis of the Seas	Royal Caribbean Int.	220,000	2009
Freedom of the Seas	Royal Caribbean Int.	154,407	2006
Independence of the Seas	Royal Caribbean Int.	154,407	2008
Liberty of the Seas	Royal Caribbean Int.	154,407	2007
Queen Mary 2	Cunard Line	148,528	2004
Explorer of the Seas	Royal Caribbean Int.	137,308	2000
Voyager of the Seas	Royal Caribbean Int.	137,280	1999
Adventure of the Seas	Royal Caribbean Int.	137,276	2001
Mariner of the Seas	Royal Caribbean Int.	137,276	2004
Navigator of the Seas	Royal Caribbean Int.	137,276	2003
MSC Fantasia	MSC Cruises	135,000	2008
MSC Splendida	MSC Cruises	133,000	2009
Celebrity Solstice	Celebrity Cruises	122,000	2008
Crown Princess	Princess Cruises	116,000	2006
Emerald Princess	Princess Cruises	116,000	2007
Ventura	P&O Cruises	116,000	2008
Diamond Princess	Princess Cruises	113,000	2004
Sapphire Princess	Princess Cruises	113,000	2005
Caribbean Princess	Princess Cruises	112,894	2004
Carnival Splendor	Carnival Cruise Lines	112,000	2008
Costa Concordia	Costa Cruises	112,000	2006
Costa Serena	Costa Cruises	112,000	2007
Carnival Conquest	Carnival Cruise Lines	110,319	2004
Carnival Freedom	Carnival Cruise Lines	110,000	2007
Carnival Glory	Carnival Cruise Lines	110,000	2003
Carnival Liberty	Carnival Cruise Lines	110,000	2005
Carnival Valor	Carnival Cruise Lines	110,000	2004
Star Princess	Princess Cruises	108,977	2002
Golden Princess	Princess Cruises	108,865	2001
Grand Princess	Princess Cruises	108,806	1998
Costa Fortuna	Costa Cruises	105,000	2003
Costa Magica	Costa Cruises	105,000	2004
Carnival Triumph	Carnival Cruise Lines	101,509	1999
Carnival Victory	Carnival Cruise Lines	101,509	2000
Carnival Destiny	Carnival Cruise Lines	101,353	1996

Striking ceiling art aboard the 158,000-ton *Freedom of the Seas*.

THE SHIP'S COMPANY

Captain

- Staff Captain
  - Chief Officer
  - First Officer
  - Second Officer
  - Junior Officers
  - Deck & Engine Staff Seamen (All Ranks)

- Chief Engineer
  - Deputy Chief Engineer
  - Second Engineer
  - Third Engineer
  - Junior Engineers

- Chief Electrician
  - First Electrician
  - Second Electrician
  - Junior Electricians

- Chief Radio Officer
  - First Radio Officer
  - Radio Officers

- Principal Medical Officer
  - Doctor
  - Nurses
  - Medical Orderlies

Hotel Manager or Chief Purser

- Deputy Hotel Manager (Food & Beverage)
  - Executive Chef
    - Head Chefs
    - Sous-Chefs
    - Pastry Chefs
    - Butcher
    - Galley Staff
    - Storekeeper Pantrymen
  - Restaurant Manager
    - Maître d'Hôtel
    - Head Waiters
    - Wine Stewards
    - Restaurant Waiters
  - Food Manager
    - Bar Manager
    - Assistant Food Manager
    - Assistant Bar Manager
    - Bartenders/ Bar Waiters

- Cruise Director
  - Shore Excursion Manager/Deputy Cruise Director
  - Social Hostess
  - Assistant Cruise Director
  - Cruise Staff

  Entertainment
  - Headliners
  - Cabaret Acts
  - Bands
  - Musicians
  - Lecturers
  - Instructors

- Purser
  - Hotel Purser
  - Purser's Staff/ Concierge
  - Crew Purser
  - Printer
  - Stewards/ Stewardesses

  Concessions
  - Photography
  - Casino
  - Hairdressing
  - Shops
  - Video Games
  - Massage

WHAT THE SMALLER LINES OFFER

While the major cruise lines dominate the mass market, dozens of other companies cater for more specialist tastes and take in some exotic destinations

The international cruise industry is comprised of around 80 companies with ocean-going cruise ships providing vacations to more than 16 million passengers each year. Most major cruise lines are owned and operated by large corporations. Other operators are family-owned cruise lines. Still others are small, with just a couple of really compact ships. Some cruise companies don't own their own ships, but charter them from ship owning and ship management companies for year-round or seasonal operation – for example, specialized ships outfitted for Arctic and Antarctic expedition cruises only.

Some cruise lines are actually tour operators – vacation packagers, mostly in Europe, that put together airlines, hotels, car rentals, and cruises. Some own their own charter airlines. Tour operators have transferred some of their land-based tourists to the sea, aboard ships that move the destinations for them. These are the equivalent of the package vacation that first became popular in Europe in the 1970s – for example, Thomson Cruises.

These mini-profiles, alphabetical order, include cruise lines with small- or mid-size ships and small fleets, those with a small number of large resort ships, those with tall ships (with either real working sail propulsion or computer-controlled assistance), those that specialize in hardy or "soft" expedition cruises, and those which cruise along coastal and inland waterways.

The major cruise companies are profiled on pages 112–144 and so are not included in this section.

Abercrombie & Kent (A&K)

Geoffrey Kent started A&K as a safari company in 1962 – there was no Mr Abercrombie, it just sounded good – and then specialized in upscale train journeys around the globe for small groups. The company got started in the cruise business when it went into a marketing agreement with the long-defunct Society Expeditions in 1990.

Two years later it bought the little expedition ship *Society Explorer* (formerly *Lindblad Explorer*) when Society Expeditions ceased operations. The ship, renamed *National Geographic Explorer*, now belongs to Lindblad Expeditions. Today, A&K charters various ships, such as those of Clipper Cruise Lines, for its cruise programs, taking passengers to the more remote destinations such as the Antarctic.

African Safari Club (Star Line Cruises)

Founded in 1967, African Safari Club specializes in vacations to Kenya and the Indian Ocean. The company owns and operates one ship, the 200-passenger *Royal Star*, and owns a charter airline to fly participants from the UK to Africa. The company also owns and operates safari lodges and hotels in Kenya and cruise/safari packages for passengers who want to combine different experiences in one vacation. While the standards of food and service aboard the ship are not high, the ship is a comfortable reminder of life in relax mode.

AIDA ships are noted for providing excellent entertainment.

AIDA Cruises

The former East German shipping company Deutsche Seereederei (DSR) was assigned the traditional cruise ship *Arkona* as part of the east-west integration in 1985, which included a contractual agreement with the Treuhandanstalt to build a new ship. It did this in 1996 with the newly built *Aida*, designed to appeal to young, active German-speaking families. The concept was to create a seagoing version of the popular Robinson Clubs – a sort of German Club Med concept. When *Aida* first debuted, there were almost no passengers and the company struggled.

In 1998 the company sold itself to Norwegian Cruise Line, who sold it back to its original Rostock-based owners. Now a very successful multi-ship brand belonging to the Carnival Corporation, it is well-known in German-speaking countries for its ultra-casual cruising, with two main self-serve buffet restaurants instead of the

American Cruise Lines runs Cape Cod itineraries.

traditional sit-down-and-be-served method of cruising. The entertainment is extremely good, and is provided in conjunction with the Schmidt Theatre in Hamburg.

American Canadian Caribbean Line

Founded in 1966 by the late Luther H. Blount, who built his ships in his own shipyard in Warren, Rhode Island, ACCL started as, and continues today, as a family-run company. Today, the company is run by his daughter, Nancy Blount.

Cruises are operated like private family outings, using two unpretentious ships that were specially constructed to operate in close-in coastal areas and inland waterways of the eastern US seaboard, with forays to the Bahamas and Caribbean during the winter.

The onboard experience is strictly no-frills cruising in very, very basic, down-to-earth surroundings that have a 1950s feel. Its early-to-bed passengers – average age 72 years – are typical of those who don't like glitz or trendy, and don't need much other than basic American food. Bring your own if you want a drink – the line supplies only tonic and soft drinks – so forget wine with dinner unless you supply your own bottle.

American Cruise Lines

ACL was originally formed in 1974, although it went bankrupt in 1989, the ships were sold off, and the company lay dormant. That is, until the original owner, Charles Robertson, a renowned yachtsman who used to race 12-meter America's Cup yachts resurrected the company in 2000, and built its own ships in its own small shipyard in Salisbury, Maryland, on the Chesapeake Bay.

ACL's four ships ply the inter-coastal waterways and rivers of the USA's east coast (between Maine and Florida), and provide an up-close, intimate experience for passengers who don't need luxury or much pampering, but do like American history

and culture. The company also formed Pearl Seas Cruises, whose ships are being built in Canada.

Aurora Expeditions

This Australian company was founded in 1993 by Australian Mount Everest veteran and geologist Greg Mortimer and adventure travel specialist Margaret Werner. The company uses the chartered expedition ship *Marina Svetaeva* for its Antarctic expedition cruise programs. Other destinations include Papua New Guinea and Russia's Far East.

Azamara Cruises

Azamara Cruises is an offshoot of Celebrity Cruises, and was created in 2007. It consists of two 700-passenger ships, taking people to smaller ports that some of the large resort ships cannot get into. The company specializes in providing high-quality dining. Its ships

ACCL serves up fresh New England corn on its ships.

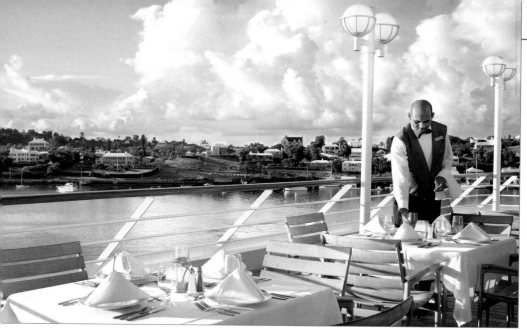

Setting up dinner aboard *Azamara Journey*.

are in direct competition with those of Oceania Cruises.

The onboard experience is similar to that aboard the ships of parent company Celebrity Cruises, but modified to suit those who want a more personal cruise experience aboard smaller ships. The company's strengths are its food and service, and each ship has two extra-charge restaurants, in addition to the main dining venues.

CDF Croisières de France

Founded and wholly owned by Royal Caribbean International, CDF Croisières de France was founded in 2007, with headquarters in Paris. It devotes all its resources to cruising for French-speaking passengers, with one ship, *Bleu de France* (the former *Europa*).

CIP Cruises

CIP Cruises (La Compagnie des Iles du Ponant) is a subsidiary of CMA CGM, the world's third largest container shipping company. The Company, whose head office is in Marseille, France, was created in April 1988, and presently operates three boutique-sized ships (*Le Diamant, Le Levant,* and *Le Ponant*) for the French-speaking market. In 2004, the company acquired the Paris-based tour operator, Tapis Rouge International, which specializes in upscale travel.

Classic International Cruises

This small, family-owned company is based in Lisbon, Portugal. It buys or charters older (pre-owned) deep-draft ships that have "traditional" decor and lovingly refurbishes them. George Potamianos and his two sons run the company, which either operates the ships itself, or charters them to various cruise/tour operators. Nautical officers and most service staff are Portuguese.

Club Med Cruises

Club Med itself became renowned for providing hassle-free vacations for the whole family. The first Club Med village was started in 1950 on the island of Mallorca, but the concept became so popular that it grew to over 100 vacation villages throughout the world.

Club Med Cruises began as an offshoot of the French all-inclusive vacation clubs, and in 1990 when it introduced its first ocean-going cruise vessel, the computer-controlled sail-cruise ship *Club Med II*. Aboard the all-inclusive ship, it's the Gentils Ordinaires, who serve as both super-cruise staff and "rah-rah" cheerleaders for the mainly French-speaking passengers. *Club Med II* has a sister ship, Wind Star Cruises' *Wind Surf*, which provides a more relaxed onboard experience.

Cruceros Australis

Cruceros Australis, based in Santiago, Chile, operates cruise ships on soft expedition cruises to the Chilean fjords, Patagonia and Tierra del Fuego. Catering increasingly to an international clientele, with Spanish as the official onboard language, cruising with this company is all about Chile and its dramatic coastline. But don't expect high standards aboard its two ships.

Cruise West

Former bush pilot Chuck West founded Cruise West in 1954. He chartered two small ships, *Glacier Queen* and *Yukon Star*, for Alaska cruises. The cruises were marketed by Alaska Cruise Line, with offices in Seattle, Washington. Their hulls – they were converted ex-Canadian Navy corvettes – were painted black, and the superstructure blue and gold.

In 1971, he sold Westours to Holland America Line. In 1973, he set up Alaska Sightseeing, dedicated to small ship travel; this became Cruise West in 1983. The young, mostly college-age service staff are willing, but lack finesse and knowledge about the food served.

Because, under US maritime procedures, its ships measure under 100 tons, the company is allowed to enter Alaska's Glacier Bay without having to bargain for the limited number of entry permits granted each year.

Crystal Cruises

Crystal Cruises was founded in 1988 by Nippon Yusen Kaisha (NYK), the world's largest freighter and transportation logistics companies, which currently have more than 700 ships. The American-managed company is based in Century City, Los Angeles. *Crystal Harmony*, the company's first ship, was built in Japan, and debuted in New York in May 1990 to great acclaim. Meanwhile, Crystal Cruises introduced two new ships, *Crystal Symphony* in 1995, and *Crystal Serenity* in 2000, one built in Finland, the other in France.

In 2006 *Crystal Harmony* was transferred to parent company NYK as *Asuka II* for its Asuka Cruise division, for Japanese-speaking passengers. Crystal Cruises continues to provide fine food and service aboard its ships, which operate worldwide.

Delphin Cruises

Founded by Herbert Hey, and based in Offenbach, Germany, this small cruise line specializes in providing superb itineraries for its German-speaking passengers. The company owns one ship, *Delphin*, and operates another ship, *Delphin Voyager*, under a long-term charter agreement. Passengers like the friendly staff and ser-

Cruise West's 39-cabin *Spirit of Alaska*.

vice, as well as the destination-rich itineraries, coupled with the fact that most cruises are of 14 days or longer.

Disney Cruise Line

In 1932, a Disney cartoon, Steamboat Willy, depicted Micky Mouse at the wheel of a ship, but it took 60 years until Disney decided to get into the cruise business, as an extension of its resort stay business, offering a "seamless vacation package."

Its two large resort ships (*Disney Magic* and *Disney Wonder*) cater to loyal Disney followers, and everything aboard the ships is Disney – every song, every piece of artwork, every movie and production show. Its first ship debuted in 1998, the second, in 1999. The company has two more ships on order to keep Mickey's fans happy. Disney is all about families with children, and the ships cater to both. One innovation is that passengers dine in three different restaurants, in rotation. You can buy a package combining a short stay at a Disney resort and a cruise. Disney also has its own cruise terminal at Port Canaveral, and Mickey's ears can be found on the funnels of the company's ships.

easyCruise.com

Sir Stelios Haji-Iouannou, founder of many "easy" businesses including the successful airline easyJet, started easyCruise.com as an antidote to regular cruise lines. The company's current ship, *easyCruise Life,* operates in the Mediterranean, particularly around the Greek Islands, and in the Caribbean. It provides no-frills cruises, with a two-night minimum stay.

The ship is second-hand and has been refitted to easyCruise.com's minimalist design, although the original concept has been somewhat modified recently, and *easyCruise Life* now operates more in a traditional cruise manner. But, with minimal soft furnishings, it's all noise and no poise – more of a bus service, really.

You can't escape Mickey's ears on Disney cruises.

Elegant Cruises & Tours

New York-based Elegant Cruises & Tours was founded in 1989 by Captain Mato Stanovich, initially to provide cruises and tours to Croatia. The company has two small vessels: the 35-cabin *Monet*, for cruises along the Dalmatian coast in Croatia; and the 57-cabin *Andrea*, a former Hurtigruten ship aimed at the "soft" adventure and expedition cruise market.

Fred Olsen Cruise Line

This is a Norwegian family-owned and family-run company which was founded in Hvitstein, a town on Oslofjord, Norway, in 1848. Today, a fifth-generation Olsen, Fred Jr., runs the company from its headquarters in Suffolk, England. The group also has interests in the hotels, aviation, shipbuilding, ferries, and offshore industries. The company specializes in cruises for adults who are usually retired and of senior years – typically over 65. Aboard the ships, interior design reflects traditional design features. The ships cruise year-round out of UK ports (Dover, Southampton, Liverpool, Newcastle, Greenock, Leith, Belfast and Dublin), with some ships operating out of Caribbean ports during the winter.

Galápagos Cruises

Metropolitan Touring, Ecuador's foremost tour and travel company, is based in Quito, Ecuador, and sells its cruises through general sales agents such as the USA's Dallas-based Adventure Associates. Its boutique ships, the well-run *Isabella* and *Santa Cruz*, visit the Galápagos Islands, with all-Ecuadorean crew and food.

Hansa Touristik

Founded in the late 1990s, Hansa Touristik is based in Bremen, Germany. It charters low-budget cruise ships for cruises for a cost-conscious German-speaking clientele. The ships have basic but comfortable facilities, with adequate and reasonable food. The service is limited by the low cruise fares, but provide good value for money.

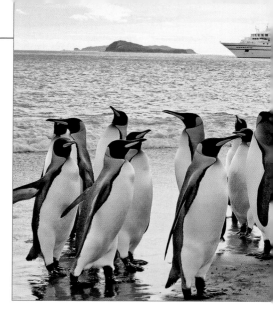

Hapag-Lloyd Cruises views Antarctica's wildlife.

Hapag-Lloyd Cruises

Germany's two most famous ocean liner companies, the Bremen-based Norddeutscher Lloyd and the Hamburg-based Hamburg America Line, merged in 1970 to become Hapag-Lloyd. Today, Hapag-Lloyd operates four ships. Two small ships are in the specialized expedition cruise market (*Bremen* and *Hanseatic*); one is in the mid-priced market (*C. Columbus*), and one ship (*Europa*) is in the luxury market. All feature destination-intensive cruises aimed at the German-speaking market, with occasional cruises for the English-speaking market.

Hebridean International Cruises

Hebridean International Cruises (formerly Hebridean Island Cruises) was set up under the Thatcher government's British Enterprise Scheme in 1989. Its headquarters is in Skipton, Yorkshire. The company operates two all-inclusive boutique ships, *Hebridean Princess* and *Hebridean Spirit*, that convey the atmosphere of English country-house life, and specialize in cruises for mature adults. Gratuities and all port taxes are included, as are most excursions. One ship operates cruises around the Scottish islands, while the other offers cruises in the Aegean, Mediterranean and Indian Ocean.

Hurtigruten

The company is an amalgamation of two shipping companies (OVDS and TVDS) and provides year-round service along the Norwegian coast, calling at 33 ports in 11 days. Hurtigruten has also recently developed expedition-style cruises, albeit aboard ships that have been converted for the purpose, rather than aboard ships specifically built for expedition cruises. So, as

Aboard Fred Olsen Cruise Lines' 868-passenger *Black Watch*.

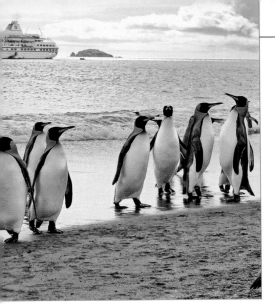

long as you think utilitarian and modest decor, you'll get the idea of life aboard one of the Hurtigruten ships, which are practical rather than beautiful. Crown Princess Mette-Marit of Norway was the godmother of the company's newest ship, the *Fram*, a 318-berth expedition vessel built for cruising in Greenland.

Iberocruceros

Founded originally as one of the Iberojet (tour-operator) companies, 75% of the company is now owned by the Carnival Corporation. The company's ships feature all-inclusive cruises for the Spanish-speaking market, in direct competition to Pullmantur Cruises.

Imperial Majesty Cruise Line

The company's single ship, *Imperial Majesty*, operates two-night cruises from Florida to the Bahamas. Despite the company's claims to international gourmet dining, *Regal Empress* provides a highly programmed, but basic party getaway cruise, with friendly staff and service. The setting is that of a traditional old ship that has been well maintained, but is now approaching its sell-by date.

Indian Ocean Cruises

Indian Ocean Cruises was formed in 2006 to offer cruises to the Lakshadweep Islands, a union territory of India off the coast of Kerala in the Arabian Sea, and the Malabar Coast. The cruise company is owned by the Foresight Group, an Indian operation set up in 1984 and based in the UK. The company's only ship, the 1965-built *Ocean Odyssey*, is an aging vessel that has been quite nicely refurbished.

Island Cruises

Island Cruises was founded as a joint venture between Royal Caribbean Cruises and the British tour operator First Choice Holidays. Its first ship

started operations in 2002. In 2007, First Choice merged with travel company TUI to become TUI Travel. The fleet's two ships, *Island Escape* and *Island Star*, provide mainly British passengers with an active cruise experience in casual surroundings. Its self-serve buffet meals are the mainstay of its culinary offerings.

Kristina Cruises

This Finnish Partanan family-owned company was founded in 1985 as Rannikkolinjat to operate short cruises on Lake Saimaa. In 1987 the company purchased its first ship and started to open Baltic and Russian-owned ports on the Gulf of Finland to international cruise passengers. Today, Kristina Cruises owns and operates two vintage-style ships, principally on cruises in the Baltic and Mediterranean, and continues to preserve nautical traditions on board.

Lindblad Expeditions

Lars-Eric Lindblad started the whole concept of expedition cruising with a single ship, *Lindblad Explorer*, in 1969, taking adventurous travellers to remote regions of the world. Today, his son, Sven-Olof Lindblad, runs the company, but with an array of small ships. It's all about wilderness, wildlife, off-the-beaten-path adventures, and learning. Zodiac inflatable craft are used to ferry participants ashore in remote areas such as the Arctic and Antarctic sub-continents.

The ships carry excellent lecturers, who are more academic than entertaining. In partnership with the National Geographic Society, the company operates the wholly owned *National Geographic Endeavour*, *National Geographic Explorer*, *National Geographic Islander* and *National Geographic Polaris*, together with other small ships for coastal or soft expedition-style cruising.

Louis Cruise Lines

In the 1930s and '40s, Louis Loizou became the undisputed father of tourism in Cyprus. He founded Louis

Hurtigruten passengers view the Midnight Sun in the Arctic.

Cruise Lines to provide inexpensive but comfortable short cruises to and from Cyprus. The Louis Organization today, run by sons Costakis and Vakis Louizou, owns hotels on the island, provides the duty-free shopping at Moscow's Sheremetrevo Airport, and operates resort hotels in Cyprus and Greece, buses in Cyprus and "meet and greet" services for other cruise lines and tour operators. The fleet consists of mainly older, small- and mid-size ships under charter to other companies, such as the tour operator Thomson Cruises, or operated by its two brands, Louis Cruise Lines, and Louis Hellenic Cruises.

Mitsui OSK Passenger Line

Osaka Shosen Kaisha was founded in 1884 in Osaka, Japan. In 1964 it merged with Mitsui Steamship, to become Mitsui OSK. It is now one of the oldest and largest shipping companies in the world.

It entered cruise shipping in 1989 with *Fuji Maru,* the first cruise ship in the Japanese-speaking domestic market. The company specialized in incentive, meetings and groups at sea rather than cruising for individuals. But the company (now known as MOPAS) steadily changed to more cruises for individuals and caters to passengers seeking low-cost cruises aboard ships that are comfortable but lack the facilities of more upscale ships. The company operates two ships, *Fuji Maru* and *Nippon Maru*, both based in Japan for Japanese-speaking passengers, with *Fuju Maru* dedicated exclusively to the charter market.

Monarch Classic Cruises

The company, formerly Majestic International Cruises, was formed in 2006; it is a Greek-owned company, based in Piraeus. The company has older, more traditional mid-

NCL's *Pride of America* leaves New York City.

size ships carrying up to 800 passengers, with service by a Greek crew. Cruises aboard the company's two ships, *Blue Monarch* and *Ocean Countess*, are typically sold by numerous international tour operators.

NCL America

NCL America is a subsidiary of NCL Corporation, owners of Norwegian Cruise Line, or NCL *(profiled on pages 131–3)*, but with a single ship (*Pride of America*) specifically constructed for inter-island family cruises in Hawaii, based year-round in Honolulu. The ship flies the US flag, and is crewed mainly by American officers and hotel staff. Resort casual cruising is featured, as well as an extensive shore excursion program, with everything tailored to Hawaii.

Noble Caledonia

Based in London, Noble Caledonia owns one boutique-sized ship, *Corinthian II*, but sells cruises aboard a wide range of small and specialist expedition cruise companies, specifically for British passengers of mature years, featuring cruises with cultural interest themes.

NYK Line

Nippon Yusen Kaisha (NYK Line) is the largest shipping company in the world, and owns the well-known US-based upscale brand, Crystal Cruises. It created its own NYK Cruise division – today called Asuka Cruise – in 1989 with one Mitsubishi-built ship, *Asuka,* for Japanese-speaking passengers. In 2006, the company sold the original *Asuka* to Germany's Phoenix Reisen, and the former *Crystal Harmony* was transferred from Crystal Cruises to become *Asuka II*.

The ship, known for its excellent Japanese and western food, includes an authentic sushi bar as well as a main restaurant, and a Shiseido health spa. It operates

Athens' Parthenon, an Oceania Cruises port of call.

an annual around-the-world cruise, together with an array of short cruises in the Asia-Pacific region.

Ocean Village

Ocean Village was founded in 2003 as a casual cruising division of P&O Cruises. With headquarters in Southampton, England, the company operates two ships, offering fly-cruises from Palma de Mallorca and Heraklion in the summer and Barbados in the winter.

This is really like the UK equivalent of AIDA Cruises, with large self-serve buffet-style restaurants, and one or two extra-cost dining venues under the watchful eye of celebrity chef James Martin. It's a youthful product, with more potential for growth as the demand for casual unstuffy cruises increases.

Oceania Cruises

Oceania Cruises was founded by Frank del Rio (ex-Renaissance Cruises) and Joe Watters (ex-Royal Viking Line), with substantial investment from Apollo Catering. The ships provide faux English charm in a country-club atmosphere – ideal for middle-aged and older couples looking for a relaxing week at sea. Fine dining, comfortable accommodations and warm, attentive service are its trademarks.

In 2006, Oceania Cruises was bought by Apollo Management (no relation to Apollo Catering), a private equity company that owns Regent Seven Seas Cruises, and 50% of NCL. The brand was placed under the umbrella of Apollo's brand, Prestige Cruise Holdings.

With *Insignia, Nautica* and *Regatta* now operating, and three new ships on order, the company is set to grow. With multiple-choice dining at no extra cost, the present 700-passenger ships suit people who prefer this size of ship to the large resort vessels.

Orion Expedition Cruises

This Australia-based expedition cruise company was created in 2004 by Sarina Bratton, specifically for soft expedition-style cruises to Antarctica, Australia's Kimberley region, and Papua New Guinea and its islands. The ship, *Orion*, built in Germany, is a little gem, with hand-crafted cabinetry in every cabin, together with marble bathrooms and a health spa and gymnasium.

P&O Cruises (Australia)

This Australian division of P&O Cruises was founded in 1932. Today it provides fun in the sand and sun cruises for the beer and bikini brigade and their families. With a maturing market, the company has larger, more contemporary hand-me-down ships from Carnival Corporation companies, and continues to thrive, specializing in cruises in the Pacific and to New Zealand.

Page & Moy Cruises

This Leicester-based British company does not own any ships, but charters *Ocean Majesty* for its many loyal passengers who want to travel widely aboard a ship with intimate dimensions. The company has long been booking and providing cruises for low-budget passengers of mature years, and today acts as a booking agency for cruises on many different lines.

Pearl Seas Cruises

Connecticut-based Pearl Seas Cruises is a sister company to American Cruise Lines, and was founded to build and operate two ships for the upscale coastal cruising sector, but also usable in international waters. Being SOLAS compliant, they will carry more passengers and be more luxurious than the ACL ships. Pearl Seas Cruises' first ship, *Pearl,* makes its debut in 2009.

Onboard service is provided by an all-American crew, consisting of well-educated youngsters who smile a lot.

Peter Deilmann Ocean Cruises

An ex-ship navigation officer, the late Peter Deilmann saw an opportunity when he "came ashore." He started by chartering rivercruise boats for cruises along some of Europe's grand rivers and waterways.

He branched into ocean-going cruise ships in 1982, buying *Berlin*. This ship was sold when the company introduced *Deutschland*. Peter Deilmann's love of music and art translated into much personal artwork being placed aboard his ships. The legacy of this self-made man lives on in the company, based in Neustadt in Holstein, Germany, under the direction of his two daughters.

Phoenix Reisen

Based in Bonn, Germany, the company for many years operated low-budget, tour-operator-style destination-intensive cruises for its German-speaking clientele. It now has a loyal, more upscale audience and more contemporary ships. It provides extremely good itineraries, and represents excellent value for money.

Plantours & Partner

This company provides low-budget cruises aboard its single small cruise ship, *Vistamar*, for German speakers.

Pullmantur Cruises

The company was set up as part of Pullmantur, the Spain-based holiday tour operator. Its cruising division was established in 2000 when it bought *Oceanic* from the long-defunct Florida-based operator Premier Cruise Lines. In 2006, Pullmantur Cruises was purchased by Royal Caribbean Cruises. The company serves the Spanish-speaking market, and operates all-inclusive cruises for families with children, to the Caribbean and Europe.

Quark Expeditions

The company was founded in 1991 by Lars Wikander, and silent-partner Christer Salen (formerly of Salen-Lindblad Cruises). It is based in Darien, Connecticut, and specializes in providing up-close-and-personal expedition cruises to some of the world's most remote regions and inaccessible areas.

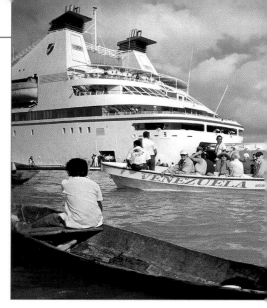

A Seabourn cruise ship meets the locals.

In its formative years, Quark Expeditions chartered Russian ice-breakers to take adventurous, hardy outdoor types to the Polar regions, and has perhaps the most experience in taking participants to Antarctica. Quark Expeditions has always been committed to minimising the environmental impact of operating in ecologically sensitive areas.

In 2007, it was sold to the UK's First Choice Holidays (founded in 1973), merged with Peregrine Shipping, and then in 2007 was bought, along with First Choice, by the large German travel company TUI.

Cruising with Quark Expeditions is all about being close to nature, wilderness, wildlife, off-the-beaten-path adventures, and learning. The company still specializes in chartering nuclear- and diesel-powered Russian ice-breakers, the most powerful in the world, to provide participants with a truly memorable expedition experience. This is adventure cruising for toughies.

Regent Seven Seas Cruises

Part of the Carlson group of companies, it was formerly called Radisson Seven Seas Cruises. Carlson Hospitality Worldwide ventured into cruising via its Radisson Hotels International division – hence, Radisson Diamond Cruises. Regent Seven Seas Cruises strives to pay close attention to detail and provide high-quality service aboard its small fleet of mid-sized cruise ships. One ship is based year-round in Tahiti, while the others operate world-wide itineraries.

In 2007 the company was purchased by US-based Apollo Management, an investment group, and, together with Oceania Cruises, was placed under the umbrella of its Prestige Cruise Holdings.

Saga Rose and *Saga Ruby* cater for the over-50s.

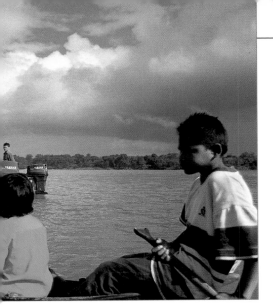

Seabourn Cruise Line

Originally founded in 1986 as Signet Cruise Line, the company, then owned by Norwegian businessman Atle Brynestad, was forced to change its name in 1988 as a result of a lawsuit brought by a Texas company that had already registered the name Signet Cruise Lines (no ships were ever built). The Carnival Corporation acquired 100% of Seabourn Cruise Line in 1999.

The company aims its product at affluent, sophisticated, well travelled North Americans, with small ships providing a high level of European-style service, open-seating dining, all-inclusive drinks, great attention to detail and personal pampering.

SeaDream Yacht Cruises

Larry Pimentel and his business partner Atle Brynestad jointly created the cruise line (Brynestad formerly founded Seabourn Cruise Line), purchasing the former Sea Goddess Cruises' ships and introducing them in 2001 to an audience anxious for exclusivity, personal pampering, and cuisine that is prepared à la minute.

The two ships, *SeaDream I* and *SeaDream II*, have been refreshed several times, and are often chartered by companies or private individuals who appreciate the refined, elegant, but casual atmosphere on board. The 100-passenger ships operate year-round in the Caribbean and Mediterranean, and provide all-inclusive beverages and open-seating dining at all times, and a high degree of personalized service, all in a cozy, club-like atmosphere, with great attention to detail and personal idiosyncracies.

Saga Cruises

Saga, based in Folkestone, England, was created by Sydney de Haan as a company offering financial services and holidays to the over-60s (reduced to the over-50s in 1995 as the company's success grew). Its popular travel flourished because it was good at providing extra personal attention and competent staff. Instead of sending passengers to ships operated by other companies, it decided to purchase its own ships and market its own product under the Saga Holidays brand.

Saga Shipping (Saga Cruises), the cruising division of Saga Holidays, was set up in 1997 when it purchased *Saga Rose* (ex-*Sagafjord*), followed not long after by *Saga Ruby* (ex-*Vistafjord*). Another brand, Spirit of Adventure, was added in 2006. The cruise company is run mainly by former Cunard executives, with strong British seamanship and training, and its fleet of three ships manages to retain the feel of traditional, elegant, child-free cruising.

A "Balinese Dream Bed" on the night deck of *SeaDream I*.

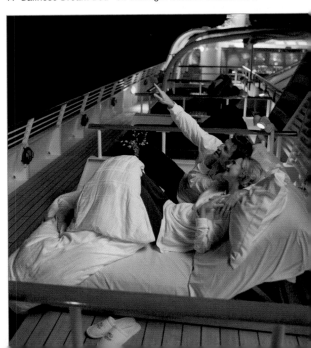

Sea Cloud Cruises

The company was founded in 1979 by a consortium of shipowners and investors known as the Hansa Treuhand (active in commercial vessel management, engineering, and construction), and has its headquarters in Hamburg, Germany. It owns and operates two tall ships (sailing vessels), the legendary *Sea Cloud* and *Sea Cloud II*, and two European rivercruise boats, *River Cloud I* and *River Cloud II*. It has another tall ship, *Sea Cloud Hussar*, on order.

The company has many corporate clients who charter the two tall ships, while a number of upscale cruise and travel companies sell cruises to individuals. The onboard style and product delivery is quite upscale, with elegant retro decor and fine food and service.

Silversea Cruises

Silversea Cruises is a mostly privately owned cruise line. It was founded in 1992 by the Lefebvre D'Ovidio family from Rome (previously co-owners of Sitmar Cruises: 90% partners being the Lefebvre D'Ovidio; 10% by V-Ships), and is based in Monaco.

Antonio Lefebvre D'Ovidio was a maritime lawyer and professor of maritime law before acquiring and operating cargo ships and ferries in the Adriatic. He took the family into partnership with Boris Vlasov's Vlasov Group (V-Ships) to co-own Sitmar Cruises until that company merged with Princess Cruises in 1988.

Silversea Cruises has generated a tremendous amount of loyalty from its frequent passengers, who view the ships as their own. All four Silversea ships feature teak verandas, and all-inclusive beverages. Open-seating dining prevails at all times, and the company is known for its partnership with the hospitality organization, Relais et Châteaux.

A new, larger, 540-passenger all-suite luxury ship, *Silver Spirit*, is expected to debut in early 2010.

Star Clippers

Swedish-born yachtsman Mikhail Krafft founded Star Cruises in 1991 with *Star Flyer* and then *Star Clipper*, both true tall ships. The company went on to build the largest tall ship presently sailing, the five-mast *Royal Clipper*. It is now building an even bigger tall ship. Good food and service in a laid-back setting, under the romance of sail, is what Star Clippers are all about. The company's *Star Flyer* is on a four-year charter to the government of Tahiti, where the ship is based year-round.

Swan Hellenic Cruises

Founded in 1954 By R.K. Swan, the company chartered small cruise ships for years. The company was purchased by P&O Cruises in 1982, and then it changed hands when Carnival Corporation merged with P&O in

Rio de Janeiro is a Voyages of Discovery port of call.

April 2004. In 2007, the Carnival Corporation disbanded Swan Hellenic, and its single ship (*Minerva II*) was transferred to the Princess Cruises fleet to become *Royal Princess*. Some months later, a semi-retired Lord Sterling purchased the brand from the Carnival Corporation and joined partners with the UK's Voyages of Discovery to be operated as a separate brand. So, the "swanners," as its intellectual passengers are called, now have their very own ship (*Minerva*).

The company's strengths are its program of highly academic lecturers and speakers, in a small ship setting that is unpretentious but comfortable, and includes gratuities, drinks (on Antarctic voyages), tailor-made shore excursions, and entrance fees to museums and places of interest. The company operates special-interest themes such as archaeology, history, nature and wildlife.

Thomson Cruises

Thomson Cruises' first foray into cruising was in 1973 when it chartered two ships, *Calypso* and *Ithaca* (Ulysses Line). It was not a success, and the company withdrew from cruising two years later. Ulysses Line became known as Useless Line.

The company started again in 2002 after seeing rival tour operator Airtours operate ships successfully. Unlike Airtours' Sun Cruises, which no longer exists, Thomson Cruises charters its ships instead of owning them outright, preferring instead to leave ship operations, management and catering to specialist maritime companies. The company operates cruises for the whole family aboard its small fleet of ships (exception: *The Calypso*, a child-free ship). The onboard currency is the British pound, and basic gratuities are included. The company owns its own airline, Thomsonfly.

Transocean Tours

Founded in 1954, Transocean Tours headquarters are in Bremen, Germany. The company specializes in providing low-cost but high-

Champagne welcome aboard a Silversea cruise.

value cruises aboard ships that are under long-term charter, with traditional decor and excellent itineraries. Gratuities and port charges are included. In 2008, *Marco Polo*, a ship known for operating destination-intensive "soft-expedition" style cruises, was introduced.

Travel Dynamics International

Founded by brothers George and Vasos Papagapitos, the company specializes in providing small and boutique cruise ships to culturally minded passengers. Long a provider of vacations and cruises to university alumni, cultural associations, and museum groups, the company seeks out unusual itineraries and destinations according to a group's interest or travel theme.

Venus Cruise

Founded in 1988, the company's headquarters are in Osaka, Japan. Venus Cruise was first known as Japan Cruise Line, which is owned by four ferry companies: Shin Nipponkai Ferry, Kyowa Shoji, Hankyu Ferry, and Kanko Kisen. As Japan Cruise Line, the company at first operated company and incentive charter cruises before branching out into cruises for individuals. The company presently has one ship, *Pacific Venus*, and caters exclusively to Japanese speakers, operating an annual around-the-world cruise as well as shorter Asia-Pacific cruises.

Vision Cruises

Spain-based Vision Cruises was founded in the late 1980s to provide low-cost, all-inclusive tour operator-style cruises for Spanish-speaking families with children. It doesn't own any ships, but charters them from other owners such as Classic International Cruises and Club Cruise. The company charters small ships and provides popular destination cruises in a casual setting, with food and service that is adequate, but nothing more.

Voyages of Discovery

UK-based Roger Allard and Dudley Smith jointly founded the company to offer low-cost cruises aboard comfortable, roomy mid-sized ships, to UK-based passengers, but with good food and service. The company's *Discovery* is one of the former "Love Boats" of US television fame. The company went public in 2006 and, with the help of Lord Sterling of Plaistow, purchased Swan Hellenic Cruises. It now operates both brands from its headquarters in the south of England.

Windstar Cruises

Founded by New York-based Karl Andren in 1984 as Windstar Sail Cruises, the company's concept was to build high-class sail-cruise ships with computer-controlled sails, and outfit them in a contemporary decor designed by Marc Held. The first ship, *Wind Star*, debuted in 1986 to much acclaim, and was followed by *Wind Spirit* (1988) and *Wind Surf* (1990).

Windstar Cruises was sold to Holland America Line in 1988. The company, with headquarters in Seattle, USA, was sold again in 2007 to the Ambassadors Cruise Group, wholly owned by Ambassadors International.

The onboard style is casual and totally unregimented, but smart, with service by Indonesian and Filipino crew. The ships carry watersports equipment, accessed from a retractable stern platform.

Zegrahm Expeditions

This small expeditions cruise company was founded in 1990 to take inquisitive travelers to remote or unusual destinations, including the Arctic and Antarctica. Although it doesn't own any ships, it charters high-quality specialized vessels, and it also sells cruises operated by other expedition companies. Two- or three-week expedition cruises are headed by experienced leaders and expert naturalists. ❏

The 347-passenger *Wind Surf* has computer-controlled sails.

CRUISING IN THE LAP OF LUXURY

Of the 75-plus cruise lines operating internationally, only a handful provide the kind of ships and onboard experience that can truly be called "luxury"

Luxury cruises versus premium and standard (large resort ship) cruises are like the difference between a Bentley and a Hyundai. "Luxury cruising" should be a flawless combination of ship, facilities, food and service. Unfortunately, the word "luxury" has been degraded by marketing people, but the panel below tells you what the term ought to mean in a cruise ship.

Little and large

Size is important. Boutique and small ships can get into ports that larger ships can't. They can also get closer to the center of large cities. For example, in St. Petersburg, Russia large and mid-sized ships (such as those of Crystal Cruises and Regent Seven Seas Cruises) dock about one hour from the city center, while boutique ships such as those of Hapag-Lloyd Cruises or Silversea Cruises can dock right next to the Hermitage Museum in the heart of the city.

One area where "luxury" ships differ least from large resort ships is in shore excursions, particularly in the Caribbean and Alaska, where almost all cruise operators are obliged to use the same specialist tour operators ashore – simply because "luxury" is virtually unknown in these regions and local tour operators consider all cruise passengers to be the same. For example, when I checked a fleet of minivan vehicles in the Caribbean island of Grenada, several vehicles had wheel nuts missing; and when I checked two 45-passenger tour buses in Philadelphia, neither had a first aid kit on board. I have a whole bagful of similar examples from around the world.

Large resort ships (those carrying more than 1,600

passengers) simply cannot provide the kind of personal service and attention to detail that the boutique/small ships can. Although you can book one of the largest suites afloat aboard a large ship, once you leave your "private living space" you'll have to mix with all other passengers, particularly if you want to go to a show, disembark at ports of call (think of the long lines at the gangway security checkpoint), or go on organized shore excursions. That's when you appreciate the fact that smaller may suit you better.

These are ships suited to those not seeking the active, family- and entertainment-driven cruise experiences that large ships resort offer. The ships, companies, and comparisons in this section provide ships, facilities and service levels hard to find elsewhere. While most of them boast about being the best, or boast the awards they receive annually from various magazines (whose respondents are almost never global in scope), not all provide the same degree of luxury, and there *are* differences in the cruise product delivered.

THE CRÈME DE LA CRÈME

These 16 ships (listed alphabetically, by company) belong to seven cruise lines, and are the "cream" of the cruise industry in terms of style, finesse, staff training, cuisine, service, hospitality and finesse. Their individual facilities are fully reviewed in the ratings section of this book, and the Berlitz ratings awarded for accommodation, food, service, entertainment and so on indicate their particular strengths.

- **CRYSTAL CRUISES**
  Crystal Serenity, Crystal Symphony
- **HAPAG-LLOYD CRUISES**
  Europa
- **HEBRIDEAN INTERNATIONAL CRUISES**
  Hebridean Spirit
- **REGENT SEVEN SEAS CRUISES**
  Seven Seas Mariner, Seven Seas Navigator, Seven Seas Voyager
- **SEABOURN CRUISE LINE**
  Seabourn Legend, Seabourn Pride, Seabourn Spirit
- **SEADREAM YACHT CRUISES**
  SeaDream I, SeaDream II
- **SILVERSEA CRUISES**
  Silver Cloud, Silver Shadow, Silver Whisper, Silver Wind

SeaDream I is the next best thing to a private yacht.

So, what are the differences?

Once you know the main differences, you'll be better equipped to choose the right cruise line and ship to provide the level of onboard food and service you are looking for. While most of the differences are immediately visible when you sail aboard (and compare) them all, some of the variations in style and service are more subtle.

Some have more crew per passenger. Some have more expensive European crew than others. Some have better food and service. Some have entertainment, some don't. Some have more public space per passenger. It's important to weigh up the differences, so that you choose the right ship for the right reasons.

For example, the following facilities and services are found aboard the ships of Hapag-Lloyd Cruises, Sea-Dream Yacht Cruises and Seabourn Cruise Line, but not aboard the ships of Crystal Cruises, Regent Seven Seas Cruises, or Silversea Cruises.

- Anticipation is more widely practiced aboard the smaller ships, where staff training is better in terms of passenger recognition (remembering your name).
- Waiters escort female guests (waitresses escort male guests) to the dining table and to the dining room exit after meals.
- Relaxed embarkation and disembarkation is at your leisure.
- Cabin stewardesses leave hand-written notes.
- There are no announcements, and no mindless background music in public rooms, accommodation hallways or elevators.
- The chef invites passengers to accompany him on visits to local food markets.

More space, better service

All 16 ships have an excellent amount of open deck and lounging space, and a high Passenger Space Ratio (almost all are above 40) when compared to large resort ships (which are typically under 35), the two Sea-Dreams being the exception.

The Argyll Restaurant aboard *Hebridean Spirit*.

Almost all have a better Crew to Passenger Ratio than the large resort ships. In warm weather areas, the ships of SeaDream Yacht Cruises and Seabourn Cruise Line (all have fold-down platforms at the stern of each ship) provide jet skis, kayaks, snorkeling gear, windsurfers and the like at no extra cost, typically for one day each cruise (the others do not).

WHAT YOU SHOULD EXPECT

- Flawless personal service and attention to detail.
- Champagne at embarkation.
- European hotel service crew.
- Personalized stationery.
- A crew that anticipates your needs, responds quickly to your requests, and don't say "no" or "impossible".
- Zero announcements (except for emergencies).
- No background music in public rooms, hallways and elevators.
- A high Passenger Space Ratio (35 to 70 gross tons per passenger).
- A high Crew to Passenger Ratio (1.5 to 1 or greater).
- Creative cuisine that excels in presentation, taste, variety, and ingredients.
- Highly qualified sommeliers to discuss and serve wines.
- Connoisseur wines and premium spirits.
- The finest quality bed linens, duvets, towels, bathrobes.
- High-quality personal toiletries (e.g. Aveda, Bulgari).
- Gratuities that are included in the fare.
- No extra charge for on-demand movies or music.
- No machinery vibration (engines/propulsion equipment).
- No lines anywhere.
- More overnight port stays.
- Separate gangway for passengers and crew.
- Shoe-shine service.
- No signing for drinks or other items.
- Your fellow passengers are unlikely to flaunt ostentatious tattoos and body piercings.

Hapag-Lloyd's *Europa* also has a fleet of Zodiac rigid inflatable craft for in-depth exploration and shore adventures, plus an ice-hardened hull and a crew who understand the culture of the passengers. And mattresses that are 7 ft (2.1 meters) long.

Dining

Fine dining is the highlight of the 16 ships in this category, and is more of an entertainment feature than the entertainment itself – if there is any. Good company and conversation make dining a pleasurable social occasion.

You can expect to find plenty of tables for two, a calm refined dining atmosphere, open or one seating dining, by candlelight, high-quality china and silverware, large wine glasses, fresh flowers, a connoisseur wine list, and sommeliers who understand and can discuss fine wines.

It's really about non-repetitive, highly creative menus, high-quality ingredients, moderate portions and attractive presentation, with fresh local fish and other items provided (when available) and cooked à la minute (not in batches), and meat of the highest grade. Caviar, foie gras, black/white truffles and other exotic foods, and fresh green vegetables (instead of frozen or canned vegetables) are provided.

Almost all the ships provide cloches for extra "wow" effect in the dining room service of main courses. Additionally, passengers are often invited to visit local markets with the chef aboard the ships of Hapag-Lloyd Cruises, SeaDream Yacht Cruises, and Seabourn Cruise Line.

Some luxury ships provide even more special touches. *Europa,* for example, makes its own breakfast preserves, while *Hebridean Spirit* provides its own bottled water.

Typically, lunch and dinner menus are provided in your suite/cabin in advance, and special orders (ordering off menu) are often possible. Room service menus are extensive, and meals can be served, course by course, in your suite/cabin, either on the balcony or inside on special portable tables (some ships do this better than others). It is also possible to have a special dinner set up on deck (wonderful in the right location), with all the finery and individual service you would expect of private dining.

Drinks: included or not?

Hebridean International Cruises, Regent Seven Seas Cruises, SeaDream Yacht Cruises, Seabourn Cruise Line, and Silversea Cruises provide wine with dinner (Seabourn and Silversea also include wine with lunch). However, real premium (connoisseur) brands and classic vintage wines will be at extra cost.

Crystal Cruises and Hapag-Lloyd Cruises charge for all alcoholic beverages. Crystal Cruises includes soft drinks. Hebridean, Regent, SeaDream, Seabourn and Silversea include all drinks (but for mostly standard brands). Hapag-Lloyd Cruises does not include alcoholic drinks, because its passengers know and want their favorite

HOW THE LUXURY SHIPS COMPARE

Ship	Company	Tonnage	Size	Pod Propulsion	Passenger space ratio
Crystal Serenity	Crystal Cruises	68,870	Mid-Size	Yes	62.6
Crystal Symphony	Crystal Cruises	51,044	Mid-Size	No	53.1
Europa	Hapag-Lloyd Cruises	28,437	Small	Yes	69.6
Hebridean Spirit	Hebridean International Cruises	4,200	Boutique	No	51.8
*Seabourn Legend**	Seabourn Cruise Line	9.961	Boutique	No	46.9
*Seabourn Pride**	Seabourn Cruise Line	9,975	Boutique	No	46.9
*Seabourn Spirit**	Seabourn Cruise Line	9,975	Boutique	No	46.9
SeaDream I	SeaDream Yacht Cruises	4,253	Boutique	No	39.4
SeaDream II	SeaDream Yacht Cruises	4,253	Boutique	No	39.4
Seven Seas Mariner	Regent Seven Seas Cruises	48,015	Mid-Size	Yes	67.8
Seven Seas Navigator	Regent Seven Seas Cruises	28,550	Mid-Size	No	58.2
Seven Seas Voyager	Regent Seven Seas Cruises	41,827	Mid-Size	Yes	59.0
Silver Cloud	Silversea Cruises	16,927	Small	No	57.1
Silver Shadow	Silversea Cruises	28,258	Small	No	72.8
Silver Whisper	Silversea Cruises	28,258	Small	No	72.8
Silver Wind	Silversea Cruises	16,927	Small	No	57.1

* These ships also have a number of "French" balcony cabins with floor-to-ceiling doors that ope

brands, many of which are well above the level of standard brands carried by those cruise lines that do include alcoholic beverages, which are normally tailored to suit North American tastes.

Other differences

Aboard the ships of Regent Seven Seas Cruises and Seabourn Cruise Line, white plastic deck lounge chairs are provided. Aboard the ships of Hebridean International Cruises and SeaDream Yacht Cruises they are made of teak (or other hardwood), and aboard Hapag-Lloyd Cruises' *Europa* they are made of aluminum and wood, and aboard the ships of Silversea Cruises they are made of aluminum.

Crystal Serenity, Crystal Symphony, Seven Seas Mariner, Seven Seas Navigator, and *Seven Seas Voyager* are mid-size ships (600–1,600 passengers) that include entertainment with production shows and cabaret acts.

To a lesser extent, so do the Seabourn ships and Hapag-Lloyd's *Europa*, but the other ships do not have entertainment as such, but instead rely on their intimacy and friendliness, and promote after-dinner conversation or, aboard the ships of Silversea Cruises, individual specialist cabaret acts.

Regrettably, *Crystal Serenity* and *Crystal Symphony* hold art auctions, which seriously detract from the otherwise fine facilities, food and service, although they do have good-quality bistros (which none of the other ships do). ❏

Europa provides its own bicycles for tours on shore.

Crew to passenger ratio	Cabins (double)	Cabins w/balcony	Largest Suite (sq. m)	Smallest Cabin (sq. m)	Plastic deck chairs	Tips incl.	Water Sports Toys	Hand-held showers	Toiletries
1.7	550	466	125.0	21.0	Yes	No	No	Yes	Aveda
1.7	480	276	91.2	18.7	Yes	No	No	Yes	Aveda
1.5	204	168	85.0	33.0	No	Yes	No	Yes	Own brand
1.1	31	8	34.0	20.0	No	Yes	No	No	Molton Brown
1.3	106	6	53.5	25.7	Yes	Yes	Yes	Yes	Molton Brown
1.3	106	6	53.5	25.7	Yes	Yes	Yes	Yes	Molton Brown
1.3	106	6	53.5	25.7	Yes	Yes	Yes	Yes	Molton Brown
1.2	54	0	45.5	18.1	No	Yes	Yes	Yes	Bulgari
1.2	54	0	45.5	18.1	No	Yes	Yes	Yes	Bulgari
1.6	354	354	142.0	28.0	Yes	Yes	No	Yes	Own brand (Regent)
1.5	245	196	109.0	28.0	Yes	Yes	No	Yes	Own brand (Regent)
1.6	354	354	130.0	33.0	Yes	Yes	No	Yes	Own brand (Regent)
1.4	148	110	122.0	22.2	Yes	Yes	No	No	Acqua di parma
1.3	194	157	133.3	26.6	Yes	Yes	No	No	Acqua di parma
1.3	194	157	133.3	26.6	Yes	Yes	No	No	Acqua di parma
1.4	148	110	122.0	22.2	Yes	Yes	No	No	Acqua di parma

for fresh air (the actual "balcony" is only about 12 inches/30 cm deep)

THE BEST SHORE EXCURSIONS

Guided tours in ports of call cost extra, but they are often the best way to get a nutshell view of a destination and make the most efficient use of your limited time ashore

Shore excursions used to be limited to city tours and venues that offered folkloric dances by local troupes. Today's excursions are almost limitless, and include flightseeing, floatplane rides, cross-country four-wheel drive trips, mountain biking, ziplining, dog sledding and overland safaris. It's possible to spend far more on shore excursions than the price of the cruise.

Most excursions are escorted by ship's staff, who will usually carry first-aid kits. If you explore independently and need medical help, you could risk missing the ship when it sails. Unless the destination is a familiar one, first-time cruisegoers are probably safer booking excursions organized by the ship and vetted by the cruise line. Also, if you have a problem during a tour, the cruise line should be able to sort it out on the spot.

If you do go it alone, always take the ship's port agent and telephone numbers with you, in case of emergencies (they are normally printed in the Daily Program). Allow plenty of time to get back to your ship before sailing time – the ship won't wait. Make sure your travel insurance covers you fully.

How tiring are excursions?

Most tours will involve some degree of walking, and some require extensive walking. Most cruise lines grade their excursions with visual symbols to indicate the degree of fitness required.

Waterfront and Table Mountain, Cape Town, South Africa.

Are there private excursions?

Yes, aboard some of the more upscale ships such as those of Hebridean International Cruises, Hapag-Lloyd Cruises, Regent Seven Seas Cruises, SeaDream Yacht Cruises, Seabourn Cruise Line and Silversea Cruises, you can have shore excursions tailored to your specific needs. But even large resort ship lines like Norwegian Cruise Line (NCL) can book something special under its Freestyle Private Touring program.

What if my first choice is sold out?

Some excursions do sell out, owing to limited space or transport, but there can be last-minute cancellations. Check with the shore excursion manager on board.

What should I take with me?

Only what's necessary; leave any valuables aboard ship, together with any money and credit cards you do not plan to use. Groups of people are often targets for pickpockets in popular sightseeing destinations. Also, beware of excursion guides who give you a colored disk to wear for "identification" – they may be marking you as a "rich" tourist for local shopkeepers. It's always prudent to wear comfortable rubber-soled shoes, particularly in older ports when there may be cobblestones or other uneven surfaces.

How can I make a booking?

Aboard some ships, where shore excursions can be booked before the sailing date via the internet, they can sell out fast. So book early. Payment aboard ship is normally made via a ship's central billing system.

If you need to cancel a shore excursion, you usually need to do so at least 24 hours before its advertised departure time. Otherwise, refunds are at the discretion of the cruise line. In many cases, you will be able to sell your ticket to

The dynamic port of Hong Kong, gateway to China.

another passenger. Tickets do not normally have names or cabin numbers on them, except those that involve flights or overland arrangements. Check with the shore excursion manager to make sure it's okay to resell.

How can I know which are good?

If it's your first cruise, try to attend the shore excursion briefing. Read the excursion literature and circle tours that appeal. Then go to the shore excursion office and ask any other questions you may have before you book. A few helpful tips:

● Shore excursions are put together for general interest. If you want to see something that is not described in the excursion literature, do not take it. Go on your own or with friends.

● Brochure descriptions of shore excursions, often written by personnel who haven't visited the ports of call, can be imprecise. All cruise lines should adopt the following definitions in their descriptive literature and for their lectures and presentations: The term "visit" should mean actually entering the place or building concerned. The term "see" should mean viewing from the outside – as from a bus, for example.

● City excursions are basically superficial. To get to know a city intimately, go alone or with a small group. Go by taxi or bus, or explore on foot.

● If you do not want to miss the major sightseeing attractions in each port, organized shore excursions provide a good solution. They also allow you to meet fellow passengers with similar interests.

● In the Caribbean, many sightseeing tours cover the same ground, regardless of the cruise line you sail with. Choose one and then do something different in the next port. The same is true of the history and archaeology excursions in the Greek Isles.

What if I lose my ticket?

Report lost or misplaced tickets to the shore excursion manager. Aboard most ships, excursion tickets, once sold, become the sole responsibility of the purchaser, and the cruise line is not generally able to issue replacements.

Going ashore independently

If you hire a taxi for sightseeing, negotiate the price in advance, and don't pay until you get back to the ship or to your destination. If you are with friends, hiring a taxi for a full- or half-day sightseeing trip can often work out far cheaper than renting a car – and it's probably safer. Try to find a driver who speaks your language.

Exploring independently is ideal in the major cruise ports of Alaska, the Bahamas, Bermuda, the Caribbean, the Mexican Riviera, the Canary Islands, the Mediterranean, Aegean ports, and the South Pacific's islands.

If you don't speak the local language, carry some identification (but not your passport, unless required), the name of your ship and the area in which it is docked. If the ship is anchored and you take a launch tender ashore, observe landmarks near the landing place, and write down the location. This will help if you get lost and need to take a taxi back to the launch.

Some small ships provide an identification tag or boarding pass at the reception desk or gangway, to be handed in each time you return to the ship. Remember that ships have schedules – and sometimes tides – to meet, and they won't wait for you if you return late.

If you are in a launch port in a tropical area and the weather changes for the worse, the ship's captain could well make a decision to depart early to avoid being hemmed in by an approaching storm; it has happened, especially in the Caribbean. If it does, locate the ship's agent in the port – he's likely to be carrying a walkie-talkie – who will try to get you back.

Planning on going to a quiet, secluded beach to swim? First check with the cruise director or shore excursion manager, as certain beaches may be considered off-limits because of a dangerous undertow, drug pushers, or persistent hawkers. And don't even think of going diving alone – even if you know the area well. ❑

The Bibi-ka-Maqbara tomb, Aurangabad, near Mumbai, India.

100 POPULAR SHORE EXCURSIONS AROUND THE WORLD

THE CARIBBEAN

Antigua
① Tour to Shirley Heights and Nelson's Dockyard

Aruba, Netherlands Antilles
② Full-day Jeep eco-adventure trip

Barbados
Party cruise aboard the *Jolly Roger* pirate boat

Grand Cayman
③ Go snorkeling with the sting rays at Sting Ray City

Grenada
④ Eco-hiking tour to the Seven Sisters waterfall

Hamilton, Bermuda
⑤ Guided Walking Tour of the former capital, St. George's

Jamaica
⑥ Excursion to Dunn's River Falls and Prospect Plantation (Ocho Rios)
⑦ Horseback riding on the beach (Montego Bay, Ocho Rios)
⑧ Zip-line forest canopy tour

Nassau, Bahamas
⑨ Go swimming with the dolphins

San Juan, Puerto Rico
⑩ El Yunque Rain Forest Tour & Hike

St Lucia
⑪ Jungle Eco-Tour by Jeep

St. Maarten, Netherlands Antilles
⑫ Join the America's Cup Regatta Adventure tour and compete in an actual yacht race

St. Thomas, US Virgin Islands
⑬ The Coral World Underwater Aquarium and Island Drive Tour
⑭ "Screemin' Eagle" Jet Boat thrill ride

Tortola, British Virgin Islands
⑮ Hiking tour to the peak of Sage Mountain (National Park)

Virgin Gorda, British Virgin Islands
⑯ Trip to "The Baths" in Virgin Gorda

MEXICO / CENTRAL AMERICA

MEXICO AND CENTRAL AMERICA

Acapulco, Mexico
⑰ Excursion to see the rock divers
⑱ Tour to the Silver City of Taxco

Belize, Central America
⑲ Horseback riding and more in the jungles of Belize

Cabo San Lucas, Mexico
⑳ Personal dolphin encounter (for children) at the Cabo Dolphin Center

Dunn's River Falls in Jamaica.

Cozumel, Mexico
㉑ Tour to 12th-century Mayan ruins of Tulum and Xel-Ha national park

EUROPE AND THE BALTIC

Amsterdam, Holland
㉒ Go to the Anne Frank Museum

Athens (Piraeus, the port for Athens), Greece
㉓ Tour to the Acroplis and museums of ancient Athens

Barcelona, Spain
㉔ City tour to see Gaudi's architecture, the Sagrada Familia cathedral, and the Ramblas

Casablanca, Morocco
㉕ Casablanca, including the Hassan II Grand Mosque, and Rabat

Catania/Messina, Sicily
㉖ Visit to Mt. Etna and Taormina
㉗ Sicilian Cooking Class tour

Copenhagen, Denmark
㉘ Guided walking tour of the famed Tivoli Gardens

Dublin, Ireland
㉙ Visit the original Guinness brewery

Dubrovnik, Croatia
㉚ Walking tour of the old walled city

Edinburgh, Scotland
㉛ Visit Edinburgh Castle and the city
㉜ The Whisky Distillery Tour

Flam/Gudvangen
㉝ Take the mountain railway excursion from Flam to Gudvangen

Helsinki, Finland
㉞ Art, city highlights and Sibelius concert tour

Istanbul, Turkey
㉟ Tour to Topkapi Palace and the Grand Bazaar

Kusadasi
㊱ Tour to historic Ephesus, and the house of the Virgin Mary

La Coruna, Spain
㊲ Tour to Santiago de Compostela, home to the mystery of St. James

Lisbon, Portugal
㊳ Tour to the Alfama (old) quarter of Lisbon and the Maritime Museum

Livorno, Italy
㊴ Full-day tour to Florence and the Leaning Tower of Pisa

London, England
㊵ River cruise along the historic River Thames for a different view of London
㊶ London by Night, including a West End musical or play

Madeira, Portugal
㊷ The toboggan ride excursion

Monte Carlo, Monaco
㊸ Tour to the Royal Palace and Grand Casino (jacket and tie required)

Naples, Italy
㊹ Tour to the Isle of Capri by boat to visit the famous Blue Grotto caves

Nice, France
㊺ Tour to Ez and the Corniche

Oslo, Norway
㊻ Tour to the Viking Museum and the warship Wasa

Palma de Mallorca
㊼ Tour to former Carthusian monastery of Valldemosa (Frederick Chopin and George Sand lived here in 1838)

Rhodes, Greece
⑯ Follow in the footsteps of St. Paul
Rome (Civitavecchia, the port for Rome), Italy
⑲ Guided "Roman Holiday" walking tour, including the Colosseum
⑳ Visit the Vatican's Sistine Chapel
Santorini, Greece
㉑ Donkey ride tour up the hillside
Sorrento, Italy
㉒ Visit to the ruins of Pompeii and the Amalfi Coast
St. Petersburg, Russia
㉓ Guided walking tour through the Hermitage Museum
㉔ Excursion to St. Catherine's Summer Palace
㉕ Night tour to a ballet or classical music concert at the Mariinsky Theater
Stockholm, Sweden
㊱ Tour to the Nobel Prize Museum
Venice, Italy
㊲ Romantic gondola ride excursion
㊳ Guided walking tour to the Guggenheim Museum
Warnemunde, Germany
㊴ Excursion to Berlin

ICELAND

Reykyavik, Iceland
㊵ Tour to the warm geothermal waters of the Blue Lagoon

INDIAN OCEAN AND THE MIDDLE EAST

Aqaba, Jordan
㊶ Tour to the "Rose Red City" of Petra
Dubai, United Arab Emirates
㊷ 4 x 4 Dune Drive Safari Tour
Male, Seychelles
㊸ Flightseeing of the atolls and inlets
Mumbai, India
㊹ Mumbai City Sights
㊺ Buddhist Trail tour to the Kanheri Caves
Alexandria or Port Said, Egypt
㊻ Tour to the amazing temple of Karnak in Luxor
Sharm el Sheik, Egypt
㊼ Go diving and snorkeling
Tripoli, Libya
㊽ Tour to historic Leptis Magna and Tripoli's Medina

THE UNITED STATES

Hilo, Hawaii
㊹ Kilauea Volcano tour in Volcanoes National Park

Juneau, Alaska
⑳ Flightseeing trip to Mendenhall Glacier, and Alaska salmon bake
Ketchikan, Alaska
㉑ Misty Fjords flightseeing trip
Key West, Florida
㉒ The Conch Train Tour in Ernest Hemingway's favorite city
Los Angeles, California
㉓ Tour past the Hollywood homes of top movie stars
New York City
㉔ Take a Circle Line boat cruise around Manhattan
Skagway, Alaska
㉕ The historic White Pass & Yukon Route Railway train tour
Sitka, Alaska
㉖ Sea Otter and Wildlife Quest

AUSTRALIA, NEW ZEALAND AND THE SOUTH PACIFIC

Auckland, New Zealand
㉗ Tour to one of West Auckland's wineries and micro-breweries
Hamilton Island, Australia
㉘ Cruise/tour to Great Barrier Reef
Melbourne, Australia
㉙ Guided walking and tram tour, including the Gold Treasury
㉚ Shark diving in the aquarium tour on the banks of the Yarra River

Floatplane rides are popular in Alaska.

Sydney, Australia
㉛ Full-day catamaran tour taking in the Blue Mountains and Featherdale Wildlife Park

SOUTHEAST ASIA

Bali, Indonesia
㉜ Balinese music and dance show
Bangkok (Laem Chabang, the port for Bangkok), Thailand
㉝ Tour to the Royal Palace and the sacred halls of Wat Phra Kaew
Ha Long Bay, Vietnam
㉞ Junk tour through the misty waters and limestone monuments
Ho Chi Minh City, Vietnam
㉟ Tour to the (Vietnam) War Museum
Hong Kong, China
㊱ The Harbour Bay cruise tour
Kuala Lumpur, Malaysia
㊲ Visit the Petronas Twin Tower building and night market
Osaka, Japan
㊳ Tour to Kyoto, Japan's former capital, and the monuments of the ancient city, now a Unesco World Heritage site
Singapore
㊴ The Night Safari Tour
Yokohama, Japan
㊵ Tour to the famous Ginza shopping area in Tokyo
㊶ Kabuki Theater Performance tour

SOUTH AMERICA

Rio de Janeiro, Brazil
㊷ Tour to Sugar Loaf Mountain
㊸ Corcovado Tour & Christ the Redeemer Monument
Buenos Aires, Argentina
㊹ Steak and Tango night tour
Ushuaia, Argentina
㊺ Ride world's southernmost train
Puerto Madryn, Chile
㊻ The Penguin Safari tour (encounter 250,000 penguins, and the landscape of Patagonia)

SOUTH AFRICA

Cape Town, South Africa
㊼ Cape Town/Table Top Mountain
㊽ Vintage car tour to Mount Nelson Hotel for afternoon tea
Mombasa, Kenya
㊾ Tour to Tsavo National Park (Kenya's oldest game preserve)
Walvis Bay, Namibia
⑩ Moon landscape and Welwitschia Plains Tour

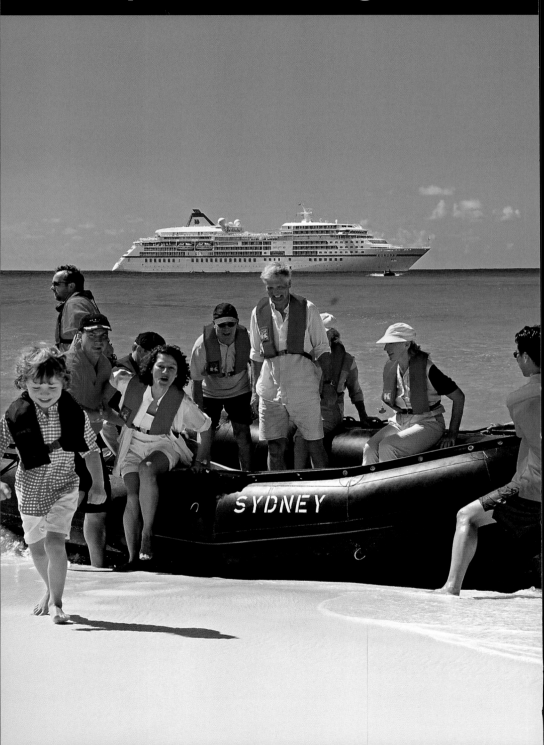

THIS YEAR'S WORLD BEATERS

Having reviewed 272 cruise ships, Berlitz names
the best performers for 2009 and explains
why they scored as highly as they did

THE WORLD'S HIGHEST RATED CRUISE SHIP

Despite constant cruise company claims that theirs has been named the "Best Cruise Line" or "Best Cruise Ship," *there really is no such thing* – only what's right for you. Most ship owners want to be a "luxury" cruise operator, and most passengers want to sail aboard one of the top-rated "luxury" ships. But few operators can really deliver a ship, product, and crew worthy of five Berlitz stars. For this 2009 edition, only one ship has achieved the score required for it to be awarded membership in this most exclusive club.

Europa   (Hapag Lloyd Cruises)   1,852 points   ★★★★★+

Why? Because there is outstanding cuisine and attentive, friendly, very attentive, yet unobtrusive personal service from a staff dedicated to working aboard the world's finest cruise ship. But it's not just the ship itself and its facilities and appointments that contribute to the ship's high rating – it's also in the extensive array of details and personal attention from a fine, dedicated crew. It all adds up to the very best cruise ship and cruise experience available today – unless you own a private motor yacht. Also, thanks to the pod propulsion system, there is absolutely no vibration anywhere.

Naturally, *Europa* is not a cheap ship, but one of the reasons for its continuing success is that the food is creatively produced using high-quality ingredients. The ship also delivers excellent itineraries, taking passengers to many ports of call off the beaten track and inaccessible to larger cruise ships. Although *Europa* is now 10 years old, it looks almost new, thanks to the dedication of its crew and owners.

THE TOP 10 LARGE RESORT SHIPS

(1,600–6,400 passengers)

Ship	Points	Rating
Queen Mary 2 (Grill Class)	1,709	★★★★★
Queen Victoria (Grill Class)	1,692	★★★★★
Celebrity Millennium	1,666	★★★★★
Celebrity Constellation	1,665	★★★★★
Celebrity Infinity	1,663	★★★★★
Celebrity Summit	1,661	★★★★★
Celebrity Century	1,615	★★★★★
Emerald Princess	1,546	★★★★
Queen Mary 2 (Britannia Class)	1,546	★★★★
Crown Princess	1,545	★★★★

THE TOP 10 MID-SIZE SHIPS

(600–1,600 passengers)

Ship	Points	Rating
Crystal Serenity	1,702	★★★★★
Crystal Symphony	1,701	★★★★★
Seven Seas Voyager	1,698	★★★★★
Seven Seas Mariner	1,695	★★★★★
Asuka II	1,685	★★★★★
Prinsendam	1,662	★★★★★
Amadea	1,600	★★★★★
Nautica	1,575	★★★★★
Insignia	1,574	★★★★★
Regatta	1,572	★★★★★

THE TOP 10 SMALL SHIPS

(200–600 passengers)

Ship	Points	Rating
Europa	1,852	★★★★★+
Silver Shadow	1,760	★★★★★
Silver Whisper	1,760	★★★★★
Silver Wind	1,669	★★★★★
Silver Cloud	1,664	★★★★★
Seven Seas Navigator	1,653	★★★★★
Royal Clipper	1,540	★★★★
Club Med 2	1,477	★★★★
Paul Gauguin	1,547	★★★★
C. Columbus	1,396	★★★★

THE TOP 10 BOUTIQUE SHIPS

(50–200 passengers)

SeaDream II	1,788	★★★★★
SeaDream I	1,786	★★★★★
Seabourn Legend	1,779	★★★★★
Seabourn Spirit	1,770	★★★★★
Seabourn Pride	1,769	★★★★★
Hanseatic	1,740	★★★★★
Sea Cloud	1,704	★★★★★
Sea Cloud II	1,703	★★★★★
Hebridean Spirit	1,697	★★★★★
Hebridean Princess	1,671	★★★★★

ABOVE: pomp and circumstance for diners aboard *Queen Mary 2*.

LEFT: shore excursion by zodiac from 2009's top-rated *Europa*.

HOW WE EVALUATE THE SHIPS

Their facilities count, of course, but just as important are the standards of food, service, staff and hospitality

I have been evaluating and rating cruise ships and the onboard product professionally since 1980. In addition, I receive regular reports from my team of five trained assessors. The ratings are conducted with *total objectivity*, from a set of predetermined criteria and a modus operandi designed to work *globally*, not just regionally, across the entire spectrum of ocean-going cruise ships today, in all segments of the marketplace.

There really is no "best cruise line in the world" or "best cruise ship" – only the ship and cruise that is right for you. After all, it's the overall enjoyment of a cruise as a vacation that's really important. Therefore, different criteria are applied to ships of different sizes, styles, and market segments throughout the world (people of different nationalities seek different things in their vacation).

This section includes 2xx oceangoing cruise ships in service (or due to enter service) and chosen by the author for inclusion when this book was completed. Almost all except the newest ships have been carefully evaluated, taking into account around 400 separate items based on personal cruises, visits and revisits to ships, as well as observations and comments from my team. These are channeled into 20 major areas, each with a possible 100 points. The maximum possible score for any ship is therefore 2,000 points.

For the sake of clarity and user-friendliness, scores are further channeled into five main sections (Ship, Accommodation, Food, Service, and Cruise Operation).

Cruise lines, ship owners, and operators should note that the ratings may be adjusted annually as a result of increased competition, the introduction of newer ships with better facilities, and other market- or passenger-driven factors.

The ratings more reflect the *standards* of the cruise product delivered to passengers (the software: dining experience, and the service and hospitality aspects of the cruise), and less the physical plant (the hardware).

Thus, although a ship may be the latest, most stunning vessel in the world in terms of design and decor, if the food, service, staff, and hospitality are not so good, the scores and ratings will reflect these aspects more clearly.

The stars beside the name of the ship at the top of each page relate directly to the Overall Rating. The highest number of stars awarded is **five stars** (★★★★★), and the lowest is one star. This system is universally recognized throughout the hospitality industry. A plus (+) indicates that a ship deserves just that little bit more than the number of stars attained. However, I must emphasize that it is the number of points achieved rather than the number of stars attained that perhaps is more meaningful to anyone comparing ships.

The star system

★★★★★+	1,851–2,000 points
★★★★★	1,701–1850 points
★★★★+	1,551–1,700 points
★★★★	1,401–1,550 points
★★★+	1,251–1,400 points
★★★	1,101–1,250 points
★★+	951–1,100 points
★★	801–950 points
★+	650–800 points
★	501–650 points

What the ratings mean

1,851–2,000 points   ★★★★★ +

You can expect an outstanding luxury cruise experience – it doesn't get any better than this. It should be truly memorable, and with the highest attention to detail, finesse, and personal service (how important you are made to feel is critical). The decor must be elegant and tasteful, measured by restraint and not flashiness, with fresh flowers and other decorative touches in abundance,

Hapag-Lloyd's *Europa* sets the standard for luxury.

Europa visits the popular island of Sylt in Germany.

and the layout of the public rooms might well follow *feng shui* principles.

Any ship with this rating must be just about unsurpassable in the cruise industry, and it has to be very, very special, with service and hospitality levels to match. There must be the very highest quality surroundings, comfort and service levels, the finest and freshest quality foods, including all breads and rolls baked on board. Highly creative menus, regional cuisine, and dining alternatives should provide maximum choice and variety, and special orders will be part of the dining ritual.

Dining room meals (particularly dinners) are expected to be grand, memorable affairs, correctly served on the finest china, with a choice of wines of suitable character and vintage available, and served in the correct-sized sommelier glasses of the highest quality (Riedel or Schott).

The service staff will take pleasure in providing you with the ultimate personal, yet unobtrusive, attention with the utmost of finesse, and the word "no" should not be in their vocabulary. This really is the very best of the best in terms of refined, unstructured living at sea, but it is seriously expensive.

1,701–1,850 points ★★★★★

You can expect a truly excellent and memorable cruise experience, with the finesse and attention to detail commensurate with the amount of money paid. The service and hospitality levels will be extremely high from all levels of officers and staff, with strong emphasis on fine hospitality training (all service personnel members *must* make you feel important).

The food will be commensurate with the high level expected from what is virtually the best possible, while the service should be very attentive yet unobtrusive. The

cuisine should be memorable, with ample taste. Special orders should never be a problem, with a creative cuisine of a very high standard. There must be a varied selection of wines, which should be served in glasses of the correct size (not simply a standard size glass for white and one for red wines).

Entertainment is expected to be of prime quality and variety. Again, the word "no" should not be in the vocabulary of any member of staff aboard a ship with this rating. A cruise aboard a ship with this high rating may well cause damage to your bank statement, particularly if you choose the most spacious grades of accommodation. Few things will cost extra once you are on board, and brochures should be more "truthful" than those for ships with a lower rating.

1,551–1,700 points ★★★★ +

You should expect to have a high-quality cruise experience that will be quite memorable, and just a little short of being excellent in all aspects. Perhaps the personal service and attention to detail could be slightly better, but, nonetheless, this should prove to be a fine all-round cruise experience, in a setting that is extremely clean and comfortable, with few lines anywhere, a caring attitude from service personnel, and a good standard of entertainment that appeals to a mainstream market. The cuisine and service will be well rounded, with mostly fresh ingredients and varied menus that should appeal to almost anyone, served on high quality china.

All in all, this should prove to be an extremely well rounded cruise experience, probably in a ship that is new or almost new. There will probably be less "extra cost" items than ships with a slightly lower rating, but you get what you pay for these days.

1,401–1,550 points ★★★★

You should expect to have a very good quality all-round cruise experience, most probably aboard a modern, highly comfortable ship that will provide a good range of facilities and services. The food and service will be quite decent overall, although decidedly not as "gourmet" and fanciful as the brochures with the always-smiling faces might have you believe.

The service on board will be well organized, although it may be a little robotic and impersonal at times, and only as good as the cruise line's training program allows. You may notice a lot of things cost extra once you are on board, although the typically vague brochure tells you that the things are "available" or are an "option." However, you should have a good time, and your bank account will be only moderately damaged.

1,251–1,400 points ★★★ +
You should expect to have a decent quality cruise experience, from a ship where the service levels should be good, but perhaps without the finesse that could be expected from a more upscale environment. The crew aboard any ship achieving this score should reflect a positive attitude with regard to hospitality, and a willingness to accommodate your needs, up to a point. Staff training will probably be in need of more attention to detail and flexibility.

Food and service levels in the dining room(s) should be reasonably good, although special or unusual orders might prove more difficult. There will probably be a number of extra-cost items you thought were included in the price of your cruise – although the brochure typically is vague and tells you that the things are "available" or are an "option."

1,101–1,250 points ★★★
You can expect a reasonably decent, middle-of-the-road cruise experience, with a moderate amount of space and quality in furnishings, fixtures, and fittings. The cabins are likely to be a little on the small side

When action matters: RCI simulates surfing.

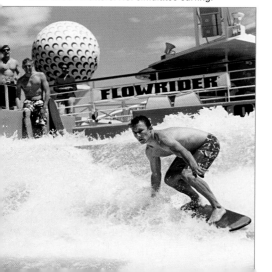

(dimensionally challenged). The food and service levels will be quite acceptable, although not at all memorable, and somewhat inflexible with regard to special orders, as almost everything is standardized.

Crew attitude could certainly be improved, the level of hospitality and cleanliness will be moderate but little more, and the entertainment provided will probably be weak. A good option, however, for those looking for the reasonable comforts of home without pretentious attitudes, and little damage to their bank statement.

951–1,100 points ★★ +
You should expect to have a cruise experience that will be average in terms of accommodation (typically with cabins that are dimensionally challenged), quality of the ship's facilities, food, wine list, service, and hospitality levels, in surroundings that are unpretentious. In particular, the food and its service will probably be disappointing.

There will be little flexibility in the levels of service, hospitality, staff training and supevision, which will be no better than poor. Thus, the overall experience will be commensurate with the small amount of money you paid for the cruise.

801–950 points ★★
You should expect to have a cruise experience of modest quality aboard a ship that is probably in need of more attention to maintenance and service levels, not to mention hospitality. The food is likely to be quite tasteless and homogenized, and of low quality, and service will leave much to be desired in terms of attitude, which will tend to be mediocre at best. Staff training is likely to be minimal, and turnover will probably be high. The "end-of-pier" entertainment could well leave you wanting to read a good book.

651–800 points ★ +
You can expect to have only the most basic cruise experience, with little or no attention to detail, from a poorly trained staff that is probably paid low wages and to whom you are just another body. The ship will, in many cases, probably be in need of much maintenance and upgrading, and will probably have few facilities.

Cleanliness and hygiene may well be questionable, and there will be absolutely no finesse in personal service levels, with poor attitude from the crew, and dismal entertainment as significant factors in the low score and rating. On the other hand, the price of a cruise is probably alluringly low.

501–650 points ★
You can expect to have a cruise experience that is the absolute bottom of the barrel, with almost nothing in terms of hospitality or finesse. You can forget about attention to detail – there won't be any. This will be the kind of experience that would equal a stay in the most

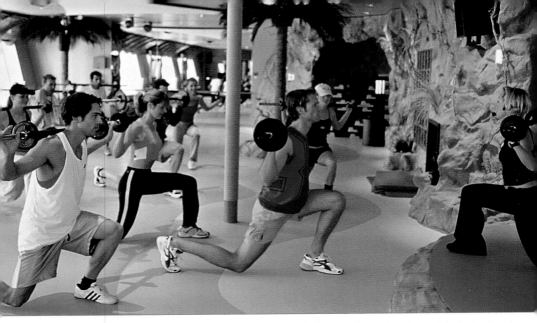

Fitness facilities have become increasingly important.

basic motel, with few facilities, a poorly trained, uncaring staff, and a ship that is in need of better maintenance and upgrading.

The low cost of a cruise aboard any cruise ship with this rating should provide a clue to the complete lack of any quality. This will be particularly true in the areas of food, service, and entertainment. In other words, this could well be a totally forgettable cruise experience.

Distribution of points

These are the percentage of the total points available which are allocated to each of the main areas evaluated:

- The Ship 25%
- Accommodation 10%
- Cuisine 20%
- Service 20%
- Entertainment 5%
- The Cruise Experience 20%

This last two categories may be combined for boutique ships, tall ships, and expedition ships.

The Ship

Hardware/Maintenance/Safety
This score reflects the general profile and condition of the ship as hardware, its age and maintenance, hull condition, exterior paint, decking and caulking, swimming pool and surrounds, deck furniture, shore tenders, lifeboats, life rafts, and other safety items. It also reflects interior cleanliness (public restrooms, elevators, floor coverings, wall coverings, stairways, passageways, and doorways), food preparation areas, refrigerators, garbage handling, compacting, and incineration, and waste disposal facilities.

Outdoor Facilities/Space
This score reflects the overall space per passenger on open decks, crowding, swimming pools/ whirlpools and their surrounds, lido deck areas, number and type of deck lounge chairs (with or without cushioned pads) and other deck furniture, outdoor sports facilities, shower enclosures and changing facilities, towels, and quiet areas (those without music).

Interior Facilities/Space/Flow
This score reflects the use of common interior public spaces, including enclosed promenades; passenger flow and points of congestion; ceiling height; lobby areas, stairways, and all passenger hallways; elevators; public restrooms and facilities; signage, lighting, air-conditioning and ventilation; and degree of comfort and density.

Decor/Furnishings/Artwork
This score reflects the overall interior decor and color scheme; hard and soft furnishings, wood (real, imitation, or veneer) paneling, carpeting (tuft density, color, and practicality), fit and finish (seams and edging), chairs (comfort, height, and support), ceilings and decor treatments, reflective surfaces, artwork (paintings, sculptures, and atrium centerpieces), and lighting.

Spa/Fitness Facilities
This score reflects any health spa, wellness center, and fitness facilities; location, accessibility and noise levels; lighting and flooring materials; fitness and muscle-training machines and other equipment; fitness programs; sports and games facilities; indoor swimming pools; whirlpools; grand baths; aqua-spa pools; saunas and steam rooms; rasul, the various types of massage (Swedish Remedial, Shiatsu, Ayurvedic, Reflexology), and other treatment rooms; changing facilities; jogging and walking tracks; and promenades.

Accommodation

Cabins: Suites and Deluxe Grades
This score reflects the design and layout of all grades of suites and deluxe grade cabins, private balconies

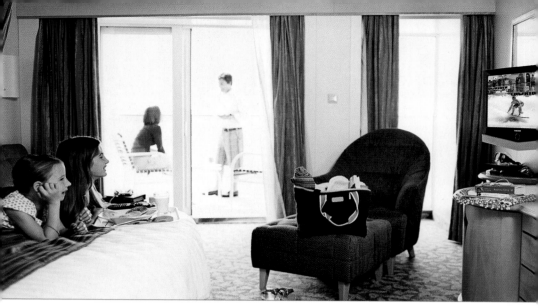

A stateroom aboard RCI's *Freedom of the Seas*.

(whether full floor-to-ceiling partition or part partitions, balcony lighting, balcony furniture). Also beds/berths, furniture (its placement and practicality), cabinetry, and other fittings; closets and other hanging space, drawer space, and bedside tables; vanity unit, bathroom facilities, washbasin, cabinets, and toiletries storage; lighting, air-conditioning, and ventilation; audiovisual facilities; quality and degree of luxury; artwork; bulkhead insulation, noise, and vibration levels. Suites should not be so designated unless the sleeping room is completely separate from the living area.

Some large resort ships now have whole decks devoted to superior grade accommodation, with a significant difference between this accommodation and that of "standard" cabins.

Also the soft furnishings and details such as the information manual (list of services); paper and postcards (including personalized stationery); telephone directory; laundry lists; tea- and coffee-making equipment; flowers (if any); fruit (if any); bathroom personal amenities kits, bathrobes, slippers, and the size, thickness, quality, and material content of towels.

Cabins: Standard Sizes

This score reflects the design and layout (whether outside or inside), beds/berths, furniture (its placement and practicality), and other fittings. Also taken into account: closets and other hanging space, drawer space, bedside tables, and vanity unit; bathroom facilities, washbasin, cabinets, and toiletries storage; lighting, air-conditioning and ventilation; audiovisual facilities; quality and degree of fittings and furnishings; artwork; bulkhead insulation, noise, and vibration levels.

In addition, we have taken into account the usefulness of the information manual (directory of services); paper and postcards (including stationery); telephone directory;

laundry lists; tea- and coffee-making equipment; flowers (if any); fruit (if any); and bathroom amenities kits, bathrobes, slippers, and the size, thickness, quality, and material content of towels.

Cuisine

Food is one of the main features of most vacations. Cruise lines put maximum emphasis on promising passengers how good their food will be, often to the point of being unable to deliver what is promised. Generally, the standard of food is good. The rule of thumb is: if you were to eat out in a good restaurant, what would you expect? Does the ship meet your expectations? Would you come back again for the food?

There are perhaps as many different tastes as there

Production shows are sometimes dated.

are passengers. The "standard" market cruise lines cater to a wide range of tastes, while the more exclusive cruise lines can offer better quality food, cooked individually to your taste. As in any good restaurant, you get what you pay for.

Dining Room/Cuisine

This score reflects the physical structure of dining rooms; window treatments; seating (alcoves and individual chairs, with or without armrests); lighting and ambience; table set-ups; the quality and condition of linen, china, and cutlery; and table centerpieces (flowers). It also reflects menus, food quality, presentation, food combinations, culinary creativity, variety, design concepts, appeal, taste, texture, palatability, freshness, color, balance, garnishes, and decorations; appetizers, soups, pastas, flambeaus, tableside cooking; fresh fruit and cakes; the wine list (and connoisseur wine list), price range, and wine service. Alternative dining venues are also checked for menu variety, food and service quality, decor, seating and noise levels.

Informal Dining/Buffets

This score reflects the hardware (including the provision of hot and cold display units, sneeze guards, "active" stations, tongs, ice containers and ladles, and serving utensils); buffet displays (which have become quite disappointing and institutionalized); presentation; trays and set-ups; correct food temperatures; food labeling; breakfast, luncheon, deck buffets, midnight buffets, and late-night snacks; decorative elements such as ice carvings; and staff attitude, service, and communication skills.

Quality of Ingredients

This score reflects the overall quality of ingredients used, including consistency and portion size; grades of meat, fish, and fowl; and the price paid by the cruise line for its food product per passenger per day. It is the quality of ingredients that most dictates the eventual presentation and quality of the finished product as well as its taste. Also included is the quality of tea and coffee (better quality ships are expected to provide more palatable tea and coffee).

Tea/Coffee/Bar Snacks

This score reflects the quality and variety of teas and coffees available (including afternoon teas/coffees and their presentation); whether mugs or cups and saucers are presented or available; whether milk is served in the correct open containers or in sealed packets; whether self-service or graciously served. The quality of such items as cakes, scones, and pastries, as well as bar/lounge snacks, hot and cold canapés, and hors d'oeuvres also forms part of this section.

Service

Dining Room

This score reflects the professionalism of the restaurant staff: the maître d'hotel, dining room managers, head section waiters, waiters and assistant waiters (busboys), and sommeliers and wine waiters. It includes place settings and correct service (serving, taking from the correct side), communication skills, attitude, flair, dress sense (uniform), and finesse. Waiters should note whether passengers are right- or left-handed and, aboard ships with assigned table places, make sure that the cutlery and glasses are placed on the side of preference. Cutlery and wine glasses are also included.

Bars

This score reflects the lighting and ambience; overall service in bars and lounges; seating, noise levels; communication skills (between bartenders and bar staff and passengers); staff attitude, personality, flair and finesse; correct use of glasses (and correct size of glasses); billing and attitude when presenting the bill (aboard those ships where a charge is made).

Cabins

This score reflects the cleaning and housekeeping staff, butlers (for penthouse and suite passengers), cabin stewards/stewardesses and their supervisory staff, attention to detail and cleanliness, in-cabin food service, linen and bathrobe changes, and language and communication skills.

Open Decks

This score reflects steward/stewardess service for beverages and food items around the open decks; service for placement and replacement of towels on deck lounge chairs, self-help towels, and emptying of used towel bins; general tidiness of all associated deck equipment; and the availability of service at nonstandard times (in the evening or early morning, for example).

Gratuities

In the Other Comments section at the end of each rating, all gratuities are usually at extra cost unless specifically included in the price. Likewise, insurance and port taxes are also at extra cost unless they are specifically stated as included.

Entertainment

Aboard specialist ships, such as those offering expedition cruises, or tall ships, where entertainment is not a feature, it is the lecture program that forms this portion of the evaluations.

The score reflects the overall entertainment program and content as designed and targeted to specific passenger demographics. The entertainment has to appeal to passengers of widely varying ages and types. Included is the physical plant (stage/ bandstand) of the main showlounge; technical support, lighting, follow spotlight operation and set/ backdrop design; sound and light systems (including laser shows); recorded click-tracks and all special effects; variety and quality of large-scale production shows (including story, plot, content, cohesion, creativeness of costumes, relevancy, quality, choreography, and vocal content); cabaret; variety shows; game shows; singers; visual acts; bands and solo musicians.

The cruise experience
Activities Program
This score reflects the variety, quality, and quantity of daytime activities and events. It includes the cruise director and staff (their visibility, availability, ability, and professionalism), sports programs, participation games, special interest programs, port and shopping lecturers, and mind-enrichment lecturers. This score also reflects the extent and quality of any water sports equipment carried), instruction programs, overall staff supervision, the marina or side-retractable water sports platforms, and any enclosed swimming area.

Movies/Television Programming
This score reflects movies screened in onboard theaters, including screen, picture and sound quality; videos screened on the in-cabin system; other televised programming, including a ship's own television station programming; content; and entertainment value. Cabin TV audio channels are included.

Hospitality Standard
This score reflects the level of hospitality of the crew and their attention to detail and personal satisfaction. It includes the professionalism of senior officers, middle management, supervisors, cruise staff, and general crew; social contact, appearance, and dress codes or uniforms; atmosphere and ambience; motivation; communication skills (most important); the general ambience and the attention to detail.

WHAT THE DESCRIPTIONS MEAN

Ship Size
● Large Resort Ship (1,600–6,000+ passengers)
● Mid-Size Ship (600–1,600 passengers)
● Small Ship (200–600 passengers)
● Boutique Ship (50–200 passengers)

Lifestyle
Designated as Standard, Premium, or Luxury, according to a general classification into which segment of the market the ship falls. This should help you choose the right size ship and cruise experience to fit your lifestyle.

● **Standard**: the least expensive, offering the basic amenities, food and service.

● **Premium**: more expensive than Standard, have generally better food, service, facilities, amenities, more attention to detail, and differentiation of suites (with butler service) and standard accommodation.

● **Luxury**: more expensive than Premium or Standard, and provide more personal comfort, space, open or one-seating dining, much better food (no processed items, more menu creativity, and everything made fresh), and highly trained staff.

The Oatmeal Factor: Luxury by Degree
The Oatmeal Factor shows how various cruise ships will provide a passenger with a basic item such as a bowl of oatmeal. The difference can be found in its presentation. In the cruise industry, there are ships that provide one of four levels of oatmeal presentation, as follows.

Standard: Hot oatmeal (supermarket brand oats) mixed with water, with little or no chance of obtaining tahini to add taste to the oatmeal. You get it from a soup tureen at the buffet, and put it into a plastic or inexpensive china bowl yourself (or it may be served in the dining room by a waiter/waitress); it is eaten with plastic or basic canteen cutlery. In other words, it's basic, basic, basic.

Premium: Hot oatmeal, water, salt and little olive oil; served in a higher quality bowl, by a waiter or waitress, with hotel-quality (or better) cutlery. It's possible that the ship will have tahini, to add taste and creaminess. It's also possible that the waiter/waitress will ask if you'd like hot or cold milk with your oatmeal. There may even be a doily between the oatmeal bowl and base plate.

Luxury: Hot oatmeal (medium or large flakes), water, salt, tahini, a little (extra virgin) olive oil and nutmeg, with a dash of blended Scotch (whisky); served in a high quality brand name bowl (Versace), with base plate and doily, and Hepp- or Robbe & Berking-quality silverware. Naturally, the waiter/waitress will ask if you'd like hot or cold milk with your oatmeal.

Incomparable: Hot Scottish (large flakes, hand ground) oatmeal, water, sea salt, tahini, and nutmeg (grated at the table), high-quality cold-pressed olive oil and a layer of rare single malt Scotch; served in small production hand-made china, with base plate and doily, and sterling silver cutlery. The waiter/waitress will ask if you'd like hot or cold milk (or anything else) with your oatmeal.

Naturally, there are variations and some crossover depending on the ship, supplies available, staff training, etc. Also, the setting and presentation play a large part in determining quality. Noise level, decor, chairs, table height, table settings, and overall comfort are all part of the total equation, and thus the evaluation process.

Cruise Line
The cruise line and the operator may be different if the company that owns the vessel does not market and operate it (tour operators often charter cruise ships for their exclusive use – Thomson Cruises is one example).

First Entered Service
Where two dates are given, the first is the ship's maiden passenger voyage when new, and the second is the date it began service for the current operator.

Pod Propulsion
The azimuthing pod propulsion system is a relatively recent high-tech installation. It replaces conventional

Overall Product Delivery

This score reflects the quality of the overall cruise as a vacation experience – what the brochure states and promises (real or implied), which reflects on the level of expectation versus the onboard product delivery of hospitality and services received.

Notes on the rating results

Cruise ship evaluations and ratings have become much more complex. Although a ship may be the newest, with all the latest high-tech facilities possible, it is the onboard food and service that often disappoints, as well as standing in lines and signing up for activities.

Cruise companies say that food quality is a trade-off against lower prices. However, this attitude only results in a downward spiral that affects food quality as well as service, quality of personnel, crew training, safety, maintenance, and other related items.

Cruise companies hope that passengers won't notice cuts in food quality and employing cheaper crew members. However, in the final analysis, it is the little things that add to points lost on the great scorecard.

The ratings are intended to help the cruise companies evaluate their product, listen to their income-generating passengers, and return some of the items and the finesse missing in the overall cruise experience, while adjusting fares to better reflect long-term growth of this good value-for-money vacation. ❏

propeller shafts, propellers and rudders, negates the need for stern thrusters, and saves valuable machinery space. The "pods" (typically two for most ships, although some ships have three, or even four pods), which resemble huge outboard motors with an externally mounted propeller, replace shaft lines, rudders and their machinery, and are compact, self-contained units powered by an internal electric propulsion motor.

The pods are turned by the hydraulic motors of the steering gear, and are capable of turning through 360 degrees (azimuthing).

Each pod typically weighs about 170 tons each (the four pods attached to *Queen Mary 2* weigh 250 tons each – more than an empty Boeing 747 jumbo jet; two are fixed, two are of the azimuthing variety). Although they are at the stern, pod units *pull*, rather than *push*, a ship through the water, thanks to their forward facing propellers, and provide greater maneuvrability.

Ships with a pod propulsion system should have no noticeable vibration or engine noise at the stern, unlike ships with conventional propulsion systems. Different manufacturers have different names for their pod systems (examples: Azipod, Mermaid).

Propulsion

The type of propulsion is given (i.e. gas turbine, diesel, diesel-electric, or steam turbine), together with the output (at 100 percent), expressed as MW (megawatts) or kW (kilowatts) generated.

Propellers

Number of propellers or azimuthing pods *(see above)*.

Passenger Capacity

The number of passengers is based on:
● Two lower beds/berths per cabin, plus all cabins for single occupancy.
● All available beds/berths filled (Note: This figure may not always be accurate, as cruise lines often make changes by adding or taking away third/fourth berths according to demand).

Passenger Space Ratio (Tons Per Passenger)

Achieved by dividing the gross tonnage by the number of passengers.

Crew to Passenger Ratio

Achieved by dividing the number of passengers by the number of crew (lower beds/all possible beds and berths filled).

Cabin Size Range

From the smallest cabin to the largest suite (including "private" balconies/verandahs), these are provided in square feet and square meters, rounded up to the nearest number.

Wheelchair-accessible Cabins

Cabins designed to accommodate passengers with limited mobility.

Dedicated Cinema/seats

A "yes" means that there is a separate cinema dedicatedly solely to showing large-screen movies throughout the day and during the evening. This is distinct from a show lounge that may be used to screen movies during the day (afternoon) and live shows in the evening. The number of seats is provided where known.

A Note About Prices

Some price examples are given throughout the ship reviews (for massage, the cover price for "alternative" restaurants, for internet access, or gratuities added to your onboard account, for example), but please note that these are provided *only* as a guideline, and may have changed since this book was completed. Always check with the cruise line, onboard concession or your travel provider for the latest prices.

KEEPING TRACK OF THE SEA CHANGES

At a time when many cruise ships are changing hands – and changing names – it's easy for regular cruisegoers to lose track. Below, we highlight some of the confusing revamps

You have fond memories of a cruise a few years ago and you are about to book a cabin aboard the same ship for your next vacation. Then you suddenly find that, although the name is the same, the ship is entirely different. Alternatively, you might find yourself aboard a ship, supposedly for the first time – but then it begins to look strangely familiar and you find you have sailed aboard this ship before when it had a different name, and probably a different owner.

Welcome to the volatile world of the cruise industry, in which ships keep changing hands, are shuffled from one company to another, or are sold for scrap – often just as the next edition of this book is going to press. That's one reason why I provide readers with updates by email *(see page 688)* and why I encourage them to invest in a new edition of the book each year. Below is a summary of just a few of the recent changes.

The name of the game

Princess Cruises' *Tahitian Princess* has changed its name to *Ocean Princess*, to reflect its wider range of itineraries. *Jules Verne* (Club Cruise) has become the new *Alexander von Humboldt* for Phoenix Reisen. And Phoenix Reisen's former *Alexander von Humboldt* is now Swan Hellenic's *Minerva*.

Pullmantur Cruises' *Holiday Dream* has been transferred to new French company CDF Croisières de France to become *Bleu de France* (sounds like a cheese), its 100% French onboard product aimed squarely at French-speaking passengers. Pullmantur Cruises will take possession of *Sovereign of the Seas* from Royal Caribbean International and will rename it *Sovereign* (now *that's* easy – they can just remove "*of the Seas*" from the ship's bows).

The New York-based Travel Dynamics International has chartered *Clelia II* (one of the 100-passenger former Renaissance Cruises ships). Carnival Cruise Lines' *Celebration* has been transferred to Spain's Iberocruceros, 75% of which is owned by the Carnival Corporation. Quark Expeditions' ex-Greenland ship *Sarpik Ittuk* now has the more mellifluous name of *Ocean Nova*.

Aegean II, operated by Golden Star Cruises, has been transferred to Louis Cruise Lines, to become *Ivory*. And Louis Cruise Lines' *Perla* has been transferred to Golden Star Cruises to become *Aegean Pearl*. *Aegean I* was sold to Gerry Herod, the owner of the former Ocean Cruise Lines, and is being totally refitted and refurbished for further service to new operators.

Meanwhile, Fred Olsen Cruise Lines' *Braemar* has just undergone a "chop and stretch" operation which saw a new 102.4-ft (31.2-meter) mid-section inserted into the ship, increasing its length by 19%. The ship gained more suites and balcony cabins, plus a new British pub, and the main restaurant was completely refurbished. Now it looks like a real stretched limo.

The new behemoth

But it's Royal Caribbean International's *Oasis of the Seas* that promises to be 2009's most newsworthy ship as, at 220,000 tons, it takes the title of the world's largest cruise ship. It will carry 5,400 passengers (two per cabin), and a maximum of 6,400 (with all beds/berths filled), so it is unlikely to be an oasis of calm.

One of its most notable aspects will be the development of the Royal Promenade concept, expanded from the *Freedom*- and *Voyager*-class ships. Aboard *Oasis of the Seas*, this rather large horizontal central area will be open to the skies – so even the seabirds can drop in. Trees and benches will be a feature of the "park," which includes dining venues, shops, an art gallery, and spaces to wander, sit, play chess, or simply look at the vegetation. Interior promenade cabins have balconies that look down into the promenade. At one end, a Rising Tide Bar will move through three floors, providing a dramatic view of the atrium, called Central. What a ship! ❑

Oasis of the Seas takes shape in Turku, Finland.

Adventure of the Seas
★★★★

Large Resort Ship:	.......137,276 tons	Passenger Decks:	14
Lifestyle:	..................Standard	Total Crew:	1,185
Cruise Line:	..........Royal Caribbean	Passengers	
	International	(lower beds/all berths):	.....3,114/3,838
Former Names:	..................none	Passenger Space Ratio	
Builder:	...Kvaerner Masa-Yards (Finland)	(lower beds/all berths):	.......44.0/35.7
Original Cost:	.............$500 million	Crew/Passenger Ratio	
Entered Service:	............Nov 2001	(lower beds/all berths):	..........2.6/3.2
Registry:	................The Bahamas	Navigation Officers:	......Scandinavian
Length (ft/m):	.............1,020.6/311.1	Cabins (total):	1,557
Beam (ft/m):	.............155.5/47.4	Size Range (sq ft/m):	.....151.0–1,358.0/
Draft (ft/m):	..................28.8/8.8		14.0–126.1
Propulsion/Propellers:	.....diesel-electric	Cabins (outside view):	939
	(75,600kW)/3 pods	Cabins (interior/no view):	618

Cabins (for one person):	0
Cabins (with private balcony):	765
Cabins (wheelchair accessible):	26
Cabin Current:	...............110 volts
Elevators:	.........14 (6 glass-enclosed)
Casino (gaming tables):	...........Yes
Slot Machines:	....................Yes
Swimming Pools (outdoors):	3
Swimming Pools (indoors):	0
Whirlpools:	6
Self-Service Launderette:	..........No
Dedicated Cinema/Seats:	..........No
Library:	.........................Yes

OVERALL SCORE: 1,477 (OUT OF A POSSIBLE 2,000 POINTS)

OVERVIEW. *Adventure of the Seas* is a large, floating, family-friendly leisure resort (sister to *Explorer of the Seas, Mariner of the Seas, Navigator of the Seas,* and *Voyager of the Seas*). The propulsion is derived from three pod units (two azimuthing, and one fixed at the centerline), powered by electric motors instead of conventional rudders and propellers, in the latest configuration of high-tech propulsion systems *(see page 174 for details).*

BERLITZ'S RATINGS		
	Possible	Achieved
Ship	500	419
Accommodation	200	150
Food	400	237
Service	400	283
Entertainment	100	83
Cruise	400	305

With large proportions, the ship provides an abundance of facilities and options, rather like a small town, yet it manages to have a healthy passenger space ratio (the amount of space per passenger). It is too large to go through the Panama Canal, thus limiting its itineraries almost exclusively to the Caribbean (where only a few islands can accept it), or for use as a floating island resort. Spend the first few hours exploring all the many facilities and public spaces aboard this vessel and it will be time well spent.

Although *Adventure of the Seas* is a large ship, the cabin hallways are warm and attractive, with artwork cabinets and wavy lines to lead you along and break up the monotony. In fact, there are plenty of colorful, even whimsical, decorative touches to avoid what could be a very clinical environment.

Embarkation and disembarkation typically take place through two access points, designed to minimize the inevitable lines (that's over 1,500 people for each access point). Once inside the ship, you'll need good walking shoes – it really is quite a long way from one end to the other.

A four-decks-high Royal Promenade is the main interior focal point; it's a good place to hang out, to meet someone, or to arrange to meet someone. The length of two football fields (American football, that is), it has two internal lobbies that rise through 11 decks. Cafés, shops, and entertainment locations front this winding street and interior "with-view" cabins look into it from above. It is an imaginative piece of design work, and those who like shopping malls enjoy it immensely.

The long super-atrium houses a "traditional" pub. There is also a Champagne Bar, a Sidewalk Café (for continental breakfast, all-day pizzas, speciality coffees, and desserts), Sprinkles (for round-the-clock ice cream and yoghurt), and a sports bar. There are also several shops – jewelry shop, gift shop, liquor shop, perfume shop, and a logo souvenir shop. Comedy art has its place here, too, for example in the *trompe l'oeil* painter climbing up the walls.

The Guest Reception and Shore Excursion counters are located at the aft end of the promenade, as is an ATM machine. Things to watch for: look up to see the large moving, asteroid-like sculpture (constantly growing and contracting). At times, street entertainers appear, and parades are staged, while at other (carefully orchestrated) times it's difficult to walk through the area as it is filled to the brim with tacky shopping items – like a cheap bazaar.

Arched across the promenade is a captain's balcony, and in the center of the promenade a stairway connects you to the deck below, where you'll find the Schooner Bar (a piano lounge that is a feature of all RCI ships) and the flashy Casino Royale. Gaming includes blackjack, Caribbean stud poker, roulette, and craps, as well as 300 slot machines.

Aft of the casino is the Aquarium Bar, while close by are some neat displays of oceanographic interest. Royal Caribbean International has teamed up with the University of Miami's Rosenstiel School of Marine and Atmospheric

Science to study the ocean and the atmosphere. A small onboard laboratory is part of the project.

There's also a regulation-size ice-skating rink (Studio B), featuring real, not fake, ice, with "bleacher" seating for up to 900, and the latest in broadcast facilities. Superb Ice Follies shows are presented here. A stunning two-deck library is open 24 hours a day. A grand $12 million was spent on permanent artwork. Drinking places include a neat Aquarium Bar, complete with 50 tons of glass and water in four large aquariums.

Other drinking places include the small and intimate Champagne Bar, Crown & Anchor Pub, and Connoisseur Club – for cigars and cognacs. Lovers of jazz might appreciate Blue Moon, an intimate room for cool music atop the ship in the Viking Crown Lounge. Golfers might enjoy the 19th Hole – a golf bar, as they play the Adventure Links.

There is a television studio with high-tech broadcast facilities, located adjacent to rooms that can be used for trade show exhibit space, with conference center seating 400 and a multi-media screening room that seats 60. High atop the ship, lovers could tie the knot in a wedding chapel in the sky, the Skylight Chapel; located on the upper level of the Viking Crown Lounge, it has wheelchair access via an electric stairlift. Outdoors, the pool and open deck areas provide a resort-like environment.

Families with children are also well catered for, as facilities for children and teenagers are quite extensive. "Aquanauts" is for 3–5 year olds; "Explorers" is for 6–8 year olds; "Voyagers" is for 9–12 year olds. Optix is a dedicated area for teenagers, including a daytime club (with several computers), soda bar, and dance floor. "Challenger's Arcade" features an array of the latest video games. Paint and Clay is an arts and crafts center for younger children. Adjacent is Adventure Beach, an area for all the family; it includes swimming pools, a water slide and game areas outdoors.

ACCOMMODATION. There is an extensive range of 22 cabin categories in four major groupings: Premium ocean-view suites and cabins, Promenade-view (interior-view) cabins, Ocean-view cabins, and Interior (no view) cabins. Many cabins are of a similar size – good for incentives groups and other large groups, and 300 have interconnecting doors – good for families. For a more detailed explanation, see entry for *Voyager of the Seas*.

CUISINE. The main dining room (total capacity 1,919) is massive, and is set on three levels, each named after a composer (Mozart, Strauss, Vivaldi). A dramatic staircase connects all three levels, and huge, fat support pillars obstruct the sight lines. All three levels have exactly the same menus.

There are also two small private wings for private groups: La Cetra and La Notte, each seating 58 persons. The dining room is totally non-smoking, there are two seatings, and tables are for four, six, eight, 10 or 12. The place settings, china and cutlery are of good quality.

Alternative Dining Options: These are for casual and informal meals, and include:

● *Café Promenade:* for continental breakfast, all-day

pizzas, pastries, desserts and specialty coffees (sadly provided in paper cups).

● *Windjammer Café:* for casual buffet-style breakfast, lunch and light dinner (except the last night of the cruise).

● *Island Grill:* (this is actually a section inside the Windjammer Cafe), for casual dinner (no reservations necessary) featuring a grill and open kitchen.

● *Portofino:* this is the ship's "upscale" (non-smoking) Euro-Italian restaurant, open for dinner only. Reservations are required, and a $6 gratuity per person is charged). The food and its presentation are better than the food in the dining room, although the restaurant is not large enough for all passengers to try even once during a cruise. Choices include: antipasti, soup, salad, pasta, main dish, dessert, cheese and coffee.

● *Johnny Rockets*, a retro 1950s all-day, all-night diner-style eatery that features hamburgers, malt shakes (at extra cost), and jukebox hits, with both indoor and outdoor seating seating (all indoor tables feature a mini-jukebox; dimes are provided for you to make your selection of vintage records), and all-singing, all-dancing waitresses that'll knock your socks off, if you can stand the high volume.

● *Sprinkles:* for round-the-clock ice cream and yoghurt.

ENTERTAINMENT. The 1,350-seat Lyric Showlounge is really a stunning room that could well be the equal of many such rooms on land. It is located at the forward end of the ship and spans the height of five decks (with only a few slim pillars and almost no disruption of sight lines from almost any seat in the house).

The ship also features an array of up-and-coming cabaret acts and late-night adults-only comedy.

Entertainment is always upbeat. There is even background music in all corridors and elevators, and constant music outdoors on the pool deck. If you want a quiet relaxing holiday, this is not the right ship for you.

SPA/FITNESS. The ShipShape health spa is reasonably large, and measures 15,000 sq. ft (1,400 sq. meters). It includes an aerobics room, fitness center (with the usual stairmasters, treadmills, stationary bikes, weight machines and free weights), treatment rooms, men's and women's sauna/ steam rooms, while another 10,000 sq. ft (930 sq. meters) is devoted to a Solarium (with magrodome sliding glass-domed roof) for relaxation after you've exercised.

There is a rock-climbing wall that's 32.8 ft high (10 meters), with five separate climbing tracks. It is located outdoors at the aft end of the funnel. You'll get a great "buzz" being 200 ft (60 meters) above the ocean while the ship is moving. Other sports facilities include a roller-blading track, a dive-and-snorkel shop, a full-size basketball court and 9-hole, par 26 golf course. A dive-and-snorkel shop provides equipment for rental, and diving classes.

● **For more extensive general information about a Royal Caribbean cruise experience, see pages 137–42, and for more detailed information about the Voyager-class ships, see *Voyager of the Seas*.**

Aegean Pearl
★★

Mid-Size Ship:...............16,710 tons	Passenger Decks:..................7	Cabins (for one person):..............9
Lifestyle: ....Standard	Total Crew:.....................334	Cabins (with private balcony):.........0
Cruise Line: ....Golden Star Cruises	Passengers	Cabins (wheelchair accessible): 0
Former Names: *Perla, Seawing, Southward*	(lower beds/all berths): 781/1,000	Cabin Current: ....110 volts
Builder: .....Cantieri Navale del Tirreno	Passenger Space Ratio	Elevators: 4
et Riuniti (Italy)	(lower beds/all berths):.......21.3/16.7	Casino (gaming tables): ....Yes
Original Cost:....................n/a	Crew/Passenger Ratio	Slot Machines: ....Yes
Entered Service: ....Nov 1971/Mar 1995	(lower beds/all berths):.........2.5/3.2	Swimming Pools (outdoors): 1
Registry: ....Cyprus	Navigation Officers: ....International	Swimming Pools (indoors): 0
Length (ft/m): 536.4/163.50	Cabins (total): 395	Whirlpools: 0
Beam (ft/m): 74.7/22.79	Size Range (sq ft/m): 89.3–255.1/8.3–23.7	Self-Service Launderette: ....No
Draft (ft/m): 21.3/6.50	Cabins (outside view): 261	Dedicated Cinema/Seats: Yes/198
Propulsion/Propellers: diesel (13,400kW)/2	Cabins (interior/no view): 134	Library: ....Yes

OVERALL SCORE: 918 (OUT OF A POSSIBLE 2,000 POINTS)

OVERVIEW. Originally built for Norwegian Cruise Lines, the ship has a clean, if dated profile, with rakish superstructure, and dual swept-back funnels. Owned by Louis Cruise Lines since 1995, it is under charter to Golden Star Cruises. The open deck and sunbathing space is very limited, and the swimming pool is small (it's just a dip pool), and there are no cushioned pads for the sunloungers.

Inside, there is a reasonable selection of comfortable public rooms with bright, fairly contemporary and upbeat decor. Perhaps the favorite is the nightclub, set high atop adjacent to the ship's forward mast. There is also a cinema with a balcony. Families with children will find lots to do, and staff is on hand to provide activities and entertainment for youngsters.

This high-density ship shows its age when compared to newer ships, but will provide a reasonably sound cruise experience for those wanting a no-frills short holiday in pleasant surroundings, at very attractive prices. Onboard drinks prices are reasonable. The onboard currency is the euro.

SUITABLE FOR: *Aegean Pearl* is best suited to younger couples, singles, and families on tight budgets who are used to package holidays and the inclusive aspects they offer.

ACCOMMODATION. There are three cabin grades (Standard, Superior and Deluxe) and several price categories. The 10 Boat Deck deluxe cabins are reasonably spacious for the size of the vessel, although the two forward-facing units overlook the mooring deck; these can be noisy, and are much smaller than the other eight suites. All suites and deluxe cabins have bathtubs.

All other outside-view and interior (no view) cabins are dimensionally challenged, yet they are basically clean and

BERLITZ'S RATINGS

	Possible	Achieved
Ship	500	192
Accommodation	200	94
Food	400	177
Service	400	200
Entertainment	100	50
Cruise	400	205

tidy, with enough closet space for a short cruise. Some cabins adjacent to the engine casing suffer from throbbing diesel engine noise.

CUISINE. The 500-seat Eldorado dining room is reasonably charming, with warm colors. There are tables for four, six, eight or 10, in two seatings. The cuisine is international in scope, but rather more like basic, no-frills fare – quantity, not quality, and definitely not memorable. Like anything, you get what you pay for. If you enjoy going out to eat well, and like being adventurous, then you might be disappointed. There is a limited wine list, but the wines are almost all quite young – typical of those found in supermarkets. Wine prices are modest, as are the prices for most alcoholic beverages.

There is a self-serve buffet for casual breakfasts and luncheons, although the selection is quite limited, and the presentation is repetitive (particularly for breakfast).

ENTERTAINMENT. The single-level Clipper Lounge is the venue for entertainment events and major social functions. The room really was designed to be a room for cabaret acts, and nothing more. The ceiling height is low (no jugglers), and sight lines are poor from many seats (too many pillars in the way). Entertainment consists mainly of low-cost production shows and second-rate cabaret acts. The ship has a main band and small musical units to provide live music for dancing and listening.

SPA/FITNESS. Although the spa and fitness facilities are small and minimal, there is a beauty salon, and a small sauna. You can, however, book a massage, an aromatherapy facial, manicure or pedicure.

AIDAaura
★★★★

Mid-size Ship:	42,289 tons
Lifestyle:	Standard
Cruise Line:	AIDA Cruises
Former Names:	none
Builder:	Aker MTW (Germany)
Original Cost:	$350 million
Entered Service:	April 2003
Registry:	Italy
Length (ft/m):	665.5/202.8
Beam (ft/m):	92.2/28.1
Draft (ft/m):	20.3/6.2
Propulsion/Propellers:	diesel-electric (27,150kW)/2
Passenger Decks:	10
Total Crew:	389
Passengers (lower beds/all berths):	1,266/1,582
Passenger Space Ratio (lower beds/all berths):	33.4/26.7
Crew/Passenger Ratio (lower beds/all berths):	3.0/3.7
Navigation Officers:	German
Cabins (total):	633
Size Range (sq ft/m):	145.3–344.4/ 13.5–32.0
Cabins (outside view):	422
Cabins (interior/no view):	211
Cabins (for one person):	0
Cabins (with private balcony):	60
Cabins (wheelchair accessible):	4
Cabin Current:	220 volts
Elevators:	6
Casino (gaming tables):	No
Slot Machines:	No
Swimming Pools (outdoors):	2
Swimming Pools (indoors):	0
Whirlpools:	5
Self-Service Launderette:	Yes
Dedicated Cinema/Seats:	No
Library:	Yes

OVERALL SCORE: 1,403

BERLITZ'S RATINGS

	Possible	Achieved
Ship	500	366
Accommodation	200	131
Food	400	276
Service	400	274
Entertainment	100	70
Cruise	400	286

Because the facilities and cruise experience offered aboard the AIDA Cruises fleet are reasonably similar, we have combined our assessment for all six ships.

OVERVIEW.

The growing fleet of ships of AIDA Cruises have a smart, contemporary profile that is quite well proportioned, each with a swept-back funnel and wedge-shaped stern. The bows display the red lips, as well as the blue eyes, of *Aïda* (from Verdi's opera, written to commemorate the opening of the Suez Canal in 1871). AIDA Cruises is part of Costa Cruises, which is itself part of the giant Carnival Corporation.

The AIDA-class ships (known as AIDA Clubships) all evolved from the first, and smallest ship, *AIDA* (over 10 years old and now named *AIDAcara*), in which the central idea was to get passengers into the public areas to participate in activities together, as in the Robinson Club concept on land. This led to "open plan" interiors and the feeling that the ship is one large space, but cleverly split into intimate rooms, although, in reality, rooms "flow" into each other at each fire zone section (a length of 157ft/48 meters).

One thing that is really noticeable aboard these ships is the fact that most of the chairs, counter stools and bar seats are really quite small, designed for thin young passengers, typically under the age of 40. There is constant high street music everywhere, so these ships are not for those wanting a "quiet escape" vacation, even though volume levels are well controlled.

AIDA Cruises has really grown up over the past few years, and no longer focuses on summer-camp style participation events. The ships have become more sophisticated, entertaining venues, and the old animateurs (somewhat like the *gentils ordinaires* of Club Med, but better) have grown up and morphed into what is now known as Club Teams. They, along with other staff, also interact with passengers throughout the ship.

About 20 nationalities are represented among the crew, who are upbeat and cheerful. Staff hospitality training is now at a high level in all departments, and AIDA Cruises has its own training schools in several countries, plus a recognized training academy in Rostock.

The company's brochure accurately describes the casual, active urban lifestyle. Sport biking is part of its youthful image, with three different levels of cycling to suit differing fitness levels. AIDA Cruises has also successfully embraced golfing, with special golf-theme packages, cruises, and golfing excursions ashore in many ports of call.

The open deck space is very tight, but sunbathing space includes some rather pleasant, reasonably quiet space above the navigation bridge. Dip pools and hot tubs, plus seating areas, are provided in a cascading, tiered setting atop the ship on the pool deck, providing a decent amount of sunbathing space. It's all designed to be in a "beach-like" environment, with splash and play areas.

There are three pricing levels – Aida Premium, Aida Vario, and Just Aida – depending on what you want to be included in your cruise vacation, plus differences in price according to the accommodation size and grade you choose, and the itinerary. Choose the basic, price-driven Just Aida package and the cruise line chooses the ship, itinerary and accommodation for you – sort of a pot luck cruise, based on or close to the dates you choose.

AIDAbella
★★★★

Large Resort Ship:	.69,200 tons
Lifestyle:	.Standard
Cruise Line:	.AIDA Cruises
Former Names:	.none
Builder:	.Meyer Werft (Germany)
Original Cost:	.$390 million
Entered Service:	.Apr 2008
Registry:	.Italy
Length (ft/m):	.826.7/252.0
Beam (ft/m):	.105.6/32.2
Draft (ft/m):	.24.6/7.5
Propulsion/Propellers:	.diesel-electric (36,000 kW)/2
Passenger Decks:	.13
Total Crew:	.646
Passengers (lower beds/all berths):	.2,050/2,500
Passenger Space Ratio (lower beds/all berths):	.33.7/27.6
Crew/Passenger Ratio (lower beds/all berths):	.3.1/3.8
Navigation Officers:	.German
Cabins (total):	.1,025
Size Range (sq ft/m):	.145.3–473.2/ 13.5–44
Cabins (outside view):	.666
Cabins (interior/no view):	.359
Cabins (for one person):	.0
Cabins (with private balcony):	.480
Cabins (wheelchair accessible):	.11
Cabin Voltage:	.110 volts
Lifts:	.10
Casino (gaming tables):	.Yes
Slot Machines:	.No
Swimming Pools (outdoors):	.3
Swimming Pools (indoors):	.0
Whirlpools:	.0
Self-Service Launderette:	.Yes
Dedicated Cinema/Seats:	.No
Library:	.Yes

The dress code is simple: casual (no ties) at all times, and there are no formal nights on board. All port taxes and gratuities are included in all packages, and, with very attractive rates, a cruise provides much better value than almost any land-based vacation. The euro is the onboard currency.

These really are family-friendly ships. Children are split into four age groups: Seepferdchen (4–6 years), Delfin (7–9), Orcas (10–12), and Teens (14–17). Each group has its own dedicated play areas. There is a diverse selection of children's and youth programs in a holiday camp atmosphere, and special Club Team members dedicated to making at all happen. Supervised by a chef, children can make their own menus for the week, and visit the galley to make cookies and other items – a novel idea more ships could adopt.

A growing fleet of ships means that AIDA Cruises can offer a wide choice of itineraries that now include the Middle East and Asia. There are some differences between the various ships, due to their size and configuration, but all share the same basic concept, with self-service eateries being the mainstay of the concept. The oldest (*AIDAcara*) was the first ship, and the company has developed subsequent ships after observing the popularity of certain areas and the flow of passengers through the public rooms, and the needs of those new to cruising.

Overall, this really is cruising for high street and urban dwellers, and for those that don't mind busy places and lines. An AIDA cruise isn't cheap, but you do get a lot of high-tech entertainment, and there's always plenty of food. Some frustration occurs when shore excursions are sold out, when lines form after shore excursion buses return to the ship and you are required to go through the slow security check – and at peak times in the self-serve restaurants, and for shore tenders.

● *AIDAcara*. The original ship, from whence the concept developed. The open deck space is tight and there's not enough restaurant seating capacity at peak times, making a cruise aboard this ship a comfortable, but slightly cramped, experience.

● *AIDAaura, AIDAvita*. These ships' layout is much the same as for *AIDAcara*, but in a slightly rearranged manner that provides more space and seating in the Markt Restaurant, and adds more seating to the balcony level of Das Theater (the showlounge).

● *AIDAbella, AIDAdiva, AIDAluna* have a small casino with blackjack, roulette and poker gaming tables and slot machines. There are many more balcony cabins, a separate sports deck (located aft), a "no music" observation lounge, art gallery. The embarkation entryway is really innovative, and has a bar, balcony, and is cheerfully painted to look like a street scene in a city such as Copenhagen (*AIDAbella*). It is totally different to the utilitarian area found aboard regular cruise ships – it's a very welcoming environment and helps to calm tempers after waiting in a line to go through the security process for embarkation or in ports of call.

SUITABLE FOR:

The ships of AIDA Cruises are for youthful German-speaking couples, singles, and particularly families seeking good value for money in a fun, upbeat party-like environment, with excellent entertainment.

OVERALL SCORE: 1,495

BERLITZ'S RATINGS

	Possible	Achieved
Ship	500	406
Accommodation	200	144
Food	400	290
Service	400	284
Entertainment	100	73
Cruise	400	298

AIDAcara
★★★★

Mid-size Ship:.	38,557 tons
Lifestyle:	Standard
Cruise Line:	AIDA Cruises
Former Names:.	*Aida*
Builder:. . . Kvaerner Masa-Yards (Finland)	
Original Cost:	DM300 million
Entered Service:	June 1996
Registry:	Italy
Length (ft/m):	634.1/193.3
Beam (ft/m):	90.5/27.6
Draft (ft/m):	19.6/6.0
Propulsion/Propellers: diesel(21,720kw)/2	
Passenger Decks:	9
Total Crew:	369
Passengers	
(lower beds/all berths):	1,180/1,339
Passenger Space Ratio	
(lower beds/all berths):	32.6/27.5
Crew/Passenger Ratio	
(lower beds/all berths):	3.1/3.7
Navigation Officers:	German
Cabins (total):	590
Size Range (sq ft/m):	145.3–376.7/
. . . .	13.5–35.0
Cabins (outside view):	390
Cabins (interior/no view):	200
Cabins (for one person):	0
Cabins (with private balcony):	48
Cabins (wheelchair accessible):	6
Cabin Current:	110 and 220 volts
Elevators:	5
Casino (gaming tables):	No
Slot Machines:	No
Swimming Pools (outdoors):	1
Swimming Pools (indoors):	0
Whirlpools:	2
Self-Service Launderette:	Yes
Dedicated Cinema/Seats:	No
Library:	Yes

OVERALL SCORE: 1,401

BERLITZ'S RATINGS

	Possible	Achieved
Ship	500	364
Accommodation	200	131
Food	400	276
Service	400	274
Entertainment	100	70
Cruise	400	286

/continued from previous page

THE SHIPS.
In all the ships, several decks of public rooms and facilities are positioned above the accommodation decks. Public rooms that have become common aboard all the ships are: Aida Bar, the main social gathering place, whose principal feature is a star-shaped bar (whose combined length per ship makes them the longest at sea).

The ships have good sport and wellness facilities, and each has a bike excursion counter, dive or golf excursion counter, golf simulator (not *AIDA-bella, AIDAluna*), shore excursion counter, library, seminar rooms, duty-free shop, Nordic Walking machines, several bars and lounges, and eateries.

ACCOMMODATION.
There are eight or nine grades of accommodation, from deluxe suites to interior (no view) cabins, depending on the ship. Accommodation ranges in size, as follows:

> *AIDAaura* (145.3–344.4 sq.ft/13.5–32 sq. meters)
> *AIDAcara* (145.3–376.7 sq. ft/13.5–35 sq. meters)
> *AIDAbella* (145.3–473.6/13.5–44 sq. meters)
> *AIDAcara* (145.3–344.4/13.5–32 sq. meters)
> *AIDAdiva* (145.3–473.6/13.5–44 sq. meters)
> *AIDAluna* (145.3–473.6/13.5–44 sq. meters)
> *AIDAvita* (145.3–344.4 sq.ft/13.5–32 sq. meters)

Contrary to maritime traditions (even-numbered cabins on the port side, odd-numbered cabins on the starboard side), cabin numbers progress numerically (example: 8201–8276 on the port side; 8101–8176 on the starboard side).

All suites and cabins have two beds (convertible to queen-sized bed). Some cabins also have two extra beds/berths for children, and some cabins have interconnecting doors (useful for families).

The decor in all accommodation grades is bright, youthful, rather minimalist, and slightly whimsical. All are accented with multi-patterned fabrics, wood-trimmed cabinetry (with nicely rounded edges) and rattan or wood-look furniture. Beds have duvets and a colorful fabric canopy that goes from the headboard to the ceiling. The windows have full pull-down blackout blinds (useful in destinations with long daylight hours). Some cabins in the ship's center (*AIDAaura, AIDAcara, AIDAvita*) may have views obstructed by lifeboats.

The bathrooms are compact, practical units; they have a shower enclosure, small washbasin, and small toilet. As in the most basic hotels and motels, only a wall-mounted body wash/shampoo dispenser is provided, so take your own conditioner, hand lotion, and other personal toiletries if you use them.

Thick 100% cotton bathrobes are provided for all grades of accommodation (*AIDAbella, AIDAdiva, AIDAluna*) and for suite-grade accommodation only (*AIDAaura, AIDAcara, AIDAvita*, although non-suite grade passengers can obtain one from the spa). Two towels are provided – a face towel and a "bath" towel, in two different colors. The "bath" towels are not very large, at 54 by 27 inches – compared to 72 by 36 inches aboard the P&O Cruises' *Ventura*, for example. Although the bathrooms do not have a hairdryer, one is located in the vanity unit in the cabin. Note that night-time turn-down service is *not* provided, and there is no cabin service after 3pm.

Large Resort Ship:	.69,200 tons
Lifestyle:	.Standard
Cruise Line:	.AIDA Cruises
Former Names:	.none
Builder:	.Meyer Werft (Germany)
Original Cost:	.$390 million
Entered Service:	.Apr 2007
Registry:	.Italy
Length (ft/m):	.826.7/252.0
Beam (ft/m):	.105.6/32.2
Draft (ft/m):	.24.6/7.5
Propulsion/Propellers:	.diesel-electric (36,000 kW)/2
Passenger Decks:	.13
Total Crew:	.646
Passengers (lower beds/all berths):	.2,050/2,500
Passenger Space Ratio (lower beds/all berths):	.33.7/27.6
Crew/Passenger Ratio (lower beds/all berths):	.3.1/3.8
Navigation Officers:	.German
Cabins (total):	.1,025
Size Range (sq ft/m):	.145.3–473.2/ 13.5–44
Cabins (outside view):	.666
Cabins (interior/no view):	.359
Cabins (for one person):	.0
Cabins (with private balcony):	.480
Cabins (wheelchair accessible):	.11
Cabin Voltage:	.110 volts
Lifts:	.10
Casino (gaming tables):	.Yes
Slot Machines:	.No
Swimming Pools (outdoors):	.3
Swimming Pools (indoors):	.0
Whirlpools:	.0
Self-Service Launderette:	.Yes
Dedicated Cinema/Seats:	.No
Library:	.Yes

Cabins with balconies have a sliding door that is easy to open and does not impinge on balcony space; a small drinks table and two small, light chairs are provided. Note that balconies on the lowest deck can be overlooked by anyone occupying a balcony on the decks above. Balcony cabins aboard AID-Abella, AIDAdiva, AIDAluna) have a hammock as standard, although it only accommodates just one (thin) person. Some cabins (forward on Deck 5 – Nos 5103, 5104, 5105, 5106, 5203, 5204, 5206) aboard these ships have cabins with an outside view (well, outside light), but they are totally obstructed by steel bulkheads that form the front section of the ship.

Naturally, suite-grade accommodation offers more space, including more drawer and storage space, better quality furniture and furnishings (as one would expect), a larger lounge area and a slightly larger bathroom with a tub – and, of course, a larger balcony (those at the front and stern of the ship have the best).

CUISINE.

Principal restaurants:

Aboard AIDAaura, AIDAcara and AIDAvita two standard (included) eateries are the self-serve Markt and Karibik restaurants, plus Rossini – a fine à la carte (extra charge) tablecloth dining spot that serves high-quality meals cooked à la minute, and has friendly waiter service.

Aboard the larger AIDAbella, AIDAdiva and AIDAluna there are three self-serve eateries: Markt (Market), Bella Vista, and Weite Welt (Wide World) restaurants plus a Buffalo Steakhouse (for excellent steaks), Rossini, a Sushi Bar, and a Pizzeria. The restaurants are open at set times only (there are no 24 hours a day outlets, because there is no demand), although in the evening, the Pizzeria is typically open until midnight.

Beverage stations are open only during restaurant opening hours, unless you go to the extra-cost coffee bar. Aboard AIDAbella, AIDAdiva and AIDAluna there are also some vending machines for out-of-hours snacks.

The meal concept is simple: main meals are taken when you want them in one of the large self-serve buffet-style restaurants, with open seating at tables (of four, six or eight) where cutlery is provided hanging in a rack (but there are no soup spoons, only dessert spoons). Beer is available at the push of a button or a pull of the tap, and table wine is typically provided in carafes set on each table for lunch and dinner. It's all very casual and easy-going.

The standard of food at the self-serve buffet islands ranges from adequate to very good, with creative displays and presentation, and table-clearing service that is sometimes efficient, sometimes not.

The many food islands and active stations cut down on the waiting time for food, as is common aboard most other cruise ships of a similar size. There is always a big selection of breads, cheeses, cold cuts, fruits and make-your-own teas – with a choice of more than 30 types of loose-leaf regular and herbal teas – and coffee.

A wide range of food, comprising more than 1,200 items, is offered. The fish section of AIDAbella, AIDAdiva, AIDAluna has its own fish smoking unit (which resembles a wine cabinet).

In addition, one à la carte option is available in all the ship: the "Rossini Restaurant", with waiter and sommelier service.

OVERALL SCORE: 1,494

BERLITZ'S RATINGS

	Possible	Achieved
Ship	500	406
Accommodation	200	144
Food	400	290
Service	400	284
Entertainment	100	73
Cruise	400	297

AIDAluna
NOT YET RATED

Large Resort Ship:	69,200 tons
Lifestyle:	Standard
Cruise Line:	AIDA Cruises
Former Names:	none
Builder:	Meyer Werft (Germany)
Original Cost:	$390 million
Entered Service:	Apr 2009
Registry:	Italy
Length (ft/m):	826.7/252.0
Beam (ft/m):	105.6/32.2
Draft (ft/m):	24.6/7.5
Propulsion/Propellers:	diesel-electric (36,000 kW)/2
Passenger Decks:	13
Total Crew:	646
Passengers	
(lower beds/all berths):	2,050/2,500
Passenger Space Ratio	
(lower beds/all berths):	33.7/27.6
Crew/Passenger Ratio	
(lower beds/all berths):	3.1/3.8
Navigation Officers:	German
Cabins (total):	1,025
Size Range (sq ft/m):	145.3 –473.2/13.5–44
Cabins (outside view):	666
Cabins (interior/no view):	359
Cabins (for one person):	0
Cabins (with private balcony):	480
Cabins (wheelchair accessible):	11
Cabin Voltage:	110 volts
Lifts:	10
Casino (gaming tables):	Yes
Slot Machines:	No
Swimming Pools (outdoors):	3
Swimming Pools (indoors):	0
Whirlpools:	0
Self-Service Launderette:	Yes
Dedicated Cinema/Seats:	No
Library:	Yes

OVERALL SCORE: NYR

BERLITZ'S RATINGS

	Possible	Achieved
Ship	500	NYR
Accommodation	200	NYR
Food	400	NYR
Service	400	NYR
Entertainment	100	NYR
Cruise	400	NYR

/continued from previous page

You can sit where you want, when you want, and with whom you want, so eating is a socially interactive occasion (in fact it's hard to be a couple and have a table for only two). However, at peak times, the venues may remind you of roadside cafés (albeit elegant ones), with all their attendant noise. Because of the large buffet rooms and self-serve dining concept, the crew to passenger ratio looks poor; but this is because there are no waiters as such (except in the à la carte venues), only staff for clearing tables.

Alternative (Extra Cost) Dining:
The **Rossini Restaurant** (à la carte), with mostly high-back seats, has an intimate atmosphere. It is open for dinner only, and has a set five- or six-course menu (plus daily specials). There is no cover charge, but an extra charge applies to everything on the à la carte menu (such as caviar, chateaubriand, rib-eye steak), and for wines. Reservations are needed. Tablecloths are provided, and the food is excellent.

Buffalo Steakhouse (*AIDAbella, AIDAdiva, AIDAluna*) has an open "display" kitchen, and features various steak cuts and sizes (Delmonico, New York Strip Loin, Porterhouse and Filet, plus bison steaks), and roast lamb rack. There is also a daily special – a prize-fix meal (example: a 180 kg filet steak, house salad, and dessert). It's just like going out to eat in a decent restaurant ashore – but there are no tablecloths. Wine is extra.

Sushi Bar (*AIDAbella, AIDAdiva, AIDAluna*). The 12-seater sushi counter is for Japanese-style sushi and sashimi dishes. While the counter provides stool seating, two low-slung tables with well-type seating are difficult to sit at and get up from (notice to females: wearing a short skirt is not advisable). The sushi is "commercial" and uninspiring, but it's typical of what you'd expect in a sushi bar not run by Japanese sushi masters. While the presentation is appetizing, the actual fare is mediocre and light on taste.

Vinotheque. The wine bar, located in front of the Weide Welt (Wide World) Restaurant, has a good list of premium wines, and Davidoff cigars (although you can't smoke them at the bar – or indeed anywhere inside the ship).

Pizzeria provides ever popular – and overcooked – pizzas

ENTERTAINMENT.
The Theater, the main venue for all shows and most cabaret, is two decks high aboard *AIDAaura, AIDAcara, AIDAvita*. It has a raised stage, and amphitheater-style bench seating on all levels. The benches have back rests, and are quite comfortable, and sight lines are good from most seats, with the exception of port and starboard balcony sections, where sight lines are interrupted by thick safety railings.

Aboard *AIDAbella, AIDAdiva, AIDAluna* the Theater (called a Theatrium) is in the center of the ship, is open to the main foyer and other public areas, on three levels (Decks 9, 10, 11), and topped by a glass dome. It has amphitheater-style seating on three decks (the bench seating on the two upper levels has back supports, but not on the lower level), plus standing tables, although sight lines to the raised thrust stage area are less than good from many seats.

Also, the layout means that people constantly walk through the area, distracting you from what's on the stage. For the performers, it's a bit like being in a TV studio, and trying to perform in front of the cameras, but with the audience in a different location. It doesn't really work well (passengers can watch the rehearsals), but, hey, this is really all about an active/interactive lifestyle, and it's a fresh way of presenting professional entertainment.

The shows are produced by AIDA Cruises' in-house department in a joint venture with SeeLive (Hamburg's Schmidt's Tivoli Theater), and typically consist of 12 performers. All vocals in the shows are performed live, to pre-recorded backing tracks that provide a mix of recorded live music and synthesized sound. The shows are trendy, upbeat, fun, and very entertaining. The whole entertainment experience is lively and fun – in fact, it's a little like going to the circus.

In addition, there is a live band in the Aida Bar, the only room with a large dance floor (except for the disco).

SPA/FITNESS.

The Wellness spas, fitness and sports programming are among the most extensive in the cruise industry. Several types of massage and body pampering treatments are offered. Examples of prices: Swedish Massage, €69 for 50 minutes; Shiatsu Massage, €79 for 50 minutes; Hot Stone Massage, €119 for 90 minutes.

"Sport Bikes" (mountain bikes with tough front and rear suspension units) are provided for conducted biking excursions in each port of call, a concession run by of Austrian downhill champion skier Erwin Resch. You can book biking, diving, and golfing excursions.

● *AIDAaura, AIDAcara, AIDAvita:*
The Body and Soul Spa, is located forward on Deck 11. It measures 11,840 sq. ft (1,100 sq. meters), and contains two saunas (one dry, one wet, both with seats for more than 20 persons, and glass walls that look onto the deck), massage and other treatment rooms, and a large lounging area. There are also showers, and two whole "ice walls" to use when you come out of the saunas (simply lean into the ice wall for maximum effect). Forward and outside the wellness center, is an FKK (FreiKoerperKultur) nude sunbathing deck, on two levels. A beauty and hair salon is located just behind the balcony level of the showlounge (*AIDAcara*).

● *AIDAbella, AIDAdiva, AIDAluna:*
The Body and Soul wellness/oasis area is located on two decks (connected by a stairway), and encompasses some 2,300 sq. meters (24,757 sq. ft). There is also an open air wellness deck for (FKK) relaxation/nude sunbathing in an area atop the ship forward of the ship's mast. In keeping with the times, all the trendy treatments are featured in an appealing contemporary setting. Each ship has a different design decor theme (*AIDAbella* is Africa, *AIDAdiva* is the Tropics, while *AIDAluna* is India).

There are saunas and steam rooms, and 14 rooms for massage and other treatments (most named after places associated with the design theme), neat showers, funky changing rooms and a tropical garden with real (waxed) palm trees and relaxation loungers.

Sporting types can play golf in the electronic simulator, or billiards, or volleyball, or squash, or go jogging.

Mid-size Ship:	42,289 tons
Lifestyle:	Standard
Cruise Line:	AIDA Cruises
Former Names:	none
Builder:	Aker MTW (Germany)
Original Cost:	$350 million
Entered Service:	Apr 2002
Registry:	Italy
Length (ft/m):	666.5/202.85
Beam (ft/m):	92.2/28.1
Draft (ft/m):	20.7/6.3
Propulsion/Propellers:	diesel-electric/2
Passenger Decks:	10
Total Crew:	389
Passengers	
(lower beds/all berths):	1,266/1,582
Passenger Space Ratio	
(lower beds/all berths):	33.4/26.7
Crew/Passenger Ratio	
(lower beds/all berths):	3.0/3.7
Navigation Officers:	German
Cabins (total):	633
Size Range (sq ft/m):	145.3–344.4/ 13.5–32.0
Cabins (outside view):	422
Cabins (interior/no view):	211
Cabins (for one person):	0
Cabins (with private balcony):	60
Cabins (wheelchair accessible):	4
Cabin Current:	220 volts
Elevators:	6
Casino (gaming tables):	No
Slot Machines:	No
Swimming Pools (outdoors):	2
Swimming Pools (indoors):	0
Whirlpools:	5
Self-Service Launderette:	Yes
Dedicated Cinema/Seats:	No
Library:	Yes

OVERALL SCORE: 1,402

BERLITZ'S RATINGS

	Possible	Achieved
Ship	500	366
Accommodation	200	131
Food	400	276
Service	400	274
Entertainment	100	70
Cruise	400	285

Albatros
★★★

Mid-Size Ship: . . . . .28,078 tons	Passenger Decks: 8	Cabins (for one person): 0
Lifestyle: . . . . .Standard	Total Crew: 340	Cabins (with private balcony): 9
Cruise Line: . . . . .Phoenix Reisen	Passengers	Cabins (wheelchair accessible): 0
Former Names: . . . . . .*Crown, Norwegian*	(lower beds/all berths): 884/1,100	Cabin Current: . . . . .110 and 220 volts
Star I, Royal Odyssey, Royal Viking Sea	Passenger Space Ratio	Elevators: 5
Builder: . . . . .Wartsila (Finland)	(lower beds/all berths): 31.7/25.5	Casino (gaming tables): . . . . .Yes
Original Cost: . . . .$22.5 million	Crew/Passenger Ratio	Slot Machines: . . . . .Yes
Entered Service: . . . . .Nov 1973/Apr 2004	(lower beds/all berths): 2.6/3.2	Swimming Pools (outdoors): 1
Registry: . . . . .The Bahamas	Navigation Officers: . . . . .European	Swimming Pools (indoors): 0
Length (ft/m): 674.2/205.50	Cabins (total): .442	Whirlpools: 3
Beam (ft/m): 82.0/25.00	Size Range (sq ft/m): 123.7– 679.2/	Self-Service Launderette: . . . . .No
Draft (ft/m): 23.9/7.30	11.8–63.1	Dedicated Cinema/Seats: Yes/156
Propulsion/Propellers: . . . . .diesel	Cabins (outside view): 380	Library: . . . . .Yes
(13,400 kW)/2	Cabins (interior/no view): 57	

OVERALL SCORE: 1,269 (OUT OF A POSSIBLE 2,000 POINTS)

OVERVIEW. *Albatros* was built for long-distance cruising for the long-defunct Royal Viking Line and is now under long-term charter to Germany's Phoenix Reisen. It was refurbished in 2004 prior to replacing Phoenix Reisen's much loved but outdated *Albatros*. There is plenty of open deck and sunbathing space, although the popular aft swimming pool can become crowded.

The ship has a wide array of public rooms, including many lounges and bars, most of which are quite elegant and have high, indented ceilings. The Observation Lounge is a particularly pleasant place. Wide stairways and foyers give a sense of space, even when the ship is full.

Phoenix Reisen offers extensive destination-intensive itineraries. Friendly staff help with shore excursions and onboard activities. There is a very informal atmosphere aboard, and a relaxed, casual dress code.

Albatros performs well in most sea conditions, and the onboard product is very good value for money. Where passengers are required to fly to join their cruises, the airline most used by Phoenix Reisen is LTU. The onboard currency is the euro. A 7% gratuity is added to bar accounts.

SUITABLE FOR: *Albatros* is best suited to older German-speaking adults and families who seek a low-budget value-for-money vacation in fairly contemporary surroundings rather than in a brand new cruise ship.

ACCOMMODATION. There are more than 20 price grades, from expansive suites with private balcony to standard outside-view cabins and small interior (no view) cabins. A Captain's Suite is located at the front, directly under the navigation

BERLITZ'S RATINGS	Possible	Achieved
Ship	500	332
Accommodation	200	133
Food	400	225
Service	400	240
Entertainment	100	61
Cruise	400	278

bridge, with fine forward-facing views. Nine other Penthouse Suites include a private balcony (with separate bedroom and living area). Most other cabins have an outside view and are quite well appointed, and there is a good amount of storage space; however, some bathrooms in the lower categories have awkward access. All cabins have a TV, bathrobe, and personal safe. Suites and "comfort cabins" also have a minibar.

Occupants of eight (mostly suite) accommodation grades receive Phoenix VIP service.

CUISINE. Two dining rooms (Mowe and Pelikan) have high ceilings, and are quite spacious. Dining is in one seating, at assigned tables for two, four, six or eight. Breakfast and luncheon can be taken in the dining room or outdoors in a self-service buffet by the swimming pool. Mid-morning bouillon is a Phoenix seagoing tradition, as is a Captain's Dinner (formal night), and Buffet Magnifique.

The service, by mainly Filipino waiters, is friendly and attentive, although there is little finesse. Table wines are included for lunch and dinner, although the quality is not good. Slightly better quality wines can be purchased.

The food itself is best described as "down home" simple. Casual eateries include a pizzeria at the (aft) pool bar.

ENTERTAINMENT. The large Pacific Lounge seats about 500, but thick pillars obstruct some sightlines. The entertainment consists of small-scale production shows presented by a small team of resident singers/dancers, and cabaret acts.

SPA/FITNESS. There's a gymnasium and sauna, two steam rooms, body treatment rooms, and a beauty salon.

Alexander von Humboldt
★★★

Small Ship:	15,343 tons	Passenger Decks:	7	Cabins (for one person):	0

Small Ship: ....15,343 tons	Passenger Decks: 7	Cabins (for one person): 0
Lifestyle: ....Standard	Total Crew: 240	Cabins (with private balcony): 10
Cruise Line: ....Phoenix Reisen	Passengers	Cabins (wheelchair accessible): 0
Former Names: ....*Jules Verne, Walrus,*	(lower beds/all berths): 508/560	Cabin Voltage: ....110 volts
Crown Monarch	Passenger Space Ratio	Lifts: 4
Builder: ....Union de Levante (Spain)	(lower beds/all berths): 30.2/27.3	Casino (gaming tables): ....Yes
Original Cost: ....$95 million	Crew/Passenger Ratio	Slot Machines: ....Yes
Entered Service: ....Dec 1990/May 2008	(lower beds/all berths): 2.3/2.6	Swimming Pools (outdoors): 1
Registry: ....The Bahamas	Navigation Officers: ....European	Swimming Pools (indoors): 0
Length (ft/m): 494.4/150.72	Cabins (total): 254	Whirlpools: 2
Beam (ft/m): 67.6/20.62	Size Range (sq ft/m):139.9–398,2/13.0–37	Self-Service Launderette: ....No
Draft: 18.7/5.7	Cabins (outside view): 225	Dedicated Cinema/Seats: ....No
Propulsion/Propellers: ....diesel	Cabins (interior/no view): 30	Library: ....Yes

BERLITZ'S OVERALL SCORE: 1,248 (OUT OF A POSSIBLE 2,000 POINTS)

OVERVIEW. Bought and refurbished by the Dutch company Club Cruise, *Alexander von Humboldt* serves the German-speaking market under charter to Phoenix Reisen until 2015. Its profile is decent and balanced, though angular, and it has a squat, swept-back funnel. The "swimming pool" is really a dip pool, but it is flanked by two hot tubs, although there is little open deck space. There's more sunbathing space on the deck above. The Passenger Space Ratio is quite good for the ship's size. The ship carries several zodiac inflatable craft for shore landings and explorations.

Most public rooms are located on one deck. The focal point of the social life is the elegant Harry's Bar – a high-ceilinged lifestyle lounge/bar, off to one side of which is the Jules Verne library/card playing area, but the library is poor.

In typical Phoenix style, it's an almost all-inclusive product and excellent value-for-money, particularly because the food and service are really good for the price. Although wine is included for lunch and dinner, bar and other personal drinks are not. There should be enough space per passenger, because Phoenix keeps the capacity to 470. Most of the hotel service crew is Filipino. The onboard currency is the euro, and all gratuities are included. Those who want a little extra can buy silver and gold packages.

SUITABLE FOR: The ship is best suited to adult German-speaking couples and singles seeking soft-adventure and enrichment-style cruising in a small ship environment.

ACCOMMODATION. There are 18 cabin price grades – a lot for this small ship. Aft of the bridge are 10 fairly spacious suites, each with a private balcony. The sleeping area, which includes a small sofa and drinks table, and ample drawer space, can be curtained off from the lounge area, which includes a mini-

BERLITZ'S RATINGS

	Possible	Achieved
Ship	500	315
Accommodation	200	128
Food	400	232
Service	400	243
Entertainment	n/a	n/a
Cruise	500	330

fridge. There are two balcony doors (one each from the bedroom and the lounge). The small bathrooms have a Jacuzzi tub/shower combination.

The standard cabins have all the basics, including twin beds that convert to a double, a small vanity desk and small chair, and flat-screen television. Bathrooms have a shower enclosure, toilet, and washbasin. However, there is not much drawer space, and the soundproofing between cabins could be better. Many cabins close to the engine casing are noisy. Cabins on the lowest decks have portholes, while those on upper decks have windows.

CUISINE. The 280-seat Fier Jahreszeiten (Four Seasons Restaurant) is quite attractive, with a slightly raised center section. Seating is at tables for two, four, six, or eight. It's an open, one seating arrangement. Table wines are included for lunch and dinner. Alternatively, casual, serve-yourself buffet-style meals (including dinner) can be taken in the Veranda indoor-outdoor eatery, although in the indoor section, windows have views obstructed by lifeboats and other safety equipment. In warm weather conditions, the seating at tables outdoors will prove very popular.

ENTERTAINMENT. The Music Lounge seats around 300 in banquette-style seating, and has decent sightlines to the wooden dance floor/stage, except for seats that are located behind the substantial support columns. A discotheque/late night spot is located adjacent to the fitness centre.

SPA/FITNESS. A wellness center is located aft of the discotheque on the uppermost deck overlooking the stern, while a beauty salon is located several decks below, as is a small unisex sauna and relaxation area.

Amadea
★★★★ +

Mid-Size Ship: . . . . .28,856 tons	Total Crew: 292	Cabins (with private balcony): 108
Lifestyle: . . . . .Standard	Passengers	Cabins (wheelchair accessible): 2
Cruise Line: . . . . .Phoenix Reisen	(lower beds/all berths): 606/624	Cabin Current: . . . . .110 volts
Former Names: . . . . .Asuka	Passenger Space Ratio	Elevators: 5
Builder: . .Mitsubishi Heavy Industries (Japan)	(lower beds/all berths): 48.0/46.6	Casino (gaming tables): . . . . .No
Original Cost: . . . .$150 million	Crew/Passenger Ratio	Slot Machines: .No
Entered Service: . . . . . .Dec 1991/Mar 2006	(lower beds/all berths): 2.3/2.3	Swimming Pools (outdoors): 1
Registry: . . . . .The Bahamas	Navigation Officers: . . . . .European	Swimming Pools (indoors): 0
Length (ft/m): 632.5/192.81	Cabins (total): 303	Whirlpools: 3
Beam (ft/m): 81.0/24.70	Size Range (sq ft/m): 182.9–649.0/	Self-Service Launderette: . . . . .Yes
Draft (ft/m): 21.6/6.6	17.0–60.3	Dedicated Cinema/Seats: Yes/97
Propulsion/Propellers: . . . . .diesel	Cabins (outside view): 300	Library: . . . . .Yes
(17,300kW)/2	Cabins (interior/no view): 3	
Passenger Decks: 8	Cabins (for one person): 0	

BERLITZ'S OVERALL SCORE: 1,600 (OUT OF A POSSIBLE 2,000 POINTS)

OVERVIEW. When introduced in 1991 as *Asuka*, it was the first all-new large ship specially designed for the domestic market, and the largest cruise ship built in Japan for the local market. The ship was sold to Phoenix Reisen in 2005 and started cruising for German-speaking passengers in March 2006.

The ship, which is a more upscale vessel compared to the other ships in the Phoenix Reisen fleet, has pleasing exterior styling and a contemporary profile, with a large, rounded, but squat funnel. There is a generous amount of open deck and sunbathing space, plus a wide walk-around teakwood promenade deck outdoors, good for strolling.

The "cake-layer" stacking of the public rooms hampers passenger flow and makes it somewhat disjointed, although passengers will like the separation of public rooms from the accommodation areas. There are many intimate public rooms, plenty of space and lots of light. So, because the ship absorbs people well, so there is never a feeling of crowding.

The interior decor is understated but elegant, with pleasing color combinations, quality fabrics and fine soft furnishings. Some fascinating Japanese artwork is featured, including a four-deck-high mural located on the wall of the main foyer staircase by Noriko Tamura, called "Song of the Seasons".

Harry's Bar is a bar and lounge decorated in the style of a contemporary gentleman's club with wood paneled walls, burgundy leather chairs, and a bar. This popular drinking spot has a light, airy feel.

As for the dress code, there is a mix of formal and informal nights, while during the day the dress code is very

BERLITZ'S RATINGS		
	Possible	Achieved
Ship	500	398
Accommodation	200	160
Food	400	336
Service	400	327
Entertainment	100	77
Cruise	400	302

casual. In case you want to do your own laundry, there is a self-service launderette, which has 8 washing machines (useful for long voyages). The ship provides an extremely comfortable and serene environment in which to cruise.

The onboard currency is the euro, and all gratuities are included.

SUITABLE FOR: *Amadea* is best suited to German-speaking couples, single travelers and families with children, who enjoy cruising in very comfortable surroundings aboard a contemporary ship.

ACCOMMODATION. There are several price categories, although in reality there are just five types of suites and cabins. Three decks (8, 9 and 10) have suites and cabins with a private balcony (note that the floor is laid with green simulated turf, and there is no outside light). No matter what grade you choose, all suites and cabins have ocean views, although some are slightly obstructed by the ship's gangway, when it is in the raised (stowed) position; there are no interior (no view) cabins.

In all grades, cherry wood cabinetry (which is in beautiful condition) has nicely rounded edges. Cabin soundproofing is excellent, and there is a good amount of closet and drawer space (including lockable drawers), refrigerator, and personal safe.

All grades have bathrooms with full, deep bathtubs (while the suite bathrooms are of generous proportions, the "standard" bathrooms are practical but small), and all have a tiled floor and bath/shower area.

Two suites provide the largest accommodation (one is decorated in blue, the other in salmon); these are larger versions of the "A" grade cabins. Each has a separate bedroom, with walk-in closet that includes a luggage deck, and twin beds that convert to a queen-sized bed), sofa, two chairs and coffee table, large vanity desk, plenty of drawer space, and large color TV set. The marble-clad bathroom is large and has a whirlpool bathtub set alongside large ocean-view windows overlooking the private balcony, and twin washbasins set in a marble surround; a living room, and separate guest bathroom. The private balcony is quite large and has a tall tropical plant set in a glass display enclosure.

The top grade cabins are excellent living spaces, and have twice the size and space of the standard cabins. They are very nicely decorated and outfitted, and have twin beds (convertible to a queen-sized bed), sofa, two chairs and coffee table, large vanity desk, plenty of drawer space, and large color television. However, when in its twin bed configuration, the room's *feng shui* is poor, as one of the beds is facing a large mirror at the writing/vanity desk – a negative. Many cabins have a private balcony (with full floor-to-ceiling partition and a green synthetic turf floor (but no outside light) with floor-to-ceiling sliding door (the door handles are awkward).

There's also an illuminated walk-in closet (with long hanging rail and plenty of drawer space). The bathrooms are partly tiled and of generous proportions, and include a glass-fronted (plastic) toiletries cabinet, and two washbasins set in a thick marble surround.

CUISINE. There are two principal restaurants (Four Seasons and Amadea); both are non-smoking and both operate an open-seating basis for all meals. The Four Seasons Restaurant has two sections; there are ocean-view windows along one side of the aft section, and along two sides of the forward section. The (newly constructed) Amadea Restaurant is located on a higher deck, with ocean view windows on two sides. The cuisine is the same in both venues.

For casual breakfasts and lunches, an informal self-serve Lido Café is provided, with plenty of outdoor seating adjacent to a small pool and hot tub.

With this ship, Phoenix Reisen has taken its cuisine and service to a much higher level in relation to that served aboard the company's other ships, by spending more money per passenger per day (this is also reflected in the cruise fare).

ENTERTAINMENT. The Atlantic Lounge is the venue for most entertainment events, including shows, social functions, and lectures. The room spans two decks, with seating on both main and balcony levels, and an extra-large wooden dance floor is provided for social dancing.

SPA/FITNESS. There is a spacious wellness center. It has large ocean-view windows, two baths, one hot tub, a sauna, steam room with wood floor and wood ceiling; there are several shower enclosures, plus a changing area with vanity counter. Two massage rooms, however, are in a different location, although they are on the same deck.

LATITUDE AND LONGITUDE

Latitude signifies the distance north or south of the equator, while **longitude** signifies distance east or west of the 0 degree at Greenwich Observatory in London ("where time begins"). Both are recorded in degrees, minutes, and seconds. At the equator, one minute of longitude is equal to one nautical mile, but as the meridians converge after leaving the equator and meeting at the poles, the size of a degree becomes smaller. It was in 1714 that an Act of Parliament established a Board of Commissioners for the Discovery of Longitude at Sea. A prize of £20,000, then a huge sum, was set. The English clockmaker John Harrison (1693–1776) won it for his highly accurate chronometer. Indeed, none other than Captain Cook used a Harrison-designed chronometer on one of his voyages to the Pacific in 1775.

American Eagle
★ ★

Boutique Ship: . . . . .1,287 tons	Total Crew: 22	Cabins (for one person): 5
Lifestyle: . . . . .Standard	Passengers	Cabins (with private balcony): 6
Cruise Line: . . . . . .American Cruise Lines	(lower beds/all berths): 49/49	Cabins (wheelchair accessible): 2
Former Names: . . . . .none	Passenger Space Ratio	Cabin Current: . . . . .110 volts
Builder: . .Chesapeake Shipbuilding (USA)	(lower beds/all berths): 26.2/26.2	Elevators: 1
Original Cost: . . . . .n/a	Crew/Passenger Ratio	Casino (gaming tables): . . . . .No
Entered Service: . . . . .Apr 2000	(lower beds/all berths): 2.2/2.2	Slot Machines: .No
Registry: . . . . .USA	Navigation Officers: . . . . .American	Swimming Pools (outdoors): 0
Length (ft/m): 174.0/53.00	Cabins (total): .27	Swimming Pools (indoors): 0
Beam (ft/m): 40.5/12.30	Size Range (sq ft/m): 176.0–382.0/	Whirlpools: 0
Draft (ft/m): 6.5/1.98	16.3–35.4	Self-Service Launderette: . . . . .No
Propulsion/Propellers: diesel/2	Cabins (outside view): 27	Dedicated Cinema/Seats: . . . . .No
Passenger Decks: 4	Cabins (interior/no view): 0	Library: . . . . .No

OVERALL SCORE: 830 (OUT OF A POSSIBLE 2,000 POINTS)

OVERVIEW. American Cruise Lines is the resurrection of a company with the same name that existed between 1974 and 1989. It now features intra-coastal waterway cruising, as well as sailings in New England and the Hudson River Valley. *American Eagle* was built specifically for coastal cruising and cannot venture far into open seas away from the coastline (a sister vessel is planned, with more balcony cabins). The ship's uppermost deck is open (good for scenery observation), and there are tables and chairs, a few sunloungers, and a small putting green.

There are just two public lounges. The larger – the observation lounge – is located forward, with windows on three sides (an open bar is set up each afternoon). This is the main meeting place for passengers. A second, smaller lounge is sandwiched between cabins on the same deck.

The whole point of a cruise aboard this ship is to get close to the inland areas, cities and town of America's intra-coastal waterways and coastline. There's no waiting in line – you can board whenever you want. The ship docks in the center, or within walking distance of most towns on the itineraries. The dress code is "no ties casual".

It really is *extremely* expensive for what you get, compared even to ships of a similar size and purpose (although this is a new ship and the cabins are of a larger size and are slightly better equipped). There is an elevator, but it doesn't go to the uppermost deck (Sun Deck). The limited choice of food is very disappointing.

SUITABLE FOR: *American Eagle* is best suited to couples and single travelers sharing a cabin who are of mature years and want to cruise in an all-American environment aboard

BERLITZ'S RATINGS

	Possible	Achieved
Ship	500	249
Accommodation	200	110
Food	400	199
Service	400	170
Entertainment	n/a	n/a
Cruise	500	102

a small ship where the itineraries and destinations are more important than food, service or entertainment.

ACCOMMODATION. There are cabins for couples and singles, six suites, and two wheelchair-accessible cabins. All cabins have twin beds, color TV, a small desk with chair, and clothes hanging space. The six suites also have a VCR and compact disc (audio) player. All cabins have a private bathroom with separate shower enclosure, washbasin and toilet (none of the cabins has a bathtub), as well as windows that open.

CUISINE. The dining salon has large, panoramic picture windows on three of its sides. It has open seating (no assigned tables). There are no tables for two, and the chairs do not have armrests. The cuisine is very much American fare – good and wholesome, featuring regional cuisines, and presented and served in a basic, unfussy manner. Note that there is little choice of entrées, appetizers, or soups, although it has been improved in the past year. There is no wine list, although basic white and red low-quality American table wines are included in the cruise fare. On the last morning of each cruise, only continental breakfast is available.

ENTERTAINMENT. There is no formal entertainment, although dinner and after-dinner conversation with fellow passengers in the ship's lounge/bar really becomes the entertainment each evening.

SPA/FITNESS. There are no health spa facilities. Also, there are no medical facilities (but then the vessel is always close to land).

American Glory
★★

Boutique Ship:	.1,287 tons	Total Crew:	.22	Cabins (for one person):	.5
Lifestyle:	.Standard	Passengers		Cabins (with private balcony):	.14
Cruise Line:	.American Cruise Lines	(lower beds/all berths):	.49/49	Cabins (wheelchair accessible):	.3
Former Names:	.none	Passenger Space Ratio		Cabin Current:	.110 volts
Builder:	.Chesapeake Shipbuilding (USA)	(lower beds/all berths):	.26.2/26.2	Elevators:	.1
Original Cost:	.n/a	Crew/Passenger Ratio		Casino (gaming tables):	.No
Entered Service:	.July 2002	(lower beds/all berths):	2.2/2.2	Slot Machines:	.No
Registry:	.USA	Navigation Officers:	.American	Swimming Pools (outdoors):	.0
Length (ft/m):	.174.0/53.00	Cabins (total):	.27	Swimming Pools (indoors):	.0
Beam (ft/m):	.40.5/12.30	Size Range (sq ft/m):	.176.0–382.0/	Whirlpools:	.0
Draft (ft/m):	.6.5/1.98		16.3–35.4	Self-Service Launderette:	.No
Propulsion/Propellers:	.diesel/2	Cabins (outside view):	.27	Dedicated Cinema/Seats:	.No
Passenger Decks:	.4	Cabins (interior/no view):	.0	Library:	.No

OVERALL SCORE: 835 (OUT OF A POSSIBLE 2,000 POINTS)

OVERVIEW. American Cruise Lines is the resurrection of a company with the same name that existed between 1974 and 1989. It now features intra-coastal waterway cruising, as well as sailings in New England and the Hudson River Valley. *American Glory* was built specifically for coastal cruising and cannot venture far from the coastline. The ship's uppermost deck is open (good for views), and there are tables and chairs, a few sunloungers, and a small putting green.

There are two public lounges. The main one – the observation lounge – is located forward, with windows on three sides (an open bar is set up each afternoon). A second, smaller lounge is sandwiched between cabins on the same deck.

The point is to get close to the inland areas, cities and town of America's intra-coastal waterways and coastline. There's no waiting in line – you can board whenever you want. The ship docks in the center, or within walking distance of most towns on the itineraries. The dress code is "no ties casual". The score is marginally better than for sister ship *American Eagle* due to some improvements in construction and the addition of more balcony cabins.

It really is *extremely* expensive for what you get, compared even to ships of a similar size and purpose (although this is a new ship and the cabins are of a better size and are slightly better equipped). There is an elevator, which goes to all decks.

SUITABLE FOR: *American Glory* is best suited to couples and single travelers sharing a cabin who are of mature years and want to cruise in an all-American environment aboard a small ship where the itineraries and destinations are more important than food, service or entertainment.

BERLITZ'S RATINGS

	Possible	Achieved
Ship	500	257
Accommodation	200	110
Food	400	196
Service	400	170
Entertainment	n/a	n/a
Cruise	500	102

ACCOMMODATION. There are cabins for couples and singles, seven suites, and five wheelchair-accessible cabins. All cabins have twin beds (which can be converted to a king-size bed), color TV, a small desk with chair, and clothes hanging space. The seven most expensive cabins also have a VCR and compact disc (audio) player. All cabins have a private bathroom with separate shower enclosure, washbasin and toilet (none of the cabins has a bathtub), as well as windows that open. Accommodation designated as suites also have a private balcony; although this is narrow, it does have two chairs and a small drinks table.

CUISINE. The dining salon, located in the latter third of the vessel, has large, panoramic picture windows on three of its sides. There's open seating (no assigned tables). There are no tables for two, and the chairs do not have armrests The food is very much American fare – good and wholesome, featuring regional cuisines.

There is little choice of entrées, appetizers, or soups, although it has been improved in the past year. There is no wine list, although basic white and red low-quality American table wines are included. On the last morning of each cruise, only continental breakfast is available.

ENTERTAINMENT. There is no formal entertainment, although dinner and after-dinner conversation with fellow passengers in the ship's lounge/bar really becomes the entertainment each evening. Otherwise, take a good book.

SPA/FITNESS. There are no health spa facilities, and no medical facilities (the ship is almost always close to land).

American Spirit
★★

Boutique Ship: . . . . .99 tons	Total Crew: 27	Cabins (for one person): 5
Lifestyle: . . . . .Standard	Passengers	Cabins (with private balcony): 23
Cruise Line: . . . . . .American Cruise Lines	(lower beds/all berths): 92/92	Cabins (wheelchair accessible): 1
Former Names: . . . . .none	Passenger Space Ratio	Cabin Current: . . . . .110 volts
Builder: . .Chesapeake Shipbuilding (USA)	(lower beds/all berths): 1.0/1.0	Elevators: 1
Original Cost: .n/a	Crew/Passenger Ratio	Casino (gaming tables): . . . . .No
Entered Service: . . . . .June 2005	(lower beds/all berths): 3.4/3.4	Slot Machines: .No
Registry: . . . . .USA	Navigation Officers: . . . . .American	Swimming Pools (outdoors): 0
Length (ft/m): 220.0/67.0	Cabins (total): .51	Swimming Pools (indoors): 0
Beam (ft/m): 46.0/14.0	Size Range (sq ft/m): 204.0-240.0/	Whirlpools: 0
Draft (ft/m): 8.2/2.5	18.9-22.2	Self-Service Launderette: . . . . .No
Propulsion/Propellers: diesel/2	Cabins (outside view): 51	Dedicated Cinema/Seats: . . . . .No
Passenger Decks: 4	Cabins (interior/no view): 0	Library: . . . . .Yes

---

BERLITZ'S OVERALL SCORE: 922 (OUT OF A POSSIBLE 2,000 POINTS)

OVERVIEW. *American Spirit* is the third vessel in the growing fleet of American Cruise Lines (which builds the vessels in its shipyard in Chesapeake, Maryland). It is the resurrection of a company with the same name that existed between 1974 and 1989. The company features intra-coastal waterway cruising, as well as sailings in New England and the Hudson River Valley. *American Spirit* is built specifically for coastal cruising and cannot venture far from the coastline. Its uppermost deck is open (good for views) behind the forward windbreaker, and the expansive open deck sports many sun-loungers, and a small putting green.

Inside, the public rooms include an observation lounge, with views forward and to port and starboard side (complimentary cocktails and hors d'oeuvres are offered before dinner); a library/lounge; a small midships lounge; and an elevator that goes to all decks.

Cruises are typically of seven days' duration. There's no waiting in line – you can board whenever you want. The ship docks in the center, or within walking distance of most towns on the itineraries. The dress code is "no ties casual". It really is extremely expensive for what you get (although this is a new ship and the cabins are of a better size and are slightly better equipped than those of smaller half-sisters *American Eagle* and *American Glory*). A sister ship, *American Star*, is entered service in June 2007.

SUITABLE FOR: *American Spirit* is best suited to couples and single travelers sharing a cabin who are of mature years and want to cruise in an all-American environment aboard a small ship where the itineraries and destinations are more important than food, service or entertainment.

BERLITZ'S RATINGS

	Possible	Achieved
Ship	500	287
Accommodation	200	125
Food	400	210
Service	400	175
Entertainment	n/a	n/a
Cruise	500	125

ACCOMMODATION. There are five cabin price grades (four are doubles, one is for singles). All cabins have twin beds (convertible to a king-size bed), a small desk with chair, color TV, and clothes hanging space. The seven most expensive cabins also have a DVD and CD player. All cabins have a private (modular) bathroom with separate shower enclosure, washbasin and toilet (none has a tub), plus windows that open, and satellite-feed TV sets. Accommodation designated as suites also have a private balcony; although this is narrow, it has two chairs and a small drinks table. Some 23 cabins have a French balcony (you can open the door for fresh air, but it's too narrow to place chairs on).

CUISINE. The dining salon, in the latter third of the vessel, has large, panoramic picture windows on three of its sides. There's open seating (no assigned tables) and all passengers dine at a single seating, at large tables, allowing you to get to know your fellow passengers. The food is very much American fare – good and wholesome, with regional cuisines. There is a limited choice of entrées, appetizers, and soups. There is no wine list, although basic white and red low-quality US table wines are included. On the last morning of each cruise, only continental breakfast is available.

ENTERTAINMENT. There is no formal entertainment, although dinner and after-dinner conversation with fellow passengers in the ship's lounge/bar really becomes the entertainment each evening. Otherwise, take a good book.

SPA/FITNESS. There is a small fitness room with a few bicycles and other exercise machines.

American Star
★★

Boutique Ship: . . . . .99 tons	Total Crew: 27	Cabins (for one person): 5
Lifestyle: . . . . .Standard	Passengers	Cabins (with private balcony): 23
Cruise Line: . . . . .American Cruise Lines	(lower beds/all berths): 94/100	Cabins (wheelchair accessible): 1
Former Names: . . . . .none	Passenger Space Ratio	Cabin Current: . . . . .110 volts
Builder: . .Chesapeake Shipbuilding (USA)	(lower beds/all berths): 1.0/0.9	Elevators: 1
Original Cost: . . . . .n/a	Crew/Passenger Ratio	Casino (gaming tables): . . . . .No
Entered Service: . . . . .June 2007	(lower beds/all berths): 3.4/3.4	Slot Machines: .No
Registry: . . . . .USA	Navigation Officers: . . . . .American	Swimming Pools (outdoors): 0
Length (ft/m): 220.0/67.0	Cabins (total): .52	Swimming Pools (indoors): 0
Beam (ft/m): 46.0/14.0	Size Range (sq ft/m): 204.0-240.0/	Whirlpools: 0
Draft (ft/m): 8.2/2.5	18.9-22.2	Self-Service Launderette: . . . . .No
Propulsion/Propellers: diesel/2	Cabins (outside view): 51	Dedicated Cinema/Seats: . . . . .No
Passenger Decks: 4	Cabins (interior/no view): 0	Library: . . . . .Yes

BERLITZ'S OVERALL SCORE: 925 (OUT OF A POSSIBLE 2,000 POINTS)

OVERVIEW. *American Star* is the fourth vessel in the growing fleet of American Cruise Lines (which builds the ships in its own shipyard in Chesapeake, Maryland), and the company's best vessel by far. The company features intra-coastal waterway cruising, as well as sailings in New England and the Hudson River Valley. *American Star* is built specifically for coastal and inland cruising to destinations unreachable by large cruise ships, in a relaxed, unregimented environment. The uppermost deck is open (good for views) behind a forward windbreaker; many sunloungers are provided, as is a small golf putting green.

The public rooms include an observation lounge, with views forward and to port and starboard side (complimentary cocktails and hors d'oeuvres are offered before dinner); a library/lounge; a small midships lounge, and an elevator that goes to all decks (including the outdoor sun deck).

Cruises are typically of 7–14 days' duration. The ship docks in the center, or within walking distance of most towns and ports. The dress code is "no ties casual." It is extremely expensive for what you get – although this is a new ship and the cabins are larger and slightly better equipped than those of smaller half-sisters *American Eagle* and *American Glory*. There are no additional costs, except for gratuities and port charges, because it's all included (quite different to big-ship cruising).

SUITABLE FOR: Couples and single travelers of mature years sharing a cabin and wishing to cruise in an all-American environment aboard a small ship where the destinations are more important than food, service or entertainment.

BERLITZ'S RATINGS

	Possible	Achieved
Ship	500	287
Accommodation	200	125
Food	400	210
Service	400	178
Entertainment	n/a	n/a
Cruise	500	125

ACCOMMODATION. There are five cabin price grades (four are doubles, one is for singles). All cabins have twin beds (convertible to a king-size bed), a small desk with chair, flat-screen TV set, DVD player and internet access, and clothes hanging space. All cabins have internet access, a private (modular) bathroom with separate shower enclosure, washbasin and toilet (no cabin has a bathtub), windows that open, and satellite-feed television sets. Accommodation incorrectly designated as suites (23) also have a private balcony; although narrow, it does have two chairs and a small drinks table.

CUISINE. The dining salon, in the latter third of the vessel, has large, panoramic picture windows on three of its sides. All passengers dine at a single (open) seating – there are no assigned tables – at large tables, so you can get to know your fellow passengers. The cuisine is American: simple, honest food featuring regional specialties. The choice of entrées, appetizers, and soups is limited, however. There is no wine list, although basic white and red American table wines are included. On the last morning of each cruise, only continental breakfast is available.

ENTERTAINMENT. There is no formal entertainment, although dinner and after-dinner conversation with fellow passengers in the ship's lounge/bar really becomes the entertainment each evening. Otherwise, take a good book.

SPA/FITNESS. There is a tiny fitness room with a few bicycles and other exercise machines.

Amsterdam
★★★★

Mid-size Ship: . . . . .61,000 tons	Passenger Decks: 12	Cabins (for one person): 0
Lifestyle: . . . . .Premium	Total Crew: 600	Cabins (with private balcony): 172
Cruise Line: . . . . . . .Holland America Line	Passengers	Cabins (wheelchair accessible): 20
Former Names: . . . . .none	(lower beds/all berths): 1,380/1,653	Cabin Current: . . . . .110 and 220 volts
Builder: . . . . .Fincantieri (Italy)	Passenger Space Ratio	Elevators: 12
Original Cost: . . . .$400 million	(lower beds/all berths): 44.2/36.9	Casino (gaming tables): . . . . .Yes
Entered Service: . . . . .Oct 2000	Crew/Passenger	Slot Machines: . . . . .Yes
Registry: . . . . .The Netherlands	Ratio (lower beds/all berths): 2.3/2.7	Swimming Pools (outdoors): 1
Length (ft/m): 780.8/238.00	Navigation Officers: . . . . .Dutch	Swimming Pools (indoors): 1
Beam (ft/m): 105.8/32.25	Cabins (total): 690	(magrodome cover)
Draft (ft/m): 25.5/7.80	Size Range (sq ft/m): 184.0–1,124.8/	Whirlpools: 2
Propulsion/Propellers: . . . . .diesel-electric	17.1–104.5	Self-Service Launderette: . . . . .Yes
(37,500 kW)/2 azimuthing pods	Cabins (outside view): 557	Dedicated Cinema/Seats: Yes/235
(15.5 MW each)	Cabins (interior/no view): 133	Library: . . . . .Yes

OVERALL SCORE: 1,537 (OUT OF A POSSIBLE 2,000 POINTS)

OVERVIEW. *Amsterdam*, a close sister ship to *Rotterdam*, has a nicely raked bow, as well as the familiar interior flow and design style. It was the first ship in the Holland America Line fleet to feature an azimuthing pod propulsion system *(see page 174 for details)*. The pods are powered by a diesel-electric system.

The decor retains much of the traditional ocean liner detailing so loved by frequent Holland America Line passengers, with some use of medium and dark wood panelling. However, some color combinations – particularly for the chairs and soft furnishings – are rather wacky. Much of the artwork reflects Holland America Line's glorious past, as well as items depicting the city of Amsterdam's history.

The interior focal point is a three-deck high atrium, in an oval, instead of circular, shape. A whimsical "Astrolobe" is the featured centerpiece in this atrium. Also clustered in the atrium lobby are the reception desk, shore excursion desk, photo shop and photo gallery.

The ship has three principal passenger stairways – so much better than two from the viewpoint of safety, flow and accessibility. There is a magrodome-covered pool on the Lido Deck between the mast and the twin funnels, watched over by a sculpture of a brown bear catching salmon.

There are children's and teens' play areas (token gestures by a company that traditionally does not cater well to children). Popcorn is available at the Wajang Theater for moviegoers, while adjacent is the popular Java Cafe. The casino, in the middle of a major passenger flow on one of the entertainment decks, has blackjack, roulette, poker and dice tables alongside the requisite rows of slot machines. *Amsterdam* is an extremely comfortable ship, with some

BERLITZ'S RATINGS

	Possible	Achieved
Ship	500	430
Accommodation	200	165
Food	400	281
Service	400	273
Entertainment	100	78
Cruise	400	310

fine, elegant and luxurious decorative features. However, these are marred by the poor quality of food and service and the lack of understanding of what it takes to make a "luxury" cruise experience, despite what is touted in the company's brochures.

Holland America Line also provides cappuccino and espresso coffees and free ice cream during certain hours of the day aboard its ships, as well as hot hors d'oeuvres in all bars – something other major lines seem to have dropped, or charge extra for.

The onboard currency is the US dollar. Perhaps the ship's best asset is its friendly and personable Filipino and Indonesian crew, although communication can prove frustrating at times.

With one whole deck of suites (and a dedicated, private concierge lounge, with preferential passenger treatment), the company has in effect created a two-class ship. The charge to use the washing machines and dryers in the self-service launderette is petty and irritating, particularly for the occupants of high-priced cabins. Communication (in English) with many of the staff, particularly in the dining room and informal buffet areas, can prove frustrating. The room service menu is limited, and room service is very basic.

ACCOMMODATION. This is spread over five decks (some cabins have full or partially obstructed views), and is in 16 grades: 11 with outside views, and 5 interior grades (no view). There are four penthouse suites, and 50 suites (14 more than aboard sister ship *Rotterdam*). No cabin is more than 130 feet (40 meters) from a stairway, which makes it very easy to find your way from your cabin to the public rooms. Although 81% of cabins have outside views, only 25% of those have balconies.

All of the "standard" interior and outside-view cabins are tastefully furnished, and have twin beds that convert to a queen-sized bed (but the space is a little tight for walking between beds and the vanity unit). There is a decent amount of closet and drawer space, although this will prove tight for longer voyages. The fully tiled bathrooms are disappointingly small (particularly on long cruises), the shower tubs are very small, and the storage for one's personal toiletries is quite basic. There is little detailing to distinguish the bathrooms from those aboard the *Statendam*-class ships. All cabin televisions carry CNN and TNT, as well as movies, and ship information and shopping channels.

There are 50 Verandah Suites and four Penthouse Suites on Navigation Deck. The suites all share a private Concierge Lounge with a concierge to handle such things as special dining arrangements, shore excursions and special requests, although strangely there are no butlers for these suites, as aboard ships with similar facilities. The lounge, with its wood detailing and private library is accessible only by private key-card.

Four Penthouse Suites are extremely civilized. Each has a separate steward's entrance, as well as a separate bedroom with king-sized bed, vanity desk, large walk-in closet with excellent drawer and hanging space, living room, dining room (seating up to eight), wet bar, and pantry. The bathroom is large, and has a big oval Jacuzzi bathtub, separate shower enclosure, two washbasins, separate toilet and bidet. There is also a guest bathroom with toilet and washbasin. There is a good-sized private balcony. Suite occupants get personal stationary, complimentary laundry and ironing, cocktail-hour hors d'oeuvres and other goodies, as well as priority embarkation and disembarkation.

CUISINE. The La Fontaine Dining Room seats 747, spans two decks, and has a huge stained-glass ceiling measuring almost 1,500 sq. ft (140 sq. meters), with a floral motif and fibre-optic lighting. There are tables for two, four, six or eight (there are few tables for two). Both open seating and fixed (assigned tables and times) seating are available, while breakfast and lunch are open-seating (you'll be seated by restaurant staff when you enter). Rosenthal china and fine cutlery are provided. The dining room is a non-smoking venue.

Alternative (Reservations Required) Dining Spot
The 88-seat Pinnacle Grill is available to all passengers on a reservation-only basis (priority reservations are given to those in suite grades). There is an extra charge for dining here ($10 for lunch, $20 for dinner), but there's better food and presentation than in the main dining room (it's open for lunch and dinner). The whimsically surreal artwork features scenic landscapes. The cuisine is California-Italian in style, with small portions and few vegetables. The wine list is good (and wines are served in the correct stemware).

Another alternative, the Lido Buffet Restaurant, is open for casual dinners on all except the last night of each cruise, in an open-seating arrangement. Tables are set with crisp linens, flatware and standard stemware. A set menu is featured, and this includes a choice of four entrées.

For casual breakfasts and lunches, the Lido Buffet Restaurant provides old-style, stand-in-line serve-yourself canteen food – adequate for anyone used to TV dinner food, but most definitely not as lavish as the brochures claim. Although the salad items appear adequate when displayed, they are too cold and quite devoid of taste. The constant supply of iceberg lettuce doesn't seem to go away (but there is little choice of other, more suitable, lettuces and greens).

ENTERTAINMENT. The 577-seat Queen's Lounge is the venue for all production shows, strong cabaret, and other entertainment. It is two decks high (with main and balcony level seating). The stage has hydraulic lifts and three video screens, and closed-loop system for the hearing-impaired.

While Holland America Line is not known for its fine entertainment (the budgets aren't high enough), what the line does offer is a consistently good, tried and tested array of cabaret acts. The production shows, while a good attempt, fall short on storyline, choreography and performance, with colorful costuming and lighting hiding the weak spots.

A number of bands, a string ensemble and solo musicians present live music for dancing and listening in many of the lounges and bars. There's dancing in the Crows Nest (atop the navigation bridge), and serenading string music in the Explorer's Lounge, among other venues.

SPA/FITNESS. The Ocean Spa is located one deck above the navigation bridge at the very forward part of the ship. It includes a gymnasium (with all the latest muscle-pumping exercise machines, including an abundance of treadmills) with forward views over the ship's bows, an aerobics exercise area, large beauty salon with ocean-view windows to the port side, several treatment rooms, and men's and women's saunas, steam rooms and changing areas.

The spa is operated by Steiner, a specialist concession, whose young staff will try to sell you Steiner's own-brand Elemis beauty products. Some fitness classes are free, while some, such as yoga, and kick-boxing, cost $10 per class. Massage facials, pedicures, and beauty salon treatments cost extra (massage, for example, costs about $2 per minute, plus gratuity).

For the sports-minded, two paddle-tennis courts are located at the aft of the Sports Deck.

● **For more extensive general information about a Holland America Line cruise, see pages 126–28.**

Andrea
★★

Boutique Ship: . . . . .2,632 tons	Total Crew: 48	Cabins (with private balcony): 0
Lifestyle: . . . . .Standard	Passengers	Cabins (wheelchair accessible): 1
Cruise Line: . . . . .Elegant Cruises & Tours	(lower beds/all berths): 107/110	Cabin Current: . . . . .220 volts
Former Names: . . . .*Harald Jarl*	Passenger Space Ratio	Elevators: 1
Builder: . . . . . .Trondheims Mek (Norway)	(lower beds/all berths): 24.5/23.9	Casino (gaming tables): 0
Original Cost: .n/a	Crew/Passenger Ratio	Slot Machines: 0
Entered Service: 1960/2003	(lower beds/all berths): 1.8/1.9	Swimming Pools (outdoors): 0
Registry: .Liberia	Navigation Officers: . . . . .European	Swimming Pools (indoors): 0
Length (ft/m): 286.0/87.4	Cabins (total): 57	Whirlpools: 0
Beam (ft/m): 43.6/13.2	Size Range (sq ft/m): .66.0-236.8/6.1-22.0	Self-Service Launderette: 0
Draft (ft/m): 15.5/4.7	Cabins (outside view): 52	Dedicated Cinema/Seats: 0
Propulsion/Propellers: diesel/2	Cabins (interior/no view): 5	Library: . . . . .Yes)
Passenger Decks: 5	Cabins (for one person): 4	

BERLITZ'S OVERALL SCORE: 927 (OUT OF A POSSIBLE 2,000 POINTS)

OVERVIEW. This small ship (formerly operated as one of the Norwegian Coastal Voyages fleet) was extensively refurbished solely for cruise activities in 2003. It has a deep blue hull with white superstructure. During the winter the ship operates cruises in the Antarctic Peninsula (and Amazon regions), and in the summer in the Baltic and Mediterranean regions. The ship, which has a good amount of outdoors space (including a forward viewing and observation platform), carries a small fleet of Zodiac inflatable shore boats, but does not have stabilizers.

The tasteful interior decor follows the 18th-century Gustavian (Swedish) style. There is an observation area (Cormorant Lounge), an aft-facing lounge (Kittiwake Lounge, which incorporates a small library, and two internet computer stations), used also for recaps and lectures. Smoking is permitted only on open decks. Gratuities are suggested at $10–$12 per person, per day, and are divided among all crew members. The onboard currency is the US dollar.

SUITABLE FOR: *Andrea* is best suited to couples and single travelers of mature years who enjoy nature and wildlife at close range, and who would not dream of cruising in the mainstream sense aboard ships with large numbers of people. This is for the hardy, adventurous types who don't need constant entertainment or mind-numbing parlor games.

ACCOMMODATION. There are nine accommodation price

BERLITZ'S RATINGS

	Possible	Achieved
Ship	500	221
Accommodation	200	108
Food	400	196
Service	400	209
Entertainment	n/a	n/a
Cruise	500	193

grades, from two owner's suites to standard (small) interior (no-view) cabins, spread across five decks. Note that passengers occupying cabins on the lowest deck have portholes that are closed during poor weather conditions (example: Drake Passage crossings).

The Owner's Suites are located at the front, directly under the navigation bridge, with forward-facing views.

Most cabins have twin beds (13 cabins have beds connected to make a double bed); most cabins have tiny bathrooms with showers (some suites have a bathtub). All suites/cabins have satellite television and telephone, hairdryer, personal safe (personal amenities include shampoo, conditioner, and body lotion), and underbed space for luggage.

CUISINE. The Shearwater Restaurant operates one seating, but the chairs do not have armrests. The food is tasty and well presented, and there is a good variety. Casual eats can be taken in the aft-facing open-deck Northern Lights Café.

ENTERTAINMENT. There is no formal entertainment, but recaps of the day's experiences and after dinner conversation are all that's needed.

SPA/FITNESS. A small fitness center has only a limited amount of equipment (treadmills, bicycles and free weights), and an adjacent massage therapy room.

Aquamarine
★★ +

Mid-Sized Ship: .... 23,149 tons	Passenger Decks: 7
Lifestyle: .... Standard	Total Crew: 432
Cruise Line: .... Louis Cruise Lines	Passengers
Former Names: .... *Arielle, Aquamarine,*	(lower beds/all berths): 1,050/1,158
Carousel, Nordic Prince	Passenger Space Ratio
Builder: .... Wartsila (Finland)	(lower beds/all berths): 22.0/19.9
Original Cost: .... $13.5 million	Crew/Passenger Ratio
Entered Service: ... July 1971/May 2008	(lower beds/all berths): 2.4/2.6
Registry: .... Cyprus	Navigation Officers: ...... International
Length (ft/m): 6357.34/1934.6530	Cabins (total): 525
Beam (ft/m): 78.8/24.03	Size Range (sq ft/m): 119.4–482.2/
Draft (ft/m): 21.9/6.70	11.1–44.8
Propulsion/Propellers: .... diesel	Cabins (outside view): 339
(13,400kW)/2	Cabins (interior/no view): 186

Cabins (for one person): 0
Cabins (with private balcony): 0
Cabins (wheelchair accessible): 0
Cabin Current: .... 110/220 volts
Elevators: 4
Casino (gaming tables): .... Yes
Slot Machines: .... Yes
Swimming Pools (outdoors): 1
Swimming Pools (indoors): 0
Whirlpools: 0
Self-Service Launderette: .... No
Dedicated Cinema/Seats: .... No
Library: .... Yes

BERLITZ'S OVERALL SCORE: 1,084 (OUT OF A POSSIBLE 2,000 POINTS)

OVERVIEW. *Aquamarine* was originally built for Royal Caribbean International and, as *Nordic Prince,* underwent a "shop and stretch" operation in 1980 that added a mid-section. It began its present life with Louis Cruise Lines in 2005, and in April 2006 operated a two-year charter to Transocean Tours.

There is a polished walk-around promenade deck outdoors and wooden railings. The open deck space for sunbathing is limited and noisy when the ship is full. The interior layout and passenger flow is sound, with rather dated and tired 1970s decor, including some wood paneling and bright metal accenting. But note that the accommodation deck hallways are extremely narrow and poorly lit. The major public rooms – showlounge, restaurant, buffet restaurant, card room/library and small casino – are conveniently located on one deck – the horizontal flow making it easy to find your way around.

The onboard currency is the euro, and all gratuities to staff are included in the fare. There are many children aboard during peak holiday periods, and under-17s cruise free (when in the same cabin as two adults), although children's facilities are extremely limited.

Aquamarine is all about no-frills destination-intensive cruising, with the ship essentially a floating hotel.

SUITABLE FOR: *Aquamarine* is best suited to younger couples, singles, and young families who are used to package holidays and tight budgets. Good for a first cruise, in reasonably comfortable, but almost basic surroundings, with a fair array of facilities plus low cost food and entertainment.

ACCOMMODATION. The cabins are divided into several price

BERLITZ'S RATINGS

	Possible	Achieved
Ship	500	258
Accommodation	200	104
Food	400	221
Service	400	241
Entertainment	100	48
Cruise	400	212

categories. Most are extremely small, and soundproofing between them is poor, but do remember that this ship will soon be 40 years old. The cabins also have mediocre closet and storage space, although all have a small TV (larger in accommodation designated as suites), radio, personal safe, and telephone. Many cabins have pull-down upper berths (good, but tight, for families with children). The bathrooms are tiny. Only the two top grades have bathrooms with bathtub; all other cabins have showers.

There are two L-shaped suites, both located on Promenade Deck; these consist of a lounge/living area, bedroom, and bathroom, but there is no private balcony.

CUISINE. The 610-seat Aquamarine Restaurant, which operates two seatings, is quite large, with tables for four, six or eight. The food is basic, no-frills cuisine, but there's plenty of it. There is an adequate, but limited, wine list. Casual meals can be taken in the self-serve Bistro buffet, located aft, or at the poolside Taverna.

ENTERTAINMENT. The Arielle Lounge has a "thrust" stage and hardwood dance floor, but many seats have obtructed sight lines. The single-level room best suits cabaret acts. Shows are typically revue or variety style, with an energetic troupe of young singers and dancers who double as cruise staff. There are also professional cabaret acts.

SPA/FITNESS. There is a beauty salon, fitness room, and sauna (all in different locations). You can book a massage, have an aromatherapy facial, or pedicure. Treatment prices are quite moderate.

Arcadia
★★★★

Large Resort Ship: ....82,972 tons	Passenger Decks: 10	Cabins (for one person): 0
Lifestyle: ....Standard	Total Crew: 886	Cabins (with private balcony): 677
Cruise Line: ....P&O Cruises	Passengers	Cabins (wheelchair accessible): 30
Former Names: ....none	(lower beds/all berths): 1,996/2,556	Cabin Current: ....110/220 volts
Builder: ....Fincantieri (Italy)	Passenger Space Ratio	Elevators: 14
Original Cost: ....$400 million	(lower beds/all berths): 41.5/32.4	Casino (gaming tables): ....Yes
Entered Service: ....April 2005	Crew/Passenger Ratio	Slot Machines: ....Yes
Registry: ....Bermuda	(lower beds/all berths): 2.2/2.8	Swimming Pools (outdoors): 2
Length (ft/m): 936.0/285.3	Navigation Officers: ....British	Swimming Pools (indoors): 0
Beam (ft/m): 105.0/32.0	Cabins (total): 998	Whirlpools: 5
Draft (ft/m): 25.5/7.8	Size Range (sq ft/m): ..170–516.6/15.7–48	Self-Service Launderette: ....Yes
Propulsion/Propellers: ....diesel-electric	Cabins (outside view): 674	Dedicated Cinema/Seats: ....No
(34,000 kW)/ 2 azimuthing pods	Cabins (interior/no view): 324	Library: ....Yes

OVERALL SCORE: 1,490 (OUT OF A POSSIBLE 2,000 POINTS)

OVERVIEW. P&O's *Arcadia* was intended to be Cunard Line's *Queen Victoria* for the British cruise market, but was transferred to the P&O Cruises brand (both are owned by the Carnival Corporation). *Arcadia* can also transit the Panama Canal.

Outdoors facilities include a wrap-around promenade deck (covered in the ship's forward section), with plenty of sunloungers (and cushioned pads). A large Lido Deck pool has a moveable glass domed cover – useful in poor weather. Panoramic exterior glass-wall elevators grace the central foyer to port and starboard and travel between all 10 passenger decks. Pod propulsion is provided (*see page 171*).

The layout provides a horizontal flow, with most public rooms, shops, bars and lounges set open-plan style on two principal decks, so finding your way around is relatively easy. However, the layout of upper public room decks is not so good. The interior decor is geared towards those with youthful, contemporary – even trendy British – tastes, and can best be described as "traditionally modern." It is, however, restrained and welcoming (if a bit bland), and has many warm, earthy pastel colors, assisted by 3,000 works of art (some outstanding) by contemporary British artists, at a cost of $4 million. Although *Arcadia* is one of the Carnival Corporation's Vista-class ships, the decor is the most refined of them all, and the passenger flow is generally good, as is the signage.

Facilities include a forward-facing Crow's Nest observation lounge high atop the ship (in a contemporary setting); a florist; a gift shop arcade; and a Monte Carlo casino, a library (with leather armchairs and a Waterstone's section for paperback sales), an internet center (Cyb@space), and The Retreat (a good place to meet and chill out). Drinking places (there

BERLITZ'S RATINGS

	Possible	Achieved
Ship	500	420
Accommodation	200	150
Food	400	258
Service	400	292
Entertainment	100	81
Cruise	400	289

are 14 bars) include the Spinnaker Bar (good for ship buffs, with its superb display of ship models, a "traditional" English pub (The Rising Sun, with Boddington's draught beer), plus a bar overlooking a very modest three decks-high atrium lobby. The lobby (there isn't one, really) is small and disappointing, particularly when compared to *Oceana*.

Arcadia, strictly a child-free ship for grown-ups (no under-18s allowed), blends traditional British cruising with contemporary facilities for adults, although it really is a completely different type of ship to the more traditional *Artemis, Aurora, Oceana* or *Oriana*. The ship is registered in Bermuda, so UK and US passport holders can be legally married by the ship's captain (check with P&O Cruises for the latest requirements). You can also renew your vows in a special ceremony (£250 per couple).

The New Horizons lecture program provides an array of lectures on a range of subjects (introductory sessions at no charge; more in-depth subject matter study in smaller groups, at an additional cost, typically £5 or £10 per class).

Arcadia is the latest generation of trendy, contemporary cruise ships, based year-round in Southampton, England (so there's no flying involved for UK passengers). The onboard currency is the UK pound. A 15% gratuity is added to all bar and wine accounts. Note that many extra onboard revenue centers have now appeared aboard P&O Cruises' ships, including *Arcadia* (such as paying for lectures and thalassotherapy pool use). Some niggles: there is no separate cinema, or room for card games such as bridge; the ship's dance floor space is pitiful; and the embarkation system keeps people waiting in a lounge after lines at the check-in desks and security until boarding card letters are called.

Other niggles include dining room waiters lacking in personality or finesse (robotic service); small public toilets (lacking in touches like flowers and hand towels); poolside gala reception lacks atmosphere (and "nibbles"); robotic pre-dinner announcements; no towels at poolside (you must take them from your cabin).

SUITABLE FOR: *Arcadia* is best suited to couples and singles seeking to cruise in a large, modern, child-free ship, with entertainment geared for British tastes, with an informal setting and plenty of public rooms to play in.

ACCOMMODATION. There are 26 price grades of accommodation (in seven types of suites/cabins); the choice includes 23 suites, 24 mini-suites, and 685 outside view cabins with a private balcony. While there are plenty of price grades, there are really only five types of accommodation: suites, mini-suites, cabins with private balcony, and twin-bedded cabins with or without a window. All cabin doors and elevators have numbers in Braille.

There are 67 suites and mini-suites. All accommodation has duvets as standard (blankets and pillows if you prefer), flat-screen televisions, tea/coffee making sets (Tetley teabags and long-life milk are provided), small refrigerator, vanity/writing desk, personal safe, hairdryer; bathrooms have half-sized bathtubs/shower/washbasin and toilet. High quality personal toiletries are by Temple Spa, an upgrade from what was previously provided aboard the ships of P&O Cruises (with larger bottles and more selection choice provided for suite occupants).

Also standard are stylish bed runners, Slumberland 8-inch sprung mattresses, 10.5 tog duvets (blankets and pillows if you prefer), Egyptian cotton towels and robes, improved tea/coffee making facilities with speciality teas (long-life is provided) and a Nick Munro-designed bespoke tray, as well as in-cabin toning and fitness facilities for passengers who would prefer to exercise in private.

In twin-bedded cabin grades (approximately 170 sq.ft.), when the beds are pushed together, there's little room to maneuver, but they are otherwise quite practical units.

Accommodation designated as suites (approximately 516 sq.ft. including balcony) and mini-suites (approximately 384 sq.ft. including balcony) benefit from more space, king-sized bed, trouser press, ironing board and iron, three-seat sofa (suites) or two-seat sofa (mini-suites), wall clock, binoculars. The bathrooms are larger, and include an aqua-jet bathtub, two washbasins, toilet, and separate shower enclosure (suites only), and a boxed set of Molton Brown personal toiletry items (but no shampoo). Butler service is provided, but, unlike most lines with these kinds of grades, bottled water costs extra, as do soft drinks.

Passenger niggles include the space-hogging coffee/tea-making set on the small vanity desk in standard cabin grades. Other gripes (standard cabins) include: closets with hanging space too narrow for the width of a man's jacket; little drawer space; poor quality plastic hangers and the hanging system, and no hooks for belts. Other niggles include noisy cabin air-conditioning (it can't be turned off).

Room service breakfast delivery costs £2 per person (even in suites/mini-suite grades); the choice is minimal (available between 7am and 11am).

CUISINE. The Meridian Restaurant, located aft, is two decks high (the two decks are connected by a spiral staircase); it has 11 superb glass/fibre optic ceiling chandeliers (created by Neil Wilkin), and a podium with grand piano graces the upper level. There are two seatings in both restaurants, and tables are for two, four, six, or eight.

Alternative (extra charge) restaurants. Arcadian Rhodes (£15 per person), and the Orchid Restaurant (£10 per person) provide smaller, more intimate dining settings as an escape from the main dining rooms. Arcadian Rhodes was Gary Rhodes's first seagoing restaurant; he created the menu and the chefs/cooks were trained in his London restaurant. The decor is rather uninspiring, however, and banquette seating doesn't suit fine dining. The Orchid Restaurant (on Deck 11) has fine panoramic views, and is an alternative, eatery with Asian-fusion (heavy on the spices) cuisine, and its own bar for pre-meal drinks. Reservations are required in both venues.

For casual meals and snacks, there's a self-serve 24-hour food-court-style eatery (Belvedere), a section of which becomes another dining venue at night, featuring Indian cuisine. There's also an open deck Neptune Grill (for burgers and other fast food items), and Caffe Vivo (for coffees and pastries, at extra cost).

ENTERTAINMENT. The Palladium show lounge is an entertainment palace with three seating tiers and the latest in high-tech staging, lighting, techno-effects and sound systems. Seating is in both banquette-style and individual tub chairs, and the sightlines to the stage are generally good. There are several major production shows –some with a Cirque du Soleil feel to them – complete with major bungee-diving acrobatics and fine adagio dancers. In addition, the ship has an array of cabaret acts. Classical concerts are scheduled for many cruises (typically in the Crows Nest).

Ballroom dance aficionados should note that there are few wooden dance floors aboard this ship (P&O Cruises typically carries professional dance hosts and teachers).

SPA/FITNESS/RECREATION. The Ocean Spa includes a gymnasium with great forward ocean views, 10 body-pampering treatment rooms, a thermal suite that incorporates a hydrotherapy pool, sauna and steam room, for which there is an extra charge (£10 for two hours, in five timed sessions per day), and two very small multi-gender saunas at no charge, but in a location that discourages their use (the thermal suite is better), well away from the changing rooms. Additionally, The Retreat is a cool space for relation, and for calming classes like tai chi, and yoga (£5 per class).

The spa is operated by Harding Brothers, a UK-based concession. Sports facilities include a sports court for racquet or football games, a golf driving range, and, of course, the traditional shuffleboard and ring toss.

Arion
★★

Small Ship:	.5,885 tons	Passenger Decks:	.5	Cabins (with private balcony):	.0
Lifestyle:	.Standard	Total Crew:	.120	Cabins (wheelchair accessible):	.0
Cruise Line:	.Classic International Cruises	Passengers (lower beds/all berths):	.334/340	Cabin Current:	.220 volts
Former Names:	.Astra I, Istra	Passenger Space Ratio		Elevators:	.1
Builder:	.Brodgradiliste (Yugoslavia)	(lower beds/all berths):	.17.6/17.3	Casino (gaming tables):	.Yes
Original Cost:	.n/a	Crew/Passenger Ratio		Slot Machines:	.Yes
Entered Service:	.1965/1999	(lower beds/all berths):	.2.7/2.8	Swimming Pools (outdoors):	.1
Registry:	.Madeira	Navigation Officers:	.Portuguese	Swimming Pools (indoors):	.0
Length (ft/m):	.387.1/118.0	Cabins (total):	.169	Whirlpools:	.0
Beam (ft/m):	.54.1/16.5	Size Range (sq ft/m):	80.7–161.4/7.5–15.0	Self-Service Launderette:	.No
Draft (ft/m):	.18.3/5.6	Cabins (outside view):	.142	Dedicated Cinema/Seats:	.No
Propulsion/Propellers:	.diesel	Cabins (interior/no view):	.27	Library:	.Yes
	(11,030kW)/2	Cabins (for one person):	.4		

OVERALL SCORE: 902 (OUT OF A POSSIBLE 2,000 POINTS)

OVERVIEW. *Arion* is a charming little ship, originally built for weekly service between Venice and Egypt. It underwent a $15 million reconstruction by Classic International Cruises (even the navigation bridge was relocated forward) after the company bought the ship at auction in Haifa in 1999, and emerged in its present form in May 2000.

The ship is operated under charter to various tour operators, and thus attracts an international mix of passengers who like smaller ships with some character.

The ship features interesting itineraries, at low prices. It is particularly suited to the "nooks and crannies" style of cruising along the Dalmatian coast. The dress code is extremely casual, there is a relaxed ambiance, and the crew is very friendly and warm.

This is a small, but charming, lovingly reconstructed ship, but there are few public rooms and facilities, and little open deck space (although sunloungers do have cushioned pads). The interior passageways are narrow, the public rooms are always busy and it is difficult to avoid smokers. The ship is not suitable for disabled passengers.

SUITABLE FOR: *Arion* is best suited to adult couples (typically over 50) looking for a basic cruise holiday, in a traditional ship. This could be good for your first cruise experience, in a setting that provides basic comforts, and at a price that provides fair value for money.

ACCOMMODATION. There are 12 cabin price grades (though this may depend on tour operators that charter the vessel). Except for the top two grades, the cabins are modest in size and features, and one would not want to spend much time

BERLITZ'S RATINGS

	Possible	Achieved
Ship	500	186
Accommodation	200	90
Food	400	182
Service	400	225
Entertainment	100	40
Cruise	400	179

in them. Cabins 1–8, which have windows, have lifeboat-obstructed views. Cabins on the higher decks have windows, while others have portholes.

Each cabin has a small TV set, personal safe, and hairdryer. There is little closet and storage space (so take the minimal amount of clothing), although each cabin does have a set of bedside drawers. Some cabins have a twin bed arrangement (side by side), while others are "L"-shaped (only 13 cabins have a double bed). Some cabins have a third, or third and fourth berth. The bathrooms are tiny and basic, yet adequate.

CUISINE. The 352-seat restaurant is warm and cosy; there are ocean-view windows on two sides, and standard place settings. There are tables (quite close together) for four, six or eight. The chairs do not have armrests. All passengers dine together in one seating.

The menus are limited, although there is a good choice of breads and bread rolls. Dinner menus typically consist of one or two appetizers, two soups, and three entrées. The wine list is quite basic, and the wine glasses are small. The all-Portuguese waiters are friendly and attentive. Casual breakfasts and luncheons can be taken in the Lido Lounge, just forward of the swimming pool and the open deck aft.

ENTERTAINMENT. There is little entertainment, and what is provided is of the cabaret variety. There is a band for dancing and a pianist in the piano bar, located just aft of the main lounge, and Lido Bar.

SPA/FITNESS. None, although there is a small beauty salon. The small swimming pool is really only a "dip" pool.

Mid-Size Ship: ....44,348 tons	Passengers		Cabins (wheelchair accessible): 4
Lifestyle: ....Standard	(lower beds/all berths): 1,200/1,260		Cabin Current: ....110 & 220 volts
Cruise Line: ....P&O Cruises	Passenger Space Ratio		Elevators: 6
Former Names: ....Royal Princess	(lower beds/all berths): 36.9/35.1		Casino (gaming tables): ....Yes
Builder: ....Wartsila (Finland)	Crew/Passenger Ratio		Slot Machines: ....Yes
Original Cost: ....$165 million	(lower beds/all berths): 2.3/2.4		Swimming Pools (outdoors): 2
Entered Service: .... Nov 1984/Jun 2005	Navigation Officers: ....British		(+2 splash pools)
Registry: ....Bermuda	Cabins (total): 600		Swimming Pools (indoors): 0
Length (ft/m): 754.5/230.0	Size Range (sq ft/m): 186.0–1,126.0/		Whirlpools: 2
Beam (ft/m): 95.8/29.2	17.2–104.5		Fitness Center: ....Yes
Draft (ft/m): 25.5/7.8	Cabins (outside view): 600		Self-Service Launderette: ....Yes
Propulsion/Propellers:diesel (29,160kW)/2	Cabins (interior/no view): 0		Dedicated Cinema/Seats: Yes/150
Passenger Decks: 9	Cabins (for one person): 0		Library: ....Yes
Total Crew: 520	Cabins (with private balcony): 152		

BERLITZ'S OVERALL SCORE: 1,385 (OUT OF A POSSIBLE 2,000 POINTS)

OVERVIEW. *Artemis* (formerly Princess Cruises' *Royal Princess*) is named after the Greek goddess Artemis and was dedicated in November 1984 by Diana, Princess of Wales. The ship has reasonably contemporary outer styling that is almost handsome. In May 2005, *Artemis* underwent a name change and a £10.5 million transformation from its former self as *Royal Princess*. The ship is now committed to the British child-free cruise market, to which the ageing ship is perhaps more ideally suited. In the refit, the Monte Carlo casino was made smaller in order to accommodate a new internet center; a Future Cruise Sales office and Portunus Club room replaced what was formerly a business center. The outdoor deck and sunbathing space is moderate, and there is a traditional wrap-around teak deck.

The well-designed, though slightly unconventional, interior layout features passenger cabins located above the public room decks. The interior decor is not the least bit garish, but rather reflects the feeling of space, openness and light; the passenger flow is good. For fans of P&O Cruises' "smaller" ships, *Artemis* has replaced the much loved *Victoria*, and, if you've cruised aboard *Aurora* and/or *Oriana*, you'll probably really like *Artemis*, which combines the traditions of cruising with the bonus of a child-free environment. There are several large, nicely appointed public rooms, spacious passageways and imposing staircases. Overall, however, the ship is well worn, and looks tired in several places.

A Horizon Lounge, set around the funnel base, has fine views and a peaceful environment during the day, while at night it transforms into a disco for the late-night set. When this ship debuted, it was state-of-the-art, but now lags behind the latest ships in several ways, and looks tired.

BERLITZ'S RATINGS

	Possible	Achieved
Ship	500	346
Accommodation	200	141
Food	400	256
Service	400	279
Entertainment	100	72
Cruise	400	291

One nice feature is the dedicated movie theater (few new ships have them). *Artemis*, the smallest ship in the P&O Cruises fleet, will provide you with a decent cruise experience in reasonably spacious, almost elegant surroundings, at a decent price.

Many of the cruises are themed, and carry out the theme in the form of the company's New Horizons program (introductory classes are at no charge, but more in-depth classes are at extra cost, typically £5 or £10).

The ship is registered in Bermuda, so UK and USA passport holders can be legally married by the ship's captain (do check with P&O Cruises for the latest requirements and details). You can also renew your vows in a special ceremony (it costs £250 per couple).

SUITABLE FOR: *Artemis* is best suited to couples and singles seeking to cruise in a modern *child-free* ship, with entertainment geared specifically for British tastes in a large ship, with an informal setting and plenty of public rooms to play in.

ACCOMMODATION. The all-outside view cabins (152 with private balcony) represent just four accommodation types (including suites), although there are 25 price categories. All cabins (most have twin beds) are comfortable and well appointed, although they are a trifle bland. Note that many cabins have mirrors placed opposite beds (which will not please *feng shui* practitioners).

All cabins have a combination bathtub and shower, three-sided mirrors, color TV set, and British three-pin sockets. Also standard are stylish bed runners, Slumberland

8-inch sprung mattresses, 10.5 tog duvets (blankets and pillows if you prefer), Egyptian cotton towels and robes, improved tea/coffee making facilities with speciality teas (long-life is provided) and a Nick Munro-designed bespoke tray, as well as in-cabin toning and fitness facilities for passengers who would prefer to exercise in private. High quality personal toiletries are by Temple Spa, an upgrade from what was previously provided aboard the ships of P&O Cruises (with larger bottles and more selection choice provided for suite occupants).

Molton Brown personal toiletries are provided (suite occupants get more, of course), as are bathrobes and chocolates on your pillow each night. Prompt, attentive room service is available 24 hours a day. Some cabins on both Baja Deck and "C" Deck have full or partial lifeboat and safety equipment-obstructed views. Some cabins have extra berths fitted. Note that the in-cabin service menu is really quite basic.

The *Canberra* and *Oriana* suites are the largest, and they are quite attractive, although not that large by today's standards (the balcony is also small). All suite occupants get butler service, an expanded range of personal toiletries, complimentary mineral water, a larger breakfast menu, and the possibility of ordering anything from the full restaurant menu for lunch and dinner.

CUISINE. The elegant, non-smoking Coral Dining Room is set low down, and is conveniently adjacent to the lobby. There are two seatings for dinner, at tables for two, four, six or eight. The well-orchestrated service, by staff from India and Goa, is friendly. The Conservatory is an indoor-outdoor Lido Deck self-serve eatery for casual meals and snacks, and is open 24 hours a day; at night one section becomes The Grill at The Conservatory.

ENTERTAINMENT. The International Lounge is the venue for shows, drama presentations, main cabaret acts, and some social functions. It is an amphitheater-shaped room with good sightlines from the majority of seats, although it is only one deck high – more for cabaret acts than large-scale production shows. P&O Cruises always provides plenty of live music for the various bars and lounges, and volume is normally kept to an acceptable level.

SPA/FITNESS. The Oasis Spa is located on one of the uppermost decks, clustered around the base of the funnel housing. It contains a gymnasium with some decent muscle-toning equipment and large picture windows that overlook one of the swimming pools, saunas and changing rooms for men and women, and beauty salon (on a different deck), as well as a display of exercise clothing for sale.

The spa is operated by Harding Brothers, a UK-based concession that provides the staff and a wide range of beauty and wellness treatments. Examples of treatments include: Body Toning (detox for the body); Seaweed Wrap; Collagen Velvet Facial Mask, and a range of aromatherapy treatments.

Examples of prices: a full body massage is £60 (50 minutes); an Indian head massage is £42 (45 minutes); a holistic facial is £45 (75 minutes). A manicure is £24 (45 minutes), while a pedicure is £35 (45 minutes).

Note that if you want to book spa treatments (massage, facial, hairdressing), it is wise to do so as soon after you embark as possible, as time slots do fill up quickly aboard large ships such as this – particularly on the shorter cruises.

● **For more extensive general information about a P&O cruise experience, see pages 133–34.**

WIND SPEEDS

A navigational announcement to passengers is normally made once or twice a day, giving the ship's position, temperature, and weather information.

Various winds affect the world's weather patterns. Such well-known winds as the Bora, Mistral, Northwind, and Sirocco, among others, play an important part in the makeup of weather at and above sea level. Wind velocity is measured on the Beaufort scale, a method that was devised in 1805 by Commodore Francis Beaufort, later Admiral and Knight Commander of the Bath, for measuring the force of wind at sea. Originally, it measured the effect of the wind on a fully rigged man-of-war (which was usually laden with cannon and heavy ammunition). It became the official way of recording wind velocity in 1874, when the International Meteorological Committee adopted it.

Mid-Size Ship: . . . . .20,606 tons	Passenger Decks: 7	Cabins (with private balcony): 0
Lifestyle: . . . . .Standard	Total Crew: .300	Cabins (wheelchair accessible): 0
Cruise Line: . . . . .Transocean Tours	Passengers	Cabin Current: . . . . .220 volts
Former Names: . . . . .Fedor Dostoyevskiy,	(lower beds/all berths): 590/650	Elevators: 3
Astor (II)	Passenger Space Ratio	Casino (gaming tables): . . . . .Yes
Builder: . . . . . . .Howaldtswerke Deutsche	(lower beds/all berths): 34.9/31.7	Slot Machines: . . . . .Yes
Werft (Germany)	Crew/Passenger Ratio	Swimming Pools (outdoors): 1
Original Cost: . . . .$65 million	(lower beds/all berths): 1.9/2.1	Swimming Pools (indoors): 1
Entered Service: . . . . . Feb 1987/Apr 1997	Navigation Officers: . . .Russian/Ukrainian	Whirlpools: 0
Registry: . . . . .The Bahamas	Cabins (total): 295	Self-Service Launderette: . . . . .No
Length (ft/m): 579.0/176.50	Size Range (sq ft/m): 140.0–280.0/	(ironing room)
Beam (ft/m): 74.1/22.61	13.0–26.0	Dedicated Cinema/Seats: . . . . .No
Draft (ft/m): 20.0/6.10	Cabins (outside view): 199	Library: . . . . .Yes
Propulsion/Propellers: . . . . .diesel	Cabins (interior/no view): 96	
(15,400kW)/2	Cabins (for one person): 0	

OVERALL SCORE: 1,370 (OUT OF A POSSIBLE 2,000 POINTS)

OVERVIEW. *Astor* was the original name for this ship, the larger of two ships bearing this same name in the 1980s (the other being the present Transocean Tours ship *Astoria*), originally built for the now-defunct Astor Cruises. Its previous owners, the also defunct Aqua-Marin Cruises, again brought back the ship's name to *Astor* from its previous name *Fedor Dostoyevskiy*.

This is an attractive modern ship with a raked bow, a large square funnel and a nicely balanced almost contemporary profile. The ship is slightly larger than the first *Astor* (presently renamed *Astoria*), and has been well maintained and refurbished throughout the years. Introduced by Transocean Tours in 1997, this ship was placed under a long-term charter agreement until 2011 (when the ship will be almost 30 years old) from its present owners, Premicon.

Astor and its (slightly smaller) sister ship *Astoria* now operate in tandem as one product – two ships of a similar size and with very similar facilities (even built in the same shipyard, with the same bathroom fittings and washbasins), the same conservative decor and ambiance.

This ship represents a good mix of traditional and modern styling, with restful decor that does not jar the senses in any way (though some say it's a little too dark). Built to a high standard in Germany, fine teakwood decking and polished wood railings are seen outside almost everywhere.

There is an excellent amount of open deck and sunbathing space, as well as cushioned pads for the sun-loungers. There is a basketball court for active passengers, as well as a large deck chess game on an aft deck, and the usual shuffleboard courts.

BERLITZ'S RATINGS

	Possible	Achieved
Ship	500	354
Accommodation	200	139
Food	400	257
Service	400	286
Entertainment	100	62
Cruise	400	272

The interior fittings are of extremely fine quality. There is a supremely comfortable and varied array of public rooms and conference facilities, most of which have high ceilings. Apart from a show lounge, public rooms include a Captain's Club lounge, a library and card room, and two large boutiques. The wood-paneled Hanse Bar (with good German lager on draft) is a fine retreat, and extremely popular as a late-night drinking club.

Transocean Tours has interesting and well-designed destination-intensive worldwide itineraries, and cruises are provided at a very attractive price. The mainly European hotel staff are friendly without being obtrusive.

This ship, which caters exclusively to German-speaking passengers, provides a certain degree of style, comfort and elegance, and a fine leisurely cruise experience in a relaxed, spacious setting that is less formal than a ship such as *Europa*. There is no crowding anywhere and no annoying background music in hallways or elevators.

The ship represents a good choice for those people who are looking for a well-packaged cruise in traditional ship surroundings. Transocean Tours staff can be found aboard every cruise, some of which are designated as special-theme cruises. As aboard all German-speaking ships, Fruhschoppen (free beer, sausages and carved meats) is one event not to be missed.

The currency aboard *Astor* is the euro. Port taxes, insurance and gratuities to staff are all included in the cruise fare. The drinks prices are inexpensive, particularly when compared to land-based prices.

A service provided by ABX Logistics will collect your

luggage from your house, and transport it to the ship for you; when you return, the service will collect it from the ship and bring it to your house – all for a nominal fee (this service is only available to/from certain ports).

SUITABLE FOR: *Astor* is best suited to German-speaking couples, and single travelers of mature years who seek a good value for money holiday in a traditional cruise ship setting, with appealing itineraries and destinations, good food and friendly service.

ACCOMMODATION. The accommodation, spanning 18 price categories, is spread over three decks, and comprises 32 suites and 263 outside-view and interior (no view) cabins. No matter what grade of accommodation is chosen, rosewood cabinetry and plain beige walls is the norm – a restful environment. All suites and cabins with outside-view windows have blackout blinds (good for cruises to the land of the midnight sun).

Suites: The suites (279.8 sq.ft/26 sq. meters) are tastefully decorated in pastel colors, and have rosewood cabinetry and accents. Each has a separate bedroom (with brass clock), lounge/living room (another brass clock), with mini-bar/refrigerator and personal safe (in a user-unfriendly position, almost at floor level). The bathroom is small but has a decent-sized cabinet for personal toiletry items, as well as a sit-in bathtub/shower combination, toilet, and a white enamel washbasin. A wide array of bathroom amenities is provided, including built-in hairdryer, soap, shampoo, shower cap, comb, sewing kit, shoe polish, shoehorn, clothes lint collector, nail file, matches, and a basket of fruit, replenished daily.

Outside-view and Interior (No View) Cabins: These cabins (139.9 sq. ft/13 sq. meters) are well appointed and tastefully decorated in fresh pastel colors, and have dark wood accents and cabinetry, making them very restful. There is plenty of closet and drawer space, as well as some under-bed storage space for luggage. The bathrooms are very practical, and each has a decent sized cabinet for personal toiletry items, as well as all the necessary fittings, including a white enamel washbasin.

Outside-view Family (4-Berth) Cabins: These large cabins (258.3 sq.ft/24 sq. meters) have two lower beds, one upper berth and one sofa bed – good for families with children. The tiled bathroom has a shower enclosure, white enamel washbasin and toilet.

No matter what grade of accommodation you choose, all passengers get European duvets, 100% cotton towels, 100% cotton bathrobe, soap, shampoo, shower cap, sewing kit and a basket of fruit. The cabin service menu is very limited and could be better, although German-speaking passengers in general seldom use room service for food items. There is an extra charge for sandwiches, and little else is available. However, there is plenty of food elsewhere around the ship. Note that there is an extra charge for freshly-squeezed orange juice, as aboard all ships in the German-speaking market. The bathroom towels are too small.

CUISINE. The no-smoking Waldorf Dining Room is reasonably elegant, well laid-out, and operates two seatings. It also has one small wing (good for private parties or groups of up to 30). The service throughout is friendly and unpretentious, and the food quality and presentation has received some attention from the food caterer, although remember that you get what you pay for, and food is not a particularly high priority for Transocean Tours. The menus are reasonably attractive, and both quality and presentation are acceptable standard fare, but nothing special – there's certainly no "wow" factor. In addition to the regular entrées (typically three entrées for dinner), there may also be a pasta dish, and a vegetarian specialty dish. The wine list contains a decent selection of wines from many regions, and all at inexpensive to moderate price levels, but wine glasses are small.

A small alternative dining venue featuring Italian cuisine is a reservations-only, extra-cost dining spot for those wanting something a little more special and as an alternative to the main dining room. Larger wine glasses are provided.

Casual breakfast and lunch buffets (both in the restaurant and another lounge) are reasonably well presented, and constantly refreshed, although they tend to be somewhat repetitive; the choice of foods is limited and there is room for improvement. In typical German style, a Fruhschoppen with the appropriate music, Bavarian sausages and complimentary beer is presented on the open lido deck once each cruise.

ENTERTAINMENT. The Showlounge is a single-level room (14 pillars unfortunately obstruct the sight lines) better suited to cabaret and mini-concerts than large-scale staged production shows. The stage itself is also the dance floor, (it cannot be raised for shows). The entertainment possibilities, therefore, are limited, with singers, magicians, and other visual acts providing the bulk of the shows.

SPA/FITNESS. The Wellness Oasis is located on the lowest passenger deck, and contains a sauna (there is no steam room), solarium, indoor swimming pool, beauty salon, treatment rooms and changing areas. Massage, facials, manicures and pedicures are some of the services offered. A separate fitness center, equipped with techno-machinery and exer-cycles, is located on an upper deck (Bridge Deck), complete with ocean views.

Astoria
★★★ +

Mid-Size Ship: . . . . .18,591 tons	Passenger Decks: 8	Cabins (for one person): 0
Lifestyle: . . . . .Standard	Total Crew: 243	Cabins (with private balcony): 0
Cruise Line: . . . . .Transocean Tours	Passengers	Cabins (wheelchair accessible): 0
Former Names: . . . .*Arkona, Astor*	(lower beds/all berths): 500/618	Cabin Current: . . . . .220 volts
Builder: . . . . . . .Howaldtswerke Deutsche	Passenger Space Ratio	Elevators: 3
Werft (Germany)	(lower beds/all berths): 36.0/30.0	Casino (gaming tables): . . . . .No
Original Cost: . . . .$55 million	Crew/Passenger Ratio	Slot Machines: .No
Entered Service: . . . . .Dec 1981/Feb 2002	(lower beds/all berths): 2.1/2.5	Swimming Pools (outdoors): 1
Registry: . . . . .The Bahamas	Navigation Officers: . . .Russian/Ukrainian	Swimming Pools (indoors): 1
Length (ft/m): 539.2/164.35	Cabins (total): 259	Whirlpools: 0
Beam (ft/m): 74.1/22.60	Size Range (sq ft/m): 150.0–725.0/	Self-Service Launderette: . . . . .No
Draft (ft/m): 20.0/6.11	13.4–65.3	Dedicated Cinema/Seats: . . . . .No
Propulsion/Propellers: . . . . .diesel	Cabins (outside view): 177	Library: . . . . .Yes
(13,200kW)/2	Cabins (interior/no view): 82	

OVERALL SCORE: 1,309 (OUT OF A POSSIBLE 2,000 POINTS)

OVERVIEW. *Astoria* is a traditional style of cruise ship (slightly smaller than sister ship *Astor*), originally constructed for the now defunct Astor Cruises. In February 2002, it started in service for Transocean Tours. The ship underwent a slight name change, to *Astoria*. Some minor modifications took place so that *Astor* and *Astoria* have been operating in tandem – two ships of a similar size and with very similar facilities (even built in the same shipyard), and the same conservative decor and ambiance. From July 2009, *Astoria* will be operated by the UK's Saga Cruises.

It is a well-constructed modern vessel with a nicely balanced profile. There is a very good amount of open deck and sunbathing space for its size, with some excellent teakwood decking and polished railings, and cushioned pads for the sunloungers. Note that there is no walk-around promenade deck outdoors. For the sports-minded, there is a volleyball court.

Astoria, like its sister ship *Astor*, has beautifully appointed interior fittings and decor, with a great deal of rosewood paneling and wood accents throughout. The ship has been maintained extremely well. Subdued lighting and soothing ambiance, highlighted by fine artwork throughout, make for a pleasant, relaxing cruise experience. There are good meetings facilities, and a well-stocked library. The late-night meeting-place is the the intimate Hanse Bar (with draft German lager) looking aft over the sun deck.

Passengers who use dialysis machines will find that Transocean Tours operates several special cruises, complete with specially trained medical personnel (dialysis equipment is installed aboard *Astoria*).

The ship has good traditional European-style hotel ser-

BERLITZ'S RATINGS

	Possible	Achieved
Ship	500	318
Accommodation	200	134
Food	400	252
Service	400	275
Entertainment	100	60
Cruise	400	270

vice, with mainly Ukrainian navigation and engineering officers and a mostly European service staff. The reception desk is open 24 hours daily.

Astoria provides good value for money cruising in comfort, and is best recommended for passengers who appreciate quality, fine surroundings, and excellent destination-intensive itineraries, all packaged neatly in an informal ambiance. Many cruises have special themes. Transocean Tours staff, available aboard every cruise, go out of their way to ensure you have an excellent cruise experience in very comfortable surroundings. The ship has many repeat passengers, who enjoy the extremely friendly, mostly German crew (who provide a fun crew show). The currency aboard *Astoria* is the euro. Port taxes, insurance and gratuities to staff are all included in the cruise fare.

A service by ABX Logistics will collect your luggage from your house, and transport it to the ship for you; when you return, the service will collect it from the ship and take it to your house – all for a nominal fee.

SUITABLE FOR: *Astoria* is best suited to German-speaking couples, and single travelers of mature years who seek a good value for money holiday in a traditional cruise ship setting, with appealing itineraries and destinations, good food and friendly service.

ACCOMMODATION. The accommodation, of which there are 18 price categories, is spread over three decks. There are no balcony cabins (the ship having been built before they became popular).

Senator Suite (one): This Boat Deck suite (725 sq. ft/65.3

sq. meters) is simply lovely, and has just about everything needed for refined, private living aboard this ship. There is a separate bedroom with double bed, living room with sofa, dining table and chairs. The tiled bathroom has a large bathtub, separate shower enclosure, and plenty of storage space for personal toiletry items.

Suites: 34 Suites (269.1 sq. ft/25 sq. meters) have a separate bedroom with twin beds, living room with sofa, dining table and chairs. The tiled bathroom has a large bathtub, separate shower enclosure, and plenty of storage space for personal toiletry items.

Outside-view Cabins/Interior (No View) Cabins: The standard cabins (139.9 sq. ft/13 sq. meters) are quite well appointed and decorated, and all feature crisp, clean colors (some might find them plain). The bathrooms are quite compact units, although there is a decent-sized shower enclosure. They are fully tiled, however, and have a decent cabinet for storing personal toiletry items.

No matter what grade of accommodation you choose, all passengers get 100% cotton towels, and bathrobe. The cabin service menu is very limited and could be better, although German-speaking passengers in general seldom use room service for food items. There is an extra charge for sandwiches, and little else is available; however, there is plenty of food elsewhere around the ship. Note that there is an extra charge for fresh-squeezed orange juice, as aboard all ships in the German-speaking market.

CUISINE. The no-smoking Astoria Restaurant, located high in the ship, has big, ocean-view picture windows and is reasonably attractive, with dark wood paneling and restful decor; there are two seatings. The food varies from adequate to very good, though choice is somewhat limited, but the service, by some charming waitresses, does help.

Do remember that, when it comes to food and ingredients, you get what you pay for, and food is not a particularly high priority for Transocean Tours. There's certainly no "wow" factor in this food or its presentation. The occasional formal candlelight dinners provide a romantic ambiance. The wine list contains a decent selection of wines from many regions, and all at inexpensive to moderate price levels.

The self-serve buffets (for breakfast and luncheon) are varied, although the presentation could be improved. The cabin service food menu is very limited.

ENTERTAINMENT. The showlounge is a single-level room. However, there are 14 pillars to obstruct the sight lines from some seats. The stage is also the dance floor and cannot be raised for shows. The entertainment, therefore, consist mostly of cabaret-style shows typically with singers, magicians and other visual acts.

SPA/FITNESS. The Wellness Oasis is located on the lowest passenger deck, and contains a sauna (there is no steam room), solarium, indoor swimming pool, treatment rooms and changing areas. Massage, facials, manicures and pedicures are some of the services offered. The beauty salon is located one deck higher, while a fitness center can be found on Bridge Deck. In addition, sophisticated hospital facilities include oxygen multi-step therapy.

WHERE NAUTICAL EXPRESSIONS COME FROM

If you've ever wondered where some terms or phrases came from, you have only to look to the sea, ships, and seamen.

Above board

This term for honesty originated in the days when pirates would hide most of their crews below decks, to trick an unsuspecting victim. A ship that sh6wed its crew openly on the deck, aboveboard, was obviously an honest merchantman.

All Above Board

"All above board referred to the fact that boards or planking which made up the decks are in plain view; hence, anything that was stored above board was in plain view of everyone. T6day we tend to use "going overboard" in the sense of going to far in our reaction or in some venture. "All above board" has come to be synonymous with honest dealings.

All hands on deck

Everyone should gather together to their positions and prepare for action. It is used nowadays to mean "to gather together for some task or other."

As the crow flies

British coastal vessels customarily carried a cage of crows. These birds hate wide expanses of water and head, "as straight as the crow flies," to the nearest land when released at sea. This was useful to vessels lost in foggy coastal weather before the days of radar. The lookout perch on sailing vessels became known as the crow's nest.

Bale out

The term is typically used in the sense of getting out of some situation - particularly a financial one. However, the verb to bale out, means to remove water, and comes from the old name 'boyle' for a bucket.

Asuka II
★★★★ +

Mid-Size Ship: . . . . .50,142 tons	Total Crew: 460	Cabins (with private balcony): 260
Lifestyle: . . . . .Luxury/Premium	Passengers	Cabins (wheelchair accessible): 4
Cruise Line: . . . . .Asuka Cruises	(lower beds/all berths): 964/1,010	Cabin Current: . . . . .115 and 220 volts
Former Names: . . . . . . .Crystal Harmony	Passenger Space Ratio	Elevators: 8
Builder:Mitsubishi Heavy Industries, Japan	(lower beds/all berths): 52.0/45.2	Casino (gaming tables): . . . . .Yes
Original Cost: . . . .$240 million	Crew/Passenger Ratio	Slot Machines: . . . . .Yes
Entered Service: July1990/May 2006	(lower beds/all berths): 1.7/1.8	Swimming Pools (outdoors): 1
Registry: . . . . .Japan	Navigation Officers: . . . . .Japanese	Swimming Pools (indoors): 0
Length (ft/m): 790.5/240.96	Cabins (total): 462	Whirlpools: 2
Beam (ft/m): 97.1/29.60	Size Range (sq ft/m): 198.1–949.4/	Self-Service Launderette: . . . . .Yes
Draft (ft/m): 24.6/7.50	18.4–88.2	Dedicated Cinema/Seats: Yes/263
Propulsion/Propellers: . . . .diesel-electric	Cabins (outside view): 462	Library: . . . . .Yes
(32,800kW)/2	Cabins (interior/no view): 0	
Passenger Decks: 8	Cabins (for one person): 0	

BERLITZ'S OVERALL SCORE: 1,685 (OUT OF A POSSIBLE 2,000 POINTS)

OVERVIEW. *Asuka II* (formerly *Crystal Harmony*) is a handsome, well-balanced contemporary ship with raked clipper bow and sleek lines. There is almost no sense of crowding anywhere aboard this ship, a good example of form follows function (comfort by design). There is a wrap-around teakwood deck for walking, and an abundance of open deck and sunbathing space. Although now 18 years old, *Asuka II* underwent a four-month long drydocking and refit between December 2005 and April 2006. A larger ship (more passengers), it replaces the first *Asuka*.

Inside, the layout is completely different to the previous *Asuka* in that there is a horizontal flow of passengers through public rooms (aboard the former *Asuka* they were mostly aft in a vertical format) with a design that combines some large ship facilities with the intimacy of rooms found aboard many smaller ships. There is a wide assortment of public entertainment lounges and small intimate rooms, and passenger flow is excellent. Fine-quality fabrics and soft furnishings, china, flatware and silver are used throughout.

Outstanding are the Vista (observation) Lounge and the tranquil, elegant Palm Court, one of the nicest rooms afloat, while adjacent are a computer (internet) room and a Washitsu (Japanese 12-tatami mat room). Other public rooms and facilities include the Mariner's Club Lounge (piano bar/lounge), Cigar Bar, Bistro Café, Casino Corner, Mahjong Room, Compass Room (meeting/activities room), a book/video library, and Stars karaoke bar. The theater is a dedicated room with high-definition video projection. There is a self-service launderette on each deck (practical for long voyages).

It is the attention to detail that makes a cruise aboard this ship so pleasant, such as almost no announcements, and lit-

BERLITZ'S RATINGS

	Possible	Achieved
Ship	500	427
Accommodation	200	160
Food	400	341
Service	400	337
Entertainment	100	83
Cruise	400	337

tle background music. The company pays attention to its repeat passengers, particularly those in Deck 10 accommodation. Although longer than the previous *Asuka*, the horizontal (rather than vertical) passenger flow (public rooms laid out horizontally) is better for NYK's typical passenger age range.

Asuka II is a hotel afloat and provides abundant choices and flexibility. It has just about everything for the discerning traveler prepared to pay for high style, space, and the comfort and the facilities of a mid-size vessel capable of long voyages. This is cruising in a well-tuned, well-run service-oriented ship, approximately the equivalent of Tokyo's Imperial Hotel. Unfortunately, dining is in two seatings, which makes it highly structured in terms of timing (although this works well in the Japanese market). The onboard currency is the Japanese Yen, and all gratuities are included.

Your evenings will be necessarily time-structured due to the fact that there are two seatings for dinner (unless you eat in the alternative dining spot), and two shows (the showlounge cannot seat all passengers at once). This detracts from the otherwise fine setting of the ship and the professionalism of its staff.

SUITABLE FOR: *Asuka II* is best suited to Japanese-speaking travellers (typically over 60) seeking a sophisticated ship with fine-quality fittings and furnishings, a wide range of public rooms and facilities, and excellent food and service from a well trained staff that enjoys providing hospitality.

ACCOMMODATION. There are five categories of suites and cabins (including four Royal Suites with private balcony;

26 Asuka Suites with balcony; 32 Suites with balcony; 198 Cabins with balcony; 202 Cabins without balcony. Regardless of the category you select, duvets and down pillows are provided, as are lots of other niceties, together with a data socket for personal laptop computer connection. All cabins have a color television, VCR, mini-refrigerator, personal safe, small couch and coffee table, excellent soundproofing, a refrigerator and mini-bar, full tea-making set, satellite-linked telephone, and hairdryer. A full range of personal toiletries (including Shiseido shampoo, hair rinse, shower cap, soap, toothbrush/toothpaste, cotton pads, razor set, hairbrush, and more) is provided, as are a plush cotton bathrobe and yukata, and plenty of cotton towels

Deck 10 Penthouses: Four Crystal penthouses measure 949.4 sq. ft (88.2 sq. meters) and have a large private balcony and lounge with audio-visual entertainment center, separate master bedroom with king-sized bed and electric curtains, large walk-in closets, and excellent ocean-view bathrooms that come with jet bathtub, bidet, two wash-basins, and plenty of storage space for one's personal toiletry items. These really are fine, private, pampered living spaces at sea, and come with all the best priority perks, including priority service, free laundry service, a wide variety of alcoholic beverages and other goodies – in fact, almost anything you require.

Other Deck 10 Suites: All the other suites on this deck are worth the asking price, have plenty of space (all have a private balcony, with outside light), including a separate lounge with large couch, coffee table and chairs, large television/VCR, and a separate sleeping area that can be curtained off (thick drapes mean you can sleep totally in the dark). The bathrooms are quite large, and extremely well appointed. All deck 10 suites/cabins are attended by social officers, and complimentary in-room dining service is offered.

Deck 9/8/7/5 Cabins: Many of the cabins have a private balcony (in fact, 50 percent of all cabins have private balconies, with outside lights), and are extremely comfortable, although a little tight for space. They are very compact units, with one-way traffic past the bed, but there is a reasonable amount of drawer and storage space (the drawers are small, however) although the closet hanging space (as well as storage space for shoes) is extremely limited for long voyages. Some cabins have lifeboat-obstructed views, so it's best to check the deck plan carefully.

The bathrooms (except for those in Deck 10 accommodation), although well appointed, are of the "you first, me next" variety (and size), but they do come with generously sized personal toiletry items and amenities, and all bathrooms are fitted with electric "washlet" high-cleanse toilets.

CUISINE. There are several choices. The non-smoking Four Seasons Dining Room is quite elegant, with plenty of space around each table, well-placed waiter service stations and a number of tables for two, as well as tables for four, six or eight. It can be noisy (particularly in the raised, center section), making it hard to carry on a conversation.

Dinner in the main dining room is in two seatings and table assignments are fixed; the advantage of these is that your waiters get to know your personal preferences, likes and dislikes (unlike dining rooms with open seating, where you may be seated with different people each evening, and your waiter changes constantly).

Afternoon tea (and coffee) can be taken in the Palm Court – a restful venue.

Alternative (extra charge) Dining: Umihiko is a Japanese specialty restaurant (reservations are necessary), complete with a real, totally authentic sushi bar and two live fish tanks (for absolutely fresh sashimi). Umihiko specializes in sushi and (authentic) sashimi dishes, and provides a refined, intimate dining experience with fine ocean views.

For casual meals, beverages and ice cream, the Lido Café, which was completely reconstructed in the refit, has an extensive self-serve buffet area; it is located high up in the ship, and with ocean views from large picture windows. For casual meals, there is also a Lido Garden Grill, a large area with wooden tables and chairs, and bar.

Additionally, The Bistro (located on the upper level of the two-deck-high lobby) is a casual spot for coffees and pastries, served in the style and atmosphere of a European street café.

ENTERTAINMENT. The Grand Hall is the ship's showlounge; it is a large room on one level (with a tiered floor). The sightlines are good from most seats, although there are a few pillars that obstruct the view from some seats. Both banquette and individual seating is provided.

In addition, there are often good-caliber cabaret acts that change constantly. The bands and musical units are also, for the most part, of a high standard, and there is plenty of music for social dancing.

SPA/FITNESS. The Grand Spa includes a large Grand Bath/cleansing center (one for men, one for women), with integral sauna and steam room. Other facilities include the first Shiseido Salon and Spa at sea, with five treatment rooms (longevity, water, wind, prosperity, harmony) including one for couples; other facilities include a separate sauna, steam rooms, changing rooms for men and women, a beauty salon, and a relaxation area. Another part of the spa houses the gymnasium, with ocean-view windows on one side.

Shiseido operates the spa and the staff offers a wide range of body pampering treatments using the brand products of Qi Estherapy, Carita and Decleor. Sample prices: Qi Energy Full Body Massage: 120 minutes, ¥21,000 (about $182); Qi Tenderness Body Massage: 90 minutes, ¥21,000 (about $182); Decleor Aromatic Body Massage: 120 minutes, ¥24,150 (about $210); Carita Body Treatment: 90 minutes, ¥29,400 (about $255); Carita Facial: 70 minutes, ¥14,700 (about $127). The spa also offers a kimono dressing service, which costs ¥12,600 (about $110).

There is an excellent amount of open deck space (including a swimming pool that is one of the longest aboard any cruise ship), and sports facilities that include a full-size paddle tennis court, putting green, and golf driving range.

Large Resort Ship: ....76,152 tons	Total Crew: 816	Cabins (with private balcony): 406
Lifestyle: ....Standard	Passengers	Cabins (wheelchair accessible): 22
Cruise Line: ....P&O Cruises	(lower beds/all berths): 1,868/1,975	(8 with private balcony)
Former Names: ....none	Passenger Space Ratio	Cabin Current: ....110 and 220 volts
Builder: ....Meyer Werft (Germany)	(lower beds/all berths): 40.7/38.5	Elevators: 10
Original Cost: ....$375 million	Crew/Passenger Ratio	Casino (gaming tables): ....Yes
Entered Service: ....May 2000	(lower beds/all berths): 2.2/2.4	Slot Machines: ....Yes
Registry: ....Great Britain	Navigation Officers: ....British	Swimming Pools (outdoors): 3
Length (ft/m): 885.8/270.0	Cabins (total): 934	(1 with magrodome)
Beam (ft/m): 105.6/32.2	Size Range (sq ft/m): 150.6–953.0/	Swimming Pools (indoors): 0
Draft (ft/m): 25.9/7.9	14.0–88.5	Whirlpools: 5
Propulsion/Propellers: .....diesel-electric	Cabins (outside view): 655	Self-Service Launderette: ....Yes
(40,000kW)/2	Cabins (interior/no view): 279	Dedicated Cinema/Seats: Yes/200
Passenger Decks: 10	Cabins (for one person): 0	Library: ....Yes

OVERALL SCORE: 1,507 (OUT OF A POSSIBLE 2,000 POINTS)

OVERVIEW. *Aurora* is named after the goddess of the dawn in Greek, Melanesian and Slavonic mythologies. Or perhaps the carnation Dianthus Aurora. Or it could be the famous Northern and Southern Lights, aurora borealis and aurora australis. At any rate, it was built specifically for Britain's growing traditional cruise market.

As ships evolve, slight differences in layout occur, as is the case with *Aurora* compared to earlier close sister *Oriana*. One big difference can be found in the addition of a large, magrodome-covered indoor/outdoor swimming pool (good in all weathers). The stern superstructure is nicely rounded and has several tiers that overlook the aft decks, pool and children's outdoor facilities. There is a good amount of open deck and sunbathing space, an important plus for the outdoors-loving mainly British passengers. There is an extra-wide wrap-around promenade deck outdoors, with plenty of white (plastic) sunloungers (cushioned pads are available).

The ship's interiors are gentle, welcoming and restrained, with warm colors and combinations that don't clash. The public rooms and areas have been designed in such a way that each room is individual, and yet there appears to be an open, yet cohesive flow throughout all of the public areas – something difficult to achieve when a number of designers are involved. There is good horizontal passenger flow, and wide passageways help to avoid congestion. Very noticeable are the fine, detailed ceiling treatments.

As it is a ship for all types of people, specific areas have been designed to attract different age groups and lifestyles. The focal point is a four-decks-high atrium lobby and a dramatic, calming, 35-ft (10.6-meter) high, Lalique-style sculpture (it's actually made of fiberglass) of two mythical

BERLITZ'S RATINGS		
	Possible	Achieved
Ship	500	407
Accommodation	200	161
Food	400	258
Service	400	307
Entertainment	100	76
Cruise	400	298

figures behind a veil of water. At the top of the atrium is the ship's library.

The carpeting throughout is of an excellent quality, much of it custom designed and made of long-lasting 100% wool. Original artworks by British artists include several tapestries and sculptures. For a weird experience, try standing on the midships staircase and look at the oil on canvas paintings by Nicholas Hely Hutchinson – they are curved – this has a dramatic effect on one's ability not to be seasick while cruising through the Bay of Biscay.

Other features include a virtual reality games room, 12 lounges/bars (among the nicest are Anderson's – similar to Anderson's aboard *Oriana*, with a fireplace and mahogany paneling, and the Crow's Nest – complete with a lovely one-sided model of one of P&O's former liners: *Strathnaver* of 1931, scrapped in Hong Kong in 1962. There is also a cinema that doubles as a concert and lecture hall.

There are special facilities and rooms for children and teens. Toybox is the playroom for 2–5 year olds, Jumpin' Jack's for 6–9 year olds, Quarterdeck for 10–13 year olds, and Decibels for 14–17 year olds, and a whole deck outdoors to play on (swimming pools and whirlpools included just for the youngsters). Children and teens have "Club Aurora" programs with their own rooms and their own outdoor pool. Children can be entertained until 10pm, which gives parents time to have dinner and go dancing. All cabins also have a baby-listening device. A night nursery for small children (ages 2–5) is available (6pm–midnight, no charge; from midnight to 2am there is a charge), as well as slumber parties for 6–9 year olds, In addition, 16 passenger cabins have interconnecting doors – good for families with children (or maid). Note that at peak holiday times (summer, Christmas, Easter) there could be 400 or more children on board. However, the ship absorbs them well, and the children's programming helps keep them occupied.

The library has several writing desks, large leather audio listening chairs, a good range of hardbacks (and a librarian), and skillfully crafted inlaid wood tables. On the second day of almost any cruise, however, it will have been almost stripped of books by word-hungry passengers. The library also sells some nautical books. An internet-connect center is located on the port side, aft of the popular Crow's Nest observation lounge (but sending emails can be expensive).

In this ship, P&O Cruises has improved on the facilities of older sister ship *Oriana*, with larger cabins and suites and with more dining options and choice of public areas. *Aurora* provides a decent, standardized cruise experience – good value for the money – for its mainly British passengers (of all dialects) and may be ideal for those who don't want to fly to join a cruise, as the ship sails from Southampton. Each year, the *Aurora* undertakes an around-the-world cruise; this is excellent value for money.

However, in the quest for more onboard revenue (and shareholder value), even birthday cakes now cost extra, as do espressos and cappuccinos (fake ones, made from instant coffee, are available in the dining rooms). Also at extra cost are ice creams, and bottled water (this can add up to a considerable amount on an around-the-world cruise). The onboard currency is the British pound. For gratuities, you should typically allow £3.50 ($5.25) per person, per day.

A British brass band send-off accompanies all sailings. Other touches include church bells that sound throughout the ship for the interdenominational Sunday church service. A coach service for passengers embarking or disembarking in Southampton covers much of the UK. Car parking is available (one rate for undercover parking, one rate for an open compound).

The ship's layout is a little disjointed in certain places, and there are several dead-ends and some poor signage. The reception desk's opening hours (7am–8pm) are too short. Shuttle buses, once provided in the various ports, are no longer free when provided (except on the around-the-world cruise). Standing in line for embarkation, disembarkation, shore tenders, and for self-serve buffet meals is inevitable. "Cashless Cruising" doesn't include tips (for an around-the-world cruise, this means carrying more than $750 in cash).

The final word: *Aurora* is the new *Canberra*, and there will typically be lots of smokers aboard, many driven to smoking in cabins and on balconies.

SUITABLE FOR: *Aurora* is best for adults of all ages (although most cruises attract the over-50s), and families with children of all ages who want a cruise that starts and ends in the UK, aboard a large ship with all the facilities of a small resort, with food and service that are very acceptable, though not as good as aboard some other cruise ships.

ACCOMMODATION. There are five main grades of cabins, in 26 price categories (location and size govern price).

Included are 2 two-level penthouses, 10 suites with balconies, 18 mini-suites with balconies, 368 cabins with balconies, 225 standard outside-view cabins, 16 interconnecting family cabins, and 279 interior (no view) cabins.

All grades, from the largest to the smallest, provide the following common features: polished cherry wood laminate cabinetry, full-length mirror, personal safe, refrigerator, television, individually controlled air conditioning; twin beds that convert to a queen-size double bed, sofa and coffee table. Also standard are stylish bed runners, Slumberland 8-inch sprung mattresses, 10.5 tog duvets (blankets and pillows if you prefer), Egyptian cotton towels and robes, improved tea/coffee making facilities with speciality teas (long-life is provided) and a Nick Munro-designed bespoke tray, as well as in-cabin toning and fitness facilities for passengers who prefer to exercise in private.

There are four whole decks of cabins with private balconies (about 40% of all cabins), and these feature easy-to-open sliding glass floor-to-ceiling doors; the partitions are of the almost full floor-to-ceiling type – so they really are quite private – and cannot be overlooked from above.

Cabin insulation could better (the magnetic catches in drawers and on the closet doors are noisy). Also, the TV sets provide only monaural sound. Although most doorways are 26 inches (66 cm) wide, the measurement of actual access is 2 inches (5 cm) less because of the doorframe; however, some doorways are only 21.5 inches (55 cm) wide.

A good range of Molton Brown products (shampoo, body lotion, shower gel) is provided for those in penthouse suites, suites or mini-suites. For all other cabins, only soap is provided, plus a "sport wash" combination soap and shampoo in a dispenser in the shower (so take your favorite shampoo and conditioner), and a small pouch of assorted personal-care items. All grades get thick, 100% cotton bathrobes, and 100% cotton towels. Except for the suites, no cabins have illuminated closets, and cabin ceilings are very plain.

Penthouse Suites: The largest cabins consist of two penthouse suites (named Library Suite and Piano Suite), each 953 sq. ft (88.5 sq. meters). They have forward-facing views, being located directly underneath the navigation bridge (the blinds must be drawn at night so as not to affect navigation). Each is spread over two decks in height, and connected by a beautiful wood curved staircase. One suite has a baby grand piano (which can be played manually or electronically), while the other has a private library. The living area is on the lower deck (Deck 10), and incorporates a dining suite (a first in a P&O ship) and a small private balcony. In the bedroom, upstairs, there is a walk-in closet, while the bathroom is decked out in porcelain and polished granite, with twin basins, bathtub and separate shower enclosure. There is also a small private balcony.

Suites: The suites (there are 10 of them) measure about 445 sq. ft (41.3 sq. meters). They have a separate bedroom with two lower beds that convert to a queen-sized bed. There is a walk-in dressing area and closet, with plenty of drawer space, a trouser press and ironing board. The lounge has a sofa, armchairs, dining table and chairs, writing desk, television, radio and stereo system. The marble-clad bathroom has a whirlpool bath, shower and toilet. The private balcony has space for two sunloungers, plus two chairs and two tables. Butler service is provided.

Mini-Suites: These measure 325 sq. ft (30.1 sq. meters), and have a separate bedroom area with two lower beds that convert to a queen-sized bed. There's one double and two single closets, a good amount of drawer space, binoculars, a trouser press and ironing board. Each private balcony has a blue plastic deck covering, one deck lounge chair, one chair and table, and exterior light.

Standard Outside-view/Interior (No View) Cabins: Any cabin designated as a double with private balcony measure about 175 sq. ft (16.2 sq. meters). They have two lower beds that convert to a queen-sized bed. The sitting area has a sofa and table. There's also a vanity table/writing desk, and a private balcony with blue plastic deck covering, two chairs (with only a small recline) and a small table. Note that a 110-volt (American) socket is located underneath the vanity desk drawer – in a difficult to access position.

Outside-view or Interior (with no view) Cabins have two lower beds that convert to a queen-sized bed, closet (but few drawers), and are 150 sq. ft (14 sq. meters). The bathroom has a mini-bath/shower and toilet, or shower and toilet.

All bathrooms in all grades (except those designated as suites) are compact, modular units, and have mirror-fronted cabinets, although the lighting is quite soft, and, in cabins with bathtubs, the retractable clothesline is located too high for most people to reach. High-quality personal toiletries are by Temple Spa.

There are 22 wheelchair-accessible cabins, well outfitted for the physically challenged passenger and almost all within easy access to lifts. However, one cabin (D165 on Deck 8) is located between forward and mid-ships stairways, and it is difficult to access the public rooms on Deck 8 without first going to the deck below, due to several steps and tight corners. All other wheelchair-accessible cabins are well positioned, and eight have a private balcony.

CUISINE. The two main dining rooms (each seats about 525) have tables for 2, 4, 6, 8 and 10, in two seatings. Medina, the midships restaurant, has a vaguely Moorish theme, while Alexandria, with windows on three sides, has Egyptian decor. Both are non-smoking, and both have more tables for two than in the equivalent restaurants aboard close sister ship *Oriana*. The china is Wedgwood, the silverware is by Elkington, the food by P&O.

The typical menu cycle is 14 days; anyone on a long voyage may find it quite repetitive). The cuisine is very British – a little adventurous at times, but always with plenty of curry dishes and other standard British items. Presentation is better than on other ships in the P&O Cruises fleet.

You should not expect exquisite dining, though – this is British hotel catering that doesn't pretend to offer caviar and other gourmet foods. But what it does present is attractive and tasty, with some excellent gravies and sauces to accompany all dining room meals. In keeping with the Britishness of P&O Cruises, the desserts and cakes are good. The service is provided by a team of friendly stewards

from India, with which P&O has had a long relationship.

There are several other dining options. You can, for example, also have dinner in the 24-hour, 120-seat French bistro-style restaurant, Cafe Bordeaux, for which there is a cover charge (for dinner only), with menus designed by Marco Pierre-White. Breakfasts and lunches are also served here, as are several coffees: espresso, cappuccino, latte, ristretto, as well as flavored coffees. So, if you want a croque-monsieur (a toasted ham and Gruyère cheese sandwich) at 5am, you can have it. For £9.50 you can try the "Tasting Menu" – a selection of small cosmopolitan dishes, with three different menus per cruise.

Casual, self-serve breakfasts and lunches can be taken from the buffet in a dazzlingl colorful eatery named "The Orangery", which has fine ocean views. Other casual dining spots include the Sidewalk Cafe (for fast food items poolside), champagne bar and, in a first for a P&O cruise ship, Raffles coffee and chocolate bar (but without the ceiling fans). All casual eateries are non-smoking.

ENTERTAINMENT. There is a wide variety of mainly British entertainment, from production shows to top British "name" and lesser name cabaret artists. The Stadium Theater Company is a group of resident actors, singers and dancers. They provide theater-style presentations such as mini versions of well-known musicals, "book" shows, revues, and drama presentations. There is also a program of theme cruises (antiques, art appreciation, classical music, comedy, cricket, gardening, jazz, Scottish dance, etc).

Ballroom dance fans will make use of the four good-sized wooden dance floors. The ship always carries a professional dance couple as hosts and teachers, and plenty of dancing time is included in the programming.

SPA/FITNESS. The Oasis Spa is midships on Lido Deck – almost at the top of the ship, just forward of the Crystal swimming pool. It is moderately large, and facilities include a gymnasium with the latest high-tech muscle-pumping and body toning toning equipment. There is also a sauna and steam room (both unisex, so you'll need a bathing suit). There's a beauty salon, a spiral staircase, and a relaxation area overlooking the forward Riviera swimming pool.

The spa is operated by Harding Brothers, a UK concession that provides the staff and a wide range of beauty and wellness treatments. Examples of treatments include: Body Toning (detox for the body); Seaweed Wrap; Collagen Velvet Facial Mask, and a range of aromatherapy treatments. Book spa treatments as soon after you embark as possible, as time slots fill up quickly aboard large ships such as this. Examples of prices: a full body massage is £60 for 50 minutes; an Indian head massage is £42 for 45 minutes; a holistic facial is £45 for 75 minutes; a manicure is £24 for 45 minutes, while a pedicure is £35 for 45 minutes.

A sports court incorporates a golf practice cage and a golf simulator (for which an extra charge applies).

● **For more extensive general information about a P&O cruise experience, see pages 133–34.**

Azamara Journey
★★★★

Mid-Size Ship: . . . . .30,277 tons	Passenger Decks: 9	Cabins (for one person): 0
Lifestyle: . . . . .Premium	Total Crew: 390	Cabins (with private balcony): 249
Cruise Line: . . . . .Azamara Cruises	Passengers	Cabins (wheelchair accessible): 6
Former Names: . . .*Blue Star, Blue Dream,*	(lower beds/all berths): 676/866	Cabin Current: . . . . .110 and 220 volts
R. Six	Passenger Space Ratio	Elevators: 4
Builder: .Chantiers de l'Atlantique (France)	(lower beds/all berths): 42.7/34.9	Casino (gaming tables): . . . . .Yes
Original Cost: . . . .$150 million	Crew/Passenger Ratio	Slot Machines: . . . . .Yes
Entered Service: . . . .Feb 2000/May 2007	(lower beds/all berths): 1.8/2.2	Swimming Pools (outdoors): 1
Registry: . . . . .Malta	Navigation Officers: . . . . .European	Swimming Pools (indoors): 0
Length (ft/m): 593.7/181.0	Cabins (total): 338	Whirlpools: 2 (+ 1 thalassotherapy hot tub)
Beam (ft/m): 95.1/29.0	Size Range (sq ft/m):	Self-Service Launderette: . . . . .Yes
Draft (ft/m): 19.85/6.0	. . . . .151.0–818.0/14.0–76.0	Dedicated Cinema/Seats: . . . . .No
Propulsion/Propellers:	Cabins (outside view): 312	Library: . . . . .Yes
. . . . .diesel 18,600kW)/2	Cabins (interior/no view): 26	

BERLITZ'S OVERALL SCORE: 1,465 (OUT OF A POSSIBLE 2,000 POINTS)

OVERVIEW. The all-white *Azamara Journey* was originally *R6*, one of a series of eight almost identical ships in the now defunct Renaissance Cruises fleet. It was purchased by Pullmantur in 2006, but transferred to Celebrity Cruises' new mid-sized ship brand, Azamara Cruises, in 2007. The ship has a sister in *Azamura Quest* (ex-*R7*).

The ship underwent a $17.5 million make-over that converted 48 cabins into 32 suites. A new Sunset Bar was added on the aft deck, and the ship received the Celebrity signature venue, Cova Café. New decking, carpets and soft furnishings, bedding and artwork were added, as was ship-wide wi-fi access. Being sister ships, the two Amazara vessels are virtually identical in features and fittings.

Azamara Journey is a contemporary ship, whose exterior design balances the ship's high sides by combining a deep blue hull with the white superstructure and large, square blue funnel. A lido deck has a tiny – and I mean tiny – swimming pool, and good sunbathing space. There is no outdoor walk-around promenade deck, although a short jogging track encircles the pool deck (but one deck above it). The uppermost outdoors deck includes a golf driving net and shuffleboard court. There are no wooden decks outdoors; instead, they are covered by a sand-colored rubberized material.

The interior decor is quite elegant, in good taste, and is a throwback to ship decor of the ocean liners of the 1920s and '30s. The overall feel is of a members-only country club. The main staircase in the two-deck-high foyer will remind you of something similar in the 1997 movie *Titanic*.

The public rooms are spread over three decks. The reception hall (lobby) has a staircase with intricate wrought-

BERLITZ'S RATINGS

	Possible	Achieved
Ship	500	417
Accommodation	200	157
Food	400	256
Service	400	283
Entertainment	100	72
Cruise	400	280

iron railings. A large observation lounge (The Looking Glass) is high atop the ship. This has a long bar with forward views (for the barmen, that is, as passengers sitting at the bar face aft). There's a bar in each of the restaurant entrances, as well as a Martini Bar. There's also a Michael's Club – a jazz/piano lounge, and, of course, a Luxe Casino, and a shop (Boutique C). Internet connectivity is provided at Online@Celebrity. Unfortunately, the tacky art auctions spoil the whole experience.

The Library is a beautiful, grand, restful room (perhaps the nicest public room), and is designed in the Regency style. It has a fireplace, a high, indented, *trompe l'oeil* ceiling, and a good selection of books, comfortable wingback chairs with footstools, and sofas you could sleep on.

The onboard currency is the US dollar, and gratuities of $12.50 are charged to your onboard SeaPass account.

SUITABLE FOR: Mature couples seeking to get away from the crowds aboard a contemporary ship with a wide range of bars and lounges, in the setting of a mid-size ship.

ACCOMMODATION. There are eight cabin price grades; three suite-grades and five other grades. All have so-called butler service. All of the standard interior (no view) and outside-view cabins (the lowest four grades) are extremely compact units, and rather tight for two persons (particularly for cruises longer than seven days).

For the extra money, it's wise to choose a suite or cabin with its own balcony. Some cabins have interconnecting doors (good for families with children) while 18 cabins on Deck 6 have lifeboat-obstructed views. No matter what grade of accommodation you choose, all have color televisions that carry European news and sports channel (where obtainable), and several movie channels.

Standard Interior (No View)/ Standard Outside-view Cabins: These have twin beds (convertible to a queen-size bed), with good under-bed storage areas, safe, vanity desk with large mirror, good closet and drawer space.

Ocean-view Cabins: Features: two lower beds convertible to queen size (some have an extra sofa bed); flat-screen TV; refrigerator with mini-bar; thermostat-controlled air conditioning; direct-dial telephone and voicemail; desk; in-room safe; hand-held hairdryer. Approximate size: 161 sq.ft.

Note that some cabins have a panorama window with an obstructed view, while those on the lowest deck have a porthole instead of a window.

Deluxe Ocean-view Cabins with Balcony: Features two lower beds convertible to queen size; floor-to-ceiling sliding glass doors; sitting area with sofa bed; private veranda; flat-screen television; refrigerator with mini-bar; thermostat-controlled air conditioning; direct-dial telephone and voicemail; desk; in-room safe; hand-held hairdryer. Approximate size: 215 sq.ft.; balcony 38 sq.ft.

Sunset Verandah Cabins: Features two lower beds convertible to queen size; floor-to-ceiling sliding glass doors; sitting area with sofa bed; private veranda; flat-screen television; refrigerator with mini-bar; thermostat-controlled air conditioning; direct-dial telephone and voicemail; desk; in-room safe; hand-held hairdryer. Approximate size: 215 sq.ft.; balcony 154 sq.ft.

Sky Suites: Superior Exterior View Cabins with Balcony: The cabins with private balconies, have partial, and not full, balcony partitions, sliding glass doors, and, due to good design and layout, only 14 cabins on Deck 6 have lifeboat-obstructed views. The bathrooms, which have tiled floors and plain walls, are compact units, and include either a bathtub/shower or a shower stall with a strong, removable hand-held shower unit, hairdryer, 100 percent cotton towels, toiletries storage shelves and retractable clothesline. Approximate size: 323 sq.ft.; balcony 57 sq.ft.

Royal Suites (Decks 6, 7): In reality these are large cabins, as the sleeping and lounge areas are not divided. While not overly large, the bathrooms have a good-sized bathtub and ample space for storing personal toiletry items. The living area has a refrigerated mini-bar, lounge area with breakfast table, and a balcony with two plastic chairs and a table. Approximate size: 538 sq.ft.; balcony 173 sq.ft.

Penthouse De-Luxe Suite with Balcony: These provide the most spacious accommodation, and are fine, large living spaces located in the forward-most and aft-most sections of the accommodation decks (particularly nice are those that overlook the stern, on Deck 6, Deck 7 and Deck 8). An entrance foyer leads to a living room, bedroom (the bed faces the sea, which can be seen through the floor-to-ceiling windows and sliding glass door), CD player (with selection of audio discs), bathroom with Jacuzzi bathtub, and a small guest bathroom. They have more extensive private balconies that really are private. Approximate size: 603 sq.ft.; balcony 215 sq.ft.

CUISINE. Discoveries, the ship's main dining room, has around 340 seats, a raised central section (conversation at these tables may be difficult, due to its low ceiling height), and open-seating dining. There are large ocean-view windows on three sides, several prime tables overlooking the stern, and a small bandstand for live dinner music. The menu changes daily for lunch and dinner. Adjacent to the restaurant is a cosy Martini Bar.

Alternative Dining Spots:

● The (extra-cost) *Aqualina Restaurant* is located at the aft of the ship on the port side of Deck 10; it has 96 seats, windows along two sides, and features Mediterranean cuisine. Reservations are required. Cost: $20 per person, or $50 per person for the special Tasting Menu, including wine.

● *Prime C* (extra cost), at the aft of the ship on the starboard side of Deck 10, has grill food items such as steaks and seafood. It has 98 seats, windows along two sides and a set menu. Reservations are required. Extra cost: $25 per person.

● The *Windows Cafe* has indoor seating for just over 150 (not really enough when cruising in cold areas or in the winter months), and 186 seats outdoors. Many tables do, however, have ocean views. It is open for breakfast, lunch and casual dinners, and incorporates a small Sushi Cafe.

All dining venues have open-seating dining, although reservations are necessary in the Aqualina Restaurant and Prime C, where there are mostly tables for four or six (there are few tables for two). Suite-grade occupants get two nights free, while other accommodation categories get one night free in one of the two alternative venues. In addition, there is a Poolside Grill and Bar. All cappuccino and espresso coffees are at extra cost, even in the restaurants.

A Cova Café (from Milan, exclusive to Azarama Crusies and Celebrity Cruises) serves fine Italian coffees, as well as teas and pastries. And a Wine Bar with an extensive cellar features wine-and-food pairings, wine tasting sessions, and wines by the glass or bottle.

ENTERTAINMENT. Celebrity Cabaret, located forward, is the venue for all main entertainment events. While this is not the ideal ship for large-scale production shows, in the evenings, the entertainment consists of a mix of classical concerts, revues, as well as comedy and drama.

The entertainment has a cultural tone to it. Additionally, local entertainers are brought on board in various destinations, providing a taste of the local traditions.

SPA/FITNESS. The AquaSpa has a gymnasium with some high-tech muscle toning equipment, a thalassotherapy pool (outside, forward on deck), and several treatment rooms. Outside on deck, there is a small swimming pool, two hot tubs, and a jogging track (one deck above the pool). The spa is staffed and operated by Steiner Leisure, a specialist concession. An "Acupuncture at Sea" clinic provides treatments that are operated independently of the spa (but also as a concession). Spa treatments are possible in your suite, too. Outside on the Lido Deck, there is a small swimming pool, two hot tubs, and a jogging track (one deck above the pool).

Azamara Quest
★★★★

Mid-Size Ship: . . . . .30,277 tons	Total Crew: 306	Cabins (with private balcony): 232
Lifestyle: . . . . .Premium	Passengers	Cabins (wheelchair accessible): 4
Cruise Line: . . . . .Azamara Cruises	(lower beds/all berths): 716/777	Cabin Current: . . . . .110 and 220 volts
Former Names: . . . . . .*Blue Moon, Delphin*	Passenger Space Ratio	Elevators: 4
Renaissance, R7	(lower beds/all berths): 42.2/38.9	Casino (gaming tables): . . . . .No
Builder: .Chantiers de l'Atlantique (France)	Crew/Passenger Ratio	Slot Machines: .No
Original Cost: . . . .$150 million	(lower beds/all berths): 2.3/2.5	Swimming Pools (outdoors): 1
Entered Service: . . . . .Oct 2000/Oct 2007	Navigation Officers: . . . . .European	Swimming Pools (indoors): 0
Registry: . . . . .Malta	Cabins (total): .358	Whirlpools: 2 (+ 1 thalassotherapy hot tub)
Length (ft/m): 591.8/180.4	Size Range (sq ft/m): 156.0–484.3/	Self-Service Launderette: . . . . .Yes
Beam (ft/m): 83.3/25.4	14.5–45.0	Dedicated Cinema/Seats: . . . . .No
Draft (ft/m): 19.0/5.8	Cabins (outside view): 332	Library: . . . . .Yes
Propulsion/Propellers: diesel 18,600kW)/2	Cabins (interior/no view): 26	
Passenger Decks: 9	Cabins (for one person): 0	

BERLITZ'S OVERALL SCORE: 1,466 (OUT OF A POSSIBLE 2,000 POINTS)

OVERVIEW. *Azamara Quest* was originally *R7*, one of a series of eight almost identical ships in the now defunct Renaissance Cruises fleet (when it was in operation, between 1998 and 2001, it was the cruise industry's only totally no-smoking cruise line). It was purchased by Pullmantur in 2006, but transferred to Celebrity Cruises' new mid-sized ship brand Azamara Cruises, in 2007. Before entering service, the ship underwent an almost $20 million make-over. The ship has a sister in *Azamura Journey* (ex-*R6*).

An outdoors lido deck has a swimming pool, and good sunbathing space, while one of the aft decks has a thalassaotherapy pool. The exterior decks are covered with a rubber and sand-like surface (teak, although very expensive, would be much better, and more in keeping with the decor of the ship). The uppermost outdoors deck includes a golf driving net and shuffleboard court.

The interior decor is quite elegant, in the style of the ocean

BERLITZ'S RATINGS

	Possible	Achieved
Ship	500	418
Accommodation	200	157
Food	400	256
Service	400	283
Entertainment	100	72
Cruise	400	280

liner decor of the 1920s and '30s. This includes detailed ceiling cornices, both real and faux wrought-iron staircase railings, leather paneled walls, *trompe l'oeil* ceilings, rich carpeting in hallways with an Oriental rug-look center section, and other interesting (and expensive-looking, but faux) decorative touches.

The overall ambiance is that of an old-world country club. The staircase in the main, two-deck-high foyer will remind you of something similar in a blockbuster hit about a certain ship in which movie stars Kate Winslet and Leonardo di Caprio met. Passengers should be pleased with the ship's tasteful, traditional-style interiors, and with the variety of public rooms (basically spread over three decks) that are featured.

For other comments regarding this ship, see the preceding entry for *Azamara Journey*. Some public rooms have different names to those of *Azamara Journey* (Breeze instead of Windows Café, for example)

Mid-Size Ship: . . . . .43,537 tons	Total Crew: 471	Cabins (for one person): 91
Lifestyle: . . . . .Standard	Passengers	Cabins (with private balcony): 121
Cruise Line: . . . . .Fred Olsen Cruise Lines	(lower beds/all berths): 1,397/1,397	Cabins (wheelchair accessible): 9
Former Names: . . . . . .*Norwegian Crown,*	+ 350 (after stretch)	Cabin Current: . . . . .110 AC
Crown Odyssey	Passenger Space Ratio	Elevators: 4
Builder: . . . . .Meyer Werft (Germany)	(lower beds/all berths): 31.1/31.1	Casino (gaming tables): . . . . .Yes
Original Cost: . . . .$178 million	Crew/Passenger Ratio	Slot Machines: . . . . .Yes
Entered Service: . . . . .Jun 1988/Jan 2008	(lower beds/all berths): 3.03/3.03	Swimming Pools (outdoors): 1
Registry: . . . . .The Bahamas	Navigation Officers: .European/Norwegian	Swimming Pools (indoors): 1
Length (ft/m): 715.2/218.0	Cabins (total): 744	Whirlpools: 2
Beam (ft/m): 92.5/28.2	Size Range (sq ft/m):	Self-Service Launderette: . . . . .Yes
Draft (ft/m): 23.8/7.26	153.9–613.5/14.3–57.0	Dedicated Cinema/Seats: . . . . .No
Propulsion/Propellers: diesel (21,330kW)/2	Cabins (outside view): 562	Library: . . . . .Yes
Passenger Decks: 10	Cabins (interior/no view): 182	

BERLITZ'S OVERALL SCORE: 1,398 (OUT OF A POSSIBLE 2,000 POINTS)

OVERVIEW. *Balmoral* (formerly *Norwegian Crown*) is a well-designed and built ship, originally constructed for the now defunct Royal Cruise Line. Norwegian Cruise Line then operated the ship for many years, before it was transferred to Orient Lines in 2000, and then back to Norwegian Cruise Line in September 2003.

Fred Olsen Cruise Lines bought the ship in 2007 and, after a major refurbishment, including a "chop and stretch" operation involving the addition of a 99-ft (30.2-meter) mid-section, it entered service in January 2008.

The all-white ship has a relatively handsome exterior profile, and one plus feature is its full, walk-around teak promenade deck outdoors, although it becomes a little narrow in the forward section of the vessel; a jogging track is also to be found on the uppermost deck outdoors. Atop the ship is the Horizon Lounge, with fine ocean views, central dance floor, and bar. Out on deck, there is a heated saltwater pool, but little shade (no glass dome for inclement weather).

The main public room spaces are on Lounge Deck. At the front of the ship is the Neptune Lounge, (the main show lounge, with an integral bar at the back of the room; the raised stage and wood dance floor is surrounded by amphitheatre-style seating in banquettes with small drinks tables. Aft of the showlounge are the shops – a spiral staircase connects this deck with the reception lobby on the deck below.

Next is the Braemar Lounge, which is combined in to a lifestyle room that includes a decent internet center with good separation for privacy, library, and card room. Aft of the Braemar Lounge is the Morning Light Pub. Aft is the

BERLITZ'S RATINGS

	Possible	Achieved
Ship	500	387
Accommodation	200	150
Food	400	258
Service	400	265
Entertainment	100	65
Cruise	400	273

Palms Café, the ship's casual self-service buffet-style café.

The two-deck high lobby has a large gold sculpture in the shape of a globe of the world by the famous sculpture artist Arnaldo Pomodoro; it used to revolve.

The onboard currency is the British pound and port taxes are included for UK passengers. Gratuities of £4 ($7) per passenger, per day, are suggested.

A piece of trivia for ship buffs: a bar at the back of the showlounge was originally named Theo's bar after one of the Royal Cruise Line's most popular bartenders.

SUITABLE FOR: *Balmoral* is best suited to British couples and single travelers wanting destination-intensive cruising in a ship that has European quality, style, and character, a sense of space, comfortable surroundings, decent facilities, realistic pricing and good value for money, with British food and entertainment. A friendly and accommodating, mostly-Filipino crew should help to make a cruise aboard the ship a pleasant, no-hassle experience.

ACCOMMODATION. There are 21 price categories; typically the higher the deck, the more expensive will be your accommodation. Most cabins are of the same size and layout, have blond wood cabinetry and accents, an abundance of mirrors, and closet and drawer space, and are very well equipped. All accommodation grades have a color television, a hairdryer, thin 100% cotton bathrobe, music console (plus a button that can be used to turn announcements on or off), personal safe, and private bathroom with shower (many upper-grade cabins have a good-sized bathtub). All towels are 100% cotton, although they could be larger;

soap, shampoo, body lotion, shower cap and sewing kit are the amenities provided.

The cabin soundproofing is generally good. Some cabins have interconnecting doors, so that they can connect to make a two-room suite. You should note that almost all cabins on Deck 8 have lifeboat-obstructed views.

The largest accommodation: 28 suites on Highland Deck 10. Each is decorated in a different style, in accordance with the name of the suite (from fore to aft they are: Edinburgh, Inverness, Balmoral, Sandringham, Shalimar, Taj Mahal, Mykonos, Portofino, Bel Air, Hollywood, Bali, Tahiti, Imperial, Shangri-La, Dynasty, Mandarin). They are quite spacious units, and provide a sleeping area and separate living room (including some nicely finished wood cabinetry and a huge amount of drawer space), together with a large, white marble-clad bathroom with a full-sized tub and integral shower), and a semi-private balcony (the balcony can be overlooked from the open deck above).

Other spacious accommodation can be found in cabins with bay windows. These include a separate sleeping area with twin beds, a huge amount of drawer space in a large vanity/writing desk, and a lounge typically with two sofas, tub chairs and heavy glass table, refrigerator and TV set. Electrically operated window blinds, together with the curtains that front them provide good blackouts for the bay windows. The white marble-clad bathroom is also large and features a full-sized bathtub with integral shower.

There are several wheelchair-accessible cabins; these provide plenty of space to maneuver, and all four include a bathroom with roll-in shower. But wheelchair accessibility in some ports on the many itineraries operated by this ship (particularly in Europe) may prove quite frustrating and wheelchair-accessible transportation will be very limited.

Cabins in the new mid-section have attractive, contemporary decor that is light and airy, but they are a little smaller than comparable grade cabins in the "old" sections. Bathrooms have shower enclosures rather than tub/shower combinations (some have two washbasins), and less storage space for personal toiletries.

CUISINE. The Ballindalloch Restaurant is the principal dining room. It has ocean-view windows on port and starboard sides, is operated in two seatings. It has comfortable seating at tables for two, four, six or eight.

Two intimate dining spots: Avon Restaurant and Spey Restaurant, are located aft on Highland Deck 10 (the deck that contains all the higher-priced suites). The floor-to-ceiling windows provide lots of light, and the decor is contemporary and minimalist.

The 70-seat Palms Cafe is an alternative, more intimate venue for informal dinners (reservations only; a cover charge applies). The intimate room has wood banquette seating, and the decor colors are coral, green and gold.

The outdoors 40-seat Marquee Grill, on an open aft deck, is a casual, al-fresco dining spot, adjacent to a sunbathing and whirlpool area, and an open-air bar. This may also be also used as a casual outdoors eatery on selected nights.

ENTERTAINMENT. The Showlounge is the venue for all entertainment shows, cabaret acts, lectures, and some social functions. It is a single level room with tiered seating levels. Sightlines are generally good, but could be better.

Revue-style production shows are staged by a resident troupe of singer/dancers) and there are cabaret acts. The quality of the shows is so-so. Cabaret acts (typically singers, magicians, ventriloquists, comedy jugglers, and comedians) perform individually or as part of the revues.

SPA/FITNESS. There is a decent indoor spa, pool, gymnasium, and several beauty treatment rooms.

Black Prince
★ ★ +

Small Ship: . . . . .11,209 tons	Total Crew: 200	Cabins (with private balcony): 0
Lifestyle: . . . . .Standard	Passengers	Cabins (wheelchair accessible): 2
Cruise Line: . . . . .Fred Olsen Cruise Lines	(lower beds/all berths): 439/472	Cabin Current: . . . . .230 volts
Former Names: . . . . .none	Passenger Space Ratio	Elevators: 2
Builder: . . . . .Fender Werft (Germany)	(lower beds/all berths): 25.3/23.7	Casino (gaming tables): . . . . .Yes
Original Cost: . . . .$20 million	Crew/Passenger Ratio	Slot Machines: .No
Entered Service: 1966	(lower beds/all berths): 2.2/2.3	Swimming Pools (outdoors): 1
Registry: . . . . .The Bahamas	Navigation Officers: . . . . .European	Swimming Pools (indoors): 1
Length (ft/m): 470.4/143.40	Cabins (total): .234	Whirlpools: 2
Beam (ft/m): 66.6/20.30	Size Range (sq ft/m): 80.7–226.0/	Self-Service Launderette: . . . . .No
Draft (ft/m): 20.0/6.10	7.5–21.0	Dedicated Cinema/Seats: . . . . .No
Propulsion/Propellers: . . . . .diesel	Cabins (outside view): 167	Library: . . . . .Yes
(12,310kW)/2	Cabins (interior/no view): 67	
Passenger Decks: 7	Cabins (for one person): 29	

OVERALL SCORE: 1,014 (OUT OF A POSSIBLE 2,000 POINTS)

OVERVIEW. *Black Prince* is a traditional style of ship (the name is 14th-century, originally referring to the son of Edward III), owned and operated as a family-run business. With its thick hull, it is as solidly built as a battleship. Originally used for winter cruising and summer North Sea crossings, the ship has been well maintained, though it has a rather ungainly profile, and tends to pitch in unkind seas (but probably less so than any new ship would). One nice feature of this old-style ship is that it has many nooks and crannies around its open decks (most of which are either painted steel decks or decks covered with blue "turf"; among them is one forward observation deck that lets you look over the bows and navigation bridge.

There are few public rooms, the principal one being the Neptune Lounge – a two-deck high room (with bars on both levels) that is the ship's main show lounge.. Another room, the Aquitaine Lounge, sits in the front part of the ship, and tends to be the quiet room – good for reading an absorbing book. There is a small, little used casino section located on the starboard side of this lounge. Additionally, a passageway that was formerly part of two restaurants is now a photo gallery and lounge area.

The decor has a very homely, restrained feel and ambiance, with soft lighting and no glitz anywhere. Many of the soft furnishings are hand-tailored on board by Filipino upholsterers. The ship has good wooden stairways throughout, although the steps are a little steep. An ironing room is provided – another useful addition for the ship's mainly British passengers. This is one solidly built ship (they don't make them like this anymore) that plods along at teenage speeds, but will always arrive on time, no matter what.

BERLITZ'S RATINGS

	Possible	Achieved
Ship	500	231
Accommodation	200	99
Food	400	201
Service	400	225
Entertainment	100	51
Cruise	400	207

Although it was really constructed as a dual purpose cruise-ferry (it used to carry tomatoes from the Canary Islands below decks, and passengers above decks), over the years it has been converted into a handy-sized vessel that will give you a comfortable ride. Actually, coming into (and leaving from) port reminds me of those Holiday Inn beds years ago that vibrated for you when you inserted a quarter (25 cents) into a little box by its side. Still, there are other ships of the same era that do the same thing.

Although the names sound similar, *Black Prince* is not at all like the larger sister ships *Black Watch* and *Boudicca*, which have many more facilities and are better ships. *Black Prince* does have an unstuffy, unpretentious feel, an almost totally Filipino staff, and is well suited to the informal, older British passenger. However, standards of cleanliness, food and service have been allowed to become sloppy. While there are many repeat passengers who would not dream of trying another ship, some newcomers will feel that this is an old, tired ship that should be heading for retirement – soon, particularly in light of the increased competition from other, newer, better ships.

The artwork aboard this ship is eclectic; it is quite uncoordinated and not looked after, but there are a few interesting pieces if you seek them out – one, a huge wood carving in the Lido Lounge (it was originally in a house in Oslo), has five bullet holes in it (but to get the full story, you'll need to book a cruise).

So, what are the good points about cruising aboard *Black Prince*? You'll have a good, well-rounded cruise experience, with well organized cruises, interesting itineraries, very few announcements, complimentary shuttle buses in many ports of call (few companies offer this service today), a reasonably comfortable (but quite basic and dated) ship, a decent standard of food, and with friendly service from (mostly Filipino) crew members who smile and mean well. Cruising aboard *Black Prince* also means that drinks prices are quite reasonable (below those of most other ships operating from UK ports) and you won't be fleeced and poked for onboard revenue at every turn. It also means cruising with experienced Norwegian navigation officers and itineraries that are well planned, with long port stays. So, for all I have said about the ship being of the old ilk, cruising aboard it is a comfortable, cosseting experience.

Port taxes are included for UK passengers. For the ship's (mainly) British passengers, the National Express bus operator works in conjunction with Fred Olsen Cruise Lines to provide a dedicated Cruiselink service via London's Victoria Coach Station to the UK departure ports of Dover or Southampton.

The crew is extremely friendly by nature, although the feeling that many passengers have is that the ship now operates more for the crew than for its passengers. Standards of product delivery and professionalism have fallen over the past few years (a stronger onboard middle management with properly recognized training is needed). The onboard currency is the British pound.

It is often hard to get away from smokers, and the service has become overly casual of late. The company lists recommended gratuities of £4 (around $6) per passenger per day, which, to some, seems a lot. The air-conditioning is inconsistent; in particular in many cabins it is not good (the ship was built when forced air circulation was the norm). Handrails throughout the ship are topped with black plastic (reminiscent of old schools and ferries) and would look and feel so much better in wood.

Despite all the negatives, it's the friendly ambiance and caring crew that make passengers want to come back again and again (rather like going back to a favourite B&B). However, the ship will be withdrawn from service in 2010 because it will not comply with the new SOLAS regulations.

SUITABLE FOR: *Black Prince* is best suited to the British passenger who enjoys seeking out the world's duty-free shops, with British-style entertainment and cabaret acts. This ship is for people who like Morris Minor cars, who don't want the latest high-tech plastic laminate cruise ship, and couldn't care less about things like having a telephone in each cabin, or internet connectivity, and for those who really like the intimacy that only small ships can provide.

ACCOMMODATION. There is a wide range of cabin sizes and configurations (the brochure lists 14) to choose from (from dimensionally challenged to quite adequate), and a good percentage of cabins are particularly reserved for single passengers. Do note, however, that many cabins have poor air-conditioning, and hard beds, and some cabins have second-person beds that fold down at night and are used as seating by day. If your accommodation is in the aft third of the ship, you won't need an alarm clock to get you out of bed in the mornings when the ship is coming into port, because the ship's vibration performs that function for you.

Duvets are provided in all grades of cabin, the bathroom towels are 100% cotton and reasonably sized (not large). A hairdryer is also supplied. A package of Gilchrist & Soames personal toiletry items (bath gel, shampoo/conditioner, sewing kit, shower cap) is provided for all passengers.

The outside-view suites are reasonably decent (particularly comfortable are the Gran Canaria and Lanzarote suites, with their wood-paneled walls) and nicely appointed. Other cabins are small, but reasonably well equipped (except for the lowest grades, which are very small and rather utilitarian), and tastefully decorated, for a smaller ship. There is a charge for some room service items. The upper-grade cabins also have a refrigerator.

CUISINE. The dining room has two sections, Fleur de Lys and Royal Garter, both non-smoking and with big picture windows along one side. There are two seatings (sometimes, first- and second-seating diners exchange seatings, a pleasant arrangement). The Balblom Restaurant (with wood/glass ceiling and patio-style tables and chairs), is located atop the ship, and provides another choice for dining (reservations required for dinner when featured).

Fred Olsen Cruise Lines has above-average cuisine that is attractively presented, with a good range of fish, seafood, meat and chicken dishes, and vegetarian options. The food is generally of good quality, with a decent selection of main course items to suit most British tastes. Breakfast buffets tend to be repetitious, although they appear to satisfy most.

Communication with the Filipino waiters can prove a little frustrating at times (although it is better now than it has been in the past, and smiles can compensate). There is a very decent range of wines, at moderate prices, but few of the wine stewards have much knowledge of wines.

ENTERTAINMENT. The Neptune Lounge is the name of the ship's showlounge. It has two levels (although sight lines to the stage are quite restricted from many seats due to the configuration of the room).

The entertainment mainly consists of small revue shows by a small team of resident singers/dancers, and cabaret acts of questionable quality (they seem to rotate around many ships of the same style and size in the cruise industry), although, to be fair, passengers who cruise aboard this ship are not really looking for first-rate entertainment, but rather something to fill the time after dinner, which is the main event for most passengers.

SPA/FITNESS. The one facility that is extremely good (for a small ship) is the indoor fitness/leisure center, complete with an indoor swimming pool and health spa area with gymnasium, sauna, and small beauty salon. To get to it, though, you have to negotiate asteep staircase with short steps. The spa is operated by Harding Brothers, a concession. Some fitness classes are free, while some, such as yoga (£5 per class or £15 for four classes), cost extra.

Black Watch
★★★ +

Mid-Size Ship: . . . . .28,613 tons	Passenger Decks: 8	Cabins (for one person): 38
Lifestyle: . . . . .Standard	Total Crew: .350	Cabins (with private balcony): 43
Cruise Line: . . . . .Fred Olsen Cruise Lines	Passengers	Cabins (wheelchair accessible): 4
Former Names: . . . .*Star Odyssey,*	(lower beds/all berths): 804/868	Cabin Current: . . . . .110 and 220 volts
Westward, Royal Viking Star	Passenger Space Ratio	Elevators: 4
Builder: . . . . .Wartsila (Finland)	(lower beds/all berths): 35.5/32.9	Casino (gaming tables): . . . . .Yes
Original Cost: . . . .$22.5 million	Crew/Passenger Ratio	Slot Machines: . . . . .Yes
Entered Service: . . .June 1972/Nov 1996	(lower beds/all berths): 2.2/2.4	Swimming Pools (outdoors): 2
Registry: . . . . .The Bahamas	Navigation Officers: . . . . .European	Swimming Pools (indoors): 0
Length (ft/m): 674.1/205.47	Cabins (total): 421	Whirlpools: 3
Beam (ft/m): 82.6/25.20	Size Range (sq ft/m): 135.6–819.1/	Self-Service Launderette: . . . . .Yes
Draft (ft/m): 24.7/7.55	12.6–76.1	Dedicated Cinema/Seats: Yes/156
Propulsion/Propellers: . . . . .diesel	Cabins (outside view): 383	Library: . . . . .Yes
(13,400kW)/2	Cabins (interior/no view): 48	

OVERALL SCORE: 1,339 (OUT OF A POSSIBLE 2,000 POINTS)

OVERVIEW. Acquired by Fred Olsen Cruise Lines in late 1996, this ship, originally built for long-distance cruising for the now-defunct Royal Viking Line (it was built for one of the three original shipping partners who formed the line – Bergenske Dampskibsselskab), has a sharply raked bow and a sleek appearance that was "stretched" in 1981 with the addition of a mid section. The ship's name is taken from the famous Scottish Black Watch regiment, although the ship itself is all-white. There is a good amount of open deck and sunbathing space, and a decent health-fitness area high atop the ship, as well as a wide wrap-around teakwood promenade deck (with wind-breaker on the aft part of the deck).

The interior decor is quiet and restful, with wide stairways and foyers, soft lighting and no glitz anywhere, although many passengers find the artwork a little drab (it is, in reality, rather more Scandinavian eclectic than anything). In general, good materials, fabrics (including the use of the Black Watch tartan) and soft furnishings add to a pleasant ambiance and comfortable feeling experienced throughout the public rooms, most of which are quite spacious and have high, indented ceilings.

There is a wide selection of public rooms, most of which (including the main dining room) are located on one deck in a user-friendly horizontal layout. An observation lounge (called The Observatory) high atop the ship, is decorated in nautical memorabilia, and has commanding views (draft beers are available, as in all bars).

There is a good cinema (few ships today have a dedicated cinema) with a steeply tiered floor, and a pleasant library (with an adjacent computer/internet access room

BERLITZ'S RATINGS

	Possible	Achieved
Ship	500	346
Accommodation	200	141
Food	400	248
Service	400	273
Entertainment	100	63
Cruise	400	268

containing two computer terminals), and a card room.

A popular meeting place is the Braemar Room, a large lounge close to the restaurant; it has a self-help beverage corner for coffees and teas (open 24 hours a day, although it does become overly busy during afternoon tea time), comfortable chairs, and large ocean-view windows along one side. On one wall is an old iron figurehead from a ship called *Braemar Castle* (it's one of several iron figureheads found aboard this ship, from a collection owned by the Olsen family).

Smokers will appreciate a special, small, cigar and pipe smoking room (The Cove), as well as a bar (Pipers Bar) for general smoking (the only two locations inside the ship where smoking is permitted).

The casino consists of two blackjack tables and a roulette table, and is presently located opposite the Starlite Nightclub; a separate room houses a clutch of slot machines. A self-serve launderette (useful on the longer cruises) has four washing machines, five dryers, and a couple of irons in a large user-friendly room.

Black Watch is a comfortable (not luxurious) ship in which to cruise, with a moderate standard of food and service from a friendly, mostly Filipino staff that provides decent (though not faultless) service, and should provide you with a good, well-rounded cruise experience. There is ample space per passenger, even when the ship is full. Cruises are well organized, with interesting itineraries, and complimentary shuttle buses in many ports of call. The onboard currency is the British pound.

Fred Olsen Cruise Lines offers good value for money cruises in a relaxed environment that provides passengers with many of the comforts of home. Port taxes are included for UK passengers.

The National Express bus operator works in conjunction with Fred Olsen Cruise Lines to provide a dedicated Cruiselink service via London's Victoria Coach Station to the UK departure ports of Dover or Southampton.

Although it is being well maintained, do remember that this ship is more than 30 years old, which means that little problems such as gurgling plumbing, creaking joints, and other idiosyncrasies can occur, and air conditioning may not be all that it should be (this is particularly true in some cabins). The company lists recommended gratuities of £4 ($6) per passenger per day, which, to some, seems a lot. Only a few suites have private balconies.

Passenger gripes include: noticeable cutbacks in food variety and quality, an increase in the use of paper napkins, packets of butter, margarine and preserves, the lack of choice of sugar, very poor coffee, long lines at the cramped buffet, and poor wine service (not enough wine waiters). Other gripes: the smell of stale cigarette smoke in lounges and bars, not enough staff for the increased passenger numbers following the addition of more cabins, and a poor selection of hardback books in the library (many paperbacks), poor service levels.

SUITABLE FOR: *Black Watch* is best suited to the older UK traveler who enjoys seeking out the world's duty-free shops, and wants a British cruise environment, in comfortable surroundings, with British food and entertainment, and more formal attire than is found aboard the smaller ships in the fleet: *Black Prince* and *Braemar*.

ACCOMMODATION. There are 18 price categories of cabins (plus one for the owner's suite, whose price is not listed in the brochure), including four grades of cabin for those traveling solo (these are spread across most of the cabin decks, and not just the lower decks, as some lines do). The wide range of cabins provides something for everyone, from spacious suites with separate bedrooms, to small (interior – no view) cabins. While most cabins are for two persons, some can accommodate a third, fourth, or even a fifth person.

In all grades, duvets are provided, the decently sized bathroom towels are 100% cotton, and a hairdryer is provided. A package of Gilchrist & Soames personal toiletry items (bath gel, shampoo/conditioner, sewing kit, shower cap) is supplied to all passengers. Occupants of suite grades also get a cotton bathrobe and cold canapes each evening (as well as priority seating in the dining rooms).

The room service menu is quite limited and could be improved (although there is an abundance of food available at most times of the day). The suites and cabins on Decks 7, 8, and 9 are quiet units. A number of cabins located in the aft section of Decks 3, 4 and 5 can prove to be uncomfortable, with noise from throbbing engines and generator units a major distraction (particularly from those cabins adjacent to the engine casing).

Outside-view/Inside (No View) Cabins: Spread across Decks 3, 4, 5, 7 and 8, all cabins are quite well equipped,

and there is plenty of good (illuminated) closet, drawer and storage space (the drawers are metal and tinny, however, and in some closets they consist of wire baskets – like you might find in inexpensive hotels in Europe). No-smoking cabins are available. Some cabin bathrooms have awkward access, and insulation between some of the lower grade cabins could be better. The bathrooms are of a decent size. All have had a facelift, with new toiletries cabinets, washbasin facings, and re-tiled floors. Some cabins have a small bathtub, although many have only a shower enclosure.

Deluxe/Bridge/Junior Suites: These suites, on Decks 7 and 8, have a large sleeping area and lounge area with ocean-view picture windows and refrigerator, plenty of hooks for hanging bathrobes, outerwear and luggage; and a bathroom with bathtub and shower (cabin 8019 is the exception, with a shower instead of a bathtub).

Marquee Suites: These suites have a large sleeping area and lounge area with bigger ocean view picture windows and a refrigerator, more hooks for hanging bathrobes, outerwear and luggage; and a bathroom with bathtub and shower.

Premier Suites: Anyone wanting the largest cabins on board (apart from one owner's suite), should consider one of nine suites, each of which is named after a place: Amalfi (9006), Lindos (9002), Nice (9004), each measuring 547.7 sq. ft/50.8 sq. meters; Seville (9001), Singapore (9003), Carmel (9005), Bergen (9007), Waterford (9009), each measuring 341.7 sq ft/31.7 m2; and Windsor (9008), measuring 574.8 sq. ft/53.4 sq. meters. These suites feature a separate bedroom with ample closet and other storage space, a lounge with large windows (with large television and VCR, refrigerator and mini-bar), and bathroom with full-size bathtub and shower, and separate toilet.

Owner's Suite: This measures 819.1 sq. ft/76.1 sq. meters (including a large balcony). It consists of a foyer leading into a lounge, with sofa, table and chairs, audio center (television, CD player, video player), refrigerator and mini-bar. A separate bedroom has a double bed, and ample closet and drawer space. A second bedroom has two bunk beds (good for families with children). The bathroom is large and has a full-size bathtub, separate shower enclosure, toilet, and two washbasins. The balcony has space enough for a table and six chairs, plus a couple of sunloungers. It is located just aft of the navigation bridge on the starboard side of the ship.

CUISINE. The Glentanar Dining Room has a high ceiling, a white sail-like focal point at its center, and ample space at each table. It is a non-smoking dining room; the chairs have armrests, and are quite comfortable. The Orchid Room is a smaller offshoot of the dining room, which can be reserved for a more intimate, quieter dining experience (suite occupants get first choice for seats in this room). While breakfast is typically in an open seating arrangement, there are two seatings for lunch and dinner. Two cold food display counters are provided for passengers to help themselves during breakfast and lunch.

The Garden Cafe is a small, more casual dining spot

with a light, breezy decor that will remind you of a garden conservatory. It sometimes has special themed dinners, such as French, Indian, or Thai. There is a self-help salad bar and hot food display so you can eat with the minimum of fuss from waiters, although they are available for service when you need them. The room is also the location for late-night snacks.

Fred Olsen Cruise Lines has above-average cuisine that is attractively presented, with a good range of fish, seafood, meat and chicken dishes, and has a good selection of cheeses as well as vegetarian options. The food is generally of good quality, with a decent selection of main course items to suit most British tastes. Breakfast buffets tend to be quite repetitive, although they appear to satisfy most.

Communication with the Filipino waiters can prove a little frustrating at times (although it is better now than it has been in the past, and smiles can compensate to some extent). There is a reasonably decent range of wines, at moderate prices, but few of the wine stewards have much knowledge of wines. All food venues are non-smoking.

Coffee and tea are always available in the Braemar Room (adjacent to, and aft of, the Glentanar Restaurant).

ENTERTAINMENT. The Neptune Lounge is the ship's show-lounge. It seats about 400, although some pillars do obstruct sight lines from several seats.

The entertainment mainly consists of small-scale production shows presented by a small team of resident singers/dancers, and cabaret acts. The production shows try hard, but the standards are quite poor in reality, and the cast self-congratulatory. Apart from the production shows, cabaret acts that typically rotate around many cruise ships of the same standard fill in the time after dinner. To be fair, passengers who cruise aboard this ship are not really looking for first-rate entertainment, but rather something to fill the time after dinner, which is the main event for most.

There is plenty of live music for dancing (many of the musicians are Filipino) and listening in several lounges, and good British sing-alongs are a feature on each cruise.

SPA/FITNESS. The spa/fitness facilities are located at the top and front of the ship (inaccessible for wheelchair users). There is a combined gymnasium/aerobics room, while a door provides access to steam rooms, saunas, and changing rooms. Sample treatment prices: Elemis Aromapure facial: £29; Well-being massage (50 minutes): £35; Personal Training Session (60 minutes): £20. Sports facilities include a large paddle tennis court, golf practice nets, shuffleboard, and ring toss.

Steiner's staff will try to sell their own-brand Elemis beauty products (spa girls have sales targets). Some fitness classes are free, while some, such as yoga and kick-boxing, cost extra.

Do make appointments as early as possible, as treatment time slots go quickly, so the day you board is the best time to book your preferred treatments.

WHERE NAUTICAL EXPRESSIONS COME FROM

Ilf you've ever wondered where some terms or phrases came from, you have only to look to the sea, ships, and seamen.

Bamboozle

Today, when you intentionally deceive someone, usually as a joke, you are said to have bamboozled them. The word also was used in the days of sail, but then it meant to deceive a passing vessel as to your ship's origin or nationality by flying an ensign other than your own – a common practice by pirates. From the 17th century, it described the Spanish custom of hoisting false flags to deceive (bamboozle) enemies.

Batten down the hatches

The real hatches are the things that cover the hatchways: gratings and close-hatches. A great deal of water can come aboard either from the sea of the sky or both, so they used to cover those hatches with tarpaulins. The crew typically took battens – stout laths of wood that fit against the coaming (the raised rim of the hatchway) – and pinned the tarpaulin down to cleats on the deck, drum tight.

Barge in

The word barge has two nautical meanings. First as a term applied to a flag officer's boat or highly decorated vessel used for ceremonial occasions. The second usage refers to the more common, flat-bottomed work boat which is hard to maneuver and difficult to control. Hence the term "barge in."

Bigwigs

The senior officers in the English Navy, who once wore huge wigs, were referred to a "bigwigs."

Bitter End

If a sailor were to lay out all of the anchor warp (chain or rope) until he reached the bitter end, then he would have no more to give out. The bitter end also refers to the end of the "starter" (a short rope knotted at on end) used for punishment. Today we talk of having reached the "bitter end" when we mean that we can go no further in a task. The landlubber's phrase "stick it to the bitter end" and "faithful to the bitter end" are derivations of the nautical term and refer to anyone who insists in adhering to a course of action without regard to consequences.

Bleu de France
★★★★

Mid-Size Ship: . . . . .37,301 tons	Total Crew: 406	Cabins (with private balcony): 6
Lifestyle: . . . . .Standard	Passengers	Cabins (wheelchair accessible): 2
Cruise Line: . . . .CDF Croisieres de France	(lower beds/all berths): 752/1,158	Cabin Current: . . . . . . .110 and 220 volts
Former Names: *Holiday Dream, SuperStar*	Passenger Space Ratio	Elevators: 4
Aries, SuperStar Europe, Europa	(lower beds/all berths): 49.6/32.2	Casino (gaming tables): . . . . .Yes
Builder: . . . . . .Bremer Vulkan (Germany)	Crew/Passenger Ratio	Slot Machines: . . . . .Yes
Original Cost: . . . .$120 million	(lower beds/all berths): 1.8/2.8	Swimming Pools (outdoors): 2
Entered Service: . . . . Jan 1982/May 2008	Navigation Officers: . . . . .European	(1 magrodome)
Registry: . . . . .The Bahamas	Cabins (total): .374	Swimming Pools (indoors): 1 (fresh water)
Length (ft/m): 654.9/199.63	Size Range (sq ft/m): 161.4–678.1/	Whirlpools: 0
Beam (ft/m): 93.8/28.60	15.0–63.0	Self-Service Launderette: . . . . .Yes
Draft (ft/m): 27.6/8.42	Cabins (outside view): 309	Dedicated Cinema/Seats: . . . . .No
Propulsion/Propellers: diesel(21,270 kW)/2	Cabins (interior/no view): 65	Library: . . . . .Yes
Passenger Decks: 10	Cabins (for one person): 0	

BERLITZ'S OVERALL SCORE: 1,402 (OUT OF A POSSIBLE 2,000 POINTS)

OVERVIEW. The ship's name, *Bleu de France*, sounds more like a cheese than a ship. Originally sailing as the former *Europa* for Hapag-Lloyd Cruises, it was for many years the flagship of the German cruise industry. Star Cruises, having bought it in April 1998, leased it back to Hapag-Lloyd until 1999, when the new, current *Europa* debuted; it went into drydock for a $15 million refit and renovation.

In 2002, as *SuperStar Aries,* it was moved into Southeast Asia for cruises to Thailand and China. In 2004 it was sold to Spain-based tour operator Pullmantur Cruises, who kept it for four years, and then to CDF Croisières de France (owned by Royal Caribbean Cruises). After a €30 million refit/transformation program that included facelifts to public rooms, and dining facilities were adapted to the growing French-speaking market, it made its latest debut in 2008, with the hospitality and the range and variety of food tailored to its new clientele.

The ship has a deep blue hull and white upper structure, and a sponson stern – a kind of "skirt" added in order to comply with stability regulations. But it still maintains its moderately handsome, balanced profile. There is a good amount of outdoor deck and sunbathing space, including a solarium on what was previously a nude bathing deck (perhaps it still is), and the ship has both outdoor and outdoor/indoor pools; the latter, which includes a Lido Deck bar, can be covered by a glass dome. While there is no walk-around outdoors promenade deck, there are half-length teak port and starboard promenades.

Bleu de France has a wide range of good-sized public rooms. Facilities include a casino, library/internet center,

BERLITZ'S RATINGS		
	Possible	Achieved
Ship	500	382
Accommodation	200	143
Food	400	260
Service	400	286
Entertainment	100	64
Cruise	400	267

karaoke room, and children's play room. Restful colors were applied to many public rooms and cabins, and subtle, hidden lighting was used throughout, particularly on the wide, spacious stairways. The public rooms are located aft in a "cake-layer" stacking, with accommodation located forward, thus separating noisy areas from quieter ones.

The interior decor has splashes of bright colors, motifs, and helpful signage. The ship, which has an all drinks-inclusive policy, provides an informal, relaxed, yet quite elegant setting, with a casual dress code. You will typically find a lot of smokers aboard. *Bleu de France* operates 7-day Caribbean (winter) and Mediterranean (summer) cruises, with all-inclusive pricing (drinks are included in all venues). The busiest period is July and August, when French nationals have their holidays. Children are split into age groups: P'tits Loupes (ages 4–7); Club des Grands Loupes (7–11); D'jeunes Club (12–17).

The crew is all-French-speaking, and the highlight is definitely the cuisine. The onboard currency is the euro.

SUITABLE FOR: This ship is totally geared to French-speaking couples, singles, and families with children of all ages who want a first cruise experience in a traditional (not new) ship, with plenty of public rooms and a lively atmosphere, food that is quantity rather than quality, at low cost.

ACCOMMODATION. There is a wide range of suites and cabins, in 14 price grades. All of the original cabins are quite spacious, and all have illuminated closets, dark wood cabinetry with rounded edges, full-length mirrors, color TV/DVD player, mini-bar/refrigerator, personal safe, hairdryer, and good cabin insulation. Most cabins can accommodate one or two additional persons, which mean the ship's original spacious feel has been greatly eroded in order to cater more to families with children. The port and starboard passenger hallways have different colors, and so do the fore and aft foyers, making it easy for first-time passengers to find their way around.

Most bathrooms have deep tubs (cabins without bathtub have a large shower enclosure), a three-head shower unit, two deep washbasins (not all cabins), large toiletries cabinet and handsome personal toiletries.

The largest living spaces are the suites added during the 1999 refit. However, because of their location – they were created from former bridge officers' cabins – they have lifeboat-obstructed views. Six other suites had private balconies added; all provide generous living spaces. There is a separate bedroom (with either queen-sized or twin beds), illuminated closets, and vanity desk. The lounge includes a wet bar with refrigerator and glass cabinets and large audio-visual center complete with large-screen TV/DVD player. The marble-clad bathroom has a large shower enclosure, with retractable clothesline.

CUISINE. Le Flamboyant, the main restaurant, is large, with ocean-view windows on two sides, and a good amount of space around each table. There are two seatings for meals; dinner is at 7:15pm and 9:30pm. There is also a large, extremely varied self-serve cold table for all meals, with colorful displays of a wide variety of foods. All meals are included in the price, as is table wine (white, red or rosé). The cuisine is decidedly French, as is the chef. The extra-cost wine list is very good (mostly French wines), and euro prices are reasonable.

For casual meals, self-serve breakfasts, luncheons and supper buffets are provided at Le Panorama self-serve buffet, located aft, with excellent ocean views.

Additionally, there is the Olive Bistro for light Mediterranean fare, located at the glass dome-covered center pool (open 11am–10pm), as well as Millesime (for cigars and quality spirits), and the Le Café Crème Bar.

ENTERTAINMENT. The main lounge (Le Grand Salon) is the venue for major events. The sightlines in the show lounge are quite poor from many seats – the room was originally built more for use as a single-level concert salon than a room for shows – although the setting is elegant.

The shows consist of a troupe of showgirl dancers, together with a host of cabaret acts, including singers, magicians, and comedians, among others, and are very much geared to the family audience that this ship carries. There is also plenty of live music for listening or dancing to in various bars and lounges, and there is the inevitable discotheque. A delightful observation lounge, Acajou, also hosts music and special acts.

SPA/FITNESS. The 800-sq. meter (8,611 sq. ft) Aqua-Marine Spa is really an extremely good indoor wellness center, and is located together with an indoor swimming pool that is larger than most outdoor pools aboard new, much bigger ships. Adjacent facilities include three saunas (Finnish, hammam, herbal), fitness/exercise centre, hydrotherapy bath, 12 treatment rooms, and beauty salon. A solarium is located outdoors atop the ship.

Blue Monarch
★★

Small Ship: ....11,429 tons	Passenger Decks: 8	Cabins (with private balcony): 0
Lifestyle: ....Standard	Total Crew: 230	Cabins (wheelchair accessible): 0
Cruise Line: ....Monarch Classic Cruises	Passengers	Cabin Voltage: ....110 volts
Former Names: ....*World Renaissance,*	(lower beds/all berths): 484/500	Lifts: 1
Awani dream, World Renaissance,	Passenger Space Ratio	Casino (gaming tables): ....Yes
Renaissance, Homeric Renaissance	(lower beds/all berths): 23.6/22.8	Slot Machines: ....Yes
Builder: .....Chantiers de l'Atlantique (France)	Crew/Passenger Ratio	Swimming Pools (outdoors): 2
Original Cost: ....n/a	(lower beds/all berths): 2.1/2.1	Swimming Pools (indoors): 0
Entered Service: ......May 1966/Apr 2007	Navigation Officers: ....Greek	Whirlpools: 0
Registry: ....Greece	Cabins (total): 242	Self-Service Launderette: ....No
Length (ft/m): 492.4/150.1	Size Range (sq ft/m): ....n/a	Dedicated Cinema/Seats: Yes/110
Beam (ft/m): 68.8/21.0	Cabins (outside view): 178	Library: ....Yes
Draft (ft/m): 22.6/6.3	Cabins (interior/no view): 63	
Propulsion/Propellers: ...diesel (10,060 kW)/2	Cabins (for one person): 1	

BERLITZ'S OVERALL SCORE: 929 (OUT OF A POSSIBLE 2,000 POINTS)

OVERVIEW. This ship has traditional 1960s styling and profile and is topped by a pencil-slim funnel. It was operated for many years by the now-defunct Epirotiki Lines/Royal Olympic Cruises. There is a reasonable amount of open deck and sunbathing space for its size.

The interior layout, however, is a little disjointed, although it's a small ship, and so it won't take you long to find your way around. The decor can be said to be somewhat "colonial" and rather eclectic, with some touches that still remind one of its original days as a French-owned ship. Although the main lounge is comfortable, there are few other public rooms, and therefore the ship's public spaces always feel crowded. The library, as a room, is a restful place to relax. Has a friendly, mainly Greek staff and service that can be said to be basic but sound, although there is little refinement.

Note that there is no walk-around outdoor promenade deck, and no cushioned pads for the sunloungers.

SUITABLE FOR: *Blue Monarch* is best suited for anyone seeking a short cruise to the Greek Isles and Turkey in fairly basic, modestly comfortable surroundings.

BERLITZ'S RATINGS		
	Possible	Achieved
Ship	500	209
Accommodation	200	90
Food	400	187
Service	400	191
Entertainment	100	46
Cruise	400	206

ACCOMMODATION. Some of the cabins have some nice wood paneling. They are homey and reasonably spacious, though definitely not luxurious; a few cabins have interconnecting doors (good for families with children). The cabin bathrooms are tiled (a few cabins have a bathtub, while most have shower only), but are very small, and there is little space for toiletries.

CUISINE. The 276-seat dining room is mildly attractive, although there are no tables for two, the tables are close together, and there are two seatings. The cuisine is basic – very basic.

There is thus a limited selection of breads, pastry, fruit and cheeses. The service is selectively friendly, but there is little finesse.

ENTERTAINMENT. Again, it's basic, but the showlounge seats 350, and is really best for cabaret-style performances.

SPA/FITNESS. There is a small fitness room (just forward of the funnel), and a separate beauty salon (inside, on a lower deck), but no sauna or steam room.

Boudicca
★★★ +

Mid-Size Ship:	.28,388 tons	Propulsion/Propellers: diesel 13,400kW)/2 (CP)	Cabins (for one person):	.35
Lifestyle:	Standard	Passenger Decks:	.8	Cabins (with private balcony):	.59
Cruise Line:	Fred Olsen Cruise Lines	Total Crew:	.320	Cabins (wheelchair accessible):	.4
Former Names:	Grand Latino, SuperStar	Passengers		Cabin Current:	.110 and 220 volts
Capricorn, Hyundai Keumgang, SuperStar	(lower beds/all berths):	.839/900	Elevators:	.5
Capricorn, Golden Princess, Sunward,	Passenger Space Ratio		Casino (gaming tables):	Yes
Birka Queen, Sunward, Royal Viking Sky	(lower beds/all berths):	.33.8/31.5	Slot Machines:	Yes
Builder:	Wartsila (Finland)	Crew/Passenger Ratio		Swimming Pools (outdoors):	.2
Original Cost:	$22.5 million	(lower beds/all berths):	.2.3/2.5	Swimming Pools (indoors):	.0
Entered Service:	June 1973/Feb 2006	Navigation Officers:	European	Whirlpools:	.2
Registry:	The Bahamas	Cabins (total):	.437	Self-Service Launderette:	Yes
Length (ft/m):	.674.1/205.47	Size Range (sq ft/m):	.135.6–579.1/12.6–53.8	Dedicated Cinema/Seats:	No
Beam (ft/m):	.82.6/25.20	Cabins (outside view):	.363	Library:	Yes
Draft (ft/m):	.24.7/7.55	Cabins (interior/no view):	.39		

BERLITZ'S OVERALL SCORE: 1,357 (OUT OF A POSSIBLE 2,000 POINTS)

OVERVIEW. Acquired by Fred Olsen Cruise Lines in 2005, this well-proportioned ship, originally built for long-distance cruising for the now-defunct Royal Viking Line (it was built for one of the three original shipping partners who formed the line – Bergenske Dampskibsselskab), has a sharply raked bow and a sleek appearance. The ship was "stretched" in 1982 with the addition of a 27.7-meter (91-ft) mid section.

The outer styling is quite handsome for an early 1970s-built vessel. The single funnel bears the company's starfish logo, and balances the profile of this attractive (now contemporary-classic) ship. The name *Boudicca* (pronounced Boodicker) comes from the Queen of the Iceni tribe that occupied England's East Anglia; she led a dramatic revolt against the Romans in AD61, and her body is supposedly buried under Platform 10 of London's King's Cross Station.

The ship has a good amount of open deck and sunbathing space; in fact, there is plenty of space everywhere and little sense of crowding because the ship absorbs passengers well. There are port and starboard walking teak promenade decks outdoors, although they no longer wrap around the front of the ship. Before the ship commenced cruising as *Boudicca*, and extensive refit (included was the creation of a number of cabins for those travelling solo) and re-engining took place.

The interior decor is restful, with a mix of English and Norwegian styles (particularly the artwork) with wide stairways and foyers, good passenger flow, soft lighting and no glitz anywhere. In general, good materials, fabrics and soft furnishings add to a pleasant ambiance and comfortable feeling experienced throughout the public rooms, most of

BERLITZ'S RATINGS		
	Possible	Achieved
Ship	500	342
Accommodation	200	154
Food	400	258
Service	400	274
Entertainment	100	65
Cruise	400	264

which are quite spacious and have high, indented ceilings. There are lots of (small) public rooms, bars and lounges to play in, unlike the newer (larger) ships built today, including a delightful observation lounge, a small casino, card room, large library, and the Secret Garden Lounge (with its integral café).

Boudicca is an extremely comfortable ship in which to cruise, with a moderate standard of food and service from a friendly, mostly Filipino staff, featuring extremely good value for money cruises in a relaxed environment that provides passengers with many of the comforts of home.

For the ship's mainly British passengers, the National Express bus operator works in conjunction with Fred Olsen Cruise Lines to provide a dedicated Cruiselink service via London's Victoria Coach Station to the UK departure ports of Dover or Southampton.

Although the ship has benefited from an extensive refit and refurbishment, do remember that it is more than 30 years old, which means that little problems such as gurgling plumbing, creaking joints, and other idiosyncrasies can occur, and air conditioning may not be all that it should be. The onboard currency is the British pound and port taxes are included for UK passengers. Gratuities of £4 ($7) per passenger, per day, are suggested.

Passenger gripes include: noticeable cutbacks in food variety and quality, an increase in the use of paper napkins, packets of butter, margarine and preserves, the lack of choice of sugar, very poor coffee, long lines at the cramped buffet, and poor wine service (not enough wine waiters). Other gripes: the smell of stale cigarette smoke in lounges and bars, not enough staff for the increased passenger numbers following the addition of more cabins, and a poor selection of hardback books in the library (many paperbacks), poor service levels.

SUITABLE FOR: *Boudicca* is best suited to British couples and single travelers looking for a ship with some sense of space, comfortable surroundings, decent facilities, realistic pricing and good value for money, with British food and entertainment. Good for passengers without tattoos.

ACCOMMODATION. There is something for every taste and wallet, from spacious family suites to small interior (no view) cabins. While most cabins are for two persons, some can accommodate a third, fourth, or even a fifth person. There are 20 price categories of cabins (plus one for the owner's suite, whose price is not listed in the brochure), including four grades of cabin for those traveling solo (these are spread across most of the cabin decks, and not just the lower decks, as is the case with some cruise lines), and three of these have a private balcony. While most cabins have bathtubs, some lower grades have only a shower enclosure.

Some of quietest cabins are those located just under the navigation bridge, on Lido Deck, as well as those suites and cabins on Bridge Deck. In the refit, a vacuum toilet system was fitted.

In all grades, duvets are provided, the bathroom towels are 100% cotton and are quite large, and a hairdryer is provided. A package of Gilchrist & Soames personal toiletry items (bath gel, shampoo/conditioner, sewing kit, shower cap) is supplied to all passengers. Occupants of suite grades also get a cotton bathrobe and cold canapés each evening, as well as priority seating in the dining rooms.

The room service menu is quite limited and could be improved (although there is an abundance of food available at most times of the day). All cabins have had a facelift. Only a few suites have private balconies.
Outside-view/Inside (No View) Cabins: These quite well equipped, and there is plenty of good (illuminated) closet, drawer and storage space, but insulation between some of the lower grade cabins could be better. While most cabins bathrooms are of a decent size, some have awkward access. Some have a small bathtub, although many have only a shower enclosure.
Deluxe/Bridge/Junior Suites: These suites, on Decks 7 and 8, have a large sleeping area and lounge area with ocean-view picture windows and refrigerator, plenty of hooks for hanging bathrobes, outerwear and luggage; and a bathroom with bathtub and shower.
Marquee Suites: These suites have a large sleeping area and lounge area with bigger ocean view picture windows and a refrigerator, more hooks for hanging bathrobes, outerwear and luggage; and a bathroom with tub and shower.
Premier Suites: Anyone wanting the most space should consider one of these suites (each is named after a place). These have a separate bedroom with ample closet and other storage space, a lounge with large windows (with large television/video player, refrigerator/mini-bar), and bathroom with full-size bathtub and shower, and a separate toilet.

CUISINE. The main dining room is divided into three venues: Heligan, Tintagel, and Four Seasons; each has a high ceiling, and ample space at each table. The Heligan Room is for suite-grade occupants.

All are non-smoking venues, with restful, but rather bland decor; the chairs, which have armrests, are quite comfortable. Window-side tables for two are the most sought after, naturally.

While breakfast is typically in an open seating arrangement, there are two seatings for lunch and dinner. Cold food display counters are provided for passengers to help themselves to breakfast and lunch items.

Fred Olsen Cruise Lines has above-average cuisine that is attractively presented, with a good range of fish, seafood, meat and chicken dishes, as well as vegetarian options, and a good selection of cheeses, to suit most British tastes. You'll find popular British standards such as bangers and mash, toad in the hole, and spotted dick. Breakfast buffets tend to be quite repetitive, although they appear to satisfy most. There is a reasonably decent range of wines, at moderate prices.

Coffee and tea are available round-the-clock in the Secret Garden Café (part of the Secret Garden Lounge), just aft of the main dining venues.

Casual self-serve deck buffets are provided outdoors at the Poolside Café, while fast food items can be obtained from the Marquee Bar (also outdoors).

ENTERTAINMENT. The Neptune Lounge is the venue for shows, cabaret acts, and lectures. It is a large room that seats about 400, although some pillars obstruct sight lines from some seats. The entertainment consists of small-scale production shows presented by a small team of resident singers/dancers, and cabaret acts (these typically rotate around many cruise ships of the same standard).

There is plenty of live music for social dancing (many of the musicians are Filipino) and listening in several lounges, and good British sing-alongs are a feature on each cruise.

SPA/FITNESS. A decent amount of (window-less) space is given to providing health and fitness facilities (on Atlantic Deck). However, they are split in three separate areas (on Atlantic Deck). Forward are the sauna/steam rooms; the center section contains a gymnasium/aerobics room, changing rooms; while the aft section houses a beauty salon.

Some fitness classes are free, while some, such as yoga and kick-boxing, cost extra.

It's best to make appointments as early as possible as treatment time slots go quickly (the day you board is the best time to book your preferred treatments). Sports facilities include a large paddle tennis court, golf practice nets, shuffleboard, and ring toss.

Braemar
★★★ +

Mid-Size Ship: . . . . .23,000 tons	Passenger Decks: 7	Cabins (for one person): 21
Lifestyle: . . . . .Standard	Total Crew: .400	Cabins (with private balcony): 70
Cruise Line: . . . . .Fred Olsen Cruise Lines	Passengers	Cabins (wheelchair accessible): 4
Former Names: . . . . .Crown Dynasty,	(lower beds/all berths): 977/977	Cabin Current: . . . . .110 and 220 volts
Norwegian Dynasty, Crown Majesty,	Passenger Space Ratio	Elevators: 5
Cunard Dynasty, Crown Dynasty	(lower beds/all berths): 23.5/23.5	Casino (gaming tables): . . . . .Yes
Builder: . .Union Navale de Levante (Spain)	Crew/Passenger Ratio	Slot Machines: . . . . .Yes
Original Cost: . . . .$100 million	(lower beds/all berths): 2.4/2.4	Swimming Pools (outdoors): 1
Entered Service: . . . .July 1993/Aug 2001	Navigation Officers: . . . . . .Scandinavian	Swimming Pools (indoors): 0
Registry: . . . . .The Bahamas	Cabins (total): 377	Whirlpools: 2
Length (ft/m): 639.7/195.01	Size Range (sq ft/m): 139.9–349.8/	Self-Service Launderette: . . . . .No
Beam (ft/m): 73.8/22.50	13.0–32.5	Dedicated Cinema/Seats: . . . . .No
Draft (ft/m): 17.7/5.40	Cabins (outside view): 251	Library: . . . . .No
Propulsion/Propellers: diesel (13,200kW)/2	Cabins (interior/no view): 126	

OVERALL SCORE: 1,312 (OUT OF A POSSIBLE 2,000 POINTS)

OVERVIEW. This ship was purchased by Fred Olsen Cruise Lines in spring 2001 and renamed *Braemar*. Following an extensive refurbishment, it started operating cruises targeted mostly at British and Scandinavian passengers.

A handsome-looking mid-sized ship for casual cruising, it has attractive exterior styling, and a lot of glass space. It's a refreshing change for those who don't want to cruise aboard larger (warehouse-size) ships. But the ship does roll somewhat, probably due to its shallow draft design (meant for warm weather cruise areas).

There is a good amount of open deck and sunbathing space for its size, and this includes two outdoors bars – one aft and one midships adjacent to the swimming pool – that feature Boddington's and Stella Artois beers on draught. Four open decks, located aft of the funnel, provide good, quiet, places to sit and read, and teak chairs add a nice touch.

The teak promenade deck is a complete walk-around deck. Passengers can also go right to the ship's bow (good for photographs). Blue plastic mat-style floor covering is used on the deck where the swimming pool is located; it looks tacky, but works well in the heat of the Caribbean, where the ship was meant to spend much of its time.

Inside, there is a pleasant five-deck-high, glass-walled atrium on the starboard side. Off-center stairways appear to add a sense of spaciousness to a clever interior design that surrounds passengers with light. The interior decor in public spaces is warm and inviting, with contemporary, but not brash, art-deco color combinations. The artwork is quite colorful and pleasant, in the Nordic manner.

In what was once a casino, the Braemar Room is now an open-plan style of lounge, with its own bar, split by a walk-

BERLITZ'S RATINGS

	Possible	Achieved
Ship	500	356
Accommodation	200	135
Food	400	235
Service	400	252
Entertainment	100	61
Cruise	400	273

way that leads to the showlounge (forward) and the shops (midships). Despite being open, it has cozy seating areas and is very comfortable, with a tartan carpet; one section is for smokers, the other for non-smokers. A model of the first Fred Olsen ship named *Braemar* (4,775 tons) is displayed in the center of the room, as is a large carved wood plaque bearing the name Braemar Castle in Scotland. There is a baby grand piano (typically played during cocktail hours); otherwise this lounge is good for reading as there is no piped music to disturb you.

The (mostly) Filipino staff is friendly and attentive, and the hospitality factor is good, although the standard of service and attention to detail is poor when compared with ships staffed with Europeans. This is noticeable in the restaurant and other food service areas. Fred Olsen Cruise Lines has come a long way from its humble beginnings, and now offers extremely good value for money cruises in a relaxed environment that provides passengers with many of the comforts of home. The dress code is casual. The onboard currency is the British pound.

In 2008, a 102.3-ft (31.2-meter) mid-section extension was added, providing additional cabins and balcony "suites" and a capacity increase to 977. New facilities include a second swimming pool and deck space, an observatory lounge, a new restaurant and a pub-style bar.

Do expect some crowding for the self-serve buffets, tenders, and the few elevators aboard this ship. British passengers should note that no suites or cabins have bathtubs. Non-smokers should be aware that the typical passenger mix may include many passengers who smoke.

Passenger gripes include: lines at the cramped self-service buffet, poor wine service (not enough wine waiters), stale smoke smell in some lounges and bars, and not enough staff. Other gripes include poor book selection in the library (many paperbacks), dumbing down in the variety and presentation of cuisine offered, poor service levels, an increase in the use of paper napkins, packets of butter, margarine and preserves, the lack of choice of sugar, and very poor coffee. There is also no self-service launderette (although there is one ironing room), and the company charges for shuttle buses in many ports of call.

SUITABLE FOR: *Braemar* is geared specifically toward the middle-aged and older British passenger who wants to cruise in a casual, unstuffy environment, and who appears to enjoy seeking out the world's duty-free shops, in a ship with British food and entertainment.

ACCOMMODATION. There are 16 cabin price categories, and, the higher the deck, the higher the price. All grades have a small television and hairdryer (some are awkward to retract from their wall-mount holders), plus European duvets. The large bathroom towels are 100% cotton (bathrobes are available upon request in suite-grade cabins). Gilchrist & Soames toiletry items are provided. There is no separate audio system in the cabin, so the only music you can obtain is from one of the TV channels, but you'll have to leave the picture on (suites, however, do have a CD music system). **Standard (Outside-view)/Inside (No View) Cabin Grades:** The standard outside-view and interior (no view) cabins, almost all of which are the same size, are really quite small, although they are nicely furnished. Most have broad picture windows (some deluxe cabins on Deck 6 and Deck 7 have lifeboat-obstructed views). They are practical and comfortable, with blond wood-trimmed accents and multi-colored soft furnishings, but there is very little drawer space, and the closet (hanging) space is extremely limited (the ship was purpose-built originally for 7-day cruises). So, as there is little room for luggage, take only the clothing that you think necessary. Each of the outside-view cabins on Deck 4 has a large picture window, while those on the lower Decks 2 and 3 have a porthole. They are quite well equipped, with a small vanity desk unit, a minimal amount of drawer space, curtained windows, and personal safe (hard to reach).

Each cabin has a private bathroom (of the "me first, you next" variety) with a tiled floor, small shower enclosure, toiletries cupboard, washbasin, and low-height toilet (of the barking dog vacuum variety), and some under-basin storage space, and an electrical socket for shavers.

When the ship was bought by Fred Olsen Cruise Lines a number of cabins were changed from double-occupancy units to cabins for the single traveler.

Some cabins do unfortunately suffer from inadequate soundproofing; passengers in cabins on Deck 4 in particular are disturbed by anyone running or jogging on the promenade deck above. Note that cabins on the lowest deck (Deck 2) in the center of the ship are subject to some noise from the adjacent engine room.

Suites: On Deck 7, accommodation designated as suites have city names such as Rio de Janeiro and Toronto. While they are not large, the suites do feature a sleeping area that can be curtained off from the living area. All of the suites are decorated in individual styles befitting their name, and each has its own small CD player/music system.

CUISINE. The Thistle Restaurant is a pleasing and attractive no-smoking venue, with large ocean-view windows on three sides and a focal point of a large oil painting on a wall behind the buffet food display counter. However, space is tight, and tables are extremely close together, making proper service difficult. There are tables for two, four, six or eight; the Porsgrund china has the familiar Venus pattern. The ambiance, however, is warm, and service is friendly and attentive.

There are two seatings for dinner, and an open seating for breakfast and lunch. The menu is varied. Salad items are quite poor and very basic, with little variety, although there is a decent choice of dessert items. For breakfast and lunch the dual food counters are functional, but at peak times these create much congestion (the layout is not ideal).

Casual breakfasts and luncheons can also be taken in the self-service buffet located in the Palms Cafe, although these tend to be repetitive and poorly supervised (dishes not replaced or refreshed properly), with indoor and outdoor seating. Although it is the casual dining spot, tablecloths are provided. The indoor flooring is wood, which makes it rather a noisy room, and some tables adjacent to the galley entrance are to be avoided at all costs.

Out on the pool deck, there is a barbecue grill, for casual eating – welcome when the ship is in warm weather areas.

ENTERTAINMENT. The Neptune Showlounge sits longitudinally along one side of the ship, with amphitheater-style seating in several tiers, but its layout is less than ideal for either shows or cocktail parties. There are smoking and no-smoking sections (most being no-smoking), and there is often congestion between first- and second-seating passengers at the entrance.

Unfortunately, 15 pillars obstruct sightlines to the stage, and the banquet and individual tub chair seating arrangement is actually quite poor.

The entertainment mainly consists of small-scale production shows and mini-musicals presented by a small troupe of resident singers/dancers, and cabaret acts. The production shows are amateurish and self-congratulatory, with a (mainly Filipino) cast. Apart from the production shows, there are the typical cabaret acts which are found on the cruise ship circuit.

SPA/FITNESS. The health spa facilities are limited. It includes a combined gymnasium/aerobics room, and a separate room for women and men, with sauna, steam room and small changing area. Spa Rituals treatments are provided by Steiner. Some fitness classes are free; others, such as yoga and kick-boxing, cost extra.

Bremen
★★★★

Boutique Ship: . . . . .6,752 tons	Total Crew: 94	Cabins (with private balcony): 18
Lifestyle: . . . . .Premium	Passengers	Cabins (wheelchair accessible): 2
Cruise Line:Hapag-Lloyd Expedition Cruises	(lower beds/all berths): 164/184	Cabin Current: . . . . .110 and 220 volts
Former Names: . . . .*Frontier Spirit*	Passenger Space Ratio	Elevators: 2
Builder: . . . . .Mitsubishi Heavy Industries	(lower beds/all berths): 41.1/36.6	Casino (gaming tables): . . . . .No
(Japan)	Crew/Passenger Ratio	Slot Machines: .No
Original Cost: . . . .$42 million	(lower beds/all berths): 1.7/1.9	Swimming Pools (outdoors): 1
Entered Service: . . . . .Nov 1990/Nov 1993	Navigation Officers: . . . . .European	Swimming Pools (indoors): 0
Registry: . . . . .The Bahamas	Cabins (total): 82	Whirlpools: 0
Length (ft/m): 365.8/111.51	Size Range (sq ft/m): 174.3–322.9/	Self-Service Launderette: . . . . .No
Beam (ft/m): 55.7/17.00	16.2–30.0	Lecture/Film Room: . . . . . .Yes (seats 164)
Draft (ft/m): 15.7/4.80	Cabins (outside view): 82	Library: . . . . .Yes (open 24 hours)
Propulsion/Propellers: .diesel (4,855kW)/2	Cabins (interior/no view): 0	Zodiacs: 12
Passenger Decks: 6	Cabins (for one person): 0	Helicopter Pad: . . . . .Yes

OVERALL SCORE: 1,461 (OUT OF A POSSIBLE 2,000 POINTS)

OVERVIEW. This purpose-built all-white expedition cruise vessel (formerly *Frontier Spirit*, for the now defunct US-based Frontier Cruises) has a handsome, wide, though squat, contemporary profile and decent equipment. Its wide beam provides decent stability and the vessel's long cruising range and ice-hardened hull provides the ship with access to remote destinations. The ship carries the highest ice classification for passenger vessels. In 1993 Hapag-Lloyd spent $2 million to reconfigure the restaurant and make other changes to the ship.

Zero-discharge of waste matter is fiercely practiced; this means that absolutely nothing is discharged into the ocean that does not meet with the international conventions on ocean pollution (MARPOL). Equipment for in-depth marine and shore excursions is provided, including a boot-washing station with three water hoses and boot cleaning brushes.

An "invitation to the bridge" policy applies. There is almost a walk-around deck (you must go up and down steps at the front of the deck to complete the "walk"). A large open deck aft of the mast provides a good viewing platform (also useful for sunbathing on warm-weather cruises).

The ship has a good number of public rooms for its size, including a forward-facing observation lounge/lecture room, and a main lounge (the Club) with a high ceiling, bandstand, dance floor and large bar, and an adjacent library with 12 bookcases (most books are in German).

Bremen has superb, well-planned destination-intensive itineraries, with good documentation, port information, and maps. It provides a good degree of comfort (although it is not as luxurious as the slightly larger sister ship *Hanseatic*). There is a reception desk (open 24 hours a

BERLITZ'S RATINGS

	Possible	Achieved
Ship	500	349
Accommodation	200	150
Food	400	298
Service	400	311
Entertainment	n/a	n/a
Cruise	500	353

day), a fine array of expert lecturers, and a friendly crew. The ship has two microscopes, and a plankton-collection net for in-depth studies.

Bremen is a practical expedition cruise vessel, nicely refurbished in 2006–7, when internet-connect computers were added. Another makeover will take place in 2008–9. Perhaps it is arguably a better expedition vessel than *Hanseatic*, and, although not as luxurious in its interiors and appointments, the ship has a very loyal following. Its cruises will provide you with a fine learning and expedition experience, particularly its Antarctic cruises (all shore landings and tours are included, as is seasickness medication).

The onboard ambiance is completely casual, comfortable, unstuffy (no tux needed), friendly, and very accommodating. Passengers also appreciate the fact that there is no television (on expedition cruises, although there are videos daily) and no music in hallways or on open decks.

Arctic/Antarctic Cruises: Red parkas (waterproof outdoor jackets) are supplied, as are waterproof rubber (Wellington) boots. You should, however, take some waterproof trousers and several pairs of thick socks, plus "thermal" underwear. Each of the fleet of 12 Zodiacs (rubber-inflatable landing craft) is named after a place or region: Amazon, Antarctic, Asmat, Bora Bora, Cape Horn, Deception, Jan Mayen, Luzon, Pitcairn, San Blas, Spitzbergen, and Ushuaia. On Arctic and Antarctic cruises, it is particularly pleasing to go to the bridge wings late at night to stargaze under pollution-free skies (the watch officers will be pleased to show you the night skies).

Special sailings may be under the auspices of various tour operators, although the ship is operated by Hapag-Lloyd

Expedition Cruises. Thus, your fellow passengers (I prefer to refer to them as expedition voyage participants) may well be from many different countries. Insurance, port taxes and all staff gratuities are typically included in the cruise fare, and an expedition cruise logbook is provided at the end of each expedition cruise for all participants – a reminder of what's been seen and done during the course of the adventure. The onboard currency is the euro.

The ship does not have a "bulbous bow" and so is liable to pitching in some sea conditions; it does, however, have stabilizers. The swimming pool is small, as is the open deck space around it, although there are both shaded and open areas. In-cabin announcements cannot be turned off (on cruises in the Arctic and Antarctic regions, announcements are often made at or before 7am on days when shore landings are permitted). Sadly, the ship was not built with good cabin soundproofing. Bathrooms are subject to gurgling plumbing noises (between the washbasin and shower enclosure) as a result of their design and construction.

SUITABLE FOR: *Bremen* is best suited to travelers (rather than cruise passengers) who would not dream of cruising aboard large, glitzy cruise ships. This is for anyone who enjoys nature and the natural world, and traveling off the beaten path to sample what the world has to offer in the more remote and unspoiled (a relative term) regions of the world, in moderate comfort, yet venturing on the wild side of cruising. It is for those who do not need entertainment, bingo, horse racing, art auctions, or parlour games.

ACCOMMODATION. There are just four different configurations. All cabins have an outside view (the cabins on the lowest deck have portholes; all others have good-sized picture windows). All cabins are well equipped for the size of the vessel. Each has wood accenting, a color TV (small) for videos, telephone, refrigerator (soft drinks are provided free and replenished daily), vanity desk (with 110v American-style and 220v European-style electrical sockets) and sitting area with small drinks table.

Cabins have either twin beds (convertible to a queen-sized bed, but with individual European cotton duvets) or double bed, according to location, bedside reading lights and alarm clock. There is also a small indented area for outerwear and rubber boots, while a small drawer above the refrigerator unit provides warmth when needed for such things as wet socks and gloves.

Each cabin has a private bathroom (of the "me first, you next" variety) with a tiled floor, shower enclosure (with curtain), toiletries cupboard, washbasin (located quite low) and low-height toilet (vacuum type, with delay), a decent amount of under-basin storage space, and an electrical socket for shavers). Large towels and 100% cotton bathrobes are provided, as is a range of personal toiletries (shampoo, body lotion, shower gel, soap, and shower cap).

Each cabin has a moderate amount of (illuminated) closet space (large enough for two weeks for two persons,

but tight for longer cruises), although the drawer space is limited (suitcases can be stored under the beds). Some Sun Deck and Bridge Deck cabins also have a small balcony (the first expedition cruise vessel to have them) with blue plastic (easily cleanable) decking and wooden handrail, but no exterior light. The balconies have two teak chairs and a small drinks table, but are small and narrow, with partial partitions and doors that open outwards onto the balcony (taking up space).

Two Sun Deck suites have a separate lounge area with sofa and coffee table, bedroom (with large wall clock), large walk-in closet, and bathroom with a bathtub and two washbasins.

CUISINE. The dining room has open seating when operating for mixed German and international passenger cruises, and open seating for breakfast and lunch, with one seating for dinner (assigned seats) when operated only as German-speaking cruises. It is fairly attractive, with pleasing decor and pastel colors; it also has big picture windows and 12 pillars placed in inconvenient positions (the result of old shipbuilding techniques).

The food, made with high-quality ingredients, is extremely good. Although the portions are small, the presentation is appealing to the eye – and you can always ask for more. There is an excellent choice of freshly made breads and pastries, and a good selection of cheeses and fruits.

Dinner typically includes a choice of two appetizers, two soups, an entremets (in-between course), two entrées (main courses) and two or three desserts, plus a cheese board (note that Europeans typically have cheese before dessert). There is always a vegetarian specialty, as well as a healthy (light) eating option. The service is also good, with smartly dressed bi-lingual (German- and English-speaking) waiters and waitresses.

As an alternative to the dining room, breakfast and luncheon buffets are available in "The Club", or outside on the Lido Deck (weather permitting), where "The Starboard Bar/Grill" provides items of grilled food.

ENTERTAINMENT. Although there is a small main lounge, this is used as a gathering place after meals (and before expedition landings ashore). There is no formal entertainment as such, lectures being the principal feature of any expedition cruise aboard this ship (unless under charter), as are after-dinner recaps of the day. Occasionally, the crew may put on a little amateur dramatics event, or a seaman's choir. And at the end of each expedition cruise, the ship's chart is auctioned off one evening to the highest bidder, and profits are sent to a charity organization.

SPA/FITNESS. There is a small fitness room, a large sauna, and beauty salon (with integral massage table). Out on the open deck is a small swimming pool, which is heated when the ship is sailing in cold weather regions such as the Arctic or Antarctica.

Brilliance of the Seas
★★★★

Large Resort Ship: ....90,090 tons	Total Crew: 869	Cabins (with private balcony): 577
Lifestyle: ....Standard	Passengers	Cabins (wheelchair accessible): 24
Cruise Line: Royal Caribbean International	(lower beds/all berths): 2,112/2,500	Cabin Current: ....110/220 volts
Former Names: ....none	Passenger Space Ratio	Elevators: 9
Builder: ....Meyer Werft (Germany)	(lower beds/all berths): 42.6/36.0	Casino (gaming tables): ....Yes
Original Cost: ....$350 million	Crew/Passenger Ratio	Slot Machines: ....Yes
Entered Service: ....July 2002	(lower beds/all berths): 2.5/2.8	Swimming Pools (outdoors): 2
Registry: ....The Bahamas	Navigation Officers: ....Norwegian	Swimming Pools (indoors): 0
Length (ft/m): 961.9/293.2	Cabins (total): 1,056	Whirlpools: 3
Beam (ft/m): 105.6/32.2	Size Range (sq ft/m): 165.8–1,216.3/	Self-Service Launderette: ....No
Draft (ft/m): 27.8/8.5	15.4–113.0	Dedicated Cinema/Seats: Yes/40
Propulsion/Propellers: ......Gas turbine/	Cabins (outside view): 818	Library: ....Yes
2 pods (19.5 MW each)	Cabins (interior/no view): 238	
Passenger Decks: 12	Cabins (for one person): 0	

OVERALL SCORE: 1,501 (OUT OF A POSSIBLE 2,000 POINTS)

OVERVIEW. This is a streamlined contemporary ship (built in 66 blocks), and has a two-deck-high wrap-around structure in the forward section of the funnel. Along the ship's port side, a central glass wall protrudes, giving great views (cabins with balconies occupy the space directly opposite on the starboard side). The gently rounded stern has nicely tiered decks, which gives the ship an extremely well-balanced look. As is common aboard all Royal Caribbean International vessels, the navigation bridge is of the fully enclosed type (good for cold-weather areas). One of two swimming pools can be covered by a large glass dome (called a magrodome) for use as an indoor/outdoor pool.

The interior decor is contemporary, yet elegant, bright and cheerful, designed for active, young and trendy types. The artwork is abundant and truly eclectic. A nine-deck high atrium lobby has glass-walled lifts (on the port side) that travel through 12 decks, face the sea and provide a link with nature and the ocean. The Centrum (as the atrium is called) has several public rooms connected to it: the guest relations (the erstwhile purser's office) and shore excursions desks, a Lobby Bar, Champagne Bar, the Library, Royal Caribbean Online, the Concierge Club, and a Crown & Anchor Lounge. A great view can be had of the atrium by looking down through the flat glass dome high above it.

There's also a Champagne Bar, and a large Schooner Bar that houses maritime art in an integral art gallery, not to mention the Casino Royale. There's also a small, deeply tiered, dedicated movie screening room (with space for two wheelchairs), as well as a 194-seat conference center, a business center, and several conference rooms.

A Viking Crown Lounge is set around the ship's funnel.

BERLITZ'S RATINGS

	Possible	Achieved
Ship	500	422
Accommodation	200	159
Food	400	244
Service	400	285
Entertainment	100	81
Cruise	400	310

This functions as an observation lounge during the daytime; in the evening, the space hosts Starquest, a futuristic, high-energy dance club, and Hollywood Odyssey, a more intimate and relaxed entertainment venue for softer mood music and "black-box" theater.

Youth facilities include Adventure Ocean, an "edutainment" area with four separate age-appropriate sections for junior passengers: Aquanaut Center (for ages 3–5); Explorer Center (6–8); Voyager Center (9–12); and the Optix Teen Center (13–17). Adventure Beach includes a splash pool with waterslide; Surfside has computer lab stations with entertaining software; and Ocean Arcade is a video games hangout.

This second of a new generation of RCI ships (more are to follow) has been constructed for longer itineraries, with more space and comfortable public areas, larger cabins and more dining options – for the young, active, and trendy set. A computer business center has 12 PCs with high-speed internet access for sending and receiving emails. The onboard currency is the US dollar.

ACCOMMODATION. A wide range of suites and standard outside-view and interior (no view) cabins comes in 10 categories and 19 price groups.

Apart from the six largest suites (called owner's suites), which have king-sized beds, almost all other cabins have twin beds that convert to a queen-sized bed (all sheets are 100% Egyptian cotton, although the blankets are of nylon). All cabins have rich (faux) wood cabinetry, including a vanity desk (with hairdryer), faux wood drawers that close silently (hooray), television, personal safe, and three-sided mirrors. Some cabins have ceiling recessed, pull-down berths for third and fourth persons, although closet and drawer space would be extremely tight for four persons (even if two are children), and some have interconnecting doors. Audio channels are available through the TV set, so if you want to go to sleep with soft music playing you'll need to put a towel over the television screen.

Most bathrooms have tiled accenting and a terrazzo-style tiled floor, and a half-moon shower enclosure (it is rather small, however), 100% Egyptian cotton towels, a small cabinet for personal toiletries and a small shelf. There is little space to stow personal toiletries for two (or more).

The largest cabins consist of a family suite with two bedrooms. One bedroom has twin beds (convertible to queen-sized bed), while a second has two lower beds and two upper Pullman berths, a combination that can sleep up to eight persons (good for large families).

Occupants of cabins designated as suites also get the use of a private Concierge Lounge (where priority dining room reservations, shore excursion bookings and beauty salon/spa appointments can be made).

Many of the "private" balcony cabins are not very private, as they can be overlooked from the port and starboard wings of the Solarium, and from other locations.

CUISINE. Minstrel, the main dining room, spans two decks (the upper deck level has floor-to-ceiling windows, while the lower deck level has windows). It seats 1,104, and has Middle Ages music as its themed decor. There are tables for two, four, six, eight or 10 in two seatings for dinner. Two small private dining rooms (Zephyr, with 94 seats and Lute, with 30 seats) are located off the main dining room. Smoking is banned in all dining venues.

The cuisine in the main dining room is typical of mass banquet catering that offers standard fare comparable to that found in American family-style restaurants ashore – mostly disappointing and without much taste. However, a decent selection of light meals is provided, and a vegetarian menu is available. Caviar (once a standard menu item) incurs a hefty extra charge. Special orders, tableside carving and flambéed items are not offered. Menus typically include a "Welcome Aboard" Dinner, French Dinner, Italian Dinner, International Dinner, Captain's Gala Dinner.

There are two alternative dining spots: "Portofino", with 112 seats, has Italian-American cuisine (choices include antipasti, soup, salad, pasta, main dish, dessert, cheese and coffee); and "Chops Grille Steakhouse", with 95 seats and an open (show) kitchen, has premium veal chops and steaks (New York Striploin Steak, Filet Mignon, Prime Rib of Beef). Both these spots have food that is of a much higher quality than in the main dining room. There is an additional charge of $20 per person (including gratuities), and reservations are required for both dining spots, which are typically open between 6pm and 11pm.

Be prepared to eat a lot of food (perhaps this justifies the cover charge), as these are Texas-sized portions presented on large plates. Menus don't change throughout the cruise. The dress code is smart casual.

Also, casual meals can be taken (for breakfast, lunch and dinner) in the self-serve, buffet-style Windjammer Cafe, which can be accessed directly from the pool deck.

Additionally, the Seaview Cafe is open for lunch and dinner. Choose from the self-serve buffet, or from the menu for fast-food seafood items, hamburgers and hot dogs. The decor, naturally, is marine- and ocean related.

ENTERTAINMENT. The Pacifica Theatre, the main show-lounge, is three decks high, has 874 seats (including 24 stations for wheelchairs), and good sight lines from most seats.

SPA/FITNESS. The ShipShape Spa's health, fitness and spa facilities have themed decor, and include a 10,176 sq.-ft (945 sq.-meter) solarium with whirlpool and counter current swimming under a retractable magrodome roof, a gymnasium (with 44 cardiovascular machines), 50-person aerobics room, sauna and steam rooms, and therapy treatment rooms. All are located on two of the uppermost decks of the ship, forward of the mast.

Examples of treatment prices include Swedish Massage ($99 for 50 mins); Aroma Stone Massage ($159 for 75 mins); Lime and Ginger Salt Glow with half body massage ($127 for 50 mins); Aromapure Facial $99 for 50 mins); Cellulite Reduction Program ($132 for 50 mins).

For the more sporting, youthful passengers, there is activity galore – including a rock-climbing wall that's 30-ft (9 meters) high, with five separate climbing tracks. It is located outdoors at the aft end of the funnel. Other sports facilities include a golf course, jogging track, basketball court, 9-hole miniature golf course (with novel decorative ornaments), and an indoor/outdoor country club with golf simulator. There is also an exterior jogging track.

● **For more extensive general information about a Royal Caribbean cruise experience, see pages 137–42.**

Caribbean Princess
★★★★

Large Resort Ship: ....112,894 tons	Total Crew: 1,163	Cabins (with private balcony): 881
Lifestyle: ....Standard	Passengers	Cabins (wheelchair accessible): 25
Cruise Line: ....Princess Cruises	(lower beds/all berths): 3,114/3,782	Cabin Voltage: ....110 volts
Former Names: ....None	Passenger Space Ratio	Elevators: 14
Builder: ....Fincantieri (Italy)	(lower beds/all berths): 36.2/29.8	Casino (gaming tables): ....Yes
Original Cost: ....$500 million	Crew/Passenger Ratio	Slot Machines: ....Yes
Entered Service: ....Apr 2004	(lower beds/all berths): 2.6/3.2	Swimming Pools (outdoors): 4
Registry: ....Bermuda	Navigation Officers: .....British/European	Swimming Pools (indoors): 0
Length (ft/m): 951.4/290.0	Cabins (total): 1,557	Whirlpools: 9
Beam (ft/m): 118.1/36.0	Size Range (sq ft/m): 163-1,279/	Self-Service Launderette: ....Yes
Draft (ft/m): 26.2/8.0	15.1-118.8	Dedicated Cinema/Seats: ....No
Propulsion/Propellers: .....diesel-electric	Cabins (outside view): 1,105	Library: ....Yes
(42,000kW)/2	Cabins (interior/no view): 452	
Passenger Decks: 15	Cabins (for one person): 0	

OVERALL SCORE: 1,539 (OUT OF A POSSIBLE 2,000 POINTS)

OVERVIEW. Designed to be a (somewhat smaller) competitor to Royal Caribbean International's *Voyager*-class ships (but with a similar passenger carry), *Caribbean Princess* has the same profile as half-sisters *Golden Princess, Grand Princess,* and *Star Princess.* This ship accommodates many more passengers than half-sisters due to an additional extra deck (Riviera Deck) full of cabins, and the fact that two of the ship's 17 upper decks are made of aluminum (although lighter than steel, it does tend to "harden" over time).

Although the ship accommodates over 500 more passengers, the outdoor deck space remains the same, as do the number of elevators (so waiting time increases during peak usage). The Passenger Space Ratio is also reduced considerably compared to that of its half-sisters. *Caribbean Princess* is built for year-round service in Caribbean cruises.

There is a good sheltered teakwood promenade deck, which almost wraps around (three times round is equal to one mile) and a walkway which goes to the (enclosed, protected) bow of the ship. The outdoor pools have various beach-like surroundings, and "Movies Under the Skies" and major sporting events are shown on a 300-sq-ft (28-sq-meter) movie screen located at the pool in front of the large funnel structure in what, aboard *Golden, Grand* and *Star Princess* would be The Conservatory. Movies afloat in the open are a big hit with passengers (they remind many of drive-in movies, which have mostly disappeared from land-based venues).

Unlike the outside decks, there is plenty of space inside (but there are also plenty of passengers), and a wide array of public rooms to choose from, with many "intimate" (a relative word) spaces and places to play. The passenger

BERLITZ'S RATINGS		
	Possible	Achieved
Ship	500	431
Accommodation	200	165
Food	400	254
Service	400	293
Entertainment	100	82
Cruise	400	314

flow is well thought-out, and there is little congestion.

High atop the stern of the ship is a ship-wide glass-walled disco pod. It looks like an aerodynamic "spoiler" and is positioned high above the water, with spectacular views from the extreme port and starboard side windows (it would make a great penthouse).

The interior decor is attractive, with lots of earth tones (well suited to both American and European tastes). In fact, this is a culmination of the best of all that Princess Cruises has to offer from its many years of operating what is now a well-tuned, good-quality product.

An extensive collection of artworks has been chosen, and this complements the interior design and colors well. If you see something you like, you will probably be able to purchase it on board – it's almost all for sale.

Caribbean Princess also includes a Wedding Chapel (a live web-cam can relay ceremonies via the internet). The ship's captain can legally marry (American) couples, thanks to the ship's Bermuda registry and a special dispensation (which should be verified when in the planning stage, according to where you reside). But to get married and take your close family members and entourage with you on your honeymoon is going to cost a lot. The "Hearts & Minds" chapel is also useful for "renewal of vows" ceremonies.

For children, there is a two-deck-high playroom, teen room, and a host of specially trained counselors. Children have their own pools, hot tubs, and open deck area at the stern of the ship, thankfully away from adult areas. There are good netted-in areas; one section has a dip pool, while another has a mini-basketball court.

Gamblers should enjoy what is presently one of the

largest casinos at sea (Grand Casino), with more than 260 slot machines, and blackjack, craps and roulette tables, plus newer games such as Let It Ride Bonus, Spanish 21 and Caribbean Draw Progressive. But the highlight could well be the specially linked slot machines that provide a combined payout.

Other features include a decent library/CD-Rom computer room, and a separate card room. Ship lovers should enjoy the wood-paneled Wheelhouse Bar, finely decorated with memorabilia and ship models tracing part of parent company P&O's history (this ship highlights the 1950-built cargo ship *Ganges*). Churchill's cigar/sports bar has several television screens. A high-tech hospital is provided, with SeaMed tele-medicine link-ups to specialists at the Cedars-Sinai Medical Center in Los Angeles, who are available for emergency help.

The ship is a stunning, grand resort playground in which to roam when you are not ashore. Princess Cruises delivers a consistently fine, well-packaged vacation product, always with a good degree of style, at an attractive, highly competitive price. Whether this really can be considered a relaxing holiday is a moot point, but with so many choices and "small" rooms to enjoy, the ship has been extremely well designed, and the odds are that you'll have an enjoyable cruise vacation.

If you are not used to large ships, it will take you some time to find your way around this one, despite the company's claim that it offers passengers a "small ship feel, big ship choice."

Caribbean Princess is a year-round Caribbean cruise ship, but the company competes with Carnival Cruise Lines and Royal Caribbean International in the same segment, the world's most popular but over-tonnaged and discounted cruise region – the Caribbean. However, *Caribbean Princess* is among the best in the standard market segment.

ACCOMMODATION. There are six principal types of cabins and configurations: (a) grand suite, (b) suite, (c) mini-suite, (d) outside-view double cabins with balcony, (e) outside-view double cabins, and (f) interior (no view) double cabins. These come in 35 different brochure price categories. The choice is quite bewildering for both travel agents and passengers; pricing will depend on two things, size and location. By comparison, the largest suite is slightly smaller, and the smallest interior (no-view) cabin is slightly larger than the equivalent suite/cabins aboard *Golden, Grand* and *Star Princess*.

Cabin bath towels are small, and drawer space is very limited. There are no butlers – even for the top-grade suites (which are not really large in comparison to similar suites aboard some other ships). Cabin attendants have too many cabins to look after (typically 20), which does not translate to fine personal service.

(a) The largest, most lavish suite is the Grand Suite (A750, located at the ship's stern). It has a large bedroom with queen-sized bed, huge walk-in (illuminated) closets, two bathrooms, a lounge (with fireplace and sofa bed) with wet bar and refrigerator, and a large private balcony on the port side (with hot tub that can be accessed from both balcony and bedroom).

(b/c) Suites (with a semi-private balcony) have a separate living room (with sofa bed) and bedroom (with a television in each). The bathroom is quite large and has both a tub and shower stall. The mini-suites also have a private balcony, and a separate living and sleeping area (with a television in each). The differences between the suites and mini-suites are basically in the size and appointments, the suite being more of a square shape while mini-suites are more rectangular, and have few drawers. Both suites and mini-suites have plush bathrobes, and fully tiled bathrooms with ample open shelf storage space. Suite and mini-suite passengers receive greater attention, including priority embarkation and disembarkation privileges. What is not good is that the most expensive accommodation has only semi-private balconies that can be seen from above and so there is little privacy (Suites C401, 402, 404, 406, 408, 410, 412, 401, 405, 411, 415 and 417 on Riviera Deck 14). Also, the suites D105 and D106 (Dolphin Deck 9), which are extremely large, have balconies that are overlooked from above.

(d/e/f). Both interior (no view) and outside-view (the outsides come either with or without private balcony) cabins are of a functional, practical, design, although almost no drawers are provided. They are quite attractive, with warm, pleasing decor and fine soft furnishing fabrics; 80 percent of the outside-view cabins have a private balcony. Interior (no view) cabins measure 163 sq. ft (15.1 sq. meters).

The 28 wheelchair-accessible cabins measure 250–385 sq. ft (23.2–35.7 sq. meters); surprisingly, there is no mirror for dressing, and no full-length hanging space for long dresses (yes, some passengers in wheelchairs do also use mirrors and full-length clothing). Additionally, two family suites consist of two suites with an interconnecting door, plus a large balcony. These can sleep up to 10 (if at least four are children) or up to eight people (if all are adults).

All cabins receive turndown service and chocolates on pillows each night, bathrobes (on request) and toiletry amenity kits (larger, naturally, for suite/mini-suite occupants) that typically include soap, shampoo, conditioner, and hand/body lotion. A hairdryer is provided in all cabins, sensibly located at the vanity desk unit in the living area. All bathrooms have tiled floors, and there is a decent amount of open shelf storage space for personal toiletries, although the plain beige decor is very basic and unappealing.

Most outside-view cabins on Emerald Deck have views obstructed by the lifeboats. There are no cabins for singles. Your name is placed outside your suite or cabin in a documents holder – making it simple for delivery service personnel but also diminishing privacy. There is 24-hour room service (but some items on the room service menu are not available during early morning hours).

Some cabins can accommodate a third and fourth person in upper berths. However, in such cabins, the lower beds cannot then be pushed together to make queen-sized bed.

Almost all balcony suites and cabins can be overlooked both from the navigation bridge wing, as well as from the port and starboard sections of the ship's discotheque – high above the ship at the stern. Cabins with balconies on Dolphin, Caribe and Baja decks can be overlooked by passengers on balconies on the deck above. They are, therefore, not private. However, perhaps the least desirable balcony cabins are eight balcony cabins located forward on Emerald Deck, as the balconies do not extend to the side of the ship and can be passed by walkers and gawkers on the adjacent Upper Promenade walkway (so occupants need to keep their curtains closed most of the time).

Also, passengers occupying some the most expensive suites with balconies at the stern of the vessel may experience considerable vibration during certain ship maneuvers. Note that most cabins on Emerald Deck 8 have a lifeboat-obstructed view.

CUISINE. As befits the size of the ship, there are a variety of dining options. There are three main dining rooms, plus Sterling Steakhouse, and Sabatini's Trattoria.

The three principal dining rooms for formal dining are Coral, Island, and Palm. The Palm Dining Room has traditional two seating dining, while "anytime dining" (you choose when and with whom you want to eat) is featured in Coral and Island. All are no-smoking and split into multi-tier sections in a non-symmetrical design that breaks what are quite large spaces into smaller sections for better ambiance. Each dining room has its own galley. While four elevators go to Fiesta Deck, where the Coral and Island restaurants are located, only two go to Plaza Deck 5, where the Palm Restaurant is located (this can cause waiting problems at peak times, particularly for anyone in a wheelchair).

Specially designed dinnerware (by Dudson of England), high-quality linens and silverware, Frette Egyptian cotton table linens, and silverware by Hepp of Germany are used in the main dining rooms. Note that 15% is added to all beverage bills, including wines.

Alternative (Extra Charge) Dining Options: There are three: Sabatini's Trattoria, Tequila's, and Sterling Steakhouse. All are open for lunch and dinner on days at sea. Sabatini's is an Italian eatery, with colorful tiled Mediterranean-style decor; it is named after Trattoria Sabatini, the 200-year old institution in Florence (where there is no cover charge). It has Italian-style pizzas and pastas, with a variety of sauces, as well as Italian-style entrées (including tiger prawns and lobster tail – all provided with flair and entertainment from by the staff of waiters (by reservation only, with a cover charge of $15 per person, for lunch or dinner).

Sterling Steakhouse is located just aft of the upper level of the Princess Theater, adjacent to the Internet Café and shops, in a somewhat open area, to tempt you as you pass by, with people walking through as you eat – not a particularly comfortable arrangement. The cover charge is $20.

The cuisine in the alternative dining spots is decidedly better than in the three main dining rooms, with better quality ingredients and more attention to presentation and taste.

Casual eateries include a poolside hamburger grill and pizza bar (no additional charge), while extra charges do apply if you order items to eat at the coffee bar/ patisserie, or the caviar/champagne bar. Other casual meals can be taken in the Horizon Court, which is open 24 hours a day. It has large ocean-view on port and starboard sides and direct access to the two principal swimming pools and lido deck. There is no real finesse in presentation, however, as plastic plates are provided.

Ultimate Balcony Dinner/Breakfast: For something different, you could try a private dinner on your balcony, an all-inclusive evening featuring cocktails, fresh flowers, champagne and a deluxe four-course meal including Caribbean lobster tail – all served by a member of the dining staff; of course, it costs extra - $50 per person (or $25 per person for the Ultimate Balcony Breakfast).

ENTERTAINMENT. The Princess Theater (showlounge) is the main entertainment venue; it spans two decks and has comfortable seating on both main and balcony levels. It has $3 million worth of sound and light equipment, plus a 9-piece orchestra, and a scenery loading bay that connects directly from stage to a hull door for direct transfer to the dockside.

A special show called "Caribbean Caliente" (highlighting contemporary and classic artists, ranging from Ricky Martin to Bob Marley) is featured. The ship carries its own resident troupe of 19 singers and dancers, plus audio-visual support staff.

Club Fusion is a second entertainment lounge (located aft). It features cabaret acts (magicians, comedy jugglers, ventriloquists and others) at night, and lectures, bingo and horse racing during the day. Explorers, a third entertainment lounge, can also host cabaret acts and dance bands. A variety of other lounges and bars have live music, and Princess Cruises employs a number of male dance hosts as partners for women traveling alone.

SPA/FITNESS/RECREATION. The Lotus Spa is located forward on Sun Deck – one of the uppermost decks. Separate facilities for men and women include a sauna, steam room, and changing rooms; common facilities include a relaxation/waiting zone, body-pampering treatment rooms, and a gymnasium with packed with the latest high-tech muscle-pumping, cardio-vascular equipment, and great ocean views. Some fitness classes are free, while some cost extra.

● **For more extensive general information on what a Princess Cruises cruise is like, see pages 134–37.**

Carnival Conquest
★★★ +

Large Resort Ship:	........110,329 tons	Passengers	
Lifestyle:	..................Standard	(lower beds/all berths):	.....2,974/3,700
Cruise Line:	......Carnival Cruise Lines	Passenger Space Ratio	
Former Names:	.................none	(lower beds/all berths):	.......36.9/29.7
Builder:	.............Fincantieri (Italy)	Crew/Passenger Ratio	
Original Cost:	.............$500 million	(lower beds/all berths):	.........2.5/3.1
Entered Service:	.............Dec 2002	Navigation Officers:	.............Italian
Registry:	....................Panama	Cabins (total):	1,487
Length (ft/m):	.........951.4/290.0	Size Range (sq ft/m):	......179.7–482.2/
Beam (ft/m):	..............116.4/35.5		16.7–44.8
Draft (ft/m):	.................27.0/8.2	Cabins (outside view):	917
Propulsion/Propellers:	.....diesel-electric	Cabins (interior/no view):	570
	(63,400kW)/2	Cabins (for one person):	0
Passenger Decks:	13	Cabins (with private balcony):	574
Total Crew:	1,160	Cabins (wheelchair accessible):	25

Cabin Current:	..............110 volts
Elevators:	18
Casino (gaming tables):	...........Yes
Slot Machines:	...................Yes
Swimming Pools (outdoors):	3
(+1 with magrodome)	
Swimming Pools (indoors):	0
Whirlpools:	7
Fitness Center:	...................Yes
Sauna/Steam Room:	...........Yes/Yes
Massage:	........................Yes
Self-Service Launderette:	..........Yes
Dedicated Cinema/Seats:	..........No
Library:	.........................Yes

OVERALL SCORE: 1,385 (OUT OF A POSSIBLE 2,000 POINTS)

OVERVIEW. *Carnival Conquest* is the 19th new-build for this very successful cruise line. It has the same well-balanced profile as its sisters: *Carnival Destiny, Carnival Freedom, Carnival Glory, Carnival Liberty, Carnival Triumph* and *Carnival Victory*. The ship, whose bows are extremely short, has the distinctive, large, swept-back wing-tipped funnel that is the trademark of Carnival Cruise Lines, in the company colors of red, white and blue. However, due to its size, the ship is unable to transit the Panama Canal, and is thus dedicated to itineraries in the Caribbean.

This is quite a stunning ship, built to impress at every turn. Amidships on the open deck is a long water slide (200 ft/60 meters in length), as well as tiered sunbathing decks positioned between two swimming pools and several hot tubs. The layout of the ship is quite logical, so finding your way around is not difficult. The decor is all about the world's great Impressionist painters, such as Degas, Monet and Van Gogh. You'll also find large Murano glass flowers on antiqued brass stems in several public areas. It is very imaginative, and a fantasy land for the senses (though it isn't as glitzy as the *Fantasy*-class ships).

As for public areas, there are three decks full of lounges, 10 bars and lots of rooms to play in. There are two atriums: the largest, the Atelier Atrium (in the forward third of the ship) goes through nine decks, while the aft atrium goes through three decks. The ship has a doublewide indoor promenade, nine-deck-high, and a glass-domed rotunda atrium lobby.

For those who like to gamble, the Tahiti casino is certainly large and action-packed; there are also more than

BERLITZ'S RATINGS		
	Possible	Achieved
Ship	500	412
Accommodation	200	157
Food	400	218
Service	400	259
Entertainment	100	82
Cruise	400	257

320 slot machines. There are several other nightspots for just about every musical taste (except for opera, ballet and classical music lovers).

Children are provided with good facilities, including their own two-level Children's Club (with an outdoor pool), and are well cared for with "Camp Carnival", the line's extensive children's program.

It is difficult to escape from noise and loud music (it's even played in cabin hallways and lifts), not to mention smokers, and masses of people walking around in unsuitable clothing, clutching plastic sport drinks bottles, at any time of the day or night. You have to carry a credit card to operate the personal safes, which is inconvenient.

The many pillars in the dining room make it difficult for proper food service by the waiters. The public toilets are spartan and could do with some cheering up.

ACCOMMODATION. There are 20 cabin price categories, in 7 different grades: suites with private balcony; deluxe outside-view cabin with private balcony; outside-view cabin with private balcony; outside-view cabin with window; cabin with a porthole instead of a window; interior (no-view) cabin; interior (no-view cabin) with upper and lower berths. The price you pay will depend on the grade, location and size you choose.

There are five decks of cabins with private balcony – over 150 more than *Carnival Destiny, Carnival Triumph* or *Carnival Victory*, for example. Many of the private balconies are not so private, and can be overlooked from various public locations.

There are even "fitness" cabins aboard this ship – in a block of 18 cabins located directly around and behind the SpaCarnival; so, fitness devotees can get out of bed and go straight to the treadmill without having to go through any of the public rooms first.

The standard cabins are of good size and come equipped with all the basics, although the furniture is rather angular, with no rounded edges. Three decks of cabins (eight on each deck, each with private balcony) overlook the stern. Most cabins with twin beds can be converted to a queen-size bed format. A gift basket is provided in all grades of cabins; it includes aloe soap, shampoo, conditioner, deodorant, breath mints, candy, and pain relief tablets (albeit all in sample sizes).

Note: If you book one of the suites (Category 11 or 12 in the Carnival Cruise Lines brochure) you automatically qualify for "Skipper's Club" priority check-in at any US homeland port – useful for getting ahead of the crowd.

CUISINE. There are two principal dining rooms: the Renoir Restaurant, with 744 seats, and the larger Monet Restaurant, with 1,044 seats. Both are two decks high, and both have a balcony level for diners (the balcony level in the Monet Restaurant is larger). Two additional wings in the Renoir Restaurant, named Cassat and Pissaro, provide room to accommodate large groups in a private dining arrangement. Dining is in four seatings, for greater flexibility: 6pm, 6.45pm, 8pm and 8.45pm (these times are approximate but equal two seatings per restaurant). Although the menu choice looks good, the actual cuisine delivered is typically adequate, but quite unmemorable.

The Cezanne Restaurant is the ship's casual self-serve international food court-style lido deck eatery, which has a capacity of over 1,200. Its decor reflects the style of a 19th-century French cafe. It has two main serving lines; it is adjacent to the aft pool and can be covered by a magrodome glass cover in inclement weather. Included in this eating mall are Paul's Deli, PC's Wok (Chinese cuisine, with wok preparation), a 24-hour pizzeria, and a patisserie (there's an extra charge for yummy pastries, however), as well as a grill for fast foods such as hamburgers and hot dogs. Each night, the Cezanne Restaurant is turned into the "Seaview Bistro", and provides a casual (dress down) alternative to eating in the main dining rooms, serving pasta, steaks, salads and desserts (typically between 6pm and 9pm). And, if you are still hungry, there's always a midnight buffet around the corner.

Alternative (Reservations-Only, Extra Cost) Dining: The Point is the name of the reservations-only, extra cost, alternative dining spot. The decor includes wall murals in the style of Seurat's famous Le Cirque (The Circus). Fine table settings, china and silverware are featured, as well as leather-bound menus.

ENTERTAINMENT. The Toulouse-Lautrec Showlounge is a multi-deck showroom seating 1,400, and serves as the main entertainment venue. It has a revolving stage, hydraulic orchestra pit, superb sound, and seating on three levels (the upper levels being tiered through two decks). There is a proscenium over the stage that acts as a scenery loft.

SPA/FITNESS. SpaCarnival is a large health, fitness and spa complex that spans two decks (the walls display hand-painted reproductions of the artist's poster work). It is located directly above the navigation bridge in the forward part of the ship (and is accessed from the forward stairway).

Facilities on the lower level include a solarium, eight treatment rooms, lecture rooms, sauna and steam rooms for men and women, and a beauty parlor. The upper level consists of a large gymnasium with floor-to-ceiling windows on three sides, including forward-facing ocean views, and an aerobics room with instructor-led classes (some at extra cost).

● **For more extensive general information on what a Carnival cruise is like, see pages 113–18.**

Carnival Destiny
★★★ +

Large Resort Ship: ....101,353 tons	Total Crew: 1,000	Cabins (with private balcony): 418
Lifestyle: ....Standard	Passengers	Cabins (wheelchair accessible): 25
Cruise Line: ....Carnival Cruise Lines	(lower beds/all berths): 2,642/3,400	Cabin Current: ....110 volts
Former Names: ....none	Passenger Space Ratio	Elevators: 18
Builder: ....Fincantieri (Italy)	(lower beds/all berths): 38.3/29.8	Casino (gaming tables): ....Yes
Original Cost: ....$400 million	Crew/Passenger Ratio	Slot Machines: ....Yes
Entered Service: ....Nov 1996	(lower beds/all berths): 2.6/3.4	Swimming Pools (outdoors): 3
Registry: ....The Bahamas	Navigation Officers: ....Italian	(+1 with magrodome)
Length (ft/m): 892.3/272.0	Cabins (total): 1,321	Swimming Pools (indoors): 0
Beam (ft/m): 116.0/35.3	Size Range (sq ft/m): 179.7–482.2/	Whirlpools: 7
Draft (ft/m): 27.0/8.2	16.7–44.8	Self-Service Launderette: ....Yes
Propulsion/Propellers: .....diesel-electric	Cabins (outside view): 806	Dedicated Cinema/Seats: ....No
(63,400kW)/2	Cabins (interior/no view): 515	Library: ....Yes
Passenger Decks: 12	Cabins (for one person): 0	

OVERALL SCORE: 1,361 (OUT OF A POSSIBLE 2,000 POINTS)

OVERVIEW. *Carnival Destiny* is the 11th new ship for this very successful cruise line. However, because of its size, the ship is unable to transit the Panama Canal, and is thus dedicated to itineraries in the Caribbean. The ship, whose bows are extremely short, has the distinctive, large, swept-back wing-tipped funnel that is the trademark of Carnival Cruise Lines, in the company colors of red, white and blue.

This is quite a stunning ship, built to impress at every turn, with the most balanced profile of all the ships in the Carnival fleet. Amidships on the open deck is a very long water slide (200 ft/60 meters in length), as well as tiered sunbathing decks positioned between two swimming pools and several hot tubs.

Inside, Joe Farcus, the designer who creates all the interiors for the ships of Carnival Cruise Lines, has done a fine job. The decor is a fantasyland for the senses (though nowhere near as glitzy as the *Fantasy*-class ships). The layout is logical, so finding your way around is easy. As for public areas, there are three decks full of lounges, 10 bars and lots of rooms to play in. The ship has a double-wide indoor promenade, nine decks high, and a glass-domed rotunda atrium lobby. For those who like to gamble, the Millionaire's Club Casino is certainly large and action-packed; there are also more than 320 slot machines.

An additional feature that this ship has which the *Fantasy*-class ships do not have is the Flagship Bar, located in the Rotunda (atrium), which faces forward to glass-walled lifts. Another feature is the All Star Bar – a sports bar with tables that include sporting memorabilia.

Youngsters are provided with good facilities, including their own two-level Children's Club (including an outdoor

BERLITZ'S RATINGS		
	Possible	Achieved
Ship	500	399
Accommodation	200	157
Food	400	218
Service	400	253
Entertainment	100	81
Cruise	400	253

pool), and are well cared for with "Camp Carnival", the line's extensive children's program.

From the viewpoint of safety, passengers can embark directly into the lifeboats from their secured position without having to wait for them to be lowered, thus saving time in the event of a real emergency.

The terraced pool deck is really cluttered, and there are no cushioned pads for the deck chairs. Getting away from people and noise is difficult. The Photo Gallery, adjacent to the atrium/purser's office, becomes extremely congested when photos are on display.

There is no escape from repetitious announcements (for activities that bring revenue, such as art auctions, bingo, and horse racing) that intrude constantly into your cruise. There is also much hustling for drinks, although accomplished with a knowing smile.

ACCOMMODATION. There are 18 price grades. The price you pay depends on grade, size and location. Over half of all cabins have an ocean-view, and at 225 sq. ft./21 sq. meters they are the largest in the standard market. The cabins spread over four decks and have private balconies (with glass rather than steel balustrades, for better, unobstructed ocean views), extending over the ship's side. The balconies have bright fluorescent lighting.

The standard cabins are of good size and come equipped with all the basics, although the furniture is rather angular, with no rounded edges. Three decks of cabins (eight on each deck, each with private balcony) overlook the stern (with three days at sea on each of two alternating itineraries, vibration is kept to a minimum).

There are eight penthouse suites, and each has a large private balcony. Although they are quite lavish in their appointments, at only 483 sq. ft (44.8 sq. meters), they are really quite modest when compared to the best suites even in many smaller ships. There are also 40 other suites, each of which has a decent sized bathroom, and a good amount of lounge space, although they are nothing special.

In those cabins with balconies (more cabins have balconies aboard this ship than those that do not), the partition between each balcony is open at top and bottom, so you can hear noise from neighbors (or smell their cigarettes). It is disappointing to see three categories of cabins (both outside and interior) with upper and lower bunk beds (lower beds are far more preferable, but this is how the ship accommodates an extra 600 people over and above the lower bed capacity).

The cabins have soft color schemes and soft furnishings in more attractive fabrics than some other ships in the fleet. Interactive "Fun Vision" technology lets you choose movies on demand (for a fee). The bathrooms, which have good-sized showers, have good storage space in the toiletries cabinet. A gift basket is provided in all grades; it includes aloe soap, shampoo, conditioner, deodorant, breath mints, candy, and pain relief tablets (albeit all in sample sizes).

If you book one of the suites (Category 11 or 12 in the Carnival Cruise Lines brochure) you automatically qualify for "Skipper's Club" priority check-in at any US homeland port – useful for getting ahead of the crowd.

CUISINE. The ship has two dining rooms: the Galaxy, forward, with windows on two sides, has 706 seats; and the Universe, aft, with windows on three sides, has 1,090 seats). Both are non-smoking. Each spans two decks (a first for any Carnival ship), and incorporate a dozen pyramid-shaped domes and chandeliers, and a soft, mellow peachy color scheme.

The Universe dining room has a two-deck-high wall of glass overlooking the stern. There are tables for four, six and eight (and even a few tables for two that the line tries to keep for honeymooners). Dining is in four seatings, for greater flexibility: 6pm, 6.45pm, 8pm and 8.45pm (these times are approximate but equal two seatings per restaurant). Although the menu choices look good, the actual cuisine delivered is adequate, but quite unmemorable.

Casual eaters will find a serve-yourself Lido Buffet – open for breakfast and lunch, while for dinner this turns into the Seaview Bistro for use as an alternative eatery – for those that do not want to dress to go to the formal dining rooms (between 6pm and 9pm). These include specialty stations where you can order omelets, eggs, fajitas, Chicken Caesar salad, pasta and stir-fry items. If you are still hungry, there's always a midnight buffet around the corner.

The dining room entrances have comfortable drinking areas for pre-dinner cocktails. There are also many options for casual dining, particularly during the daytime. The Sun and Sea Restaurant is two decks high; it is the ship's informal international food court-style eatery, which is adjacent to the aft pool and can be covered by a magrodome glass cover in inclement weather. Included in this eating mall are a Trattoria (for Italian cuisine, with made-to-order pasta dishes), Happy Valley (Chinese cuisine, with wok preparation), a 24-hour pizzeria, and a patisserie (extra charge for pastries), as well as a grill (for fast foods such as hamburgers and hot dogs).

At night, the area becomes the "Seaview Bistro" (it typically operates 6pm–9pm), providing a casual (dress down) alternative to eating in the main dining rooms. It serves pasta, steaks, salads and desserts. The good thing is that, if you really want to eat 24 hours a day, you can do it aboard this ship, which has something for (almost) everyone.

ENTERTAINMENT. The three-level (non-smoking) Palladium showlounge, the setting for all production shows and large-scale cabaret acts, is quite stunning, and has a revolving stage, hydraulic orchestra pit, superb sound, and seating on three levels (the upper levels being tiered through two decks). There is a proscenium over the stage that acts as a scenery loft.

SPA/FITNESS. SpaCarnival spans two decks (with a total area of 13,700 sq. ft/1,272 sq. meters), and is located directly above the navigation bridge in the forward part of the ship (it is accessed from the forward stairway). Facilities on the lower level include a solarium, eight treatment rooms, lecture rooms, sauna and steam rooms for men and women, and a beauty parlor; the upper level consists of a large gymnasium with floor-to-ceiling windows on three sides, including forward-facing ocean views, and an aerobics room with instructor-led classes (some at extra cost).

● **For more extensive general information on what a Carnival cruise is like, see pages 113–18.**

Carnival Ecstasy
★★★

Large Resort Ship:	........70,367 tons	Passenger Decks:	10	Cabins (for one person):	0
Lifestyle:	.................Standard	Total Crew:	920	Cabins (with private balcony):	54
Cruise Line:	......Carnival Cruise Lines	Passengers		Cabins (wheelchair accessible):	22
Former Names:	..............Ecstasy	(lower beds/all berths):	.....2,052/2,594	Cabin Current:	..............110 volts
Builder:	...Kvaerner Masa-Yards (Finland)	Passenger Space Ratio		Elevators:	14
Original Cost:	............$275 million	(lower beds/all berths):	.......34.2/27.1	Casino (gaming tables):	............Yes
Entered Service:	...........June 1991	Crew/Passenger Ratio		Slot Machines:	.......................Yes
Registry:	....................Panama	(lower beds/all berths):	.........2.2/2.8	Swimming Pools (outdoors):	3
Length (ft/m):	.............855.8/260.6	Navigation Officers:	............Italian	Swimming Pools (indoors):	0
Beam (ft/m):	...............103.0/31.4	Cabins (total):	1,026	Whirlpools:	6
Draft (ft/m):	.................25.9/7.9	Size Range (sq ft/m):	..173.2–409.7/16–38	Self-Service Launderette:	..........Yes
Propulsion/Propellers:	.....diesel-electric	Cabins (outside view):	618	Dedicated Cinema/Seats:	..........No
	(42,240kW)/2	Cabins (interior/no view):	408	Library:	.......................Yes

---

OVERALL SCORE: 1,248 (OUT OF A POSSIBLE 2,000 POINTS)

OVERVIEW. Open deck areas are reasonable (although there is no walk-around open promenade deck), but they quickly become inadequate when it is full and everyone wants to be out on deck. The aft decks tend to be less noisy, whereas all the activities are focused around the main swimming pool and hot tubs – one of which has a thatched roof to provide shade. There is also a "banked" jogging track outdoors on the deck above a large, glass-enclosed enclosed health spa that's always busy. There's a well-defined "topless" sunbathing area.

A new nine-hole miniature golf course was added in 2007, as was a 1,600 sq.ft. (148 sq.meter) Children's World play area, an "art" gallery, and a 1,200 sq.ft. (111 sq.meter) conference room. Additionally, all suites/cabins were completely refurbished, with flat-screen TV and remodelled bathroom. Also included was an atrium lobby bar, coffee bar, and a New York-style deli counter.

The passenger flow is good, and the interior design is clever, functional, and extremely colorful. A six-deck-high atrium is topped by a large colored glass dome. The library has delightful decor, but few books. The Chinatown Lounge has Oriental decor, hanging lanterns and a smoking dragon.

ACCOMMODATION. There are 13 grades. The standard outside-view and interior (no view) cabins have decor that is quite plain and non-memorable. See the *Carnival Fantasy* entry for more details.

CUISINE. Wind Star and Wind Song are the two main dining rooms (the galley is between them). They have attractive decor and colors, but they are large, crowded and very noisy. The food is adequate. Dining is in four seatings, for

BERLITZ'S RATINGS		
	Possible	Achieved
Ship	500	319
Accommodation	200	138
Food	400	213
Service	400	262
Entertainment	100	73
Cruise	400	243

greater flexibility: 6pm, 6.45pm, 8pm and 8.45pm.

While the menu items sound good, their presentation is simple, and few garnishes are used. Many meat and fowl dishes are disguised with gravies and sauces. The selection of fresh green vegetables, breads, rolls, cheeses and fruits is limited, and there is much use of canned fruit and jellied desserts. There is a decent wine list, but no wine waiters. The waiters sing and dance, and there are constant waiter parades.

The Lido Cafe features the usual casual serve-yourself buffet foods. At night, the Lido Café becomes the "Seaview Bistro" and provides a casual alternative to the main dining rooms, serving pasta, steaks, salads and desserts.

ENTERTAINMENT. The Blue Sapphire Showlounge is the venue for production shows and major cabaret acts (although 20 pillars obstruct the views from several seats). With all the audio-visual support staff, dressers, and stage managers, the personnel count comes to just over 40.

SPA/FITNESS. SpaCarnival is a large, glass-wrapped health, fitness and spa complex, consisting of a gymnasium with muscle-pumping machines, an aerobics exercise room, men's and women's changing rooms, sauna and steam rooms, and beauty salon. The spa is operated by Steiner. Some fitness classes are free, while some, such as yoga, and kick-boxing, cost $10 per class.

● **For more extensive information on what a Carnival cruise is like, see pages 113–18, and for more information on the Fantasy-class ships, see *Carnival Fantasy*.**

Carnival Elation
★★★

Large Resort Ship: . . . . .70,367 tons	Passenger Decks: 10	Cabins (for one person): 0
Lifestyle: . . . . .Standard	Total Crew: .920	Cabins (with private balcony): 54
Cruise Line: . . . . . . .Carnival Cruise Lines	Passengers	Cabins (wheelchair accessible): 22
Former Names: . . . . .Elation	(lower beds/all berths): 2,052/2,594	Cabin Current: . . . . .110 volts
Builder: . . .Kvaerner Masa-Yards (Finland)	Passenger Space Ratio	Elevators: 14
Original Cost: . . . .$300 million	(lower beds/all berths): 34.2/27.1	Casino (gaming tables): . . . . .Yes
Entered Service: . . . . .Mar 1998	Crew/Passenger Ratio	Slot Machines: . . . . .Yes
Registry: . . . . .Panama	(lower beds/all berths): 2.2/2.8	Swimming Pools (outdoors): 3
Length (ft/m): 855.0/260.6	Navigation Officers: . . . . .Italian	Swimming Pools (indoors): 0
Beam (ft/m): 103.3/31.5	Cabins (total): 1,026	Whirlpools: 6
Draft (ft/m): 25.9/7.9	Size Range (sq ft/m): 173.2–409.7/	Self-Service Launderette: . . . . .Yes
Propulsion/Propellers: . . . . .diesel-electric	16.0–38.0	Dedicated Cinema/Seats: . . . . .No
42,842 kW)/2 azimuthing pods	Cabins (outside view): 618	Library: . . . . .Yes
(14 MW each)	Cabins (interior/no view): 408	

OVERALL SCORE: 1,225 (OUT OF A POSSIBLE 2,000 POINTS)

OVERVIEW. Externally angular and not particularly handsome, *Carnival Elation* is the seventh in a series of eight ships of the same Fantasy-class series. The expansive open deck areas (there is no walk-around open promenade deck) are inadequate when it is full and everyone wants to be on deck. The aft decks tend to be less noisy, whereas all the activities are focused around the main swimming pool and hot tubs (one with a thatched shade). There's a well-defined "topless" sunbathing area around the funnel base on Verandah Deck. The ship was the first in the cruise industry to be fitted with a "pod" propulsion system *(see page 174)*.

Inside, the general passenger flow is good, and the interior design is clever, functional, and extremely colorful. The theme of the decor is mythical muses, and composers and their compositions (many of the public rooms have musical names), and the colors, while bright, are less so than aboard previous ships in this series.

As in its sister ships, there is a six-deck-high open atrium appropriately dressed to impress, topped by a large glass dome; it includes a lobby bar with live music.

There are public entertainment lounges, bars and clubs galore, and a large children's playroom. Busy colors and design themes abound in the public rooms, most of which are connected by wide indoor boulevards and beg your attention and indulgence. There is also an eclectic art collection, much of it bright, vocal, and tacky. The library is a fine room, but there are few books.

This ship is not for those who want a quiet, relaxing cruise experience. There are simply too many annoying announcements, and a great deal of hustling for drinks. Shore excursions are booked via the in-cabin "Fun Vision"

BERLITZ'S RATINGS

	Possible	Achieved
Ship	500	295
Accommodation	200	138
Food	400	213
Service	400	262
Entertainment	100	73
Cruise	400	244

television system, so obtaining advice and suggestions is not easy.

ACCOMMODATION. There are 13 grades of accommodation. See *Carnival Fantasy* for more details.

CUISINE. There are two dining room, Imagination and Inspiration, with attractive decor and colors, but they are large, crowded and very noisy. The food is adequate, but no more. Dining in each restaurant is in four seatings, for greater flexibility: 6pm, 6.45pm, 8pm and 8.45pm (times are approximate).

For casual meals, there's The Lido, which, aboard this ship, has some improvements and additions worthy of note, such as: orange juice machine, where you put in oranges and out comes fresh juice. There's also a token sushi bar.

At night, the "Seaview Bistro," as the Lido Cafe becomes known, provides a casual (dress down) alternative to eating in the main dining rooms, serving pasta, steaks, salads and desserts (it typically operates 6pm–9pm).

ENTERTAINMENT. The Mikado Showlounge seats 1,010 and is the principal venue for large-scale production shows. Almost every lounge and bar has live music.

SPA/FITNESS. The large SpaCarnival complex consists of a gymnasium with muscle-pumping electronic machines), an aerobics exercise room, men's and women's changing rooms, sauna and steam rooms, and beauty salon.

● **For more extensive information on what a Carnival cruise is like, see pages 113–18, and for more information on the Fantasy-class ships, see *Carnival Fantasy*.**

Carnival Fantasy
★★★

Large Resort Ship:	.........70,367 tons	Total Crew:	920	Cabins (with private balcony):	54
Lifestyle:	...................Standard	Passengers		Cabins (wheelchair accessible):	22
Cruise Line:	.......Carnival Cruise Lines	(lower beds/all berths):	.....2,056/2,634	Cabin Current:	..............110 volts
Former Names:	...............*Fantasy*	Passenger Space Ratio		Elevators:	14
Builder:	...Kvaerner Masa-Yards (Finland)	(lower beds/all berths):	........34.4/26.7	Casino (gaming tables):	...........Yes
Original Cost:	.............$225 million	Crew/Passenger Ratio		Slot Machines:	....................Yes
Entered Service:	..............Mar 1990	(lower beds/all berths):	..........2.2/2.8	Swimming Pools (outdoors):	3
Registry:	.....................Panama	Navigation Officers:	.............Italian	Swimming Pools (indoors):	0
Length (ft/m):	..............855.8/263.6	Cabins (total):	1,028	Whirlpools:	6
Beam (ft/m):	................103.0/31.4	Size Range (sq ft/m):	......173.2–409.7/	Self-Service Launderette:	...........Yes
Draft (ft/m):	..................25.9/7.9		16.0–38.0	Dedicated Cinema/Seats:	...........No
Propulsion/Propellers:	.....diesel-electric	Cabins (outside view):	620	Library:	.........................Yes
	(42,240kW)/2	Cabins (interior/no view):	408		
Passenger Decks:	10	Cabins (for one person):	0		

BERLITZ'S OVERALL SCORE: 1,247 (OUT OF A POSSIBLE 2,000 POINTS)

OVERVIEW. Externally angular and not at all handsome, *Carnival Fantasy* (previously *Fantasy*) was the first of eight almost identical, very successful ships built for Carnival Cruise Lines, and the company's fifth new ship (others in the same series are *Carnival Ecstasy, Carnival Elation, Carnival Fascination, Carnival Imagination, Carnival Inspiration, Carnival Paradise* and *Carnival Sensation*). Except for *Carnival Elation* and *Carnival Paradise*, which feature pod propulsion systems *(see page 174)*, almost vibration-free service is provided by the diesel electric propulsion system (using the pod system negates the need for stern thrusters). It has proven to be a successful design for this company that targets the mainstream first-time cruise market.

The lifeboats (six of which double as twin screw shore tenders) are positioned high atop the ships in this series. Most of the *Carnival Fantasy*-class ships operate cruises shorter than a week (there are fewer of the much sought-after balcony cabins than in the company's newer ships).

The ship, whose bows are extremely short, has the distinctive, large, swept-back wing-tipped funnel that is the trademark of Carnival Cruise Lines, in the company colors of red, white and blue. The ship has reasonable open deck areas, but they quickly become inadequate when it is full and everyone wants to be out on deck. The aft decks tend to be less noisy, whereas all the activities are focused around the main swimming pool and hot tubs (one with a thatched shade). There's also a topless sunbathing area for those who prefer European-style sunning. There is no walk-around open promenade deck, although there is a short jogging track.

The interior spaces are well utilized. The general passenger flow is good, and the interior design (the work of

BERLITZ'S RATINGS		
	Possible	Achieved
Ship	500	318
Accommodation	200	138
Food	400	213
Service	400	262
Entertainment	100	73
Cruise	400	243

Miami-based creative genius Joe Farcus) is clever, functional, and extremely colourful. He calls it "entertainment architecture," and considers every part of a ship as a piece of a giant jigsaw puzzle.

Each of the ships has an interior design theme. *Carnival Fantasy*'s is mythical muses, and composers and their compositions (many of the public rooms have musical names), and the colors, while bright, are less so than aboard some other ships in this series.

The interior focal (and gathering) point is an "open" atrium lobby, whose balconied shape may remind you of some of the world's great opera houses; it spans six decks, and is topped by a large glass dome. The lowest level is where you'll find the Purser's Desk and Shore Excursion Desk. The original neon lighting in the lobby has gone, replaced by softer, more elegant design elements; the sculpture has also gone, replaced by a lobby bar (and live music); it's the most central place to meet.

There are public entertainment lounges, bars and clubs galore, with something for everyone (except quiet space). The public rooms, connected by a double-width indoor boulevard called "Via Marina" – with decor inspired by the ancient Roman city of Pompeii, beat a colorful mix of classic and contemporary design elements that beg your indulgence. Most public rooms and attractions lead off from this boulevard – a sort of shipboard "Main Street" which runs between the showlounge (forward) and lounge/nightclub (aft).

A large casino has almost non-stop action, as one would expect aboard any Carnival Cruise Lines ship. Conversely, there is also a fine-looking library and reading room, but few books.

Kids will, I am sure, enjoy "Children's World", a 2,500 sq. ft (230 sq. meter) play-area with games and fun stuff for youngsters of all ages, including Apple computers loaded with educational software, and an arts and crafts area with spin and sand art machines. A group babysitting service is available ($6 per hour for the first child; $4 per hour for each additional child of the same immediate family).

While the cuisine is just so-so, the real fun begins at sundown when Carnival really excels in sound, lights, razzle-dazzle shows and late-night high volume sounds. From the futuristic Electricity Disco to the ancient Cleopatra's Bar, this ship will entertain you well. This ship is not for those who want a quiet, relaxing cruise experience. There are simply too many annoying announcements, and the never-ending hustling to get you to buy drinks and many other things. Shore excursions can be booked via the in-cabin "Fun Vision" television system, but obtaining advice and suggestions is not easy. In fact, getting anyone to answer your questions can prove frustrating.

Onboard enhancements for all eight of the "Carnival Fantasy"-class ships (to be completed during 2007–8 refurbishments) include: an expansive children's water park; updated design style and features for pool areas, and the creation of the Serenity adults-only deck area; a nine-hole miniature golf course on Sun Deck as well as a new Café (a patisserie serving specialty coffees and sweets, located along the Promenade Deck); a teen club (for the line's popular "Club 02" teen program), plus a new 1,600-sq-ft (149-sq-meter) Children's World play area, located on Verandah Deck, to enhance the Camp Carnival children's program.

Other additions include an art gallery, a photo gallery, an Atrium Bar, a New York-style deli in the Lido restaurant, a better internet café, and a 1,200-sq-ft (111-sq-meter) conference room. Suites/cabins now include flat screen TVs, new décor and remodeled bathrooms. Spa Carnival receives new private treatment rooms, updated exercise equipment, and other cosmetic enhancements to the facility. Some modifications to the layout of the aft lounge and casino area (to accommodate larger groups) are also being made

ACCOMMODATION. There are 13 grades of accommodation. The price you pay will depend on grade, size and location. The standard outside-view and interior (no view) cabins have decor that is rather plain and unmemorable. They are marginally comfortable, yet spacious enough and practical (most are of the same size and appointments), with good storage space and practical, well-designed no-nonsense bathrooms. However, if you have a queen-bed configuration instead of the standard twin-bed layout, note that one person has to clamber over the bed – an ungainly exercise for those of a heavier build.

Anyone booking one of the outside suites will find more space, whirlpool bathtubs, and some fascinating, rather eclectic decor and furniture. These are mildly attractive, but nothing special, and they are much smaller than those aboard the ships of a similar size of several competing companies. A gift basket is provided in all grades of accommodation; it includes aloe soap, shampoo, conditioner, deodorant, breath mints, candy, and pain relief tablets (albeit all in sample sizes).

If you book accommodation in a suite (Category 11 or 12 in the Carnival Cruise Lines brochure), you automatically qualify for "Skipper's Club" priority check-in at any US homeland port – useful for getting ahead of the crowd.

Room service items are available 24 hours a day, although in standard cabins, only cold food is available, while those in suite-grade accommodation get a greater range of items (both hot and cold) to choose from.

CUISINE. There are two large dining rooms: Celebration, located midships, and Jubilee, located aft, with the galley between them. Both have ocean-view windows; both are non-smoking, and noisy, but the decor is attractive, although it is rather vivid. There are four seatings (5:45 and 8pm in the Jubilee Restaurant; 6:15 and 8:30pm in the Celebration Restaurant), for greater flexibility.

At night, the "Seaview Bistro", as the Windows on the Sea lido self-serve buffet restaurant is known in the evenings, provides a casual (dress down) alternative to eating in the main dining rooms, serving pasta, steaks, salads and desserts (it typically is in operation only between 6pm and 9pm). Although the food selection is very limited, it does make a change from the large, crowded main dining rooms.

A patisserie (Piazza Café) offers specialty coffees and sweets (extra charge), and a so-called sushi bar on Promenade Deck is open prior to dinner (if you know anything about sushi, don't expect any revelations – it's really basic).

Note that the *Carnival Fantasy*-class ships do not have an "alternative" dining spot.

ENTERTAINMENT. The Universe Showlounge is the principal venue for large-scale production shows and major cabaret acts (although 20 pillars obstruct the views from several seats). In a typical 3- or 4-day cruise, there will be one or two, large-scale, trend-setting production shows, with a cast of two lead singers and a clutch of dancers, backed by a 10-piece live orchestra.

SPA/FITNESS. The Nautica Spa is a large, glass-wrapped health, fitness and spa complex that is located on the uppermost interior deck, forward of the ship's mast, and accessed from the forward stairway; it is typically open from 6am to 8pm daily. It consists of a gymnasium with oceanview windows that look out over the ship's bow (it has a large array of the latest in muscle-pumping electronic machines), an aerobics exercise room, men's and women's changing rooms, sauna and steam rooms, and beauty salon. A common complaint is that there are not enough staff to keep the area clean and tidy, and used towels are often strewn around the changing rooms (particularly on the men's side).

Sporting types can play basketball or volleyball, or ping-pong. There is also a "banked" jogging track outdoors on the deck above the spa.

● **For more extensive general information on what a Carnival cruise is like, see pages 113–18.**

Carnival Fascination
★★★

Large Resort Ship: . . . . .70,367 tons	Total Crew: 920	Cabins (with private balcony): 54
Lifestyle: . . . . .Standard	Passengers	Cabins (wheelchair accessible): 22
Cruise Line: . . . . . . .Carnival Cruise Lines	(lower beds/all berths): 2,056/2,634	Cabin Current: . . . . .110 volts
Former Names: . . . . .Fascination	Passenger Space Ratio	Elevators: 14
Builder: . . .Kvaerner Masa-Yards (Finland)	(lower beds/all berths): 34.4/26.7	Casino (gaming tables): . . . . .Yes
Original Cost: . . . .$315 million	Crew/Passenger Ratio	Slot Machines: . . . . .Yes
Entered Service: . . . . .July 1994	(lower beds/all berths): 2.2/2.8	Swimming Pools (outdoors): 3
Registry: . . . . .The Bahamas	Navigation Officers: . . . . .Italian	Swimming Pools (indoors): 0
Length (ft/m): 855.0/260.60	Cabins (total): 1,028	Whirlpools: 6
Beam (ft/m): 103.0/31.40	Size Range (sq ft/m): 173.2–409.7/	Self-Service Launderette: . . . . .Yes
Draft (ft/m): 25.7/7.86	16.0–38.0	Dedicated Cinema/Seats: . . . . .No
Propulsion/Propellers: . . . . .diesel-electric	Cabins (outside view): 620	Library: . . . . .Yes
(42,240kW)/2	Cabins (interior/no view): 408	
Passenger Decks: 10	Cabins (for one person): 0	

OVERALL SCORE: 1,247 (OUT OF A POSSIBLE 2,000 POINTS)

OVERVIEW. Although externally angular and not handsome, *Carnival Fascination* is the fourth in a series of eight almost identical, successful ships built for Carnival Cruise Lines, and the company's eighth new ship (others in the series are *Carnival Ecstasy, Carnival Elation, Carnival Fantasy, Carnival Imagination, Carnival Inspiration, Carnival Paradise* and *Carnival Sensation*). Almost vibration-free service is provided by the diesel electric propulsion system. It has proven to be a successful design for this fun company that targets the first-time passenger.

The ship has short bows, and Carnival's distinctive, large, swept-back wing-tipped funnel in the company colors of red, white and blue. The ship has good open deck areas, but these are inadequate because is the ship is almost always full and everyone wants to be out on deck at the same time – the aft decks tend to be less noisy, whereas all the activities are focused around the main swimming pool and hot tubs (one has a thatched roof for shade).

Inside, the general passenger flow is good, and the interior design is functional, and extremely colorful. The neon lighting and color combinations are quite vivid (think total sensory stimulation).

There are public entertainment lounges, bars and clubs galore, with something for everyone (except peace and quiet). Most public rooms lead off from a wide indoor boulevard, and feature a colorful mix of classic and contemporary design elements that beg your indulgence.

As in its sister ships, there is a six-deck-high atrium (whose balconied shape may remind you of some of the world's great opera houses), appropriately dressed to impress, topped by a large glass dome. The large casino has

BERLITZ'S RATINGS

	Possible	Achieved
Ship	500	292
Accommodation	200	138
Food	400	213
Service	400	262
Entertainment	100	73
Cruise	400	243

almost non-stop action, as one would expect aboard any Carnival Cruise Lines ship. There is a fine-looking library and reading room, but few books, and a large shop, stuffed to the gills with low-quality, tacky merchandise.

This is another ship that reflects the fine creative interior design work of Joe Farcus. The interior decor aboard all Carnival ships is themed; this one has a sophisticated Hollywood motif. Excellent photo opportunities exist with some 24 superb life-like figures from the movies. Look for Marilyn Monroe and James Dean outside the casino at Stars Bar, while Humphrey Bogart and Ingrid Bergman are seated at the piano at Bogart's Café; Sophia Loren and Paul Newman are close by, and Vivien Leigh and Clark Gable can be found in Tara's Library. Meanwhile, John Wayne is for some reason at the entrance to the Passage to India Lounge, while Edward G. Robinson is inside. Outside the Diamonds Are Forever discotheque are Elizabeth Taylor and Elvis Presley. Lena Horne and Sydney Poitier can be found outside the Beverly Hills Bar, while Katherine Hepburn and Spencer Tracy are inside. Just in case you want to gamble, you'll find Lucille Ball outside the casino. Incidentally, all the slot machines aboard all Carnival ships are linked into a big prize, called, naturally, Megacash.

Following a six-month charter to the US government as emergency housing after Hurricane Katrina, the ship underwent an extensive refurbishment program in 2007 which provided a face-lift for the ship's tired interiors. A new nine-hole miniature golf course was also added, as was a 1,600-sq-ft (148-sq-meter) Children's World play area, an "art" gallery, and a 1,200-sq-ft (111-sq-meter) conference room.

Additionally, all suites/cabins were completely refurbished, with flat-screen television and remodelled bathroom. Also included was an atrium lobby bar, coffee bar, and a New York-style deli counter.

ACCOMMODATION. There are 13 price grades. The price you pay will depend on the grade, size and location you choose. See *Carnival Fantasy* for more details.

CUISINE. There are two large, noisy dining rooms (Sensation, located midships, and Imagination, located aft, with the galley between them). Both are non-smoking, and with Carnival's typically usual efficient, fast but assertive service. The buffets are rather run-of-the-mill, with little creativity, and only basic supermarket foods. Dining is now in four seatings, for greater flexibility: 6pm, 6.45pm, 8pm and 8.45pm (times are approximate).

At night, the "Seaview Bistro", as the Lido Cafe becomes known, provides a casual (dress down) alternative to eating in the main dining rooms, serving pasta, steaks, salads and desserts (it typically is in operation between 6pm and 9pm).

ENTERTAINMENT. The Palace Showlounge is the principal venue for large-scale production shows and major cabaret acts (although 20 pillars obstruct the views from several seats). In a typical 3- or 4-day cruise, there will be one or two, large-scale, trend-setting production shows, with a cast of two lead singers and a clutch of dancers, backed by a 10-piece live orchestra.

SPA/FITNESS. SpaCarnival is a large, glass-enclosed health, fitness and spa complex that is located on the uppermost interior deck, forward of the ship's mast, and accessed from the forward stairway.

It consists of a gymnasium with oceanview windows that look out over the ship's bow (it has a large array of the latest in muscle-pumping electronic machines to choose from), an aerobics exercise room, men's and women's changing rooms, sauna and steam rooms, and beauty salon.

There is also a "banked" jogging track outdoors on the deck above the spa.

● **For more extensive information on what a Carnival cruise is like, see pages 113–18, and for more information on the Fantasy-class ships, see *Carnival Fantasy*.**

WHERE NAUTICAL EXPRESSIONS COME FROM

If you've ever wondered where some terms or phrases came from, you have only to look to the sea, ships, and seamen.

Booby Hatch

A booby hatch is a small, covered compartment under the deck, toward the bow. Sailors were punished by confinement in the booby hatch. The term has come to mean a mental institution.

Carry on

In the days of sail, the officer of the deck kept a weather eye constantly on the slightest change in the wind so sail could be reefed or added as necessary to ensure the fastest headway. Whenever a good breeze came along, the order to "carry on" would be given. It meant to hoist every bit of canvas the yards could carry. Pity the poor sailor whose weather eye failed him and the ship

was caught partially reefed when a good breeze arrived. Through the centuries the term's connotation has changed somewhat usually meaning an order to resume work.

Clean Slate

It was the custom in sailing ships to record the vessel's courses, distances and tacks on a log slate. The new watch would start with a clean slate if things had been growing fine, disregarding what had gone before and starting anew. In a similar way, today, we refer to a new beginning or a second chance in life as starting with a "clean slate."

Davy Jones's Locker

This is seamen's slang for the bottom of the sea. There are several theories as to its origin: One is that Davy Jones was the owner of a sixteenth-century London pub where unwary sailors were drugged and

put in lockers, and then awoke aboard ship to find they had been press-ganged into the Navy.

Devil to pay

Devil and the deep blue sea: In traditional wooden ships, the sailors had to caulk or pay the seams with hot tar between the planks of the deck to prevent leakage into the bilge. The devil seam was topmost on the hull next to the scuppers at the edge of the deck and the longest and most difficult seam to caulk. Hence, if there was the "devil to pay," then this was the most difficult and dangerous job since the sailor might be knocked down (scuppered) by a large wave and find himself between the "devil and the deep blue sea." The former phrase has come to mean that there will be a big price to pay for a particular action; the latter now refers to being on the horns of a dilemma.

Carnival Freedom
★★★ +

Large Resort Ship: . . . . .110,239 tons	Total Crew: .1,150	Cabins (with private balcony): 574
Lifestyle: . . . . .Standard	Passengers	Cabins (wheelchair accessible): 25
Cruise Line: . . . . . . .Carnival Cruise Lines	(lower beds/all berths): 2,974/3,700	Cabin Current: . . . . .110 volts
Former Names: . . . . .none	Passenger Space Ratio	Elevators: 18
Builder: . . . . .Fincantieri (Italy)	(lower beds/all berths): 37.0/29.7	Casino (gaming tables): . . . . .Yes
Original Cost: . . . .$500 million	Crew/Passenger Ratio	Slot Machines: . . . . .Yes
Entered Service: . . . . .Feb 2007	(lower beds/all berths): 2.5/3.1	Swimming Pools (outdoors): 3
Registry: . . . . .Panama	Navigation Officers: . . . . .European	(+1 with magrodome)
Length (ft/m): 951.4/290.0	Cabins (total): 1,487	Swimming Pools (indoors): 0
Beam (ft/m): 105.6/32.2	Size Range (sq ft/m): 179.7–484.2/	Whirlpools: 7
Draft (ft/m): 27.2/8.3	16.7–44.8	Self-Service Launderette: . . . . .Yes
Propulsion/Propellers: . . . . .diesel-electric	Cabins (outside view): 917	Dedicated Cinema/Seats: . . . . .No
(63,400kW)/2	Cabins (interior/no view): 570	Library: . . . . .Yes
Passenger Decks: 13	Cabins (for one person): 0	

OVERALL SCORE: 1,390 (OUT OF A POSSIBLE 2,000 POINTS)

OVERVIEW. *Carnival Freedom* is the 24th new ship ordered by this incredibly successful cruise line that bases its success on the "Fun Ship" concept. It shares the same generally balanced profile as sisters *Carnival Conquest, Carnival Destiny, Carnival Glory, Carnival Liberty, Carnival Triumph, Carnival Valor*, and *Carnival Victory*. Being a non-Panamax ship, it is unable to transit the Panama Canal, due to its size. Immediately recognizable is the ship's swept-back, red, white and blue wingtip funnel – the trademark of all Carnival's ships.

The ship's interior decor is a kaleidoscopic blend of colors that stimulate and excite the senses, and is dedicated to time, and the decades. The deck and public room layout is logical, and finding your way around is quite easy. Most of the public rooms are located on one deck off a main interior boulevard, above a deck which contains the two main dining rooms. The public rooms include a large casino (gaming includes blackjack, craps, roulette, three-card poker, Caribbean Stud poker, Face Up, Let it Ride, Bonus, and Wheel of Madness, and more than 300 slot machines).

If you like movies on big screens in the open air (remember drive-in movie theaters?), Carnival's Seaside Theatre for movies on deck should do it for you (seating is in tiered rows and the movie screen faces forward). The ship has bow-to-stern wi-fi internet access (including all passenger cabins).

Youngsters are provided with their own Camp Carnival children's club (with its own small outdoor pool), and are well cared for with the line's extensive children's program. Camp Carnival is located on Sun Deck (out of the way of older passengers).

Minor niggles include the fact that many pillars obstruct

BERLITZ'S RATINGS

	Possible	Achieved
Ship	500	414
Accommodation	200	157
Food	400	218
Service	400	260
Entertainment	100	82
Cruise	400	259

passenger flow (particularly in the dining room, where they make it difficult for the waiters to serve food properly).

ACCOMMODATION. There are 20 cabin price categories, in 7 different suite/cabin types, sizes and grades. These include suites with private balcony; deluxe outside-view cabins with private balcony; outside-view cabins with private balcony; outside-view cabins with window; cabins with a porthole instead of a window; interior (no-view) cabins; and interior (no-view cabins) with upper and lower berths. There are five decks of cabins with private balconies. Standard cabins are of good size and come equipped with all the basics, although the furniture is rather square and angular, with no rounded edges. Three decks of cabins (eight on each deck, each with private balcony) overlook the stern. Most cabins with twin beds can be converted to a queen-size bed format.

Book one of the suites (Category 11 or 12 in the Carnival Cruise Lines brochure) and you'll get "Skipper's Club" priority check-in at any US homeland port – useful for getting ahead of the crowd.

There are even "spa" cabins aboard this ship – a grouping of 18 cabins that are located directly around and behind SpaCarnival; so fitness devotees can get out of bed and go straight to the treadmill without having to go through any of the public rooms first.

A gift basket of personal toiletry items is provided in all grades of cabins; it includes aloe soap, shampoo, conditioner, deodorant, breath mints, candy, and pain relief tablets (all in sample sizes – and most in paper packets that are difficult, sometimes frustrating, to open).

CUISINE. There are two principal dining rooms (Chic 744, located midships; and Posh, aft, seating 1,122). Both are two decks high and have a balcony level (the balcony level in Posh is larger than the one in Chic). Dining is in four seatings, for greater flexibility: 6pm, 6.45pm, 8pm and 8.45pm (these times are approximate, and equal two seatings per restaurant). There are few tables for two, but my favourites are the two tables for two right at the very back of the restaurant, with ocean views astern.

Alternative (Reservations-Only, Extra Cost) Dining: There is one reservations-only, extra-cost dining spot, the Sun King Supper Club. It features fine table settings, china and silverware, as well as leather-bound menus. The featured specialties are steaks and seafood items. It's worth paying the cover charge to get a taste of what Carnival can really deliver in terms of food that is of better quality than that served in the main dining rooms.

Casual Eateries: The Freedom Restaurant is a casual self-serve international food court-style lido deck eatery. It has two main serving lines. Included in this eating mall are a deli, an Asian eatery (with wok preparation), a 24-hour pizzeria, and a grill for fast foods such as hamburgers and hot dogs. Each night, the Freedom Restaurant morphs into the "Seaview Bistro," and provides a casual (dress down) alternative to eating in the main dining rooms, serving pasta, steaks, salads and desserts (typically between 6pm and 9pm).

Other "nooks and crannies" (extra cost) food and drink-related places include the Nouveau Wine Bar, the Viennese Café, and the cute little Meiji Sushi Bar. All are located on Promenade Deck.

ENTERTAINMENT. The Victoriana Theater (named after England's Queen Victoria) is the ship's multi-deck showroom. This large showlounge seats up to 1,400, and serves as the principal entertainment venue for the ship's colourful large-scale entertainment, including Las-Vegas-style production shows and major cabaret acts. It has a revolving stage, hydraulic orchestra pit, superb sound, and seating on three levels (the upper levels being tiered through two decks). A proscenium over the stage acts as a scenery loft.

The decor is medieval (drinks tables are made to look like shields, for example; and towers with stained-glass windows, shields, and coats of armor flank the stage).

An alternative entertainment venue is the aft lounge, which seats 425 and typically features live music and late-night cabaret acts including smutty adult comedy.

Body-throbbing loud music sensations can be found in the ship's discotheque; it includes a video wall with live projections from the dance floor. Meanwhile piano bar lovers should enjoy the 100-seat Lindy Hop piano bar.

SPA/FITNESS. SpaCarnival spans two decks (with a total area of approximately 13,300 sq. ft/1,235 sq. meters), and is located directly above the navigation bridge in the forward part of the ship (it is accessed from the forward stairway. Facilities on the lower level include a solarium, eight treatment rooms, lecture rooms, sauna and steam rooms for men and women, and a beauty parlor; the upper level consists of a large gymnasium with floor-to-ceiling windows on three sides, including forward-facing ocean views, and an aerobics room with instructor-led classes (some at extra cost) for which you'll need to sign up.

● **For more extensive general information on what a Carnival cruise is like, see pages 113–18.**

Carnival Glory
★★★ +

Large Resort Ship: ....110,000 tons	Total Crew: 1,160	Cabins (with private balcony): 574
Lifestyle: ....Standard	Passengers	Cabins (wheelchair accessible): 25
Cruise Line: ......Carnival Cruise Lines	(lower beds/all berths): 2,974/3,700	Cabin Current: ....110 volts
Former Names: ....none	Passenger Space Ratio	Elevators: 18
Builder: ....Fincantieri (Italy)	(lower beds/all berths): 36.9/29.7	Casino (gaming tables): ....Yes
Original Cost: ....$500 million	Crew/Passenger Ratio	Slot Machines: ....Yes
Entered Service: ....July 2003	(lower beds/all berths): 2.5/3.1	Swimming Pools (outdoors): 3
Registry: ....Panama	Navigation Officers: ....Italian	(+1 with magrodome)
Length (ft/m): 951.4/290.0	Cabins (total): 1,487	Swimming Pools (indoors): 0
Beam (ft/m): 116.4/35.5	Size Range (sq ft/m): 179.7–482.2/	Whirlpools: 7
Draft (ft/m): 27.0/8.2	16.7–44.8	Self-Service Launderette: ....Yes
Propulsion/Propellers: .....diesel-electric	Cabins (outside view): 917	Dedicated Cinema/Seats: ....No
(63,400kW)/2	Cabins (interior/no view): 570	Library: ....Yes
Passenger Decks:..................13	Cabins (for one person): 0	

OVERALL SCORE: 1,380 (OUT OF A POSSIBLE 2,000 POINTS)

OVERVIEW. *Carnival Glory* is the 20th new ship for this very successful cruise line. It is, together with sister ship *Carnival Conquest*, the largest ship in the Carnival Cruise Lines fleet, and has the same generally well-balanced profile profile as its sisters: *Carnival Destiny Carnival Freedom, Carnival Glory, Carnival Liberty, Carnival Triumph* and *Carnival Victory*.

The ship is unable to transit the Panama Canal, due to its size. With extremely short bows, it has the distinctive, large, swept-back wing-tipped funnel that is the trademark of Carnival Cruise Lines, in the company colors of red, white and blue.

The ship's interior decor is truly a fantasyland of colors (the central design theme), and every hue of the rainbow (and a few more) is represented in the public rooms and hallways throughout this ship. Also, the layout is logical, so finding your way around is easy. Most public rooms are located off the Kaleidoscope Boulevard, or main interior promenade (great for strolling and people-watching).

As for public areas, there are three decks full of lounges, 10 bars and lots of rooms to play in. There are two atriums: the largest, called The Colors Lobby, in the forward third of the ship (check out the interpretative paintings of US flags at the Color Bar) goes through nine decks – the colors on the towering atrium wall really are kaleidoscopic – while the aft atrium goes through three decks.

There are nightspots for just about every musical taste (except for opera, ballet and classical music lovers), and for those who like to gamble, the Camel Club Casino, with its Egyptian motif, is certainly large and action-packed; there are also more than 320 slot machines.

Youngsters are provided with good facilities, including

BERLITZ'S RATINGS

	Possible	Achieved
Ship	500	408
Accommodation	200	157
Food	400	218
Service	400	259
Entertainment	100	82
Cruise	400	256

their own two-level Children's Club (including an outdoor pool), and are well cared for with "Camp Carnival", the line's extensive children's program. Note that soft-drinks packages can be purchased for children (and adults).

Many pillars obstruct passengers flow. Those in the dining room, for example, make it difficult for the waiters to serve food properly. The public toilets are spartan and could do with some cheering up.

ACCOMMODATION. There are 20 cabin price categories, in 7 different grades: suites with private balcony; deluxe outside-view cabins with private balcony; outside-view cabins with private balcony; outside-view cabins with window; cabins with a porthole instead of a window; interior (no-view) cabins; and interior (no-view cabins) with upper and lower berths. There are five decks of cabins with private balcony – like sister ship *Carnival Conquest*. The price will depend on the grade, location and size you choose.

The standard cabins are of good size and come equipped with all the basics, although the furniture is rather square and angular, with no rounded edges. Three decks of cabins (eight on each deck, each with private balcony) overlook the stern. Most cabins with twin beds can be converted to a queen-size bed format.

If you book one of the suites (Category 11 or 12 in the Carnival Cruise Lines brochure) you automatically qualify for "Skipper's Club" priority check-in at any US homeland port – useful for getting ahead of the crowd.

There are even "fitness" cabins – in a block of 18 cabins located directly around and behind the SpaCarnival; so, fitness devotees can get out of bed and go straight to the treadmill without having to go through any of the public rooms.

A gift basket is provided in all grades of cabins; it includes aloe soap, shampoo, conditioner, deodorant, breath mints, candy, and pain relief tablets (albeit all in sample sizes).

CUISINE. There are two principal dining rooms (Golden and Platinum). Both are two decks high, and both have a balcony level for diners (the balcony level in the aft dining room is larger than the other). The decor is interesting and includes wall coverings featuring a pattern of Japanese bonsai trees. Two additional wings provide room to accommodate large groups in a private dining arrangement.

Dining is in four seatings, for greater flexibility: 6pm, 6.45pm, 8pm and 8.45pm (these times are approximate but equal two seatings per restaurant). Although the menu choice looks good, the actual cuisine delivered is typically adequate, and quite unmemorable.

There is also a casual self-serve international food court-style lido deck eatery, the two-level Red Sail Restaurant. It has two main serving lines; it is adjacent to the aft pool and can be covered by a magrodome glass cover in inclement weather. Included in this eating mall are Paul's Deli, PC's Wok (Chinese cuisine, with wok preparation), a 24-hour pizzeria, and a patisserie (there's an extra charge for yummy pastries, however), as well as a grill for fast foods such as hamburgers and hot dogs. Each night, the Cézanne Restaurant is turned into the "Seaview Bistro," and provides a casual (dress down) alternative to eating in the main dining rooms, serving pasta, steaks, salads and desserts (typically between 6pm and 9pm).

Alternative (Reservations-Only, Extra Cost) Dining: There is one reservations-only, extra cost, alternative dining spot, the Emerald Room. Fine table settings, china and silverware are featured, as well as leather-bound menus, cobalt-blue walls and lighting fixtures resembling giant emeralds.

ENTERTAINMENT. The Amber Palace Showlounge (named after Russia's great Amber Room, a gift by Frederick the Great in 1715) is a multi-deck showroom seating up to 1,400, and serves as the principal entertainment venue for large-scale entertainment, including Las-Vegas-style production shows and major cabaret acts. It has a revolving stage, hydraulic orchestra pit, superb sound, and seating on three levels (the upper levels being tiered through two decks). There is a proscenium over the stage that acts as a scenery loft.

For those who enjoy the body-throbbing sensations of loud music, the White Heat Dance Club is the ship's discotheque, with its "Liberace-like" tall candelabra, and a video wall with projections live from the dance floor. Jazz lovers should enjoy the Bar Blue, while those whoe enjoy the sounds of the piano can do so in the Cinn-A-Bar, with its curved aluminum walls.

SPA/FITNESS. SpaCarnival spans two decks (with a total area of approximately 13,300 sq. ft/1,235 sq. meters), and is located directly above the navigation bridge in the forward part of the ship (it is accessed from the forward stairway). The area's decor is Polynesian in style, a theme that incorporates lush foliage, teak flooring, and a waterfall.

Facilities on the lower level include a solarium, eight treatment rooms, lecture rooms, sauna and steam rooms for men and women, and a beauty parlor; the upper level consists of a large gymnasium with floor-to-ceiling windows on three sides, including forward-facing ocean views, and an aerobics room with instructor-led classes (some at extra cost).

● **For more extensive general information on what a Carnival cruise is like, see pages 113–18.**

PLIMSOLL MARK

The safety of ships at sea and all those aboard owes much to the 19th-century social reformer Samuel Plimsoll, a member of the British Parliament concerned about the frequent loss of ships due to overloading. In those days, some shipowners would load their vessels down to the gunwales to squeeze every ounce of revenue out of them. They gambled on good weather, good fortune, and good seamanship to bring them safely into port. Consequently, many ships went to the bottom of the sea – the result of their buoyancy being seriously impaired by overloading.

Plimsoll helped to enact legislation that came to be known as the Merchant Shipping Act of 1875. This required shipowners to mark their vessels with a circular disc 12 inches (30 cm) long bisected by a line 18 inches (46 cm) long, as a measure of their maximum draft; that is, the depth to which a ship's hull could be safely immersed at sea.

The Merchant Shipping Act of 1890 went even further, and required the Plimsoll mark (or line) to be positioned on the sides of vessels in accordance with tables drawn up by competent authorities.

The Plimsoll mark is now found on the ships of every nation. The Plimsoll mark indicates three different depths: the depth to which a vessel can be loaded in fresh water, which is less buoyant than salt water; the depth in summer, when seas are generally calmer; and the depth in winter, when seas are much rougher.

Carnival Imagination
★★★

Large Resort Ship: ....70,367 tons	Passenger Decks: 10	Cabins (for one person): 0
Lifestyle: ....Standard	Total Crew: 920	Cabins (with private balcony): 54
Cruise Line: ......Carnival Cruise Lines	Passengers	Cabins (wheelchair accessible): 22
Former Names: ....*Imagination*	(lower beds/all berths): 2,056/2,634	Cabin Current: ....110 volts
Builder: ...Kvaerner Masa-Yards (Finland)	Passenger Space Ratio	Elevators: 14
Original Cost: ....$330 million	(lower beds/all berths): 34.4/26.7	Casino (gaming tables): ....Yes
Entered Service: ....July 1995	Crew/Passenger Ratio	Slot Machines: ....Yes
Registry: ....The Bahamas	(lower beds/all berths): 2.2/2.8	Swimming Pools (outdoors): 3
Length (ft/m): 855.0/260.6	Navigation Officers: ....Italian	Swimming Pools (indoors): 0
Beam (ft/m): 103.0/31.4	Cabins (total): 1,028	Whirlpools: 6
Draft (ft/m): 25.9/7.9	Size Range (sq ft/m): .173.2–409.7/16–38	Self-Service Launderette: ....Yes
Propulsion/Propellers: .....diesel-electric	Cabins (outside view): 620	Dedicated Cinema/Seats: ....No
(42,240 kW)/2	Cabins (interior/no view): 408	Library: ....Yes

OVERALL SCORE: 1,226 (OUT OF A POSSIBLE 2,000 POINTS)

OVERVIEW. *Carnival Imagination* has an angular appearance typical of today's space-creative designs. This is the fifth in a series of eight identically sized Fantasy-class Carnival ships. Almost vibration-free service is provided by the diesel electric propulsion system.

The ship has expansive open deck areas (sadly, there is no walk-around open promenade deck), but they are inadequate when it is full and everyone wants to be out on deck. The aft decks tend to be less noisy, whereas all the activities focus on the main swimming pool and hot tubs (one with a thatched roof for shade). There is a "banked" jogging track outdoors on the deck above a large, glass-enclosed health spa.

The general passenger flow is good, and the interior design is clever, functional, and extremely colorful. The theme of the interior decor is musical muses and classical mythology. There is also a $1 million art collection. There are public entertainment lounges, bars and clubs galore, with something for everyone (except quiet space).

The public rooms, connected by a wide indoor boulevard, are a colorful mix of classic and contemporary design elements. There is a dramatic six-deck-high atrium, topped by a large glass dome. The large casino has almost non-stop action; an ATM machine is located outside it.

The Victorian-style library is a curious room, with intentionally mismatched furnishings (it reminds one of *Alice in Wonderland*), fine oriental rugs, and even a few books.

ACCOMMODATION. There are 13 price grades, linked to grade, size and location. See *Carnival Fantasy* for details.

CUISINE. There are two large, colorful, noisy dining rooms (Pride, located midships, and Spirit, located aft, with the

BERLITZ'S RATINGS

	Possible	Achieved
Ship	500	297
Accommodation	200	138
Food	400	213
Service	400	262
Entertainment	100	73
Cruise	400	243

galley between the two). Both are non-smoking. Shorts are permitted in the dining room for one dinner each cruise. Dining in each restaurant is now in four seatings, for greater flexibility: 6pm, 6.45pm, 8pm and 8.45pm (times are approximate) – this should give you some idea what to expect from your dining experience.

The Lido Cafe self-serve buffets are very basic, as is the selection of breads, rolls, fruit and cheeses. At night, the "Seaview Bistro", as the Lido Cafe becomes known, provides a casual (dress down) alternative to eating in the main dining rooms, serving pasta, steaks, salads and desserts (it typically is in operation between 6pm and 9pm).

There's also a Pizzeria (this one is open 24 hours a day and typically serves over 500 every single day).

ENTERTAINMENT. The Dynasty Showlounge is the principal venue for large-scale production shows and major cabaret acts (but 20 pillars obstruct the views from several seats).

SPA/FITNESS. The Nautica Spa is a large glass-wrapped health, fitness and spa complex consisting of a gymnasium with oceanview windows, an aerobics exercise room, men's and women's changing rooms, sauna and steam rooms, and beauty salon.

A common complaint from passengers is that there are not enough staff to keep the area clean and tidy, and used towels are often strewn around the changing rooms (particularly on the men's side).

● **For more extensive information on what a Carnival cruise is like, see pages 113–18, and for more information on the Fantasy-class ships, see** *Carnival Fantasy.*

Carnival Inspiration
★★★

Large Resort Ship: . . . . .70,367 tons	Passenger Decks: 10	Cabins (for one person): 0
Lifestyle: . . . . .Standard	Total Crew: 920	Cabins (with private balcony): 54
Cruise Line: . . . . . . .Carnival Cruise Lines	Passengers	Cabins (wheelchair accessible): 22
Former Names: . . . .*Inspiration*	(lower beds/all berths): 2,056/2,634	Cabin Current: . . . . .110 volts
Builder: . . .Kvaerner Masa-Yards (Finland)	Passenger Space Ratio	Elevators: 14
Original Cost: . . . .$270 million	(lower beds/all berths): 34.4/26.7	Casino (gaming tables): . . . . .Yes
Entered Service: . . . . .Apr 1996	Crew/Passenger Ratio	Slot Machines: . . . . .Yes
Registry: . . . . .The Bahamas	(lower beds/all berths): 2.2/2.8	Swimming Pools (outdoors): 3
Length (ft/m): 855.0/260.6	Navigation Officers: . . . . .Italian	Swimming Pools (indoors): 0
Beam (ft/m): 103.0/31.4	Cabins (total): 1,028	Whirlpools: 6
Draft (ft/m): 25.9/7.9	Size Range (sq ft/m): .173.2–409.7/16–38	Self-Service Launderette: . . . . .Yes
Propulsion/Propellers: . . . . .diesel-electric	Cabins (outside view): 620	Dedicated Cinema/Seats: . . . . No
(42,240 kW)/2	Cabins (interior/no view): 408	Library: . . . . .Yes

OVERALL SCORE: 1,223 (OUT OF A POSSIBLE 2,000 POINTS)

OVERVIEW. The ship has expansive open deck areas (sadly, there is no walk-around open promenade deck), but they quickly become inadequate when it is full and everyone wants to be out on deck (the aft decks are less noisy, because all the activities are focused on the main swimming pool and hot tubs). Almost vibration-free service is provided by the diesel electric propulsion system.

The general passenger flow is good, and the interior design is clever, functional, and extremely colorful. There is lots of neon lighting, and the color combinations are quite vivid. The decor itself is themed after the arts (in an art nouveau style) and literature. There is also a $1 million art collection. Particularly interesting is an avant-garde rendition of the famed *Mona Lisa*, in Pablo's Lounge. There are public entertainment lounges, bars and clubs galore. Most lead off from a wide indoor boulevard.

As in its sister ships, there is a six-deck-high atrium, topped by a large glass dome. The atrium has scrolled shapes resembling the necks and heads of violins, and a marble staircase. The Shakespeare Library is a fine, stately room (25 of his quotations adorn the oak veneer), but there are few books. Another dazzling room is the Rock and Roll Discotheque, with its guitar-shaped dance floor and video dance club and dozens of video monitors.

ACCOMMODATION. There are 13 grades. The price you pay will depend on the grade, size and location you choose. For a detailed explanation, see the entry for *Carnival Fantasy*.

CUISINE. There are two large, rather noisy – or perhaps one should say "lively" – dining rooms (Mardi Gras, located

BERLITZ'S RATINGS

	Possible	Achieved
Ship	500	295
Accommodation	200	138
Food	400	213
Service	400	262
Entertainment	100	73
Cruise	400	242

midships, and Carnival, located aft, with the galley between them), both of which are non-smoking. The service is attentive, but far too fast and assertive, and lacks any kind of finesse. Dining in each restaurant is now in four seatings, for greater flexibility: 6pm, 6.45pm, 8pm and 8.45pm (these times are approximate).

Carnival meals stress quantity, not quality, although the company constantly works hard to improve the cuisine. However, food and its taste are still not the company's strongest points (you get what you pay for, remember).

Casual meals can be taken at informal food outlets such as the Brasserie Bar and Grill, which also includes an always-open Pizzeria (it serves over 500 every single day). At night, the "Seaview Bistro", as the Lido Café becomes known, provides a casual (dress down) alternative to eating in the main dining rooms, serving pasta, steaks, salads and desserts (it typically is in operation from 6pm to 9pm).

ENTERTAINMENT. The Paris Showlounge is the principal venue for large-scale production shows and major cabaret acts (although 20 pillars obstruct views from some seats).

SPA/FITNESS. The Nautica Spa is a large glass-enclosed complex consisting of a gymnasium with a large array of the latest in muscle-pumping electronic machines), an aerobics exercise room, men's and women's changing rooms, sauna and steam rooms, and beauty salon.

● **For more extensive information on what a Carnival cruise is like, see pages 113–18, and for more information on the Fantasy-class ships, see *Carnival Fantasy*.**

Carnival Legend
★★★ +

Large Resort Ship: . . . . .85,920 tons	Total Crew: .1,030	Cabin Current: . . . . .110 volts
Lifestyle: . . . . .Standard	Passengers	Elevators: 15
Cruise Line: . . . . . . .Carnival Cruise Lines	(lower beds/all berths): 2,124/2,680	Casino (gaming tables): . . . . .Yes
Former Names: . . . . .none	Passenger Space Ratio	Slot Machines: . . . . .Yes
Builder: . . . . .Kvaerner Masa-Yards	(lower beds/all berths): 40.4/32.0	Swimming Pools (outdoors): . . . . .2+1
Original Cost: . . . .$375 million	Crew/Passenger Ratio	children's pool
Entered Service: . . . . .Aug 2002	(lower beds/all berths): 2.2/2.6	Swimming Pools (indoors): 1
Registry: . . . . .Panama	Navigation Officers: . . . . .Italian	(indoor/outdoor)
Length (ft/m): 959.6/292.5	Cabins (total): 1,062	Whirlpools: 5
Beam (ft/m): 105.6/32.2	Size Range (sq ft/m): .185–490/17.1–45.5	Fitness Center: . . . . .Yes
Draft (ft/m): 25.5/7.8	Cabins (outside view): 849	Sauna/Steam Room: . . . . .Yes/Yes
Propulsion/Propellers: . . . . .diesel-electric	Cabins (interior/no view): 213	Massage: . . . . .Yes
(62,370 kW)/2 azimuthing pods	Cabins (for one person): 0	Self-Service Launderette: . . . . .Yes
(17.6 MW each)	Cabins (with private balcony): 750	Dedicated Cinema/Seats: . . . . .No
Passenger Decks: 12	Cabins (wheelchair accessible): 16	Library: . . . . .Yes

OVERALL SCORE: 1,388 (OUT OF A POSSIBLE 2,000 POINTS)

OVERVIEW. *Carnival Legend* (sister ship to *Carnival Miracle, Carnival Pride* and *Carnival Spirit*) is the 18th new ship for this very successful cruise line. Its launch made headlines in 2002 when actress Dame Judi Dench, the celebrity chosen to break the traditional bottle of champagne on its hull, had difficulty doing so; a final hefty heave smashed the bottle, drenching Dame Judi with champagne. The ship, whose bows are extremely short, has the distinctive, large, swept-back wing-tipped funnel that is the Carnival's trademark, in the company colors of red, white and blue.

This ship is longer than the company's larger quintet (*Carnival Conquest, Carnival Destiny, Carnival Glory, Carnival Triumph,* and *Carnival Victory*). The colourful atrium lobby, spanning eight decks, has a wall decoration best seen from any of the multiple viewing balconies on any deck above the main lobby floor level. Take a drink from the lobby bar and look upwards – the surroundings are stunning, with a mural of the Colossus of Rhodes the focal point.

The interior decor is dedicated to the world's great legends, from wonders of the ancient world and heroes of antiquity to 20th-century jazz masters and great athletes – an eclectic mix that somehow works well. There are two entertainment/public room decks, the upper with an exterior promenade deck – something new for this fun cruise line.

Without doubt, the most dramatic room aboard this ship is the Follies Showlounge. Spanning three decks in the forward section of the ship, it recalls the movie palaces of the 1920s. Spiral stairways at the back of the lounge connect all three levels. Stage shows are best seen from the upper three levels, from where the sight lines are reasonably good.

BERLITZ'S RATINGS	Possible	Achieved
Ship	500	401
Accommodation	200	148
Food	400	229
Service	400	252
Entertainment	100	81
Cruise	400	277

Directly underneath is the Firebird Lounge, which has a bar in its starboard aft section.

A small wedding chapel is forward of the uppermost level of the two main entertainment decks, adjacent to the library and internet center. Other facilities include a winding shopping street with several boutique stores, photo gallery, video games room, an observation balcony in the center of the vessel (at the top of the multi-deck atrium), and the large Club Merlin Casino, with its castle-like atmosphere (damsels, knights and wizards are painted on the walls).

In the medical department, Tele-Radiology is installed. This system enables shipboard physicians to digitally transmit X-rays and other patient information to shore-side facilities – useful for peace of mind for passengers and crew.

The information desk in the lobby is quite small, and can become congested. It is hard to escape from noise and loud music (it's even played in cabin hallways and lifts), not to mention smokers, and masses of people walking around in unsuitable clothing, clutching plastic sport drinks bottles, at any time of the day or night. Many private balconies are not so private, and can be overlooked from public locations.

Many pillars obstruct passenger flow (those in the dining room, for example, make it difficult for proper food service by the waiters). Books and computers are cohabitants in the ship's library/internet center, but anyone wanting a book has to lean over others who may be using a computer – an awkward arrangement.

ACCOMMODATION. There are 20 cabin categories, priced by grade, location and size. The range of cabins includes suites (with private balcony), outside-view cabins with private balcony, 68 ocean view cabins with French doors (pseudo balconies that have doors which open, but no balcony to step out onto), and a healthy proportion of standard outside-view to interior (no view) cabins.

All cabins have spy-hole doors, and have twin beds that can be converted into a queen-sized bed, individually controlled air-conditioning, television, and telephone. A number of cabins on the lowest deck have views that are obstructed by lifeboats. Some cabins can accommodate a third and fourth person, but have little closet space, and there's only one personal safe. There is no separate radio in each cabin – instead, audio channels are provided on the in-cabin TV system, but you can't turn the picture off. A gift basket of (sample sized) personal amenities is provided in all grades.

If you book one of the suites (Category 11 or 12 in the Carnival Cruise Lines brochure), you automatically qualify for "Skipper's Club" priority check-in at any US homeland port – useful for getting ahead of the crowd.

Among the most desirable suites and cabins are those on five of the aft-facing decks; these have private balconies overlooking the stern and ship's wash. You might think that these units would suffer from vibration, but they don't – a bonus provided by the pod propulsion system (see page 174).

For the ultimate in extra space, it would be worth your while trying one of the large deluxe balcony suites on Deck 6, with its own private teakwood balcony. These tend to be quiet suites, with a large lounge and sleeping areas, a good-sized bathroom with twin washbasins, toilet and bidet, and whirlpool bathtub. They have twin beds that convert to a queen-sized bed, three (illuminated) closets, and a huge amount of drawer space. The balcony has an outside light, and a wide teakwood deck with smoked glass and wood railing (you could easily seat 10 people here).

Even the largest suites, however, are quite small compared with suites aboard other ships of a similar size – for example, Celebrity Cruises' *Constellation, Infinity, Millennium,* and *Summit,* where penthouse suites measure up to 2,530 sq. ft (235 sq. meters). Carnival Cruise Lines has fallen behind in the move to larger living spaces, and, with this ship, lost an opportunity to provide more space. But Carnival's philosophy has always been to get its passengers out into public areas to socialize and spend money.

CUISINE. This ship has a single, large, two-decks-high, 1,300-seat main dining room, Truffles Restaurant, with seating on both upper and main levels. Its huge ceiling has large murals of a china pattern made famous by Royal Copenhagen, and wall-mounted glass display cases contain fine china. The galley is located underneath the restaurant, with waiter access by escalators. There are tables for two, four, six or eight, and small rooms on both upper and lower levels can be closed off for groups of up to 60. Dining is in two seatings (main and late) for lunch and dinner, while breakfast is in an open-seating arrangement.

For casual eaters, while there is no lido cafe, the Unicorn Cafe is an extensive eatery that forms the aft third of Deck 9 (part of it also wraps around the upper section of the huge atrium). Murals of unicorns are everywhere. The cafe includes a central area with small buffet counters (deli sandwich corner, Asian corner, rotisserie, and International counter); there are salad counters, a dessert counter, and a 24-hour Pizzeria counter, all of which form a large eatery with both indoor and outdoor seating. Movement around the buffet area is slow, and you have to stand in line for everything. Each night, the Unicorn Cafe becomes Seaview Bistro, for casual, serve-yourself dinners (typically open 6pm–9.30pm).

Alternative (Reservations-Only, Extra Cost) Dining: The Golden Fleece Supper Club is a more upscale dining spot atop the ship, with just 156 seats and a show kitchen. It is located on two of the uppermost decks of the ship, above the Unicorn, in the lower, forward section of the funnel housing, with great views over the multi-deck atrium. The decor is set around the Greek legend of Jason and the Argonauts. The bar is the setting for a large sculpture of the Golden Fleece. Fine table settings, china and silverware are featured, as well as leather-bound menus.

ENTERTAINMENT. The Follies Showlounge is the ship's principal venue for large-scale production shows and cabaret shows. Stage shows are best seen from the upper three levels. Directly underneath the showlounge is the Firebird Lounge, which has a bar in its starboard aft section.

Almost every lounge/bar, including Billie's Bar (a piano lounge), and Satchmo's Club (a nightclub with bar and dance floor) has live music in the evening. Finally, for the very lively, there's the disco; and there's always karaoke as well as a Passenger Talent Show during each cruise.

SPA/FITNESS. SpaCarnival spans two decks, is located directly above the navigation bridge in the forward part of the ship and has 13,700 sq. ft (1,272 sq. meters) of space. Facilities on the lower level include a solarium, eight treatment rooms, lecture rooms, sauna and steam rooms for men and women, and a beauty parlor; the upper level consists of a large gymnasium with floor-to-ceiling windows on three sides, including forward-facing ocean views, and an aerobics room with instructor-led classes.

There are two centrally located swimming pools outdoors, and one can be used in inclement weather due to its retractable glass dome. There are two whirlpool tubs, adjacent to the swimming pools. A winding water slide that spans two decks in height is located at an aft, upper deck. Another smaller pool is available for children. An outdoor jogging track is located around the ship's mast and the forward third of the ship; it doesn't go around the whole ship, but it's long enough for some serious walking.

● **For more extensive general information on what a Carnival cruise is like, see pages 113–18.**

Carnival Liberty
★★★ +

Large Resort Ship:	110,000 tons	Total Crew:	1,160	Cabins (with private balcony):	574
Lifestyle:	Standard	Passengers		Cabins (wheelchair accessible):	25
Cruise Line:	Carnival Cruise Lines	(lower beds/all berths):	2,974/3,700	Cabin Current:	110 volts
Former Names:	none	Passenger Space Ratio		Elevators:	18
Builder:	Fincantieri (Italy)	(lower beds/all berths):	36.9/29.7	Casino (gaming tables):	Yes
Original Cost:	$500 million	Crew/Passenger Ratio		Slot Machines:	Yes
Entered Service:	July 2005	(lower beds/all berths):	2.5/3.1	Swimming Pools (outdoors):	3
Registry:	Panama	Navigation Officers:	Italian		(+1 with magrodome)
Length (ft/m):	951.4/290.0	Cabins (total):	1,487	Swimming Pools (indoors):	0
Beam (ft/m):	116.4/35.5	Size Range (sq ft/m):	179.7–482.2/	Whirlpools:	7
Draft (ft/m):	27.0/8.2		16.7–44.8	Self-Service Launderette:	Yes
Propulsion/Propellers:	diesel-electric	Cabins (outside view):	917	Dedicated Cinema/Seats:	No
	(63,400kW)/2	Cabins (interior/no view):	570	Library:	Yes
Passenger Decks:	13	Cabins (for one person):	0		

OVERALL SCORE: 1,383 (OUT OF A POSSIBLE 2,000 POINTS)

OVERVIEW. *Carnival Liberty* is the 23rd new ship for this incredibly successful cruise line. It shares the same generally well-balanced profile as sisters *Carnival Conquest, Carnival Destiny, Carnival Freedom, Carnival Glory, Carnival Triumph, Carnival Valor* and *Carnival Victory*. The ship is unable to transit the Panama Canal, due to its size (so it's called a non-Panamax ship). With extremely short bows, it has the distinctive, large, swept-back wing-tipped funnel that is the trademark of Carnival Cruise Lines, in the company colors of red, white and blue.

The ship's decor, in the public rooms, hallways and atrium, features a design theme that salutes the master trades, like ironwork, masonry, pottery and painting. The layout is logical, so finding your way around is easy. Most public rooms are located off one main boulevard (an interior promenade that is great for strolling and people watching – particularly from the Jardin Café or Promenade Bar). Other hangouts and drinking places include The Stage (live music/karaoke lounge), the Flower Bar (main lobby), Gloves Bar (sports Bar), Paparazzi (wine bar), and The Cabinet.

As for public areas, there are three decks full of lounges, 10 bars and lots of rooms to play in. There are two atriums: the largest, in the forward third of the ship goes through nine decks (the Grand Villa Garden Atrium combines all four of the design themes), while a small aft atrium spans three decks.

There are nightspots for just about every musical taste (except for opera, ballet and classical music lovers), and for those who like to gamble, the Czar's Palace Casino, with its Russian motifs and theme, is certainly large and action-packed; there are more than 320 slot machines.

BERLITZ'S RATINGS

	Possible	Achieved
Ship	500	411
Accommodation	200	157
Food	400	218
Service	400	257
Entertainment	100	82
Cruise	400	258

Youngsters are provided with good facilities, including their own two-level Children's Club (including an outdoor pool), and are well cared for with "Camp Carnival", the line's extensive children's program. Soft-drinks packages can be purchased for children (and adults).

Many pillars obstruct passenger flow (those in the two main restaurants make it difficult for the waiters to serve properly). The public toilets are spartan and could do with some cheering up.

ACCOMMODATION. There are 20 cabin price categories, in 7 different grades: suites with private balcony; deluxe outside-view cabins with private balcony; outside-view cabins with private balcony; outside-view cabins with window; cabins with a porthole instead of a window; interior (no-view) cabins; and interior (no-view cabins) with upper and lower berths. There are five decks of cabins with private balconies. The price depends on the grade, location and size you choose.

The standard cabins are of good size and come equipped with all the basics, although the furniture is rather square and angular, with no rounded edges. Three decks of cabins (eight on each deck, each with private balcony) overlook the stern. Most cabins with twin beds can be converted to a queen-size bed format.

Book one of the suites (Category 11 or 12 in the Carnival Cruise Lines brochure) and you qualify for "Skipper's Club" priority check-in at any US homeland port – useful for getting ahead of the crowd.

There are even "fitness" cabins aboard this ship – in a block of 18 cabins located directly around and behind SpaCarnival; so, fitness devotees can get out of bed and go straight to the treadmill without having to go through any of the public rooms first.

A gift basket is provided in all grades; it includes aloe soap, shampoo, conditioner, deodorant, breath mints, candy, and pain relief tablets (albeit all in sample sizes).

CUISINE. There are two principal dining rooms (Golden Olympian Restaurant, forward, seating 744: and Silver Olympian Restaurant, aft, seating 1,122). Both are two decks high, and both include a balcony level for diners (the balcony level in the aft dining room is larger than the other). Two additional wings (the Persian Room and Satin Room) have room to accommodate large groups in a private dining arrangement. Dining is in four seatings, for greater flexibility: 6pm, 6.45pm, 8pm and 8.45pm (these times are approximate, but equal two seatings per restaurant). Although the menu choice looks good, the actual cuisine delivered is typically adequate, and quite unmemorable.

There is also a casual self-serve international food court-style lido deck eatery, the two-level Emile's. It has two main serving lines; it is adjacent to the aft pool and can be covered by a magrodome glass cover in inclement weather. Included in this eating mall are a deli, Chinese cuisine eatery, with wok preparation, a 24-hour pizzeria, and a patisserie (there's an extra charge for yummy pastries, however), as well as a grill for fast foods such as hamburgers and hot dogs. Each night, Emilie's morphs into the "Seaview Bistro", and provides a casual (dress down) alternative to eating in the main dining rooms, serving pasta, steaks, salads and desserts (typically 6pm–9pm).

Alternative (Reservations-Only, Extra Cost) Dining: There is one reservations-only, extra cost, alternative dining spot, Harry's. Fine table settings, china and silverware are featured, as well as leather-bound menus, cobalt-blue walls and lighting fixtures resembling giant emeralds.

ENTERTAINMENT. The Venetian Palace Showlounge is a multi-deck showroom seating up to 1,400, and serves as the principal entertainment venue for large-scale entertainment, including Las-Vegas-style production shows and major cabaret acts. It has a revolving stage, hydraulic orchestra pit, superb sound, and seating on three levels (the upper levels being tiered through two decks). There is a proscenium over the stage that acts as a scenery loft.

The Victoria Lounge, located aft, seats 425 and typically features live music and late-night cabaret acts, including adult comedy.

Body-throbbing loud music sensations can be found in the Tattooed Lady Dance Club is the ship's discotheque; it includes a video wall with projections live from the dance floor. Piano bar lovers should enjoy the 100-seat Piano Man piano bar.

SPA/FITNESS. SpaCarnival spans two decks (with a total area of approximately 13,300 sq. ft/1,235 sq. meters), and is located directly above the navigation bridge in the forward part of the ship (it is accessed from the forward stairway). The decor is Polynesian in style, a theme that incorporates lush foliage, teak flooring, and a waterfall.

Facilities on the lower level include a solarium, eight treatment rooms, lecture rooms, sauna and steam rooms for men and women, and a beauty parlor; the upper level consists of a large gymnasium with floor-to-ceiling windows on three sides, including forward-facing ocean views, and an aerobics room with instructor-led classes (some cost extra).

● **For more extensive general information on what a Carnival cruise is like, see pages 113–18.**

Carnival Miracle
★★★ +

Large Resort Ship: ....85,920 tons	Total Crew: 961
Lifestyle: ....Standard	Passengers
Cruise Line: ......Carnival Cruise Lines	(lower beds/all berths): 2,124/2,680
Former Names: ....none	Passenger Space Ratio
Builder: ....Kvaerner Masa-Yards	(lower beds/all berths): 40.4/32.0
Original Cost: ....$375 million	Crew/Passenger Ratio
Entered Service: ....April 2004	(lower beds/all berths): 2.2/2.7
Registry: ....Panama	Navigation Officers: ....Italian
Length (ft/m): 959.6/292.5	Cabins (total): 1,062
Beam (ft/m): 105.6/32.2	Size Range (sq ft/m): 185.0–490.0/
Draft (ft/m): 25.5/7.8	17.1–45.5
Propulsion/Propellers: ....diesel-electric	Cabins (outside view): 849
(62,370 kW)/2 azimuthing pods	Cabins (interior/no view): 213
(17.6 MW each)	Cabins (for one person): 0
Passenger Decks: 13	Cabins (with private balcony): 750

Cabins (wheelchair accessible): 16
Cabin Current: ....110 volts
Elevators: 15
Casino (gaming tables): ....Yes
Slot Machines: ....Yes
Swimming Pools (outdoors): ....2+1
children's pool
Swimming Pools (indoors): 1
(indoor/outdoor)
Whirlpools: 5
Self-Service Launderette: ....Yes
Dedicated Cinema/Seats: ....No
Library: ....Yes)

OVERALL SCORE: 1,387 (OUT OF A POSSIBLE 2,000 POINTS)

OVERVIEW. *Carnival Miracle* (sister to *Carnival Legend, Carnival Pride* and *Carnival Spirit*) is the 21st new ship for this very successful cruise line. Built from more than 100 blocks (each weighing up to 450 tons), the ship, whose bows are extremely short, has the distinctive, large, swept-back wing-tipped funnel that is the trademark of Carnival Cruise Lines, in the company colors of red, white and blue. The ship is longer than the company's larger quintet (*Carnival Conquest, Carnival Destiny, Carnival Glory, Carnival Triumph,* and *Carnival Victory*).

The interior decor is very artistic (and overwhelmingly colorful – there are no restful colors), with "fictional icons" as the design theme, with such luminaries as the Phantom of the Opera, Sherlock Holmes, Philip Marlowe, and Captain Ahab among the many art images (bronze statues of Orpheis, Sirenes, and Ulysses adorn the swimming pools).

The dramatic atrium lobby space spans eight decks and presents a stunning wall decoration best seen from any of the multiple viewing balconies on each deck above the main lobby floor level. Take a drink from the lobby bar and look upwards – the surroundings are simply stunning, with a mural of the Colossus of Rhodes (one of the seven wonders of the world). The interior decor is dedicated to the world's great legends, from wonders of the ancient world and heroes of antiquity to 20th-century jazz masters and great athletes – an eclectic mix of "entertainment architecture" that somehow works well.

There are two whole entertainment/public room decks, the upper of which also has an exterior promenade deck – something new for this fun cruise line. A small wedding

BERLITZ'S RATINGS		
	Possible	Achieved
Ship	500	401
Accommodation	200	148
Food	400	229
Service	400	251
Entertainment	100	81
Cruise	400	277

chapel is forward of the uppermost level of the two main entertainment decks, adjacent to the library and internet center. Other facilities include a winding shopping street with several boutique stores (including those selling the usual Carnival logo items), photo gallery, video games room, an observation balcony in the center of the vessel (at the top of the multi-deck atrium), and a large Club Merlin Casino, with its castle-like atmosphere (damsels, knights and wizards are painted on the walls).

In the medical department, Tele-Radiology is installed. This system enables shipboard physicians to digitally transmit X-rays and other patient information to shore-side facilities – useful for peace of mind for passengers and crew.

The information desk in the lobby is really quite small, and can become quite congested. It is difficult to escape from noise and loud music (it's even played in cabin hallways and lifts), not to mention smokers, and masses of people walking around in unsuitable clothing, clutching plastic sport drinks bottles, at any time of the day or night. Many of the private balconies aren't so private, and can be overlooked from public locations. A stream of flyers advertises daily art auctions and other promotions, while "artworks" for auction are strewn throughout the ship.

Many pillars obstruct passengers flow. Those in the dining room, for example, make it hard for proper food service by the waiters. Books and computers are cohabitants in the ship's library/internet center, but anyone wanting a book has to lean over others who may be using a computer – a very awkward arrangement. Public toilets are spartan and could do with cheering up.

ACCOMMODATION. There are 20 cabin categories, priced according to grade, location and size. The range of cabins includes suites (with private balcony), outside-view cabins with private balcony, 68 ocean view cabins with French doors (pseudo balconies that have doors which open, but no balcony to step out onto), and a healthy proportion of standard outside-view to interior (no view) cabins. All cabins have original motifs of nature, plant life and lake views.

All cabins have spy-hole doors, and twin beds that can be converted into a queen-sized bed, individually controlled air-conditioning, TV, and telephone. Some cabins on the lowest deck have views obstructed by lifeboats. Some cabins that can accommodate a third and fourth person have very little closet space, and there's only one personal safe. There is no separate radio in each cabin – instead, audio channels are provided on the in-cabin television system (however, you can't turn the picture off). A gift basket of (sample sized) personal amenities is provided in all grades.

If you book one of the suites (Category 11 or 12 in the Carnival Cruise Lines brochure), you automatically qualify for "Skipper's Club" priority check-in at any US homeland port – useful for getting ahead of the crowd.

Among the most desirable suites and cabins are those on five of the aft-facing decks; these have private balconies overlooking the stern and ship's wash. You might think that these units would suffer from vibration, but they don't – a bonus provided by the pod propulsion system (*see page 155*).

For the ultimate in extra space, it would be worth your while trying one of the large deluxe balcony suites on Deck 6, with its own private teakwood balcony. These tend to be quiet suites, with a large lounge and sleeping areas, a good-sized bathroom with twin (his 'n' hers) washbasins, toilet and bidet, and whirlpool bathtub. These suites have twin beds that convert to a queen-sized bed, three (illuminated) closets, and a huge amount of drawer space. The balcony has an outside light, and a wide teakwood deck with smoked glass and wood railing (you could easily seat 10 people with comfort and still have space left over).

Even the largest suites are quite small, however, compared with suites aboard other ships of a similar size – for example, Celebrity Cruises' *Constellation, Infinity, Millennium,* and *Summit,* where penthouse suites measure up to 2,530 sq. ft (235 sq. meters). Carnival Cruise Lines has fallen behind in the move to larger living spaces, and, with this ship, lost an opportunity to provide more space for those seeking it.

CUISINE. This ship has a single, large, two-decks-high, 1,300-seat main dining room called the Bacchus Restaurant, with seating on both upper and main levels. Its huge ceiling has large murals of a china pattern made famous by Royal Copenhagen, and wall-mounted glass display cases feature fine china. There are tables for two, four, six or eight, and small rooms on both upper and lower levels can be closed off for groups of up to 60. Dining is in two seatings (main and late) for lunch and dinner, while breakfast is in an open-seating arrangement.

For casual eaters, while there is no lido cafe, Horatio's Cafe is an extensive eatery that forms the aft third of Deck 9 (part of it also wraps around the upper section of the huge atrium). Murals of unicorns are everywhere. The cafe includes a central area with small buffet counters (deli sandwich corner, Asian corner, rotisserie, and International counter); there are salad counters, a dessert counter, and a 24-hour Pizzeria counter, all of which form a large eatery with both indoor and outdoor seating. Movement around the buffet area is slow, and you have to stand in line for everything. At night, the cafe becomes Seaview Bistro, for casual, serve-yourself dinners (typically open 6pm–9.30pm). **Alternative (Reservations-Only, Extra Cost) Dining:** Nick and Nora's Supper Club is a more upscale dining spot, with just 156 seats and a show kitchen. It is located on two of the uppermost decks of the ship, above the Unicorn Grille, in the lower, forward section of the funnel housing, with great views over the multi-deck atrium. The decor is set around the Greek legend of Jason and the Argonauts. Fine table settings, china and silverware are featured, as well as leather-bound menus.

ENTERTAINMENT. The Mad Hatter's Ball Showlounge is the ship's principal venue for large-scale production shows and other evening cabaret shows. Stage shows are best seen from the upper three levels, from where the sight lines are reasonable. Directly underneath the showlounge is the Phantom Lounge, which has a bar in its starboard aft section. Stage smoke appears to be in constant use during the production shows, and volumes are of the ear-splitting type.

SPA/FITNESS. SpaCarnival spans two decks, is located directly above the navigation bridge in the forward part of the ship, and has 13,700 sq. ft (1,272 sq. meters) of space. Facilities on the lower level include a solarium, eight treatment rooms, lecture rooms, sauna and steam rooms for men and women, and a beauty parlor; the upper level consists of a large gymnasium with floor-to-ceiling windows on three sides, including forward-facing ocean views, and an aerobics room with instructor-led classes.

There are two centrally located swimming pools outdoors, and one of the pools can be used in inclement weather due to its retractable glass dome. There are two whirlpool tubs, located adjacent to the swimming pools. A winding water slide that spans two decks in height is located at an aft, upper deck. Another smaller pool is available for children. There is an additional whirlpool tub outdoors. A jogging track is located around the mast and the forward third of the ship. Although it doesn't go around the whole ship, it's long enough for some serious walking.

● **For more extensive general information on what a Carnival cruise is like, see pages 113–18.**

Carnival Paradise
★★★

Large Resort Ship: . . . . .70,367 tons	Passenger Decks: 10	Cabins (for one person): 0
Lifestyle: . . . . .Standard	Total Crew: 920	Cabins (with private balcony): 26
Cruise Line: . . . . . .Carnival Cruise Lines	Passengers	Cabins (wheelchair accessible): 22
Former Names: . . . . .Paradise	(lower beds/all berths): 2,052/2,594	Cabin Current: . . . . .110 volts
Builder: . . .Kvaerner Masa-Yards (Finland)	Passenger Space Ratio	Elevators: 14
Original Cost: . . . .$300 million	(lower beds/all berths): 34.2/26.7	Casino (gaming tables): . . . . .Yes
Entered Service: . . . . .Nov 1998	Crew/Passenger Ratio	Slot Machines: . . . . .Yes
Registry: . . . . .Panama	(lower beds/all berths): 2.2/2.8	Swimming Pools (outdoors): 3
Length (ft/m): 855.0/260.6	Navigation Officers: . . . . .Italian	Swimming Pools (indoors): 0
Beam (ft/m): 103.3/31.5	Cabins (total): 1,026	Whirlpools: 6
Draft (ft/m): 25.9/7.9	Size Range (sq ft/m): .173.2–409.7/16–38	Self-Service Launderette: . . . . .Yes
Propulsion/Propellers: . . . . .diesel-electric	Cabins (outside view): 618	Dedicated Cinema/Seats: . . . . .No
(42,842 kW)/2 azimuthing pods	Cabins (interior/no view): 408	Library: . . . . .Yes

OVERALL SCORE: 1,222 (OUT OF A POSSIBLE 2,000 POINTS)

OVERVIEW. *Carnival Paradise* is the eighth (and final) in a series of eight ships of the same series of eight *Carnival Fantasy*-class ships, with the same internal configuration and layout. It is good for first-time passengers and those seeking party-style cruising. The ship has a forthright, angular appearance typical of today's space-creative designs. It is one of only two of the *Carnival Fantasy*-class ships (the other is *Carnival Elation*) to have been provided with a "pod" propulsion system *(technical details: page 174)*.

The ship has expansive open deck areas (there is no walk-around open promenade deck), but they quickly become inadequate when it is full and everyone wants to be out on deck (the aft decks tend to be less noisy, whereas all the activities are focused around the main swimming pool and hot tubs).

The interior decor includes splashy, showy, public rooms and interior colors – pure Las Vegas, ideal for some tastes. Public entertainment lounges, bars and clubs galore offer something for everyone, including a large children's playroom. Some busy colors and design themes abound in the handsome public rooms. Much of the eclectic art collection is bright and eye-catching. The Blue Riband library: nice room, few books, but there are models of ocean liners.

Good hangout place: the atrium lobby bar, with live music. Facilities include a shop stuffed with low-quality merchandise; a large casino with gaming tables for blackjack, craps, roulette, Caribbean stud poker, plus slot machines.

ACCOMMODATION. There are 13 grades, priced according to grade, size and location. See *Carnival Fantasy* for a more detailed description.

BERLITZ'S RATINGS	Possible	Achieved
Ship	500	296
Accommodation	200	138
Food	400	213
Service	400	260
Entertainment	100	73
Cruise	400	242

CUISINE/DINING. There are two dining rooms (Destiny, aft; and Elation, midships), both non-smoking. They have splashy decor, and are large, crowded and very noisy. While menu descriptions sound inviting, the food may prove disappointing. You get what you pay for, and this company pays very little for food. Dining in each restaurant is in four seatings: 6pm, 6.45pm, 8pm and 8.45pm (times are approximate).

For casual meals, there's the Lido Cafe, which, aboard this ship, has some improvements and additions worthy of note, such as: an orange juice machine, where you put in oranges and out comes fresh juice (better than the concentrate stuff supplied in the dining room). The Pizzeria is open 24 hours a day. There's also a small sushi bar. At night, the "Seaview Bistro", as the Lido Cafe becomes known, provides a casual (dress down) venue.

ENTERTAINMENT. The Normandie Showlounge seats 1,010, and is the principal venue for large-scale production shows and cabaret acts (20 pillars obstruct some sightlines).

SPA/FITNESS. SpaCarnival is a large health, fitness and spa complex on the uppermost interior deck, forward of the ship's mast. It consists of a gymnasium with ocean-view windows that look out over the ship's bow (it has the latest in muscle-pumping electronic machines), an aerobics exercise room, men's and women's changing rooms, sauna and steam rooms, and beauty salon.

● For more extensive information on what a Carnival cruise is like, see pages 113–18, and for more information on the Fantasy-class ships, see *Carnival Fantasy*.

Carnival Pride
★★★ +

Large Resort Ship: ....85,920 tons	Total Crew: 1,029	Cabins (wheelchair accessible): 16
Lifestyle: ....Standard	Passengers	Cabin Current: ....110 volts
Cruise Line: ......Carnival Cruise Lines	(lower beds/all berths): 2,124/2,680	Elevators: 15
Former Names: ....none	Passenger Space Ratio	Casino (gaming tables): ....Yes
Builder: ....Kvaerner Masa-Yards	(lower beds/all berths): 40.4/32.0	Slot Machines: ....Yes
Original Cost: ....$375 million	Crew/Passenger Ratio	Swimming Pools (outdoors): ....2+1
Entered Service: ....Jan 2002	(lower beds/all berths): 2.2/2.6	children's pool
Registry: ....Panama	Navigation Officers: ....Italian	Swimming Pools (indoors): 1
Length (ft/m): 959.6/292.5	Cabins (total): 1,062	(indoor/outdoor)
Beam (ft/m): 105.6/32.2	Size Range (sq ft/m): 185.0–490.0/	Whirlpools: 5
Draft (ft/m): 25.5/7.8	17.1–45.5	Self-Service Launderette: ....Yes
Propulsion/Propellers: .....diesel-electric	Cabins (outside view): 849	Dedicated Cinema/Seats: ....No
(62,370 kW)/2 azimuthing pods	Cabins (interior/no view): 213	Library: ....Yes
(17.6 MW each)	Cabins (for one person): 0	
Passenger Decks: 12	Cabins (with private balcony): 750	

OVERALL SCORE: 1,386 (OUT OF A POSSIBLE 2,000 POINTS)

OVERVIEW. *Carnival Pride* (sister to *Carnival Legend, Carnival Miracle* and *Carnival Spirit*, all of which can transit the Panama Canal) is the 17th new ship for this very successful cruise line. The ship, whose bows are extremely short, has the distinctive, large, swept-back wing-tipped funnel that is the trademark of Carnival Cruise Lines, in the company colors of red, white and blue. The ship is longer than the company's larger quintet (*Carnival Conquest, Carnival Destiny, Carnival Glory, Carnival Triumph,* and *Carnival Victory,* all of which measure over 100,000 tons).

The lobby is immense, spanning eight decks, and the decor includes lots of larger than life women's breasts, bums, and nude men – all reproductions from the Renaissance period. The atrium lobby has a stunning 37-ft high (11-meter) reproduction of Raphael's Nymph Galatea that is best seen from any of the multiple viewing balconies on each deck above the main lobby floor level. There's no question about it – the surroundings are quite stunning.

The decor is extremely artistic (eclectic, in fact), with art being the theme throughout the ship – even elevator doors and interiors display reproductions (blown-up, over-grainy photographic copies) of some of the great Renaissance masters such as Gauguin, Matisse and Vignali.

There are two whole entertainment/public room decks, the upper of which also has an exterior promenade deck – something new for this cruise line. Although it doesn't go around the whole ship, it's long enough to do some serious walking on. There is also a jogging track outdoors, located around the ship's mast and the forward third of the ship.

A small wedding chapel is forward of the uppermost level

BERLITZ'S RATINGS

	Possible	Achieved
Ship	500	401
Accommodation	200	148
Food	400	229
Service	400	251
Entertainment	100	81
Cruise	400	276

of the two main entertainment decks, adjacent to the library and internet center. Other facilities include a winding shopping street with boutique sections for brands such as Fendi, Fossil, Tommy Hilfiger, plus Carnival logo items. There's a photo gallery, video games room, an observation balcony in the center of the vessel (at the top of the multi-deck atrium), and a large casino, with gaming tables, slot machines, bar and entertainment.

The information desk in the lobby is quite small, and can become congested. You need a credit card to operate the personal safe, an inconvenience. You'll endure a stream of flyers advertising daily promotions, while "artworks" for auction are strewn throughout the ship. Many pillars obstruct passenger flow. Those in the dining room, for example, make it difficult for proper food service by the waiters.

Books and computers are cohabitants in the library/internet center, but to get a book you have to lean over those using a computer – an awkward arrangement. Public toilets are spartan and could do with some cheering up.

ACCOMMODATION. There are 20 cabin price categories, in 6 different grades, with the price depending on grade, location and size. The range of cabins includes suites (with private balcony), outside-view cabins with private balcony (many are not really private, and can be overlooked from above), 68 ocean view cabins with French doors (pseudo-balconies that have doors which open, but no balcony to step out onto – although you do get fresh air), and a healthy proportion of standard outside-view to interior (no view) cabins. While the smallest cabin measures a very decent 185 sq. ft (17.1 sq.

meters), the largest suite measures only 490 sq. ft (45.5 sq. meters) – small when compared with many other ships of a similar size, although still a healthy chunk of living space.

While the bathrooms are quite compact, they do include a shower enclosure, several shelves, a shaving mirror, and 100% cotton towels. A gift basket of (sample sized) personal amenities is provided in all grades; it includes aloe soap, shampoo and conditioner sachets, deodorant, breath mints, candy, and pain relief tablets.

All cabins have spy-hole doors, and have twin beds that can be converted into a queen-sized bed, individually controlled air-conditioning, TV, telephone, hairdryer (in the vanity desk), and neat, yellow glass bedside lights that might remind you of Tin Man in *The Wizard of Oz*. Some cabins on the lowest cabin deck (Main Deck) have views obstructed by lifeboats. Some cabins that can accommodate a third and fourth person have very little closet space, and there's only one personal safe. There is no separate radio in each cabin – instead, audio channels are provided on the in-cabin television system (but you can't turn the picture off).

Among the most desirable suites and cabins are those on five of the aft-facing decks; these have private balconies with views over the stern and ship's wash. You might think that these units would suffer from vibration, but they don't, thanks to the two-pod propulsion system *(see page 174)*.

For the ultimate in extra space, try one of the large deluxe balcony suites on Deck 6 with large private teak deck balcony. These tend to be quiet suites, with a large lounge and sleeping areas, large bathroom with twin (his 'n' hers) washbasins, toilet and bidet, and whirlpool bathtub. These suites have twin beds that convert to a queen-sized bed, three (illuminated) closets, and a huge amount of drawer space. The balcony has an outside light, and wide teak deck with smoked glass and wood railing (you could seat 10 people with comfort and still have space left over).

To keep things in perspective, note that even the largest suites are small compared with suites aboard other ships of a similar size – for example, Celebrity Cruises' *Constellation, Infinity, Millennium,* and *Summit,* where penthouse suites measure up to 2,530 sq. ft (235 sq. meters). Carnival Cruise Lines has fallen behind in the move to larger living spaces. However, Carnival's philosophy has always been to get its passengers out into public areas to socialize, and spend money (this is, after all, a holiday).

If you book one of the suites (Category 11 or 12 in the Carnival Cruise Lines brochure) you automatically qualify for "Skipper's Club" priority check-in at any US homeland port – useful for getting ahead of the crowd.

CUISINE. This ship has a single, large, two-decks-high, 1,300-seat main dining room called the Normandie Restaurant, with seating on both upper and main levels. The decor is designed to give the impression that you are dining in the grand style of the famous French liner *Normandie,* although ship buffs would probably be critical of the results. The galley is located underneath the restaurant, with waiter access by escalators. There are tables are for two, four, six or eight, and small rooms on both upper and lower levels can be closed off for groups of up to 60. Dining is in two seatings, main and late, for lunch and dinner, while breakfast is in an open seating arrangement.

For casual meals, there is the extensive Mermaid's Grille is the equivalent of a lido cafe – which is an eatery that forms the aft third of Deck 9 (part of it also wraps around the upper section of the huge atrium). It includes a central area with small buffet counters (deli sandwich corner, Asian corner, rotisserie, and International counter) in an eclectic mix; there are salad counters, a dessert counter, and a 24-hour Pizzeria counter, all of which form a large eatery with both indoor and outdoor seating. There is plenty of variety, although it's uninspiring. Movement around the buffet area is very slow. Each night, Mermaid's Grille changes its name to Seaview Bistro, for casual, serve-yourself dinners in a dress-down setting (typically open 6pm–9.30pm).

Alternative (Reservations-Only, Extra Cost) Dining: David's Supper Club is a more upscale dining spot located on two of the uppermost decks, under a huge glass dome, with seating for approximately 150. It has a show kitchen where chefs can be seen preparing their masterpieces. It is directly above Mermaid's Grille (the self-serve buffet area), in the lower, forward section of the funnel housing, with superb views over the multi-deck atrium, as well as to the sea. The decor includes a 12-ft (3.7-meter) replica of Michaelangelo's *David.* Fine table settings, china and silverware are featured, as are well as leather-bound menus.

ENTERTAINMENT. The 1,170-seat Taj Mahal Showlounge (the venue for large-scale production shows and major cabaret acts) is a dramatic room that spans three decks in the forward section. Spiral stairways at the back of the lounge connect all three levels. Stage shows are best seen from the upper three levels. Directly underneath the showlounge is Butterflies, a large lounge with its own bar.

SPA/FITNESS. SpaCarnival is quite large, spans two decks, is located directly above the navigation bridge in the forward part of the ship and has 13,700 sq. ft (1,272 sq. meters) of space. Facilities on the lower level include a solarium, eight treatment rooms, lecture rooms, sauna and steam rooms for men and women, and a beauty parlor; the upper level consists of a large gymnasium with floor-to-ceiling windows on three sides, including forward-facing ocean views, and an aerobics room with instructor-led classes.

One of the two centrally located outdoor swimming pools can be used in inclement weather due to its retractable glass dome. There are two whirlpool tubs, located adjacent to the swimming pools. A winding water slide that spans two decks in height is located at an aft, upper deck. Another smaller pool is available for children. There is also an additional whirlpool tub outdoors.

● **For more extensive general information on what a Carnival cruise is like, see pages 113–18.**

Carnival Sensation
★★★

Large Resort Ship: . . . . .70,367 tons	Passenger Decks: 10	Cabins (for one person): 0
Lifestyle: . . . . .Standard	Total Crew: 920	Cabins (with private balcony): 54
Cruise Line: . . . . . . .Carnival Cruise Lines	Passengers	Cabins (wheelchair accessible): 20
Former Names: . . . . .Sensation	(lower beds/all berths): 2,040/2,594	Cabin Current: . . . . .110 volts
Builder: . . . . .Kvaerner Masa-Yards	Passenger Space Ratio	Elevators: 14
(Finland)	(lower beds/all berths): 34.4/26.7	Casino (gaming tables): . . . . .Yes
Original Cost: . . . .$300 million	Crew/Passenger Ratio	Slot Machines: . . . . .Yes
Entered Service: . . . . .Nov 1993	(lower beds/all berths): 2.2/2.8	Swimming Pools (outdoors): 3
Registry: . . . . .The Bahamas	Navigation Officers: . . . . .Italian	Swimming Pools (indoors): 0
Length (ft/m): 855.0/260.6	Cabins (total): 1,020	Whirlpools: 6
Beam (ft/m): 104.0/31.4	Size Range (sq ft/m): 173.2–409.7/	Self-Service Launderette: . . . . .Yes
Draft (ft/m): 25.9/7.9	16.0–38.0	Dedicated Cinema/Seats: . . . . .No
Propulsion/Propellers: . . . . .diesel-electric	Cabins (outside view): 618	Library: . . . . .Yes
(42,240kW)/2	Cabins (interior/no view): 402	

OVERALL SCORE: 1,244 (OUT OF A POSSIBLE 2,000 POINTS)

OVERVIEW. *Carnival Sensation*, whose bows are extremely short, has a distinctive, large, swept-back wing-tipped funnel, the trademark of Carnival Cruise Lines. The ship, which is almost vibration-free, has expansive open deck areas (sadly, there is no walk-around open promenade deck), but they quickly become inadequate when it is full and everyone wants to be out on deck.

After a six-month charter to the US government as emergency housing in the wake of Hurricane Katrina, the ship was extensively refurbished in 2007, which provided a facelift for the ship's tired interiors. A new nine-hole miniature golf course was added, as was a 1,600-sq-ft (148-sq-meter) Children's World play area, a new "art" gallery, photo gallery, and a 1,200-sq-ft (111-sq-meter) conference room. Additionally, all cabins were completely refurbished and given flatscreen TVs (the bathrooms were also updated). A new New York-style deli counter and a patisserie were added to the Lido Café, and the internet café was redesigned.

Inside, the general passenger flow is good, and the interior design is clever, functional, and extremely colorful. A dramatic six-deck-high atrium, with cool marble and hot neon, is topped by a large colored glass dome.

The library is a lovely room, but there are few books. The Michelangelo Lounge is a creative thinker's delight, while Fingers Lounge is sheer sensory stimulation. The casino has plenty of gaming tables and slot machines.

ACCOMMODATION. There are 13 price grades. See *Carnival Fantasy* for more detailed information.

BERLITZ'S RATINGS

	Possible	Achieved
Ship	500	317
Accommodation	200	138
Food	400	213
Service	400	261
Entertainment	100	73
Cruise	400	242

CUISINE. There are two huge, noisy dining rooms (Ecstasy and Fantasy, both no-smoking) with the usual efficient, assertive service. Dining in each restaurant is now in four seatings, for greater flexibility.

The Lido Cafe self-serve buffets are very basic, as is the selection of breads, rolls, fruit and cheeses. At night, the "Seaview Bistro", as the Lido Cafe becomes known, provides a casual (dress down) alternative to the main dining rooms, serving pasta, steaks, salads and desserts (typically between 6pm and 9pm). The Pizzeria is open 24 hours a day.

ENTERTAINMENT. The Fantasia Showlounge is the main venue for large-scale production shows and cabaret acts (although 20 pillars obstruct the views from several seats).

SPA/FITNESS. The Nautica Spa is a large health, fitness and spa complex that is located on the uppermost interior deck, forward of the ship's mast, and accessed from the forward stairway. It consists of a gymnasium with oceanview windows that look out over the ship's bow, an aerobics exercise room, men's and women's changing rooms, sauna and steam rooms, and beauty salon.

There is a "banked" jogging track outdoors on the deck above the spa.

● **For more extensive information on what a Carnival cruise is like, see pages 113–18, and for more information on the Fantasy-class ships, see *Carnival Fantasy*.**

Carnival Spirit
★★★ +

Large Resort Ship: ....85,920 tons	Total Crew: 930	Cabins (wheelchair accessible): 16
Lifestyle: ....Standard	Passengers	Cabin Current: ....110 volts
Cruise Line: ......Carnival Cruise Lines	(lower beds/all berths): 2,124/2,680	Elevators: 15
Former Names: ....none	Passenger Space Ratio	Casino (gaming tables): ....Yes
Builder: ....Kvaerner Masa-Yards	(lower beds/all berths): 40.4/32.0	Slot Machines: ....Yes
Original Cost: ....$375 million	Crew/Passenger Ratio	Swimming Pools (outdoors): ....2+1
Entered Service: ....Apr 2001	(lower beds/all berths): 2.2/2.6	children's pool
Registry: ....Panama	Navigation Officers: ....Italian	Swimming Pools (indoors): 1
Length (ft/m): 959.6/292.5	Cabins (total): 1,062	(indoor/outdoor)
Beam (ft/m): 105.6/32.2	Size Range (sq ft/m): 185.0–490.0/	Whirlpools: 5
Draft (ft/m): 25.5/7.8	17.1–45.5	Self-Service Launderette: ....Yes
Propulsion/Propellers: .....diesel-electric	Cabins (outside view): 849	Dedicated Cinema/Seats: ....No
(62,370 kW)/2 azimuthing pods	Cabins (interior/no view): 213	Library: ....Yes
(17.6 MW each)	Cabins (for one person): 0	
Passenger Decks: 12	Cabins (with private balcony): 750	

OVERALL SCORE: 1,390 (OUT OF A POSSIBLE 2,000 POINTS)

OVERVIEW. *Carnival Spirit* is the 16th new ship for this very successful cruise line. It has Carnival's trademark large wing-tipped funnel in the Miami-based company's red, white and blue colors. The design makes the ship look much sleeker than any other in the Carnival Cruise Lines fleet (except for its sister ships), a process of continuing ship design and evolvement.

Sister ships in the same class and internal layout and design are *Carnival Legend, Carnival Miracle* and *Carnival Pride*, and all can transit the Panama Canal.

There are two centrally located swimming pools outdoors, and one can be used in inclement weather due to its retractable glass-dome cover. Two whirlpool tubs, located adjacent to the swimming pools, are abridged by a bar. Another smaller pool is available for children; it incorporates a winding water slide that spans two decks in height. There is also a whirlpool tub outdoors.

The interior design theme is a tribute to the world's great architecture, from art nouveau to postmodern. The immense lobby space spans eight decks. The atrium lobby, with its two grand stairways, presents a stunning wall decoration best seen from any of the multiple viewing balconies on each deck above the main lobby floor level.

There are two entertainment/public room decks, the upper of which also has an exterior promenade deck – something new for this fun cruise line. Although it doesn't extend around the whole ship, it's long enough for some serious walking. There is also a jogging track outdoors, around the ship's mast and the forward third of the ship.

There is a winding shopping street with several boutique

BERLITZ'S RATINGS		
	Possible	Achieved
Ship	500	402
Accommodation	200	148
Food	400	229
Service	400	252
Entertainment	100	81
Cruise	400	278

stores (selling all the usual Carnival logo items). A small wedding chapel is located forward of the uppermost level of the two main entertainment decks, adjacent to the combined library and internet center. Other facilities include a photo gallery, video games room, an observation balcony in the center of the vessel (at the top of the multi-deck atrium), a large casino, and a piano lounge/bar. The casino is large (one has to walk through it to get from the restaurant to the showlounge on one of the entertainments decks), and it has all the gaming paraphernalia and array of slot machines you can imagine.

There is a "tele-radiology" system that enables shipboard physicians to digitally transmit X-rays and other patient information to shore-side facilities – useful for peace of mind for passengers and crew.

The information desk in the lobby is quite small, and can become quite congested. It is difficult to escape from smokers, noise and loud music (it's even played in cabin hallways and elevators). Many private balconies are not so private, being overlooked from various public locations. You'll need to carry a credit card to operate the personal safe in your suite or cabin – an inconvenience. You'll endure a stream of flyers advertising various products.

Books and computers are cohabitants in the ship's library/internet center, but anyone wanting a book has to lean over others who may be using a computer – a very awkward arrangement. Public toilets are spartan and could do with some cheering up.

ACCOMMODATION. There are 20 cabin categories, priced according to grade, location and size. The range of cabins includes suites (with private balcony), outside-view cabins with private balcony, 68 ocean view cabins with French doors (pseudo balconies that have doors which open, but no balcony to step out onto), and a healthy proportion of standard outside-view to interior (no view) cabins. While the smallest cabin measures a very decent 185 sq. ft (17.1 sq. meters), the largest suite measures only 490 sq. ft (45.5 sq. meters) – small compared with many similar ships.

The bathrooms are quite compact, but include a circular shower enclosure, several shelves, a shaving mirror, and 100% cotton towels. A gift basket of (sample sized) personal amenities is provided in all grades; it includes aloe soap, shampoo, conditioner, deodorant, breath mints, candy, and pain relief tablets.

Regardless of the grade of cabin chosen, all cabins have spy-hole doors, and have twin beds that can be converted into a queen-sized bed, individually controlled air-conditioning, television, and telephone. A number of cabins on the lowest cabin deck have views obstructed by lifeboats. Some cabins that can accommodate a third and fourth person have very little closet space, and there's only one personal safe. There is no separate radio in each cabin – instead, audio channels are provided on the in-cabin television system (however, you can't turn the picture off).

If you book one of the suites (Category 11 or 12 in the Carnival Cruise Lines brochure), you automatically qualify for "Skipper's Club" priority check-in at any US homeland port – useful for getting ahead of the crowd.

Among the most desirable suites and cabins are those on five of the aft-facing decks; these have private balconies overlooking the stern and ship's wash. You might think that these units would suffer from vibration, but they don't – a bonus provided by the pod propulsion system (see page 174).

For the ultimate in extra space, try one of the large deluxe balcony suites on Deck 6 with large private teak balcony. These tend to be quiet, with a large lounge and sleeping areas, a large bathroom with twin (his 'n' hers) washbasins, toilet and bidet, and whirlpool bathtub. These suites have twin beds that convert to a queen-sized bed, three (illuminated) closets, and a huge amount of drawer space. The balcony has an outside light, and a wide teak deck with smoked glass and wood railing (you could seat 10 people with comfort and still have space left over).

To keep things in perspective, note that even the largest suites are small compared with suites aboard other ships of a similar size – for example, Celebrity Cruises' *Constellation*, *Infinity*, *Millennium*, and *Summit*, where penthouse suites measure up to 2,530 sq. ft (235 sq. meters). Carnival Cruise Lines has fallen behind in the move to larger living spaces, and, with this ship, lost an opportunity to provide more space for those seeking it.

CUISINE. This ship has a single, large, two-decks-high, 1,300-seat main dining room called the Empire Restaurant, with seating on both upper and main levels. The decor is heavily "Napoleonic" (early 19th-century French) style. The galley is located underneath the restaurant, with waiter access by escalators. There are tables for two, four, six or eight, and small rooms on both upper and lower levels can be closed off for groups of up to 60. Dining is in two seatings, main and late, for lunch and dinner, while breakfast is in an open seating arrangement.

For casual eaters, while there is no lido cafe, there is the extensive La Playa Grille, which forms the aft third of Deck 9 (part of it also wraps around the upper section of the huge atrium). It includes a central area with small buffet counters (deli sandwich corner, Asian corner, rotisserie, and International counter); there are salad counters, a dessert counter, and a 24-hour Pizzeria counter, all forming a large eatery with both indoor and outdoor seating. Movement around the buffet area is very slow, with frequent lines. Each night, La Playa Grille becomes Seaview Bistro, for casual, serve-yourself dinners (typically open 6pm–9.30pm).

There is an outdoor self-serve buffet (adjacent to the fantail pool), which serves fast-food items such as hamburgers and hot dogs, chicken and fries, as well as two smaller buffets adjacent to the midships pool area. If you want to eat 24 hours a day, you can do it aboard this ship, which has something for (almost) everyone.

Alternative (Reservations-Only, Extra Cost) Dining: The Nouveau Supper Club is a more upscale dining spot located on two of the uppermost decks of the ship under a huge glass dome, with seating for approximately 150. It has a open-view kitchen where chefs can be seen preparing their masterpieces. It is located directly above La Playa Grille Mermaid's Grille, in the lower, forward section of the funnel housing, with some superb views over the multi-deck atrium, as well as to the sea. Fine table settings, china and silverware are used, as well as leather-bound menus. The decor has a floral pattern and there is a stained-glass balcony on the upper level. There is also a stage and dance floor.

ENTERTAINMENT. The 1,170-seat Pharaoh's Palace Showlounge is a dramatic room which spans three decks in the forward section of the ship. Spiral stairways at the back of the lounge connect all levels. Stage shows are best seen from the upper three levels, from where the sight lines are reasonably good. Directly underneath the showlounge is the Versailles Lounge (in the highy decorative manner of 18th-century France), a large lounge with its own bar.

SPA/FITNESS. A large Nautica health spa, spanning two decks, is located directly above the navigation bridge in the forward part of the ship and has 13,700 sq. ft (1,272 sq. meters) of space. Facilities on the lower level include a solarium, eight treatment rooms, lecture rooms, sauna and steam rooms for men and women, and a beauty parlor; the upper level consists of a large gymnasium with floor-to-ceiling windows on three sides, including forward-facing ocean views, and an aerobics room with instructor-led classes (some at extra cost).

● **For more extensive general information on what a Carnival cruise is like, see pages 113–18.**

Carnival Splendor
★★★ +

Large Resort Ship:	........110,239 tons	Total Crew:	1,150
Lifestyle:	...................Standard	Passengers	
Cruise Line:	.......Carnival Cruise Lines	(lower beds/all berths):	.....2,974/3,700
Former Names:	................none	Passenger Space Ratio	
Builder:	.............Fincantieri (Italy)	(lower beds/all berths):	.......37.0/29.7
Original Cost:	...........$500 million	Crew/Passenger Ratio	
Entered Service:	...........July 2008	(lower beds/all berths):	.........2.5/3.1
Registry:	....................Panama	Navigation Officers:	.........European
Length (ft/m):	............951.4/290.0	Cabins (total):	1,487
Beam (ft/m):	.............105.6/32.2	Size Range (sq ft/m):	......179.7–484.2/
Draft (ft/m):	.................27.2/8.3		16.7–44.8
Propulsion/Propellers:	.....diesel-electric	Cabins (outside view):	917
	(63,400kW)/2	Cabins (interior/no view):	570
Passenger Decks:	13	Cabins (for one person):	0

Cabins (with private balcony):	574
Cabins (wheelchair accessible):	25
Cabin Current:	...............110 volts
Elevators:	18
Casino (gaming tables):	...........Yes
Slot Machines:	....................Yes
Swimming Pools (outdoors):	3
	(+1 with magrodome)
Swimming Pools (indoors):	0
Whirlpools:	7
Self-Service Launderette:	...........Yes
Dedicated Cinema/Seats:	..........No
Library:	........................Yes

BERLITZ'S OVERALL SCORE: 1,393 (OUT OF A POSSIBLE 2,000 POINTS)

OVERVIEW. *Carnival Splendor* is the 25th new ship ordered by this "Fun Ship" cruise line. It shares the same generally balanced profile as sisters *Carnival Conquest, Carnival Destiny, Carnival Freedom, Carnival Glory, Carnival Liberty, Carnival Triumph, Carnival Valor,* and *Carnival Victory.* It is unable to transit the Panama Canal, due to its size. Immediately recognizable is the ship's swept-back, red, white and blue wingtip funnel – the trademark of all Carnival's ships.

The ship's interior decor contains a vivid palette of colors that stimulate and excite the senses. The deck and public room layout is logical, and finding your way around is relatively easy. Most of the public rooms are located on one deck off a main interior boulevard, above a deck which contains the two main dining rooms. The public rooms include the large Royal Flush Casino (gaming includes blackjack, craps, roulette, three-card poker, Caribbean Stud poker, Face Up, Let it Ride, Bonus, and Wheel of Madness, and more than 300 slot machines).

If you like movies on big screens in the open air (remember drive-in movie theaters?), Carnival's Seaside Theater for movies on deck should do it for you (seating is in tiered rows and the movie screen faces forward). The ship has bow-to-stern wi-fi internet access (including all passenger cabins).

Youngsters are provided with their own Camp Carnival children's club (with its own small outdoor pool), and are well cared for with the line's extensive children's program. Camp Carnival is located on Sun Deck (out of the way of older passengers).

Minor niggles include the fact that many pillars obstruct passenger flow (particularly in the dining room, where they

BERLITZ'S RATINGS

	Possible	Achieved
Ship	500	414
Accommodation	200	157
Food	400	218
Service	400	260
Entertainment	100	82
Cruise	400	262

make it difficult for the waiters to serve food properly).

ACCOMMODATION. There are 20 cabin price categories, in 7 different suite/cabin types, sizes and grades. These include suites with private balcony; deluxe outside-view cabins with private balcony; outside-view cabins with private balcony; outside-view cabins with window; cabins with a porthole instead of a window; interior (no-view) cabins; and interior (no-view cabins with upper and lower berths. There are five decks of cabins with private balconies.

The standard cabins are of good size and come equipped with all the basics, although the furniture is rather square and angular, with no rounded edges. Three decks of cabins (eight on each deck, each with private balcony) overlook the stern. Most cabins with twin beds can be converted to a queen-size bed format. Book one of the suites (Category 11 or 12 in the Carnival Cruise Lines brochure) and you'll get "Skipper's Club" priority check-in at any US home-land port – useful for getting ahead of the crowd.

There are even "spa" cabins aboard this ship – a grouping of 18 cabins that are located directly around and behind SpaCarnival; so fitness devotees can get out of bed and go straight to the treadmill without having to go through any of the public rooms first.

A gift basket of personal toiletry items is provided in all grades of cabins; it includes aloe soap, shampoo, conditioner, deodorant, breath mints, candy, and pain relief tablets (all in sample sizes – and most in paper packets that are difficult, sometimes frustrating, to open).

CUISINE. There are two principal dining rooms (Black Pearl, seating 744, located midships; and Gold Pearl, located aft, seating 1,122). Both are two decks high and have a balcony level (the balcony level in Gold Pearl is larger than the one in Black Pearl). Dining is in four seatings, for greater flexibility: 6pm, 6.45pm, 8pm and 8.45pm (these times are approximate, and equal two seatings per restaurant). There are few tables for two, but my favourites are the two tables for two right at the very back of the Gold Pearl restaurant, with ocean views astern.

Alternative (Reservations-Only, Extra Cost) Dining: There is one reservations-only, extra-cost dining spot, the Pinnacle. It has fine table settings, china and silverware, as well as leather-bound menus. The featured specialties are USDA dry-aged prime steaks and seafood items. It's worth paying the cover charge to get a taste of what Carnival can really deliver in terms of food that is of better quality than that served in the main dining rooms.

Casual Eateries: The Lido Restaurant is a casual self-serve international food court-style eatery. It has two main serving lines and several stand-alone sections. Included in this eating mall are a New York-style deli, a 24-hour pizzeria, and a grill for fast foods such as hamburgers and hot dogs; one section has a Tandoori oven for Indian-themes items. Each night, the venue morphs into the "Seaview Bistro," and provides a casual (dress down) alternative to eating in the main dining rooms, serving pasta, steaks, salads and desserts (typically between 6pm and 9pm). An upstairs Rotisserie offers chicken.

ENTERTAINMENT. The large, multi-deck Spectacular Showlounge seats up to 1,400, and serves as the principal entertainment venue for the ship's colourful large-scale entertainment including Las-Vegas-style production shows and major cabaret acts. It has a revolving stage, hydraulic orchestra pit, superb sound, and seating on three levels (the upper levels being tiered through two decks).

An alternative entertainment venue is the El Morocco, a 425-seat lounge located aft; this typically features live music and late-night cabaret acts including smutty adult comedy. Adjacent is the Grand Piano Lounge/Bar.

SPA/FITNESS. The Cloud 9 Spa spans two decks (with a total area of approximately 40,000 sq. ft/3,715 sq. meters including the 16 spa suites – or 13,000 sq.ft./1,235 sq. m excluding the spa suites), and is located directly above the navigation bridge in the forward part of the ship (it is accessed from the forward stairway.

Facilities on the lower level include a gymnasium, solarium, a thermal suite (a number of saunas and steam rooms – some infused with herbal aromas), thalassotherapy pool (check out the huge Chinese dogs), and a beauty salon; the upper level houses 17 treatment rooms including two VIP suites (one for couples, one specially configured for wheelchair access), rasul (Mediterranean mud treatment – best for couples) chamber, floatation therapy room, several treatment rooms and outdoor relaxation areas (on both port and starboard sides) with integrated massage cabana.

This is Carnival's most extensive spa, and using it will cost you lots of pennies if you have several treatments – or even if you simply want to use the thermal suite – there's a charge for everything.

● **For more extensive general information on what a Carnival cruise is like, see pages 113–18.**

DID YOU KNOW...

● that when sailing from England to the Caribbean in "the old days" a rule of thumb was to sail south until the butter melts, then proceed west?

● that the word "buccaneer" comes from the French word *boucanier*, which means: "to cure meat on a bucan (barbeque)?" Since pirates often used this method of cooking, they became known as buccaneers. The word buccaneer, strictly speaking, was used to denote pirates in the Caribbean.

● that in 1992 Carnival Cruise Lines used its original ship *Mardi Gras* as an accommodation ship? It was for senior executives and staff who were made homeless when Hurricane Andrew hit Miami in August that year.

Carnival Triumph
★★★ +

Large Resort Ship: ....101,509 tons	Passenger Decks: 13	Cabins (for one person): 0
Lifestyle: ....Standard	Total Crew: 1,100	Cabins (with private balcony): 508
Cruise Line: ......Carnival Cruise Lines	Passengers	Cabins (wheelchair accessible): 25
Former Names: ....none	(lower beds/all berths): 2,758/3,473	Cabin Current: ....110 volts
Builder: ....Fincantieri (Italy)	Passenger Space Ratio	Elevators: 18
Original Cost: ....$420 million	(lower beds/all berths): 36.8/29.2	Casino (gaming tables): ....Yes
Entered Service: ....Oct 1999	Crew/Passenger Ratio	Slot Machines: ....Yes
Registry: ....The Bahamas	(lower beds/all berths): 2.3/3.0	Swimming Pools (outdoors): 3
Length (ft/m): 893.0/272.2	Navigation Officers: ....Italian	(+1 with magrodome)
Beam (ft/m): 116.0/35.3	Cabins (total): 1,379	Swimming Pools (indoors): 0
Draft (ft/m): 27.0/8.2	Size Range (sq ft/m): 179.7–482.2/	Whirlpools: 7
Propulsion/Propellers: .....diesel-electric	16.7–44.8	Self-Service Launderette: ....Yes
(34,000 kW)/2 azimuthing pods	Cabins (outside view): 853	Dedicated Cinema/Seats: ....No
(17.6 MW each)	Cabins (interior/no view): 526	Library: ....Yes

OVERALL SCORE: 1,379 (OUT OF A POSSIBLE 2,000 POINTS)

OVERVIEW. *Carnival Triumph* is the 14th new ship for this very successful cruise line. It is unable to transit the Panama Canal due to its size. The ship, whose bows are extremely short, has the distinctive, large, swept-back wing-tipped funnel that is the trademark of Carnival Cruise Lines, in the company colors of red, white and blue.

This is quite a stunning ship, built to impress at every turn, and has the most balanced profile of all the ships in the Carnival Cruise Lines fleet. Amidships on the open deck is the longest water slide at sea (200ft /60 meters in length, it travels from just aft of the ship's mast), as well as tiered sunbathing decks positioned between two small swimming pools and several hot tubs. The Lido Deck space is more expansive than aboard earlier sister ship *Carnival Destiny* (the swim-up bar has been eliminated), and the pool is larger, as it is aboard close sister *Carnival Victory*.

The ship is a fantasy land for the senses (though nowhere near as glitzy as the "Fantasy"-class ships). The layout is logical, so finding your way around is fairly simple. There are three decks full of lounges, 10 bars and lots of rooms to play in. Like her smaller (though still large) predecessors, this ship has a doublewide indoor promenade, and a deck-high, glass-domed rotunda atrium lobby. For those that like to gamble, the Club Monaco is certainly a large (and noisy) casino. There are more than 320 slot machines.

An additional feature that this ship has which the Fantasy-class ships do not have is the Flagship bar, located in the Rotunda (atrium), which faces forward to the glass-walled lifts. A sports bar (Olympic Bar) has tables that feature sports memorabilia.

Children are provided with good facilities, including

BERLITZ'S RATINGS

	Possible	Achieved
Ship	500	409
Accommodation	200	157
Food	400	218
Service	400	259
Entertainment	100	82
Cruise	400	255

their own two-level Children's Club (including an outdoor pool), and are well cared for with "Camp Carnival", the line's extensive children's program.

From the viewpoint of safety, passengers can embark directly into the lifeboats from their secured position without having to wait for them to be lowered, thus saving time in the event of a real emergency. Well done.

The terraced pool deck is really cluttered, and there are no cushioned pads for the deck chairs. Although the outdoor deck space has been improved, there is still much crowding when the ship is full and at sea. Getting away from people and noise is difficult. The Photo Gallery becomes extremely congested when photos are on display.

ACCOMMODATION. There are 20 categories, the price depending on grade, location and size. Over half of all cabins are of the outside view type (and at 225 sq. ft./21 sq. meters they are among the largest in the mainstream cruise market). They are spread over four decks and have private balconies (with glass rather than steel balustrades, for unobstructed ocean views) extending from the ship's side. The balconies have bright fluorescent lighting.

The standard cabins are of good size and come equipped with all the basics, although the furniture is rather angular, with no rounded edges. Three decks of cabins (eight cabins on each deck, each with private balcony) overlook the stern.

There are eight penthouse suites, and each has a large private balcony. Although they are quite lavish in their appointments, at only 483 sq. ft (44.8 sq. meters), they are really quite small when compared to the best suites even in many smaller ships. There are also 40 other suites, each of which has a decent sized bathroom, and a good amount of lounge space, although they are nothing special.

In the cabins with balconies (more cabins have balconies aboard this ship than those that do not), the partition between each balcony is open at top and bottom, so you may well hear noise from neighbors (or smell their cigarettes. It is disappointing to see three categories of cabins (both outside and interior) with upper and lower bunk beds (lower beds are far more preferable, but this is how the ship accommodates an extra 600 people over and above the lower bed capacity).

The cabins feature soft color schemes and soft furnishings in more attractive fabrics than other ships in the fleet. Interactive "Fun Vision" technology lets you choose movies on demand (and for a fee). The bathrooms, which have good-sized showers, feature good storage space in the toiletries cabinet. A gift basket is provided in all grades; it includes aloe soap, shampoo, conditioner, deodorant, breath mints, candy, and pain relief tablets (albeit all in sample sizes).

If you book one of the suites (Category 11 or 12 in the Carnival Cruise Lines brochure) you automatically qualify for "Skipper's Club" priority check-in at any US homeland port – useful for getting ahead of the crowd.

CUISINE. The ship's two dining rooms (the London, forward, with windows on two sides, has 706 seats; the Paris, aft, with windows on three sides, has 1,090 seats), and both are non-smoking. Each dining room spans two decks, and incorporates a dozen domes and chandeliers. The Paris dining room has a two-deck-high wall of glass overlooking the stern. There are tables for four, six and eight (and even a few tables for two that the line tries to keep for honeymooners).

Dining is in four seatings, for greater flexibility: 6pm, 6.45pm, 8pm and 8.45pm (times are approximate but equal two seatings per restaurant). Although the menu choice looks good, the cuisine delivered is adequate, but quite unmemorable.

The ship also has a serve-yourself casual Lido Buffet – for breakfast and lunch, while for dinner this turns into the Sea View Bistro for use as a casual alternative eatery – for those that do not want to dress to go to the formal dining rooms. The buffet and bistro include speciality stations where you can order omelets, eggs, fajitas, Chicken Caesar salad, and pasta and stir-fry items. And, if you're still hungry, there's a midnight buffet around the corner.

The dining room entrances have comfortable drinking areas for pre-dinner cocktails. There are also many options for casual dining, particularly during the day.

The South Beach Club (a lido cafe) is the ship's informal international self-serve buffet-style eatery, with seating on two levels. Included in this eatery are the New York Deli (typically open 11am–11pm), and the Hong Kong Noodle Company (for Chinese cuisine, with wok preparation), and a 24-hour pizzeria (this ship typically serves an average of more than 800 pizzas every day).

There is a grill for fast foods (such as chicken, hamburgers and hot dogs), and a salad bar – all part of the poolside South Beach Club. In addition, there is a self-serve ice cream and frozen yogurt station (no extra charge).

At night, the South Beach Club is turned into the "Seaview Bistro" (typically in operation between 6pm and 9pm) and provides a casual (dress down) alternative to eating in the main dining rooms, serving pasta, steaks, salads and desserts. The good thing is that, if you want to eat 24 hours a day, you can do it aboard this ship, which has something for (almost) everyone.

ENTERTAINMENT. The three-level (non-smoking) Rome Showlounge is quite a stunning room, and has a revolving stage, hydraulic orchestra pit, superb sound, and seating on three levels (the upper levels being tiered through two decks). There is also a proscenium over the stage that acts as a scenery loft.

SPA/FITNESS. SpaCarnival spans two decks (with a total area of 13,700 sq. ft/1,272 sq. meters), and is located directly above the navigation bridge in the forward part of the ship (it is accessed from the forward stairway). Facilities on the lower level include a solarium, eight treatment rooms, lecture rooms, sauna and steam rooms for men and women, and a beauty parlor; the upper level consists of a large gymnasium with floor-to-ceiling windows on three sides, including forward-facing ocean views, and an aerobics room with instructor-led classes (some at extra cost).

● **For more extensive general information on what a Carnival cruise is like, see pages 113–18.**

Carnival Valor
★★★ +

Large Resort Ship: ....110,239 tons	Total Crew: 1,160	Cabins (with private balcony): 574
Lifestyle: ....Standard	Passengers	Cabins (wheelchair accessible): 25
Cruise Line: ......Carnival Cruise Lines	(lower beds/all berths): 2,974/3,700	Cabin Current: ....110 volts
Former Names: ....none	Passenger Space Ratio	Elevators: 18
Builder: ....Fincantieri (Italy)	(lower beds/all berths): 37.0/29.7	Casino (gaming tables): ....Yes
Original Cost: ....$500 million	Crew/Passenger Ratio	Slot Machines: ....Yes
Entered Service: ....December 2004	(lower beds/all berths): 2.5/3.1	Swimming Pools (outdoors): 3
Registry: ....Panama	Navigation Officers: ....Italian	(+1 with magrodome)
Length (ft/m): 951.4/290.0	Cabins (total): 1,487	Swimming Pools (indoors): 0
Beam (ft/m): 116.4/35.5	Size Range (sq ft/m): 179.7–482.2/	Whirlpools: 7
Draft (ft/m): 27.0/8.2	16.7–44.8	Self-Service Launderette: ....Yes
Propulsion/Propellers: .....diesel-electric	Cabins (outside view): 917	Dedicated Cinema/Seats: ....No
(63,400kW)/2	Cabins (interior/no view): 570	Library: ....Yes
Passenger Decks: 13	Cabins (for one person): 0	

OVERALL SCORE: 1,380 (OUT OF A POSSIBLE 2,000 POINTS)

OVERVIEW. *Carnival Valor* is the 22nd new ship for this very successful cruise line. It shares the same generally well-balanced profile a sisters *Carnival Conquest, Carnival Destiny, Carnival Freedom, Carnival Glory, Carnival Liberty, Carnival Triumph* and *Carnival Victory*. The ship is unable to transit the Panama Canal, due to its size. With extremely short bows, it has the distinctive, large, swept-back wing-tipped funnel that is the trademark of Carnival Cruise Lines, in the company colors of red, white and blue.

The ship's interior decor is truly a fantasyland of colors; just about every hue of the rainbow (and a few more) is represented in the public rooms and hallways throughout this ship. The layout is logical, so finding your way around is easy. Most public rooms are located off a main boulevard, or main interior promenade (good for strolling and people watching, particularly from the Dream Bar or Java café – check out the "cup" lights above the bar). The interior design theme is that of famous names and heroes, with public rooms named and themed after them. Look for some of them. Examples include: the Lindy Hop Piano Bar (Charles Lindbergh); Paris Hot Jazz Club (Josephine Baker); Jeanne's Wine Bar (there's a sculpture of Joan of Arc behind the bar); One Small Step disco (Neil Armstrong). The ship was also the first Carnival ship to have bow-to-stern Wi-Fi internet access (including cabins)

There are three decks full of public rooms, 10 bars and lots of rooms to play in. There are two atriums: the larger (American Atrium), located in the forward third of the ship goes through nine decks (the decor here is stars and stripes), while a small aft atrium spans three decks.

Good hangouts and drinking places include Paris Hot

BERLITZ'S RATINGS		
	Possible	Achieved
Ship	500	410
Accommodation	200	157
Food	400	218
Service	400	260
Entertainment	100	82
Cruise	400	253

(live music/karaoke lounge), the American Bar (main lobby), Bronx Bar (sports Bar), Jeanne's (wine bar), and Hero's Club lounge. There are nightspots for just about every musical taste (except for opera, ballet and classical music lovers). For gamblers, the Shogun Club casino, with its Japanese motif and theme, is certainly large and action-packed; there are also more than 320 slot machines. Gaming includes blackjack, craps, roulette, three-card poker, Caribbean Stud poker, Face Up, Let it Ride, Bonus, and Wheel of Madness.

Youngsters are provided with good facilities, including their own two-level Children's Club (with its own small outdoor pool), and are well cared for with "Camp Carnival", the line's extensive children's program. Note that soft-drinks packages can be purchased for children (and adults).

Many pillars obstruct passengers flow. Those in the dining room, for example, make it difficult for the waiters to serve food properly. The public toilets are spartan and could do with some cheering up.

ACCOMMODATION. There are 20 cabin price categories, in 7 different grades: suites with private balcony; deluxe outside-view cabins with private balcony; outside-view cabins with private balcony; outside-view cabins with window; cabins with a porthole instead of a window; interior (no-view) cabins; and interior (no-view cabins) with upper and lower berths. There are five decks of cabins with private balconies. Standard cabins are of good size and come equipped with all the basics, although the furniture is rather square and angular, with no rounded edges. Three decks of cabins (eight on each deck, each with private balcony) overlook the stern. Most cabins with twin beds can be converted to a queen-size bed format.

Book one of the suites (Category 11 or 12 in the Carnival Cruise Lines brochure) and you'll get "Skipper's Club" priority check-in at any US homeland port – useful for getting ahead of the crowd.

There are even "fitness" cabins aboard this ship – in a block of 18 cabins located directly around and behind SpaCarnival; so fitness devotees can get out of bed and go straight to the treadmill without having to go through any of the public rooms first.

A gift basket is provided in all grades of cabins; it includes aloe soap, shampoo, conditioner, deodorant, breath mints, candy, and pain relief tablets (all in sample sizes).

CUISINE. There are two principal dining rooms (Lincoln Restaurant, forward, seating 744: and Washington Restaurant, aft, seating 1,122). Both are two decks high and have a balcony level for diners (the balcony level in the aft dining room is larger than the other). The decor is interesting and includes wall coverings featuring a pattern of Japanese bonsai trees. Two additional wings (the Betsy Ross Room and the John Paul Jones Room) provide room to accommodate large groups in a private dining arrangement. Dining is in four seatings, for greater flexibility: 6pm, 6.45pm, 8pm and 8.45pm (these times are approximate, but equal two seatings per restaurant). Although the menu choice looks good, the actual cuisine delivered is typically adequate, and quite unmemorable.

There is also a casual self-serve international food court-style lido deck eatery, the two-level Rosie's Restaurant. It has two main serving lines; it is adjacent to the aft pool and can be covered by a magrodome glass cover in inclement weather. Included in this eating mall are a deli, a Chinese eatery, with wok preparation), a 24-hour pizzeria, and a patisserie (there's an extra charge for yummy pastries, however). There's also a grill for fast foods such as hamburgers and hot dogs. Each night, Rosie's Restaurant morphs into the "Seaview Bistro", and provides a casual (dress down) alternative to eating in the main dining rooms, serving pasta, steaks, salads and desserts (typically between 6pm and 9pm).

Alternative (Reservations-Only, Extra Cost) Dining: There is one reservations-only, extra-cost dining spot, Scarlett's. It has fine table settings, china and silverware, as well as leather-bound menus, and a design theme set around Scarlett O'Hara, the heroine of Margaret Mitchell's classic novel *Gone With the Wind*.

ENTERTAINMENT. The Ivanhoe Theater is a multi-deck show-room seating up to 1,400, and serves as the principal entertainment venue for large-scale entertainment, including Las-Vegas-style production shows and major cabaret acts. It has a revolving stage, hydraulic orchestra pit, superb sound, and seating on three levels (the upper levels being tiered through two decks). There is a proscenium over the stage that acts as a scenery loft. The decor is medieval (drinks tables are made to look like shields, for example; and towers with stained-glass windows, shields, and coats of armor flank the stage).

The Eagles Lounge, located aft, seats 425 and typically features live music and late-night cabaret acts including adult comedy.

Body-throbbing loud music sensations can be found in the One Small Step Dance Club is the ship's discotheque; it includes a video wall with projections live from the dance floor. Piano bar lovers should enjoy the 100-seat Lindy Hop piano bar.

SPA/FITNESS. SpaCarnival spans two decks (with a total area of approximately 13,300 sq. ft/1,235 sq. meters), and is located directly above the navigation bridge in the forward part of the ship (it is accessed from the forward stairway). The decor is Polynesian in style, a theme that incorporates lush foliage, teak flooring, and a waterfall. Facilities on the lower level include a solarium, eight treatment rooms, lecture rooms, sauna and steam rooms for men and women, and a beauty parlor; the upper level consists of a large gymnasium with floor-to-ceiling windows on three sides, including forward-facing ocean views, and an aerobics room with instructor-led classes (some at extra cost).

● **For more extensive general information on what a Carnival cruise is like, see pages 113–18.**

Carnival Victory
★★★ +

Large Resort Ship: ....101,509 tons	Passenger Decks: 13	Cabins (for one person): 0
Lifestyle: ....Standard	Total Crew: 1,100	Cabins (with private balcony): 508
Cruise Line: ......Carnival Cruise Lines	Passengers	Cabins (wheelchair accessible): 25
Former Names: ....none	(lower beds/all berths): 2,758/3,473	Cabin Current: ....110 volts
Builder: ....Fincantieri (Italy)	Passenger Space Ratio	Elevators: 18
Original Cost: ....$410 million	(lower beds/all berths): 36.8/29.2	Casino (gaming tables): ....Yes
Entered Service: ....Aug 2000	Crew/Passenger Ratio	Slot Machines: ....Yes
Registry: ....Panama	(lower beds/all berths): 2.3/3.0	Swimming Pools (outdoors): 3
Length (ft/m): 893.0/272.2	Navigation Officers: ....Italian	(+1 with magrodome)
Beam (ft/m): 116.0/35.3	Cabins (total): 1,379	Swimming Pools (indoors): 0
Draft (ft/m): 27.0/8.2	Size Range (sq ft/m): 179.7–482.2/	Whirlpools: 7
Propulsion/Propellers: .....diesel-electric	16.7–44.8	Self-Service Launderette: ....Yes
(34,000 kW)/2 azimuthing pods	Cabins (outside view): 853	Dedicated Cinema/Seats: ....No
(17.6 MW each)	Cabins (interior/no view): 526	Library: ....Yes

OVERALL SCORE: 1,369 (OUT OF A POSSIBLE 2,000 POINTS)

OVERVIEW. *Carnival Victory* is the 15th new ship for this very successful cruise line. It shares the same generally well-balanced profile as sisters *Carnival Conquest, Carnival Destiny, Carnival Freedom, Carnival Glory, Carnival Liberty, Carnival Triumph* and *Carnival Valor*. It is unable to transit the Panama Canal due to its size. The ship, whose bows are extremely short, has the distinctive, large, swept-back wing-tipped funnel that is the trademark of Carnival Cruise Lines, in the company colors of red, white and blue.

This is quite a stunning ship, built to impress at every turn, has the most balanced profile of all the ships in the Carnival Cruise Lines fleet. Amidships on the open deck is the longest water slide at sea (200 ft /60 meters in length, it travels from just aft of the ship's mast), as well as tiered sunbathing decks positioned between two small swimming pools and several hot tubs. The Lido Deck space is more expansive than aboard the earlier sister ship *Carnival Destiny* (the swim-up bar has been eliminated), and the pool is larger, as aboard sister ship *Carnival Triumph*.

The ship's decor is actually quite tasteful – the theme being a tribute to the oceans of the world (although nowhere near as glitzy as the "Fantasy"-class ships). Seahorses (no, you can't race them), corals and shells are prominent throughout the design. The layout is logical, so finding your way around is a fairly simple matter.

There are three decks full of lounges, 10 bars and lots of rooms to play in (their names all relating to oceans or seas). Like its smaller (though still large) predecessors, this ship has a doublewide indoor promenade, nine-deck-high, with statues of Neptune at both ends, and a glass-domed rotunda

BERLITZ'S RATINGS

	Possible	Achieved
Ship	500	407
Accommodation	200	157
Food	400	218
Service	400	249
Entertainment	100	81
Cruise	400	257

atrium lobby. For those who like to gamble, the South China Sea Club is certainly a large (and noisy) casino, with more than 320 slot machines.

An additional feature that the Fantasy-class ships do not have is the square-shaped Capitol bar, located in the Rotunda (atrium), which faces forward to the glass-walled lifts and sits under the 10-deck-high atrium dome. A sports bar (Aegean Bar) has tables that feature sports memorabilia.

Children are provided with good facilities, including their own two-level Children's Club (including an outdoor pool), and are well cared for with "Camp Carnival," the line's extensive children's program.

From the viewpoint of safety, passengers can embark directly into the lifeboats from their secured position without having to wait for them to be lowered, thus saving time in the event of a real emergency. Well done.

Note that the terraced pool deck is really cluttered, and there are no cushioned pads for the deck chairs. Although the outdoor deck space has been improved, there is still much crowding when the ship is full and at sea. Getting away from people and noise is extremely difficult. The Photo Gallery becomes extremely congested when photos are on display.

ACCOMMODATION. There are 20 price categories (the price you pay will depend on the grade, location and size you choose). Over half of all cabins are outside (and at 225 sq. ft./21 sq. meters they are among the largest in the standard market). They are spread over four decks and have private balconies (with glass rather than steel balustrades, for unobstructed ocean views) extending from the ship's side. The balconies have bright fluorescent lighting.

The standard cabins are of good size and have all the basics, although the furniture is angular, with no rounded edges. Three decks of cabins (eight on each deck, each with private balcony) overlook the stern (with three days at sea on each of two alternating itineraries, vibration is kept to a minimum).

There are eight penthouse suites, and each has a large private balcony. Although they are quite lavish in their appointments, at only 483 sq. ft (44.8 sq. meters), they are really quite small when compared to the best suites even in many smaller ships. There are also 40 other suites, each of which has a decent sized bathroom, and a good amount of lounge space, although they are nothing special.

In cabins with balconies (more cabins have balconies aboard this ship than those that do not), the partition between each balcony is open at top and bottom, so you may well hear noise from neighbors or smell their cigarettes. It is disappointing to see three categories of cabins (both outside and interior) with upper and lower bunk beds (lower beds are far more preferable, but this is how the ship accommodates an extra 600 over and above the lower bed capacity).

The cabins have soft color schemes and more soft furnishings in more attractive fabrics than other ships in the fleet. Interactive "Fun Vision" technology lets you choose movies on demand (and for a fee). The bathrooms, which have good-sized showers, feature good storage space in the toiletries cabinet. A gift basket is provided in all grades; it includes aloe soap, shampoo, conditioner, deodorant, breath mints, candy, and pain relief tablets (albeit all in sample sizes).

If you book one of the suites (Category 11 or 12 in the Carnival Cruise Lines brochure) you automatically qualify for "Skipper's Club" priority check-in at any US homeland port – useful for getting ahead of the crowd.

CUISINE. The ship's two main dining rooms (the Atlantic, forward, with windows on two sides, has 706 seats; the Pacific, aft, with windows on three sides, has 1,090 seats), and both are non-smoking. Each dining room spans two decks, and incorporate a dozen domes and chandeliers. The Pacific dining room has a two-deck-high wall of glass overlooking the stern. There are tables for four, six and eight (and even a few tables for two that the line tries to keep for honeymooners).

Dining is in four seatings, for greater flexibility: 6pm, 6.45pm, 8pm and 8.45pm (these times are approximate but equal two seatings per restaurant). Note that this gives you very little time to "dine" – although it should give you some idea of what to expect from your dining experience. Although the menu choice looks good, the actual cuisine delivered is adequate, but quite unmemorable.

The dining room entrances have comfortable drinking areas for pre-dinner cocktails. There are also many options for casual dining, particularly during the day.

The Mediterranean Restaurant, the ship's informal international self-serve buffet-style eatery, has seating on two levels. Included in this eatery are the East River Deli (a New York-style deli, open 11am–11pm), the Yangtse Wok (for Chinese cuisine, with wok preparation), and a 24-hour pizzeria (this ship typically serves an average of more than 800 pizzas every day).

At night, the Mediterranean Restaurant is turned into the "Seaview Bistro" and provides a casual (dress down) alternative to eating in the main dining rooms, serving pasta, steaks, salads and desserts. If you want to eat 24 hours a day, you can do it aboard this ship, which has something for (almost) everyone.

There is also the Mississippi Barbecue for fast grilled foods (such as chicken, hamburgers and hot dogs), and a salad bar. In addition, there is a self-serve ice cream and frozen yogurt station (at no extra charge).

ENTERTAINMENT. The three-level (non-smoking) Caribbean Showlounge is stunning, and has a revolving stage, hydraulic orchestra pit, superb sound, and seating on three levels (the upper levels being tiered through two decks). There is a proscenium over the stage that acts as a scenery loft.

SPA/FITNESS. SpaCarnival spans two decks (with a total area of 13,700 sq. ft/1,272 sq. meters), and is located directly above the navigation bridge in the forward part of the ship (it is accessed from the forward stairway). Facilities on the lower level include a solarium, eight treatment rooms, lecture rooms, sauna and steam rooms for men and women, and a beauty parlor; the upper level consists of a large gymnasium with floor-to-ceiling windows on three sides, including forward-facing ocean views, and an aerobics room with instructor-led classes (some at extra cost).

● **For more extensive general information on what a Carnival cruise is like, see pages 113–18.**

Celebrity Century
★★★★ +

Large Resort Ship: . . . . .71,545 tons	Total Crew: 858	Cabins (with private balcony): 386
Lifestyle: . . . . .Premium	Passengers	Cabins (wheelchair accessible): 8
Cruise Line: . . . . .Celebrity Cruises	(lower beds/all berths): 1,750/2,150	Cabin Current: . . . . . . .110 and 220 volts
Former Names: . . . .*Century*	Passenger Space Ratio	Elevators: 9
Builder: . . . . .Meyer Werft (Germany)	(lower beds/all berths): 40.8/33.2	Casino (gaming tables): . . . . .Yes
Original Cost: . . . .$320 million	Crew/Passenger Ratio	Slot Machines: . . . . .Yes
Entered Service: . . . . .Dec 1995	(lower beds/all berths): 2.0/2.5	Swimming Pools (outdoors): 2
Registry: . . . . .Malta	Navigation Officers: . . . . .Greek	Swimming Pools (indoors): . . .1 hydropool
Length (ft/m): 807.1/246.0	Cabins (total): 907	Whirlpools: 4
Beam (ft/m): 105.6/32.2	Size Range (sq ft/m): 168.9–1,514.5/	Self-Service Launderette: . . . . .No
Draft (ft/m): 24.6/7.5	15.7–140.7	Dedicated Cinema/Seats: Yes/190
Propulsion/Propellers: . . . . .diesel	Cabins (outside view): 590	Library: . . . . .Yes
(29,250kW)/2	Cabins (interior/no view): 317	
Passenger Decks: 10	Cabins (for one person): 0	

OVERALL SCORE: 1,615 (OUT OF A POSSIBLE 2,000 POINTS)

OVERVIEW. This ship's exterior profile is quite well balanced despite its squared-off stern, and carries the distinctive Celebrity Cruises' "X" funnel ("X" being the Greek letter "C" – for Chandris, the former owning company, before Royal Caribbean purchased it). With a high passenger space ratio for such a large ship, there is no real sense of crowding, passenger flow is very good, and the high crew/passenger ratio provides a sound basis for good passenger service.

There is a good amount of open deck space, a three-quarter, two-level teak wood promenade deck, and a wrap-around jogging track atop the ship. The interior decor is elegant and understated, and the ship absorbs passengers really well. A small, dedicated cinema also doubles as a conference and meeting center with the latest audio-visual technology. The atrium is calm and refreshing, and not glitzy.

The former cigar club (Michael's Club) has been converted into a piano lounge; this triangular-shaped room, a favorite watering hole, has large comfortable chairs and the feel of a real gentlemen's club. Those who like gambling will find a large casino tightly packed with slot machines and gaming tables.

Children and teens are well catered for, too. X-Treme, within the Kid's Fun Factory area, is a new hangout for teens. Children's counselors are aboard for every cruise.

Outstanding are the 500 pieces of art that adorn the ship – a $3.8 million art collection that includes many Warhol favorites and fascinating contemporary sculptures (look for the colored violins on Deck Seven). The "Century Collection" includes a comprehensive survey of the most important artists and the major developments in art since the 1960s, and embraces Abstract Expressionism, Pop, Conceptualism,

BERLITZ'S RATINGS		
	Possible	Achieved
Ship	500	427
Accommodation	200	177
Food	400	310
Service	400	317
Entertainment	100	72
Cruise	400	312

Minimalism and Neo-Expressionism.

Overall, this is a fine vessel for a big-ship cruise vacation, but some instances of wear and tear and sloppy maintenance show in some areas, although general cleanliness is excellent. Gratifyingly, there are few annoying announcements. Gratuities are charged to your onboard account daily, and a 15% gratuity is added to all bar and wine accounts. The onboard currency is the US dollar.

Embarkation and disembarkation remain weak links in the Celebrity Cruises operation, and the cruise staff is unpolished and has little finesse. Standing in line for embarkation, disembarkation, shore tenders and for self-serve buffet meals is an inevitable aspect of cruising aboard all large ships. The interactive TV system is frustrating to use, and the larger suites have three remotes for TV/audio equipment (one would be better).

In 2006, *Celebrity Century* underwent a $55 million make-over that added 314 balconies, 14 new "Sky Suites" and 10 other cabins. The self-serve buffet area was expanded; an "Acupuncture at Sea" facility has been added, as has Murano – a specialty extra-charge restaurant, more shop space, an art gallery for art auctions, more internet-?connect computers plus ship-wide wi-fi, and a neat ice-walled bar that is part of the Martini Bar. In short, the refit makes the ship more like the larger Millennium-class ships.

ACCOMMODATION. There are 12 different grades. The price depends on the grade, size and location. The wide variety of cabin types includes 18 family cabins, each with two lower beds, two foldaway beds and one upper berth.

All cabins have wood cabinetry and accenting, personal

safe, mini-bar/refrigerator (there is a charge if you use anything, of course), and interactive flat-screen TVs and entertainment systems (you can shop, book shore excursions or play casino games interactively in English, German, French, Italian or Spanish). Bathrooms have hairdryers, 100% cotton towels and large shower enclosures. However, the standard 24-hour cabin menu is disappointing, and very limited. There are no cabins for single occupancy.

The cabins are nicely equipped and decorated, with warm wood-finish furniture, and none of the boxy feel of cabins in many ships, due to the angled placement of vanity and audio-video consoles. In addition, all suites on Deck 10 (and the Sky Deck suites on Deck 12) have butler service and in-cabin dining facilities. Suites that have private balconies also have floor-to-ceiling windows and sliding doors to balconies (a few have outward opening doors).

For the largest living space aboard, choose one of two beautifully decorated Presidential Suites, each 1,173 sq. ft (109 sq. meters). These are located amidships in the most desirable position (each can be combined with the adjacent mini-suite via an inter-connecting door, to provide a living space of 1,515 sq. ft (140.7 sq. meters). Each suite has a marble-floored foyer, a living room with mahogany wood floor and hand-woven rug. Other features include a separate dining area with six-seat dining table; butler's pantry with wet bar; a wine bar with private label stock, refrigerator and microwave. A large private balcony has a dining table for two, chaise lounge chairs with cushioned pads, hot tub and dimmer-controlled lighting; master bedroom with king-sized bed, dressed with fine fabrics and draperies, and walk-in closet with abundant storage space. The all-marble bathroom has a jet-spray shower and whirlpool bath.

All cabins designated as suites have European duvets instead of sheets/blankets, fresh flowers, VCR, and butler service. Electrically operated blinds and other goodies are also standard in some suites.

CUISINE. A grand staircase connects the upper and lower levels of the splendid two-level, no-smoking Grand Dining Room. Huge windows overlook the stern. Each of the two levels has a separate finishing galley. There are two seatings for dinner (open seating for breakfast and lunch), at tables for two, four, six, eight or 10. The design of the two galleys is good, so food that should be hot does arrive hot at the table. The heavy dining room chairs should, but do not, have armrests.

All meals, including full dinners, can be served, course-by-course, in all suites and cabins, no matter what grade you choose. For those who can't live without them, freshly baked pizzas (boxed) can be delivered, in an insulated pouch, to your cabin.

Celebrity Cruises has an enviable reputation for fine dining aboard its ships. All meals are made from scratch, with nothing pre-cooked or pre-packaged ashore. However, the food served as room-service items is decidedly below the standard of food featured in the dining room.

There is also a large indoor/outdoor Lido Café (called "Islands") with four separate self-service buffet lines (included is a 76-seat sushi café), as well as two-grill serving stations located adjacent to the swimming pools outdoors. **Alternative Dining.** Murano, a new reservations-only specialty restaurant off the main lobby, is a fine dining experience that takes about three hours, in a small, intimate setting – ideal for celebrating a birthday or anniversary, with refined service and specializing in à la minute tableside cooking and flambé items. The wine list is extensive.

Cova Café di Milano. This is a signature item aboard all the ships of Celebrity Cruises, and a seagoing version of the original Café di Milano opened in 1817 next to La Scala Opera House in Milan. The café is placed in a prominent position, on the second level of the atrium lobby, and a display case shows off the extensive range of Cova coffee, chocolates and alcoholic digestives. It is a fine meeting place for those who appreciate fine Italian coffees, pastries and superb cakes in an elegant, refined setting.

ENTERTAINMENT. The Celebrity Theater is a two-level, 1,000-seat showlounge/theater with side balconies. It has a large stage, a split orchestra pit (hydraulic), and the latest in high-tech lighting and sound equipment. Unfortunately, the production shows are not nearly as lavish. In fact, compared to some of the other major cruise lines, the shows are a letdown, and not in keeping with the elegant nature of the interior decor. Bar service, supplied continuously during shows, can prove irritating.

While there are some good cabaret acts, they are the same ones seen aboard many ships of the major cruise lines. In other words, it is disappointing to note that there is absolutely nothing to distinguish Celebrity Cruises in the entertainment department. The ship does have a number of bands, although there is very little music for social dancing, other than disco and pop music.

SPA/FITNESS. The AquaSpa has 9,040 sq. ft (840 sq. meters) of space dedicated to well-being and body treatments, all set in a calming environment. It includes a large fitness/exercise area, complete with all the latest high-tech muscle machines, thalassotherapy pool, and 10 treatment rooms. The spa has some of the more unusual wellness treatments, including an Acupuncture at Sea clinic, and a Rasul – a mud and gentle steam bathing room.

The spa is operated by Steiner, a specialist concession, whose young staff will try to sell you their Elemis beauty products. Some fitness classes are free, while some, such as yoga and kick-boxing, cost $10 per class. However, being aboard will allow you to try some of the more exotic treatments (particularly massages). Massage (including Aroma Stone massage, Chakra Balancing massage and other well-being massages), facials, manicures, pedicures, and beauty salon treatments cost extra. Examples of treatment costs: Hot Stone Massage, $175 for 75 minutes; facial, $130 for 50 minutes; plus a 10% gratuity.

● **For more extensive general information on what a Celebrity cruise is like, see pages 118–21.**

Celebrity Constellation
★★★★ +

Large Resort Ship: . . . . .90,228 tons	Total Crew: 999	Cabins (wheelchair accessible): 26
Lifestyle: . . . . .Premium	Passengers	(17 with private balcony)
Cruise Line: . . . . .Celebrity Cruises	(lower beds/all berths): 1,950/2,450	Cabin Current: . . . . .110 and 220 volts
Former Names: . . . . .Constellation	Passenger Space Ratio	Elevators: 10
Builder: . . . . .Chantiers de l'Atlantique	(lower beds/all berths): 46.2/36.8	Casino (gaming tables): . . . . .Yes
(France)	Crew/Passenger Ratio	Slot Machines: . . . . .Yes
Original Cost: . . . .$350 million	(lower beds/all berths): 1.9/2.4	Swimming Pools (outdoors): 2
Entered Service: . . . . .May 2002	Navigation Officers: . . . . .Greek	Swimming Pools (indoors): 1
Registry: . . . . .Malta	Cabins (total): 975	(with magrodome)
Length (ft/m): 964.5/294.0	Size Range (sq ft/m): 165.1–2,530.0/	Whirlpools: 4
Beam (ft/m): 105.6/32.2	15.34–235.0	Self-Service Launderette: . . . . .No
Draft (ft/m): 26.2/8.0	Cabins (outside view): 780	Dedicated Cinema/Seats: Yes/368
Propulsion/Propellers: . . . . .gas turbine/2	Cabins (interior/no view): 195	Library: . . . . .Yes
azimuthing pods (39,000kW)	Cabins (for one person): 0	
Passenger Decks: 11	Cabins (with private balcony): 590	

BERLITZ'S OVERALL SCORE: 1,665 (OUT OF A POSSIBLE 2,000 POINTS)

OVERVIEW. *Celebrity Constellation* is a sister ship to *Celebrity Infinity, Celebrity Millennium,* and *Celebrity Summit* (the *Celebrity Millennium*-class ships). Jon Bannenberg, the famous mega-yacht designer, dreamed up the exterior featuring a royal blue and white hull, and racy lines in red, blue and gold – although it has turned out to look quite ungainly. This is the fourth Celebrity Cruises ship to be fitted with the "pod" propulsion system *(see page 174)* coupled with a quiet, smokeless, energy-efficient gas turbine powerplant (two GE gas turbines provide engine power while a single GE steam turbine drives the electricity generators).

On one side of Sky Deck, there is a huge bronze sculpture of a gorilla holding a fish under its arm; created by Angus Fairhurst, it is titled "A couple of differences between thinking and feeling."

One delightful feature is a large conservatory located in a glasshouse and spreading across a whole foyer. It includes a botanical environment with flowers, plants, tress, mini-gardens and fountains, all designed by the award-winning floral designer Emilio Robba of Paris. It is directly in front of the main funnel and a section of it has glass walls overlooking the ship's side.

Inside, the ship has a similar standard of decor and materials, and public rooms that have made the existing ships in the fleet so user-friendly. The atrium (with separately enclosed room for shore excursions) is three decks high and houses the reception desk, tour operator's desk, and bank. Four dramatic glass-walled elevators travel through the ship's exterior (port) side, connecting the atrium with another seven decks, thus traveling through 10 passenger

BERLITZ'S RATINGS

	Possible	Achieved
Ship	500	443
Accommodation	200	180
Food	400	326
Service	400	322
Entertainment	100	76
Cruise	400	318

decks, including the tender stations – a nice ride.

Facilities include a combination Cinema/Conference Center, an expansive shopping arcade with 14,447 sq. ft (1,300 sq. meters) of retail store space (with trendy brand name labels such as Fendi, Fossil, Hugo Boss, and Versace), a lavish four-decks-high showlounge with the latest in staging and lighting equipment, a two-level library (one level for English-language books; a second for books in other languages and reference material), card room, music listening room, and an observation lounge/ discotheque with outstanding views. Michael's Club (originally a cigar smoker's haven), is now a piano lounge/ bar. An internet cafe has almost 20 computers with custom-made wood-surround flat-screen monitors and internet access.

The artwork throughout the ship (particularly the sculptures) is eclectic, provocative, thoughtful, and intelligent, and at almost every turn another piece appears to break the monotony associated with large spaces.

Gaming sports include the ship's overly large Fortunes Casino, with blackjack, roulette, and slot machines, and lots of bright lights and action. Families with children will appreciate the Fun Factory (for children) and The Tower (for teenagers). Children's counselors and youth activities staff provide a wide range of supervized activities.

After the downturn in business following 2001's terrorist attacks on the US, new management was brought in to restore Celebrity Cruises to the premium product envisioned when the company first started. Improvements introduced in 2003 have restored the art of hospitality and provide a taste of luxury for all. For example, on days at sea (in warm weather areas) if you are sunbathing on deck, someone will bring you a cold towel, and a sorbet, ice water and iced tea. Little touches like this differentiate Celebrity Cruises from other major cruise lines.

A cruise aboard a large ship such as this provides a wide range of choices and possibilities. If you travel in one of the suites, the benefits include the highest level of personal service, while cruising in non-suite accommodation is almost like in any large ship. One thing really is certain: cruising in a hassle-free environment such as this is hard to beat no matter how much or how little you pay. The onboard currency is the US dollar. A 15% gratuity is added to all bar and wine accounts.

Note that there is, sadly, no wrap-around wooden promenade deck outdoors. Standing in line for embarkation, disembarkation, shore tenders and for self-serve buffet meals is an inevitable aspect of cruising aboard all large ships (however, more flexible embarkation hours do help to spread the flow), but the worst time is when large numbers of passengers return from shore excursions and have to wait to go through a security check; the result being long lines outside the ship. The ship's two seating dining and two shows detract from an otherwise excellent product, and this ship (together with sister ships *Celebrity Infinity*, *Celebrity Millennium* and *Celebrity Summit*) can be said to provide the very best of the ships in the Premium segment of the marketplace, providing a taste of luxury for those who book in the largest suites.

ACCOMMODATION. There are 20 different grades from which to choose, depending on your preference for the grade, size and location of your living space. Almost half of the ship's cabins feature a "private" balcony; approximately 80 percent are outside-view suites and cabins, and 20 percent are interior (no view) cabins. The cabins are extremely comfortable throughout this ship, regardless of which cabin grade you choose. Suites, naturally, have more space, butler service (whether you want it or not), more and better amenities and more personal service than if you choose any of the standard cabin grades. There are several categories of suites, but those at the stern of the ship are in a prime location and have huge balconies that are really private and not overlooked from above.

Regardless of the grade you choose, all suites and cabins have wood cabinetry and accenting, interactive television and entertainment systems (you can go shopping, book shore excursions, play casino games interactively, and even watch soft porn movies). The bathrooms have hairdryers and 100 % cotton towels.

Penthouse Suites: Two Penthouse Suites (on Penthouse Deck) are the largest cabins aboard this ship. Each occupies one half of the beam (width) of the ship, overlooking the ship's stern. Each measures a huge 2,530 sq. ft (235 sq. meters), consisting of 1,431.6 sq. ft (133 sq. meters) of living space, plus a huge wrap-around terrace measuring 1,098 sq. ft (102 sq. meters) with 180-degree views. This terrace includes a wet bar, hot tub and whirlpool tub – but much of

it can be overlooked by passengers on other decks above. Features include a marble foyer, a separate living room (complete with ebony baby grand piano – bring your own pianist if you don't play yourself – and a formal dining room. The master bedroom has a large walk-in closet, personal exercise equipment, dressing room with vanity desk, exercise equipment, marble-clad master bathroom with twin washbasins, deep whirlpool bathtub, separate shower, toilet and bidet areas, flat-screen televisions (one in the bedroom and one in the lounge), and electronically controlled drapes. Butler service is standard, and a butler's pantry, with separate entry door, has a full-size refrigerator, temperature-controlled wine cabinet, microwave oven and good-sized food preparation and storage areas. For even more space, an interconnecting door can be opened into the adjacent suite (ideal for multi-generation families).

Royal Suites: Eight Royal Suites, each measuring 733 sq ft (68 sq. meters), are located towards the aft of the ship (four each on the port and starboard sides). Each has a separate living room with dining and lounge areas (with refrigerator, mini-bar and Bang & Olufson CD sound system), and a separate bedroom. There are two entertainment centers with DVD players, and two flat-screen televisions (one in the living area, one in the bedroom), and a large walk-in closet with vanity desk. The marble-clad bathroom has a whirlpool bathtub with integral shower, and there is also a separate shower enclosure, two washbasins and toilet. The teakwood decked balcony is extensive (large enough for on-deck massage) and also has a whirlpool hot tub.

Celebrity Suites: Eight Celebrity Suites, each 467 sq. ft (44 sq. meters), have floor-to-ceiling windows, a separate living room with dining and lounge areas, two entertainment centers with flat-screen televisions (one in the living room, one in the bedroom), and a walk-in closet with vanity desk. The marble-clad bathroom has a whirlpool bathtub with integral shower (a window with movable blind lets you look out of the bathroom through the lounge to the large ocean-view windows). Interconnecting doors allow two suites to be used as a family unit (as there is no balcony, these suites are ideal for families with small children). These suites overhang the starboard side of the ship (they are located opposite a group of glass-walled lifts), and provide stunning ocean views from the glass-walled sitting/dining area, which extends out from the ship's side. A personal computer with wood-surround screen allows direct internet connectivity. Butler service is standard.

Sky Suites: There are 30 Sky Suites, each 308 sq. ft (28.6 sq. meters), including the private balcony (note that some balconies may be larger than others, depending on the location). Although these are designated as suites, they are really just larger cabins that feature a marble-clad bathroom with bathtub/shower combination. The suites also have a VCR player in addition to a TV set, and have a larger lounge area (than standard cabins) and sleeping area. Butler service is standard.

Butler Service: Butler service (in all cabins designated as suites) includes full breakfast, in-suite lunch and dinner service (as required), afternoon tea service, evening hors d'oeuvres, complimentary espresso and cappuccino, daily news delivery, shoeshine service, and other personal touches.

Suite occupants in Penthouse, Royal, Celebrity and Sky suites also get welcome champagne; a full personal computer in each suite, including a printer and internet access (on request in the Sky Suites); choice of films from a video library; personalized stationery; tote bag; priority dining room seating preferences; private portrait sitting, bathrobe; and in-suite massage service.

Standard Outside-View/Interior (No View) Cabins: All other outside-view and interior (no view) cabins have a lounge area with sofa or convertible sofa bed, sleeping area with twin beds that can convert to a double bed, a good amount of closet and drawer space, personal safe, mini-bar/refrigerator (extra cost), interactive television, and private bathroom. The cabins are nicely decorated with warm wood-finish furniture, and there is none of the boxy feel of cabins in so many ships, due to the angled placement of vanity and audio-video consoles. Even the smallest cabin has a good-sized bathroom and shower enclosure.

Wheelchair-Accessible Suites/Cabins: Wheelchair accessibility is provided in six Sky Suites, three premium outside-view, eight deluxe ocean-view, four standard ocean-view and five interior (no view) cabins measuring 347–362 sq. ft (32.2–33.6 sq. meters). They are located in the most practical parts of the ship and close to lifts for good accessibility – all have doorways and bathroom doorways, and showers are wheelchair-accessible. Some cabins have extra berths for third or third and fourth occupants (note, however, that there is only one safe for personal belongings, which must be shared).

CUISINE. The 1,198-seat San Marco Restaurant is the ship's formal dining room. It is two decks high, has a grand staircase connecting the two levels (on the upper level of which is a musicians' gallery), and a huge glass wall overlooking the sea at the stern of the ship (electrically operated blinds provide several different backdrops). There are two seatings for dinner (with open seating for breakfast and lunch), at tables for two, four, six, eight or 10. The dining room, like all large dining halls, can be extremely noisy.

The menu variety is good, the food is tasty, and it is very attractively presented and served in a well orchestrated operation that displays fine European traditions and training. Full service in-cabin dining is also available for all meals (including dinner).

For casual eating, the Seaside Cafe & Grill is a self-serve buffet area, with six principal serving lines, and around 750 seats; there is also a grill and pizza bar. Each evening, casual alternative dining takes place here (reservations are needed, although there's no additional charge), with tablecloths on tables and a modicum of service.

Alternative (Reservations-Only, Extra Cost) Dining: Ocean Liners Restaurant is the ship's alternative dining salon; it is adjacent to the main lobby. The decor includes some lacquered paneling from the famed 1920s French ocean liner *Ile de France*. Fine tableside preparation is the feature of this alternative dining room, whose classic French cuisine and service is very good. This is haute cuisine at the height of professionalism, for this is, indeed, a room for a full savoring, and not merely for dinner, featuring the French culinary arts of découpage and flambé. However, with just 115 seats, not all passengers are able to experience it even once during a one-week cruise (reservations are necessary, and a cover charge of $30 per person applies). There's a dine-in wine cellar (with more than 200 labels from around the world).

Cova Café di Milano: The Cova Café di Milano is a signature item aboard all the ships of Celebrity Cruises, and a seagoing version of the original 1756 Café di Milano, located next to La Scala Opera House in Milan. The café is in a prominent position, on the third level of the atrium lobby. It is a delightful meeting place, and the place to see and be seen, for those who appreciate fine Italian coffees (for espresso, espresso macchiato, cappuccino, latte), pastries and superb cakes in an elegant, refined setting. The breakfast pastries are really superb (the favourite seems to be Pane con Cioccolata – chocolate pastry).

ENTERTAINMENT. The 900-seat Celebrity Theatre is the three-deck-high venue for the ship's production shows and major cabaret acts. It is located in the forward part of the ship, with seating on the main level and two balcony levels. The large stage is equipped with a full fly loft behind its traditional proscenium.

SPA/FITNESS. Wellness facilities include a large AquaSpa measuring 24,219 sq. ft (2,250 sq. meters). It has a large thalassotherapy pool under a huge solarium dome, complete with health bar for light breakfast and lunch items and fresh squeezed fruit and vegetable juices.

There are 16 treatment rooms, plus eight treatment rooms with showers and one treatment room specifically designed for wheelchair passengers, an aerobics room, gymnasium (complete with over 40 exercise machines), large male and female saunas (with a large ocean-view porthole window), a unisex thermal suite (containing several steam and shower mist rooms with different fragrances such as chamomile, eucalyptus and mint, and a glacial ice fountain), and beauty salon.

Sports facilities include a full-size basketball court, compact football, paddle tennis and volleyball, golf simulator, shuffleboard (on two different decks) and a jogging track.

● **For more extensive general information on what a Celebrity cruise is like, see pages 118–21.**

Celebrity Galaxy
★★★★

Large Resort Ship: ....77,713 tons	Total Crew: 909	Cabins (with private balcony): 220
Lifestyle: ....Premium	Passengers	Cabins (wheelchair accessible): 8
Cruise Line: ....Celebrity Cruises	(lower beds/all berths): 1,870/2,681	Cabin Current: ....110 and 220 volts
Former Names: ....Galaxy	Passenger Space Ratio	Elevators: 10
Builder: ....Meyer Werft (Germany)	(lower beds/all berths): 41.5/28.9	Casino (gaming tables): ....Yes
Original Cost: ....$320 million	Crew/Passenger Ratio	Slot Machines: ....Yes
Entered Service: ....Dec 1996	(lower beds/all berths): 2.0/2.9	Swimming Pools (outdoors): 2
Registry: ....Malta	Navigation Officers: ....Greek	Swimming Pools (indoors): 1
Length (ft/m): 865.8/263.9	Cabins (total): 935	indoor/outdoor (magrodome)
Beam (ft/m): 105.6/32.20	Size Range (sq ft/m): 1,219.0/	Whirlpools: 4
Draft (ft/m): 25.2/7.70	15.7–113.2	Self-Service Launderette: ....No
Propulsion/Propellers: ....diesel	Cabins (outside view): 639	Dedicated Cinema/Seats: Yes/200
(31,500kW)/2	Cabins (interior/no view): 296	Library: ....Yes
Passenger Decks: 10	Cabins (for one person): 0	

OVERALL SCORE: 1,542 (OUT OF A POSSIBLE 2,000 POINTS)

OVERVIEW. *Celebrity Galaxy* will be withdrawn in March 2009 and transferred to TUI Cruises, a joint-venture company between RCI and Germany's TUI Cruises, for whom the ship will enter service two months later for the German-speaking family market.

Slightly longer than sister ship *Celebrity Century* (by 45.9 ft/14 meters), *Celebrity Galaxy*'s extra length provides room for a third swimming pool, which is covered by a retractable glass magrodome. Although there are more than 4.5 acres (1.8 hectares) of space on the open decks, it does seem a little small and crowded when the ship is full. This ship also has excellent tender loading platforms.

Inside, the decor takes a clean, minimalist approach. There are two atriums; one is a four-deck-high main foyer, and the second is a three-deck-high atrium. There is a small, dedicated cinema, which doubles as a conference and meeting center with all the latest audio-visual technology, including simultaneous translation in three languages and headsets for the hearing-impaired.

The ship has a superb, somewhat whimsical collection of artwork, which casts an eclectic look at life in some of its many forms. The collection is the result of the personal work of Christina Chandris. The company's "zero announcement" policy is appreciated by its passengers.

Apart from the "front of house" aspects of this ship, it is the "back of house" facilities, the design and flow of the main galley (23,700 sq. ft/2,200 sq. meters), where the ship really shines.

"Stratosphere," the large combination observation lounge (with forward-facing as well as wrap-around views) and discotheque, provides what is probably the best viewing room when the ship operates Alaska cruises.

BERLITZ'S RATINGS

	Possible	Achieved
Ship	500	410
Accommodation	200	165
Food	400	282
Service	400	308
Entertainment	100	71
Cruise	400	306

For a big-ship cruise experience, this one has just about all you need to have an enjoyable and rewarding cruise experience. *Celebrity Galaxy* delivers a fine product that is worth much more than the cruise fare charged when compared to several other large-ship cruise lines. A 15% gratuity is added to bar and wine accounts. The onboard currency is the US dollar.

Although this is a fine ship, the shore excursion operation, embarkation and disembarkation remain weak links in the Celebrity Cruises operation, and the cruise staff has little finesse. Standing in line for embarkation, disembarkation, shore tenders and for self-serve buffet meals is an inevitable aspect of cruising aboard all large ships.

The interactive TV system is frustrating to use, and the largest suites have several remotes for television/audio equipment (one would be better). The one area of congestion is the Photo Gallery, when passenger flow at peak evening times is impeded.

SUITABLE FOR: This ship is best suited to well traveled couples and singles of 40 and above (not particularly recommended for children and teenagers). They will be seeking a large ship with a sophisticated environment, good itineraries, fine food and good European-style service from a reliable crew that delivers a well-above-average product.

ACCOMMODATION. There are 15 category/price grades, depending on your preference for the size and location of your living space, but the accommodation is extremely comfortable throughout. Occupants of all accommodation designated as suites get gold cards to open their doors (and priority service throughout the ship, free cappuccino/espresso coffees when served by a butler, welcome champagne, flowers, and video recorder. Occupants of standard (interior no view and outside-view) cabins have white cards. Suites with private balconies have floor-to-ceiling windows and sliding doors to balconies (a few suites have outward opening doors).

All suites and cabins have interactive television for booking shore excursions, ordering room service, playing electronic casino games and buying goods from the ship's boutiques (available in English, French, German, Italian and Spanish). So you don't have to leave your quarters if you don't wish to, especially if you dislike the ports of call.

Most of the suites with private balconies have floor-to-ceiling windows and sliding doors to balconies (a few have outward opening doors). All accommodation designated as suites has duvets on the beds instead of sheets/blankets. In-suite massage service is available (with the right balcony, such as those in the Sky Suites, this is an excellent service). **Penthouse Suites:** These two suites, located amidships, are the largest. Each is 1,173 sq. ft (108.9 sq. meters), and comes with its own butler's pantry. There is an inter-connecting door so that it can link to the suite next door to become an impressive 1,515-sq. ft (141-sq. meter) apartment.

Most of the Deck 10 suites and cabins are of generous proportions, are beautifully equipped, and have balconies with full floor-to-ceiling partitions, as well as VCRs. The Sky Deck suites are also excellent, and have huge balconies (sadly, the partitions are not quite of the floor-to-ceiling type, so you can hear your neighbors). Also included are wall clock, large floor-to-ceiling mirrors, marble-topped vanity/writing desk, excellent closet and drawer space, and even dimmer-controlled ceiling lights.

Standard Outside-view/Interior (No View) Cabins: All of the standard interior and outside cabins are of a good size and come nicely furnished with twin beds that convert to a queen-sized unit. The bathrooms are spacious and well equipped (with generous-size showers, hairdryers, and space for personal toiletry items). Baby-monitoring telephones are in all cabins. There are no cabins for singles.

The room service menu is poor, and room service items are below the standard of food served in the dining room.

CUISINE. The no-smoking Orion Restaurant is a large two-level dining hall. It is reminiscent of the dining halls aboard the ocean liners of the 1930s, with a grand staircase that flows between both levels and perimeter alcoves that provide more intimate dining spaces. Each level of the dining room has its own separate galley, and the noise level in the two sections is quite acceptable (more noise is noticeable on the larger, lower level, however). There are two seatings for dinner (open seating for breakfast and lunch), at tables for two, four, six, eight or 10. The cuisine is based on menus created originally by top chef Michel Roux. The food has lots of taste (in particular, the sauces accompanying many of the main dishes); it also has fine color balance, and is nicely presented.

Just outside the lower-level entrance to the dining room, a champagne and caviar bar has ossetra and sevruga caviar – well presented with all the trimmings, and, of course, champagne and vodka to go with it.

For informal breakfasts and lunches, there is a two-level Oasis (lido) Cafe with several serving lines (it has a warm wood-accented decor), and eight bay windows provide some really prime seating spots. There are also two poolside grills – one located adjacent to the midships pools, the other wedged into the aft pool.

Tastings is a coffee lounge and bar for specialty coffees and pastries. For passengers in the two Presidential and 48 other suites, in-cabin dining is an option. However, the food served as room-service items is decidedly below the standard of food featured in the dining room.

ENTERTAINMENT. The 927-seat Celebrity Theater is the ship's principal showlounge. It spans two decks, with seating on both main and cantilevered balcony levels (with excellent sight lines from all seats). There is a revolving stage, "hard" curtain and large fly tower.

The production shows are just so-so – not at all in keeping with the elegant nature of the interior decor. Most consist mainly of running, jumping, smoke, colored laser lighting, very loud music and click tracks, and little story line intelligence. Bar service, supplied continuously during shows, can prove irritating.

While there are some good cabaret acts, they are the same ones seen aboard many ships of the major cruise lines. The ship has a number of bands, although there is little music for social dancing, other than disco and pop music.

SPA/FITNESS. The AquaSpa, containing 9,040 sq. ft (840 sq. meters) of space, includes a large fitness/exercise area, complete with all the latest high-tech muscle machines and video cycles, thalassotherapy pool, and seven treatment rooms. The spa has some of the more unusual wellness treatments (including a steamy Rasul room – for Mediterranean mud and gentle steam bathing).

The spa is operated by Steiner, a specialist concession, whose staff will try to sell you Steiner's own-brand Elemis beauty products. Personal training sessions in the gymnasium cost $83 for one hour. Some fitness classes are free, while some, such as yoga and kick-boxing, cost $10 per class. Massage (including exotic massages such as Aroma Stone massage, Chakra Balancing massage and other well-being massages), facials, pedicures, and beauty salon treatments cost extra. Examples of treatment costs: massage $109 for 50 minutes, facial $109, seaweed wrap $190 for 75 minutes – all plus a "gratuity" of 10 percent. Make appointments early – aboard a ship so large, time slots go quickly.

● **For more extensive general information on what a Celebrity cruise is like, see pages 118–21.**

Celebrity Infinity
★★★★ +

Large Resort Ship:	.90,228 tons	Total Crew:	.999
Lifestyle:	.Premium	Passengers	
Cruise Line:	.Celebrity Cruises	(lower beds/all berths):	.1,950/2,450
Former Names:	.Infinity	Passenger Space Ratio	
Builder:	.Chantiers de l'Atlantique	(lower beds/all berths):	.46.2/36.8
	(France)	Crew/Passenger Ratio	
Original Cost:	.$350 million	(lower beds/all berths):	.1.9/2.4
Entered Service:	.Mar 2001	Navigation Officers:	.Greek
Registry:	.Malta	Cabins (total):	.975
Length (ft/m):	.964.5/294.0	Size Range (sq ft/m):	.165.1–2,530.0/
Beam (ft/m):	.105.6/32.2		15.34–235.0
Draft (ft/m):	.26.2/8.0	Cabins (outside view):	.780
Propulsion/Propellers:	.gas turbine/2	Cabins (interior/no view):	.195
	azimuthing pods (39,000 kW)	Cabins (for one person):	.0
Passenger Decks:	.11	Cabins (with private balcony):	.590

Cabins (wheelchair accessible):	.26
	(17 with private balcony)
Cabin Current:	.110 and 220 volts
Elevators:	.10
Casino (gaming tables):	.Yes
Slot Machines:	.Yes
Swimming Pools (outdoors):	.2
Swimming Pools (indoors):	.1
	(with magrodome)
Whirlpools:	.4
Self-Service Launderette:	.No
Dedicated Cinema/Seats:	.Yes/368
Library:	.Yes

OVERALL SCORE: 1,663 (OUT OF A POSSIBLE 2,000 POINTS)

OVERVIEW. *Celebrity Infinity* is a sister ship to *Celebrity Constellation, Celebrity Millennium* and *Celebrity Summit.* Jon Bannenberg (famous for his mega-yacht designs) designed the exterior that features a royal blue and white hull, and racy lines in red, blue and gold. This is the second Celebrity Cruises ship to be fitted with a "pod" propulsion system *(see page 174)* coupled with a quiet, smokeless, energy-efficient gas turbine powerplant (two GE gas turbines provide engine power while a single GE steam turbine drives the electricity generators).

One neat feature is a conservatory that includes seating, set in a botanical environment of flowers, plants, trees, mini-gardens and fountains, designed by the award-winning floral designer Emilio Robba of Paris. It is located directly in front of the main funnel and has glass walls that overlook the ship's side. It has fresh flowers for any occasion, and a selection of Emilio Robba glass and flower creations, as well as pot pourri and other flora and fauna items.

Inside, the ship features the same high-class decor and materials, and public rooms that have made the existing ships in the fleet so popular and user-friendly. The atrium (with separately enclosed room for shore excursions) is three decks high and houses the reception desk, tour operator's desk, and bank. Four dramatic glass-walled elevators travel through the ship's exterior (port) side, connecting the atrium with another seven decks, thus traveling through 10 passenger decks, including the tender stations – a nice ride.

Facilities include a combination Cinema and Conference Center, an expansive shopping arcade with a 14,447 sq.-ft (1,300 sq.-meter) retail store space (including H. Stern,

BERLITZ'S RATINGS		
	Possible	Achieved
Ship	500	443
Accommodation	200	180
Food	400	326
Service	400	322
Entertainment	100	76
Cruise	400	316

Donna Karan, Fossil), a lavish four-decks-high showlounge with the latest in staging and lighting equipment, two-level library (one level for English-language books; a second level for books in other languages); card room; compact disc listening room; art auction center (with seating that look rather more like a small chapel); Cosmos, a combination observation lounge/discotheque; an Internet Center with 18 computer stations. Michael's Club (originally a cigar smoker's haven), is now a piano lounge/bar.

Gaming sports include the ship's overly large Fortunes Casino, with blackjack, roulette, and slot machines, and lots of bright lights and action. Families with children will like the Fun Factory (for young children) and The Tower (for teenagers). Children's counselors and youth activities staff provide a wide range of supervised activities.

New management was brought in during the past couple of years to restore Celebrity Cruises to the premium product envisioned when the company first started, and the improvements introduced in 2003 have restored the art of hospitality and provide a taste of luxury for all. For example, on days at sea (in warm weather areas) if you are sunbathing on deck, someone will bring you a cold towel, and a sorbet, ice water and iced tea. Little touches like this differentiate Celebrity Cruises from other major cruise lines.

A cruise aboard a large ship such as this provides a wide range of choices and possibilities. If you travel in one of the suites, the benefits provide you with the highest level of personal service, while cruising in non-suite accommodation is almost like in any large ship – you'll be one of a number, with little access to the niceties and benefits of "upper class" cruising. It all depends how much you are willing to pay. The onboard currency is the US dollar. A 15% gratuity is added to bar and wine accounts. The ship's two-seating dining and two shows sadly detract from an otherwise excellent product.

There is, sadly, no walk-around wooden promenade deck outdoors. There are cushioned pads for poolside sun-loungers only, but not for chairs on other outside decks. Trying to reach Cabin Service or the Guest Relations Desk to answer the phone (to order breakfast, for example, if you don't want to do so via the interactive television) is a matter of luck, timing and patience.

ACCOMMODATION. There are 20 different price grades. Almost half of the ship's accommodation features a "private" balcony; approximately 80% are outside-view suites and cabins, and 20 percent are interior (no view) cabins. The accommodation is extremely comfortable throughout this ship. Suites, naturally, have more space, butler service (whether you want it or not), more and better amenities and more personal service than any of the standard cabin grades. There are several categories of suites, but those at the stern of the ship are in a prime location and have huge balconies that are very private and not overlooked from above.

All suites and cabins have wood cabinetry and accenting, interactive television and entertainment systems (you can go shopping, book shore excursions, play casino games, interactively, and even watch soft porn movies). Bathrooms have hairdryers, and 100% cotton towels.

Penthouse Suites: Two Penthouse Suites (on Penthouse Deck) are the largest accommodation aboard. Each occupies one half of the beam (width) of the ship, overlooking the ship's stern. Each measures a huge 2,530 sq. ft (235 sq. meters): 1,431.6 sq. ft (133 sq. meters) of living space, plus a huge wrap-around balcony measuring 1,098 sq. ft (102 sq, meters) with 180° views, which occupies one half of the beam (width) of the ship, overlooking the stern (it includes a wet bar, hot tub and whirlpool tub); however, much of this terrace can be overlooked from other decks above.

Features include a marble foyer, a separate living room (complete with ebony baby grand piano – bring your own pianist if you don't play yourself) and a formal dining room. The master bedroom has a large walk-in closet; personal exercise equipment; dressing room with vanity desk; exercise equipment; marble-clad master bathroom with twin washbasins; deep whirlpool bathtub; separate shower; toilet and bidet areas; flat-screen televisions (one in the bedroom and one in the lounge); and electronically controlled drapes. Butler service is standard, and a butler's pantry, with separate entry door, features a full-size refrigerator, temperature-controlled wine cabinet, microwave oven and good-sized food preparation and storage areas. For even more space, an interconnecting door can be opened into the adjacent suite.

Royal Suites: Eight Royal Suites, each measuring 733 sq. ft (68 sq. meters), are located towards the aft of the ship (four each on the port and starboard sides). Each features a separate living room with dining and lounge areas (with refrigerator, mini-bar and a Bang & Olufsen CD sound system), and a separate bedroom. There are two entertainment centers

with DVD players, and two flat-screen televisions (one in the living area, one in the bedroom), and a large walk-in closet with vanity desk. The marble-clad bathroom has a whirlpool bathtub with integral shower, and there is also a separate shower enclosure, two washbasins and toilet. The teakwood decked balcony is extensive (large enough for on-deck massage) and also features a whirlpool hot tub.

Celebrity Suites: Eight Celebrity Suites, each measuring 467 sq. ft (44 sq. meters), have floor-to-ceiling windows, a separate living room with dining and lounge areas, two entertainment centers with flat-screen televisions (one in the living room, one in the bedroom), and a walk-in closet with vanity desk. The marble-clad bathroom has a whirlpool bathtub with integral shower (a window with movable shade lets you look out of the bathroom through the lounge to the large ocean-view windows). Interconnecting doors allow two suites to be used as a family unit (as there is no balcony, these suites are ideal for families with small children). These suites overhang the starboard side of the ship (they are located opposite a group of glass-walled elevators), and provide stunning ocean views from the glass-walled sitting/dining area, which extends out from the ship's side. A personal computer with wood-surround screen allows direct internet connectivity. Butler service is standard.

Sky Suites: There are 30 Sky Suites, each measuring 308 sq. ft (28.6 sq. meters), including the private balcony (some balconies may be larger than others, depending on the location). Although these are designated as suites, they are really just larger cabins that feature a marble-clad bathroom with bathtub/shower combination. The suites also have a VCR player in addition to a television, and have a larger lounge area and sleeping area than standard cabins. Butler service is standard.

Butler Service: Butler service (in all accommodation designated as suites) includes full breakfast, in-suite lunch and dinner service (as required), afternoon tea service, evening hors d'oeuvres, complimentary espresso and cappuccino, daily news delivery, and shoeshine service.

Suite occupants in Penthouse, Royal, Celebrity and Sky suites also get welcome champagne; a full personal computer in each suite, including a printer and internet access (on request in the Sky Suites); choice of films from a video library; personalized stationery; tote bag; priority dining room seating preferences; private portrait sitting; bathrobe; and in-suite massage service.

Concierge Class: In 2003, Celebrity Cruises added a third service "class" to some of the accommodation grades aboard this ship. Positioned between the top grade suite grades and standard cabin grades, Concierge Class adds value to these "middle-class" cabins.

Enhanced facilities include priority embarkation, disembarkation, tender tickets, alternative dining and spa reservations. Here's what you get in the Concierge Class cabins that others don't (except for the suites): European duvet; double bed overlay (no more falling "between the cracks" for couples); choice of four pillows (goose down pillow, isotonic pillow, body pillow, conformance pillow); eight-vial flower vase on vanity desk; throw pillows on sofa; fruit basket; binoculars; golf umbrella; leather telephone notepad; larger beach towels; hand-held hairdryer. The balcony gets better furniture. In the bathrooms: plusher Frette bathrobes; larger towels in sea green and pink (alternating days); flower in silver vase. It all adds up to excellent value for money.

Standard Outside-View/Interior (No View) Cabins: All other outside-view and interior (no view) cabins feature a lounge area with sofa or convertible sofa bed, sleeping area with twin beds that can convert to a double bed, a good amount of closet and drawer space, personal safe, minibar/refrigerator (extra cost), interactive television, and private bathroom. The cabins are nicely decorated with warm wood-finish furniture, and there is none of the boxy feel of cabins in so many ships, due to the angled placement of vanity and audio-video consoles. Even the smallest cabin has a good-sized bathroom and shower enclosure.

Wheelchair-Accessible Accommodation: Wheelchair-accessible accommodation is available in six Sky Suites, three premium outside-view, eight deluxe ocean-view, four standard ocean-view and five interior (no view) cabins measure 347 sq. ft to 362 sq. ft (32.2–33.6 sq. meters) and are located in the most practical parts of the ship and close to elevators for good accessibility (all doorways and bathroom doorways and showers are wheelchair-accessible). Some cabins have extra berths for third or third and fourth occupants (note, however, that there is only one safe for personal belongings, which must be shared).

CUISINE. The Thellis Restaurant is the ship's 1,170-seat formal dining room. It is two decks high, has a grand staircase connecting the two levels, a huge glass wall overlooking the sea at the stern of the ship (electrically operated shades provide several different backdrops), and a musician's gallery on the upper level (typically for a string quartet/quintet). There are two seatings for dinner (open seating for breakfast and lunch), at tables for two, four, six, eight or 10. The dining room is a totally no-smoking area, and, you should note, that, like all large dining halls, it can prove to be extremely noisy. The menu variety is good, the food has taste, and it is very attractively presented and served in a well orchestrated operation that displays fine European traditions and training. Full service in-cabin dining is also available for all meals (including dinner).

Besides this principal restaurant, there are several other dining options, particularly for those seeking more casual dining, or for an extra-special (extra cost) meal in a more intimate (and quiet) setting. Full service in-cabin dining is also available for all meals (including dinner).

For casual eating, the Las Olas Café and Grill is a self-serve buffet area, with six principal serving lines, and seating for 754; there is also a grill and pizza bar. For champagne and caviar lovers, not to mention martinis, Carlisle's is the place to see and be seen.

Alternative (Reservations-Only, Extra Cost) Dining Option: The United States Restaurant is the ship's alternative dining salon, located adjacent to the main lobby. Actual glass panelling from the former United States Lines liner *United States* is featured (in 1952, the *United States* gained renown for the fastest transatlantic crossing by a passenger ship, and took the famed "Blue Riband" from the Cunard liner *Queen Mary*). The United States Restaurant is not nearly as luxurious as the alternative dining salons aboard sister ships *Celebrity Constellation*, *Celebrity Millennium* or *Celebrity Summit*.

A team of 10 chefs prepares the cuisine exclusively for this restaurant. Fine tableside preparation is the attraction of this alternative dining room, whose classic French cuisine (but including some menu items from the *United States*) and service are very good. This is haute cuisine at the height of professionalism, for this is, indeed, a room for a full degustation, and not merely a dinner. However, with just 134 seats, not all passengers will be able to experience it even once during a one-week cruise (reservations are necessary, and a cover charge of $30 per person applies). A dine-in wine cellar is also a feature, as is a demonstration galley.

Additionally, a Cova Café di Milano (with 92 seats) is a signature item aboard all the ships of Celebrity Cruises, and a seagoing version of the real Café di Milano that was originally located next to La Scala Opera House in Milan. It is located in a prominent position, on the second level of the atrium lobby, and several display cases show off the extensive range of Cova coffee, chocolates and alcoholic digestives; this is the place to see and be seen. The Cova Café is for anyone who appreciates fine Italian coffees (for espresso, espresso macchiato, cappuccino, and latte), pastries and superb cakes in an elegant, refined setting. The breakfast pastries are really superb (the favorite seems to be Italy's pane con cioccolata – chocolate pastry).

ENTERTAINMENT. The 900-seat Celebrity Theater is the three-deck-high venue for production shows and major cabaret acts. It is located in the forward part of the ship, with seating on main, and two balcony levels. The large stage has a full fly loft behind its traditional proscenium.

SPA/FITNESS. There is a large AquaSpa measuring 24,219 sq. ft (2,250 sq. meters). It features a large thalassotherapy pool under a huge solarium dome, complete with health bar for light breakfast and lunch items and fresh squeezed fruit and vegetable juices. Spa facilities include 16 treatment rooms, plus eight treatment rooms with showers and one treatment room specifically designed for wheelchair passengers, aerobics room, gymnasium (complete with over 40 exercise machines), large men's and women's saunas (with large ocean-view porthole window), a unisex thermal suite (containing several steam and shower mist rooms with different fragrances such as chamomile, eucalyptus and mint, and a glacial ice fountain), and beauty salon.

The spa is operated by Steiner, a specialist concession. Sports facilities include a full-size basketball court, compact football, paddle tennis and volleyball, golf simulator, shuffleboard (on two different decks) and a jogging track.

● **For more extensive general information on what a Celebrity cruise is like, see pages 118–21.**

Celebrity Mercury
★★★★

Large Resort Ship: ....77,713 tons	Total Crew: 909	Cabins (with private balcony): 220
Lifestyle: ....Premium	Passengers	Cabins (wheelchair accessible): 8
Cruise Line: ....Celebrity Cruises	(lower beds/all berths): 1,870/2,681	Cabin Current: ....110 and 220 volts
Former Names: ....*Mercury*	Passenger Space Ratio	Elevators: 10
Builder: ....Meyer Werft (Germany)	(lower beds/all berths): 41.5/28.9	Casino (gaming tables): ....Yes
Original Cost: ....$320 million	Crew/Passenger Ratio	Slot Machines: ....Yes
Entered Service: ....Nov 1997	(lower beds/all berths): 2.0/2.9	Swimming Pools (outdoors): 2
Registry: ....Malta	Navigation Officers: ....Greek	Swimming Pools (indoors): 1
Length (ft/m): 865.8/263.90	Cabins (total): 935	indoor/outdoor (magrodome)
Beam (ft/m): 105.6/32.20	Size Range (sq ft/m): 171.0–1,219.0/	Whirlpools: 4
Draft (ft/m): 25.2/7.70	15.8–113.2	Self-Service Launderette: ....No
Propulsion/Propellers: ....diesel	Cabins (outside view): 639	Dedicated Cinema/Seats: Yes/183
(31,500 kW)/2	Cabins (interior/no view): 296	Library: ....Yes
Passenger Decks: 10	Cabins (for one person): 0	

OVERALL SCORE: 1,544 (OUT OF A POSSIBLE 2,000 POINTS)

OVERVIEW. *Celebrity Mercury* is a fine ship, inside and outside. The profile is quite well-balanced despite its squared-off stern. It has the distinctive Celebrity Cruises' "X" funnel ("X" being the Greek letter "C" which stands for Chandris, the former owning company, before Royal Caribbean bought it). With a high passenger space ratio for such a large ship, there is no real sense of crowding, and the passenger flow is very good.

Facilities include a three-deck-high main foyer with marble floored lobby and waterfall; more than 190,000 sq. ft (18,000 sq. meters) of open deck space (poolside lounge chairs have cushioned pads, those on other decks do not); a magrodome-covered indoor-outdoor pool; AquaSpa thalassotherapy pool (with several "active" water jet stations), and assorted treatment rooms including a "rasul" mud treatment room.

Other facilities include "Michael's Club", a cigar/cognac room on Promenade Deck that overlooks the atrium, a small but luxurious cinema, a large casino (this is extremely glitzy, with confusing and congested layout). The children's facilities are good. As well as the "Fun Factory," there's an outdoor play area and a paddling pool.

The interior decor is elegant and understated. It includes plenty of wood (or wood-look) paneling and accenting throughout, and many refinements have been made during the three-ship "Century Series" that Celebrity Cruises has introduced in the past few years.

The ship also houses a $3.5 million living art collection with true, museum-quality pieces. The health and fitness facilities are among the nicest aboard any ship, and have been well thought-out and designed for quiet, effi-

BERLITZ'S RATINGS

	Possible	Achieved
Ship	500	412
Accommodation	200	165
Food	400	282
Service	400	308
Entertainment	100	71
Cruise	400	306

cient operation, with everything in just the right place.

This ship will provide you with a finely packaged cruise holiday in elegant surroundings. It is efficiently run. There are more crew members per passenger than would be found aboard other ships of the same size in the premium category, and hence service in general is very good indeed. Note that a 15% gratuity is added to all bar and wine accounts.

After Celebrity Cruises was purchased by Royal Caribbean International, the standard of product delivery aboard all the ships in the Celebrity Cruises fleet went down as cuts were made by the new owner. However, new management has been brought in to put things right, and I (and many passengers) look forward to experiencing the improvements. The onboard currency is the US dollar.

Trying to reach Cabin Service or the Guest Relations Desk to answer the phone (to order breakfast, for example, if you don't want to do so via the interactive television) is a matter of luck, timing and patience (a sad reminder of the automated age, and lack of personal contact). The library is disappointingly small, and poorly located away from the main flow of passengers. There is a charge for using the Aquaspa/sauna/steam room complex. The room-service menu is poor, and food items are below the standards of food featured in the dining room. Standing in line for embarkation, disembarkation, shore tenders and for self-serve buffet meals is an inevitable aspect of cruising aboard all large ships.

While under the direction of its former owner, John Chandris, Celebrity Cruises managed to create a superb quality cruise holiday product virtually unbeatable at the prices charged in the Alaska and Caribbean markets, representing outstanding value for money. However, given the subtle changes that have occurred since Celebrity Cruises was integrated into the Royal Caribbean Cruises family in 1997, it has become evident that some slippage of product delivery standards and staff have occurred, and the latest score reflects these changes. Passenger participation activities are amateurish and should be upgraded. The officers have become more aloof lately, with far less contact with passengers than when the company first commenced operations.

SUITABLE FOR: *Mercury* is best suited to well-traveled couples and singles of 40 and above (not particularly recommended for children and teenagers) seeking a large ship with a sophisticated environment, good itineraries, fine food and good European-style service from a well-trained crew that cares and delivers an onboard product that is well above average.

ACCOMMODATION. There are 13 different grades. The price you pay will depend on the grade, size and location. The accommodation is extremely comfortable, regardless of which cabin grade you choose. Naturally, if you select a suite, you will find more space, butler service (whether you want it or not), more and better amenities and more personal service than if you choose any of the standard cabin grades.

Occupants of all accommodation designated as suites get gold cards to open their doors (and priority service throughout the ship, free cappuccino/espresso coffees when served by a butler, welcome champagne, flowers, and video recorder. All occupants of standard (interior no view and outside-view) cabins have white cards. Suites that have private balconies also have floor-to-ceiling windows and sliding doors to balconies (a few suites have outward opening doors).

Two Presidential Suites are located amidships. These provide spectacular living spaces, perhaps even better than those in *Celebrity Century* and *Celebrity Galaxy*, depending on your personal taste. There is a separate bedroom (with high-tech Sony multimedia entertainment center), large lounge (complete with dining table), huge walk-in closet with mountains of drawers, and king-sized marble-tiled bathroom with every appointment necessary.

There is in-suite dining for the two Presidential and 12 Century Suites, as well as for the 24 Sky Suites (1202, 1203, 1236 and 1237 have enormous fully private balconies, while the others are only semi-private). All suites feature full butler service, personalized stationery, and business cards. If you choose one of the forward-most Sky Deck suites, however, be warned that you may well be subject to constant music and noise from the pool deck (one deck below) between 8am and 6pm (not good if you want to relax). The closet and drawer space provided in these suites is superb. In the bathrooms of the Sky Suites, the shaving mirror is positioned too high, and in the bedroom, the TV set cannot be viewed from the bed. Push-button bell and privacy curtains should be provided, but are not. In-suite massage is available (this really is pleasant when provided on the balcony of the Sky Suites).

The standard (interior and outside) cabins are quite spacious and nicely decorated with cheerful fabrics, and marble-topped vanity unit. The bathrooms are generous with space, tiled from floor to ceiling, and the power showers are extremely practical units.

All cabins have interactive TV for booking shore excursions, ordering cabin service items and purchasing goods from the ship's boutiques, so you don't have to leave your quarters, especially if you dislike the ports of call. The system works in English, French, German, Italian and Spanish. There are five channels of music – all available from the TV set (therefore you cannot have music without having a picture). All cabins are also equipped with a "baby monitoring telephone system" which allows you to telephone your cabin whilst you are elsewhere, and have a two-way intercom to "listen in". Automatic "wake-up" calls can also be dialed in. All accommodation designated as suites has duvets on the beds instead of sheets and blankets.

CUISINE. The two-level formal Manhattan Restaurant, located at the ship's stern, is quite grand and elegant (each level has its own full galley); a grand staircase connects the two levels. Large picture windows provide sea views on three sides; at night, large shades (with scenes of Manhattan, the name of the dining room) roll down electronically to cover the stern-facing windows. There are two seatings for dinner (open seating for breakfast and lunch), at tables for two, four, six, eight or 10, and the dining room is a totally no-smoking area.

Fine cuisine made Celebrity Cruises the shining star of the contemporary cruise industry. The menus are creative and the food is very attractively presented. There is also an excellent wine list, and real wine waiters (unlike so many other large cruise companies), although prices are high (particularly for good champagne) and the wine vintages are quite young.

There are also several informal dining spots as an alternative to the main dining room: a Lido Cafe, with four main serving lines; a poolside grill, and another indoor/outdoor grill located behind the aft swimming pool. The Lido Cafe has fine wood paneling and is much more elegant than the informal dining areas found aboard most ships, and has some seating in bay window areas with great ocean views.

In the center of the ship is Tastings, a delightful coffee/tea lounge; in one corner is a presentation of goodies made by COVA, the Milanese chocolatier – an exclusive to Celebrity Cruises (the original Cova Cafe di Milano is adjacent to the La Scala Opera House in Milan). This is the place to see and be seen. It is a delightful setting (as well as a good meeting place) for those who appreciate fine Italian coffees (espresso, espresso macchiato, cappuccino, and latte), pastries, and superb cakes.

Finally, for those who cannot live without them, freshly baked pizzas can be ordered and delivered to your cabin inside an insulated pouch.

ENTERTAINMENT. As aboard its identical sister *Galaxy*, there is a 1,000-seat showlounge, with side balconies, and no pillars to obstruct views (there are three high-tech "dazzle and sizzle" production shows per 7-night cruise.

Unfortunately, the production shows are not nearly as lavish as the showlounge they play in. In fact, compared to those mounted by some of the other major cruise lines, the shows are a letdown, and not in keeping with the elegant nature of the interior decor. Most consist mainly of running, jumping, smoke, colored laser lighting, very loud music and click tracks, and very little storyline. Bar service, supplied continuously during shows, can prove irritating.

While there are some good cabaret acts, they are the same ones seen aboard many ships of the major cruise lines. In other words, it is disappointing to note that there is absolutely nothing to distinguish Celebrity Cruises in the entertainment department. The ship does have a number of bands, although there is very little music for social dancing, other than disco and pop music.

SPA/FITNESS. The AquaSpa contains 9,040 sq. ft (840 sq. meters) of space dedicated to well-being and body treatments, and includes a large fitness/exercise area, complete with all the latest high-tech muscle machines and video cycles, thalassotherapy pool, and seven treatment rooms. The spa features some of the more unusual wellness treatments (including a steamy rasul room – for Mediterranean mud and gentle steam bathing).

The spa is operated by Steiner, a specialist concession, whose enthusiastic staff will try to and sell you Steiner's own-brand Elemis beauty products (spa girls have sales targets). Personal training sessions in the gymnasium cost $83 for one hour.

Some fitness classes are free, while some, such as yoga, and kickboxing, cost $10 per class. However, being aboard will give you an opportunity to try some of the more exotic treatments (particularly some of the massages available). Massage (including exotic massages such as Aroma Stone massage, Chakra Balancing massage and other well-being massages), facials, pedicures, and beauty salon treatments are at extra cost.

Examples of treatment costs: massage at $109 (50 minutes), facial at $109, seaweed wrap (75 minutes) $190 – all plus a gratuity of 10 percent. Do make appointments as early as possible – aboard large ships, time slots go quickly, so the day you board is the best time to book treatments.

● **For more extensive general information about the Celebrity Cruises experience, see pages 118–21.**

WHERE NAUTICAL EXPRESSIONS COME FROM

If you've ever wondered where some terms or phrases came from, you have only to look to the sea, ships, and seamen.

In the doldrums

Doldrums is the name of a place in the ocean that is located either side of, and near, the equator. It is characterized by unstable trade winds or even lack of winds for days, if not weeks, at a time. A sailing ship caught in the Doldrums can be stranded due to lack of wind. If the situation was bad enough, or if danger threatened, the boats might be launched in order to tow the ship until the wind picked up. Today, if we are in the doldrums, we feel stagnated or even morose.

Mind your P's and Q's

Sailors would get credit at the waterfront taverns until they were paid. The innkeeper kept a record of their drinks, and he had to mind that no pints or quarts were left off of their accounts. Today, the term usually refers to manners.

Passed with flying colors

This comes from sailing ships that, when passing other ships at sea, would fly their colors (pennants, flags) if they wanted to be identified. Today we tend to mean by this phrase that a person has passed an exam or test or trial with great marks.

Pipe down

A boatswain's call denoting the completion of an all hands evolution, and that you can go below. This expression is now used to mean "keep quiet" or "quiet down."

Port and Starboard

Originally, the old sailing ships (like the Vikings), didn't have a rudder, and were steered by a board on the right side. This came to be the "steerboard" side or starboard. The other side was called "larboard" at first, but since the side with the board could not be against the dock, the left when facing forward, it became known as the "port" side.

Round robin

The term originated in the British nautical tradition. Sailors wishing to mutiny would sign their names in a circle so the leader could not be identified. Today the term is often used in sports and competitions to denote a series of games in which all members of a league play each other one time.

Celebrity Millennium
★★★★ +

Large Resort Ship: ....90,228 tons	Total Crew: 999	Cabins (wheelchair accessible): 26
Lifestyle: ....Premium	Passengers	(17 with private balcony)
Cruise Line: ....Celebrity Cruises	(lower beds/all berths): 1,950/2,450	Cabin Current: ....110 and 220 volts
Former Names: ....*Millennium*	Passenger Space Ratio	Elevators: 10
Builder: ....Chantiers de l'Atlantique	(lower beds/all berths): 46.2/36.8	Casino (gaming tables): ....Yes
(France)	Crew/Passenger Ratio	Slot Machines: ....Yes
Original Cost: ....$350 million	(lower beds/all berths): 1.9/2.4	Swimming Pools (outdoors): 2
Entered Service: ....June 2000	Navigation Officers: ....Greek	Swimming Pools (indoors): 1
Registry: ....Malta	Cabins (total): 975	(with magrodome)
Length (ft/m): 964.5/294.0	Size Range (sq ft/m): 170.0–2,350.0/	Whirlpools: 4
Beam (ft/m): 105.6/32.2	15.7–235.0	Self-Service Launderette: ....No
Draft (ft/m): 26.2/8.0	Cabins (outside view): 780	Dedicated Cinema/Seats: Yes/368
Propulsion/Propellers: .....gas turbine/2	Cabins (interior/no view): 195	Library: ....Yes
azimuthing pods (39,000 kW)	Cabins (for one person): 0	
Passenger Decks: 11	Cabins (with private balcony): 590	

OVERALL SCORE: 1,666 (OUT OF A POSSIBLE 2,000 POINTS)

OVERVIEW. This was the first Celebrity Cruises ship to be fitted with a "pod" propulsion system coupled with a gas turbine powerplant. Indeed, this is the first cruise ship in the world to be powered by quiet, smokeless, energy-efficient gas turbines (two GE gas turbines provide engine power while a single GE steam turbine drives the electricity generators). The ship was dogged by technical problems in its early days.

One delightful feature is a large conservatory located in a glasshouse environment and spreading across a whole foyer. It includes a botanical environment with flowers and plants. It is directly in front of the main funnel and a section of it has glass walls overlooking the ship's side. Facilities outdoors include two outdoor pools, one indoor/outdoor pool, and six whirlpools.

Inside, the ship has an understated elegance, with the same high-class decor and materials (including lots of wood, glass and marble) and public rooms that have made other ships in the fleet so popular. The atrium (with separately enclosed room for shore excursions) is four decks high and houses the reception desk, tour operator's desk, and bank. Four glass-walled elevators travel through the ship's exterior (port) side, connecting the atrium with another seven decks, thus traveling through 10 passenger decks, including the tender stations – a nice ride.

Other facilities include a combination cinema/conference center, an expansive shopping arcade, with more than 14,450 sq. ft (1,300 sq. meters) of retail store space (including some trendy brand names, a lavish four-decks-high showlounge with the latest in high-tech staging and lighting equipment, two-level library (one level for English-language

BERLITZ'S RATINGS

	Possible	Achieved
Ship	500	443
Accommodation	200	180
Food	400	326
Service	400	323
Entertainment	100	76
Cruise	400	318

books; a second level for books in other languages); card room; CD listening room; art auction center (with seating that makes it look more like a small chapel); Cosmos, a combination observation lounge/ discotheque; an Internet Center with 19 computer stations (with custom-made wood-surround flat screens).

Gaming sports include the ship's overly large Fortunes Casino, with blackjack, roulette, and slot machines, and lots of bright lights and action. Michael's Club, originally a cigar smoker's haven, is now a piano lounge/bar.

Families cruising with children will appreciate the Fun Factory (for children) and The Tower (for teenagers). Children's counselors and youth activities staff are on hand.

Celebrity Millennium delivers a well-defined North American cruise experience at a very modest price. The "zero announcement policy" means there is little intrusion. My advice is to book a suite-category cabin for all the extra benefits it brings – it really is worth it. The ship's two seating dining and two shows sadly detract from an otherwise excellent product, and this ship (together with sister ships *Celebrity Constellation*, *Celebrity Infinity* and *Celebrity Summit*) can be said to provide the very best of the ships in the Premium segment of the marketplace.

There is, sadly, no wrap-around wooden promenade deck outdoors. There are cushioned pads for poolside deck lounge chairs only, but not for chairs on other outside decks. Passenger participation activities are amateurish and should be upgraded. Although the officers have become more aloof lately, with far less contact with passengers than when the company first started, new management has done much to restore the art of hospitality. One thing is certain: cruising in a hassle-free, crime-free environment such as this is hard to beat, no matter how much or how little you pay.

ACCOMMODATION. There are 20 different grades. Almost half of the ship's accommodation has a "private" balcony. The accommodation is extremely comfortable. Suites, naturally, have more space, butler service (whether you want it or not), more and better amenities and more personal service than if you choose any of the standard cabin grades. There are several categories of suites, but those at the stern of the ship are in a prime location and have huge balconies that really are private and not overlooked from above.

All suites and cabins have wood cabinetry and accenting, interactive television and entertainment systems (you can go shopping, book shore excursions, play casino games, interactively, and even watch soft porn movies). Bathrooms have hairdryers, and 100% cotton towels.

Penthouse Suites: Two Penthouse Suites (on Penthouse Deck) are the largest accommodation aboard. Each occupies one half of the beam (width) of the ship, overlooking the ship's stern. Each measures a huge 2,530 sq. ft. (235 sq. meters): 1,432 sq. ft. (133 sq. meters) of living space, plus a huge wrap-around balcony measuring 1,098 sq. ft. (102 sq. meters) with 180° views, which occupies one half of the beam (width) of the ship, overlooking the ship's stern (it includes a wet bar, hot tub and whirlpool tub); however, note that much of this terrace can be overlooked by passengers on other decks above.

Features include a marble foyer, a separate living room (complete with ebony baby grand piano) and a formal dining room. The master bedroom has a large walk-in closet; personal exercise equipment; dressing room with vanity desk, exercise equipment; marble-clad master bathroom with twin washbasins; deep whirlpool bathtub; separate shower; toilet and bidet areas; flat-screen televisions (one in the bedroom and one in the lounge) and electronically controlled drapes. Butler service is standard, and a butler's pantry, with separate entry door, has a full-size refrigerator, temperature-controlled wine cabinet, microwave oven and good-sized food preparation and storage areas. For even more space, an interconnecting door can be opened into the adjacent suite.

Royal Suites: Eight Royal Suites, each measuring 733 sq. ft (68 sq. meters), are located towards the aft of the ship (four each on the port and starboard sides). The decor in each is different, and is in the style of a country (Africa, China, Mexico, France, India, Italy, Morocco and Portugal). Each features a separate living room with dining and lounge areas (with refrigerator, mini-bar and Bang & Olufsen CD sound system), and a separate bedroom. There are two entertainment centers with DVD players, and two flat-screen televisions (one in the living area, one in the bedroom), and a large walk-in closet with vanity desk. The marble-clad bathroom has a whirlpool bathtub with integral shower, and there is also a separate shower enclosure, two washbasins and toilet. The teakwood decked balcony is extensive (large enough for on-deck massage) and also has a whirlpool hot tub.

Celebrity Suites: Eight Celebrity Suites, each 467 sq ft (44 sq. meters), feature floor-to-ceiling windows, a separate living room with dining and lounge areas, two entertainment centers with flat-screen televisions (one in the living room, one in the bedroom), and a walk-in closet with vanity desk. The marble-clad bathroom features a whirlpool tub with integral shower (a window with movable shade lets you look out of the bathroom through the lounge to the large ocean-view windows). Interconnecting doors allow two suites to be used as a family unit (as there is no balcony, these suites are ideal for families with small children).

These suites overhang the starboard side of the ship (they are located opposite a group of glass-walled lifts), and provide stunning ocean views from the glass-walled sitting/dining area, which extends out from the ship's side. A personal computer with wood-surround screen allows direct internet connectivity. Butler service is standard.

Sky Suites: There are 30 Sky Suites, each 308 sq ft (28.6 sq. meters), including the private balcony (some balconies may be larger than others, depending on location). Although these are designated as suites, they are really just larger cabins with a marble-clad bathroom with bathtub/shower combination. The suites also have a VCR player in addition to a television, and have a larger lounge area (than standard cabins) and sleeping area. Butler service is standard.

Butler Service: Butler service (in all accommodation designated as suites) includes full breakfast, in-suite lunch and dinner service (as required), afternoon tea service, evening hors d'oeuvres, free espresso and cappuccino, daily news delivery, shoeshine service, and other personal touches. Suite occupants in Penthouse, Royal, Celebrity and Sky suites also get welcome champagne; a full personal computer in each suite, including a printer and internet access (on request in the Sky Suites); choice of films from a video library; personalized stationery; tote bag; priority dining room seating preferences; private portrait sitting, and bathrobe; and in-suite massage service.

Concierge Class: In 2003, Celebrity Cruises added a third service "class" to some of the accommodation grades aboard this ship. Positioned between the top grade suite grades and standard cabin grades, Concierge Class offers added value to purchasers of these "middle-class" cabins.

Enhanced facilities include priority embarkation, disembarkation, tender tickets, alternative dining and spa reservations. Here's what you get in the Concierge Class cabins that others don't (except for the suites): European duvet; double bed overlay (no more falling "between the cracks" for couples); choice of four pillows (goose down pillow, isotonic pillow, body pillow, conformance pillow); eight-vial flower vase on vanity desk; throw pillows on sofa; fruit basket; binoculars; golf umbrella; leather telephone notepad; larger beach towels; hand-held hairdryer. The balcony gets better furniture. In the bathrooms: plusher Frette bathrobes; larger towels in sea green and pink (alternating days); flower in silver vase. It all adds up to excellent value for money.

Standard Outside-View/Interior (No View) Cabins: All other outside-view and interior (no view) cabins (those not designated as suites) have a lounge area with sofa or convertible sofa bed, sleeping area with twin beds that can convert to a double bed, a good amount of closet and drawer space, personal safe, mini-bar/refrigerator (all items are at extra cost), interactive television, and private bathroom. The cabins are nicely decorated with warm wood-finish furniture, and there is none of the boxy feel of cabins in so many ships, due to the angled placement of vanity and audio-video consoles. Even the smallest interior (no view) cabin has a good-sized bathroom and shower enclosure.

Wheelchair-Accessible Accommodation: This is available in six Sky Suites, three premium outside-view cabins, eight deluxe ocean-view cabins, four standard ocean-view and five interior (no view) cabins measure 347 sq. ft to 362 sq. ft (32.2 to 33.6 sq. meters) and are located in the most practical parts of the ship and close to lifts for good accessibility (all have doorways and bathroom doorways and showers that are wheelchair-accessible.

CUISINE. The Metropolitan Dining Room, which seats 1,224 passengers, is the principal dining hall. It is two decks high, has a grand staircase connecting the two levels, a huge glass wall overlooking the sea, and a musician's gallery on the upper level (typically for a string quartet or quintet). There are two seatings for dinner (open seating for breakfast and lunch), at tables for two, four, six, eight or 10. The menu variety is good, the food has taste, and it is attractively presented. Full service in-cabin dining is also available for all meals (including dinner).

For casual meals, the self-serve buffet-style Ocean Cafe is an extensive area that features six principal serving lines, and can seat 754. At the after end of the Ocean Buffet, a separate pasta bar, sushi counter, grill/rotisserie and pizza servery provide freshly created items. Note that all pizzas are made aboard from pizza dough and do not come ready made for reheating, as with many cruise lines. On selected evenings, alternative dinners can be taken here (reservations are necessary). There is also an outdoors grill, for fast food items, adjacent to the swimming pool.

For champagne and caviar lovers, the Platinum Club has a platinum and silver *belle-époque* decor reminiscent of a 1930s gentleman's club.

Cova Cafe di Milano: This is in a prominent position, on the second level of the atrium lobby, and display cases show off the extensive range of Cova coffee, chocolates and alcoholic digestives; this is the place to see and be seen. It is a delightful setting (and meeting place) for anyone who appreciates fine Italian coffees, pastries and superb cake.

Alternative (Reservations-Only, Extra Cost) Dining: Celebrity Cruises created its first true alternative restaurant aboard this ship. The Olympic Restaurant is named after White Star Line's transatlantic ocean liner of the same name, *Olympic* (sister ship to the ill-fated *Titanic*). It is adjacent to the atrium lobby, and has a dining lounge that is rather like an ante-room that contains figured French walnut wood paneling from the à la carte dining room of the

1911 ship, which was decorated in Louis XVI splendor. When the panelling, sold by the scrapyard, was found in a house in Southport, northern England, Celebrity Cruises bought the house in order to obtain it.

A team of chefs prepares the cuisine exclusively for this restaurant. Fine tableside preparation is the feature of this alternative dining room, whose classic French cuisine and service are very good; this is, indeed, a room for a full dégustation, and not merely a dinner.

A wine cellar, in which it is possible to dine, is also a feature, as is a demonstration galley. The wine list is extremely extensive (with more than 400 labels represented). But the real treat for rare wine lovers is an additional list of rare vintage wines, including (when I was last aboard) a magnum of 1949 Château Petrus (at $12,400), a 1907 Heidsieck Monopole Champagne (a mere $7,000 and brought to the surface from a sunken German ship), and a Château Lafite-Rothschild Pouillac from 1890 (a snip at $2,160).

To enjoy classic French cuisine and service in this fine setting – it's rather like dining in a living museum – takes a minimum of three hours of culinary excellence and faultless service, and is among the very finest dining experiences at sea today. However, with just 134 seats, not all passengers will be able to experience it even once during a one-week cruise (reservations are needed, and a cover charge of $30 per person applies). A dine-in wine cellar is also provided, as is a demonstration galley, and tableside preparation is a feature of this alternative dining venue.

ENTERTAINMENT. The 900-seat Celebrity Theater is the three-deck-high venue for the ship's production shows and major cabaret acts. It is located in the forward part of the ship, with seating on main, and two balcony levels. The large stage is equipped with a full fly loft behind its traditional proscenium.

SPA/FITNESS. Wellness facilities include a large AquaSpa measuring 24,219 sq. ft (2,250 sq. meters). It has a large thalassotherapy pool under a huge solarium dome, complete with health bar for light breakfast and lunch items and fresh squeezed fruit and vegetable juices. There are 16 treatment rooms, plus eight treatment rooms with showers and one treatment room specifically designed for wheelchair passengers, aerobics room, gymnasium (complete with over 40 exercise machines), large men's and women's saunas, a unisex thermal suite (containing several steam and shower mist rooms with fragrances such as chamomile, eucalyptus and mint, and a glacial ice fountain), and beauty salon.

Sports facilities include a full-size basketball court, compact football, paddle tennis and volleyball, golf simulator, shuffleboard (on two different decks) and a jogging track. A 70-person capacity sports bar called Extreme (a first for a Celebrity Cruises' ship, although it just doesn't, somehow, belong) is located directly in front of the main funnel and has glass walls that overlook the ship's side.

● **For more extensive general information on what a Celebrity cruise is like, see pages 118–21.**

Celebrity Solstice
NOT YET RATED

Large Resort Ship: ....122,000 tons	Total Crew: 1,253	Cabins (with private balcony): 1,216
Lifestyle: ....Premium	Passengers	Cabins (wheelchair accessible): 30
Cruise Line: ....Celebrity Cruises	(lower beds/all berths): 2,852/3,145	Cabin Voltage: ....110/220 volts
Former Names: ....none	Passenger Space Ratio	Lifts: 12
Builder: ....Meyer Werft (Germany)	(lower beds/all berths): 42.7/38.7	Casino (gaming tables): ....Yes
Original Cost: ....$641 million	Crew/Passenger Ratio	Slot Machines: ....Yes
Entered Service: .... Nov 2008	(lower beds/all berths): 2.2/2.5	Swimming Pools (outdoors): 2
Registry: ....Malta	Navigation Officers: ....European	Swimming Pools (indoors): 1
Length (ft/m): 1,033.4/315.0	Cabins (total): 1,426	Whirlpools: 6
Beam (ft/m): 120.7/36.8	Size Range (sq ft/m): 182.9–1,668.4/	Self-Service Launderette: ....Yes
Draft (ft/m): 27.2/8.3	17.0/155.0	Dedicated Cinema/Seats: ....No
Propulsion/Propellers: ....diesel	Cabins (outside view): 1,286	Library: ....Yes
(67,200kW)/2 pods	Cabins (interior/no view): 140	
Passenger Decks: 14	Cabins (for one person): 0	

OVERALL SCORE: NYR (OUT OF A POSSIBLE 2,000 POINTS)

OVERVIEW. Since it was founded in 1989, Celebrity Cruises has favored celestial names for its ships. *Celebrity Solstice,* its first new ship over 100,000 tons, is the first in a quartet of non-Panamax Solstice-class ships; the others are: *Celebrity Equinox* (2010), *Celebrity Eclipse* (2011), and an as-yet-unnamed ship in 2012. The distinctive "X" now shows on both sides of the ship, as part of a design that highlights the cruise line's origins as a Greek family-owned company.

Two funnels, set one behind the other, distinguish the new ship from previous (single-funnel) Celebrity ships. Between the two funnels a real grass outdoor area, the Lawn Club. This is the real stuff – not green Astroturf – so let's hope it likes the salty air. The Lawn Club is open to all, so you can go putting, play croquet or bocce ball (like bowling or French boules), or have a picnic on the grass (picnic baskets not included), or perhaps sleep on it. Several pool and water-play areas are positioned on Resort Deck: one in a solarium (with glass roof), a sports pool, a family pool, and a wet zone.

Inside, the decor is elegant, yet contemporary. Several firmly established Celebrity "signature" rooms are featured. One such is Michaels Club, an intimate, quiet lounge with classic English leather club chairs, a dramatic black glass chandelier, a grand Michelangelo marble fireplace and some contemporary artwork. Rich furnishings help create a warm atmosphere, amidst a backdrop of piano and jazz music, as well as single malt scotch and cognacs for tastings.

Other features include a wine bar with a sommelier, a pre-dinner cocktail lounge that reflects the jazz music period of Duke Ellington and Count Basie (1930s and

BERLITZ'S RATINGS		
	Possible	Achieved
Ship	500	NYR
Accommodation	200	NYR
Food	400	NYR
Service	400	NYR
Entertainment	100	NYR
Cruise	400	NYR

'40s); a bar with the look of an ocean-going yacht; Quasar, a bar with designs from the 1960s and '70s and large screens that create a nightly light show synchronized to music; and an observation lounge with a dance floor.

Celebrity's signature Martini Bar, which has a frosted bar – and more than 100 varieties of vodka as well as martinis – has a new addition, a small alcove called Crush that has an ice-filled table where you can participate in caviar and vodka tasting, or host a private party.

Fortunes Casino has 16 gaming tables and 200 slot machines. The ship also has a delightful two-deck library; a card room (located, unusually, in the center of the ship, with no ocean view windows to distract players).

An innovative Hot Glass Show, created in collaboration with Corning Museum of Glass, includes demonstrations and a narrated performance of glass-blowing, housed in an outdoor studio on the open deck as part of the Lawn Club. Three resident glass-blowing artists will host workshops.

The onboard currency is the US Dollar, and gratuities are charged to your onboard account.

CHILDREN. Play areas include the Fun Factory (for 3–12 year-olds, featuring Leapfrog Schoolhouse's educational programs); and "X Club" – a high-tech teens-only chill-out room with a night-time dance club, and an integral coffee bar.

ACCOMMODATION. About 90% of the accommodation is in outside-view cabins. Of these, 85% have a balcony; indeed, this ship has more balcony cabins than any other cruise ship to date and, due to its slender width, there are very few interior (no-view) cabins. There are four suite-grade categories: Royal Suite, Celebrity Suite, Sky Suite, and Penthouse Suite. If you can afford it, book a suite-category cabin for all the extra benefits it brings – it really is worth it.

Some 130 cabins designated as AquaClass accommodation get unlimited access to the AquaSpa's Thermal Relaxation Room and a Persian Garden (with aromatherapy/steam rooms) on the same deck, as well as complimentary dining in Blu, an intimate 130-seat specialty restaurant.

Features in all grades of accommodation include: twin beds convertible to a queen-sized bed, sitting area, vanity desk with hairdryer, flat-screen TV; bathroom with shower enclosure, toilet, and washbasin. Also standard in all cabins: 32-inch flat-screen TVs (larger screens in suites), wireless internet access (for a fee), premium bedding, shower enclosure with a useful foot-rail for leg-shaving. The suites, of course, have more space, larger balconies, and more personal amenities and goodies.

Like other cruise lines, Celebrity has added "Spa-Class" accommodation. AquaSpa-class cabins share the relaxation room of the AquaSpa itself, incorporate select spa elements into the cabins, and allow for specialized access to spa amenities. Occupants also get assigned seating at the exclusive Restaurant Blu. Features include: a choice of four pillows (conformance, body, goose, Isotonic); express luggage delivery; shoeshine; Frette bathrobes; dining and seating preferences; and early embarkation/disembarkation. Bathrooms include a tub plus a separate shower enclosure.

Other accommodation grades are named Veranda-class; Sunset-Veranda-class; Concierge-class; Family oceanview with veranda; Deluxe Oceanview with veranda; Standard Oceanview; and Standard Interior (no view) cabins.

CUISINE. This ship has a number of restaurants and trendy dining options (reservations are needed for some, and most cost extra).

Grand Epernay, the ship's balconied principal dining room and included in the cruise price, is located towards the aft section of the ship close to the main lobby, and has ocean views on the port and starboard sides. The decor is beige and contemporary. However, the tub-style chairs are not particularly comfortable because they lack a separate armrest. At the forward end, a two-deck high wine tower glistens (one hopes the wine is kept at the right temperature).

The following four dining venues are all located one deck above the main restaurant and galley (on Deck 5), and occupy the aft section of the ship:

● Murano is an extra-cost, reservations required venue offering high-quality traditional dining with a French flair and exquisite table settings, including Reidel wine glasses.

● Blu is a 130-seat specialty restaurant designated just for the occupants of AquaClass cabins. The room has pleas-

ing (but rather cold) blue decor. The beige chairs don't have armrests, but the ambiance is cool. The wine glasses are, however, small.

● The Tuscan Grille, an extra-cost venue, serves Kobe beef and premium quality steaks.

● Silk Harvest is a Southeast Asian dining venue serving pan-Asian fusion cuisine. This venue has wood-topped tables (no tablecloths).

For snacks and less ambitious meals, the options are:

● Bistro on Five (Deck 5, that is) is for coffee, cakes, pastries, and more.

● Café al Bacio & Geleteria is a coffeehouse (not Cova) situated on one side of the main lobby.

● Oceanview Café and Grill is the expansive, casual self-serve buffet venue. There are a number of food "islands" rather than those awful straight buffet counters, but let's hope the signage is good.

● The AquaSpa Café is for light, healthier options (solarium fare), while the Mast Bar Grill and Bar is an outside venue that offers fast-food items

ENTERTAINMENT. The 1,115-seat Solstice Theater, the ship's principal showlounge, has a main level and two balconied sections positioned amphitheatre-style around a stage with music lofts set on either side. There are three circus-themed production shows.

Colorful theme nights are held in the Observation Lounge (whose daytime bland and minimalist decor comes alive at night thanks to mood lighting effects). The 200-seat Celebrity Central hosts stand-up comedy, cooking demonstrations, enrichment lectures and feature films. Quasar is Celebrity's first nightclub, per se.

An Entertainment Court showcases street performers, psychics and caricaturists, and is in the center of the ship, linked to the adjacent Quasar nightclub, with its decor harking back to the 1960s and '70s.

The Ensemble Lounge is a big-band era cocktail lounge with live jazz-styled music, set adjacent to the Murano, the specialty restaurant.

SPA/FITNESS. The AquaSpa is the largest spa aboard a Celebrity Cruises ship, and is operated by Steiner Leisure. The fitness center includes kinesis (pulleys against gravity) workout equipment, plus the familiar favorite muscle-pumping cardio-vascular machinery. There's also a relaxation area, AquaSpa station, and acupuncture center.

Massages include fashionable things such as a Herbal Poultice massage and a Bamboo Massage (using bamboo shoots and essential oils).

● **For more extensive general information on what a Celebrity cruise is like, see pages 118–21.**

Celebrity Summit
★★★★ +

Large Resort Ship:	.91,000 tons	Total Crew:	.999	Cabins (wheelchair accessible):	.26
Lifestyle:	.Premium	Passengers		(17 with private balcony)	
Cruise Line:	.Celebrity Cruises	(lower beds/all berths):	.1,950/2,450	Cabin Current:	.110 and 220 volts
Former Names:	.Summit	Passenger Space Ratio		Elevators:	.10
Builder:	.Chantiers de l'Atlantique	(lower beds/all berths):	.46.6/37.1	Casino (gaming tables):	.Yes
	(France)	Crew/Passenger Ratio		Slot Machines:	.Yes
Original Cost:	.$350 million	(lower beds/all berths):	.1.9/2.4	Swimming Pools (outdoors):	.2
Entered Service:	.Nov 2001	Navigation Officers:	.Greek	Swimming Pools (indoors):	.1
Registry:	.Malta	Cabins (total):	.975		(with magrodome)
Length (ft/m):	.964.5/294.0	Size Range (sq ft/m):	.165.1–2,530.0/	Whirlpools:	.4
Beam (ft/m):	.105.6/32.2		15.34–235.0	Self-Service Launderette:	.No
Draft (ft/m):	.26.2/8.0	Cabins (outside view):	.780	Dedicated Cinema/Seats:	.Yes/368
Propulsion/Propellers:	.gas turbine/2	Cabins (interior/no view):	.195	Library:	.Yes
	azimuthing pods (39,000kW)	Cabins (for one person):	.0		
Passenger Decks:	.11	Cabins (with private balcony):	.590		

OVERALL SCORE: 1,661 (OUT OF A POSSIBLE 2,000 POINTS)

OVERVIEW. *Celebrity Summit* is a sister ship to *Celebrity Constellation, Celebrity Infinity* and *Celebrity Millennium.* Jon Bannenberg (famous as a mega-yacht designer) designed the exterior that has a royal blue and white hull, although it has actually turned out to look extremely ungainly. This is the third Celebrity Cruises ship to be fitted with a "pod" propulsion system (and controllable pitch propellers) coupled with a quiet, smokeless gas turbine power-

BERLITZ'S RATINGS		
	Possible	Achieved
Ship	500	443
Accommodation	200	180
Food	400	326
Service	400	320
Entertainment	100	76
Cruise	400	316

plant; two GE gas turbines provide engine power while a single GE steam turbine drives the electricity generators.

One neat feature is a conservatory which includes many seats set in a botanical environment of flowers, plants, tress, mini-gardens and fountains, designed by the award-winning floral designer Emilio Robba of Paris. It is located directly in front of the main funnel and has glass walls that overlook the ship's side.

Inside, the ship has the high-class decor and materials and public rooms that have made the existing ships in the fleet so popular and user-friendly. The atrium (with separately enclosed room for shore excursions) is three decks high and houses the reception desk, tour operator's desk, and bank. Four dramatic glass-walled elevators travel through the ship's exterior (port) side, connecting the atrium with another seven decks, thus traveling through 10 passenger decks, including the tender stations – a nice ride.

Facilities include a combination Cinema/Conference Center, an expansive shopping arcade, with 14,500 sq. ft (1,300 sq. meters) of retail store space, a lavish four-decks-high showlounge with the latest in staging and lighting equipment, a two-level library (one level for English-language books; a

second level for books in other languages), a card room, a music room, and a combination observation lounge/discotheque. Michael's Club (originally a cigar smoker's haven), is now a piano lounge/bar. Gaming facilities include the ship's overly large Fortunes Casino, with blackjack, roulette, and slot machines, and lots of bright lights and action. Families will appreciate the Fun Factory (for children) and The Tower (for teenagers). Children's counselors and youth activities staff provide a wide range of supervised activities.

The ship's two seating dining and two shows detract from an otherwise excellent product, but this ship provides a taste of luxury to those who book the largest suites.

There is no walk-around wooden promenade deck outdoors. There are cushioned pads for poolside sunloungers only, but not for chairs on other outside decks. Trying to reach Cabin Service or the Guest Relations Desk to answer the phone (to order breakfast, for example, if you don't want to do so via the interactive television) is a matter of luck, timing and patience.

ACCOMMODATION. There are 20 different grades, giving you a wide choice of size and location (the price you pay will depend on the grade, location and size chosen).

Almost half the accommodation has a "private" balcony; approximately 80 percent are outside-view suites and cabins, and 20 percent are interior (no view) cabins. The accommodation is extremely comfortable throughout this ship, regardless of which grade you choose. Suites, naturally, have more space, butler service (whether you want it or not), more and better amenities and more personal service than if you choose any of the standard cabin grades. There are several categories of suites, but those at the stern of the ship are in a prime location and have huge balconies that are really private and not overlooked from above.

All suites and cabins have wood cabinetry and accenting, interactive television and entertainment systems (you can go shopping, book shore excursions, play casino games, interactively, and even watch soft-porn movies). Bathrooms have hairdryers, and 100% cotton towels.

Penthouse Suites: Two Penthouse Suites (on Penthouse Deck) are the largest accommodation aboard. Each occupies one half of the beam (width) of the ship, overlooking the ship's stern. Each measures a huge 2,530 sq. ft (235 sq. meters) – 1,432 sq. ft (133 sq. meters) of living space, plus a huge wrap-around balcony measuring 1,098 sq. ft (102 sq. meters) with 180° views, which occupies one-half of the beam (width) of the ship, overlooking the ship's stern (it includes a wet bar, hot tub and whirlpool tub); however, note that much of this terrace can be overlooked by passengers on other decks above.

Features include a marble foyer, a separate living room (complete with ebony baby grand piano – bring your own pianist if you don't play yourself) and a formal dining room. The master bedroom has a large walk-in closet; personal exercise equipment; dressing room with vanity desk, exercise equipment; marble-clad master bathroom with twin washbasins; deep whirlpool bathtub; separate shower; toilet and bidet areas; flat-screen televisions (one in the bedroom and one in the lounge) and electronically controlled drapes. Butler service is standard, and a butler's pantry, with separate entry door, has a full-sized refrigerator, temperature-controlled wine cabinet, microwave oven and good-sized food preparation and storage areas. For even more space, an interconnecting door can be opened into the adjacent suite (ideal for multi-generation families).

Royal Suites: Eight Royal Suites, each measuring 733 sq. ft (68 sq. meters), are located towards the aft of the ship (four each on the port and starboard sides). Each has a separate living room with dining and lounge areas (with refrigerator, mini-bar and Bang & Olufsen CD sound system), and a separate bedroom. There are two entertainment centers with DVD players, and two flat-screen televisions (one in the living area, one in the bedroom), and a large walk-in closet with vanity desk. The marble-clad bathroom has a whirlpool bathtub with integral shower, and there is also a separate shower enclosure, two washbasins and toilet. The teakwood decked balcony is extensive (large enough for on-deck massage) and also has a whirlpool hot tub.

Celebrity Suites: Eight Celebrity Suites, each measuring 467 sq. ft (44 sq. meters), have floor-to-ceiling windows, a separate living room with dining and lounge areas, two entertainment centers with flat-screen televisions (one in the living room, one in the bedroom), and a walk-in closet with vanity desk. The marble-clad bathroom has a whirlpool bathtub with integral shower (a window with movable shade lets you look out of the bathroom through the lounge to the large ocean-view windows). Interconnecting doors allow two suites to be used as a family unit (as there is no balcony, these suites are ideal for families with small children). These suites overhang the starboard side of the ship (they are located opposite a group of glass-walled elevators), and provide stunning ocean views from the glass-walled sitting/dining area, which extends out from the ship's side. A personal computer with wood-surround screen allows direct internet connectivity. Butler service is standard.

Sky Suites: There are 30 of these, each measuring 308 sq. ft (28.6 sq. meters), including the private balcony (some balconies may be larger than others, depending on the location). Although these are designated as suites, they are really just larger cabins that feature a marble-clad bathroom with bathtub/shower combination. The suites also have a VCR player in addition to a TV set, and have a larger lounge area (than standard cabins) and sleeping area. Butler service is standard.

Butler Service: Butler service (in all accommodation designated as suites) includes full breakfast, in-suite lunch and dinner service (as required), afternoon tea service, evening hors d'oeuvres, free espresso and cappuccino, daily news delivery, shoeshine service, and other personal touches.

Suite occupants in Penthouse, Royal, Celebrity and Sky suites also get welcome champagne; a full personal computer in each suite, including a printer and internet access (on request in Sky Suites); choice of films from a video library; personalized stationery; tote bag; priority dining room seating preferences; private portrait sitting, and bathrobe; and in-suite massage service.

Concierge Class: In 2003, Celebrity Cruises added a third service "class" to some of the accommodation grades aboard this ship. Positioned between the top grade suite grades and standard cabin grades, Concierge Class adds value to purchasers of these "middle-class" cabins.

Enhanced facilities include priority embarkation, disembarkation, tender tickets, alternative dining and spa reservations. Here's what you get in the Concierge Class cabins that others don't (except for the suites): European duvet; double bed overlay (no more falling "between the cracks" for couples); choice of four pillows (goose down pillow, isotonic pillow, body pillow, conformance pillow); eight-vial flower vase on vanity desk; throw pillows on sofa; fruit basket; binoculars; golf umbrella; leather telephone notepad; larger beach towels; hand-held hairdryer. The balcony gets better furniture. In the bathrooms: plusher Frette bathrobe; larger towels in sea green and pink (alternating days); flower in silver vase in bathroom. It all adds up to an excellent value for money, as well as better recognition from staff.

Standard Outside-View/Interior (No View) Cabins: All other outside-view and interior (no view) cabins have a lounge area with sofa or convertible sofa bed, sleeping area with twin beds that can convert to a double bed, a good amount of closet and drawer space, personal safe, mini-bar/refrigerator (extra cost), interactive television, and private bathroom. The cabins are nicely decorated with warm wood-finish furniture, and there is none of the boxy feel of cabins in so many ships, due to the angled placement of vanity and audio-video consoles. Even the smallest cabin has a good-sized bathroom and shower enclosure.

Wheelchair-Accessible Accommodation: This is available in six Sky Suites, three premium outside-view, eight deluxe ocean-view, four standard ocean-view and five interior (no view) cabins measuring from 347 to 362 sq. ft (32.2 to 33.6 sq. meters) and are located in the most practical parts of the ship and close to elevators for good accessibility. All have doorways and bathroom doorways and showers are wheelchair-accessible. Some cabins have extra berths for third or third and fourth occupants (note, however, that there is only one safe for personal belongings, which must be shared).

CUISINE. The 1,170-seat Cosmopolitan Restaurant, the ship's formal dining room. It is two decks high, has a grand staircase connecting the two levels, a huge glass wall overlooking the sea at the stern of the ship; electrically operated shades provide several different backdrops, and a musician's gallery on the upper level, typically for a string quartet/quintet. There are two seatings for dinner (open seating for breakfast and lunch), at tables for two, four, six, eight or 10. The dining room is a no-smoking area, and, you should note that, like all large dining halls, it can prove to be extremely noisy.

The menu variety is good, the food has taste, and it is very attractively presented and served in a well-orchestrated operation that displays fine European traditions and training. Full service in-cabin dining is also available for all meals (including dinner). As a tribute to the French Line ship *Normandie*, a statue created by Leon-Georges Baudry, called "La Normandie", that once overlooked the ship's grand staircase and for the past 47 years graced the Fontainebleu Hotel in Miami, was purchased for $250,000 and can now be seen in this dining room.

For casual eating, the Waterfall Cafe is a self-serve buffet area, with six principal serving lines and 754 seats. There is also a grill and pizza bar.

For champagne and caviar lovers, the Platinum Club has a platinum and silver art-deco decor that is reminiscent of a 1930s gentleman's club. It includes a diamond-pane reflective mirror wall. There's also a Martini Bar.

Alternative (Reservations-Only, Extra Cost) Dining Option: The Normandie Restaurant is an alternative dining room, adjacent to the conference center. It has gold lacquered paneling from the smoking room of the original French Line ship. Fine tableside preparation is the feature of this alternative dining room, whose classic French cuisine and service are very good indeed. This is haute cuisine at the height of professionalism. However, with just 134 seats, not all passengers can experience it even once during a one-week cruise (reservations are necessary, and a cover charge of $30 per person applies). There is a dine-in wine cellar (with more than 200 labels from around the world), and a demonstration galley. A team of 10 chefs prepares the cuisine exclusively for this restaurant. Tableside preparation is a feature of this alternative dining spot.

Cova Cafe di Milano: The Cova Cafe di Milano is a signature item aboard all Celebrity Cruises ships, and a seagoing version of the 200-year-old Cafe di Milano originally located next to La Scala Opera House in Milan. It is in a prominent position, on the second level of the atrium lobby, and several display cases show off the extensive range of Cova coffee, chocolates and alcoholic digestives; this is the place to see and be seen. It is a delightful setting (and meeting place) for those who appreciate fine Italian coffees (for espresso, espresso macchiato, cappuccino, latte), pastries and superb cakes in an elegant, refined setting. The breakfast pastries are really superb (the favorite seems to be the Italian pane con cioccolata – chocolate pastry).

ENTERTAINMENT. The 900-seat Celebrity Theater is the three-deck-high venue for the ship's production shows and major cabaret acts. It is located in the forward part of the ship, with seating on main, and two balcony levels. The large stage is equipped with a full fly loft behind its traditional proscenium.

SPA/FITNESS. Facilities include an AquaSpa (a multi-station thalassotherapy pool), 16 treatment rooms, plus eight treatment rooms with showers and one treatment room specifically designed for wheelchair passengers, aerobics room, gymnasium (complete with over 40 machines), large male and female saunas (with large ocean-view porthole window), a unisex thermal suite (containing several steam and shower mist rooms with different fragrances such as chamomile, eucalyptus and mint, and a glacial ice fountain), and beauty salon.

Sports facilities include a full-size basketball court, compact football, paddle tennis and volleyball, golf simulator, shuffleboard (on two different decks) and a jogging track.

● **For more extensive general information on what a Celebrity cruise is like, see pages 118–21.**

Celebrity Xpedition
★★★★

Boutique Ship: . . . . .2,842 tons	Passengers	Cabins (wheelchair accessible): 0
Lifestyle: . . . . .Premium	(lower beds/all berths): 94/98	Cabin Voltage: 220
Cruise Line: . . . . .Celebrity Cruises	Passenger Space Ratio	Elevators: 0
Former Names: . . . . .Sun Bay	(lower beds/all berths): 30.2/29.0	Casino (gaming tables): . . . . .No
Builder: . . . . . .Cassens-Werft (Germany)	Crew/Passenger Ratio	Slot Machines: .No
Original Cost: . . . . .DM 35 million	(lower beds/all berths): 1.4/1.4	Swimming Pools (outdoors): . . . . .No
Entered Service: . . .June 2001/June 2004	Navigation Officers: . . . . .European	Swimming Pools (indoors): . . . . .No
Registry: . . . . .The Bahamas	Cabins (total): .47	Whirlpools: 1
Length (ft/m): 290.3/88.5	Size Range (sq ft/m): 156.0–460.0/	Fitness Center: . . . . .Yes
Beam (ft/m): 45.9/14.0	14.5–42.7	Sauna/Steam Room: . . . . .Yes/No
Draft (ft/m): 11.4/3.5	Cabins (outside view): 47	Massage:. . . . . .Yes
Propulsion/Propellers: .diesel (3,000kW)/2	Cabins (interior/no view): 0	Self-Service Launderette: . . . . .No
Passenger Decks: 4	Cabins (for one person): 0	Dedicated Cinema/Seats: . . . . .No
Total Crew: 64	Cabins (with private balcony): 9	Library: . . . . .Yes

OVERALL SCORE: 1,404 (OUT OF A POSSIBLE 2,000 POINTS)

OVERVIEW. This is the first specialist boutique ship for Celebrity Cruises and is like a small private club. The brochure rates may or may not include the Galápagos Islands visitor tax (about $100), which must be paid in cash at Guayaquil or Quito airports or in the islands.

There is a surprisingly good amount of open deck space – better, in proportion – than many larger ships, and much of it with teakwood decking, as well as teak sunloungers and patio furniture. Although there is no swimming pool (the ship's too small for one), there is a whirlpool tub on the uppermost open deck. Stabilizers were installed in 2004.

All accommodation is located forward half, with public rooms aft. The ambience is unhurried, yet subtly elegant. Except for the dining room (which can double as a conference room), there is only one public room: the main lounge, complete with bar, dance floor and bandstand.

This is ecotourism of the best kind. Shore excursions (by Zodiac inflatable boats) are in small groups led by Ecuadorian guides. On your return, waiters greet you with refreshing drinks and towels. Included in the fare: excursions, gratuities to shipboard staff, beverages including house wine, champagne, liquor, beer and soda.

SUITABLE FOR: *Celebrity Xpedition* is best suited to mature adults who want an intimate and casual cruise experience without the crowds, and would enjoy learning about the nature and wildlife of the Galápagos Islands.

ACCOMMODATION. There are four price categories in two cabin types: 9 Suites, measuring 247 sq. ft (23 sq. meters);

BERLITZ'S RATINGS

	Possible	Achieved
Ship	500	336
Accommodation	200	139
Food	400	281
Service	400	302
Entertainment	n/a	n/a
Cruise	500	346

34 Comfort Cabins, 172 sq. ft (16 sq. meters); and 3 Comfort cabins, 156 sq. ft (14.5 sq. meters). All suites and cabins have twin beds (four comfort cabins have a double bed), TV, sofa, drinks table, vanity desk with hairdryer, mini-bar/refrigerator, and personal safe. Bathrooms all have a good-sized shower enclosure (there are no tubs) with soap/shampoo dispenser, black granite washbasin, and white marble-clad walls.

The largest accommodation is in nine suites, each with a private balcony. One suite is located forward, with forward-facing views, and has a sloping ceiling with character. Balcony partitions are almost private; the balcony deck is teak covered. Two of the suites can be joined together. One bedroom has two pull-down Murphy beds.

CUISINE. The Darwin Dining Room is an intimate room that operates on an open-seating basis. Nicely decorated, it has ocean-view windows along one side. A self-serve buffet offers salads, cold cuts and cheeses. House wines and beer are included in the fare; a few better wines can be bought. The cuisine depends on local suppliers; meat quality is poor, fish seafood and fruit good, vegetables inconsistent.

The casual, self-serve Seagull Buffet is just behind the main lounge on the open deck, with teak tables and chairs.

ENTERTAINMENT. Dinner and after-dinner conversation with fellow passengers is the main entertainment each evening.

SPA/FITNESS. There is a small fitness room, and adjacent unisex sauna located inside on the uppermost deck, while a small beauty salon is located on the lowest deck.

Clelia II
★★★★

Boutique Ship: ....4,077 tonnes	Passenger Decks: 5	Cabins (with private balcony): 16
Lifestyle: ....Premium	Total Crew: 60	Cabins (wheelchair accessible): 0
Cruise Line: Travel Dynamics International	Passengers	Cabin Current: ....110 volts
Former Names: ......*Renaissance Four*	(lower beds/all berths): 100/100	Elevators: 1
Builder: ....Cantieri Navale Ferrari (Italy)	Passenger Space Ratio	Casino (gaming tables): ....No
Original Cost: ....$20 million	(lower beds/all berths): 40.7/40.7	Slot Machines: ....No
Entered Service: ....Jan 1991/Mar 2009	Navigation Officers: ....European	Swimming Pools (outdoors): 0
Registry: ....Bahamas	Cabins: 50	Swimming Pools (indoors): 0
Length (ft/m): 289.0/88.1	Size Range (sq ft/m): 215.0–258.3/	Whirlpools: 1
Beam (ft/m): 50.1/15.3	20.0–24.0	Self-Service Launderette: ....No
Draft (ft/m): 13.4/4.1	Cabins (outside view): 50	Dedicated Cinema/Seats: ....No
Propulsion/Propellers: ....diesel	Cabins (interior/no view): 0	Library: ....Yes
(3,514kW)/2 (CP)	Cabins (for one person): 0	

BERLITZ'S OVERALL SCORE: 1,404 (OUT OF A POSSIBLE 2,000 POINTS)

OVERVIEW. Nicely refurbished in early 2009 and renamed after its owner, this charming and comfortable little ship provides a destination-intensive, refined, and relaxed cruise for those who don't like crowds or organized entertainment.

It has the contemporary look and feel of a private yacht, with handsome interior styling, although the exterior profile isn't overly attractive. There are two teakwood walk-around promenade decks outdoors. A "Baby Clelia" water jet-propelled shore tender hangs over the stern. A fleet of Zodiac inflatable craft for shore landings is carried. The open deck and sunbathing space is quite limited, however.

The accommodation is located forward, with public rooms aft. The pleasing colors and a refined and attractive interior decor reflect Greek design elements, and Greek artists are responsible for many pieces of art around the ship.

Public rooms include a small library, a lounge that can accommodate all passengers (good for lectures), and a piano bar/lounge. Smoking is allowed only on open decks.

The onboard currency is the US dollar, and all gratuities are included.

SUITABLE FOR: *Clelia II* is all about themes, and onboard lecturers who are academic and experts in their field. It is best suited to mature adults who want a small ship environment that offers a high degree of comfort, but with excellent lecturers, decent cuisine, and no entertainment.

ACCOMMODATION. The all-outside cabins, called "suites" in the brochure, combine highly polished (imitation) rosewood paneling with lots of mirrors, and fine, hand crafted Italian furniture. All suites have twin beds that can convert to a queen-sized bed, a sitting area with three-person sofa,

BERLITZ'S RATINGS		
	Possible	Achieved
Ship	500	378
Accommodation	200	154
Food	400	245
Service	400	278
Entertainment	n/a	n/a
Cruise	500	349

one individual chair, coffee table, mini-bar-refrigerator (all drinks cost extra), a color TV/DVD combo unit, and direct-dial satellite telephone. Closet space is good, but space for stowing luggage is tight, and there is little drawer space. There are no music channels in the cabins, and there is no switch to turn off announcements.

The marble bathrooms are compact units that have showers (no bathrooms have a tub) with fold-down (plastic) seat, real teakwood floor, marble vanity, large mirror, recessed towel rail (good for storing personal toiletries), and built-in hairdryer. There is a high "lip" into the bathroom.

There are also 16 balcony suites providing a little more space that includes an office desk.

CUISINE. The Restaurant, with single-seating dining, is bright, elegant and welcoming. It is on the lowest deck and has portholes rather than windows, due to maritime regulations. The open-seating arrangement offers tables for two, four, six, or eight. Dinners are normally sit-down affairs, although, depending on the itinerary and length of cruise, there could be an occasional self-serve buffet. Breakfast and lunch are usually buffets and can be taken at the poolside (weather permitting), in your suite, or in the restaurant.

The cuisine consists of continental dishes complemented by local (regional) delicacies. The food quality, choice and presentation are all good.

ENTERTAINMENT. Lecturers and recaps provide the main after-dinner entertainment.

SPA/FITNESS. There is a small fitness room, a beauty salon, and a sauna.

Clipper Adventurer
★★ +

Boutique Ship: . . . . .5,750 tons	Total Crew: 72	Cabins (with private balcony): 0
Lifestyle: . . . . .Standard	Passengers	Cabins (wheelchair accessible): 0
Cruise Line: . . . . .Quark Expeditions	(lower beds/all berths): 122/122	Cabin Current: . . . . .220 volts
Former Names: . . . . .Alla Tarasova	Passenger Space Ratio	Elevators: 0
Builder: . . . . .Brodgradiliste Uljanik	(lower beds/all berths): 47.1/47.1	Casino (gaming tables): . . . . .No
(Yugoslavia)	Crew/Passenger Ratio	Slot Machines: .No
Original Cost: .n/a	(lower beds/all berths): 1.4/1.4	Swimming Pools (outdoors): . . . . .No
Entered Service: 1976/Apr 1998	Navigation Officers: . . . . .European	Swimming Pools (indoors): . . . . .No
Registry: . . . . .The Bahamas	Cabins (total): .61	Whirlpools: . . . . .No
Length (ft/m): 328.1/100.01	Size Range (sq ft/m): 119.0–211.0/	Self-Service Launderette: . . . . .No
Beam (ft/m): 53.2/16.24	11.0–19.6	Dedicated Cinema/Seats: . . . . .No
Draft (ft/m): 15.2/4.65	Cabins (outside view): 61	Library: . . . . .Yes
Propulsion/Propellers: diesel (3,884kW)/2	Cabins (interior/no view): 0	
Passenger Decks: 5	Cabins (for one person): 0	

OVERALL SCORE: 1,098 (OUT OF A POSSIBLE 2,000 POINTS)

OVERVIEW. *Clipper Adventurer* is a solidly built small ship. It has an ice-strengthened (A-1 ice classification), and a royal blue hull and white funnel, bow-thruster and stabilizers. But, even with an ice classification, it got stuck in an ice field in the Bellings-hausen Sea in 2000. Fortunately, the Argentine Navy icebreaker *Almirante Irizar* freed it. The ship had a $15 million refit/conversion in 1997–98, and meets international safety codes and requirements. It specializes in operating close-in expedition-style cruising. There are 10 Zodiac rubber inflatable landing craft for in-depth excursions, and a covered promenade deck.

This cozy ship caters to travelers rather than mere passengers. The dress code is casual during the day, although at night many passengers wear jacket and tie. For trekking ashore, take long-sleeved garments. The public spaces are a little limited, with just one main lounge and bar. There is a small but decent library, with high wingback chairs.

There is no observation lounge with forward-facing views, although there is an outdoor observation area directly below the bridge. Quark Expeditions provides its own expedition staff, and experienced geologists and naturalist lecturers accompany all cruise expeditions. Smoking is permitted only on the outside decks. The onboard currency is the US dollar.

The passageways are narrow (it is difficult to pass housekeeping carts), and the stairs are steep on the outer decks.

SUITABLE FOR: *Clipper Adventurer* is best suited to couples and single travelers who enjoy nature and wildlife up close and personal, and who would wish to cruise in the

BERLITZ'S RATINGS		
	Possible	Achieved
Ship	500	269
Accommodation	200	106
Food	400	230
Service	400	232
Entertainment	100	40
Cruise	400	221

mainstream sense aboard large resort ships. This is for hardy, adventurous types who don't need vacuous entertainment or mindless parlor games.

ACCOMMODATION. All cabins (there are seven grades, including a dedicated price for single cabin occupancy) have outside views and twin lower beds, with private bathroom with shower, and toilet. The bathrooms are really tiny, although they are tiled, and have all the basics. Several double-occupancy cabins can be booked by single travelers (but special rates apply).

All cabins have a lockable drawer for valuables, telephone, and individual temperature control. Some have picture windows, while others have portholes. Two larger cabins (called suites in the brochure, which they really are not) are quite well equipped for the size of the vessel.

CUISINE. The dining room, with deep ocean-view windows, seats all passengers at a single seating. The food is a combination of American and Continental cuisine, prepared freshly by chefs trained at some of America's finest culinary institutions. There are limited menu choices, but the food is wholesome, and simply and attractively presented, but certainly not gourmet. Casual, self-service breakfast and luncheon buffets are taken in the main lounge, as are cocktail-hour hors d'oeuvres and other snacks.

ENTERTAINMENT. Dinner and after-dinner conversation in the ship's lounge/bar is the main entertainment.

SPA/FITNESS. There is a small sauna.

Clipper Odyssey
★★★ +

Boutique Ship: . . . . .5,218 tons	Passenger Decks: 5	Cabins (for one person): 0
Lifestyle: . . . . .Standard	Total Crew: 52	Cabins (with private balcony): 8
Cruise Line: . . . . . .Zegrahm Expeditions	Passengers	Cabins (wheelchair accessible): 1
Former Names: . . . .*Oceanic Odyssey,*	(lower beds/all berths): 128/128	Cabin Current: . . . . .115 volts
Oceanic Grace	Passenger Space Ratio	Elevators: 1
Builder: . . . . . . .NKK Tsu Shipyard (Japan)	(lower beds/all berths): 43.4/43.4	Casino (gaming tables): . . . . .No
Original Cost: . . . .$40 million	Crew/Passenger Ratio	Slot Machines: .No
Entered Service: . . . . . Apr 1989/Jun 2008	(lower beds/all berths): 2.4/2.4	Swimming Pools (outdoors): 1
Registry: . . . . .The Bahamas	Navigation Officers: . . . . .European	Swimming Pools (indoors): 0
Length (ft/m): 337.5/102.9	Cabins (total): .64	Whirlpools: 1
Beam (ft/m): 50.5/15.4	Size Range (sq ft/m): . .182.9–258.3/17–24	Self-Service Launderette: . . . . .No
Draft (ft/m): 14.1/4.3	Cabins (outside view): 64	Dedicated Cinema/Seats: . . . . .No
Propulsion/Propellers: diesel (5,192kW)/2	Cabins (interior/no view): 0	Library: . . . . .Yes

OVERALL SCORE: 1,396 (OUT OF A POSSIBLE 2,000 POINTS)

OVERVIEW. *Clipper Odyssey* has a somewhat square, angular, but contemporary profile, with twin outboard funnels. The ship, designed in Holland and built in Japan, was an attempt to copy the original *Sea Goddess* small ship/ ultra-yacht concept specifically for the Japanese market. Operated by Japan's Showa Line, the ship was not particularly successful for Japan's often choppy seas. After 10 years, the company withdrew from passenger cruises, and Clipper Cruise Line (owned by International Shipping Partners) bought the ship as an ideal addition to its small ship fleet. In June 2008 the ship began a five-year charter to Seattle-based Zegrahm Expeditions.

Considering the size of this ship, there are expansive areas outdoors, excellent for sunbathing or for viewing wildlife. The small swimming pool is just a "dip" pool, however. There is a wide teakwood outdoor jogging track. A decompression chamber for divers, originally included, is no longer used due to insurance requirements. But free snorkeling equipment is available, as is a small fleet of Zodiacs (inflatable landing craft for "soft" expedition use).

Inside, nothing jars the senses, as the interior design concept successfully balances East–West color combinations with some Indonesian accents. The ambiance is warm and intimate, and is for those who seek a small ship where entertainment and loud music isn't a priority. *Clipper Odyssey* will provide a pleasing antidote to cruising aboard large ships. The onboard currency is the US dollar.

There are lots of pillars in almost all public areas, which spoil the decor and sightlines.

SUITABLE FOR: *Clipper Odyssey* is best suited to couples and single travelers who enjoy nature and wildlife up close

BERLITZ'S RATINGS		
	Possible	Achieved
Ship	500	401
Accommodation	200	147
Food	400	259
Service	400	240
Entertainment	n/a	n/a
Cruise	500	349

and personal, and who would not dream of cruising in the mainstream sense aboard ships with large numbers of people. This is for hardy, adventurous types who don't need entertainment or parlor games.

ACCOMMODATION. There are six cabin categories. The ship has all-outside cabins that are quite tastefully furnished and feature blond wood cabinetry, twin- or queen-sized beds, living area with sofa, personal safe, mini-bar/refrigerator, TV set and VCR, and three-sided mirror. All bathrooms have a deep, half-sized tub. Some cabins have private balconies; but these are very small, with awkward door handles. The bathroom toilet seats are extremely high. There is one suite, which is actually the size of two cabins. It provides more room, of course, with a lounge area, and more storage space.

CUISINE. The dining room has large ocean view picture windows. It is quite warm and inviting, and all passengers eat in a single seating. The cuisine includes fresh foods from local ports, in a mix of regional and some Western cuisine, with open seating. A young, friendly American staff provides the service.

ENTERTAINMENT. There is no formal entertainment, although dinner and after-dinner conversation with fellow passengers in the ship's lounge/bar really becomes the entertainment each evening. Otherwise, it might be a good idea to bring a good book or two.

SPA/FITNESS. There is a tiny beauty salon, and an adjacent massage/body treatment room, while a small fitness room is located on a different deck.

Club Med 2
★★★★

Small Ship: . . . . .14,983 tons	Sail Area (sq ft/m2): 26,910/2,500	Cabins (outside view): 197
Lifestyle: . . . . .Premium	Main Propulsion: . . . . . .a) engines/b) sails	Cabins (interior/no view): 0
Cruise Line: . . . . .Club Med Cruises	Propulsion/Propellers: diesel (9,120kW)/2	Cabins (for one person): 0
Former Names: . . . . .none	Passenger Decks: 8	Cabins (with private balcony): 0
Builder: . . . .Ateliers et Chantiers du Havre	Total Crew: .200	Cabins (wheelchair accessible): 0
(France)	Passengers	Cabin Current: . . . . .110 and 220 volts
Original Cost: . . . .$125 million	(lower beds/all berths): 394/409	Elevators: 2
Entered Service: . . . . Dec 1992	Passenger Space Ratio	Casino (gaming tables): . . . . .No
Registry: . . . . .Wallis & Fortuna	(lower beds/all berths): 38.0/36.6	Slot Machines: . . . . .No
Length (ft/m): 613.8/187.10	Crew/Passenger Ratio	Swimming Pools (outdoors): 2
Beam (ft/m): 65.6/20.00	(lower beds/all berths): 1.9/2.0	Whirlpools: 0
Draft (ft/m): 16.4/5.00	Navigation Officers: . . . . .French	Self-Service Launderette: . . . . .No
Type of Vessel: . . . . .high-tech sail-cruiser	Cabins (total): 197	Library: . . . . .Yes
No. of Masts: . . . . .5 (164 ft high)/	Size Range (sq ft/m): 193.8–322.0/	
7 computer-controlled sails	18.0–30.0	

OVERALL SCORE: 1,477 (OUT OF A POSSIBLE 2,000 POINTS)

OVERVIEW. *Club Med 2* is one of a pair of the world's largest high-tech sail-cruisers ever built (the other is *Wind Surf*, operated by Windstar Cruises), part-cruise ship, part-yacht. Five huge masts rise 221 ft (67.5 meters) above sea level; they carry seven triangular, self-furling Dacron sails with a total surface area of 26,881 sq. ft (2,497 sq. meters). No human hands touch the sails, as everything is controlled by computer from the bridge. The system computer also keeps the ship on an even keel (via the movement of a hydraulic ballast system, so there is no heeling (rolling) over 6 degrees. When the ship is not using the sails, four diesel-electric motors propel it at up to 12 knots.

An extensive array of water sports facilities is provided (all except scuba gear are included in the cruise fare), and there's an aft marina platform (equipment includes 12 windsurfers, 3 sailboats, 2 water ski boats, several kayaks, 20 single scuba tanks, snorkels, and 4 motorized water sport boats. There are two small saltwater swimming pools (really dip pools); one is located amidships on the uppermost deck of the ship, while the other is located aft, together with two hot tubs, and an adjacent bar. There is an open bridge policy.

Inside, facilities include a main lounge, meeting room and a golf simulator (extra charge) as well as a fitness and beauty center, and piano bar. The onboard activities come under the direction of a large team of young, energetic GOs (*gentils ordinaires*). No gratuities are expected or accepted. The onboard currency is the euro.

SUITABLE FOR: *Club Med 2* is best suited to youthful couples and singles who want contemporary facilities and some

BERLITZ'S RATINGS

	Possible	Achieved
Ship	500	390
Accommodation	200	162
Food	400	280
Service	400	284
Entertainment	100	72
Cruise	400	289

watersports in a very relaxed but quite chic and trendy setting that is different to "normal" cruise ships, with good food and service, but with little or no entertainment.

ACCOMMODATION. There are five suites and 192 standard cabins (all of equal size). All cabins are nicely equipped and very comfortable, and have an inviting decor that includes much blond wood cabinetry. They all feature a mini-bar/refrigerator, 24-hour room service (but you pay for food), a personal safe, color television, plenty of storage space, bathrobes, and a hairdryer. There are six, four-person cabins, and some 35 doubles are fitted with an extra Pullman berth – good for young families but cramped.

CUISINE. The two main rooms have tables for one, two or more. There is open seating, so you can sit with whom you wish. The Odyssey Restaurant has a delightful open terrace for informal meals. Complimentary wines and beers are available with lunch and dinner (there is also an à la carte wine list, at a price). Afternoon tea is a delight. The cuisine provides French, continental and Japanese specialties, and the creativity and presentation are good.

ENTERTAINMENT. This is limited to occasional cabaret acts. There is live music for dancing and listening each evening

SPA/FITNESS. The Health Spa has a unisex sauna, beauty salon, and treatment rooms for massage, facials and body wraps; there is also a decent fitness room, and a beauty salon. The spa facilities are split on three separate decks.

C. Columbus
★★★ +

Small Ship: ....14,903 tons	Total Crew: 170	Cabins (with private balcony): 2
Lifestyle: ....Standard	Passengers	Cabins (wheelchair accessible): 0
Cruise Line: ....Hapag-Lloyd Cruises	(lower beds/all berths): 410/423	Cabin Current: ....110 volts
Former Names: ....none	Passenger Space Ratio	Elevators: 3
Builder: ....MTW Schiffswerft (Germany)	(lower beds/all berths): 36.3/35.2	Casino (gaming tables): ....No
Original Cost: ....$69 million	Crew/Passenger Ratio	Slot Machines: ....No
Entered Service: ....July 1997	(lower beds/all berths): 2.4/2.4	Swimming Pools (outdoors): 1
Registry: ....The Bahamas	Navigation Officers: ....German	Swimming Pools (indoors): 0
Length (ft/m): 472.8/144.13	Cabins (total): 205	Whirlpools: 0
Beam (ft/m): 70.5/21.50	Size Range (sq ft/m): 139.9–339.0/	Self-Service Launderette: ....No
Draft (ft/m): 16.8/5.15	13.0–31.5	Dedicated Cinema/Seats: ....No
Propulsion/Propellers: ....diesel	Cabins (outside view): 158	Library: ....Yes
(10,560kW)/2	Cabins (interior/no view): 47	
Passenger Decks: 6	Cabins (for one person): 0	

BERLITZ'S OVERALL SCORE: 1,396 (OUT OF A POSSIBLE 2,000 POINTS)

OVERVIEW. *C. Columbus* has a smart contemporary profile, with a single, large funnel (painted in Hapag-Lloyd's orange/blue colors). The Hamburg-based Hapag-Lloyd Cruises has chartered the ship from the German company Conti Reederei, the owner.

The ship also has an ice-hardened hull, which is useful for cold-weather cruise areas. In addition, the bridge "wings" can be folded inwards (as can the overhang lights) flush with the ship's side so that the vessel can enter the locks in the US/Canada Great Lakes region, including the St. Lawrence Seaway and Welland Canal, for which the ship was specifically built.

The ship has a good passenger space ratio. Each deck has a distinctly different color scheme and carpeting, making it easy to find one's way around. There is a reasonable range of public rooms to choose from, most of which are located in a "cake-layer" vertical stacking aft of the accommodation. Although the ceilings in the public rooms are plain and unimaginative (except for the Palm Garden), the decor is really bright and upbeat, and very different to all other ships in the Hapag-Lloyd fleet. The most popular room is arguably the delightful multi-function Palm Garden, which is also the ship's forward-facing observation lounge.

The fit and finish of the ship's interiors can best be described as a little utilitarian (the mottled gray walls are somewhat cold, but a contrast to the splashes of color found in carpeting and other decorative touches). The artwork chosen is, for the most part, minimal and uncoordinated, yet it all works together to provide cheerful surroundings. Ship buffs will be pleased to find some superb original photographs from the Hapag-Lloyd archives adorning the stairways.

BERLITZ'S RATINGS

	Possible	Achieved
Ship	500	342
Accommodation	200	145
Food	400	282
Service	400	297
Entertainment	100	61
Cruise	400	269

You should know that the level of "luxury" is well below that of Hapag-Lloyd's *Europa*, and the experience on this very informal ship is completely different (so, of course, is the cruise price). The onboard currency is the euro. Gratuities are extra and are recommended at €5–€6 per person per day.

First-time cruise passengers in particular will find this a fresh, comfortable, casual and unpretentious ship for a cruise vacation. You don't need to buy a new wardrobe, and you can leave your tuxedo at home; for this ship you need only informal and casual clothes.

Well-planned itineraries and destination-intensive cruises are featured. Of particular note are the Great Lakes cruises, which are only possible because of the pencil-slim design of *C. Columbus* (previously, the last ocean-going cruise vessel to operate Great Lakes cruises was *World Discoverer* in 1974).

While it's a comfortable, trendy ship, note that the swimming pool is small (it's more like a "dip" pool), as is the open deck space, and there is no wrap-around promenade deck outdoors. One of the main reasons to cruise aboard this ship is the excellent dining experience in a relaxed, one-seating environment.

SUITABLE FOR: *C. Columbus* is best suited to youthful-minded German-speaking couples and single travelers who are seeking good value for money on a first cruise, aboard a ship with contemporary, comfortable (but not pretentious or luxurious) surroundings, and good itineraries, at a very modest price.

ACCOMMODATION. The standard cabins are really small, and many are interior (no view) cabins. All but 10 cabins have lower berths, but the 16 price grades established really are a lot for this size of ship. Except for two forward-facing suites, there are no balcony cabins, and no room service (except for accommodations designated as suites).

The cabin decor is bright and upbeat, and a good amount of closet and shelf space is provided. The bathrooms are fully tiled and have large shower stalls (none have bathtubs). All cabins feature a mini-bar/refrigerator (all items are at extra cost, as in hotels ashore), personal safe, and hairdryer (bathrobes are available on request, incurring a small surcharge).

There are eight suites (each is at least double the size of a standard cabin), and each has a curtained partition between its lounge and sleeping areas, with a wall unit that houses a television that can be turned 360 degrees for viewing from either the lounge or bedroom. Two of the suites located at the bow each have a narrow private veranda (with two teak lounge chairs and coffee table), bedroom (with large wall clock) and lounge area separated by a curtain, two televisions, and an excellent amount of closet, drawer and shelf space. The cabinetry, with its walnut-finish and birds-eye pattern, makes these suites feel warm and luxurious. All the suites have a small room service menu. The bathrooms have a large shower (it is big enough for two), hairdryer, and under-sink storage space.

CUISINE. There is one large main dining room, located at the stern, with large ocean-view windows on three sides, and all passengers can be seated in a single seating, at assigned tables. There are just two tables for two, but other tables can accommodate up to 16 – good for family reunions. The cuisine, which is presented in an unstuffy way, is extremely good, though the menu choice is small (there are typically two or three entrée options for dinner). There is an excellent selection of fresh-baked breads and rolls every day, and a good selection of cold cuts and cheeses daily. Creatively themed dinners, as well as an extensive array of late-night snacks, make dining a delight, and well beyond most passengers' expectations.

Breakfast and lunch can be taken in the bright, but casual, setting of the Palm Garden, which is also the ship's very comfortable observation lounge. Light dinners also can be taken in the Palm Garden, where a small dance floor adds another dimension.

ENTERTAINMENT. The Columbus Lounge is a single level, H-shaped room that is quite large, with banquette and individual seating in tub chairs, and a bar is situated on the port side in the aft corner of the room. Because the apron stage is in the center of the room, the sightlines from many seats are not that good. Entertainment consists mainly of cabaret acts typical of the cruise ship circuit. Plenty of live music, for dancing, is also provided.

SPA/FITNESS. A fitness room is located forward on the uppermost deck of the ship. A sauna is located on the lowest passenger deck, next to the beauty salon, and massage/facial treatments are available.

KNOTS AND LOGS

A knot is a unit of speed measuring one nautical mile. (A nautical mile is equal to one-60th of a degree of the earth's circumference and measures exactly 6,080.2 ft (1,852 km). It is about 800 ft (243 meters) longer than a land mile. Thus, when a ship is traveling at a speed of 20 knots (note: this is never referred to as 20 knots per hour), it is traveling at 20 nautical miles per hour (1 knot equals 1.151 land miles).

This unit of measurement has its origin in the days prior to the advent of modern aids, when sailors used a log and a length of rope to measure the distance that their boat had covered, as well as the speed at which it was advancing. In 1574, a tract by William Bourne, entitled A Regiment for the Sea, records the method by which this was done. The log was weighted down at one end while the other end was affixed to a rope. The weighted end, when thrown over the stern, had the effect of making the log stand upright, thus being visible. Sailors believed that the log remained stationary at the spot where it had been cast into the water, while the rope unraveled. By measuring the length of rope used, they could ascertain how far the ship had traveled, and were thus able to calculate its speed.

Sailors first tied knots at regular intervals, eventually fixed at 47 ft 3 inches (14.4 meters) along a rope, then counted how many knots had passed through their hands in a specified time (later established as 28 seconds), and measured by the amount of sand that had run out of an hourglass. They then used simple multiplication to calculate the number of knots their ship was traveling at over the period of an hour.

The data gathered in this way were put into a record, called a logbook. Today, a logbook is used to record the day-to-day details of the life of a ship and its crew as well as other pertinent information.

Coral
★★

Mid-Size Ship: . . . . .14,155 tons	Passenger Decks: 7	Cabins (for one person): 0
Lifestyle: . . . . .Standard	Total Crew: 265	Cabins (with private balcony): 0
Cruise Line: . . . . .Louis Hellenic Cruises	Passengers	Cabins (wheelchair accessible): 2
Former Names: . . .*Triton, Cunard Adventurer,*	(lower beds/all berths): 756/945	Cabin Current: . . . . .110 and 220 volts
Sunward II	Passenger Space Ratio	Elevators: 2
Builder: . .Rotterdamsche Dry Dock (Holland)	(lower beds/all berths): 18.7/14.9	Casino (gaming tables): . . . . .Yes
Original Cost: . . . . .n/a	Crew/Passenger Ratio	Slot Machines: . . . . .Yes
Entered Service: . . . . . .Oct 1971/May 2005	(lower beds/all berths): 2.8/3.5	Swimming Pools (outdoors): 1
Registry: . . . . .Greece	Navigation Officers: . . . . .Greek	Swimming Pools (indoors): 0
Length (ft/m): 491.1/149.70	Cabins (total): 378	Whirlpools: 0
Beam (ft/m): 70.5/21.50	Size Range (sq ft/m): 118.4–131.3/11.0–12.2	Self-Service Launderette: . . . . .No
Draft (ft/m): 19.22/5.86	Cabins (outside view): 142	Dedicated Cinema/Seats: Yes/96
Propulsion/Propellers: .diesel (19,860kW)/2	Cabins (interior/no view): 0	Library: . . . . .No

OVERALL SCORE: 944 (OUT OF A POSSIBLE 2,000 POINTS)

OVERVIEW. The ship has a smart, but dated profile, a deep clipper bow, and twin funnels. It has been fairly well maintained, although it is showing its age. There is a wrap-around painted steel outdoors promenade deck, a decent amount of open deck space for sunbathing, and small "kidney-shaped" pool. Much of the open space outdoors is covered by canvas awnings (providing shelter from the summer sun).

Inside, it's easy to find your way around. The few public rooms are dressed in cheerful, warm colors, although ceilings are low, which provides a cramped feeling. Decor and artwork are eclectic, and deck names are Greek. There's a small nightclub with forward observation views. There is no library (except for some old paperbacks). On one of the upper decks, a dance floor is provided outdoors, with a bar called Jailhouse Rock.

Expect lines for buffets and shore excursions. There are many announcements. The onboard currency is the euro, and gratuities are not included in the fare. The dress code is casual throughout (no formal nights).

SUITABLE FOR: *Coral* is best suited to first-time passengers who simply want to cruise the Greek Islands in a modicum of comfort, and at a bargain price.

ACCOMMODATION. Cabins are in eight grades, priced by grade, location and size. Most are very small and narrow, with only the most basic appointments. The closet and drawer space is minimal, and cabin soundproofing is very poor. There are 32 cabins (in the two highest grades) with a tub/shower; otherwise the cabin bathrooms have very small shower enclosures, and little space for toiletries.

BERLITZ'S RATINGS

	Possible	Achieved
Ship	500	231
Accommodation	200	91
Food	400	194
Service	400	216
Entertainment	100	40
Cruise	400	172

CUISINE. While the Dining Room is quite attractive and has contemporary colors and ambiance, it is very noisy. There are two seatings for dinner on most nights (typically an open seating for the first night), and open seating for breakfast and lunch. Dining room seating and table assignments (except for the first night) are handled by the maître d' upon embarkation.

The cuisine is predominantly Continental, with some regional (Greek) specialties (much use of oil and salt). Spa and vegetarian dishes are also available on lunch and dinner menus. Overall, the food has little taste. Service is hurried and indifferent.

Casual breakfast and lunch (with limited choices) can also be taken outside on deck poolside (or in the main lounge when the weather is not good). Additional light refreshments are available indoors at the Cafe Brazil.

ENTERTAINMENT. The Main Lounge is a single deck height, rectangular-shaped room (no sloping floor) designed for cabaret acts. Banquette and individual seating is set around a "thrust" stage, but six pillars obstruct sightlines: only passengers seated in the first few rows can see below waist level.

SPA/FITNESS. A small gymnasium is located aft, close to the swimming pool (it's really only a "dip" pool); adjacent is a sauna and massage room. A beauty salon is located indoors on another deck (there is no natural light, which makes tinting and coloring difficult).

Massages, aromatherapy facials, manicures, pedicures, and hair beautifying treatments are available, but facilities are minimal.

Coral Princess
★★★★

Large Resort Ship:	........91,627 tons	Passengers	
Lifestyle:	.................Standard	(lower beds/all berths):	.....1,974/2,590
Cruise Line:	.........Princess Cruises	Passenger Space Ratio	
Former Names:	.................none	(lower beds/all berths):	.......46.4/35.3
Builder: Chantiers de l'Atlantique (France)		Crew/Passenger Ratio	
Original Cost:	.............$360 million	(lower beds/all berths):	..........2.1/2.8
Entered Service:	.............Dec 2002	Navigation Officers:	.............British
Registry:	...................Bermuda	Cabins (total):	987
Length (ft/m):	.............964.5/294.0	Size Range (sq ft/m):	.......156–470.0/
Beam (ft/m):	..............105.6/32.2		14.4–43.6
Draft (ft/m):	....................26/7.9	Cabins (outside view):	879
Propulsion/Propellers:	.....gas turbine/2	Cabins (interior/no view):	108
Passenger Decks:	11	Cabins (for one person):	0
Total Crew:	900	Cabins (with private balcony):	727

Cabins (wheelchair accessible):	20
Cabin Current:	...............110 volts
Elevators:	14
Casino (gaming tables):	...........Yes
Slot Machines:	....................Yes
Swimming Pools (outdoors):	2
	(+ 1 splash pool)
Swimming Pools (indoors):	0
Whirlpools:	5
Self-Service Launderette:	.........Yes
Dedicated Cinema/Seats:	..........No
Library:	............................Yes
Classification Society:	. . .Lloyd's Register

OVERALL SCORE: 1,544 (OUT OF A POSSIBLE 2,000 POINTS)

OVERVIEW. *Coral Princess* has an instantly recognizable funnel due to two jet engine-like pods that sit high up on its structure but really are mainly for decoration. Four diesel engines provide the generating power. Electrical power is provided by a combination of four diesel and one gas turbine (CODAG) unit; the diesel engines are located in the engine room, while the gas turbine unit is located in the ship's funnel housing. The ship also has three bow thrusters and three stern thrusters.

The ship's interior layout is similar to that of the *Grand Princess*-class ships (but with two decks full of public rooms, lounges and bars instead of just one), and sensibly has three major stair towers for passengers (good from the safety and evacuation viewpoint), with plenty of lifts for easy access. For a large ship, the layout is quite user-friendly, and less disjointed than many ships of a similar size and, because of its slim beam, the ship is able to transit the Panama Canal, thus providing greater flexibility in deployment than the *Grand Princess*-class ships.

New facilities not before incorporated into a Princess Cruises ship include a flower shop (where you can order flowers and Godiva chocolates for cabin delivery – good for a birthday or anniversary), cigar lounge (Churchill Lounge), and martini bar (Crooners). Also different is a casino with a London theme.

What is very civilized is the fact that sunbathers who use the "quiet" deck forward of the mast have their own splash pool, so they won't have to go down two decks to get to the two main pools. Strollers will like the ship's full wrap-around exterior promenade deck.

Surfers can find an AOL Internet Cafe conveniently

BERLITZ'S RATINGS

	Possible	Achieved
Ship	500	436
Accommodation	200	154
Food	400	261
Service	400	294
Entertainment	100	85
Cruise	400	314

located on the top level of the four-deck-high lobby. The dreaded "fine arts" get their own room, so that paintings to be sold during the art auctions are not spread all over the ship. Adjacent is the Wedding Chapel (a live web-cam can relay ceremonies via the internet). The ship's captain can legally marry (American) couples, due to the ship's registry and a special dispensation (this should, however, be verified when in the planning stage, and may depend on where you live). Princess Cruises offers three wedding packages – Pearl, Emerald, Diamond; the fee includes registration and official marriage certificate. The Wedding Chapel can also host "renewal of vows" ceremonies (there is a fee).

ACCOMMODATION. There are 33 price categories, in six types: 16 Suites with balcony (470 sq. ft/43.6 sq. meters); 184 Mini-Suites with balcony (285–302 sq. ft/26.4–28.0 sq. meters); 8 Mini-Suites without balcony (300 sq. ft/27.8 sq. meters); 527 Outside-View Cabins with balcony (217–232 sq. ft/ 20.1–21.5 sq. meters); 144 Standard Outside-view Cabins (162 sq. ft/15 sq. meters); Interior (no view) Cabins (156 sq. ft/144.5 sq. meters). There are also 20 wheelchair-accessible cabins (217–374 sq. ft/20.1–34.7 sq. meters). Note that all measurements are approximate. Almost all of the outside-view cabins have a private balcony. Some cabins can accommodate a third, or third and fourth person (good for families with children). Some cabins on Emerald Deck (Deck 8) have a view obstructed by lifeboats.

Suites: There are just 16 suites and, although none are really that large (when compared to such ships as *Norwegian Dawn* and *Norwegian Star*, where the largest suites measure a whopping 5,350 sq. ft/497 sq. meters, for example), each has a private balcony. All are named after islands (mostly coral-based islands in the Indian Ocean and Pacific Ocean). All suites are located on either Deck 9 or Deck 10. In a departure from many ships, *Coral Princess* does not have any suites or cabins with a view of the ship's stern. There are also four Premium Suites, located sensibly in the center of the ship, adjacent to a bank of six lifts. Six other suites (called Verandah Suites) are located further aft.

All Accommodation: All suites and cabins are equipped with a refrigerator, personal safe, television (with audio channels), hairdryer, satellite-dial telephone, and twin beds that convert to a queen-sized bed (there are a few exceptions). All accommodation has a bathroom with shower enclosure and toilet. Accommodation designated as suites and mini-suites (there are seven price categories) has a bathtub and separate shower enclosure, and two televisions.

All passengers receive turndown service and chocolates on pillows each night, bathrobes (on request) and toiletry amenity kits (larger, naturally, for suite/mini-suite occupants). There are no cabins for singles. Princess Cruises typically includes CNN, CNBC, ESPN and TNT on the in-cabin color television system (when available). There are no butlers – even for the top-grade suites. Cabin attendants have too many cabins to look after (typically 20), which does not translate to fine personal service.

CUISINE. The two main dining rooms, Bordeaux and Provence, are located in the forward section of the ship on the two lowest passenger decks, with the galley all the way forward so it doesn't intersect public spaces. Both are almost identical in design and layout (the ceilings are quite low and make the rooms appear more cramped than they are), and have plenty of intimate alcoves and cozy dining spots, with tables for two, four, six, or eight. There are two seatings for dinner, while breakfast and lunch are on an open-seating basis; you may have to stand in line at peak times, just as in almost any large restaurant ashore. Both dining rooms are non-smoking.

Horizon Court is the ship's casual 24-hour eatery, and is located in the forward section of Lido Deck, with superb ocean views. Several self-serve counters provide an array of food for breakfast and lunch buffets, and offer bistro-style casual dinners in the evening.

Alternative (Extra Charge) Eateries: There are two "alternative" dining rooms (Sabatini's and the Bayou Cafe), both enclosed (i.e. not open areas which passengers can walk through, as in some Princess Cruises ships). Both cost extra, and you must make a reservation.

Sabatini's is an Italian eatery, with colorful tiled Mediterranean-style decor; it is named after Trattoria Sabatini, the 200-year old institution in Florence (where there is no cover charge). It has Italian-style pizzas and pastas, with a variety of sauces, as well as Italian-style entrées (including tiger prawns and lobster tail – all provided with flair and entertainment by the waiters). The food is both creative and tasty (with seriously sized portions). Sabatini's is by reservation only, and there is a cover charge of $15 per person, for lunch or dinner (on sea days only).

The Bayou Cafe is open for lunch and dinner, and has a cover charge of $10 per person (including a free Hurricane cocktail), and evokes the charm of New Orleans' French Quarter, complete with wrought-iron decoration. The Bayou Cafe has Creole food (with platters such as Peel 'n' Eat Shrimp Piquante, Sausage Grillades, Oysters Sieur de Bienville and N'Awlins Crawfish "Mud Bug" Bisque delivered to the table when you arrive). Popular entrées include Seafood Gumbo, and Chorizo Jambalaya with fresh seafood and traditional dried spice mixes, as well as Cajun Grill items such as Smothered Alligator Ribs, Flambeaux Grilled Jumbo Prawns, Corn Meal Fried Catfish, Blackened Chicken Brochette, and Red Pepper Butter Broiled Lobster; desserts include sweet potato pie and banana whiskey pound cake. The room sports a small stage, with baby grand piano, and live jazz is also part of the dining scenario.

Other outlets include La Pâtisserie, in the ship's reception lobby coffee, cakes and pastries spot; a good place for informal meetings; there's also a Pizzeria, hamburger grill, and an ice cream bar (extra charge for the ice cream). Meanwhile, puffers and sippers should enjoy Churchill's, a neat cigar and cognac lounge, cleverly sited near a little hideaway bar called the Rat Pack Bar.

ENTERTAINMENT. The Princess Theatre is two decks high, and, unusually, there is much more seating in the upper level than on the main floor below. There are typically two production shows on a 7-day cruise, and three on a 10-day cruise. These are colorful, glamorous shows with well designed costumes and good lighting.

A second entertainment lounge (Universe Lounge) is designed more for cabaret-style features. It also has two levels (a first for a Princess Cruises ship), and three separate stages – so nonstop entertainment can be provided without constant set-ups. Some 50 of the room's seats are equipped with a built-in laptop computer. The room is also used for cooking demonstrations (it has a full kitchen set), and other life-enrichment participation activities. There is a good mix of music in the various bars and lounges.

For self-improvement, Princess Cruises' new "Scholar-Ship@Sea" program offers about 20 courses per cruise (six on any given day at sea). Although all introductory classes are free, if you want to continue any chosen subject in a smaller setting, charges apply. There are four core subjects: Culinary Arts, Visual/Creative Arts, Photography, and Computer Technology. There is a full culinary demonstration kitchen and a pottery studio complete with kiln.

SPA/FITNESS. The Lotus Spa is located aft on one of the ship's uppermost decks. It contains men's and women's saunas, steam rooms, changing rooms, relaxation area, beauty salon, aerobics exercise room and gymnasium with ocean-views packed with the latest high-tech muscle-pumping, cardio-vascular equipment. There are several large rooms for individual treatments.

● **For more extensive general information about a Princess Cruises cruise experience, see pages 134–37.**

Corinthian II
★★★★

Boutique Ship: . . . . 4,280 tons	Total Crew: 66
Lifestyle: . . . . .Standard	Passengers
Cruise Line: . . .Travel Dynamics International	(lower beds/all berths): 112/122
Former Names: . . . .*Island Sun, Regina*	Passenger Space Ratio
Renaissance, Renaissance VIII	(lower beds/all berths): 38.2/38.2
Builder: . . . . .Nuovi Cantieri Appaunia (Italy)	Crew/Passenger Ratio
Original Cost: . . . .$25 million	(lower beds/all berths): 1.7/1.8
Entered Service: . . . . . .Dec 1991/May 2005	Navigation Officers: . . .Norwegian/European
Registry: . . . . .Mauritius	Cabins (total): 61
Length (ft/m): 297.2/90.6	Size Range (sq ft/m): 234.6–353.0/
Beam (ft/m): 50.1/15.3	21.8–32.8
Draft (ft/m): 12.9/2.95	Cabins (outside view): 61
Propulsion/Propellers: . . .diesel (5000kW)/2	Cabins (interior/no view): 0
Passenger Decks: 5	Cabins (for one person): 0

Cabins (with private balcony): 4
Cabins (wheelchair accessible): 0
Cabin Current: . . . . .110 volts
Elevators: 1
Casino (gaming tables): . . . . .No
Slot Machines: . . . . .No
Swimming Pools (outdoors): 0
Swimming Pools (indoors): 0
Whirlpools: 1
Self-Service Launderette: . . . . .No
Dedicated Cinema/Seats: . . . . .No
Library: . . . . .Yes

OVERALL SCORE: 1,546 (OUT OF A POSSIBLE 2,000 POINTS)

OVERVIEW. *Corinthian II* (originally built as one of a series of eight similar ships for the now-defunct Renaissance Cruises) has mega-yacht looks, a smart profile and handsome styling, with twin flared funnels and a "ducktail" (sponson) stern to provide good stability and seagoing comfort. This charming ship is operated by Travel Dynamics International year-round on "soft" destination-intensive" discovery cruises. The ship (upgraded in 2004) has a teak wrap-around promenade deck outdoors, and decent amount of open deck and sunbathing space.

A baby shore tender hangs off the aft deck and acts as ship-to-shore transportation. Some equipment for watersports is carried, and active types can enjoy wind surfing, scuba diving and snorkeling, deep sea fishing, mountain biking, golfing, and hiking.

Inside, you will find an elegant interior design, with polished wood-finish paneling throughout. There is also a very small book and video library.

This vessel is very comfortable and totally inviting, and features warm-weather cruising in regions devoid of large cruise ships. Although this intimate ship is not up to the standard of a Seabourn or Silversea ship, it will provide a good cruise experience at a moderate cost. Gratuities are appreciated but not required.

The onboard currency is the US dollar.

SUITABLE FOR: Mature adults who want to discover small ports, in a relaxed lifestyle combined with good food and

BERLITZ'S RATINGS

	Possible	Achieved
Ship	500	392
Accommodation	200	159
Food	400	309
Service	400	306
Entertainment	n/a	n/a
Cruise	500	380

service, and itineraries that say "get away from it all, but in comfort."

ACCOMMODATION. The spacious cabins combine highly polished imitation rosewood paneling with lots of mirrors and hand-crafted Italian furniture, lighted walk-in closets, three-sided vanity mirrors (in fact, there are a lot of mirrored surfaces in the decor), and just about everything you need, including a TV set and VCR, and a refrigerator).

The bathrooms are extremely compact units; they have real teakwood floors and marble vanities, and shower enclosures (none have tubs, not even the owner's suite).

CUISINE. The dining room operates with an open seating for all meals. It is small but quite smart, with tables for two, four, six, and eight. You simply sit where you like, with whom you like, and at what time you like.

The meals are self-service, buffet-style cold foods for breakfast and lunch, with hot foods chosen from a table menu and served properly, and sit down service for dinner. The food quality, choice, and presentation are all very good.

ENTERTAINMENT. There is no formal entertainment in the main lounge, the venue for all social activities (six pillars obstruct the sightlines to the small stage area anyway).

SPA/FITNESS. Water sports facilities include an aft platform, sailfish, snorkel equipment, and Zodiacs.

Costa Allegra
★★ ✛

Mid-Size Ship: . . . . .28,430 tons	Total Crew: 450	Cabins (with private balcony): 10
Lifestyle: . . . . .Standard	Passengers	Cabins (wheelchair accessible): 8 (interior)
Cruise Line: Costa Crociere (Costa Cruises)	(lower beds/all berths): 820/1,072	Cabin Current: . . . . . . .110 and 220 volts
Former Names: . . . .*Annie Johnson*	Passenger Space Ratio	Elevators: 4
Builder: . . . . . . .Mariotti Shipyards (Italy)	(lower beds/all berths): 34.7/26.5	Casino (gaming tables): . . . . Yes
Original Cost: . . . .$175 million	Crew/Passenger Ratio	Slot Machines: . . . . .Yes
Entered Service: . . . . .Dec 1992	(lower beds/all berths): 2.0/2.6	Swimming Pools (outdoors): 1
Registry: . . . . .Italy	Navigation Officers: . . . . .Italian	Swimming Pools (indoors): 0
Length (ft/m): 616.1/187.8	Cabins (total): 410	Whirlpools: 2
Beam (ft/m): 83.9/25.6	Size Range (sq ft/m): 105.4–575.8/	Self-Service Launderette: . . . . .No
Draft (ft/m): 23.9/7.3	9.8–53.5	Dedicated Cinema/Seats: . . . . .No
Propulsion/Propellers: . . . . .diesel	Cabins (outside view): 218	Library: . . . . .Yes
(19,200kW)/2	Cabins (interior/no view): 192	
Passenger Decks: 8	Cabins (for one person): 0	

OVERALL SCORE: 1,092 (OUT OF A POSSIBLE 2,000 POINTS)

OVERVIEW. *Costa Allegra* originally began life as a container ship built for Sweden's Johnson Line, then underwent a skilful transformation into contemporary cruise ship, which resulted in a jazzy, angular-looking vessel with a low-slung appearance (fine when it debuted, but now it looks outdated). There are three bolt-upright yellow funnels that have become a signature item for almost all Costa Cruises' ships. Slightly longer and larger than its sister ship *Costa Marina* (after the addition of a 44ft/13.4-meter section), this vessel has a much better standard of interior fit and finish, and more outdoors space than its sister ship. It has an interesting glass-enclosed stern.

There is a high glass-to-steel ratio for the size of the ship, with numerous glass domes and walls admitting light, as well as Murano glass light fixtures in some places. There is a good amount of outdoor deck and sunbathing space, although there is no observation lounge with forward-facing views over the ship's bows. bows. No cushioned pads are provided for the sunloungers outdoors.

The decks are named after famous painters. The decor underwent a change in 2006 to provide more of an Asian ambiance, while still retaining a European feel; this was done before the ship was sent to China for local market cruising. There are few public restrooms.

The many loud and extended announcements (in several languages) quickly become tiresome. The opening hours for the small library are poor. Gratuities are added to your onboard account.

SUITABLE FOR: *Costa Allegra* provides a decent first cruise experience for young adults who enjoy European-style ser-

BERLITZ'S RATINGS		
	Possible	Achieved
Ship	500	275
Accommodation	200	120
Food	400	192
Service	400	226
Entertainment	100	57
Cruise	400	222

vice and a real upbeat, almost elegant atmosphere with an Italian accent and lots of noise.

ACCOMMODATION. There are several categories (the price will depend on grade, location and size). The standard cabins are quite light and airy, with splashes of fabric colors, and wood accenting, and are laid out in a practical manner. However, they are small, and there is little closet and drawer space, so take only casual clothing. There are many small interior (no view) cabins, and all cabins suffer from poor soundproofing. Many cabins also have pull-down (Pullman-style) berths for a third or fourth occupant. The bathrooms are compact, although they do have good shower enclosures, with sliding circular door instead of the usual limp curtain. The cabin service menu is extremely limited.

On Rousseau Deck there are three forward-facing suites (the largest accommodation on board), each of which has a living room, dinette and wet bar. A further 10 slightly smaller mini-suites feature a small, very narrow balcony, but it is really not private, as it can be seen from the walking track on the deck above.

CUISINE. The Montmartre Restaurant has 310 seats. It operates two seatings and has an international menu. It is fairly spacious (but noisy) and has expansive glass windows that look out over the stern, while the port side and starboard side have large portholes. It has tables for four, six, eight or 10 (there are no tables for two). Adjacent is the 134-seat Montemartre Verandah Restaurant is an à la carte, pay-to-eat venue with an Italo-Asian menu.

Four small dining venues were added in the 2006 refit.

These include Piazzetta Allegra, a pay-to-eat sushi and sashimi bar seating 110 with a karaoke area, and Almalfi, an Italian pay-to-eat à la carte restaurant with that seats 76 indoors and 52 outside, and has a dance floor. Excellent cappuccino and espresso coffees are always available in various bars around the ship, served in the right sized china cups.

ENTERTAINMENT. The Folies Bergères Showroom is a single level room. The sight lines are adequate, but could be better (14 pillars obstruct sight lines from several seats). Because it is only a single-level room, its poor ceiling height precludes jugglers and the like from working, and limits what can be achieved. In other words, don't expect much. The room is quite adequate, however, as a cabaret lounge.

For live dance music and listening music, head to the Flamenco Ballroom, located at the aft end of the ship. In addition, the Crystal Club Discotheque, one deck above the Flamenco Ballroom, is the place for the young at heart, late of night, and hard of hearing.

SPA/FITNESS. A new (Caracalla Spa) wellness center was created in 2006 from a 30-ton aluminum superstructure that houses a gymnasium, eight treatment rooms, two locker rooms, two saunas and a relaxation area.

The spa is operated by Steiner, a specialist concession, whose young staff will try to sell you Steiner's own-brand Elemis beauty products (spa girls have sales targets). fitness classes are free, while some cost extra. Do make appointments early as time slots can go quickly. There is also a jogging track outdoors.

● **For more extensive general information on what a Costa Cruises cruise is like, see pages 121–24.**

SHIP TALK

Gross Tons (gt): not the weight of a ship but the total volume measurement of all permanently enclosed spaces above and below decks, with certain exceptions, such as the bridge, radio room, galleys, washing facilities, and other specified areas. It is the basis for harbor dues. International regulations introduced in 1982 required shipowners to re-measure the grt (formerly gross register tons) of their vessels (1 grt = 100 cubic ft of enclosed space/2.8 cubic meters). This unit of measure was invented in England centuries ago for taxation purposes, when wine shipped from France was stored in standard-size casks, called tonneaux. Thus a ship carrying 20 casks measured 20 tons, and taxes were applied accordingly. Gross tonnage measurements may or may not include balconies.

Helm: the apparatus for steering a ship.

House Flag: the flag denoting the company to which a ship belongs.

Hull: the frame and body of the ship exclusive of masts or super-structure.

Leeward: the side of a ship that is sheltered from the wind.

Luff: the side of a ship facing the wind

Manifest: a list of the ship's passengers, crew, and cargo.

Nautical Mile: one-sixtieth of a degree of the circumference of the Earth.

Pilot: a person licensed to navigate ships into or out of a harbor or through difficult waters, and to advise the captain on handling the ship during these procedures.

Pitch: the rise and fall of a ship's bow that may occur when the ship is under way.

Port: the left side of a ship when facing forward.

Quay: berth, dock, or pier.

Rudder: a finlike device astern and below the waterline, for steering the vessel.

Screw: a ship's propeller.

Stabilizer: a gyroscopically operated retractable "fin" extending from either or both sides of the ship below the waterline to provide a more stable ride.

Starboard: the right side of the ship when facing forward.

Stern: the aftmost part of the ship that is opposite the bow.

Tender: a smaller vessel, often a lifeboat, used to transport passengers between ship and shore when the vessel is at anchor.

Wake: the track of agitated water left behind a ship when in motion.

Waterline: the line along the side of a ship's hull corresponding to the water surface.

Windward: the side of a ship facing the direction in which the wind blows.

Yaw: the erratic deviation from the ship's set course, usually caused by a heavy sea.

● *More Ship Talk, page 379.*

Costa Atlantica
★★★★

Large Resort Ship: ....85,700 tons	Passenger Decks: 12	Cabins (with private balcony): 742
Lifestyle: ....Standard	Total Crew: 920	Cabins (wheelchair accessible): 8
Cruise Line: ....Costa Crociere	Passengers	Cabin Current: ....110 volts
(Costa Cruises)	(lower beds/all berths): 2,112/2,680	Elevators: 12
Former Names: ....none	Passenger Space Ratio	Casino (gaming tables): ....Yes
Builder: ....Kverner Masa-Yards (Finland)	(lower beds/all berths): 40.5/31.9	Slot Machines: ....Yes
Original Cost: ....$335 million	Crew/Passenger Ratio	Swimming Pools (outdoors): 2
Entered Service: ....July 2000	(lower beds/all berths): 2.3/2.9	(+1 indoor/outdoor)
Registry: ....Italy	Navigation Officers: ....Italian	Swimming Pools (indoors): ....No
Length (ft/m): 959.6/292.5	Cabins (total): 1,056	Whirlpools: ....Yes
Beam (ft/m): 105.6/32.2	Size Range (sq ft/m): 161.4–387.5/	Self-Service Launderette: ....No
Draft (ft/m): 25.5/7.8	15.0–36.0	Dedicated Cinema/Seats: ....No
Propulsion/Propellers: .....diesel-electric	Cabins (outside view): 843	Library: ....Yes
(34,000 kW)/2 azimuthing pods	Cabins (interior/no view): 213	
(17.6 MW each)	Cabins (for one person): 0	

OVERALL SCORE: 1,436 (OUT OF A POSSIBLE 2,000 POINTS)

OVERVIEW. *Costa Atlantica* (sister: *Costa Mediterranea*) has basically the same exterior design and internal layout as that of parent company Carnival Cruise Lines' *Carnival Legend, Miracle, Pride* and *Spirit*. There are two centrally located swimming pools outdoors, one of which can be used in poor weather due to its retractable magrodome cover. A bar abridges two adjacent whirlpool tubs. There's a smaller pool for children, and a winding water slide that spans two decks in height (it starts on a platform bridge at the aft funnel). There is an additional whirlpool tub outdoors.

Inside, the layout is somewhat of an extension of that found in previous newbuilds for Costa Cruises – particularly that of *Costa Victoria*. The deck names are inspired by Federico Fellini movies (Roma Deck, Le Notte di Cabiria, La Voce della Luna, La Strada, La Luci del Varieta). There's even a deck named after a Fellini TV movie, Ginger and Fred. The interior design is, however, bold and brash – a mix of classical Italy and contemporary features. Good points include the fact that the interior design allows good passenger flow from one public space to another, and there are several floor spaces for dancing, and a range of bars and lounges for socializing.

You'll be struck by the immense size of the lobby space spanning eight decks. Take a drink from the lobby bar and look upwards – the surroundings are stunning. A small chapel is located forward of the uppermost level.

Other facilities include a winding shopping street with boutique stores (Fendi, Gianni Versace, Paul & Shark Yachting – as well as a shop dedicated to selling Caffe Flo-

BERLITZ'S RATINGS		
	Possible	Achieved
Ship	500	427
Accommodation	200	152
Food	400	240
Service	400	273
Entertainment	100	64
Cruise	400	280

rian products), photo gallery, video games room, an observation balcony, a casino and library (with internet access).

Costa Cruises has updated its image, and is retraining its staff. With the debut of *Costa Atlantica* came many new, better, uniforms for many departments, as well as more choice in a ship that is designed to wow the hip and trendy as well as pay homage to many of Italy's great art and past masters.

Food and service levels have been raised to a better standard than that found aboard most other Costa Cruises ships to date. All printed materials (room service folio, menus, etc.) are in six languages (Italian, English, French, German, Portuguese, Spanish). The onboard currency is the US dollar or euro, depending on the region of operation.

Some tables in the Tiziano Dining Room have a less than comfortable view of the harsh lighting of the escalators between the galley and the two decks of the dining room. Too many pillars obstruct passenger flow and sight lines throughout the ship. The many pillars in the dining room make it difficult for waiters to provide proper food service. The fit and finish of some interior decoration is quite poor. The hospitality levels and service are inconsistent, and below the standard of several other "major" cruise lines.

SUITABLE FOR: *Costa Atlantica* is best suited to young (and young at heart) couples and singles (plus families with children) that enjoy big city life, piazzas and outdoor cafes, constant activity accompanied by lots of noise (some call it ambiance), late nights, entertainment that is consistently loud, and an international mix of fellow passengers.

ACCOMMODATION. There are 14 categories. There is a healthy (78 percent) proportion of outside-view to interior (no view) cabins. All cabins have twin beds that convert into a queen-sized bed, individually controlled air-conditioning, television, and telephone. Many cabins have views obstructed by lifeboats on Deck 4 (Roma Deck), the lowest of the accommodation decks, as well as some cabins on Deck 5. Some cabins have pull-down (Pullman-style) berths that are fully hidden in the ceiling when not in use. There is too much use of fluorescent lighting in the suites and cabins, and the soundproofing could be much better. Some bathroom fixtures – bath and shower taps in particular – are frustrating to use until you get the hang of them.

Some of the most desirable suites and cabins are those with private balconies on five aft-facing decks (Decks 4, 5, 6, 7, and 8) with views overlooking the stern and ship's wash. Other cabins with private balconies will find the balconies not so private – the partition between one balcony and the next is not a full partition – so you might be able to hear your neighbors.

However, these balcony occupants all have good views through glass and wood-topped railings, and the deck is made of teak. The cabins are well laid out, typically with twin beds that convert to a queen-sized bed, vanity desk (with built-in hairdryer), large TV set, personal safe, and one closet that has moveable shelves – providing more space for luggage storage. However, the lighting is fluorescent, and much too harsh. The bathroom is a simple, modular unit that has shower enclosures with soap dispenser.

The largest suites are designated Penthouse Suites, although they are really quite small when compared with suites aboard other ships of a similar size. However, they do at least offer more space to move around in, and a slightly larger, better bathroom.

CUISINE. The large Tiziano Dining Room is located in the aft section of the ship on two levels, with a spiral stairway between them. There are two seatings, with tables for two, four, six or eight. Dinner on European cruises is typically scheduled at 7pm and 9pm to accommodate the later eating habits of Europeans. Themed evenings are a part of the Costa Cruises tradition, and three different window blinds help create a different feel. However, the artwork is placed at table height, so the room seems more closed-in than it should.

Alternative Dining: A reservations-only alternative for dinner, Ristorante Club Atlantica, with menus by Gualtiero Marchesi, is available six nights a week. There is a cover/service charge of €20 per person (passengers occupying suite-grade accommodation get a free pass for one evening). The food is decidedly better than in the main dining room, although it's nothing special.

Undoubtedly the place that most people will want to see and be seen is in the informal Caffe Florian – a replica of the famous indoor/outdoor cafe that opened in 1720 in St. Mark's Square, Venice. There are four separate salons (Sala delle Stagioni, Sala del Senato, Sala Liberty, and Sala degli Uomini Illustri), and the same fascinating mosaic, marble and wood floors, opulent ceiling art, and special lampshades. Even the espresso/cappuccino machine is a duplicate of that found in the real thing. The only problem is that the chairs are much too small.

Casual breakfast and luncheon self-serve buffet-style meals can be taken in the Botticelli Buffet Restaurant, adjacent to the swimming pools, with seating both indoors and outdoors. A grill (for hamburgers and hot dogs) and a pasta bar are conveniently adjacent to the second pool, while indoors is the Napoli Pizzeria.Excellent cappuccino and espresso coffees are always available in various bars around the ship, served in the right-sized china cups.

ENTERTAINMENT. A three-deck-high showlounge (the Caruso Theater) is an imposing room, with just over 1,000 seats. Spiral stairways at the back of the lounge connect all levels. Stage shows are best seen from the upper three levels, from where the sight lines are reasonably good. Directly underneath the showlounge is the Coral Lounge, a large lounge complete with its own bar. An onboard resident troupe of singers and dancers provides the cast members for colorful, high-energy production shows. However, the production shows are loud and quite poor. For nights when there are no production shows, the showlounge presents cabaret acts such as singers, comedy jugglers, magicians, ventriloquists, and so on. These are generally ho-hum, however.

A number of bands and small musical units provide a variety of live music in many of the ship's lounges and bars, and there is a discotheque.

SPA/FITNESS. The Ischia Spa is quite expansive, spanning two decks. Facilities include a solarium, eight treatment rooms, lecture rooms, sauna and steam rooms for men and women, a beauty parlor. A large gymnasium has floor-to-ceiling windows on three sides, including forward-facing ocean views, and an aerobics room with instructor-led classes. There is also a jogging track outdoors.

The spa is operated by Steiner, a specialist concession, whose young staff will try to sell you Steiner's own-brand Elemis beauty products. Some fitness classes are free, while some, such as yoga, and kick-boxing, cost $10 per class.

Massage (including exotic massages such as Aroma Stone massage, Chakra Balancing massage and other well-being massages), facials, pedicures, and beauty salon treatments are at extra cost (massage, for example, costs about $2 per minute, plus gratuity). Do make appointments as early as possible since time slots go quickly.

● **For more extensive general information on what a Costa Cruises cruise is like, see pages 121–24.**

Costa Classica
★★★

Mid-Size Ship: . . . . .52,950 tons	Passenger Decks: 10	Cabins (for one person): 0
Lifestyle: . . . . .Standard	Total Crew: 650	Cabins (with private balcony): 10
Cruise Line: . . . . .Costa Crociere	Passengers	Cabins (wheelchair accessible): 6
(Costa Cruises)	(lower beds/all berths): 1,308/1,766	(interior)
Former Names: . . . . .none	Passenger Space Ratio	Cabin Current: . . . . . . .110 and 220 volts
Builder: . . . . .Fincantieri (Italy)	(lower beds/all berths): 40.4/29.9	Elevators: 8
Original Cost: . . . .$287 million	Crew/Passenger Ratio	Casino (gaming tables): . . . . .Yes
Entered Service: . . . . .Jan 1992	(lower beds/all berths): 2.0/2.7	Slot Machines: . . . . .Yes
Registry: . . . . .Italy	Navigation Officers: . . . . .Italian	Swimming Pools (outdoors): 2
Length (ft/m): 718.5/220.61	Cabins (total): 654	Swimming Pools (indoors): 0
Beam (ft/m): 98.4/30.80	Size Range (sq ft/m): 185.1–430.5/	Whirlpools: 4
Draft (ft/m): 25.0/7.60	17.2–40.0	Self-Service Launderette: . . . . .No
Propulsion/Propellers: . . . . .diesel	Cabins (outside view): 438	Dedicated Cinema/Seats: . . . . .No
(22,800kW)/2	Cabins (interior/no view): 216	Library: . . . . .Yes

OVERALL SCORE: 1,245 (OUT OF A POSSIBLE 2,000 POINTS)

OVERVIEW. *Costa Classica* is an all-white ship (now over 10 years old) with a straight slab-sided unflattering profile, which is topped by Costa Cruises' unmistakable trademark trio of tall yellow funnels. This was the ship that brought Costa into the mainstream of cruising, Italian-style, and was part of a multi-million plan to modernize the Costa Cruises (Costa Crociere) fleet.

Inside, the ship has contemporary, innovative Italian design and styling that is best described as befitting European tastes. The design incorporates much use of circles (large portholes instead of windows can be found in cabins on lower decks, and in the dining room, self-serve buffet area, coffee bar, and discotheque, for example). There is an excellent range of public rooms, lounges and bars. A number of specially designed business and meeting facilities can be found; the rooms provide multi-flexible configurations.

Some fascinating artwork includes six hermaphrodite statues in one lounge. There is a fine, if unconventional multi-tiered amphitheater-style showlounge, but the seats are bolt upright and downright uncomfortable for more than a few minutes. The multi-level atrium is stark, angular, and cold. The marble-covered staircases look pleasant, but are uncarpeted and a little dangerous if water or drinks are spilled on them when the ship is moving).

Perhaps the interior is best described as an innovative design project that almost works. A forward observation lounge/nightclub sits atop ship like a lump of cheese, and, unfortunately, fails to work well as a nightclub. Internet access is available from one of several computer terminals in the Internet Cafe.

BERLITZ'S RATINGS

	Possible	Achieved
Ship	500	331
Accommodation	200	133
Food	400	214
Service	400	267
Entertainment	100	60
Cruise	400	240

In November 2002 the ship was scheduled to enter dry-dock for a $10 million "chop-and-stretch" operation to increase its tonnage to 78,000, its length to 870.7 ft (265.4 meters), and its passenger capacity to 2,516. However, this was shelved due to a dispute over the quality of workmanship of the mid-section that was produced by British shipyard Cammell Laird.

There is no wrap-around promenade deck outdoors. The ship's rather slow service speed (19.5 knots) means that itineraries have to be carefully chosen, as the ship cannot compete with the newer ships with faster service speeds.

The air-conditioning system in the Tivoli Dining Room is noisy. There are too many loud, repetitious and irritating announcements. Shore excursions are very expensive. Tipping envelopes provided in your cabin state the amount you are expected to give. The onboard currency is the euro.

SUITABLE FOR: *Costa Classica* is best suited to young (and young at heart) couples and singles (plus families with children) that enjoy big city life, piazzas and outdoor cafes, constant activity accompanied by lots of noise (some call it ambiance), late nights, and entertainment that is consistently loud, and an international mix of fellow passengers.

ACCOMMODATION. There are 11 categories, the price depending on grade, size and location). These include 10 suites, while other cabins are fairly standard in size, shape, and facilities, a higher price being asked for cabins on the highest decks. All suites and cabins have twin lower beds, color television, and telephone.

Suites: The 10 suites, located in the center of Portofino Deck, each have a private rounded balcony, marble-clad bathrooms with Jacuzzi bathtub, and separate shower enclosure. There is plenty of space in the living and sleeping areas, and for the storage of luggage, as these really are very spacious suites.

Standard Outside-View/Interior (No View) Cabins: In general, the cabins are of a fairly generous size, and are laid out in a practical manner. They have cherry wood veneered cabinetry and accenting, and include a vanity desk unit with a large mirror. There are useful (unusual, for a cruise ship) sliding doors to the bathroom and closets, and the good cabin soundproofing is much appreciated. The soft furnishings are of good quality, but the room service menu is disappointing. The suites have more space (although they are not large by any means), and hand-woven bedspreads.

Some cabins have one or two extra pull-down (Pullman-style) berths – useful for families with small children.

CUISINE. The Tivoli Dining Room has a lovely indented clean white ceiling, although it is extremely noisy (there are two seatings, with dinner typically at 7pm and 9pm to accommodate the later eating habits of Europeans), and there are a good number of tables for two, as well as tables for four, six or eight. Changeable wall panels help create a European Renaissance atmosphere, albeit at the expense of blocking off windows (but during dinner, it's dark outside anyway – unless you are in the far North). Romantic candlelight dining is provided on formal nights.

For casual outdoor eating, the Alfresco Cafe, with its teak deck and traditional canvas sailcloth awning, is moderately good, depending on what you expect. Unfortunately, breakfast and luncheon buffets are repetitive, quite poor and uncreative; there is little variety, and long lines are typical. The selection of bread rolls, fruits and cheeses is disappointing.

Excellent cappuccino and espresso coffees are always available in various bars around the ship, served in the right-sized china cups.

ENTERTAINMENT. The Colosseo Theater, the ship's main showlounge, has an interesting amphitheatre-like design. However, the seats are bolt upright, and quite uncomfortable for any length of time. The Galileo discotheque, located atop the ship, for the young at heart, late of night, and hard of hearing.

SPA/FITNESS. The Caracalla Spa, located on one of the ship's uppermost decks, contains a gymnasium (with good forward-facing views over the ship's bows) with some high-tech muscle-pump machines, an aerobics exercise area, two hot tubs, Roman bath, health bar, sauna and steam rooms, and beauty salon.

The spa is operated by Steiner, a specialist concession, whose young staff will try to sell you Steiner's own-brand Elemis beauty products (spa girls have sales targets). Some fitness classes are free, while some, such as yoga and kick-boxing, cost $10 per class. However, being aboard will give you an opportunity to try some of the more exotic treatments (particularly some of the massages available). Massage (including exotic massages such as Aroma Stone massage, Chakra Balancing massage and other well-being massages), facials, pedicures, and beauty salon treatments are at extra cost (massage, for example, costs about $2 per minute, plus gratuity). Do make appointments as early as possible as time slots can go quickly.

● **For more extensive general information on what a Costa Cruises cruise is like, see pages 121–24.**

THE BRIDGE

A ship's navigation bridge is manned at all times, both at sea and in port. Besides the captain, who is master of the vessel, other senior officers take "watch" turns for four- or eight-hour periods. In addition, junior officers are continually honing their skills as experienced navigators, waiting for the day when they will be promoted to master. The captain is always in command at times of high risk, such as when the ship is entering or leaving a port, when the density of traffic is particularly high, or when visibility is severely restricted by poor weather.

Navigation has come a long way since the days of the ancient mariners, who used only the sun and the stars to calculate their course across the oceans. The space-age development of sophisticated navigation devices (using satellites) has enabled us to eliminate the guesswork of early navigation (the first global mobile satellite system came into being in 1979).

A ship's navigator today uses a variety of sophisticated instruments to pinpoint the ship's position at any time and establish its course.

Costa Concordia
★★★★

Large Resort Ship:	.........112,000 tons	Total Crew:	1,090	Cabins (with private balcony):	571
Lifestyle:	..................Standard	Passengers		Cabins (wheelchair accessible):	12
Cruise Line:	..............Costa Cruises	(lower beds/all berths):	......3,000/3,800	Cabin Current:	.......110 and 220 volts
Former Names:	.................none	Passenger Space Ratio		Elevators:	14
Builder:	.............Fincantieri (Italy)	(lower beds/all berths):	.......37.3/29.4	Casino (gaming tables):	............Yes
Original Cost:	.............$565 million	Crew/Passenger Ratio		Slot Machines:	....................Yes
Entered Service:	.............July 2006	(lower beds/all berths):	.........2.7/3.4	Swimming Pools (outdoors):	3
Registry:	........................Italy	Navigation Officers:	.............Italian	Swimming Pools (indoors):	0
Length (ft/m):	..............951.4/290.2	Cabins (total):	1,500	Whirlpools:	4
Beam (ft/m):	.................123.0/37.5	Size Range (sq ft/m):	......482.2/179.7	Self-Service Launderette:	..........No
Draft (ft/m):	................26.4/8.05		44.8/16.7	Dedicated Cinema/Seats:	..........No
Propulsion/Propellers:	......diesel-electric	Cabins (outside view):	914	Library:	........................Yes
	(34,000kW)/2 azimuthing pods	Cabins (interior/no view):	586		
Passenger Decks:	14	Cabins (for one person):	2		

OVERALL SCORE: 1,450 (OUT OF A POSSIBLE 2,000 POINTS)

OVERVIEW. This a slightly larger, extended version of *Costa Fortuna/Costa Magica*. One of the three pools can be covered by a sliding glass dome in case of poor weather (the ship operates Mediterranean cruises year-round), while one pool has a long water slide (great for kids). There is not a lot of open deck space, but *Costa Concordia* does absorb passengers well.

There are three decks full of bars and lounges plus lots of other public rooms. This ship has a nine-decks-high, glass-domed rotunda atrium lobby, with a lively bar on the lowest deck, adjacent to the reception and shore excursion desks. The Barcelona Casino is large and glitzy. There's also a chapel, and a small library that could be better, an internet center, card room, art gallery, and video game room. Most passengers are Italian.

SUITABLE FOR: *Costa Concordia* is best suited to those who enjoy entertainment that is consistently loud.

ACCOMMODATION. There are 20 price grades, from 2-bed interior (no view) cabins to 10 grand suites with private balcony, although in reality there are only three different sizes: Suites with balcony, 2- or 4-bed outside view cabins, and 2- or 4-bed interior (no-view) cabins, most of which measure about 160 sq.ft /15 sq.m. There are also two single cabins. The largest accommodation is provided in 8 Grand Suites (360 sq.ft/33.5 sq.m). They have a queen-sized bed; bathrooms have a tub and two washbasins. As suites go, they are not large.

CUISINE. There are two main dining rooms, allocated by accommodation grade and location. Both Milano and Roma restaurants have two seatings. Costa specializes in pasta – 50

BERLITZ'S RATINGS

	Possible	Achieved
Ship	500	426
Accommodation	200	152
Food	400	251
Service	400	375
Entertainment	100	64
Cruise	400	282

types are typically provided. Almost all the wines (the majority Italian) are young. The two 100-seat Samsara dining spots are for those seeking spa food; this features food prepared with reduced calories, fat and salt.

Alternative (Reservations Required) Dining Option: The Club Concordia is an 80-seat upscale dining venue with seating under a large glass dome. There's a cover charge of €23 per person, and it's worth it. Molecular Gastronomy, interpreted by famed Italian chef Ettore Bocchia, is featured. Molecular cooking consists of using liquid nitrogen in order to make food produced with more taste.

Casual Eatery: The Parigi Buffet Restaurant is a self-serve eatery for breakfast, lunch, afternoon pizzas, and beverages (coffee and tea) at any time. Good cappuccino and espresso coffees are always available in various bars (at extra cost).

Additionally, Caffeteria Helsinki (which has Nordic decor) is the place to go for decent (extra cost) coffees.

ENTERTAINMENT. The Athena Theater, spanning three decks, is quite stunning, and has a revolving stage, hydraulic orchestra pit, superb sound, and seating on three levels.

SPA/FITNESS. The The ship's Samsara Spa has more than 22,600 sq. ft (2,100 sq. meters) of spa/wellness facilities, spread over two decks. It includes a large fitness room, separate saunas, steam rooms, UVB. Samsara cabin and suite occupants get unlimited access to the spa plus two treatments and fitness or meditation lessons.

● **For more extensive general information on what a Costa Cruises cruise is like, see pages 121–24.**

Costa Europa
★★★

Large Resort Ship: . . . . .53,872 tons	Total Crew: 650	Cabins (with private balcony): 6
Lifestyle: . . . . .Standard	Passengers	Cabins (wheelchair accessible): 4
Cruise Line: . . . . .Costa Crociere	(lower beds/all berths): 1,506/1,756	Cabin Current: . . . . .110/220 volts
(Costa Cruises)	Passenger Space Ratio	Elevators: 7
Former Names: . . . .Westerdam, Homeric	(lower beds/all berths): 35.7/30.6	Casino (gaming tables): . . . . .Yes
Builder: . . . . .Meyer Werft (Germany)	Crew/Passenger Ratio	Slot Machines: . . . . .Yes
Original Cost: . . . .$150 million	(lower beds/all berths): 2.4/2.7	Swimming Pools (outdoors): 2
Entered Service: . . . . .May 1986/Apr 2002	Navigation Officers: . . . . .Italian	(1 with magrodome)
Registry: . . . . .Italy	Cabins (total): 753	Swimming Pools (indoors): 0
Length (ft/m): 797.9/243.23	Size Range (sq ft/m): 129.1–425.1/	Whirlpools: 2
Beam (ft/m): 95.1/29.00	12.0–39.5	Self-Service Launderette: . . . . .Yes (5)
Draft (ft/m): 23.6/7.20	Cabins (outside view): 501	Dedicated Cinema/Seats: Yes/237
Propulsion/Propellers: diesel (23,830kW)/2	Cabins (interior/no view): 252	Library: . . . . .Yes
Passenger Decks: 9	Cabins (for one person): 18	

OVERALL SCORE: 1,244 (OUT OF A POSSIBLE 2,000 POINTS)

OVERVIEW. *Costa Europa* was originally the Home Lines cruise ship *Homeric*, which underwent an $84 million "chop and stretch" operation in 1990 after being purchased by Holland America Line. You don't even have to look closely to tell where the mid-section was inserted, because the windows are larger than the fore and aft sections. The ship was moved to Costa Cruises (a cruise line wholly owned by Carnival Corporation) in 2002.

When Costa Cruises took over the ship, no structural changes were made, although some of the soft furnishings were changed and the decor was made brighter and more European in style, although, after a £5 million refit, surprisingly few changes are really noticeable. The funnel, however, looks surprisingly good in Costa Cruises' trademark yellow.

The ship has good teak outside decks and a wrap-around promenade deck with real wooden sunloungers. There is also a good amount of open deck space for sunbathing. There is a magrodome-covered swimming pool deck, but unfortunately it is rather small for the number of passengers carried.

The ship has elegant, functional, and restful interior decor. The public rooms are decorated in pastel tones, although some decor looks dated. The ship absorbs passengers well, and has good passenger flow, but the layout is a little awkward to learn at first.

Most of the public entertainment rooms are located on one deck, which makes access a simple matter. An addition, made when Costa Cruises took over the ship, is the Medusa Ballroom, with stage and proper hardwood dance floor. Also added were more children's facilities, for the

BERLITZ'S RATINGS

	Possible	Achieved
Ship	500	326
Accommodation	200	124
Food	400	239
Service	400	256
Entertainment	100	61
Cruise	400	238

increase in families that now choose this ship. There are several bars and lounges to choose from, some small and intimate, others larger and noisier. However, there are, fortunately, lots of nooks and crannies to play in – much nicer than the warehouse-style public rooms of the latest, larger, ships.

Costa Europa is a well-run, modern ship (comfortable, but certainly not luxurious) that provides a satisfactory cruise experience, particularly for families with children. There are few Italians among the crew, however (except in key positions), as many are from the Philippines.

Passenger gripes: communication with staff is not easy; room service is poor; there are many loud, repetitive and irritating announcements (typically, in at least four languages); shore excursions are expensive; there is some noticeable vibration in some areas. The onboard currency is the euro. Envelopes for gratuities are provided in your cabin and state the amount expected.

ACCOMMODATION. There are 13 cabin price categories; these include suites, mini-suites, outside-view cabins, and inside (no view) cabins (the price will depend on the grade, size and location you choose).

Except for the suite category cabins (there are five suites, each with king-sized beds, separate lounge area and bathroom with full size bathtub), almost all other cabins are of a similar size. In general, they are generously proportioned units that are well appointed and equipped with almost everything you need. Features include ample closet, drawer and storage space, hairdryer, and good-sized bathrooms (the towels are quite small, however). Unfortunately, there are far too many interior (no view) cabins (over 50 percent of all cabins), and the cabin soundproofing is rather poor – so you really can hear your neighbors brushing their hair. All cabin televisions receive European news channels.

Most cabins have twin beds, although there are a number that have the old-style upper and lower berths, so do make sure you request (and get) the kind of cabin with the sleeping arrangements you want when you book. Some of the larger cabins also have a sofa that turns into a bed – good for families with small children. There are four cabins for the disabled, suitably located, on higher decks, close to lifts.

CUISINE. The Orion Restaurant (enlarged by 345 sq.ft./32 sq.m. in 2006) is a traditional dining room that has a raised central, cupola-style dome, and port and starboard side portholes are highlighted at night by pleasing lighting. There are two seatings for all meals; note that on European cruises, dinner is typically at 7pm and 9pm to accommodate the later eating habits of Europeans. Also, do take note that dining room tables are extremely close together, and, except for the center section, the ceiling is quite low (being only one deck high), and so the noise level is extremely high. The service is reasonable, but communication can prove frustrating sometimes, and smiles from the waiters and assistants can only do so much.

The cuisine is Continental in nature, but, although there is plenty of food, its quality and presentation often proves disappointing. While the quality of meats is adequate, it could be better, and is often disguised with gravies and rich sauces. Fish and seafood tend to be lacking in taste and are typically overcooked, and green vegetables are hard to come by. However, good pasta dishes are served each day (the pasta is made fresh on board daily), although quantity, not quality, is what appears from the galley. Breads and rolls are typically good, but desserts tend to be past their sell-by date.

The Andromeda Restaurant and Sirens Restaurant (both located in the aft section of the ship) provide breakfast and lunch in self-serve buffet style, but lines and a crowded environment are noisy and not really enjoyable.

Excellent cappuccino and espresso coffees are always available in various bars around the ship, served in the right-sized china cups.

ENTERTAINMENT. Entertainment facilities include the Atlantic Theater, the ship's two-decks-high showlounge, with seating on both main and balcony levels. However, several pillars obstruct sightlines from a number of seats.

An onboard resident troupe of singers and dancers provides the cast members for colorful, high-energy production shows. However, these are quite poor compared to many of the shows aboard similar sized ships, and there seems to be little consistency when it comes to entertainment strategy. Stage smoke is used a lot during the production shows, and the volume is ear-splitting. For nights when production shows are not featured, the showlounge presents cabaret acts such as singers, comedy jugglers, magicians, ventriloquists, and so on. These are generally ho-hum, however, and are more based on price rather than coherent themes.

A number of bands and small musical units provide live music in many of the ship's lounges and bars – so there is always plenty of music to dance to or listen to, from light classical to jazz to pop, dance and rap. In addition, there is a discotheque for the young at heart and hard of hearing.

SPA/FITNESS. The Nereidi Fitness Center (located on an upper deck, aft of the ship's mast) includes a gymnasium, saunas and massage rooms, although there is no steam room. The facility is rally small, considering the number of passengers carried – although, to be fair, such facilities were not very popular when the ship was built.

The spa is operated by Steiner, a specialist concession, whose young staff will try to sell you Steiner's own-brand Elemis beauty products (spa girls have sales targets). Some fitness classes are free, while some, such as yoga and kick-boxing, cost $10 per class.

However, being aboard will give you an opportunity to try some of the more exotic treatments (particularly some of the massages available). Massage (including Aroma Stone massage, Chakra Balancing massage and other well-being massages), facials, pedicures, and beauty salon treatments cost extra (massage, for example, costs about $2 per minute, plus gratuity). Do make appointments as early as possible – aboard a ship so large, time slots go quickly, so the day you board is the best time to book your treatments.

● **For more extensive general information on what a Costa Cruises cruise is like, see pages 121–24.**

Costa Fortuna
★★★★

Large Resort Ship: ....102,587 tons	Passenger Decks: 13	Cabins (for one person): 0
Lifestyle: ....Standard	Total Crew: 1,068	Cabins (with private balcony): 522
Cruise Line: Costa Crociere (Costa Cruises)	Passengers	Cabins (wheelchair accessible): 8
Former Names: ....none	(lower beds/all berths): 2,716/3,470	Cabin Current: ....220 volts
Builder: ....Cantieri Sestri Navale (Italy)	Passenger Space Ratio	Elevators: 14
Original Cost: ....$381 million	(lower beds/all berths): 37.7/29.5	Casino (gaming tables): ....Yes
Entered Service: ....November 2003	Crew/Passenger Ratio	Slot Machines: ....Yes
Registry: ....Italy	(lower beds/all berths): 2.5/3.2	Swimming Pools (outdoors): 3
Length (ft/m): 892.3/272.0	Navigation Officers: ....Italian	Swimming Pools (indoors): 0
Beam (ft/m): 124.6/38.0	Cabins (total): 1,358	Whirlpools: 5
Draft (ft/m): 27.2/8.3	Size Range (sq ft/m): 179.7–482.2/	Self-Service Launderette: ....No
Propulsion/Propellers: ....diesel-electric		16.7–44.8	Dedicated Cinema/Seats: ....No
34,000kW/2 azimuthing pods	Cabins (outside view): 857	Library: ....Yes
(17.6 MW each)	Cabins (interior/no view): 501	

OVERALL SCORE: 1,444 (OUT OF A POSSIBLE 2,000 POINTS)

OVERVIEW. The design of *Costa Fortuna* (together with sister ship *Costa Magica*, which made its debut in 2004) is based on the platform of *Carnival Triumph* and, although the bow is extremely short, the ship presents a well balanced profile. The name Fortuna is an interesting one: in Greek mythology, Fortuna is the daughter of Poseidon (it's also the name of the Temple Fortuna, located along one of the conserved streets of Pompeii).

The aft decks are tiered, with cut off quarters that make the ship look less square than it otherwise would. There are three pools, one of which can be covered by a sliding glass dome (magrodome) in case of inclement weather, while one pool has a long water slide. There is not a lot of open deck space for the number of passengers carried, so sunloungers tend to be crammed together (there are no cushioned pads).

Costa Fortuna is built to impress the trendy city-dweller at every turn, and the ship absorbs passengers quite well, with a good passenger space ratio. The interior decor focuses on the Italian passenger ships of yesteryear, so much of the finishing detail replicates the Art Deco interiors fitted aboard ocean liners such as the *Conte de Savoia*, *Michaelangelo*, *Neptunia*, *Rafaello*, *Rex*, etc., although in the kind of contemporary colors not associated with such ships (their interiors were rather subdued). Deck names are those of major cities in Europe and South America (examples: Barcelona, Buenos Aires, Caracas, Lisbon, Genoa, Miami). Passenger flow is generally good, with few congestion points.

There are three decks full of lounges, and 11 bars. The interior focal point is a nine-deck high, glass-domed rotunda

BERLITZ'S RATINGS

	Possible	Achieved
Ship	500	426
Accommodation	200	146
Food	400	251
Service	400	275
Entertainment	100	64
Cruise	400	282

atrium lobby: it houses the Costa Bar on the lower level, a bank of four glass-walled elevators, and, in a tribute to ship buffs, some 26 models of Italian ships past and present, glued upside down on the ceiling – it's a weird feeling to look at them and then look at your feet. The lowest three decks connect the public rooms, the upper levels being mainly for accommodation decks. For those who like to gamble, the Neptunia 1932 Casino is the place to go. There's also a chapel – standard aboard all Costa ships – and a small library that's a bit of a token gesture, an internet center, card room, art gallery, and video game room.

The greater percentage of passengers are Italian, so the ship is lively, but quite noisy, with lots of children running around (particularly during school holiday periods). There are few Italians among the crew, however (except in key positions), as many are from the Philippines.

ACCOMMODATION. There are 15 price grades, from 2-bed interior cabins to grand suites with private balcony, although in reality there are only three different sizes: Suites with balcony, 2- or 4-bed outside view cabins (some 335 of which have portholes rather than windows), and 2- or 4-bed interior (no-view) cabins. There are also two single cabins – quite unusual for a large ship. In an example of good design, no cabins have lifeboat obstructed views – something not easy with large ships such as this.

The largest accommodation can be found in 8 Grand Suites, located in the center of the ship on one of the higher decks. They have a queen-sized bed; bathrooms have a bathtub and two washbasins.

Wheelchair-accessible cabins: Note that 12 of the most

desirable (outside-view) wheelchair-accessible cabins are rather idiotically located a long way from elevators, while 8 interior (no view) cabins are located close to elevators.

CUISINE. There are two dining rooms: the Michelangelo 1965 Restaurant (aft), whose ceiling features frescoes by the Great Masters, and the Rafaello 1965 Restaurant (mid-ships), are both two decks high and have two seatings. Dinner on European cruises is typically scheduled at 7pm and 9pm. Over 50 types of pasta are available during a typical one-week cruise. There is a wine list, although there are no wine waiters, and nearly all the wines (mostly Italian) are young.

Alternative (Reservations Required) Dining Option: The Conte Grande 1927 Club is an upscale dining spot with seating for around 150 under a huge glass dome (if the lights were turned out, you might be able to see the stars). In its show kitchen, chefs can be seen preparing their masterpieces. Fine table settings, china, silverware and leather-bound menus are used. Reservations are required and there is a cover charge of $18.75 per person (for service and tip).

The Christoforo Columbus 1954 Buffet Restaurant is a self-serve eatery for breakfast, lunch, afternoon pizzas, and beverages at any time. Excellent cappuccino and espresso coffees are always available in the various bars aboard the ship.

ENTERTAINMENT. The Rex 1932 Theater spans three decks in the ship's forwardmost section. It is the setting for all production shows and large-scale cabaret acts, is quite stunning, and has a revolving stage, hydraulic orchestra pit, superb sound, and seating on three levels (the upper levels being tiered through two decks). Volume levels are high.

SPA/FITNESS. Facilities in the two-deck high Saturnia Spa (it measures about 14,424 sq. ft/1,340 sq. meters) include a large solarium, eight treatment rooms, sauna and steam rooms for men and women, and a beauty parlor. The gymnasium (it's full of techno-gym equipment for those into muscle-pumping and exertion) has floor-to-ceiling windows on three sides, including forward-facing ocean views, and there's an aerobics section with instructor-led classes (some, such as yoga, kick-boxing, cost extra). If you want to be near the spa, note that there are 18 two-bed cabins (with ocean view windows) located adjacent (aft) of the spa.

● **For more extensive general information on what a Costa Cruises cruise is like, see pages 121–24.**

STEERING

Two different methods can be used to steer a ship:

Electrohydraulic steering uses automatic (telemotor-type) transmission from the wheel itself to the steering gear aft. This is generally used when traffic is heavy, during maneuvers into and out of ports, or when there is poor visibility.

Automatic steering (gyropilot) is used only in the open sea. This system does not require anyone at the wheel because it is controlled by computer. However, aboard all ships, a quartermaster is always at the wheel, for extra safety, and just in case a need should arise to switch from one steering system to another.

Satellite Navigator

Using this latest high-tech piece of equipment, ship's officers can read, on a small television screen, the ship's position in the open ocean anywhere in the world, any time, and in any weather with pinpoint accuracy.

Satellite navigation systems use the information transmitted by a constellation of orbiting satellites. Each is in a normal circular polar orbit at an altitude of 450 to 700 nautical miles, and orbits the Earth in about 108 minutes.

Data from each gives the current orbital position every two minutes. Apart from telling the ship where it is, it continuously provides the distance from any given point, calculates the drift caused by currents and so on, and tells the ship when the next satellite will pass.

The basis of the satellite navigation is the US Navy Satellite System (NNSS). This first became operational in January 1964 as the precision guidance system for the Polaris submarine fleet and was made available for commercial use in 1967.

The latest (and more accurate) system is the GPS (Global Positioning System), which is now fitted to an increasing number of ships. This uses 24 satellites (18 of which are on-line at any given time) that provide accuracy in estimating a ship's position to plus or minus 6 ft. Another variation is the NACOS (Navigational Command System), which collects information from a variety of sources: satellites, radar, gyroscopic compass, speed log, and surface navigational systems as well as engines, thrusters, rudders, and human input. It then displays relevant computations and information on one screen, controlled by a single keyboard.

Costa Luminosa
NOT YET RATED

Large Resort Ship: ....92,700 tons	Total Crew: 1,050	Cabins (with private balcony): 772
Lifestyle: ....Standard	Passengers	Cabins (wheelchair accessible): 12
Cruise Line: ....Costa Cruises	(lower beds/all berths): 2,260/2,828	Cabin Voltage: ....110 volts
Former Names: ....-	Passenger Space Ratio	Elevators: 12
Builder: ....Fincantieri (Italy)	(lower beds/all berths): 41.0/32.7	Casino (gaming tables): ....Yes
Original Cost: ....€420 million	Crew/Passenger Ratio	Slot Machines: ....Yes
Entered Service: ....May 2009	(lower beds/all berths): 2.1/2.6	Swimming Pools (outdoors): 2
Registry: ....Italy	Navigation Officers: ....Italian	Swimming Pools (indoors): 1
Length (ft/m): 958.0/292.0	Cabins (total): 1,130	(with retractable roof)
Beam (ft/m): 111.5/34.0	Size Range (sq ft/m): 134.5-534.0/	Whirlpools: ....
Draft (ft/m): 26.2/8.0	12.5-49.6	Self-Service Launderette: ....No
Propulsion/Propellers: .....diesel-electric	Cabins (outside view): 951	Dedicated Cinema/Seats: ....No
(42,000 kW)/2 pods	Cabins (interior/no view): 179	Library: ....Yes
Passenger Decks: 13	Cabins (for one person): 0	

OVERALL SCORE: NYR (OUT OF A POSSIBLE 2,000 POINTS)

OVERVIEW. *Costa Luminosa* (a sister ship to Cunard Line's *Queen Elizabeth*, set to debut in 2010) is the new flagship of Costa Cruises, and constructed as what is termed a Vista-class ship. A 4-D cinema features sound and lighting effects, with scent pumped in to heighten the experience.

Its two-deck midships Lido area swimming pool can be covered with a sliding glass roof. There's also a large 193.7-sq ft (18-sq meter) poolside movie screen. Other sporting features include a large Samsara Spa and a roller skating track.

The interior decor, which includes fine marble, wood and mother of pearl , pays tribute to light and lighting, as you might expect from a ship called *Costa Luminosa*, so it feels a little like cruising in a special effects bubble, albeit an elegant one. The public rooms include 11 bars, a large Vega Casino, and lots of lounges and entertainment venues.

Printed materials such as room service folio and menus are in six languages (Italian, English, French, German, Portuguese, Spanish). The onboard currency is the euro, and gratuities are not included in the cruise price.

ACCOMMODATION. About 68% of all accommodation suites and cabins have an ocean view. Four suites and 52 Samsara Spa cabins are located adjacent to (and considered part of) the designated wellness area. Samsara suite/cabin occupants get unlimited access to the spa plus two treatments and fitness or meditation lessons as part of their package, and dine in one of the two Samsara restaurants. All Samsara-designated accommodation grades receive Samsara bathroom personal amenities.

A pillow menu, with five choices, is available to suite-grade accommodation occupants, who also get bathrobes, better

BERLITZ'S RATINGS		
	Possible	Achieved
Ship	500	NYR
Accommodation	200	NYR
Food	400	NYR
Service	400	NYR
Entertainment	100	NYR
Cruise	400	NYR

amenities than standard-grade cabin occupants, a shaving mirror, and walk-in closets – although the hangers are plastic. Note that background music is played 24 hours a day in all hallways and elevators, so you may well be aware of it if you are a light sleeper.

CUISINE. The Taurus Restaurant is the large, main restaurant. It is located at the aft of the ship and there are two seatings for dinner. The Samsara Restaurant is for occupants of Samsara-grade accommodation, and is located adjacent to the Taurus Restaurant.

The Club Luminosa is a reservations-only, intimate restaurant that features à la carte dining with a show kitchen as part of the venue. The food is cooked à la minute and so it is fresher, looks better, and tastes better than food in the main dining room. It's a good idea to go for a meal in this venue, particularly to celebrate a special occasion.

The Andromeda Buffet is the self-serve casual eatery. While there appears to be a decent choice of food, the layout of the venue invites congestion due to some narrow passageways

ENTERTAINMENT. The Phoenix Theater, with over 800 seats, spans three decks and is the ship's principal showlounge; it will appear as if lit by a rainbow of lighting effects.

SPA/FITNESS. This area contains 37,674 sq ft (3,500 sq meters) of Samsara Spa space. Not far away, a Grand Prix Formula One simulator is housed in a glass enclosure. For tee-time, a golf simulator provides a choice of 37 18-hole courses.

● **For more extensive general information on what a Costa Cruises cruise is like, see pages 121–24.**

Costa Magica
★★★★

Large Resort Ship: ....102,587 tons	Passenger Decks: 13	Cabins (with private balcony): 522
Lifestyle: ....Standard	Total Crew: 1,068	Cabins (wheelchair accessible): 8
Cruise Line: Costa Crociere (Costa Cruises)	Passengers	Cabin Current: ....220 volts
Former Names: ....none	(lower beds/all berths): 2,718/3,788	Elevators: 14
Builder: ....Fincantieri (Italy)	Passenger Space Ratio	Casino (gaming tables): ....Yes
Original Cost: ....$418.5 million	(lower beds/all berths): 37.7/27.0	Slot Machines: ....Yes
Entered Service: ....November 2004	Crew/Passenger Ratio	Swimming Pools (outdoors): 3
Registry: ....Italy	(lower beds/all berths): 2.5/3.2	Swimming Pools (indoors): 0
Length (ft/m): 893.3/272.3	Navigation Officers: ....Italian	Whirlpools: 5
Beam (ft/m): 124.6/38	Cabins (total): 1,359	Self-Service Launderette: ....No
Draft (ft/m): 27.2/8.3	Size Range (sq ft/m): 179.7/482.2	Dedicated Cinema/Seats: ....No
Propulsion/Propellers: ....diesel-electric	Cabins (outside view): 857	Library: ....Yes
34,000kW/2	Cabins (interior/no view): 501	
azimuthing pods (17.6 MW each)	Cabins (for one person): 0	

OVERALL SCORE: 1,445 (OUT OF A POSSIBLE 2,000 POINTS)

OVERVIEW. *Costa Magica* is built to impress at every turn. The ship absorbs passengers quite well, with a good passenger space ratio. Passenger flow is generally good. There is not a lot of open deck space for the number of passengers carried, so sunloungers tend to be crammed together. The interior decor is inspired by some of Italy's "magic" places (examples include Costa Smerelda, Isola Bella, Portofino, Spoleto).

There are three decks full of lounges (all named after Italian places), 11 bars, and lots of rooms to play in. The ship's life center features a nine-deck high, glass-domed rotunda atrium lobby which houses the Costa Bar on the lower level. The Sicily Casino (look out for the shiny armor, helmets and shields) is big, glitzy and noisy. There's also a chapel. The Bressanone Library is a nice room, although it is only open about an hour each day.

Most passengers are Italian, so the ship is lively (noisy), with lots of children running around (particularly during school holidays). There are few Italians among the crew, (except in key positions), as many are from the Philippines.

ACCOMMODATION. There are 15 price grades, from two-bed interior cabins to grand suites with private balcony. There are also two single cabins (unusual for a large ship). No cabins have lifeboat obstructed views. The largest accommodation can be found in 8 Grand Suites, located in the center of the ship on one of the higher decks. They have a queen-sized bed; bathrooms have a tub and two washbasins.
Wheelchair-accessible cabins: Note that 12 of the most desirable (outside-view) wheelchair-accessible cabins are rather idiotically located a long way from elevators, while 8 interior (no view) cabins are located close to elevators.

BERLITZ'S RATINGS		
	Possible	Achieved
Ship	500	427
Accommodation	200	146
Food	400	251
Service	400	275
Entertainment	100	64
Cruise	400	282

CUISINE. The two dining rooms, Costa Smeralda Restaurant (aft) and the Portofino Restaurant (midships), are both two decks high, and both have two seatings. Dinner on European cruises is typically scheduled at 7pm and 9pm. Almost all the wines are young.
Alternative (Reservations Required) Dining Option: The Vincenza Tavernetta Club is an upscale dining spot with seating for around 150 under a huge glass dome. Fine table settings, Versace china, woven cloth napkins, fine silverware and leather-bound menus are used. The recipes, from Belloni and Belloni, are excellent. There is a cover charge of $18.75 per person.

The Bellagio Buffet Restaurant is a self-serve eatery for breakfast, lunch, afternoon pizzas, and beverages at any time. The bars serve excellent cappuccino and espresso coffees.

ENTERTAINMENT. The Urbino Theater spans three decks in the forwardmost section of the ship. It is the setting for all production shows and large-scale cabaret acts, is quite stunning, and has a revolving stage, hydraulic orchestra pit, superb sound, and seating on three levels.

SPA/FITNESS. Facilities in the two-deck high Saturnia Spa include a large solarium, eight treatment rooms, sauna and steam rooms for men and women, and a beauty parlor. The gymnasium is full of techno-gym equipment. There's an aerobics section with instructor-led classes (some, such as yoga, kick-boxing, cost extra).

● **For more extensive general information on what a Costa Cruises cruise is like, see pages 121–24.**

Costa Marina
★★ +

Mid-Size Ship: . . . . .25,441 tons	Passenger Decks: 8	Cabins (for one person): 0
Lifestyle: . . . . .Standard	Total Crew: 400	Cabins (with private balcony): 8
Cruise Line: . . . . .Costa Crociere	Passengers	Cabins (wheelchair accessible): 0
(Costa Cruises)	(lower beds/all berths): 772/1,005	Cabin Current: . . . . .110 and 220 volts
Former Names: . . . . .Axel Johnson	Passenger Space Ratio	Elevators: 8
Builder: . . . . . . .Mariotti Shipyards (Italy)	(lower beds/all berths): 32.9/25.3	Casino (gaming tables): . . . . .Yes
Original Cost: . . . .$130 million	Crew/Passenger Ratio	Slot Machines: . . . . .Yes
Entered Service: . . . . .July 1990	(lower beds/all berths): 1.9/2.5	Swimming Pools (outdoors): 1
Registry: . . . . .Italy	Navigation Officers: . . . . .Italian	Swimming Pools (indoors): 0
Length (ft/m): 571.8/174.25	Cabins (total): 386	Whirlpools: 3
Beam (ft/m): 84.6/25.75	Size Range (sq ft/m):104.4–264.8/9.7–24.6	Self-Service Launderette: . . . . .No
Draft (ft/m): 26.1/8.20	Cabins (outside view): 183	Dedicated Cinema/Seats: . . . . .No
Propulsion/Propellers: diesel (19,152kW)/2	Cabins (interior/no view): 205	Library: . . . . .Yes

---

OVERALL SCORE: 1,090 (OUT OF A POSSIBLE 2,000 POINTS)

OVERVIEW. This angular-looking vessel, converted from a container carrier, has a contemporary, cutaway stern that is virtually replaced by a glass wall (in fact, the dining room windows), and a stark cluster of three yellow funnels. Today the design seems dated.

Most of the public rooms are above the accommodation decks and include several bars and lounges. There is generally good passenger flow throughout its public room spaces, although congestion occurs between first and second dinner seatings.

In 2002, *Costa Marina* underwent a considerable amount of interior redecoration and emerged as an Italian ship for German-speaking passengers ("La Deutsche Vita"). The onboard currency is the euro.

The fit and finish of this vessel, when it debuted as a cruise ship, were well below standard. There is a very limited amount of open deck and sunbathing space, and no observation lounge with forward-facing views. The swimming pool is very small. There are simply too many interior (no view) cabins. The library is really poor. Tipping envelopes in your cabin state the level of tip expected.

SUITABLE FOR: *Costa Marina* is best suited to young (and young at heart) German-speaking couples and singles (plus families with children) that enjoy European city life, plenty of activities, and entertainment that is consistently loud.

ACCOMMODATION. There are 12 categories, ranked by grade, size and location. Both the outside view and interior (no view) cabins are quite comfortable, but have plain, almost clinical, decor. Bathrooms are functional, but there is little space for toiletry items. The room service menu is poor.

BERLITZ'S RATINGS

	Possible	Achieved
Ship	500	275
Accommodation	200	120
Food	400	192
Service	400	226
Entertainment	100	58
Cruise	400	219

CUISINE. The 452-seat Cristal Restaurant is fairly spacious and has expansive glass windows overlooking the stern, while port and starboard sides have large portholes. There are two seatings but few tables for two, most of the tables being for four, six or eight. Romantic candlelight dining is typically featured on a formal night.

The cuisine is Continental in nature (with some German regional specialties). The quality of meats is good, although it is often disguised with gravies and rich sauces. Fish and seafood tend to be lacking in taste and are typically overcooked, and green vegetables are hard to come by. However, good pasta dishes are served each day (the pasta is made fresh on board daily), although quantity, not quality, is what appears from the galley. While the breads and rolls are typically good, the desserts are not. There is a wine list, although almost all wines are young – very young.

Excellent cappuccino and espresso coffees are always available in various bars, served in proper china cups.

ENTERTAINMENT. The Tropicana Showroom is a single level room; however, 14 pillars obstruct many sight lines from many seats. The room is adequate as a cabaret lounge.

SPA/FITNESS. The spa/fitness facilities are not large, but they include a solarium, several treatment rooms, sauna and steam rooms for men and women, beauty salon and gymnasium with floor-to-ceiling windows on three sides. There is also a jogging track outdoors.

● **For more extensive general information on what a Costa Cruises cruise is like, see pages 121–24.**

Costa Mediterranea
★★★★

Large Resort Ship: ....85,700 tons	Passenger Decks:..................11	Cabins (with private balcony): 742
Lifestyle: ....Standard	Total Crew: 920	Cabins (wheelchair accessible): 8
Cruise Line: ....Costa Crociere	Passengers	Cabin Current: ....110 volts
(Costa Cruises)	(lower beds/all berths): 2,112/2,680	Elevators: 12
Former Names: ....none	Passenger Space Ratio	Casino (gaming tables): ....Yes
Builder: ...Kvaerner Masa-Yards (Finland)	(lower beds/all berths): 40.5/31.9	Slot Machines: ....Yes
Original Cost: ....$335 million	Crew/Passenger Ratio	Swimming Pools (outdoors): 2
Entered Service: ....May 2003	(lower beds/all berths): 2.2/2.9	(+1 indoor/outdoor)
Registry:......................Italy	Navigation Officers: ....Italian	Swimming Pools (indoors): ....No
Length (ft/m): 959.6/292.5	Cabins (total): 1,056	Whirlpools: ....Yes
Beam (ft/m): 105.6/32.2	Size Range (sq ft/m): 161.4–387.5/	Self-Service Launderette: ....No
Draft (ft/m): 25.5/7.8	15.0–36.0	Dedicated Cinema/Seats: ....No
Propulsion/Propellers: .....diesel-electric	Cabins (outside view): 843	Library: ....Yes
(34,000 kW)/2 azimuthing pods	Cabins (interior/no view): 213	
(17.6 MW each)	Cabins (for one person): 0	

OVERALL SCORE: 1,437 (OUT OF A POSSIBLE 2,000 POINTS)

OVERVIEW. The first thing that regular passengers will notice is the length of this ship, which gives it an attractive sleekness. There are two centrally located swimming pools outdoors, one of which can be used in poor weather due to its retractable glass dome (magrodome) cover. A bar abridges two adjacent whirlpool tubs. Another smaller pool is for children; there is also a winding water slide that spans two decks in height (it starts on a platform bridge located at the aft funnel). There is also an additional whirlpool tub outdoors.

Inside, the layout is just the same as in sister ship *Costa Atlantica*. The interior design is, however, bold and brash – a mix of classical Italy and contemporary features. There is good passenger flow from one public space to another, several floor spaces for dancing, and a range of bars and lounges for socializing. The dramatic eight-deck atrium lobby, with two grand stairways, presents a stunning wall decoration consisting of two huge paintings and 25-piece wall sculpture by Gigi Rigamonte (called *Danza*) that is best seen from any of the multiple viewing balconies on each deck above the main lobby-floor level (the squid-shaped wall lighting sconces are neat, too). But pillars throughout the ship obstruct passenger flow and pillars in the dining room provide an obstacle course for waiters.

The decor is said to be inspired by many Italian palaces (some known, many not) and by a profound live for art and architecture. It is extremely upbeat, bright, glitzy, and in-your-face wherever you go – I was amused by one of three larger-than-life digital faces of Dionisio in the Dionisio Lounge, with a door handle that sticks out of his mouth

BERLITZ'S RATINGS		
	Possible	Achieved
Ship	500	426
Accommodation	200	152
Food	400	240
Service	400	273
Entertainment	100	64
Cruise	400	282

in a style that recalls Monty Python. A small chapel is located forward of the uppermost level. Other facilities include a winding shopping street with boutique stores (typically including Fendi, Fossil, Paul & Shark Yachting), a photo gallery, video games room, observation balcony, a large Grand Canal Casino, and a library (with internet access but very few books). Food and service levels have been raised to a better standard than that found aboard most other Costa Cruises ships to date. But do expect irritating announcements (particularly for activities that bring in revenue, such as art auctions, bingo, horse racing), and much hustling for drinks. All printed materials (room service folio, menus, etc.) are in six languages (Italian, English, French, German, Portuguese, Spanish). The onboard currency is the euro or US dollar, depending on region of operation.

SUITABLE FOR: The vessel is best suited to young (and young at heart) couples and singles (plus families with children) that enjoy big city life, piazzas and outdoor cafes, constant activity accompanied by lots of noise, late nights, loud entertainment, and an international mix of passengers.

ACCOMMODATION. There are 14 price grades. There is a healthy (78 percent) proportion of outside-view to interior (no view) cabins. All of the cabins have twin beds that can be converted into a queen-sized bed, individually controlled air-conditioning, television, and telephone. Some many cabins have their views obstructed by lifeboats – on Deck 4 (Roma Deck), the lowest of the accommodation decks, as well as some cabins on Deck 5. Some cabins have pull-down Pullman berths that are fully hidden in the ceiling when not in use. There is too much use of fluorescent lighting in the suites and cabins, and the soundproofing could be much better. Some bathroom fixtures – bath and shower taps in particular – are frustrating to use until you get the hang of them.

Some of the most desirable suites and cabins are those with private balconies on the five aft-facing decks (Decks 4, 5, 6, 7, and 8) with views overlooking the stern and ship's wash. The other cabins with private balconies will find the balconies not so private – the partition between one balcony and the next is not a full partition, so you will be able to hear your neighbors (or smell their smoke).

However, these balcony occupants all have good views through glass and wood-topped railings, and the deck is made of teak. The cabins are well laid out, typically with twin beds that convert to a queen-sized bed, vanity desk (with built-in hairdryer), large television, personal safe, and one closet that has moveable shelves – thus providing more space for luggage storage. However, note that the lighting is fluorescent, and much too harsh (the bedside control is for a master switch only – other individual lights cannot be controlled). The bathroom is a simple, modular unit that has shower enclosures with soap dispenser; there is a good amount of stowage space for personal toiletry items.

The largest suites are those designated as Penthouse Suites, although they are really quite small when compared with suites aboard other ships of a similar size. However, they do at least offer more space to move around in, and a slightly larger, better bathroom.

CUISINE. The Ristorante degli Argentiere, the ship's main dining room, is extremely large and is located at the aft section of the ship on two levels with a spiral stairway between them. There are two seatings, with tables for two, four, six or eight. Dinner on European cruises is typically scheduled at 7pm and 9pm. Some tables in the dining room have a less than comfortable view of the harsh lighting of the escalators between the galley and the two decks of the dining room.

Alternative (Reservations-Only, Extra Cost) Dining: The Medusa Supper Club (with menu by Zeffirino – a famous restaurant in Genoa) is a more upscale dining spot located on two of the uppermost decks of the ship under a huge glass dome, with seating for approximately 150. It has an open kitchen where chefs can be seen preparing their masterpieces. Fine table settings, china and silverware are featured, as are leather-bound menus. Reservations are required and there is a cover charge of €20 per person (for service and tip). But you may think it's worth it in order to have dinner in a setting that is quieter and more refined than the main dining room.

The Perla del Lago Buffet is an extensive eatery that forms the aft third of Deck 9 (part of it also wraps around the upper section of the huge atrium). It includes a central area with several small buffet counters; there are salad counters, a dessert counter, and a 24-hour Posillipo Pizzeria counter, all forming a large eatery with indoor and outdoor seating. Movement around the buffet area is very slow, and requires you to stand in line for everything. Venture outdoors and you'll find a grill (for hamburgers and hot dogs) and a pasta bar, both conveniently located adjacent to the second of two swimming pools on the lido deck.

Other Venues: The place that most people will want to see and be seen is at the casual Oriental Cafe; there are four separate salons, which provide intimate spaces for drinks, conversation, and people-watching. Excellent cappuccino and espresso coffees are always available in various bars around the ship, served in the right-sized china cups.

ENTERTAINMENT. The Osiris Theater is the principal venue for all production shows and major cabaret acts. It spans three decks, and seating on all three levels. Sightlines to the stage are better from the second and third levels. Spiral stairways at the back of the lounge connect all three levels.

SPA/FITNESS. The expansive Ischia Spa spans two decks, is located directly above the navigation bridge in the forward part of the ship (accessed by the forward stairway elevators) and has approximately 13,700 sq. ft (1,272 sq. meters) of space. Facilities on the lower level include a solarium, eight treatment rooms, lecture rooms, sauna and steam rooms for men and women, a beauty parlor; the upper level consists of a large gymnasium with floor-to-ceiling windows on three sides, including forward-facing ocean views, and an aerobics room with instructor-led classes (the aerobics room and gymnasium together measure almost 6,000 sq. ft (557 sq. meters). There is also a jogging track outdoors, around the ship's mast and the forward third of the ship, as well as a multi-purpose court for basketball, volleyball and deck tennis.

● **For more extensive general information on what a Costa Cruises cruise is like, see pages 121–24.**

Costa Pacifica
NOT YET RATED

Large Resort Ship: . . . . 114,500 tons	Passenger Decks: 13	Cabins (for one person): 0
Lifestyle: . . . . Standard	Total Crew: 1,110	Cabins (with private balcony): 579
Cruise Line: . . . . Costa Cruises	Passengers	Cabins (wheelchair accessible): 12
Former Names: . . . . none	(lower beds/all berths): 3,012/3,780	Cabin Voltage: . . . . 110/220 volts
Builder: . . . . Fincantieri (Italy)	Passenger Space Ratio	Elevators: 14
Original Cost: . . . . €510 million	(lower beds/all berths): 38.0/30.2	Casino (gaming tables): . . . . Yes
Entered Service: . . . . Apr 2009	Crew/Passenger Ratio	Slot Machines: . . . . Yes
Registry: . . . . Italy	(lower beds/all berths): 2.7/3.4	Swimming Pools (outdoors): 2
Length (ft/m): 952.0/290.0	Navigation Officers: . . . . Italian	Swimming Pools (indoors): . . . . 2 (glass dome)
Beam (ft/m): 116.4/35.5	Cabins (total): 1,506	Whirlpools: 5
Draft (ft/m): 27.2/8.3	Size Range (sq ft/m): . . 179.7–482.2/16.7–44.8	Self-Service Launderette: . . . . No
Propulsion/Propellers: . . . . diesel-electric	Cabins (outside view): 926	Dedicated Cinema/Seats: . . . . No
(34,000kW)/2 azimuthing pods	Cabins (interior/no view): 580	Library: . . . . Yes

OVERALL SCORE: NYR (OUT OF A POSSIBLE 2,000 POINTS)

OVERVIEW. Sporting a single, large funnel, *Costa Pacifica* is a sister to the popular *Costa Concordia* and *Costa Serena*. Two pool areas can be covered with retractable glass domes – good in case of inclement weather – and one of the pools has a water slide (great for kids). There is also a huge screen for poolside movies. A Grand Prix simulator is available on one of the upper decks.

However, the open deck space is cramped when the ship is full, so sunloungers tend to be crammed together, and they do not have cushioned pads.

This ship has a musical interior design theme featuring the "greatest hits." The lobby, for example, appears to be covered in musical symbols and instruments. The passenger flow inside is quite good, and the ship absorbs passengers reasonably well. It also provides a decent passenger space ratio, which means that it won't feel too crowded.

There are three decks full of bars and lounges plus many other public rooms. This ship has a glass-domed rotunda atrium lobby that is nine decks high, with great upward views from the lobby bar, as well as from its four glass panoramic elevators. The casino is large and glitzy, always lively and entertaining (slot machines occupy a separate area to gaming tables, so serious gamers can concentrate). There's also a very small library, an internet-connection center, card room, art gallery, and video game room, together with several other bars and lounges. A chapel is a standard aboard all Costa ships.

Although Costa Cruises is noted for its "Italian" style, ambience and spirit, there are few Italian crew members on board its ships. While many of the officers are Italian, most of the crew members – particularly the dining room and housekeeping staff – are from the Philippines. The

BERLITZ'S RATINGS		
	Possible	Achieved
Ship	500	NYR
Accommodation	200	NYR
Food	400	NYR
Service	400	NYR
Entertainment	100	NYR
Cruise	400	NYR

lifestyle on board is, however, perceived to be Italian – lively, noisy, with lots of love for life and a love of all things casual – even on so-called "formal" nights. Most passengers will be Italian, with a sprinkling of other European nationals. One night, at the end of each cruise, is typically reserved for a "Roman Bacchanal" night on Europe/Mediterranean cruises – when it's fun to dress up toga-style for dinner and beyond.

Printed materials such as room service folio and menus will typically be in six languages (Italian, English, French, German, Portuguese, and Spanish). During peak European school holiday periods, particularly Christmas and Easter, expect to be cruising with a lot of children of all ages.

Costa Cruises is a cruise line for those who like to enjoy life and party. As aboard other Costa ships, note that for embarkation, few staff members are on duty at the gangway when you arrive; they merely point you in the direction of your deck, or to the ship's elevators and do not escort you to your cabin.

SUITABLE FOR: Costa Cruises does a good job of providing first-time cruise passengers with a well-packaged holiday, particularly for families with children, that is a mix of sophistication and chaos, accompanied by loud music everywhere. This is a cruise line for those who like to enjoy life and party.

ACCOMMODATION. There are 20 price grades, from 2-bed interior cabins to grand suites with private balcony, although in reality there are only three different sizes: Suites with "private" balcony (which are really not particularly large in comparison with some other large ships), 2- or 4-bed outside view cabins, and 2- or 4-bed interior (no-view) cabins. Fortunately, no cabins have views obstructed by lifeboats or other safety equipment views, and, in all cabins, twin beds can be changed to a double/queen-bed configuration.

A total of eight Grand Suites comprise the largest accommodation. These are located in the center of the ship on one of the uppermost decks. They have a queen-sized bed and larger living area with vanity desk; the bathrooms have a tub and two washbasins.

If you like wellness treatments, there are 12 "Samsara Spa Suites" located just aft of the spa (although 99 cabins, including the 12 suites, are designated as Samsara-grade). Samsara suite/cabin occupants get unlimited access to the spa plus two treatments and fitness or meditation lessons as part of their package, and dine in one of the two Samsara restaurants. All Samsara-designated accommodation grades have an Oriental decorative theme, and special Samsara bathroom personal amenities.

A pillow menu, with five choices, is available in all suite accommodation grades. Note that only suite grades get bathrobes and better amenities, shaving mirror, and walk-in closets – although the hangars are plastic. Music is played 24 hours a day in all hallways and elevators, so you may well hear it if you are a light sleeper.

CUISINE. There are two main dining rooms (New York, New York, and My Way), allocated according to your accommodation grade and location. There are two seatings in each for dinner.

Two 100-seat Samsara Restaurants (spa cuisine spots) are provided with separate entrances, adjacent to the restaurant My Way. These two dining spots are for those seeking spa food (reduced calories, fat and salt, with menu creations under the direction of dietary consultant and Michelin-star chef Ettore Boccia and his molecular Italian cuisine), while the two main restaurants offer traditional cruise fare. These dining venues are open for lunch and dinner to those in Samsara-grade suites and cabins, and to anyone else (for dinner only) for an extra charge of €20 per day, or €120 for a 7-day cruise package.

Alternative (Reservations Required) Dining Option: Club Blue Moon is an elegant dining venue with seating under a huge glass dome. Fine table settings, china, silverware and leather-bound menus are provided. There's a cover charge of $20 per person, for service and gratuity.

Casual Eatery: The La Paloma Buffet Restaurant is a self-serve eatery for breakfast, lunch, afternoon pizzas, and coffee and tea)at any time. A balcony level provides additional seating (you'll need to carry your own food plates – there are no trays). Decent quality cappuccino and espresso coffees are always available in various bars (at extra cost)

Additionally, the Caffeteria is the place to go for decent (extra cost) coffees and Italian pastries.

ENTERTAINMENT: The showlounge seats more than 800, and utilizes the latest in LED technology. It is three decks high and is decorated in a Baroque style, with warm colors and a Murano glass chandelier. It is the venue for all production shows and large-scale cabaret acts, is quite stunningly glitzy, and has a revolving stage, hydraulic orchestra pit, superb sound, and seating on three levels (the upper levels are tiered through two decks).

Typical fare consists of revue-style shows performed by a small troupe of resident onboard singers/ dancers, with fast-moving action and busy lighting and costume changes that all add up to a high-energy performance.

SPA/FITNESS. The Samsara Spa is a large facility that occupies 23,186 sq.ft/2,154 sq. meters of space, spread over two decks. It includes a large fitness room, separate saunas, steam rooms, UVB solarium, and changing rooms for men and women, 10 body treatment rooms, and two VIP treatment rooms, which are available to couples for half-day rentals, are located on the upper level.

The spa/fitness facilities are staffed and operated by Steiner Leisure, a specialist spa/beauty concession, whose young staff will try to sell you Steiner's own-brand beauty products. Some fitness classes are free, while some, such as Pathway to Yoga, Pathway to Pilates, and Pathway to Meditation, cost €9 per class. Make appointments early as time slots can go quickly.

You can purchase a day pass in order to use the sauna/steam rooms, thermal suite and relaxation area, at a cost of €35 per person. However, there is an additional no-charge sauna for men and women, but to access it you must walk through an active fitness area – maybe with your bathrobe on (some women may not feel comfortable with this arrangement).

Treatment price examples: Samsara Aroma Stone Massage (75 mins, €146); Asian Stone Therapy (50 mins, €91); Swedish Massage (50 mins, €91); Samsara Frangipani Body Wrap (120 mins, including a full body massage, €199); Elemis Pro-Collagen Facial (50 mins, €108).

● **For more extensive general information on what a Costa Cruises cruise is like, see pages 121–24.**

Costa Romantica
★★★

Mid-Size Ship: . . . . .53,049 tons	Total Crew: 610	Cabins (for one person): 0
Lifestyle: . . . . .Standard	Passengers	Cabins (with private balcony): 10
Cruise Line: . . . . .Costa Crociere	(lower beds/all berths): 1,356/1,779	Cabins (wheelchair accessible): 6 (interior)
Former Names: . . . . .none	Passenger Space Ratio	Cabin Current: . . . . .110 volts
Builder: . . . . .Fincantieri (Italy)	(lower beds/all berths): 39.1/29.8	Elevators: 8
Original Cost: . . . .$325 million	Crew/Passenger Ratio	Casino (gaming tables): . . . . .Yes
Entered Service: . . . . .Nov 1993	(lower beds/all berths): 2.2/2.9	Slot Machines: . . . . .Yes
Registry: . . . . .Italy	Navigation Officers: . . . . .Italian	Swimming Pools (outdoors): 2
Length (ft/m): 718.5/220.61	Cabins (total): 678	Swimming Pools (indoors): 0
Beam (ft/m): 98.4/30.89	Size Range (sq ft/m): 185.1–430.5/	Whirlpools: 4
Draft (ft/m): 25.0/7.60	17.2–40.0	Self-Service Launderette: . . . . .No
Propulsion/Propellers: diesel (22,800kW)/2	Cabins (outside view): 462	Dedicated Cinema/Seats: . . . . .No
Passenger Decks: 10	Cabins (interior/no view): 216	Library: . . . . .Yes

OVERALL SCORE: 1,247 (OUT OF A POSSIBLE 2,000 POINTS)

OVERVIEW. *Costa Romantica* is a bold, contemporary ship with an upright yellow funnel cluster of three typical of Italian styling today. Sadly, there is no wrap-around promenade deck outdoors, and so contact with the sea is minimal, although there is some good open space on several of the upper decks. Being Italian, the ship is chic and very tasteful, and will appeal to the sophisticated. The layout and flow are somewhat disjointed, however. The ship has a good number of business and conference facilities, with several flexible meeting rooms. The multi-level atrium is open and spacious, and has a revolving mobile sculpture. There is a small chapel and an internet café.

ACCOMMODATION. There are 11 price categories. These include 16 suites, 10 of which have a private semi-circular balcony, while six suites command views over the ship's bows. The other cabins are fairly standard in size, shape, and facilities; the ones on the highest decks cost more.
Suites/Mini-Suites: The 16 suites (with floor-to-ceiling windows) and 18 mini-suites are quite pleasant (except for the rounded balconies of the 10 suites on Madrid Deck, where a solid steel half-wall blocks the view). A sliding door separates the bedroom from the living room, and bathrooms are of a decent size. Cherry wood walls and cabinetry help make these suites warm and attractive.
The six suites at the forward section of Monte Carlo Deck are the largest, and have huge glass windows with commanding forward views, but no balconies.
Standard Outside-View/Interior (No View) Cabins: All other cabins are of a moderately generous size, and all have nicely finished cherry wood cabinetry and walls. However,

BERLITZ'S RATINGS

	Possible	Achieved
Ship	500	333
Accommodation	200	133
Food	400	214
Service	400	267
Entertainment	100	60
Cruise	400	240

the cabin bathrooms and shower enclosures are quite small. There are a good number of triple and quad cabins, ideal for families with children. The company's in-cabin food service menu is extremely basic.

CUISINE. The 728-seat Botticelli Restaurant is of a superior design. There are several tables for two, four, six or eight. There are two seatings (dinner on European cruises is typically at 7pm and 9pm), and there are both smoking and non-smoking sections. Romantic candlelight dining is typically featured on a formal night.
For casual meals and snacks, try the Giardino Buffet, but note that the buffet layout is extremely tight, and the buffet items are very much standard fare, with the exception of some good commercial pasta dishes. One would expect Italian waiters, but, sadly, this is not the case now, with most of the waiters coming from countries other than Italy.

ENTERTAINMENT. The L'Opera Theater, the main show-lounge, is an interesting amphitheater-like design that spans two decks, with seating on both main and balcony levels. However, the seats are bolt upright, and quite uncomfortable and 10 large pillars obstruct many sightlines.

SPA/FITNESS. The Caracalla Spa contains a gymnasium with some high-tech muscle-pump machines, an aerobics exercise area, two hot tubs, Roman bath, health bar, sauna and steam rooms, and beauty salon.

● **For more extensive general information on what a Costa Cruises cruise is like, see pages 121–24.**

Costa Serena
★★★★

Large Resort Ship:	.......114,147 tons	Total Crew:	1,090

Large Resort Ship: ....114,147 tons
Lifestyle: ....Standard
Cruise Line: Costa Crociere (Costa Cruises)
Former Names: ....none
Builder: ....Fincantieri (Italy)
Original Cost: ....€475 million
Entered Service: ....May 2007
Registry: ....Italy
Length (ft/m): 952.0/290.2
Beam (ft/m): 116.4/35.50
Draft (ft/m): 27.2/8.3
Propulsion/Propellers: ...diesel-electric
34,000kW/2 azimuthing pods
Passenger Decks: 13

Total Crew: 1,090
Passengers
(lower beds/all berths): 3,000/3,780
Passenger Space Ratio
(lower beds/all berths): 38.0/30.1
Crew/Passenger Ratio
(lower beds/all berths): 2.7/3.4
Navigation Officers: ....Italian
Cabins (total): 1,500
Size Range (sq ft/m): 482.2–179.7/
44.8–16.7
Cabins (outside view): 914
Cabins (interior/no view): 586
Cabins (for one person): 0

Cabins (with private balcony): 575
Cabins (wheelchair accessible): 12
Cabin Current: ....110 and 220 volts
Elevators: 14
Casino (gaming tables): ....Yes
Slot Machines: ....Yes
Swimming Pools (outdoors): 4
Swimming Pools (indoors): 0
Whirlpools: 5
Self-Service Launderette: ....No
Dedicated Cinema/Seats: ....No
Library: ....Yes)

OVERALL SCORE: 1,452 (OUT OF A POSSIBLE 2,000 POINTS)

OVERVIEW. *Costa Serena* is the sister ship to *Costa Concordia* (debuted 2006), which is itself a slightly larger, extended version of *Costa Fortuna/ Costa Magica*, but with an additional 17 meters in length that allows for more cabins to accommodate another 300 passengers.

Two of the ship's four swimming pools can be covered by a sliding glass dome (magrodome) in case of poor weather, while one pool has a long water slide (great for kids), and there is a huge screen for poolside movies. There is not a lot of open deck space, so sunloungers tend to be crammed together (there are no cushioned pads). *Costa Serena* absorbs passengers reasonably well, and provides a decent passenger space ratio that means that it won't feel too crowded (except, perhaps, on the open decks).

There are three decks full of bars and lounges plus lots of other public rooms. This ship has a glass-domed rotunda atrium lobby (with four panoramic elevators providing great views) that is nine decks high, with great upward views from the lobby bar. Ride up in the glass elevators and you'll think you're cruising in the heavens – well, the clouds, anyway – due to the delightful interior design, which is themed around the heavens and astrology (ship deck names are those of the Zodiac).

The Casino is large and glitzy, but always lively and entertaining (slot machines occupy a separate area to gaming tables, so serious gamers can concentrate). There's also a very small library, an internet-connection center, card room, art gallery, and video game room, together with several other bars and lounges to play in, plus a chapel (a standard aboard all Costa Cruises' ships).

Costa Cruises is noted for its "Italian" style, ambience

BERLITZ'S RATINGS

	Possible	Achieved
Ship	500	427
Accommodation	200	152
Food	400	252
Service	400	275
Entertainment	100	64
Cruise	400	282

and spirit. To be truthful, however, there are few Italian crew members on board its ships (while many of the officers are Italian, most of the crew members – particularly the dining room and housekeeping staff – are from the Philippines). The lifestyle on board is, however, perceived to be Italian – lively, noisy, with lots of love for life and a love of all things casual – even on so-called "formal" nights. Most passengers will be Italian, with a sprinkling of other European nationals. One night (at the end of each cruise) is typically reserved for a "Roman Bacchanal" (or Venetian Carnival night on Europe/Mediterranean cruises), when it's fun to dress up toga-style for dinner and beyond.

Costa Cruises does a good job of providing first-time cruise passengers with a well-packaged holiday – particularly for families with children – that is a mix of sophistication and basic fare, albeit accompanied by loud music everywhere.

All printed materials (room service folio, menus, etc.) will typically be in six languages (Italian, English, French, German, Portuguese, and Spanish). You can expect to be cruising with a lot of children of all ages during peak European holiday periods (such as Easter and Christmas). Costa Cruises is a cruise line for those who like to enjoy life and party. As aboard other Costa ships, note that for embarkation, few staff members are on duty at the gangway when you arrive; they merely point you in the direction of your deck, or to the ship's elevators and do not escort you to your cabin.

ACCOMMODATION. There are 20 price grades, from 2-bed interior cabins to grand suites with private balcony, although in reality there are only three different sizes: Suites with balcony (which are really not particularly large in comparison with some other large ships), 2- or 4-bed outside view cabins, and 2- or 4-bed interior (no-view) cabins. Fortunately, there are no cabins with lifeboat obstructed views, and, in most cabins, twin beds can be changed to a double/queen-bed configuration.

Eight Grand suites comprise the largest accommodation. These are located in the center of the ship on one of the uppermost decks. They have a queen-sized bed and larger living area with vanity desk; the bathrooms have a tub and two washbasins.

For anyone who likes to take wellness (spa) treatments, there are 12 "Samsara Spa Suites" located just aft of the spa itself (although 99 cabins, including the 12 suites, are designated as Samsara-grade. Samsara suite/cabin occupants get unlimited access to the spa plus two treatments and fitness or meditation lessons as part of their package, and dine in one of the two Samsara restaurants. All Samsara-designated accommodation grades have an Oriental decorative theme, and special Samsara bathroom personal amenities.

As this book was going to press, a 5-choice pillow menu was being introduced in all suite-grade accommodation. Note that only suite-grades get bathrobes and better amenities, shaving mirror, and walk-in closets – although the hangars are plastic. Music is played 24 hours a day in all hallways (and elevators), so you may well hear it if you are a light sleeper (I receive many complaints and letters of frustration about this annoyance).

CUISINE. There are two main dining rooms (Ceres, located aft, and Vesta, in the ship's center), allocated according to your accommodation grade and location. There are two seatings.

Two 100-seat Samsara Restaurants (spa cuisine spots) are provided with separate entrances, adjacent to the Vesta Restaurant. These two dining spots are for those seeking spa food (reduced calories, fat and salt, with menu creations under the direction of dietary consultant and Michelin-star chef Ettore Boccia and his molecular Italian cuisine), while the two main restaurants offer traditional cruise fare. These dining venues are open for lunch and dinner to those in Samsara-grade suites and cabins, and to anyone else not in Samsara-grade accommodation (for dinner only) for an extra charge of €20 per day, or €120 for a 7-day cruise package.

Alternative (Reservations Required) Dining Option: Club Bacco is an upscale dining venue with seating under a huge glass dome. Fine table settings, china, silverware and leather-bound menus are provided. There's a cover charge of $20 per person (for service and gratuity). Ettore Boccia has also created the menus in this venue, with small portion dishes that present a delightful array and variety of new flavours (some traditional chefs call it "foam food").

Casual Eatery: The The Promotea Buffet Restaurant is a self-serve eatery for breakfast, lunch, afternoon pizzas, and beverages (coffee and tea) at any time. A balcony level provides additional seating (you'll need to carry your own food plates – there are no trays). Decent quality cappuccino and espresso coffees are always available in various bars (at extra cost).

Additionally, the Caffeteria will be the place to go for decent (extra cost) coffees and Italian pastries.

ENTERTAINMENT. The 1,287-seat Giove Theater spans three decks in the forward section of the ship. It is the venue for all production shows and large-scale cabaret acts, is quite stunningly glitzy, and has a revolving stage, hydraulic orchestra pit, superb sound, and seating on three levels (the upper levels are tiered through two decks).

Typically, revue-style shows (performed by a small troupe of resident onboard singers/ dancers) are presented, with fast moving action and busy lighting and costume changes that all add up to a high-energy performance.

SPA/FITNESS. The ship's Samsara Spa (presently the largest spa at sea) has more than 23,186 sq. ft (2,154 sq. meters) of spa/wellness facilities, spread over two decks. It includes a large fitness room, separate saunas, steam rooms, UVB solarium, and changing rooms for men and women, 10 body treatment rooms, and two VIP treatment rooms, which are available to couples for half-day rentals, are located on the upper level.

The Spa/fitness facilities are staffed and operated by Steiner Leisure, a specialist spa/beauty concession, whose young staff will try to sell you Steiner's own-brand beauty products. Some fitness classes are free, while some, such as Pathway to Yoga, Pathway to Pilates, and Pathway to Meditation, cost €9 per class. Make appointments early as time slots can go quickly.

Note that to use the sauna/steam rooms, thermal suite and relaxation area, you'll need to purchase a day pass at a cost of €35 per person. However, there is an additional no-charge sauna for men and women, but to access it you'll need to walk through the active fitness area – maybe with your bathrobe on (not comfortable, especially for women).

Treatment price examples: Samsara Aroma Stone Massage (75 mins, €146); Asian Stone Therapy (50 mins, €91); Swedish Massage (50 mins, €91); Samsara Frangipani Body Wrap (120 mins, including a full body massage, €199); Elemis Pro-Collagen Facial (50 mins, €108).

● **For more extensive general information on what a Costa Cruises cruise is like, see pages 121–24.**

Costa Victoria
★★★+

Large Resort Ship:	.75,200 tons	
Lifestyle:	Standard	
Cruise Line:	Costa Crociere	
	(Costa Cruises)	
Former Names:	none	
Builder:	Bremer Vulkan (Germany)	
Original Cost:	$388 million	
Entered Service:	July 1996	
Registry:	Italy	
Length (ft/m):	823.0/251.00	
Beam (ft/m):	105.5/32.25	
Draft (ft/m):	25.6/7.8	
Propulsion/Propellers: diesel (30,000kW)/2		
Passenger Decks:	10	
Total Crew:	800	
Passengers		
(lower beds/all berths):	1,928/2,464	
Passenger Space Ratio		
(lower beds/all berths):	39.0/30.5	
Crew/Passenger Ratio		
(lower beds/all berths):	2.4/3.0	
Navigation Officers:	Italian	
Cabins (total):	964	
Size Range (sq ft/m):	120.0–430.5/	
	11.1–40.0	
Cabins (outside view):	573	
Cabins (interior/no view):	391	
Cabins (for one person):	0	
Cabins (with private balcony):	246	
Cabins (wheelchair accessible):	6	
Cabin Current:	110 and 220 volts	
Elevators:	12	
Casino (gaming tables):	Yes	
Slot Machines:	Yes	
Swimming Pools (outdoors):	2	
Swimming Pools (indoors):	1	
Whirlpools:	4	
Self-Service Launderette:	Yes	
Dedicated Cinema/Seats:	No	
Library:	Yes	

OVERALL SCORE: 1,384 (OUT OF A POSSIBLE 2,000 POINTS)

OVERVIEW. *Costa Victoria* has an outdoor walk-around promenade deck (full of sunloungers) and a wrap-around jogging track. Inside is a lovely four-deck-high forward-facing observation lounge with a "beam-me-up" glass elevator; in the center is a cone-shaped waterfall. It is a stunning space, and has its own bar.

The seven-deck-high "planetarium" atrium has four glass lifts that travel up to a clear crystal dome. The uppermost level of the atrium is the deck where two outside swimming pools are located, together with four blocks of showers, and an ice cream bar and grill.

Unusual for a new ship is a pleasant (but tiny) indoor swimming pool and a sauna. Adjacent is a steam room, and gymnasium (limited assortment of equipment), as well as a covered walking/jogging track. There is also a tennis court.

Where this ship differs from most large ships is in its distinct European interior decor, with decidedly Italian styling. When inside, there is absolutely no feeling that this is a ship. Internet access is available from computer terminals in the Teens Center. The onboard currency is the euro or US dollar, depending on the region of operation.

ACCOMMODATION. There are 13 price categories. The six large Panorama suites (each with third/ fourth Pullman berths in tiny, train-like compartments) and 14 mini-suites have butler service; 65 percent of all other cabins have outside views, but they are small (for two). While the suites are not large, all other cabins are of rather mean dimensions. Only 16 of the interior (no view) cabins accommodate four people, while all other cabins are for two or three.

All cabins have wood cabinetry. There is a decent amount of closet and drawer space for two for a one-week

BERLITZ'S RATINGS

	Possible	Achieved
Ship	500	402
Accommodation	200	152
Food	400	220
Service	400	273
Entertainment	100	73
Cruise	400	264

cruise, excellent air-conditioning, mini-bar/refrigerator, and electric blackout window blind (no curtains). The ocean-view cabins have large picture windows. The cabin bathrooms are small but well appointed. There are six cabins for the disabled.

CUISINE. This ship has two main dining rooms: the 594-seat Minuetto Restaurant, and the 506-seat Fantasia Restaurant. There are two seatings, with smoking and no-smoking sections in both restaurants. They are expansive and feature marble and pine walls. The cuisine is good basic fare, and the presentation is adequate, but nothing special. Pasta is freshly made on board daily. **Alternative (reservations-only) dining:** Ristorante Magnifico by Zeffirino, is available six nights each week, with a service charge of €20 per person (passengers occupying suites will get a free pass for one evening).

The ship also has casual breakfast and lunch buffets with indoor/outdoor seating, although the buffet displays are very disappointing. There is also a pizzeria.

ENTERTAINMENT. The Festival Showlounge, spanning two decks, is the venue for production shows, major cabaret, and social functions.

SPA/FITNESS. The congested spa/fitness area, on a lower deck, is much too small for the size of the ship. It has a beauty salon, indoor swimming pool, treatment rooms, sauna and steam room, but cramped changing areas.

● **For more extensive general information on what a Costa Cruises cruise is like, see pages 121–24.**

Cristal
★★★

Mid-Size Ship: . . . . .25,611 tons	Passenger Decks: 7	Cabins (for one person): 0
Lifestyle: . . . . .Standard	Total Crew: 400	Cabins (with private balcony): 10
Cruise Line: . . . . . .Louis Hellenic Cruises	Passengers	Cabins (wheelchair accessible): 6
Former Names: . . . . Silja Opera,	(lower beds/all berths): 966/1,278	Cabin Voltage: 110/220
SuperStar Taurus, Leeward,	Passenger Space Ratio	Elevators: 4
Sally Albatross, Viking Saga	(lower beds/all berths): 26.5/20.0	Casino (gaming tables): . . . . .Yes
Builder: . . . . .Wartsila (Finland)	Crew/Passenger Ratio	Slot Machines: . . . . .Yes
Original Cost: .n/a	(lower beds/all berths): 2.4/3.1	Swimming Pools (outdoors): 1
Entered Service: 1980/Jul 2007	Navigation Officers: . . . . .European	Swimming Pools (indoors): 0
Registry: .Greece	Cabins (total): 483	Whirlpools: 1
Length (ft/m): 530.5/161.7	Size Range (sq ft/m): . . . . .107.6 – 462.8/	Self-Service Launderette: . . . . .No
Beam (ft/m): 100.0/30.5	10.0 – 43.0	Dedicated Cinema/Seats: . . . . .No
Draft (ft/m): 19.3/5.9	Cabins (outside view): 318	Library: . . . . .No
Propulsion/Propellers: diesel (19,120kW/2	Cabins (interior/no view): 165	

BERLITZ'S OVERALL SCORE: 1,236 (OUT OF A POSSIBLE 2,000 POINTS)

OVERVIEW. This ship has undergone a number of changes, modifications and mishaps during its busy life so far. Originally constructed as a passenger ferry, it was extensively reconstructed in 1995 to the tune of $60 million, after which it was operated under charter to Norwegian Cruise Line (as *Leeward*). It was bought by Louis Cruise Lines as a replacement for the ill-fated *Sea Diamond*, at a cost of almost $50 million.

Cristal has a smart wedge-shaped profile, with a squared-off stern and short, stubby bows, and the enclosed bridge looks like it's really one deck lower than it should be. The ship does, however, benefit from a good, walk-around teakwood promenade deck. The pool deck is very cramped, although the pool itself can be covered by a sliding glass dome roof (magrodome). There is no forward-facing observation lounge atop the ship, but there is a reasonable array of public rooms, lounges, bars and meeting places to choose from.

The onboard currency is the euro, and gratuities are not included in the fare. The dress code is casual throughout (no formal nights).

Note that, as this book was being completed, plans for the ship's refit/refurbishment had not been announced.

SUITABLE FOR: *Cristal* is best suited to first-time passengers who simply want to cruise the Greek Islands in a modicum of comfort, and at a bargain price.

ACCOMMODATION. There are three suite categories (Grand, Imperial, and Royal, plus an interior "suite"), and a mix of several outside-view cabins (some of which have bal-

BERLITZ'S RATINGS

	Possible	Achieved
Ship	500	321
Accommodation	200	131
Food	400	230
Service	400	246
Entertainment	100	65
Cruise	400	243

conies) and interior (no view) cabins.

The top-grade suites have neatly-angled private balconies and provide a decent amount of space for short cruises; the bathrooms feature a bathtub, separate shower, and good storage facilities for personal toiletry items.

Most of the standard cabins, however, are really quite small, but adequate enough for the 3- and 4-day Greek Isles cruises that this ship operates. The bathrooms, however, really are dimensionally-challenged (dancing with the shower curtain comes to mind). Also, note that some cabins have views obstructed by safety equipment.

CUISINE. There are two principal dining rooms, plus a number of other dining spots and casual eateries. There are two seatings for dinner on most nights (typically an open seating for the first night), and open seating for breakfast and lunch. Seating and table assignments are made by the maître d' during embarkation.

The cuisine is predominantly Continental, with some regional (Greek) specialties (much use of oil and salt). Spa and vegetarian dishes are also available on lunch and dinner menus.

ENTERTAINMENT. The showlounge has tiered seating and decent sightlines.

SPA/FITNESS. Facilities include a beauty salon, fitness room, and sauna. Massages, aromatherapy facials, manicures, pedicures, and hair beautifying treatments are available.

Crown Princess
★★★★

Large Resort Ship: . . . . .116,000 tons	Passenger Decks: 15	Cabins (for one person): 0
Lifestyle: . . . . .Standard	Total Crew: 1,163	Cabins (with private balcony): 881
Cruise Line: . . . . .Princess Cruises	Passengers	Cabins (wheelchair accessible): 25
Former Names: . . . . .none	(lower beds/all berths): 3,114/3,782	Cabin Current: . . . . .110 volts
Builder: . . . . .Fincantieri (Italy)	Passenger Space Ratio	Elevators: 14
Original Cost: . . . .$500 million	(lower beds/all berths): 37.2/30.6	Casino (gaming tables): . . . . .Yes
Entered Service: . . . . .May 2006	Crew/Passenger Ratio	Slot Machines: . . . . .Yes
Registry: . . . . .Bermuda	(lower beds/all berths): 2.6/3.2	Swimming Pools (outdoors): 4
Length (ft/m): 951.4/290.0	Navigation Officers: . . . . .British/European	Swimming Pools (indoors): 0
Beam (ft/m): 118.1/36.0	Cabins (total): 1,557	Whirlpools: 9
Draft (ft/m): 26.2/8.0	Size Range (sq ft/m): .163-1,279/15.1-118.8	Self-Service Launderette: . . . . .Yes
Propulsion/Propellers: gas turbine (25 MW)/2	Cabins (outside view): 1,105	Dedicated Cinema/Seats: . . . . .No
azimuthing pods (21,000 kW each)	Cabins (interior/no view): 452	Library: . . . . .Yes

OVERALL SCORE: 1,545 (OUT OF A POSSIBLE 2,000 POINTS)

OVERVIEW. *Crown Princess* has the same profile as half-sisters *Caribbean Princess, Golden Princess, Grand Princess,* and *Star Princess,* but it accommodates many more passengers than half-sisters (except *Caribbean Princess* and *Emerald Princess*) due to an additional extra deck (Riviera Deck) full of cabins, and the fact that two of the ship's 17 upper decks are made of aluminum (although lighter than steel, it does tend to "harden" over time).

Although the ship accommodates over 500 more passengers, the outdoor deck space remains the same, as do the number of elevators (so waiting time could increase during peak usage). The Passenger Space Ratio is also considerably reduced compared to that of its half-sisters.

One nice feature is The Sanctuary, an extra-cost adults-only retreat located forward on the uppermost deck. It provides a "private" place to relax and unwind and includes attendants to provide chilled face towels and deliver light bites; there are also two outdoor cabanas for massages. It's a plush, outdoor spa-inspired setting for relaxation with attentive service.

There is a good sheltered teakwood promenade deck, which almost wraps around (three times round is equal to one mile) and a walkway which goes to the (enclosed, protected) bow of the ship. The outdoor pools have various beach-like surroundings, and "Movies Under the Skies" and major sporting events are shown on a 300-sq-ft (28-sq-meter) movie screen located at the pool in front of the large funnel structure. Movies afloat in the open are a big hit with passengers (they remind many of drive-in movies, which mostly have disappeared from land-based venues).

Unlike the outside decks, there is plenty of space inside (but there are also plenty of passengers), and a wide array

BERLITZ'S RATINGS

	Possible	Achieved
Ship	500	435
Accommodation	200	168
Food	400	255
Service	400	292
Entertainment	100	82
Cruise	400	313

of public rooms, with many "intimate" (this being a relative word) spaces and places to play. The passenger flow has been well thought-out, and there is little congestion.

Atop the stern of the ship is a ship-wide glass-walled disco called Sky-walkers. It's in a lower position than in sister ships of the same series, but still with spectacular views from the extreme port and starboard side windows (it would make a great penthouse).

The interior decor is attractive, with lots of earth tones (well suited to both American and European tastes). In fact, this is a culmination of the best of all that Princess Cruises has to offer from its many years of operating what is now a well-tuned, good-quality product.

An extensive collection of artworks complements the interior design and colors well. If you see something you like, you will probably be able to purchase it on board – it's almost all for sale.

Crown Princess also includes a Wedding Chapel (a live web-cam can relay ceremonies via the internet). The ship's captain can legally marry (American) couples, thanks to the ship's Bermuda registry and a special dispensation (which should be verified when in the planning stage, according to where you reside). But to get married and take your close family members and entourage with you on your honeymoon may prove expensive. The "Hearts & Minds" chapel is also useful for "renewal of vows" ceremonies.

For children, there is a two-deck-high playroom, teen room, and a host of trained counsellors. Children have their own pools, hot tubs, and open deck area at the stern of the ship, thankfully away from adult areas. There are good net-ted-in areas; one section has a dip pool, while another has a mini-basketball court. There's a video games arcade, too.

Gamblers should enjoy the large casino, with more than 260 slot machines, and blackjack, craps and roulette tables, plus newer games such as Let It Ride Bonus, Spanish 21 and Caribbean Draw Progressive. A highlight may be the specially linked slot machines that provide a combined payout.

Other features include a decent library/computer room, and a separate card room. Ship lovers should enjoy the wood-paneled Wheelhouse Bar, finely decorated with memorabilia and ship models tracing part of parent company P&O's history. A sports bar, has two billiard tables, and several television screens.

Crown Princess is a grand resort playground in which to roam when you are not ashore, and Princess Cruises delivers a consistently fine, well-packaged vacation product, always with a good degree of style, at an attractive, highly competitive price.

With many choices and "small" rooms (a relative term) to enjoy, the ship has been extremely well designed, and the odds are that you'll have an enjoyable cruise vacation. If you are not used to large ships, it will take you some time to find your way around this one, despite the company's claim that it offers passengers a "small ship feel, big ship choice."

ACCOMMODATION. There are six principal types of cabins and configurations: (a) grand suite, (b) suite, (c) mini-suite, (d) outside-view double cabins with balcony, (e) outside-view double cabins, and (f) interior (no view) double cabins. These come in 35 different brochure price categories (the choice is bewildering for both travel agents and passengers), and pricing depends on size and location.

Cabin bath towels are small, and drawer space is very limited. There are no butlers – even for the top-grade suites (which are not really large in comparison to similar suites aboard some other ships). Cabin attendants have too many cabins to look after (typically 20), which does not translate to fine personal service.

(a) The largest, most lavish suite is the Grand Suite. It has a large bedroom with queen-sized bed, huge walk-in (illuminated) closets, two bathrooms, a lounge (with fireplace and sofa bed) with wet bar and refrigerator, and a large private balcony on the port side (with hot tub that can be accessed from both balcony and bedroom).

(b/c) Suites (with a semi-private balcony) have a separate living room (with sofa bed) and bedroom (with a TV set in each). The bathroom is quite large and has both a tub and shower stall. The mini-suites also have a private balcony, and a separate living and sleeping area (with a television in each). The differences between the suites and mini-suites are basically in the size and appointments, the suite being more of a square shape while mini-suites are more rectangular, and have few drawers. Both suites and mini-suites have plush bathrobes, and fully tiled bathrooms with ample open shelf storage space. Suite and mini-suite passengers receive greater attention, including priority embarkation and disembarkation privileges. What is not good is that the most expensive accommodation has only semi-private balconies that can be seen from above and so there is little privacy.

(d/e/f). Both interior (no view) and outside-view (the outsides come either with or without private balcony) cabins are of a functional, practical, design, although almost no drawers are provided. They are quite attractive, with warm, pleasing decor and fine soft furnishing fabrics; 80 percent of the outside-view cabins have a private balcony. Interior (no view) cabins measure 163 sq. ft (15.1 sq. meters).

The 28 wheelchair-accessible cabins measure 250–385 sq. ft (23.2–35.7 sq. meters); surprisingly, there is no mirror for dressing, and no full-length hanging space for long dresses (yes, some passengers in wheelchairs do also use mirrors and full-length clothing). Additionally, two family suites consist of two suites with an interconnecting door, plus a large balcony. These can sleep up to 10 (if at least four are children) or up to eight people (if all are adults).

All cabins receive turndown service and chocolates on pillows each night, bathrobes (on request) and toiletry amenity kits (larger, naturally, for suite/mini-suite occupants) that typically include soap, shampoo, conditioner, and hand/body lotion. A hairdryer is provided in all cabins, sensibly located at the vanity desk unit in the living area. All bathrooms have tiled floors, and there is a decent amount of open shelf storage space for personal toiletries, although the plain beige decor is very basic and unappealing.

Most outside-view cabins on Emerald Deck have views obstructed by the lifeboats. There are no cabins for singles. Your name is placed outside your suite or cabin in a documents holder – making it simple for delivery service personnel but also diminishing privacy. There is 24-hour room service (but some items on the room service menu are not available during early morning hours).

Some cabins can accommodate a third and fourth person in upper berths. However, in such cabins, the lower beds cannot then be pushed together to make queen-sized bed.

Almost all balcony suites and cabins can be overlooked both from the navigation bridge wing, as well as from the port and starboard sections of the ship's discotheque – high above the ship at the stern. Cabins with balconies on Dolphin, Caribe and Baja decks can be overlooked by passengers on balconies on the deck above. They are, therefore, not private.

However, perhaps the least desirable balcony cabins are eight balcony cabins located forward on Emerald Deck, as the balconies do not extend to the side of the ship and can be passed by walkers and gawkers on the adjacent Upper Promenade walkway (so occupants need to keep their curtains closed most of the time). Also, passengers occupying some the most expensive suites with balconies at the stern of the vessel may experience considerable vibration during certain ship maneuvers.

Note that most cabins on Emerald Deck 8 have a lifeboat-obstructed view.

CUISINE. As befits the size of the ship, there's a variety of options. There are three main dining rooms, plus Sterling

Steakhouse, and Sabatini's Trattoria. Of the three principal dining rooms for formal dining, one has traditional two-seating dining, while the other two offer "anytime dining" (you choose when and with whom you want to eat). All are no-smoking and split into multi-tier sections in a non-symmetrical design that breaks what are quite large spaces into smaller sections for better ambiance. Each dining room has its own galley. While four elevators go to Fiesta Deck, where two of the restaurants are located, only two go to Plaza Deck 5, where the Palm Restaurant is located (this can cause waiting problems at peak times, particularly for anyone in a wheelchair).

Specially designed dinnerware, high-quality linens and silverware, Frette Egyptian cotton table linens, and silverware by Hepp of Germany are used in the main dining rooms. Note that 15% is added to all beverage bills, including wines.

Alternative (Extra Charge) Dining Options: There are two: Sabatini's Trattoria, and Crown Grill. Both are open for lunch and dinner on days at sea. Sabatini's is an Italian eatery, with colorful tiled Mediterranean-style decor; it is named after Trattoria Sabatini, the 200-year old institution in Florence (where there is no cover charge). It has Italian-style pizzas and pastas, with a variety of sauces, as well as Italian-style entrées (including tiger prawns and lobster tail – all provided with flair and entertainment from by the staff of waiters (by reservation only, with a cover charge of $20 per person, for lunch or dinner).

The 160-seat Crown Grill is located just aft of the upper level of the Princess Theater, adjacent to the Internet Café and shops, in a somewhat open area, to tempt you as you pass by, with people walking through as you eat – not a particularly comfortable arrangement. The cover charge is $10.

The cuisine in the alternative dining spots is decidedly better than in the three main dining rooms, with better quality ingredients and more attention to presentation and taste.

Casual eateries include a poolside hamburger grill and pizza bar (no additional charge), while extra charges do apply if you order items to eat at the coffee bar/patisserie or the caviar/champagne bar. Other casual meals can be taken in the Horizon Court, which is open 24 hours a day. It has large ocean-view on port and starboard sides and direct access to the two principal swimming pools and lido deck. There is no real finesse in presentation, however, as plastic plates are provided.

Ultimate Balcony Dinner/Breakfast: For something different, you could try a private dinner on your balcony, an all-inclusive evening featuring cocktails, fresh flowers, champagne and a deluxe four-course meal including Caribbean lobster tail – all served by a member of the dining staff on your private balcony; of course, it costs extra – $50 per person (or $25 per person for the Ultimate Balcony Breakfast).

ENTERTAINMENT. The Princess Theater (showlounge) is the main entertainment venue; it spans two decks and has comfortable seating on both main and balcony levels. It has $3 million worth of sound and light equipment, plus a 9-piece orchestra, and a scenery loading bay that connects directly from stage to a hull door for direct transfer to the dockside. The ship carries its own resident troupe of almost 20 singers and dancers, plus and audio-visual support staff.

Club Fusion is a second entertainment lounge (located aft). It features cabaret acts (magicians, comedy jugglers, ventriloquists and others) at night, and lectures, bingo and horse racing during the day. Explorers, a third entertainment lounge, can also host cabaret acts and dance bands. A variety of other lounges and bars have live music, and Princess Cruises employs a number of male dance hosts as partners for women traveling alone.

SPA/FITNESS. The Lotus Spa is located forward on Sun Deck – one of the uppermost decks. Separate facilities for men and women include a sauna, steam room, and changing rooms; common facilities include a relaxation/waiting zone, body-pampering treatment rooms, and a gymnasium with packed with the latest high-tech muscle-pumping, cardio-vascular equipment, and great ocean views. Some fitness classes are free, while some cost extra.

Above the spa, The Sanctuary, an adults-only retreat, offers shade and solitude, although MP3 players are provided, pre-loaded with a variety of music, at a cost of $15 per person per half-day.

● **For more extensive general information on what a Princess Cruises cruise is like, see pages 134–37.**

Crystal Serenity
★★★★★

Mid-Size Ship: . . . . .68,870 tons	Total Crew: 650	Cabins (with private balcony): 466
Lifestyle: . . . . .Luxury/Premium	Passengers	Cabins (wheelchair accessible): 8
Cruise Line: . . . . .Crystal Cruises	(lower beds/all berths): 1,100/1,100	Cabin Current: . . . . .110/220 volts
Former Names: . . . . .none	Passenger Space Ratio	Elevators: 8
Builder: Chantiers de l'Atlantique (France)	(lower beds/all berths): 62.6/62.6	Casino (gaming tables): . . . . .Yes
Original Cost: . . . .$350 million	Crew/Passenger Ratio	Slot Machines: . . . . .Yes
Entered Service: . . . . .June 2003	(lower beds/all berths): 1.7/1.7	Swimming Pools (outdoors): 1
Registry: . . . . .The Bahamas	Navigation Officers: . . . . . . .Scandinavian	Swimming Pools (indoors): 1
Length (ft/m): 820.2/250.0	Cabins (total): 550	(indoor/outdoor)
Beam (ft/m): 111.5/34.0	Size Range (sq ft/m): 226–1,345.5/	Whirlpools: 2
Draft (ft/m): 24.9/7.6	21–125	Self-Service Launderette: . . . . .Yes
Propulsion/Propellers: . . . . .2 pods/	Cabins (outside view): 550	Dedicated Cinema/Seats: Yes/202
diesel power	Cabins (interior/no view): 0	Library: . . . . .Yes
Passenger Decks: 9	Cabins (for one person): 0	

OVERALL SCORE: 1,702 (OUT OF A POSSIBLE 2,000 POINTS)

OVERVIEW. *Crystal Serenity* is the latest (slightly larger but still mid-size) close sister ship to the company's first ship, the former *Crystal Harmony* (now *Asuka II*) and to *Crystal Symphony*. This ship carries forward the same look, and profile. *Crystal Serenity* is a contemporary ship with a nicely raked clipper bow and well-balanced lines. While some might not like the "apartment block" look of the ship's exterior, it is the contemporary, "in" look, with balconies having become important standard features aboard almost all new cruise ships built today.

The latest in podded propulsion is provided *(see page 174 for details)*. Electrical power is provided by the latest generation of environmentally friendly diesel engines.

This ship has an excellent amount of open deck, sunbathing space, and sports facilities. The aft of two outdoor swimming pools can be covered by a magrodome (retractable glass dome) in poor weather. There is no sense of crowding in this superb example of comfort by design, high-quality construction and engineering. There is also a wide wrap-around teakwood deck for walking, pleasingly uncluttered by sunloungers.

With the exception of a gray, clinical photo gallery passageway, the decor in most areas is warm, inviting and contemporary. There is much use of rich wood paneling and detailing. The main lobby houses the reception desk (staffed 24 hours a day), concierge and shore excursion desks, and a lounge/bar (Crystal Cove) with baby grand piano. However, there are no passenger cabins forward of the lobby (they have instead become accommodation for officers and staff, a more sensible arrangement since this area really is considered to be "back of house").

BERLITZ'S RATINGS		
	Possible	Achieved
Ship	500	431
Accommodation	200	165
Food	400	341
Service	400	339
Entertainment	100	84
Cruise	400	342

Some of the most elegant public rooms include Palm Court (evoking images of Colonial-style grand hotel lounges); the Avenue Saloon (a favorite watering hole of the late-night crowd and a throwback to the gentlemen's clubs of yesteryear); the Connoisseur Club (for cigar and cognac enthusiasts); and the Stardust Club (cabaret entertainment lounge). Other new additions include a dedicated room for viewing art for auction, computer-learning center (24 terminals), an internet center, and Vintage Room (private dining room where 12 invited diners can enjoy exclusive vintage wines from around the world in special wine-tasting dinners).

The casino is centrally located, with no outside views to distract passengers who are intent on gaming. Instead, the location is adjacent to lifeboats on both sides (in this arrangement, the lifeboats do not obstruct either cabins or public rooms).

This ship has just about everything for the discerning, seasoned traveler who is prepared to pay for fine style, abundant space and the comfort and the facilities of a large vessel, including an excellent program of guest lecturers. The one thing that lets the product down is the fact that the dining room operation is in two seatings (however, many older passengers do want to eat early, while the line's younger passengers prefer to dine later, so there is some balance).

Your evenings will be necessarily rather structured due to the fact that there are two seatings for dinner (unless you eat in one of the alternative dining spots), and two shows (the showlounge cannot seat all passengers at once). This detracts from the otherwise luxurious setting of the ship and the fine professionalism of its staff. Many passengers feel that gratuities should really be included on a ship that is rated this highly (they can, however, be pre-paid).

The ship achieves a high rating because of its fine facilities, service and crew. It is the extra attention to detail that makes a cruise with this ship so special. The passenger mix is usually 85% North American (half from California) and 15% other nationalities. The ship should provide you with announcement-free cruising in a well-tuned, very professionally run, service-oriented ship, roughly the equivalent of a Four Seasons or Ritz Carlton hotel. All bottled water and (non-alcoholic) soft drinks are included in the price. The onboard currency is the US dollar, and gratuities are at your discretion (15% is added to bar accounts, however).

SUITABLE FOR: *Crystal Serenity* is best suited to sophisticated travelers (typically over 50) who seek contemporary ship surroundings, with fine quality fittings and furnishings, a wide range of public rooms and facilities, and excellent food and service from a well trained staff.

ACCOMMODATION. This consists of: four Crystal Penthouses with balcony; 32 Penthouse Suites with Balcony; 66 Penthouses with balcony; 78 superior outside-view cabins with balcony; 286 outside-view cabins with balcony; 84 outside-view cabins without balcony but with large picture windows. Two whole decks of accommodation are designated as suites (Deck 11, and Deck 10), while all other accommodation is located on Decks 9, 8 and 7. .

Duvets and down pillows are provided, as are lots of other niceties, together with a data socket for connecting a laptop computer. All accommodation has a refrigerator and mini-bar, television, satellite-linked telephone, and hairdryer. There's a full range of Aveda personal toiletry amenities, a plush, full-length cotton bathrobe, and plenty of cotton towels (the largest of which measures a generous 70 by 34 inches/180 by 85cm). The in-cabin TV programming is excellent (although why it starts at Channel 53, and not Channel 1, is unclear), and close-captioned videos are provided for the hearing-impaired. The air-conditioning in bathrooms and walk-in closets is extremely loud. In suites/cabins with "private" balcony, the balcony partition is of the partial, not full, type, and so noisy neighbors (particularly if using mobile phones in ports of call) can prove intrusive. The balcony decking is teak, however.

Butlers provide excellent service in all the top category suites on Decks 10 and 11, where room service food arrives on silver trays. Afternoon tea trolley service and evening hors d'oeuvres are standard fare in "butler service" suites.

Crystal Penthouses (with balcony): There are four Crystal Penthouses with private balcony (1,345 sq. ft/125 sq. meters). These are ideally located in the center of the ship on Penthouse Deck 11, each with outstanding views and large private balconies with outside lighting (they are a slightly different shape to those of the other ships in the fleet). There is a lounge with audio-visual entertainment center, separate master bedroom with king-sized bed and electric curtains, large walk-in closets, and large vanity desk.

The marble-clad bathrooms have ocean views; they are stunning and come with a whirlpool bathtub with integral shower, two washbasins, separate large shower enclosure, bidet and toilet, and plenty of storage space for toiletries.

Penthouse Suites (with balcony): There are 32 of these (538 sq. ft/50 sq. meters), all on Penthouse Deck 11. Each has a separate bedroom, walk-in closet and en-suite bathroom with full-size bathtub with integral shower, two washbasins, separate shower enclosure, bidet, toilet, and ample space for toiletries. The lounge has a large couch, coffee table and several armchairs, and there is a dining table and four chairs.

Penthouse Deck Cabin (with balcony): These are 66 of these, located on Penthouse Decks 10 and 11. They measure 403.6 sq. ft/37.5 sq. meters. All come with a private balcony, although eight that are located at the aft of Deck 11 have larger balconies. These units are really large cabins that have a sleeping area that can be curtained off from the lounge area, with its large, long vanity desk. The bathroom is large, and has a full-size bathtub (with integral shower), separate shower enclosure, and a bidet and toilet.

Superior Deluxe Outside-View Cabins (with balcony): This really is a standard outside-view cabin that is larger than any standard cabin aboard most other ships, and measures 269 sq. ft (25 sq. meters). The 78 cabins are longer than cabins that don't have a private balcony. They have a sleeping area with clothes closets, small couch, and drinks table, vanity desk with hairdryer. The bathroom has a bathtub with integral shower, two washbasins, and toilet. Large patio doors open onto a private balcony.

Deluxe Outside-View Cabins (with balcony): This is really a standard outside-view cabin that is larger than any standard cabin aboard most other ships, and measures 269 sq. ft (25 sq. meters). The 286 cabins, about the same size and shape as the "Deluxe" version but on a "superior" deck (Penthouse Deck 10), are longer than cabins that don't have a private balcony. They have a sleeping area with clothes closets, small couch, and drinks table, vanity desk with hairdryer. The bathroom has a tub with integral shower, two basins, and toilet. Patio doors open to a private balcony.

Deluxe Outside-View Cabins (no balcony): This is really a standard outside-view cabin (located on Deck 7, with the wrap-around promenade deck outside each cabin) that is larger than any standard cabin aboard most ships. The 84 cabins measure 226 sq. ft (21 sq. meters), and have a large window, sleeping area with clothes closets, small sofa and drinks table, vanity desk with hairdryer. The small bathroom has a bathtub with integral shower, two washbasins, and toilet.

Wheelchair Accessible Accommodation: This includes two penthouse grades, two cabins with balconies, and four cabins with large picture windows.

CUISINE. There is one main dining room (the Crystal Dining Room), two alternative dining rooms (reservations are required), and a sushi bar. The Crystal Dining Room is quite elegant, with a crisp, clean "California Modern" style that includes plenty of space around each table. It is well laid-out, and has a raised, circular central section, although it is noisy at times, and not conducive to a fine dining experience. There are tables for two (many positioned adjacent to large windows), four, six or eight. All restaurants are non-smoking areas. At dinner, a wandering trio serenades passengers at their tables, but this is tacky and not representative of fine dining.

The food is very attractively presented on large plates, and well served (using both plate service and silver service). It is of a very high standard with fine quality (high cost) ingredients. European dishes are predominantly featured (but in an American style). The menus are extremely varied, and feature a fine selection of meat, fish and vegetarian dishes. Special (off-menu) orders are available, as are caviar and other culinary niceties. Kosher meals are also available (frozen when brought on board); Kosher pots, pans and utensils are sterilized in salt water, and all plates used during service are hand-washed separately.

Overall, the food is really good for the size of ship, and, with the choice of the two alternative dining spots, receives high praise. Sadly, dinner in the main dining room is in two seatings and has fixed-table assignments, the company having used the space that could have provided a second main dining room, for public areas. While the early seating is simply too rushed for many, with two alternative restaurants, off-menu choices, a hand-picked European staff and excellent service, dining is often memorable. Fresh pasta and dessert flambeau specialties are made at the table each day by accommodating headwaiters.

Alternative Dining Spots (reservations required, no extra charge): There are two alternative restaurants (one Italian, the other Asian). Both are aft on Deck 7, and both have excellent views from large picture windows. Prego is for Italian food, Italian wines, and service with a flair. Silk Road has Asian-California "fusion" food. Although there is no extra charge, a "gratuity" is added to your account.

There is a separate sushi bar, with items selected by superb Los-Angeles-based Japanese super-chef Nobu Matsuhisa, and skillfully prepared on board by a Nobu-trained chef; the high-cost ingredients are flown regularly to the ship. The alternative dining spots provide an excellent standard of culinary fare – with food cooked to order at no extra charge (although many Crystal regulars feel the recommended $6 waiter gratuity per meal should be included in the cruise fare). To eat in one of Nobu's restaurants ashore costs a considerable amount; aboard the ship, not only is the food free, it is outstanding.

The Bistro: Located on the upper level of the two-deck-high lobby, this is a casual spot for coffees and pastries, served in the style and atmosphere of a European street cafe. The Bistro has unusual Crystal Cruises-logo china that can be bought in one of the ship's boutiques.

Casual Eateries: For casual meals, the Lido Cafe has an extensive self-serve buffet area. It's high up in the ship, with great views from its large picture windows. For casual poolside lunches, there is also the Trident Grill, as well as an ice cream/frozen yoghurt counter (no extra charge). Special themed luncheon buffets, with appropriate decor and service staff dressed accordingly, are provided at the Trident indoor/outdoor pool area. These include the popular Asian Buffet and Follow the Sun (Mediterranean) buffet.

ENTERTAINMENT. The Galaxy Lounge is the ship's principal showlounge. It is quite a large room with a high ceiling, but on one level (with a nicely sloping floor) for good visibility. Indeed, the sightlines are good from almost all seats. Both banquette and individual seating is provided. The stage, lighting, and sound equipment are all excellent.

The shows are elegant, with excellent costuming (though not much in the way of scenery), but some are seriously dated, too long, and Crystal Cruises' many repeat passengers know them all. In addition, many nights feature cabaret acts and classical artistes that are of a good caliber, and constantly changing. The bands and musical units are also, for the most part, of a high caliber, and there is plenty of music for social dancing. The ship also provides gentlemen hosts (called Ambassador Hosts) for the many single ladies that enjoy traveling with Crystal Cruises.

SPA/FITNESS. The Crystal Spa is located aft on Lido Deck 12, one of the ship's uppermost decks. Facilities include men's and women's changing rooms with sauna (which has a large porthole-shaped window) and steam rooms, gymnasium with high-tech muscle-pumping equipment, an aerobics exercise area, and reception/relaxation area.

Treatments are provided under the aegis of Steiner Platinum Service (Steiner being the concession). Facilities include one room dedicated to yoga and pilates classes (no extra charge), an aerobics/exercise room, plus separate sauna, steam rooms, and changing rooms for both men and women. There are seven treatment rooms (including one for couples, and one with a "dry float bed") for massage, facials, and other treatments, and a separate beauty salon.

Some staff will try to sell you Steiner's own-brand Elemis beauty products). Massage (including exotic massages such as Aroma Stone massage, Chakra Balancing massage and other well-being massages), facials, pedicures, and beauty salon treatments cost extra. Examples: Swedish Massage ($109 for 50 minutes); Deep Tissue Massage ($116 for 50 minutes). There are also some excellent multi-therapy packages that provide you with hours of pampering. Example: Ceremony of Precious Metal (exotic lime and ginger salt glow, aroma spa ocean wrap, well-being massage) lasting 3 hours 30 minutes, for $323. A simple hair cut (for men) costs $25, while it is $57 for women with short hair for a shampoo, cut and blow-dry.

The ship has excellent open deck and sunbathing space, and sports facilities that include two full-size paddle tennis courts, electronic golf simulator, and golf driving range. One of two outdoor swimming pools has a magrodome (retractable glass dome) cover, while the one that is in the open is one of the longest aboard any ship today. Anyone trying to sunbathe quietly on the deck under and close to the paddle tennis courts will hear the noise of play (bat against ball) when the court is in use.

Crystal Symphony
★★★★★

Mid-Size Ship: ....51,044 tons	Total Crew: 545	Cabins (with private balcony): 276
Lifestyle: ....Luxury/Premium	Passengers	Cabins (wheelchair accessible): 7
Cruise Line: ....Crystal Cruises	(lower beds/all berths): 960/1,010	Cabin Current: ....110 and 220 volts
Former Names: ....none	Passenger Space Ratio	Elevators: 8
Builder: ....Masa-Yards (Finland)	(lower beds/all berths): 53.1/50.5	Casino (gaming tables): ....Yes
Original Cost: ....$300 million	Crew/Passenger Ratio	Slot Machines: ....Yes
Entered Service: ....Mar 1995	(lower beds/all berths): 1.7/1.8	Swimming Pools (outdoors): 2
Registry: ....The Bahamas	Navigation Officers: ......Scandinavian	(1 with magrodome)
Length (ft/m): 777.8/237.10	Cabins (total): 480	Swimming Pools (indoors): 0
Beam (ft/m): 98.0/30.20	Size Range (sq ft/m): 201.2–981.7/	Whirlpools: 2
Draft (ft/m): 24.9/7.60	18.7–91.2	Self-Service Launderette: ....Yes
Propulsion/Propellers: .....diesel-electric	Cabins (outside view): 480	Dedicated Cinema/Seats: Yes/143
(33,880kW)/2	Cabins (interior/no view): 0	Library: ....Yes
Passenger Decks: 8	Cabins (for one person): 0	

OVERALL SCORE: 1,701 (OUT OF A POSSIBLE 2,000 POINTS)

OVERVIEW. *Crystal Symphony* is a contemporary ship with a nicely raked clipper bow and well-balanced lines. While some might not like the "apartment block" look of its exterior, it is the contemporary, "in" look, balconies having become standard aboard almost all new cruise ships. This ship has an excellent amount of open deck, sunbathing space, and sports facilities. The aft of two outdoor swimming pools can be covered by a magrodome in inclement weather. There is no sense of crowding anywhere – a fine example of comfort by design (form follows function) and high-quality construction. The ship combines large ship facilities with the intimacy of rooms found aboard many small vessels. There is a wide wrap-around teakwood deck for walking, uncluttered by lounge chairs.

The interior decor is restful, with color combinations that don't jar the senses. It has a good mixture of public entertainment lounges and small intimate rooms. Outstanding is the Palm Court, an observation lounge with forward-facing views over the ship's bows – it is tranquil, and one of the nicest rooms afloat (it is larger than aboard the sister ship).

There is an excellent book, video and CD-ROM library (combined with a Business Center). The theater has high-definition video projection and headsets for the hearing-impaired. Useful self-service launderettes are provided on each deck. Fine-quality fabrics and soft furnishings, china, flatware and silver are used. Excellent in-cabin television programming (including CNN) is transmitted, as well as close-captioned videos for the use of the hearing-impaired.

The Connoisseurs Club, adjacent to the Avenue Saloon, serves fine premium brands of liquor and cigars for those

BERLITZ'S RATINGS

	Possible	Achieved
Ship	500	430
Accommodation	200	163
Food	400	340
Service	400	342
Entertainment	100	84
Cruise	400	342

who appreciate them. The Computer Learning Center, with more than 20 stations, is a popular venue. Private lessons are available (but expensive).

This ship has just about everything for the discerning, seasoned traveler who wants and is prepared to pay good money for fine style, abundant space and the comfort and the facilities of a large vessel capable of extended voyages, including an excellent program of guest lecturers.

The one thing that lets the product down is the fact that the dining room operation is in two seatings (however, having said that, there are many older passengers who want to eat early, while the line's younger passengers prefer to dine later, so there is some semblance of balance).

Crystal Cruises takes care of its ships, and its staff, and it is the staff that make the cruise experience special. They are a well-trained group that stress hospitality at all times. The ship achieves a high rating because of its fine facilities, service and crew. It is the extra attention to detail that really counts. The passenger mix is approximately 85 percent North American (typically half will be from California) and 15% other nationalities.

This is announcement-free cruising in a well-tuned, very professionally run, service oriented, ship, the approximate equivalent of a Four Seasons hotel. However, note that the score has gone downwards a little recently, the result of the fact that, in comparison to other ships available in the discounted marketplace, this is still a two-seating ship, which makes it more highly structured in terms of timing than it really should be. All bottled water and (non-alcoholic) soft drinks are included in the cost of your cruise (this feature was introduced with the debut of *Crystal Serenity*, but has now been applied fleet-wide). The onboard currency is the US dollar, and gratuities are at your discretion (15% is added to bar accounts, however).

In 2007, *Crystal Symphony* was given a $23 million refurbishment that included making the ship's main entertainment deck more contemporary. All suites/cabins received flat-screen televisions, new Murano bedside table lamps and Rubelli fabrics, and oval glass washbasins set in granite surrounds were introduced, together with a raft of other behind-the-scenes items that have helped bring the ship right up to date.

Your evenings will be necessarily rather structured due to the fact that there are two seatings for dinner (unless you eat in one of the alternative dining spots), and two shows (the showlounge cannot seat all passengers at once). This detracts from the otherwise luxurious setting of the ship and the fine professionalism of its staff. Many passengers feel that gratuities should really be included on a ship that is rated this highly (they can, however, be pre-paid).

Plastic patio furniture on suite and cabin balconies would be better replaced with the more elegant teak variety, to go with the teak decking.

SUITABLE FOR: *Crystal Symphony* is best suited to discerning adult travelers (typically over 50) that seek contemporary ship surroundings, with fine-quality fittings and furnishings, a wide range of public rooms and facilities, and excellent food and service from a well trained staff.

ACCOMMODATION. There are eight categories, with the most expensive suites located on the highest accommodation deck (Deck 10). There are two Crystal Penthouses with private balcony; 18 Penthouse Suites with private balcony; 44 Penthouse Cabins with balcony; 214 Cabins with balcony; 202 Cabins without balcony. Some cabins (grades G and I) have obstructed views. Except for the suites on Deck 10, most other cabin bathrooms are very compact units.

Regardless of the accommodation category you select, duvets and down pillows are provided, as are lots of other niceties, together with a data socket for connecting a personal laptop computer. All accommodation has a refrigerator and mini-bar, television, satellite-linked telephone, and hairdryer. A full range of Aveda personal toiletry amenities is provided, as is a plush cotton bathrobe, and plenty of cotton towels (the largest of which measures a generous 70 by 34 inches (180 by 85cm). The in-cabin television programming is excellent, and close-captioned videos are provided for the hearing-impaired.

Deck 10 Penthouses: Two delightful Crystal Penthouses measure 982 sq. ft (91 sq. meters) and have a huge private balcony (with outside light) and lounge with audio-visual entertainment center, separate master bedroom with king-sized bed and electric curtains, large walk-in closets, and stunning ocean-view marble bathrooms with a whirlpool bathtub, bidet, two washbasins, and plenty of storage space for one's personal toiletry items. These really are among the best in fine, private, pampered living spaces at sea, and come with all the best priority perks, including laundry service.

Other Deck 10 Suites: All of the other suites on this deck have plenty of space (all feature a private balcony, with outside light), including a lounge with large sofa, coffee table and chairs, a sleeping area and walk-in closet. Rich wood cabinetry provides much of the warmth of the decor. The bathrooms are quite large, and are extremely well appointed, with full-sized bathtub and separate shower enclosure, two washbasins, bidet and toilet. In fact, any of the suites on this deck are equipped with everything necessary for refined, private living at sea.

Five butlers provide the best in personal service in all the top category suites on Deck 10 (with a total of 132 beds), where all room service food arrives on silver trays. Afternoon tea trolley service and evening hors d'oeuvres are standard fare in the "butler service" suites.

Decks 5/6/7/8/9: More than 50 percent of all cabins have private balconies. All are well equipped, and extremely comfortable, with excellent sound insulation. The balcony partitions, however, do not go from floor to ceiling, so you can hear your neighbors. Even in the lowest category of standard cabins, there is plenty of drawer space, but the closet hanging space may prove somewhat limited for long voyages. There are generously sized personal bathroom amenities, duvets and down pillows. European stewardesses provide excellent service and attention.

CUISINE. The Crystal Dining Room (totally non-smoking) is quite an elegant room, with crisp design, plenty of space around each table, and well-placed waiter service stations. It is well laid out, and has a raised, circular central section, although it is somewhat noisy at times, and not conducive to a fine dining experience. There are tables for two (many of them positioned adjacent to large windows), four, six or eight. Each evening at dinner, a wandering trio serenades passengers at their tables, but this is tacky and not representative of fine dining.

The food is very attractively presented on large plates, and well served (using both plate service as well as silver service in the best European traditions). It is of a very high standard with fine quality (high cost) ingredients. European dishes are predominantly featured (but in an American style). The menus are extremely varied, and feature a fine selection of meat, fish and vegetarian dishes. Special (off-menu) orders are available, as are caviar and other culinary niceties. Kosher meals are also available (frozen when brought on board). Kosher pots, pans and utensils are sterilized in salt water, and all plates used during service are hand-washed separately.

Overall, the food is really good for the size of ship, and, with the choice of the two alternative dining spots, receives high praise. Sadly, dinner in the main dining room is in two seatings (with fixed table assignments), the company having used the space that could have provided a second main dining room, for public areas. While the early seating is simply too rushed for many, with two alternative restaurants, off-menu choices, a hand-picked European staff and excellent service, dining is often memorable. The advantage of fixed table assignments is that your waiters get to know your personal preferences, likes and dislikes (unlike dining rooms with open seating, where you may be seated with different people each evening, and your waiter changes constantly). Fresh pasta and dessert flambeau specialties are made at the table each day by accommodating headwaiters.

The wine list is excellent (though pricey), with an outstanding collection of across-the-board wines, including a mouthwatering connoisseur selection.

Afternoon tea in the Palm Court is a civilized daily event. The Lido provides breakfast and luncheon buffets that are fairly standard fare.

Alternative Dining Spots (reservations required, no extra charge): Two alternative dining spots are the 75-seat Prego (featuring fine Italian cuisine, and specializing in good Italian wines), and the revamped 100-seat Jade Garden (featuring five contemporary Chinese/French fusion dishes in association with Wolfgang Puck's Chinois on Main restaurant in Santa Monica). These rooms are located on Deck 6; each restaurant has a separate entrance and themed decor. Both provide an excellent standard of culinary fare, with food cooked to order at no extra charge (although many feel that the recommended $6 waiter gratuity per meal should be included in the cruise fare).

The Bistro (on the upper level of the two-deck-high lobby) is a casual spot for coffees and pastries, served in the style and atmosphere of a European street cafe. The Bistro has unusual, Crystal Cruises-logo china that can also be purchased in one of the ship's boutiques.

For casual meals, the Lido Cafe has an extensive self-serve buffet area, located high up in the ship, and with great views from its large picture windows. For casual poolside lunches, there is also the Trident Grill, as well as an ice cream/frozen yoghurt counter (all at no extra charge). Several special themed luncheon buffets, with appropriate decor and service staff dressed accordingly, are provided at the Trident indoor/outdoor pool area. These include the popular Asian Buffet and Follow the Sun (Mediterranean) buffet.

ENTERTAINMENT. The Galaxy Lounge is the ship's principal showlounge. It is quite a large room with a high ceiling, but on one level (with a tiered floor) for good visibility. The sightlines are good from most seats, although there are a few pillars that obstruct sight lines from some seats. Both banquette and individual seating is provided. The stage, lighting, and sound equipment are all excellent.

The shows are elegant, with excellent costuming and scenery, but they are now seriously dated, too long, and

Crystal Cruises' many repeat passengers know them all. In addition, many nights feature cabaret acts that are of a good caliber, and constantly changing. The bands and musical units are also, for the most part, of a high caliber, and there is plenty of music for social dancing. The ship also provides male hosts (called Ambassador Hosts) for the many single women who enjoy traveling with Crystal Cruises.

SPA/FITNESS. In 2000 an expanded range of Spa facilities and treatments was introduced, under the aegis of Steiner Platinum Service (Steiner being the concession). Facilities include one room dedicated to yoga and pilates classes (no extra charge), an aerobics/exercise room, plus separate sauna, steam rooms, and changing rooms for both men and women. There are seven treatment rooms (including one for couples, and one room featuring a "dry float bed") for various types of massage, facials, and other treatments, as well as a separate beauty salon.

Some staff will try to sell you Steiner's own-brand Elemis beauty products (spa girls have sales targets). Being aboard this ship will give you an opportunity to try some of the more exotic treatments (particularly some of the massages available). Massage (including exotic massages such as Aroma Stone massage, Chakra Balancing massage and other well-being massages), facials, pedicures, and beauty salon treatments are at extra cost. Examples: Swedish Massage ($109 for 50 minutes); Deep Tissue Massage ($116 for 50 minutes); Yin Yang Facial ($109 for 50 minutes).

There are also some excellent multi-therapy packages that provide you with hours of pampering. Some examples: Ceremony of Precious Metal (exotic lime and ginger salt glow, aroma spa ocean wrap, well-being massage) lasting 3 hours 30 minutes, for $323; Ceremony of Water (aroma stone therapy, Japanese silk booster facial, Japanese eye zone therapy) lasting 3 hours 30 minutes, for $365; Ceremony of Earth (frangipani body nourish ritual, absolute spa ritual, frangipani hair and scalp conditioning with style dry, exotic hand ritual with paraffin wax, sole delight foot treatment with paraffin wax) lasting 6 hours and 30 minutes, for $561. A simple hair cut (for men) costs $25, while it is $57 for women with short hair for a shampoo, cut and blow-dry.

The ship also has excellent open deck and sunbathing space, and sports facilities that include a full-sized paddle tennis court, electronic golf simulator, and golf driving range. One of two outdoor swimming pools has a magrodome (retractable glass dome) cover, while the one that is in the open is one of the longest aboard any ship today.

Dawn Princess
★★★★

Large Resort Ship:	........77,499 tons	Total Crew:	900
Lifestyle:	..................Standard	Passengers	
Cruise Line:	..........Princess Cruises	(lower beds/all berths):	.....1,950/2,250
Former Names:	................none	Passenger Space Ratio	
Builder:	............Fincantieri (Italy)	(lower beds/all berths):	.......39.7/34.4
Original Cost:	............$300 million	Crew/Passenger Ratio	
Entered Service:	...........May 1997	(lower beds/all berths):	.........2.1/2.5
Registry:	................Great Britain	Navigation Officers:	......British/Italian
Length (ft/m):	............857.2/261.3	Cabins (total):	975
Beam (ft/m):	...........105.6/32.2	Size Range (sq ft/m):	......135.0–635.0/
Draft (ft/m):	..................26.5/8.1		12.5–59.0
Propulsion/Propellers:	.....diesel-electric	Cabins (outside view):	603
	(46,080kW)/2	Cabins (interior/no view):	372
Passenger Decks:	10	Cabins (for one person):	0

Cabins (with private balcony):	446
Cabins (wheelchair accessible):	19
Cabin Current:	.......110 and 220 volts
Elevators:	11
Casino (gaming tables):	............Yes
Slot Machines:	....................Yes
Swimming Pools (outdoors):	4
Swimming Pools (indoors):	0
Whirlpools:	5
Self-Service Launderette:	...........Yes
Dedicated Cinema/Seats:	...........No
Library:	.........................Yes

OVERALL SCORE: 1,532 (OUT OF A POSSIBLE 2,000 POINTS)

OVERVIEW. *Dawn Princess* is an all-white ship with a decent contemporary profile, well balanced by a large funnel that contains a deck tennis/basketball/volleyball court in its sheltered aft base. There is a wide, teakwood walk-around promenade deck outdoors, some real teak steamer-style deck chairs (complete with royal blue cushioned pads), and 93,000 sq. ft (8,640 sq. meters) of space outdoors. A great amount of glass area on the upper decks provides plenty of light and connection with the outside world.

The ship absorbs passengers well, and has an almost intimate feel to it. The interiors are very pretty and warm, with attractive colors and welcoming decor that includes some very attractive wall murals and other artwork. The signage throughout the ship could be better, however. There are a number of dead ends in the interior layout, so it's not as user-friendly as a ship this size could be. The cabin numbering system is extremely illogical, with numbers going through several hundred series on the same deck.

There is a wide range of public rooms, with several intimate rooms and spaces so that you don't get the feel of being overwhelmed by large spaces. The interior focal point is a huge four-deck-high atrium lobby with winding, double stairways, and two panoramic glass-walled elevators.

There are two showlounges, one at each end of the ship; one is a superb 550-seat, theater-style showlounge (movies are also shown here) and the other is a 480-seat cabaret-style lounge, complete with bar.

The library, a very warm room, has six large butter-colored leather chairs for listening to compact audio discs, with ocean-view windows. There is a conference center for up to 300, as well as a business center with computers, copy

BERLITZ'S RATINGS		
	Possible	Achieved
Ship	500	424
Accommodation	200	161
Food	400	266
Service	400	291
Entertainment	100	86
Cruise	400	304

and fax machines. The collection of artwork is good, particularly on the stairways, and helps make the ship feel smaller than it is, although in places it doesn't always seem coordinated. The casino, while large, is not really in the main passenger flow and so it does not generate the "walk-through" factor found aboard so many ships.

The most traditional room is the Wheelhouse Lounge/Bar, which is decorated in the style of a late 19th-century gentleman's club, with wood paneling and comfortable seating. The focal point is a large ship model from the P&O collection archives: aboard *Dawn Princess* it is *Kenya*.

One nice feature is the captain's cocktail party – it is typically held in the four-deck-high main atrium – so you can come and go as you please, and there's no standing in line to have your photograph taken with the captain if you don't want to. However, note that cruising aboard large ships such as this one has become increasingly an onboard revenue-based product. The in-your-face art auctions are simply overbearing, and the paintings, lithographs and faux, framed pictures that are strewn throughout the ship (and clash irritatingly with the ship's interior decor) are an annoying intrusion into what should be a holiday, not a cruise inside a floating "art" emporium. There are no cushioned pads for the sunloungers on the open lido decks.

The swimming pools are small for so many passengers, and the pool deck is cluttered with white, plastic sunloungers, without cushioned pads. Waiting for tenders in anchor ports can prove irritating, but typical of large ship operations. Charging for use of the machines and washing powder in the self-service launderette is trifling.

As is the case aboard most large ships today, if you live

in the top suites, you will be well attended; if you do not, you will merely be one of a large number of passengers. *Dawn Princess* (like sister *Sun Princess*) is now dedicated to the Australian cruise region.

ACCOMMODATION. The brochure shows that there are 28 different cabin grades: 20 outside-view and 8 interior (no view) cabins. Although the standard outside-view and interior (no view) cabins are a little small, they are well designed and functional in layout, and have earth tone colors accentuated by splashes of color from the bedspreads. Proportionately, there are quite a lot of interior (no view) cabins. Many of the outside-view cabins have private balconies, and all seem to be quite well soundproofed, although the balcony partition is not the floor-to-ceiling type, so you can hear your neighbors clearly (or smell their smoke). Note that the balconies are very narrow, only just large enough for two small chairs, and there is no dedicated lighting.

A reasonable amount of closet and abundant drawer and other storage space is provided in all cabins – adequate for a 7-night cruise, as are a television and refrigerator. Each night a chocolate will appear on your pillow. The cabin bathrooms are practical, and come complete with most of the things needed, although they really are tight spaces, and are best described as one person at-a-time units. They do, however, have a decent shower enclosure, a small amount of shelving for your personal toiletries, real glasses, a hairdryer and a bathrobe.

The largest accommodation is in six suites, two on each of three decks located at the stern of the ship, with large private balcony (536–754 sq.ft/49.8–21.3 sq.meters, including balcony). These are well laid out, and have large bathrooms with two sinks, a Jacuzzi bathtub, and a separate shower enclosure. The bedroom has generous amounts of wood accenting and detailing, indented ceilings, and television sets in both bedroom and lounge areas. The suites also have a dining room table and four chairs.

The 32 mini-suites (374–536 sq.ft/34.7–49.7 sq.meters) typically have two lower beds that convert into a queen-sized bed. There is a separate bedroom/sleeping area with vanity desk, and a lounge with sofa and coffee table, indented ceilings with generous amounts of wood accenting and detailing, walk-in closet, and larger bathroom with Jacuzzi bathtub and separate shower enclosure.

There are 19 wheelchair-accessible cabins, which measure 213–305 sq. meters/19.7–28.2 sq.ft and are a mix of 7 outside view and 12 interior (no view) cabins.

Princess Cruises has CNN, CNBC, ESPN and TNT on the in-cabin TV system (when available, depending on area).

CUISINE. There are two main dining rooms of asymmetrical design (each seats about 500), Florentine and Venetian (both non-smoking, as are all dining rooms aboard the ships of Princess Cruises), located adjacent to the two lower levels of the four-deck high atrium lobby. Each has its own galley and each is split into multi-tier sections, which help create a feeling of intimacy, although there is a lot of noise from the waiter stations, which are adjacent to many tables.

Breakfast and lunch are provided in an open seating arrangement, while dinner is in two seatings.

On any given 7-day cruise, a typical menu cycle will include a Sailaway Dinner, Captain's Welcome Dinner, Chef's Dinner, Italian Dinner, French Dinner, Captain's Gala Dinner, and Landfall Dinner. The wine list is reasonable, but not good, and the company has, sadly, seen fit to eliminate all wine waiters. Note that 15% is added to all beverage bills, including wines.

For some really good meat, however, consider the Sterling Steakhouse; it's for those who want to taste four different cuts of Angus beef from the popular "Sterling Silver" brand of USDA prime meats – Filet Mignon, New York Strip, Porterhouse, and Rib-Eye – all presented on a silver tray.

There is also a barbecue chicken option, plus the usual baked potato or French fries as accompaniments. This is available as an alternative to the dining rooms, between 6.30pm and 9.30pm only, at an additional charge of $8 per person. However, it is not, as you might expect, a separate, intimate dining room, but is located in a section of the Horizon Buffet, with its own portable bar and some decorative touches to set it apart (from the regular Horizon Buffet).

The Horizon Buffet is open 24 hours a day, and, at night, has an informal dinner setting with sit-down waiter service; a small bistro menu is also available. The buffet displays are, for the most part, quite repetitious, but better than they have been in the past few years (there is no real finesse in presentation, however, as plastic plates are provided, instead of trays). The cabin service menu is very limited, and presentation of the food items featured is poor.

There is also a patisserie (for cappuccino/espresso coffees and pastries), a wine/caviar bar, and a pizzeria with cobblestone floors and wrought-iron decorative features, and excellent pizzas (there are six to choose from).

ENTERTAINMENT. There are two showlounges (both theatre and cabaret style). The main one, Princess Theater, has a sloping floor, with aisle-style seating (as found in shoreside movie theaters) that is well tiered, and with good sight lines to the raised stage from most of the 500 seats.

The second showlounge (Vista Lounge), located at the aft end of the ship, has cabaret entertainment, and also acts as a lecture and presentation room. Princess Cruises has a good stable of regular cabaret acts to draw from, so there should be something for almost all tastes.

SPA/FITNESS. A glass-walled health spa complex is located high atop the ship and includes a gymnasium with the latest high-tech machines. One swimming pool is "suspended" aft between two decks (there are two other pools, although they are not large for the size of the ship).

Sports facilities are located in an open-air sports deck positioned inside the ship's funnel and adaptable for basketball, volleyball, badminton or paddle tennis. Joggers can exercise on the wrap-around open Promenade Deck.

● **For more extensive general information about the Princess Cruises experience, see pages 134–37.**

Delphin
★★ +

Small Ship: . . . . .16,214 tons	Passengers		Cabin Voltage: . . . . .220 volts
Lifestyle: . . . . .Standard	(lower beds/all berths): 466/556		Elevators: 2
Cruise Line: . . . . .Delphin Seereisen/	Passenger Space Ratio		Casino (gaming tables): . . . . .No
Hansa Touristilk	(lower beds/all berths): 35.6/29.8		Slot Machines: .No
Former Names: *Kazakhstan II/Belorussiya*	Crew/Passenger Ratio		Swimming Pools (outdoors): 1
Builder: . . . . .Wartsila (Finland)	(lower beds/all berths): 1.9/2.3		Swimming Pools (indoors): 0
Original Cost: . . . .$25 million	Navigation Officers: . . . . .Ukrainian		Whirlpools: 0
Entered Service: . . . .Jan 1975/Dec 1993	Cabins (total): .233		Fitness Center: . . . . .Yes
Registry: . . . . .Malta	Size Range (sq ft/m): 150.0–492.0/		Sauna/Steam Room: . . . . .Yes/Yes
Length (ft/m): 512.5/156.24	14.0–45.7		Massage: . . . . .Yes
Beam (ft/m): 71.8/21.90	Cabins (outside view): 128		Self-Service Launderette: . . . . .Yes
Draft (ft/m): 20.3/6.20	Cabins (interior/no view): 105		Dedicated Cinema/Seats: . . . . .No
Propulsion/Propellers: diesel (13,250kW)/2	Cabins (for one person): 0		Library: . . . . .Yes
Passenger Decks: 8	Cabins (with private balcony): 0		
Total Crew: 234	Cabins (wheelchair accessible): 0		

OVERALL SCORE: 1,092 (OUT OF A POSSIBLE 2,000 POINTS)

OVERVIEW. *Delphin* is a reasonably smart-looking cruise ship (originally built as one of a series of five vessels in the same class), and is topped by a square funnel. It was refitted and refurbished throughout following a shipyard rollover incident (when it was named *Belorussiya*). The ship's original car decks have long been converted into useful public rooms and additional cabins and the former car loading ramps on the vessel's stern have been fully sealed.

When the ship last underwent a major refurbishment, several new facilities were added; these improved almost all the public areas and added better health/fitness and spa facilities and an improved lido deck (the circular "swimming" pool is small, however, and is really only useful as a "dip" pool.

The promenade decks outdoors are quite reasonable, although there are "lips" which you have to step over in the forward section.

The interior decor is quite tasteful and warm, with colors that do not jar the senses. Flower bouquets and colorful artwork enhance the otherwise plain decor throughout.

Delphin will provide a very comfortable cruise experience for those German-speaking passengers looking for destination-intensive cruises, in comfortable, though not luxurious surroundings, at an extremely attractive price. It is not a luxury product, nor does it pretend to be. This is a good, basic product, and decent value for money. The ship's interiors are always in excellent shape and spotlessly clean,.

Hansa Touristik attracts many repeat passengers because of the destination-intensive itineraries and decent level of service. The company continues to spend money on little

BERLITZ'S RATINGS

	Possible	Achieved
Ship	500	252
Accommodation	200	111
Food	400	218
Service	400	227
Entertainment	100	57
Cruise	400	227

refinements throughout the ship, which are appreciated by the many loyal repeat passengers. Note that all port taxes and insurance are included. The currency on board is the euro.

A negative point is that there are many pillars throughout the public rooms, and these inhibit sight lines. The ceiling height is quite low in most public rooms, and the stairways are quite steep, with steps that are short and difficult to replace without major structural changes (a leftover from the ship's former life as a passenger ferry). The gangway is quite narrow. There is no wraparound promenade deck outdoors and no observation lounge/bar with forward-facing views over the ship's bows.

SUITABLE FOR: *Delphin* is best suited to German-speaking couples and single travelers of mature years who are seeking good value for money in a ship with traditional, quite comfortable (but not pretentious or luxurious) surroundings, at a modest price, with well planned itineraries.

ACCOMMODATION. There are several grades of accommodation to choose from. Typically, the higher the deck, the more expensive will be the accommodation.

The Boat Deck suites (located forward) are spacious and well equipped, with an abundance of drawers and good closet space, and all feature blond wood furniture, and a refrigerator. The bathrooms are very spacious, and come with full-sized bathtubs and large toiletries cabinet; bathrobes are also provided.

All the other outside-view and interior (no view) cabins are very compact units, yet adequate (but not for an around-the-world cruise), although there is little drawer space, and storage space is tight on the long cruises which this ship often undertakes. All of the beds have European duvets, and all cabins receive fresh flowers each cruise. The bathrooms are small, but there is a decent amount of space for toiletry items.

CUISINE. There is one large main dining room – the Pacific Restaurant, which has 554 seats. It has a high ceiling, large ocean-view picture windows, pleasing decor, and seats all passengers in one seating – so there is no need to hurry over meals.

In general, the food is attractively presented (better now that the catering is actively managed in-house), and the variety of foods featured is quite sound. The choice is good (with a heavy reliance on meat and game dishes), although selections for vegetarians are also available. While standard white and red table wines are included for lunch and dinner, there is also an additional wine list with a reasonably good selection at moderate prices. The gala buffet is very good. Service comes with a smile from attractive Ukrainian waitresses, although communicating with them can prove frustrating at times.

For casual meals, breakfast and lunch buffets can be taken in The Lido. The food featured is decent enough, with reasonable choice, although there is some degree of repetition, particularly of breakfast items.

ENTERTAINMENT. The showlounge is a single level room that is really designed for cabaret-style entertainment. Sight lines are quite good from most seats, although it is obstructed in some seats by some pillars.

SPA/FITNESS. The spa facilities are located on the lowest deck of the ship, while a fitness room and beauty salon are located on different decks, so there is no cohesive spa as such. However, in the facility on the lowest deck is a sauna, steam room, solarium, and massage rooms. In addition, there is a dialysis station for up to 26 persons (for special cruises when dialysis technicians are provided – they are not available on all cruises). Sports participants will find volleyball, basketball, and table tennis.

WHERE NAUTICAL EXPRESSIONS COME FROM

If you've ever wondered where some terms or phrases came from, you have only to look to the sea, ships, and seamen.

In the doldrums

Doldrums is the name of a place in the ocean that is located either side of, and near, the equator. It is characterized by unstable trade winds or even lack of winds for days, if not weeks, at a time. A sailing ship caught in the Doldrums can be stranded due to lack of wind. If the situation was bad enough, or if danger threatened, the boats might be launched in order to tow the ship until the wind picked up. Today, if we are in the doldrums, we feel stagnated or even morose.

Mind your P's and Q's

Sailors would get credit at the waterfront taverns until they were paid. The innkeeper kept a record of their drinks, and he had to mind that no pints or quarts were left off of their accounts. Today, the term usually refers to manners.

Passed with flying colors

This comes from sailing ships that, when passing other ships at sea, would fly their colors (pennants, flags) if they wanted to be identified. Today we tend to mean by this phrase that a person has passed an exam or test or trial with great marks.

Pipe down

A boatswain's call denoting the completion of an all hands evolution, and that you can go below. This expression is now used to mean "keep quiet" or "quiet down."

Port and Starboard

Originally, the old sailing ships (like the Vikings), didn't have a rudder, and were steered by a board on the right side. This came to be the "steerboard" side or starboard. The other side was called "larboard" at first, but since the side with the board could not be against the dock, the left when facing forward, it became known as the "port" side.

Round robin

The term originated in the British nautical tradition. Sailors wishing to mutiny would sign their names in a circle so the leader could not be identified. Today the term is often used in sports and competitions to denote a series of games in which all members of a league play each other one time.

Delphin Voyager
★★★

Small Ship: . . . . .21,884 tons	Passenger Decks: 8	Cabins (for one person): 0
Lifestyle: . . . . .Standard	Total Crew: 250	Cabins (with private balcony): 177
Cruise Line: . . . . .Delphin Cruises	Passengers	Cabins (wheelchair accessible): 2
Former Names: . . . . .Orient Venus	(lower beds/all berths): 650/650	Cabin Current: . . . . .110 volts
Builder: . . . . .Ishikawajima Heavy	Passenger Space Ratio	Elevators: 4
. . . . .Industries (Japan)	(lower beds/all berths): 33.6/33.6	Casino (gaming tables): . . . . .No
Original Cost: . . . .$150 million	Crew/Passenger Ratio	Slot Machines: .No
Entered Service: . . . . .July 1990/Apr 2007	(lower beds/all berths): 2.6/2.6	Swimming Pools (outdoors): 1
Registry: . . . . .The Bahamas	Navigation Officers: . . . . .European	Swimming Pools (indoors): 0
Length (ft/m): 570.8/174.00	Cabins (total): 325	Whirlpools: 0
Beam (ft/m): 78.7/24.00	Size Range (sq ft/m): 182.9–592.0/	Self-Service Launderette: . . . . .Yes
Draft (ft/m): 21.3/6.52	17.0–55.0	Dedicated Cinema/Seats: . . . . .No
Propulsion/Propellers: . . . . .diesel	Cabins (outside view): 269	Library: . . . . .Yes
(13,830 kW)/2	Cabins (interior/no view): 56	

BERLITZ'S OVERALL SCORE: 1,243 (OUT OF A POSSIBLE 2,000 POINTS)

OVERVIEW. *Delphin Voyager* was the first cruise ship built (as *Orient Venus*) for its former Japanese owners, Venus Cruise. This is a conventional-shaped ship with a pleasant enough profile. There is a reasonable amount of open deck and sunbathing space, including an expansive amount of open deck space for sunbathing, aft of funnel.

Great views can be had from the new Panorama observation lounge, which is wrapped around the funnel housing (although there is no elevator access for disabled passengers, a chair-lift is provided). There is a good array of public rooms with tasteful, European decor, including a three-deck-high entrance lobby, the focal point of communication. Most public rooms are set on one deck, providing good horizontal flow. The onboard currency is the euro.

SUITABLE FOR: *Delphin Voyager* is best suited to German-speaking couples and single travelers of mature years who enjoy traveling in very comfortable surroundings, and who enjoy good food and service, all at a moderate cost. It offers a superb cruise and seminar/learning experience.

ACCOMMODATION. There are seven cabin grades. The standard cabins have decor that is best described as light, but plain, with a reasonable amount of closet space; however, the drawer space is quite limited.

The largest suites (there are three) have an expansive lounge area with large, plush armchairs, coffee table, and window-side chairs and drinks table, large windows, and a larger private balcony. There is a separate sleeping room

BERLITZ'S RATINGS

	Possible	Achieved
Ship	500	331
Accommodation	200	128
Food	400	229
Service	400	241
Entertainment	100	61
Cruise	400	253

(curtained off from the living room) with twin- or queen-sized bed, vanity/office desk, and larger bathroom.

All grades have a flat-screen color television set, telephone, hairdryer, and refrigerator. All cabins have a shower, with the exception of the three suites, which feature a bathtub and separate shower. 36 cabins have life-boat obstructed vviews.

When the ship was refitted in 2007, new cabins were installed but the original cabins didn't receive much attention. Consequently, it is best to book one of the new cabins.

CUISINE/DINING. The main dining room (single seating with assigned tables) is quite attractive, and there is plenty of space around the dining tables. The aft section is perhaps the most desirable, with its views over the stern.

An alternative Romanesque Grill is unusual, with its classic period Roman decor and a high, elegant ceiling. The ship offers reasonably good, but commercial Japanese cuisine *(washoku)* exclusively.

ENTERTAINMENT. The horseshoe-shaped Carnival Main Lounge is a single level room, and has good sightlines to the platform stage. On most cruises, special featured entertainers are brought on board from ashore (singers, instrumentalists, storytellers, dance champions, and others).

SPA/FITNESS. There is a small spa, which consists of a gymnasium, saunas, and treatment rooms. There is also a special room with five fully-equipped dialysis stations for special cruises, when a dialysis technician is on board.

Deutschland
NOT RATED

Mid-Size Ship: . . . . .22,400 tons	Passenger Decks: 7	Cabins (for one person): 36
Lifestyle: . . . . .Premium	Total Crew: 270	Cabins (with private balcony): 2
Cruise Line: . . . .Peter Deilmann Reederei	Passengers	Cabins (wheelchair accessible): 1
Former Names: . . . . .none	(lower beds/all berths): 548/560	Cabin Current: . . . . .230 volts
Builder: . . . . .Howaldswerke Deutsche	Passenger Space Ratio	Elevators: 3
Werft	(lower beds/all berths): 40.8/40.0	Casino (gaming tables): . . . . .No
Original Cost: . . . . .DM 212 million	Crew/Passenger Ratio	Slot Machines: .No
Entered Service: . . . . .May 1998	(lower beds/all berths): 2.0/2.0	Swimming Pools (outdoors): 1
Registry: .Germany	Navigation Officers: . . . . .European	Swimming Pools (indoors): 1
Length (ft/m): 574.1/175.0	Cabins (total): 294	Whirlpools: 0
Beam (ft/m): 75.4/23.0	Size Range (sq ft/m): 129.1–365.9/	Self-Service Launderette: . . . . .No
Draft (ft/m): 19.0/5.8	12.0–34.0	Dedicated Cinema/Seats: Yes/83
Propulsion/Propellers: . . . . .diesel	Cabins (outside view): 220	Library: . . . . .Yes
(12,300 kW)/2	Cabins (interior/no view): 74	

OVERALL SCORE: NYR (OUT OF A POSSIBLE 2,000 POINTS)

OVERVIEW. *Deutschland,* now over 10 years old but in fine condition, is an important vessel for German-speaking passengers seeking a traditional ship. It has an angular, low-in-the-water profile that is not particularly handsome, and a large, single, squat, traditional funnel. The ship, built in sections by four shipyards, was assembled in Kiel, Germany. It is well maintained and kept very clean.

Although there is no wrap-around promenade deck outdoors as such (it's full of chairs around the central section where a swimming pool is located), you can walk along some of the open space (although there are windbreakers to negotiate). There are also port and starboard mid-ship walking decks under the inboard lifeboats. There is, in fact, a decent amount of open deck and sunbathing space for a ship of this size, including three aft decks for open-air lovers, and real teakwood deck chairs, with thick royal blue cushioned pads.

The Lido Deck has sides covered by canvas shading and white support pillars – like the ones you would find on seaside piers in England – as a setting for the outdoor swimming pool. The Lido Deck is a self-contained deck that has not only the pool, but also the casual Lido Buffet restaurant and Lido Terrasse Cafe. One could spend all day outdoors on this deck without having to dress to go indoors to eat. There is also a small waterfall aft of the pool.

The ship is laid out in a classic symmetrical pattern, and the interior decor has been successfully designed to re-create and reproduce the atmosphere of the ocean liners of the 1920s. The ship is beautifully decorated throughout (some might say overly decorated), with rich, dark woods and intricate brass and wrought-iron staircases that remind one of what were once called "gentlemen's clubs." There

BERLITZ'S RATINGS		
	Possible	Achieved
Ship	500	NYR
Accommodation	200	NYR
Food	400	NYR
Service	400	NYR
Entertainment	100	NYR
Cruise	400	NYR

is so much detail in the decoration work, and especially in the ornate ceilings, and cleaning it all is rather labor-intensive. There are quite a number of real statues, which don't seem to fit well aboard a cruise ship, but there are also many works of art on display.

There's a good range of public rooms and spaces, although these have been possible only by making the cabins smaller than one would expect of a ship of this size. The ship has an interesting, eclectic decor from different periods, as well as a wide assortment of cabin sizes, configurations and grades. The passenger mix is also somewhat varied.

There are two favorite drinking places: Zum Alten Fritz (Old Fritz) Bar, with dark wood interiors and Belle Epoque ambiance; and the Lili Marleen Salon (adjacent to the Berlin Restaurant), with mahogany channeled ceiling. Another nice public room is the Lido Terrace, which would have made a superb observation lounge had the designers extended it to the forward extremes of the deck. It is reminiscent of the winter gardens aboard the early transatlantic liners, and a delightful place to read or take afternoon tea.

The late Peter Deilmann's personal touch in the heavily detailed interiors is evident everywhere. *Deutschland* is registered under the German flag, but is actually placed under a second German register, which allows for the employment of many non-German staff. Thus, you will find Filipinos and other nationalities in the hotel service areas (the friendliness of the staff is good). The currency aboard is the euro, and the ship operates cashless cruising – charges must be settled on the last day of the cruise, when all purchases must, inconveniently, be made in cash.

Although the ship absorbs passengers well, the space

ratio could be better. The onboard product is generally sound, with attentive service, but the food and catering side of the operation could be improved. While the interiors are very attractive, the vessel does not come close to ships such as *Europa, Silver Shadow*, and *Silver Whisper*, with their much larger suites/cabins, open-seating dining (except *Europa*, which has open seating for breakfast and lunch, and assigned tables for dinner), and their abundance of cabins with private balconies. Smoking is permitted only on open decks. There is no internet center.

Just two suites have private balconies; most other cabins are very small when compared to other ships in the luxury and premium sectors of the international market. International passengers should note that the entertainment is almost totally in German; in fact, the whole ship is geared almost exclusively to German tastes.

SUITABLE FOR: *Deutschland* is best suited to German-speaking couples, and single travelers of mature years who seek a good value for money holiday in a very traditional cruise ship setting, with appealing itineraries and destinations, good food and attentive service. It could also appeal to English-speaking travelers used to being in European surroundings with a heavy German-speaking influence, and who can do without entertainment, onboard activities or shore excursions in English. I would not recommend the ship for children, due to the lack of facilities for them.

ACCOMMODATION. There are 10 categories (the higher the deck, the higher the cost). There are 18 outside view suites, 189 outside view doubles, 17 outside view single cabins; 12 interior (no view) doubles, 50 interior (no view) single cabins.

While many cabins are disappointingly small, all are furnished in fancy bird's-eye maple, and all the ceilings are fine, one-piece units, unlike the metal strip ceilings of most contemporary cruise vessels, and come with molded coving and ornamentation. The closet and drawer space is quite generous, and the attention to detail is very good. All beds have duvets and pillows. All cabins have a TV set, direct-dial satellite telephone, mini-bar/refrigerator, and real cabin keys (not plastic cards) are provided for all passengers. Many cabins have only one electrical outlet.

The bathrooms are also generously appointed, with a pink marble sink, gold anodized fittings, gilt-edged mirrors, hairdryer, and ample space for one's personal toiletry items. There is an electrical power outlet for shavers, with both 110 and 230 volts. Bathrobes are provided for all passengers.

Accommodations designated as suites (of which there are two grades) are reasonably large, with a living area that contains a couch, coffee table and two chairs; the bathroom has a full-size tub (all other cabins have showers only). Only the Executive Suites and Owner's Suites are (sensibly) located in the center of the ship, and each has a small private balcony. There is one wheelchair-accessible cabin (8042).

CUISINE. The main restaurant (Berlin), with 300 seats (and two seatings), is a very pleasant room, and all the chairs

have armrests, although space for serving at window-side tables is limited, and the hard backs of the chairs are not really very comfortable.

There are tables for two, four, six or eight, and two seatings for dinner. Two cold buffet bars for cold cuts of meat, cheese and salad items (either your waiter can obtain the food for you or you can choose it yourself) are featured for breakfast and lunch. Overall, the cuisine is quite creative (with lots of courses, with small portions of nouvelle cuisine), with a wide variety of choice and good taste, although it is not really memorable (the desserts, however, are extremely good). The place settings are extensive.

The Restaurant Vierjahreszeiten (Four Seasons), with 104 seats, is an intimate dining room (principally for suite occupants and for à la carte dining, for which a reservation is necessary). There is much detailing and ornamentation in the decor, and the ornate ceiling lamps and indented ceiling coving create an elegant ambiance that is relatively intimate.

There are tables for two, four or six. There is also a small private dining room (the Chancellor Room) with a large oval table which seats 10–12 (ideal for those special occasions and celebrations).

The extensive wine list includes a fine selection of wines from Germany and Austria, although the choice of wines from other countries is very limited. Eating in this restaurant takes considerably longer than in the Berlin Restaurant, and is best for those seeking an evening of fine dining and conversation.

The Lido Restaurant is the ship's casual dining venue. It has large ocean-view windows on two sides and a centrally located, multi-section self-serve buffet station. Additionally, there is a Lido Terrasse, at the stern, with windows on three sides. It is set on two slightly different levels, houses the ship's library, and has statuary and a relaxing, garden conservatory-like setting. This room also has a bar, plus elegant tea (and coffee) service.

ENTERTAINMENT. The Kaisersaal (Emperor's Saloon) is the ship's showlounge. It is a galleried period room with red velveteen chairs and is more like a ballroom than showlounge. It is reminiscent of a small opera house, and has a beautiful, huge central chandelier.

However, sight lines are obstructed from some seats (on both upper and lower seating levels) by many large marble-effect pillars. The entertainment is geared to German tastes, and is mostly in German.

SPA/FITNESS. The main spa area is on Deck 3, and this includes a small indoor swimming pool (with a statue of a female diver at one end), sauna, solarium, thalassotherapy baths, and massage/body therapy rooms; there is also a dialysis station.

Deck 6 has a fitness/sport center (with a few exercise machines), a sauna with a sea view, and a steam room. A beauty salon is in yet another location, on Deck 7.

Diamond Princess
★★★★

Large Resort Ship:	115,875 tons	Passenger Decks:	13
Lifestyle:	Standard	Total Crew:	1,238
Cruise Line:	Princess Cruises	Passengers	
Former Names:	none	(lower beds/all berths):	2,674/3,100
Builder:	Mitsubishi Heavy Industries (Japan)	Passenger Space Ratio (lower beds/all berths):	43.3/37.3
Original Cost:	$400 million	Crew/Passenger Ratio	
Entered Service:	February 2004	(lower beds/all berths):	2.1/2.5
Registry:	Bermuda	Navigation Officers:	British/Italian
Length (ft/m):	951.4/290.00	Cabins (total):	1,337
Beam (ft/m):	123.0/37.50	Size Range (sq ft/m):	168–1,329.3/ 15.6–123.5
Draft (ft/m):	26.4/8.05	Cabins (outside view):	1,000
Propulsion/Propellers:	gas turbine (25 MW)/2 azimuthing pods (21,000 kW each)	Cabins (interior/no view):	337

Cabins (for one person):	0
Cabins (with private balcony):	750
Cabins (wheelchair accessible):	28 (18 outside/10 interior)
Cabin Current:	110 volts
Elevators:	14
Casino (gaming tables):	Yes
Slot Machines:	Yes
Swimming Pools (outdoors):	4
Swimming Pools (indoors):	0
Whirlpools:	9
Self-Service Launderette:	Yes
Dedicated Cinema/Seats:	No
Library:	Yes

OVERALL SCORE: 1,544 (OUT OF A POSSIBLE 2,000 POINTS)

OVERVIEW. *Diamond Princess* has an instantly recognizable funnel due to two jet engine-like pods that sit high up on its structure but really are mainly for decoration. This is the first ship to be constructed by a Japanese shipyard for Princess Cruises (sister ship: *Sapphire Princess*). The ship is similar in size and internal layout to *Golden Princess, Grand Princess* and *Star Princess* (although of a slightly greater beam). Unlike its half-sister ships, however, all of which had a "spoiler" (containing a discotheque) located aft of the funnel, this has thankfully been removed from both *Diamond Princess* and *Sapphire Princess*, and has been replaced by a more sensible (and less weighty) aft-facing nightclub/discotheque structure (Skywalkers Nightclub) set around the base of the adjoining the funnel structure. The view from the nightclub overlooks aft-facing cascading decks and children's pool.

In December 2002, while the ship was under construction in the shipyard, a fire broke out on Deck 5. This lasted for 20 hours and burned some (548,980 sq ft (51,000 sq. meters) from Deck through Deck 13. The ship's hull was switched with that of identical sister *Sapphire Princess*, which was also under construction in the same yard at the same time. Consequently, the ship's debut was delayed from July 2003 to February 2004.

Diamond Princess is the first of the "Grand Class" ships to have a "pod" propulsion system installed (*for details, see page 171*). Electrical power is provided by a combination of four diesel and one gas turbine (CODAG) unit; the diesel engines are located in the engine room, while the gas turbine unit is located in the ship's funnel housing, on each side of which is a cosmetic pod that resembles a jet

BERLITZ'S RATINGS

	Possible	Achieved
Ship	500	431
Accommodation	200	168
Food	400	256
Service	400	293
Entertainment	100	82
Cruise	400	314

aircraft engine. Four areas focus on swimming pools; one of these is two decks high and is covered by a retractable glass dome, itself an extension of the funnel housing.

Unlike the outside decks, there is plenty of space inside the ship (but there are also plenty of passengers), and a wide array of public rooms, with many "intimate" (this being a relative word) spaces and places to play and enjoy. The passenger flow has been well thought out, and works with little congestion. The decor is attractive, with lots of earth tones. An extensive collection of art works has been chosen, and this complements the interior design and colors well.

Like half-sisters *Golden Princess, Grand Princess* and *Star Princess*, this ship also has a Wedding Chapel (a live web-cam can relay ceremonies via the internet). The ship's captain can legally marry (American) couples, due to the ship's Bermuda registry and a special dispensation (which should be verified when in the planning stage, according to where you reside). Princess Cruises offers three wedding packages – Pearl, Emerald, Diamond; the fee includes registration and official marriage certificate. The "Hearts & Minds" chapel is useful for "renewal of vows" ceremonies.

Gaming lovers should enjoy what is one of the largest casinos at sea (Grand Casino), with more than 260 slot machines; there are blackjack, craps and roulette tables, plus newer games such as Let It Ride Bonus, Spanish 21 and Caribbean Draw Progressive. But the highlight could well be the specially linked slot machines that provide a combined payout.

Other features include a library/CD-Rom computer room, and a separate card room. Ship lovers should enjoy the wood-paneled Wheelhouse Bar, finely decorated with memorabilia and ship models tracing part of parent company P&O's history. Aft of the International Dining Room is the Wake View Bar, with a spiral stairway that leads down to a great viewing spot for those who want to watch the ship's wake (like the one aboard the rivercruise stern paddle-wheeler *American Queen*); it is reached from the back of Club Fusion, on Promenade Deck. A high-tech hospital is provided, with live SeaMed tele-medicine link-ups with specialists at the Cedars-Sinai Medical Center in Los Angeles available for emergency help.

For youngsters and teenagers there is a two-deck-high playroom, teen room, and a host of specially trained counselors. Children have their own pools, hot tubs, and open deck area at the stern of the ship (away from adult areas).

If you are not used to large ships, it will take you some time to find your way around this one, despite the company's claim that this vessel offers passengers a "small ship feel, big ship choice."

The cabin bath towels are small, and drawer space is limited. There are no butlers – even for the top grade suites (which are not really large in comparison to similar suites aboard some other ships). Cabin attendants have too many cabins to look after (typically 20), which does not translate to fine personal service.

You'll have to live with the many extra charge items (such as for ice cream, and freshly squeezed orange juice) and activities (such as yoga, group exercise bicycling and kick boxing classes at $10 per session, not to mention $4 per hour for group babysitting services – at the time this book was completed). There's also a charge for using the washers and dryers in the self-service launderettes.

ACCOMMODATION. All passengers receive turndown service and chocolates on pillows each night, as well as bathrobes (on request) and toiletry amenity kits (larger for suite/mini-suite occupants). A hairdryer is provided in all cabins, sensibly located at the vanity desk unit in the living area. All bathrooms are tiled and have a decent amount of open shelf storage space for personal toiletries. Princess Cruises has BBC World, CNN, CNBC, ESPN and TNT on the in-cabin color TV system (when available, depending on cruise area).

The majority of the outside cabins on Emerald Deck have views obstructed by the lifeboats. Sadly, there are no cabins for singles. Your name is typically placed outside your suite or cabin – making it simple for delivery service personnel but also limiting your privacy. There is 24-hour room service (but some items on the room service menu are not available during early morning hours). Most balcony suites and cabins can be overlooked both from the navigation bridge wing. Cabins with balconies on Baja, Caribe, and Dolphin decks are also overlooked by passengers on balconies on the deck above.

CUISINE. All dining rooms are located on one of two decks. There are five principal dining rooms with themed decor and cuisine – smaller than the three dining rooms on the similarly sized *Golden Princess*, *Grand Princess* and *Star Princess*

because two dining rooms have been halved to become four; they are Sterling Steakhouse (for steak and grilled meats), Vivaldi (Italian fare), Santa Fe (southwestern USA cuisine), Pacific Moon (Asian cuisine) and International (the largest, located aft, with two seatings and "traditional" cuisine). These offer a mix of two seatings (with seating assigned according to the location of your cabin) and "anytime dining" (where you choose when and with whom you want to eat).

All dining rooms are non-smoking and are split into sections in a non-symmetrical design that breaks what are quite large spaces into many smaller sections, for better ambience and less noise pollution.

Specially designed dinnerware and good quality linens and silverware are featured: Dudson of England (dinnerware), Frette Egyptian cotton table linens, and silverware by Hepp of Germany.

Alternative dining options: Trattoria Sabatini is an informal eatery (reservations required; cover charge $20 per person). It features an eight-course meal, including Italian-style pizzas and pastas, with a variety of sauces, as well as Italian-style entrées (including tiger prawns and lobster tail – all provided with flair and entertainment by the waiters (by reservation only; the cover charge is $20 per person). The cuisine in this eatery is potentially better than in all the other dining rooms, with better quality ingredients and more attention to presentation, taste and delivery.

A poolside hamburger grill and pizza bar (no additional charge) are additional dining spots for casual bites, while extra charges will apply if you order items to eat at either the coffee bar/patisserie, or the caviar/champagne bar.

Other casual meals can be taken in the Horizon Court, open 24 hours a day, with large ocean-view on port and starboard sides and direct access to the two main swimming pools and lido deck (there is no finesse in presentation, however, and plastic plates, not trays, are provided).

ENTERTAINMENT. The Princess Theatre (showlounge) spans two decks and has comfortable seating on both main and balcony levels. It has $3 million in sound and light equipment, plus a 9-piece orchestra.

A second large entertainment lounge, Club Fusion, features cabaret acts acts at night, and lectures, bingo and horse racing during the day. A third entertainment lounge can also host cabaret acts and dance bands. Many other lounges and bars have live music, and a number of male dance hosts act as partners for women traveling alone.

SPA/FITNESS. The Lotus Spa complex, which has Japanese-style decor, surrounds one of the swimming pools (you can have a massage or other spa treatment in an ocean-view treatment room). Lotus Spa treatments include Chakra hot stone massage, Asian Lotus ritual (featuring massage with reflexology, reiki and shiatsu massage), deep-tissue sports therapy massage, lime and ginger salt glow, wild strawberry back cleanse, and seaweed mud wraps.

● **For more extensive general information about the Princess Cruises experience is like, see pages 134–37.**

Mid-Size Ship: . . . . .21,186 tons	Total Crew: 350
Lifestyle: . . . . .Standard	Passengers
Cruise Line: . . . . .Discovery World Cruises	(lower beds/all berths): 710/796
Former Names: .*Platinum, Hyundai Pungak,*	Passenger Space Ratio
Island Princess, Island Venture	(lower beds/all berths): 29.8/26.6
Builder: Rheinstahl Nordseewerke (Germany)	Crew/Passenger Ratio
Original Cost: . . . .$25 million	(lower beds/all berths): 2.4/2.6
Entered Service: . . . . . .Feb 1972/May 2003	Navigation Officers: . . . . .European
Registry: . . . . .Bermuda	Cabins (total): 355
Length (ft/m): 553.6/168.74	Size Range (sq ft/m): . . . . . . .125.9 – 441.3/
Beam (ft/m): 80.7/24.6	11.7 – 41.0
Draft (ft/m): 80.8/24.64	Cabins (outside view): 283
Propulsion/Propellers: diesel (13,400 kW)/2	Cabins (interior/no view): 72
Passenger Decks: 8	Cabins (for one person): 0

Cabins (with private balcony): 0
Cabins (wheelchair accessible): 2
Cabin Current: . . . . .110 and 220 volts
Elevators: 4
Casino (gaming tables): . . . . .Yes
Slot Machines: . . . . .Yes
Swimming Pools (outdoors): 2
Swimming Pools (indoors): 0
Whirlpools: 2
Self-Service Launderette: . . . . .No
Dedicated Cinema/Seats: Yes/129
Library: . . . . .Yes

OVERALL SCORE: 1,245 (OUT OF A POSSIBLE 2,000 POINTS)

OVERVIEW. *Discovery*, formerly operated from 1972 to 1999 by Princess Cruises, has a very attractive traditional ship profile and well balanced, somewhat rounded exterior styling. As the former *Island Princess*, it was, together with sister ship *Pacific Princess* (presently *Pacific*), one of the pair of original "Love Boats" in the American television series *The Love Boat*. Hyundai Asan Cruises acquired the ship in 1999, and operated cruises from South Korea to North Korea.

In 2001, the entrepreneur Gerry Herrod, who formerly founded the long defunct Ocean Cruise Lines, and Orient Lines bought the ship. He then spent $10 million refurbishing and updating it for its present cruising role under the brand name of Voyages of Discovery, principally for the UK market. For the winter season, the ship carries five Zodiac inflatable shore landing craft.

One of the ship's two outdoor swimming pools has a glass dome (magrodome) cover, which can be used in inclement weather conditions. There is no walk-around promenade deck outdoors, however.

Inside, the public areas are quite spacious considering the size of the ship, and there are numerous public rooms (some with high ceilings), with reasonably wide passageways. These include a lobby with mezzanine level and curved staircase (several shops and offices are on the upper level), and the Discovery Lounge, located aft, has a two-deck high glass wall overlooking the aft deck. There's an internet center, equipped with six computer stations, and a library with 5,000 books provided by the Marine Society. Tasteful decor is featured throughout, with pastel colors and fine artwork that is pleasing to the eye, if a little bland.

BERLITZ'S RATINGS		
	Possible	Achieved
Ship	500	293
Accommodation	200	113
Food	400	279
Service	400	261
Entertainment	100	56
Cruise	400	243

The forward observation lounge also acts as an indoor dining area.

The ship, which has been well maintained, and is quite elegant, with comfortable surroundings for the older passenger who wants plenty of space and does not want to be part of larger, more impersonal ships. *Discovery* competes directly with *Marco Polo* (Transocean Tours), which is an older ship with the same type of passengers and following that *Discovery* seeks to attract, in this limited, but growing, marketplace. Concessions run the hotel operations, dining, spa/beauty services, and shops. The onboard currency is the British pound. All gratuities are included. Perhaps a self-serve launderette or ironing room (missed by many British passengers) would be a useful addition.

SUITABLE FOR: *Discovery* is best suited to couples and single travelers of mature years who enjoy being transported to interesting destinations in the comfort of a ship that is now considered to be traditional in style, unpretentious and with a casual dress code, and without the trappings of much entertainment or organized parlor games.

ACCOMMODATION. There are as many as 15 price categories (rather a lot for a mid-sized ship). The price you pay will depend on the grade, location and size of the cabin.

There are five suites; these are of quite a decent size, and well designed, with plenty of space to move around in. Two of the suites are located forward, just under the navigation bridge, and command good views.

Most other cabins have ample room, are quite well appointed, and there is plenty of closet and drawer space.

The top category cabins (on Bridge Deck and Promenade Deck) have a full bathtub, while all others have a shower enclosure (although many have obstructed views). None of the suites or cabins has a private balcony (the ship was built before private balconies came into vogue).

No matter what category of suites or cabin you choose, there is a television, telephone, personal safe and hairdryer in each. Some cabins have interconnecting doors, and some can accommodate a third/fourth person.

CUISINE. The Seven Continents Dining Room is a reasonably comfortable room, and is operated in two seatings (note that there are few tables for two, most being for four, six or eight). The cuisine (upgraded from previous Voyages of Discovery ships) includes many classic favorites, and the presentation and service are good. The wine list is adequate, and prices are reasonable, although the selection is small and consists mostly of younger wines. Casual breakfasts and lunches can be taken in the Yacht Club (an observation lounge), with fine ocean views on three sides or outdoors on the Lido Deck, adjacent to the swimming pool.

Alternative (Reservations Only) Dining Option: Alternative dinners can also be taken in the Yacht Club, with its observation lounge views on three sides, adjacent to the Lido; Continental and Italian specialties are featured, and there is no cover charge. A late-riser's breakfast is always popular; you can also opt for Continental Breakfast to be served in your cabin if you wish.

All dining areas are non-smoking.

ENTERTAINMENT. The "theater-in-the-round" Carousel Showlounge has banquette-style seating in several tiers, set around a "thrust" stage. The entertainment is low-key, which means only the occasional cabaret act is featured. There is live music throughout the ship for dancing.

SPA/FITNESS. The Spa Atlantis is positioned aft on two of the uppermost decks (a stairway connects the two). A beauty salon is on the upper deck, while a gymnasium (with aft-facing ocean-view windows), three treatment rooms, and male and female saunas are on the lower level. It is operated by a UK-based concession, Harding Brothers, and has products from Guinot and Thalgo), but do be aware that staff often try to sell beauty products aggressively.

Sample prices include: full body massage, €45 (50 minutes); back, neck and shoulder massage, €30 (30 minutes); reflexology, €25; course of four yoga classes, €15; Pilates class, €5 (30 minutes); hairdressing services which include a shampoo, cut and finish for €15.

RULES OF THE ROAD

Ships, the largest moving objects made by man, are subject to stringent international regulations. They must keep to the right in shipping lanes, and pass on the right (with certain exceptions). When circumstances raise some doubt, or shipping lanes are crowded, ships use their whistles in the same way an automobile driver uses directional signals to show which way he will turn. When one ship passes another and gives a single blast on its whistle, this means it is turning to starboard (right). Two blasts mean a turn to port (left).

The other ship acknowledges by repeating the same signal. Ships switch on navigational running lights at night — green for starboard, red for port, plus two white lights on the masts, the forward one lower than the aft one.

Flags and pennants form another part of a ship's communication facilities and are displayed for identification purposes. Each time a country is visited, its national flag is shown. While entering and leaving a port, the ship flies a blue-and-white vertically striped flag to request a pilot, while a half-red, half-white flag (divided vertically) indicates that a pilot is on board. Cruise lines also display their own "house" flag from the mast.

A ship's funnel (smokestack) is one other means of identification, each line having its own design and color scheme. The size, height, and number of funnels were all points worth advertising at the turn of the 20th century. Most ocean liners of the time had four funnels and were called "four-stackers."

There are numerous customs at sea, many of them older than any maritime law. Superstition has always been an important element, as in the following example quoted from the British Admiralty Manual of Seamanship: "The custom of breaking a bottle of wine over the stem of a ship when it is being launched originates from the old practice of toasting prosperity to a ship with a silver goblet of wine, which was then cast into the sea in order to prevent a toast of ill intent being drunk from the same cup. This was a practice that proved too expensive, and it was replaced in 1690 by the breaking of a bottle of wine over the stem."

Disney Magic
★★★★

Large Resort Ship:	.........83,338 tons	Passengers		Cabins (wheelchair accessible): 12
Lifestyle:	...................Standard	(lower beds/all berths): 1,750/3,325		Cabin Current: ....110 volts
Cruise Line:	........Disney Cruise Line	Passenger Space Ratio		Elevators: 12
Former Names:	..................none	(lower beds/all berths): 47.6/25.0		Casino (gaming tables): ....No
Builder:	.............Fincantieri (Italy)	Crew/Passenger Ratio		Slot Machines: ....No
Original Cost:	.............$350 million	(lower beds/all berths): 1.8/3.5		Swimming Pools (outdoors): 3
Entered Service:	.............July 1998	Navigation Officers: ....European/		Swimming Pools (indoors): 0
Registry:	.................The Bahamas	Scandinavian		Whirlpools: 6
Length (ft/m):	.............964.5/294.00	Cabins (total): 875		Fitness Center: ....Yes
Beam (ft/m):	.............105.7/32.22	Size Range (sq ft/m): 180.8–968.7/		Sauna/Steam Room: ....Yes/Yes
Draft (ft/m):	..................26.2/8.0	16.8–90.0		Massage: ....Yes
Propulsion/Propellers: .....diesel-electric		Cabins (outside view): 720		Self-Service Launderette: ....Yes (3)
	(38,000kW)/2	Cabins (interior/no view): 155		Dedicated Cinema/Seats: Yes/270
Passenger Decks:	11	Family Cabins: 80		Library: ....No
Total Crew:	945	Cabins (with private balcony): 388		

OVERALL SCORE: 1,508 (OUT OF A POSSIBLE 2,000 POINTS)

OVERVIEW. *Disney Magic*'s 10-year-old profile combines streamlining with tradition and nostalgia, and has two large red and black funnels designed to remind you of the ocean liners of the past. *Disney Magic* is the first cruise ship built with two funnels since the 1950s. However, one of the funnels is a dummy, and contains a variety of public spaces, including a neat teen center called Aloft (with big-screen TV, MP3 players, computers with hi-tech games, and video games). The ship was actually constructed in two halves, which were then joined together in the shipyard in Venice, Italy. The ship's whistle even plays "When You Wish Upon a Star" (or a sort of sickly version of it). The bow has handsome gold scrollwork that more typically seen adorning the tall ships of yesteryear. There is a walk-around promenade deck outdoors for strolling.

Disney Cruise Line did not add ostentatious decoration to the exterior. However, Mickey Mouse's ears are painted on the funnels; there is also a special 85-ft (26-meter) long paint stripe that cleverly incorporates Disney characters into the whimsical yellow paintwork along each side of the hull at the bow. Cute. The exterior colors are also those of Mickey himself. Also of note is a 15-ft (4.5-meter) Goofy hanging upside down in a bosun's chair, painting the stern.

A sports deck has a paddle tennis court, table tennis, basketball court, shuffleboard, and golf driving range. There are three outdoor pools: one pool for adults only (in theory), one for children, and one for families, complete with a large poolside movie screen (guess which one has Mickey's ears painted into the bottom?). However, there's music everywhere (four different types), and it's impossible to find a

BERLITZ'S RATINGS		
	Possible	Achieved
Ship	500	428
Accommodation	200	166
Food	400	207
Service	400	295
Entertainment	100	90
Cruise	400	322

quiet spot (in fact, you can sit in many places a get two types of music blaring at you at the same time). The children's pool has a long yellow water slide (available at specified times), held up by the giant hand of Mickey Mouse, although the pool itself really is too small considering the number of small children typically carried.

A 24-by-14-ft Goofy Pool Jumbo Screen is positioned by the family pool area (just behind the forward funnel); it shows classic Disney animated and live-action movies, TV shows and sporting events. Also added during an October 2005 refit were additional space for spa/fitness facilities, and Ocean Quest, *Disney Magic*'s fifth dedicated space for children. Ocean Quest has a scale replica of the ship's bridge and LCD screen "windows" that let youngsters look out over the bridge via live video feed from the actual bridge. Kids can sit in a captain's chair and participate in a simulation game where they steer into and out of various ports. Older children can go to Aloft – a teens-only dorm-like chill-out zone.

Inside, the ship is quite stunning, but is poorly finished in several places. The Art Deco theme of the old ocean liners or Radio City Music Hall has been tastefully carried out (check out the stainless steel/pewter Disney detailing on the handrails and balustrades in the three-deck-high lobby).

Most public rooms have high ceilings. Much of the interior detailing is whimsical – pure Disney. The lobby provides a real photo opportunity, with a 6-ft (1.8-meter) high bronze statue of Mickey in the role of a ship's helmsman (there is probably some pixie dust around somewhere, too). Mickey is also visible in many other areas, albeit subtly (for Disney). If you can't sleep, try counting the number of times Mickey's logo appears.

There are two large shops and an abundance of Disney-theme clothing, soft toys, collectibles and specialty items. Other facilities include a superb, 1,040-seat Walt Disney Theater (spread over four decks but without a balcony), piano bar, adults-only nightclub/disco, family lounge, and a dedicated cinema (where classic Disney films are shown, as well as first-run movies).

The children's entertainment areas measure 13,000 sq. ft (1,200 sq. meters); more than 30 children's counselors run the extensive programmes. There is also a separate teen club and video game arcade. A child drop-off service is available in the evenings, and private babysitting services are available ($11 per hour), as are character "tuck-ins" for children, and character breakfasts and lunches. Strollers are available, at no charge, and parents can be provided with beepers, so that they can also enjoy their time alone, away from their offspring for much of the day.

Other Disney exclusives include the game show "Who Wants to be a Mouseketeer?" The prizes include free cruises and onboard credits of up to $1,000 and Tea with Wendy Darling (from Disney's version of *Peter Pan*).

Apart from the ports of call, the highlight for most is a day spent on Disney's private island, Castaway Cay. It is an outstanding private island (perhaps the benchmark for all private islands for families with children), with its own pier so that the ship can dock alongside – a cruise industry first. There is a post office with its own special Bahamas/Disney stamp, and a whole host of dedicated, well thought-out attractions and amenities for all ages (including a large adults-only beach, complete with massage cabanas).

Disney characters are aboard for all cruises and lots of photo opportunities; they come out to play mainly when children's activities are scheduled. All the artwork in public areas comes from Disney films or animation features, with many original drawings dating from the early 1930s.

Disney Magic operates 7-day cruises to the Eastern Caribbean (and Castaway Cay in the Bahamas), offering three different itineraries.

At Port Canaveral, the Disney terminal is a $27 million copy of the original Ocean Terminal used by the transatlantic liners *Queen Elizabeth* and *Queen Mary* in Southampton, England. Transfers between Walt Disney World resorts in Orlando and the ship are included. Special buses feature vintage 1930s/1940s style interior decor (30 sets of Mickey's face and ears can be found in the blue fabric of each seat). Five of the 45 custom-made buses are outfitted to carry wheelchair passengers.

Embarkation and disembarkation is an entertainment event rather than the hassle-laden affair that it has become for many cruise lines with large ships (if all the buses do not arrive together), and it's quite slick. The cruise terminal's second floor has a neat 13,000 sq.ft. terrazzo tile map of Florida's east coast and The Bahamas.

Disney Magic is like a floating theme park – a sea-going Never-Never Land. In reality, it is a highly programmed, strictly timed and regimented onboard experience, with tick-ets, lines and reservations necessary for almost everything. Since its introduction, the product has been fine-tuned. Security is very good, and all registered children must wear an ID bracelet (showing name, cabin number and muster station number), and parents are given pagers for emergencies.

Take mainly casual clothing (casual with a capital "C"), although there are two "formal" nights on the 7-day cruise, and wish upon a star – that's really all you'll need to do to enjoy yourself aboard this stunning ship. The onboard currency is the US dollar. Members of Disney's Holiday Club can exchange points for cruises. It is expensive (but so is a stay at any Disney resort), gratuities are extra (suggested at about $10 per person, per day), and 15% is added to all bar/beverage/wine and spa accounts.

Lines at various outlets can prove irritating (some creative Disney Imagineering is needed), as can trying to get through to Guest Services by telephone. Gripes include: poky elevators; lines and signing up for activities; the food product and delivery falls short of less expensive cruise products; there is no proper library – something many adult passengers miss; and the early morning disembarkation and customs inspection is a definite turn-off for many.

Onboard airline check-in for post-cruise flights from Orlando is now offered, with luggage transfer directly from ship to flight on any one of seven airlines: AirTran, Alaska, American, Continental, Delta, Northwest and United. You'll need to complete pre-registration information (from Orlando Airport or a hospitality desk at the Disney World Resort).

SUITABLE FOR: *Disney Magic* is great for families with children (or grandchildren), although couples and singles are also welcome (there are few activities for couples during the daytime, but enough entertainment at night). Whether cruising with 1,000 (or more) kids aboard will make for a relaxing holiday for those without kids will depend on how much noise they can absorb. You will, however, need to be a real Disney fan, as *everything* revolves around Disney and the family theme; this means an emphasis on entertainment and good times, while food takes a back step into the world of "theme park" cuisine. For children of all ages (minimum 12 weeks old and above), it's hard to beat *Disney Magic* or *Disney Wonder*.

ACCOMMODATION. There are 12 grades (price will depend on grade, size and location). Spread over six decks, all suites/cabins have been designed for practicality and have space-efficient layouts. Most cabins have common features such as a neat vertical steamer trunk for clothes storage, illuminated closets, a hairdryer located at a vanity desk (or in the bathroom), and bathrobes for all passengers. Many cabins have third- and fourth pull-down berths that rise and are totally hidden in the ceiling when not in use, but the standard interior and outside cabins, while acceptable for two, are extremely tight with three or four. The decor is practical, creative, and colorful, with lots of neat styling touches. Cabins with refrigerators can have them stocked with one of several packages (at extra cost).

The bathrooms, although compact (due to the fact that

the toilet is separate), are really functional units, designed with split-use facilities so that more than one person can use them at the same time (good for families). Many have bathtubs (really shower tubs).

Accommodation designated as suites offers much more space, and extra goodies such as VCRs, CD players, large screen TVs, and extra beds (useful for larger families). Some of the suites are beneath the pool deck, teen lounge, or informal cafe, so there could be noise as the ceiling insulation is poor (but the cabin to cabin insulation is good).

Wheelchair-bound passengers have a variety of cabin sizes and configurations, including suites with a private balcony (unfortunately you cannot get a wheelchair through the balcony's sliding door) and extra-large bathrooms with excellent roll-in showers, and good closet and drawer space (almost all the vessel is accessible). For the sight-impaired, cabin numbers and elevator buttons are braille-encoded.

A 24-hour room service is available (suite occupants also get concierge service); but the room service menu and cabin breakfast menu are limited. There is a 15% service charge for all beverage deliveries (including tea and coffee).

CUISINE. There are three main dining rooms (all non-smoking), each with over 400 seats, two seatings, and unique themes. Lumiere's has Beauty and the Beast; Parrot Cay has a tacky, pseudo-Caribbean theme; Animator's Palate (the most visual of the three) has food and electronic art that makes the evening decor change from black and white to full-color. You will eat in all three dining rooms in rotation (twice per 7-day cruise), and move with your assigned waiter and assistant waiter to each dining room in turn, thus providing a different dining experience (each has a different decor, different menus). As you will have the same waiter in each of the three restaurants, any gratuities go only to "your" waiter. Parrot Cay and Lumiere's have open seating for breakfast and lunch (the lunch menu is pitiful). The noise level in all three dining rooms is extremely high. If the formal nights happen to fall on the evening you are due to eat in Parrot Cay, formal wear and the decor of Parrot Cay Restaurant just don't mix.

Alternative Dining Venue: Palo is an elegant 140-seat reservations-only alternative restaurant (with a $5 cover/gratuity charge) featuring Italian cuisine. It has a 270° view, and is for adults only (no "Munchkins" allowed); the à la carte cuisine is cooked to order, and the wine list is good (although prices are high). Make your reservations as soon as you board or miss out on the only decent food aboard this ship. Afternoon High Tea is also presented here, on days at sea.

Casual Dining Venue: Topsider's is an indoor/outdoor cafe featuring low-quality self-serve breakfast and lunch buffets with limited choice and presentation, and a buffet dinner for children (consisting mostly of fried foods). However, Topsider's is often overcrowded at lunchtime, so it may be better to go to the Parrot Cay dining room, which offers breakfast and lunch buffet, too. A newly added poolside Goofey's Galley has grilled panini sandwiches and wraps, and soft drinks are complimentary.

An ice cream and frozen yogurt bar (Scoops) opens infrequently; other fast food outlets include Pluto's (for hamburgers, hot dogs), Pinocchio's, which is open throughout the day but not in the evening (for basic pizza and sandwiches). On one night of the cruise, there is also an outdoor self-serve "Tropicalifragilisticexpialidocious" buffet.

Vegetarians and those seeking light cuisine will be totally underwhelmed by the lack of green vegetables. Guest chefs from Walt Disney World Resort prepare signature dishes each cruise, and also host cooking demonstrations.

ENTERTAINMENT. The entertainment and activities programming for families and children are extremely good. There are three large-scale stage shows (in the stunning 977-seat showlounge) featuring original Disney musicals; *Disney Dreams, Hercules – The Muse-ical,* and *The Golden Mickeys.* Sadly, there is no live orchestra, although the lighting, staging and technical effects are excellent. There is also a Disney-themed Trivia Game Show.

For grown-ups, there is "Route 66" – an adult entertainment area that includes a wacky Hollywood-style street, complete with three entertainment rooms. "Cadillac" is a jazz piano lounge, with private headphones for listening to music of all types when no live music is scheduled; "Wavebands" (for ear-splitting rock 'n' roll and country music); and "Barrel of Laughs" (for improvisational comedy involving the audience). During the day, creative enrichment programs have been added. Once each cruise, a "Pirates In the Caribbean" poolside party takes place; this late-night event even includes fireworks.

SPA/FITNESS. The Vista Spa is a fitness/wellbeing complex that measures 10,700 sq ft/994 sq metres. The fitness/workout room (with high-tech Cybex muscle-toning equipment) has ocean-view windows overlooking the navigation bridge on the deck below. There are 11 rooms for spa/beauty treatments – but note that the pounding from the basketball court directly above makes spa treatments less than relaxing.

Three spa "villas" have indoor treatment suites connected to private outdoor verandahs with personal hot tub, open-air shower and chaise lounge. There's an area for spinning classes and a couple of private salons for Pilates instruction and one-on-one beauty and fitness consultations.

Thermal bath rooms feature a "tropical rain shower", sauna, mild steam room, aromatic steam room and a fog shower. Aromatic scents such as eucalyptus, lime, peppermint, rose and sage can be infused into the mild steam room, while chamomile is used in the aromatic steam room.

Massage (including exotic massages such as Aroma Stone massage and other well-being massages, as well as underwater massage in a hydrotherapy bath), aromatherapy facials, pedicures, and beauty salon treatments are at extra cost (massage, for example, costs about $2 per minute, plus gratuity). The Rasul mud and steam room is an absolute delight for couples. Make appointments early.

For something extra special, consider booking a massage at Castaway Cay – in a private beach hut on the beach that is open to the sea. It's magical.

Disney Wonder
★★★★

Large Resort Ship: ....85,000 tons	Total Crew: 945	Cabins (with private balcony): 388
Lifestyle: ....Standard	Passengers	Cabins (wheelchair accessible): 12
Cruise Line: ....Disney Cruise Line	(lower beds/all berths): 1,750/3,325	Cabin Current: ....110 volts
Former Names: ....none	Passenger Space Ratio	Elevators: 12
Builder: ....Fincantieri (Italy)	(lower beds/all berths): 48.5/25.5	Casino (gaming tables): ....No
Original Cost: ....$350 million	Crew/Passenger Ratio	Slot Machines: ....No
Entered Service: ....Aug 1999	(lower beds/all berths): 1.8/3.5	Swimming Pools (outdoors): 3
Registry: ....The Bahamas	Navigation Officers: European/Norwegian	Swimming Pools (indoors): 0
Length (ft/m): 964.5/294.00	Cabins (total): 875	Whirlpools: 6
Beam (ft/m): 105.7/32.22	Size Range (sq ft/m): 180.8–968.7/	Self-Service Launderette: ....Yes (3)
Draft (ft/m): 26.2/8.0	16.8–90.0	Dedicated Cinema/Seats: Yes/270
Propulsion/Propellers: .....diesel-electric	Cabins (outside view): 720	Library: ....Yes
(38,000kW)/2	Cabins (interior/no view): 155	
Passenger Decks: 11	Family Cabins: 80	

OVERALL SCORE: 1,509 (OUT OF A POSSIBLE 2,000 POINTS)

OVERVIEW. Zip-a-Dee-Do-Dah, Zip-a-Dee-Day! *Disney Wonder*'s profile has managed to combine streamlining with tradition and nostalgia, and has two large red and black funnels designed to remind you of the ocean liners of the past. *Disney Wonder* is only the second cruise ship built with two funnels since the 1950s (the first was *Disney Magic*). However, one of the funnels is a dummy, and contains a variety of public spaces, including a neat ESPN sports bar and a broadcast center. The ship was actually constructed in two halves, which were then joined together in the shipyard in Venice, Italy. The ship's whistle even plays "When You Wish Upon a Star" (or a sort of sickly version of it). The bow has handsome gold scrollwork that more typically seen adorning the tall ships of yesteryear. There is a walk-around promenade deck outdoors for strolling.

Disney Cruise Line did not add ostentatious decoration to the ship's exterior, although Mickey Mouse's ears are painted on the funnels. There is also a special 85-ft (26-meter) long paint stripe that cleverly incorporates Disney characters into the whimsical yellow paintwork along each side of the hull at the bow. Cute. The ship's exterior colors are also those of Mickey himself. Also of note is a whimsical, 15-ft (4.5-meter) tall Donald Duck and Huey hanging upside down in a bosun's chair, painting the stern.

On deck, a sports deck has a paddle tennis court, table tennis, basketball court, shuffleboard, and golf driving range. An ESPN Skybox Bar has 12 TV sets of differing sizes for live (by satellite) sports events and noisy conversation (cigar smokers welcome). There are three outdoor pools: one pool for adults only (in theory), one for children, and one for families – guess which one has Mickey's

BERLITZ'S RATINGS		
	Possible	Achieved
Ship	500	429
Accommodation	200	166
Food	400	207
Service	400	295
Entertainment	100	90
Cruise	400	322

ears painted into the bottom? – which benefited from the addition of a large 24-ft x 14-ft poolside-movie screen in 2006. Note that there's music everywhere (four different types), and it's impossible to find a quiet spot (in fact, you can sit in many places a get two types of music blaring at you at the same time). The children's pool has a long yellow water slide (available at specified times), held up by the giant hand of Mickey Mouse, although the pool itself really is too small considering the number of small children typically carried.

Inside, the ship is quite stunning, although poorly finished in several places. The Art Deco theme of the old ocean liners has been tastefully carried out (check out the stainless steel/pewter Disney detailing on the handrails and balustrades in the three-deck-high lobby). Most public rooms have high ceilings. The decor is reminiscent of New York's Radio City Music Hall. Much of the interior detailing is whimsical – pure Disney. The lobby provides a photo opportunity that should not be missed: a 6-ft (1.8-meter) bronze statue of "The Little Mermaid." Mickey himself is visible in many areas, albeit subtly (for Disney). If you can't sleep, try counting the number of times Mickey's logo appears – it's an impossible task.

There are two large shops and an abundance of Disney-theme clothing, soft toys, collectibles and specialty items. There's a superb 1,040-seat Walt Disney Theater (spread over four decks but without a balcony), piano bar, adults-only nightclub/disco, family lounge, and a cinema (where classic Disney films are shown, as well as first-run movies).

The children's entertainment areas measure 13,000 sq. ft (1,200 sq. meters); more than 30 children's counselors run the extensive programmes. There is also a separate teen club and video game arcade. A child drop-off service is available in the evenings, and private babysitting services are available ($11 per hour), as are character "tuck-ins" for children, and character breakfasts and lunches. Free strollers are available, and parents can be provided with beepers, so that they can also enjoy their time alone, away from their offspring for much of the day.

Although Nassau is decidedly unappealing and not tourist-friendly, the highlight of the itinerary is Disney's private island, Castaway Cay. It is an outstanding private island (perhaps the benchmark for all private islands), with its own pier so that the ship can dock alongside – a cruise industry first. The post office has its own special Bahamas/Disney stamp, and a whole host of dedicated, well thought out attractions and amenities for all ages (including a large adults-only beach, complete with massage cabanas). Watersports equipment (floats, paddleboats, kayaks, hobie cats, aqua fins, aqua trikes, and snorkels) can be rented.

Disney characters are aboard for all cruises and lots of photo opportunities; they come out to play mainly when children's activities are scheduled. All the artwork in public areas comes from Disney films or animation features, with many original drawings dating from the early 1930s.

Disney Wonder has year-round 3- and 4-day cruises to The Bahamas – part of a 7-night vacation package that includes a 3- or 4-day stay at a Walt Disney World resort hotel in Orlando; the cruise then forms the second half of the vacation. It's all tied up in one encapsulated, well-controlled, seamless, and crime-free environment that promises escape and adventure. You can also book just the cruise without the resort stay. American Express cardholders get special treatment and extra goodies. Members of Disney's Vacation Club can exchange points for cruises.

At Port Canaveral, a special terminal has been constructed; it's a copy of the original Ocean Terminal used by the transatlantic liners *Queen Elizabeth* and *Queen Mary* in Southampton, England. Transfers between Walt Disney World resorts in Orlando and the ship are included. Special buses feature vintage 1930s/1940s style interior decor (30 sets of Mickey's face and ears can be found in the blue fabric of each seat). Five of the 45 custom-made buses are outfitted to carry wheelchair passengers. Embarkation and disembarkation is an entertainment event rather than the hassle-laden affair that it has become for many cruise lines with large ships (if all the buses do not arrive together).

Disney Wonder (and sister ship *Disney Magic*) are the cruise industry's floating theme parks – sea-going Never-Never Lands that are rated on their own, in common with all other ships. The rating does not include any additional 3- or 4-day stay at a Disney World resort, which forms part of the total Disney Cruise Line vacation (although it is now possible to book just the cruise). Be aware, however, that this is a highly programmed, strictly timed and regimented onboard experience, with tickets, lines and reservations necessary for almost everything. Since its introduction, the product has improved almost to the point that Disney now understands that cruise ships are different to operate than its theme parks. Parents can relax knowing that security is very good, and all registered children must wear an ID bracelet (showing name, cabin number and muster station number), and parents are given pagers for emergencies.

Take mainly casual clothing (casual with a capital "C"), although there are two formal nights on the 7-day cruise, and wish upon a star – that's really all you'll need to do to enjoy yourself aboard this stunning ship. The onboard currency is the US dollar. Members of Disney's Holiday Club can exchange points for cruises.

There is no observation lounge with forward-facing views over the ship's bows. There is no dance floor with live orchestra for adults (other than "Rockin Bar D" in Beat Street for throbbing disco/country-style music). The elevators are very small, and so is the gymnasium (for such a large ship). It is expensive (but then so is a week at any Disney resort), gratuities are extra (suggested at about $10 per person, per day), and 15% is added to all bar, beverage and wine and spa accounts.

Standing in line for embarkation, disembarkation, shore tenders and for self-serve buffet meals is an inevitable aspect of cruising aboard all large ships. Lines at various outlets can prove irritating (some creative Disney Imagineering is needed, including a large sprinkling of pixie dust). Other gripes include: poky elevators; lines and signing up for activities; getting through to "guest services" (the reception desk) by telephone; the food product and delivery falls short of less expensive cruise products; there is no proper library – something many adult passengers miss; and the early morning disembarkation and customs inspection is a definite turn-off for many.

Onboard airline check-in for post-cruise flights from Orlando is now offered, with luggage transfer directly from ship to flight on any one of seven airlines: AirTran, Alaska, American, Continental, Delta, Northwest and United. You'll need to complete pre-registration information (from Orlando Airport or a hospitality desk at the Disney World Resort).

SUITABLE FOR: *Disney Wonder* is ideally suited to families with children (or grandchildren), although couples and singles are also welcome (there are few activities for couples during the daytime, but plenty of entertainment at night). Whether cruising with 1,000 (or more) kids aboard will make for a relaxing holiday for those without kids will depend on how much noise they can absorb. You will, however, need to be a real Disney fan, as *everything* revolves around Disney and the family theme; this means that everything is based on entertainment and good times, while food takes a back step into the world of "theme park" cuisine. For children of all ages, there's simply nothing better than *Disney Magic* or *Disney Wonder*.

ACCOMMODATION. There are 12 price grades for accommodation (price will depend on grade, size and location you choose). Spread over six decks, all suites/cabins have been designed for practicality and have space-efficient layouts. Most cabins have common features such as a neat vertical steamer trunk for clothes storage, illuminated closets, a hairdryer located at a vanity desk (or in the bathroom), and bathrobes for all passengers. Many cabins have third- and fourth pull-down berths that rise and are totally hidden in the ceiling when not in use, but the standard interior and outside cabins, while acceptable for two, are extremely tight with three or four. The decor is practical, creative, and colorful, with lots of neat styling touches. Cabins with refrigerators can have them stocked with one of several packages (at extra cost).

The bathrooms, although compact (due to the fact that the toilet is separate from the rest of the bathroom), are really functional units, designed with split-use facilities so that more than one person can use them at the same time – good for families. Many have bathtubs (really shower tubs).

Accommodation designated as suites offers much more space, and extra goodies such as VCRs, CD players, large screen TVs, and extra beds (useful for larger families). But some suites are beneath the pool deck, teen lounge, or informal cafe, so there could be lots of noise as the ceiling insulation is poor (but the cabin to cabin insulation is good).

Wheelchair-bound passengers have a variety of cabin sizes and configurations, including suites with a private balcony (unfortunately you cannot get a wheelchair through the balcony's sliding door) and extra-large bathrooms with excellent roll-in showers, and good closet and drawer space (almost all the vessel is accessible). For the sight-impaired, cabin numbers and elevator buttons are braille-encoded.

A 24-hour room service is available (suite occupants also get concierge service); but the room service menu and cabin breakfast menus are limited. There is a 15% service charge for all beverage deliveries (including tea and coffee).

CUISINE. There are three main dining rooms (all non-smoking), each with over 400 seats, two seatings, and unique themes. Lumiere's has Beauty and the Beast; Parrot Cay has a tacky, pseudo-Caribbean theme; Animator's Palate (the most visual of the three) has food and electronic art that makes the evening decor change from black and white to full-color. You will eat in all three dining rooms in rotation (twice per 7-day cruise), and move with your assigned waiter and assistant waiter to each dining room in turn, thus providing variety (each has a different decor, different menus). As you will have the same waiter in each restaurant, any gratuities go only to "your" waiter. Parrot Cay and Lumiere's have open seating for breakfast and lunch (the lunch menu is pitiful). The noise level in all three dining rooms is extremely high. If the formal nights happen to fall on the evening you are due to eat in Parrot Cay, formal wear and the decor of Parrot Cay Restaurant do not go together at all.

In addition, Palo is an elegant 140-seat reservations-only alternative restaurant (with a $5 cover/gratuity charge) serving Italian cuisine. It has a 270° view, and is for adults only (no "Munchkins" allowed); the à la carte cuisine is cooked to order, and the wine list is good (although prices are high). Make your reservations as soon as you board or miss out on the only decent food aboard this ship. Afternoon High Tea is also presented here, on days at sea.

For casual eating, Topsider's is an indoor/outdoor café

featuring low-quality self-serve breakfast and lunch buffets with very poor choice and presentation, and a buffet dinner for children (consisting mostly of fried foods). There is also an ice cream and frozen yogurt bar (Scoops) that opens infrequently; other fast food outlets include Pluto's (for hamburgers, hot dogs), Pinocchio's, which is open throughout the day but not in the evening (for basic pizza and sandwiches). On one night of the cruise, there is also an outdoor self-serve "Tropicalifragilisticexpialidocious" buffet.

Overall, the food has improved since the ship was first introduced (it needed to, it was of a very low quality), and is now more attractively presented, although there are still so few green vegetables. Vegetarians and those seeking light cuisine will be totally underwhelmed. Guest chefs from Walt Disney World Resort prepare signature dishes each cruise, and also host cooking demonstrations.

ENTERTAINMENT. The entertainment and activities programming for families and children are extremely good. There are three large-scale stage shows (in the stunning 977-seat showlounge) featuring original Disney musicals such as *Disney Dreams, Hercules – The Muse-ical,* and *The Golden Mickeys.* Sadly, they are performed without a hint of a live orchestra, although the lighting, staging and technical effects are excellent. There is also a Disney-themed Trivia Game Show.

For grown-ups, there is "Route 66" – an adult entertainment area that includes a wacky Hollywood-style street. "Cadillac" is a jazz piano lounge, with private headphones for listening to music of all types when no live music is scheduled; "Wavebands" (for ear-splitting rock 'n' roll and country music); and "Barrel of Laughs" (for improvisational comedy involving the audience). During the day, creative enrichment programs have been added.

SPA/FITNESS. Fancy a little pampering? The Vista Spa is a fitness/wellbeing complex that measures 8,500 sq. ft/790 sq. meters. The fitness/workout room (with high-tech Cybex muscle-toning equipment) has ocean-view windows that overlook the navigation bridge on the deck below. There are 11 rooms for spa/beauty treatments (however, note that the pounding from the basketball court located directly above makes relaxing spa treatments almost impossible).

Thermal bath rooms have a "tropical rain shower", sauna, mild steam room, aromatic steam room and a fog shower. Aromatic scents such as eucalyptus, lime, peppermint, rose and sage can be infused into the mild steam room, while camomile is used in the aromatic steam room.

Massage (including exotic massages such as Aroma Stone massage and other well-being massages, as well as underwater massage in a hydrotherapy bath), aromatherapy facials, pedicures, and beauty salon treatments are at extra cost (massage, for example, costs about $2 per minute, plus gratuity). For something different, try the Rasul mud and steam room (great for couples).

For something extra special, consider booking a massage at Castaway Cay – in a private beach hut on the beach that is open to the sea. It's magical.

Emerald Princess
★★★★

Large Resort Ship: ....113,561 tons	Total Crew: 1,200	Cabins (with private balcony): 881
Lifestyle: ....Standard	Passengers	Cabins (wheelchair accessible): 25
Cruise Line: ....Princess Cruises	(lower beds/all berths): 3,114/3,782	Cabin Current: ....110 volts
Former Names: ....none-	Passenger Space Ratio	Elevators: 14
Builder: ....Fincantieri (Italy)	(lower beds/all berths): 36.2/29.8	Casino (gaming tables): ....Yes
Original Cost: ....$500 million	Crew/Passenger Ratio	Slot Machines: ....Yes
Entered Service: ....May 2007	(lower beds/all berths): 2.5/3.1	Swimming Pools (outdoors): 4
Registry: ....Bermuda	Navigation Officers: .....British/European	Swimming Pools (indoors): 0
Length (ft/m): 951.4/290.0	Cabins (total): 1,557	Whirlpools: 9
Beam (ft/m): 118.1/36.0	Size Range (sq ft/m): 163–1,279/	Self-Service Launderette: ....Yes
Draft (ft/m): 26.2/8.0	15.1–118.8	Dedicated Cinema/Seats: ....No
Propulsion/Propellers: gas turbine (25MW)	Cabins (outside view): 1,105	Library: ....Yes
/2 azimuthing pods (21,000 kW each)	Cabins (interior/no view): 452	
Passenger Decks: 15	Cabins (for one person): 0	

OVERALL SCORE: 1,546 (OUT OF A POSSIBLE 2,000 POINTS)

OVERVIEW. *Emerald Princess* has the same profile as sister *Crown Princess* (similar to half-sisters, *Diamond Princess, Golden Princess, Grand Princess, Ruby Princess, Sapphire Princess* and *Star Princess*. Although the ship takes over 500 more passengers than the half-sisters, the outdoor deck space remains the same, as do the number of elevators (so waiting time could increase during peak usage). The Passenger Space Ratio is also considerably reduced.

One nice feature that's worth booking on days at sea is The Sanctuary (an extra-cost adults-only retreat), located forward on the uppermost deck. It provides a "private" place to relax and unwind and includes attendants to provide chilled face towels and deliver light bites; there are also two outdoor cabanas for massages.

There is a good sheltered teakwood promenade deck, which almost wraps around (three times round is equal to one mile) and a walkway which goes to the (enclosed, protected) bow of the ship. The outdoor pools have various beach-like surroundings, and "Movies Under the Skies" and major sporting events are shown on a 300-sq-ft (28-sq-meter) movie screen located at the pool in front of the large funnel structure. Movies afloat in the open are a big hit with passengers – reminding many of drive-in movies, now virtually extinct in North America.

Unlike the outside decks, there is plenty of space inside (but there are also plenty of passengers), and a wide array of public rooms, with many "intimate" (this being a relative word) spaces and places to play. The passenger flow has been well thought-out, and there is little congestion.

Just aft of the funnel housing is a ship-wide glass-walled disco called Skywalkers. It's in a lower position than in the

BERLITZ'S RATINGS

	Possible	Achieved
Ship	500	435
Accommodation	200	168
Food	400	255
Service	400	292
Entertainment	100	82
Cruise	400	314

half-sister ships, but still has fine views from the port and starboard side windows (it would make a great penthouse).

The interior decor is attractive, with lots of earth tones (well suited to both American and European tastes). In fact, this is a culmination of the best of all that Princess Cruises has to offer from its many years of operating what is now a well-tuned, good-quality product.

An extensive collection of artworks has been chosen, and this complements the interior design and colors well. If you see something you like, you will probably be able to purchase it on board – it's almost all for sale.

Emerald Princess also includes a wedding chapel (a live web-cam can relay ceremonies via the internet). The ship's captain can legally marry (American) couples, thanks to the ship's Bermuda registry and a special dispensation (which should be verified when in the planning stage, according to where you reside). But to get married and take your close family members and entourage with you on your honeymoon may prove expensive. The "Hearts & Minds" chapel is also useful for "renewal of vows" ceremonies.

For children, there is a two-deck-high playroom, teen room, and a host of trained counselors. Children have their own pools, hot tubs, open deck and sports court area at the stern of the ship, away from the adults.

Gamblers should enjoy the large Gatsby's Casino, with more than 260 slot machines, and blackjack, craps and roulette tables, plus games such as Let It Ride Bonus, Spanish 21 and Caribbean Draw Progressive. But the highlight could well be the linked slot machines that provide a combined payout.

Other features include a decent library/computer room,

and a separate card room. Ship lovers should enjoy the wood-paneled Wheelhouse Bar, finely decorated with memorabilia and ship models tracing part of parent company P&O's history; while sports lovers should enjoy the sports bar, with its two billiard tables, and several television screens.

The ship is a fine, grand resort playground in which to roam when you are not ashore, and Princess Cruises delivers a consistently fine, well-packaged vacation product, always with a good degree of style, at an attractive, highly competitive price. Whether this really can be considered a relaxing holiday is a moot point, but with so many choices and "small" rooms to enjoy, the ship has been extremely well designed, and the odds are that you'll have an enjoyable cruise vacation.

If you are not used to large ships, it will take you some time to find your way around this one, despite the company's claim that it offers passengers a "small ship feel, big ship choice." And there are several points of congestion, particularly outside the shops when bazaar tables are set up outside on the upper level of the atrium lobby.

ACCOMMODATION. There are six principal types of cabins and configurations: (a) grand suite, (b) suite, (c) mini-suite, (d) outside-view double cabins with balcony, (e) outside-view double cabins, and (f) interior (no view) double cabins. These come in 35 different brochure price categories (the choice is bewildering for both travel agents and passengers), and pricing depends on size and location.

Cabin bath towels are small, and drawer space is very limited. There are no butlers – even for the top-grade suites (which are not really large in comparison to similar suites aboard some other ships). Cabin attendants have too many cabins to look after (typically 20), which does not translate to fine personal service.

(a). The largest, most lavish suite is the Grand Suite. It has a large bedroom with queen-sized bed, huge walk-in (illuminated) closets, two bathrooms, a lounge (with fireplace and sofa bed) with wet bar and refrigerator, and a large private balcony on the port side (with hot tub that can be accessed from both balcony and bedroom).

(b/c). Suites (with a semi-private balcony) have a separate living room (with sofa bed) and bedroom (with a TV set in each). The bathroom is quite large and has both a tub and shower stall. The mini-suites also have a private balcony, and a separate living and sleeping area (with a TV set in each). The differences between the suites and mini-suites are basically in the size and appointments, the suite being more of a square shape while mini-suites are more rectangular, and have few drawers. Both suites and mini-suites have plush bathrobes, and fully tiled bathrooms with ample open shelf storage space. Suite and mini-suite passengers receive greater attention, including priority embarkation and disembarkation privileges. What is not good is that the most expensive accommodation has only semi-private balconies that can be seen from above and so there is little privacy.

(d/e/f). Both interior (no view) and outside-view (the outsides come either with or without private balcony) cabins are of a functional, practical, design, although almost no drawers are provided. They are quite attractive, with warm, pleasing decor and fine soft furnishing fabrics; 80 percent of the outside-view cabins have a private balcony. Interior (no view) cabins measure approximately 163 sq. ft (15.1 sq. meters).

The 28 wheelchair-accessible cabins measure 250–385 sq. ft (23.2–35.7 sq. meters); surprisingly, there is no mirror for dressing, and no full-length hanging space for long dresses (yes, some passengers in wheelchairs do also use mirrors and full-length clothing). Additionally, two family suites consist of two suites with an interconnecting door, plus a large balcony. These can sleep up to 10 (if at least four are children) or up to eight people (if all are adults).

All cabins receive turndown service and chocolates on pillows each night, bathrobes (on request) and toiletry amenity kits (larger, naturally, for suite/mini-suite occupants) that typically include soap, shampoo, conditioner, and hand/body lotion. A hairdryer is provided in all cabins, sensibly located at the vanity desk unit in the living area. All bathrooms have tiled floors, and there is a decent amount of open shelf storage space for personal toiletries, although the plain beige decor is very basic and unappealing.

Most outside-view cabins on Emerald Deck have views obstructed by the lifeboats. There are no cabins for singles. Your name is placed outside your suite or cabin in a documents holder – making it simple for delivery service personnel but also diminishing privacy. There is 24-hour room service (but some items on the room service menu are not available during early morning hours).

Some cabins can accommodate a third and fourth person in upper berths. However, in such cabins, the lower beds cannot then be pushed together to make queen-sized bed.

Almost all balcony suites and cabins can be overlooked both from the navigation bridge wing, as well as from the port and starboard sections of the ship's discotheque – high above the ship at the stern. Cabins with balconies on Dolphin, Caribe and Baja decks can be overlooked by passengers on balconies on the deck above. They are, therefore, not private. However, perhaps the least desirable balcony cabins are eight balcony cabins located forward on Emerald Deck, as the balconies do not extend to the side of the ship and can be passed by walkers and gawkers on the adjacent Upper Promenade walkway (so occupants need to keep their curtains closed most of the time).

Also, passengers occupying some the most expensive suites with balconies at the stern of the vessel may experience considerable vibration during certain ship maneuvers.

Note that most cabins on Emerald Deck 8 have a lifeboat-obstructed view.

CUISINE. As befits the size of the ship, there's a variety of options. There are three main dining rooms (Botticelli, Da Vinci, and Michaelangelo), plus Crown Steakhouse, and Sabatini's Trattoria. All are no-smoking.

Of the three principal dining rooms for formal dining, one has traditional two-seating dining, while the other two have "anytime dining" (you choose when and with whom you want to eat). All are split into multi-tier sections in a non-symmetrical design that breaks what are quite large spaces into smaller sections for better ambiance.

While four elevators go to the deck where two of the restaurants are located, only two go to Plaza Deck 5, where the Palm Restaurant is located (this can cause waiting problems at peak times, particularly for anyone in a wheelchair).

Specially designed dinnerware, high-quality linens and silverware, Frette Egyptian cotton table linens, and silverware by Hepp of Germany are used in the main dining rooms. Note that 15% is added to all beverage bills, including wines.

Alternative (Extra Charge) Dining Options: There are two: Sabatini's Trattoria, and Crown Grill. Both are open for lunch and dinner on days at sea. Sabatini's is an Italian eatery located on a high deck aft of the funnel housing, with colorful tiled Mediterranean-style decor; it is named after Trattoria Sabatini, the 200-year old institution in Florence (where there is no cover charge). It includes Italian-style multi-course antipasti and pastas, as well as Italian-style entrées, including tiger prawns and lobster tail. All are provided with flair and entertainment from by the staff of waiters. It's by reservation only; cover charge $20 per person, for dinner.

The Crown Grill, located aft on Promenade Deck, is a reservation-only steakhouse, offering prime quality steaks and seafood. The cover charge is $25 (plus an additional charge for lobster).

The cuisine in these two dining spots is decidedly better than in the three main dining rooms, with better quality ingredients and more attention to presentation and taste. **Casual Eateries:** These include a poolside hamburger grill and pizza bar (no additional charge), while extra charges do apply if you order items to eat either at the International Cafe (a coffee bar/ patisserie), or in Vines seafood/wine bar in the atrium lobby. Other casual meals can be taken in the Horizon Court (open 24 hours a day). It has large ocean-view on port and starboard sides and direct access to the two principal swimming pools and lido deck. Although

there is a wide variety of food, there is no real finesse in presentation, however, as plastic plates are provided **Ultimate Balcony Dinner/Breakfast:** For something different, you could try a private dinner on your balcony, an all-inclusive evening featuring cocktails, fresh flowers, champagne and a deluxe four-course meal including Caribbean lobster tail – all served by a member of the dining staff on your private balcony; of course, it costs extra – $50 per person (or $25 per person for the Ultimate Balcony Breakfast).

ENTERTAINMENT. The 800-seat Princess Theater (show-lounge) is the main entertainment venue; it spans two decks and has comfortable seating on both main and balcony levels. It has $3 million worth of sound and light equipment, plus a nine-piece orchestra, and a scenery loading bay that connects directly from stage to a hull door for direct transfer to the dockside. The ship has its own resident troupe of almost 20 singers and dancers, plus and audio-visual support staff.

There is also a second entertainment lounge, Club Fusion, located aft. It features cabaret acts at night, and lectures, bingo and horse racing during the day. Explorers Lounge, a third entertainment lounge, can also host cabaret acts and dance bands.

A variety of other lounges and bars have live music, including a string quartet, and street performers that appear in the main atrium lobby

SPA/FITNESS. The Lotus Spa is located forward on Sun Deck – one of the uppermost decks. Separate facilities for men and women include a sauna, steam room, and changing rooms; common facilities include a relaxation/waiting zone, body-pampering treatment rooms, and a gymnasium with packed with the latest high-tech muscle-pumping, cardio-vascular equipment, and great ocean views. Some fitness classes are free, while some cost extra.

● **For more extensive general information on what a Princess Cruises cruise is like, see pages 134–37.**

Empress
★★★

Large Resort Ship: . . . . .48,563 tons	Total Crew: 685	Cabins (with private balcony): 69
Lifestyle: . . . . .Standard	Passengers	Cabins (wheelchair accessible): 4
Cruise Line: . . . . .Pullmantur Cruises	(lower beds/all berths): 1,600/2,020	Cabin Current: . . . . .110 volts
Former Names: . . . .*Empress of the Seas,*	Passenger Space Ratio	Elevators: 7
Nordic Empress	(lower beds/all berths): 30.2/24.0	Casino (gaming tables): . . . . .Yes
Builder: .Chantiers de l'Atlantique (France)	Crew/Passenger Ratio	Slot Machines: . . . . .Yes – 220
Original Cost: . . . .$170 million	(lower beds/all berths): 2.3/2.9	Swimming Pools (outdoors): 1
Entered Service: . . .June 1990/May 2008	Navigation Officers: . . . . .European	(+1 wading pool)
Registry: . . . . .The Bahamas	Cabins (total): 800	Swimming Pools (indoors): 0
Length (ft/m): 692.2/211.00	Size Range (sq ft/m): 117.0–818/	Whirlpools: 4
Beam (ft/m): 100.7/30.70	10.8–76	Self-Service Launderette: . . . . .No
Draft (ft/m): 24.9/7.60	Cabins (outside view): 471	Dedicated Cinema/Seats: . . . . .No
Propulsion/Propellers: diesel (16,200 kW)/2	Cabins (interior/no view): 329	Library: . . . . .No
Passenger Decks: 9	Cabins (for one person): 0	

BERLITZ'S OVERALL SCORE: 1,246 (OUT OF A POSSIBLE 2,000 POINTS)

OVERVIEW. This contemporary ship has a short bow and squared-off stern, and yet it manages to look reasonably well balanced. Originally known as *Nordic Empress*, it was designed specifically for the short-cruise market, for which the ship is quite well suited. In March 2008 the ship was transferred from the RCI fleet to Pullmantur Cruises, to operate as *Empress* for Spanish-speakers.

There is a polished wood walk-around promenade deck outdoors, and a dramatic use of glass-enclosed viewing spaces that provide good contact from the upper, open decks to the sea. Although the outdoor pool is decent enough (good at night for evenings under the stars), the two swimming pools provided are very small considering the number of passengers carried when the ship is full. In other words, there's not a lot of open deck space, and sunloungers are crammed together with little room to maneuver around them on sunny days at sea.

A nine-deck-high atrium is the focal point of the interior design, which tends to have many Scandinavian influences. Lots of crystal and brass have been used to good effect to reflect light. Indeed, the clever use of lighting effects provides illuminating interiors that make it feel warm. Passenger flow is generally good, although, because two seatings and two show times are operated, some congestion is inevitable adjacent to the entrance foyer at show time. A small library was added a few years ago – a needed facility that was not included when the ship was built.

A three-level casino has a sailcloth ceiling, but it is a noisy room. The Viking Crown Lounge, aft of the funnel, is a two-level nightclub-disco for the late-night set.

Empress is a fairly smart ship with a high passenger den-

BERLITZ'S RATINGS

	Possible	Achieved
Ship	500	332
Accommodation	200	121
Food	400	222
Service	400	261
Entertainment	100	66
Cruise	400	244

sity, and you won't be bored – there is an adequate array of activities for all ages. In the final analysis, you may be overwhelmed by the public spaces, and underwhelmed by the size of the cabins. However, this is basically a well-run, fine-tuned, highly structured cruise product geared particularly to those seeking an action-packed cruise vacation at a moderately good price, with lots of fellow passengers to keep you company. The onboard currency is the euro.

Standing in line for embarkation, disembarkation, shore tenders and for self-serve buffet meals is an inevitable aspect of cruising aboard all large ships.

SUITABLE FOR: *Empress* is best suited to young, and young-at-heart Spanish-speaking couples and singles seeking an all-inclusive cruise, and those who want a good basic getaway cruise aboard a ship that offers some good drinking places, lots of noise and good cheer, in fairly comfortable surroundings.

ACCOMMODATION. There are 15 different price categories. The largest accommodation is in the Royal Suite, located just under the navigation bridge on the port side. This has a queen-sized bed, walk-in closet, separate living area with bar, refrigerator and entertainment center; the bathroom has a whirlpool tub, and vanity dressing area. There is a private balcony.

Nine cabins have private balconies that overlook the ship's stern; these consist of two large owner's suites and seven "superior" ocean-view cabins. The other cabins with private balconies also have a decent amount of living space, and a small sofa, coffee table and chair, and vanity desk.

Almost all the other cabins are really dimensionally challenged, and only moderately comfortable. All grades of accommodation have twin beds that can convert to a queen-size configuration. The bathrooms (all refurbished in 2004) are nicely laid-out, and have a decent amount of space for personal toiletry items.

CUISINE. The Hollywood musical-themed Carmen Dining Room is non-smoking. It is two decks high, with both a main and balcony level, as well as large windows that overlook the stern of the ship, but it really is a noisy room. There are two seatings, at tables for four, six, eight or 10.

The cuisine is typical of mass banquet catering that offers standard fare comparable to that found in family-style restaurants ashore. While the menu descriptions provide a tempting read, the food, when it arrives, has little taste – many items are pre-prepared ashore to keep down costs. Special orders, tableside carving and flambeau items are not offered.

Alternative Dining Option: There is one à la carte extra-charge restaurant (reservations are required). However, it's worth the extra money, as the food is so much better than in the dining room, and the room's intimacy makes it a nice, romantic place – it has a good number of tables for two.

Casual Dining Option: For casual breakfasts and lunches, the Windjammer Café, with its two buffet display lines, provides an alternative to the dining room, although there are often lines at peak times, and the selection is at best very average. There are no "active stations" – where items such as omelets could be made to order.

ENTERTAINMENT. The two-level Strike Up the Band show-lounge has poor sight lines in the upper lateral balconies. It has a main floor level as well as a balcony level. However, the sightlines from the balcony are almost useless as they are ruined by railings. Strong cabaret acts are also featured in the main showlounge.

The entertainment throughout is upbeat – in fact, it is difficult to get away from music and noise – but is typical of the kind of resort hotel found ashore in Las Vegas. There is even background music in all corridors and lifts, and constant music outdoors on the pool deck. If you want a quiet relaxing holiday, choose another ship.

SPA/FITNESS. The ShipShape Fitness Center is a two-deck-high facility, and contains a gymnasium with some good muscle-pump equipment, men's and women's saunas and changing areas, and massage treatment rooms. The beauty salon is located on the port side of Showtime Deck 6, and has ocean-view windows.

WHERE NAUTICAL EXPRESSIONS COME FROM

If you've ever wondered where some terms or phrases came from, you have only to look to the sea, ships, and seamen.

Scuttlebutt

A small drinking ladle with scuttles or holes in it to discourage sailors from idle chit chat (scuttlebutt) around the water barrel while their water ration dribbled back into the barrel. Today the usually refers to gossip or the latest news concerning a given situation or person.

Shape up

A helmsman working off a lee shore would point up and "shape up" to his course in order to avoid the danger. In modern-day usage it is used similar sense to "smarten up" or "pull yourself together."

Showing your true colors

Early warships often carried flags from many nations on board in order to elude or deceive the enemy. The rules of civilized warfare called for all ships to hoist their true national ensigns before firing a shot. Someone who finally "shows his true colors" is acting like a warship, which hails another ship flying one flag, but then hoisted its own flag when the vessel got within firing range.

Skyscraper

A small, triangular shaped sail that was set above the mains on the old square-riggers to try to scrape (catch) more wind in areas of calm air. The term came ashore to represent anything that was tall enough to "scrape" the sky.

Slush fund

The fat obtained by "scraping the bottom of the barrel" by the ship's cook and secreted away in his "slush fund" for selling ashore to candle makers, tanneries, etc. Today the words describe a rainy-day fund or cash reserve. Another version of the term's derivation is that the grease (slush) from frying the salt pork on a voyage was kept and sold when the ship returned to port. The money raised was put into a "fund" for the crew.

Enchantment of the Seas ★★★★

Large Resort Ship: . . . . .81,500 tons
Lifestyle: . . . . .Standard
Cruise Line: . . . . .Royal Caribbean
International
Former Names: . . . . .none
Builder: . . .Kvaerner Masa-Yards (Finland)
Original Cost: . . . .$300 million
Entered Service: . . . . .July 1997
Registry: . . . . .The Bahamas
Length (ft/m): 990.1/301.8
Beam (ft/m): 105.6/32.2
Draft (ft/m): 25.5/7.6
Propulsion/Propellers: . . . . .diesel-electric
(50,400kW)/2
Passenger Decks: 11

Total Crew: 840
Passengers
(lower beds/all berths): 2,252/2,730
Passenger Space Ratio
(lower beds/all berths): 36.1/29.8
Crew/Passenger Ratio
(lower beds/all berths): 2.6/3.2
Navigation Officers: . . . . . .Scandinavian/
International
Cabins (total): 1,126
Size Range (sq ft/m): 158.2–1,267.0/
14.7–117.7
Cabins (outside view): 663
Cabins (interior/no view): 463
Cabins (for one person): 0

Cabins (with private balcony): 248
Cabins (wheelchair accessible): 20
Cabin Current: . . . . . . .110 and 220 volts
Elevators: 9
Casino (gaming tables): . . . . .Yes
Slot Machines: . . . . .Yes
Swimming Pools (outdoors): 2
Swimming Pools (indoors): 1
(indoor/outdoor w/sliding glass roof)
Whirlpools: 4
Self-Service Launderette: . . . . .No
Dedicated Cinema/Seats: . . . . .No
Library: . . . . .Yes

OVERALL SCORE: 1,491 (OUT OF A POSSIBLE 2,000 POINTS)

OVERVIEW. This is one of a pair of ships for this popular cruise line (sister to *Grandeur of the Seas*). It has a long profile, with a single funnel located well aft (almost a throwback to designs used during the 1950s). The stern is nicely rounded (rather like the older *Monarch of the Seas*-class ships), and a Viking Crown Lounge is set amidships. This, together with the forward mast, provides three distinct focal points in its exterior profile. There is a wrap-around promenade deck outdoors (but no cushioned pads for the tacky home patio-style plastic sunloungers).

A large Viking Crown Lounge (a trademark of all Royal Caribbean International ships) sits between funnel and mast at the top of the atrium lobby, and overlooks the forward section of the swimming pool deck, as aboard *Legend of the Seas* and *Splendour of the Seas*, with access provided from stairway of the central atrium.

The principal interior focal point is a seven-deck-high Centrum (atrium lobby), which provides a good meeting point (the Purser's Desk and Shore Excursion Desk are located on one of the lower levels). Many public entertainment rooms and facilities are located off the atrium.

This ship has good passenger flow inside. There is a good, varied collection of artworks (including several sculptures), principally by British artists, with classical music, ballet and theater themes. The casino is large and glitzy, and has a fascinating, theatrical glass-covered, but under-floor exhibit. The children's and teens' facilities are good, much expanded from previous ships in the fleet.

A delightful champagne terrace bar sits forward of the lower level of the two-deck-high dining room. There is a

BERLITZ'S RATINGS		
	Possible	Achieved
Ship	500	429
Accommodation	200	166
Food	400	238
Service	400	285
Entertainment	100	81
Cruise	400	292

good use of tropical plants throughout the public rooms, which helps to counteract the rather plain and clinical pastel wall colors, while huge murals of opera scenes adorn several stairways.

Enchantment of the Seas has quite attractive interiors, and will provide a good cruise vacation, particularly for first-time passengers seeking comfortable surroundings similar to those in a Hyatt Hotel, with fabrics and soft furnishings that blend together to provide a contemporary resort environment. This company provides a well organized, but rather homogenous cruise experience, with the same old passenger participation activities and events that have been provided for more than 25 years. The onboard currency is the US dollar.

In 2005, the ship underwent a $60 million "chop-and-stretch" operation that added a 72.8-ft (22.2-meter) midsection. It took six days to slice the ship in two before the mid-section was slotted in, increasing the ship's overall length to 990.1 ft (301.8 meters). The ship's tonnage was increased to 81,500 tons. The upgrade added another 151 passenger cabins (including two "family" cabins that can sleep six), and some public rooms were given a make-over at the same time. Sports facilities were augmented; these included two "ball zones," each with three basketball hoops of different heights to accommodate youth, teen and adult shooters. The pool deck was given more space plus soaring "suspension" bridges. Special handicap lifts were provided for the two pools, as was a new Splash Deck (children will love the 64 water jets) with a decorative night-time fiber-optic light show. "Bungee" trampolines were added to Deck 10 (above the Windjammer Café). The main dining room and Windjammer Café (casual eatery) were enlarged to handle the extra capacity, and so was the art auction gallery.

ACCOMMODATION. There are 16 price grades (the price depends on the grade, size and location, with location and grade perhaps more important, since so many of the cabins are of the same, or a very similar size).

There are five grades of suites: Royal Suite (1), Owner's Suite (5), Royal Family Suite (4), Grand Suite (12), and Superior Suite (44, including two superior suites for the disabled). All are well appointed and have pleasing decor (best described as Scandinavian Moderne), with good wood and color accenting (the largest has a baby grand piano).

Royal Suite. The largest accommodation can be found in the Royal Suite, located directly aft of the ship's navigation bridge on the starboard side. It has a separate bedroom with kind-size bed, walk-in closet and vanity dressing area, living room with queen-sized sofa bed, baby grand piano, refrigerator and wet bar, dining table, entertainment center, and large private balcony. The bathroom has a whirlpool tub, separate shower enclosure, two washbasins, and toilet.

Owner's Suite. The five owner's suites are at the forward end of the ship, just behind the navigation bridge (close to the Royal Suite). They have a queen-sized bed, separate living area with queen-size sofa bed, vanity dressing area, refrigerator and wet bar. The bathroom has a full-size tub, separate shower enclosure, toilet and two washbasins.

Royal Family Suite. These have two bedrooms with twin beds that convert to queen-size beds, living area with double sofa bed and Pullman bed, refrigerator, two bathrooms (one with tub), and private balcony. This suite can accommodate eight, and might suit families.

Grand Suite. Features include twin beds that can be convert to a queen-size bed, vanity dressing area, lounge area with sofa bed, refrigerator, and a bathroom with bathtub. There's also a private balcony.

Superior Suite. Features include twin beds that can be convert to a queen-size bed, vanity dressing area, lounge area with sofa bed, refrigerator, and a bathroom with tub. Private balcony. Note that although this is called a suite, it really is little more than a larger standard cabin with balcony.

Other Grades. All standard cabins have twin beds that convert to a queen-size bed, ample closet space for a one-week cruise, and a good amount of drawer space, although under-bed storage space is not good for large suitcases. The

bathrooms have nine mirrors. Plastic buckets are provided for champagne/wine and are really tacky.

All grades of suite/cabin are provided with a hairdryer. The room service menu has only the most basic selection.

CUISINE. The 1,195-seat, no-smoking My Fair Lady Dining Room spreads over two decks, connected by a grand, sweeping staircase. There are two seatings for dinner. **Alternative dining option ($20 per person cover/gratuity charge):** Chops Grill Steakhouse, added during the 2005 "stretch," is an à la carte steakhouse featuring steaks and veal chops; reservations are necessary (think big steaks, better service, an unhurried and more comfortable dining experience).

Casual, self-serve breakfasts and luncheons can be taken in the 790-seat informal Windjammer Marketplace. It has a great expanse of ocean-view glass windows, the decor is bright and cheerful, and buffet "islands" feature food from around the world. An intimate Champagne/Caviar Bar terrace is forward of the lower level of the two-deck-high dining room and just off the atrium for those who might like to taste something a little bit out of the ordinary, in a setting that is both bright and contemporary.

ENTERTAINMENT. The Orpheum Theater, the ship's the principal showlounge, is a grand room located at the forward part of the ship, and has 875 seats. This is where the big production shows and major cabaret acts are staged.

A second showlounge, the 575-seat Carousel Lounge, is located aft, and is for smaller shows and adult cabarets, including late-night adult (blue) comedy. A variety of other lounges and bars feature almost constant live music; there's no real quiet (no music) bar to have a drink in.

There is even background music in all corridors and elevators, and constant music outdoors on the pool deck. If you want a quiet relaxing holiday, choose another ship.

SPA/FITNESS. The ShipShape Spa is aft of the funnel and spans two decks. Facilities include an expanded gymnasium (with all the latest machines), aerobics exercise room, sauna and steam rooms, a beauty salon, and 13 treatment rooms, including a couples massage room.

● **For more extensive general information about the Royal Caribbean cruise experience, see pages 137–42.**

Eurodam
NOT YET RATED

Large Resort Ship: . . . . .86,700 tons	Total Crew: 929	Cabins (with private balcony): 708
Lifestyle: . . . . .Standard	Passengers	Cabins (wheelchair accessible): 30
Cruise Line: . . . . . . .Holland America Line	(lower beds/all berths): 2,104/2,671	Cabin Voltage: . . . . .110 volts
Former Names: . . . . .none	Passenger Space Ratio	Elevators: 14
Builder: . . . . .Fincantieri (Italy)	(lower beds/all berths): 41.2/32.4	Casino (gaming tables): . . . . .Yes
Original Cost: . . . .$450 million	Crew/Passenger Ratio	Slot Machines: . . . . .Yes
Entered Service: . . . . .July 2008	(lower beds/all berths): 2.2/2.8	Swimming Pools (outdoors): 2
Registry: . . . . .The Netherlands	Navigation Officers: . . . . .European	+ 1 children's pool
Length (ft/m): 935.0/285.0	Cabins (total): 1,052	Swimming Pools (indoors): 1
Beam (ft/m): 105.6/32.2	Size Range (sq ft/m): 170.0–1,318.6/	(indoor/outdoor with retractable dome)
Draft (ft/m): 25.5/7.8	15.7–122.5	Whirlpools: 5
Propulsion/Propellers: . . . . .diesel-electric	Cabins (outside view): 897	Self-Service Launderette: . . . . .Yes
(34,000kW/2 pods (17.6 MW each)	Cabins (interior/no view): 155	Dedicated Cinema/Seats: Yes/170
Passenger Decks: 12	Cabins (for one person): 0	Library: . . . . .Yes

Ⓞ   BERLITZ'S OVERALL SCORE: NYR (OUT OF A POSSIBLE 2,000 POINTS)

OVERVIEW. *Eurodam* was the newest ship in the HAL fleet when it debuted in summer 2008. With one deck more than close sister *Noordam*, it has more cabins than *Noordam* (which itself had 35 more cabins than close sisters *Oosterdam, Westerdam* and *Zuiderdam*) but still the same number of elevators, and open deck space.

The ship has two funnels, positioned close together – one behind the other instead of side by side – the result of the machinery configuration. The ship has, in effect, two engine rooms – one with three diesels, and one with two diesels. A "pod" propulsion system is provided *(see page 174 for explanation of the technicalities)*.

One neat feature consists of 22 private (rent by the day) cabanas, with goodies such as champagne, chocolate strawberries, an iPod pre-stocked with music, bathrobes, fresh fruit and chilled towels (for two adults and two children, so they may not be the promised "quiet" spaces, after all). They are located in an area on observation deck and around the Lido Pool, with a daily charge for the 14 cabanas in The Retreat – $75 for sea days and $45 on port days; for the 8 Lido Deck cabanas it's $50 on sea days and $30 on port days. My recommendation: book a cabana in The Retreat – it will be less busy, and thus more relaxing.

The ship is designed to appeal to younger, more vibrant, multi-generational holidaymakers. There is a complete walk-around exterior teak promenade deck, and real teak "steamer" style sunloungers are provided. Additionally, there is a jogging track outdoors, located around the ship's mast and the forward third of the ship.

Exterior glass elevators, mounted midships on both port and starboard sides, provide fine ocean views from any one

BERLITZ'S RATINGS

	Possible	Achieved
Ship	500	NYR
Accommodation	200	NYR
Food	400	NYR
Service	400	NYR
Entertainment	100	NYR
Cruise	400	NYR

of the 11 passenger decks. There are two centrally located swimming pools outdoors, one of which can be used in inclement weather due to its retractable sliding glass roof. Two whirlpool tubs, adjacent to the swimming pools, are abridged by a bar. A smaller (swimming) pool is available for children, and this incorporates a winding water slide that spans two decks in height. There is an additional whirlpool tub outdoors.

The intimate lobby (which has its own bar) spans three decks. Adjacent are interior elevators, and glass wall elevators with exterior views. The interior decor is bright in many areas (in order to attract a younger clientele). In keeping with the traditions of Holland America Line, a large collection of artwork will be a standard feature, and pieces reflect the former Dutch East Indies.

There are two whole entertainment/ public room decks. Perhaps the most dramatic room aboard this ship is the showlounge, spanning four decks in the forward section of the ship. Other facilities include a winding shopping street with several boutique stores and logo shops, card room, an art gallery, photo gallery, and several small meetings rooms.

The casino is large (one has to walk through it to get from the restaurant to the showlounge on Lower Promenade Deck), and is equipped with all the necessary gaming paraphernalia and slot machines.

"Explorations" is a combination coffee bar (coffees and other drinks are at extra cost), lounge, an extensive library and internet-connect center, all in one attractive, open "lifestyle" environment adjacent to the Crows Nest Lounge.

For families with children, Club HAL's KidZone provides a whole area dedicated to children's facilities and extensive programming for different age groups (5–17), with one counselor for every 30 children. Free ice cream is provided at certain hours, plus hot hors d'oeuvres in all bars.

While this formula doesn't work so well for loyal repeat passengers used to the line's smaller ships, *Eurodam* offers a wide range of public rooms. Dutch artefacts and museum pieces from the 16th and 17th centuries are displayed.

The information desk in the lobby is small and somewhat removed from the main passenger flow on the two decks above it. Several pillars obstruct the passenger flow and lines of sight throughout the ship. There are no self-service launderettes – something families with children miss, even though special laundry packages are available.

ACCOMMODATION. Of the total 1,022 suites/cabins, 86% have an outside view, while 67 of these have a private balcony. Note that many cabins on Upper Promenade Deck have lifeboat-obstructed views. For an explanation of suites/cabins, see the entry for *Noordam*. A total of 37 cabins have inter-connecting doors. All balconies have solid steel railings instead of glass.

All suites/cabins feature Signature of Excellence premium amenities: plush Mariner's Dream beds, waffle/terry cloth robes, Egyptian cotton towels, flat panel TVs, DVD players, make-up mirrors with halo lighting, massage shower heads, large hair dryers, fresh flowers and complimentary fruit baskets.

CUISINE. The two-deck-high Rembrandt main dining room is located at the aft of the ship, with seating at tables for two, four, six or eight on both main and upper levels (the galley is located under the restaurant, accessed by port and starboard escalators). It provides a traditional Holland America Line dining experience, with friendly service from smiling Indonesian and Filipino stewards.

Both open seating and fixed seatings (assigned tables and time) are available, plus an open-seating arrangement for breakfast and lunch; you'll be seated by restaurant staff when you enter. The dining room is a non-smoking venue. **Alternative themed dining spots** include the reservations-only Pinnacle Grill – the premium Sterling Silver steak and seafood restaurant and adjacent Pinnacle Bar; Tamarind, a 144-seat Pan-Asian restaurant (no charge for lunch; $15 for dinner); and the 72-seat Canaletto, an Italian eatery created nightly in a section of the Lido Cafe.

ENTERTAINMENT. Theatre-style seating in the ship's main showlounge.

SPA/FITNESS. The Greenhouse Spa is the largest yet for HAL, and includes a thermal suite (wet steam rooms with various herbal mists, plus dry saunas), and a large gymnasium. Sports enthusiasts can enjoy a basketball court, volleyball court, golf simulator.

● **For more extensive general information about Holland America Line, see pages 126–28.**

WHERE NAUTICAL EXPRESSIONS COME FROM

If you've ever wondered where some terms or phrases came from, you have only to look to the sea, ships, and seamen.

Square meal

This derives from the meals served on square wooden platters used on board ship. The platters could be easily stowed in racks between meals. Any substantial meal is now described as a "square meal."

Three Sheets to the Wind

A term said of a man under the influence of drink. A ship with three sheets in the wind would "stagger to and fro like a drunken man." Conversely, a drunken man behaves like a ship with three sheets in the wind.

To Know the ropes

There were miles and miles of cordage in the rigging of a square rigged ship. The only way of keeping track of and knowing the function of all of these lines was to know their locations. It took an experienced seaman to know the ropes.

Under the weather

Refers to a sailor being in the uncomfortable position of having his station at the weather bow and being subject to the pitching of the boat and constant spray blown in his face. Used today to mean feeling

Europa
★★★★★ +

Small Ship: . . . . .28,890 tons	Total Crew: .280	Cabins (wheelchair accessible): 2
Lifestyle: . . . . .Utterly Exclusive	Passengers	Cabin Current: . . . . .110 and 220 volts
Cruise Line: . . . . . . .Hapag-Lloyd Cruises	(lower beds/all berths): 408/450	Elevators: 4
Former Names: . . . . .none	Passenger Space Ratio	Casino (gaming tables): . . . . .No
Builder: . . .Kvaerner Masa-Yards (Finland)	(lower beds/all berths): 70.4/64.2	Slot Machines: . . . . .No
Original Cost: . . . . .DM260 million	Crew/Passenger Ratio	Swimming Pools (outdoors): 1
Entered Service: . . . . .Sept 1999	(lower beds/all berths): 1.4/1.6	Swimming Pools (indoors): 1
Registry: . . . . .The Bahamas	Navigation Officers: . . . . .German	(indoor/outdoor with magrodome)
Length (ft/m): 651.5/198.6	Cabins (total): 204	Whirlpools: 1
Beam (ft/m): 78.7/24.0	Size Range (sq ft/m): 355.2–914.9/	Self-Service Launderette: . . . . .Yes
Draft (ft/m): . .r. 20.0/6.1	33.0–85.0	(ironing room)
Propulsion/Propellers: . . . . .diesel-electric	Cabins (outside view): 204	Dedicated Cinema/Seats: Yes/60
(21,600 kW)/2 azimuthing pods	Cabins (interior/no view): 0	Library: . . . . .Yes
(13.3 MW each)	Cabins (for one person): 0	
Passenger Decks: 7	Cabins (with private balcony): 168	

OVERALL SCORE: 1,852 (OUT OF A POSSIBLE 2,000 POINTS)

OVERVIEW. *Europa* has a sleek appearance, with sweeping lines, a graceful profile, and Hapag-Lloyd's orange/ blue funnel. Look down from the aft Lido Deck fantail and you will see a rounded, graceful stern – unlike the box-like rears of so many contemporary ships.

This is a very stable ship in the open sea, and there is absolutely no vibration or noise – thanks partly to its "pod" propulsion system *(for further details, see page 174).* It carries 14 Zodiac landing craft for use during close-up shore excursions; and bootwashing areas are also provided. There is a walking/jogging area with rubberized deck (plus a wrap-around outdoors teak promenade deck outdoors), as well as a small FKK (Frei-KörperKultur) deck for those who enjoy nude sunbathing. The sunloungers are aluminum with teak armrests, and have thick cushioned pads.

There is one swimming pool, in a long, rectangular in shape (it was modified from its original "bottle"-shaped design in December 2000), and, while not the widest, it is longer than the pools aboard many other cruise ships; it measures 56.7 by 16.8 ft (17.3 by 5.15 meters). Movies are shown poolside on a large screen on selected evenings, and themed events are held here.

With this ship, Hapag-Lloyd has been able to reach and maintain the high standards that its passengers demand, due to the fact that most of *Europa's* hotel service crew are German-speaking nationals who understand the culture and can talk in depth about German/Swiss/Austrian life, unlike an international crew that can barely communicate.

The space per passenger is high, there is never a hint of a line anywhere, and both restaurant and show lounge seat a

BERLITZ'S RATINGS

	Possible	Achieved
Ship	500	477
Accommodation	200	183
Food	400	371
Service	400	359
Entertainment	100	90
Cruise	400	372

full complement of passengers. *Europa* is one of the world's most spacious purpose-built cruise ships – an exquisite retreat. Step aboard this ship and you'll find a world of relaxed, contemporary cruising that is intensely welcoming.

Europa is finely appointed, in the contemporary style usually described as "minimalism" in hotel-speak. Only the very best quality soft furnishings have been chosen for the ship's interiors, subtly blending traditional with modern designs and materials. Most public rooms and hallways have extremely high ceilings, providing an enhanced sense of space and grandeur. The colors used in the ship's interior decor are light and contemporary – there is no hint of glitz, garish colors, or neon, anywhere.

Public rooms include the Club Belvedere (the venue for afternoon tea and intimate music recitals), the Europa Lounge (the main showlounge), which has a U-shaped seating configuration and a proper stage, although there are several pillars. In addition, there is a Clipper Lounge/Bar (with high ceilings), an Atrium Piano Bar with Steinway baby grand piano. When the ship first debuted there was a casino, although this proved to be so little used that Hapag-Lloyd Cruises turned it into a multi-functional space for small cocktail parties, and as a high-class art gallery.

There is also a fine sidewalk Havana Bar cigar lounge. This clubby room is equipped with three large glass-fronted, fully temperature-controlled and conditioned humidor cabinets, and carries an extensive range of cigars from Cuba and other countries. Cigars stocked include a range (from 102mm to 232mm) of top brands. The bar also serves a fine range of armagnacs, calvados and cognacs, all poured tableside, as well as Cuban beer. Embedded in a wall adjacent to the bar is a digital MP3 jukebox, with a push-button selection of 15,000 songs and instrumental music of every description, so you can choose what you want to hear.

What's really nice in this intimate spot – with its buttery soft leather chairs and sofas – is Irish Coffee, correctly presented (the glass should be rotated while the sugar is blended with the alcohol and heated gently over a candle flame, the liquor set alight before coffee and cream are added).

Other features include a business center, an electronic golf simulator room (there is also a golf driving range, and a shuffleboard court), and dedicated rooms for hobbies (arts and crafts), and for children. The nicely stocked library has an illuminated globe of the world, and is open 24 hours. There's also a small cinema/meeting/function room.

In 2004, an indoor/outdoor bar (Sansibar) was added above the Lido Café (with great aft-facing views), and is the "in" place for the late-night set. Just forward of Sansibar is a new electronic golf simulator, golf club, and teaching facility (the ship carries a PGA golf pro on all cruises).

There is a seven-deck-high central atrium, plus two glass-walled elevators (operated by "piccolos" on embarkation day), and a lobby on the lower level with a Steinway grand piano and lobby bar, reception desk, concierge desk, shore excursion desk and a future cruise sales desk.

Wheelchair passengers should note that a special ramp is provided from the swimming pool/outdoors deck down to where the lifeboats are located; only three other ships have them. When the ship was delivered there were several small lips at door thresholds (particularly at fire zone doors) throughout the ship. Some of these have been ramped or replaced with airtight-sealing rubber strips, so that wheelchair access is now good everywhere.

This ship should appeal to all those who desire to be aboard what is arguably the most luxurious and finest of all the smaller cruise ships. For the German-speaking market, nothing else comes close (the crew also speaks English for the few British and American passengers, and some cruises are designated as bi-lingual English/German language voyages). Combined with an enthusiastic and well-trained crew, whose aim is to serve and please passengers in the most sumptuous but unobtrusive manner, the tradition of luxury cruising in a contemporary setting is taken to its highest expression. Although a children's playroom is provided, *Europa* really is a ship for adults to cruise in a quiet, refined setting that mixes formality and informality well.

The reason that *Europa* scores so highly, even though it is 10 years old, lies in the little details that most other cruise lines have long left behind in the age of discounts, the extras and the meticulous attention to personal comfort and service (there is no charge for in-suite movies on demand, for example, whereas Silversea Cruises charges extra). If you are relaxing at the swimming pool in a hot climate, deck stewards will set your sunlounger and cover the mattress pad with a towel, serve you drinks, give you a cold herbal towel, and spray you with Evian water to keep you cool while you take the sun. Naturally, only real glasses are used at the swimming pool and on the open decks – no plastic

glasses would ever be considered. When drinks are served, they are placed on cotton doilies (not paper or cork – a luxurious touch not found aboard any other cruise ship). Real flowers, pot pourri and cloth towels (paper towels are not permissible at this rating level) are provided in all public restrooms. Indeed, fresh flowers are everywhere.

Details, details, details – that's what *Europa* cruising is all about, and what the ship's many repeat passengers expect. The prices for drinks and wines are also very reasonable (they are not included for the simple reason that ships that include drinks typically have a much more restricted selection, including young table wines that may not be to all tastes); also, the ship provides many special functions and parties where drinks *are* provided free. Birthdays and anniversaries are quietly celebrated in one's suite – there are no singing waiters in the dining room to disturb other passengers.

Excellent port information is provided (both in written form and via the TV infotainment system). All port taxes and gratuities are included, although further tipping is not prohibited. The currency on board is the euro. The ship's voyage chart is auctioned each cruise, with the money collected going directly to charity.

When taking all things into account – the unhurried lifestyle of single seating dining, plenty of suites with private balconies, a fine array of classical music artists and lecturers, absolutely no vibration anywhere, and the outstanding cuisine and friendly, very attentive personal service from a staff dedicated to working aboard the world's finest cruise ship – it all adds up to the very best luxurious cruise ship and cruise experience available today (unless you have your own private motor yacht). While most cruise lines have been engaged in dressing down, Hapag-Lloyd has done the opposite: in 2003, dining room staff donned stunning new uniforms for formal nights, consisting of tails and trousers.

It has to be said that there *are* ships with more grandiose penthouse suites, larger balconies, show lounges, health spas and other appointments – but aboard *Europa*, everything is in scale, and in relation to the requirements of its passengers. At present, while there are plenty of imitators, there are no equals. There are few weak points, although perhaps an indoor swimming pool might be welcome. The balcony partitions are part-partitions, but would be more private if they were of the full (floor-to-ceiling) type – although this rarely presents a problem for passengers.

While *Europa* is not for everyone, the ship, which provides a more formal cruise experience than some might seek, provides the setting for the highest expression of the art of unobtrusive service and hospitality.

SUITABLE FOR: *Europa* is best suited to well-traveled, discerning passengers who simply want the best at sea in an uncluttered, utterly refined setting, with superb food, creature comforts, and a caring, very professional and pampering staff that has been well trained, and enjoys practising the fine art of hospitality in a chic, trendy setting.

ACCOMMODATION. This is provided in five configurations

and 10 price categories. It consists of all-outside-view suites: 2 Penthouse Grand Suites (Hapag, and Lloyd) and 10 Penthouse Deluxe Suites (Bach, Beethoven, Brahms, Handel, Lehar, Haydn, Mozart, Schubert, Strauss, Wagner, with each suite containing a large framed picture of the composer), 156 suites with private balcony, and 36 standard suites. There are two suites (with private balcony) for the disabled and 8 suites with interconnecting doors (good for families). Almost all suites have a private balcony (with wide teakwood deck, and lighting), and come complete with a smoked glass screen topped by a teakwood rail. However, 12 suites that overlook the stern are among the most sought-after accommodation (six on each of two decks, each suite having private balconies with canvas "ceilings" for shade and privacy).

General Information: Each suite has a wood floor entryway, and each has a sleeping area with twin beds that can convert to a queen-sized bed, and two bedside tables with lamps and two drawers. There is a separate lounge area (with curtain divider) and bird's-eye maple wood cabinetry and accenting (with rounded edges). Facilities include a refrigerator/mini-bar (beer and soft drinks are supplied at no extra charge), a writing/vanity desk and couch with large table in a separate lounge area. An illuminated walk-in closet provides ample hanging rail space, six drawers, personal safe (this can be opened with a credit card), umbrella, shoehorn, and clothes brush. European duvets are provided, and, in another cruise industry first, so is a full-color free daily newspaper (there's a wide choice). Almost all suites have totally unobstructed views and excellent soundproofing. All passengers receive a practical blue/beige shoulder travel bag, insulated lunch bag for shore excursions, leather keycard holder, and a generous supply of personal toiletries.

In what was a cruise industry first, a superb integrated color TV/computer monitor and "CIN" (Cruise Infotainment System) – 24 hours per day video and audio on-demand – is provided free, so you choose when you want to watch any one of up to 100 movies, or when you want to listen to a specific compact audio disc (there are more than 1,000 to choose from). The infotainment system includes large flat screens and direct, 24 hours-a-day internet connection via a full wireless keyboard located in a drawer in an adjacent vanity unit (each passenger has an assigned email address), Restaurant seating plans, menus, ship's position and chart, deck plan, shore excursion video clips, plus other informational video clips and items are featured. Your private email address is provided with your tickets and other documentation (there is no charge for incoming or outgoing emails, only for attachments, and for internet access). A modem (data) socket is also provided should you decide to bring your own laptop computer (the ship can also provide a laptop for your use).

All suites have a 100% air-circulation system, illuminated walk-in closets and a generous amount of hanging and storage space. Western European butlers and cabin stewardesses are employed (butlers for the 12 premium suites on Deck 10, cabin stewardesses for all other suites). The white/gray/sea green marble-tiled bathrooms are

very well designed, have light decor, and include two good size cabinets for personal toiletries. All bathrooms have a full tub (plus an integral shower and a retractable clothesline) and separate glass-fronted shower enclosure. Thick, 100% cotton bathrobes are provided, as are slippers and an array of personal toiletry amenities.

Penthouses (Deck 10): There are two Penthouse Grand suites, and 10 Penthouse Deluxe suites. These have a teakwood entrance hall, spacious living room with full-size dining table and four chairs, fully stocked drinks cabinet with refrigerator butler service, complimentary bar set-up (replenished with whatever you need), laundry and ironing service included, priority spa reservations, caviar or other canapés daily before dinner, hand-made chocolates, petit-fours and other niceties at no extra charge. Balconies have teakwood decking, and white canvas ceiling shades. For the ultimate in exclusivity, the two Penthouse Grand suites also have even larger bathrooms (each with its own private sauna), and extensive forward views from their prime, supremely quiet location one deck above the navigation bridge; a very large wrap-around private balcony; larger walk-in closet (with its own window), and large flat-screen TVs. Well-trained butlers provide the highest level of unobtrusive service for these suites.

Spa suites: Newly created in 2007 are four delightful spa suites, located just forward to the Futuresse Spa on Deck 7. These are fine new suites, and incorporate a large private teak-decked balcony (good for massages); twin or queen-sized bed; walk-in closet; dark wood cabinetry housing a refrigerator (stocked with fruit juices and different mineral waters) and bar set-up, personal computer, flat-screen TV, and storage space including a jewelry drawer, with pull-around doors that can close off everything to view; writing/vanity desk, and floor-to-ceiling windows. The decor colors are warm reds, yellow and gold. There is a large window (with wooden blond) between the living/sleeping area and the bathroom. The bathroom itself has warm Asian decor, underwater lighted Jacuzzi bath, separate large shower enclosure (with rain shower), toilet and gold, thick-glass washbasin, hand-held hairdryer, and plenty of storage space. A range of special toiletry amenities is provided, and special teas and other services are provided by spa personnel. And, for cruises longer than 10 days, a customized spa package (including treatments) is included in the price.

Suites for the Disabled (Deck 7): These spacious suites have one electronically operated bed with hydraulic elevator plus one regular bed, while a non-walk-in closet with drawers replaces the walk-in closet in all other suites. The bathroom has a roll-in shower area. All fittings are at the correct height, and there are several grab handles, plus an emergency call-for-help button. Wheelchair-accessible public toilets are provided on the main restaurant/entertainment deck.

CUISINE. With over 5,000 separate food ingredients carried at any one time, the executive chef can produce menus that don't repeat even for around-the-world and other long voyages for which this ship excels. The cuisine is outstanding, always full of surprises, and never boring. Seasonal and regional ingredients are featured, with much totally fresh fish and seafood as standard. This is as good as it gets. There are four restaurants to choose from.

The Europa Restaurant is a beautiful dining room that is two decks high, and can accommodate all passengers in one seating, with tables assigned for dinner only (breakfast and lunch are open seating). Passengers thus keep their favorite waiter throughout each cruise (for dinner). In common with most German ships, a small smoking sections is provided. There are tables for two (quite a few), four, six or eight. For superb service, there is a *chef de rang* and an assistant waiter, so that the *chef de rang* is always at the station, with the assistant waiter acting as runner.

The cuisine is superb, and very varied. Plated presentation of food is provided for entrées with silver service for additional vegetables, as well as tableside flambeaux. The size of portions is sensible – never overwhelming. On days at sea, in addition to the regular, extensive breakfast, a Gourmet Breakfast menu includes such things as beef tartare, carpaccio of smoked tuna with wasabi cream, gooseliver tureen with orange confit, and other specialties rarely found aboard cruise ships today. In 2006 a new Cuisine Legeré menu was added (light, healthy, but very tasty spa cuisine).

Table settings include Dibbern china, 150-gram weight Robbe & Berking silverware and Riedel wine glasses (these are delicate and have to be hand-washed). The cuisine is very international, but includes German favorites as well as regional dishes from around the world. The quality of food is extremely high. Although top-grade caviar is found on dinner menus at least once each week, it is always available on request (at extra cost). An extensive wine list is provided, and includes a good selection of vintage French wines, as well as a well-balanced selection of Austrian, German and Swiss wines.

Alternative dining options: There are two, non-smoking intimate alternative dining spots: the Oriental Restaurant, for Euro-Asian cuisine that is extremely creative and beautifully presented, and Venezia, for Italian cuisine (and a wide variety of olive oils and grappa). Both are adjacent to and forward of the main restaurant, and provide the setting for a truly intimate dining experience, in nicely appointed surroundings. These are available by reservation, and there is no extra charge. The Oriental Restaurant has stunning, hand-made Meissen china (the famous porcelain manufacturer reanimated and modernized an old "Flying Fish" pattern especially for *Europa*; the idea for the original pattern came from a Hapag steamer in 1904). In Venezia, Rosenthal china is featured. Both venues are open for lunch and dinner.

For more casual dining, there is an elegant Lido Cafe for serve-yourself breakfasts (the ship even makes its own preserves), luncheons and dinners, with both indoor and outdoor seating and adjacent indoor/outdoor bar. New, colorful Dibbern china (in three patterns) was added in 2003. Themed evening dining is also featured here, with full waiter service. There is a wide variety of food, and many special lunch buffets have a number of popular themes and regional specialties.

Europa is famous for its real German sausages, available in the Clipper Bar, and at a special Bavarian Fruschoppen featured once each cruise in the Lido Cafe. Late each night, "light bites", beautifully presented on silver trays, are taken around the various bars and lounges.

Afternoon tea is a sheer delight, with a selection of about 30 teas (loose tea, of course, never teabags). There are also several types of coffee and impeccably made liqueur coffees, heated in a hand-turned glass enclosure, and a superb selection of cakes (made fresh every day). Nautical tradition is kept up with bouillon service each morning at sea, and other daily niceties include fresh waffles and ice cream each afternoon around the pool.

ENTERTAINMENT. The Europa Lounge, whose decor is a rich red, is the main showlounge; it has a sloping floor, providing good sightlines from almost every seat. The ship excels in its fine, intellectual entertainment program (it is tailored more to the theme of the cruise), which includes a constant supply of high-quality classical and contemporary musical artistes, a variety of cabaret acts, as well as a programme of expert lecturers, poetry readers, and so on, together with an occasional colorful production show, and local shows brought on board in various ports.

The smaller, more intimate Clipper Lounge is the setting for late-night cabaret (vocalists, magicians, ballroom dance specialists, comedians). The ship carries a main showband, plus a number of small musical units to provide live music for listening or dancing. Classical concerts and recitals are provided in the Belvedere Lounge, with its dropped central circular floor and white Steinway grand piano.

SPA/FITNESS. The Ocean Spa has a wide range of beauty services and treatments, including hot stone massage, and an array of other rejuvenating treatments (including full-day spa packages. Shiseido cosmetics are the featured cosmetic/spa products for sale. The entire spa area was completely refitted and redecorated in May 2007 and is now a well integrated and very welcoming wellness and treatment area.

Facilities include a steam room and sauna (mixed), two shower enclosures and two foot-washing stations, relaxation room with 3 hot tiled beds and 3 wicker relax beds, and male and female changing/dressing rooms. There is also a separate gymnasium and a beauty salon. A Japanese Spa is featured (treatments include a cream body massage, gentle steam room and a two-tatami mat relaxation area), which is booked individually for a special 90-minute treatment.

Other treatment samples and prices: Asian style spa special (hot aroma body wrap with head, shiatsu and food reflex massages) (€90 for 60 minutes); Pacific style spa special – Lomi Lomi massage with warm aroma oils and body pack (€90 for 60 minutes); Classic Massage (€40 for 30 minutes); Shiatsu Massage (€60 for 30 minutes); Shiseido Intensive Facial (€110 for 90 minutes); Goddess of the Sea total indulgence program (€290 for three hours of pampering including a Lomi Lomi massage, body pack, and facial).

A nice touch is that the treatment rooms have music menus, so you can choose what music you wish to hear.

Explorer of the Seas
★★★★

Large Resort Ship: ....137,308 tons	Total Crew: 1,181	Cabins (with private balcony): 757
Lifestyle: ....Standard	Passengers	Cabins (wheelchair accessible): 26
Cruise Line: Royal Caribbean International	(lower beds/all berths): 3,114/3,840	Cabin Current: ....110 volts
Former Names: ....none	Passenger Space Ratio	Elevators: ....14 (6 glass-enclosed)
Builder: ...Kvaerner Masa-Yards (Finland)	(lower beds/all berths): 44.0/35.7	Casino (gaming tables): ....Yes
Original Cost: ....$500 million	Crew/Passenger Ratio	Slot Machines: ....Yes
Entered Service: ....Oct 2000	(lower beds/all berths): 2.6/3.2	Swimming Pools (outdoors): 3
Registry: ....The Bahamas	Navigation Officers: ......Scandinavian	Swimming Pools (indoors): 0
Length (ft/m): 1,020.6/311.1	Cabins (total): 1,557	Whirlpools: 6
Beam (ft/m): 155.5/47.4	Size Range (sq ft/m): 151.0–1,358.0/	Self-Service Launderette: ....No
Draft (ft/m): 28.8/8.8	14.0–126.1	Dedicated Cinema/Seats: ....No
Propulsion/Propellers: .....diesel-electric	Cabins (outside view): 939	Library: ....Yes
(75,600kW)/3 pods	Cabins (interior/no view): 618	
Passenger Decks: 14	Cabins (for one person): 0	

OVERALL SCORE: 1,476 (OUT OF A POSSIBLE 2,000 POINTS)

OVERVIEW. This large, stunning, floating leisure resort is sister to *Adventure of the Seas, Mariner of the Seas, Navigator of the Seas* and *Voyager of the Seas*). The ship's propulsion is derived from three pod units, powered by electric motors (two azimuthing, and one fixed at the centerline) in the latest configuration of high-tech propulsion systems *(for details, see page 174).*

With its large proportions, the ship provides more facilities and options, yet it has a healthy amount of space per passenger. It is too large to go through the Panama Canal, thus limiting itineraries almost exclusively to the Caribbean (where few islands can accept it), or for use as a floating resort. Spend the first few hours exploring the many facilities and public spaces and it will be time well spent.

Although *Explorer of the Seas* is large, the cabin hallways are warm and attractive, with artwork cabinets and wavy lines to lead you along and break up the monotony. There are plenty of colorful, even whimsical, decorative touches to prevent the environment being too clinical.

Embarkation and disembarkation take place through two access points, designed to minimize the inevitable lines (that's over 1,500 people for each access point). Take good walking shoes, particularly to go from one end to the other – it really is a long way.

The four-decks-high Royal Promenade, which is 394 ft (120 meters) long, is the main interior focal point (it's a good place to hang out, to meet someone, or to arrange to meet someone). The length of two American football fields, it has two internal lobbies (atria) that rise as many as 11 decks high. Restaurants, shops and entertainment locations front this winding street and interior "with-view" cabins look into it from above. The Guest Reception and Shore Excursion

BERLITZ'S RATINGS		
	Possible	Achieved
Ship	500	418
Accommodation	200	150
Food	400	237
Service	400	281
Entertainment	100	83
Cruise	400	307

counters are located at the aft end of the promenade, as is an ATM machine. Look up to see the large moving, asteroid-like sculpture (constantly growing and contracting), parades and street entertainers.

Arched across the promenade is a captain's balcony. Meanwhile, a stairway in the center of the promenade connects you to the deck below, where you'll find Schooner Bar (a piano lounge that is a feature of all RCI ships) and the colorful Casino Royale. This is naturally large and full of flashing lights and noises. Casino gaming includes blackjack, Caribbean stud poker, roulette, and craps, as well as 300 slot machines.

Aft of the casino is the Aquarium Bar; adjacent are some neat displays of oceanographic interest. Royal Caribbean International has teamed up with the University of Miami's Rosenstiel School of Marine and Atmospheric Science to study the ocean and the atmosphere. To this end, a small onboard laboratory is part of the project.

There is a regulation-size ice-skating rink (Studio B), with real ice, and stadium-style seating for up to 900, plus the latest in broadcast facilities. Ice Follies shows are also presented here. Slim pillars obstruct clear-view arena stage sightlines, however. If ice-skating in the Caribbean doesn't appeal, perhaps you'd like the stunning two-deck library (open 24 hours a day). A grand $12 million has been spent on permanent artwork.

Drinking places include a neat Aquarium Bar, which comes complete with 50 tons of glass and water in four large aquariums (whose combined value is more than $1 million). Other drinking places include the intimate Champagne Bar, Crown & Anchor Pub, a Sidewalk Cafe (for continental breakfast, all-day pizzas, specialty coffees and desserts), Sprinkles (for round-the-clock ice cream and yoghurt), and Weekend Warrior (a sports bar), and a Connoisseur Club (for cigars and cognacs). Lovers of jazz might like Dizzy's, an intimate room for cool music within the Viking Crown Lounge, or the Schooner Bar piano lounge. Golfers might enjoy the 19th Hole, a golf bar, as they play the Explorer Links.

There are also several shops on the Royal Promenade (jewelry shop, gift shop, liquor shop and a logo souvenir shop). At times, street entertainers appear, and parades happen, while at other (carefully orchestrated) times it's difficult to walk through the area as it is filled to the brim with shopping items – like a cheap bazaar.

A TV studio is adjacent to rooms useable for trade show exhibit space, with a 400-seat conference center and a multi-media screening room that seats 60. Lovers can tie the knot in a wedding chapel in the sky, the Skylight Chapel (it's located on the upper level of the Viking Crown Lounge, and even has wheelchair access via an electric stairlift). Meanwhile, outdoors, the pool and open deck areas provide a resort-like environment.

Families with children are also well catered to, as facilities for children and teenagers are quite extensive. "Aquanauts" is for 3–5 year olds; "Explorers" (6–8); "Voyagers" (9–12). Optix is a dedicated area for teenagers, including a daytime club (with computers), soda bar, disco with disc jockey and dance floor. Challenger's Arcade has the latest video games. Paint and Clay is an arts and crafts center for younger children. Adjacent to these indoor areas is Adventure Beach, an area for all the family to enjoy: it includes swimming pools, a water slide and game areas outdoors.

In terms of sheer size, this ship dwarfs most other ships in the cruise industry, but in terms of personal service, the reverse is the case, unless you have one of the top suites. Royal Caribbean International does try hard to provide a good standard of programmed service from its hotel staff. But this is impersonal city life at sea, and a superb, well-designed alternative to a land-based resort, which is what the company wanted to build. Perhaps if you dare to go outside, you might even be able to see the sea. Remember to take lots of extra pennies – you'll need them to pay for all the additional-cost items.

Passenger gripes: cabin bath towels and explosively noisy (vacuum) toilets; few quiet places to sit and read – almost everywhere there is intrusive background music. And if you have a cabin with a door that interconnecting door to another cabin, be aware that you'll be able to hear everything your next-door neighbours say and do.

ACCOMMODATION. There are 22 cabin categories, in four major groupings: Premium ocean-view suites and cabins, Promenade-view (interior-view) cabins, Ocean-view cabins, and Interior (no view) cabins. Many cabins are of a similar size – good for incentives and large groups, and 300 have interconnecting doors – good for families. Prices depend on grade, size and location.

Some 138 interior (no view) cabins have bay windows that look into a horizontal atrium, with interior cabins that look into a central shopping plaza. However, all cabins except for the Royal Suite and Owner's Suite have twin beds that convert to a queen-sized unit, television, radio and telephone, personal safe, vanity unit, mini-bar, hairdryer and private bathroom.

The largest accommodation includes luxurious penthouse suites (whose occupants, sadly, must share the rest of the ship with everyone else, except for their own exclusive, and private, concierge club). The grandest is the Royal Suite, positioned on the port side of the ship, and measures 1,146 sq. ft (106.5 sq. meters). It has a king-sized bed in a separate, large bedroom, a living room with an additional queen-sized sofa bed, baby grand piano, refrigerator/wet bar, dining table, entertainment center, and large bathroom.

The slightly smaller, but still highly desirable Owner's Suites (there are 10, all in the center of the ship, on both port and starboard sides, each measuring 468 sq. ft (43 sq. meters)) and four Royal Family suites (each measures 574 sq. ft (53 sq. meters), all of which feature similar items. However, the four Royal Family suites, which have two bedrooms (including one with third/ fourth upper Pullman berths) are located at the stern of the ship and have magnificent views over the ship's wake (and seagulls).

All cabins have a private bathroom with shower enclosure (towels are 100% cotton), plus interactive television and pay-per-view movies. Cabins with "private balconies" are not so private, as the partitions are only partial, leaving you exposed to your neighbor's smoke or conversation. The balcony decking is made of Bolidt – a sort of rubberized sand – and not wood, while the balcony rail is of wood.

CUISINE. The large main dining room is set on three levels, named after explorers (Christopher Columbus, Da Gama and Magellan). A dramatic staircase connects all three levels, and huge, fat support pillars obstruct the sight lines. All three feature exactly the same menus and food. The dining room is totally non-smoking, there are two seatings, and tables are for four, six, eight 10 or 12.

Alternative Dining Options: Alternative dining options for casual and informal meals at all hours (according to company releases) include:
● Cafe Promenade, for continental breakfast, all-day pizzas and speciality coffees (provided in paper cups).
● Windjammer Cafe, for casual buffet-style breakfast, lunch and light dinner (except on a cruise's last night).
● Island Grill (actually a section inside the Windjammer Cafe), for casual dinner (no reservations needed), with a grill and open kitchen.
● Portofino: the ship's "upscale" (non-smoking) Italian restaurant, open for dinner only. Reservations are required, and there's a $6 gratuity per person. The food and its presentation are better than the food in the dining room, although the restaurant is not large enough for all passengers to try even once during a cruise. Choices include antipasti, soup, salad, pasta, main dish, dessert, cheese and coffee. The menu does not change throughout the cruise.

● Johnny Rockets, a retro 1950s all-day, all-night diner-style eatery, has hamburgers, malt shakes (at extra cost), and jukebox hits, with both indoor and outdoor seating (all indoor tables feature a mini-jukebox; dimes are provided for you to make your selection of vintage records), and all-singing, all-dancing waitresses.

● Sprinkles, for round-the-clock ice cream and yogurt, pastries and coffee.

ENTERTAINMENT. The 1,350-seat Palace Showlounge is a stunning room that could well be the equal of many such rooms on land. It is located at the forward end of the ship and spans the height of five decks (with only a few slim pillars and almost no disruption of sight lines from almost any seat in the house).

The room has a hydraulic orchestra pit and huge stage areas, together with sonic-boom loud sound, and some superb lighting equipment.

The ship also has an array of cabaret acts. Although many are not what you would call headliners (the strongest cabaret acts are featured in the main showlounge, while others are presented in the Maharaja's Lounge, also the site for late-night adults-only comedy), they regularly travel the cruise ship circuit.

SPA/FITNESS. The ShipShape health spa is large, and measures 15,000 sq. ft (1,400 sq. meters). It includes a large aerobics room, fitness center (with the usual techno-gym equipment for muscle pumping), several treatment rooms, men's and women's sauna/steam rooms, while another 10,000 sq. ft (930 sq. meters) is devoted to a Solarium (with magrodome sliding glass roof) for relaxation after you've exercised too much.

There is a rock-climbing wall that's 32.8 ft high (10 meters), with five separate climbing tracks. It is located outdoors at the aft end of the funnel.

Other sports facilities include a roller-blading track, a dive-and-snorkel shop, a full-size basketball court and 9-hole, par 26 golf course.

● **For more extensive general information about the Royal Caribbean cruise experience, see pages 137–42.**

A PASSENGER'S PRAYER

"Heavenly Father, look down on us, Your humble, obedient passengers who are doomed to travel the seas and waterways of this earth, taking photographs, mailing postcards, buying useless souvenirs, and walking around in ill-fitting swimwear.

"We beseech You, oh Lord, to see that our plane is not hijacked, our luggage is not lost, and that our over-sized carry-ons go unnoticed.

"Protect us from surly and unscrupulous taxi drivers, avaricious porters, and unlicensed, English-speaking guides in foreign places.

"Give us this day Divine guidance in the selection of our cruise ships and our travel agents — so that we may find our bookings and dining room reservations honored, our cabins of generous proportions, that our luggage arrives before the first evening meal, and that our beds are made up.

"We humbly ask that our shower curtains and personal safes do not provoke us into meaningless frustration and destructive thoughts.

"We pray for art auction-free cruise ships, duty-free-free zones, and mobile phone-free restaurants and open decks.

"We pray that our cabin telephones work, the operator (human or electrical) speaks our tongue, and that there are no phone calls from our children forcing us to abandon our cruise early.

"Lead us, dear Lord, to good, affordable restaurants in the world ashore, where the food is superb, the waiters friendly, and the wine included in the price of a meal.

"Please grant us a cruise director who does not "cream" excessively from the spoils of bingo or horse racing, or does not stress only those jewelry stores from which he accepts an offering.

"Grant us the strength to take shore excursions – to visit the museums, cathedrals, spice stalls, and gift shops listed in Berlitz Pocket Guides.

"And if on our return journey by non-air-conditioned buses we slip into slumber, have mercy on us for our flesh is weak, hot, and tired.

"Give us the wisdom to tip correctly at the end of our voyage. Forgive us for under-tipping out of ignorance, and over-tipping out of fear. Please make the chief purser and ship's staff loves us for what we are and not for what we can contribute to their worldly goods or company comment forms.

"Dear God, keep our wives from shopping sprees and protect them from bargains they do not need or cannot afford. Lead them not into temptation in St. Thomas or Hong Kong for they know not what they do.

"Almighty Father, keep our husbands from looking at foreign women and comparing them to us. Save them from making fools of themselves in cafés and nightclubs. Above all, please do not forgive them their trespasses for they know exactly what they do.

"And when our voyage is over and we return home to our loved ones, grant us the favor of finding someone who will look at our home videos and listen to our stories, so our lives as tourists will not have been in vain. This we ask you in the name of our chosen cruise line, and in the name of American Express, Visa, MasterCard, and our banks. Amen."

Freedom of the Seas
★★★★

Large Resort Ship:	154,407 tons	Total Crew:	1,397
Lifestyle:	Standard	Passengers	
Cruise Line:	Royal Caribbean International	(lower beds/all berths):	3,634/4,375
Former Names:	none	Passenger Space Ratio	
Builder:	Kvaerner Masa-Yards (Finland)	(lower beds/all berths):	42.0/35.32
Original Cost:	$590 million	Crew/Passenger Ratio	
Entered Service:	June 2006	(lower beds/all berths):	2.6/3.1
Registry:	The Bahamas	Navigation Officers:	European
Length (ft/m):	1,112.2/339.0	Cabins (total):	1,817
Beam (ft/m):	183.7/56.0	Size Range (sq ft/m):	153.0–2,025.0/
Draft (ft/m):	27.8/8.5		14.2–188.1
Propulsion/Propellers:	diesel-electric	Cabins (outside view):	1,084
	(75,600 kW)/3 pods (42,000 kW)	Cabins (interior/no view):	733
Passenger Decks:	15	Cabins (for one person):	0

Cabins (with private balcony):	842
Cabins (wheelchair accessible):	32
Cabin Current:	110 volts
Elevators:	14
Casino (gaming tables):	Yes
Slot Machines:	Yes
Swimming Pools (outdoors):	2
Swimming Pools (indoors):	0
Whirlpools:	6
Self-Service Launderette:	No
Dedicated Cinema/Seats:	No
Library:	Yes

OVERALL SCORE: 1,530 (OUT OF A POSSIBLE 2,000 POINTS)

OVERVIEW. Bring your boxing gloves. Why? Because there's a full-sized boxing ring on board. Now read on... *Freedom of the Seas* (with sisters *Independence of the Seas* and *Liberty of the Seas*) is the largest purpose-built cruise ship ever constructed. An extension of the highly successful Voyager-class of ships, which Royal Caribbean International introduced in 1999 with *Voyager of the Seas*, this latest behemoth is at the cutting edge of contemporary resort ship design. The ship's length and beam were extended, enabling an increase in the number of cabins and passenger capacity, as well as a combined pool area 43 percent larger than the Voyager-class (but with 500 more passengers).

The extra length (at 1,112 ft/339 meters long, the ship is the length of 37 London double-decker buses; and with a beam of 185 ft/56 meters, it is wider than the Washington's White House, at 165 ft/50 meters) has enabled more innovative designs to be incorporated. These include two 16-person hot tubs cantilevered 12 ft (3.7 meters) over the sides of the ship in an adults-only Solarium area (although the Solarium's pool itself is small).

The ship's "pod" propulsion is powered by electric motors (two azimuthing, and one fixed at the centerline) instead of conventional rudders and propellers, in the latest configuration of high-tech systems that virtually eliminates vibration *(for further details, see page 174)*.

Perhaps the "wow" factor aboard this ship is its connection with water (of the seas), including a 40ft x 32ft (12.2 x 9.7 meters) "Flowrider" (wave simulator) surfing zone that is the ship's stern; a wall of water, flowing at 35,000 gallons per minute, provides the backdrop for board or body surfers – but no more than two at a time (don't

BERLITZ'S RATINGS

	Possible	Achieved
Ship	500	430
Accommodation	200	161
Food	400	245
Service	400	294
Entertainment	100	83
Cruise	400	317

worry if you get wiped out, the landing is soft). Then there's the H$_2$O Zone forward of the funnel, an interactive water-themed play area for families that includes a pool fed by a waterfall, and two hot tubs. Included are water cannons and spray fountains, water jets and ground gushers; by night the "water park" turns into a colorfully-lit "Sculpture Garden." Twin central pools consist of a main pool and a sports pool, with grandstand-style seating and competitive games including pole jousting.

Other active sports facilities include a rock-climbing wall, in-line skating area, an ice-skating rink, golf simulators, and that full-sized boxing ring (sparring partners included in the session) in the spa.

The same facilities (public rooms, bars and lounges) featured in the Voyager-class ships have been incorporated, but with the addition of substantial conference facilities, extensive wi-fi coverage and connectivity for cell phones. The four elements (earth, air, fire, and water) provide the decorative theme for the artwork aboard this ship.

Although this is the world's largest cruise ship (take your GPS unit with you!), the cabin hallways have an extremely warm, attractive feel, with some neat whimsical interactive artwork cabinets and asymmetrical flow that leads you along and breaks up the monotony. In fact, there are plenty of colorful, whimsical, decorative touches typical of Scandinavian designers. Note that, if you meet someone somewhere, and want to meet them again, it's best to make an appointment and location, for this really is a large, Las Vegas-style American floating resort-city.

There are 16 bars and lounges. There's a whole promenade of shops, munching and drinking spots along an indoor mall-like environment called The Royal Promenade that is four decks high (some interior cabins have great views into the promenade-mall). The Royal Promenade is home to fashion, jewelry and perfume shops, a general store, logo shop, Promenade Cafe, Ben & Jerry's ice cream outlet, a Book Nook, a barber shop called A Close Shave (a razor shave "experience" costs $72), a pizzeria, and an English pub called The Bull and Bear (and do watch out for the stilt walkers and inflatable elephants when the circus is in town). Look at the ceiling in this large atrium and you'll see Vittoria Alata ("Winged Victory") flowing down towards you – an exact replica of the sculpture in the Piazza Venetia in Rome.

The forward section of this large space leads neatly into a large nightclub called Pharaoh's Palace (typically used for late-night adult comedy). One deck down from the Royal Promenade houses a large Casino Royale, The Crypt (discotheque), Schooner Bar (piano bar), Boleros (Latin hangout), and a photo gallery, while the forward section leads you into the three-decks high 1, 350-seat Arcadia Theatre. A whimsical piece of artwork on the forward starboard stairway includes a musical line whose tune is: "My Bonnie Lies Over the Ocean…"

There is also a regulation-size ice-skating rink (Studio B), featuring real, not fake, ice, with "bleacher" seating, and the latest in broadcast facilities. Superb "Ice Follies" shows are also presented here (but a number of slim pillars obstruct clear-view arena stage sight lines). Almost at the top of the ship is RCI's trademark Viking Crown Lounge, the cutely named Olive or Twist jazz lounge, and a wedding chapel.

Other facilities include a cigar smoker's lounge, conference center, a concierge lounge (for suite occupants only), and the comfortable 3,600-book Wilhemsen Library.

Children are also well catered to, with Adventure Ocean (for kids of 6 months to 17 years of age). In fact, children will love this ship and all the fun activities and sports.

Freedom of the Seas is fresh, exciting and very comfortable, with tasteful decor and many bars and lounges. It is certainly a great ship for young, active families with children, as long as you don't mind lines and signing up for popular activities like the "Flowrider" surf area (about a year ahead should do it), rock-climbing wall and boxing ring. Note also that there are only four banks of elevators (two forward and two aft) totaling 14, so if you have a cabin in the center of the ship, you'll need to walk forward or aft in order to travel vertically between decks; and there are only two major stairways – one forward, one aft – for such a large ship. On disembarkation day, you'll need to allow plenty of time to get an elevator, and, probably, for your luggage (there are no seats in the luggage hall in Maimi).

ACCOMMODATION. There is a wide range of suites and cabins in 14 categories and 21 price grades, from a Presidential Family Suite that can sleep up to 14 to twin-bed two person interior (no view) cabins, and interior cabins that look into an interior shopping/strolling atrium promenade. Price depends on grade. There are many family-friendly cabins, good for family reunions, but there are no single

occupancy cabins. All outside-view cabins have even numbers; all interior (no view) cabins have odd numbers.

Some accommodation examples (from large to small): **Presidential Family Suite:** Located in the aft section, this suite (there is just one) comprises five rooms. These include two master bedrooms, each with twin beds that convert to a queen-size bed and ensuite bathroom with bathtub/shower (the toiletries cabinets are the same as in all other cabins); two other (very small) bedrooms that can sleep four; private balcony (sand-colored rubberized decking, not teak) with loungers, tables, chairs, a bar, and a decent view aft (although part of the balcony is overlooked by balconies on the decks above, and there is a lot of wasted space aft of the balcony because it doesn't extend to the very stern); lounge with two sofa beds, bar. The suite can accommodate eight to 14 (that's odd numbers breathing in, even numbers breathing out!), located aft (at the opposite end of the ship to the showlounge). Size: 1,215 sq. ft. (113 sq. meters), plus Balcony: 810 sq. ft (75 sq. meters). It's a pleasant enough apartment, but nothing special (it's really quite cramped and the ceilings are plain), but it could be good value for a large family (provided everyone gets on well in a confined space).

Owner's Suite: Features include a queen-sized bed, private balcony, separate living area with queen-sized sofa bed, wet bar, vanity area, walk-in closet; bathroom with tub and shower. Sleeps up to five. Size: 506 sq. ft. (46 sq. meters) plus Balcony: 131 sq. ft. (12.1 sq. meters).

Royal Suite: Perhaps the nicest decor of all the suites, the Royal Suite has a very spacious lounge (with black baby grand player piano, queen-sized sofa and entertainment center), wet bar, dining table. The bedroom is quite spacious and has a queen-sized bed; the bathroom has a jacuzzi bath, large walk-in shower, and two (rather gaudi gold) washbasins. Sleeps up to four. Size: 1,406 sq.ft. (130.6 sq. meters) plus 377 sq.ft. (35 sq. meters).

Grand Suite: This has two twin beds convertible to queen-size, a private balcony, sitting area (some with sofa bed), vanity area; bathroom with tub and shower. Sleeps up to four. Size: 381 sq. ft. (35.3 sq. meters) plus Balcony: 89 sq. ft. (8.2 sq. meters)

Junior Suite: Two twin beds convertible to queen-size, a private balcony, sitting area (some with sofa bed), vanity area; bathroom with tub and shower. Sleeps up to four. Size: 277 sq. ft. (25.7 sq. meters) plus Balcony: 65 sq. ft. (6.0 sq. meters).

Superior Oceanview Cabin: Two twin beds convertible to queen-size, a private balcony, sitting area (some with sofa bed), vanity area; bathroom with shower. Sleeps 2 (some rooms sleep three or four). Size: 202 sq. ft. (18.7 sq. meters) + Balcony: 42 sq. ft. (3.9 sq. meters).

Deluxe Oceanview Cabin: Two twin beds convertible to queen-size, a private balcony, sitting area (some with sofa bed), vanity area; bathroom with shower. Sleeps 2 (some rooms sleep three or four). Size: 173 sq. ft. (16.0 sq. meters) + Balcony: 46 sq. ft. (4.2 sq. meters).

Interior (promenade-view) Cabin: These 172 cabins, on three decks, are interior cabins but with bay windows that allow occupants to look into the Royal Promenade. They have two twin beds convertible to queen-size; private bath-room with shower.

Interior (no view) Cabin: Two twin beds convertible to queen-size; private bathroom with shower. Sleeps two (some rooms sleep three or four). Size: 160 sq. ft. (14.8 sq.meters).

Family Ocean-view Cabin: Located at the front of the ship, it contains two twin beds (convertible to queen-size), sofa and/or Pullman beds, sitting area; bathroom, with shower. Accommodates six, and has 48-inch round windows. Size: 265 sq. ft. (24.6 sq. meters).

All grades of accommodation have a private bathroom (with tub and shower, or shower only, washbasin and toiletries cabinet – although they are disappointingly basic, modular and akin to bathrooms found in caravans/mobile homes), vanity desk with hairdryer, mini-bar, personal safe, flat-screen TV, radio, satellite-dial telephone, 9-inch thick mattresses and duvets. A room service menu is provided. Suite occupants have access to a Concierge Lounge, for more personal service (this saves going down to the reception desk and standing in line). Occupants of suite-grade accommodation have access to a Concierge Club lounge and its preferential services.

CUISINE. The extremely large main dining room is set on three levels (each has a theme and different name: Leonardo, Isaac, and Galileo). A dramatic staircase connects all three levels, but huge, fat support pillars obstruct the sight lines from many seats. All three have exactly the same menus and food. The dining room is non-smoking, there are two seatings, and tables are for four, six, eight 10 or 12.

Alternative (extra-charge) Dining Options: These venues, all non-smoking, provide casual and informal meals at all hours (according to company statements):

● *Chops Grill*: for steaks, chops and special seafood, set in a great location. Open for dinner only, reservations required; cover charge $20.

● *Portofino*: this Euro-Italian restaurant is open for dinner only. Reservations required; cover charge $20. Choices include: antipasti, soup, salad, pasta, main dish, dessert, cheese and coffee (menu doesn't change during the cruise).

● *Promenade Café*: for continental breakfast, all-day pizzas, sandwiches and coffees (provided in paper cups).

● *Sprinkles*: for round-the-clock ice cream and yoghurt, pastries and coffee.

● *Windjammer Café*: self-serve casual buffet breakfast, lunch and dinner (except for the cruise's last night).

● *Jade Restaurant* (a section of the Windjammer Café): self-serve casual buffet breakfasts, lunch and dinner (no reservations necessary).

● *Johnny Rockets*, a retro 1950s all-day, all-night diner-style eatery that features hamburgers, hot dogs and other fast-food items, malt shakes and sodas (at extra cost) with indoor and outdoor seating (all indoor tables have a mini-jukebox; dimes are provided for you to make your selection of vintage records), and all-singing, all-dancing waitresses. Cover charge: $3.95.

You'll need to make reservations for Chops Grill or Portofino as early as you can in the cruise, because seating is limited and sells out quickly – not surprising when there are typically over 4,000 passengers on each cruise.

ENTERTAINMENT. The stunning Arcadia Theater is located on three decks at the forward end of the ship (actually five decks including orchestra pit and scenery storage space). It has only a few pillars and little disruption of sightlines. The room has a hydraulic orchestra pit and huge stage areas, together with sonic-boom loud sound, and some superb lighting equipment. A cast of 18 perform three production shows each cruise: "Marquee," a medley of performances, the musical "Now You See It!" magic show and "Once Upon a Time," a narrative based on the Brothers Grimm's fairytales.

Most of the cabaret acts are not what you would call headliners. The strongest acts perform in the main show-lounge, while others are presented in the Nightclub, the venue for late-night adults-only comedy. The most entertaining shows, however, are the Ice Spectaculars. There is also a TV studio, adjacent to rooms that can also be used for trade show exhibit space (good for conventions at sea).

Royal Caribbean's production shows are colorful spectaculars that will remind you of Las Vegas casino hotels, fast-moving, razzle-dazzle shows that have little or no story line, and often poor linkage between themes and scenes, and choreography that is more stepping in place rather than dancing.

One "show" not to be missed is the "Greatest Show at Sea" Parade – a superbly executed 15-minute fun extravaganza that bumbles along the Royal Promenade at turtle speed; it replicates the parade of stars and animals at a circus of yesteryear (Barnum and Bailey's meets cruise ship). This is when it's really good to have one of those interior-view atrium cabins (sadly, the windows don't open, so you can't take photographs); otherwise, get a position early along the Royal Promenade.

SPA/FITNESS. The ShipShape health spa is large. It includes a large aerobics room, fitness center (with the usual stairmasters, treadmills, stationary bikes, weight machines and free weights), treatment rooms, and men's and women's sauna/steam rooms and relaxation areas. Sample prices: AromaStone Therapy massage, $195 (75 mins); Swedish Massage, $119 (50 mins); Couples massage, $260 (50 mins); facial, $119 (50 mins), plus tip.

The spa facility is operated by Steiner, whose staff will try to hard-sell you Elemis products. Some (basic) exercise classes are free, but the good ones (examples: yoga, personal training) cost extra.

More active passengers can bodyboard, go boxing (in the full-size boxing ring in the middle of the spa; the cost is $83 for a personal session, or $10 as part of a Power-boxing class), climb (the rock-climbing wall at the back of the funnel housing), jog, putt, swim, skate, step, surf, workout and more (including play basketball and volleyball) in the sports area of the ship, located mostly aft of the funnel.

● **For more extensive general information on what a Royal Caribbean cruise is like, see pages 137–42.**

Fuji Maru
★★★

Small Ship:	.23,340 tons	Total Crew:	.190	Cabins (with private balcony):	.0
Lifestyle:	.Standard	Passengers		Cabins (wheelchair accessible):	.2
Cruise Line:	.Mitsui OSK Passenger Line	(lower beds/all berths):	.328/603	Cabin Current:	.100 volts
Former Names:	.none	Passenger Space Ratio		Elevators:	.5
Builder:	.Mitsubishi (Japan)	(lower beds/all berths):	.71.1/38.7	Casino (gaming tables):	.Yes
Original Cost:	.$63.5 million	Crew/Passenger Ratio		(no cash can be won, only gifts)	
Entered Service:	.Apr 1989	(lower beds/all berths):	.1.7/3.1	Slot Machines:	.No
Registry:	.Japan	Navigation Officers:	.Japanese	Swimming Pools (outdoors):	.1
Length (ft/m):	.547.9/167.00	Cabins (total):	.164	Swimming Pools (indoors):	.0
Beam (ft/m):	.78.7/24.00	Size Range (sq ft/m):	.182.9–376.7/	Whirlpools:	.0 (4 Japanese Baths)
Draft (ft/m):	.21.4/6.55		17.0–35.0	Self-Service Launderette:	.Yes
Propulsion/Propellers:	.diesel	Cabins (outside view):	.164	Dedicated Cinema/Seats:	.Yes/142
	(15,740kW)/2	Cabins (interior/no view):	.0	Library:	.Yes
Passenger Decks:	.8	Cabins (for one person):	.0		

OVERALL SCORE: 1,195 (OUT OF A POSSIBLE 2,000 POINTS)

OVERVIEW. When *Fuji Maru* was completed in 1989, it was Japan's largest cruise ship. It has a well thought-out, and flexible, design for multifunctional uses, but its main use is for incentives, conventions, as a seminar and training ship, and only occasionally for individual passengers. The utilitarian outdoor decks are little used. The interiors are plain and a little clinical, although there is some good artwork throughout to brighten things up. There are extensive lecture and conference facilities. The largest lecture hall is two decks high, seats 600, and converts into a sports stadium or exhibition hall for industrial product introductions. The lobby is quite elegant and open and is part of a two-level atrium.

The ship has a classic, wood-paneled library. Other features include Japanese grand baths and a traditional Washitsu tatami mat room, and lecture room. A Hanaguruma owner's room is reasonably elegant for small formal functions. The Sakura Salon is soothing, with a blend of Western and traditional Japanese design. The media and TV systems include much high-tech equipment.

There are many more modern ships in the international marketplace (also serving Japanese passengers), with better facilities, more dining choices, and a less utilitarian ambience, and so the score for this ship has been lowered slightly.

A specialist courier company will collect your luggage from your home before the cruise, and deliver it back after the cruise (this service available only in Japan). The onboard currency is the Japanese yen. As in any ship for Japanese passengers, tipping is not allowed.

There is a complete waste of open deck space, and maintenance of it is poor. The deck furniture is plastic. The lighting is too bright, which also increases the noise level.

BERLITZ'S RATINGS

	Possible	Achieved
Ship	500	274
Accommodation	200	114
Food	400	252
Service	400	268
Entertainment	100	65
Cruise	400	222

SUITABLE FOR: Japanese-speaking couples and single travelers looking for modestly comfortable surroundings, decent food and service, all at low cost.

ACCOMMODATION. There are seven price grades. There are two suites that are quite lovely, with separate bedroom and living room. The deluxe cabins are also of a good standard, and come with a vanity/writing desk, mini-bar/refrigerator, and full-sized, deep bathtub. Almost all the other (standard) cabins are furnished very simply, but they are good for seminar and school cruises, with many accommodating three or four persons. The cabin insulation is reasonable, but could be better. The bathrooms are small and utilitarian. The folded blankets, a MOPAS (Mitsui OSK Passenger Line) tradition, are lovely.

CUISINE. The single, large dining room is quite attractive and has a high ceiling, but rather bright lighting. Both Japanese and Western cuisines are featured for all meals, in a single seating. The food itself is good, with simple, but colorful, presentation, and a good variety.

ENTERTAINMENT. The Pacific Lounge is the venue for entertainment events, social functions, and social dancing. It is a two deck high room, with seating on both main and balcony levels. On most cruises, special featured entertainers are brought on board from ashore.

SPA/FITNESS. There is no spa, but there are two Japanese Grand Baths (men's and women's) with ocean-view windows. These include washing stations and two small communal baths. There is a sauna, and massage is available.

Funchal
★★ +

Small Ship . . . . .9,563 tons	Total Crew: .155	Cabins (with private balcony): 0
Lifestyle: . . . . .Standard	Passengers	Cabins (wheelchair accessible): 0
Cruise Line: Classic International Cruises	(lower beds/all berths): 430/524	Cabin Current: . . . . .220 volts
Former Names: . . . . .none	Passenger Space Ratio	Elevators: 3
Builder: . . .Helsingor Skibsvog (Denmark)	(lower beds/all berths): . . . . . . .22.2\18.2	Casino (gaming tables): . . . . .Yes
Original Cost: . . . . .n/a	Crew/Passenger Ratio	Slot Machines: . . . . .Yes
Entered Service: . . . . .Oct 1961/May 1986	(lower beds/all berths): 2.7/3.3	Swimming Pools (outdoors): 1
Registry: . . . . .Madeira	Navigation Officers: . . . . .Portuguese	Swimming Pools (indoors): 0
Length (ft/m): 503.6/153.51	Cabins (total): 222	Whirlpools: 0
Beam (ft/m): 62.5/19.05	Size Range (sq ft/m): 102.2–252.9/	Self-Service Launderette: . . . . .No
Draft (ft/m): 20.6/6.40	9.5–23.5	Dedicated Cinema/Seats: . . . . .No
Propulsion/Propellers: . . . . .diesel	Cabins (outside view): 151	Library: . . . . .Yes
(7,356kW)/2	Cabins (interior/no view): 71	
Passenger Decks: 6	Cabins (for one person): 14	

OVERALL SCORE: 1,045 (OUT OF A POSSIBLE 2,000 POINTS)

OVERVIEW. *Funchal* has a classic 1960s small ship profile with well balanced, rounded lines, and pleasing real wooden decks, including one outdoor deck with two sheltered promenades, although they do not completely encircle the ship. Originally, the ship was built as a dual-purpose mail/passenger ship, but was rebuilt as a one-class cruise ship in 1972–73 and has since undergone regular refurbishments. Its interior has lots of fine woodwork and heavy-duty fittings. One deck houses the main public rooms, the most appealing of which is the Porto Bar, reminiscent of a classy 19th-century drinking club. A highly polished wooden spiral stairway is a beautiful, classic piece of decoration not found in today's ships.

The mostly Portuguese staff is warm, friendly and quite attentive. This ship is popular with Europeans and Scandinavians during the summer and winter. It provides destination-intensive cruises in a pleasant, old-world atmosphere.

Funchal is like an old, well-worn shoe – comfortable, but in need of a little spit and polish, and so it hovers just a tad under the three-star level (a two-and-a-half star vessel with a three-star heart). The ship and overall product is actually quite good if you enjoy small, vintage vessels with all their accompanying eccentricities. While the ship cannot be compared to the latest brand new, larger ships, *Funchal* has a delightful character and charm. The feeling of camaraderie and friendliness from the loyal crew (many of whom have been aboard the ship for many years) offsets some of the hardware negatives. The ship often operates under charter to various tour packagers and operators. The

BERLITZ'S RATINGS		
	Possible	Achieved
Ship	500	203
Accommodation	200	101
Food	400	242
Service	400	240
Entertainment	100	55
Cruise	400	204

onboard currency, typically, is the euro.

SUITABLE FOR: *Funchal* is best suited to couples and single travelers seeking a first cruise aboard a small ship of vintage character and charm, with few facilities, but at a low price.

ACCOMMODATION. The cabins are extremely compact but tasteful, and come in both twin and double-bedded configurations. Each has a private bathroom, and there is just enough closet and drawer space providing you don't pack too many clothes. All bathrooms are typically provided with soap, shampoo, shower cap, shoeshine, sewing kit, and bathrobe (suites only).

CUISINE. There are two tastefully decorated dining rooms, Lisboa and the smaller Coimbra (which doubles as a video screening room after dinner). Both have ocean-view picture windows on port and starboard sides. There is just one seating, and tables are for four, six or eight (there are no tables for two). The food is European in style (it includes plenty of fresh fish) and is surprisingly good. The wine list includes Portuguese wines at modest prices.

ENTERTAINMENT. The Main Lounge is the showlounge, an H-shaped room that extends to the sides of the ship. The room has a flat floor, and the sight lines to the stage are poor from some seats. As this is a small and older vessel, entertainment is a low priority (and has a low budget).

SPA/FITNESS. There is a small beauty salon.

Galapagos Explorer II
★★★

Boutique Ship: ....4,077 tons	Total Crew: 72	Cabins (with private balcony): 4
Lifestyle: ....Standard	Passengers	Cabins (wheelchair accessible): 0
Cruise Line: ....Canodros	(lower beds/all berths): 106/111	Cabin Current: ....110 volts
Former Names: ......*Renaissance Three*	Passenger Space Ratio	Elevators: 1
Builder: .....Cantieri Navale Ferrari (Italy)	(lower beds/all berths): 38.4/36.7	Casino (gaming tables): ....Yes
Original Cost: ....$20 million	Crew/Passenger Ratio	Slot Machines: ....Yes
Entered Service: .....Aug 1990/Feb 1998	(lower beds/all berths): 1.4/1.5	Swimming Pools (outdoors): 1
Registry: ....Liberia	Navigation Officers: ....International	Swimming Pools (indoors): 0
Length (ft/m): 293.1/89.35	Cabins (total): 53	Whirlpools: 1
Beam (ft/m): 50.1/15.30	Size Range (sq ft/m): 231.4–282.0/	Self-Service Launderette: ....No
Draft (ft/m): 11.9/3.65	21.5–26.2	Dedicated Cinema/Seats: ....No
Propulsion/Propellers: ....diesel	Cabins (outside view): 53	Library: ....No
(3,514kW)/2	Cabins (interior/no view): 0	
Passenger Decks: 5	Cabins (for one person): 0	

OVERALL SCORE: 1,244 (OUT OF A POSSIBLE 2,000 POINTS)

OVERVIEW. This is a comfortable and inviting ship (built as one of a series of eight similar small ships for the defunct Renaissance Cruises). While it is in good condition, the maintenance could be better. Its looks are quite contemporary in the style of a mega-yacht, with handsome styling. There is a wooden promenade deck outdoors. The limited number of public rooms have smart and restful, non-glitzy decor. The main lounge doubles as a lecture room, but perhaps it is the piano bar that provides the best place to relax after dinner in the evening. A doctor is carried at all times.

This ship provides a destination-intensive, refined, quiet and relaxed cruise for those who don't like crowds or dressing up. Naturalist guides trained at the Darwin Station lead the shore excursions (included in the fare), and the ship carries two glass-bottom boats. Take your passport, short and long-sleeve cotton shirts, good walking shoes, windbreaker, mosquito repellent, sunglasses with retaining strap, and personal medication. You will need to fly from Quito to San Cristobal (via Guayaquil) to join your cruise.

Galapagos Explorer II operates three-, four-, and seven night Galápagos cruises year-round from San Cristobal. Liquor, beer, cocktails, bottled water and soft drinks are included in the fare, but wine and champagne are not. Also included are guided visits to the islands. The brochure rates may or may not include the Galápagos Islands visitor tax (about $100), which must be paid in cash at Guayaquil or Quito airports or in the islands. Shore visits take place in "pangas" (local lingo for "dinghies").

Gratuities for shipboard staff are excessive, at a recommended $80 per person, per seven-night cruise. The onboard currency is the US dollar.

BERLITZ'S RATINGS

	Possible	Achieved
Ship	500	325
Accommodation	200	154
Food	400	209
Service	400	245
Entertainment	n/a	n/a
Cruise	500	311

The tiny "dip" pool is not a swimming pool. Sunbathing space is cramped. Plastic wood is everywhere (but looks good). The service is without finesse, but the crew is willing. The small library is attractive, but the book selection is poor. The ship does not sail well in inclement weather. It has not been cared for, and maintenance is poor.

SUITABLE FOR: The ship is best for couples and single travelers who want to cruise around the primitive Galápagos Islands, but want to do so in comfortable, stylish surroundings.

ACCOMMODATION. This is located forward, with public rooms aft. Pleasant, all-outside suites have a large picture window and combine gorgeous, highly polished imitation rosewood paneling with lots of mirrors, hand-crafted Italian furniture, and wet bar. All cabins have a queen-sized bed, a sitting area, a mini-bar/refrigerator, TV set, VCR and hairdryer. The small bathrooms have showers with a fold-down seat, real teakwood floors and marble vanities.

CUISINE. The small, elegant dining room has open seating, and tables for two, four, six, and eight. The meals are self-service buffet-style cold foods for breakfast and lunch (sometimes lunch will be on deck), with local delicacies. There is limited choice.

ENTERTAINMENT. Dinner and after-dinner conversation with fellow passengers forms the entertainment each evening.

SPA/FITNESS. There is a sauna. Water sports facilities include an aft platform, sailfish, snorkel gear, and Zodiacs.

Golden Princess
★★★★

Large Resort Ship: ....108,865 tons	Passengers	Cabins (wheelchair accessible): 28
Lifestyle: ....Standard	(lower beds/all berths): 2,600/3,100	(18 outside/10 interior)
Cruise Line: ....Princess Cruises	Passenger Space Ratio	Cabin Current: ....110 and 220 volts
Former Names: ....none	(lower beds/all berths): 41.8/35.1	Elevators: 14
Builder: ....Fincantieri (Italy)	Crew/Passenger Ratio	Casino (gaming tables): ....Yes
Original Cost: ....$450 million	(lower beds/all berths): 2.3/2.8	Slot Machines: ....Yes
Entered Service: ....May 2001	Navigation Officers: ......British/Italian	Swimming Pools (outdoors): 4
Registry: ....Bermuda	Cabins (total): 1,300	Swimming Pools (indoors): 0
Length (ft/m): 951.4/290.0	Size Range (sq ft/m): 161.4–764.2/	Whirlpools: 9
Beam (ft/m): 118.1/36.0	15.0–71.0	Self-Service Launderette: ....Yes
Draft (ft/m): 26.2/8.0	Cabins (outside view): 928	Dedicated Cinema/Seats: ....No
Propulsion/Propellers: .....diesel-electric	Cabins (interior/no view): 372	Library: ....Yes
(42,000kW)/2	Cabins (for one person): 0	
Passenger Decks: 13	Cabins (with private balcony): 710	
Total Crew: 1,100		

OVERALL SCORE: 1,541 (OUT OF A POSSIBLE 2,000 POINTS)

OVERVIEW. *Golden Princess* (sister to *Grand Princess* and *Star Princess*) presents a bold, forthright profile, with a racy "spoiler" effect at the stern that I do not consider handsome (this acts as an observation lounge with aft-facing views by day, and a noisy discotheque by night). The ship has a flared snub-nosed bow and a galleon-like transom stern. At 118 ft/36 meters (but more than 43 ft/13 meters wider than the canal, including the navigation bridge wings) *Golden Princess* is too wide to transit the Panama Canal, with many balcony cabins overhanging the ship's hull.

There is a good sheltered teakwood promenade deck, which almost wraps around (three times round is equal to one mile) and a walkway that goes right to the (enclosed, protected) bow of the ship. The outdoor pools have various beach-like surroundings. One lap pool has a pumped "current" to swim against.

Unlike the outside decks, there is plenty of space inside the ship (but also plenty of passengers), and a wide array of public rooms, with many "intimate" (this being a relative word) spaces and places to play. The passenger flow has been well thought-out, and works with little congestion, except at the photo gallery on Promenade Deck (Deck 7), where there is congestion at peak times when passengers try to go through the gallery to get to the Vista Lounge. The decor is very attractive and warm, with lots of earth tones. In fact, this ship is the culmination of the best of all that Princess Cruises has to offer from its many years of operating what is now a well-tuned, good quality product.

Four areas center on swimming pools, one of which is two decks high and is covered by a magrodome, itself an

BERLITZ'S RATINGS

	Possible	Achieved
Ship	500	430
Accommodation	200	166
Food	400	256
Service	400	293
Entertainment	100	82
Cruise	400	314

extension of the funnel housing. High atop the stern of the ship is a ship-wide glass-walled disco pod. It looks like an aerodynamic "spoiler" and is positioned high above the water, with spectacular views from the extreme port and starboard side windows.

There is an extensive collection of art works, which complement the elegant, non-glitzy interior design and colors. If you see something you like, you'll probably be able to buy it.

This ship also has a Wedding Chapel (a live web-cam can relay ceremonies via the internet). The ship's captain can legally marry (American) couples, due to the ship's Bermuda registry and a special dispensation (this should, however, be verified when in the planning stage, and may vary according to where you reside). Princess Cruises offers three wedding packages: Pearl, Emerald, Diamond – the fee includes registration and official marriage certificate. However, to get married and take your close family members and entourage with you on your honeymoon is going to cost a lot. The "Hearts & Minds" chapel can also be used for "renewal of vows" ceremonies.

Teenagers (and others) might like the array of video games (50 cents to $3 per game), while photo enthusiasts should find "FX" (the digital photo shop) of interest – you can have your photo morphed into almost any setting. For youngsters there is a two-deck-high playroom and teen room located in the forward section of the ship (although the video games room is located at the opposite end of the ship), and a host of trained counselors.

Gamblers should enjoy the large casino, with more than 260 slot machines. There are blackjack, craps and roulette tables, plus games such as Let It Ride Bonus, Spanish 21 and Caribbean Draw Progressive.

Ship lovers should enjoy the wood-paneled Wheelhouse Bar, finely decorated with memorabilia and ship models tracing part of parent company P&O's history. There is an Internet Cafe, with a couple of dozen AOL-linked computer terminals ($7.50 per 15 minutes when this book was completed); but it should be called an Internet Center, as there is no cafe – not even any coffee.

Princess Cays – Princess Cruises' own "private island" in the Caribbean – is "yours" (along with other passengers, of course) for a day on Caribbean itineraries; however, you will need to take a shore tender to get to and from it, and this can take some time. A high-tech hospital is provided, with live SeaMed tele-medicine link-up to specialists at the Cedars-Sinai Medical Center in Los Angeles available for emergency help (hardly useful for international passengers who don't reside in the USA).

The automated telephone system is frustrating to use, and luggage delivery is inefficient. Lines form for many things, but particularly for the purser's desk, and for open-seating breakfast and lunch in the three main dining rooms.

You'll have to live with the many extra charge items (such as for ice cream, and freshly squeezed orange juice) and activities (such as yoga, group exercise bicycling and kick boxing classes at $10 per session, not to mention $4 per hour for group babysitting services). There is a charge for using the washers and dryers in the self-service launderettes (coins are needed).

Whether all this really can be considered a relaxing holiday is a moot point, but with many choices and "small" rooms to enjoy, the ship has been extremely well designed, and the odds are that you'll have a fine time, in a controlled, well packaged way.

ACCOMMODATION. There are six principal types of cabins and configurations: (a) grand suite, (b) suite, (c) mini-suite, (d) outside double with balcony, (e) outside double, and (f) interior (no view) double. There are, however, 35 different brochure price categories, making the choice bewildering for both travel agents and passengers. The price depends on grade, size and location. Many cabins have additional upper berths (there are 609), good for those with children.

(a) The largest, most lavish suite is the Grand Suite (B748, which is at the ship's stern – a different position to the two Grand Suites aboard sister ship *Grand Princess*). Although large for Princess Cruises, it does not compare with much larger suites (three times the size, in fact) aboard such ships as *Constellation, Infinity, Millennium, Norwegian Dawn, Norwegian Star, Summit*. It has a large bedroom with a queen-sized bed, huge walk-in (illuminated) closets, a large bathroom with full-size tub and separate shower enclosure, toilet, and washbasin, and a hot tub (accessed from the bedroom), a lounge (with sofa bed, dining table and chairs, wet bar and refrigerator, a guest bathroom (with toilet and washbasin), and a large private balcony.

(b/c) Suites (with a semi-private balcony) have a separate living room (with sofa bed) and bedroom (with a TV set in each). The bathroom is quite large and has both a tub and shower stall. The mini-suites also have a semi-private balcony, and a separate living and sleeping area (with a television in each). The bathroom is also quite spacious, with both a bathtub and shower stall. The differences between the suites and mini-suites are basically in the size and appointments, the suite being more of a square shape while mini-suites are more rectangular, and have few drawers. Plush bathrobes and fully tiled bathrooms with ample open shelf storage space are provided. Passengers occupying the best suites receive greater attention, including priority embarkation and disembarkation privileges. What is not good is that some of the most expensive accommodation has only semi-private balconies that can be seen from above, so there is no privacy whatsoever (Suites C401, 402, 409, 410, 414, 415, 420, 421, 422, 423, 424 and 425 on Caribe Deck in particular). Also, the suites D105 and D106 (Dolphin Deck), which are extremely large, have balconies that can be seen from above.

(d/e/f) The standard interior and outside-view (the outsides come either with or without private balcony) cabins are of a functional, practical, design, although almost no drawers are provided. They are very attractive, with warm, pleasing decor and fine soft furnishing fabrics.

Additionally, two family suites consist of two suites with an interconnecting door, plus a large balcony. These can sleep up to 10 (if at least four are children), or up to eight people (if all are adults).

All passengers receive turndown service and chocolates on pillows each night, bathrobes (on request) and toiletry amenity kits (larger, naturally, for suite/mini-suite occupants) that typically include soap, shampoo, conditioner, and hand/body lotion. A hairdryer is provided in all cabins. All bathrooms are tiled and have a decent amount of open shelf storage space for personal toiletries. Princess Cruises receives BBC World, CNN, CNBC, ESPN and TNT on the in-cabin color television system (when available, depending on cruise area).

Most outside cabins on Emerald Deck have views obstructed by lifeboats. Your name is placed outside your suite or cabin – making it simple for delivery service personnel but also making it intrusive with regard to your privacy. Some cabins can accommodate a third and fourth person in upper berths. However, in such cabins, the lower beds cannot then be pushed together to make queen-sized bed. There are no cabins for singles.

Almost all balcony suites and cabins can be overlooked both from the navigation bridge wing, as well as from the port and starboard sections of the ship's discotheque – located high above the ship at the stern. Cabins with balconies on Dolphin, Caribe and Baja decks are also overlooked by passengers on balconies on the deck above; they are, therefore, not at all private. However, perhaps the least desirable balcony cabins are the eight located forward on Emerald Deck, as the balconies do not extend to the side of the ship and can be passed by walkers and gawkers on the adjacent Upper Promenade walkway (so occupants need to keep their curtains closed most of the time). Also, passengers occupying some the most expensive suites with balconies at the stern of the vessel may experience considerable vibration during certain ship maneuvers.

Cabin bath towels are too small, and drawer space is limited. There are no butlers – even for the top-grade suites. Cabin attendants have too many cabins to look after (typically 20), which cannot translate to fine personal service.

CUISINE. There are a number of "Personal Choice" dining options. For formal meals there are three principal dining rooms (Bernini, Canaletto, and Donatello). There are two seatings in one restaurant, while "anytime dining" (where you choose when and with whom you want to eat) is typically featured in the other two. All three are non-smoking and split into multi-tier sections in a non-symmetrical design that breaks what are quite large spaces into many smaller sections, for better ambience. Each dining room has its own galley. While four elevators go to Fiesta Deck where the Canaletto and Donatello restaurants are located, only two go to Plaza Deck 5 where the Bernini Restaurant is located (this can cause long wait problems at peak times, particularly for anyone in a wheelchair). Note that 15% is added to beverage bills, including wines.

Alternative (Extra Charge) Dining: There are two alternative informal dining areas: Sabatini's Trattoria and Desert Rose. Both serve lunch and dinner. Sabatini's is an Italian eatery, with colorful tiled Mediterranean-style decor; it is named after Trattoria Sabatini, the 200-year-old institution in Florence. It has Italian-style pizzas and pastas, with a variety of sauces, as well as Italian-style entrées (including tiger prawns and lobster tail). Sabatini's is by reservation only, and there is a cover charge of $15 per person, for lunch or dinner (on sea days only).

Desert Rose has "southwestern American food"; by reservation only, with a cover charge of $8 per person, for lunch or dinner on sea days only. However, do note that Desert Rose is spread over the whole beam (width) of the ship, and two walkways intersect it, which means that it's a very open area, with people walking through it as you eat. The cuisine in both of these spots is decidedly better than in the three main dining rooms.

A poolside hamburger grill and pizza bar (no additional charge) are additional dining spots for casual bites, while extra charges will apply if you order items to eat at either the coffee bar/patisserie, or the caviar/champagne bar.

Other casual meals can be taken in the Horizon Court – open 24 hours a day, with large ocean-view on port and starboard sides and direct access to the two principal swimming pools and lido deck. Plastic plates are used.

ENTERTAINMENT. The Princess Theatre (showlounge) spans two decks and has comfortable seating on both main and balcony levels. It has a 9-piece orchestra, and a scenery loading bay that connects directly from stage to a hull door for direct transfer to the dockside). Princess Cruises prides itself on its glamorous all-American production shows (there are typically two or three shows each 7-day cruise).

The Vista Lounge is a second entertainment lounge. It has cabaret acts at night, and lectures, bingo and horse racing during the day. Explorers, a third entertainment lounge, can host cabaret acts and dance bands. Many other lounges and bars have live music, and there are male dance hosts as partners for women traveling alone.

SPA/FITNESS. The Lotus Spa is a large complex that surrounds one of the swimming pools at the forward end of the ship. It comprises a large gymnasium with all the usual equipment, an aerobics room, sauna and steam rooms, beauty salon, treatment rooms, and a relaxation area.

● **For more extensive general information about the Princess Cruises experience, see pages 134–37.**

Grand Celebration
★★★

Large Resort Ship:................47,262 tons	Passenger Decks: 10	Cabins (for one person):.........................0
Lifestyle: ....Standard	Total Crew: 620	Cabins (with private balcony):..............10
Cruise Line: ....Iberocruceros	Passengers	Cabins (wheelchair accessible): 14
Former Names: ....*Celebration*	(lower beds/all berths):.......1,494/1,896	Cabin Current: ....110/220 volts
Builder:.....................Kockums (Sweden)	Passenger Space Ratio	Elevators: 8
Original Cost:........................$130 million	(lower beds/all berths):.....,.......31.6/24.9	Casino (gaming tables): ....Yes
Entered Service: ....Mar 1987/Jun 2008	Crew/Passenger Ratio	Slot Machines:....................................Yes
Registry:.....................................Panama	(lower beds/all berths):..............2.4/3.0	Swimming Pools (outdoors): 3
Length (ft/m):.....................732.6/223.30	Navigation Officers: ....European	Swimming Pools (indoors): 0
Beam (ft/m):..........................92.5/28.20	Cabins (total): 747	Whirlpools: 2
Draft (ft/m): 25.5/7.80	Size Range (sq ft/m): 184.0/17.1	Self-Service Launderette:....................Yes
Propulsion/Propellers: ....diesel	Cabins (outside view):........................453	Dedicated Cinema/Seats: ....No
(23,520kW)/2	Cabins (interior/no view):..................296	Library: ....Yes

BERLITZ'S OVERALL SCORE: 1,182 (OUT OF A POSSIBLE 2,000 POINTS)

OVERVIEW. First introduced as the fourth new ship for Carnival Cruise Lines, the ship has a rather angular exterior, typical of the space-conscious designs introduced in the early 1980s to try to maximize interior (revenue-generating) space. It is now operating for Iberocruceros, and the white hull is adorned with splashed of color, with the Iberocruceros name on the forward section.

This all-white ship, now over 20 years old, has extremely short bows, and a distinctive, large, swept-back wing-tipped blue and white funnel. The swimming pools are smaller than one would expect, but the open deck space can be extremely crowded.

Inside, this ship features a double-width indoor promenades and a good selection of public rooms, including a large casino. The flamboyant interior decor in public rooms is bright, bold and stimulating, not relaxing, as is the colorful artwork. Facilities include a library and internet-connect center. Children are split into two age categories, with facilities for each: Club 5 (5–10 year olds), or Club 10 (10 years and older).

There's no escape from repetitious announcements – particularly for activities that bring revenue, such as bingo, or horse racing. Standing in line for embarkation, disembarkation, shore tenders and for self-serve buffet meals is inevitable when cruising aboard all large ships. The onboard currency is the euro, and all gratuities to staff are included.

SUITABLE FOR: This ship is a floating playground for young, Spanish-speaking active adults who enjoy constant stimulation, close contact with lots and lots of others. There is a wide range of entertainment and passenger participation activities from which to choose, and it should prove a good choice for families with children (there are many places for kids to explore).

BERLITZ'S RATINGS		
	Possible	Achieved
Ship	500	297
Accommodation	200	121
Food	400	216
Service	400	247
Entertainment	100	66
Cruise	400	235

ACCOMMODATION. The ship has a range of suites, outside-view cabins and interior (no view) cabins in 13 price grades. The cabins are quite standard and mostly identical in terms of layout and decor (which means they are good for large groups who generally like to have identical cabins for their participants), are of fairly generous proportions, except for the interior (no view) cabins, which are quite small. They are reasonably comfortable and well equipped, but nothing special. A 24-hour room service menu is also provided.

The best living spaces on board are in 10 suites, each of which has much more space, its own private balcony, a larger bathroom and more closet, drawer and storage space (good for families).

CUISINE/DINING. There are two dining rooms (Vista Hermoza, with 550 seats, and Riazor, with 450 seats). They are quite cramped when full, and extremely noisy (both are non-smoking), and they have low ceilings in the raised sections of their centers. There are tables for four, six or eight (none for two). The decor is bright and extremely colorful, to say the least. Dining is in two seatings: 8:30pm and 10:30pm. Meals for vegetarians and special children's menus are also available, as is a snack at midnight.

Presentation is simple, and few garnishes are used. Many meat and fowl dishes are disguised with gravies and sauces. There is much use of canned fruit and jellied desserts. This is all about banquet catering, with all its attendant standardization and production cooking.

Although there is a decent wine list, there are no wine waiters and so the regular waiters are expected to serve both food and wine. The service is highly programmed, although the waiters are willing and reasonably friendly.

Casual meals can be taken as self-serve buffets in the

280-seat Buffet Triana, although the meals provided are very basic, and quite disappointing, with much repetition (particularly for breakfast).

ENTERTAINMENT. The Astoria Showlounge is the main venue for large-scale production shows and major cabaret acts (although several pillars obstruct the views from some seats). Large-scale, high volume production shows are featured, together with a number of European cabaret acts.

Almost every lounge/bar has live bands and musical units, so there is always plenty of live music happening each evening.

SPA/FITNESS. The Spa is located on the ship's uppermost deck, just aft of the mast, and accessed by the center stairway and lifts. It has a gymnasium (with some muscle-pumping cardiovascular machines) and views over the ship's main swimming pool, men's and women's changing rooms and saunas. The beauty salon is located in another spot.

Massage (including exotic massages such as Aroma Stone massage and Swedish Remedial Massage, facials, pedicures, and beauty salon treatments are at extra cost. Do make appointments as early as possible as time slots on can go quickly.

SHIP TALK

Abeam: off the side of the ship, at a right angle to its length.

Aft: near, toward, or in the rear of the ship.

Ahead: something that is ahead of the ship's bow.

Alleyway: a passageway or corridor.

Alongside: said of a ship when it is beside a pier or another vessel.

Amidships: in or toward the middle of the ship; the longitudinal center portion of the ship.

Anchor Ball: black ball hoisted above the bow to show that the vessel is anchored.

Astern: is the opposite of Ahead (i.e., meaning something behind the ship).

Backwash: motion in the water caused by the propeller(s) moving in a reverse (astern) direction.

Bar: sandbar, usually caused by tidal or current conditions near the shore.

Beam: width of the ship between its two sides at the widest point.

Bearing: compass direction, expressed in degrees, from the ship to a particular objective or destination.

Below: anything beneath the main deck.

Berth: dock, pier, or quay. Also means bed on board ship.

Bilge: lowermost spaces of the infrastructure of a ship.

Boat Stations: allotted space for each person during lifeboat drill or any other emergency when lifeboats are lowered.

Bow: the forward most part of the vessel.

Bridge: navigational and command control center.

Bulkhead: upright partition (wall) dividing the ship into compartments.

Bunkers: the space where fuel is stored; "bunkering" means taking on fuel.

Cable Length: a measured length equaling 100 fathoms or 600 feet.

Chart: a nautical map used for navigating.

Colors: refers to the national flag or emblem flown by the ship.

Companionway: interior stairway.

Course: direction in which the ship is headed, in degrees.

Davit: a device for raising and lowering lifeboats.

Deadlight: a ventilated porthole cover to prevent light from entering.

Disembark (also debark): to leave a ship.

Dock: berth, pier, or quay.

Draft (or draught): measurement in feet from the ship's waterline to the lowest point of its keel.

Embark: to join a ship.

Fantail: the rear or overhang of the ship.

Fathom: distance equal to 6 ft.

Flagstaff: a pole at the stern of a ship where the flag of its country of registry is flown.

Free Port: port or place free of customs duty and regulations.

Funnel: chimney from which the ship's combustion gases are propelled into the atmosphere.

Galley: the ship's kitchen.

Gangway: the stairway or ramp that provides the link between ship and shore.

● *More Ship Talk, page 305.*

Grand Mistral
★★★ +

Mid-Size Ship:	48,2006 tons	Passenger Decks:	.8	Cabins (for one person):	.0
Lifestyle:	Standard	Total Crew:	.470	Cabins (with private balcony):	.80
Cruise Line:	Iberocruceros	Passengers		Cabins (wheelchair accessible):	.2
Former Names:	*Mistral*	(lower beds/all berths):	1,196/1,600	Cabin Current:	110 and 220 volts
Builder:	Chantiers de l'Atlantique (France)	Passenger Space Ratio		Elevators:	.6
Original Cost:	$245 million	(lower beds/all berths):	39.5/30.1	Casino (gaming tables):	Yes
Entered Service:	July 1999/May 2005	Crew/Passenger Ratio		Slot Machines:	Yes
Registry:	Marshall Islands	(lower beds/all berths):	2.4/3.4	Swimming Pools (outdoors):	.2
Length (ft/m):	709.9/216.4	Navigation Officers:	European	Swimming Pools (indoors):	.0
Beam (ft/m):	94.6/28.84	Cabins (total):	.598	Whirlpools:	.2 (thalassotherapy)
Draft (ft/m):	22.4/6.85	Size Range (sq ft/m): 139.9–236.8/13.0–22.0		Self-Service Launderette:	No
Propulsion/Propellers:	diesel-electric	Cabins (outside view):	.375	Dedicated Cinema/Seats:	No
	(31,680 kW)/2	Cabins (interior/no view):	.223	Library:	Yes

OVERALL SCORE: 1,315 (OUT OF A POSSIBLE 2,000 POINTS)

OVERVIEW. *Grand Mistral*, an all-white ship with a single blue funnel, was the first brand-new ship for the now defunct Festival Cruises (Mistral is the name of a famous desert wind; it's also the name of a violin concerto).

Grand Mistral is owned by a consortium of French investors and banks, and chartered to Iberocruceros, a vibrant tour operator (75% of which is owned by the giant Carnival Corporation) for the Spanish-speaking family market. The ship's profile is similar to that of most new cruise ships, although the built-up stern makes it look bulky and less than handsome.

The lido deck surrounding the outdoor swimming pools (these are small, and regulated for use by various age groups in several time of day zones), has whirlpool tubs and a large bandstand is set in raised canvas-covered pods. Sunloungers have cushioned pads. There is no full walk-around promenade deck outdoors, although there is a partial walking deck on port and starboard sides under the lifeboats, plus an oval jogging track atop ship. The interior layout and passenger flow is good, as are the "you are here" deck signs, and the ship absorbs passengers quite well.

The interior layout and passenger flow is good, as are the "you are here" deck signs, and the ship absorbs passengers quite well. It is light and cheerful without being glitzy in any way (with not even a hint of colored neon), and there is much use of blonde/cherry wood paneling and rich, textured soft furnishings.

Public rooms, bars and lounges have names inspired by European places or establishments (examples: San Remo Casino, San Marco Lounge, Cafe Guon and Richlieu Library). There is a smoking room (Le Diplomate), with all the hallmarks of a gentleman's club of former times, a

BERLITZ'S RATINGS

	Possible	Achieved
Ship	500	369
Accommodation	200	135
Food	400	240
Service	400	252
Entertainment	100	58
Cruise	400	261

piano bar, and a library that has real writing desks (something many ships seem to omit).

Atop the ship is an observation lounge with a twist – it faces aft, instead of forward; it doubles as a discotheque for the late-night set. A conference center provides facilities that are useful for meetings.

There is also a decent-sized spa/beauty complex, set forward of the mast. This includes a fitness center with lots of muscle-toning equipment and lifecycles and life-rowing machines and a view over the bow of the ship through large floor-to-ceiling windows. There are six rooms for massage and other body treatments, as well as a sauna each for men and women, plus an aerobics exercise room. Adjacent to the spa is a video game room for teens, and a children's center.

Smokers are difficult to avoid, towels are small, and the square chairs in the Cafe Navona are uncomfortabl and impractical. Standing in line for embarkation, disembarkation, shore tenders and for self-serve buffet meals is inevitable aboard all ships of this size. The onboard currency is the euro. Gratuities are included.

SUITABLE FOR: *Grand Mistral* is best suited to youthful Spanish-speaking couples and singles, and families with children that enjoy big city life and outdoor cafes, constant activity accompanied by lots of noise, late nights, entertainment that is loud, and food that focuses on quantity rather than quality.

ACCOMMODATION. There are three basic cabin types, in nine different price grades. There are 80 "suites" (each has a private balcony, although partitions are of the partial, and not the full type), ocean-view standard cabins and interior (no view) standard cabins. The price you pay will depend on grade, size and location.

The cabins on Deck 10 are subject to noise from the Lido Deck above. Good planning and layout means that no outside-view cabins have lifeboat-obstructed views. The cabin numbering system goes against maritime tradition, where even-numbered cabins are on the port side and odd-numbered cabins on the starboard; in *Grand Mistral*, the opposite is in effect.

All cabins have twin beds that convert to a queen-sized unit, bold, colorful bedspreads (with blankets and sheets, not duvets), a personal safe, a combination colour TV/VCR, telephone, a personal safe, and a good amount of closet and drawer space for a one-week cruise. The bathrooms, although not large, do have a good-sized shower enclosure, and there is a decent amount of stowage space for personal toiletries.

Accommodation designated as suites (these are really only larger cabins and not suites, as there is no separation of lounge and sleeping space), quite naturally, have more space, larger (walk-in) closets, more drawers and better storage space, plus a two-person sofa, coffee table and additional armchair, vanity desk, floor-to-ceiling mirrors and hairdryer; bathrooms have a bathtub/shower combination.

Six Grand Suites, added in 2007 at the ship's stern, are well-designed units that feature a separate bedroom (flat-screen TV), bedside tables, vanity desk, floor-to-ceiling windows, and door to balcony; the lounge has an audio-visual center, sofa, dining table, and lots of space, plus a balcony door. A large bathroom has contemporary styling, two Villeroy & Boch washbasins, dark hardwood storage cabinets, large Jacuzzi bathtub, separate shower enclosure (hand-held shower), and bathrobes.

In addition, there are two interior (no view) wheelchair accessible cabins for the handicapped, which provide more spacious interiors than standard cabins.

CUISINE. There are two dining rooms (and two seatings for meals), which can be configured in any of several different ways. Both have ocean-view windows. The principal dining room (Restaurant Mallorca, with 610 seats) has round tables for two, four, six or eight, and a small podium with baby grand piano.

A second dining venue – Restaurant Formentor, with 380 seats (chairs have no armrests), is on a different deck. Smaller and more intimate, it is for passengers occupying Deck 10 accommodation; it has tables for two, four or six, and ocean-view windows.

The food is quite sound, and, with varied menus and decent presentation, should prove a highlight for most passengers. The wine list features a good variety of standard wines at reasonable prices, but almost all are young.

There's also a casual Bahia de Palma cafeteria for al fresco self-serve buffet-style breakfasts and lunches, with ocean-view windows, but the flow is awkward and cramped. Additionally, there's an outdoor pool bar; plus a pleasant little coffee bar ((Café Navona, serving Brazilian coffee) on the upper level of the two-deck high lobby, with lifeboat-restricted ocean views.

ENTERTAINMENT. The Grand Theatre Ibiza, the showlounge, spans two decks, has a sloping floor, and good sight lines from most seats (there is banquette-style seating), and there is a small balcony level at the rear. Sadly, the designer forgot to include space for a live band, and the lighting facilities are less than high-tech. There's also a bar/lounge (Salon Formentera) on the lower (main) level at the entrance to the showlounge. Entertainment is, without doubt, the weak link in the chain of Iberocruceros.

SPA/FITNESS. The Santai Spa health/fitness facilities, located forward of the mast, are quite decent. Included is a gymnasium with high-tech muscle-pump equipment, lifecycles and life-rowing machines and a view over the bow of the ship through large floor-to-ceiling windows.

Other facilities include a thalassotherapy room, and beauty salon, six rooms for massage and other body treatments, as well as a sauna each for men and women, plus an aerobics exercise room. It's best to make appointments early, as the best time slots can go fairly quickly.

Sample prices: Balinese Massage or Shiatsu Massage, €74 for 45 minutes or €90 for 60 minutes; Cranial (head) Massage, €20.

Grand Princess
★★★★

Large Resort Ship:	.......108,806 tons	Total Crew:	1,100
Lifestyle:	..................Standard	Passengers	
Cruise Line:	.........Princess Cruises	(lower beds/all berths):	.....2,600/3,100
Former Names:	..................none	Passenger Space Ratio	
Builder:	..............Fincantieri (Italy)	(lower beds/all berths):	.......41.8/35.0
Original Cost:	............$450 million	Crew/Passenger Ratio	
Entered Service:	.............May 1998	(lower beds/all berths):	.........2.3/2.8
Registry:	...................Bermuda	Navigation Officers:	......British/Italian
Length (ft/m):	...........951.4/290.0	Cabins (total):	1,300
Beam (ft/m):	................118.1/36.0	Size Range (sq ft/m):	......161.4–764.2/
Draft (ft/m):	..................26.2/8.0		15.0–71.0
Propulsion/Propellers:	.....diesel-electric	Cabins (outside view):	928
	(42,000kW)/2	Cabins (interior/no view):	372
Passenger Decks:	13	Cabins (for one person):	0

Cabins (with private balcony):	710
Cabins (wheelchair accessible):	28
(18 outside/10 interior)	
Cabin Current:	........110 and 220 volts
Elevators:	14
Casino (gaming tables):	............Yes
Slot Machines:	.......................Yes
Swimming Pools (outdoors):	4
Swimming Pools (indoors):	0
Whirlpools:	9
Self-Service Launderette:	...........Yes
Dedicated Cinema/Seats:	...........No
Library:	...........................Yes

OVERALL SCORE: 1,541 (OUT OF A POSSIBLE 2,000 POINTS)

OVERVIEW. *Grand Princess* (sister to *Golden Princess* and *Star Princess*) presents a bold, forthright profile, with a racy "spoiler" effect at the stern that many do not consider handsome (this acts as an observation lounge with aft-facing views by day, and a stunning discotheque by night). The ship has a flared snub-nosed bow and a galleon-like transom stern. At 118 ft/36 meters (but more than 43 ft/13 meters wider than the canal, including the navigation bridge wings) *Grand Princess* is too wide to transit the Panama Canal, with many balcony cabins overhanging the ship's hull.

There is a good sheltered teakwood promenade deck, which almost wraps around (three times round is equal to one mile) and a walkway that goes right to the (enclosed, protected) bow of the ship. The outdoor pools have various beach-like surroundings. One lap pool has a pumped "current" to swim against.

Unlike the outside decks, there is plenty of space inside the ship (but also plenty of passengers), and a wide array of public rooms, with many "intimate" (this being a relative word) spaces and places to play. The passenger flow has been well thought-out, and works with little congestion, except at the photo gallery on Promenade Deck (Deck 7), where there is congestion at peak times when passengers try to go through the gallery to get to the Vista Lounge. The decor is very attractive and warm, with lots of earth tones. In fact, this ship is the culmination of the best of all that Princess Cruises has to offer from its many years of operating what is now a well-tuned, good-quality product.

Four areas center on swimming pools, one of which is two decks high and is covered by a magrodome, itself an

BERLITZ'S RATINGS

	Possible	Achieved
Ship	500	430
Accommodation	200	166
Food	400	256
Service	400	293
Entertainment	100	82
Cruise	400	314

extension of the funnel housing. High atop the stern of the ship is a ship-wide glass-walled disco pod. It looks like an aerodynamic spoiler and is positioned some 150 ft (45 meters) above the water-line, with spectacular views from the extreme port and starboard side windows (you can look along the ship's side and onto lots of "private" balconies).

There's an extensive collection of art works, which complements the interior design and colors well. If you see something you like, you'll probably be able to buy it on board.

This ship also has a Wedding Chapel (a live web-cam can relay ceremonies via the internet). The ship's captain can legally marry (American) couples, due to the ship's Bermuda registry and a special dispensation (this should, however, be verified when in the planning stage, and may vary according to where you reside). Princess Cruises offers three wedding packages: Pearl, Emerald, Diamond – the fee includes registration and official marriage certificate. However, to get married and take your close family members and entourage with you on your honeymoon is going to cost a lot. The "Hearts & Minds" chapel can also be used for "renewal of vows" ceremonies.

Another neat feature is the motion-based "virtual reality" room with its enclosed motion-based rides, and a "blue screen" studio, where passengers can star in their own videos. There is an excellent library/CD-Rom computer room, and a separate card room. Youngsters have a two-deck-high playroom, teen's room, and specially trained counselors.

Gamblers should enjoy what is one of the largest casinos at sea, with more than 260 slot machines (all with dolphin-shaped handles); there are blackjack, craps and roulette tables, plus games such as Let It Ride Bonus, Spanish 21 and Caribbean Draw Progressive. A highlight is Neptune's Lair, a multimedia gaming extravaganza.

Ship lovers should enjoy the wood-paneled Wheelhouse Bar, finely decorated with memorabilia and ship models tracing part of parent company P&O's history.

Princess Cays – Princess Cruises' own "private island" in the Caribbean – is "yours" (along with a couple of thousand other passengers) for a day; however, you will need to take a shore tender to get to and from it, and this can take some time. A high-tech hospital is provided with live SeaMed tele-medicine link-ups with specialists at the Cedars-Sinai Medical Center in Los Angeles available for emergency help (hardly useful for international passengers that do not reside in the USA).

This ship is full of revenue centers, designed to help you part with more money. The dress code has been simplified – reduced to formal or smart casual. Gratuities are automatically added to your account, at $10 per person, per day (gratuities for children are charged at the same rate). If you want to pay less, you'll have to line up at the reception desk to have these charges adjusted. The onboard currency is the US dollar.

Whether this really can be considered a relaxing holiday is a moot point, but with so many choices and "small" rooms to enjoy, the ship has been extremely well designed; the odds are that you'll have a fine time, in a controlled, well-packaged way. If you are not used to large ships, it will probably take you some time to find your way around (take good walking shoes), despite the company's claim that this vessel offers a "small ship feel, big ship choice".

The automated telephone system frustrates many passengers, and luggage delivery needs to be more efficient.

ACCOMMODATION. There are six types of cabins and configurations: (a) grand suite, (b) suite, (c) mini-suite, (d) outside double with balcony, (e) outside double, and (f) interior (no view) double. There are, however, 35 different brochure price categories; the choice is bewildering for both travel agents and passengers. Price depends on grade, size and location. Many cabins have additional upper berths (there are 609 of them), good for families with children.

(a) The plushest suite is the Grand Suite, which has a hot tub accessible from both the private balcony and from the bedroom, two bedrooms, lounge, two bathrooms, a huge walk-in closet, and plenty of drawer and storage space.

(b/c) Suites (with a semi-private balcony) have a separate living room (with sofa bed) and bedroom (with a TV set in each). The bathroom is quite large and has both a bathtub and shower stall. The mini-suites also have a private balcony, and feature a separate living and sleeping area (with a television in each). The differences between the suites and mini-suites are basically in the size and appointments, the suite being more of a square shape while mini-suites are more rectangular, and have few drawers. Both suites and mini-suites feature really plush bathrobes, fully tiled bathrooms with ample open shelf storage space. Suite and mini-suite passengers receive priority attention, including speedy embarkation and disembarkation privileges. What is

really unacceptable is that the most expensive accommodation aboard this ship has only semi-private balconies that can be seen from above and so there is absolutely no privacy whatsoever (Suites C401, 402, 409, 410, 414, 415, 420, 421/422, 423, 424 and 425 on Caribe Deck). Also, the suites D105 and D106 (Dolphin Deck) are extremely large, but their balconies can be seen from above.

(d/e/f) Both interior and outside-view (the outsides come either with or without private balcony) cabins are functional and practical, although almost no drawers are provided. They are attractive, with warm, pleasing decor and fine soft furnishing fabrics; 80% of the outside cabins have a private balcony. The tiled bathrooms have a good amount of open shelf storage space for personal toiletries.

There are also two family suites. These consist of two suites with an interconnecting door, plus a large balcony, and can sleep up to 10 (if at least four are children), or up to eight people (if all are adults).

Most outside cabins on Emerald Deck have views obstructed by lifeboats. Sadly, there are no cabins for singles. Your name is placed outside your suite or cabin – making it simple for delivery service personnel but compromising privacy. Some cabins can accommodate a third and fourth person in upper berths – but in such cabins, the lower beds cannot then be pushed together to make queen-sized bed.

Almost all balcony suites and cabins can be overlooked both from the navigation bridge wing, as well as from the port and starboard sections of the ship's discotheque – located high above the ship at the stern. Perhaps the least desirable balcony cabins are the eight located forward on Emerald Deck, as the balconies do not extend to the side of the ship and can be passed by walkers and gawkers on the adjacent Upper Promenade walkway (so occupants need to keep their curtains closed most of the time). Also, passengers occupying some the most expensive suites with balconies at the stern of the vessel may experience considerable vibration during certain ship maneuvers.

The cabin bath towels are small, and drawer space is very limited. There are no butlers – even for the top grade suites. Cabin attendants have too many cabins to look after (typically 20), which cannot translate to fine personal service.

CUISINE. There is a variety of "Personal Choice" dining options. For formal meals, there are three principal dining rooms, Botticelli, with 504 seats, Da Vinci (486), and Michelangelo (486). There are two seatings in one restaurant, while the other two have "anytime dining" (where you choose when and with whom you want to eat). All three are non-smoking and split into multi-tier sections in a non-symmetrical design that breaks what are quite large spaces into many smaller sections, for better ambiance. Each dining room has its own galley. While four elevators go to Fiesta Deck where the Botticelli and Da Vinci restaurants are located, only two go to Plaza Deck 5 where the Michaelangelo Restaurant is located (this can cause long waits at peak times, particularly for anyone in a wheelchair).

Alternative (Extra Charge) Dining: There are two alternative informal dining areas: Sabatini's Trattoria and Painted Desert. Both are open for lunch and dinner. Sabatini's is an Italian eatery, with colorful tiled Mediterranean-style decor; it is named after Trattoria Sabatini, the 200-year old institution in Florence. It has Italian-style pizzas and pastas, with a variety of sauces, as well as Italian-style entrées (including tiger prawns and lobster tail). Sabatini's is by reservation only, and there is a cover charge of $15 per person, for lunch or dinner (on sea days only). Painted Desert has "southwestern American food"; by reservation only, with a cover charge of $8 per person, for lunch or dinner on sea days only. However, do note that Painted Desert is spread over the whole beam (width) of the ship, and two walkways intersect it, which means that it's a very open area, with people walking through it as you eat. The cuisine in both of these spots is decidedly better than in the three main dining rooms.

The poolside hamburger grill and pizza bar (no additional charge) are additional dining spots for casual bites, while extra charges will apply if you order items to eat at either the coffee bar/patisserie, or the caviar/champagne bar.

Other casual meals can be taken in the Horizon Court – open 24 hours a day, with large ocean-view on port and starboard sides and direct access to the two principal swimming pools and lido deck. Plastic plates are used.

ENTERTAINMENT. The Princess Theater (showlounge) spans two decks and has comfortable seating on both main and balcony levels. It has a 9-piece orchestra, and a scenery loading bay that connects directly from stage to a hull door for direct transfer to the dockside.

The Vista Lounge is a second entertainment lounge. It has cabaret acts at night, and lectures, bingo and horse racing during the day. Explorers, a third entertainment lounge, can also host cabaret acts and dance bands. Many lounges and bars have live music, and a number of gentlemen dance hosts act as partners for women traveling alone.

SPA/FITNESS. The Lotus Spa is a large complex that surrounds one of the swimming pools at the forward end. It comprises a large gymnasium with all the usual equipment, an aerobics room, sauna and steam rooms, beauty salon, ocean-view treatment rooms, and a relaxation area.

● **For more extensive general information about the Princess Cruises experience, see pages 134–37.**

Grand Voyager
★★★ +

Mid-Size Ship:	.24,391 tons	Passenger Decks:	.8	Cabins (for one person):	.0
Lifestyle:	.Standard	Total Crew:	.360	Cabins (with private balcony):	.12
Cruise Line:	.Iberocruceros	Passengers		Cabins (wheelchair accessible):	.4
Former Names:	.Olympia Voyager,	(lower beds/all berths):	.840/920	Cabin Current:	.110 and 230 volts
	Olympic Voyager	Passenger Space Ratio		Elevators:	.4
Builder:	.Blohm & Voss (Germany)	(lower beds/all berths):	.29.0/26.5	Casino (gaming tables):	.Yes
Original Cost:	.$150.8 million	Crew/Passenger Ratio		Slot Machines:	.Yes
Entered Service:	.July 2000 /June 2004	(lower beds/all berths):	.2.3/2.5	Swimming Pools (outdoors):	.1
Registry:	.The Bahamas	Navigation Officers:	.European	Swimming Pools (indoors):	.0
Length (ft/m):	.590.5/180.0	Cabins (total):	.420	Whirlpools:	.0
Beam (ft/m):	.83.6/25.5	Size Range (sq ft/m):	.140.0–375.0/	Self-Service Launderette:	.No
Draft (ft/m):	.23.2/7.1		13.0–34.8	Dedicated Cinema/Seats:	.No
Propulsion/Propellers:	.diesel	Cabins (outside view):	.294	Library:	.Yes
	(37,800 kW)/2	Cabins (interior/no view):	.126		

OVERALL SCORE: 1,314 (OUT OF A POSSIBLE 2,000 POINTS)

OVERVIEW. *Grand Voyager* (original name *Olympic Voyager*) was the first new ship ordered by Royal Olympia Cruises. However, the ship's high building cost was a problem, and it was put up for auction in March 2003. Having been bought by Horizon Navigation, it was placed under charter to Iberocruceros (75%-owned by the giant Carnival Corporation) and dedicated to the Spanish-speaking market.

The exterior hull design (called a "fast monohull") is similar to that of naval frigates, with a slender fore-body, and two engine rooms (forward and amidships) that can provide a 28-knot speed (and even some additional power in reserve). The ship is well suited to destination-intensive itineraries, allowing passengers more time in each port (or more ports per cruise). Its funnel is of a streamlined, swept-back design.

There is a limited amount of open deck space, although there are not many sunloungers. All exterior railings are made – unusually – of stainless steel (topped with thick, beautifully polished wood). The seawater swimming pool is located aft, and is quite small (most passengers will be enjoying the destinations served by this cruise line); adjacent are two shower enclosures.

The interior design combines contemporary touches with restrained decor, intended to remind one of the Mediterranean region the ship is designed for, with warm colors and an abundance of wood and opaque glass paneling. Perhaps the most striking, yet subtle, features in terms of design and decoration can be found in the artwork. Of particular note are two flowing poems etched in backlit opaque glass panels on the stairways (these poems are from Greece and Cyprus). However, to read the poems, you'll need to walk

BERLITZ'S RATINGS

	Possible	Achieved
Ship	500	369
Accommodation	200	135
Food	400	240
Service	400	252
Entertainment	100	58
Cruise	400	260

down the complete set of stairways. One poem, from 1911 (Ithaca) by the Greek poet Constantinos Petrou Kavafis, complements the other poem, Let's Say, by Cypriot poet Yannis Papadopoulos.

Most public rooms are located on one principal deck in a horizontal-flow layout that makes it easy to quickly find your way around, with a slightly winding open passageway that links several leisure lounges in one neat "street scene." There's a smoking room, adjacent to the main show lounge (Sala de Fiestas), for cigar and cognac devotees (with a black fireplace from the 1890s). In the popular Piano Bar, three ship models are cleverly displayed behind large glass wall panels. There's also a nightclub, a small library and a card room. Additionally, a casino (with its own bar) has table games, as well as slot machines.

There is no full wrap-around promenade deck, although you can walk around parts of the vessel outdoors. There is considerable vibration when the ship is underway at high speed, and when maneuvering at slow speeds. There are no dedicated facilities or rooms for the large numbers of children or teens that are typically carried during the July/August summer holidays. None of the public toilets is accessible by wheelchair. There are not enough sunloungers considering the number of passengers carried, and not enough open deck space.

While service isn't perfect, it comes with a smile. The onboard currency is the euro.

SUITABLE FOR: *Grand Voyager* is best suited to Spanish-speaking couples and single travelers who want to see as much as possible (in terms of destinations), in contemporary, comfortable, but not luxurious surroundings, and with food and service that are acceptable, but nothing special, all at a very modest cruise fare.

ACCOMMODATION. There are 9 price grades (including one for wheelchair accessible cabins with spacious bathrooms and roll-in showers). The price will depend on grade, location and size.

Standard Cabins: The standard interior (no view) and outside-view cabins are quite compact, but practically laid-out, and the decor includes warm blond wood cabinetry, accents and facings, and pleasing soft furnishings. The bathrooms are small, but have a decent-sized shower enclosure, and good storage facilities for personal toiletry items. All cabins include TV set, hairdryer, mini-bar/refrigerator and personal safe. You should note that only one personal safe is provided in each cabin, although there could be as many as four persons sharing a cabin.

Outside-View Superior Cabins: These simply have a little more room than the standard interior (no view) and outside-view cabins (some have bay windows that extend over the side of the ship). The bathrooms are small, but have a decent-sized shower enclosure, and good storage facilities for personal toiletries.

Balcony Suites: The largest accommodation can be found in 12 Sky Suites located high atop the ship and in the forward-most section. They have large private balconies (some are more like large terraces), floor-to-ceiling windows, limited butler service, and 24-hour dining service.

Some suites have walk-in closets, while others have closets facing the entranceway, but all have an abundance of drawer and hanging space, and a chrome pullout shoe rack and tie rack. The bathroom has a combination tub/shower (although the bathtub is extremely small and is really only for sitting in) and retractable clothesline.

All suites have wood paneled walls with vanity desk, mini-bar/refrigerator, sofa, drinks table (it's fixed, and cannot be raised), and sleeping area partly separated from the lounge area by a wood/glass divider. Four of the suites have large structures above their balconies that are the port side and starboard side gangway lowering mechanisms; they are noisy in ports of call and anchor ports, and thus the balconies cannot be considered very private.

Also, when the ship is traveling at speed, considerable wind sweeps across the balconies, and renders them almost useless. The balconies have (expensive) stainless steel railings instead of glass, topped with a thick wood railing. Outside-view and interior (no-view) cabins located aft on Deck 3 (Neptune Deck: Numbers 3120–3138 and 3121–3151) are subject to a substantial amount of throbbing noise from the diesel engines, and should be avoided (unless you like throbbing engine noise, that is).

CUISINE. The 470-seat Main Restaurant is located aft (one deck below the main "street" of public rooms and thus out of the main flow), and has picture windows on three sides. It has a semi-circular walkway, with minimalist decor, as its entrance.

The decor in the dining room itself is warm and welcoming, and quite tasteful, finished in what is best described as a "Greek Moderne" style; the chairs, however, do not have armrests. There are two seatings, and there are tables for two, four, six or eight. A few tables close to the entrance to the galley's escalators suffer from the service area, and, because of the single deck ceiling height and open waiter stations, the noise level can be considerable at times (depending on the nationalities of your fellow passengers).

For casual breakfast and lunch self-service buffets, the Garden Buffet is a pleasant but basic room, with large picture windows and an open feel. It has seating for 210 indoors and about 200 outdoors (where smokers congregate), and a bar outdoors is covered with a sailcloth-style cover. The two self-service buffet lines are small, and have a user-unfriendly layout that invites congestion – a victim of poor design.

Additional munching outlets include a pizza serving area/salad bar, and an ice cream bar.

ENTERTAINMENT. The Main Lounge is the venue for entertainment events. It is a single-level room with 420 seats although there are many pillars to obstruct the sight lines from many of those seats (about 40 per cent are almost useless). Entertainment is limited aboard this ship, whose show lounge is best for cabaret-style shows. There's a disco.

SPA/FITNESS. One of the nicest and most useful facilities aboard this ship can be found in the Spa. It includes a large fitness room, several massage/treatment rooms, sauna, steam room, and rest/changing area.

Grande Caribe
★ +

Boutique Ship: ....99 tons	Total Crew: 17	Cabins (with private balcony): 0
Lifestyle: ....Standard	Passengers	Cabins (wheelchair accessible): 0
Cruise Line: ....American Canadian	(lower beds/all berths): 100/100	Cabin Current: ....110 volts
Caribbean Line	Passenger Space Ratio	Elevators: 0
Former Names: ....none	(lower beds/all berths): 0.99/0.99	Casino (gaming tables): ....No
Builder: ....Blount Industries (USA)	Crew/Passenger Ratio	Slot Machines: ....No
Original Cost: ....$8 million	(lower beds/all berths): 5.8/5.8	Swimming Pools (outdoors): 0
Entered Service: ....June 1997	Navigation Officers: ....American	Swimming Pools (indoors): 0
Registry: ....USA	Cabins (total): 50	Whirlpools: 0
Length (ft/m): 183.0/55.7	Size Range (sq ft/m): 72.0–96.0/	Self-Service Launderette: ....No
Beam (ft/m): 40.0/12.1	6.6–8.9	Dedicated Cinema/Seats: ....No
Draft (ft/m): 6.5/1.9	Cabins (outside view): 41	Library: ....Yes
Propulsion/Propellers: diesel (1,044kW)/2	Cabins (interior/no view): 9	
Passenger Decks: 3	Cabins (for one person): 0	

OVERALL SCORE: 744 (OUT OF A POSSIBLE 2,000 POINTS)

OVERVIEW. *Grande Caribe* is the largest and the most contemporary of the Blount-built vessels. During passenger emergency drill, passengers are taught how to use fire extinguishers – a useful piece of training.

This vessel's shallow draft enables it to cruise into off-the-beaten-path destinations well out of reach of larger ships, and also has a retractable navigation bridge – practical for those low bridges along inland waterways. *Grande Caribe*, together with sister vessel *Grande Mariner*, has stabilizers. An underwater video camera allows passengers, while seated in (dry) comfort in the lounge, to view on large-screen TV monitors what a scuba diver might see underneath the ship. Underwater lights, which attract fish and other marine life, are also fitted.

The style is casual (no jackets or ties) by day and night. There are two 24-passenger launches (one of which is a glass-bottomed boat), and some snorkeling equipment.

There is one lounge/bar, located on a different deck to the dining room. Water sports facilities include a glass-bottom boat, sunfish sailboat and snorkeling equipment.

This basic, no-glitz vessel will be good for anyone who does not want crowds, or a high standard of service. An electric stairway chair-lift is provided for those who do not walk well. Gratuities given by passengers (high at the suggested $10–$15 per person, per day) are pooled and shared by all the staff. The onboard currency is the US dollar.

SUITABLE FOR: *Grande Caribe* is best suited to couples and single travelers who enjoy nature and wildlife up close and personal, and who would not dream of cruising in the mainstream sense aboard the large, warehouse-sized ships. This

BERLITZ'S RATINGS

	Possible	Achieved
Ship	500	157
Accommodation	200	67
Food	400	155
Service	400	181
Entertainment	n/a	n/a
Cruise	500	184

is for outdoors types who don't need entertainment or mindless parlor games, but do want an all-American cruise experience, albeit at a high price. It's not for children.

ACCOMMODATION. The cabins are all extremely small, relatively utilitarian units, with very little closet space (but just enough drawers) and very small bathrooms. The twin beds convert to queen-sized beds (there is good storage space under the beds). There is no room service menu, and only soap is supplied (bring your own shampoo and other toiletries). Each cabin has its own air conditioner, so passengers do not have to share air with the rest of the ship (and other passengers). Refreshingly, there are no cabin keys. Be prepared for noise from the generators.

CUISINE. The dining room seats all passengers in one open seating, so you dine with whomever you wish, making new friends and enjoying different conversation each day (it is also good for small groups). The tables convert to card tables for use between meals. Passengers are welcome to bring their own alcohol, as the company does not sell it aboard ship. Effervescent, young American waitresses provide the service, although there is no finesse.

ENTERTAINMENT. There is no formal entertainment, although dinner and after-dinner conversation with fellow passengers in the ship's lounge/bar really becomes the entertainment each evening. So, if you don't want to talk to your fellow passengers, take a good book.

SPA/FITNESS. No facilities.

Grande Mariner
★ +

Boutique Ship: . . . . .99 tons	Passenger Decks: 3	Cabins (for one person): 0
Lifestyle: . . . . .Standard	Total Crew: 17	Cabins (with private balcony): 0
Cruise Line: . . . . .American Canadian	Passengers	Cabins (wheelchair accessible): 0
Caribbean Line	(lower beds/all berths): 100/100	Cabin Current: . . . . .110 volts
Former Names: . . . . .none	Passenger Space Ratio	Elevators: 0
Builder: . . . . .Blount Industries (USA)	(lower beds/all berths): 0.99/0.99	Casino (gaming tables): . . . . .No
Original Cost: . . . .$8 million	Crew/Passenger Ratio	Slot Machines: . . . . .No
Entered Service: . . . . .June 1998	(lower beds/all berths): 5.8/5.8	Swimming Pools (outdoors): 0
Registry: . . . . .USA	Navigation Officers: . . . . .American	Swimming Pools (indoors): 0
Length (ft/m): 183.0/55.7	Cabins (total): 50	Whirlpools: 0
Beam (ft/m): 40.0/12.1	Size Range (sq ft/m): . .72.0–96.0/6.6–8.9	Self-Service Launderette: . . . . .No
Draft (ft/m): 6.5/1.9	Cabins (outside view): 41	Dedicated Cinema/Seats: . . . . .No
Propulsion/Propellers: .diesel (1,044kW)/2	Cabins (interior/no view): 9	Library: . . . . .Yes

OVERALL SCORE: 747 (OUT OF A POSSIBLE 2,000 POINTS)

OVERVIEW. *Grande Mariner* is another example of a Blount-built vessel. During passenger emergency drill, passengers are taught how to use fire extinguishers – useful training.

This vessel has a shallow draft, which enables it to cruise into off-the-beaten-path destinations well out of reach of larger ships, and also has a retractable navigation bridge – practical for those low bridges along the inland waterways. *Grande Mariner*, together with sister vessel *Grande Caribe*, has stabilizers. An underwater video camera allows passengers, while seated in (dry) comfort in the lounge, to view on large-screen TV monitors what a scuba diver might see underneath the ship. Underwater lights, which attract fish and other marine life, are also fitted.

The style is unpretentious and extremely casual (definitely no jackets or ties) both day and night. There are two 24-passenger launches (one of which is a glass bottom boat), sunfish sailboat, and some snorkeling equipment.

There is one lounge/bar, located on a different deck to the dining room – a departure for ACCL from the company's former vessels. An electric chair-lift is provided at all stairways for those who do not walk well. Water sports facilities include a glass-bottom boat, and sunfish sailboat.

All gratuities are pooled and shared by the staff (although the suggested daily rate is very high for the product delivered). The onboard currency is the US dollar.

SUITABLE FOR: *Grande Mariner* is best suited to couples and single travelers who enjoy nature and wildlife up close and personal and would not dream of cruising in the mainstream sense aboard ships with large numbers of people.

BERLITZ'S RATINGS

	Possible	Achieved
Ship	500	159
Accommodation	200	67
Food	400	155
Service	400	181
Entertainment	n/a	n/a
Cruise	500	185

This is for outdoors types who don't need entertainment, but do want an all-American cruise experience, albeit at a high price. It's not for children.

ACCOMMODATION. The cabins are all extremely small, relatively utilitarian units, with very little closet space (but just enough drawers) and very small bathrooms. There are 50 cabins, each with twin beds that convert to queen-sized beds (there is good storage space under the beds). There is no room service menu, and only soap is supplied (bring your own shampoo and other toiletries). Each cabin has its own air conditioner, so passengers do not have to share air with the rest of the ship (and other passengers). Refreshingly, there are no cabin keys.

CUISINE. The dining room seats all passengers in a single, open seating, so you dine with whomever you wish. The advantage of this is that you can make new friends and enjoy different conversation each day (it is also good for small groups). The dining tables convert to card tables for use between meals. Passengers are welcome to bring their own alcohol, as the company does not sell it aboard ship. Effervescent, young American waitresses provide the service, although there is no finesse.

ENTERTAINMENT. There is no formal entertainment, although dinner and after-dinner conversation with fellow passengers in the ship's lounge/bar really provides the entertainment each evening. So, if you don't want to talk to your fellow passengers, take a good book.

SPA/FITNESS. No spa facilities.

Grandeur of the Seas
★★★★

Large Resort Ship: ....74,137 tons	Total Crew: 760	Cabins (with private balcony): 212
Lifestyle: ....Standard	Passengers	Cabins (wheelchair accessible): 14
Cruise Line: Royal Caribbean International	(lower beds/all berths): 1,950/2,446	Cabin Current: ....110 and 220 volts
Former Names: ....none	Passenger Space Ratio	Elevators: 9
Builder: . . .Kvaerner Masa-Yards (Finland)	(lower beds/all berths): 38.0/30.3	Casino (gaming tables): ....Yes
Original Cost: ....$300 million	Crew/Passenger Ratio	Slot Machines: ....Yes
Entered Service: ....Dec 1996	(lower beds/all berths): 2.5/3.2	Swimming Pools (outdoors): 1
Registry: ....The Bahamas	Navigation Officers: ......International	Swimming Pools (indoors): 1
Length (ft/m): 916.0/279.6	Cabins (total): 975	(indoor/outdoor w/sliding glass roof)
Beam (ft/m): 105.6/32.2	Size Range (sq ft/m): 158.2–1,267.0/	Whirlpools: 6
Draft (ft/m): 25.5/7.6	14.7–117.7	Self-Service Launderette: ....No
Propulsion/Propellers: .....diesel-electric	Cabins (outside view): 576	Dedicated Cinema/Seats: ....No
(50,400kW)/2	Cabins (interior/no view): 399	Library: ....Yes
Passenger Decks: 11	Cabins (for one person): 0	

OVERALL SCORE: 1,492 (OUT OF A POSSIBLE 2,000 POINTS)

OVERVIEW. This is one of a pair of ships for this popular cruise line (sister to *Enchantment of the Seas*). The vessel has an attractive contemporary profile, with a single funnel located well aft (almost a throwback to some ship designs used in the 1950s), and has a nicely rounded stern (rather like the older *Monarch of the Seas*-class ships), and a Viking Crown Lounge is set amidships. This, together with the forward mast, provides three distinct focal points in its exterior profile. There is a walk-around promenade deck outdoors (there are no cushioned pads for the tacky home patio-style plastic sunloungers, however).

A large Viking Crown Lounge (a trademark of all Royal Caribbean International ships) sits between funnel and mast at the top of the atrium lobby, and overlooks the forward section of the swimming pool deck, with access provided from stairway off the central atrium.

The principal interior focal point is a seven-deck-high Centrum (atrium lobby), which provides a good meeting point (the Purser's Desk and Shore Excursion Desk are located on one of the lower levels). Many public entertainment rooms and facilities can be located off the atrium.

This ship has good interior passenger flow. There is a good, varied collection of artworks (including several sculptures), principally by British artists, with classical music, ballet and theater themes. The casino is large and glitzy, and has a fascinating, somewhat theatrical glass-covered, but under-floor exhibit. The children's and teens' facilities are good, much expanded from previous ships in the fleet.

A neat champagne terrace bar sits forward of the lower level of the two-deck-high dining room. There is a good use of tropical plants throughout the public rooms, which

BERLITZ'S RATINGS

	Possible	Achieved
Ship	500	429
Accommodation	200	166
Food	400	238
Service	400	286
Entertainment	100	81
Cruise	400	292

helps counteract the rather plain and clinical pastel wall colors, while huge murals of opera scenes adorn several stairways. There are good children's and teens' facilities – larger than those of previous ships in the fleet. The onboard currency is the US dollar.

ACCOMMODATION. There are 16 price grades (the price depending on grade, size and location, with location and grade perhaps more important, since so many of the cabins are of the same, or a very similar size).

There are five grades of suites: Royal Suite (1), Owner's Suite (5), Royal Family Suite (4), Grand Suite (12), and Superior Suite (44, including two superior suites for the disabled). All are well appointed and have pleasing decor (best described as Scandinavian Moderne), with good wood and color accenting (the largest has a baby grand piano).

Royal Suite. The largest accommodation can be found in the Royal Suite, located directly aft of the ship's navigation bridge on the starboard side. It has a separate bedroom with king-sized bed, walk-in closet and vanity dressing area, living room with queen-sized sofa bed, baby grand piano, refrigerator and wet bar, dining table, entertainment center, and large private balcony. The bathroom has a whirlpool tub, separate shower enclosure, two washbasins, and toilet.

Owner's Suite. The five owner's suites are at the forward end of the ship, just behind the navigation bridge (close to the Royal Suite). They have a queen-sized bed, separate living area with queen-sized sofa bed, vanity dressing area, refrigerator and wet bar. The bathroom has a full-size bathtub, separate shower enclosure, toilet and two washbasins.

Royal Family Suite. Features include two bedrooms with twin beds that convert to queen-sized beds, living area with double sofa bed and Pullman bed, refrigerator, two bathrooms (one with bathtub), and private balcony. This suite can accommodate eight, and might be suitable for families.

Grand Suite. Twin beds convert to a queen-sized bed. Vanity dressing area, lounge area with sofa bed, refrigerator, and a bathroom with bathtub, plus a private balcony.

Superior Suite. Twin beds that convert to a queen-sized bed. Vanity dressing area, lounge area with sofa bed, refrigerator, plus private balcony, and a bathroom with bathtub. Although this is called a suite, it really is little more than a larger standard cabin with balcony.

Other Grades. All standard cabins have twin beds that convert to a queen-sized bed, ample closet space for a one-week cruise, and a good amount of drawer space, although under-bed storage space is not good for large suitcases. The bathrooms have nine mirrors. Plastic buckets are provided for champagne/wine and are really tacky.

All grades of suite/cabin include a hairdryer. The room service menu is minimal, with only the most basic selection.

CUISINE. The 1,195-seat (non-smoking) Great Gatsby Dining Room is a large dining hall that is spread over two decks, with both levels connected by a grand, sweeping staircase. There are two seatings.

The cavernous, 790-seat informal Windjammer Cafe is the ship's casual eatery. It has a great expanse of ocean-view glass windows, and is where breakfast and lunch buffets are available as an alternative to the dining room.

An intimate terrace Champagne Bar is located forward of the lower level of the two-deck-high dining room and just off the atrium for those who might like to taste something a little out of the ordinary, in a setting that is bright and contemporary.

ENTERTAINMENT. The Palladium Theater is the ship's principal showlounge. It is located at the forward part of the ship (accessed by the forward stairway/lift bank), and is used for big production shows. It has excellent sightlines from 98 percent of the 875 seats. Another showlounge, the 575-seat South Pacific Lounge, is used for smaller shows and cabaret acts, including late-night adult (blue) comedy.

SPA/FITNESS. The ShipShape Spa is located aft of the funnel and spans two decks. Facilities include a gymnasium (with all the latest muscle-pumping exercise machines), aerobics exercise room, sauna and steam rooms, a beauty salon, and a clutch of treatment rooms.

For the sporting, there is activity galore – including a rock-climbing wall, with several separate climbing tracks. It is located outdoors at the aft end of the funnel.

● **For more extensive general information about the Royal Caribbean experience, see pages 137–42.**

Hanseatic
★★★★★

Boutique Ship: . . . . .8,378 tons	Passenger Decks: 7
Lifestyle: . . . . .Luxury	Total Crew: 122
Cruise Line: . . . . . . .Hapag-Lloyd Cruises	Passengers
Former Names: . . . . . .Society Adventurer	(lower beds/all berths): 184/194
Builder: . . . . .Rauma Yards (Finland)	Passenger Space Ratio
Original Cost: . . . .$68 million	(lower beds/all berths): 45.5/43.1
Entered Service: . . . . .Mar 1993	Crew/Passenger Ratio
Registry: . . . . .The Bahamas	(lower beds/all berths): 1.5/1.5
Length (ft/m): 402.9/122.80	Navigation Officers: . . . . .German
Beam (ft/m): 59.1/18.00	Cabins (total): .92
Draft (ft/m): 16.1/4.91	Size Range (sq ft/m): 231.4–470.3/
Propulsion/Propellers: . . . . .diesel	21.5–43.7
(5,880kW)/2	Cabins (outside view): 92

Cabins (interior/no view): 0
Cabins (for one person): 0
Cabins (with private balcony): 0
Cabins (wheelchair accessible): 2
Cabin Current: . . . . .220 volts
Elevators: 2
Swimming Pools (outdoors): 1
Whirlpools: 1
Self-Service Launderette: . . . . .No
Lecture/Film Room: . . . . . .Yes (seats 160)
Library: . . . . .Yes
Zodiacs: 14
Helicopter Pad: . . . . .Yes

OVERALL SCORE: 1,740 (OUT OF A POSSIBLE 2,000 POINTS)

OVERVIEW. Originally ordered for Society Cruises as *Society Adventurer* (although it never actually sailed under that name, because the company declared itself bankrupt and didn't take possession of the ship), *Hanseatic* was well designed and constructed specifically to operate worldwide expedition-style cruises in contemporary, but quite luxurious, surroundings. The ship is extremely environmentally friendly and has the latest "zero-discharge", non-polluting waste disposal system including a pollution-filtered incinerator, full biological sewage treatment plant, and a large storage capacity. This is one of only very few ships that will allow you to sign up for a tour of the engine room.

This is an outstanding ship for the best in destination-intensive exploration voyages, and is under long-term charter to Hapag-Lloyd Cruises. It has a fully enclosed bridge and an ice-hardened hull with the highest passenger vessel ice classification. The ship also has the very latest in high-tech navigation equipment.

A fleet of 14 Zodiac inflatable craft, each named after a famous explorer, is used for in-depth shore landings. These craft provide the ship with tremendous flexibility in itineraries, and provide excellent possibilities for up-close wildlife viewing in natural habitats, with small numbers of passengers. Rubber boots, parkas, boot-washing and storage rooms are provided for passengers, particularly useful for Arctic and Antarctic cruises.

Inside, the ship is equipped with fine quality luxury fittings and soft furnishings. There is a choice of several public rooms (most are located aft, with accommodation forward), all of them well-furnished and decorated, and all of them have high ceilings, which help to provide an

BERLITZ'S RATINGS

	Possible	Achieved
Ship	500	434
Accommodation	200	172
Food	400	345
Service	400	343
Entertainment	N/A	N/A
Cruise	500	446

impression of space; the result is that the ship feels much larger than its actual size. The library/observation lounge provides a good selection of hardback books and videos in both the English and German languages; it has a sunken bar, and a warm, inviting atmosphere.

Hanseatic provides destination-intensive, nature and life-enrichment cruises and expeditions in elegant, but unstuffy surroundings, to some of the world's most fascinating destinations, at a suitably handsome price. The passenger maximum is generally kept to about 150, which means plenty of comfort, no lines, and lots of space.

The ship is at its best when operating in Arctic and Antarctic regions (however, infirm passengers would be well advised to be wary of the difficult conditions for shore landings in these areas). Safety is paramount, particularly in the Antarctic and, in this regard, the ship excels with professionalism, pride and skilled seamanship. It always operates in two languages, English and German (many staff speak several languages), and caters well to both sets of passengers. All port taxes, insurance, staff gratuities, Zodiac trips and most shore excursions (except when the ship operates in Europe) are included. A relaxed ambience prevails on board. The onboard currency is the euro.

Hapag-Lloyd Cruises specializes in providing outstanding, well-planned itineraries. Where this ship really scores, however, is in its Antarctic sailings, where the experience of the captain, the cruise director and the crew really shine, because the hotel service crew understands the culture of the passengers. The lectures, briefings, and the amount of information provided about the itinerary and ports of call are outstanding. Well-qualified lecturers and naturalists accompany each cruise, and a discreet crew and unobtrusive service are hallmarks of the cruise experience. An expedition cruise logbook is provided at the end of each cruise for all passengers – a superb reminder of what's been seen and done during the course of your cruise.

Note that there are few negative things about this ship. It is principally marketed to German-speaking and English-speaking passengers, so other nationalities may find it hard to integrate. Marine quality telescopes, mounted outdoors, would be a useful addition.

SUITABLE FOR: *Hanseatic* is best suited to well-traveled couples and single travelers who are adventurous and enjoy learning about nature and the natural sciences, geography, history, gardening, art, architecture, and want to be aboard a very small ship with almost no entertainment or mindless parlor games. This ship is ideal for those who would never wish to set foot aboard one of the big "floating resort" ships which go on highly programmed cruises, and for those who want to experience destinations that are probably out of the ordinary (such as Antarctica) in style and a high degree of comfort.

ACCOMMODATION. There are no bad cabins, and accommodation is priced in seven grades. The price will depend on the grade, size and location you choose. The all-outside cabins, located in the forward section of the ship, are large and very well equipped, and include a separate lounge area next to a large picture window (which has a pull-down blackout blind as well as curtains) and refrigerator.

All furniture is in warm woods such as beech, and everything has rounded edges. Wood trim accents the ceiling perimeter, and acts as a divider between bed and lounge areas. Each cabin has a mini-bar, television, VCR, two locking drawers, and plenty of closet and drawer space, as well as two separate cupboards and hooks for all-weather outerwear. There really should be (but there isn't, at present) a privacy curtain between the cabin door and the sleeping area of the cabin (passengers can be seen from the hallway when the cabin door is opened).

In 2003 a complete, high-tech in-cabin infotainment system was added to all suites/cabins (similar to the one aboard *Europa* and *Queen Mary 2*), which provides a large selection of on-demand videos (at no charge) and audio tracks.

All cabin bathrooms have a large shower enclosure, toiletries cabinets, wall-mounted hairdryer, and bathrobe. There are only two types of cabins; 34 have double beds, others have twin beds. Towels, bed linens and pillowcases are 100% cotton, and individual cotton-filled duvet covers are provided.

The suites and cabins on Bridge Deck have impeccable butler service and full in-cabin dining privileges, as well as personalized stationery, larger flat-screen televisions and DVD player. Soft drinks are supplied in the cabin refrigerator, and replenished daily, at no charge (all liquor is at extra cost, however).

CUISINE. The 186-seat Marco Polo restaurant is elegant, warm and welcoming, and has large picture windows on two sides as well as aft, and table settings are graced with fine Rosenthal china and silverware. There is one seating for dinner, and open seating for breakfast and lunch. The cuisine and service are absolutely first-rate, but are more informal than, for example, aboard the larger *Europa* (which is at or close to the same price level). Top-quality ingredients are always used, and most items are purchased fresh when available.

The meals are very creative and nicely presented, and each is appealing to the eye as well as to the palate. There is always an excellent selection of breads, cheeses, desserts and pastry items. Note that when operating in the Arctic or Antarctic, table set-ups are often minimal, due to the possible movement of the ship (stabilizers cannot be used in much of the Antarctic region), so cutlery is provided and changed for each course.

The Columbus Lounge, with 74 seats, is an informal, open seating, self-serve (or waiter service) buffet-style eatery by day, changes into a second dining room night, with themed dinners and barbeques featuring ethno (regional) food. Reservations are required (you make them in the morning of the day you want to dine there), but there is no extra charge, and there is no tipping at any time. Also, on each cruise a full Viennese teatime is featured, as well as a daily teatime.

ENTERTAINMENT. There is no showlounge as such, although there is a lecture room. Entertainment is certainly not a priority aboard this ship, but the itinerary and destinations are the main show. There is no formal entertainment (except on some cruises in the summer, when, typically, a little classical music ensemble may be carried), nor does the ship normally carry a band. Lectures, by some of the foremost authorities and experts in various fields associated with expeditions and nature are a principal attraction of any cruise aboard this ship (unless under charter for special theme cruises during the summer), as are after-dinner recaps of the day.

Occasionally, the ship's crew may put on a little amateur dramatics event, or a seamen's choral presentation. And on one evening at the end of each expedition cruise, the ship's chart is auctioned off to the highest bidder, with any profits being sent to a charity organisation.

SPA/FITNESS. The spa facilities, expanded in 2004, include a decently-sized gymnasium (with up-to-date cardiovascular and muscle-toning equipment, treadmills and exercycles), a sauna, and massage facilities, all located forward on the Sun Deck in an area that also includes a solarium and hot tub. Nothing more is really needed on this kind of expedition-style cruising as most of each day is taken up with being ashore, and evenings mainly consist of dinner and daily recaps. Massage is also available, at €46 for 60 minutes, and €38 for 45 minutes.

Hebridean Princess
★ ★ ★ ★ +

Boutique Ship: . . . . .2,112 tons	Total Crew: 37	Cabins (with private balcony): 4
Lifestyle: . . . . .Luxury	Passengers	Cabins (wheelchair accessible): 0
Cruise Line:Hebridean International Cruises	(lower beds/all berths): 49/49	Cabin Current: . . . . .240 volts
Former Names: . . . .*Columba*	Passenger Space Ratio	Elevators: 0
Builder: . . . . .Hall Russell (Scotland)	(lower beds/all berths): 43.1/43.1	Casino (gaming tables): . . . . .No
Original Cost: . . . . .n/a	Crew/Passenger Ratio	Slot Machines: .No
Entered Service: 1964/Apr 1989	(lower beds/all berths): 1.3/1.3	Swimming Pools (outdoors): 0
Registry: . . . . .Great Britain	Navigation Officers: . . . . .British	Swimming Pools (indoors): 0
Length (ft/m): 235.0/71.6	Cabins (total): .30	Whirlpools: 0
Beam (ft/m): 46.0/14.0	Size Range (sq ft/m): 144.0–340.0/	Self-Service Launderette: . . . . .No
Draft (ft/m): 10.0/3.0	13.4–31.6	Dedicated Cinema/Seats: . . . . .No
Propulsion/Propellers: . . . . .diesel	Cabins (outside view): 24	Library: . . . . .Yes
(1,790kW)/2	Cabins (interior/no view): 6	
Passenger Decks: 5	Cabins (for one person): 11	

OVERALL SCORE: 1,671 (OUT OF A POSSIBLE 2,000 POINTS)

OVERVIEW. Small can be beautiful. *Hebridean Princess*, originally one of three Scottish ferries built for for David MacBayne Ltd – although actually owned by the British government – was skillfully converted into a gem of a cruise ship in order to operate island-hopping itineraries in Scotland, together with the occasional jaunt to Norway. It was renamed in 1989 by the Duchess of York. There is an outdoors deck for occasional sunbathing and al fresco meals, as well as a bar (occasionally, formal cocktail parties are held here when the weather conditions are right). There is no wrap-around promenade deck, although there is a useful open deck atop ship. The ship carries a Zodiac inflatable runabout, as well as a rowing boat (for passenger use) and two Hardy shore tenders (*Scarba* and *Shona*).

Use of the ship's small boats, speedboat, bicycles (about a dozen), and fishing gear are included in the price, as are entrance fees to gardens, castles, other attractions, and the occasional coach tour (depending on the itinerary). The destination-intensive cruises have very creative itineraries and there really is plenty to do, despite the lack of big-ship features. Specialist guides, who give daily talks about the destinations to be visited and some fascinating history and the local folklore, accompany all cruises.

The principal public room inside the ship is the charming Tiree Lounge, which has a real brick-walled inglenook fireplace, as well as a very cozy bar with a wide variety of whiskies (the selection of single malts is excellent) and cognacs for connoisseurs (naturally, the ship specializes in Scottish spirits).

This charming little ship has a warm, totally cosseted, traditional Scottish country house ambiance and stately

BERLITZ'S RATINGS

	Possible	Achieved
Ship	500	410
Accommodation	200	174
Food	400	348
Service	400	337
Entertainment	n/a	n/a
Cruise	500	402

home service that is unobtrusive but always at hand when you need it. Agatha Christie's Inspector Hercule Poirot would be very much at home here (particularly in the Tiree Lounge) – although he may be wary of the secret and intrigue that "Glen Etive" (a figure that dates from 1911– you'll need to go aboard to find it) holds. Who needs megaships when you can take a retro-cruise aboard this little gem of a ship? Direct bookings are accepted.

What is so appreciated by passengers is the fact that the ship does not have photographers or some of the trappings found aboard larger ships. Passengers also love the fact that there is no bingo, art auctions, or mindless parlor games. The onboard currency is the UK pound.

Hebridean Princess has UK officers and an excellent Latvian service crew; all are discreet and provide unobtrusive service. This little ship remains one of the world's best-kept travel secrets (indeed, Queen Elizabeth II chartered the ship for a family-only celebration of her 80th birthday in 2006).

A polished gem (although with a few rough edges), it is especially popular with single passengers. More than 50 percent of the ship's passengers are repeaters. Children under nine are not accepted. Despite the shortcomings of the ship itself, it's the food that rates highly.

If you cruise from Oban, you can be met at Glasgow station (or airport) and taken to/from the ship by private motor coach. Passengers are "piped aboard" at embarkation by a Scottish bagpiper – a neat touch. All drinks (except premium brands, which incur a small extra charge), soft drinks and bottled (Scottish) mineral water are included in the fare, as are gratuities (the company requests that no additional gratuities be given).

Although this vessel is strong, it does have structural limitations and noisy engines that cause some vibration (however, the engines do not run at night because the ship anchors before bedtime, providing soul-renewing tranquility – except for the sound of a single generator). The ship does not have an elevator, so anyone with walking disabilities may find it challenging (and there may be several tender ports on each itinerary). It is often cold and very wet in the Scottish highlands and islands (flexible weather), so take plenty of warm clothing for layering.

Hebridean International Cruises has a slightly larger sister ship, *Hebridean Spirit* (acquired in 2001), which offers the same sort of style and comfort, but in a more contemporary setting; the ship features more international itineraries to warm weather regions

SUITABLE FOR: *Hebridean Princess* is best suited to adult couples and single travelers of mature years who enjoy learning about nature and the natural sciences, geography, history, gardening, art, architecture, and want to be aboard a very small ship with almost no entertainment. This is ideal for those who would abhor big ship cruising.

ACCOMMODATION. The price will depend on the grade, size and location you choose. All cabins have different color schemes and names (there are no numbers, and, refreshingly, no door keys, although cabins can be locked from the inside). All are individually designed (no two cabins are identical) and created, with delightfully eclectic curtains, sweeping drapes over the beds, and lots of cushions. They really are quite delightful (and quite different to almost all other cruise ships) and come in a wide range of configurations (some with single, some with double, some with twin beds), including four that have a private balcony (a delightfully private and self-indulgent bonus).

All except two cabins have a private bathroom with bath or shower (two cabins share a bathroom); all have a refrigerator, ironing board with iron, trouser press, brass clock, and tea/coffee making set. All towels and bathrobe are 100% cotton, as is the bed linen. Molton Brown personal toiletry items are provided.

All cabins come with Victorian-style bathroom fittings (many are gold-plated), and some have brass cabin portholes or windows that actually open. Three of the newest

cabins added are outfitted in real Scottish Baronial style. Some cabins in the front of the ship are subject to the noise of the anchor being weighed each morning.

CUISINE. The Columba Restaurant is a non-smoking dining room with ocean-view windows, and tables that are laid with crisp white linen, and sometimes with lace overlays (note that, while days are casual, dinner means jackets and ties, and formal attire typically twice per cruise). Classic white Schonwald china is provided. There is a single seating, at assigned tables. Some chairs have armrests while some do not.

The cuisine is extremely creative, and at times outstanding – and about the same quality and presentation as *SeaDream I* and *SeaDream II*, although, typically, menus feature one meat and one fish dish (a different fish each day), plus an alternative, casual option. Fresh, taste-filled ingredients are sourced and purchased locally (supporting Scottish suppliers) – a welcome change from the mass catering of most ships. Although there are no flambeau items (the galley has electric, not gas, ranges), what is created is beautifully presented and of the highest standard. The desserts are also worth saving space for.

The breakfast menu is standard each day, although you can always ask for any favorites you may have, and each day a speciality item is featured. Try the "porridge and a wee dram (Scotch whisky)" – it's lovely on a cold morning, and it sets you up for the whole day. Although there is waiter service for most things, there is also a good buffet table display during breakfast and luncheon. Wines are provided at lunch and dinner, although an additional connoisseur's list is available for those seeking fine vintage wines. Highly personal and attentive service from an attentive Latvian service staff completes the picture.

ENTERTAINMENT. The Tiree Lounge is the equivalent of a main lounge aboard this very small ship. Dinner is *the* entertainment of the evening. Occasionally, there might be after-dinner drinks, poetry readings, and an occasional storyteller, but little else (passengers neither expect nor need it).

SPA/FITNESS. There is no spa, as the ship is too small. The only concessions to fitness are an exercycle, treadmill, power stepper and slide (row) machine.

DID YOU KNOW...

Should staff name badges be on the left or right side of the body?

In the hospitality industry, name badges are worn on the left side of the body. There are two principal reasons for this:
● Typically 81 percent of humans are right-handed, and

the human eye naturally goes towards the right (that is, the left side of the body of the person facing you).
● The right side of the body is considered reserved for the military, whose name badges are always worn on the right side of

the body (medals being worn on the left, or most important, side).

You may also notice that when cameras pan in a documentary film made by painstaking professionals (such as in nature films), it is normal procedure to pan from right to left.

Hebridean Spirit
★★★★ +

Boutique Ship:	4,200 tons	Total Crew:	72
Lifestyle:	Luxury	Passengers	
Cruise Line:Hebridean International Cruises		(lower beds/all berths):	81/97
Former Names:	*Sun Viva II,*	Passenger Space Ratio	
MegaStar Capricorn, Renaissance Six		(lower beds/all berths):	51.8/43.2
Builder:	Nuovi Cantieri Apuania (Italy)	Crew/Passenger Ratio	
Entered Service:	Mar 1991/July 2001	(lower beds/all berths):	1.1/1.3
Registry:	Great Britain	Navigation Officers:	British
Length (ft/m):	297.2/90.60	Cabins (total):	49
Beam (ft/m):	50.1/15.30	Size Range (sq ft/m):	215.0–365.9/
Draft (ft/m):	13.7/4.20		20.0–34.0
Propulsion/Propellers:	diesel	Cabins (outside view):	49
	(5,000kW)/2	Cabins (interior/no view):	0
Passenger Decks:	5	Cabins (for one person):	18

Cabins (with private balcony):	8
Cabins (wheelchair accessible):	0
Cabin Current:	110/220 volts
Dining Rooms:	1
Elevators:	1
Casino (gaming tables):	No
Slot Machines:	No
Swimming Pools (outdoors):	1
Swimming Pools (indoors):	0
Whirlpools:	0
Self-Service Launderette:	No
Dedicated Cinema/Seats:	No
Library:	Yes

OVERALL SCORE: 1,697 (OUT OF A POSSIBLE 2,000 POINTS)

OVERVIEW. *Hebridean Spirit* has a contemporary look, although there is also a traditional single funnel. The navigation bridge is a well-rounded half-moon design. It was one of four identical vessels originally built for Renaissance Cruises, and acquired by Hebridean International Cruises in November 2000. After being chartered to Star Cruises until March 2001, the ship underwent an extensive redesign and refurbishment program. Its exterior design has been altered somewhat with the addition of an enclosed lounge deck forward of the single funnel, which has been made to look similar to that of smaller (and quite different) and much older sister ship *Hebridean Princess*.

There is one wrap-around teakwood promenade deck outdoors, and a very reasonable amount of open deck and sunbathing space. All of the deck furniture – the tables and chairs – are made of teak and the sunloungers have thick cushioned pads. All exterior handrails are of beautifully polished wood. There is also a teakwood water sports platform at the stern of the ship, where two fine, water-jet driven shore tenders (*Ardbeg* and *Talisker*) are located (these have high central rails inside for passengers to hold when standing up). The ship also carries a number of lightweight bicycles (helmets are also provided, and required), for those who like to be independent explorers in ports of call.

You will find elegant interior design and the touches reminiscent of a small, lavish country house hotel (most of its original furnishings and fittings were removed in a multi-million pound refurbishment program when the ship was delivered to Hebridean International Cruises in 2001). The Skye Lounge is the ship's main lounge, and it has the unmistakable feel of a traditional drawing room; it

BERLITZ'S RATINGS

	Possible	Achieved
Ship	500	432
Accommodation	200	176
Food	400	350
Service	400	339
Entertainment	N/A	N/A
Cruise	500	405

includes a large, white, Bath stone fireplace with an imitation log fire (safety regulations prohibit a one), and is the focal point for all social activities and cocktail parties.

Smokers can enjoy their very own (small) Lookout Room, adjacent to the Panorama Lounge (where you'll find internet-connect computer stations), located forward of the funnel, atop the ship. A humidor is provided, with a small selection of Cuban cigars. There is also a good travel library/reading room.

For passengers who want to explore independently, 18 bicycles are available on board; otherwise, shore excursions are typically included, and well arranged. Destination lecturers are provided during the cruise.

The ship's itineraries take participants mostly to quiet, off-the-beaten-track ports not often visited by larger cruise ships. So, what is so good about a cruise aboard this ship? It's the faultless, friendly but unobtrusive service, and the attention to detail so lacking in most large ships today. This utterly charming little vessel has a warm, totally cosseted, traditional country house ambience that is unobtrusive but always at hand when you need it. Inspector Hercule Poirot would be very much at home here, as it is rather like a small, exclusive club. The fact that the ship does not have photographers and some of the trappings found aboard larger ships does not matter one bit.

Although the dress code is casual and comfortable, most passengers dress well for dinner; there are typically two formal evenings each cruise.

Mid-morning bouillon, afternoon tea with homemade cakes and biscuits (cookies) are a delightful fact of lifestyle aboard this floating (English) country house hotel.

All in all, a cruise aboard *Hebridean Spirit* should prove to be ideal for those who don't like large cruise ships. The service is friendly but unobtrusive; the atmosphere is quiet (no music in passageways or elevator) and refined, and the ship is well run by a crew (British officers, Ukrainian hotel staff) who are proud to provide the kind of personal service expected by passengers who are intellectual and well-traveled. In fact, a discreet crew and unobtrusive service are hallmarks of the cruise experience aboard this ship.

During the winter season, rates are quoted as cruise-only; during the summer season, passengers are flown in a privately chartered aircraft from Stansted, near London and prices are cruise and air inclusive. Also included are all guided shore excursions. The onboard currency is the British pound. All alcoholic drinks (including wines and champagne), soft drinks and bottled water are included in the fare, as are all gratuities (the company requests that no additional gratuities be given).

Hebridean International Cruises also operates a much smaller, even more intimate sister ship, mainly in the western islands off the coast of Scotland, *Hebridean Princess*. The company's brochure uses only real passengers in its photographs. Children under nine are not accepted on board (the ship really is too small to provide children's facilities).

Several pillars (needed for structural support) provide obstructions in some public rooms and hallways. The interior decor consists of plastic woods instead of real woods (it looks almost too perfect in places), although it does work in providing a warm, welcoming ambiance.

SUITABLE FOR: *Hebridean Spirit* is best suited to couples and singles who enjoy learning about the natural sciences, geography, history, gardening, art, architecture, and want to be aboard a very small ship with little or no entertainment. This is ideal for those who would abhor big ship cruising.

ACCOMMODATION. There are five grades of double or twin-bedded cabins and four grades of cabins for single travellers. The price you pay will depend on the grade, size and location you choose. The cabins (named after glens, isles, castles, and clans) are quite spacious units, measuring between 215 and 365 sq. ft (20–34 sq. meters), including bathrooms and balconies. Castle and clan grades have portholes; isles have windows; glens have private balconies.

This is quite generous for a small ship such as this one. All are decorated in a similar fashion to those aboard *Hebridean Princess*. All have outside views, and most feature wallpapered walls, lighted walk-in closets (one of the two large suites and 24 other cabins only), full-length mirror, dressing table with three-sided vanity mirrors, tea/coffee-making equipment, combination large-screen color television and DVD player, refrigerator/mini-bar (always stocked with fresh milk and mineral water), direct-dial satellite telephone, personal safe, ironing board, and electric trouser press. The two suites and 14 other cabins have an additional sofa bed.

Naturally, all towels and thick, plush bathrobe are 100% cotton, as is the bed linen, which has traditional sheets and blankets (not duvets), and thick, patterned bedspread. There are no music channels, and there is no switch to turn announcements off in your cabin.

The bathrooms are of a reasonably decent size, and all are marble clad; they have tiled floors, marble vanities, and shower enclosures (except for "Suite", "Glen" and "Isle" grade cabins, which have a tub/shower combination). Molton Brown personal toiletry items are provided. Note that there is a small step between bedroom and bathroom.

The two largest suites (Saint Columba and Saint Oran, which don't have balconies) and all balcony cabins feature a combination color television and integral DVD player.

CUISINE. The Argyll Restaurant is a non-smoking dining room with ocean-view portholes, and operates with table assignments for dinner, in a single seating, and an open seating arrangement for breakfast and lunch. It is a very elegant and pleasant room, with wood paneling, fine furnishings, subtle lighting, and plenty of space around each table. A mix of chairs with and without armrests is provided. There are many tables for two, although there are also tables for four, six, and eight. Tables are always laid with crisp white linen, and ship's officers eat with passengers each night. Schonwald china is used. Dinner is typically at 7.30pm. The cuisine is quite creative – at times outstanding – but not quite up to the quality and presentation (although not quite the variety) as can be found aboard *SeaDream I* and *SeaDream II*. Haggis (and neeps), a Hebridean Cruises tradition, is presented with fanfare and ceremony on the final gala night of each cruise.

Fresh ingredients are often purchased locally when possible – a welcome change from the mass catering of most ships. The desserts are worth saving space for. Note that Hebridean International Cruises operates within European Union regulations concerning genetically modified foods, which are not used aboard *Hebridean Spirit*.

Breakfasts and lunches can also be taken outdoors at the alfresco Mizzen Deck Brasserie, particularly when the ship is operating in warm weather areas. Morning coffee and afternoon tea can be taken in the lounge areas or (weather permitting) on the open decks.

ENTERTAINMENT. The Skye Lounge is the equivalent of a main lounge aboard this small ship. Passengers really like the fact that there is no formal entertainment (the ship does not carry a band), game shows, bingo, horse racing, art auctions, or mindless parlor games – just good company and easy conversation, and very soft, gentle live piano (or piano/accordion) music in the lounge each evening.

SPA/FITNESS. The Asian-style spa, at the aft end of Promenade Deck, is a haven of tranquility and peace. It contains a hairdressing salon, gymnasium, steam room shower, and a relaxation area. It is operated by hand-picked staff from Mandara Spa (owned by Steiner Leisure) that are more mature than those found aboard the large cruise ships. Several types of massage are offered, as well as aromatherapy facials, pedicures, manicures, and hairdressing services.

Holiday
★★★

Mid-Size Ship: . . . . .46,052 tons	Total Crew: .660	Cabins (with private balcony): 10
Lifestyle: . . . . .Standard	Passengers	Cabins (wheelchair accessible): 15
Cruise Line: . . . . . . .Carnival Cruise Lines	(lower beds/all berths): 1,452/1,800	Cabin Current: . . . . .110 volts
Former Names: . . . . .none	Passenger Space Ratio	Elevators: 8
Builder: . . . . . .Aalborg Vaerft (Denmark)	(lower beds/all berths): 31.7/25.5	Casino (gaming tables): . . . . .Yes
Original Cost: . . . .$170 million	Crew/Passenger Ratio	Slot Machines: . . . . .Yes
Entered Service: . . . . .July 1985	(lower beds/all berths): 2.2/2.7	Swimming Pools (outdoors): 3
Registry: . . . . .The Bahamas	Navigation Officers: . . . . .European	Swimming Pools (indoors): 0
Length (ft/m): 726.9/221.57	Cabins (total): 726	Whirlpools: 2
Beam (ft/m): 92.4/28.17	Size Range (sq ft/m): 189.2–420.0/	Self-Service Launderette: . . . . .Yes
Draft (ft/m): 25.5/7.77	17.0–39.0	Dedicated Cinema/Seats: . . . . .No
Propulsion/Propellers: . . . . .diesel	Cabins (outside view): 447	Library: . . . . .Yes
(22,360kW)/2	Cabins (interior/no view): 279	
Passenger Decks: 9	Cabins (for one person): 0	

OVERALL SCORE: 1,134 (OUT OF A POSSIBLE 2,000 POINTS)

OVERVIEW. *Holiday* was the second new ship ordered by Carnival Cruise Lines, and is now the fleet's oldest. It is a bold, high-sided, all-white contemporary ship with short, rakish bow and stubby stern typical of so many recently built vessels. The ship, whose bows are extremely short, has the distinctive, large, swept-back wing-tipped funnel that is Carnival Cruise Lines' trademark, in the company colors of red, white and blue.

Inside, the passenger flow is quite good. There are numerous public rooms on two entertainment decks to choose from and play in, and these flow from a double-width indoor promenade. A real red-and-cream bus is located right in the middle of one of the two promenades, and this is used as a snack Cafe.

The bright (very bright) interior decor has a distinct Broadway theme. The Carnegie Library (which has very few books) is the only public room that is not bright. The casino is good, and there is around-the-clock action. There is plenty of dazzle and sizzle entertainment, while "Camp Carnival" takes care of the junior cruisers (facilities include virtual-reality machines).

This ship, now more than 20 years old, is ideal for a first cruise experience in glitzy, very lively surroundings, and for the active set who enjoy constant stimulation, loud music, and a fun-filled atmosphere, at an attractive price. The line does not provide finesse, nor does it claim to. But, forget fashion – having fun is the *sine qua non* of a Carnival cruise. There is no doubt that Carnival does a great job of providing a fun venue, but many passengers say that once is enough, and afterwards you will want to move to a more upscale experience.

Gratuities are automatically added to your onboard

BERLITZ'S RATINGS

	Possible	Achieved
Ship	500	280
Accommodation	200	121
Food	400	206
Service	400	238
Entertainment	100	64
Cruise	400	225

account at $9.75 per person, per day; you can have this amount adjusted, although you'll have to visit the information desk to do so. The onboard currency is the US dollar.

A cruise aboard this ship can be noisy and not relaxing at all (although it is good if you enjoy big-city nightlife), with little chance to escape from announcements that intrude (particularly those that bring revenue, such as art auctions, bingo, horse racing), and much hustling for drinks (although this is often done with a knowing smile from the bar waiters, working for gratuities).

SUITABLE FOR: *Holiday* is best suited to first-time young (and young at heart) couples, single passengers, tots, children and teenagers (anyone under 21 must be accompanied by a parent, relative or guardian). They should enjoy big city nightlife, be looking for contemporary, upbeat surroundings, and the latest in facilities, plenty of entertainment lounges and bars and high-tech sophistication. This should come in a highly programmed, well-packaged cruise holiday, with plenty of music, constant activity, and fairly brash entertainment including adult late-night smutty comedy, and food that is acceptable but nothing more (unless you are prepared to pay extra for dining in the "alternative" restaurant), all delivered with friendly service that lacks any kind of polish.

ACCOMMODATION. There are 11 different grades. The price will depend on the grade, size and location you choose. Carnival Cruise Lines has always tried to provide an adequate amount of space in passenger cabins, and the cabins aboard *Holiday* are no exception. They are quite functional and provide all the basics; bathrooms are practical units, with decent-sized shower stalls.

A gift basket is provided in all grades of accommodation; it includes aloe soap, shampoo, conditioner, deodorant, breath mints, candy, and pain relief tablets (in sample sizes).

If you book accommodation in one of the suites (Category 11 or 12 in the Carnival Cruise Lines brochure) you qualify for "Skipper's Club" priority check-in at any US homeland port – useful for getting ahead of the crowd.

CUISINE. There are two dining rooms (Four Winds, and Seven Seas); both are large and have low ceilings, making the raised center sections seem crowded (intimate?) and noisy because they are always full. Dining in each restaurant is now in four seatings, for greater flexibility: 6pm, 6.45pm, 8pm and 8.45pm (times are approximate).

Carnival meals stress quantity, not quality, although the company constantly works hard to improve the cuisine. However, food is still not the company's strongest points (you get what you pay for, remember).

While the menu items sound good, their presentation and taste may prove disappointing. Meats are of a high quality, but fish and seafood are not. Presentation is simple, and few garnishes are used. Many meat and fowl dishes are disguised with gravies and sauces. The selection of fresh green vegetables, breads, rolls, cheeses and fruits is limited, and there is too much canned fruits and jellied desserts. However, do remember that this is banquet catering, with all its attendant standardization and production cooking (it is, therefore, difficult to ask for anything remotely unusual or off-menu).

Although there is a decent wine list, there are no wine waiters. The service is highly programmed, although the waiters are willing and reasonably friendly. However, the waiters do sing and dance, and there are constant waiter parades; the dining room is show business – all done in the name of eventual gratuities.

The Lido Cafe self-serve buffets are very basic, as is the selection of breads, rolls, fruit and cheeses. At night, the "Seaview Bistro", as the Lido Cafe becomes known, provides a casual (dress down) alternative to eating in the main dining rooms, serving pasta, steaks, salads and desserts (it typically is in operation between 6pm and 9pm).

ENTERTAINMENT. The American Showlounge is the principal venue for large-scale production shows and major cabaret acts (although some pillars obstruct the views from several seats). In a typical 4- or 5-day cruise, there will be one or two, large-scale, trend-setting production shows, with a cast of two lead singers and a clutch of dancers, backed by a live orchestra. These have been the mainstay of Carnival's "we've got the fun" entertainment theme for years. They are of the razzle-dazzle, Las Vegas-style revues that have little or no story line or flow (there's lots of running around on stage and stepping in place, but very little dancing). However, the skimpy costumes are very colorful, as is the lighting (with extensive use of "color mover" lights). Stage smoke appears to be in constant use during the production shows, and volumes are ear-splitting.

With all the audio-visual support staff, dressers, and stage managers, the personnel count comes to almost 40. Other speciality acts take center stage on nights when there is no production show, and late-night adults-only comedy (typically with very blue material and language) is also standard aboard the ships of Carnival Cruise Lines. Carnival rotates entertainers aboard its ships, so passengers see different acts each night.

Almost every lounge/bar has live bands and musical units, so there is always plenty of live music happening (mostly in the evenings).

SPA/FITNESS. SpaCarnival is located on the ship's uppermost deck (Verandah Deck), just aft of the mast, and is accessed by the center stairway and lifts. It has a gymnasium (with some high-tech muscle-pumping cardio-vascular machines) with views over the ship's only swimming pool, men's and women's changing rooms and saunas. The beauty salon is located in another spot, on America Deck, just aft of the Americana Showlounge.

The spa is operated by Steiner, a specialist concession, whose staff will try to sell you Steiner's own-brand Elemis beauty products (spa girls have sales targets). Some fitness classes are free, while some, such as yoga, and kickboxing, cost $10 per class. However, being aboard will give you an opportunity to try some of the more exotic treatments (particularly some of the massages available).

Massage (including exotic massages such as Aroma Stone massage, Chakra Balancing massage and other well-being massages), facials, pedicures, and beauty salon treatments are at extra cost (massage, for example, costs about $2 per minute, plus gratuity).

Do make appointments as early as possible – aboard a ship so large, time slots go quickly.

● **For more extensive general information on what a Carnival cruise is like, see pages 113–18.**

Independence of the Seas
★★★★

Large Resort Ship: . . . . .154,407 tons	Total Crew: .1,397	Cabins (with private balcony): 842
Lifestyle: . . . . .Standard	Passengers	Cabins (wheelchair accessible): 32
Cruise Line: Royal Caribbean International	(lower beds/all berths): 3,634/4,376	Cabin Current: . . . . .110 volts
Former Names: . . . . .none	Passenger Space Ratio	Elevators: 14
Builder: . . .Kvaerner Masa-Yards (Finland)	(lower beds/all berths): 42.0/35.2	Casino (gaming tables): . . . . .Yes
Original Cost: . . . .$590 million	Crew/Passenger Ratio	Slot Machines: . . . . .Yes
Entered Service: . . . . .May 2008	(lower beds/all berths): 2.6/3.1	Swimming Pools (outdoors): 2
Registry: . . . . .The Bahamas	Navigation Officers: . . . . .European	Swimming Pools (indoors): 0
Length (ft/m): 1,112.2/339.0	Cabins (total): 1,817	Whirlpools: 6
Beam (ft/m): 184.0/56.0	Size Range (sq ft/m): 149.0–2,025.0/	Self-Service Launderette: . . . . .No
Draft (ft/m): 27.8/8.5	13.8–188.1	Dedicated Cinema/Seats: . . . . .No
Propulsion/Propellers: . . . . .diesel-electric	Cabins (outside view): 1,084	Library: . . . . .Yes
(kW)/4 pods	Cabins (interior/no view): 733	
Passenger Decks: 15	Cabins (for one person): 0	

OVERALL SCORE: 1,532 (OUT OF A POSSIBLE 2,000 POINTS)

OVERVIEW. *Independence of the Seas* (together with sister ships *Freedom of the Seas* and *Liberty of the Seas*) is the largest-ever purpose-built cruise ship, although it will be superseded in 2009 by RCI's first Genesis-class ship, *Oasis of the Seas*. It is an extension of the highly successful Voyager-class of ships, which Royal Caribbean International introduced in 1999 with the now 10-year-old *Voyager of the Seas*.

The ship's length and beam were extended. This enabled an increase in the number of cabins and passenger capacity, as well as a combined pool area 43 percent larger than the Voyager-class (but with 500 more passengers). The extra length has enabled more innovative design elements to be incorporated, such as two 16-person hot tubs cantilevered 12 feet (3.7 meters) over the sides of the ship in an adults-only Solarium. The ship's pod propulsion virtually eliminates vibration *(for further details, see page 174).*

This Freedom-class ship is essentially split into three separate areas, rather (like the Disney cruise ships – adults-only, family, or main).

The "wow" factor aboard the ship is its connection with water (of the seas) in the design of a dramatic water theme park afloat. By day, the H2O Zone (aft of the funnel) has an interactive water-themed play area for families that includes water cannons and spray fountains, water jets and ground gushers; by night the "water park" turns into a colourfully-lit sculpture garden. Meanwhile, the ship's central pool has become a sports pool, with grandstand seating and competitive games that include pole jousting. Other active sports facilities include an Everlast boxing ring, rock-climbing wall (10 ft/3 meters taller than in the Voyager-class

BERLITZ'S RATINGS

	Possible	Achieved
Ship	500	430
Accommodation	200	161
Food	400	245
Service	400	294
Entertainment	100	83
Cruise	400	319

ships), in-line skating area, an ice-skating rink, and golf simulators.

This ship has the same layout and facilities as *Freedom of the Seas* and *Liberty of the Seas.*

ACCOMMODATION. There is a wide range of suites and cabins in 14 categories and 21 price grades; the price you pay depends on the grade, from the 14-person Presidential Suite to twin-bed two person interior (no view) cabins, and interior cabins that look into an inside shopping/strolling atrium promenade. There are many family-friendly cabins, good for family reunions. For a detailed description of the accommodation, see *Freedom of the Seas.*

CUISINE. The main dining room is large and is set on three levels (each has a theme and different name: Galileo, Isaac, and Leonardo). A dramatic staircase connects all three levels, and huge, fat support pillars obstruct the sightlines from many seats. All three have the same menus and food. The dining room is all non-smoking, there are two seatings, and tables are for four, six, eight 10 or 12.

Alternative Dining Options: Alternative dining options for casual and informal meals at all hours (according to company statements) include:

● *Promenade Café*: for continental breakfast, all-day pizzas (Sorrento's), sandwiches and coffees (provided in paper cups).

● *Windjammer Café*: for casual buffet-style breakfast, lunch and light dinner (except for the cruise's last night).

● *Island Grill* (a section of the Windjammer Café): for casual dinner (no reservations necessary) featuring a grill and open kitchen.

● *Portofino:* this is the ship's "upscale" (non-smoking) Euro-Italian restaurant, open for dinner only. Reservations are required, and a there's a gratuity of $6 per person). Choices include: antipasti, soup, salad, pasta, main dish, dessert, cheese and coffee (the menu does not change during the cruise).

● *Chops Grill:* an intimate restaurant for steaks and seafood. A cover charge applies.

● *Johnny Rockets,* a retro 1950s all-day, all-night diner-style eatery that features hamburgers, hot dogs and other fast-food items, malt shakes, and jukebox hits, with both indoor and outdoor seating (all indoor tables have a mini-jukebox; dimes are provided for you to make your selection of vintage records), and all-singing, all-dancing waitresses that'll knock your socks off, if you can stand the volume. There is a cover charge.

● *Sprinkles:* for round-the-clock ice cream and yoghurt, pastries and coffee.

ENTERTAINMENT. The Showlounge is a stunning space, located at the forward end of the ship and spanning the height of five decks (with only a few slim pillars and almost no disruption of sightlines). The room has a hydraulic orchestra pit and huge stage area, together with sonic-boom loud sound, and superb lighting equipment.

In addition, the ship has an array of cabaret acts. The strongest are featured in the main showlounge, while others are presented in the Nightclub, the venue for late-night adults-only smutty comedy.

The most entertaining shows, however, are the Spectaculars on ice. There is also a television studio (in case you thought you'd need one aboard a cruise ship), located adjacent to rooms that could be used, for example, for trade show exhibit space (good for conventions at sea).

SPA/FITNESS. The Independence Day Spa is large. It includes a large aerobics room, ShipShape fitness center (with the usual stairmasters, treadmills, stationary bikes, weight machines and free weights), treatment rooms, and men's and women's sauna/steam rooms and relaxation areas.

Sample prices: AromaStone Therapy massage, $195 (75 mins); Swedish Massage, $119 (50 mins); Couples massage, $269 (50 mins); facial, $119 (50 mins), plus tip. The spa facility is operated by Steiner, whose staff will try to hard-sell you Elemis products. Some (basic) exercise classes are free, but the good ones (examples: yoga, personal training) cost extra.

More active passengers can bodyboard, go boxing (in the full-size boxing ring in the middle of the spa; the cost is $83 for a personal session, or $10 as part of a Power-boxing class), climb (the rock-climbing wall at the back of the funnel housing), jog, putt, swim, skate, step, surf, workout and more (including play basketball and volleyball) in the sports area of the ship, located mostly aft of the funnel.

● **For more extensive general information on what a Royal Caribbean cruise is like, see pages 137–42.**

Insignia
★★★★ +

Mid-Size Ship:	.30,277 tons	Passengers	Cabin Voltage:	.110 and 220
Lifestyle:	.Premium	(lower beds/all berths): .684/824	Elevators:	.4
Cruise Line:	.Oceania Cruises	Passenger Space Ratio	Casino (gaming tables):	.Yes
Former Names:	.R One	(lower beds/all berths): .44.2/36.7	Slot Machines:	.Yes
Builder:	.Chantiers de l'Atlantique	Crew/Passenger Ratio	Swimming Pools (outdoors):	.1
Original Cost:	.$150 million	(lower beds/all berths): .1.7/2.1	Swimming Pools (indoors):	.0
Entered Service:	.July 1998/Apr 2004	Navigation Officers: .European	Whirlpools: .2 (+ 1 thalassotherapy)	
Registry:	.Marshall Islands	Cabins (total): .342	Fitness Centre:	.Yes
Length (ft/m):	.593.7/181.0	Size Range (sq ft/m): .145.3 – 968.7/	Sauna/Steam Room:	.No/Yes
Beam (ft/m):	.83.5/25.5	13.5 – 90.0	Massage:	.Yes
Draft (ft/m):	.19.5/6.0	Cabins (outside view): .317	Self-Service Launderette:	.Yes
Propulsion/Propellers:	.diesel	Cabins (interior/no view): .25	Dedicated Cinema/Seats:	.No
	(18,600 kW)/2	Cabins (for one person): .0	Library:	.Yes
Passenger Decks:	.9	Cabins (with private balcony): .232		
Total Crew:	.386	Cabins (wheelchair accessible): .3		

OVERALL SCORE: 1,574 (OUT OF A POSSIBLE 2,000 POINTS)

OVERVIEW. *Insignia* (sister ships: *Nautica* and *Regatta*) was one of a series of almost identical ships originally built for the now-defunct Renaissance Cruises. The exterior design manages to balance the ship's high sides by painting the whole ship white (it previously had a dark blue hull), with a large, square white funnel. The addition of teak overlaid decking and teak lounge chairs has greatly improved what was a bland pool deck outdoors.

The interior decor is quite stunning, a throwback to ship decor of the ocean liners of the 1920s and '30s, with dark woods and warm colors, all carried out in fine taste (but a bit faux in places). This includes detailed ceiling cornices, both real and faux wrought-iron staircase railings, leather-paneled walls, trompe l'oeil ceilings, rich carpeting in hallways with an Oriental rug-look center section, and many other interesting (and expensive-looking) decorative touches. It feels like an old-world country club.

The public rooms are spread over three decks. The reception hall (lobby) features a staircase with intricate wrought-iron railings. A large observation lounge, the Horizon Bar, is located high atop ship. This has a long bar with forward views (for the barmen, that is).

There are plenty of bars – including one in each of the restaurant entrances. Perhaps the nicest is the casino bar/lounge, a beautiful room which is reminiscent of London's grand hotels and includes a martini bar. It has an inviting marble fireplace, comfortable sofas and individual chairs.

The Library is a grand Regency-style room, with a fireplace, a high, indented, trompe l'oeil ceiling, and an excellent selection of books, plus very comfortable wingback

BERLITZ'S RATINGS

	Possible	Achieved
Ship	500	417
Accommodation	200	160
Food	400	312
Service	400	295
Entertainment	100	77
Cruise	400	313

chairs with footstools, and sofas you could sleep on. Oceania@Sea is the ship's internet connect center.

There may not be marble bathroom fittings, or caviar and other expensive niceties, but the value for money is good. The dress code is "smart casual." The onboard currency is the US dollar. Gratuities are added at $10.50 per person, per day (accommodation designated as suites have an extra $3 per person charge for the butler). A 15% gratuity is added to bar and spa accounts.

There is no wrap-around promenade deck outdoors (there is, however, a small jogging track around the perimeter of the swimming pool, and port and starboard side decks). Stairways, though carpeted, are tinny. The staircase in the main, two-deck-high foyer will remind you of something similar in the 1998 blockbuster movie *Titanic*.

Oceania Cruises is a young company with a refreshing vision and desire to provide an extremely high level of food and service in an informal setting that is at once elegant yet comfortable, and that is exactly what it has achieved in a short space of time.

SUITABLE FOR: *Insignia* is best suited to couples who like good food and style, but want informality with no formal nights on board, and interesting itineraries, all at a very reasonable price well below what the luxury ships charge.

ACCOMMODATION. There are six cabin categories, and 10 price grades: 3 suite price grades; 5 outside-view cabin grades; 2 interior (no view) cabin grades. All of the standard interior (no view) and outside-view cabins (the lowest four grades) are extremely compact units, and extremely tight for two persons, particularly for cruises longer than five days. They have twin beds (or queen-sized bed), with good under-bed storage areas, personal safe, vanity desk with large mirror, good closet and drawer space (in rich, dark woods), 100% cotton bathrobe and towels, slippers, clothes brush and shoe horn. Color TVs carry a major news channel (where obtainable), plus a sports channel and round-the-clock movie channels.

Certain cabin categories (about 100 of them) qualify as "Concierge Level" accommodation, and occupants get extra goodies such as enhanced bathroom amenities, complimentary shoeshine, tote bag, cashmere throw blanket, bottle of champagne on arrival, hand-held hairdryer, priority restaurant reservations, priority embarkation and dedicated check-in desk,

Owner's Suites. The six Owner's Suites, measuring 962 sq.ft/89.3 sq.meters, provide the most spacious accommodation. They are fine, large living spaces located aft overlooking the stern on Decks 6, 7, and 8 (they are, however, subject to more movement and some vibration). They have extensive teak-floor private balconies that really are private and cannot be overlooked from the decks above. Each has an entrance foyer, living room, separate bedroom (the bed faces the sea, which can be seen through the floor-to-ceiling windows and sliding glass door), CD player (with selection of audio discs), fully tiled bathroom with Jacuzzi bathtub, and a small guest bathroom.

Vista Suites. There are four, each around 785.7 sq.ft/73 sq.meters, and located forward on Decks 5 and 6. They have extensive teak-floor private balconies that cannot be overlooked from the decks above. Each has an entrance foyer, living room, separate bedroom (the bed faces the sea, which can be seen through the floor-to-ceiling windows and sliding glass door), CD player (with selection of audio discs), and fully tiled bathroom with Jacuzzi bathtub.

Penthouse Suites. There are 52 of these (actually, they are not suites at all, but large cabins as the bedrooms aren't separate from the living areas). They do, however, measure around 322.9 sq.ft (30 sq. meters), and have a good-sized teak-floor balcony with sliding glass door (but with partial, and not full, balcony partitions) and teak deck furniture. The lounge area has a proper dining table and there is ample clothes storage space. The bathroom has a tub, shower enclosure, washbasin and toilet.

Cabins with Balcony. Cabins with private balconies (around 216 sq.ft/20 sq. meters), comprise about 66% of all cabins. They have partial, not full, balcony partitions, sliding glass doors, and only 14 cabins on Deck 6 have lifeboat-obstructed views. The living area has a refrigerated mini-bar, lounge area with breakfast table, and a balcony with teak floor, two teak chairs and a drinks table. The bathrooms, with tiled floors and plain walls, are compact, standard units, and include a shower stall with a strong, removable hand-held shower unit, hairdryer, toiletries storage shelves and retractable clothesline.

Outside View and Interior (No View) Cabins. These measure around 160–165 sq.ft (14.8–15.3 sq.meters), and have twin beds (convertible to a queen-sized bed), vanity desk, small sofa and coffee table, and bathroom with a shower enclosure with a strong, removable hand-held shower unit, hairdryer, toiletries storage shelves, retractable clothesline, washbasin, and toilet. Although they are not large, they are quite comfortable, with decent storage space.

CUISINE. Flexibility and choice are what the dining facilities aboard the Oceania ships are all about. There are four different restaurants:

● The **Grand Dining Room** has around 340 seats, and a raised central section, but the problem is the noise level: it's atrocious when the dining room is full – the effect of the low ceiling height. Being located at the ship's stern, there are large ocean-view windows on three sides (prime tables overlook the stern). The chairs are comfortable and have armrests. The menus change daily for lunch and dinner.

● The **Toscana Italian Restaurant** has 96 seats, windows along two sides, and a set menu (plus daily chef's specials).

● The cozy **Polo Grill** has 98 seats, windows along two sides and a set menu including prime steaks and seafood.

● The **Terrace Cafe** has seats for 154 indoors – not enough during cruises to cold-weather areas – and 186 outdoors. It is open for breakfast, lunch and casual dinners, when it has tapas (Tapas on the Terrace) and other Mediterranean food. As the ship's self-serve buffet restaurant, it incorporates a small pizzeria and grill. There are basic salads, a meat carving station, and a reasonable selection of cheeses.

All restaurants have open-seating dining, so you can dine when you want, with whom you wish. Reservations are needed in Toscana Restaurant and Polo Grill (but there's no extra charge), where there are mostly tables for four or six; there are few tables for two. There is a Poolside Grill Bar. All cappuccino and espresso coffees cost extra.

The food and service staff is provided by Apollo, a respected maritime catering company that has an interest in Oceania Cruises. The consultant chef is Jacques Pepin (well-known as a TV chef in America). Oceania Cruises' brochure reference to "cuisine so extraordinary it's unrivalled at sea" is hogwash – it's good, but not that good.

ENTERTAINMENT. The Regatta Lounge has entertainment, lectures and some social events. There is little entertainment due to the intensive nature of the itineraries. However, there is live music in several bars and lounges.

SPA/FITNESS/RECREATION. A lido deck has a swimming pool, and good sunbathing space, plus a thalassotherapy tub. A jogging track circles the swimming pool deck (but one deck above). The uppermost outdoors deck includes a golf driving net and shuffleboard court. The Oceania Spa consists of a beauty salon, three treatment rooms, men's and women's changing rooms, and steam room (there is no sauna). Harding Brothers operates the spa and beauty salon, and provides the staff. Note that 15% is added to your spa account, whether you like it or not.

Island Escape
★★★

Mid-Size Ship: . . . . .40,132 tons	Total Crew: 540	Cabins (with private balcony): 5
Lifestyle: . . . . .Standard	Passengers	Cabins (wheelchair accessible): 3
Cruise Line: . . . . .Island Cruises	(lower beds/all berths): 1,504/1,710	Cabin Current: . . . . .110 volts
Former Names: . . . .*Viking Serenade,*	Passenger Space Ratio	Elevators: 5
Stardancer, Scandinavia	(lower beds/all berths): 26.6/23.4	Casino (gaming tables): . . . . .Yes
Builder: . . .Dubigeon-Normandie (France)	Crew/Passenger Ratio	Slot Machines: . . . . .Yes
Original Cost: . . . .$100 million	(lower beds/all berths): 2.7/3.1	Swimming Pools (outdoors): 1
Entered Service: . . . . .Oct 1982/Mar 2002	Navigation Officers: . . . . . . .International	(magrodome)
Registry: . . . . .Bahamas	Cabins (total): 757	Swimming Pools (indoors): 0
Length (ft/m): 623.0/189.89	Size Range (sq ft/m): 143.1–398.2/	Whirlpools: 0
Beam (ft/m): 88.6/27.01	13.3–37.0	Self-Service Launderette: . . . . .No
Draft (ft/m): 23.6/7.20	Cabins (outside view): 462	Dedicated Cinema/Seats: . . . . .No
Propulsion/Propellers: diesel (19,800 kW)/2	Cabins (interior/no view): 295	Library: . . . . .Yes
Passenger Decks: 10	Cabins (for one person): 0	

OVERALL SCORE: 1,193 (OUT OF A POSSIBLE 2,000 POINTS)

OVERVIEW. This ship, built for the long-defunct Scandinavian World Cruises to operate a cruise-ferry service between New York and Freeport, Bahamas, has been extensively reconstructed to operate as a cruise ship. It has only a token bow, a fairly decent amount of open deck and sunbathing space, and a pool (more a "dip" pool) with a sliding glass dome (called a magrodome) that can be used in case of inclement weather. The ship suffers from having an extremely boxy, angular shape with a short, stubby funnel, and has a "sponson" skirt that goes around the stern at the waterline (this is required for stability reasons). *Island Escape* underwent a $75 million reconstruction in 1991, when Royal Caribbean International (then Royal Caribbean Cruise Line) took over the ship.

In 2001 it transferred to Island Cruises, a new joint venture between the UK's First Choice Holidays and Royal Caribbean International, and began cruising in 2002 as *Island Escape*. Inside, the accommodation is mostly located forward, while the public rooms are mostly located in the aft third of the ship. There is a decent enough array of public rooms and facilities, including six bars and a lounge/ discotheque that is cantilevered around the funnel with excellent ocean views. The decor features tasteful colors and furnishings of decent quality, but some have seen better days. Other facilities include a cyber center (for internet connection and email), and a coffee/pastry shop with three internet computer stations. The ceilings in many public areas and accommodation hallways are quite low (a legacy of the ship's original role as a cruise-ferry).

The ship, now more than 20 years old, has a dual existence: in summer it operates specifically for the British

BERLITZ'S RATINGS		
	Possible	Achieved
Ship	500	293
Accommodation	200	111
Food	400	219
Service	400	259
Entertainment	100	60
Cruise	400	251

family market, providing one-week cruises. In other words, this is cruising in utterly casual, comfortable, unpretentious surroundings that are quite upbeat, with a "totally relaxed" ambience that appeals to the young at heart. Children should enjoy themselves with "Palmy" is a children's character they can even eat with), and there are lots of well-supervised activities.

Vacations can be extended with a "cruise-and-stay" package, with special pricing to make your extended break more affordable. If you book two cruises back-to-back, however, some of the entertainment may be repeated for the second week.

Island Cruises provides scheduled or charter air service (through its own Air 2000 fleet – but do expect cramped "knees-up" seats) to get you to and from the ship (from the UK). Island Cruises' airport transfer and baggage handling/delivery operation makes for a hassle-free start to your cruise vacation. Gratuities are included. The onboard currency is the British pound.

The ship spends winters in Brazil (operating short cruises for the young, mainly Brazilian market), when the locals arise late, dance and gyrate (and smoke) until dawn (the onboard currency being the Brazilian real). Some onboard concessions and entertainment change for the winter season.

Background music is played almost everywhere inside the ship (and on deck around the pool), making it difficult to find quiet spots to relax, chill out and simply read a book. Passenger participation events tend to be quite amateurish (although this opinion depends on what you compare them to). Smokers are everywhere.

Standing in line for embarkation, disembarkation, shore tenders and for self-serve buffet meals can be an inevitable aspect of cruising aboard all ships carrying more than 1,000 passengers.

SUITABLE FOR: *Island Escape* is best suited to young (and young-minded) couples and singles of all ages, families with children and teenagers, who like to mingle in a fairly large ship setting with plenty of life and entertainment for everyone, with food that is quantity rather than quality, delivered with friendly service that lacks polish, but the price is right – particularly for a first cruise.

ACCOMMODATION. There are just six categories, so choosing the right one for you shouldn't be difficult. The price will depend on grade, size and location. The cabins, however, are quite small, with little closet space, so take as few clothes as possible. They are moderately appointed with soft furnishings that are very cheerful, with upbeat colors.

Almost all cabins have twin beds that can be pushed together to form a queen-sized bed (some cabins have an L-shaped arrangement, with immovable beds). No matter what grade of accommodation you choose, all feature a television, telephone, and three-channel radio, dressing table and mirror. There are many interior (no view) cabins, and drawers and other storage space is extremely limited. If you'd like to have more space, it's best to go for one of the suite categories.

The cabin bathrooms are really small, so you can expect to dance with the shower curtain, particularly if you have a larger than average sized body (only some of the accommodation designated as suites have a bathtub). Eleven outside-view cabins have even numbers, and all interior (no view) cabins have odd numbers. Also, if you are cruising with young children, there's almost no space for baby strollers. If, after looking at the deck plans, you want to book a specific cabin number, it currently costs £20 per cabin extra. Some cabins have extra Pullman upper berths (good for families with young children). An in-cabin room service menu is available, but all items cost extra.

Island Suite: The "Island Suite", towards the aft of the ship on the port side, provides the largest accommodation. Although it doesn't have a balcony, it's relatively spacious. A bathtub and shower are provided in the bathroom, and there's a walk-in closet, and mini-bar/refrigerator.

Club Suites: Five other cabins (with balconies) are designated as suites. These are at the stern and have great views over the wash created by the ship's propellers, although they may be subject to a little vibration now and then. A bathtub and shower are provided in the marble-clad bathroom, and there's a walk-in closet in the sleeping area, and mini-bar/refrigerator and entertainment center in the living room. Additionally, another two suites (without balcony or bathtub) are located in the forward third of the ship one deck lower than the aft-facing suites, but with the same facilities.

CUISINE. The Island Restaurant, the ship's main dining room, has ocean-view windows on two sides, and upbeat decor (there are tables for two, four, six or eight). It is open for breakfast, lunch and dinner; you can serve yourself from the buffets, or be served by a waiter. It's a very casual open-seating arrangement, and so waiters do not get to know your preferences. Although there is much repetition of salad items (for lunch), there are plenty of main dish and dessert choices. The menus contain a wide variety of foods, most of which is well presented and has taste.

Oasis, a smaller (more intimate and exclusive, and quieter) restaurant, is located one deck below the Island Restaurant. This à la carte (extra cost) dining spot, with seats for two or four, is open only for dinner, with full waiter service for all courses. Reservations are required; the ship's officers eat here, and you are welcome to join them, or invite them to your table. The wine list is quite typical of a high street eatery, with European prices that provide quite good value for money.

The ceiling is quite low in both restaurants, which provides a sense of intimacy, but can increase the noise level.

For breakfast, lunch and dinner (in fact, 24 hours a day), there is another place to go – the Beachcomber Cafe. This is even more casual, and is ideal for grabbing a bite to eat while "taking the sun" on the open decks. Again, it's a self-serve buffet, with food constantly being refreshed. Tea and coffee are provided at a beverage station, with plastic cups and mugs. Additionally, there's the Café Brazil for pastries, extremely sinful cakes and pastries, and a range of espresso/cappuccino coffees, all at extra cost.

ENTERTAINMENT. The Ocean Theater is a single level showlounge, with banquette and individual seating surrounding a "thrust" stage. Although it is a comfortable room, several pillars obstruct sight lines from some seats.

A resident troupe of young, enthusiastic singer/dancers provide the low-budget revue-style "shows" that are, at best, slightly amateurish, with weak click tracks but lots of color. In addition, visiting cabaret acts (typically strong singers, magicians, comedians and others) are presented, both in their own shows and as the middle of a "pie" that includes the ship's resident troupe.

There is a main ship's band and several small musical units and pianists to provide live music for dancing and listening in the bars and lounges. In addition, a throbbing discotheque is provided for those who enjoy such things.

SPA/FITNESS. The Ship Shape Hair and Beauty Spa is surprisingly good for the size of the ship. There are treatment rooms for massage, separate saunas and changing rooms for men and women, and a large beauty salon. The gymnasium itself is quite large and contains lots of muscle-pumping, body toning equipment. It is located just aft of the main swimming pool on the port side of the ship, and contains some high-energy muscle-pumping equipment.

Spa staff are provided by Harding Brothers (a concession), and treatments offered include massages, aromatherapy facials, manicures, pedicures, and hair beautifying treatments. Examples: Massage, £45 (50 minutes); Back, Neck and Shoulders Massage, £30 (20 minutes); Marine Algae Body Wrap, £40; Hydrodermie Facial, £45 (75 minutes). Do book appointments for beauty/body treatments early, as time slots go quickly.

Island Princess
★★★★

Large Resort Ship: ....91,627 tons	Total Crew: 900	Cabins (with private balcony): 727
Lifestyle: ....Standard	Passengers	Cabins (wheelchair accessible): 20
Cruise Line: ....Princess Cruises	(lower beds/all berths): 1,974/2,590	Cabin Current: ....110 volts
Former Names: ....none	Passenger Space Ratio	Elevators: 14
Builder: Chantiers de l'Atlantique (France)	(lower beds/all berths): 46.4/35.3	Casino (gaming tables): ....Yes
Original Cost: ....$360 million	Crew/Passenger Ratio	Slot Machines: ....Yes
Entered Service: ....June 2003	(lower beds/all berths): 2.1/2.8	Swimming Pools (outdoors): 2
Registry: ....Bermuda	Navigation Officers: ....British	(+ 1 splash pool)
Length (ft/m): 964.5/294.0	Cabins (total): 987	Swimming Pools (indoors): 0
Beam (ft/m): 105.6/32.2	Size Range (sq ft/m): 156–470.0/14.4–43.6	Whirlpools: 5
Draft (ft/m): 26/7.9	Cabins (outside view): 879	Self-Service Launderette: ....Yes
Propulsion/Propellers: .....gas turbine/2	Cabins (interior/no view): 108	Dedicated Cinema/Seats: ....No
Passenger Decks: 11	Cabins (for one person): 0	Library: ....Yes

---

BERLITZ'S OVERALL SCORE: 1,542 (OUT OF A POSSIBLE 2,000 POINTS)

OVERVIEW. *Island Princess* (sister ship to *Coral Princess*) has an instantly recognizable funnel due to two jet engine-like pods that sit high up on its structure. Four diesel engines provide the generating power. Electrical power is provided by a combination of four diesel and one gas turbine (CODAG) unit; the diesel engines are located in the engine room, while the gas turbine unit is located in the ship's funnel housing. The ship also has three bow thrusters and three stern thrusters.

The ship's interior layout is similar to that of the *Grand Princess*-class ships (but with two decks full of public rooms, lounges and bars instead of just one), and sensibly features three major stair towers for passengers (good from the safety and evacuation viewpoint), with plenty of elevators for easy access. For a large ship, the layout is quite user-friendly, and less disjointed than many ships of a similar size. Because of its slim beam, the ship is able to transit the Panama Canal, thus providing greater flexibility in deployment than the *Grand Princess*-class ships.

New facilities for a Princess Cruises ship include a flower shop (where you can order flowers and Godiva chocolates for cabin delivery – good for a birthday or anniversary), cigar lounge (Churchill Lounge), martini bar (Crooners). Also different is a casino with a London theme.

What is very civilized is the fact that sunbathers who use the "quiet" deck forward of the mast have their own splash pool, so they won't have to go down two decks to get to the two main pools. Strollers will like the ship's full walk-around exterior promenade deck.

Surfers can find an AOL Internet Cafe conveniently located on the top level of the four-deck-high lobby. Meanwhile, it's good to see that the dreaded "fine arts" get

BERLITZ'S RATINGS

	Possible	Achieved
Ship	500	434
Accommodation	200	154
Food	400	261
Service	400	294
Entertainment	100	85
Cruise	400	314

their own room, so that paintings to be sold during the art auctions are not spread all over the ship. Adjacent is the Wedding Chapel (a live web-cam can relay ceremonies via the internet). The ship's captain can legally marry (American) couples, due to the ship's registry and a special dispensation (this should, however, be verified when in the planning stage, and may depend on where you live). Princess Cruises offers three wedding packages – Pearl, Emerald, Diamond; the fee includes registration and official marriage certificate. The Wedding Chapel can host "renewal of vows" ceremonies (there is a charge for these).

ACCOMMODATION. There are 33 price categories, in six types: 16 Suites with balcony (470 sq. ft/43.6 sq. meters); 184 Mini-Suites with balcony (285–302 sq. ft/26.4–28.0 sq. meters); 8 Mini-Suites without balcony (300 sq. ft/27.8 sq. meters; 527 Outside-View Cabins with balcony (217–232 sq. ft/ 20.1–21.5 sq. meters); 144 Standard Outside-view Cabins (162 sq. ft/15 sq. meters); Interior (no view) Cabins (156 sq. ft/144.5 sq. meters). There are also 20 wheelchair-accessible cabins (217–374 sq. ft/20.1–34.7 sq. meters). The price you pay will depend on grade, size and location. Note that all measurements are approximate. Almost all of the outside-view cabins have a private balcony. Some cabins can accommodate a third, or third and fourth person (good for families with children). Some cabins on Emerald Deck (Deck 8) have a view obstructed by lifeboats.

Suites: There are just 16 suites and, although none are really that large (compared to such ships as *Norwegian Dawn* and *Norwegian Star*, where the largest measure a whopping 5,350 sq. ft/497 sq. meters, for example), each has a private balcony. All are named after islands (mostly coral-based islands in the Indian Ocean and Pacific Ocean). All suites are located on either Deck 9 or Deck 10. In a departure from many ships, *Island Princess* does not have any suites or cabins with a view of the ship's stern. There are also four Premium Suites, located sensibly in the center of the ship, adjacent to a bank of six lifts. Six other suites (called Verandah Suites) are located further aft.

All Accommodation: Suites and cabins have a refrigerator, personal safe, television (with audio channels), hairdryer, satellite-dial telephone, and twin beds that convert to a queen-sized bed (there are a few exceptions). All accommodation has a bathroom with shower enclosure and toilet. Accommodation designated as suites and mini-suites (there are seven price categories) have a bathtub and separate shower enclosure, and two TV sets.

All passengers receive turndown service and chocolates on pillows each night, bathrobes (on request) and toiletry kits. Most "outside-view" cabins on Emerald Deck have views obstructed by the lifeboats. There are no cabins for singles. Princess Cruises typically includes CNN, CNBC, ESPN and TNT on the in-cabin color television system (when available). There are no butlers – even for the top-grade suites. Cabin attendants have too many cabins to look after (typically 20), which does not translate to fine personal service.

CUISINE. There are two main dining rooms, named Bordeaux and Provence; they are located in the forward section of the ship on the two lowest passenger decks, with the galley all the way forward so it doesn't intersect public spaces (an example of good design). Both are almost identical in design and layout (the ceilings are quite low and make the rooms appear more cramped than they are), and have plenty of intimate alcoves and cozy dining spots, with tables for two, four, six, or eight. There are two seatings for dinner, while breakfast and lunch are on an open seating basis; you may have to stand in line at peak times. Both dining rooms are non-smoking.

Horizon Court is the ship's casual 24-hour eatery, and is located in the forward section of Lido Deck, with superb ocean views. Several self-serve counters provide an array of food for breakfast and lunch buffets, while each evening, bistro-style casual dinners are available.

Alternative (Extra Charge) Eateries: There are two "alternative" dining rooms, Sabatini's and the Bayou Cafe, both enclosed. They incur an extra charge, and you must make a reservation. Sabatini's is an Italian eatery, with colorful tiled Mediterranean-style decor; it has Italian-style pizzas and pastas, with a variety of sauces, as well as Italian-style entrées (including tiger prawns and lobster tail), all provided with flair and entertainment by the waiters. The food that is both creative and tasty (with seriously sized portions). There is a cover charge of $15 per person, for lunch or dinner (on sea days only).

The Bayou Cafe is open for lunch and dinner, and has a cover charge of $10 per person (including a free Hurricane cocktail), and evokes the charm of New Orleans' French Quarter, complete with wrought-iron decoration. The

Bayou Cafe serves Creole food (with platters such as Peel 'n' Eat Shrimp Piquante, Sausage Grillades, Oysters Sieur de Bienville and N'Awlins Crawfish "Mud Bug" Bisque delivered to the table when you arrive). Popular entrées include Seafood Gumbo, and Chorizo Jambalaya with fresh seafood and traditional dried spice mixes, as well as Cajun Grill items such as Smothered Alligator Ribs, Flambeaux Grilled Jumbo Prawns, Corn Meal Fried Catfish, Blackened Chicken Brochette, and Red Pepper Butter Broiled Lobster; desserts include sweet potato pie and banana whiskey pound cake. The room has a small stage, with baby grand piano, and live jazz is also part of the dining scenario.

Other outlets include La Pâtisserie, in the ship's reception lobby, a coffee, cakes and pastries spot and good for informal meetings. There's also a Pizzeria, hamburger grill, and an ice cream bar (extra charge for the ice cream). Meanwhile, puffers and sippers should enjoy Churchill's, a neat cigar and cognac lounge, cleverly sited near a neat little hideaway bar called the Rat Pack Bar.

ENTERTAINMENT. The Princess Theatre is two decks high, and, unusually, there is much more seating in the upper level than on the main floor below. A second entertainment lounge (Universe Lounge) is designed more for cabaret-style features. It also has two levels, and three separate stages – so non-stop entertainment can be provided without constant set-ups. Some 50 of the room's seats are equipped with a built-in laptop computer. The room is also used for cooking demonstrations (it has a full kitchen set), and other life enrichment participation activities.

Princess Cruises always provides plenty of live music in bars and lounges, with a wide mix of light classical, jazz, and dance music, from solo entertaining pianists to showbands, and volume is normally kept to an acceptable level.

Feel in need of education? Now you can learn aboard ship, with "ScholarShip@Sea," a new Princess Cruises program, which debuted aboard this vessel. It includes about 20 courses per cruise (six on any given day at sea). Although all introductory classes are free, if you want to continue any chosen subject in a smaller setting, there are fees. There are four core subjects: Culinary Arts, Visual/Creative Arts, Photography, and Computer Technology. A full culinary demonstration kitchen set has been built into the Universe Lounge (this can also play host to wine tasting), and a pottery studio complete with kiln has been built into the ship as part of the facilities.

SPA/FITNESS. The Lotus Spa is located aft on one of the ship's uppermost decks. It contains men's and women's saunas, steam rooms, changing rooms, relaxation area, beauty salon, aerobics exercise room and gymnasium with aft-facing ocean-views packed with the latest high-tech muscle-pumping, cardio-vascular equipment. There are several large rooms for individual treatments.

● **For more extensive general information about the Princess Cruises experience, see pages 134–37.**

Island Sky
★★★★

Boutique Ship: . . . . .4,280 tons	Passenger Decks: 5	Cabins (for one person): 0
Lifestyle: . . . . .Standard	Total Crew: 66	Cabins (with private balcony): 4
Cruise Line: . . . . .Noble Caledonia	Passengers	Cabins (wheelchair accessible): 0
Former Names: . . . . .Regina Renaissance,	(lower beds/all berths): 112/122	Cabin Voltage: .110
Renaissance VII	Passenger Space Ratio	Lifts: 1
Builder: . . . . . . .Nuovi Cantieri Appaunia	(lower beds/all berths): 38.2/38.2	Casino (gaming tables): . . . . .No
(Italy)	Crew/Passenger Ratio	Slot Machines: .No
Original Cost: . . . .$25 milltion	(lower beds/all berths): 1.7/1.8	Swimming Pools (outdoors): 0
Entered Service: . . . .Dec 1991/May 2004	Navigation Officers: . . . . .Norwegian/	Swimming Pools (indoors): 0
Registry: . . . . .Mauritius	European	Whirlpools: 1
Length (ft/m): 297.2/90.6	Cabins (total): .59	Self-Service Launderette: . . . . .No
Beam (ft/m): 50.1/15.3	Size Range (sq ft/m): . . . . . 234.6 – 353.0/	Dedicated Cinema/Seats: . . . . .No
Draft (ft/m): 12.9/2.95	21.8 – 32.8	Library: . . . . .Yes
Propulsion/Propellers: . . . . .diesel	Cabins (outside view): 59	
(5000kW)/2	Cabins (interior/no view): 0	

OVERALL SCORE: 1,540 (OUT OF A POSSIBLE 2,000 POINTS)

OVERVIEW. *Island Sky*, refurbished in 2004 before being chartered to Noble Caledonia, has contemporary mega-yacht looks and handsome styling, with twin flared funnels give this ship a smart profile, and a "ducktail" (sponson) stern provides good stability and seagoing comfort. This ship was originally built as one of a series of eight similar ships for the now-defunct Renaissance Cruises. The ship is owned by a Bahamas-based company, and operated by Noble Caledonia year-round in an attractive destination-specific region renowned for wildlife. There is one teak walk-around promenade deck outdoors, and a reasonable amount of open deck and sunbathing space.

A "baby island" tender hangs off the aft deck and acts as ship-to-shore transportation. Some equipment for watersports is carried, and active types can enjoy wind surfing, scuba diving and snorkeling, deep sea fishing, mountain biking, golfing, and hiking.

Inside, you will find an elegant interior design, with polished wood-finish paneling throughout. There is also a very small library with two internet-connect workstations.

This vessel is very comfortable and totally inviting, and features warm-weather cruising in an area devoid of large cruise ships (the South Indian Ocean). The itinerary includes two uninhabited islands in the Cargados group. Although this intimate ship is not up to the standard of a Seabourn or Silversea vessel, it will provide a good cruise experience at a moderate cost. Gratuities are appreciated but not required. The onboard currency is the US dollar.

SUITABLE FOR: Best suited to seasoned travelers who like

BERLITZ'S RATINGS		
	Possible	Achieved
Ship	500	392
Accommodation	200	159
Food	400	303
Service	400	306
Entertainment	n/a	n/a
Cruise	500	380

a relaxed lifestyle combined with good food and service, and an itinerary that says "get away from it all, but in comfort."

ACCOMMODATION. The spacious cabins (four were added in the 2003 refit) combine highly polished imitation rosewood paneling with lots of mirrors and hand-crafted Italian furniture, lighted walk-in closets, three-sided vanity mirrors (in fact there are a lot of mirrored surfaces in the decor), and just about everything you need, including a TV set and VCR, and a refrigerator).

The bathrooms are extremely compact units; they have real teakwood floors and marble vanities, and shower enclosures (none have bathtubs, not even the owner's suite).

CRUISE. The dining room operates with an open seating for all meals. It is small but quite smart, with tables for two, four, six, and eight. You simply sit where you like, with whom you like, and at what time you like.

The meals are self-service, buffet-style cold foods for breakfast and lunch, with hot foods chosen from a table menu and served properly. The dining room operation works well. The food quality, choice, and presentation are all very decent.

ENTERTAINMENT. There is no formal entertainment in the main lounge, the venue for all social activities (six pillars obstruct the sightlines to the small stage area anyway).

SPA/FITNESS/RECREATION. Water sports facilities include an aft platform, sailfish, snorkel equipment, and zodiacs.

Island Star
★★★ +

Mid-Size Ship:	46,811 tons	Total Crew:	.573	Cabins (with private balcony):	.68
Lifestyle:	.Standard	Passengers		Cabins (wheelchair accessible):	.5
Cruise Line:	.Island Cruises	(lower beds/all berths):	.1,506/1,875	Cabin Current:	.110 volts
Former Names:	.*Horizon*	Passenger Space Ratio		Elevators:	.7
Builder:	.Meyer Werft (Germany)	(lower beds/all berths):	.31.0/24.9	Casino (gaming tables):	.Yes
Original Cost:	.$185 million	Crew/Passenger Ratio		Slot Machines:	.Yes
Entered Service:	.May 1990/Dec 2005	(lower beds/all berths):	.2.6/3.2	Swimming Pools (outdoors):	.2
Registry:	.The Bahamas	Navigation Officers:	.International	Swimming Pools (indoors):	.0
Length (ft/m):	.681.1/207.6	Cabins (total):	.753	Whirlpools:	.0
Beam (ft/m):	.95.1/29.0	Size Range (sq ft/m):	.114.1–383.2/	Self-Service Launderette:	.No
Draft (ft/m):	.23.6/7.2		10.6/35.6	Dedicated Cinema/Seats:	.No
Propulsion/Propellers:	.diesel	Cabins (outside view):	.587	Library:	.Yes
	(19,960kW)/2	Cabins (interior/no view):	.165		
Passenger Decks:	.10	Cabins (for one person):	.0		

OVERALL SCORE: 1,328 (OUT OF A POSSIBLE 2,000 POINTS)

OVERVIEW. *Island Star* is a reasonably handsome, contemporary ship (it was the first brand-new ship ordered by former owners Celebrity Cruises), its sharp angles softened by an all-white exterior and large logo. There is a good amount of open deck space, two swimming pools (one designated for children), and cushioned pads are provided for poolside sunloungers. The ship underwent an extensive refit program in 2005, when more cabins were added, and balconies were added to cabins on Sapphire Deck (10).

Inside, the ship has good passenger flow, the public rooms (there are several lounges and bars to choose from) are quite spacious and many have high ceilings. The Sundowner Casino is for gaming, and there are duty-free shops for jewelry, liquor, and perfumes. The decor is fresh and upbeat, with plenty of color, and wood paneling creates a warm ambiance. A two-deck-high lobby (housing the reception desk, and shore excursion desk, has a contemporary, yet "retro" feel to it.

Island Star delivers a well-defined British cruise experience during the summer, when the onboard currency is the British pound at a very modest price. During the winter, the ship sails in South America, catering to Argentinian and Brazilian passengers. Vacations can be extended with a "cruise-and-stay" package, with special pricing to make your extended break more affordable.

If you book two cruises back-to-back, however, some of the entertainment may be repeated for the second week. Note also that doors to public restrooms and the outdoor decks are heavy (the public restrooms themselves are plain and could do with some warmer decor). Background music is played almost everywhere inside the ship (and on deck

BERLITZ'S RATINGS		
	Possible	Achieved
Ship	500	346
Accommodation	200	150
Food	400	236
Service	400	263
Entertainment	100	63
Cruise	400	270

around the pool), making it difficult to find quiet spots to relax, chill out and simply read a book.

Passenger participation events tend to be quite amateurish (although this opinion depends on what you compare them to). Smokers are everywhere. You may need to take converters for any electrical appliances, because the current is 110 volts (US flat-pin plugs).

Basic gratuities are included, and 15% is automatically added to all bar and wine accounts.

SUITABLE FOR: *Island Star* is best suited to adult couples, singles and families with children seeking a large contemporary ship with good itineraries, decent food and good service from a well-trained crew that cares and delivers an onboard product that is above average.

ACCOMMODATION. There are 12 price grades, including outside-view suites and cabins, and interior (no view) cabins, but even the smallest cabin is .quite spacious and well appointed. The price will depend on the grade, size and location (the higher the deck, the higher the cost); note that several outside view cabins have lifeboat-obstructed views. Strangely, cabin numbers are the opposite of normal maritime tradition (which dictates that even-numbered cabins are on the port, or left side of the ship – but here they are on the starboard, or right side). Note that room service typically incurs an extra charge (example: £4.50 for Continental Breakfast, and no hot food items). There's also a weekly charge of £10 for use of the personal safe in your cabin.

Standard Cabins: All standard outside-view and interior (no view) cabins have good quality fittings with wood accenting, are tastefully decorated and of an above-average size, with an excellent amount of closet and drawer space, and reasonable insulation between cabins (depending on the location). All have twin beds that convert to a queen-sized bed, and a good amount of closet and drawer space.

The bathrooms have a generous shower area, although the bathroom towels are a little small, as is storage space for personal toiletry items. The lowest-grade outside-view cabins have a porthole, but all others have picture windows. **Grand Island Suites:** Located on Platinum Deck (Deck 11), these two suites have a private balcony. The suites have a separate bedroom (with European duvet), lounge with sofa bed and audio-visual control center. The bathroom is large and comes with a whirlpool bathtub and an integral shower. **Island Suites/Junior Suites** (on Deck 10/11) are tastefully furnished, but a little smaller than the Grand Island Suites. They have a generous amount of drawer and other storage space, separate sleeping area plus a lounge area. They also have large bathrooms.

CUISINE. The Island Restaurant is set on a single level, but its central section, which houses the self-serve buffet counters and food islands, is raised. It is large, yet there is also a sense of intimacy; there are tables for two, four, six or eight, and open seatings. The chairs do not have armrests, due to space limitations.

The wine list is quite typical of a high street eatery, with European prices that provide quite good value for money. Two small alternative (extra cost items) dining spots adjacent to the Island Restaurant are Oasis, and The Steak House (reservations are required in these extra-cost dining spots; both have full waiter service for all courses.

The Beachcomber Café is the place for al fresco, bistro-like eating (open 24 hours a day – although, as in most buffets, hot food items are seldom hot). There's also The Grill, an alfresco outdoors eatery for fast-food items. The Harbour Café is the place to go for informal coffees and pastries.

ENTERTAINMENT. The two-level Ocean Theatre is a two-deck high showlounge that doubles as a movie theater; it has side balconies on the upper level, and good sightlines from most seats. The room has a large stage (for this size of ship), decent lighting and sound equipment, and shows are aimed at a general family audience.

A resident troupe of young, enthusiastic singer/dancers provide the low-budget revue-style "shows" that are, at best, slightly amateurish, with weak click tracks but lots of color. In addition, visiting cabaret acts (typically strong singers, magicians, comedians and others) are presented, both in their own shows and as the middle of a "pie" that includes the ship's resident troupe.

There is a main ship's band and several small musical units and pianists to provide live music for dancing and listening in the bars and lounges. In addition, a throbbing discotheque is provided for the hearing-impaired.

SPA/FITNESS. The Island Spa/Fitness Center is located aft of the funnel, and facilities include a gymnasium with ocean views and the high-tech muscle-pump equipment, an exercise area, several therapy treatment rooms, and men's/women's sauna.

Ivory
★★

Small Ship: . . . . 12,609 tons	Passenger Decks: 8	Cabins (for one person): 1
Lifestyle: . . . . Standard	Total Crew: 280	Cabins (with private balcony): 0
Cruise Line: . . . . Louis Cruise Lines	Passengers	Cabins (wheelchair accessible): 0
Former Names: . . . . Aegean II, Ivory,	(lower beds/all berths): 496/701	Cabin Current: . . . . 220 volts
Ithaca, Ausonia	Passenger Space Ratio	Elevators: 1
Builder: Cantieri Riuniti dell' Adriatico (Italy)	(lower beds/all berths): 25.4/17.9	Casino (gaming tables): . . . . Yes
Original Cost: . . . . n/a	Crew/Passenger Ratio	Slot Machines: . . . . Yes
Entered Service: . . . Sept 1957/Apr 2007	(lower beds/all berths): 1.8/2.5	Swimming Pools (outdoors): 1
Registry: . . . . Greece	Navigation Officers: . . . . Greek	Swimming Pools (indoors): 0
Length (ft/m): 522.5/159.26	Cabins (total): 248	Whirlpools: 1
Beam (ft/m): 69.8/21.29	Size Range (sq ft/m): 69.9–269.1/	Self-Service Launderette: . . . . No
Draft (ft/m): 21.4/6.54	6.5–25.0	Dedicated Cinema/Seats: Yes/125
Propulsion/Propellers: . . . . steam turbine	Cabins (outside view): 152	Library: . . . . Yes
(12,799kW)/2	Cabins (interior/no view): 96	

BERLITZ'S OVERALL SCORE: 885 (OUT OF A POSSIBLE 2,000 POINTS)

OVERVIEW. This all-white ship, a former ocean liner, has a classic 1950s steamship profile, with a large, single funnel placed amidships. There is a decent amount of open deck and sunning space although the swimming pool is tiny; it's really just a "dip" pool. The ship was bought by Louis Cruise Lines in 1997, and underwent extensive refurbishing and upgrading in 1998.

Most public rooms are on one deck, and so it's easy to find one's way around. The number of public lounges and rooms is, however, limited: main lounge, library, cinema, boutique. The Majorca Lounge – the main showlounge – is pleasantly decorated, although the sight lines to the stage are poor; the seats on the raised sections on the port and starboard sides are slightly better.

There is a small nightclub, casino, duty-free shop, an enclosed "winter garden" lounge/reading area on the starboard side, and a cinema.

Public rooms have many small, uncomfortable "tub" chairs. Many passengers are heavy smokers and it is difficult to avoid them. The ship has a narrow gangway, which can be quite steep in some ports.

SUITABLE FOR: Ivory is best suited to adult couples and singles looking for a basic cruise holiday, in a ship that is more traditional than modern, and doesn't have the latest facilities. This could be good for a first cruise experience, in a setting that is comfortable, not luxurious, and at a price that is low but provides fair value for money.

BERLITZ'S RATINGS

	Possible	Achieved
Ship	500	190
Accommodation	200	87
Food	400	184
Service	400	212
Entertainment	100	44
Cruise	400	168

ACCOMMODATION. From "suites" to standard interior and outside-view cabins, all are small and compact, yet reasonably comfortable, in 10 price grades. They have all the basics including a private bathroom and adequate closet space for frugal packers, and drawer space is limited. The uppermost grades have a full-sized bathtub (two suites have whirlpool baths); others have showers. There are several family cabins. Some interior and outside standard cabins have upper and lower berths.

CUISINE. The no-smoking Pharaoh's Restaurant, high up on the same deck as most of the few public rooms, has good ocean views from large picture windows. There are tables for four, six or eight, and meals are in two seatings. The international cuisine provides a good mix of Continental fare, with some regional Mediterranean specialties and British favorites. The selection of fruits and cheeses is limited. The basic wine list provides an inexpensive range and a decent choice.

ENTERTAINMENT. The Discovery Showlounge is a single-level room designed for cabaret acts and lectures, not lavish shows. Pillars obstruct some sightlines. The entertainment is low-key and low-budget. Several musical units provide music for dancing and listening.

SPA/FITNESS. There is a tiny fitness room with old equipment, and a sauna.

Jewel of the Seas
★★★★

Large Resort Ship: ....90,090 tons	Passenger Decks: 12	Cabins (for one person): 0
Lifestyle: ....Standard	Total Crew: 858	Cabins (with private balcony): 577
Cruise Line: ....Royal Caribbean	Passengers	Cabins (wheelchair accessible): 14
International	(lower beds/all berths): 2,110/2,500	(8 with private balcony)
Former Names: ....none	Passenger Space Ratio	Cabin Voltage: 110
Builder: ....Meyer Werft (Germany)	(lower beds/all berths): 42.9/36.0	Elevators: 9
Original Cost: ....$350 million	Crew/Passenger Ratio	Casino (gaming tables): ....Yes
Entered Service: ....June 2004	(lower beds/all berths): 2.4/2.9	Slot Machines: ....Yes
Registry: ....The Bahamas	Navigation Officers: ....Norwegian	Swimming Pools (outdoors): 2
Length (ft/m): 961.9/293.2	Cabins (total): 1,055	Swimming Pools (indoors): 0
Beam (ft/m): 105.6/32.2	Size Range (sq ft/m): 165.8–1,216.3/	Whirlpools: 3
Draft (ft/m): 27.8/8.5	15.4–113.0	Self-Service Launderette: ....No
Propulsion/Propellers: .....Gas turbine/2	Cabins (outside view): 817	Dedicated Cinema/Seats: Yes/40
azimuthing pods (20 MW each)	Cabins (interior/no view): 238	Library: ....Yes

OVERALL SCORE: 1,522 (OUT OF A POSSIBLE 2,000 POINTS)

OVERVIEW. *Jewel of the Seas* is the fourth Royal Caribbean International ship to use gas and steam turbine power (sister ships: *Brilliance of the Seas, Radiance of the Seas* and *Serenade of the Seas*) instead of the conventional diesel or diesel-electric combination. Pod propulsion power *(see page 174 for description)* is also provided. As is common aboard almost all new cruise ships today, the navigation bridge is of the fully enclosed type. In the very front of the ship is a helipad, which also acts as a viewing platform.

Jewel of the Seas is a streamlined, contemporary ship, and has a two-deck-high wrap-around structure in the forward section of the funnel. Along the starboard side, a central glass wall protrudes, giving great views (cabins with balconies occupy the space directly opposite on the port side). The gently rounded stern has nicely tiered decks, which gives the ship an extremely well-balanced look.

Inside, the decor is contemporary, yet elegant, bright and cheerful, designed for young, active, hip types. The artwork is quite eclectic (so there should be something for all tastes), and provides a spectrum and a half of color works.

The ship's interior focal point is a nine-deck high atrium lobby that has glass-walled elevators (on the port side of the ship only) that travel through 12 decks, face the sea and provide a link with nature and the ocean. The Centrum (as the atrium is called) has several public rooms connected to it: the guest relations and shore excursions desks, a Lobby Bar, Champagne Bar, the Library, Royal Caribbean Online (an internet-connect center), the Concierge Club, and a Crown & Anchor Lounge. A great view can be had of the atrium by looking down through the flat glass dome high above it.

Other facilities include a delightful but very small library,

BERLITZ'S RATINGS

	Possible	Achieved
Ship	500	428
Accommodation	200	158
Food	400	248
Service	400	298
Entertainment	100	81
Cruise	400	309

a Champagne Bar, and a large Schooner Bar that houses maritime art in an integral art gallery. Gambling devotees should enjoy the rather large, noisy and colorful Casino Royale. There's also a small dedicated screening room for movies (with space for two wheelchairs), as well as a 194-seat conference center, and a business center.

This ship also contains a Viking Crown Lounge (a Royal Caribbean International trademark), a large structure set around the base of the ship's funnel. It functions as an observation lounge during the daytime (with views forward over the swimming pool). In the evening, the space becomes a futuristic, high-energy dance club, as well as a more intimate and relaxed entertainment venue for softer mood music and "black box" theater.

Royal Caribbean Online is a dedicated computer center that has 12 PCs with high-speed internet access for sending and receiving email, located in a semi-private setting.

Youth facilities include Adventure Ocean, an "edu-tainment" area with four separate age-appropriate sections for junior passengers: Aquanaut Center (for ages 3–5); Explorer Center (6–8); Voyager Center (9–12); and the Optix Teen Center (13–17). There is also Adventure Beach, which includes a splash pool complete with waterslide; Surfside, with computer lab stations with entertaining software; and Ocean Arcade, a video games hangout.

The onboard product delivery is more casual and unstructured than RCI has previously been delivering. *Jewel of the Seas* offers more space and more comfortable public areas (and several more intimate spaces), slightly larger cabins and more dining options than most of the larger ships in the RCI fleet.

While the ship is quite delightful in many ways, the onboard operation is less spectacular, and suffers from a lack of service staff. There are no cushioned pads for the sunloungers, and the deck towels provided are quite thin and small. Spa treatments are extravagantly expensive (as they are aboard most ships today, in line with land-based spa prices in the U.S.). It is virtually impossible to escape background music anywhere. The onboard currency is the US dollar, and 15 percent is added to all bar and spa bills.

SUITABLE FOR: *Jewel of the Seas* is best suited to young-minded adult couples and singles of all ages, families with toddlers, tots, children, and teenagers who like to mingle in a large ship setting with plenty of life and high-energy entertainment for everyone, with food that is acceptable quantity rather than quality (unless you are prepared to pay extra for dining in the "alternative" restaurant), all delivered with friendly service that lacks polish.

ACCOMMODATION. There is a wide range of suites and standard outside-view and interior (no view) cabins to suit different tastes, requirements, and depth of wallet, in 10 different categories and 19 different price groups.

Apart from the largest suites (six owner's suites), which have king-sized beds, almost all other cabins have twin beds that convert to a queen-sized bed (all sheets are of 100% Egyptian cotton, although blankets are of nylon). All cabins have rich (but faux) wood cabinetry, including a vanity desk (with hairdryer), faux wood drawers that close silently (hooray), TV set, personal safe, and three-sided mirrors. Some cabins have ceiling-recessed, pull-down berths for third and fourth persons, although closet and drawer space would be extremely tight for four (even if two are children), and some have interconnecting doors (so families with children can cruise together, in adjacent cabins. Note that audio channels are available through the TV set, so you can't switch off its picture while listening. Data ports are provided in all cabins.

Many of the "private" balcony cabins are not very private, as they can be overlooked by anyone standing in the port and starboard wings of the Solarium, and from other locations.

Most cabin bathrooms have tiled accenting and a terrazzo-style tiled floor, and a shower enclosure in a half-moon shape (it is rather small, however, considering the size of some passengers), 100 % Egyptian cotton towels, a small cabinet for personal toiletries and a small shelf. There is little space to stow toiletries for two (or more).

The largest accommodation consists of a family suite with two bedrooms. One bedroom has twin beds (convertible to queen-sized bed), while a second has two lower beds and two upper Pullman berths, a combination that can sleep up to eight persons (this would be suitable for large families).

Occupants of accommodation designated as suites also get the use of a private Concierge Lounge (where priority dining room reservations, shore excursion bookings and beauty salon/spa appointments can be made).

CUISINE. Reflections, the principal dining room, spans two decks; the upper deck level has floor-to-ceiling windows, while the lower deck level has picture windows. It is a fine, but inevitably noisy dining hall, and eight huge, thick pillars obstruct the sightlines. Reflections seats 1,104, and its decor has a cascading water theme. There are tables for two, four, six, eight or 10 in two seatings. Two small private dining rooms (Illusions and Mirage) are located off the main dining room. No smoking is permitted in dining venues. There is an adequate wine list, with moderate prices.

Alternative Restaurants: Portofino, with 112 seats, offers Italian cuisine, and Chops Grille Steakhouse, with 95 seats and an open "show" kitchen, serves premium meats in the form of chops and steaks. Both have food that is of a much higher quality than in the main dining room and are typically open 6pm–11pm. There is an additional charge of $20 per person (including gratuities), and reservations are required. The dress code is smart casual.

Casual Eateries: Casual meals (for breakfast, lunch and dinner) can be taken in the self-serve, buffet-style Windjammer Cafe, which can be accessed directly from the pool deck. It has about 400 seats, and islands dedicated to specific foods, and indoors and outdoors seating. Additionally, there is the Seaview Cafe, open for lunch and dinner. Choose from the self-serve buffet, or from the menu for casual, fast-food seafood items including fish sandwiches, popcorn shrimp, fish 'n' chips, as well as non-seafood items such as hamburgers and hot dogs.

ENTERTAINMENT. Entertainment facilities include the three-level Coral Reef Theater, with 874 seats (including 24 wheelchair stations) and good sightlines from most seats due to steep tiers. A second entertainment venue is the Safari Club, which hosts cabaret shows, late-night adult (blue) comedy, and dancing to live music. All the ship's entertainment is upbeat – so much so that it's virtually impossible to get away from music and noise.

SPA/FITNESS. The ShipShape health, fitness and spa facilities have themed decor, and include a 10,176 sq.-ft (945 sq.-meter) solarium with whirlpool and counter current swimming under a retractable magrodome roof, a gymnasium (with 44 cardiovascular machines), 50-person aerobics room, sauna and steam rooms, and therapy treatment rooms.

For the more sporting, there is activity galore – including a rock-climbing wall that's 30 ft (9 meters) high, with five separate climbing tracks. It's free, and all safety gear is included, but you'll need to sign up.

Other sports facilities include a 9-hole miniature golf course, and an indoor/outdoor country club with golf simulator, a jogging track, and basketball court. Want to play pool? You can, thanks to two special tables whose technology adjusts automatically to the movement of the ship.

● **For more extensive general information about Royal Caribbean International cruises, see pages 137–42.**

Kapitan Dranitsyn
★★★

Boutique Ship: . . . . .12,288 tons	Passenger Decks: 6	Cabins (for one person): 0
Lifestyle: . . . . .Standard	Total Crew: 90	Cabins (with private balcony): 0
Cruise Line: . . . . . . .Murmansk Shipping/	Passengers	Cabins (wheelchair accessible) 0
Quark Expeditions	(lower beds/all berths): 106/113	Cabin Current: . . . . .220 volts
Former Names: . . . . .none	Passenger Space Ratio	Elevators: 0
Builder: . . . . .Wartsila (Finland)	(lower beds/all berths): 115.9/108.7	Casino (gaming tables): . . . . .No
Original Cost: .n/a	Crew/Passenger Ratio	Slot Machines: .No
Entered Service: . . . . .Dec 1980	(lower beds/all berths): 1.1/1.2	Swimming Pools (outdoors): 0
Registry: . . . . .Russia	Navigation Officers: . . . . .Russian	Swimming Pools (indoors): 1
Length (ft/m): 434.6/132.49	Cabins (total): .53	Whirlpools: 0
Beam (ft/m): 86.9/26.50	Size Range (sq ft/m): 150.6–269.0/	Lecture/Film Room: . . . . .No
Draft (ft/m): 27.8/8.50	14.0–25.0	Library: . . . . .Yes
Propulsion/Propellers: . . . . .diesel-electric	Cabins (outside view): 53	Zodiacs: 4
(18,270 kW)/3	Cabins (interior/no view): 0	Helicopter Pad: . . . . . . .Yes (1 helicopter)

OVERALL SCORE: 1,162 (OUT OF A POSSIBLE 2,000 POINTS)

OVERVIEW. *Kapitan Dranitsyn* is a working icebreaker, one of 10 built in Finland to exacting Russian specifications for the challenging seas and conditions in the Arctic. Converted to passenger use in 1994 (and since upgraded), it has a very thick hull, forthright profile, and a bow like an inverted whale head. An open bridge policy allows passengers to visit the bridge. Strong diesel-electric engines (delivering 24,000 HP) allow it to plow through ice several feet thick. There is plenty of open deck and observation space, and a heated (but very small) indoor swimming pool.

There is always a team of excellent naturalists and lecturers aboard. A helicopter is usually (but not always) carried and can be used by all passengers for sightseeing forays, as is a fleet of Zodiac rubber landing craft for in-your-face shore landings and wildlife spotting. Light but warm parkas are provided for passengers.

Kapitan Dranitsyn is good for tough expedition cruising, and will provide thoroughly practical surroundings, a friendly, experienced and dedicated group of crew members, and excellent value for the money. An expedition cruise logbook is typically provided at the end of each cruise for all passengers – a superb keepsake.

The ship offers only basic cruise amenities and very spartan, no-frills decor. Also, be prepared for some tremendous roaring noise when the ship breaks through pack ice.

SUITABLE FOR: This type of cruising suits adventurous, hardy outdoors types of mature years who enjoy being with nature in some of the earth's most inhospitable places. Suggested gratuities: $9–12 per day.

BERLITZ'S RATINGS

	Possible	Achieved
Ship	500	265
Accommodation	200	113
Food	400	237
Service	400	224
Entertainment	n/a	n/a
Cruise	500	311

ACCOMMODATION. The cabins, in four price categories, are spread over four decks in an accommodation block, and all have private facilities and plenty of storage space. Although nothing special, the cabins are quite comfortable, with two lower beds (typically one is a fixed bed, the other being a convertible sofa bed, either in a twin or an L-shaped format), large closets, storage for outerwear and boots, and portholes that actually open. The bathrooms are practical units, although storage space for personal toiletries is tight. Four of the accommodation units are designated as "suites" that have more room, including a larger bathroom.

CUISINE. The one dining room is plain and unpretentious, yet quite comfortable. It is non-smoking; there is a single seating, with assigned tables, formally laid with white tablecloths and full place settings. The food is hearty fare, with generous portions (and an emphasis on fish and potatoes). Fruits, vegetables and international cheeses tend to be in limited supply. Quark Expeditions has its own catering team and so European chefs oversee the cuisine and its presentation, and only the best ingredients are provided. The wine list is pretty basic.

ENTERTAINMENT. Dinner is the main event of the evening, followed by discussion of what lies ahead for the next day. You might actually do a shore landing at night.

SPA/FITNESS. There is a gymnasium with some basic equipment, a small (heated) indoor swimming pool (really a "dip" pool), and a sauna.

Kapitan Khlebnikov
★★★

Boutique Ship: . . . . .12,288 tons	Passenger Decks: 6	Cabins (for one person): 0
Lifestyle: . . . . .Standard	Total Crew: 60	Cabins (with private balcony): 0
Cruise Line: . . . . . . .Murmansk Shipping/	Passengers	Cabins (wheelchair accessible): 0
Quark Expeditions	(lower beds/all berths): 108/114	Cabin Current: . . . . .220 volts
Former Names: . . . . .none	Passenger Space Ratio	Elevators: 1
Builder: . . . . .Wartsila (Finland)	(lower beds/all berths): 113.7/107.7	Casino (gaming tables): . . . . .No
Original Cost: .n/a	Crew/Passenger Ratio	Slot Machines: .No
Entered Service: 1981	(lower beds/all berths): 1.8/1.9	Swimming Pools (outdoors): 0
Registry: .Russia	Navigation Officers: . . . . .Russian	Swimming Pools (indoors): 1
Length (ft/m): 434.6/132.49	Cabins (total): .54	Whirlpools: 0
Beam (ft/m): 87.7/26.75	Size Range (sq ft/m): 150.6–269/	Lecture/Film Room: . . . . .No
Draft (ft/m): 27.8/8.50	14.0–25.0	Library: . . . . .Yes
Propulsion/Propellers: . . . . .diesel-electric	Cabins (outside view): 54	Zodiacs: 4
(18,270 kW)/3	Cabins (interior/no view): 0	Helicopter Pad: . . . . .Yes (1 helicopter)

OVERALL SCORE: 1,164 (OUT OF A POSSIBLE 2,000 POINTS)

OVERVIEW. *Kapitan Khlebnikov* is a real, working icebreaker, one of a fleet of 10 built in Finland to exacting Russian specifications for the challenging seas and conditions in the Arctic. Converted to exclusive passenger use in 1994 (and since upgraded), it has an incredibly thick hull, forthright profile, a bow like an inverted whale head, and much technical equipment. In 1997, *Kapitan Khlebnikov* became the first vessel ever to circumnavigate Antarctica with passengers. An open bridge policy allows passengers to visit the bridge at almost any time. Strong diesel-electric engines (delivering 24,000 horsepower) allow it to plow through ice several feet thick. There is plenty of open deck and observation space, and a heated (but very small) indoor swimming pool.

There is always a team of excellent naturalists and lecturers aboard. A helicopter, when carried, can be used for sightseeing forays, as is a fleet of Zodiac rubber landing craft for in-your-face shore landings and wildlife spotting.

Kapitan Khlebnikov is particularly good for tough expedition cruising, and will provide thoroughly practical surroundings, a friendly, experienced and dedicated group of crew members, and excellent value for the money. An expedition cruise logbook is typically provided at the end of each cruise for all passengers – a superb keepsake.

The ship offers only basic cruise amenities and very spartan, no-frills decor. Also, be prepared for some tremendous roaring noise when the ship breaks through pack ice.

SUITABLE FOR: This type of cruising suits adventurous, hardy outdoors types of mature years who enjoy being with

BERLITZ'S RATINGS		
	Possible	Achieved
Ship	500	267
Accommodation	200	113
Food	400	237
Service	400	224
Entertainment	n/a	n/a
Cruise	500	311

nature in some of the earth's most inhospitable places. Suggested gratuities: $9–$12 per day.

ACCOMMODATION. The cabins, in four price categories, are spread over four decks in an accommodation block, and all have private facilities and plenty of storage space. Although nothing special, the cabins are quite comfortable, with two lower beds (typically one is a fixed bed, the other being a convertible sofa bed, either in a twin or an L-shaped format), large closets, storage for outerwear and boots, and portholes that actually open. The bathrooms are practical units, although storage space for personal toiletries is tight. Four of the accommodation units are designated as "suites" that have more room, including a larger bathroom.

CUISINE. The one dining room is plain and unpretentious, yet quite comfortable. It is non-smoking; there is a single seating, with assigned tables. The food is hearty fare, with generous portions (and an emphasis on fish and potatoes). Fruits, vegetables and international cheeses tend to be in limited supply. Quark Expeditions has its own catering team. The wine list is pretty basic.

ENTERTAINMENT. Dinner is the main event of the evening, followed by discussion of what lies ahead for the next day. You might actually do a shore landing at night.

SPA/FITNESS. There is a gymnasium with some basic equipment, a small (heated) indoor swimming pool (really a "dip" pool), and a sauna.

Kristina Regina
★★ +

Boutique Ship:	.4,295 tons	Total Crew:	.55	Cabins (with private balcony):	.0
Lifestyle:	.Standard	Passengers		Cabins (wheelchair accessible):	.0
Cruise Line:	.Kristina Cruises	(lower beds/all berths):	.186/245	Cabin Current:	.220 volts
Former Names:	.Borea, Bore	Passenger Space Ratio		Elevators:	.0
Builder:	.Oskarshamn Shipyard (Sweden)	(lower beds/all berths):	.14.8/11.6	Casino (gaming tables):	.No
Original Cost:	.n/a	Crew/Passenger Ratio		Slot Machines:	.No
Entered Service:	.1960/1987	(lower beds/all berths):	.5.2/6.7	Swimming Pools (outdoors):	.0
Registry:	.Finland	Navigation Officers:	.Finnish	Swimming Pools (indoors):	.0
Length (ft/m):	.327.5/99.83	Cabins (total):	.119	Whirlpools:	.0
Beam (ft/m):	.50.0/15.25	Size Range (sq ft/m):	.64.5–150.6/ 6.0–14.0	Self-Service Launderette:	.No
Draft (ft/m):	.18.0/5.50			Dedicated Cinema/Seats:	.No
Propulsion/Propellers:	.diesel (3,233 kW)/2	Cabins (outside view):	.98	Library:	.Yes
		Cabins (interior/no view):	.21		
Passenger Decks:	.6	Cabins (for one person):	.30		

OVERALL SCORE: 1,052 (OUT OF A POSSIBLE 2,000 POINTS)

OVERVIEW. *Kristina Regina*, a lovely family-owned old-world ship, originally a coastal ferry, was converted for close-in northern European coastal and archipelago cruises, and was extensively refurbished in 2000. It originally had steam turbines powerplant, but this was converted to diesel in 1987. This is one of the few ships left today that has two funnels, and is owned by a single family, many of whose members work aboard the ship. Passengers can visit the navigation bridge at any time (conditions permitting).

Exterior features include a wrap-around wooden promenade deck outdoors. There are few public rooms (there are, however, two small conference rooms), but the ship does have some beautiful hardwoods throughout its interiors, plus lots of brass accents. The Scandinavian artwork is also fascinating. The ship has a good-sized auditorium that doubles as a cinema and lecture hall, built into what was formerly a car deck. During the 2000 refit and refurbishment, a small gymnasium was installed.

Unusually, the fare includes only breakfast. However, meal packages (for lunch and dinner) can be purchased for the principal restaurant. The onboard currencies are the US dollar and the euro. Non-alcoholic drinks are free; alcoholic drinks are expensive. The ship's itineraries take it to the Baltic States and Russia, into White Sea ports, and to many ports in Europe and the Mediterranean.

SUITABLE FOR: *Kristina Regina* is best suited to couples and solo travellers who would not dream of stepping foot aboard a regular (large) cruise ship, but want a highly personalized vacation aboard a very traditional ship that is reminiscent of how ship travel used to be.

BERLITZ'S RATINGS

	Possible	Achieved
Ship	500	233
Accommodation	200	110
Food	400	238
Service	400	233
Entertainment	100	42
Cruise	400	196

ACCOMMODATION. There is a wide assortment of cabin sizes and configurations, from "suites" to cabins that are small (compartments, really). Some cabins have a queen-sized bed; others have two lower beds, or a single bed. All grades have a shower and toilet, radio, telephone (for internal calls only), but not much else, and they are really tiny, as are the bathrooms.

As the cabins have very little storage space, you should take only what's really necessary. There are also five allergy-free cabins, as well as several cabins with interconnecting doors – good for families with children.

CUISINE. The principal dining room, Restaurant Regina, is quite charming and features Continental (European) cuisine, with much emphasis on fresh fish, seafood, and fresh berries (in season). The breads and cheeses are also good. There is single seating at assigned tables, and fine, hearty, and friendly service comes with a smile.

A second dining spot, the Kotka Restaurant, has an à la carte menu (everything is cooked to order), although all items are at extra cost. Additionally, continental breakfast and light snack foods can be found in the cafe.

ENTERTAINMENT. There is no formal entertainment, although dinner and after-dinner conversation with fellow passengers in the ship's lounge/bar really becomes the entertainment each evening.

SPA/FITNESS. There are none, except, of course, for a sauna (this *is* a Finnish cruise company, after all) and a small fitness room.

Le Diamant
★★★ +

Boutique Ship: . . . . .8,282 tons	Passenger Decks: 6	Cabins (for one person): 0
Lifestyle: . . . . .Premium	Total Crew: 140	Cabins (with private balcony): 10
Cruise Line: . . . . .Ponant Cruises	Passengers	Cabins (wheelchair accessible): 0
Former Names: . . . .*Song of Flower,*	(lower beds/all berths): 198/198	Cabin Current: . . . . .220 volts
Explorer Starship	Passenger Space Ratio	Elevators: 2
Builder: . . . . .KMV (Norway)	(lower beds/all berths): 41.8/41.8	Casino (gaming tables): . . . . .Yes
Original Cost: . . . . .n/a	Crew/Passenger Ratio	Slot Machines: .Yes
Entered Service: 1986/May 2004	(lower beds/all berths): 1.4/1.4	Swimming Pools (outdoors): 1
Registry: . . . . .Wallis and Fortuna	Navigation Officers: . . . . .European	Swimming Pools (indoors): 0
Length (ft/m): 407.4/124.2	Cabins (total): 99	Whirlpools: 1
Beam (ft/m): 52.4/16.0	Size Range (sq ft/m): 183.0-398.0/	Self-Service Launderette: . . . . .No
Draft (ft/m): 16.0/4.9	17.0-37.0	Dedicated Cinema/Seats: . . . . .No
Propulsion/Propellers: . . . . .diesel	Cabins (outside view): 99	Library: . . . . .Yes
(5,500kW)/2 (CP)	Cabins (interior/no view): 0	

OVERALL SCORE: 1,340 (OUT OF A POSSIBLE 2,000 POINTS)

OVERVIEW. *Le Diamant* is a charming boutique-sized cruise ship (originally built as the ro-ro vessel *Begonia* in 1974 and fully converted for cruising in 1986). Operated for many years by Radisson Seven Seas Cruises, the ship was sold to the French company, Compagnie des Isles du Ponant/Tapis Rouges, a joint venture. The ship has rather tall, twin funnels (with a platform between them) that give a somewhat squat profile. If only the foredeck and bow could be a little longer, it would provide a more sleek appearance! The ship has been well maintained and cared for and is very clean throughout, although its interiors now look rather tired. There is a good amount of sheltered open deck and sunbathing space. Water sports facilities include snorkel equipment.

The interior decor is warm, with pastel colors, accented by splashes of color are used throughout the public rooms, passageways, and stairways. Good quality soft furnishings and fabrics are provided, and make the ship feel chic and comfortable, though not luxurious.

The ship has a warm and caring crew that really tries hard to make you feel at home and comfortable and at home during your cruise vacation. Totally understated elegance and a warm, informal lifestyle are the hallmarks of a cruise aboard this nice ship. *Le Diamant* should provide you with a pleasing, destination-intensive, yet relaxing cruise experience, delivered with a decent amount of style and panache. The tender is in poor shape and needs replacing.

SUITABLE FOR: *Le Diamant* is for young-minded French-speaking couples and singles who want fairly contemporary

BERLITZ'S RATINGS

	Possible	Achieved
Ship	500	315
Accommodation	200	128
Food	400	291
Service	400	281
Entertainment	100	62
Cruise	400	263

facilities in a very relaxed but chic, yacht-like small ship setting that is different to "normal" cruise ships, with very good food and decent service.

ACCOMMODATION. There are 10 elegant suites; 10 cabins are strictly non-smoking. All others are well equipped, complete with bathrobes and slippers, refrigerator, and VCR. All come with excellent closet and drawer space.

Many have bathtubs, but they are tiny (shower tubs would be a better description). Disabled passengers should choose a cabin with a shower instead of a bath. There are no in-cabin dining facilities for dinner. When compared with the Seabourn and Silversea ships, the cabins are really rather plain.

CUISINE. The dining room is really most charming and has warm colors, a welcoming ambience, and one seating, with no assigned tables (tables are for two, four or six. Dining is in open seating. Free wines accompany lunch and dinner. The cuisine is, naturally, classic French, with small portions that are attractively presented. The personal service is good, from the warm, highly personable and attentive staff.

ENTERTAINMENT. The well-tiered show lounge is a good, comfortable room, and there are good sight lines from almost all the banquette-style seating.

SPA/FITNESS. The health spa facility is very compact and short on space, but is reasonably adequate, and includes a beauty salon and sauna.

Le Levant
★★★★

Boutique Ship:	.3,504 tons	Passenger Decks:	.5	Cabins (for one person):	.0
Lifestyle:	.Premium	Total Crew:	.50	Cabins (with private balcony):	.0
Cruise Line:	.Ponant Cruises	Passengers		Cabins (wheelchair accessible):	.0
Former Names:	.none	(lower beds/all berths):	.90/90	Cabin Current:	.110 and 220 volts
Builder:	.Leroux & Lotz (France)	Passenger Space Ratio		Elevators:	.1
Original Cost:	.$35 million	(lower beds/all berths):	.38.9/38.9	Casino (gaming tables):	.No
Entered Service:	.Jan 1999	Crew/Passenger Ratio		Slot Machines:	.No
Registry:	.Wallis and Fortuna	(lower beds/all berths):	.1.8/1.8	Swimming Pools (outdoors):	.1
Length (ft/m):	.328.0/100.00	Navigation Officers:	.French	Swimming Pools (indoors):	.0
Beam (ft/m):	.45.9/14.00	Cabins (total):	.45	Whirlpools:	.0
Draft (ft/m):	.11.4/3.50	Size Range (sq ft/m):	.199.1/18.5	Self-Service Launderette:	.No
Propulsion/Propellers:	.diesel	Cabins (outside view):	.45	Dedicated Cinema/Seats:	.No
	(3,000 kW)/2	Cabins (interior/no view):	.0	Library:	.Yes

OVERALL SCORE: 1,434 (OUT OF A POSSIBLE 2,000 POINTS)

OVERVIEW. *Le Levant* is a high-class vessel that has the looks of a stream-lined private mega-yacht. It has two slim funnels that extend over port and starboard sides to carry any soot away from the vessel. It was built in a specialist yacht-building yard in St Malo, France. There is an "open bridge" policy, so passengers may visit the bridge at any time (except when the ship is maneuvering in difficult conditions).

A stern "marina" platform is used for scuba diving, snorkeling or swimming. Two special landing craft are carried for shore visits, hidden in the stern, as well as six inflatable Zodiacs runabouts for landings in "soft" expedition areas such as the Amazon.

Inside, the vessel features contemporary, clean and uncluttered decor, and all the facilities of a private yacht. The public rooms are elegant and refined, with much use of wood trim and accenting. Particularly pleasing is the wood-paneled library. There is one grand salon, which accommodates all passengers, and is used by day as a lecture room, and by night as the main lounge/bar. A resident scuba dive master is aboard for all Caribbean sailings. Each cruise has life-enrichment lecturers aboard, as well as tour leaders.

This ship is often under charter to the New York-based Classical Cruises, which operates it in some offbeat destinations and cruise regions. In summer it may be in the Great Lakes, sailing between Toronto and Chicago (its pencil-slim beam allows it to navigate the locks). During the fall the ship heads to Canada/New England, and in the winter to the Caribbean and South America.

This is all-inclusive cruising, with all port charges, gratuities, and shore excursions included in the fare. The crew is almost entirely French. The onboard currency is the euro.

BERLITZ'S RATINGS

	Possible	Achieved
Ship	500	384
Accommodation	200	155
Food	400	286
Service	400	281
Entertainment	n/a	n/a
Cruise	500	328

SUITABLE FOR: *Le Levant* is best suited to young-minded couples and singles who want contemporary and sophisticated facilities in a very relaxed but chic, yacht-like small ship setting that is different to "normal" cruise ships, with very good food and decent service.

ACCOMMODATION. There are 45 ocean-view cabins (the brochure incorrectly calls them "suites") and all are midships and forward, in five price categories (a lot for such a small ship). Each cabin has a large ocean-view window, inlaid wood furniture and accenting, designer fabrics, two beds that will convert to a queen-sized bed, a television, VCR, refrigerator, personal safe, and personal amenity kits in the marble-appointed bathrooms, all of which feature a shower with a (circular) door (much better than a shower curtain); there are no bathtubs.

CUISINE. The Lafayette is a wood-panelled room that is warm and welcoming, with round and oval tables. The informal Veranda Restaurant has a panoramic view overlooking the stern (with both indoor and outdoor seating). Dining is in open seating. Free wines accompany lunch and dinner. The cuisine is, naturally, classic French.

ENTERTAINMENT. The Grand Salon, the main lounge, accommodates all passengers. It is the only room where smoking is allowed, and there are built-in video screens for showing movies. The only other entertainment is a singer/pianist (the room has a small dance floor in its center).

SPA/FITNESS. There is a small fitness room, and a steam room (there is no sauna) and shower.

Le Ponant
★★★ +

Boutique Ship:	1,489 tons	Main Propulsion:	a) engine/b) sails	Cabins (outside view):	32
Lifestyle:	Premium	Propulsion/Propellers:	diesel/	Cabins (interior/no view):	0
Cruise Line:	Ponant Cruises		sail power/1	Cabins (for one person):	0
Former Names:	none	Passenger Decks:	3	Cabins (with private balcony):	0
Builder:	SFCN (France)	Total Crew:	30	Cabins (wheelchair accessible):	0
Original Cost:	n/a	Passengers		Cabin Current:	220 volts
Entered Service:	1991	(lower beds/all berths):	64/67	Elevators:	No
Registry:	France	Passenger Space Ratio		Casino (gaming tables):	No
Length (ft/m):	288.7/88.00	(lower beds/all berths):	23.2/22.2	Slot Machines:	No
Beam (ft/m):	39.3/12.00	Crew/Passenger Ratio		Swimming Pools (outdoors):	0
Draft (ft/m):	13.1/4.00	(lower beds/all berths):	2.1/2.2	Whirlpools:	0
Type of Vessel:	high tech sail-cruiser	Navigation Officers:	French	Self-Service Launderette:	No
No. of Masts:	3	Cabins (total):	32	Library:	Yes
Sail Area (sq ft/m2):	16,150/1,500	Size Range (sq ft/m):	139.9/13.0		

OVERALL SCORE: 1,396 (OUT OF A POSSIBLE 2,000 POINTS)

OVERVIEW. Ultra sleek, and very efficiently designed, this contemporary sail-cruise ship has three masts that rise 54.7 ft (16.7 meters) above the water line, and features electronic winches that assist in the furling and unfurling of the sails. The total sail area measures approximately 1,500 sq. meters/16,140 sq. ft. This captivating ship has plenty of room on its open decks for sunbathing (although they have padded cushions, somehow the off-white plastic sunloungers are not at all elegant – teak would be so much more in keeping with the otherwise ultra-yacht look of the ship, although there probably is no room for them).

The very elegant, no-glitz interior design is clean, stylish, functional and ultra-high-tech. Three public lounges have pastel decor, soft colors and great European flair.

One price fits all. The ship is marketed mainly to young, sophisticated French-speaking passengers who love yachting and the sea. This is *très* French, and *très* chic and venturing off the beaten path is what cruising aboard *Le Ponant* is all about. The company also has a stunning mega-yacht cruise vessel, *Le Levant*. Gratuities are not "required", but they are expected. The onboard currency is the euro.

SUITABLE FOR: *Le Ponant* is best suited to young-minded couples and singles who want contemporary, sophisticated facilities in a very relaxed but chic setting that is different to "normal" cruise ships, with good food and service, no entertainment, and plenty of time for quiet relaxation.

ACCOMMODATION. There are 5 cabins on Antigua Deck (the open deck) and 27 cabins on Marie Galante Deck (the lowest deck). Crisp, clean blond woods and pristine white cab-

BERLITZ'S RATINGS

	Possible	Achieved
Ship	500	382
Accommodation	200	143
Food	400	278
Service	400	288
Entertainment	n/a	n/a
Cruise	500	305

ins have twin beds that convert to a double. There's a mini-bar, personal safe, and a private bathroom. All cabins have portholes, crisp artwork, and a refrigerator. There is limited storage space, however, and few drawers (they are also very small). The cabin bathrooms are quite small, but efficiently designed.

CUISINE. The lovely Karukera dining room has an open seating policy), so you can sit where you wish and dine with anyone you want. There is fresh fish daily (when available), and dinner is always treated as a true *affaire gastonomique*. The chef goes out to buy fresh local food items, including fresh fish, produce and fruits.

Free wines are included for lunch and dinner, and the cuisine is, naturally, classic French. Being French, the selection of cheeses and bread (and breakfast croissants) are good. Free cappuccinos and espresso are available.

For casual breakfasts and luncheons, there is also the charming outdoor café under a canvas sailcloth awning.

ENTERTAINMENT. There is no professional entertainment as such (although occasionally the crew may put on a little soirée). Dinner is the main event each evening, and, being a French product, dinner can provide several hours' worth of entertainment in itself.

SPA/FITNESS. There is no spa, fitness room, sauna, or steam room aboard *Le Ponant*. However, for recreation, there are water sports facilities, and these include an aft marina platform (from which you can swim), windsurfers, water-ski boat, scuba and snorkel equipment (scuba diving is an extra cost item, per dive).

Legend of the Seas

★★★★

Large Resort Ship:	.69,130 tons	Total Crew:	.720
Lifestyle:	Standard	Passengers	
Cruise Line: Royal Caribbean International		(lower beds/all berths):	1,800/2,076
Former Names:	none	Passenger Space Ratio	
Builder: Chantiers de l'Atlantique (France)		(lower beds/all berths):	38.3/33.2
Original Cost:	.$325 million	Crew/Passenger Ratio	
Entered Service:	May 1995	(lower beds/all berths):	.2.5/2.8
Registry:	The Bahamas	Navigation Officers:	Norwegian
Length (ft/m):	867.0/264.2	Cabins (total):	.900
Beam (ft/m):	105.0/32.0	Size Range (sq ft/m):	.137.7–1,147.4/
Draft (ft/m):	.23.9/7.3		12.8–106.6
Propulsion/Propellers:	diesel	Cabins (outside view):	.575
	(40,200 kW)/2	Cabins (interior/no view):	.325
Passenger Decks:	.11	Cabins (for one person):	.0

Cabins (with private balcony):	.231
Cabins (wheelchair accessible):	.17
Cabin Current:	110 and 220 volts
Elevators:	.11
Casino (gaming tables):	Yes
Slot Machines:	Yes
Swimming Pools (outdoors):	.2
	(1 with sliding roof)
Swimming Pools (indoors):	.0
Whirlpools:	.4
Self-Service Launderette:	No
Dedicated Cinema/Seats:	No
Library:	Yes

OVERALL SCORE: 1,497 (OUT OF A POSSIBLE 2,000 POINTS)

OVERVIEW. This vessel (sister to *Splendour of the Seas*) has a contemporary profile and a nicely tiered stern. The pool deck amidships overhangs the hull to provide an extremely wide deck, while still allowing the ship to navigate the Panama Canal. With engines placed midships, there is little noise and no noticeable vibration, and the ship has an operating speed of up to 24 knots.

The interior decor is colorful, but rather glitzy for European tastes, although it makes a change from the bland interiors of many UK-based ships (the ship is based in Britain during the summer, and features Europe/Med cruising for both American and British passengers) The outside light is brought inside in many places, with over 2 acres (8,000 sq. meters) of glass providing contact with sea and air. There's an innovative single-level sliding glass roof (not a magrodome) over the more formal setting of one of two swimming pools, providing a multi-activity, all-weather indoor-outdoor area, called the Solarium. The glass roof provides shelter for the Roman-style pool and the health and fitness facilities (which are good) and slides aft to cover the miniature golf course when required (both cannot be covered at the same time, however).

Golfers might enjoy the 18-hole, 6,000-sq. ft (560 sq.-meter) miniature golf course. It has the topography of a real course, complete with trees, foliage, grass, bridges, water hazards, and lighting for play at night. The holes themselves are 155-230 sq. ft (14.3–21.3 sq. meters).

Inside, two full entertainment decks are sandwiched between five decks full of cabins, so there are plenty of public rooms to lounge and drink in. A multi-tiered seven-deck-high atrium lobby, complete with a huge stainless steel

BERLITZ'S RATINGS

	Possible	Achieved
Ship	500	426
Accommodation	200	163
Food	400	240
Service	400	297
Entertainment	100	78
Cruise	400	293

sculpture, connects with the impressive Viking Crown Lounge via glass-walled lifts. The casino is expansive, incredibly glitzy but usually packed. The library, outside of which is a bust of Shakespeare, is a nice facility, with almost 2,000 books.

There is, sadly, no separate cinema. The casino could be somewhat disorienting, with its mirrored walls and lights flashing everywhere, although it is no different to those found in Las Vegas gaming halls, and it can be difficult to find relaxation areas without music (except for the Viking Crown Lounge in the daytime).

ACCOMMODATION. There are 17 different grades – rather too many – but no cabins for singles. Royal Caribbean International has designed a ship with much larger standard cabins than in any of the company's previous vessels (except *Splendour of the Seas*).

Some cabins on Deck 8 also have a larger door for wheelchair access in addition to the 17 cabins for the physically disabled, and the ship is very accessible, with ample ramped areas and sloping decks. All cabins have a sitting area and beds that convert to double configuration, and there is ample closet and drawer space. There is not much space around the bed, though, and the showers could have been better designed. Those cabins with balconies have glass railings rather than steel/wood to provide less intrusive sightlines.

The largest accommodation is the Royal Suite, which is beautifully designed, finely decorated, and features a baby grand piano, whirlpool bathtub, and other fine amenities. Several quiet sitting areas are located adjacent to the best cabins amidships.

CUISINE. The Romeo and Juliet Dining Room has dramatic two-deck-high glass side walls, so many passengers both upstairs and downstairs can see both the ocean and each other in reflection (it would, perhaps, have been even better located at the stern), but it is quite noisy when full (call it atmosphere). The two seatings are non-smoking, and a decent level of relaxed service is provided.

A cavernous indoor-outdoor Windjammer Café, located towards the bow and above the bridge, has good views on three sides from large ocean-view windows. A good-sized snack area provides even more informal eating options.

ENTERTAINMENT. The "That's Entertainment" Theatre seats 802 and is a single-level showlounge with tiered seating levels: sightlines are generally good from almost all seats.

Strong cabaret acts are also featured in the main showlounge. A second entertainment lounge, the Anchors Aweigh Lounge, is where cabaret acts, including late-night adult (blue) comedy are featured. Other lounges and bars have live music for listening and dancing.

The entertainment throughout is upbeat (in fact, it is difficult to get away from music and noise), but is typical of the kind of resort hotel found ashore in Las Vegas. There is even background music in all corridors and elevators, and constant music outdoors on the pool deck. If you want a quiet relaxing holiday, you should choose another ship.

SPA/FITNESS. The ShipShape Fitness Center has a gymnasium (it is located on the port side of the ship, aft of the funnel), and has a small selection of high-tech muscle-pumping equipment. There is also an aerobics studio (classes are offered in a variety of keep fit regimes), a beauty salon, and a sauna, as well as treatment rooms for such pampering things as massages, facials, etc. While the facilities are quite small when compared with those aboard the company's newer ships, they are adequate for the short cruises that this ship operates.

For more sporting passengers, there is activity galore – including a rock-climbing wall, with several separate climbing tracks. It is located outdoors at the aft end of the funnel.

● **For more extensive general information about the Royal Caribbean experience, see pages 137–42.**

FUN FACTS

● Cruise ship design is interesting. The beauty of design lies in curves, not in straight lines. Today's large resort ships, designed merely for cruising in warm weather regions and not for voyaging across the North Atlantic (heaven forbid, the delivery voyage was enough), are made of straight lines. They are boxy and cold in appearance, although they provide much more usable space inside the ship (some call it warehouse cruising). Take a look at *Saga Rose* (the former *Sagafjord*) and you won't find a straight line anywhere. Then look at *Carnival Imagination* and compare the two.

● Beatrice Muller, in her early 80s, makes her permanent home at sea. She lives year-round aboard Cunard Line's *Queen Elizabeth 2*, paying a set amount to reside in Cabin 4068. She prefers being aboard the ship rather than sit around in a retirement home in Britain's damp climate, and proves that the world is her oyster. She loves it because she doesn't have to deal with the daily drudgery of shopping, doesn't need a car, or pay electric, gas or telephone bills. She communicates with her family by using the computer center's email service.

● Cruise lines and charity go hand in hand. Cunard donated 1,500 pieces of classic furniture from the 1994 refit of *QE2* to the Salvation Army for its adult rehabilitation program. Crew aboard the same ship donate money to buy guide dogs for the blind, or an ambulance for the St. John's Ambulance Brigade in the UK. Princess Cruises made a "sizeable" contribution to UNICEF following the death of Audrey Hepburn in 1993 (she named the company's *Star Princess*, now operating as *Sea Princess* for Princess Cruises). Passengers of Hapag-Lloyd's *Europa* have donated more than 1 million euros to children's homes in Vietnam. Both Holland America Line and Princess Cruises have contributed heavily to the Raptor Center in Juneau, Alaska.

● Someone forgot to "score" the champagne bottle when Dame Judi Dench named *Carnival Legend* in Harwich, England, on August 21, 2002. On the first two tries, the bottle didn't break. Then Dame Judi took the bottle in her own hands and smashed it against the side of the ship. It broke, and the foam and champagne went all over her. She was dubbed Dame Judi Drench.

● In the mid-1960s there were 12 "bell boys" ("piccolos" in hotels-peak) aboard the Cunard Line's RMS *Queen Elizabeth* and *Queen Mary*. They manned the elevators and opened the doors to the various restaurants. Each day, before they were allowed to work, they all lined up and their fingernails were inspected. Those were the days.

Liberty of the Seas
★★★★

Large Resort Ship: ....154,407 tons	Total Crew: 1,397	Cabins (with private balcony): 842
Lifestyle: ....Standard	Passengers	Cabins (wheelchair accessible): 32
Cruise Line: Royal Caribbean International	(lower beds/all berths): 3,634/4,375	Cabin Current: ....110 volts
Former Names: ....none	Passenger Space Ratio	Elevators: 14
Builder: . . .Kvaerner Masa-Yards (Finland)	(lower beds/all berths): 42.0/35.3	Casino (gaming tables): ....Yes
Original Cost: ....$590 million	Crew/Passenger Ratio	Slot Machines: ....Yes
Entered Service: ....Spring 2007	(lower beds/all berths): 2.6/3.1	Swimming Pools (outdoors): 2
Registry: ....The Bahamas	Navigation Officers: ....European	Swimming Pools (indoors): 0
Length (ft/m): 1,112.2/339.0	Cabins (total): 1,817	Whirlpools: 6
Beam (ft/m): 184.0/56.0	Size Range (sq ft/m): 149.0–2,025.0/	Self-Service Launderette: ....No
Draft (ft/m): 27.8/8/5	13.8–188.1	Dedicated Cinema/Seats: ....No
Propulsion/Propellers: .....diesel-electric	Cabins (outside view): 1,084	Library: ....Yes
(kW)/4 azimuthing pods	Cabins (interior/no view): 733	
Passenger Decks: 15	Cabins (for one person): 0	

OVERALL SCORE: 1,532 (OUT OF A POSSIBLE 2,000 POINTS)

OVERVIEW. *Liberty of the Seas* (together with sister ships *Freedom of the Seas* and *Independence of the Seas*) is the largest ever purpose-built cruise ship. It is essentially split into three separate areas, rather like the Disney cruise ships – adults-only, family, or main.

The "wow" factor is its connection with water (of the seas) in the design of a dramatic water theme park afloat. By day, the H2O Zone (aft of the funnel) has an interactive water-themed play area for families that includes water cannons and spray fountains, water jets and ground gushers; by night the "water park" turns into a colourfully-lit sculpture garden. Meanwhile, the ship's central pool has become a sports pool, with grandstand seating and competitive games that include pole jousting. Other active sports facilities include an Everlast boxing ring, rock-climbing wall (10 ft taller than in the Voyager-class ships), in-line skating area, an ice-skating rink, and golf simulators.

The same facilities (public rooms, bars and lounges) featured in the Voyager-class ships have been incorporated, but with the addition of more conference and meetings facilities, extensive wi-fi capabilities and connectivity for cell phones. Other facilities include a large casino.

The cabin hallways have an extremely warm, attractive feel, with artwork cabinets and asymmetrical flow to lead you along and break up the monotony. In fact, there are plenty of colorful, even whimsical, decorative touches. Note that, if you meet someone you'd like to see again, you'll need to make an appointment and specify a location, for this really is a large, Las Vegas-style floating resort-city.

ACCOMMODATION. There is a wide range of cabins in 14

BERLITZ'S RATINGS		
	Possible	Achieved
Ship	500	430
Accommodation	200	161
Food	400	245
Service	400	294
Entertainment	100	83
Cruise	400	319

categories and 21 price grades. The price depends on the grade, from the 14-person Presidential Suite to twin-bed two person interior (no view) cabins, and interior cabins that look into an inside shopping/strolling atrium promenade. There are many family-friendly cabins, good for family reunions.

Some accommodation examples (from large to small):

Presidential Family Suite: Two master bedrooms, each with twin beds (convertible to queen-size), private balcony, sofa bed, bar, private bathroom, bathtub, vanity, hair-dryer, closed-circuit flat screen TV and phone. Great views over the ship's fantail (stern). Occupants have access to the Concierge Club lounge and services. There is only one Presidential Family Suite on board (it can take up to 14, but this would be quite cramped). Size: 1,215 sq. ft. (112.8 sq. meters), plus balcony: 810 sq. ft. (75.2 sq. meters), set with lounge area and dining table.

Royal Suite: Features a separate bedroom with king-size bed, private balcony, living room with queen-size sofa bed and private bathroom. Measures: 1,406 sq. ft.,(130.6 sq.meters); balcony 377 sq. ft. (35.0 sq.meters)

Royal Family Suite: Features two bedrooms with twin beds that convert to queen-size beds (one room has third and fourth Pullman beds), a private balcony, two bathrooms and living area with double sofa bed. Measures 588 sq. ft. (54.6 sq.meters); balcony 234 sq. ft. (21.7 sq.meters)

Owners Suite: Features include a queen-sized bed, private balcony, separate living area with queen-sized sofa bed, wet bar, vanity area, walk-in closet; bathroom with tub and shower, plus access to the Concierge Club lounge and attendant services. Sleeps up to five. Size: 506 sq. ft. (46 sq. meters) + Balcony: 131 sq. ft. (12.1 sq. meters).

Grand Suite: Two twin beds convertible to queen-size, a private balcony, sitting area (some with sofa bed), vanity area; bathroom with tub and shower. Access to the Concierge Club lounge and services. Sleeps up to four. Size: 381 sq. ft. (35.3 sq.meters) + Balcony: 89 sq. ft. (8.2 sq. meters).

Junior Suite: Two twin beds convertible to queen-size, private balcony, sitting area (some with sofa bed), vanity area; bathroom with tub and shower. Sleeps up to four. Size: 285.2 sq. ft. (26.5 sq.meters) + Balcony: 101 sq. ft. (9.3 sq.meters).

Superior Oceanview Cabin: Two twin beds convertible to queen-size, a private balcony, sitting area (some with sofa bed), vanity area; bathroom with shower. Sleeps 2 (some rooms sleep three or four). Size: 202 sq. ft. (18.7 sq. meters) + Balcony: 42 sq. ft. (3.9 sq. meters).

Deluxe Oceanview Cabin: Two twin beds convertible to queen-size, a private balcony, sitting area (some with sofa bed), vanity area; bathroom with shower. Sleeps 2 (some rooms sleep three or four). Size: 173 sq. ft. (16.0 sq. meters) + Balcony: 46 sq. ft. (4.2 sq. meters).

Promenade Cabin (interior, but overlooking the Royal Promenade): A view of the Royal Promenade with bay windows, two twin beds that can convert into queen-size, and private bathroom. Measures: 149 sq. ft. (13.8 sq.meters).

Promenade Family Cabin: Features two twin beds that can convert into queen-size, and private bathroom. Measures: 300 sq. ft. (27.8 sq.meters).

Interior (no view) Cabin: Two twin beds convertible to queen-size; private bathroom with shower. Sleeps two (some rooms sleep three or four). Size: 152sq. ft. (14.1 sq. meters).

Family Ocean-view Cabin: Located at the front of the ship, it contains two twin beds (convertible to queen-size), sofa and/or Pullman beds, sitting area; bathroom, with shower. Accommodates six, and features 48-inch round windows. Size: 265 sq. ft. (24.6 sq. meters).

All cabins have a private bathroom (with tub and shower, or shower only), vanity desk with hairdryer, mini-bar, personal safe, flat-screen TV, radio, and satellite telephone. A room service menu is provided. Suite occupants have access to a Concierge Lounge, for more personal service (this saves standing in line at the reception desk).

CUISINE. The main dining room is extremely large and is set on three levels (each has a theme and name: Galileo, Isaac, and Leonardo). A dramatic staircase connects all three levels, and huge, fat support pillars obstruct the sightlines from many seats. All three have the same menus and food. The dining room is all non-smoking, there are two seatings, and tables are for four, six, eight 10 or 12.

Alternative Dining Options: Alternative dining options for casual and informal meals at all hours (according to company statements) include:

● *Promenade Café:* for continental breakfast, all-day pizzas (Sorento's), sandwiches and coffee (in paper cups).

● *Windjammer Café:* for casual buffet-style breakfast, lunch and light dinner (except for the cruise's last night).

● *Island Grill* (a section of the Windjammer Café): for casual dinner (no reservations necessary) featuring a grill and open kitchen.

● *Portofino:* this is the ship's "upscale" (non-smoking) Euro-Italian restaurant, open for dinner only. Reservations are required, and a there's gratuity of $20 per person). Choices include: antipasti, soup, salad, pasta, main dish, dessert, cheese and coffee (the menu does not change during the cruise).

● *Chops Grill:* an intimate restaurant for steaks and seafood. A cover charge of $20 applies.

● *Johnny Rockets*, a retro 1950s all-day, all-night diner-style eatery that has hamburgers, hot dogs and other fast-food items, malt shakes, and jukebox hits, with both indoor and outdoor seating (indoor tables have a mini-jukebox), and all-singing, all-dancing waitresses that'll knock your socks off, if you can stand the volume. Cover charge: $3.95.

● *Sprinkles:* for round-the-clock ice cream and yoghurt, pastries and coffee.

ENTERTAINMENT. The Showlounge is a stunning space, located at the forward end of the ship and spanning the height of five decks (with only a few slim pillars and almost no disruption of sightlines). The room has a hydraulic orchestra pit and huge stage areas, together with sonic-boom loud sound, and superb lighting equipment. In addition, the ship has an array of cabaret acts. The strongest are featured in the main showlounge, while others are presented in the Nightclub, the venue for late-night adults-only comedy.

The most entertaining shows, however, are the Spectaculars on ice. There is also a television studio (in case you thought you'd need one aboard a cruise ship), located adjacent to rooms that could be used, for example, for trade show exhibit space (good for conventions at sea).

One performance not to be missed is the "Greatest Show at Sea" Parade – a superbly executed 15-minute fun extravaganza that bumbles along the Royal Promenade at turtle speed; it replicates the parade of stars and animals at a circus of yesteryear (Barnum and Bailey's meets cruise ship). This is when it's really good to have one of those interior-view atrium cabins (sadly, the windows don't open, so you can't take photographs); otherwise, get a position early along the Royal Promenade.

SPA/FITNESS. The ShipShape health spa is large. It includes a large aerobics room, fitness center, treatment rooms, and men's and women's sauna/steam rooms and relaxation areas. The spa facility is operated by Steiner. Some (basic) exercise classes are free, but the good ones (examples: yoga, personal training) cost extra. Sample prices: Swedish Massage $119 (50 mins); Couples massage $269 (50 mins); facial $119 (50 mins), plus tip.

More active passengers can bodyboard, go boxing (in the full-size boxing ring in the middle of the spa), climb (the rock-climbing wall at the back of the funnel housing), jog, putt, swim, skate, step, surf, workout and more (including play basketball and volleyball) in the sports area of the ship, located mostly aft of the funnel.

● **For more extensive general information on what a Royal Caribbean cruise is like, see pages 137–42.**

Maasdam
★★★★

Mid-Size Ship: ....55,451 tons	Total Crew: 557	Cabins (with private balcony): 150
Lifestyle: ....Premium	Passengers	Cabins (wheelchair accessible): 6
Cruise Line: ......Holland America Line	(lower beds/all berths): 1,266/1,627	Cabin Current: ....110 and 220 volts
Former Names: ....none	Passenger Space Ratio	Elevators: 8
Builder: ....Fincantieri (Italy)	(lower beds/all berths): 43.8/34.0	Casino (gaming tables): ....Yes
Original Cost: ....$215 million	Crew/Passenger Ratio	Slot Machines: ....Yes
Entered Service: ....Dec 1993	(lower beds/all berths): 2.2/2.9	Swimming Pools (outdoors): 1
Registry: ....The Netherlands	Navigation Officers: ....Dutch	Swimming Pools (indoors): 1
Length (ft/m): 719.3/219.30	Cabins (total): 632	(magrodome)
Beam (ft/m): 101.0/30.80	Size Range (sq ft/m): 186.2–1,124.8/	Whirlpools: 2
Draft (ft/m): 24.6/7.50	17.3–104.5	Self-Service Launderette: ....Yes
Propulsion/Propellers: .....diesel-electric	Cabins (outside view): 502	Dedicated Cinema/Seats: Yes/249
(34,560 kW)/2	Cabins (interior/no view): 131	Library: ....Yes
Passenger Decks: 10	Cabins (for one person): 0	

OVERALL SCORE: 1,418 (OUT OF A POSSIBLE 2,000 POINTS)

OVERVIEW. *Maasdam* is one of a series of four almost identical ships in the same series – the others are *Statendam*, *Ryndam* and *Veendam*. Although the exterior styling is rather angular (some would say boxy – the funnel certainly is), it is softened and balanced somewhat by the fact that the hull is painted black. There is a full wrap-around teak promenade deck outdoors – excellent for strolling, and, thankfully, no sign of synthetic turf anywhere. The sun-loungers on the exterior promenade deck are wood, and have comfortable cushioned pads, while those at the swimming pool on Lido Deck are of white plastic. Holland America Line keeps its ships clean and tidy, and there is good passenger flow throughout the public areas.

In the interiors of this "S" -class ship, an asymmetrical layout helps to reduce bottlenecks and congestion. Most of the public rooms are concentrated on two decks, Promenade Deck, and Upper Promenade Deck, which creates a spacious feel to the ship's interiors. In general, a restrained approach to interior styling is taken, using a mixture of contemporary materials combined with traditional woods and ceramics. There is, fortunately, little "glitz" anywhere.

What is noticeable is the array of artworks throughout the ship (costing about $2 million), assembled and nicely displayed to represent the fine Dutch heritage of Holland America Line and to present a balance between standard itineraries and onboard creature comforts. Several oil paintings of former Holland America Line ships by Stephen Card (an ex-captain) adorn stairway landings. Also noticeable are the fine flower arrangements throughout the public areas and foyers – used to good effect to brighten up what to some is dull decor.

BERLITZ'S RATINGS

	Possible	Achieved
Ship	500	372
Accommodation	200	150
Food	400	254
Service	400	287
Entertainment	100	72
Cruise	400	283

Atop the ship, with forward facing views that wrap around the sides, is the Crow's Nest Lounge. By day it makes a fine observation lounge, with large ocean-view windows, while by night it turns into a nightclub with extremely variable lighting.

The atrium foyer is three decks high, although its light-catching green glass sculpted centerpiece (*Totem* by Luciano Vistosi, composed of almost 2,000 pieces of glass) makes it look a little crowded, and leaves little room in front of the purser's office (called the Front Office). A hydraulic magrodome (glass) roof covers the reasonably-sized swimming pool/whirlpools and central Lido area (whose focal point is a large dolphin sculpture) so that this can be used in either fine or inclement weather.

Maasdam, a well-built ship, has fairly decent interior decor. Holland America Line is constantly fine-tuning its performance and its regular passengers (almost all of whom are North American – there are few international passengers) find the company's ships comfortable and well-run. The company continues its strong maritime traditions, although the food and service components still let the rest of the cruise experience down. Perhaps the ship's best asset is its friendly and personable Filipino and Indonesian crew, although communication can prove frustrating and service is inconsistent. The onboard currency is the US dollar.

This ship has a large, relaxing library (Leyden Library); there's also a cardroom, an Explorer's Lounge (good for relaxing in, for afternoon tea, and after-dinner coffee), a Crows Nest (the ship's observation lounge that doubles as a late-night spot and discotheque), an intimate Piano Bar, and, of course, a casino.

Holland America Line's many repeat passengers always seem to enjoy the fact that social dancing is always on the menu. In the final analysis, however, the score for this ship ends up just a disappointing tad under what it could be if the food and food service staff were more memorable (more professional training might help).

An escalator travels between two of the lower decks (one of which was originally planned to be the embarkation point), but it is almost pointless. The charge to use the washing machines and dryers in the self-service launderette is petty, particularly for suite occupants, as they pay high prices for their cruises. The men's urinals in public restrooms are unusually high.

ACCOMMODATION. The accommodation ranges from small interior (no view) cabins to a large penthouse suite, in 17 price categories. The price you pay will depend on the grade, size and location you choose. All cabin televisions receive CNN and TNT.

The interior (no view) and outside (with a view) standard cabins feature twin beds that convert to a queen-size bed, and there is a separate living space with sofa and coffee table. However, although the drawer space is generally good, the closet space is actually very tight, particularly for long cruises (although more than adequate for a 7-night cruise). Bathrobes are also provided for all suites/cabins, as are hairdryers, and a small range of personal toiletries (soap, conditioning shampoo, body lotion, shower cap, vanity kit). The bathrooms are quite well laid out, but the bathtubs are small units better described as shower tubs.

On Navigation Deck, 28 suites have accommodation for up to four. These suites also have in-suite dining as an alternative to the dining room, for private, reclusive meals. These are very spacious, tastefully decorated and well laid-out suites, and have a separate, good-sized living room, bedroom with two lower beds (convertible to a king-size bed), dressing room, plenty of closet and drawer space (walk-in closet), marble bathroom with Jacuzzi tub and separate toilet/washroom with bidet.

The largest accommodation of all is a penthouse suite. There is only one, on the starboard side of Navigation Deck at the forward staircase. It has a king-sized bed (TV and video player) and vanity desk; large walk-in closet with superb wardrobe space, oversize whirlpool bath (it could seat four) and separate shower enclosure, separate washroom with toilet, bidet and washbasin; living room with writing desk, large television and full set of audio equipment; dressing room, large private balcony (with teak lounge chairs and drinks tables, dining table and four chairs), pantry (with large refrigerator, toaster unit, and full coffee/tea making facilities and food preparation area, and a separate entrance from the hallway), mini-bar/refrigerator, a guest toilet and floor-to-ceiling windows. There is no bell push.

CUISINE. The Rotterdam Dining Room, which is a non-smoking venue, spans two decks. It is located at the stern of the ship, is quite dramatic, and has a grand staircase, panoramic views on three sides, and a music balcony. Both open seating and fixed (assigned tables and times) seating are available, while breakfast and lunch are open-seating (you'll be seated by restaurant staff when you enter). The waiter stations in the dining room are very noisy for anyone seated adjacent to them.

Alternative dining option: Added in 2003, the Pinnacle Grill is located just forward of the balcony level of the main dining room on the starboard side. The 66-seat dining spot features Pacific Northwest cuisine (Dungeness crab, Alaska salmon, halibut and other regional specialties). The new venue (reservations are necessary, and a cover/service charge of $20 applies) was created out of the former private dining wing of the main dining room, plus a slice of the Explorer's Lounge. A Bulgari show plate, Rosenthal china, Reidel wine glasses, and Frette table linen are used. The Pinnacle Grill is a much better dining experience than the main dining room and worth it for that special celebration.

For more casual evening eating, the Lido Buffet is open for casual dinners on all except the last night of each cruise, in an open-seating arrangement. Tables are set with crisp linens, flatware and stemware. A set menu is featured, and this includes a choice of four entreés.

The dual-line, self-serve Lido Buffet (one side is for smokers, the other side for non-smokers) is also the place for casual breakfasts and lunches. Again there is much use of canned fruits (good for older passengers with few teeth) and packeted items, although there are several commercial low-calorie salad dressings. The beverage station also lets it down, for it is no better than those found in family outlets ashore in the United States. In addition, a poolside grill provides basic American hamburgers and hot dogs.

Passengers will need to eat in the Lido Cafe on any days when the dining room is closed for lunch (this is typically once or twice per cruise, depending on the itinerary).

ENTERTAINMENT. The Rembrandt Showlounge, located at the forward part of the ship, spans two decks, with banquette seating on both main and upper levels. It is basically a well-designed room, but the ceiling is low and the sight lines from the balcony level are quite poor.

SPA/FITNESS. The Ocean Spa is located one deck below the navigation bridge at the very forward part of the ship. It includes a gymnasium (with all the latest muscle-pumping exercise machines, including an abundance of treadmills) with ocean views, an aerobics exercise area, large beauty salon with ocean-view windows to the port side, several treatment rooms, and men's and women's sauna, steam room and changing areas.

● **For more extensive general information on what a Holland America Line cruise is like, see pages 126–28.**

Majesty of the Seas
★ ★ ★

Large Resort Ship: . . . . .73,941 tons	Passenger Decks: 11	Cabins (for one person): 0
Lifestyle: . . . . .Standard	Total Crew: 827	Cabins (with private balcony): 62
Cruise Line: . . . . .Royal Caribbean	Passengers	Cabins (wheelchair accessible): 4
International	(lower beds/all berths): 2,380/2,774	Cabin Current: . . . . .110 volts
Former Names: . . . . .none	Passenger Space Ratio	Elevators: 11
Builder: .Chantiers de l'Atlantique (France)	(lower beds/all berths): 30.8/26.3	Casino (gaming tables): . . . . .Yes
Original Cost: . . . .$300 million	Crew/Passenger Ratio	Slot Machines: . . . . .Yes
Entered Service: . . . . .Apr 1992	(lower beds/all berths): 2.8/3.3	Swimming Pools (outdoors): 2
Registry: . . . . .The Bahamas	Navigation Officers: . . . . .Norwegian	Swimming Pools (indoors): 0
Length (ft/m): 879.9/268.2	Cabins (total): 1,190	Whirlpools: 2
Beam (ft/m): 105.9/32.3	Size Range (sq ft/m): 118.4–670.0/	Self-Service Launderette: . . . . .No
Draft (ft/m): 24.9/7.6	11.0–62.2	Dedicated Cinema/Seats: . . . . .No
Propulsion/Propellers: . . . . .diesel	Cabins (outside view): 732	Library: . . . . .Yes
(21,844 kW)/2	Cabins (interior/no view): 458	

OVERALL SCORE: 1,246 (OUT OF A POSSIBLE 2,000 POINTS)

OVERVIEW. When first introduced, this ship (together with its two sisters, *Monarch of the Seas* and *Sovereign of the Seas*) was an innovative vessel. Royal Caribbean International's trademark Viking Crown lounge and bar surrounds the funnel and provides a stunning view. The open deck space is very cramped when full, as aboard any large ship, although there seems to be plenty of it. There is a basketball court.

The interior layout is a little awkward, as it is designed in a vertical stack, with most of the public rooms located aft, and the accommodation located forward (this ensures quiet areas) There is, however, an impressive array of spacious and elegant public rooms, although the decor calls to mind the IKEA school of interior design. A stunning five-deck-high Centrum lobby has cascading stairways and two glass-walled elevators. The ship had a complete make-over in 2007 when all cabins were refreshed, and more casual eating options introduced.

There is a decent two-level showlounge and a decent array of shops, albeit with lots of tacky merchandise. Casino gamers will find blackjack, craps, Caribbean stud poker and roulette tables, plus an array of slot machines in Casino Royale. Among the public rooms, the library is a nice feature for quite relaxation, and there is a decent selection of books. The entertainment program is quite sound, and there is a decent range of children's/teens' programs and cheerful youth counselors.

This smart-looking resort ship provides a well tuned, yet impersonal, short cruise experience (3- and 4-day Bahamas cruises year-round from Miami) for a lot of passengers. The dress code is very casual. In the final analysis, you will probably be overwhelmed by the public spaces, and under-

BERLITZ'S RATINGS

	Possible	Achieved
Ship	500	333
Accommodation	200	119
Food	400	221
Service	400	260
Entertainment	100	66
Cruise	400	247

whelmed by the size of the cabins. Because the public rooms are mostly located aft (accommodation is located in the forward section of the ship), there is often a long wait for elevators, particularly at peak times (after dinner, shows, and talks).

ACCOMMODATION. There are 17 price categories. The price will depend on the grade, size and location you choose.

Suites: Thirteen suites on Bridge Deck are reasonably large and nicely furnished (the largest is the Royal Suite), with separate living and sleeping spaces. They provide more space, with better service and more perks than standard-grade accommodation.

Standard Cabins: The standard outside-view and interior (no view) cabins are extremely small, however, although an arched window treatment and colorful soft furnishings do give the illusion of more space. Almost all cabins have twin beds that can be converted to a queen-sized or double bed configuration, together with moveable bedside tables. All of the standard cabins have very little closet and drawer space (you will need some luggage engineering to stow your cases). You should, therefore, think of packing only minimal clothing, which is all you really need for a short cruise.

All cabins have a private bathroom, with shower enclosure, toilet and washbasin. All are provided with good mattresses, and duvets.

CUISINE. There are two main dining rooms, named Moonlight and Starlight (both are non-smoking). The Moonlight Dining Room is located on the lowest level of the atrium lobby, while the Starlight Dining Room is located one deck higher. There are tables for four, six or eight, but no tables for two. There are two seatings. The dining operation is well orchestrated, with emphasis on highly programmed (insensitive), extremely hurried service that many find intrusive.

For casual breakfasts and lunches, the Windjammer Café is the place to go, now split into various specialty areas including American, Asian, Latin, and Mediterranean fare, together with Compass Deli, a make up your own sandwich bar. Also added in a 2007 refit is a Johnny Rockets 1950s retro diner for fast foods like hamburgers and hot dogs, sodas and shakes, at extra cost; it is located on the new upper deck section of the Windjammer Café.

For coffee fans, there's Café Latte-tudes, featuring Seattle's Best Coffee brand. Coffee comes in paper cups.

ENTERTAINMENT. A Chorus Line is the ship's principal show lounge; it has both main and balcony levels, with banquette seating. On the stage is a video wall with 50 screens – good for visual presentations.

Royal Caribbean's large-scale production shows are extremely colorful spectaculars that will remind you of Las Vegas casino hotel shows, with their high-energy hype, presentation and glitz. They are fast-moving, razzle-dazzle shows that rely a lot on lighting and special effects, but have little or no storyline, often poor linkage between themes and scenes, and choreography that is more stepping in place rather than dancing. Strong cabaret acts are also featured in the main showlounge.

The entertainment throughout is upbeat (in fact, it is difficult to get away from music and noise), but is typical of the kind of resort hotel found ashore in Las Vegas. There is even background music in all corridors and lifts, and constant music outdoors on the pool deck.

SPA/FITNESS. The ShipShape Fitness Center has a gymnasium with aft-facing views (it is located at the aft of the ship, one deck lower than its pre-2007 refit location), and a selection of high-tech muscle-pumping equipment. There is also an aerobics studio, and classes are offered in a variety of keep fit regimes. There is also a beauty salon, and a sauna, and 10 treatment rooms for pampering massages, facials, etc. While the facilities are not as extensive as those aboard the company's newer ships, they are adequate for the short cruises that this ship operates.

For the more sporting, there is activity galore – including a rock-climbing wall, with several separate climbing tracks. It is located outdoors at the aft end of the funnel.

● **For more extensive general information about the Royal Caribbean cruise experience, see pages 137–42.**

WASTE DISPOSAL

Environmental concerns are taken very seriously by the cruise industry. Cruise ships must be capable of efficient handling of garbage and waste materials, as trash generated by passengers and crew must be managed, stored, and disposed of efficiently and economically. The larger the ship, the more waste is created, and the greater the need for reliable disposal systems.

The sheer magnitude of waste materials can be highly problematic, especially on long cruises. If solid waste is not burnable, or cannot be disposed of overboard (this must be biodegradable), it must be stored for later off-loading and disposal on land.

The latest cruise ships have "zero-discharge" facilities. These include incinerators and food waste handling systems that include vacuum transportation from feeding station in all galleys and food preparation areas, recycling and storage systems for ash, glass, metal and paper. But many older cruise ships have outdated garbage handling equipment.

Food waste is typically sent to a pulping machine that has been partially filled with water. Cutting mechanisms reduce the waste and allow it to pass through a special sizing ring to be pumped directly overboard or into a holding tank or an incinerator when the ship is within three-mile limits.

Marco Polo
★★★

Mid-Size Ship: . . . . .22,080 tons	Total Crew: 356	Cabins (with private balcony): 0
Lifestyle: . . . . .Standard	Passengers	Cabins (wheelchair accessible): 2
Cruise Line: . . . . .Transocean Tours	(lower beds/all berths): 848/915	Cabin Current: . . . . .110 and 220 volts
Former Names: . . . . .Aleksandr Pushkin	Passenger Space Ratio	Elevators: 4
Builder: . . . . . .VEB Mathias Thesen Werft	(lower beds/all berths): 26.0/24.1	Casino (gaming tables): . . . . .No
(Germany)	Crew/Passenger Ratio	Slot Machines: .No
Original Cost: . . . . .n/a	(lower beds/all berths): 2.3/2.5	Swimming Pools (outdoors): 1
Entered Service: . . . .Apr 1966/Apr 2008	Navigation Officers: . . . . . . .Scandinavian	Swimming Pools (indoors): 0
Registry: . . . . .The Bahamas	Cabins (total): .425	Whirlpools: 3
Length (ft/m): 578.4/176.28	Size Range (sq ft/m): 93.0–484.0/8.6–44.9	Self-Service Launderette: . . . . .No
Beam (ft/m): 77.4/23.60	Cabins (outside view): 292	Dedicated Cinema/Seats: . . . . .No
Draft (ft/m): 26.8/8.17	Cabins (interior/no view): 133	Library: . . . . .Yes
Propulsion/Propellers: .diesel(14,444 kW)/2	Cabins (for one person): . . .(many doubles	
Passenger Decks: 8	sold for single occupancy)	

OVERALL SCORE: 1,222 (OUT OF A POSSIBLE 2,000 POINTS)

OVERVIEW. This ship was built as one of five almost identical sister ships for the Russian/Ukrainian fleet. It was originally constructed to re-open the Leningrad to Montreal transatlantic route in 1966, after a long absence since 1949. The vessel has a traditional "real-ship" profile, an extremely strong ice-strengthened hull, and huge storage spaces for long voyages.

The now-defunct Orient Lines and its single ship, *Marco Polo*, was bought by Norwegian Cruise Line in 1998. In 2007 the ship was sold to Greek owners and, in April 2008, began a charter operation for Germany's Transocean Tours.

Marco Polo is fitted with the latest navigational aids and biological waste treatment center, and carries 10 Zodiac landing craft for in-depth shore trips in eco-sensitive areas.

This is a comfortable vessel throughout and, because it has a deep draft, rides well in unkind sea conditions. There are two large, forward-facing open-deck viewing areas. There is also a helicopter-landing pad atop the ship. The teakwood-decked aft swimming pool/lido deck area is kept in good condition. Joggers and walkers can circle around the ship – not on the promenade deck, but one deck above, although this goes past vast air intakes that are noisy, and the walkway is narrow.

As soon as you walk aboard, you feel a warm, welcoming, homely ambiance that is instantly comforting. There is a wide range of public rooms, most of which are arranged on one horizontal deck. A sense of spaciousness pervades, as most have high ceilings. The interior decor is very tasteful, with careful use of mirrored surfaces, as well as colors that do not clash and are relaxing but not boring; the subdued lighting helps maintain an air of calmness and relaxation.

BERLITZ'S RATINGS		
	Possible	Achieved
Ship	500	308
Accommodation	200	127
Food	400	230
Service	400	256
Entertainment	100	58
Cruise	400	243

Although this ship is more than 40 years old, it is in remarkably fine shape. Indeed, it's in better shape than many ships only 10 years old, and its interiors are constantly being refurbished and refreshed.

All in all, *Marco Polo* operates well-planned destination-intensive cruises, and offers really good value for money in very comfortable, unpretentious but tasteful surroundings, while a friendly and accommodating crew helps to make a cruise a pleasant, no-hassle experience.

There is no observation lounge with forward-facing views over the ship's bows. There are many "lips" or raised thresholds, so you need to be on your guard when walking through the ship, and particularly when negotiating the exterior stairways. This could prove difficult for mobility-limited passengers.

SUITABLE FOR: *Marco Polo* is best suited to couples and single travelers of mature years who enjoy being transported to interesting destinations in the comfort of a ship that is traditional in style, unpretentious yet pleasing, and without the trappings of much entertainment or organized parlor games.

ACCOMMODATION. The cabins, which come in many different price grades, depending on location and size, are a profusion of different sizes and configurations. All are pleasingly decorated, and have rich wood cabinetry, wood and mirror-fronted closets, adequate drawer and storage space, television set, thin cotton bathrobe (upper grades only), and hairdryer (in the bathroom) and non-vacuum (non-noisy) toilets. Carpets curtains and bedspreads are all nicely color coordinated. Weak points include extremely poor sound insulation between cabins – you can probably hear you neighbours brushing their hair – and the fact that the bathrooms are small, with little storage space for toiletries, which is a particular concern during long cruises.

The largest accommodation is found in six suites. These have a separate living room, and marble bathroom with bathtub/shower, walk-in closet, refrigerator, and a television/DVD unit.

Also quite comfortable are the Superior Deluxe ocean-view cabins that have two lower beds (some can be converted to a queen-sized bed), marble bathroom with tub/shower, and refrigerator.

Some cabins on Upper Deck and Sky Deck have lifeboat-obstructed views. It would be advisable to avoid cabins 310/312 as these are located close to the engine room doorway and the noise level is considerable. No cabins have a balcony because the ship was built for long-distance ocean/sea crossings before they became popular.

CUISINE/DINING. The Seven Seas Restaurant is nicely decorated in soft pastel colors, practical in design, and functions well, but it has a low ceiling, is noisy, and the tables are very close together.

There are two seatings, with tables for two to 10, and good place settings/china. The food itself is of an adequate standard, but presentation could be improved. The wine and prices are reasonable, although most wines are young.

Raffles is the place to head for informal self-serve break-fasts and lunches (there is seating inside as well as outdoors around the ship's swimming pool). On some evenings during each cruise it also becomes an alternative dining spot, for about 75 people. Reservations are required, but there is no extra charge. A 15% gratuity is added to all bar and wine accounts.

The onboard currency is the euro.

ENTERTAINMENT. The Ambassador Lounge is the principal venue for shows, cabaret acts, and lectures. A single-level room, it has banquette seating and fairly decent sightlines, although there are several pillars to obstruct the view from several seats. Entertainment is low-key and low-budget, and consists of a few cabaret acts (singers, magicians, comedians and others).

There's live music for social dancing and listening in several of the ship's bars and cocktail lounges.

SPA/FITNESS. This is an older ship that was built when spa and wellbeing facilities were not really thought about. A Health Spa was added in a later refit. It is located aft on Upper Deck, and contains a small gymnasium (it's not large, but there are a few treadmills, exercycles, and some muscle-toning equipment), a beauty salon, a sauna, changing facilities, and treatment rooms (for massages, facials, and other body pampering treatments).

The spa is operated by Mandara Spa, and treatments have a Far Eastern flavor (Indonesian facials, coconut body polish, aromatherapy massages).

EXPEDITIONS: DID YOU KNOW...

● that Quark Expeditions made maritime history in July/ August 1991, when its chartered Russian icebreaker, *Sovetskiy Soyuz*, made a spectacular 21-day voyage to negotiate a passage from Murmansk, Russia, to Nome, Alaska, across the North Pole? Although the polar ice cap had been navigated by the US nuclear submarines *Skate* and *Nautilus*, as well as by dirigible and airplane, this was the first passenger ship to make the hazardous crossing.

● that in 1984, Salen Lindblad Cruising made maritime history by negotiating a westbound voyage through the Northwest Pas-

sage, a 41-day epic that started from St. John's, Newfoundland, in Canada, and ended at Yokohama, Japan? The search for a Northwest Passage to the Orient attracted brave explorers for more than four centuries. Despite numerous attempts and loss of life, including Henry Hudson in 1610, a "white passage" to the East remained an elusive dream. Amundsen's 47-ton ship *Gjoa* eventually navigated the route in 1906, taking three years to do so. It was not until 1943 that a Canadian ship, *St. Roch*, became the first vessel in history to make the passage in a single season. *Lindblad Explorer*

became the 34th vessel, and the first cruise vessel, to complete the Northwest Passage.

● that the most expensive expedition cruise excursion was a cruise/dive to visit the resting place of RMS *Titanic* aboard the two deep-ocean submersibles *Mir I* and *Mir II* used in James Cameron's Hollywood blockbuster. Just 60 participants went as observers in 1998, and another 60 were taken in 1999.

● that a passenger once asked the operations director of a well-known expedition cruise ship where the best shops were in Antarctica? His reply: "On board, madam!"

Mariner of the Seas
★★★★

Large Resort Ship: . . . . . . .137,276 tons	Total Crew: 1,185	Cabins (with private balcony): 765
Lifestyle: . . . . .Standard	Passengers	Cabins (wheelchair accessible): 26
Cruise Line: Royal Caribbean International	(lower beds/all berths): 3,114/3,840	Cabin Current: . . . . .110 volts
Former Names: . . . . .none	Passenger Space Ratio	Elevators: . . . . .14 (6 glass-enclosed)
Builder: . . .Kvaerner Masa-Yards (Finland)	(lower beds/all berths): 44.0/35.7	Casino (gaming tables): . . . . .Yes
Original Cost: . . . .$500 million	Crew/Passenger Ratio	Slot Machines: . . . . .Yes
Entered Service: . . . . .Spring 2004	(lower beds/all berths): 2.6/3.2	Swimming Pools (outdoors): 3
Registry: . . . . .The Bahamas	Navigation Officers: . . . . . .Scandinavian	Swimming Pools (indoors): 0
Length (ft/m): 1,020.6/311.1	Cabins (total): 1,557	Whirlpools: 6
Beam (ft/m): 155.5/47.4	Size Range (sq ft/m): 151.0–1,358.0/	Self-Service Launderette: . . . . .No
Draft (ft/m): 28.8/8.8	14.0–126.1	Dedicated Cinema/Seats: . . . . .No
Propulsion/Propellers: . . . . .diesel-electric	Cabins (outside view): 939	Library: . . . . .Yes
(75,600kW)/3 azimuthing pods	Cabins (interior/no view): 618	
Passenger Decks: 14	Cabins (for one person): 0	

BERLITZ'S OVERALL SCORE: 1,472 (OUT OF A POSSIBLE 2,000 POINTS)

OVERVIEW. *Mariner of the Seas* is a stunning, large, floating leisure resort, sister to *Adventure of the Seas,* *Explorer of the Seas,* *Navigator of the Seas* and *Voyager of the Seas,* which debuted between 1999 and 2003, respectively. The exterior design is not unlike an enlarged version of the company's Vision-class ships.

The ship's propulsion is derived from three pod units, powered by electric motors (two azimuthing, and one fixed at the centerline) instead of conventional rudders and propellers.

With large proportions, the ship provides more facilities and options, yet the ship manages to have a healthy passenger space ratio (the amount of space per passenger). Being a "non-Panamax" ship, it is simply too large to go through the Panama Canal, thus limiting its itineraries almost exclusively to the Caribbean (where only a few islands can accept it), or for use as a floating island resort. Spend the first few hours exploring all the many facilities and public spaces aboard this vessel and it will be time well spent.

Although *Mariner of the Seas* is a large ship, the cabin hallways are warm and attractive, with artwork cabinets and wavy lines to lead you along and break up the monotony. In fact, there are plenty of colorful, even whimsical, decorative touches to help you avoid what would be a very clinical environment.

Embarkation and disembarkation take place through two stations/access points, designed to minimize lines (that's more than 1,500 people for each access point). Once inside the ship, you'll need good walking shoes, particularly when you need to go from one end to the other – it really is quite a long way.

BERLITZ'S RATINGS

	Possible	Achieved
Ship	500	418
Accommodation	200	150
Food	400	237
Service	400	277
Entertainment	100	83
Cruise	400	307

The four-decks-high Royal Promenade, which is 393.7 ft (120 meters) long, is the main interior focal point (it's a good place to hang out, to meet someone, or to arrange to meet someone). The length of two football fields (American football, that is), it has two internal lobbies (atria) that rise to as many as 11 decks high. Restaurants, shops and entertainment locations front this winding street and interior "with-view" cabins look into it from above. It is designed loosely in the image of London's fashionable Burlington Arcade – although there's not a real brick in sight, and I wonder if the designers have ever visited the real thing. It is, however, an imaginative piece of design work, and most passengers (particularly those who enjoy shopping malls) enjoy it immensely.

The super-atrium houses a "traditional" pub (the Wig & Gavel), with draft beer and plenty of "street-front" seating (North American passengers always seem to sit down, while British passengers prefer to stand at the bar). There is also a Champagne Bar, a Sidewalk Cafe (for continental breakfast, all-day pizzas, specialty coffees and desserts), Sprinkles (for round-the-clock ice cream and yoghurt), and a sports bar. There are also several shops – jewelry shop, gift shop, logo souvenir shop, and a Tommy Hilfiger signature store. Altogether, the Royal promenade is a nice place to see and be seen, and it sees action throughout the day and night. Comedy art has its place here, too, for example in the *trompe l'oeil* painter climbing up the walls. The Guest Reception and Shore Excursion counters are located at the aft end of the promenade, as is an ATM machine. Things to watch for: look up to see the large moving, asteroid-like sculpture (constantly growing and contracting). At times, street entertainers appear, and parades happen, while at other (carefully orchestrated) times it's difficult to walk through the area as it is filled to the brim with shopping items – like a cheap bazaar.

Arched across the promenade is a captain's balcony. Meanwhile, in the center of the promenade is a stairway that connects you to the deck below, where you'll find the Schooner Bar (a piano lounge that is a feature of all RCI ships) and the colorful Casino Royale. This is naturally large and full of flashing lights and noises. Gaming includes blackjack, Caribbean stud poker, roulette, and craps, as well as 300 slot machines. Aft of the casino is Bolero's Bar.

There's also a regulation-size ice-skating rink (Studio B), featuring real, not fake, ice, with "bleacher" seating for up to 900, and the latest in broadcast facilities. Ice Follies shows are presented here. Slim pillars obstruct clear-view arena stage sight lines, however. If ice-skating in the Caribbean doesn't appeal, you may enjoy the stunning two-deck library (open 24 hours a day). A grand $12 million was spent on permanent artwork. Drinking places include a neat Aquarium Bar, complete with 50 tons of glass and water in four large aquariums (whose combined value is over $1 million).

Drinking places include the small and intimate Champagne Bar, and a Connoisseur Club – for cigars and cognacs. Lovers of jazz might appreciate Ellington's, an intimate room for cool music atop the ship in the Viking Crown Lounge, or the Schooner Bar piano lounge. Golfers might enjoy the golf bar, as they play the Mariner Dunes.

There is a large television studio, adjacent to rooms that can be used for trade show exhibit space, with conference center that seats 400 and a multi-media screening room that seats 60. Lovers could tie the knot in a wedding chapel in the sky, the Skylight Chapel (it's located on the upper level of the Viking Crown Lounge, and even has wheelchair access via an electric stairway lift). Outdoors, the pool and open deck areas provide a resort-like environment.

Families with children are also well catered to, as facilities for children and teenagers are quite extensive. "Aquanauts" is for 3–5 year-olds; "Explorers" is for 6–8 year-olds; "Voyagers" is for 9–12 year-olds. Optix is a dedicated area for teenagers, including a daytime club (with several computers), soda bar, and dance floor. "Challenger's Arcade" features an array of the latest video games. Paint and Clay is an arts and crafts center for younger children. Adjacent is Adventure Beach, an area for all the family; it includes swimming pools, a water slide and game areas outdoors.

In terms of sheer size, this ship dwarfs almost all other ships in the cruise industry, but in terms of personal service, the reverse tends to be the case, unless you happen to reside in one of the top suites. Royal Caribbean International does, however, try hard to provide a good standard of programmed service from its hotel service staff. Remember to take lots of extra pennies – you'll need them to pay for all the additional-cost items.

ACCOMMODATION. There is an extensive range of 22 cabin categories in four major groupings: Premium ocean-view suites and cabins, Promenade-view (interior-view) cab-

ins, Ocean-view cabins, and Interior (no view) cabins. Many cabins are of a similar size – good for incentives and large groups, and 300 have interconnecting doors – good for families. If you do have a cabin with an interconnecting door to another cabin, be aware that you'll probably be able to hear everything your next-door neighbors say and do. Bathroom toilets are explosively noisy – like a barking dog.

A total of 138 interior (no view) cabins have bay windows that look into a horizontal atrium – first used to good effect aboard the Baltic passenger ferries *Silja Serenade* (1990) and *Silja Symphony* (1991) with interior cabins that look into a central shopping plaza. Regardless of what cabin grade you choose, however, all except for the Royal Suite and Owner's Suite have twin beds that convert to a queen-sized unit, television, radio and telephone, personal safe, vanity unit, mini-bar (called an Automatic Refreshment Center) hairdryer and private bathroom.

The largest cabins includes luxuriously appointed penthouse suites (whose occupants, sadly, must share the rest of the ship with everyone else, except for their own exclusive, and private, concierge club). The grandest is the Royal Suite, which is positioned on the port side of the ship, and measures 106.5 sq. meters/ 1,146 sq. ft). It features a king-sized bed in a separate, large bedroom, a living room with an additional queen-sized sofa bed, baby grand piano (no pianist is included, however), refrigerator/wet bar, dining table, entertainment center, and large bathroom.

Slightly smaller, but still highly desirable are the Owner's Suites (there are 10, all located in the center of the ship, on both port and starboard sides, each measuring 43 sq. meters/ 468 sq. ft) and four Royal Family suites (each 53 sq. meters/574 sq. ft), all of which feature similar items. However, the four Royal Family suites, which have two bedrooms (including one with third/fourth upper Pullman berths) are at the stern of the ship and have magnificent views over the ship's wake (and seagulls).

All cabins feature twin beds that convert to a queen-sized bed, a private bathroom with shower enclosure (towels are 100% cotton), as well as interactive, closed-circuit and satellite television, and pay-per-view movies. Cabins with "private balconies" are not so private, as the partitions are only partial, not full. The balcony decking is made of Bolidt – a sort of rubberized sand – and not wood, while the balcony rail is of wood.

CUISINE. The main dining room has a total seating capacity of 1,919); it is massive, and is set on three levels. A dramatic staircase connects all three levels, and huge, fat support pillars obstruct the sight lines. All three levels (Rhapsody in Blue, Top Hat and Tails, and Sound of Music) have exactly the same menus and food. There are also two small private wings for private groups, each seating 58 persons. The dining room is totally non-smoking, there are two seatings, and tables are for four, six, eight 10 or 12. The place settings, china and cutlery are of good quality. **Alternative Dining Options:** These are for casual and informal meals at all hours and include:

● **Cafe Promenade:** for continental breakfast, all-day pizzas, pastries, desserts and specialty coffees (sadly provided in paper cups).

● **Windjammer Cafe:** for casual buffet-style breakfast, lunch and light dinner (except the last night of the cruise).

● **Island Grill:** (this is actually a section inside the Windjammer Cafe), for casual dinner (no reservations necessary) featuring a grill and open kitchen.

● **Portofino:** this is the ship's "upscale" (non-smoking) Euro-Italian restaurant, open for dinner only. Reservations are required, and a $20 gratuity per person applies. The food and its presentation are better than the food in the dining room, although the restaurant is not large enough for all passengers to try even once during a cruise. Choices include antipasti, soup, salad, pasta, main dish, dessert, cheese and coffee. The menu does not change throughout the cruise.

● **Johnny Rockets**, a retro 1950s all-day, all-night diner-style eatery that features hamburgers, malt shakes (at extra cost), and jukebox hits, with both indoor and outdoor seating seating (all indoor tables feature a mini-jukebox; dimes are provided for you to make your selection of vintage records), and all-singing, all-dancing waitresses who'll knock your socks off, if you can stand the volume.

● **Sprinkles:** for round-the-clock ice cream and yoghurt.

ENTERTAINMENT. The 1,350-seat Savoy showlounge is a stunning room that could well be the equal of many such rooms on land. It is located at the forward end of the ship and spans the height of five decks (with only a few slim pillars and almost no disruption of sight lines from almost any seat in the house). The room features a hydraulic orchestra pit and huge stage areas, together with sonic-boom loud sound, and some superb lighting equipment.

In addition, the ship has a whole array of cabaret acts.

Although many of the cabaret acts are not what you would call headliners (the strongest cabaret acts are featured in the main showlounge, while lesser acts are presented in the Lotus Lounge, which is also the venue for late-night adults-only comedy), they regularly travel the cruise ship circuit.

The entertainment throughout is really upbeat, but is typical of the kind of resort hotel found ashore in Las Vegas. There is even background music in all corridors and lifts, and constant music outdoors on the pool deck. If you want a quiet relaxing holiday, this isn't the right ship for you.

There is also a television studio (in case you thought you'd need one aboard a cruise ship), located adjacent to rooms that could be used, for example, for trade show exhibit space (good for conventions at sea).

SPA/FITNESS. The ShipShape health and fitness spa is large, and measures 15,000 sq. ft (1,400 sq. meters). It includes a large aerobics room, fitness center (with the usual stairmasters, treadmills, stationary bikes, weight machines and free weights), treatment rooms, men's and women's sauna/steam rooms, while another 10,000 sq. ft (930 sq. meters) is devoted to a Solarium (with magrodome sliding glass roof) for relaxation after you've exercised too much.

For the more sporting, there is activity galore – including a rock-climbing wall that's 32.8 ft high (10 meters), with five separate climbing tracks. It is located outdoors at the aft end of the funnel. You'll get a great "buzz" being 200 ft (60 meters) above the ocean while the ship is moving. Other sports facilities include a roller-blading track, a dive-and-snorkel shop.

● **For more extensive general information about the Royal Caribbean experience, see pages 137–42.**

Minerva
★★★ +

Small Ship: ....12,500 tons	Passenger Decks: 6	Cabins (for one person): 4
Lifestyle: ....Standard	Total Crew: 157	Cabins (with private balcony): 12
Cruise Line: ....Swan Hellenic	Passengers	Cabins (wheelchair accessible): 2
Discovery Cruises	(lower beds/all berths): 352/474	Cabin Current: ....220 Volts
Former Names: *Explorer II, Alexander von*	Passenger Space Ratio	Elevators: 2
Humboldt, Saga Pearl, Minerva, Okean	(lower beds/all berths): 35.5/26.3	Casino (gaming tables): ....No
Builder: ....Mariotti (Italy)	Crew/Passenger Ratio	Slot Machines: ....No
Original Cost: ....n/a	(lower beds/all berths): 2.1/3.0	Swimming Pools (outdoors): 1
Entered Service: ....Apr 1996/May 2008	Navigation Officers: ....European	Swimming Pools (indoors): 0
Registry: ....The Bahamas	Cabins (total): 178	Whirlpools: 0
Length (ft/m): 436.3/133.0	Size Range (sq ft/m): 139.9–360.6/	Self-Service Launderette: ....Yes
Beam (ft/m): 65.6/20.0	13.0–33.5	Dedicated Cinema/Seats: Yes/96
Draft (ft/m): 19.6/6.0	Cabins (outside view): 126	Library: ....Yes
Propulsion/Propellers: diesel/2 (3,480 kW)/2	Cabins (interior/no view): 52	

OVERALL SCORE: 1,324 (OUT OF A POSSIBLE 2,000 POINTS)

OVERVIEW. Originally intended as a spy ship (*Okean*) for the Soviet navy, the strong, 1989-built ice-strengthened hull was constructed at Nikolajev in Ukraine; it had a stern ramp for launching submersibles for submarine tracking. The hull was bought by Monaco-based V-Ships, the present owners, who towed it to Italy for conversion into a "soft expedition" cruising vessel. The ship, under charter for six years, now operates for Swan Hellenic Discovery Cruises, part of the UK's All Leisure Group's Voyages of Discovery.

It's déja-vu for Swanners, as Swan Hellenic passengers are affectionately known. The ship has quite an angular profile, with a single, central funnel, and a slightly rounded stern. It does not handle unkind seas well, and the navigation bridge looks as if it should have been located one deck higher. There's ample open and shaded deck space for this size of ship, particularly in the aft section, and there is also a teak walk-around promenade deck. The uppermost passenger deck is artificial turf – awful when wet.

A fleet of rubber inflatable Zodiacs is carried for excursions ashore, ideal for inhospitable locations such as in Antarctica without landing piers or formal docking arrangements. The interior decor is homely and restrained, like a country house hotel, not in the slightest bit glitzy, for passengers with good taste, although cushions would be a welcome addition to the many sofas. Lectures and briefings are set in the Auditorium, the ship's main lounge. Fine wool carpets inhabit the passageways and public rooms.

Perhaps the most appreciated and used public room is the excellent library, with its great range of reference books (many of university-standard), with its classical decor and

BERLITZ'S RATINGS

	Possible	Achieved
Ship	500	311
Accommodation	200	114
Food	400	287
Service	400	288
Entertainment	n/a	n/a
Cruise	500	324

motifs, while Shackleton's Lounge, exuding a country-house atmosphere, is a fine place for a relaxing drink. Cigar smokers should appreciate the special smoking room and humidor service and high back leather chairs that provide a sense of well-being and privacy.

Despite the small cabins and tiny bathrooms, it's really the excellent food and very friendly service throughout the ship, plus a fine library, that makes a cruise aboard *Minerva* a rather special soft expedition vacation experience. The onboard currency is the pound sterling. All gratuities are included, although port charges are extra.

SUITABLE FOR: *Minerva* is for Swanners – couples and single travelers of a mature age who seek to cruise off the beaten track in comfortable surroundings, and who don't need the entertainment and organized parlor games found aboard larger ships. This ship is not recommended for children.

ACCOMMODATION. There are five different grades of cabins, in 16 price categories: Owner's Suite, Suite, Deluxe, Superior, and Standard. The price depends on the grade and location chosen rather than any great difference in the size of the accommodation. Most of the standard cabins really are quite small, particularly when compared to the "standard" cabin size on the latest ships today. There are few cabins with private balcony.

Owner's Suites (2): These Bridge Deck measure 360 sq. ft (33.5 sq. meters). Facilities include a queen-sized bed, an extra-large double closet and ample drawer space; separate lounge area with sofa, table and chair, and vanity table/writing desk, television/DVD player combo, refrigerator, hairdryer and binoculars; floor to ceiling patio doors leading to private balcony; bathroom with bath/ shower combination and toilet.

Suites (10): These suites on Bridge Deck measure 290 sq. ft (27 sq. meters). Facilities include twin beds or queen-sized bed, two double closets and ample drawer space; separate lounge area with sofa, table and chair, and vanity table/writing desk (poor lighting), small television/DVD player combo, refrigerator, hairdryer and binoculars; floor to ceiling patio doors leading to private (Astroturf-covered) balcony; bathroom with tub/shower and toilet.

Deluxe: These measure 226 sq. ft (21 sq. meters). Facilities include twin beds or queen-sized bed, two double closets and ample drawer space; separate lounge area with sofa, table and chair, and vanity table/writing desk, television and VCR, refrigerator, hairdryer and binoculars; large picture window; bathroom with bath/shower and toilet.

Superior: These measure 162 sq. ft (15 sq. meters). Facilities include twin beds or queen-sized bed, two double closets and ample drawer space; separate lounge area with sofa, table and chair, and vanity table/writing desk, television and VCR, refrigerator, hairdryer and binoculars; large picture window; bathroom with bath/shower and toilet.

Standard Outside-View or Interior (No View) Cabins: These "standard" cabins are small (140 sq. ft/13 sq. meters) when compared to the size of standard cabins aboard today's newest ships, which is around 182 sq. ft (17 sq. meters). Facilities include twin beds or queen-sized bed, two double closets and ample drawer space; separate lounge area with sofa, table and chair, and vanity table/writing desk, television and VCR, refrigerator, hairdryer and binoculars; large picture window (outside-view cabins only; or porthole, depending on deck and price category); bathroom with shower enclosure (small) and toilet.

The bathrooms have a raised "lip" to step over, are totally white, and have very small showers (except for the suites, which have bathtubs and green/black marble floors), although plumbing fixtures were poorly installed. No matter what grade of accommodation you book, all grades have

a hairdryer, 100% cotton bathrobe, TV with music channels, and a direct-dial telephone. However, there is little space for hanging outerwear parkas and other gear for expedition cruises, and some cabins on B Deck are subject to noise and vibration from the ship's engines/generators.

Because the insulation is quite poor, Bridge Deck suites suffer from noise that bleeds through from the Darwin lounge under them. This typically happens on itineraries where there is evening entertainment rather than when the ship is operating in the Antarctic region when fewer passengers are carried.

CUISINE. The Dining Room has open-seating dining, allowing you to dine with whomever you wish, in both the main restaurant and the informal indoor/outdoor café. The menus are very good, and the food itself is of a really high quality. It's also very creative, attractively presented, and has plenty of taste. In fact, it's far superior to the food aboard the previous ship of the same name. The wine list is really good, and so is the rather special champagne. The service staff really provide fine service, and they are very pleasant, friendly and willing.

Coffees and teas are available 24 hours a day from a beverage station in the self-serve Bridge Café, in which you can have casual breakfasts, luncheons, and dinners in an open-seating arrangement; for dinner, the menu is the same as in the main dining room.

ENTERTAINMENT. Although there is a main lounge, this is used principally for lectures, and occasionally for cabaret acts and classical music ensembles. The ship has a small band and solo entertaining musicians to provide live music for dancing and listening.

SPA/FITNESS. There is a small gymnasium on Funnel Deck (with side-facing views), while a beauty salon is located near the restaurant. Massages and aromatherapy facials, manicures, pedicures and hair beautifying treatments are available, and there is also a small sauna and adjacent shower, but no changing facilities.

Monarch of the Seas
★★★

Large Resort Ship: . . . . .73,937 tons	Passenger Decks: 11	Cabins (for one person): 0
Lifestyle: . . . . .Standard	Total Crew: 858	Cabins (with private balcony): 62
Cruise Line: . . . . .Royal Caribbean	Passengers	Cabins (wheelchair accessible): 4
International	(lower beds/all berths): 2,384/2,774	Cabin Current: . . . . .110 volts
Former Names: . . . . .none	Passenger Space Ratio	Elevators: 11
Builder: .Chantiers de l'Atlantique (France)	(lower beds/all berths): 31.0/26.6	Casino (gaming tables): . . . . .Yes
Original Cost: . . . .$300 million	Crew/Passenger Ratio	Slot Machines: . . . . .Yes
Entered Service: . . . . .Nov 1991	(lower beds/all berths): 2.8/3.3	Swimming Pools (outdoors): 2
Registry: . . . . .The Bahamas	Navigation Officers: . . . . .Norwegian	Swimming Pools (indoors): 0
Length (ft/m): 879.9/268.2	Cabins (total): 1,192	Whirlpools: 2
Beam (ft/m): 105.9/32.3	Size Range (sq ft/m): 118.4–670.0/	Self-Service Launderette: . . . . .No
Draft (ft/m): 24.9/7.6	11.0–62.2	Dedicated Cinema/Seats: . . . . .No
Propulsion/Propellers: . . . . .diesel	Cabins (outside view): 732	Library: . . . . .Yes
(21,844 kW)/2	Cabins (interior/no view): 460	

OVERALL SCORE: 1,248 (OUT OF A POSSIBLE 2,000 POINTS)

OVERVIEW. The ship is almost identical in size and appearance to sister ships *Majesty of the Seas* and *Sovereign of the Seas* but with an improved internal layout, better public room features, passenger flow and signage. Royal Caribbean International's trademark Viking Crown lounge and bar surrounds the funnel and provides a stunning view, although the original Scandinavian tub chairs are extremely small and have no back support. The open deck space is very cramped when full, as aboard any large ship, although there seems to be plenty of it. There is a basketball court for sports lovers.

Following a grounding just before Christmas 1998, the ship underwent the replacement of 460 tons of bottom shell plating. At the same time, a new facility for toddlers was created. The children's and teens' programs are good, overseen by enthusiastic youth counselors, and there is a busy but sound activities program for adults.

The interior layout is a little awkward, as it is designed in a vertical stack, with most public rooms located aft, and the accommodation forward. There is, however, an impressive array of spacious and elegant public rooms, although the decor definitely brings to mind the IKEA school of interior design. A stunning five-deck-high Centrum lobby has cascading stairways and two glass-walled elevators.

There is a decent two-level showlounge and decent shops, albeit with lots of tacky merchandise. Casino gamers will find blackjack, craps, Caribbean stud poker and roulette tables, plus an array of slot machines.

This floating resort provides a well-tuned, yet very impersonal, short cruise experience for a lot of passengers. The dress code is very casual. There are many public rooms

BERLITZ'S RATINGS		
	Possible	Achieved
Ship	500	334
Accommodation	200	119
Food	400	221
Service	400	260
Entertainment	100	66
Cruise	400	248

and spaces to play in, including a five-deck-high atrium, which really is the interior focal point of the ship, and has glass lifts. Among the public rooms, the library offers space for relaxation and has a decent selection of books.

The ship provides a decent enough range of facilities with consistently sound, but highly programmed service from a reasonably attentive young staff. In the final analysis, you will probably be overwhelmed by the public spaces, and underwhelmed by the size of the cabins. The ship underwent an extensive internal refurbishment in 2003 and still looks fresher for it.

ACCOMMODATION. There are 17 categories. The price you pay will depend on the grade, size and location you choose. Note that there are no cabins with private balconies.

Suites: Thirteen suites on Bridge Deck are reasonably large and nicely furnished (the largest is the Royal Suite), with separate living and sleeping spaces. They provide more space, with better service and more perks than standard-grade accommodation.

Standard Cabins: The standard outside-view and interior (no view) cabins are very small, although an arched window treatment and colorful soft furnishings do give the illusion of more space.

Almost all cabins have twin beds that can be converted to a queen-sized or double bed configuration, together with moveable bedside tables. However, when in a queen-bed configuration, the bed is typically flush against the wall, and access is from one side only. All of the standard cabins have very little closet and drawer space (you will need some luggage engineering to stow your cases). You should, therefore, think of packing only minimal clothing, which is all you really need for a short cruise.

All cabins have a private bathroom, with a shower enclosure, toilet and washbasin.

CUISINE. The two large, no-smoking dining rooms, Claude's and Vincent's, are located off the Centrum lobby (Claude's is one deck above Vincent's). There are tables for four, six or eight, but no tables for two, and there are two seatings. The dining operation is well-orchestrated, with emphasis on highly programmed service.

The cuisine is typical of mass banquet catering that offers standard fare comparable to that found in American family-style restaurants ashore. While menu descriptions are tempting, the actual food may be somewhat disappointing and unmemorable (many items are pre-prepared ashore to keep costs down).

However, a decent selection of light meals is provided, and a vegetarian menu is available. The selection of breads, rolls, fruit and cheese is quite poor, however, and could do with improvement. Caviar (once a standard menu item) now incurs a hefty extra charge. Menus typically include a Welcome Aboard Dinner, French Dinner, Italian Dinner, International Dinner, and Captain's Gala Dinner.

The wine list is not extensive, but the prices are moderate. The waiters, many from Caribbean countries, eastern Europe and Goa, are perhaps overly friendly for some tastes – particularly on the last night of the cruise, when tips are expected.

For casual breakfasts and lunches, the Windjammer Café is the place to go, although there are often long lines at peak times. Although the selection is just average, several themes, such as Mexican and Indian, are featured. On the aft of the upper level of the venue is Sorrento's Pizzeria.

ENTERTAINMENT. The Sound of Music is the name of the principal showlounge; it has both main and balcony levels, with banquette seating, although sight lines from many of the balcony seats are poor.

A smaller entertainment lounge, the April in Paris Lounge, is where cabaret acts, including late-night adult (blue) comedy are featured, as well as music for dancing.

The entertainment throughout is upbeat (in fact, it is difficult to get away from music and noise). There is even background music in all corridors and elevators, and constant music outdoors on the pool deck. If you want a quiet relaxing holiday, choose another ship.

SPA/FITNESS. The ShipShape Fitness Center has a gymnasium with aft-facing views (it is located at the aft of the ship) and a selection of high-tech muscle-pumping equipment. There is also an aerobics studio, and classes are offered in a variety of keep fit regimes. There is also a beauty salon, and a sauna, as well as treatment rooms for pampering massages, facials, etc. While the facilities are not as extensive as those aboard RCI's newer ships, they are adequate for the short cruises that this ship operates.

For the more sporting, there is activity galore – including a rock-climbing wall, with several separate climbing tracks. It is located outdoors aft of the funnel and wrap-around Viking Crown Lounge.

● **For more extensive general information about the Royal Caribbean experience, see pages 137–42.**

QUOTABLE QUOTES

These are some of the questions I have been asked by passengers cruising for the first time:

"Does the crew sleep on board?"

"How far above sea level are we?"

"Is the island surrounded by water?"

"Are all Caribbean islands the same size?"

"How does the captain know which port to go to?"

"Can we get off in the Panama Canal?"

"Does the ship generate its own electricity?"

"Does this elevator go up as well as down?"

"Will this elevator take me to my cabin?"

"Why is the sauna so hot?"

"What time's the midnight buffet?"

"Are there two seatings at the midnight buffet?"

"Do we have to stay up until midnight to change our clocks?"

"Does the chef cook himself?"

"What happens to the ice sculptures after they melt?"

"How many fjords to the dollar?"

"What time's the 2 o'clock tour?"

"Where's the bus for the walking tour?"

"Can you see the Equator from the deck?"

Monet
★★

Boutique Ship: . . . . .1,480 tons	Total Crew: 27	Cabins (with private balcony): 0
Lifestyle: . . . . .Standard	Passengers	Cabins (wheelchair accessible): 0
Cruise Line: . . . . .Elegant Cruises & Tours	(lower beds/all berths): 66/71	Cabin Current: . . . . .220 volts
Former Names: . .*Stella Dalmatiae, Yushar*	Passenger Space Ratio	Elevators: 0
Builder: . .Brodoremont Shipyard (Croatia)	(lower beds/all berths): 22.4/20.8	Casino (gaming tables): . . . . .No
Original Cost: .n/a	Crew/Passenger Ratio	Slot Machines: . . . . .No
Entered Service: 1970/2001	(lower beds/all berths): 2.0/2.2	Swimming Pools (outdoors): 1
Registry: . . . . .St Vincent	Navigation Officers: . . . . .Croatian	Swimming Pools (indoors): 0
Length (ft/m): 223.4/68.1	Cabins (total): .35	Whirlpools: 2
Beam (ft/m): 33.1/10.1	Size Range (sq ft/m): 92.0–151.0/	Self-Service Launderette: . . . . .No
Draft (ft/m): 11.5/3.5	8.5/14.0	Dedicated Cinema/Seats: . . . . .No
Propulsion/Propellers: . . . . .diesel	Cabins (outside view): 35	Library: . . . . .Yes
(1,000kW)/1 (CP)	Cabins (interior/no view): 0	
Passenger Decks: 4	Cabins (for one person): 4	

OVERALL SCORE: 941 (OUT OF A POSSIBLE 2,000 POINTS)

OVERVIEW. *Monet*, named after the French Impressionist Claude Monet (1840–1926), is a gem of a ship that inhabits the small ports of the Adriatic Sea. It is an all-white boutique ship, good for up-close coastal cruising. Originally built in Bulgaria, the vessel was extensively refitted in 1997 in Croatia, with a new superstructure built onto an existing hull. The ship is operated by New York-based Elegant Cruises & Tours (fellow passengers will typically be American and British).

The ship has smart hardwood teak decks, with hardwood tables and chairs on the open Sun Deck aft. Its interior decor is charming, with warm colors throughout the limited public spaces. There is one (small) main lounge, a restaurant, and small boutique, so the ambiance is intimate. The dress code is casual, and informality rules. The Croatian staff provides warm, well-meaning, but unsophisticated service.

Monet is a pleasant ship for those who do not like lines or crowds. Note that there is no elevator, so you must be able to negotiate steps on board and in some ports of call. Typically, 7-day cruises are the staple, with an occasional longer cruise. Shore excursions, gratuities, and port charges are extra (shore excursions may be included on special, longer itineraries). There are no medical facilities, and no doctor on board. The ship is often chartered by various groups.

SUITABLE FOR: *Monet* is best suited to adult couples and single travelers of mature years who seek a go-slow lifestyle, and who wouldn't be interested in venturing aboard those big ships with hordes of passengers. This is for passengers who want to learn about the Adriatic region's history and architecture.

BERLITZ'S RATINGS		
	Possible	Achieved
Ship	500	192
Accommodation	200	107
Food	400	211
Service	400	230
Entertainment	100	30
Cruise	400	171

ACCOMMODATION: There are five price grades for the all-outside view cabins. Cabins are located on three of the ship's four passenger decks. All have hardwood cabinetry and soft furnishings of a decent quality, color TV and video player, multiple music channels, telephone, hairdryer, and vanity desk with lighted mirror. Closet space is tight, so take only essentials. All (except for four single-occupancy cabins) have lower beds, in either a twin-bed or double-bed arrangement (two of the cabins can accommodate three persons) and all have a tiny (wet shower) bathroom with hand-held shower. The washbasins are positioned extremely low. There is no room service menu. There are also two Master Cabins, with forward-facing views, and more space.

CUISINE: The intimate Nymphea Restaurant, just forward of the reception desk, has large square ocean-view picture windows. Single seating, leisurely dining is featured (for dinner) at tables for two, four or six, while breakfasts and lunches are self-service.

The cuisine, which is reasonably varied, encompasses regional specialties, and wine, beer and soft drinks are typically included for lunch and dinner, but espresso and cappuccino coffees (from the bar) cost extra.

ENTERTAINMENT: The Giverny Bar/Piano Bar, the gathering place for after-dinner conversation, has a cozy wood-topped bar, and also has a musical unit that provides music for listening and dancing.

SPA/FITNESS: The ship really is too small to have any spa facilities, although there are two hot tubs on outside decks.

MSC Armonia
★★★★

Large Resort Ship: . . . . .58,625 tons	Passenger Decks: 10	Cabins (for one person): 0
Lifestyle: . . . . .Standard	Total Crew: 710	Cabins (with private balcony): 132
Cruise Line: . . . . .MSC Cruises	Passengers	Cabins (wheelchair accessible): 2
Former Names: . . . .*European Vision*	(lower beds/all berths): 1,566/2,223	Cabin Current: . . . . .110 and 220 volts
Builder: . . . . .Chantiers de l'Atlantique	Passenger Space Ratio	Elevators: 9
(France)	(lower beds/all berths): 37.4/26.3	Casino (gaming tables): . . . . .Yes
Original Cost: . . . .$245 million	Crew/Passenger Ratio	Slot Machines: . . . . .Yes
Entered Service: . . .June 2001/May 2004	(lower beds/all berths): 2.2/3.1	Swimming Pools (outdoors): 2
Registry: . . . . .Italy	Navigation Officers: . . . . .European	Swimming Pools (indoors): 0
Length (ft/m): 823.4/251.0	Cabins (total): 783	Whirlpools: . . . . .1 (thalassotherapy)
Beam (ft/m): 94.4/28.8	Size Range (sq ft/m): 139.9–236.8/	Self-Service Launderette: . . . . .No
Draft (ft/m): 22.4/6.85	13.0–22.0	Dedicated Cinema/Seats: . . . . .No
Propulsion/Propellers: . . . . .diesel-electric	Cabins (outside view): 511	Library: . . . . .Yes
(31,680kW)/2 azimuthing pods	Cabins (interior/no view): 272	

OVERALL SCORE: 1,434 (OUT OF A POSSIBLE 2,000 POINTS)

OVERVIEW. Built originally for the now defunct Festival Cruises, the ship was a cousin to Festival's first new ship *Mistral*, but with an additional deck that allowed for the addition of more suites with private balconies in what is really a premium real estate area. The additional deck also provided a better balance to the ship's overall profile. A 115-ft (35-meter) mid-section was added to increase the ship's length and provide more cabins and public rooms.

The ship is fitted with a high-tech azimuthing "pod" propulsion system (*see page 174 for a definition*). As *European Vision*, the ship began its working life auspiciously, having been selected to be a floating hotel to accommodate the leaders and staff of the G8 summit in 2001. In 2004, Festival Cruises ceased operations (the result of heavy discounts and competition in the marketplace which sadly resulted in many crew members losing their jobs). The ship was bought by MSC Cruises for €215 million and renamed *MSC Armonia*.

The exterior deck space is barely adequate for the number of passengers carried, no more. The lido deck surrounding the outdoor swimming pool also has whirlpool tubs and a large bandstand is set in raised canvas-covered pods (all sunloungers have cushioned pads).

Inside, the layout and passenger flow is good, as are the "you are here" deck signs. The decks are named after European cities – e.g. Oxford Deck (with British public room names), Venice Deck (with Italian public room names), and Biarritz Deck (with French public room names). The decor is "European Moderne" – whatever that means – but it does include crisp, clean lines, minimalism in furniture designs (including some chairs that look interesting but are totally

BERLITZ'S RATINGS

	Possible	Achieved
Ship	500	405
Accommodation	200	155
Food	400	235
Service	400	298
Entertainment	100	55
Cruise	400	286

impractical). However, the interior colors chosen are extremely good; nothing jars the senses, but rather calms them, unlike many ships today.

Facilities include Amadeus, the ship's nightclub, and La Gondola Theater, for production shows and cabaret, plays and other theatrical presentations. There's a cigar smoking room (called Ambassador), which has all the hallmarks of a gentleman's club; as well as Vivaldi, a piano lounge. The Goethe Library/Card Room has real writing desks (something many ships seem to omit). There is an extensive internet cafe, as well an English pub called the White Lion. Gamblers will find solace in the Lido Casino, with blackjack, poker and roulette games, plus an array of slot machines.

The onboard currency is the euro. Gratuities are recommended at $8.50 per person, per day. Additionally, 15% is added to all bar bills and heath spa treatments.

Standing in line for embarkation, disembarkation, shore tenders and for self-serve buffet meals is an inevitable aspect of cruising aboard all large ships. Heavy smokers are everywhere, and are virtually impossible to avoid (in typical European fashion, ashtrays are simply moved – if used at all – to wherever smokers happen to be sitting or standing). Announcements are in several languages.

The staff is more focused on Italian passengers than those who speak any other European language. If you are considering two back-to-back 7-day cruises, note that some ports may be duplicated, and menus and entertainment are based on a 7-day cycle, so there is much product repetition (including the cruise director's jokes). Regular passenger complaints include poor ports of call information.

The wheelchair-bound should note that there is no access

to the uppermost forward and aft decks, although access throughout most of the interior of the ship is very good. The passenger hallways are a little narrow on some accommodation decks to pass when housekeeping carts are in place, however.

The company keeps prices low by providing air transportation that may be at inconvenient times, or that involves long journeys by bus. In other words, be prepared for a little discomfort in getting to and from your cruise in exchange for low cruise rates.

SUITABLE FOR: *MSC Armonia* is best suited to adult couples and singles (plus families with children) who enjoy big city life, piazzas and outdoor cafes, constant activity accompanied by lots of noise (some call it ambiance), late nights, entertainment that is loud and of questionable quality, and food that is quantity rather than quality. It is for those who are comfortable hearing several (European) languages everywhere around them.

ACCOMMODATION. There are 11 categories, the price depending on grade, size and location. These include 132 suites with private balcony (the partitions are only of the partial and not the full type), outside-view cabins and interior (no view) cabins.

Suite grade accommodation (they are not true suites, as there is no separate bedroom and lounge) also has more room, a larger lounge area, walk-in closet, wall-to-wall vanity counter, a bathroom with combination tub and shower, toilet, and private balcony (with light). Bathrobes are provided. In general, the "suites" are well laid out and nicely furnished. However, except for the very highest category, the suite bathrooms are very plain, with white plastic washbasins and white walls, and mirrors that steam up.

Even the smallest interior (no- view) cabins are quite spacious, with plenty of space between the two lower beds. All grades of accommodation have sheets and blankets as bed linen (no duvets), and are equipped with a TV set, hairdryer, mini-bar/refrigerator, personal safe (cleverly positioned behind a vanity desk mirror), bathroom with shower and toilet, and 100% cotton towels. However, the standard grade cabins are quite small when compared to many other ships, at a modest 140 sq. ft (13 sq. meters).

CUISINE. The four dining spots are no-smoking. The principal dining room, the 610-seat Marco Polo Restaurant, typically has two seatings for dinner, and open seating for breakfast and lunch. However, for breakfast and lunch, you

may well be seated with others with whom you may not be able to communicate very satisfactorily, given the mixture of languages on board.

In general, the cuisine is acceptable, if unmemorable. The menus are varied and the presentation is generally sound, and should prove a highlight for most passengers. The wine list has a wide variety of wines at fairly reasonable prices, although most of the wines are very young.

La Pergola, the most formal restaurant, has stylish Italian cuisine. It is assigned to all passengers occupying accommodation designated as suites, although other passengers can dine in it too, on a reservations-only basis.

Chez Claude, on the starboard side aft, adjacent to the ship's funnel, is a grill area for fast-food items. La Brasserie is a casual, self-serve buffet eatery, open 24 hours a day. The selections are very standardized (minimal). Cafe San Marco, on the upper, second level of the main lobby, is available for coffee and pastry items.

ENTERTAINMENT. La Gondola Theater is two decks high, and is the main venue for production shows, cabaret acts, plays and other theatrical presentations. It is a well designed room (except for the fact that no space was allocated for a live showband), with good sight lines from most seats, and four entrances that allow easy access (and exit).

Entertainment is weak, although it could improve somewhat as more ships are brought into service by MSC Cruises. Other shows consist of unknown cabaret acts (typically singers, magicians, mime artistes, comedy jugglers, and others) doing the cruise ship circuit. The ship carries a number of bands and small musical units that provide live music for dancing or listening.

SPA/FITNESS. The Atlantica Spa has numerous body-pampering treatments, a gymnasium with ocean views, and an array of high-tech, muscle-toning and strengthening equipment. There's also a thermal suite (with different kinds of steam rooms combined with aromatherapy infusions such as chamomile and eucalyptus) and a rasul chamber (a combination of two or three different kinds of special application mud, and gentle steam shower).

The spa, operated by the Italian concession OceanView, offers a wide range of well-being treatments.

For the sports-minded, there's a simulated climbing wall outdoors, while other sports and fitness facilities include volleyball/basketball court, and mini-golf.

● **For more extensive general information about the MSC Cruises experience, see pages 129–30.**

MSC Fantasia
NOT YET RATED

Large Resort Ship: ....135,000 tons	Total Crew: 1,313	Cabins (with private balcony): 1,260
Lifestyle: ....Standard	Passengers	Cabins (wheelchair accessible): 43
Cruise Line: ....MSC Cruises	(lower beds/all berths): 3,274/3,900	Cabin Voltage: ....110 volts
Former Names: ....none	Passenger Space Ratio	Elevators: 14
Builder: ....Aker Yards (France)	(lower beds/all berths): 41.2/34.6	Casino (gaming tables): ....Yes
Original Cost: ....$550 million	Crew/Passenger Ratio	Slot Machines: ....Yes
Entered Service: ....Dec 2008	(lower beds/all berths): 2.5/3.0	Swimming Pools (outdoors): 3
Registry: ....Panama	Navigation Officers: ....European	Swimming Pools (indoors): 1
Length (ft/m): 1,093.5/333.3	Cabins (total): 1,637	(with glass dome)
Beam (ft/m): 124.1/37.9	Size Range (sq ft/m): 161.4–699.6/	Whirlpools: 13
Draft: 27.72/8.45	15.0–65.0	Self-Service Launderette: ....No
Propulsion/Propellers: .....diesel-electric	Cabins (outside view): 1,354	Dedicated Cinema/Seats: ....No
(40mW)/2	Cabins (interior/no view): 283	Library: ....Yes
Passenger Decks:..................13	Cabins (for one person): 0	

OVERVIEW. Built in 67 blocks (some of which exceed 600 tons), *MSC Fantasia* is the latest generation of large ships for this growing company. It is 10 meters longer than the Eiffel Tower is high, and the propulsion power is the equivalent of 120 Ferraris. There are four swimming pools, one of which can be covered by a glass dome (magrodome).

The interior design is really an enlargement and extension of the smaller *MSC Musica/MSC Orchestra*-class ships, but with some new additions. Included are a large show lounge, a nightclub/discotheque, numerous lounges and bars, library, card room, an internet center, virtual reality center, shopping gallery (the shops are integrated with many bars, lounges and entertainment areas so that shopping becomes a city-like environment). Gamers will like the Monte Carlo Casino, featuring blackjack, poker and roulette games, plus an array of slot machines.

Drinking places include a pub-like venue and several comfortable loungeswith live music. A neat mini-golf course is located on the port side of the funnel, while a walking/jogging track encircles th two swimming pools. The ship is designed to accommodate families with children, who have their own play centers (a children's club and jungle adventure playground), youth counselors, and programs.

SUITABLE FOR: Best suited to young adult couples, singles, and families with tots, children and teens who enjoy big-ships, a city-style life, with all its attendant noise and different nationalities and languages (mostly European).

ACCOMMODATION. Eighty percent of cabins have an outside view, and 95% of these have a balcony (a standard balcony

BERLITZ'S RATINGS		
	Possible	Achieved
Ship	500	NYR
Accommodation	200	NYR
Food	400	NYR
Service	400	NYR
Entertainment	100	NYR
Cruise	400	NYR

cabin will measure almost 172 sq. ft (16 sq. meters), plus bathroom and balcony).

There are 99 suites in a "MSC Yacht Club" VIP section, with full butler service. The private area, on two decks, a pool (with skydome) and sun deck with access via private elevators, an observation lounge/bar, direct access to the spa, a private galley for room service and a private concierge lounge with an integral library. A black marble floor leads to a magnificent Swarovski glass staircase which connects the concierge facilities between Deck 15 and 16 under a glass-domed ceiling.

CUISINE. There are four dining venues: the two-deck-high Main Restaurant; an Italian panoramic specialty restaurant; a Tex-Mex restaurant; and a restaurant for suite passengers only. The main restaurant is in the aft section, with a stairway to connect the two levels. For casual breakfasts and lunches can be taken in a self-serve buffet-style eatery.

ENTERTAINMENT. The main showlounge has 1,700 seats, and facilities rival almost any found on land today.

SPA/FITNESS. The Fantasia Wellbeing Center has a beauty salon, several treatment rooms, and a gymnasium with great ocean views. Included is a thermal suite, containing different kinds of steam rooms combined with herbal aromatherapy infusions. The center is run by Italy's OceanView. Sports facilities include deck quoits, shuffleboard courts, large tennis/basketball court, minigolf, and a jogging track.

● **For more extensive general information about the MSC Cruises experience, see pages 129–30.**

MSC Lirica
★★★★

Large Resort Ship: . . . . .59,058 tons	Passenger Decks: 10	Cabins (for one person): 0
Lifestyle: . . . . .Standard	Total Crew: 701	Cabins (with private balcony): 132
Cruise Line: . . . . .MSC Cruises	Passengers	Cabins (wheelchair accessible): 4
Former Names: . . . . .none	(lower beds/all berths): 1,560/2,065	Cabin Current: . . . . .110/220 volts
Builder: . . . . . . .Chantiers de l'Atlantique	Passenger Space Ratio	Elevators: 9
(France)	(lower beds/all berths): 37.5/28.3	Casino (gaming tables): . . . . .Yes
Original Cost: . . . .$266 million	Crew/Passenger Ratio	Slot Machines: . . . . .Yes
Entered Service: . . . . .Mar 2003	(lower beds/all berths): 2.2/2.9	Swimming Pools (outdoors): 2
Registry: .Panama	Navigation Officers: . . . . .Italian	Swimming Pools (indoors): 0
Length (ft/m): 830.7/253.25	Cabins (total): 780	Whirlpools: 2
Beam (ft/m): 94.4/28.8	Size Range (sq ft/m): 139.9–302.0/	Self-Service Launderette: . . . . .No
Draft (ft/m): 22.4/6.85	. . . . .13.0–28.0	Dedicated Cinema/Seats: . . . . .No
Propulsion/Propellers: . . . . .diesel	Cabins (outside view): 504	Library: . . . . .Yes
(31,680kW)/2 azimuthing pods	Cabins (interior/no view): 276	

OVERALL SCORE: 1,439 (OUT OF A POSSIBLE 2,000 POINTS)

OVERVIEW. Similar in size and structure to the (now defunct) Festival Cruises' sister ships *European Dream* and *European Vision*, but arguably with a more attractive exterior profile, *MSC Lirica* (sister to *MSC Opera*) is the first of a pair of newbuilds for Mediterranean Shipping Cruises (MSC), Italy's largest privately owned cruise line (its former name was Star Lauro Cruises).

The blue funnel is quite sleek, with a swept-back design that closely resembles that of the Princess Cruises ships, and carries the MSC logo. The ship is fitted with an azimuthing pod propulsion system (*for details, see page 174*).

Inside, the layout and passenger flow is quite good with the exception of a couple of points of congestion (typically when the first seating comes out of the dining room and passengers on second seating are waiting to go in. The decor has many Italian influences, and this includes clean lines, minimalism in furniture design, and an eclectic collection of colors and soft furnishings that somehow work well together, and without any hint of garishness.

Real wood and marble have been used extensively in the interiors, and the high quality reflects MSC's commitment to the vessel's future. The "fit and finish" of the interior decor, and most carpeting, is very good.

Facilities include the ship's main showlounge, a nightclub/discotheque, several lounges and bars, an internet center (Cyber Cafe, with 10 terminals), a virtual reality center, a shopping gallery named Rodeo Drive (with shops that have an integrated bar and entertainment area so that shopping becomes a city-like environment where you can shop, drink, and be entertained all in one convenient area), and a children's club. Gamblers may find solace in the Las

BERLITZ'S RATINGS

	Possible	Achieved
Ship	500	407
Accommodation	200	156
Food	400	236
Service	400	299
Entertainment	100	55
Cruise	400	286

Vegas Casino, with blackjack, poker and roulette games, together with an array of slot machines. There is also a card room, but the integral library is small and disappointing, and there are no hardback books.

The ship is designed to accommodate families with children, who have their own play center, youth counselors, and programming.

MSC Lirica features Mediterranean cruises during the summer and Caribbean cruises during the winter. The onboard currency is the euro (summer) and US$ (winter). Note that gratuities are extra, but bar drinks include a service charge.

Anyone who is wheelchair-bound should note that there is no access to the uppermost forward and aft decks, although access throughout most of the interior of the ship is very good (there are also several wheelchair-accessible public restrooms). The passenger hallways are a little narrow on some decks for you to pass when housekeeping carts are in place, however.

Some things that passengers find irritating: the ship's photographers always seem to be in your face; the telephone numbering system to reach such places as the information bureau (2224) and hospital (2360) are not easy to remember (single digit numbers would be more user-friendly).

Standing in line for embarkation, disembarkation, shore tenders and for self-serve buffet meals is an inevitable aspect of cruising aboard all large resort ships. Heavy smokers seem to be everywhere, and are virtually impossible to avoid (in typical European fashion, ashtrays are simply moved – if used at all – to wherever smokers happen to be sitting).

SUITABLE FOR: *MSC Lirica* is best suited to young adult couples, singles, and families with tots, children and teens who enjoy big ship surroundings, a big city life, with all its attendant noise (some call it ambience), and passengers of different nationalities and languages (mostly European).

ACCOMMODATION. There are 11 different price levels for accommodation, depending on the grade and location you choose: one suite category, five outside-view cabin grades, and five interior (no view) cabin grades. Included are 132 "suites" with private balcony (note that the partitions between each balcony are of the partial and not the full wall type), outside-view cabins and interior (no view) cabins.

No matter what grade of cabin you choose, all have a mini-bar and personal safe, satellite-linked television, several audio channels, and 24-hour room service (note that while tea and coffee are complimentary, snacks for room service carry a delivery charge of €2.50 each time).

Accommodation designated as Suites (they are not true suites, as there is no separate bedroom and lounge – in other words, it is not a "suite" of rooms) also has more room, a larger lounge area, walk-in closet, wall-to-wall vanity counter, a bathroom with combination bathtub and shower, toilet, and semi-private balcony with light (the partitions are of the partial, not full, type). The bathrobes are 100% cotton. However, except for the very highest category, the suite bathrooms are very plain, with white plastic wash-basins and white walls, and mirrors that steam up.

According to the rules of feng shui, it is bad luck to place any mirror in such a position that it can be seen by anyone lying in bed (there are two floor-to-ceiling mirrors opposite the bed).

Some cabins on Scarlatti Deck have views obstructed by lifeboats, while those on Deck 10 aft (10105–10159) can be subject to late-night noise from the discotheque on the deck above.

CUISINE. There are two dining rooms (La Bussola Restaurant, and the smaller, slightly more intimate L'Ippocampo Restaurant, located one deck above), both of which have large ocean-view picture windows at the aft end of the ship. There are two seatings for meals, in keeping with all other ships in the MSC fleet, and tables are for two, four, six or eight.

La Pergola is the most formal restaurant, offering stylish Italian cuisine. It is assigned to all passengers occupying accommodation designated as suites, although other passengers can dine in it too, on a reservations-only basis. As you might expect, the food and service are superior to that in the main dining room.

Casual, self-serve buffets (for breakfast and lunch) can be taken in Le Bistrot Cafeteria (there are serving lines on both port and starboard sides). For fast foods, there is also a grill and a pizzeria (both are located outside, adjacent to the swimming pool and ship's funnel).

The Coffee Corner, located on the upper, second level of the main lobby, is the place for coffees and pastry items – as well for people-watching throughout the day. Although there are windows, the view is not of the ocean, but of the stowed gangways and associated equipment.

ENTERTAINMENT. The Broadway Theater is the ship's main showlounge, located in the forward section of the ship. It has tiered seating set in a sloping floor, and sightlines are good from most seats. The room can also serve as a venue for large social functions. There is no separate bandstand, and the shows work with recorded music; hence there is little consistency in orchestration and sound balance.

High-quality entertainment has not, to date, been part of MSC's mindset. Hence, production shows and variety acts tend to be adequate at best. The Lirica Lounge (located one deck above the showlounge) is the place for social dancing, with live music provided by a band. Meanwhile, for the young and lively set, there is The Blue Club (the ship's throbbing, ear-melting discotheque).

SPA/FITNESS. The Lirica Health Center is located one deck above the navigation bridge at the forward end of the ship. The complex features a beauty salon, several treatment rooms offering massage and other body-pampering treatments, as well as a gymnasium with ocean views and an array of high-tech, muscle-toning and strengthening equipment. There's also a thermal suite, containing different kinds of steam rooms combined with aromatherapy infusions, at €12 per session, or six sessions for €60.

The health center is run as a concession by the Italian company OceanView, with European hairstylists and Balinese massage and body treatment staff. Examples of treatment prices: full body massage, shiatsu massage, both at €90 for 50 minutes; cranial massage, €20 for 20 minutes; facial, €65; shampoo and finish, €32. Gratuities are not included, and are not charged to your account.

● **For more extensive general information about the MSC Cruises experience, see pages 129–30.**

MSC Melody
★★★

Mid-Size Ship: . . . . .36,500 tons	Total Crew: 535	Cabins (with private balcony): 0
Lifestyle: . . . . .Standard	Passengers	Cabins (wheelchair accessible): . . . . . .Yes
Cruise Line: . . . . .MSC Cruises	(lower beds/all berths): 1,098/1,600	Cabin Current: . . . . .110 volts
Former Names: .Star/ShipAtlantic, Atlantic	Passenger Space Ratio	Elevators: 4
Builder: . . . . .C.N.I.M. (France)	(lower beds/all berths): 33.2/22.8	Casino (gaming tables): . . . . .Yes
Original Cost: . . . .$100 million	Crew/Passenger Ratio	Slot Machines: . . . . .Yes
Entered Service: . . . .Apr 1982/June 1997	(lower beds/all berths): 2.0/2.9	Swimming Pools (outdoors): 1
Registry: .Panama	Navigation Officers: . . . . .Italian	Swimming Pools (indoors): 1
Length (ft/m): 671.9/204.8	Cabins (total): .549	Whirlpools: 3
Beam (ft/m): 89.7/27.4	Size Range (sq ft/m): 137.0–427.0/	Self-Service Launderette: . . . . .No
Draft (ft/m): 25.5/7.8	12.7–39.5	Dedicated Cinema/Seats: Yes/227
Propulsion/Propellers: . . . . .diesel	Cabins (outside view): 392	Library: . . . . .Yes (2 book racks)
(22,070 kW)/2	Cabins (interior/no view): 157	
Passenger Decks: 9	Cabins (for one person): 0	

BERLITZ'S OVERALL SCORE: 1,248 (OUT OF A POSSIBLE 2,000 POINTS)

OVERVIEW. The ship has a short, stubby, foreshortened bow and squat funnel, and an all-white hull and superstructure, although it cannot be considered at all handsome because the lifeboats are located high above the superstructure. There is a good amount of outdoor deck space, but noise levels can be high when the ship is full (particularly in summer). The interior is quite spacious, with plenty of public rooms, mostly high-ceilinged. The decor is somber in places, and the lighting is quite subdued. There is a generous amount of stainless steel and teakwood trim. A large observation lounge (with good views from large picture windows) is rather wasted as an informal eating area.

There is a good indoor-outdoor pool area (this can be covered by a magrodome in bad weather). There is a fairly good children's program during peak periods, and several children's (and teens') counselors. Typically about 60% of passengers will be Italian. Expect lots of extra charges. The onboard currency is the euro (although during the winter the ship typically sails in South American waters, when the onboard currency may change).

The almost constant loud announcements are intrusive. There is no wrap-around promenade deck outdoors, and cushioned pads are not provided for the sunloungers. The ship has only four elevators – not nearly enough. Standing in line for embarkation, disembarkation, and buffet meals is inevitable aboard large ships.

SUITABLE FOR: Best suited to young couples, singles, and families with children and teens who enjoy big ship surroundings, a big city life, with all its attendant noise, and passengers of different nationalities and languages.

BERLITZ'S RATINGS

	Possible	Achieved
Ship	500	347
Accommodation	200	147
Food	400	215
Service	400	241
Entertainment	100	58
Cruise	400	240

ACCOMMODATION. There are 12 categories and price grades. Six suites have plenty of space for families of four, and have a decent walk-in closet. The bathroom is large and has a full-size bathtub, oversize basin, and an uncomfortable square toilet. Other outside-view and interior (no view) cabins are of a good size, and have ample closet and drawer space. Many cabins have upper berths – good for families, although with four persons there is very little space for luggage. The cabin soundproofing is extremely poor, and the room service menu is quite basic. The bathrooms are of a decent size, and quite practical in their facilities.

CUISINE. The Galaxy Restaurant, on a lower deck (Restaurant Deck), is large and quite attractive, but the tables are very close together. Also, the chairs do not have armrests, and the noise level is extremely high. There are two seatings, and the cuisine is Italian. The food quality generally is adequate for the price, but doesn't live up to menu descriptions. There is a limited wine list.

ENTERTAINMENT. The Club Universe is just forward of midships on Lounge Deck. Although the ceiling is high, it is a single-level room with banquette seating. The ship has a showband and several small musical units.

SPA/FITNESS. The SeaSport Health and Fitness Center has a gymnasium (with treadmills, exercycles, and muscle-pumping equipment), beauty salon, and massage room.

● **For more extensive general information about the MSC Cruises experience, see pages 129–30.**

MSC Musica
★★★★

Large Resort Ship:	.........92,409 tons
Lifestyle:	.................Standard
Cruise Line:	...........MSC Cruises
Former Names:	.................none
Builder:	...........Aker Yards (France)
Original Cost:	.............$360 million
Entered Service:	............July 2006
Registry:	...................Panama
Length (ft/m):	.............963.9/293.8
Beam (ft/m):	................105.6/32.2
Draft (ft/m):	...................25.2/7.7
Propulsion/Propellers:	..........diesel
	(31,680kW)/2
Passenger Decks:	13

Total Crew:	987
Passengers	
(lower beds/all berths):	....2,550/3,013
Passenger Space Ratio	
(lower beds/all berths):	.......36.2/30.6
Crew/Passenger Ratio	
(lower beds/all berths):	.........2.6/3.0
Navigation Officers:	............Italian
Cabins (total):	1,275
Size Range (sq ft/m):	.....150.6–301.3/
	14.0/28.0
Cabins (outside view):	1,000
Cabins (interior/no view):	275
Cabins (for one person):	0

Cabins (with private balcony):	827
Cabins (wheelchair accessible):	17
Cabin Voltage:	...........110/220 volts
Elevators:	13
Casino (gaming tables):	............Yes
Slot Machines:	...................Yes
Swimming Pools (outdoors):	2
Swimming Pools (indoors):	0
Whirlpools:	4
Self-Service Launderette:	..........No
Dedicated Cinema/Seats:	..........No
Library:	........................Yes

OVERALL SCORE: 1,462 (OUT OF A POSSIBLE 2,000 POINTS)

OVERVIEW. *MSC Musica* is an extension and evolution of the slightly smaller *MSC Lirica* and *MSC Opera*. The blue funnel is quite sleek, with a swept-back design and carries the MSC logo in gold lettering, and forward of the mast, additional decks provide a more balanced profile. The hull features large circular porthole-style windows instead of square or rectangular windows. From a technical viewpoint, the ship is powered by diesel motors driving electric generators to provide power to two conventional propellers.

BERLITZ'S RATINGS		
	Possible	Achieved
Ship	500	412
Accommodation	200	156
Food	400	243
Service	400	298
Entertainment	100	62
Cruise	400	291

The interior layout and passenger flow is quite good with the exception of a couple of points of congestion, typically when the first seating exits the two main dining rooms and passengers on the second seating are waiting to enter. The musically-themed decor has many Italian influences, including clean lines, minimalism in furniture design, and a collection of colors, soft furnishings and fabrics that work well together, although it's a little more garish than one would expect.

Real wood and marble have been used extensively in the interiors, and the high quality reflects the commitment that MSC Cruises has in the vessel's future.

The focal point of the ship is the main three-deck high lobby, with a water-feature backdrop and a crystal piano on a small stage that appears to float on a pond. Other facilities include a large main show lounge, a nightclub, discotheque, numerous lounges and bars (including a wine bar), library, card room, an internet center, virtual reality center, children's club, and cigar lounge. A shopping gallery, which includes an electronics store, has an integrated bar and entertainment area that flows through the main lobby so that shopping becomes a city-like environment where you can shop, drink, and be entertained all in one convenient area. Gamblers will like the expansive San Remo Casino (with blackjack, poker and roulette games, together with an array of slot machines).

Drinking places include a pub-like venue as well as several comfortable lounges with live music. A mini-golf course is on the port side of the funnel, while a walking/jogging track encircles an upper level above the two swimming pools. The ship is designed to accommodate families with children, who have their own play center, video games room, youth counselors, and activity programs.

Some of the artwork is whimsical, but fishermen will appreciate the stuffed head from a blue marlin caught by Pierfrancesco Vago, president of MSC Cruises in 2004 – weighing 588 pounds (266.7 kg), it stands at the Blue Marlin Bar on the pool deck. And do check out the "restroom with a view" – the men's/ladies toilets adjacent to the Blue Marlin pool deck bar have a great ocean view (you can even watch the passing scenery while sitting on the toilet if you leave the door open).

The on-board currency is the euro. Gratuities are charged to your onboard account, at €6 per person, per day, but bar drink prices include a service charge.

Although access throughout most of the interior of the ship is very good, anyone who is wheelchair-bound should note that the passenger hallways are a little narrow on some decks for you to pass when housekeeping carts are in place. Sadly, there is no walk-around open promenade deck.

SUITABLE FOR: *MSC Musica* is best suited to young adult couples, singles, and families with tots, children and teens who enjoy big ship surroundings, a big city life, with all its attendant noise (some call it ambience), and passengers of different nationalities and languages (mostly European).

ACCOMMODATION. There are 12 price levels, depending on grade and location: suites, outside-view cabins, and interior (no view) cabins. Included are 18 "suites" with private balcony, mini-suites, outside-view cabins and interior (no view) cabins. Contrary to nautical convention, the cabin numbering system has even numbered cabins on the starboard side, and odd numbered cabins on the port side.

All cabins have a mini-bar and personal safe, satellite flat-screen TV, several audio channels, and 24-hour room service. Note that, while continental breakfast is complimentary from 7:30 to 10am, room service snacks are available at extra cost at any other time.

Accommodation designated as "suites" (they are not true suites, as there is no separate bedroom and lounge) also has more room (although they are small compared to suites on some of the major cruise lines), a larger lounge area, walk-in closet, and vanity desk with drawer-mounted hairdryer; a bathroom with combination bathtub and shower, toilet, and semi-private balcony with light (the partitions between each balcony are of the partial, not full, type). The bathrobes and towels are 100% cotton. The suite bathrooms are plain, with white plastic washbasins and white walls, and mirrors that steam up.

Many cabins on Forte Deck have views obstructed by lifeboats. Also, cabins on the uppermost accommodation deck (Cantata Deck) may be subject to sunloungers being dragged across the deck above when it is set up or cleaned early in the morning. Some of the most popular cabins are those at the aft end of the ship, with views over the ship's stern from the balcony cabins (on Virtuoso, Adagio, Intermezzo and Forte decks).

The 17 cabins for the disabled are spacious and well equipped.

CUISINE. There are two principal dining rooms (L'Oleandro and Le Maxim's), both located aft, with large ocean-view picture windows. There are two seatings for meals, in keeping with other ships in the MSC Cruises fleet, and tables are for two, four, six or eight; seating is both banquette-style and in individual chairs; the chairs, however, are slim and do not have armrests. All dining venues are managed and supervised by Italians.

Passengers occupying accommodation designated as suites and deluxe grades are typically assigned the best tables in the quietest sections of Le Maxim's restaurant, which itself is quieter than L'Oleandro, the main dining room.

Casual, self-serve buffets (for breakfast and lunch) can be taken in the Gli Archi Cafeteria (one section of which forms the reservations-only Il Giardino; or at a pool deck outside fast-food eatery. Coffee/tea and pastries can be taken in several bars adjacent to the midships atrium lobby.
Alternative Dining Spots:
● *Il Giardino* is an à la carte dining spot; the cost is Euro18 per person for dinner.

● *Kaito* is a Japanese sushi bar with counter and table seating and a menu that has a fine array of à la carte sashimi pieces, nigiri and temaki sushi and maki rolls, tempura and teriyaki items, and a choice of several types of cold or hot sake, and Japanese beer.
● *Enoteca Wine Bar* is a very creative wine bar, and provides a selection of famous regional cheeses, hams and wine in a relaxing and entertaining bistro-style setting.

In other words, there are more dining choices than aboard other previous MSC Cruises ships, if you are willing to pay extra.

Silver trays full of late-night snacks are taken throughout the ship by waiters, and on some days, special late-night desserts, such as flambé items, are showcased in various lounges like the Il Tucana Lounge. The ship makes its own ice cream.

ENTERTAINMENT. The Theatro La Scala, the large, principal show lounge, is in the forward section of the ship. It has tiered seating on two levels (the sightlines are good from most of the plush, comfortable seats). The room can also serve as a venue for large groups or social functions.

High-quality entertainment has not, to date, been a priority for MSC Cruises. Production shows and variety acts tend to be amateurish (particularly when compared to some other major cruise lines). There is no showband, and all shows are performed to recorded music "click" tracks.

The Il Tucano (Tucan) Lounge (aft of the show lounge) is the place for social dancing and functions such as cooking demonstrations, with live music provided by a band. Another nightclub, the Crystal Lounge, provides music for the social dance set. Meanwhile, for the young and lively crowd, the ship's ear-melting G32 discotheque is the place to head for; with its floor-to-ceiling windows, it is a quiet, pleasant place to relax and read during sea days.

Additionally, big-screen movies are shown on a large screen above the forward pool, just behind the ship's mast.

SPA/FITNESS. The Aloha Beauty Farm (spa center) is one deck above the navigation bridge at the forward end of the ship. The complex has a beauty salon, several treatment rooms offering massage and other body-pampering treatments, and a gymnasium with forward ocean views and an array of high-tech, muscle-toning and strengthening equipment. There's also a Middle East-themed thermal suite, containing steam rooms and saunas with aromatherapy infusions, and a relaxation/hot tub room; to use these facilities costs €30 per day, or €150 per cruise. Examples of treatment prices: Aromaspa Massage, €158 (90 minutes); shiatsu massage, €99 (50 minutes); facial, €99 (50 minutes).

The spa is run as a concession by Steiner Leisure, with European hairstylists and massage/body treatment staff.

Sports facilities include table tennis, a tennis court mini golf course, golf practice net, two shuffleboard courts, and a jogging track.

● **For more extensive general information about the MSC Cruises experience, see pages 129–30.**

MSC Opera
★★★★

Large Resort Ship:	.59,058 tons	Passenger Decks:	.10
Lifestyle:	.Standard	Total Crew:	.701
Cruise Line:	.MSC Cruises	Passengers	
Former Names:	.none	(lower beds/all berths):	.1,756/2,200
Builder:	.Chantiers de l'Atlantique	Passenger Space Ratio	
	(France)	(lower beds/all berths):	.33.6/26.8
Original Cost:	.$266 million	Crew/Passenger Ratio	
Entered Service:	.Mar 2004	(lower beds/all berths):	.2.5/3.1
Registry:	.Italy	Navigation Officers:	.Italian
Length (ft/m):	.830.7/256.25	Cabins (total):	.878
Beam (ft/m):	.94.4/28.8	Size Range (sq ft/m):	.139.9–302.0/
Draft (ft/m):	.22.4/6.85		.13.0–28.0
Propulsion/Propellers:	.diesel	Cabins (outside view):	.504
(31,680kW)/2 azimuthing pods		Cabins (interior/no view):	.276

Cabins (for one person):	.0
Cabins (with private balcony):	.200
Cabins (wheelchair accessible):	.4
Cabin Voltage:	.110 and 220
Elevators:	.9
Casino (gaming tables):	.Yes
Slot Machines:	.Yes
Swimming Pools (outdoors):	.2
Swimming Pools (indoors):	.0
Whirlpools:	.2
Self-Service Launderette:	.No
Dedicated Cinema/Seats:	.No
Library:	.Yes

OVERALL SCORE: 1,438 (OUT OF A POSSIBLE 2,000 POINTS)

OVERVIEW. *MSC Opera* is the second of a pair of newbuilds for MSC Cruises (the first being *MSC Lirica*), Italy's largest privately owned cruise line (formerly Star Lauro Cruises), although this ship has almost 100 cabins more than *MSC Opera*. The blue funnel is quite sleek, with a swept-back design that closely resembles that of the Princess Cruises ships, and carries the MSC logo in gold lettering. The ship is similar in size and structure to *MSC Lirica,* there are many modifications (mostly in technical spaces), and improvements in the layout of public rooms; there are also more cabins with private balcony.

All decks are named after operas. The interior layout and passenger flow is quite good with the exception of a couple of points of congestion, typically when the first seating exits the dining room and passengers on second seating are waiting to enter. The decor has many Italian influences, including clean lines, minimalism in furniture design, and a collection of colors, soft furnishings and fabrics that work well together, and without any hint of garishness. Real wood and marble have been used extensively in the interiors, and the high quality reflects the commitment that MSC Cruises has in the vessel's future. The "fit and finish" of the interior decor, and most carpeting, is very good.

Facilities include the ship's main show lounge, a nightclub/discotheque, several lounges and bars, an internet center with 10 terminals, a virtual reality center, a children's club, a shopping gallery named Via Conditti (with shops that have an integrated bar and entertainment area so that shopping becomes a city-like environment where you can shop, drink, and be entertained all in one convenient area). Gamblers will find pleasure in the Monte Carlo Casino, with

BERLITZ'S RATINGS

	Possible	Achieved
Ship	500	408
Accommodation	200	156
Food	400	235
Service	400	298
Entertainment	100	55
Cruise	400	286

blackjack, poker and roulette games, together with an array of slot machines. There is also a card room, but the integral library is small and disappointing, and there are no hardback books. Possible drinking places include the Sotto Vento Pub (under the show lounge), or the La Cabala lounge. Outside on deck, a neat 8-hole mini-golf course wraps around the funnel, while a walking/jogging track encircles the ship's two swimming pools.

The ship is designed to accommodate families with children, who have their own play center, youth counselors, and programming.

MSC Opera typically features Mediterranean cruises during the summer and Caribbean cruises during the winter. The onboard currency is the euro (summer) and US$ (winter). Note that gratuities are extra, but bar drinks include a service charge.

Anyone who is wheelchair-bound should note that there is no access to the uppermost forward and aft decks, although access throughout most of the interior of the ship is very good (there are also several wheelchair-accessible public restrooms). The passenger hallways are a little narrow on some decks for you to pass when housekeeping carts are in place, however.

Minor niggles include the ship's photographers who always seem to be in your face; constant music in every lounge; and the fact that standing in line for embarkation, disembarkation, shore tenders and for self-serve buffet meals is an inevitable aspect of cruising aboard all large ships (although lines are minimal when the ship operates from Port Everglades). Smokers are everywhere, and are virtually impossible to avoid (in typical European fashion, ashtrays are simply moved – if used at all – to wherever smokers happen to be sitting). Sadly, there is no forward observation lounge.

The ship's onboard product delivery changes (for the better) when operated during the winter Caribbean season. This is because the ship operates under the auspices of MSC Cruises (USA), when the product is "tweaked" to accommodate American tastes and preferences.

SUITABLE FOR: *MSC Opera* is best suited to young adult couples, singles, and families with tots, children and teens who enjoy big ship surroundings, a big city life, with all its attendant noise (some call it ambience), and passengers of different nationalities and languages (mostly European).

ACCOMMODATION. There are 11 price levels, depending on grade and location: one suite category, five outside-view cabin grades, and five interior (no view) cabin grades. Included are 172 "suites" with private balcony, outside-view cabins and interior (no view) cabins. The cabin numbering system has even numbered cabins on the starboard side, and odd numbered cabins on the port side – contrary to nautical convention.

All cabins have a mini-bar and personal safe, satellite TV, several audio channels, and 24-hour room service (note that while tea and coffee are complimentary, snacks for room service carry a delivery charge of €2.50 each time).

Accommodation designated as Suites (they are not true suites, as there is no separate bedroom and lounge) also has more room, a larger lounge area, walk-in closet, wall-to-wall vanity counter, a bathroom with combination bathtub and shower, toilet, and semi-private balcony with light (the partitions betwen each balcony are of the partial, not full, type). 100 percent cotton bathrobes are provided. However, except for the very highest category, the suite bathrooms are very plain, with white plastic washbasins and white walls, and mirrors that steam up.

Some cabins on Othello Deck and Rigoletto Deck have views obstructed by lifeboats, while those on Turandot Deck aft (10192–10241) may be subject to late-night and early morning noise from the cafeteria on the deck above. Also, cabins on the uppermost accommodation deck are subject to deck chairs and tables being dragged across the deck when it is set up or cleaned early in the morning.

CUISINE. There is one principal dining room (La Caravella Restaurant), with large ocean view picture windows in the aft third of the ship. There are two seatings for meals, in keeping with other ships in the MSC Cruises fleet, and tables are for two, four, six or eight.

L'Approdo Restaurant is assigned to all passengers occupying accommodation designated as suites, although other passengers can dine in it too, on a reservations-only basis. As you might expect, the food and service are superior to that in the main dining room.

Casual, self-serve buffets (for breakfast and lunch) can be taken in Le Vele Cafeteria (the serving lines on both port and starboard sides are quite cramped, and the food is quite basic); or at the pool deck outside the fast food eatery, with grill and pizzeria. Coffee/tea and pastries can be taken in the Aroma Café set around the upper level of the two-deck-high atrium lobby, but annoying videos constantly play on TVsets in the forward sections.

ENTERTAINMENT. The 713-seat Theatre dell Opera is the ship's main show lounge, located in the forward section of the ship. It has tiered seating set in a sloping floor, and the sightlines are good from most seats, which are plush and comfortable. The room can also serve as a venue for large social functions. There is no separate bandstand, and the shows work with recorded music; hence there is little consistency in orchestration and sound balance.

High-quality entertainment has not, to date, been a priority for MSC Cruises. Hence, production shows and variety acts tend to be amateurish at best (when compared to some other major cruise lines).

The Opera Lounge (one deck above the show lounge) is for social dancing, with a live band. Meanwhile, for the young and lively set, there is the Byblos Discotheque (the ship's throbbing, ear-melting discotheque).

SPA/FITNESS. The Opera Health Center is located one deck above the navigation bridge at the forward end of the ship. The complex features a beauty salon, several treatment rooms offering massage and other body-pampering treatments, as well as a gymnasium with ocean views and an array of high-tech, muscle-toning and strengthening equipment. There's also a thermal suite, containing different kinds of steam rooms combined with aromatherapy infusions, at €12 per session, or six sessions for €60.

The health center is run as a concession by the Italian company OceanView, with European hairstylists and Balinese massage and body treatment staff. Examples of treatment prices: Balinese massage, €93 (45 minutes); shiatsu massage, €90 (45 minutes); hot stone therapy, €100 (45 minutes); facial, €65; pedicure, €40. Gratuities are not included, and are not charged to your account.

● **For more extensive general information about the MSC Cruises experience, see pages 129–30.**

MSC Orchestra
★★★★

Large Resort Ship: ....92,409 tons	Total Crew: 987	Cabins (with private balcony): 827
Lifestyle: ....Standard	Passengers	Cabins (wheelchair accessible): 17
Cruise Line: ....MSC Cruises	(lower beds/all berths): 2,550/3,013	Cabin Voltage: ....110/220 volts
Former Names: ....none	Passenger Space Ratio	Elevators: 13
Builder: ....Aker Yards (France)	(lower beds/all berths): 36.2/30.6	Casino (gaming tables): ....Yes
Original Cost: ....$360 million	Crew/Passenger Ratio	Slot Machines: ....Yes
Entered Service: ....May 2007	(lower beds/all berths): 2.6/3.0	Swimming Pools (outdoors): 2
Registry: ....Italy	Navigation Officers: ....Italian	Swimming Pools (indoors): 0
Length (ft/m): 963.9/293.8	Cabins (total): 1,275	Whirlpools: 4
Beam (ft/m): 105.6/32.2	Size Range (sq ft/m): 150.6–301.3/	Self-Service Launderette: ....No
Draft (ft/m): 25.2/7.7	......................14.0/28.0	Dedicated Cinema/Seats: ....No
Propulsion/Propellers: .....diesel electric	Cabins (outside view): 1,000	Library: ....Yes
(40.4MW)/2	Cabins (interior/no view): 275	
Passenger Decks: 13	Cabins (for one person): 0	

BERLITZ'S OVERALL SCORE: 1,465 (OUT OF A POSSIBLE 2,000 POINTS)

OVERVIEW. *MSC Orchestra* is a sister to *MSC Musica*, which entered service in 2006. The ship has a balanced profile. The blue funnel is of a sleek, swept-back design and carries the MSC logo in gold lettering. From a technical viewpoint, the ship is powered by diesel motors driving electric generators to provide power to two conventional propellers.

The interior layout and passenger flow is quite good with the exception of a couple of points of congestion – typically when the first seating exits the two main dining rooms and passengers on the second seating are waiting to enter. The decor is decidedly European, with many Italian influences, including clean lines, minimalism in furniture design, and a collection of high-quality soft furnishings and fabrics in warm colors that work beautifully together, and with no hint of garishness at all (arguably much nicer and softer than sister ship *MSC Musica*). Real wood and marble have been used extensively in the interiors, and the high quality reflects the commitment that MSC Cruises has in its product and the vessel's future.

Facilities include a large main show lounge, a nightclub/discotheque, numerous lounges and bars (including the stunning "Out of Africa" Savannah Lounge, library, card room, an internet center, virtual reality center, shopping gallery (the shops are integrated with many bars, lounges and entertainment areas so that shopping becomes a city-like environment where you can shop, drink, and be entertained all in one convenient area). Gamblers will find pleasure in the Monte Carlo Casino, featuring blackjack, poker and roulette games, plus an array of slot machines, and a couple of gilt female nude reclining sculptures.

BERLITZ'S RATINGS

	Possible	Achieved
Ship	500	413
Accommodation	200	156
Food	400	243
Service	400	298
Entertainment	100	62
Cruise	400	293

Drinking places include a pub-like venue as well as several comfortable lounges that have live music. Outside on deck a neat mini-golf course is locate don the port side of the funnel, while a walking/jogging track encircles the ship's two swimming pools. The ship is really designed to accommodate families with children, who have their own play centers (a children's club and jungle adventure playground), youth counselors, and programs.

MSC Orchestra operates Mediterranean cruises in summer and Caribbean cruises in winter. The onboard currency is the euro (summer) and US$ (winter). Gratuities (at a suggested €6 per person per day) are extra, but bar drink prices include a service charge. Although access throughout most of the interior of the ship is very good, anyone who is wheelchair-bound should note that the passenger hallways are a little narrow on some decks for you to pass when housekeeping carts are in place.

SUITABLE FOR: *MSC Orchestra* is best suited to young adult couples, singles, and families with tots, children and teens who enjoy big-ship surroundings, a city-style life, with all its attendant noise (some call it ambience), and passengers of different nationalities and languages (mostly European)

ACCOMMODATION. There are 12 price levels, depending on grade and location. Included are suites with private balcony, outside-view cabins, and interior (no view) cabins with private balcony; outside-view cabins)no balcony) and interior (no view) cabins. Contrary to nautical convention, the cabin numbering system has even numbered cabins on the starboard side, and odd numbered cabins on the port side.

All cabins have a mini-bar and personal safe, satellite TV, several audio channels, and 24-hour room service (note that, while tea and coffee are complimentary, snacks for room service incur a delivery charge).

Accommodation designated as "suites" (they are not true suites, as there is no separate bedroom and lounge) also has more room, a larger lounge area, walk-in closet, wall-to-wall vanity counter, a bathroom with combination bathtub and shower, toilet, and semi-private balcony with light (the partitions between each balcony are of the partial, not full, type). Bathrobes (100% cotton) are provided. However, except for the very highest category, the suite bathrooms are very plain, with white plastic washbasins and white walls, and mirrors that steam up.

Some cabins have views obstructed by lifeboats. Also, cabins on the uppermost accommodation deck may be subject to deck chairs and tables being dragged across the deck when it is set up or cleaned early in the morning.

CUISINE. There are two principal dining rooms, Villa Borghese Restaurant and L'Ibiscus. They are located in the aft section of the ship, and have large ocean-view picture windows. There are two seatings for dinner, and open seating for breakfast and lunch, in keeping with other ships in the MSC Cruises fleet. Tables are for two, four, six or eight, and some alcove banquette seating.

Anyone occupying upper-grade accommodation typically gets better tables in quieter areas.

Alternative (extra-cost) Dining Venues:

● The *Shanghai Chinese Restaurant* provides an alternative dining spot for a change from the main restaurants. This is the first real Chinese restaurant aboard any cruise ship (mainly because of the challenges of providing high-temperature wok and deep fryer preparation). Dim sum steamed dishes are also featured (typically for lunch). Food from four main cuisines is featured (Beijing, Cantonese, Shanghai and Szechzuan), as is Tsing Tao beer.

● The *Four Seasons Restaurant* is another alternative dining spot which offers à la carte Italian cuisine in a garden-like setting (cover charge: €18 per person), and fine china.

Casual, self-serve buffets (for breakfast and lunch) can be taken in the lido café-style Four Seasons Restaurant; or at a pool deck outside fast-food grill and pizzeria (La Piazzetta). Coffee/tea (at extra cost) and pastries can be taken in several bars (all fitted with coffee machines) set around the first and second levels of the atrium lobby, in which a delightful four-piece classical ensemble regularly performs.

ENTERTAINMENT. Covent Garden is the ship's stunning large show lounge. Located in the forward section of the ship, it has tiered seating set in a sloping floor, and the sightlines are good from most seats, which are plush and comfortable. The room can also serve as a venue for large social functions. High-quality entertainment has not, to date, been a priority for MSC Cruises. But providing production shows and variety acts that appeal to a multinational audience is a challenge.

The Opera Lounge (located one deck above the show lounge) is the place for social dancing, with live music provided by a band. Meanwhile, for the young and lively set, the ship's G32 discotheque is the hot place to head for.

Additionally, a large poolside movie screen provides movie-goers with more choices. Activities are provided by a team of multi-lingual animators.

SPA/FITNESS. The Orchestra Health Center (Body and Mind spa) is located one deck above the navigation bridge at the forward end of the ship. The complex has a beauty salon, several treatment rooms offering massage and other body-pampering treatments, as well as a gymnasium with ocean views and an array of high-tech, muscle-toning and strengthening equipment.

There's also a thermal suite, containing different kinds of steam rooms combined with aromatherapy infusions, at €12 per session, or six sessions for €60; there's also a neat juice/smoothie bar opposite the reception desk.

The health center is run as a concession by the Italian company OceanView, with European hairstylists and fine Balinese massage and body treatment staff. Examples of treatment prices: Balinese massage, €93 (45 minutes); shiatsu massage, €90 (45 minutes); hot stone therapy, €100 (45 minutes); facial, €65; pedicure, €40. Gratuities are not included, and are not charged to your account.

Sports facilities include deck quoites, two shuffleboard courts, large tennis/basketball court, minigolf, and a jogging track.

● **For more extensive general information about the MSC Cruises experience, see pages 129–30.**

MSC Poesia
★★★★

Large Resort Ship: ....92,490 tons	Total Crew: 987	Cabins (for one person): 0
Lifestyle: ....Standard	Passengers	Cabins (with private balcony): 827
Cruise Line: ....MSC Cruises	(lower beds/all berths): 2,550/3,013	Cabins (wheelchair accessible): 17
Former Names: ....none	Passenger Space Ratio	Cabin Voltage: ....110/220 volts
Builder: ....Fincantieri (Italy)	(lower beds/all berths): 36.2/30.6	Elevators: 13
Original Cost: ....$360 million	Crew/Passenger Ratio	Casino (gaming tables): ....Yes
Entered Service: ....Oct 2008	(lower beds/all berths): 2.6/3.0	Slot Machines: ....Yes
Registry: ....Panama	Navigation Officers: ....Italian	Swimming Pools (outdoors): 2
Length (ft/m): 963.9/293.8	Cabins (total): 1,275	Swimming Pools (indoors): 0
Beam (ft/m): 105.6/32.2	Size Range (sq ft/m): 150.6–301.3/	Whirlpools: 4
Draft (ft/m): 26.2/8.0	14.0/28.0	Self-Service Launderette: ....No
Propulsion/Propellers: diesel (58,000kW)/2	Cabins (outside view): 1,000	Dedicated Cinema/Seats: ....No
Passenger Decks: 13	Cabins (interior/no view): 275	Library: ....Yes

BERLITZ'S OVERALL SCORE: 1,467 (OUT OF A POSSIBLE 2,000 POINTS)

OVERVIEW. *MSC Orchestra* is a sister ship to *MSC Musica* and *MSC Orchestra*. The ship's blue funnel has a sleek, swept-back design and carries the MSC logo in gold lettering, and a balanced profile. The hull has large circular porthole-style windows instead of square or rectangular ones. From a technical viewpoint, the ship has a conventional rudders and propellers propulsion system, while a new anti-foul paint was applied to the ship's underwater hull – the first newly built ship to have this new sleek paint applied.

BERLITZ'S RATINGS

	Possible	Achieved
Ship	500	414
Accommodation	200	156
Food	400	243
Service	400	298
Entertainment	100	62
Cruise	400	294

The interior layout and passenger flow is quite good with the exception of a couple of points of congestion, typically when the first seating exits the two main dining rooms and passengers on the second seating are waiting to enter. The musically-themed decor has many Italian influences, including clean lines, minimalism in furniture design, and a collection of colors, soft furnishings and fabrics that work well together, although it's a little more garish than one would expect. Real wood and marble have been used extensively in the interiors, and the high quality reflects the commitment that MSC Cruises has in the vessel's future.

The focal point of the ship is the main three-deck high lobby, with a water-feature backdrop and a crystal piano on a small stage that appears to float on a pond. Other facilities include a large main show lounge, a nightclub, a discotheque, numerous lounges and bars (including a wine bar), library, card room, an internet center, virtual reality center, children's club, and cigar lounge. A shopping gallery, which includes an electronics store, has an integrated bar and entertainment area that flows through the main lobby so that shopping becomes a city-like environment where you can shop, drink, and be entertained all in one convenient area. Gamblers can find entertainment pleasure in the expansive Casino (with blackjack, poker and roulette games, together with an array of slot machines).

Drinking places include a pub-like venue as well as several comfortable lounges that have live music. On deck, a mini-golf course is on the port side of the funnel, while a walking/jogging track encircles an upper level above the ship's two swimming pools. The ship is designed to accommodate families with children, who have their own play center, video games room, youth counselors, and activity programs.

Some of the artwork is quite whimsical. And do check out the "restroom with a view" – the men's/ladies' toilets adjacent to the Blue Marlin pool deck bar have a great ocean view (you can even watch the passing scenery while sitting on the toilet if you leave the door open).

Although access throughout most of the interior of the ship is very good, anyone who is wheelchair-bound should note that the passenger hallways are a little narrow on some decks for you to pass when housekeeping carts are in place. There is no walk-around open promenade deck.

SUITABLE FOR: Best suited to young adult couples, singles, and families with tots, children and teens who enjoy big ship surroundings, a big city life, with its attendant buzz, and caters to passengers of different nationalities and languages (mostly European). The on-board currency is the euro. Gratuities are charged to your onboard account, at €6 per person, per day, but bar drink prices include a service charge.

ACCOMMODATION. There are 12 price levels, depending on grade and location: suites, outside-view cabins, and interior (no view) cabins. Included are 18 "suites" with private balcony, mini-suites, outside-view cabins and interior (no view) cabins. Contrary to nautical convention, the cabin numbering system has even numbered cabins on the starboard side, and odd numbered cabins on the port side.

All cabins have a mini-bar and personal safe, satellite flat-screen TV, several audio channels, and 24-hour room service. Note that, while continental breakfast is complimentary from 7:30 to 10am, room service snacks are available at extra cost at any other time.

Accommodation designated as "suites" (they are not true suites, as there is no separate bedroom and lounge) also has more room (although they are small compared to suites on some of the major cruise lines), a larger lounge area, walk-in closet, and vanity desk with drawer-mounted hairdryer; a bathroom with combination bathtub and shower, toilet, and semi-private balcony with light (the partitions between each balcony are of the partial, not full, type). The bathrobes and towels are 100% cotton. The suite bathrooms are plain, with white plastic washbasins and white walls, and mirrors that steam up.

Some of the most popular cabins are at the aft end of the ship, with views over the stern from the balconies. The 17 cabins for the disabled are spacious and well equipped.

CUISINE. There are two principal dining rooms, both aft with large ocean-view picture windows. There are two seatings for meals, as aboard other ships in the MSC Cruises fleet, and tables are for two, four, six or eight; seating is both banquette-style and in individual chairs; the chairs, however, are slim and do not have armrests. All dining venues are managed and supervised by Italian nationals.

Alternative Dining Spots:
● A *Tex-Mex Restaurant* is the ship's featured à la carte dining spot; reservations are necessary, and there is an extra cost.
● *Kaito* is a Japanese restaurant, incorporating a sushi bar. It has a very extensive menu.
● The *Wine Bar* provides a selection of famous regional cheeses, hams and wine in a bistro-style setting that is relaxing and entertaining.

Casual, self-serve buffets (for breakfast and lunch) can be taken in the Cafeteria, or at a pool deck outside fast-food eatery. Coffee/tea and pastries can be taken in several bars adjacent to the midships atrium lobby.

Additionally, silver trays full of late-night snacks are taken throughout the ship by waiters, and on some days, special late-night desserts, such as flambé items, are showcased in various lounges.

ENTERTAINMENT. There is one large, principal showlounge, located in the forward section of the ship. It has tiered seating on two levels (the sightlines are good from most of the plush, comfortable seats). The room can also be a venue for large groups or social functions. There is no showband, and all shows are performed to recorded music "click" tracks.

Another large lounge (aft of the show lounge) is the place for social dancing and functions such as cooking demonstrations, with live music provided by a band.

Additionally, big-screen movies are shown on a large screen above the forward pool, just behind the ship's mast.

SPA/FITNESS. The Poesia Health Center (Body and Mind spa) is located one deck above the navigation bridge at the forward end of the ship.

The facility includes a beauty salon, several treatment rooms offering massage and other body-pampering treatments, as well as a gymnasium with ocean views and an array of high-tech, muscle-toning and strengthening equipment. There's also a thermal suite, containing different kinds of steam rooms combined with aromatherapy infusions, at €12 per session, or six sessions for €60, and a juice/smoothie bar.

The health center is run as a concession by the Italian company OceanView, with European hairstylists and fine Balinese massage and body treatment staff. Examples of treatment prices: Balinese massage, €93 (45 minutes); shiatsu massage, €90 (45 minutes); hot stone therapy, €100 (45 minutes); facial, €65; pedicure, €40. Gratuities are not included, and are not charged to your account.

Sports facilities include deck quoits, two shuffleboard courts, a large tennis and basketball court, minigolf, and a jogging track.

● For more extensive general information about the MSC Cruises experience, see pages 129–30.

MSC Rhapsody
★★★

Mid-Size Ship: . . . . .16,852 tons	Passenger Decks: 8	Cabins (for one person): 0
Lifestyle: . . . . .Standard	Total Crew: .350	Cabins (with private balcony): 0
Cruise Line: . . . . .MSC Cruises	Passengers	Cabins (wheelchair accessible): 0
Former Names: . . . . . . .Cunard Princess,	(lower beds/all berths): 788/959	Cabin Current: . . . . .220 volts
Cunard Conquest	Passenger Space Ratio	Elevators: 2
Builder: . . .Burmeister & Wein (Denmark)	(lower beds/all berths): 21.3/17.5	Casino (gaming tables): . . . . .Yes
Original Cost: . . . . £12 million	Crew/Passenger Ratio	Slot Machines: . . . . .Yes
Entered Service: . . . . .Mar 1977/May1995	(lower beds/all berths): 2.2/2.7	Swimming Pools (outdoors): 1
Registry: . . . . .Panama	Navigation Officers: . . . . .Italian	Swimming Pools (indoors): 0
Length (ft/m): 541.0/164.9	Cabins (total): 394	Whirlpools: 2
Beam (ft/m): 76.1/23.2	Size Range (sq ft/m): 87.1–264.8/	Self-Service Launderette: . . . . .No
Draft (ft/m): 19.0/5.8	8.1–24.6	Dedicated Cinema/Seats: Yes/135
Propulsion/Propellers: . . . . .diesel	Cabins (outside view): 267	Library: . . . . .Yes
(15,670 kW)/2	Cabins (interior/no view): 127	

BERLITZ'S OVERALL SCORE: 1,177 (OUT OF A POSSIBLE 2,000 POINTS)

OVERVIEW. *MSC Rhapsody* is almost identical to its sister, *Ocean Countess*), with the same contemporary profile and smart looks. The ship was originally completed for Cunard Line as an informal Caribbean cruise vessel named *Cunard Princess*, although the original name (which was not used) was to have been *Cunard Conquest*.

Conceived originally by Hugh Hefner as a "floating Playboy Club," the ship was built for Cunard. It was acquired in 1995 by StarLauro Cruises, which was renamed Mediterranean Shipping Cruises (and, subsequently, MSC Cruises), as a replacement for its *Achille Lauro*, which caught fire and sank off the coast of East Africa in 1995.

There is a good amount of open deck space for sun-worshippers. There is a good selection of public rooms with attractive decor, in light, bright colors, including an observation lounge above the bridge, overlooking the bow.

The ship has an excellent indoor-outdoor entertainment nightclub and bar, which incorporates the occasional use of an aft open deck area. The show lounge, a one-deck high room with raised seating on its port and starboard sides, has eight pillars that obstruct sightlines (the ceiling height is also very low).

This ship provides a very comfortable first cruise experience, featuring destination-intensive itineraries, in a pleasing, casual, but very high-density environment.

This ship is now marketed mostly to Europeans and to Italian passengers in particular (who form about 60% of the passengers. While it still looks sharp following an extensive refit and refurbishment in 1997, the standard of food and service offered are disappointingly commonplace. There is no outdoor wrap-around promenade deck outdoors.

BERLITZ'S RATINGS

	Possible	Achieved
Ship	500	315
Accommodation	200	112
Food	400	216
Service	400	238
Entertainment	100	62
Cruise	400	234

The cabins really are very small. The onboard currency is the euro.

SUITABLE FOR: *MSC Rhapsody* is best suited to young couples, singles, and families with tots, children and teens on their first cruise. The ship is for those who would not enjoy large or palatial ships, but do enjoy being among fellow passengers of different nationalities and languages.

ACCOMMODATION. There are 11 grades, the price depending on grade, size and location.

Deluxe/Standard Outside View/Interior No View Cabins. The cabins are mostly of a standard (very compact) size, and come in light colors and plain, but pleasant decor that is adequate for short cruises. They are best described as space-efficient units with metal fixtures and poor insulation – you can talk to your neighbors without having to use the telephone. All standard cabins have two lower beds (some are in a twin shape, while others are in an L-shape; they are fixed and cannot be moved together). Many cabins also have a third upper berth. The cabins on the lowest deck suffer from vibration and the odor of diesel fuel, and have portholes (as do cabins on the deck above), while all other cabins on the upper decks have windows. The cabin bathrooms are small modular units, good for one, but quite impossible for two to be together in (they contain a shower enclosure, toilet and washbasin, but little storage space for personal toiletries).

Suites. The largest accommodation is found in the "suites" (in two price grades). These all have a double bed, a good amount of closet space, lounge area with sofa or chairs, television, and a larger bathroom with bathtub and shower, toilet and washbasin. If you are seeking more space, these are the rooms to go for.

CUISINE. The Meridian Restaurant is located in the middle of the ship. It has sea views from large picture windows, but is fairly noisy because of its open design. There are two seatings. The standard "banquet" food is reasonable and tailored mainly to Italian passengers, with typical Italian dishes including plenty of pasta (but sadly no tableside cooking). The service is bubbly, cheerful, attentive, and comes with a smile, but it lacks finesse. There is a limited selection of breads and fruits. The cabin service menu is very limited.

Additionally, a casual self-serve open-air area is available for breakfast, lunches and (sometimes, depending on the itinerary) buffet dinners.

ENTERTAINMENT. The Pisto da Ballo Lounge is the ship's main lounge, and is the principal venue for entertainment events and social functions. It is a single-level, rectangular-shaped room with a black granite dance floor, designed for cabaret acts, and not production-style shows. Although the sides of the room are raised, several pillars obstruct the sightlines.

The ship has a main showband, together with small musical units and solo pianists to provide live music for dancing and listening, in the various lounges and bars.

SPA/FITNESS. There is a small gymnasium located on one side of the funnel housing, on the pool deck, while a jogging track is provided on the deck above (difficult to use because it is narrow and passengers place their deck chairs there for sunbathing); massage facilities and changing area are provided on the opposite side to the gymnasium.

A beauty salon is located indoors on another deck, adjacent to the reception desk and shops. Body pampering treatments include various massages, facials, body wraps, manicures, pedicures, and hairdressing services.

● **For more extensive general information about the MSC Cruises experience, see pages 129–30.**

WHO'S WHO IN ON-BOARD ENTERTAINMENT

Although production companies differ in their approach, the following gives some idea of the various people involved behind the scenes.

Executive Producer
Transfers the show's concept from design to reality. First, the brief from the cruise line's director of entertainment might be for a new production show (the average being two major shows per seven-day cruise). After deciding on an initial concept, they then call in the choreographer, vocal coach, and musical arranger.

Choreographer
Responsible for auditioning the dancers and for creating, selecting, and teaching the routines.

Musical Director
Coordinates all musical scores and arrangements; trains the singers in voice and microphone techniques, projection, accenting, phrasing, memory, and general presentation; and oversees session singers and musicians for the recording sessions.

Musical Arranger
After the music has been selected, the musical arrangements must be made. Just one song can cost more than $2,000 for a single arrangement for a 12-piece orchestra.

Costume Designer
Provides creative original designs for a minimum of seven costume changes in one show lasting 45 minutes. The costumes must also be practical, as they will be used repeatedly.

Costume Maker
Buys all materials, and must be able to produce all required costumes in time for a show.

Graphic Designer
Provides all the set designs, whether they are physical one- two- or three-dimensional sets for the stage, or photographic images created on slide film, video, laser disk, or other electronic media.

Lighting Designer
Creates the lighting patterns and effects for a production show. Sequences and action on stage must be carefully lit to the best advantage. The completed lighting plot is computerized.

Bands/Musicians
Before the big production shows and artists can be booked, bands and musicians must be hired, often for long contracts. Naturally, live musicians are favored for a ship's show band, as they are excellent music readers (necessary for all visiting cabaret artists and for big production shows). Big bands are often placed in some of the larger ships for special sailings, or for world cruises, on which ballroom dancing plays a large part. Most musicians work to contracts of about six months.

MSC Sinfonia
★★★★

Large Resort Ship:	.58,600 tons	Passenger Decks:	.10
Lifestyle:	.Standard	Total Crew:	.710
Cruise Line:	.MSC Cruises	Passengers	
Former Names:	*European Stars*	(lower beds/all berths):	.1,566/2,223
Builder: Chantiers de l'Atlantique (France)		Passenger Space Ratio	
Original Cost:	.$245 million	(lower beds/all berths):	.37.4/27.6
Entered Service:	.Apr 2002/Mar 2005	Crew/Passenger Ratio	
Registry:	.Italy	(lower beds/all berths):	.2.2/3.1
Length (ft/m):	.823.4/251.0	Navigation Officers:	.European
Beam (ft/m):	.94.4/28.8	Cabins (total):	.783
Draft (ft/m):	.22.4/6.85	Size Range (sq ft/m): .139.9–236.8/13–22	
Propulsion/Propellers:	.diesel	Cabins (outside view):	.511
	(31,680 kW)/2 pods	Cabins (interior/no view):	.272

Cabins (for one person):	.0
Cabins (with private balcony):	.132
Cabins (wheelchair accessible):	.2
Cabin Current:	.110 and 220 volts
Elevators:	.9
Casino (gaming tables):	.Yes
Slot Machines:	.Yes
Swimming Pools (outdoors):	.1
Swimming Pools (indoors):	.0
Whirlpools:	.1 (thalassotherapy)
Self-Service Launderette:	.No
Dedicated Cinema/Seats:	.No
Library:	.Yes

BERLITZ'S OVERALL SCORE: 1,435 (OUT OF A POSSIBLE 2,000 POINTS)

OVERVIEW. *MSC Sinfonia* was originally built and operated by the now-defunct Festival Cruises. Like sister ship *MSC Armonia*, it was built on the platform of the *Mistral*, with an 114.8-ft long (35-meter) mid-section added to increase the ship's length and provide more space per passenger than *Mistral*. *MSC Sinfonia* has an azimuthing pod propulsion system, instead of conventional rudders and propellers, in the latest configuration of high-tech propulsion systems (*for explanation, see page 174*). The lido deck surrounding the outdoor swimming pool also has whirlpool tubs and a large bandstand is set in raised canvas-covered pods.

The interior layout is stylish. Passenger flow is good, as are the "you are here" deck signs. The decor is decidedly "European Moderne" and includes clean lines, minimalism in furniture designs (including some chairs that look interesting but are totally impractical unless you are prepared to face reconstructive surgery).

Facilities include Amadeus, the ship's show lounge, and La Gondola Theater, for plays and other theatrical presentations. There's a cigar smoking room (Ambassador), with the hallmarks of a gentleman's club of former times, as well as a piano bar. The Goethe Library/Card Room has real writing desks (something many ships seem to omit), and this ship has an internet cafe, as well an English pub called the White Lion. Those who enjoy gambling may find excitement in the Lido Casino, with blackjack, poker and roulette games, plus the usual one-armed slot machines. The onboard currency is the euro.

Standing in line for embarkation, disembarkation, shore tenders and for self-serve buffet meals is an inevitable aspect of cruising aboard all large ships. The heavy smok-

BERLITZ'S RATINGS	Possible	Achieved
Ship	500	395
Accommodation	200	155
Food	400	254
Service	400	295
Entertainment	100	54
Cruise	400	282

ers are virtually impossible to avoid (in typical European fashion, ashtrays are simply moved – if used at all – to wherever smokers happen to be sitting). All announcements are in several languages, although these are thankfully fewer than in the past. The entertainment is of a low standard, with intrusive animateurs that mean well, but who perform as one would expect to find in a holiday camp – with great energy and enthusiasm but little else.

The cruise line keeps prices low by providing air transportation that may be at inconvenient times, or transportation involving long journeys by bus. In other words, be prepared for a little discomfort in getting to and from your cruise in exchange for low cruise rates. The constant push for onboard revenue is also very irritating – you have to pay extra even for a visit to the ship's navigation bridge. The staff is much more focused on Italian passengers than those who speak any other European language (including English), although the international mix adds to the overall ambiance of the cruise experience.

If you are considering doing two back-to-back 7-day cruises, note that some ports may be duplicated, and all menus and entertainment are based on a 7-day cycle, so there is much product repetition (including the cruise director's jokes). Regular passenger complaints include poor ports of call information and rudeness of shore excursion staff.

SUITABLE FOR: *MSC Sinfonia* is best suited to young adult couples, singles, and families with tots, children and teens who enjoy big ship surroundings, a big city life, with all its attendant noise (some call it ambience), and passengers of different nationalities and languages (mostly European).

ACCOMMODATION. There are 11 price categories, the price depending on the grade, size and location. These include 132 suites with private balcony (note that the partitions are only of the partial and not the full type), outside-view cabins and interior (no view) cabins.

Suite grade accommodation has more room, a larger lounge area, walk-in closet, wall-to-wall vanity counter, a bathroom with combination tub and shower, toilet, and private balcony (with light). But they are not true suites, as there is no separate bedroom and lounge – in other words, these are not "suites" of rooms. Bathrobes are provided.

In general, the "suites" are well laid out and nicely furnished. However, except for the very highest category, the suite bathrooms are very plain, with white plastic washbasins and white walls, and mirrors that steam up. According to the rules of feng shui, however, it is bad luck to place any mirror in such a position that it can be seen by anyone lying in bed.

Even the smallest interior cabins are sensibly spacious and well designed, with plenty of space between lower beds. All grades of accommodation have sheets and blankets as bed linen (no duvets), and are equipped with a TV set, hairdryer, mini-bar/refrigerator, personal safe (cleverly positioned behind a vanity desk mirror), bathroom with shower and toilet, and 100% cotton towels (except for hand towels, which, when I last sailed, were 86% cotton and 14% polyester).

However, the standard grade cabins are quite small when compared to many other new ships, at a modest 140 sq. ft (13 sq. meters). Note that cabins located under the aft self-service buffet provoke many complaints of noise from occupants.

CUISINE. All dining spots are non-smoking venues. There are two main dining rooms, the 610-seat Il Galeone Restaurant and the Il Covo Restaurant; both have two seatings and share the same menu. The cuisine is reasonably sound, and, with varied menus and good presentation, should prove a highlight for most passengers. The wine list has a wide variety of wines at fairly reasonable prices, although almost all are very young.

La Terrazza is the ship's casual, self-serve buffet eatery, open 24 hours a day. The selections are very standardized, however, and could be better. Café del Mare, adjacent to one of two swimming pools and to the ship's funnel, is a grill area for fast food.

Meanwhile, coffee/tea and pastries can be taken in Le Baroque Café, which is set around the upper level of the two-deck high atrium lobby. It's a good location for people-watching, but annoying music videos are constantly played on TV sets in the forward sections.

ENTERTAINMENT. The Gondola Theater is two decks high, and is the main show lounge, for production shows, cabaret acts, plays and other theatrical presentations. It is a well designed room (except for the fact that no space was allocated for a live showband), with good sightlines from most seats, and four entrances that allow easy access.

Entertainment is a weak area for MSC Cruises, although this could improve as more ships are brought into service and more money is assigned to this important aspect of the company's cruise product. Other shows consist of unknown cabaret acts (typically singers, magicians, mime artistes, comedy jugglers, and others) doing the cruise ship circuit. The principal difficulty aboard this ship is that the ship operates year-round in five or six languages, making any entertainment (other than visual acts such as mime, magic or juggling) virtually impossible.

The ship carries a number of bands and small musical units that provide live music for dancing or listening in various lounges and bars throughout the ship.

SPA/FITNESS. The Atlantica Spa, one deck above the navigation bridge at the forward end of the ship, has numerous body-pampering treatments, as well as a gymnasium with ocean views and an array of high-tech, muscle-toning and strengthening equipment.

There's also a thermal suite (this contains different kinds of steam rooms combined with aromatherapy infusions such as camomile and eucalyptus) and a rasul chamber (a combination of two or three different kinds of special application mud, and gentle steam shower – highly recommended for couples).

The spa is run as a concession by the Italian company OceanView, with European hairstylists and Balinese massage and body treatment staff. Examples of treatment prices: Balinese massage, €93 (45 minutes); shiatsu massage, €90 (45 minutes); hot stone therapy, €100 (45 minutes); facial, €65; pedicure, €40. Gratuities are not included, and are not charged to your account.

For the sports-minded, there is a simulated climbing wall outdoors, while other sports and fitness facilities include volleyball/basketball court, and mini-golf.

● **For more extensive general information about the MSC Cruises experience, see pages 129–30.**

MSC Splendida
NOT YET RATED

Large Resort Ship:	.............133,500 tons	Passenger Decks:	13	Cabins (for one person):	0
Lifestyle:	....................................Standard	Total Crew:	1,313	Cabins (with private balcony):	1,260
Cruise Line:	...........................MSC Cruises	Passengers		Cabins (wheelchair accessible):	43
Former Names:	...................................none	(lower beds/all berths):	..........3,300/3,900	Cabin Voltage:	...........................110 volts
Builder:	.....................Aker Yards (France)	Passenger Space Ratio		Lifts:	14
Original Cost:	.........................$550 million	(lower beds/all berths):	..............40.4/34.2	Casino (gaming tables):	......................Yes
Entered Service:	.........................Mar 2009	Crew/Passenger Ratio		Slot Machines:	....................................Yes
Registry:	......................................Panama	(lower beds/all berths):	........................2.5/3.0	Swimming Pools (outdoors):	3
Length (ft/m):	......................1,093.5/333.3	Navigation Officers:	...................European	Swimming Pools (indoors): 1 (glass dome)	
Beam (ft/m):	...........................124.6/38.0	Cabins (total):	1,650	Whirlpools:	13
Draft:	....27.2/8.45	Size Range (sq ft/m):.161.4–699.6/15–65		Self-Service Launderette:	....................No
Propulsion/Propellers:	.....................diesel	Cabins (outside view):	1,354	Dedicated Cinema/Seats:	....................No
	(40,000 kW)/2	Cabins (interior/no view):	283	Library:	....Yes

---

BERLITZ'S OVERALL SCORE: NYR (OUT OF A POSSIBLE 2,000 POINTS)

OVERVIEW. This ship was built of 67 blocks (some exceeding 600 tons), and is a sister ship to *MSC Fantasia*. There are four swimming pools, one of which can be covered by a sliding glass dome – useful in case of poor weather.

The interior design is an enlargement of the smaller *MSC Musica* and *MSC Orchestra*-class ships, but with pleasing new additions. The public rooms include a large showlounge, a nightclub/discotheque, many lounges and bars, library, card room, an internet center, a virtual reality center, and an extensive shopping gallery. The shops are integrated with several bars, lounges and entertainment areas so that it all feels rather like a European city-center environment.

Drinking places include pub-like venues and many comfortable lounges and bars, most with live music. The ship is designed to accommodate families with children well. Children have their own play centers (a children's club and jungle adventure playground), youth counselors, and programs.

The onboard currency is the euro. Gratuities (at a suggested €6 per person per day) are extra, but bar drink prices do include a service charge.

ACCOMMODATION. Eighty percent of the cabins are outsides, of which 95% have a balcony (the standard balcony cabin will measure almost 172 sq ft (16 sq meters), plus bathroom and balcony).

A total of 99 suites are located within a VIP section called the "MSC Yacht Club," with full butler service. This private area, spread out on two decks, has its own pool with skydome, and sun deck, with access via private elevators, an observation lounge/bar, direct access to the spa, a private galley for room service, and a private concierge lounge with an integral library. A black marble floor leads to a magnifi-

BERLITZ'S RATINGS

	Possible	Achieved
Ship	500	NYR
Accommodation	200	NYR
Food	400	NYR
Service	400	NYR
Entertainment	100	NYR
Cruise	400	NYR

cent Swarovski glass staircase which connects the concierge facilities between two decks.

CUISINE. There are four dining venues: the main restaurant, an Italian specialty restaurant, a Tex-Mex restaurant, a restaurant for suite passengers only, and a large casual self-serve lido buffet-style eatery. Coffee/tea (at extra cost) and pastries are served in several bars (all with coffee machines using Italian Segafredo brand coffee) set around the first and second levels of the atrium lobby. The main restaurant has two seatings for dinner, and open seating for breakfast and lunch, like other MSC Cruises ships. Tables are for two, four, six or eight, and some alcove banquette seating.

ENTERTAINMENT. The showlounge is a very large room, with plush seating in tiers for as many as 1,700, and good sightlines from most seats.

SPA/FITNESS. The Splendida Wellbeing Center measures approximately 16,000 sq ft (1,485 sq meters), and has a beauty salon, several well-equipped treatment rooms, and a large gymnasium with ocean views. Included is a large thermal suite, containing several different kinds of steam rooms combined with herbal aromatherapy infusions, saunas, and relaxation area. The wellbeing center is run as a concession by the Italian company OceanView.

Sports facilities include deck quoits, shuffleboard courts, large tennis/basketball court, minigolf, and a jogging track, plus a Formula One simulator.

● **For more extensive general information about the MSC Cruises experience, see pages 129–30**

National Geographic Endeavour
★★

Boutique Ship:	3,132 tons	Total Crew:	64	Cabins (with private balcony):	0
Lifestyle:	Standard	Passengers		Cabins (wheelchair accessible):	0
Cruise Line:	Lindblad Expeditions	(lower beds/all berths):	113/124	Cabin Current:	110/220 volts
Former Names:	Caledonian Star,	Passenger Space Ratio		Elevators:	0
	North Star, Lindmar, Marburg	(lower beds/all berths):	27.7/25.2	Casino (gaming tables):	No
Builder:	A.G. Weser Seebeckwerft (Germany)	Crew/Passenger Ratio		Slot Machines:	No
Original Cost:	n/a	(lower beds/all berths):	1.7/1.9	Swimming Pools (outdoors):	1
Entered Service:	1966/1984	Navigation Officers:	Scandinavian	Whirlpools:	0
Registry:	The Bahamas	Cabins (total):	62	Self-Service Launderette:	No
Length (ft/m):	292.6/89.20	Size Range (sq ft/m):	191.6–269.1/	Lecture/Film Rooms:	Yes
Beam (ft/m):	45.9/14.00		17.8–25.0	Library:	Yes
Draft (ft/m):	20.3/6.20	Cabins (outside view):	62	Zodiacs:	10
Propulsion/Propellers:	diesel (3,236kW)/1	Cabins (interior/no view):	0	Helicopter Pad:	No
Passenger Decks:	6	Cabins (for one person):	14		

BERLITZ'S OVERALL SCORE: 945 (OUT OF A POSSIBLE 2,000 POINTS)

OVERVIEW. Renamed in 2005, the former *Endeavour* was originally built as a stern factory fishing trawler for North Sea service, before being morphed into a passenger ship. Today, it is tidy and well cared for as an expedition cruise vessel operating "soft" expedition cruises. There is an open bridge policy for all passengers. The vessel carries Zodiac landing craft for in-depth excursions, and there is an enclosed shore tender. An aft stairway (it is steep) leads down to the landing craft platform. The ship has a warm, intimate ambiance, and a casual dress code.

This small ship has a reasonable number of public rooms and facilities, including a lecture room/lounge/bar/library, where videos are also stocked for in-cabin use. Specialized lecturers accompanying each cruise make this a real life-enrichment experience for a clientele wanting to travel and learn, while enveloped in comfortable, unpretentious surroundings. There's a good book selection.

This likeable, homey little ship runs well-organized destination-intensive, soft expedition-style cruises, at a very reasonable price. It attracts loyal repeat passengers who don't want to sail aboard ships that look like apartment blocks. The itineraries include Antarctica, where this ship started operating in 1998. The onboard currency is the US dollar.

The interior stairways are a little steep, as is the exterior stairway to the Zodiac embarkation points. Noise from the diesel engines can be irksome, particularly on the lower decks.

Recommended gratuities are $10 per person, per day.

SUITABLE FOR: This ship and its type of soft adventure/exploration cruising are best suited to adventurous, hardy

BERLITZ'S RATINGS		
	Possible	Achieved
Ship	500	198
Accommodation	200	86
Food	400	193
Service	400	217
Entertainment	n/a	n/a
Cruise	500	251

types who enjoy being with nature and wildlife in some of the most interesting (sometimes inhospitable) places on earth, but cosseted aboard a small, modestly comfortable ship.

ACCOMMODATION. There are five categories of cabins: 1 suite category and 4 non-suite categories. The all-outside-view cabins (all above the waterline) are very compact, but reasonably comfortable, and they are decorated in warm, muted tones. All cabins have a mini-bar/refrigerator, VCR, a decent amount of closet and drawer space (but tight for long voyages), and a clock.

The bathrooms are tight, with little space for the storage of personal toiletries.

Four "suites" are basically double the size of a standard cabin, and have a wood partition separating the bedroom and lounge area. The bathroom is still small, however.

CUISINE. The dining room is small and charming, but the low-back chairs are not very comfortable. Open seating is operated in this non-smoking room. The cuisine is European in style with reasonably high quality, fresh ingredients, but not a lot of menu choice. Salad items, in particular, are rather scarce on variety, as are international cheeses. Service is attentive and friendly.

ENTERTAINMENT. The main lounge is the venue for lectures, slide shows and occasional film presentations. There are no shows (none are needed), and no facilities for them.

SPA/FITNESS. There is a small fitness room (about three people and it is full) and tiny sauna.

National Geographic Polaris
★★

Boutique Ship: . . . . .2,214 tons	
Lifestyle: . . . . .Standard	
Cruise Line: . . . . . . .Lindblad Expeditions	
Former Names: .Polaris, Lindblad Polaris, Oresund	
Builder: . . . . . .Aalborg Vaerft (Denmark)	
Original Cost: . . . . .n/a	
Entered Service: 1960/May 1987	
Registry: . . . . .Ecuador	
Length (ft/m): 236.6/72.12	
Beam (ft/m): 42.7/13.03	
Draft (ft/m): 13.7/4.30	
Propulsion/Propellers: . . . . .diesel (2,354 kW)/2	

Passenger Decks: 4	
Total Crew: 44	
Passengers (lower beds/all berths): 82/84	
Passenger Space Ratio (lower beds/all berths): 27.0/26.3	
Crew/Passenger Ratio (lower beds/all berths): 1.8/1.8	
Navigation Officers: . . . . .Ecuadorian	
Cabins (total): 41	
Size Range (sq ft/m): 99.0–229.2/ 9.2–21.3	
Cabins (outside view): 41	
Cabins (interior/no view): 0	

Cabins (for one person): 0	
Cabins (with private balcony): 0	
Cabins (wheelchair accessible): 0	
Cabin Current: . . . . .220 volts	
Elevators: 0	
Casino (gaming tables): . . . . .No	
Slot Machines: . . . . .No	
Swimming Pools (outdoors): 0	
Whirlpools: 0	
Self-Service Launderette: . . . . .No	
Lecture/Film Room: . . . . .No	
Library: . . . . .Yes	
Zodiacs: 8	
Helicopter Pad: . . . . .No	

BERLITZ'S OVERALL SCORE: 943 (OUT OF A POSSIBLE 2,000 POINTS)

OVERVIEW. This is what is often termed a "soft" expedition cruise vessel. It is of modest proportions, and has a dark blue hull and white superstructure. A "cute" vessel, it has been well maintained and operated, having been skillfully converted from a Scandinavian ferry. It sports a fantail and an aft lounge area outdoors. The ship carries several Zodiac inflatable rubber landing craft, as well as a glass-bottom boat.

Inside, there are few public rooms, although the Scandinavian-style interior furnishings and decor are very tidy and welcoming (if dated), accented by lots of wood trim. Has a friendly, very intimate atmosphere on board, with Filipino service staff. There is a good team of lecturers and nature observers, whose daily recaps are a vital part of the experience. A restful, well-stocked library helps passengers learn more about the region and the natural world.

If you are going on a Galápagos cruise, it is important to take with you: passport, short and long-sleeve cotton shirts, good walking shoes, windbreaker, mosquito repellent (mosquitoes are at their worst between December and July, particularly in Bartolome), sunglasses with retaining strap, and any personal medication. You will need to take a flight from Quito to San Cristobal (via Guayaquil) to join your cruise.

This is a decent enough small vessel, operating year-round nature-intensive "soft" expedition cruises based in and around the Galápagos Islands. It's an area to which the ship is well suited because only 90 passengers from any one ship are allowed at any one time in the islands, where tourism is managed well by the local Equadorians. In fact, this ship is among the best suited to this region.

Bottled water is provided at no extra charge. All port

BERLITZ'S RATINGS

	Possible	Achieved
Ship	500	189
Accommodation	200	85
Food	400	186
Service	400	216
Entertainment	n/a	n/a
Cruise	500	267

charges are included in this product, which is marketed by Lindblad Expeditions and Noble Caledonia. The onboard currencies are the US dollar and Ecuadorian sucre.

SUITABLE FOR: This type of cruising is best suited to adventurous, hardy outdoors types who enjoy being with nature and wildlife in one of the most interesting places on earth.

ACCOMMODATION. There are five price grades. The cabins, all above the waterline (while most have windows, a few have portholes), are fairly roomy and nicely appointed, but there is little drawer space. Some have been refurbished, and have large (lower) beds. Each cabin has either a double bed or two single beds, a small writing desk, and hairdryer. Some of the larger cabins also have a third (upper) berth. The cabin bathrooms are tiny (the towels are small, too).

CUISINE. The Dining Room has big picture windows and a wrap-around view. Seating is now at individual tables (formerly family style) in a leisurely single seating.

The ship's cuisine is basically sound, with emphasis on local fish and seafood, and other Ecuadorian regional specialties (meats are poor). Breakfast and lunch are self-serve buffet-style. The wine selection is very limited.

ENTERTAINMENT. Lectures, briefings and recaps are the main onboard entertainment events, together with dinner and after-dinner conversation.

SPA/FITNESS. There is a small fitness room (large enough for two). Beauty isn't a big concern on such cruises.

Nautica
★★★★ +

Mid-Size Ship:................30,277 tons	Total Crew: 386	Cabins (with private balcony): 232
Lifestyle: ....Premium	Passengers	Cabins (wheelchair accessible): 3
Cruise Line: ....Oceania Cruises	(lower beds/all berths): 684/824	Cabin Current: ....110/220 volts
Former Names: ....R Five	Passenger Space Ratio	Elevators: 4
Builder: ....Chantiers de l'Atlantique	(lower beds/all berths): 44.2/36.7	Casino (gaming tables): ....Yes
Original Cost: ....£150 million	Crew/Passenger Ratio	Slot Machines: ....Yes
Entered Service: Dec1998/Nov 2005	(lower beds/all berths): 1.7/2.1	Swimming Pools (outdoors): 1
Registry: ....Marshall Islands	Navigation Officers: ....European	Swimming Pools (indoors): 0
Length (ft/m): 593.7/181.0	Cabins (total): 342	Whirlpools: ....2 (+1 thalassotherapy)
Beam (ft/m): 83.5/25.5	Size Range (sq ft/m): 145.3–968.7/13.5–90.0	Self-Service Launderette: ....Yes
Draft (ft/m): 19.5/6.0	Cabins (outside view): 317	Dedicated Cinema/Seats: ....No
Propulsion/Propellers: .diesel (18,600 kW)/2	Cabins (interior/no view): 25	Library: ....Yes
Passenger Decks: 9	Cabins (for one person): 0	

OVERALL SCORE: 1,575 (OUT OF A POSSIBLE 2,000 POINTS)

OVERVIEW. *Nautica* was formerly one of a series of eight almost identical ships, originally built for the now-defunct Renaissance Cruises, the cruise industry's first totally non-smoking cruise line. The exterior design manages to balance the ship's high sides by painting the whole ship white (it previously had a dark blue hull), with a large, square white funnel.

The addition of teak overlaid decking and teak lounge chairs greatly improved what was formerly a bland pool deck outdoors. Its sister ships are *Insignia* (formerly Renaissance Cruises' *R One*) and *Regatta* (formerly *R Two*).

While there is no wrap-around promenade deck outdoors, there is a small jogging track around the perimeter of the swimming pool, and port and starboard side decks.

The interior decor is stunning and elegant, a throwback to ship decor of the ocean liners of the 1920s and '30s, with dark woods and warm colors, all carried out in fine taste (but a bit *faux* in places). This includes detailed ceiling cornices, both real and *faux* wrought-iron staircase railings, leather-paneled walls, *trompe l'oeil* ceilings, rich carpeting in hallways with an Oriental rug-look center section, and many other interesting (and expensive-looking) decorative touches. It feels like an old-world country club.

The public rooms are spread over three decks. The reception hall (lobby) has a staircase with intricate wrought-iron railings. A large observation lounge, called the Horizon Bar, is located high atop ship.

There are plenty of bars – including one in each of the restaurant entrances. Perhaps the nicest is the casino bar/lounge, a beautiful room reminiscent of London's grand hotels and includes a martini bar. It has an inviting marble fireplace, comfortable sofas and individual chairs.

BERLITZ'S RATINGS

	Possible	Achieved
Ship	500	418
Accommodation	200	160
Food	400	312
Service	400	295
Entertainment	100	77
Cruise	400	313

The Library is a grand Regency-style room, with a fireplace, a high, indented, *trompe l'oeil* ceiling, and excellent selection of books, plus very comfortable wingback chairs with footstools, and sofas you could sleep on. Oceania@Sea is the ship's internet connect center.

The dress code is "smart casual." The onboard currency is the US dollar. Gratuities are added at $10.50 per person, per day (accommodation designated as suites have an extra $3 per person charge for the butler). A 15% gratuity is added to bar and spa accounts.

Stairways, though carpeted, are tinny. Oceania Cruises is a young company with a refreshing vision and desire to provide an extremely high level of food and service in an informal setting that is at once elegant yet comfortable, and that is exactly what it has achieved.

SUITABLE FOR: *Nautica* is best suited to couples who like good food and style, but want informality with no formal nights on board, and interesting itineraries, all at a very reasonable price well below what the luxury ships charge.

ACCOMMODATION. There are six cabin categories, and 10 price grades (3 suite price grades; 5 outside-view cabin grades; 2 interior (no view) cabin grades.

All of the standard interior (no view) and outside-view cabins (the lowest four grades) are extremely compact units, and extremely tight for two persons (particularly for cruises longer than five days). They have twin beds (or queen-sized bed), with good under-bed storage areas, personal safe, vanity desk with large mirror, good closet and drawer space (in rich, dark woods), 100% cotton bathrobe and towels, slippers, clothes brush and shoe horn. Color

TVs carry a major news channel (where obtainable), plus a sports channel and round-the-clock movie channels.

Certain cabin categories (about 100 of them) qualify as "Concierge Level" accommodation, and occupants get extra goodies such as enhanced bathroom amenities, complimentary shoeshine, tote bag, cashmere throw blanket, bottle of champagne on arrival, hand-held hairdryer, priority restaurant reservations, and priority embarkation.

Owner's Suites. The six Owner's Suites, measuring around 962 sq.ft/89.3 sq.meters, provide the most spacious accommodation. They are fine, large living spaces located aft overlooking the stern on Decks 6, 7, and 8 (they are, however, subject to more movement and some vibration). They have extensive teak-floor private balconies that really are private and cannot be overlooked from the decks above. Each has an entrance foyer, living room, separate bedroom (the bed faces the sea, which can be seen through the floor-to-ceiling windows and sliding glass door), CD player (with selection of audio discs), fully tiled bathroom with Jacuzzi bathtub, and a small guest bathroom.

Vista Suites. There are four, each measuring around 785.7 sq.ft/73 sq.meters, and located forward on Decks 5 and 6. They have extensive teak-floor private balconies that cannot be overlooked by anyone from the decks above. Each has an entrance foyer, living room, separate bedroom (the bed faces the sea, which can be seen through the floor-to-ceiling windows and sliding glass door), CD player (with selection of audio discs), and fully tiled bathroom with Jacuzzi tub.

Penthouse Suites. There are 52 of these (actually, they are not suites at all, but large cabins as the bedrooms aren't separate from the living areas). They do, however, measure around 322.9 sq.ft (30 sq. meters), and have a good-sized teak-floor balcony with sliding glass door (but with partial, and not full, balcony partitions) and teak deck furniture. The lounge area has a proper dining table and there is ample clothes storage space. The bathroom has a tub, shower enclosure, washbasin and toilet.

Cabins with Balcony. Cabins with private balconies (around 216 sq.ft/20 sq. meters), comprise about 66% of all cabins. They have partial, not full, balcony partitions, sliding glass doors, and only 14 cabins on Deck 6 have lifeboat-obstructed views. The living area has a refrigerated mini-bar, lounge area with breakfast table, and a balcony with teak floor, two teak chairs and a drinks table. The bathrooms, with tiled floors and plain walls, are compact, standard units, and include a shower stall with a strong, removable hand-held shower unit, hairdryer, toiletries storage shelves and retractable clothesline.

Outside View and Interior (No View) Cabins. These measure around 160–165 sq.ft (14.8–15.3 sq.meters), and have twin beds (convertible to a queen-sized bed), vanity desk, small sofa and coffee table, and bathroom with a shower enclosure with a strong, removable hand-held shower unit, hairdryer, toiletries storage shelves, retractable clothesline, washbasin, and toilet. Although they are not

large, they are quite comfortable, with a decent amount of storage space.

CUISINE. Flexibility and choice are what the dining facilities aboard the Oceania ships are all about. There are four different restaurants:

● The **Grand Dining Room** has around 340 seats, and a raised central section, but the problem is the noise level – because of the low ceiling height, it's atrocious when the dining room is full. Being located at the stern, there are large ocean-view windows on three sides (prime tables overlook the stern). The chairs are comfortable and have armrests. The menus change daily for lunch and dinner.

● **Toscana Italian Restaurant** has 96 seats, windows along two sides, and a set menu (plus chef's daily specials).

● The cozy **Polo Grill** has 98 seats, windows along two sides and a set menu including prime steaks and seafood.

● The **Terrace Café** has seats for 154 indoors – not enough during cruises to cold-weather areas – and 186 outdoors. It is open for breakfast, lunch and casual dinners, when it offers tapas and other Mediterranean food. As the ship's self-serve buffet restaurant, it incorporates a small pizzeria and grill. There are basic salads, a meat carving station, and a reasonable selection of cheeses.

All restaurants have open-seating dining, so you can dine when you want, with whom you wish. Reservations are needed in Toscana Restaurant and Polo Grill (but there's no extra charge), where there are mostly tables for four or six; there are few tables for two. There is a Poolside Grill Bar. All cappuccino and espresso coffees cost extra.

The food and service staff is provided by Apollo, a well-known and respected maritime catering company that also has an interest in Oceania Cruises. The consultant chef is Jacques Pepin (well-known as a television chef in America), who oversees the cuisine.

ENTERTAINMENT. The Nautica Lounge has entertainment, lectures and some social events. There is little entertainment due to the intensive nature of the itineraries. However, there is live music in several bars and lounges.

SPA/FITNESS. A lido deck has a swimming pool, and good sunbathing space, plus a thalassotherapy tub. A jogging track circles the swimming pool deck (but one deck above). The uppermost outdoors deck includes a golf driving net and shuffleboard court. The Oceania Spa consists of a beauty salon, three treatment rooms, men's and women's changing rooms, and steam room (there is no sauna). Harding Brothers operates the spa and beauty salon, and provides the staff. Examples of pricing include: full body massage $99 (50 minutes); foot and ankle massage $39 (20 minutes); body contour wrap, $159 (75 minutes); botanical therapy facial, $99 (75 minutes); personal training session $75 (75 minutes); shampoo, style and dry $29 (short hair); manicure $29; pedicure $39. Note that 15% is added to your spa account, whether you like it or not.

Navigator of the Seas
★★★★

Large Resort Ship: . . . . .137,276 tons	Passenger Decks: 14	Cabins (for one person): 0
Lifestyle: . . . . .Standard	Total Crew: .1,185	Cabins (with private balcony): 765
Cruise Line: . . . . .Royal Caribbean	Passengers	Cabins (wheelchair accessible): 26
International	(lower beds/all berths): 3,114/3,835	Cabin Current: . . . . .110 volts
Former Names: . . . . .none	Passenger Space Ratio	Elevators: . . . . .14 (6 glass-enclosed)
Builder: . . .Kvaerner Masa-Yards (Finland)	(lower beds/all berths): 44.0/35.7	Casino (gaming tables): . . . . .Yes
Original Cost: . . . .$500 million	Crew/Passenger Ratio	Slot Machines: . . . . .Yes
Entered Service: . . . . .Spring 2003	(lower beds/all berths): 2.6/3.2	Swimming Pools (outdoors): 3
Registry: . . . . .The Bahamas	Navigation Officers: . . . . . .Scandinavian	Swimming Pools (indoors): 0
Length (ft/m): 1,020.6/311.1	Cabins (total): 1,557	Whirlpools: 6
Beam (ft/m): 155.5/47.4	Size Range (sq ft/m): 151.0–1,358.0/	Self-Service Launderette: . . . . .No
Draft (ft/m): 28.8/8.8	14.0–126.1	Dedicated Cinema/Seats: . . . . .No
Propulsion/Propellers: . . . . .diesel-electric	Cabins (outside view): 939	Library: . . . . .Yes
(75,600 kW)/3 pods	Cabins (interior/no view): 618	

OVERALL SCORE: 1,471 (OUT OF A POSSIBLE 2,000 POINTS)

OVERVIEW. *Navigator of the Seas* is a stunning, large, floating leisure resort (sister to *Adventure of the Seas, Explorer of the Seas*, and *Voyager of the Seas*).

The ship's propulsion is derived from three pod units, powered by electric motors (two azimuthing, and one fixed at the centerline) instead of conventional rudders and propellers, in the latest configuration of high-tech propulsion systems. With its large proportions, the ship provides more facilities and options, yet the ship manages to have a healthy passenger space ratio (the amount of space per passenger).

Being a "non-Panamax" ship, it is simply too large to go through the Panama Canal, thus limiting its itineraries almost exclusively to the Caribbean (where few islands can accept it), or for use as a floating island resort. Spend the first few hours exploring all the many facilities and public spaces aboard this vessel and it will be time well spent.

Although *Navigator of the Seas* really is a large ship, the cabin hallways are warm and attractive, with artwork cabinets and wavy lines to lead you along and break up the monotony. In fact, there are plenty of colorful, even whimsical, decorative touches to help you avoid what would otherwise be a very clinical environment.

Embarkation and disembarkation take place through two stations/access points, designed to minimize the inevitable lines at the start and end of the cruise (that's more than 1,500 people for each access point). Once inside the ship, you'll need good walking shoes, particularly when you need to go from one end to the other – it really is quite a long way.

The four-decks-high Royal Promenade, which is 394 ft (120 meters) long, is the main interior focal point of the

BERLITZ'S RATINGS		
	Possible	Achieved
Ship	500	418
Accommodation	200	150
Food	400	237
Service	400	276
Entertainment	100	83
Cruise	400	307

ship (it's also a good place to hang out, or to meet someone). The length of two football fields (American football, that is), it has two internal lobbies (atria) that rise to as many as 11 decks high. Restaurants, shops and entertainment locations front this winding street and interior "with-view" cabins look into it from above. It is designed loosely in the image of London's fashionable Burlington Arcade – although there's not a real brick in sight. It is, however, an imaginative piece of design work, and most passengers (particularly those who like shopping malls) enjoy it immensely.

The super-atrium houses a "traditional" English-style pub (Two Poets Pub), with draft beer and plenty of "street-front" seating (it's funny, but North American passengers sit down, while British passengers prefer to stand at the bar). There is also a Champagne Bar, a Sidewalk Cafe (for continental breakfast, all-day pizzas, specialty coffees and desserts), Sprinkles (for round-the-clock ice cream and yoghurt). There are also several shops – for jewelry, gifts, liquor and logo souvenirs.

Altogether, the Royal promenade is a nice place to see and be seen, and there is action throughout the day and night. The Guest Reception and Shore Excursion counters are located at the aft end of the promenade, as is an ATM, while opposite is the cozy Champagne Bar. Watch for the parades and street entertainers.

Arched across the promenade is a Captain's Balcony. Meanwhile, in the center of the promenade is a stairway that connects you to the deck below, where you'll find the Schooner Bar (a piano lounge that is a feature found aboard all RCI ships) and the colorful Casino Royale. This is naturally large and full of flashing lights and noises. Gaming includes blackjack, Caribbean stud poker, roulette, and craps, as well as 300 slot machines.

There is also a regulation-size ice-skating rink (Studio B), featuring real, not fake, ice, with "bleacher" seating for up to 900, and the latest in broadcast facilities. Ice Follies shows are also presented here. A number of slim pillars obstruct clear-view arena stage sight lines, however. If ice-skating in the Caribbean doesn't appeal, perhaps you'd like the stunning two-deck library (it's the first aboard any ship, and it is open 24 hours a day). A grand amount of money was spent on permanent artwork.

Drinking places include a neat Aquarium Bar, which comes complete with 50 tons of glass and water in four large aquariums (whose combined value is over $1 million). Other drinking places include the aforementioned Champagne Bar, the Crown & Anchor Pub, and a Connoisseur Club – for cigars and cognacs.

Lovers of jazz might appreciate the Cosmopolitan Club, an intimate room for cool music atop the ship within the Viking Crown Lounge, or the Schooner Bar piano lounge. Golfers might enjoy the 19th Hole, a golf bar, as they play the Navigator Links.

There is a large TV studio, adjacent to rooms that can be used for trade show exhibit space, with conference center that seats 400 and a multi-media screening room that seats 60. Lovers could tie the knot in a wedding chapel in the sky, the Skylight Chapel (it's located on the upper level of the Viking Crown Lounge, and even has wheelchair access via an electric stairway lift). Meanwhile, outdoors, the pool and open deck areas provide a resort-like environment.

Families with children are also well catered to, as facilities for children and teenagers are extensive (they are much larger than aboard sister ships *Adventure of the Seas, Explorer of the Seas and Voyager of the Seas*). An area called Adventure Ocean is split into age-related areas: "Aquanauts" is for 3–5 year-olds; "Explorers" is for 6–8 year-olds; "Voyagers" is for 9–12 year-olds. The Living Room and Fuel are dedicated areas for teenagers, that include a daytime club (with several computers), soda bar, and disco; there's also an array of the latest video games. Paint and Clay is an arts and crafts center for younger children. Adjacent to these indoor areas is Adventure Beach, an area for all the family; this includes swimming pools, a water slide and game areas outdoors.

In terms of sheer size, this ship dwarfs all others in the cruise industry, but in terms of personal service, the reverse is the case, unless you happen to reside in one of the top suites. Royal Caribbean International does, however, try hard to provide a good standard of programmed service from its hotel staff. This is impersonal city life at sea, millennium-style, and a superb, well-designed alternative to a land-based resort, which is what the company wanted to build. Welcome to the escapist world of highly programmed resort living aboard ship.

Remember to take plenty of extra funds – you'll need them to pay for all the additional-cost items. The onboard currency is the US dollar.

The ship is large, so remember that if you meet someone somewhere, and want to meet them again you'll need to make an appointment – for this really is a large, Las Vegas-style floating resort-city for the lively of heart and fleet of foot. The best advice I can give you is to arrange to meet somewhere along the Royal Promenade.

SUITABLE FOR: *Navigator of the Seas* is best suited to young-minded adults and couples of all ages, families with toddlers, tots, children, and teenagers who like to mingle in a large ship setting with plenty of entertainment for everyone, with food that focuses on quantity rather than quality (unless you are prepared to pay extra in the "alternative" restaurant), all delivered with friendly but unpolished service.

ACCOMMODATION. There is an extensive range of 22 cabin categories, in four major groupings: Premium ocean-view suites and cabins, Promenade-view (interior-view) cabins, Ocean-view cabins, and Interior (no view) cabins. Note that many cabins are of a similar size (good for incentives and large groups), and 300 have interconnecting doors (good for families). Suites and cabins with private balcony have Bolidt floors (a substance that looks like rubberized sand) instead of wood. If you have a cabin with an interconnecting door to another cabin, you should be aware that noise can filter through from the adjoining room. Also, the bathroom toilets are quite noisy. The price you pay will depend on the grade, size and location you choose.

A total of 138 interior (no view) cabins have bay windows that look into a horizontal atrium – first used to good effect aboard the Baltic passenger ferries *Silja Serenade* (1990) and *Silja Symphony* (1991) with interior cabins that look into a central shopping plaza. These cabins measure 157 sq. ft (15 sq. meters). Regardless of which cabin grade you choose, all except for the Royal Suite and Owner's Suite have twin beds that convert to a queen-sized unit, a TV set, radio and telephone, personal safe, vanity unit, mini-bar (called an Automatic Refreshment Center) hairdryer and private bathroom.

The largest accommodation includes luxuriously appointed penthouse suites (whose occupants, sadly, must share the rest of the ship with everyone else, except for their own exclusive, and private, concierge club). The grandest is the Royal Suite, which is positioned on the port side of the ship, and measures 1,146 sq. ft/106.5 sq. meters). It has a king-sized bed in a separate, large bedroom, a living room with an additional queen-sized sofa bed, baby grand piano (no pianist is included, however), refrigerator/wet bar, dining table, entertainment center, and large bathroom.

The slightly smaller, but still highly desirable, Owner's Suites (there are 10 of these, all located in the center of the ship, on both port and starboard sides, each measuring 468 sq. ft/43 sq. meters) and four Royal Family suites (each 574 sq. ft/53 sq. meters), all featuring similar items. However, the four Royal Family suites, which have two bedrooms (including one with third/fourth upper Pullman berths) are at the stern of the ship and have magnificent views over the ship's wake (and seagulls).

All cabins have a private bathroom with shower enclosure (towels are 100% cotton), as well as interactive, closed-circuit and satellite TV, and pay-per-view movies. Cabins with "private balconies" aren't so private, as the partitions are only partial, not full. The balcony decking is made of Bolidt and not wood, while the balcony rail is of wood.

CUISINE. The main dining room, with a capacity of almost 2,000, is large and noisy. It is set on three levels, with a dramatic staircase connecting all three levels. All three have exactly the same menus and food. There are also two small private wings for private groups, each seating about 58 persons. The dining room is totally non-smoking, there are two seatings, and tables are for four, six, eight 10 or 12. The china and cutlery are good-quality.

Alternative (Extra Cost) Dining

Alternative dining options for casual and informal meals at all hours (according to company releases) include:

● **Cafe Promenade:** for continental breakfast, all-day pizzas and specialty coffees (provided in paper cups).

● **Windjammer Cafe:** for casual buffet-style breakfast, lunch and light dinner (except for the cruise's last night).

● **Chops Grille** (a steakhouse that is actually a little section inside the Windjammer Cafe): for casual dinner (no reservations necessary) featuring a grill and open kitchen. A cover charge of $20 per person applies. Meats and steaks featured include Veal Chop, New York Striploin Steak, Filet Mignon, and Prime Rib of Beef.

● **Portofino:** this is the ship's "upscale" (non-smoking) Euro-Italian restaurant, open for dinner only. Reservations are required (a $20 cover charge/gratuity of $20 per person applies). The food and its presentation are better than the food in the dining room, although the restaurant is not large enough for all passengers to try even once during a cruise. Choices include: antipasti, soup, salad, pasta, main dish, dessert, cheese and coffee.

● **Johnny Rockets:** a retro 1950s all-day, all-night American diner-style eatery that features hamburgers, malt shakes (at extra cost), and jukebox hits, with both indoor and outdoor seating (all indoor tables have a mini-jukebox; dimes are provided for you to make your selection of vintage records), and all-singing, all-dancing waitresses

that'll knock your socks off, if you can stand the volume.

● **Sprinkles:** for round-the-clock ice cream and yoghurt (in the Royal Promenade).

ENTERTAINMENT. The 1,350-seat Metropolis Showlounge is a really stunning room that could well be the equal of many such rooms on land. It is located at the forward end of the ship and spans the height of five decks (with only a few slim pillars and almost no disruption of sight lines from almost any seat in the house). The room features a hydraulic orchestra pit and huge stage areas, together with sonic-boom loud sound, and some superb lighting equipment.

In addition, the ship has a whole array of cabaret acts. Although many of these are not what you would call headliners (the strongest cabaret acts are featured in the main showlounge, while others are presented in the Ixtapa Lounge, which is also the venue for late-night adults-only comedy), they regularly travel the cruise ship circuit.

There is also a television studio, located adjacent to rooms that could be used, for example, for trade show exhibition space (good for conventions at sea).

SPA/FITNESS. The ShipShape Spa is large, and measures 15,000 sq. ft (1,400 sq. meters). It includes a large aerobics exercise room, fitness center (with the usual stairmasters, treadmills, stationary bikes, weight machines and free weights), treatment rooms, men's and women's sauna/ steam rooms, while another 10,000 sq. ft (930 sq. meters) is devoted to a Solarium (with magrodome sliding glass roof) for relaxation after you've exercised too much.

For the more sporting, there is activity galore – including a rock-climbing wall that's 32.8 ft high (10 meters), with five separate climbing tracks. It is located outdoors at the aft end of the funnel. You'll get a great "buzz" being 200 ft (60 meters) above the ocean while the ship is moving.

Other sports facilities include a roller-blading track, a dive-and-snorkel shop, a full-size basketball court and 9-hole, par 26 golf course.

● **For more extensive general information about the Royal Caribbean experience, see pages 137–42.**

Nippon Maru
★★★ +

Small Ship: . . . . .21,903 tons	Passenger Decks: 7	Cabins (for one person): 0
Lifestyle: . . . . .Standard	Total Crew: .160	Cabins (with private balcony): 0
Cruise Line: . . .Mitsui OSK Passenger Line	Passengers	Cabins (wheelchair accessible): 2
Former Names: . . . . .none	(lower beds/all berths): 408/607	Cabin Current: . . . . .100 volts
Builder: . . . .Mitsubishi Heavy Industries	Passenger Space Ratio	Elevators: 5
(Japan)	(lower beds/all berths): 53.6/36.0	Casino (gaming tables): . . . . .Yes
Original Cost: . . . .$59.4 million	Crew/Passenger Ratio	(no cash can be won, only gifts)
Entered Service: . . . . .Sept 1990	(lower beds/all berths): 2.5/3.7	Slot Machines: . . . . .No
Registry: . . . . .Japan	Navigation Officers: . . . . .Japanese	Swimming Pools (outdoors): 1
Length (ft/m): 546.7/166.65	Cabins (total): 204	Swimming Pools (indoors): 0
Beam (ft/m): 78.7/24.00	Size Range (sq ft/m): 150.6–430.5/	Whirlpools: . . . . .4 (Japanese baths)
Draft (ft/m): 21.4/6.55	14.0–40.0	Self-Service Launderette: . . . . .Yes
Propulsion/Propellers: . . . . .diesel	Cabins (outside view): 189	Dedicated Cinema/Seats: Yes/135
(15,740 kW)/2	Cabins (interior/no view): 15	Library: . . . . .Yes

OVERALL SCORE: 1,390 (OUT OF A POSSIBLE 2,000 POINTS)

OVERVIEW. *Nippon Maru* has a single, large, orange, swept-back funnel aft of amidships, with an exterior styling that is very traditional. There is a decent amount of open outdoors space, and the teakwood decking outdoors is good.

The focal point of the interiors is an atrium lobby that spans six decks. The public rooms have very high ceilings, giving a sense of spaciousness, and are well-designed, with high-quality furnishings and soothing color combinations. Public rooms include a main lounge, main hall/lecture room, piano lounge, cinema/lecture room, and a washitsu tatami room. Organized children's activities are provided only on leisure cruises.

A specialist courier company provides an excellent luggage service and will collect your luggage from your home before the cruise, and deliver it back to your home after the cruise (this service is available only in Japan). The onboard currency is the Japanese yen.

The white cheap plastic deck furniture is difficult to keep clean and looks really shoddy. The seats in the theater are rather plain and utilitarian. Hospitality towards passengers could be improved (particularly by the officers). A big refit is planned for 2009.

SUITABLE FOR: *Nippon Maru* is best suited to Japanese-speaking couples and single travelers who want modestly comfortable surroundings, and who enjoy decent food and service, all at a low cost. There is no tipping.

ACCOMMODATION. Most cabins are located forward, with public rooms positioned aft. The suites are quite large (larger

BERLITZ'S RATINGS

	Possible	Achieved
Ship	500	348
Accommodation	200	135
Food	400	287
Service	400	289
Entertainment	100	62
Cruise	400	269

than aboard half-sister ship *Fuji Maru*), and have a separate bedroom and living room with a solid wall divider (except for the doorway, where there is a curtain but no door). A large sofa, four chairs, and coffee table occupy one section of the lounge; there is also a vanity/writing desk. The bedroom has a good amount of closet and drawer space and two beds. The bathroom is very small. Slippers and bathrobes are provided.

The deluxe cabins are nicely decorated, and the living area has a table and two chairs, and two beds (they cannot be pushed together). The standard cabins are utilitarian and clinical (adequate for convention and seminar cruise passengers). Many of these have a third (or third and fourth) pull-down upper Pullman berth.

CUISINE. The dining room, which seats around 320, is pleasing but basic. It features both traditional Japanese cuisine and some Western dishes. There is one seating dining for leisure cruises, and two seatings for when the ship is under charter. Food presentation is decent, but plain.

ENTERTAINMENT. The Main Hall has a theater-style stage, wooden dance floor, and seating in individual chairs on both the lower (main) level and the upper (balcony) level of this two-deck high room. Social dancing is on the agenda each evening. On most cruises, special featured entertainers are brought on board from ashore..

SPA/FITNESS. There is a traditional Japanese Grand Bath (one for women, one for men), with washing stations, a sauna, and beauty salon. Massages and facials are available.

Noordam
★★★★

Large Resort Ship: ....82,300 tons	Total Crew: 820	Cabins (with private balcony): 641
Lifestyle: ....Premium	Passengers	Cabins (wheelchair accessible): 28
Cruise Line: ....Holland America Line	(lower beds/all berths): 1,918/2,457	Cabin Current: ....110 volts
Former Names: ....none	Passenger Space Ratio	Elevators: 14
Builder: ....Fincantieri (Italy)	(lower beds/all berths): 42.9/33.4	Casino (gaming tables): ....Yes
Original Cost: ....$400 million	Crew/Passenger Ratio	Slot Machines: ....Yes
Entered Service: ....Feb 2006	(lower beds/all berths): 2.3/2.9	Swimming Pools (outdoors): 2
Registry: ....The Netherlands	Navigation Officers: ....European	+ children's pool
Length (ft/m): 935.0/285.0	Cabins (total): 959	Swimming Pools (indoors):1 (indoor/outdoor)
Beam (ft/m): 105.6/32.25	Size Range (sq ft/m): 170.0–1,318.6/	Whirlpools: 5
Draft (ft/m): 25.5/7.8	15.7–122.5	Self-Service Launderette: ....No
Propulsion/Propellers: .....diesel-electric	Cabins (outside view): 806	Dedicated Cinema/Seats: Yes/170
(34,000 kW)/2 pods (17.6 MW each)	Cabins (interior/no view): 153	Library: ....Yes
Passenger Decks: 11	Cabins (for one person): 0	

OVERALL SCORE: 1,519 (OUT OF A POSSIBLE 2,000 POINTS)

OVERVIEW. *Noordam* (with 35 cabins more than sister ships *Eurodam, Oosterdam, Westerdam, Zuiderdam*) is one of the Vista-class of ships in the Holland America Line fleet, designed to appeal to multi-generational holidaymakers.

The twin working funnels are the result of the slightly unusual machinery configuration; the ship has, in effect, two engine rooms – one with three diesels, and one with two diesels and a gas turbine). A pod propulsion system is provided *(see page 174 for explanation)*, powered by a diesel-electric system, with a small gas turbine located in the funnel for the reduction of emissions.

There is a complete walk-around exterior teak promenade deck, and teak "steamer" style sunloungers are provided. Additionally, there is a jogging track outdoors, located around the ship's mast and the forward third of the ship. Exterior glass elevators, mounted midships on both port and starboard sides, provide fine ocean views from any one of 10 decks. There are two centrally located swimming pools outdoors, and one can be used in inclement weather due to its retractable sliding glass roof. Two whirlpool tubs, adjacent to the swimming pools, are abridged by a bar. A smaller (swimming) pool is available for children, and this incorporates a winding water slide that spans two decks in height. There is an additional whirlpool tub outdoors.

The intimate lobby spans three decks, and is topped by a beautiful, rotating, Waterford Crystal globe of the world. Adjacent are interior and glass wall elevators with exterior views. The interior decor is bright in many areas (in order to attract a younger clientele), and the ceilings are particularly noticeable. In keeping with the traditions of Holland America Line, a large collection of artwork is a standard

BERLITZ'S RATINGS		
	Possible	Achieved
Ship	500	427
Accommodation	200	162
Food	400	269
Service	400	275
Entertainment	100	77
Cruise	400	309

feature, and pieces reflect the former Dutch East Indies.

There are two whole entertainment/public room decks. Perhaps the most dramatic room aboard this ship is the showlounge, spanning four decks in the forward section of the ship. Other facilities include a winding shopping street with several boutique stores and logo shops, card room, an art gallery, photo gallery, and several small meetings rooms. The casino is large (one has to walk through it to get from the restaurant to the showlounge on one of the entertainments decks), and is equipped with all the gaming paraphernalia and slot machines you can think of. Sports enthusiasts can enjoy a basketball court, volleyball court, golf simulator. "Explorations" is a combination coffee bar (coffees and other drinks are at extra cost), lounge, an extensive library and internet-connect center, all contained in one attractive, open "lifestyle" environment – it's a really fine, very popular area for relaxation and reading (although noise from the coffee machine can interrupt concentration).

For families with children, Club HAL's KidZone provides a whole area dedicated to children's facilities and extensive programming for different age groups (5–17), with one counselor for every 30 children. Free ice cream is provided at certain hours, plus hot hors d'oeuvres in all bars.

While this formula may not work well for the loyal repeat passengers used to the line's smaller ships, Noordam offers a wide range of public rooms with a reasonably intimate atmosphere and the overall feel of the ship is quite homely and comforting, with fresh flowers everywhere, as well as some nicely showcased Dutch artifacts and museum pieces from the 16th and 17th centuries. Perhaps the ship's best asset is its friendly and personable crew (most are from Indonesia and the Philippines).

The information desk in the lobby is small and somewhat removed from the main passenger flow on the two decks above it. Many pillars obstruct the passenger flow and lines of sight throughout the ship. There are no self-service launderettes (something families with children miss – although special laundry packages are available).

ACCOMMODATION. There are 24 price categories: 16 outside-view/8 interior (no view). Some cabins on the lowest accommodation deck (Main Deck) have views obstructed by lifeboats. Some cabins that can accommodate a third and fourth person have very little closet space, and only one personal safe. Some cabins have interconnecting doors – good for families with children. Occupants of suites also get exclusive use of the Neptune Lounge and concierge service, priority embarkation and disembarkation, and other benefits. In many of the suites/cabins with private balconies the balconies are not so private, and can be overlooked from various public locations.

Penthouse Verandah Suites: Two suites offer the largest accommodation (1,318 sq. ft/122.5 sq. meters, including balcony). These have a separate bedroom with a king-sized bed; there's also a walk-in closet, dressing room, living room, dining room, butler's pantry, mini-bar and refrigerator, and private balcony (verandah). The main bathroom has a large whirlpool bathtub, two washbasins, toilet, and plenty of storage space for personal toiletry items. Personalized stationery and free dry cleaning are included, as are hot hors d'oeuvres and other goodies daily.

DeLuxe Verandah Suites: Next in size are 60 of these suites (563 sq. ft/52.3 sq. meters). These have twin beds that convert to a king-sized bed, vanity desk, lounge area, walk-in closet, mini-bar and refrigerator, and bathroom with full-size bathtub, washbasin and toilet. Personalized stationery and complimentary dry cleaning are included, as are hot hors d'oeuvres and other goodies.

Verandah Suites: There are 100 of these (actually they are cabins, not suites, and measure (284 sq. ft/26.3 sq. meters). Twin beds can convert to a queen-sized bed; there is also a lounge area, mini-bar and refrigerator, while the bathroom has a tub, washbasin and toilet. Floor to ceiling windows open onto a private balcony (verandah).

Outside-view Cabins: Standard outside cabins (197 sq. ft/18.3 sq. meters) have twin beds that can convert to a queen-size bed. There's a small sitting area, while the bathroom has a tub/ shower combination. The interior (no view) cabins are slightly smaller (182.9 sq. ft/ 17 sq. meters).

CUISINE. The 1,045-seat Vista (main) Dining Room is two decks high, with seating (at tables for two, four, six or eight) on both main and balcony levels (the galley is underneath the restaurant, accessed by port and starboard escalators), and is at the stern. It provides a traditional Holland America Line dining experience, with friendly service from smiling Indonesian and Filipino stewards. Both open seating and

fixed (assigned tables and times) seating are available, while breakfast and lunch are open-seating (you'll be seated by restaurant staff when you enter). The dining room is a non-smoking venue.

Holland America Line can provide Kosher meals, although these are prepared ashore, frozen, and brought to your table sealed in their original containers.

Alternative Dining Option: The 148-seat Pinnacle Grill is a more upscale dining spot (with higher quality ingredients, and better presentation than in the larger main dining room). On Lower Promenade Deck, it fronts onto the second level of the atrium lobby (note that tables along the outer section of the restaurant are open to it and can suffer from noise from the Atrium Bar one deck below – but the tables are good for those who like to see and be seen). "Pacific Northwest" cuisine is featured (with items such as sesame-crusted halibut with ginger-miso; and an array of premium quality steaks). Formal table settings, china and silverware are featured, as are leather-bound menus. The wine menu (expanded in 2006) features some fine wines from around the world, including many gorgeous Bordeaux reds. Reservations are required and there is a cover charge of $30 per person for service and gratuity.

Informal Eateries: For casual eating, there is an extensive Lido Café, an eatery that wraps around the funnel, with indoor-outdoor seating and ocean views. It includes several sections including a salad bar, Asian stir-fry and sushi section, deli sandwiches, and a separate dessert buffet, although lines can form for made-to-order items (omelets for breakfast, pasta for lunch, etc.).

There's also an outdoor grill bar (adjacent to the Lido pool) with fast-food items such as hamburgers, veggie burgers, hot dogs, chicken and fries. On certain days, barbecues and other culinary specialties are available poolside.

ENTERTAINMENT. The 867-seat Vista Lounge is the principal venue for Las Vegas-style revues and major cabaret shows. The main floor level has a bar in its starboard aft section. Spiral stairways at the back of the lounge connect all levels. Stage shows are best seen from the upper levels, from where the sightlines are quite good.

SPA/FITNESS. The Greenhouse Spa is a large, two-decks-high health spa, and is located directly above the navigation bridge. Facilities include a solarium, hydrotherapy pool, unisex thermal suite – a unisex area incorporating a Laconium (gentle sauna), Hammam (mild steam), and Chamomile Grotto (small aromatic steam room).

There is also a beauty salon, 11 massage/therapy rooms (including one for couples), and a large gymnasium with floor-to-ceiling windows on three sides and forward-facing ocean views, and the latest high-tech muscle-toning equipment.

● **For more extensive general information on what a Holland America Line cruise is like, see pages 126–28.**

Norwegian Dawn
★★★★

Large Resort Ship: ....91,740 tons	Passenger Decks: 11	Cabins (for one person): 0
Lifestyle: ....Standard	Total Crew: 1,318	Cabins (with private balcony): 511
Cruise Line: .....Norwegian Cruise Lines	Passengers	Cabins (wheelchair accessible): 20
Former Names: ....none	(lower beds/all berths): 2,244/2,840	Cabin Current: ....110 AC
Gross Tonnage: 91,000	Passenger Space Ratio	Elevators: 12
Builder: ....Meyer Werft (Germany)	(lower beds/all berths): 40.8/32.0	Casino (gaming tables): ....Yes
Original Cost: ....$400 million	Crew/Passenger Ratio	Slot Machines: ....Yes
Entered Service: ....Oct 2002	(lower beds/all berths): 1.7/3.0	Swimming Pools (outdoors): 2
Registry: ....Bahamas	Navigation Officers: ......Scandinavian	Swimming Pools (indoors): 1
Length (ft/m): 964.9/294.13	Cabins (total): 1,122	Whirlpools: ...4 (+ 1 children's whirlpool)
Beam (ft/m): 105.6/32.2	Size Range (sq ft/m): 142.0–5,350.0/	Self-Service Launderette: ....No
Draft (ft/m): 26.9/8.2	13.2–497.0	Dedicated Cinema/Seats: Yes/151
Propulsion/Propellers: ...diesel-electric/2	Cabins (outside view): 787	Library: ....Yes
azimuthing pods (19.5MW each)	Cabins (interior/no view): 335	

OVERALL SCORE: 1,520 (OUT OF A POSSIBLE 2,000 POINTS)

OVERVIEW. *Norwegian Dawn* (sister to *Norwegian Star*, which debuted in 2001) was constructed in 64 sections, ("blocks"). It is a state-of-the-art vessel for Norwegian Cruise Line, and features a "pod" propulsion system (*see page 174 for a detailed explanation*).

The hull displays interesting logos on top of its white paint, depicting the ship's itineraries: the port side features the cruise itinerary from New York to the Bahamas and Florida, while the starboard side features the winter itinerary from Miami to the Caribbean. Dolphins, the Statue of Liberty, and representations of the four original paintings displayed on board (the Impressionists Matisse, Renoir, Van Gogh, and the pop artist Andy Warhol). It is a colorful concept, and makes the ship easy to spot in a sea of similar-sized ships in port.

Facilities include a large Dawn Club Casino gaming area, an Internet Cafe (with 24 computer stations and internet connection), a 1,150-seat showlounge with main floor and balcony level, a 3,000-book library, a card room, a writing and study room, a business center, conference and meeting rooms, and a retail shopping complex measuring 20,000 sq. ft (1,800 sq. meters).

As in sister ship *Norwegian Star*, a good deal of space is devoted to children's facilities (the T-Rex Kids' Center and Teen Club) – all tucked well away from adult recreation areas, at the aft end of the ship. Children of all ages will get to play in a superb wet 'n' wild space-themed water park (complete with large pool, water slide, and paddle pool). There's a room full of cots for toddlers to use for sleepovers, and even the toilets are at a special low height. Teens, too, are well catered for, and get their own cinema (with

BERLITZ'S RATINGS		
	Possible	Achieved
Ship	500	422
Accommodation	200	156
Food	400	289
Service	400	284
Entertainment	100	66
Cruise	400	303

DVD movies), discotheque with dance floor, and their own whirlpool (hot) tub.

With so many dining choices (some of which cost extra), your final cruise and dining experience will be determined by how much you are prepared to spend. To make the most of your cruise holiday, you will need to plan where you want to eat well in advance, and make the necessary reservations, or you may be disappointed.

More choices, including more dining options, add up to a very attractive holiday package, particularly suitable for families with children, in a very contemporary floating leisure center that really does provide ample facilities for you to have an enjoyable time. The dress code is casual – very casual (no jacket and tie needed, although you are welcome to dress formally if you so wish). There is no suggested dress code on the daily programme.

While the initial cruise fare seems very reasonable, the extra costs and charges soon mount up if you want to sample more than the basics. Although service levels and finesse are sometimes inconsistent, the level of hospitality is very good – made so much better and brighter by the addition of a great number of Asian female staff rather than the surly and inconsistent Caribbean Basin staff still found aboard some NCL ships.

Despite the company's name, Norwegian Cruise Line, there's almost nothing Norwegian about this product, except for some senior officers. The staff, incidentally, includes many Southeast Asians who already have service experience aboard parent company Star Cruises' big ships.

Cruising aboard large ships such as this has become increasingly an onboard revenue-based product. The ship is full of revenue centers designed to help you part with even more money than what is paid for in the price of your cruise ticket. You can expect to be subjected to a stream of flyers advertising daily art auctions, "designer" watches, "inch of gold/silver" and other promotions.

Gratuities for staff (cabin attendants, dining room waiters, etc.) are automatically added to your onboard account at $10 per person, per day; you can, however, reduce or otherwise amend these if necessary before you disembark, but in May 2005 the gratuity became a non-adjustable "service charge." In addition, a 15% gratuity is added to all bar and spa treatment accounts. The onboard currency is the US dollar.

Although the suites and junior suites are quite spacious, the standard interior (no view) and outside-view cabins are very small when compared to those of other major cruise lines such as Carnival or Celebrity, particularly when occupied by three or four persons; the bathrooms, however, are of quite a decent size, and have large shower enclosures. Music played in some areas bleeds through into others; for example, Latin music played in Salsas (on the second level of the lobby) is heard throughout the lobby and the internet café on the third level of the lobby and is most disconcerting. Communication (particularly between some of the Asian staff and passengers) is weak. Standing in line for embarkation, disembarkation, shore tenders and for self-serve buffet meals is an inevitable aspect of cruising aboard all large ships – even those designated as "Freestyle".

ACCOMMODATION. There are 29 price/grades (the price will depend on the grade, location and size). Regardless of the accommodation you choose, all cabins have tea and coffee making sets (note that only "coffee creamer" is provided, so tea drinkers who want fresh milk need to arrange this with their steward, or call room service), rich cherry wood cabinetry, bathroom with sliding door and separate toilet, shower enclosure and washbasin compartments, and European duvets. The private balconies of the top suites have teak decks, while most other cabins with balconies feature a "Bolidt" (rubberized sand-like) deck, and smoked glass/wood rail panels that provide good sightlines. Audio channels can be found on the in-cabin television system, but you cannot turn off the picture. Elemis personal amenities are provided in the bathroom.

Garden Villas. The largest living spaces are two huge Garden Villas (Vista and Horizon), high atop the ship in a pod located forward of the ship's funnel, and overlooking the main swimming pool and recreation deck. These villas have huge glass walls and landscaped private roof gardens for outdoor dining (with whirlpool tubs, naturally), and huge private sunbathing areas completely shielded from anyone. Each has three bedrooms and bathrooms, and a large living room overlooking the lido/pool deck. These units have their own private elevator access and private stairway. Each measures 5,350 sq ft. (497 sq meters) and can be combined to create a huge, double-sized "house" measuring 10,700 sq ft (994-sq-meters), including a private outdoor Italian garden. Butler service is provided, naturally.

Owner's Suites. Four Owner's Suites (each measures 750 sq.ft./69.6 sq. meters) are located in the very front of the ship. Two of these are nestled under the enclosed navigation bridge wings on Deck 11 (the other two are located in the equivalent space on the deck below). They have an entrance (with wooden door front), large lounge/dining room, and separate bedroom (with king-sized bed beneath a mirrored ceiling, and television with integral DVD player. The bathroom (almost as large as a standard cabin) has a full-sized tub with shower and TV; separate shower enclosure, separate toilet, and a dressing area with his-and-hers walk-in closets. There are forward facing (open) and side facing (enclosed) private balconies. Butler service is provided. If you don't need the entertaining space of the Garden Villas, these owner's suites are delightful living spaces. However, they do suffer occasionally from noise generated in Spinnaker's (a nightclub/disco) on the deck above. Each Owner's Suite can also be interconnected to a Penthouse Suite and balcony cabin (very useful for large families when parents want their privacy).

Penthouse Suites. There are 30 Penthouse Suites; each measures 366 sq.ft./34 sq. meters. Features include a bedroom with queen sized bed, walk-in closet, living room with dining table, and bathroom with separate shower enclosure and bathtub. Penthouse Suites on Deck 11 can be interconnected to children's cabin with double sofa bed and a pull-down Pullman-style) bed with separate bathroom and shower enclosure. These suites also have a private balcony, and butler service.

Romance Suites. There are four Romance Suites, each measuring 288 sq.ft./26.7 sq. meters. They include a separate bedroom with queen-sized bed, a sitting area with double sofa bed, and living and dining areas. The bathroom has a full-sized tub and shower. These suites also have a private balcony.

Mini Suites. There are 107 mini suites (measuring 229 sq. ft/21.2 sq. meters), each with two lower beds that convert into a queen-sized bed, and a sitting area with double sofa bed. The bathroom has a full-sized tub and shower. Floor-to-ceiling windows open onto a private balcony.

All suites are lavishly furnished (most in rich cherry wood), although closet space in some of the smaller units is tight. Some suites have extras like a trouser press, and a full range of toiletries by L'Occidentale. Suites also get butlers, who can serve all meals en-suite from the menus of a number of restaurants.

Although they are nicely furnished and quite well equipped, the standard outside-view and interior (no view) cabins are quite small, particularly when occupied by three or four persons. Some cabins have interconnecting doors (good for families with children). Many cabins have third- and fourth-person pull-down berths or trundle beds.

A small room service menu is available (all items are at extra cost, and a 15% service charge and a gratuity are added to your account). Bottled water is placed in each cabin (but a charge will be made to your account if you open the bottle).

CUISINE. With "Freestyle Dining", you can choose which restaurant to eat in, at what time, and with whom (there are no assigned dining rooms, tables or seats). While this is fine in theory, in practice it means that you have to make reservations (including the time that you want to eat), so "freestyle dining" actually turns out to be programmed dining. All restaurants and eateries are non-smoking.

Although there are three principal dining rooms, there are also a number of other themed eating establishments, giving a wide range of choice – though some cost extra, and require advance reservations (particularly for dinner). There are two entire decks of restaurants to choose from, involving 10 different restaurants and eateries. Note that NCLs dress code states that: "jeans, T-shirts, tank tops and bare feet are not permitted in restaurants."

● **Venetian:** the first main dining room (seats 472) offers traditional six-course dining (open 5.30pm–midnight). The dining room is located aft, and has good views over the ship's stern (at least in the daytime), although the sightlines from some seats are obstructed by 14 pillars. The room has a baby grand piano in the center of the forward part of the room. If you want a quieter table, I recommend being seated in one of two wings in the forward section (near the entrance/steps).

● **Aqua:** the second main dining room (seats 344) offers traditional six-courses (open 5.30pm–midnight).

● **Impressions:** the third main dining room (seats 236) offers lighter cuisine (open 5.30pm–midnight). The waiter stations are too close to the tables and are very noisy.

● **Bamboo (a Taste of Asia):** a Japanese/Thai/Chinese restaurant, with 140 seats, features a sit-up conveyor-belt style sushi/sashimi bar, sake bar, show galley, and separate room with a teppanyaki grill. In the evenings, music from Gatsby's lounge/bar (on the deck below) completely fill the restaurant (through an open lobby-like well), and a quiet meal is almost impossible. All items are at extra cost (there is an "all you can eat" sushi charge of $10).

● **Le Bistro:** a French restaurant with 72 seats, featuring Le Bistro's nouvelle cuisine (the decor includes four Impressionist paintings on loan from the private collection of the chairman of Star Cruises, parent company of NCL), although they don't really match the room's decor. A cover charge of $12.50 applies (there's also a line for you to add an *extra* gratuity – very cheeky). Best food on board and worth the extra cost.

● **Blue Lagoon:** a food court-style eatery; 68 seats; serving hamburgers, fish & chips, pot pies and wok fast dishes.

● **Garden Cafe:** an indoor/outdoor self-serve buffet eatery (seats 490). It includes "action stations" featuring made-to-order omelets, waffles, fruit, soups, ethnic specialities and pasta dishes.

● **Salsa:** a Spanish tapas eatery and bar (seats 112) with a selection of hot and cold tapas dishes and authentic entertainment, located on the second level of the atrium lobby.

● **La Trattoria;** located inside the indoor/outdoor buffet (seats 162), this eatery serves pasta, pizza and other popular Italian fare.

● **Cagney's Steak House:** arranged atop the ship (seats 112), incorporates a show kitchen, and serves US prime steaks and seafood. Be prepared for large portions, and a cover charge of $17.50.

Other eating/drinking spots include the Pearly Kings (an English pub for draft beer and perhaps a game of darts); Havanas, a cigar and cognac lounge; Java, an atrium lobby Cafe and bar (hot and frozen coffees, teas and pastries); a Beer Garden (grilled foods); a Gelato Bar (ice cream); and a Gym and Spa Bar (health food snacks and drinks).

ENTERTAINMENT. The Stardust Theatre seats 1,037, and is the venue for colorful Las-Vegas-style production shows and major cabaret acts. It is designed in the style of an opera house, spans three decks, and has a steeply tiered main floor and port and starboard balconies.

There are three production shows in a typical 7-day cruise (all ably performed by the Jean Ann Ryan Company): Bollywood, Music of the Night, and South Beach Rave. These are all very colorful, high-energy, razzle-dazzle shows (with much use of pyrotechnics, laser and color-mover lighting), with so much happening on stage that by the end of the evening, if you are a typical passenger, you will be tired and unable to remember much about the shows, which are, however, very entertaining.

The ship carries a number of bands and solo entertaining musicians, which provide live music for listening and dancing in several of the lounges and bars. Throughout the ship, loud Latin music prevails. In Spinnakers Lounge, the ship's nightclub, a Pachanga Party (a Miami South Beach rave) is featured each cruise.

SPA/FITNESS. Wellness devotees should enjoy the two-deck-high El Dorado health spa complex (operated by the Hawaii-based Mandara Spa, owned by Steiner), located at the stern of the ship (with large ocean-view windows on three sides). There are many facilities and services (almost all at extra charge), including Thai massage (in the spa, outdoors on deck, in your cabin or on your private balcony).

In addition, there is an indoor lap pool (measuring 37 ft/11.2 meters), hydrotherapy pool, two sit-in deep tubs, aromatherapy and wellness centers, and mud treatment room treatment rooms (there are 15 treatment rooms in all, including one specifically designed for couples).

The fitness and exercise rooms are located not within the spa, but at the top of the glass-domed atrium lobby (they feature the latest Cybex muscle-pumping equipment). Included is a room for exercycle classes. Some classes, such Pathway to Yoga, Body Cycling Class and Body Beat Class (cardio kick-boxing), cost extra.

Recreational sports facilities include a jogging track, golf driving range, basketball and volleyball courts, as well as four levels of sunbathing decks.

● **For more extensive general information on what an NCL cruise is like, see pages 131–33.**

Norwegian Gem
★★★★

Large Resort Ship:	93,530 tons	Total Crew:	1,100
Lifestyle:	Standard	Passengers	
Cruise Line:	Norwegian Cruise Line	(lower beds/all berths):	2,394/2,846
Former Names:	none	Passenger Space Ratio	
Builder:	Meyer Werft (Germany)	(lower beds/all berths):	39.0/32.8
Original Cost:	$390 million	Crew/Passenger Ratio	
Entered Service:	Oct 2007	(lower beds/all berths):	2.1/2.5
Registry:	Panama	Navigation Officers:	Scandinavian
Length (ft/m):	964.8/294.1	Cabins (total):	1,197
Beam (ft/m):	105.6/32.2	Size Range (sq ft/m):	142.0–4,390.0/
Draft (ft/m):	26.9/8.2		13.2–407.8
Propulsion/Propellers:	diesel-electric/	Cabins (outside view):	792
	2 pods (19.5MW each)	Cabins (interior/no view):	405
Passenger Decks:	12	Cabins (for one person):	0

Cabins (with private balcony):	540
Cabins (wheelchair accessible):	27
Cabin Current:	110 volts
Elevators:	12
Casino (gaming tables):	Yes
Slot Machines:	Yes
Swimming Pools (outdoors):	2
Swimming Pools (indoors):	0
Whirlpools:	6
Self-Service Launderette:	Yes
Dedicated Cinema/Seats:	No
Library:	Yes

BERLITZ'S OVERALL SCORE: 1,521 (OUT OF A POSSIBLE 2,000 POINTS)

OVERVIEW. This ship's design and layout is similar to that of *Norwegian Pearl*, and features a "pod" propulsion system for vibration-free cruising *(see page 174 for explanation)*. The ship's white hull has a colourful, funky string of gems along its sides as a design. There are plenty of deck lounge chairs (in fact, more than the number of passengers carried). Water slides are included for the adult swimming pools (children have their own pools at the ship's stern – out of sight of the adult areas).

BERLITZ'S RATINGS		
	Possible	Achieved
Ship	500	425
Accommodation	200	156
Food	400	287
Service	400	285
Entertainment	100	67
Cruise	400	301

Inside the ship is an entertaining mix of bright, funky, but warm colors and decor that you probably wouldn't have in your home, and yet somehow they all work extremely well in this large resort ship setting designed to attract the young, active, and trendy.

There are 11 bars and lounges, including "Bar Central," four specialty bars: martini bar, champagne and wine bar, beer and whiskey bar, and a cigar lounge; these interconnect with the lobby, yet have distinct personalities. The lobby houses a Java Bar, plus a two-deck-high movie screen, typically used to show sports events and Wii activities. One neat room is the "Bliss Ultra Lounge & Night Club," located at the aft end of the ship; rather like a South Beach club, it houses a 24-hours a day V-shaped sports bar and lounge complex, including a bowling alley with four real bowling lanes – the cost is $5 per person, including special playing shoes, and it is limited to six persons per lane. The lounge doesn't have many seats, but does have a couple of beds.

The casino is typical of larger resort ship casinos, with plenty of gaming tables, slot machines, noise, and smoke. So, if you walk through the casino to get from the showlounge to other public rooms, you'll be subject to cig-

arette smoke. A new twist in the onboard casino scene has appeared, however, with poolside blackjack now established in its own "open-air casino" on the pool deck.

Because NCL is all about cruising with families of all ages, much space is devoted to children's facilities, all of which are thoughtfully tucked well away from adult recreation areas, at the aft end of the ship. Children of all ages will get to play in a superb wet 'n' wild space-themed water park (the Aqua Kid's Club), complete with large pool, water slide, and paddle pool; there's also 30-ft by 19-ft climbing wall at the ship's funnel. There's a room full of cots for toddlers to use for sleepovers. Teens, too, are well catered for, and have their own cinema, discotheque with dance floor, and hot tub.

Plenty of choices, including many dining options, add up to a very attractive holiday package, highly suitable for families with children, in a floating leisure center that really does provide ample facilities for enjoyment.

The dress code is very casual: no jacket and tie needed, although you are welcome to dress formally – but jeans are probably essential. Although service levels and finesse may be inconsistent, the level of hospitality aboard NCL ships is good – made better and brighter by the addition of a good number of Asian staff. Despite the company's name (Norwegian Cruise Line), there's little that's Norwegian about this product, except for some senior officers. There's plenty of lively music, constant activity, entertainment, and food that is mainstream and acceptable but nothing more (even when you pay extra to eat in the "alternative" dining spots).

While the initial cruise fare is reasonable, extra costs and charges soon mount up if you want to sample more than the basics. The ship is full of revenue centers which are designed to help you part with even more money than what is paid for in the price of your cruise ticket. You can expect to be subjected to a stream of flyers advertising daily art auctions, "designer" watches, gold and silver chain by the inch, and other promotions, and long programme announcements three times daily by the cruise director.

The onboard currency is the US dollar. Gratuities for staff (cabin attendants, dining room waiters, etc.) are automatically added to your onboard account at $10 per person, per day; you can, however, reduce or otherwise amend these if necessary before you disembark. In addition, a 15% gratuity is added to all bar and spa treatment accounts.

ACCOMMODATION. There are 32 different price grades, so there's something for all tastes, from small interior (no view) cabins to lavish suites in a private courtyard setting.

Although they are nicely furnished and quite well equipped, the standard outside-view and interior (no view) cabins are quite small, particularly when occupied by three or four persons. Over 250 cabins have interconnecting doors (good for families with children). So, interior (no-view) cabins can connect; outside view cabins can connect; and outside view and balcony cabins can connect, providing families with much choice. Also for families, many cabins also have third- and fourth-person pull-down berths or trundle beds, and about 280 cabins have interconnecting doors – ideal for family cruising.

A small room service menu is available (all items are at extra cost, and a 15% service charge/gratuity is automatically added to your account). Bottled water is placed in each cabin, but you will be charged if you open the bottle.

The following suites are available:

Courtyard Villas/Garden Villas: The two Garden Villa Suites, each of which measures 4,390 sq.ft. (407.8 sq.m), and 10 Courtyard Villas share a private courtyard with its own small pool, hot tub, and small fitness room, and have butler service. These units enjoy exclusivity – rather like accommodation in a gated community – where others cannot live unless they pay the asking price.

Deluxe Owner's Suites: These two suites, named Black Pearl and Golden Pearl, are set high atop all other accommodation, have stunning ocean views, and consist of a master bedroom with king-size bed, a dining/lounge area, a decent-sized balcony, and access to the private courtyard.

Penthouse Suites: Located at the front of the ship, they have a (partly) private balcony directly under the navigation bridge.

CUISINE. There are two main dining rooms: the 304-seat Grand Palace, with its minimalist decor; and the 558-seat Magenta Restaurant. There are several other themed eating spots, giving a wide range of choice; some cost extra, and require advance reservations, particularly for dinner; all are part of NCL's "Freestyle Dining" (there are no assigned dining rooms, tables or seats, so you'll need to plan your meals and times accordingly).

With 17 video screens located around the ship, you can check how busy each dining spot is and make a booking and find out if, or how long, you'll need to wait for a table (pagers are also available, so you can go bar-hopping while you wait for a table in your chosen venue). The system generally works well (with colored bars to indicate whether a restaurant is "full," "moderately busy," or "empty;" this has cut down the frustration of waiting a long time for a table, although on "formal" nights (when you may want to see the production shows), congestion certainly does occur. Note that NCL's dress code states that: "jeans, T-shirts, tank tops and bare feet are not permitted in restaurants," and all dining venues are non-smoking.

Alternative Restaurants/Eateries ínclude *Cagney's Steak House* (serving steaks from 5oz to 48oz); *Blue Lagoon* (for trendy fast-food street snacks); *Le Bistro* for classic French cuisine; *Orchid Garden*, an Asian eatery complete with sushi bar and Teppanyaki grill (where the chef puts on a display in front of you); *La Cucina*, serving Italian cuisine; *Latin Restaurant*; the *Garden Café*, a large self-serve buffet-style restaurant, for casual meals; *Kids' Café*; and a *Java Café*, which serves Lavazza coffee, in the lobby.

ENTERTAINMENT. The Stardust Theater seats 1,042, and is the venue for colorful Las-Vegas-style production shows and major cabaret acts. It is designed in the style of an opera house, spans three decks, and has a steeply tiered main floor and port and starboard balconies.

There are three production shows in a typical 7-day cruise (all ably performed by the Jean Ann Ryan Company). They are colorful, high-energy, razzle-dazzle shows (with much use of pyrotechnics, laser and color-mover lighting.

The ship has a number of bands and solo entertaining musicians, which provide live music for listening and dancing in several lounges and bars. Throughout the ship, loud Latin music prevails. In the nightclub, a Pachanga Party (a Miami South Beach rave) is featured each cruise.

SPA/FITNESS. Wellness devotees should enjoy the two-deck-high Yin-Yang Health Spa complex (operated by the Hawaii-based Mandara Spa, owned by Steiner). It is located in the front of the ship, with large ocean-view windows on three sides. There are many facilities and services to pamper you – almost all at extra charge – including Thai massage (in the spa, outdoors on deck, in your cabin or on your private balcony), and 18 treatment rooms. There's also a 37-ft (11.2-meter) indoor lap pool, hydrotherapy pool, two sit-in deep tubs, aromatherapy and wellness centers, and mud treatment room.

The Body Waves fitness and exercise rooms are within the spa and feature the latest Cybex muscle-pumping equipment. Some classes, such as Pathway to Yoga, Body Cycling Class and Body Beat Class (cardio kick-boxing) cost extra.

Recreational sports facilities include a jogging track, golf driving range, basketball and volleyball courts, as well as several levels of sunbathing decks, plus the four bowling lanes, and a funnel-mounted rock-climbing wall.

● **For more extensive general information on what an NCL cruise is like, see pages 131–33.**

Norwegian Jade
★★★★

Large Resort Ship: ....93,558 tons	
Lifestyle: ....Standard	
Cruise Line: ......Norwegian Cruise Line	
Former Names: ....*Pride of Hawaii*	
Builder: ....Meyer Werft (Germany)	
Original Cost: ....$390 million	
Entered Service: ....May 2006/Mar 2008	
Registry: ....The Bahamas	
Length (ft/m): 964.8/294.1	
Beam (ft/m): 105.6/32.2	
Draft (ft/m): 26.9/8.2	
Propulsion/Propellers: ....diesel-electric/	
2 azimuthing pods (20.0MW each)	
Passenger Decks: 12	

Total Crew: 1,000
Passengers
(lower beds/all berths): 2,466/2,890
Passenger Space Ratio
(lower beds/all berths): 37.9/32.3
Crew/Passenger Ratio
(lower beds/all berths): 2.4/2.8
Navigation Officers: ....Scandinavian
Cabins (total): 1,233
Size Range (sq ft/m): 142.0–4,390.0/
13.2–407.8
Cabins (outside view): 834
Cabins (interior/no view): 425
Cabins (for one person): 0

Cabins (with private balcony): 763
Cabins (wheelchair accessible): 27
Cabin Current: ....110 volts
Elevators: 12
Casino (gaming tables): ....Yes
Slot Machines: ....Yes
Swimming Pools (outdoors): 2
Swimming Pools (indoors): 0
Whirlpools: 6
Self-Service Launderette: ....No
Dedicated Cinema/Seats: ....No
Library: ....Yes

BERLITZ'S OVERALL SCORE: 1,514 (OUT OF A POSSIBLE 2,000 POINTS)

OVERVIEW. Built from 67 blocks, this is a sister ship to *Norwegian Jewel*. After service as *Pride of Hawaii*, it underwent a small transformation, including the addition of a casino, to become *Norwegian Jade*, for cruising in Europe and the Caribbean; some interior decor elements from the ship's former life in Hawaii remain. The ship features a "pod" propulsion system *(see page 174 for a detailed explanation)*. The interior decor is decidedly bright and cheerful.

BERLITZ'S RATINGS

	Possible	Achieved
Ship	500	421
Accommodation	200	156
Food	400	287
Service	400	283
Entertainment	100	67
Cruise	400	300

Norwegian Jade's interior focal gathering place is "Bar Central" – three specialty bars (Magnum's Champagne/ Wine Bar, Mixers' Martini/ Cocktail Bar, and Tankard's Beer/Whiskey Bar) that are connected but have distinct personalities. They are located on the deck above the reception lobby. All told, there are a dozen bars and lounges on board). Other facilities include a casino, three meeting rooms, a chapel, card room, bridge viewing room, and the *SS United States* Library (with original photography and material about America's last ocean liner).

The dress code is casual – very casual; no jacket and tie needed, although you are welcome to dress formally if you wish. In fact, there is no suggested dress code in the daily program. Children are well provided for, and have their own facilities, including a Kids' Club; teens have their own disco, the Wipe-Out Club.

While the initial cruise fare seems very reasonable, the extra costs and charges soon mount up if you want to sample more than the basics. This ship has an all-American crew and service. It is full of revenue centers designed to help you part with more of your money. You can expect to be subjected to a stream of flyers advertising daily art auctions, "designer" watches, and many other promotions (including poolside "Inch of Gold" sales outlets).

A non-changeable service charge – this is, not a gratuity – for staff is automatically added to your onboard account at $10 per person ($5 for children aged 3–12) per day. The onboard currency is the US dollar.

Passenger niggles include waiting to use the interactive dining reservation screens in the public areas; lines for breakfast in the main dining spots (particularly before the shore excursions start); and poor service and hospitality in some areas.

SUITABLE FOR: *Norwegian Jade* is best suited to youthful adult couples, single passengers, and families with children and teenagers who want contemporary, upbeat surroundings, good facilities, plenty of entertainment lounges and bars and high-tech sophistication – all in a neat, highly programmed, well packaged cruise in an Americana setting.

ACCOMMODATION. There are 33 price grades, determined by size and location. Although they are nicely furnished and quite well equipped, the standard outside-view and interior (no view) cabins are quite small, particularly when occupied by three or four persons. Over 250 cabins have interconnecting doors (good for families with children). So, interior (no-view) cabins can connect; outside view cabins can connect; and outside view and balcony cabins can connect, providing families with much choice. Also for families, many cabins also have third- and fourth-person pull-down berths or trundle beds.

A small room service menu is available (all items are at extra cost, and a 15% service charge/gratuity is added to your account). Bottled water is placed in each cabin, but a charge is made to your account if you open the bottle.

Garden Villas: Two multi-room villas have great views over the pool deck (and ocean). Each has a roof terrace and private garden, with open-air dining, hot tub, and private sunning and relaxation areas. They are, perhaps, the most extravagant suites at sea today. Each has a living room with Bose audio-visual equipment (including a CD/DVD library), grand piano, wet bar, and refrigerator. Each has three bedrooms (king- or queen-sized bed) with ensuite bathroom, walk-in closet. Each Garden Villa measures approximately 4,390 sq ft./407.8 sq meters – the ultimate in living space, exclusivity and privacy.

Courtyard Villas: 10 Courtyard Villas (up to 660 sq.ft./61 sq.m.) share a private courtyard with its own (small) pool, hot tub, massage bed, and fitness room – all in a setting that is distinctly Asian. They also share a private concierge lounge with the two largest villas, as well as butler and concierge service. These units enjoy exclusivity – rather like accommodation in a gated community. The two Garden Villas each have three bedrooms (with ensuite bathroom), living room, dining room, and stunning views.

Owner's Suites: Each of these five units (approximately 1,195 sq.ft/111 sq.meters) has a large bedroom with king-size bed and audio-visual entertainment center, and a living room with dining area. The bathroom has a tub, separate shower enclosure and powder room. Some Owner's suites can interconnect with Penthouse Suites.

Penthouse Suites: There are 24 of these, measuring up to 600 sq.ft. (55.5 sq.meters), featuring a bedroom with queen-sized bed, living room with dining area; the bathroom has a bathtub/shower or separate shower enclosure. Some can be interconnect to a kid's room with double sofa bed and a Pullman bed with separate bathroom with shower.

All villas and suites have a private balcony, walk-in closet, rich cherry wood cabinetry, tea/coffee/espresso/cappuccino makers, plus butler and concierge service.

CUISINE. With "Freestyle Dining", you can choose which restaurant to eat in, at what time, and with whom (there are no assigned dining rooms, tables or seats). In practice, it means that you have to make reservations (including the time that you want to eat), so "freestyle dining" actually turns out to be programmed dining. All restaurants and eateries are non-smoking.

There are two entire decks of restaurants, comprising 10 restaurants and eateries. Some are included in the cruise fare, others cost extra.

The two main restaurants (included in the cruise fare) are Alizar (310 seats) and Grand Pacific (486 seats).

Cagney's Steak House (176 seats), and Blue Lagoon (a casual eatery serving American food and seating 94), and Le Bistro (a classic French restaurant, with 129 seats – check out the beautiful, and real, Van Gogh painting) are favorite NCL alternative dining venues. Paniola (100 seats) offers trendy tapas and salsa fare. Jade Garden (including a sushi counter, sake bar, and a 32-seat Teppanyaki Grill), has Southeast Asian cuisine. The 70-seat Papa's Italian Kitchen has a long wooden table that creates a farmhouse ambiance. Self-serve buffet-style meals can be taken in the Garden Café, and its outdoor section. Lavazza (Italian) coffees can be found in the Aloha Café.

You can make reservations through the Freestyle Dining information system; plasma screens showing waiting times for the various venues are located in high-traffic areas.

ENTERTAINMENT. The 1,042-seat Stardust Theatre is the venue for colorful Las-Vegas-style production shows and major cabaret acts. It is designed in the style of an opera house, spans three decks, and has a steeply tiered main floor and port and starboard balconies. Colorful, high-energy, razzle-dazzle production shows are ably performed by the Jean Ann Ryan Company.

Bands and solo entertaining musicians provide live music for listening and dancing in several lounges and bars. Throughout the ship, loud music prevails. In Spinnakers Lounge (the ship's nightclub located high atop the ship with great ocean views on three sides), a Pachanga Party (a Miami South Beach rave) is held during each cruise.

SPA/FITNESS. The two-deck-high Yin and Yang health spa complex, operated by the Steiner-owned Mandara Spa, is at the stern (with large ocean-view windows on three sides). There are many facilities and services, almost all at extra charge. In addition, there is an indoor lap pool (measuring 37 ft/ 11.2 meters), hydrotherapy pool, two sit-in deep tubs, aromatherapy and wellness centers, and mud treatment room treatment rooms, including one for couples.

The fitness and exercise rooms are located not within the spa, but at the top of the glass-domed atrium lobby (they have the latest Cybex muscle-pumping equipment). Included is a room for exercycle classes.

Recreational sports facilities include a jogging track, two golf driving nets (there's a golf pro shop, too), basketball and volleyball courts, paddle tennis, mini-golf, oversized chess, and several sunbathing decks.

● **For more extensive general information on what an NCL cruise is like, see pages 131–33.**

Norwegian Jewel
★★★★

Large Resort Ship: ....93,000 tons	Total Crew: 1,000	Cabins (with private balcony): 540
Lifestyle: ....Standard	Passengers	Cabins (wheelchair accessible): 27
Cruise Line: ......Norwegian Cruise Line	(lower beds/all berths): 2,376/2,846	Cabin Current: ....110 volts
Former Names: ....none	Passenger Space Ratio	Elevators: 12
Builder: ....Meyer Werft (Germany)	(lower beds/all berths): 39.1/32.6	Casino (gaming tables): ....Yes
Original Cost: ....$390 million	Crew/Passenger Ratio	Slot Machines: ....Yes
Entered Service: ....Aug 2005	(lower beds/all berths): 2.3/2.8	Swimming Pools (outdoors): 2
Registry: ....Panama	Navigation Officers: ....Scandinavian	Swimming Pools (indoors): 0
Length (ft/m): 964.8/294.1	Cabins (total): 1,188	Whirlpools: 6
Beam (ft/m): 105.6/32.2	Size Range (sq ft/m): 142.0–4,390.0/	Self-Service Launderette: ....No
Draft (ft/m): 26.9/8.2	13.2–407.8	Dedicated Cinema/Seats: ....No
Propulsion/Propellers: diesel-electric/2	Cabins (outside view): 783	Library: ....Yes
azimuthing pods (20.0MW each)	Cabins (interior/no view): 405	
Passenger Decks: 12	Cabins (for one person): 0	

OVERALL SCORE: 1,516 (OUT OF A POSSIBLE 2,000 POINTS)

OVERVIEW. The ship, assembled from 67 blocks, and whose basic design and layout is similar to that of *Norwegian Gem* and *Norwegian Pearl*, features a "pod" propulsion system *(see page 174 for explanation).* The white hull has a colourful, funky design on its sides featuring sparkling jewels. There are plenty of sunloungers (in fact, the number is greater than the number of passengers carried). Water slides are included for the adult swimming pools (children have their own pools at the ship's stern – out of sight of the adult areas).

Inside the ship, you'll be met by an eclectic mix of colors and decor that you probably wouldn't have in your home, and yet somehow it works extremely well in this large resort ship setting designed to attract the young, active, and trendy.

There are 13 bars and lounges to enjoy, including "Bar Central," three specialty bars that are connected but have distinct personalities. Shakers Martini and Cocktail Bar is a 1960s-inspired lounge; Magnum's Champagne and Wine Bar recalls Paris of the 1920s and the liner Normandie; and Maltings Beer and Whiskey Pub is a contemporary bar with artwork themed around whiskey and beer production.

A good deal of space is devoted to children's facilities, which are all tucked well away from adult recreation areas, at the aft end of the ship. Children of all ages will get to play in a superb wet 'n' wild space-themed water park (complete with large pool, water slide, and paddle pool). There's a room full of cots for toddlers to use for sleepovers, and even the toilets are at a special low height. Teens, too, are well catered for, and have their own cinema, discotheque with dance floor, and hot tub.

Plenty of choices, including many dining options, add up

BERLITZ'S RATINGS

	Possible	Achieved
Ship	500	424
Accommodation	200	156
Food	400	287
Service	400	283
Entertainment	100	66
Cruise	400	300

to a very attractive vacation package, particularly suitable for families with children, in a contemporary floating leisure center that really does provide ample facilities for you to have an enjoyable time. The dress code is very casual (no jacket and tie needed, although you are welcome to dress formally if you wish).

The level of hospitality aboard NCL ships is good – made so much better and brighter by the addition of a great number of Asian female staff. Despite the company's name (Norwegian Cruise Line), there's little that's Norwegian about this product, except for some senior officers. There's plenty of lively music, constant activity, entertainment, and food that is mainstream and acceptable but nothing more (unless you pay extra to eat in the "alternative" dining spots). All this is delivered by a smiling, friendly service staff that lacks polish but is willing.

While the initial cruise fare is reasonable, extra costs and charges soon mount up if you want to sample more than the basics. The ship is full of revenue centers which are designed to help you part with even more money than what is paid for in the price of your cruise ticket. You can expect to be subjected to a stream of flyers advertising daily art auctions, "designer" watches, "inch of gold/silver" and so on.

Gratuities for staff (cabin attendants, dining room waiters, etc.) are automatically added to your onboard account at $10 per person, per day; you can, however, reduce or otherwise amend these if necessary before you disembark. In addition, a 15% gratuity is added to all bar and spa treatment accounts. The onboard currency is the US dollar.

ACCOMMODATION. There are 26 price grades, so there's something for all tastes, from small interior (no view) cabins to lavish penthouse suites in a private courtyard setting.

Although they are nicely furnished and quite well equipped, the standard outside-view and interior (no view) cabins are quite small, particularly when occupied by three or four persons. Over 250 cabins have interconnecting doors (good for families with children). So, interior (no-view) cabins can connect; outside view cabins can connect; and outside view and balcony cabins can connect, providing families with much choice. Also for families, many cabins also have third- and fourth-person pull-down berths or trundle beds.

A small room service menu is available (all items are at extra cost, and a 15% service charge/gratuity are automatically added to your account). Bottled water is placed in each cabin, but a charge will be made to your account if you open the bottle.

Courtyard Penthouses/Suites: Two Garden Villas (each measures 4,390 sq ft./407.8 sq meters), and 10 Courtyard Villas share a private courtyard with its own (small) pool, hot tub, massage bed, and fitness room – all in a setting that is distinctly Asian. They also share a private concierge lounge with the two largest villas, as well as butler and concierge service. These units enjoy exclusivity – rather like accommodation in a gated community – where others cannot live unless they pay the asking price. The two largest are duplex apartments, with a spiral stairway between the upper and lower quarters.

CUISINE. There are two main dining rooms: the 552-seat Tsar's Palace, designed to look like the interior of Catherine the Great's palace in St. Petersburg (Russia), and the 310-seat Azura. There are also a number of other themed eating establishments, giving a wide range of choice – though some cost extra, and require advance reservations (particularly for dinner). There are 10 different restaurants and eateries (some are included in the cruise fare, while others incur an extra charge) that represent NCL's "Freestyle Dining," allowing you to choose which restaurant to eat in, at what time, and with whom (there are no assigned dining rooms, tables or seats).

The 17 video screens located around the ship enable you to check how long you'll have to wait for a table at each dining spot. Pagers are also available, so you can go bar-hopping while you wait for a table. The system works well, although on "formal" nights (when you may want to see the show), congestion can occur. NCL's dress code states that: "jeans, T-shirts, tank tops and bare feet are not permitted in restaurants," and all dining venues are non-smoking.

Alternative Restaurants/Eateries: Cagney's House (for fine steaks and seafood), Blue Lagoon (Asian street food), and Le Bistro (French cuisine) are NCL favorites. Tango's a contemporary spot with bright colors and Latin/tapas fare. Chin Chin is an Asian eatery (with a Teppanyaki Grill and sushi counter). Mama's Italian Kitchen is novel in that it features a long wooden table running through the room to create the ambiance of a Tuscan farmhouse. For really casual (self-serve) buffet-style eating, there's the light, airy Great Outdoors. Finally, the Garden Café incorporates an ice cream bar, and Kid's Café (wisely located opposite the children's play areas, with its own kid-height counter). For coffee, head to the Java Café in the lobby – it's a great place for people watching. Three of the "alternative" restaurants incur a cover charge, while others are free.

ENTERTAINMENT. The Stardust Theatre seats 1,037, and is the venue for colorful Las-Vegas-style production shows and major cabaret acts. It is designed in the style of an opera house, spans three decks, and has a steeply tiered main floor and port and starboard balconies.

There are two or three production shows in a typical 7-day cruise (all ably performed by the Jean Ann Ryan Company). These are all very colorful, high-energy, razzle-dazzle shows (with much use of pyrotechnics, laser and color-mover lighting), with so much happening on stage that by the end of the evening, if you are a typical passenger, you will be tired and unable to remember much about the shows, which are, however, very entertaining.

The ship carries a number of bands and solo entertaining musicians, which provide live music for listening and dancing in several of the lounges and bars. Throughout the ship, loud Latin music prevails. In Spinnakers Lounge (the ship's nightclub), a Pachanga Party is featured each cruise (a Miami South Beach rave).

SPA/FITNESS. Wellness devotees should enjoy the two-deck-high Bora Bora health spa complex (operated by the Hawaii-based Mandara Spa, owned by Steiner), located in the front of the ship (with large ocean-view windows on three sides). There are many facilities and services to pamper you (almost all at extra charge), including Thai massage (in the spa, outdoors on deck, in your cabin or on your private balcony). In addition, there is a 37 ft (11.2 meters) indoor lap pool, hydrotherapy pool, two sit-in deep tubs, aromatherapy and wellness centers, and mud treatment room treatment rooms (there are 15 treatment rooms in all, including one specifically designed for couples), and heated tile loungers in a relaxation area.

The fitness and exercise rooms are located not within the spa, but at the top of the glass-domed atrium lobby (they feature the latest Cybex muscle-pumping equipment). Included is a room for exercycle classes. Some classes, such as Pathway to Yoga, Body Cycling Class and Body Beat Class (cardio kick-boxing) cost extra.

Recreational sports facilities include a jogging track, golf driving range, basketball and volleyball courts, as well as four levels of sunbathing decks.

● **For more extensive general information on what an NCL cruise is like, see Page 131–33.**

Norwegian Majesty
★★★

Mid-Size Ship:	40,876 tons	Passenger Decks:	.9
Lifestyle:	Standard	Total Crew:	.620
Cruise Line:	Norwegian Cruise Line	Passengers	
Former Names:	*Royal Majesty*	(lower beds/all berths):	1,460/1,790
Builder:	Kvaerner Masa-Yards	Passenger Space Ratio	
	X(Finland)	(lower beds/all berths):	27.9/22.8
Original Cost:	$229 million	Crew/Passenger Ratio	
Entered Service:	Sept 1992/Nov 1997	(lower beds/all berths):	2.0/2.5
Registry:	The Bahamas	Navigation Officers:	Norwegian
Length (ft/m):	680.0/207.20	Cabins (total):	730
Beam (ft/m):	90.5/27.60	Size Range (sq ft/m):	118.4–374.5/
Draft (ft/m):	20.3/6.20		11.0–34.8
Propulsion/Propellers:	diesel	Cabins (outside view):	481
	(21,120 kW)/2	Cabins (interior/no view):	249

Cabins (for one person):	.0
Cabins (with private balcony):	.0
Cabins (wheelchair accessible):	.7
Cabin Current:	110 and 220 volts
Elevators:	.6
Casino (gaming tables):	Yes
Slot Machines:	Yes
Swimming Pools (outdoors):	.2
Swimming Pools (indoors):	.0
Whirlpools:	.3
Self-Service Launderette:	No
Dedicated Cinema/Seats:	No
Library:	Yes

OVERALL SCORE: 1,242 (OUT OF A POSSIBLE 2,000 POINTS)

OVERVIEW. This smart, stylish, contemporary cruise ship was originally built for the now defunct Majesty Cruise Line. It will end its service for NCL in December 2009, when it will be transferred to Louuis Cruise Lines.

Norwegian Majesty has an improved profile and is generally a well-designed vessel (its original lines were those of a Baltic ferry, albeit with a rounded bow, and not at all handsome). The ship underwent a $53.3 million, 110-ft (34-meter) "chop and stretch" and refurbishment operation in 1999, which added more cabins, new public rooms, much more open deck space and two new elevators, while all other existing public spaces were refreshed. For a real "wind-in-the-hair" experience, passengers can stand at the very bow of this ship (weather permitting) because all the mooring ropes and winches are on the deck below.

The open deck and sunbathing space has been improved (there are now two swimming pools, plus a splash pool for children). The ship's exterior profile is sleeker and more aerodynamic. Cutting the ship in half, however, required ingenuity, for, unlike *Norwegian Dream*, it was never designed for such a splicing operation.

Inside, it is quite a pretty ship, and is tastefully appointed, with lots of wood paneling and chrome/copper accents, reasonably discreet lighting, soothing colors, no glitz and almost no neon lighting. Wide passageways provide a feeling of inner spaciousness. The ship has a nice touch of elegance, and open walking areas provide a fine feel to it. The circular lobby is bright and classical in appearance.

There are several public rooms, bars and lounges in which to play. The Royal Observatory observation lounge has fine views, but is sometimes used as a karaoke lounge.

BERLITZ'S RATINGS

	Possible	Achieved
Ship	500	321
Accommodation	200	137
Food	400	230
Service	400	246
Entertainment	100	65
Cruise	400	243

The showlounge, while comfortable, is poorly designed, with 14 pillars obstructing the sightlines. Families with children will find "Kids' Corner" a useful place to deposit young ones for a full programme of activities.

Norwegian Majesty should provide you with a comfortable cruise experience in warm, fairly elegant surroundings, with generally good food (and plenty of it), and a modicum of hospitality from a reasonably friendly crew, although the service has little finesse. The ship is full of revenue centers, however, which are designed to help part you from your money. You can expect to be subjected to a stream of flyers advertising daily art auctions, "designer" watches and other promotions, while "artworks" for auction are strewn throughout the ship.

A non-adjustable "service charge" (gratuity) of $10 per person per day is added to your onboard account. In addition, a 15% gratuity is added to all bar and spa treatment accounts. The onboard currency is the US dollar.

There are no cushioned pads for the plastic deck chairs. The buffet area is simply too small for the extra number of passengers carried (while the ship was expanded, the buffet and seating areas were not). While adequate for 3- and 4-day cruises, the ship is only moderately comfortable for 7-day cruises. Standing in line for embarkation, disembarkation, shore tenders and for self-serve buffets is inevitable aboard all large ships.

ACCOMMODATION. There are 22 different price grades – a bewildering choice, and too many for a ship of this size. The price you pay will depend on the grade, size and location you choose. The suites have concierge service and extra goodies such as late afternoon snacks and hors d'oeuvre items. Although they cannot be considered large, they are quite well equipped, and come with VCRs as well as televisions. Bottled water is placed in each cabin (but a charge will be made if you open the bottle).

Almost all other outside-view and interior (no view) cabins are on the small side, but quite comfortable. The closets are really small, so suitcases have to be stored under the bed to keep them out of the way (this is also the best place for shoes). The bathrooms are a little tight, although there is a generous amount of room in the shower enclosures. A number of cabins are designated for non-smokers. Many cabins on Norway and Viking Decks have obstructed views; so check the deck plans carefully.

CUISINE. With what NCL calls "Freestyle Dining", you choose which restaurant you wish to eat in, at what time, and with whom (there are no assigned dining rooms, tables or seats). All restaurants and eateries are non-smoking. NCL's dress code states that: "jeans, T-shirts, tank tops and bare feet are not permitted in restaurants."

Although there are two principal dining rooms, there are also a number of other themed eating establishments, giving a wide range of choice – although it would be wise to plan in advance, particularly for dinner.

The main dining rooms are Seven Seas, with 636 seats, and the more intimate Four Seasons (added when the ship was "stretched" in 1999), with 266 seats. However, they are quite noisy and the tables are close together, which means that correct service is difficult. The food, menu, creativity and service are basically quite sound, with a good selection of breads and bread rolls, but the choice of cheeses and fruits is limited (almost all cheeses are American). Some dinners are "themed" – a popular feature.

There is also a 56-seat Le Bistro Restaurant, which serves Italian- and Continental-style cuisine for alternative dinners in an intimate environment (no reservations needed).

For casual, self-serve meals, the Cafe Royale is a small buffet dining spot with 112 seats (not nearly enough for the number of passengers now carried). It is open for breakfast, lunch and snacks. An outdoor grill (oddly named the Piazza San Marco) serves fast food items, including pizza (this can also be delivered to your cabin). A small coffee bar/lounge in an open passageway (street cafe) serves a variety of coffees, coffee-flavored drinks, "flaming" specialty drinks, and teas.

Overall, the food is best described as adequate, but lacks taste and presentation, although the menus make the dishes sound good. The wine list is quite decent and well arranged, together with moderate prices, although you won't find any good vintage wines (and the wine glasses are small). The cutlery is very ordinary (there are no fish knives). There is no formal afternoon tea, although you can make your own from various beverage stations. The service is adequate at best, which proves that good staff members that can communicate well (and know about food) are difficult to find. The breakfast and lunch buffets tend to have unimaginative presentation (more variety and better ingredients needed).

A lavish "chocoholics" buffet is featured once each cruise – this is a firm favorite among NCL passengers.

ENTERTAINMENT. The Palace Showlounge is the room for production shows and major cabaret acts. It is located aft on Majesty Deck and is shaped like an amphitheater, with banquette and individual tub chairs.

Two or three production shows are presented in a typical 7-day cruise (all ably performed by the Jean Ann Ryan Company). These are all very colorful, high-energy, high-volume razzle-dazzle shows (with much use of pyrotechnics, laser and color-mover lighting). There's so much happening that by the end of the evening, if you are a typical passenger, you'll be tired and won't remember much about the shows, which are, however, very entertaining.

The ship carries a number of bands and solo entertaining musicians. These provide live music for listening and dancing in several of the ship's lounges and bars.

SPA/FITNESS. Bodywaves, the spa/fitness center, is adjacent to the disco at the aft of Promenade Deck, and contains a small gymnasium with muscle-toning equipment, an aerobics exercise area, men's and women's saunas and changing rooms (these are extremely cramped), and Vanity Fair beauty salon. Mandara Spa (headquartered in Honolulu, but owned by Steiner Leisure) operates the spa/fitness center, and provides all staff and treatments as the concession.

● **For more extensive general information on what an NCL cruise is like, see pages 131–33.**

Norwegian Pearl
★★★★

Large Resort Ship:	.93,530 tons	Total Crew:	.1,100	Cabins (with private balcony):	.540
Lifestyle:	.Standard	Passengers		Cabins (wheelchair accessible):	.27
Cruise Line:	.Norwegian Cruise Line	(lower beds/all berths):	.2,394/2,846	Cabin Current:	.110 volts
Former Names:	.none	Passenger Space Ratio		Elevators:	.12
Builder:	.Meyer Werft (Germany)	(lower beds/all berths):	.39.0/32.8	Casino (gaming tables):	.Yes
Original Cost:	.$390 million	Crew/Passenger Ratio		Slot Machines:	.Yes
Entered Service:	.Dec 2006	(lower beds/all berths):	.2.1/2.5	Swimming Pools (outdoors):	.2
Registry:	.Panama	Navigation Officers:	.Scandinavian	Swimming Pools (indoors):	.0
Length (ft/m):	.964.8/294.1	Cabins (total):	.1,197	Whirlpools:	.6
Beam (ft/m):	.105.6/32.2	Size Range (sq ft/m):	.142.0–4,390.0/	Self-Service Launderette:	.Yes
Draft (ft/m):	.26.9/8.2		13.2–407.8	Dedicated Cinema/Seats:	.No
Propulsion/Propellers:	.diesel-electric/	Cabins (outside view):	.792	Library:	.Yes
	2 pods (19.5MW each)	Cabins (interior/no view):	.405		
Passenger Decks:	.12	Cabins (for one person):	.0		

OVERALL SCORE: 1,520 (OUT OF A POSSIBLE 2,000 POINTS)

OVERVIEW. This ship, built from 67 pre-assembled blocks, and whose basic design and layout is similar to that of *Norwegian Jewel*, has a "pod" propulsion system (*see page 174 for explanation*) for vibration-free cruising. The ship's white hull has a colourful, funky string of pearl design along its sides. There are plenty of deck lounge chairs (in fact, the number is greater than the number of passengers carried). Water slides are included for the adult swimming pools (children have their own pools at the ship's stern).

BERLITZ'S RATINGS	Possible	Achieved
Ship	500	425
Accommodation	200	156
Food	400	287
Service	400	284
Entertainment	100	67
Cruise	400	301

Inside the ship, you'll be met by an entertaining, eclectic mix of colors and decor that you probably wouldn't have in your home, and yet somehow they all work extremely well in this large resort ship setting designed to attract the young, active, and trendy.

There are 13 bars and lounges, including "Bar Central," four specialty bars: martini bar, champagne and wine bar, beer and whiskey bar, and a cigar bar; these interconnect with the lobby, yet feature distinct personalities. The lobby houses a Java Bar, plus a large movie screen, typically used to show sports events. One neat room is the "Bliss Ultra Lounge & Night Club," at the aft end of the ship; rather like a South Beach club, it houses a 24-hours a day sports bar and lounge complex. This includes a bowling alley with four real bowling lanes – the first aboard any cruise ship (it costs $5 per person, including special playing shoes, and is limited to six persons per lane). The lounge doesn't actually have many seats, but does have a couple of beds, as well as arcade games that include a Mad Wave Motion Theater, with its wild, moving seats.

Because NCL is all about cruising with families of all ages, much space is devoted to children's facilities, all thoughtfully tucked well away from adult recreation areas, at the aft end of the ship. Children of all ages will get to play in a superb wet 'n' wild space-themed water park (the Aqua Kid's Club), complete with large pool, water slide, and paddle pool; there's also 30-ft x 19-ft climbing wall at the funnel. There's a room full of cots for toddlers to use for sleepovers. Teens, too, are well catered for, and have their own cinema, discotheque with dance floor, and hot tub.

Plenty of choices, including many dining options, add up to a very attractive holiday package, highly suitable for families with children, in a contemporary floating leisure center that really does provide ample facilities for enjoyment. The dress code is very casual (no jacket and tie needed, although you are welcome to dress formally if you wish).

Although service levels and finesse may be inconsistent, the level of hospitality aboard NCL ships is good – made better and brighter by the addition of a good number of Asian female staff. Despite the company's name (Norwegian Cruise Line), there's little that's Norwegian about this product, except for some senior officers. There's plenty of lively music, constant activity, entertainment, and food that is mainstream and acceptable but nothing more (even when you pay extra to eat in the "alternative" dining spots).

While the initial cruise fare is reasonable, extra costs and charges soon mount up if you want to sample more than the basics. The ship is full of revenue centers designed to help you part with your money. You can expect to be subjected to a stream of flyers advertising daily art auctions, "designer" watches, "inch of gold/silver" and other promotions, and long program announcements three times daily by the cruise director.

The onboard currency is the US dollar. Gratuities for staff (cabin attendants, dining room waiters, etc.) are automatically added to your onboard account at $10 per person, per day; you can, however, reduce or otherwise amend these if necessary before you disembark. In addition, a 15% gratuity is added to all bar and spa treatment accounts.

ACCOMMODATION. There are 32 different price grades, so there's something for all tastes, from small interior (no view) cabins to lavish suites in a private courtyard setting.

Although they are nicely furnished and quite well equipped, the standard outside-view and interior (no view) cabins are quite small, particularly when occupied by three or four persons. Over 250 cabins have interconnecting doors (good for families with children). So, interior (no-view) cabins can connect; outside view cabins can connect; and outside view and balcony cabins can connect, providing families with much choice. Also for families, many cabins also have third- and fourth-person pull-down berths or trundle beds, and about 280 cabins have interconnecting doors – ideal for family cruising.

A small room service menu is available (all items are at extra cost, and a 15% service charge/gratuity are automatically added to your account). Bottled water is placed in each cabin, but a charge will be made to your account if you open the bottle.

The following suites are available:

Courtyard Villas/Garden Villas: The two Garden Villa Suites, each 4,390 sq.ft. (407.8 sq.m), and 10 Courtyard Villas share a private courtyard with its own small pool, hot tub, and small fitness room, and have butler service. These units enjoy exclusivity – rather like accommodation in a gated community, where others cannot live unless they pay the asking price.

Deluxe Owner's Suites: These two suites, Black Pearl and Golden Pearl, are set high atop all other accommodation, have stunning ocean views, and consist of a master bedroom with king-size bed, a dining/lounge area, a decent-sized balcony, and access to the private courtyard.

CUISINE. The two principal dining rooms are the 304-seat Indigo, with its minimalist decor; and the 558-seat Summer Palace, slightly reminiscent of a Russian tsar's palace. There are eight other themed eating spots, giving a wide range of choice; some cost extra, and require advance reservations, particularly for dinner; all are part of NCL's "Freestyle Dining." With "Freestyle Dining", you can choose which restaurant to eat in, at what time, and with whom (there are no assigned dining rooms, tables or seats).

With 17 video screens located around the ship, you can check how busy each dining spot is and make a booking and find out if, or how long, you'll need to wait for a table (pagers are also available, so you can go bar-hopping while you wait for a table in your chosen venue). The system generally works well (with colored bars to indicate whether a restaurant is "full," "moderately busy," or "empty;" this has cut down the frustration of waiting a long time for a table, although on "formal" nights (when you may want to

see the production shows), congestion certainly does occur. Note that NCL's dress code states that: "jeans, T-shirts, tank tops and bare feet are not permitted in restaurants," and all dining venues are non-smoking.

Alternative Restaurants/Eateries: Cagney's Steak House (featuring steaks from 5oz–24oz), Blue Lagoon (for trendy fast-food street snacks), and Le Bistro are NCL favorites; others include a tapas bar, and Lotus Garden, an Asian eatery complete with sushi bar and Teppanyaki grill (where the chef puts on a display in front of you).

There's also a large self-serve buffet-style restaurant, for casual meals (the Garden Café, which incorporates several active service stations).

ENTERTAINMENT. The showlounge, seating 1,042, is the venue for colorful Las-Vegas-style production shows and major cabaret acts. It is designed in the style of an opera house, spans three decks, and has a steeply tiered main floor and port and starboard balconies.

There are three production shows in a typical 7-day cruise (all ably performed by the Jean Ann Ryan Company). All are colorful, high-energy, razzle-dazzle shows (there is much use of pyrotechnics, laser and color-mover lighting), with so much happening on stage that by the end of the evening, if you are a typical passenger, you may be tired and unable to remember much about the shows, which are, however, very entertaining.

The ship carries a number of bands and solo entertaining musicians, which provide live music for listening and dancing in several of the lounges and bars. Throughout the ship, loud Latin music prevails. In the ship's nightclub, a Pachanga Party (a Miami South Beach rave) is featured each cruise.

SPA/FITNESS. Wellness devotees should enjoy the two-deck-high South Pacific Health Spa complex (operated by the Hawaii-based Mandara Spa, owned by Steiner). It is located in the front of the ship, with large ocean-view windows on three sides. There are many facilities and services to pamper you (almost all at extra charge), including Thai massage (in the spa, outdoors on deck, in your cabin or on your private balcony). There's also a 37-ft (11.2-meter) indoor lap pool, hydrotherapy pool, two sit-in deep tubs, aromatherapy and wellness centers, and mud treatment room treatment rooms. There are 15 treatment rooms in all, including one specifically designed for couples.

The Body Waves fitness and exercise rooms are located within the spa (they feature the latest Cybex muscle-pumping equipment). Some classes, such as Pathway to Yoga, Body Cycling Class and Body Beat Class (cardio kick-boxing) cost extra.

Recreational sports facilities include a jogging track, golf driving range, basketball and volleyball courts, as well as several levels of sunbathing decks, plus the four bowling lanes, and a funnel-mounted rock-climbing wall.

● **For more extensive general information on what an NCL cruise is like, see Page 131–33.**

Norwegian Sky
★★★ +

Large Resort Ship:	. . . . .77,104 tons	Passenger Decks: 12	Cabins (for one person): 0

Large Resort Ship: . . . . .77,104 tons
Lifestyle: . . . . .Standard
Cruise Line: . . . . . .Norwegian Cruise Line
Former Names: . . . .*Pride of Aloha,*
Norwegian Sky
Builder: . . . . .Lloyd Werft (Germany)
Original Cost: . . . .$332 million
Entered Service: . . . . .Aug 1999/Jun 2008
Registry: . . . . .The Bahamas
Length (ft/m): 853.0/260.00
Beam (ft/m): 105.8/32.25
Draft (ft/m): 26.2/8.00
Propulsion/Propellers: . . . . .diesel-electric
(50,000 kW)/2

Passenger Decks: 12
Total Crew: 950
Passengers
(lower beds/all berths): 2,002/2,450
Passenger Space Ratio
(lower beds/all berths): 38.5/31.4
Crew/Passenger Ratio
(lower beds/all berths): 2.6/3.2
Navigation Officers: . . . . .Norwegian
Cabins (total): 1,001
Size Range (sq ft/m): 120.5–488.6/
11.2–45.4
Cabins (outside view): 574
Cabins (interior/no view): 427

Cabins (for one person): 0
Cabins (with private balcony): 252
Cabins (wheelchair accessible): 6
Cabin Current: . . . . .110 volts
Elevators: 12
Casino (gaming tables): . . . . .Yes
Slot Machines: . . . . .Yes
Swimming Pools (outdoors): 2
Swimming Pools (indoors): 0
Whirlpools: 5
Self-Service Launderette: . . . . .No
Dedicated Cinema/Seats: . . . . .No
Library: . . . . .Yes

OVERALL SCORE: 1,387 (OUT OF A POSSIBLE 2,000 POINTS)

OVERVIEW. In 2004 *Norwegian Sky* was "Hawaiianized" and morphed into *Pride of Aloha* for NCL's Hawaii cruise operation. It withdrew from that market in May 2008 and was transferred to NCL for short cruises in the Caribbean. The outdoor space is quite generous, with an extra wide pool deck – created from port and starboard "overhangs" that resulted from balconies added to cabins on two decks beneath it – with two swimming pools and four hot tubs.

The interior decor reflects the ship's operating area, and the focal point is the ship's eight-deck high atrium lobby, with spiral sculptures and rainbow-colored sails. Public rooms include a shopping arcade, children's playroom (there is also a splash pool in a prime open deck area forward atop ship), internet center (with 14 terminals and coffee available from an adjacent bar), several lounges and bars, small conference room, the Mark Twain library; Captain Cook's for cigars and cognac. Those with a black belt in shopping should know the Black Pearl Gem Shop is a joint venture.

Norwegian Sky is a resort at sea, and caters well to a multi-generational clientele, with lots of choices for dining and entertainment. It provides a fine, comfortable base from which to explore. The onboard currency is the US dollar.

The hustling for passengers to attend art auctions is aggressive and annoying, as is the constant bombardment for revenue activities and the daily junk mail that arrives at one's cabin door. There are many announcements – particularly annoying are those that state what is already written in the daily program. There is little connection to the sea from many public rooms. Passenger hallways are quite plain.

ACCOMMODATION. There are 19 price categories: 13 for out-

BERLITZ'S RATINGS

	Possible	Achieved
Ship	500	400
Accommodation	200	149
Food	400	248
Service	400	232
Entertainment	100	79
Cruise	400	279

side-view suites and cabins, and six for interior (no view) cabins. All the standard outside-view and interior (no view) cabins have two lower beds that can convert to a queen-sized bed, a small lounge area with sofa and table, and a decent amount of closet space, but very little drawer space, and the cabins themselves are disappointingly small. However, each is decorated in colorful Hawaiian style, with an explosion of floral themes and vibrant colors.

More than 200 outside-view cabins have their own private balcony. Each cabin has a small vanity/writing desk, color television, personal safe, climate control, and a laptop computer connection socket. Audio can be obtained only through the TV set. Bottled water is placed in each cabin – but a charge will be made to your account if you open the bottle.

The largest accommodation is four Owner's Suites. Each has a hot tub, large teak table, two chairs and two sun-loungers outside on a huge, very private, forward-?facing teakwood floor balcony just under the ship's navigation bridge, with large floor-to-ceiling windows. Each suite has a separate lounge and bedroom. The lounge has a large dining table and four chairs, two two-person sofas, large television, DVD/CD player, coffee table, queen-sized pull-down Murphy's bed, guest closet, writing desk, wet bar with two bar stools, refrigerator and sink, several cupboards for glasses, and several drawers and other cupboards for storage. The bedroom, which has sliding wood half-doors that look into the lounge, has a queen-sized bed (with European duvet) under a leaf-glass chandelier, vanity desk, TV, walk-in closet with plenty of hanging rail space, five open shelves and large personal safe. The white-tiled bathroom, although not large, has a full-sized tub with retractable clothesline above, separate shower enclosure with glass doors, deep washbasin, and toiletries cabinets.

There are 10 Junior Suites, each with a private teak decked balcony; these suites face aft in a secluded position and overlook the ship's wash. They have almost the same facilities as those in the owner's suites, except for the outdoor hot tub, and the fact that there is less space.

CUISINE. You can choose which restaurant you would like to eat in, at what time, and with whom.

The main dining rooms – Palace Restaurant, with 510 seats, and Crossings Restaurant, with 556 seats – have tables for four, six or eight and an open-seating arrangement. The cuisine in both includes regional specialties However, it's best to have dinner in one of the specialty restaurants, as the food in these two large dining rooms is just so-so.

A smaller eatery, the 83-seat Plantation Club Restaurant, is an à la carte, light-eating option serving "healthy" spa dishes and tapas. It has half-moon shaped alcoves and several tables for two. The wine list is quite decent and well arranged, with moderate prices, although you won't find many good vintage wines. The cutlery is very ordinary and there are no fish knives.

For classic and nouvelle French cuisine, the 102-seat Bistro has an à la carte menu. The decor is inspired by royal and aristocratic gardens.

For premium steaks and lamb chops, there's Cagneys Restaurant, with 84 seats, intimate seating alcoves and good food (at extra cost).

Other eateries include Pacific Heights, a casual Pacific Rim/Asian Fusion eatery that has steaks plus local fish and seafood. Casual, self-serve buffet-style meals can be taken in the Garden Café.

ENTERTAINMENT. The 1,000-seat two-decks-high (main and balcony levels) Stardust Theater is the venue for production shows and major cabaret acts, although the sightlines are quite poor from some seats.

The ship has a number of bands and solo entertaining musicians, providing live music for listening and dancing in several lounges and bars.

SPA/FITNESS. Body Waves is a large health/fitness spa – including an aerobics room and a separate gymnasium, and several treatment rooms. Mandara Spa (headquartered in Honolulu, but owned by Steiner Leisure) is the operator of the spa/fitness center, and provides all staff and treatments as the concession.

Sports fans will appreciate the large basketball/volleyball court, baseball-batting cage, golf-driving net, platform tennis, shuffleboard and table tennis facilities, and sports bar (with baseball and surfing themes) with live satellite television coverage of sports events and major games on several TV screens. Joggers will find a wrap-around indoor/outdoor jogging track.

● **For more extensive general information on what an NCL cruise is like, see pages 131–33.**

Norwegian Spirit
★★★★

Large Resort Ship: ....75,338 tons
Lifestyle: ....Standard
Cruise Line: ......Norwegian Cruise Line
Former Names: ....*SuperStar Leo*
Builder: ....Meyer Werft (Germany)
Original Cost: ....$350 million
Entered Service: .....Oct 1998/May 2004
Registry: ....Panama
Length (ft/m): 879.2/268.0
Beam (ft/m): 105.6/32.2
Draft (ft/m): 25.9/7.9
Propulsion/Propellers: ....2 diesels
(50,400kW)/2
Passenger Decks: 10

Total Crew: 1,300
Passengers
(lower beds/all berths): ...1,966/2,475
Passenger Space Ratio
(lower beds/all berths): 38.1/30.4
Crew/Passenger Ratio
(lower beds/all berths): 1.5/2.1
Navigation Officers: ......Scandinavian
Size Range (sq ft/m): 150.6–638.3/
14.0–59.3
Cabins (outside view): 609
Cabins (interior/no view): 379
Cabins (for one person): 0

Cabins (with private balcony): 374
Cabins (wheelchair accessible): 4
Cabin Current: ....240 volts
Elevators: 9
Casino (gaming tables): ....Yes
Slot Machines: ....Yes
Swimming Pools (outdoors): 2
Swimming Pools (indoors): 0
Whirlpools: 4
Self-Service Launderette: ....No
Dedicated Cinema/Seats: ....No
Library: ....Yes

OVERALL SCORE: 1,495 (OUT OF A POSSIBLE 2,000 POINTS)

OVERVIEW. *Norwegian Spirit* (ex-*Super-Star Leo*), was the first brand new ship ordered by parent company Star Cruises specifically for the Southeast Asia market. It was moved to NCL in 2004 in a fleet redeployment. There is a full wrap-around promenade deck outdoors, good for strolling, and lots of outdoor space, including a whole area devoted to children's outdoor activities and pool.

Inside, there are two indoor boulevards, and a large, stunning, two-deck-high central atrium lobby, with three glass-walled lifts and ample space to peruse the shops and cafes that line its inner sanctum. The lobby itself is modeled after the lobby of the Hyatt Hotel in Hong Kong, with little clutter from the usual run of desks found aboard other cruise ships.

The interior design theme revolves around art, architecture, history and literature. The ship has a mix of both eastern and western design and decor details. Three stairways are each carpeted in a different color, which helps new cruise passengers find their way around easily.

A 450-seat room atop the ship functions as an observation lounge during the day and a nightclub at night, with live music. From it, a spiral stairway takes you down to a navigation bridge viewing area, where you can see the captain and bridge officers at work.

There is a business center (complete with conference center – good for small groups) and writing room, and a smoking room, for those who enjoy cigars and cognac. A shopping concourse is set around the second level of the lobby.

Want the casino? The casino complex is at the forward end of the atrium boulevard on Deck 7 (not between showlounge and restaurant as in most western ships). This includes a large general purpose, brightly lit casino,

BERLITZ'S RATINGS	Possible	Achieved
Ship	500	419
Accommodation	200	154
Food	400	286
Service	400	278
Entertainment	100	61
Cruise	400	297

Maharajah's, with gaming tables and slot machines.

Families with children should note that teens have their own huge video arcade, while younger children get to play in a wet 'n' wild aft pool (complete with pirate ship and caves) and two whirlpool tubs. Plus there's all the fun and facilities of Charlie's childcare center, which includes a painting room, computer learning center, and small cinema. Even the toilets are at a special low height, and there's a room full of cots for toddlers. Over 15,000 sq. ft (1,400 sq. meters) is devoted to children's facilities – all tucked well away from adult recreation areas.

The dress code is extremely casual (no jacket and tie needed). Watch out for the extra costs and charges to mount up if you order more than the basics. With many dining choices (some of which cost extra) to accommodate different tastes and styles, your cruise and dining experience will largely depend on how much you are prepared to spend. Gratuities for staff (non-adjustable from May 2005) are added to your onboard account, and 15 percent is added to all bar, wine and spa accounts. The onboard currency is the U.S. dollar.

Because this is quite a stunning ship and offers a wide choice of dining venues, keeping consistency of product delivery will depend on the quality of the service and supervisory staff. There are many extra-cost items (in addition to the à la carte/extra charge dining spots), and there is constant intrusion into your cruise experience with announcements for things such as art auctions, bingo and horse racing. Note that standing in line for embarkation, disembarkation, shore tenders and for self-serve buffet meals is an inevitable aspect of cruising aboard all large ships.

ACCOMMODATION. Three whole decks of cabins have private balconies, while two-thirds of all cabins have an outside view. Both the standard outside-view and interior (no view) cabins really are very small (particularly given that all cabins have extra berths for a third/fourth person), although the bathrooms have a good-sized shower enclosure. So, take only the smallest amount of clothing you can get away with. All cabins have a personal safe, 100% cotton towels and 100% cotton duvets or sheets. Note that, in cabins with balconies, the balconies are extremely narrow, and the cabins themselves are very small (the ship was originally constructed for 3- and 4-day cruises).

Choose one of the six largest Executive Suites (named Hong Kong, Malaysia, Shanghai, Singapore, Thailand and Tokyo) and you'll have an excellent amount of private living space, with separate lounge, and bedroom. Each has a large en-suite bathroom that is part of the bedroom and opens onto it. It has a gorgeous mosaic tiled floor, kidney bean-shaped whirlpool bathtub, two sinks, separate shower enclosure (with floor-to-ceiling ocean-view window) and separate toilet (with glass door). There are TV sets in the lounge, bedroom and bathroom. The Singapore and Hong Kong suites and the Malaysia and Thai suites can be combined to form a double suite (good for families with children). Butler service and concierge come with the territory.

Choose one of the 12 Zodiac suites (each is named after a sign of the Zodiac) and you will get the second largest accommodation aboard the ship. Each suite has a separate lounge, bedroom, and bathroom, and an interconnecting door to an ocean-view cabin with private balcony (good for families). All cabinetry features richly lacquered woods, large (stocked) wet bar with refrigerator, dining table (with a top that flips over to reveal a card table) and four chairs, sofa and drinks table, and trouser press. The bedrooms are small, but have a queen-sized bed; there is a decent amount of drawer space, although the closet space is rather tight (it contains two personal safes). The large en-suite bathrooms are similarly designed to those in the Executive Suites.

A small room service menu is available (all items are at extra cost, and both a 15% service charge as well as a gratuity are added to your account). Butler service and concierge come with the territory.

CUISINE. There is certainly plenty of choice when it comes to formal dining and casual eateries. There are, in all, eight places to eat (all are non-smoking), of which, two are at extra charge. You will, therefore, need to plan where you want to eat well in advance, or you may be disappointed.

Windows Restaurant: The equivalent of a main dining room, it seats 632 (in two seatings), is two decks high at the aft-most section, and has huge cathedral-style windows set in three sections overlooking the ship's stern and wake.

Waiter stations are tucked neatly away in side wings, which help to keep down noise levels.

Garden Room Restaurant: This has 268 seats.

Raffles Terrace Cafe: a large self-serve buffet restaurant with indoor/outdoor seating for 400 and pseudo-Raffles Hotel-like decor, with rattan chairs, overhead fans, etc.

Taipan: a Chinese Restaurant, with traditional Hong Kong-themed decor and items such as dim sum made from fresh, not frozen, ingredients (cover charge applicable, reservations necessary).

Shogun Asian Restaurant: a Japanese restaurant and sushi bar, for sashimi, sushi, and tempura. A section can be closed off to make the Samurai Room, with 22 seats, while a traditional Tatami Room has seats for eight. There's also a teppanyaki grill, with 10 seats, where the chef cooks in front of you.

Maxim's: a small à la carte restaurant with ocean-view windows; fine cuisine in the classic French style (cover charge applicable, reservations necessary).

Blue Lagoon Café: a small, casual street cafe with about 24 seats, featuring noodle dishes, fried rice and other Southeast Asian cuisine (adjacent is a street bar called The Bund).

The Café: a casual pâtisserie serving several types of coffees, teas, cakes and pastries (at extra cost), in the atrium lobby.

ENTERTAINMENT. The Moulin Rouge Showlounge, with 973 seats, is the main venue. It is two decks high, with a main and balcony levels. The room has almost no support columns to obstruct the sightlines, and a revolving stage for Broadway-style reviews and other production shows (typically to recorded music), although there's little space for an orchestra. The show lounge is also used as a large-screen cinema, and has excellent surround sound.

SPA/FITNESS. The Roman Spa and Fitness Center is located on one of the uppermost decks, just forward of the Tivoli Pool. It has a gymnasium full of high-tech muscle-toning equipment, and aerobics exercise room, hair and beauty salon, and saunas, steam rooms, and changing rooms for men and women, as well as several treatment rooms, and aqua-swim pools that provide counter-flow jets (swimming against the current). The spa facility is operated by the Hawaii-based Mandara Spa, owned by Steiner Leisure.

The fitness and exercise rooms are located not within the spa, but at the top of the glass-domed atrium lobby (they feature the latest Cybex muscle-pumping equipment). Included is a room for exercycle classes. Sports facilities include a jogging track, golf driving range, basketball and tennis courts, and there are four levels of sunbathing decks.

● **For more extensive general information on what an NCL cruise is like, see pages 131–33.**

Norwegian Star
★★★★

Large Resort Ship:	.........91,740 tons	Total Crew:	1,100	Cabins (with private balcony):	509
Lifestyle:	..................Standard	Passengers		Cabins (wheelchair accessible):	20
Cruise Line:	......Norwegian Cruise Line	(lower beds/all berths):	.....2,244/2,846	Cabin Current:	................110 AC
Former Names:	................none	Passenger Space Ratio		Elevators:	12
Builder:	........Meyer Werft (Germany)	(lower beds/all berths):	.......40.8/32.0	Casino (gaming tables):	...........Yes
Original Cost:	............$400 million	Crew/Passenger Ratio		Slot Machines:	..................Yes
Entered Service:	............Dec 2001	(lower beds/all berths):	.........2.0/3.7	Swimming Pools (outdoors):	2
Registry:	....................Panama	Navigation Officers:	......Scandinavian	Swimming Pools (indoors):	1
Length (ft/m):	...........964.9/294.13	Cabins (total):	1,122	Whirlpools: ...4 (+ 1 children's whirlpool)
Beam (ft/m):	................105.6/32.2	Size Range (sq ft/m):	.....142.0–5,350.0/	Self-Service Launderette:	...........No
Draft (ft/m):	.................26.9/8.2		13.2–497.0	Dedicated Cinema/Seats:	.......Yes/151
Propulsion/Propellers: ...diesel-electric/2		Cabins (outside view):	787	Library:	.........................Yes
azimuthing pods (19.5 MW each)		Cabins (interior/no view):	363		
Passenger Decks:	12	Cabins (for one person):	0		

OVERALL SCORE: 1,520 (OUT OF A POSSIBLE 2,000 POINTS)

OVERVIEW. *Norwegian Star* is a sister ship to *Norwegian Dawn*, which debuted in 2002. It has a "pod" propulsion system (*see page 174 for explanation*). A large structure located forward of the funnel houses a children's center, and, one deck above, the two outstanding "villa" suites described in the accommodation section above. The ship's hull is adorned with a decal consisting of a burst of colorful stars and streamers.

There are plenty of sunloungers (in fact, the number is greater than the number of passengers carried). Water slides are included for the adult swimming pools (children have their own pools at the ship's stern – out of sight of the adult areas).

Inside the ship, you'll be met by a truly eclectic mix of bright colors and decor that you probably wouldn't have in your home (unless you were color-blind) – and yet somehow it works extremely well in this large ship setting that is meant to attract young, active types.

Facilities include an Internet Cafe (with 17 computer stations), a 1,150-seat showlounge with main floor and two balcony levels, 3,000-book library, card room, writing and study room, business center, karaoke lounge, conference and meeting rooms and associated facilities, and a retail shopping complex of 20,000 sq. ft (1,800 sq. meters). In 2004, a 929-sq. meter (10,000-sq. ft) casino was added.

Children of all ages will get to play in a superb wet 'n' wild space-themed water park (complete with large pool, water slide, and paddle pool). They also get their own dedicated cinema (DVD movies are featured all day long), a jungle gym, painting area, and computer center. Even the toilets are at a special low height. Teens, too, are well

BERLITZ'S RATINGS

	Possible	Achieved
Ship	500	419
Accommodation	200	156
Food	400	293
Service	400	284
Entertainment	100	66
Cruise	400	302

catered for, and get their own cinema (with DVD movies), discotheque with dance floor, and whirlpool (hot) tub.

With so many dining choices (some costing extra) to accommodate the tastes of an eclectic mix of nationalities, the amount you are prepared to spend will determine what your final cruise and dining experience will be like. To make the most of your vacation, you will need to plan where you want to eat well in advance, and make the necessary reservations, or you may be disappointed. More choices, including more dining options, add up to a very attractive package, particularly suitable for families with children, in a very contemporary floating leisure center that really does provide ample facilities for enjoyment, as well as provide you with the opportunity to immerse yourself in all things Hawaiian. The dress code is very casual (no jacket and tie needed, although you are welcome to dress formally if you wish).

While the initial cruise fare seems very reasonable, the extra costs and charges soon mount up if you want more than the basics. Although service levels and finesse are sometimes inconsistent, the level of hospitality is very good – made so much better and brighter by the addition of a great number of Asian female staff rather than the surly and inconsistent Caribbean staff still found on some of the smaller NCL ships.

Despite the company's name (Norwegian Cruise Line), there's almost nothing Norwegian about this product, except for some of the ship's senior officers. The staff, incidentally, includes many Southeast Asians who have service experience aboard parent company Star Cruises' big ships.

Gratuities for staff (cabin attendants, dining room waiters, etc) are added to your onboard account at $10 per person, per day; you can reduce or otherwise amend these if necessary before you disembark, but in May 2005 the gratuity became a non-adjustable "service charge." In addition, a 15% gratuity is added to all bar and spa treatment accounts. The onboard currency is the US dollar.

The hustling for passengers to attend art auctions is both aggressive and annoying. Standing in line for embarkation, disembarkation, shore tenders and for self-serve buffet meals is an inevitable aspect of cruising aboard all large ships – even those designated as "Freestyle".

Reaching room service tends to be an exercise in frustration. Communication (particularly between the many new Asian staff and passengers) remains weak. Mindless "art auctions" are a real turn-off on a Hawaiian cruise.

ACCOMMODATION. With 29 price grades, this is a mix that includes something for everyone. There are 36 suites (including two of the largest aboard any cruise ship); 372 "balcony-class" standard cabins with private balconies, 415 outside-view cabins (no balcony); 363 interior (no view) cabins; 36 suites with balconies, and 20 wheelchair-accessible cabins. Suites and cabins with private balconies have easy-to-use sliding glass doors.

Regardless of the accommodation (and thus the price you pay for your cruise), all have a powerful hairdryer (located in the cabin itself, and not, thankfully, in the bathroom), and a tea and coffee making sets, rich cherry wood cabinetry, and a bathroom with a sliding door and a separate toilet, shower enclosure and washbasin compartments. There is plenty of wood accenting in all accommodation, including wood frames surrounding balcony doors – a nice touch that will be subliminally appreciated by passengers.

The largest accommodation is in two huge Garden Villas (Vista and Horizon), located high atop the ship in a pod that is located forward of the ship's funnel, and overlooks the main swimming pool. Each measures 5,350 sq ft. (497 sq meters) and can be combined to create a huge, double-sized "house" measuring 10,700 sq ft (994-sq-meters). These villas have huge glass walls and landscaped private roof gardens (one has a Japanese-style garden, the other a Thai-style garden) for outdoor dining (with whirlpool tubs, naturally), and huge private sunbathing areas that are completely shielded from anyone; the garden itself extends to 1,720 sq. ft (160 sq. meters).

Each suite has three bedrooms (one with a sliding glass door that leads to the garden) and bathrooms (one bathroom has a large corner tub, and two washbasins set in front of large glass walls that overlook the side of the ship as well as the swimming pool, although most of the view is of the overlarge waterslide), and a large living room (with Yamaha baby grand piano) with glass dining table and eight chairs, overlooking the lido/pool deck. These units have their own private elevator and private stairway, and can be combined to create a large, 10,700 sq.-ft (994 sq.-meter) "house" (the garden is included in the measurements)

There are many suites (the smallest measures 290 sq. ft/27 sq. meters) in several different configurations. Some overlook the stern, while others are in the forward part of the ship. All are lavishly furnished, although closet space in some of the smaller units is tight.

Although the suites and junior suites are quite spacious, the standard interior (no view) and outside-view cabins are very small when compared to those of other major cruise lines such as Carnival or Celebrity, particularly when occupied by three or four persons (the bathrooms, however, are of quite a decent size, and have large shower enclosures). Some cabins have interconnecting doors (good for families with children), and many cabins have third- and fourth-person pull-down berths or trundle beds.

A small room service menu is available (all items are at extra cost, and a 15% service charge and a gratuity are automatically added to your account). Bottled water is placed in each cabin, but a charge will be made to your account if you open the bottle.

CUISINE. NCL features "Freestyle Dining", so you can choose which restaurant to eat in, at what time, and with whom. You can eat in a different restaurant every night – just like going out on the town ashore – or you can eat in the same restaurant every day, even having the same waiter, as in traditional cruising. Freestyle Dining also appears to work far better for individuals rather than large groups.

All restaurants and eateries are non-smoking. The dress code states that: "jeans, T-shirts, tank tops and bare feet are not permitted in restaurants", although this is not followed in practice, particularly when families with young children are aboard at peak holiday times. On Formal Nights, many passengers want to eat in the two large main dining rooms, and this can create a logjam.

Although there are two main dining rooms (come when you want), there are several other themed eating establishments, giving a wide range of choice. It would be wise to plan in advance, particularly for dinner. In fact, there are two entire decks of dining establishments to choose from, involving 10 different restaurants and eateries, and 11 different menus nightly.

● **Versailles**, the ornate 375-seat first main dining room, is decorated in brilliant red and gold. This offers the traditional six-course dining experience (open 5.30pm–midnight). This is located aft and has excellent views through windows that span two decks.

● **Aqua:** a contemporary-styled 374-seat second main dining room, offering lighter cuisine (open 5.30pm–midnight), and an open galley where you can view the preparation of pastries and dessert items.

● **Soho:** Pacific Rim cuisine is where East meets West (California and Asian cuisine) in culinary terms. Has a live lobster tank (the first aboard a ship outside Southeast Asia). A main dining area that can seat 132, plus private dining rooms (each seats 10). A collection of pop art (including Andy Warhol prints) adorns the walls.

● **Ginza:** a Japanese restaurant, with 193 seats, a sit-up sushi bar, tempura bar, show galley, and separate "teppan-yaki grill" room.

● **Le Bistro:** a French restaurant, with 66 seats, serving nouvelle cuisine and six courses.

● **Blue Lagoon:** a funky food court-style eatery with 88 seats (both indoors and outdoors on the Promenade Deck), with hamburgers, fish and chips, potpies and fast (wok stir-fried) dishes.

● **Market Cafe**: a large indoor/outdoor self-serve buffet eatery, with almost 400 ft (120 meters) of buffet counter space. "Action Stations" has made-to-order omelets, waffles, fruit, soups, ethnic specialities and pasta dishes.

● **La Trattoria**, an Italian (evening only) dining spot located within the indoor/outdoor buffet area, has pasta, pizza and other popular Italian fare.

● **Steakhouse:** this serves prime USDA beef steaks and lamb chops.

● **Endless Summer:** a Hawaiian themed restaurant – arranged around the second level of the central atrium and incorporating a performance stage and a large movie screen.

Other eating/drinking spots include the Red Lion (an English pub for draft beer and perhaps a game of darts); Havana Club, a cigar and cognac lounge; Java Cafe, an atrium lobby Cafe and bar (for hot and frozen coffees, teas and pastries); a Beer Garden (for grilled foods); a Spinkles (an ice cream bar); a Gym and Spa Bar (for health food snacks and drinks); and Gatsby's wine bar (at the entrance to Soho).

Overall, the food provided is adequate, but lacks taste and presentation quality, although the menus make the dishes sound good. There's a reasonably decent selection of breads, rolls, cheeses and fruits. The wine list is quite decent and well arranged, together with moderate prices, although you won't find any good vintage wines (and the wine glasses are small). The cutlery is very ordinary (there are no fish knives). There is no formal afternoon tea, although you can make your own from various beverage stations. Overall service is just so-so. Breakfast and lunch buffets tend to have unimaginative presentation (more variety and better ingredients would be useful).

A lavish "chocoholics" buffet is available once each cruise – a firm favorite among regular passengers.

ENTERTAINMENT. The Stardust Theatre seats 1,037, and is the venue for colorful Las-Vegas-style production shows and major cabaret acts. It is designed in the style of an opera house, spans three decks, and has a steeply tiered main floor and port and starboard balconies.

Two or three production shows are presented in a typical 7-day cruise (all ably performed by the Jean Ann Ryan Company). These are all very colorful, high-energy, high-volume razzle-dazzle shows (with much use of pyrotechnics, laser and color-mover lighting). There's so much happening that by the end of the evening you'll be tired and may not remember a great deal about the shows – even though they're very entertaining.

The ship has a number of bands and solo entertaining musicians, which provide live music for listening and dancing in several of the ship's lounges and bars.

SPA/FITNESS. Wellness devotees should enjoy the two-deck-high Barong health spa complex (operated by the Hawaii-based Mandara Spa, owned by Steiner), located at the stern of the ship (with large ocean-view windows on three sides). There are many facilities and services to pamper you (almost all at extra charge), including Thai massage (in the spa, outdoors on deck, in your cabin or on your private balcony). In addition, there is an indoor lap pool (measuring 37 ft/11.2 meters), hydrotherapy pool, aromatherapy and wellness centers, and mud treatment room treatment rooms (there are 15 treatment rooms in all, including one specifically designed for couples).

Mandara Spa (headquartered in Honolulu, but owned by Steiner Leisure) is the operator of the spa/fitness center, and provides all staff and treatments as the concession.

The fitness and exercise rooms are not within the spa, but at the top of the atrium lobby, and have the latest Cybex muscle-pumping equipment. Included is a room for exercycle classes. Recreational sports facilities include a jogging track, golf driving range, basketball and volleyball courts, as well as four levels of sunbathing decks.

● **For more extensive general information on what an NCL cruise is like, see pages 131–33.**

Norwegian Sun
★★★★

Large Resort Ship:	.........78,309 tons	Total Crew:	980

Large Resort Ship: ....78,309 tons
Lifestyle: ....Standard
Cruise Line: ......Norwegian Cruise Line
Former Names: ....none
Builder: ....Lloyd Werft (Germany)
Original Cost: ....$332 million
Entered Service: ....Nov 2001
Registry: ....The Bahamas
Length (ft/m): 853.0/260.00
Beam (ft/m): 105.8/32.25
Draft (ft/m): 26.2/8.00
Propulsion/Propellers: ....diesel-electric
(50,000 kW)/2
Passenger Decks: 12

Total Crew: 980
Passengers
(lower beds/all berths): 2,002/2,400
Passenger Space Ratio
(lower beds/all berths): 39.1/32.6
Crew/Passenger Ratio
(lower beds/all berths): 2.0/2.4
Navigation Officers: ....Norwegian
Cabins (total): 1,001
Size Range (sq ft/m): 120.5–488.6/
11.2–45.4
Cabins (outside view): 675
Cabins (interior/no view): 326
Cabins (for one person): 0

Cabins (with private balcony): 252
Cabins (wheelchair accessible): 6
Cabin Current: ....110 volts
Elevators: 12
Casino (gaming tables): ....Yes
Slot Machines: ....Yes
Swimming Pools (outdoors): 2
Swimming Pools (indoors): 0
Whirlpools: 4
Self-Service Launderette: ....No
Dedicated Cinema/Seats: ....No
Library: ....Yes

OVERALL SCORE: 1,514 (OUT OF A POSSIBLE 2,000 POINTS)

OVERVIEW. *Norwegian Sun* is a close sister ship to *Norwegian Sky,* but with better outfitting and finishing detail, plus one additional deck of balcony cabins, and crew cabins were added to accommodate an extra 200 crew, needed for the Freestyle dining concept. The amount of outdoor space is quite good, especially the ultra-wide pool deck, with its two swimming pools and four Jacuzzi tubs, and plenty of sunloungers, albeit arranged in rows, camp-style.

A separate cabaret venue, Dazzles Lounge, has an extremely long bar. Other features include a large casino (this will operate 24 hours a day, with special facilities and rooms for high-rollers and "club" members), a shopping arcade, children's playroom (there is also a splash pool in a prime open deck area), and a video arcade.

Other facilities include a small conference room, library and beauty salon, a lounge for smoking cigars and drinking cognac, and an internet cafe, located on the Promenade Deck within the ship's atrium lobby, with 20 computer stations. Numerous shops showcase a wide range of goods, from inexpensive to very expensive.

Young passengers will find an array of facilities, which include a children's playroom called Kid's Corner (for "junior sailors" ages 3–5; (First Mates (ages 6–9); Navigators (ages 10–12); and Teens (ages 13–17).

With this ship, Norwegian Cruise Line has made an effort to provide more and better public rooms and more entertainment facilities than aboard its smaller ships. There are certainly plenty of options for eating. But the ship is full of revenue centers, designed to help you part you from your money. You can expect to be subjected to a stream of flyers advertising daily art auctions, "designer" watches, and

BERLITZ'S RATINGS

	Possible	Achieved
Ship	500	410
Accommodation	200	152
Food	400	286
Service	400	284
Entertainment	100	78
Cruise	400	304

other promotions, while "artworks" for auction are strewn throughout the ship.

Gratuities for staff are added to your onboard account at $10 per person, per day; you can, however, reduce or otherwise amend these before you disembark, but in May 2005 the gratuity became a non-adjustable "service charge." In addition, a 15% gratuity is added to bar and spa accounts. The onboard currency is the US dollar.

The standard interior (no view) and outside-view cabins are very small when compared to those of other major cruise lines. The food in the large dining rooms is a weak point. There are many plastic plates, Styrofoam and plastic cups and plastic stirrers in use in the casual eateries.

ACCOMMODATION. There are 30 different categories, including 6 grades of suites, 15 grades of outside-view cabins and nine grades of interior (no view) cabins, so choosing the right accommodation requires some thought.

All of the standard outside-view and interior (no view) cabins have common facilities, such as: two lower beds that can convert to a queen-sized bed, a small lounge area with sofa and table, and a decent amount of closet and drawer space, although the cabins themselves are disappointingly small. Over 200 outside-view cabins have a private balcony. Each cabin has a small vanity/ writing desk, color TV set, personal safe, refrigerator, climate control, and laptop computer connection socket. Bottled water is placed in each cabin (but a charge will be made to your account if you open the bottle).

There are two Honeymoon/Anniversary Suites, located at the front of the ship, with forward facing and side views.

Each suite has a separate lounge and bedroom. The lounge has a large dining table and chairs, two sofas, large television, DVD/CD player, coffee table, queen-sized pull-down Murphy's bed, guest closet, writing desk, wet bar with two bar stools, refrigerator and sink, several cupboards for glasses, and several drawers and other cupboards for storage. The sleeping area has twin beds that convert to a queen-sized bed, and walk-in closet with a good amount of hanging space. The tiled bathroom, although not large, has a full-size whirlpool tub and shower, retractable clothesline, deep washbasin, and personal toiletries cabinets.

The largest accommodation is in two Owner's Suites – each with a hot tub, large teak table, two chairs and two sun-loungers outside on a huge, private, forward-facing teak floor balcony just under the ship's navigation bridge, with large floor-to-ceiling windows. Each suite has a separate lounge and bedroom. The lounge has a large dining table and chairs, two sofas, large TV set, DVD/CD player, coffee table, queen-sized pull-down Murphy's bed, guest closet, writing desk, wet bar with two bar stools, refrigerator and sink, several cupboards for glasses, and several drawers and other cupboards for storage. The bedroom, with sliding wood half-doors that look into the lounge, has a queen-sized bed (with European duvet) under a leaf-glass chandelier, vanity desk, TV set, walk-in closet with plenty of hanging rail space, several open shelves and large personal safe. The tiled bathroom, although not large, has a full-size tub with retractable clothesline above, separate shower enclosure with glass doors, deep washbasin, and personal toiletries cabinets.

There are also a number of other suites – each with a private teakwood balcony; these suites face aft in a secluded position and overlook the ship's wash. They have some of the same facilities as found in the owner's suites, except for the outdoor hot tub, and the fact that there is less space. All cabins have tea/coffee making sets, personal safe, satellite-linked telephone, and private bathroom with bath or shower.

CUISINE. NCL has "Freestyle Dining", so you can choose which restaurant you would like to eat in, at what time, and with whom. Although there are two large dining rooms, there are also a number of other themed eating establishments – although it would be wise to plan in advance, particularly for dinner. All are non-smoking, and some incur an extra charge. The dress code states that: "jeans, T-shirts, tank tops and bare feet are not permitted in restaurants."

The two main dining rooms – the 564-seat Four Seasons Dining Room, and the 604-seat Seven Seas Dining Room, have tables for two, four, six or eight. Sandwiched between the two (rather like a train carriage) is a third, 84-seat Italian Restaurant, Il Adagio, available as an à la carte dining option (for which there is an extra charge), with window-side tables for two or four persons. Reservations are necessary.

There are also several other dining options, most located on one of the upper-most decks of the ship, with great views from large picture windows. These include:
● **Le Bistro:** a 90-seat alternative dining spot for some fine French-style meals, including tableside cooking. Reser-

vations are necessary for dinner.
● **Las Ramblas:** a Spanish/Mexican style eatery serving tapas (light snack items).
● **Ginza:** a Japanese Restaurant, with a sushi bar (all you can eat for $10) and a teppanyaki grill (show cooking in a U-shaped setting where you sit around the chef). Reservations are needed for dinner.
● **East Meets West:** a Pacific Rim Fusion Restaurant, featuring à la carte California/Hawaii/Asian cuisine. Reservations are necessary for dinner.
● **Pacific Heights:** a Healthy Living Restaurant (with 80 seats), featuring spa cuisine and Cooking Light menus. Reservations are necessary for dinner.
● **Garden Cafe:** a busy 24-hour restaurant indoor/outdoor self-serve buffet-style eatery with fast foods and salads.

Although the menus make meals sound appetizing, overall the food is rather unmemorable, lacking taste and mostly overcooked. However, the presentation is generally quite good. There is a reasonable selection of breads, rolls, and pastry items, but the selection of cheeses is very poor.

The wine list is well balanced, and there is also a connoisseur list of premium wines, although the vintages tend to be young. There are many types of beer (including some on draught in the popular Sports Bar & Grill).

There is no formal afternoon tea, although you can make your own at beverage stations (but it's difficult to get fresh milk as non-dairy "creamers" are typically supplied). The service is, on the whole, adequate, nothing more.

A lavish "chocoholics" buffet is featured once each cruise – a firm favorite among NCL passengers.

ENTERTAINMENT. The Stardust Theater is a two-level show lounge with more than 1,000 seats and a large proscenium stage. However, the sightlines are obstructed in a number of seats by several slim pillars. Two or three production shows are presented in a typical 7-day cruise (all ably performed by the Jean Ann Ryan Company). These are all very colorful, high-energy, high-volume razzle-dazzle shows (with much use of pyrotechnics, laser and color-mover lighting). The ship carries a number of bands and solo entertaining musicians. These provide live music for listening and dancing in several of the lounges and bars, including the loud Dazzles, home to musical groups.

SPA/FITNESS. Bodywaves, at the top of the atrium, is a large health/fitness spa (including an aerobics room and separate gymnasium), several treatment rooms, and men's and women's saunas/steam rooms and changing rooms.

There is a wrap-around indoor-outdoor jogging track. a large basketball/volleyball court, baseball-batting cage, golf-driving range, platform tennis, shuffleboard and table tennis facilities, and sports bar with 24-hour live satellite TV coverage of sports events and major games.

● **For more extensive general information on what an NCL cruise is like, see pages 131–33.**

Ocean Dream
★★★

Mid-Size Ship: . . . . .35,190 tons	Passenger Decks: 10	Cabins (for one person): 0
Lifestyle: . . . . .Standard	Total Crew: 550	Cabins (with private balcony): 12
Cruise Line: . . . . .Pullmantur Cruises	Passengers	Cabins (wheelchair accessible): 11
Former Names: . . . . .Pacific Star,	(lower beds/all berths): 1,022/1,350	Cabin Current: . . . . .110/220 volts
Costa Tropicale, Tropicale	Passenger Space Ratio	Elevators: 8
Builder: . . . . . . .Aalborg Vaerft (Denmark)	(lower beds/all berths): 34.4/26.0	Casino (gaming tables): . . . . .Yes
Original Cost: . . . .$100 million	Crew/Passenger Ratio	Slot Machines: . . . . .Yes
Entered Service: . . . . .Jun 1982/Mar 2008	(lower beds/all berths): 1.8/2.5	Swimming Pools (outdoors): 3
Registry: . . . . .The Bahamas	Navigation Officers: . . . . .European	Swimming Pools (indoors): 0
Length (ft/m): 671.7/204.76	Cabins (total): 511	Whirlpools: 0
Beam (ft/m): 86.7/26.45	Size Range (sq ft/m): 180.0–398.2/16.7–37.0	Self-Service Launderette: . . . . .Yes
Draft (ft/m): 23.3/7.11	Cabins (outside view): 324	Dedicated Cinema/Seats: . . . . .No
Propulsion/Propellers: diesel (19,566kW)/2	Cabins (interior/no view): 187	Library: . . . . .Yes

BERLITZ'S OVERALL SCORE: 1,110 (OUT OF A POSSIBLE 2,000 POINTS)

OVERVIEW. *Ocean Dream*, now over 25 years old, was originally the first new ship ordered by Carnival Cruise Lines. The ship was sent to Costa Cruises in 2001. Pullmantur Cruises acquired and refurbished it in 2008. It has a fairly distinctive, though boxy look and profile. The ship's open deck space is very limited, and there is no walk-around promenade deck outdoors.

The interior layout and passenger flow is generally good. The public rooms are bright and cheerful, with many bold, bright color splashes. Rooms include a card room, internet-connect center, piano bar, and several bars and lounges. Pullmantur Cruises understands and caters to young cruisers as well as their parents, particularly during school vacation periods.

This is a very standard product, with banquet catering. But families should have fun in the sun; there are plenty of opportunities for gaming and partying. The onboard currency is the euro, and all drinks and gratuities are included, so it's really a good-value, drinks-inclusive vacation for the whole family.

SUITABLE FOR: *Ocean Dream* is best suited to Spanish-speaking families, young couples, and singles seeking a standard cruise in modestly contemporary surroundings.

ACCOMMODATION. There are nine cabin price categories. Most of the "standard" interior (no view) and outside-view cabins are all of the usual cookie-cutter variety (but of a decent size), with an imaginative European-style decor, and just enough closet and drawer space for a week's cruise. A number of cabins have third and fourth person upper berths – useful for families with small children. The bathrooms are plain, but adequate for short cruises, although there's lit-

BERLITZ'S RATINGS		
	Possible	Achieved
Ship	500	271
Accommodation	200	113
Food	400	209
Service	400	246
Entertainment	100	58
Cruise	400	213

tle storage space for personal toiletry items.

The largest accommodation is in 12 "suites" – each with a small (narrow) semi-private balcony. Naturally, there is more space, with the living and sleeping areas divided. The bathrooms are marginally larger, too. However, all of these suites have their views substantially blocked by the positioning of the lifeboats. The cabin soundproofing could be better, and the room service menu is quite basic.

CUISINE. The Restaurant Principal is on the ship's lowest deck. It is colorful, very cheerful, brightly lit, but noisy and rather cramped, making proper service quite difficult. There are tables for four, six or eight (none for two), and dining is in two seatings (dinner on European cruises is typically at 7pm and 9pm).

The Buffet Panorama is a self-service buffet facility, with European selections that are quite basic, as is the selection of breads, rolls, fruit and cheeses. At night, as the Lido Café, it becomes a bistro and provides a casual (dress-down) alternative to eating in the main dining room. There's also a pizzeria. Good cappuccino and espresso coffees are available in the various bars.

ENTERTAINMENT. The Salon de Espectaculos (showlounge) is a single-level room that has bright, cheerful decor, although sightlines to the stage are obstructed from several seats. A mix of banquette and individual seating is provided, together with small drinks tables.

SPA/FITNESS. The spa/fitness area is located just behind the ship's mast, and is small. It contains a gymnasium, sauna and changing rooms for men and women.

Ocean Majesty
★★ +

Mid-Size Ship: . . . . .10,417 tons	Propulsion/Propellers: . . . . .diesel
Lifestyle: . . . . .Standard	(12,200 kW)/2
Cruise Line: . . . .Monarch Classic Cruises	Passenger Decks: 8
Former Names: . . . . . . .Homeric, Olympic,	Total Crew: .235
Ocean Majesty, Kypros Star,	Passengers
Sol Christina, Juan March	(lower beds/all berths): 535/621
Builder: . .Union Navale de Levante (Spain)	Passenger Space Ratio
Original Cost: . . . .$65 million	(lower beds/all berths): 19.4/16.7
Entered Service: 1966/Apr 1994	Crew/Passenger Ratio
Registry: .Greece	(lower beds/all berths): 2.2/2.6
Length (ft/m): 443.8/135.30	Navigation Officers: . . . . .Greek
Beam (ft/m): 62.9/19.20	Cabins (total): 273
Draft (ft/m): 19.5/5.95	Size Range (sq ft/m): .96.8–182.9/9.0–17.0
	Cabins (outside view): 186

Cabins (interior/no view): 87
Cabins (for one person): 11
Cabins (with private balcony): 8
Cabins (wheelchair accessible): 2
Cabin Current: . . . . . . .110 and 220 volts
Elevators: 3
Casino (gaming tables): . . . . .Yes
Slot Machines: . . . . .Yes
Swimming Pools (outdoors): 1
Swimming Pools (indoors): 0
Whirlpools: 1
Self-Service Launderette: . . . . .No
Dedicated Cinema/Seats: . . . . .No
Library: . . . . .Yes

OVERALL SCORE: 992 (OUT OF A POSSIBLE 2,000 POINTS)

OVERVIEW. This ship has a pleasing, balanced, almost handsome profile, with an aft funnel. Its name, *Ocean Majesty*, however, is decidedly ill-suited to such a small ship. There is a good amount of open deck space for the size of the vessel, but the plastic deck furniture looks tacky (thin blue cushioned pads are provided). There are several good public rooms, bars and lounges. The decor includes highly polished mirrored surfaces, but passageways are narrow and public rooms are only one deck high, which makes the ship feel cramped and inadequate.

BERLITZ'S RATINGS		
	Possible	Achieved
Ship	500	219
Accommodation	200	88
Food	400	217
Service	400	225
Entertainment	100	47
Cruise	400	196

The ship's size means that it can get into many ports in the Aegean and Mediterranean that larger ships cannot. It is often chartered to various tour operators and packagers, which means that the standards of product delivery can vary. In summer, it is chartered by Page & Moy for cruises to Northern Europe and the Baltic, when food and its presentation improve marginally and the onboard currency is the British pound. This is a high-density vessel, so do expect lines to form for shore excursions and buffets. Smoking is allowed only on the open decks.

SUITABLE FOR: *Ocean Majesty* is best suited to adult couples and single mature travelers, who want a basic cruise in unpretentious yet comfortable surroundings, and at a low price that offers good value for money.

ACCOMMODATION. There are 13 cabin price grades – too many for a ship of this size. Most cabins are very small and barely functional, with a reasonable amount of closet and drawer space for short cruises only (as long as you don't plan on taking many clothes). The ceilings are very plain, and the soundproofing could be better. All cabins have twin lower beds or double beds. Some also have one or two additional upper (Pullman) berths, but to accommodate three or four persons, you'd all need to be contortionists. The tiled bathrooms (all have a shower; none have a bathtub) are bright and functional, with good lighting, but do lack space for storage of toiletries.

The largest cabins are on two of the uppermost decks (Coral and Aquamarine Decks). Although there are two wheelchair-accessible cabins, wheelchair access throughout much of this small ship is quite awkward.

CUISINE. The Restaurant has two seatings. There are few tables for two; most are for eight. The cuisine is continental, with British favorites and signature dishes. There is a good selection of breads, fruits and cheeses, but the buffets are generally simple and unimaginative.

ENTERTAINMENT. The Starlight Showlounge was intended for cabaret acts and mini-revues, although some sightlines are obstructed. Audio-visual facilities are minimal.

The cabaret acts featured here are the kind that you would see aboard other cruise ships (vocalists, magicians, puppeteers, comedians and others), and are a limited in scope because of the size of the room and ship. A ship's band and small musical units provide live music for dancing and listening in the various lounges.

SPA/FITNESS. There is a tiny gym (without windows, so there's no natural light), a sauna, and a cramped, poorly lit beauty salon.

Ocean Princess
★★★★

Mid-Size Ship: . . . . .30,277 tons	Passengers	Cabin Current: . . . . .110 and 220 volts
Lifestyle: . . . . .Standard	(lower beds/all berths): 688/826	Elevators: 4
Cruise Line: . . . . .Princess Cruises	Passenger Space Ratio	Casino (gaming tables): . . . . .Yes
Former Names: .Tahitian Princess, R Four	(lower beds/all berths): 44.1/36.6	Slot Machines: . . . . .Yes
Builder: Chantiers de l'Atlantique (France)	Crew/Passenger Ratio	Swimming Pools (outdoors): 1
Original Cost: . . . .$150 million	(lower beds/all berths): 1.8/2.2	Swimming Pools (indoors): 0
Entered Service: . . . . .Nov 1999/Dec 2002	Navigation Officers: . . . . .European	Whirlpools: 2
Registry: . . . . .Gibraltar	Cabins (total): 344	(+ 1 thalassotherapy)
Length (ft/m): 593.7/181.0	Size Range (sq ft/m): . . . . .145.3 – 968.7/	Fitness Center: . . . . .Yes
Beam (ft/m): 83.5/25.5	13.5 – 90.0	Sauna/Steam Room: . . . . .No/Yes
Draft (ft/m): 19.5/6.0	Cabins (outside view): 317	Massage: . . . . .Yes
Propulsion/Propellers: . . . . .diesel-electric	Cabins (interior/no view): 27	Self-Service Launderette: . . . . .Yes
(18,600kW)/2	Cabins (for one person): 0	Dedicated Cinema/Seats: . . . . .No
Passenger Decks: 9	Cabins (with private balcony): 232	Library: . . . . .Yes
Total Crew: 373	Cabins (wheelchair accessible): 3	

OVERALL SCORE: 1,487 (OUT OF A POSSIBLE 2,000 POINTS)

OVERVIEW. *Ocean Princess* and its sister ships *Pacific Princess* and *Royal Princess* are of an ideal size for operating in the warm water regions of Tahiti and the Pacific Ocean islands. *Ocean Princess* now has an all-white hull (when owned by the now defunct Renaissance cruises, it had a black hull with white superstructure). The all-white hull makes the ship appear larger. It has a large, square-ish white funnel.

The interior decor is stunning and elegant, a throwback to ship decor of the ocean liners of the 1920s and '30s. This includes detailed ceiling cornices, both real and faux wrought-iron staircase railings, leather- and cherry wood paneled walls, *trompe l'oeil* ceilings, rich carpeting in hallways with an Oriental rug-look center section, and many other interesting (and expensive-looking) decorative touches. The overall feel is of an old-world country club. The staircase in the main, two-deck-high foyer may remind you of the one in the 1998 blockbuster movie *Titanic*.

The public rooms are basically spread over three decks. The reception hall (lobby) has a staircase with intricate wrought-iron railings. The Nightclub, with forward-facing views, sits high in the ship and has Polynesian-inspired decor and furniture.

There are plenty of bars – including one in the entrance to each of the restaurants. Perhaps the nicest can be found in the casino bar/lounge, a beautiful room reminiscent of London's grand hotels and understated gaming clubs. It has an inviting marble fireplace and comfortable sofas and individual chairs. There is also a large Card Room, which incorporates an Internet Center, with eight stations.

BERLITZ'S RATINGS		
	Possible	Achieved
Ship	500	406
Accommodation	200	155
Food	400	265
Service	400	287
Entertainment	100	72
Cruise	400	302

The Library is a grand room, designed in the Regency style (it was designed by Scottish interior designer John McNeece), and has a fireplace, a high, indented, *trompe l'oeil* ceiling, and an excellent selection of books, plus some comfortable wingback chairs with footstools, and sofas you can easily fall asleep on – it's the most relaxing room aboard.

The value for money is extremely good, and gives you with a chance to cruise in comfort aboard a mid-sized ship with some interesting dining choices. There's very little entertainment, but it is certainly not needed in these cruise areas. *Ocean Princess* is much more about relaxation than the larger ships in the fleet, and would make a good child-free vessel.

In common with all ships in the Princess Cruises fleet, 15% is added to all bar and spa accounts (drink prices are moderate, while beer prices are high), and a standard gratuity (about $10 per person, per day) is automatically added to your onboard account. If you think this is too much and want to reduce the amount, you'll need to go to the reception desk to do so.

There is no walk-around promenade deck outdoors (there is, however, a small jogging track around the perimeter of the swimming pool, and port and starboard side decks), and no wooden decks outdoors (instead, they are covered by Bolidt, a sand-colored rubberized material). There is no sauna. Stairways, although carpeted, are tinny. In order to keep the prices low, often the air routing to get to and from your ship is often not the most direct. There is a charge (tokens must be obtained from the reception desk) for using the machines in the self-service launderette (a change machine in the launderette itself would be better).

Note that getting to Tahiti is not easy (Princess Cruises mostly uses a charter airline, with very cramped seating), and flights are limited. If you make your own air travel arrangements, allow plenty of time for connections (preferably an extra day or so before your cruise).

SUITABLE FOR: *Ocean Princess* is best suited to couples (young and not so young), families with children and teenagers, and older singles who like to mingle in a mid-size ship setting with pleasing, sophisticated surroundings and lifestyle, reasonably good entertainment and fairly decent food and service, all at an affordable price.

ACCOMMODATION. There is a variety of about eight different cabin types. All of the standard interior (no view) and outside-view cabins (the lowest four grades) are extremely compact units, and extremely tight for two persons (particularly for cruises longer than seven days). Cabins have twin beds (or queen-size bed), with good under-bed storage areas, personal safe, vanity desk with large mirror, good closet and drawer space (in rich, dark woods), and bathrobe. Color TVs carry a major news channel (where obtainable), plus a sports channel and several round-the-clock movie channels. The bathrooms, which have tiled floors and plain walls, are compact, standard units, and include a shower enclosure with a removable, strong hand-held shower unit, hairdryer, 100% cotton towels, toiletries storage shelves and a retractable clothesline.

The suites/cabins that have private balconies (66 percent of all suites/cabins, or 73 percent of all outside view suites/cabins) have partial, and not full, balcony partitions, sliding glass doors, and, due to good design and layout, only 14 cabins on Deck 6 have lifeboat-obstructed views. The balcony floor is covered in thick plastic matting (teak would be nicer), and some awful plastic furniture.

Mini-Suites: The 52 accommodation units designated as mini-suites are in reality simply larger cabins than the standard varieties, as the sleeping and lounge areas are not divided. While not overly large, the bathrooms have a good-sized bathtub and ample space for storing personal toiletry items. The living area has a refrigerated mini-bar, lounge area with breakfast table, and a balcony with two plastic chairs and a table.

Owner's Suites: The 10 Owner's Suites are the most spacious accommodation, and are fine, large living spaces located in the forward-most and aft-most sections of the accommodation decks (particularly nice are those that overlook the stern, on Deck 6, 7 and 8). They have more extensive balconies that really are private and cannot be overlooked by anyone from the decks above. There is an entrance foyer, living room, bedroom (the bed faces the sea, which can be seen through the floor-to-ceiling windows and sliding glass door), CD player, bathroom with Jacuzzi bathtub, as well as a small guest bathroom.

CUISINE. Flexibility and choice are what this mid-sized ship's dining facilities are all about. There is a choice of four different dining spots (one is a casual self-serve buffet):

● **The Club Restaurant** has 338 seats (all chairs have armrests), and includes a large raised central section. There are large ocean-view windows on three sides, several prime tables overlooking the stern, and a small bandstand for occasional live dinner music. The noise level in this dining room can be high, due to its single deck height ceiling. This restaurant is operated in two seatings (the others have an open dining hours); dinner is typically 6pm and 8.15pm.

● **Sabatini's Trattoria** is an Italian restaurant, with 96 seats (all chairs have armrests), windows along two sides, and a set "Bellissima" three-hour degustation menu. The cover charge is $15 per person.

● **The Sterling Steakhouse** is an "American steak house", has 98 seats (all chairs have armrests), and windows along two sides and a set menu (together with added daily chef's specials). The cover charge is $8 per person.

● **The Lido Cafe** has seating for 154 indoors and 186 outdoors (with white plastic patio furniture). It is open for breakfast, lunch and casual dinners. It is the ship's self-serve buffet restaurant (24 hours a day), and incorporates a small pizzeria and grill. Basic salads, a meat carving station, and a reasonable selection of cheeses are served daily.

All restaurants have open-seating dining, although reservations are necessary in Sabatini's Trattoria and Sterling Steakhouse, where there are mostly tables for four or six (there are few tables for two). There is a Poolside Grill and Bar for fast food items.

ENTERTAINMENT. The 345-seat Cabaret Lounge has a stage, and circular hardwood dance floor with banquette and individual tub chair seating, and raised sections on port and starboard sides. It is not large, and not really designed for production shows, so cabaret acts form the main focus, with mini-revue style shows presented by a troupe of resident singer/dancers in a potted version of what you might experience aboard the large ships of Princess Cruises. Inevitably, art auctions and bingo are pushed almost daily. The entertainment highlight for many, however, is a song and dance show put on by locals of all ages, so you become immersed in the art and culture of the islands.

A band, small musical units, and solo entertaining pianists provide live music for shows and dancing in the various lounges and bars before and after dinner.

SPA/FITNESS. There is a gymnasium (with ocean-view windows) with some high-tech muscle-toning equipment and treadmills, steam rooms (no sauna), changing areas for men and women, and a beauty salon with ocean views. The spa is operated by Steiner, a specialist concession.

A lido deck has a swimming pool, and good sunbathing space, while one of the aft decks has a thalassaotherapy pool. A jogging track circles the swimming pool deck (but one deck above). The uppermost outdoors deck includes a golf driving net and shuffleboard court.

● **For more extensive general information about the Princess Cruises experience, see pages 134–37.**

Ocean Village
★★★ +

Large Resort Ship: ....63,524 tons	Passenger Decks: 12	Cabins (for one person): 0
Lifestyle: ....Standard	Total Crew: 514	Cabins (with private balcony): 64
Cruise Line: ....Ocean Village	Passengers	Cabins (wheelchair accessible): 8
Former Names: ...*Arcadia, Star Princess,*	(lower beds/all berths): 1,624/1,692	Cabin Current: ....220 volts
FairMajesty	Passenger Space Ratio	Elevators: 9
Builder: Chantiers de L'Atlantique (France)	(lower beds/all berths): 39.1/37.5	Casino (gaming tables): ....Yes
Original Cost: ....$200 million	Crew/Passenger Ratio	Slot Machines: ....Yes
Entered Service: .... Mar 1987/May 2003	(lower beds/all berths): 3.1/3.2	Swimming Pools (outdoors): 3
Registry: ....Great Britain	Navigation Officers: ....British	Swimming Pools (indoors): 0
Length (ft/m): 810.3/247.00	Cabins (total): 812	Whirlpools: 4
Beam (ft/m): 105.6/32.20	Size Range (sq ft/m): 148.0–538.2/	Self-Service Launderette: ....Yes
Draft (ft/m): 26.9/8.20	13.7–50.0	Dedicated Cinema/Seats: Yes/205
Propulsion/Propellers: .....diesel-electric	Cabins (outside view): 622	Library: ....No
(39,000kW)/2	Cabins (interior/no view): 190	

BERLITZ'S OVERALL SCORE: 1,351 (OUT OF A POSSIBLE 2,000 POINTS)

OVERVIEW. *Ocean Village* was originally designed and built for Sitmar Cruises, a company that was absorbed into Princess Cruises in 1988 before the ship was completed. The ship was extensively refurbished in 1997 at the Harland & Wolff shipyard in Belfast, and reconfigured specifically for British cruise passengers.

After a refurbishment intended to brighten the interior passageways, public rooms and dining spots, the former *Arcadia* morphed into *Ocean Village* in April 2003, and is now a trendy, ship that has been refreshingly designed for younger couples and families who want to take a cruise, but don't want the sedentary "eat when we tell you to and relax" image typical of traditional cruise ships.

In the 2003 refit, several new cabins were added, although the overall number of crew was reduced (not so many are needed for this more casual style of cruising, particularly in the food service areas); the casino was also relocated (it displaced the library), while the former casino has been turned into an internet center/bar, Connexions.

Ocean Village is a well proportioned ship, with a good amount of open deck space. On the open leisure deck are two pools (one has sloping steps, while the other has vertical steps; one has a sit-in bar), while the aft pool will probably be used by families with children. Four hot tubs sit on a raised platform, and two shower cubicles stand adjacent to a poolside bar.

The ship's interiors are upbeat and trendy in a high-street sort of fashion (with decor by the designers who did a good job with the ships of Aida Cruises), but also include a few items that have a link with the past, such as the art deco stainless steel balustrades and the soulless stainless steel

BERLITZ'S RATINGS		
	Possible	Achieved
Ship	500	356
Accommodation	200	138
Food	400	238
Service	400	273
Entertainment	100	72
Cruise	400	274

elevators. There aren't a lot of public rooms to play in, although one nice feature is the fact that the public rooms do have ceilings that are higher than average for contemporary cruise ships.

The focal point of the interior is a three-deck-high foyer, highlighted by a large blue and yellow painted (it's actually stainless steel underneath) kinetic sculpture resembling a Swiss Army knife (its blades move slowly) that brings one's attention to a multi-deck horseshoe-shaped staircase.

There is a domed observation lounge (the Bayside Club, which sits atop the ship, forward of the mast). It is a restful spot for cocktails; at night it turns into a night-spot/discotheque that includes not only a sunken dance floor but also exercise bicycles and step machines – a strange combination (so you can dance, drink, *and* fall off your bike!). There is an internet cafe, with five computer terminals (but no privacy screens); the charge is £7.50 for 15 minutes.

For retail therapy, several shops are clustered around the second and third decks of the three-deck high atrium lobby, plus a dedicated cinema. Other facilities include a casino (aft of the upper level of the two-deck high showlounge), The Oval lounge/bar, Connexions Bar, and the Blue Bar (a more traditional drinking lounge).

Families should enjoy the children's facilities, which are extensive. There is a children's indoor play area (Base Camp) located at the aft (blunt) end of the ship, while exterior aft decks have a paddling pool and games areas. There's also a Night Nursery for sleepovers (operates 6pm–2am, but there is a per child charge after midnight). Teenagers have their own area, The Hideout. Although supplies of disposable nappies, baby wipes and sterilizing fluids are available on board, Ocean Village recommends that you bring your own supplies and top up on board (where such things are necessarily more expensive). Babies under 6 months old are not accepted as passengers.

Ocean Village began fly-cruise operations in May 2003. The ship is based on Palma de Majorca, with flights from five UK airports (Birmingham, Edinburgh, London Gatwick, London Stansted, and Manchester). You can take a 7-day or 14-day cruise (there are two different itineraries, Palaces/Paella, and Pizzas/Pasta, which alternate each week) and add on a one-week or two-week stay at a choice of Majorcan family resort hotels (one is exclusive to Ocean Village).

The vacation includes a variety of active sports such as mountain biking, abseiling, jet skiing, jeep safaris, quad biking, parasailing, helicopter flight-seeing, and snorkeling (all are at extra cost). The ship carries a "fleet" of mountain bikes. Both active and passive cruising, therefore, are on offer.

In marketing terms, this ship and casual dress-down product is designed to compete head to head with Island Cruises and Thomson Cruises, with the same kind of itineraries and cost structure for the British market. *Ocean Village*, however, is the superior ship in terms of hardware. Basic gratuities to staff are included in the cruise/holiday price, but you'll need to budget spending money for all the little things that cost extra on board. The Cruise Comment Card is interesting, with sections for you to tick Fab, Good, OK, or Yuk!

Sadly, there is no full wrap-around promenade deck outdoors (open port and starboard walking areas stretch only partly along the sides). The elevators have a "London Underground" voice that says "mind the doors". There is no library. Standing in line for embarkation, disembarkation, shore tenders and for self-serve buffet meals tends to happen with ships of this size. Smokers are everywhere.

In spring 2007, a sister ship, *Ocean Village Two* (formerly *AIDAblu*) joined the fleet.

SUITABLE FOR: *Ocean Village* is best suited to young couples and singles of all ages, families with children and teenagers, who like to mingle in a large ship setting with plenty of life, music and entertainment for everyone, with food that is quantity rather than quality, delivered with friendly service that lacks polish, at an attractive price.

ACCOMMODATION. There are four basic types, in 14 different price grades (the price you pay will depend on the grade, location and size you choose). These include two grades of suites: 36 suites with private balcony and bathtub, plus separate shower enclosure, 2 suites with shower, but no balcony. There are also 28 suites with private balcony, and shower. All other accommodation consists of standard outside-view and interior (no view) grade cabins. Many passengers like to fall asleep with soft music playing however, because music is only available through the TV set, you can't obtain any of the music channels without having a TV picture on. When the ship was converted from *Arcadia* into

Ocean Village, the accommodation was left almost untouched. While the cabins are of modestly generous proportions, the bathroom fittings (washbasin, shower) need updating. Accommodation designated as suites did receive a facelift. Note that closets have fixed hangars; there aren't many, so you may need to ask your cabin steward for extra hangars – which will probably be of the thin wire type.

Standard Outside-view/Interior (No View) Cabins: All are equipped with twin beds that can (in most cases) be placed together to form a queen-sized bed. All have a good amount of storage space, including wooden drawer units, plus some under-bed space for luggage, and a walk-in (open) closet. A direct dial telephone is provided. However, the sound insulation between cabins is quite poor (TV sound late at night can be particularly irritating, as can loud children, or fellow passengers banging drawers). A number of cabins also have third- and fourth-person berths – good for families with children, but the drawer and storage space becomes tight, and there is only one personal safe.

The bathrooms are of a modular design, and are of quite a decent size, with good shower enclosures, and a retractable clothesline. None have tubs, except in one of the grades designated as suites, as the ship was originally built for American passengers (who prefer showers to baths). Soap is provided, and a soap/ shampoo dispenser is fitted into the shower enclosure (although there is no conditioner).

Suites: For more living space, choose one of the suite grades. Some have a small private balcony with part partition. Suite occupants also get a 100% cotton bathrobe.

Other Cabins: Lighting is very subdued, and the fittings are now quite dated (the bathroom cabinets are noisy and the washbasin is small). However, coffee and tea making facilities are provided in all cabins – a very useful item, particularly as tea/coffee costs extra in all bars.

CUISINE. The idea of Ocean Village (the company) is that the whole cruise experience should be casual, with none of the stuffiness normally associated with traditional cruise ship dining. So, the dining concept is simple: meals are taken in a self-serve buffet style setting, so you can dress as casually as you like.

To this end there are several dining spots, including two large self-serve buffet restaurants (Plantation, and Waterfront), a bistro, La Luna pizzeria on deck for lunch or dinner (there is a cover charge of £5 a person at night, when reservations are necessary). All dining spots are non-smoking.

Plantation and The Waterfront both have large ocean-view windows and self-serve buffet display counters. There are plenty of tables, most of which are for four, six or eight persons, and all cutlery is supplied in a help-yourself rack (so waiters and waitresses don't have to set tables). Plantation is open 24 hours a day, while The Waterfront (bland decor) has set opening hours, detailed in the daily program. At night, Plantation has Asian and Oriental themed buffets, with such main courses as Pork Vindaloo, Beef Biriyani, Lamb Rogan Josh, and Salmon Tikka.

For more attention, better food, and greater presentational flair, try The Bistro (located in one corner of the

Waterfront Restaurant). This dining spot features Mediterranean cuisine created by celebrity chef James Martin, who joins the occasional cruise; there's a cover charge of £8.50, and reservations are needed.

There are six main courses on The Bistro menu, including two vegetarian dishes. There is a reasonably decent selection of wines, although all are quite young.

In general, the food is typical of what you would find in a couples-only or family-style holiday village (modern British with a Mediterranean touch), with plenty of choices for families with children. It is straightforward, unfussy and unpretentious, with little use of garnishes. Vegetarian dishes are incorporated into the menu each day.

The service is warm and lighthearted, although communication in English with waiters, waitresses and bar staff (most are from Goa, in India) can be a little frustrating. You'll be able to have the "Great British Breakfast" as well as light, healthy fare.

Bar drinks are reasonably priced (there is a good range of standard brands, as well as a selection of 12 beers), and, with 35ml measures, are 40 percent larger than comparable measures on land in the UK. However, an espresso/cappuccino costs £1.35 each, and if you want bar snacks such as peanuts or crisps, you have to pay extra.

ENTERTAINMENT. The Marquee Showlounge is the venue for all of the principal entertainment events. It is a horseshoe-shaped room, with main and balcony levels (connected by two spiral staircases), and there are adequate sightlines from most of the banquette-style seating, although the sightlines from the front row seats on the upper level are obstructed by the required balcony railing.

There is a wide variety of mainly British entertainment, from production shows (accompanied by a live showband and "click" track) to cabaret-style acts that may or may not be well-known British "names" (and lesser artists). And don't be surprised if the occasional "street performer" jumps out to present an impromptu rendering in various locations.

There is plenty of live music throughout the many lounges and bars (in fact there is no bar without music, so sitting down for a quiet drink and chat is not possible).

SPA/FITNESS. Facilities include a beauty salon, gymnasium (Bayside Club), and wellness centre (called the Karma Spa), with a sauna/steam room complex, although it is located on the lowest passenger deck.

The spa is operated by Harding Brothers, a UK concession that provides the staff and a wide range of beauty and wellness treatments. Examples of treatments include: Full Body Massage, at £45 (60 minutes); Indian Head Massage, at £35; Hot/cold stone Massage, at £55; Thalgo Collagen Facial, at £50. A shampoo, cut, and blow-dry costs £28; a manicure is £15, a permanent wave £58.

It is wise to book treatments (massages, facials, etc) as soon as possible after you embark, as time slots do fill up quickly aboard large ships such as this. Some exercise classes are free, but most incur a charge (examples: Yoga at £15 for four classes, Pilates £5 per class, Fit Ball £5 per class, Personal Training £39).

Ocean Village Two
★★★ +

Large Resort Ship: ....70,285 tons	Passenger Decks: 11	Cabins (for one person): 0
Lifestyle: ....Standard	Total Crew: 621	Cabins (with private balcony): 198
Cruise Line: ....Ocean Village	Passengers	Cabins (wheelchair accessible): 10
Former Names: .....AIDAblu, A'RosaBlu,	(lower beds/all berths): 1,708/2,014	Cabin Current: ....110 and 220 volts
Crown Princess	Passenger Space Ratio	Elevators: 9
Builder: ....Fincantieri Navali (Italy)	(lower beds/all berths): 41.1/34.8	Casino (gaming tables): ....Yes
Original Cost: ....$276.8 million	Crew/Passenger Ratio	Slot Machines: ....Yes
Entered Service: ...July 1990/April 2007	(lower beds/all berths): 2.5/2.9	Swimming Pools (outdoors): 2
Registry: ....Great Britain	Navigation Officers: ....European	Swimming Pools (indoors): 0
Length (ft/m): 805.7/245.6	Cabins (total): 832	Whirlpools: 4
Beam (ft/m): 105.8/32.25	Size Range (sq ft/m): 188.3–538.2/	Self-Service Launderette: ....Yes
Draft (ft/m): 26.9/8.21	17.5–50.0	Dedicated Cinema/Seats: ....No
Propulsion/Propellers: .....diesel-electric	Cabins (outside view): 628	Library: ....No
(24,000kW)/2	Cabins (interior/no view): 197	

BERLITZ'S OVERALL SCORE: 1,365 (OUT OF A POSSIBLE 2,000 POINTS)

OVERVIEW. Originally ordered by Sitmar Cruises, the ship debuted in 1990 as *Crown Princess*. It was moved to the A'Rosa brand and in 2002, as *A'Rosa Blu*, began operating cruises for the German-speaking family market. In April 2004, it was refitted and renamed *AIDAblu* for AIDA Cruises. It became *Ocean Village Two* in 2007, a slightly larger half-sister ship to *Ocean Village One*, with a similar internal layout, but with more open deck space, and more facilities, including a superb health/fitness spa.

Ocean Village Two has a dolphin-like upper front structure made of lightweight aluminum alloy to keep the weight down in line with stability requirements (it was designed by the renowned Italian architect Renzo Piano, who designed Paris's revolutionary Centre Georges Pompidou and Japan's Kansai International Airport, Osaka). A large swept-back funnel (also made from aluminum alloy) is placed aft.

The area that received most attention in its conversion to *AIDAblu* was concentrated in what was formerly a casino; set high atop the ship in the "dolphin head". The space was been turned into an extensive, two-deck spa/wellness center *(see below)*.

Facilities that are in line with the tastes of young, active British families and single parents with children, and single travelers are provided. The interior layout is a bit disjointed, however, and takes a little getting used to (typically 60 percent of Ocean Village passengers are on their first cruise). Some innovative and elegant styling of the period is mixed with traditional features and a reasonably spacious interior layout. An understated decor of soft pastel shades is highlighted by some colorful artwork.

The atrium lobby (called the Village Square, although

BERLITZ'S RATINGS

	Possible	Achieved
Ship	500	350
Accommodation	200	140
Food	400	263
Service	400	273
Entertainment	100	72
Cruise	400	267

it's actually oval) is three decks high and is fairly elegant, with a grand staircase as its focal point, and provides a good setting for stand-up cocktail parties. However, the lobby is really a bazaar, with clothing racks, duty-free items and other items to ruin the area, as well as easels and paintings for the almost daily art auctions.

Shops, bars and lounges span out from the lobby on three decks. Other facilities include a cyber zone for internet connection, eight bars, and oodles of facilities for children, including a paddling pool for babies, a base camp and night nursery for supervised sleepovers, a chill-out room for teens (The Attic) and a noisy Sega Games Room.

This ship provides a pleasant first cruise experience in contemporary, comfortable surroundings, and the young, vibrant staff will make you feel welcome. Although the ads say "the cruise for people who don't do cruises," the reality is that it is still a cruise.

Standing in line for embarkation, disembarkation, shore tenders and for the self-serve buffet meals in the main dining spots happens aboard any large ship such as *Ocean Village Two*. There is no decent forward observation viewpoint indoors. There is no outdoors walk-around promenade deck (the only walking space being along the port and starboard sides of the ship); in fact, there is little contact with the outdoors, and sunbathing space is really limited. However, with destination-intensive itineraries, most first-time passengers will want to be off exploring the ports of call.

Other niggles include the fact that there are many support pillars throughout the public rooms that obstruct the sightlines and impede passenger flow, and there's no library (take your own reading material). Oh, by the way, leave the tux (and even your jacket) at home, this is casual cruising – tattoos and tee-shirts are *de rigueur*. Social manners and etiquette obviously do not do cruises, either, and what's missing is contact between officers and passengers.

SUITABLE FOR: *Ocean Village Two* is best suited to young UK couples, single travelers, families, and single parent families with children seeking a good value for money first cruise in a casual, large ship setting, with appealing itineraries and destinations, a range of fun-filled activities and a holiday camp party atmosphere at night. *OV Two* has more and better facilities than OV *One*, albeit in a larger ship, with many high ceilinged public rooms. Basic gratuities are included, but you can provide extra tips if you wish.

ACCOMMODATION. There are 15 price categories, including suites (with private balconies), outside view cabins and interior (no view) cabins, and special cabins for the disabled. Generally, accommodation on the higher decks will cost more, because, aboard ship, location is everything. Occupants of accommodation designated as suites (there are 14 of them) and junior suites (there are 36) also have access to an extra-cost private lounge in which to escape from the constant music and noise everywhere else.

Ocean Village has also recognized that single-parent families comprise an increasing number of today's cruise passengers, and so a good number of two-bed cabins have had a third (or third/fourth) pull-down berth added.

In general, the cabins are well designed and have large bathrooms as well as good soundproofing. Walk-in closets, refrigerator, kettle (yes, you can make tea or coffee in your cabin), personal safe, color TV and interactive video system are provided in all cabins, but chocolates on your pillow are not. Twin beds convert to queen-size beds in most cabins. Bathrobes and personal toiletry amenities are provided. The outside-view cabins for the disabled have views that are obstructed by lifeboats, as do some other cabins on the same deck (Deck 8).

Suites: The most expensive suites (there are 36) have a private balcony, and are quite well laid out to a practical design that positions most things in just about the right place. The bedroom is separated from the living room by a heavy wooden door, and there are TV sets in both rooms. The closet and drawer space is very generous, even for two back-to-back cruises.

CUISINE. There are two principal restaurants, several decks apart: Plantation, and The Waterfront (both are for self-serve buffet-style meals) There are a few tables for two, but most are for four, six or eight; the most desirable tables (seating six persons) are those overlooking the stern. Food islands break up the traditional straight line buffets, and make these casual dining venues more appetizing. Plantation is open 24 hours a day, while The Waterfront is open at times given in the daily program. Breakfasts tend to be repetitive and unimaginative; lunches and dinners are somewhat better – and there's food 24 hours a day if you need it. **Alternative Dining Options:** For a treat or special cele-

bration, extra-charge full service dining is available in a 68-seat bistro-style restaurant, with menu items designed by celebrity chef James Martin. The Bistro is forward of the main pools, on the starboard side, accessed by the forward stairway. The cover (service) charge of £15 (US$30) is worth it because the meals have lots of taste and neat flavor combinations, but the TV screens showing meals being prepared in the kitchen are intrusive and not at all appetizing.

La Luna is a small, casual deck restaurant serving Mediterranean-style food (including pizzas); it is adjacent to the aft pool and funnel, and features surf 'n' turf as well as pizzas and other Italian food. The cover (service) charge is £5 (US$10).

For coffee, tea and sweet snacks during the day, and drinks in the evening, try Charlie's Bar, an extra-cost patisserie/bar located on the lower level of the spacious lobby. Each evening, tapas are available free at the Balcony Bar.

ENTERTAINMENT. The Marquee Theatre is the venue for the ship's main entertainment events. It spans two decks, with seating on both main and balcony levels (note that several support pillars obstruct sightlines from a number of seats). There is plenty of colorful entertainment, including a song and dance troupe, and cabaret acts.

A high-energy acrobatic-cum-dance deck show is provided for warm nights under the stars, on a stage and acrobatic archway that was fitted during the conversion to *Ocean Village Two*.

Other entertainment includes comedy, and musical entertainers who sing to background tracks (Music Munus One comes to mind).

SPA/FITNESS. The Karma Spa is an extensive wellness center that spans two decks, and measures almost 14,000 sq. ft (1,300 sq. meters); a staircase connects two levels. Located at the top of the ship at the forward stairway, it occupies the space in the "dolphin head" section (the casino under the ship's first operators). Walking the treadmills or exercycling and facing out to sea (albeit on the port side) feels like you're doing so in the upper deck of a Boeing 747, with its curved surfaces.

Panoramic saunas and Hammam steam room are on the lower level (a 7-day pass for the sauna and steam rooms costs £35; a two-hour pass is £10). The reception area has a waterfall and cypress trees, and there are 11 treatment rooms for facials, massage (including hot stones and couples massage), manicure and pedicure, dry float and hydrobath; there is also a solarium, and a four-person relaxation room. One other neat feature is a small food bar with a choice of healthy spa dishes. It's a very nice spa facility.

The spa is operated by Harding Brothers, a specialist concession. Some exercise classes and health talks are free; others incur a charge. Body pampering treatments include various types of massage such as hot-stone massage (£75 for 75 minutes); OV2 facial (£99 for 90 minutes; Monticelli mud wrap (£65); £50 for 45 minutes); teeth whitening (£135); manicure (£55 for 60 minutes); men's shaving routine (£30); Cut and Blow Dry (£40).

Large Resort Ship:	........77,499 tons	Total Crew:	850
Lifestyle:	.................Standard	Passengers	
Cruise Line:	.............P&O Cruises	(lower beds/all berths):	.....1,950/2,272
Former Names:	.........Ocean Princess	Passenger Space Ratio	
Builder:	.............Fincantieri (Italy)	(lower beds/all berths):	.......39.7/34.1
Original Cost:	.............$300 million	Crew/Passenger Ratio	
Entered Service:	.....Feb 2000/Nov 2002	(lower beds/all berths):	.........2.2/2.5
Registry:	..................Bermuda	Navigation Officers:	.............British
Length (ft/m):	............857.2/261.30	Cabins (total):	975
Beam (ft/m):	............105.6/32.20	Size Range (sq ft/m):	......158.2–610.3/
Draft (ft/m):	.................25.9/7.9		14.7–56.7
Propulsion/Propellers:	.....diesel-electric	Cabins (outside view):	603
	(28,000 kW)/2	Cabins (interior/no view):	372
Passenger Decks:	10	Cabins (for one person):	0

Cabins (with private balcony): 410
Cabins (wheelchair accessible): 19
Cabin Current: ....110 and 220 volts
Elevators: 11
Casino (gaming tables): ....Yes
Slot Machines: ....Yes
Swimming Pools (outdoors): 4
Swimming Pools (indoors): 0
Whirlpools: 5
Self-Service Launderette: ....Yes
Dedicated Cinema/Seats: ....No
Library: ....Yes

OVERALL SCORE: 1,502 (OUT OF A POSSIBLE 2,000 POINTS)

OVERVIEW. The all-white *Oceana* has a pleasing profile for a large ship, and is well balanced by its large funnel, which contains a deck tennis/basketball/ volleyball court in its sheltered aft base. There is 93,000 sq. ft (8,600 sq. meters) of space and a wide, teakwood wrap-around promenade deck outdoors. A great amount of glass area on the upper decks provides plenty of light and connection with the outside world. The ship underwent a few changes to make it more user-friendly for British (rather than American) passengers.

The ship, while large, absorbs passengers well, although its open lounge architecture means bleed-through music and little sense of intimacy. Its interiors are pretty and warm, with attractive colors and welcoming decor that includes some attractive wall murals and other artwork.

There is a wide range of public rooms, with several intimate rooms and spaces, so that you don't feel overwhelmed by large spaces. The interior focal point is a large four-deck-high atrium lobby with winding, double stairways and two panoramic glass-walled lifts.

There is plenty of space throughout the public areas, and the traffic flow is quite good. The library is a warm room and has six large buttery leather chairs for listening to compact audio discs, with ocean-view windows.

The collection of artwork is decent, particularly on the stairways, and this helps make the ship feel smaller than it really is. The Monte Carlo Club Casino, while large, is not really in the main passenger flow and so it does not generate the "walk-through" factor found aboard so many ships. Without question, the most traditional room aboard is the Yacht and Compass Bar, decorated in the style of a turn-of-

BERLITZ'S RATINGS		
	Possible	Achieved
Ship	500	416
Accommodation	200	159
Food	400	258
Service	400	290
Entertainment	100	81
Cruise	400	298

the-century gentleman's club, with wood paneling and comfortable seating.

Ballroom dance fans will be pleased to note that there are several good-sized wooden dance floors. The ship usually carries a professional dance couple as hosts and teachers, and there is plenty of dancing time included in the entertainment programming.

Children have their own Treasure Chest (for ages 2–5), The Hideout (6–9 year-olds), and for older children (aged 10–13) there is The Buzz Zone. P&O Cruises provides an abundance of staff to look after the children, as well as many activities to keep them out of adult areas. A night nursery is available from 6pm to 2am (there is a per child charge after midnight). While many children don't like organized clubs, they will probably find they make new friends quickly during a cruise.

As is the case aboard most large ships, if you live in the best accommodation (a suite), you will be well attended; if you do not, you will merely be one of a very large number of passengers aboard a ship that caters to families with children (lots of them in peak vacation periods). One nice feature is the Captain's cocktail party – it is held in the four-deck-high main atrium so you can come and go as you please, with no standing in line to have your photograph taken with the captain if you don't want to.

This ship is all about British-ness and will be comfortingly familiar for families with children who want to go abroad but take their British traditions and food with them. Most cabin stewards and dining room personnel are from India, and provide service with a well-balanced smile and warmth that many other nationals find difficult to equal.

However, note that in the quest for increased onboard

revenue (and shareholder value), even birthday cakes are an extra-cost item, as are espressos and cappuccinos (fake ones, made from instant coffee, are available in the dining rooms). Also at extra cost are ice cream, and bottled water (these can add up to a considerable amount). You can expect to be subjected to a stream of flyers advertising daily art auctions, "designer" watches and other promotions. For gratuities (which are optional), you should typically allow £3.50 (about $5.50) per person, per day. The onboard currency is the British pound.

A fine British brass band send-off accompanies all sailings from Southampton. Other touches include church bells that sound throughout the ship for the interdenominational Sunday church service. A coach service for any passengers embarking or disembarking in Southampton covers much of the UK. Car parking is also available (there is one rate for undercover parking, one rate for parking in an open compound).

There are a number of dead ends in the interior layout, so it's not as user-friendly as it should be. Standing in line for disembarkation, shore tenders and for self-serve buffet meals is an inevitable aspect of cruising aboard all large ships. You may be subjected to announcements for revenue-producing activities such as art auctions, bingo, horse racing that intrude constantly into your cruise.

The swimming pools are actually rather small and will be crowded when the ship is full; also the pool deck is cluttered with white, plastic deck lounge chairs, which don't have cushioned pads (the rule about not leaving sun-loungers unattended for more than half an hour is flouted by most British passengers, who are keen to keep their favored position).

SUITABLE FOR: *Oceana* is best suited to adults of all ages (couples and single travelers, young and not so young), and families with children of all ages. The ship is particularly suitable as an excellent value for money cruise for first-time tabloid-reading passengers.

ACCOMMODATION. There are 19 different cabin grades, designated as: suites (with private balcony), mini-suites (with private balcony), outside-view twin-bedded cabin with balcony, outside-view twin bedded cabin, and interior (no view) twin-bedded cabins. The price you pay will depend on the grade, location and size you choose. Although the standard outside-view and interior (no view) cabins are a little small, they are well designed and functional in layout, and have earth tone colors accentuated by splashes of color from the bedspreads. Proportionately, there are quite a lot of interior (no view) cabins.

The cabin numbering system is illogical, with numbers going through several hundred series on the same deck. The walls of the passenger accommodation decks are very plain (some artwork would be an improvement).

Many of the outside-view cabins have private balconies, and all seem to be quite well soundproofed, although the balcony partition is not of the floor to ceiling type, so you can hear your neighbors clearly (or smell their smoke). The balconies are very narrow, and only just large enough for two small chairs, and there is no dedicated outdoor balcony lighting. Many cabins have third- and fourth-person upper bunk beds – these are good for families with children. Tea and coffee-making facilities are provided in all cabins – a comforting addition.

There is a reasonable amount of closet and abundant drawer and other storage space in all cabins; although this is adequate for a 7-night cruise, it could prove to be quite tight for longer. Also provided are a color television, and refrigerator, and each night a chocolate will appear on your pillow. The cabin bathrooms are practical units, and come complete with all the details one needs, although again, they really are tight spaces, best described as one person at-a-time units. Fortunately, they have a shower enclosure of a decent size, a small amount of shelving for your personal toiletries, real glasses, and a hairdryer.

High-quality personal toiletries are by Temple Spa; suite occupants get larger bottles and a wider selection.

Also standard in all cabins are Slumberland 8-inch sprung mattresses, 10.5 tog duvets (blankets and pillows if you prefer), Egyptian cotton towels, improved tea/coffee making facilities with speciality teas (long-life is provided) and a Nick Munro-designed bespoke tray.

Suites: The largest accommodation is in six suites, two on each of three decks at the aft of the ship (with a private balcony giving great views over the stern). Each of these suites – Oronsay, Orcades, Orion, Orissa, Orsova, Orontes, all P&O ships of yesteryear – has a large private balcony. They are well laid out, and have large, marble-clad bathrooms with two washbasins, a Jacuzzi bathtub, and a separate shower enclosure. The bedroom has generous amounts of wood accenting and detailing, indented ceilings, and TV sets in both bedroom and lounge areas, which also have a dining room table and four chairs.

Mini-Suites: Mini-suites typically have two lower beds that convert to a queen-sized bed. There is a separate bedroom/sleeping area with vanity desk, and a lounge with sofa and coffee table, indented ceilings with generous amounts of wood accenting and detailing, walk-in closet, and a larger, marble-clad bathroom with Jacuzzi bathtub and separate shower enclosure. There is a private balcony.

Standard Outside-view/Interior (No View) Cabins: A reasonable amount of closet and abundant drawer and other storage space is provided in all cabins (adequate for 7 nights but a little tight for longer cruises), as are a TV set and refrigerator. Each night a chocolate will appear on your pillow. The cabin bathrooms are practical, and come with all the details one needs, although they really are tight spaces, best as one-person at-a-time units. They do, however, have a decent shower enclosure, a small amount of shelving for personal toiletries, real glasses, and a hairdryer.

You can receive BBC World channel on the in-cabin color television system (when available, depending on cruise area), as well as movies (there is no dedicated theater aboard this ship). The cabin service menu is rather limited, and presentation of the food items could be better.

CUISINE. There are two principal asymmetrically designed dining rooms, Adriatic and Ligurian (each seats about 500), located adjacent to the two lower levels of the four-deck high atrium lobby. Both dining rooms are non-smoking, as are the dining rooms aboard all ships of P & O Cruises, and which one you are assigned to will depend on the location of your accommodation. Each has its own galley and each is split into multi-tier sections, which help create a feeling of intimacy, although there is a lot of noise from the waiter stations adjacent to many tables. Breakfast and lunch are provided in an open-seating arrangement, while dinner is in two seatings.

The cuisine is decidedly British – a little adventurous at times, but always with plenty of curry dishes and other standard British items. Don't expect exquisite dining – this is British hotel catering that doesn't pretend to offer caviar and other gourmet foods. But what it does present is attractive and tasty, with some excellent gravies and sauces to accompany meals.

In keeping with the Britishness of P&O Cruises, the desserts are always good. A statement in the onboard cruise folder states that P&O Cruises does not knowingly purchase genetically modified foods, though it makes no mention of all those commercial American cereals.

The service is provided by a team of friendly stewards – most from India, with which P&O has had a long relationship. The wine list is quite reasonable. A 15% gratuity is added to all beverage bills, including wines.

The Plaza, a self-serve buffet, is located above the navigation bridge, with some commanding views. At night, this large room (there are two food lines – one each on both port and starboard sides) is transformed into an informal dinner setting with sit-down waiter service. For an extra £9.50 you can experience the "Tasting Menu" – a selection of small cosmopolitan dishes, with three different menus per cruise.

Outdoors on deck, with a sheltered view over the Riviera Pool, the Horizon Grill has fast-food items for those who don't want to change from their sunbathing attire.

For other informal eats, there is also Café Jardin, with a Frankie's Bar & Grill-style menu serving Italian inspired dishes such as antipasti, glazed belly pork Marco Polo and rib-eye steak alla rosmarino. Upgraded in a March 2008 refit, it is on the uppermost level of the four-deck high atrium lobby.

In addition, there is Explorer's (for cappuccino, espressos and pastries), and Magnums (a champagne/ caviar bar).

ENTERTAINMENT. There are two showlounges (Footlights Theatre, and Starlights), one at each end of the ship. The Footlights, located at the forward end of the ship, is a superb 550-seat, theater-style showlounge, for production shows and theater events (movies can also be shown here), while Starlights is a 480-seat cabaret-style lounge with bar.

P&O Cruises places a big emphasis on a decent quality of entertainment. To this end, the ship has a group of actors, singers and dancers resident aboard *Oceana*. They provide theater-style presentations such as mini versions of well-known musicals. In addition, the ship features a whole array of cabaret acts. Although many of the cabaret acts are not what you would call headliners, they do regularly travel the cruise ship circuit. Classical concerts are scheduled for many of the cruises throughout the year.

Ballroom dance aficionados will be pleased to note that there are several good-sized wooden dance floors aboard this ship, and P&O Cruises carries a professional dance couple as hosts and teachers (there is plenty of dancing time included in the entertainment programming).

SPA/FITNESS. The Ocean Spa has facilities that are contained in a glass-walled complex located on one of the highest decks at the aft part of the ship. It includes a gymnasium, with all the associated high-tech muscle-pumping equipment, a combination aerobics/exercise class room, sauna, steam room, and several treatment rooms. If you want to book spa treatments (massage, facial, hair beautification), it is wise to do so as soon after you embark as possible, as time slots do fill up quickly aboard large ships such as this.

The spa is operated by Harding Brothers, a UK concession that provides the staff and range of beauty and wellness treatments. Examples of treatments include: Body Toning (detox for the body); Body Bien Etre (body scrub and massage); Seaweed Wrap; Collagen Velvet Facial Mask.

One swimming pool is "suspended" aft between two decks and forms part of the spa complex (two other pools are located in the center of the ship), although they are not large for the size of the vessel. Sports facilities are located in an open-air sports deck positioned inside the ship's funnel structure and can be adapted to basketball, volleyball, badminton or paddle tennis. Joggers can exercise on the wrap-around open Promenade Deck. There's an electronic golf simulator (no need to bring your own clubs).

● **For more extensive general information about the P&O Cruises experience, see pages 133–34.**

Oceanic
★★ +

Mid-Size Ship: . . . . .38,772 tons	Total Crew: 565	Cabins (wheelchair accessible): 1
Lifestyle: .Standard	Passengers	Cabin Current: . . . . .110 volts
Cruise Line: . . . . .Pullmantur Cruises	(lower beds/all berths): 1,124/1,800	Elevators: 5
Former Names: . . .*Big Red Boat I, Oceanic*	Passenger Space Ratio	Casino (gaming tables): . . . . .Yes
Builder: . . . .Cantieri Riuniti dell' Adriatico	(basis 2): 34.7/21.54	Slot Machines: .Yes
(Italy)	Passenger Space Ratio	Swimming Pools (outdoors): 2
Original Cost: . . . .$40 million	(all berths): 21.5/3.1	Swimming Pools (inside): 0
Entered Service: . . . . .Apr 1965/May 2001	Navigation Officers: . . . . .Spanish	Whirlpools: 3
Registry: . . . . .Spain	Cabins (total): .562	Fitness Center: .Yes
Length (ft/m): 782.1/238.40	Size Range (sq ft/m): 139.9–454.2/	Sauna/Steam Room: . . . . .No/No
Beam (ft/m): 96.5/29.44	13.0–42.2	Massage: . . . . .Yes
Draft (ft/m): 28.2/8.60	Cabins (outside view): 252	Self-Service Launderette: . . . . .No
Propulsion/Propellers: . . . . .steam turbine	Cabins (interior/no view): 310	Cinema/Seats: .No
(45,100 kW)/2	Cabins (for one person): 0	Library: . . . . .Yes
Passenger Decks: 10	Cabins (with private balcony): 21	

OVERALL SCORE: 1,047 (OUT OF A POSSIBLE 2,000 POINTS)

OVERVIEW. Constructed with a strong, riveted hull, this classic ocean liner (built for the long-defunct Home Lines), *Oceanic* (the ship's first name), underwent a successful conversion to provide cheap and cheerful family cruises following its purchase by Premier Cruise Lines in 1985. When Premier went into bankruptcy in 2000, the ship was purchased at auction, and is presently owned and operated by Spain-based tour operator Pullmantur Cruises, which has kept the ship's exterior in good shape.

There is a reasonable amount of open teakwood-covered deck space for sunbathing, but it becomes cramped and noisy when the ship is full, and there are no cushioned pads for the white plastic sunloungers (except on the sunloungers located along the inside promenade deck). The twin swimming pools atop the ship have a sliding magrodome roof that can be used in inclement weather.

The ship's interiors and public rooms have changed little since the ship was operated by Premier Cruise Lines, and some artwork (particularly on the stairways) exist from its original operator, Home Lines. *Oceanic*, however, has been well maintained – a testament to good shipbuilding.

The interiors have upbeat decor, and cheerful soft furnishing fabrics. One neat feature is the enclosed promenades (popular on the old ocean liners crossing the North Atlantic in all weather conditions) for strolling around the ship, or for just sitting; however, table tennis tables do restrict the flow around this promenade deck. During a refurbishment in May 2000, a new kids' room and teen room were built, and an Internet Cafe was installed. Framed photographs and paintings, which are for sale, are placed on the walls of the main lounge deck.

BERLITZ'S RATINGS

	Possible	Achieved
Ship	500	246
Accommodation	200	124
Food	400	204
Service	400	214
Entertainment	100	56
Cruise	400	203

One interesting feature of the former ocean liner can be found on the aft of Lounge Deck, which has a bar outdoors (with San Miguel beer on draft), and a small enclosure with original brass emergency steering equipment, made by Hastie of Greenock, Scotland, together with the ship's wheel.

Oceanic provides a family with children with a busy, fun-filled first cruise in a classic ship setting. The good thing is that all drinks are included – so there's no signing paper chits and getting a bill at the end of your cruise. But it certainly does remind me of a summer camp at sea, particularly when school vacations mean lots (and I mean lots) of children have the run of the ship, the complaints of many passengers who have cruised aboard other cruise ships. The onboard currency is the euro.

The noise pollution is high throughout the ship, with constant repetitive announcements, and music throughout all hallways and on open decks. The interiors need more attention to detail, and cleanliness could be better. Many public rooms have numerous support pillars to obstruct sight lines. Smokers are everywhere – there is no escape. One of the most popular drinking places is the Heroes and Legends pub – it's the place to see and be seen.

SUITABLE FOR: *Oceanic* is best suited to young (and young at heart) Spanish-speaking couples, singles, and families with children of all ages who want a first cruise experience in a traditional (not new) ship, with plenty of public rooms and a lively atmosphere, food that is quantity rather than quality, at low cost.

ACCOMMODATION. *Oceanic* has a wide range of suites and

standard outside-view and interior (no view) cabins, in 12 different price categories (seven for outside-view suites, junior suites and cabins, and five for interior cabins without a view). There are far more interior (no view) cabins than outside-view cabins. There are eight deluxe suites, each with a private balcony; 65 suites (13 with a private balcony), the rest being a mixture of inside (no view) and outside (sea-view) cabins. Many of the suites have views obstructed by lifeboats. Some of the larger cabins are ideal for families with small children.

The ceiling height is good, which helps give an impression of space. All cabins have heavy-duty furniture and are quite well equipped, although many are now in need of refurbishment. Many cabins have double beds. All cabins have a television, telephone, and climate control.

CUISINE. The Seven Continents Restaurant, which operates in two seatings, is large and cheerful, but it is extremely noisy when full (some might call it ambiance). The tables (for between two and eight persons) are very close together, and chairs do not have armrests (there is simply not enough room for them). All meals are included in the price.

The cuisine is adequate, no more, and dining room service is of only a very basic standard – there is absolutely no finesse in service, although the staff is warm and friendly. The food is plentiful and tastes good, but there is a limited selection of breads, cheeses and fruits. Vegetarian selections are always available. The wine list is reasonably decent (with many Spanish wines included), and the prices are reasonable.

There's also a self-service buffet restaurant, but it's popular, noisy, and always busy.

ENTERTAINMENT. The Salon Broadway is at the forward end of the ship on the main entertainment/public room deck, called Lounge Deck. Unfortunately, the thrust stage and dance floor are located as you enter the room, rather than be located where they should be, at the opposite end. The shows consist of a troupe of showgirl dancers, whose routines are mediocre – like high-school shows.

Cabaret acts are the main feature; these include singers, magicians, and comedians, among others, and very much geared to the family audience that this ship carries for much of the time.

There is also plenty of live music for listening or dancing to in various bars and lounges, and there is the inevitable discotheque, located directly above a clutch of cabins aft on Continental Deck below.

SPA/FITNESS. Although there is no spa as such, there is a fitness room (with some antiquated equipment). There is also a beauty salon, and massage is also available (but the facilities are quite primitive).

SAFETY MEASURES

Fire Control
If anyone sounds the fire alarm, an alarm is automatically set off on the bridge. A red panel light will be illuminated on a large plan, indicating the section of the ship that has to be checked so that the crew can take immediate action.

Ships are sectioned into several zones, each of which can be tightly closed off. In addition, almost all ships have a water-fed sprinkler system that can be activated at the touch of a button, or automatically activated when sprinkler vials are broken by fire-generated heat. New electronic fire detection systems are being installed aboard ships in order to increase safety further.

Emergency Ventilation Control
This automatic fire damper system also has a manual switch that is activated to stop or control the flow of air to all areas of the ship, in this way reducing the fanning effect on flame and smoke via air-conditioning and fan systems.

Watertight Doors Control
Watertight doors throughout the ship can be closed off, in order to contain the movement of water flooding the ship. A master switch activates all the doors in a matter of seconds. All water-tight doors can be operated electrically and manually, which means that nobody can be trapped in a watertight compartment.

Stabilizers Control
The ship's two stabilizing fins can be extended, housed, or controlled. They normally operate automatically under the command of a gyroscope located in the engine control room.

Oosterdam
★★★★

Large Resort Ship:	.81,769 tons	
Lifestyle:	Premium	
Cruise Line:	Holland America Line	
Former Names:	none	
Builder:	Fincantieri (Italy)	
Original Cost:	$400 million	
Entered Service:	August 2003	
Registry:	The Netherlands	
Length (ft/m):	935.0/285.0	
Beam (ft/m):	105.6/32.25	
Draft (ft/m):	25.5/7.80	
Propulsion/Propellers:	diesel-electric	
	(34,000 kW)/2 azimuthing pods	
	(17.6 MW each)	
Passenger Decks:	11	
Total Crew:	800	
Passengers		
(lower beds/all berths):	1,918/2,387	
Passenger Space Ratio		
(lower beds/all berths):	43.6/34.2	
Crew/Passenger Ratio		
(lower beds/all berths):	2.3/2.9	
Navigation Officers:	European	
Cabins (total):	924	
Size Range (sq ft/m):	185.0–1,318.6/	
	17.1–122.5	
Cabins (outside view):	788	
Cabins (interior/no view):	136	
Cabins (for one person):	0	
Cabins (with private balcony):	623	
Cabins (wheelchair accessible):	28	
Cabin Current:	110 volts	
Elevators:	14	
Casino (gaming tables):	Yes	
Slot Machines:	Yes	
Swimming Pools (outdoors):	2	
	+1 children's pool	
Swimming Pools (indoors):	1	
	(indoor/outdoor)	
Whirlpools:	5	
Self-Service Launderette:	No	
Dedicated Cinema/Seats:	Yes/170	
Library:	Yes	

OVERALL SCORE: 1,520 (OUT OF A POSSIBLE 2,000 POINTS)

OVERVIEW. *Oosterdam* (sister ships: *Eurodam, Noordam, Westerdam* and *Zuiderdam*) is one of the latest generation of "Vista"-class ships for Holland America Line, designed to appeal to younger, more vibrant, multi-generational, family-oriented holidaymakers.

The twin working funnels are the result of the slightly unusual machinery configuration; the ship has, in effect, two engine rooms – one with three diesels, and one with two diesels and a gas turbine. A pod propulsion system is provided *(see page 174)*, powered by a diesel-electric system, with a small gas turbine located in the funnel for the reduction of emissions.

There is a complete wrap-around exterior teak promenade deck, and teak "steamer" style sunloungers are provided. Additionally, there is a jogging track outdoors, located around the ship's mast and the forward third of the ship. Exterior glass elevators, mounted midships on both port and starboard sides, provide fine ocean views from any one of 10 decks. There are two centrally located swimming pools outdoors, and one can be used in inclement weather due to its retractable sliding glass roof. Two whirlpool tubs, adjacent to the swimming pools, are abridged by a bar. Another smaller pool is available for children; it incorporates a winding water slide that spans two decks in height. There is an additional whirlpool tub outdoors.

The intimate lobby spans three decks, and is topped by a beautiful, rotating, Waterford crystal globe of the world. Adjacent are interior and glass wall elevators with exterior views. The interior decor, is bright, yet comfortable – designed to attract a younger clientele. The ceilings are particularly noticeable in the public rooms. In keeping with the

BERLITZ'S RATINGS

	Possible	Achieved
Ship	500	428
Accommodation	200	162
Food	400	269
Service	400	277
Entertainment	100	76
Cruise	400	308

traditions of Holland America Line, a large collection of artwork is a standard feature. Included are some superb paintings of former Holland America Line ships on the mid-ship stairwells by maritime artist Captain Stephen Card.

Also notable are many pieces reflecting the former Dutch East Indies. The cast-aluminum elevator doors are also interesting – the design being inspired by the deco designs from New York's Chrysler Building.

There are two whole entertainment/public room decks. Without doubt, the most dramatic room aboard this ship is the showlounge, spanning four decks in the forward section of the ship. Other facilities include a winding shopping street with several boutique stores and logo shops, an internet center, library, card room, an art gallery, photo gallery, and several small meetings rooms. The casino is large (one has to walk through it to get from the restaurant to the showlounge on one of the entertainments decks), and is equipped with all the gaming paraphernalia and slot machines you can think of. Sports enthusiasts can enjoy a basketball court, volleyball court, golf simulator. For families with children, Club HAL's KidZone provides a whole area dedicated to children's facilities and extensive programming for different age groups (5–17), with one counselor for every 30 children. The company provides free coffee at the Java Bar, and free ice cream at certain hours, as well as hot hors d'oeuvres in all bars.

This formula may not work well for those loyal repeat passengers used to the line's smaller ships. However, *Oosterdam* does offer a range of public rooms with a reasonably intimate atmosphere and the overall feel of the ship is quite homely and comforting. Perhaps the ship's best asset is its friendly and personable Filipino and Indonesian crew, although communication (in English) can be frustrating.

The information desk in the lobby is small and somewhat removed from the main passenger flow on the two decks above it. Many pillars obstruct the passenger flow and lines of sight throughout the ship. There are no self-service launderettes (something families with children might miss – although special laundry packages are available).

ACCOMMODATION. There are 24 price categories: 16 outside-view/8 interior (no view). Some cabins on the lowest accommodation deck (Main Deck) have views obstructed by lifeboats. Some cabins that can accommodate a third and fourth person have very little closet space, and only one personal safe. Some cabins have interconnecting doors – good for families with children. Occupants of suites also get exclusive use of the Neptune Lounge and concierge service, priority embarkation and disembarkation, and other benefits. In many of the suites/cabins with private balconies the balconies are not so private, and can be overlooked from various public locations.

Penthouse Verandah Suites: Two suites offer the largest accommodation (1,318 sq. ft/122.5 sq. meters, including balcony). These have a separate bedroom with a king-sized bed; there's also a walk-in closet, dressing room, living room, dining room, butler's pantry, mini-bar and refrigerator, and private balcony (verandah). The main bathroom has a large whirlpool bathtub, two washbasins, toilet, and plenty of storage space for personal toiletry items. Personalized stationery and free dry cleaning are included, as are hot hors d'oeuvres and other goodies daily.

DeLuxe Verandah Suites: Next in size are 60 of these suites (563 sq. ft/52.3 sq. meters). These have twin beds that convert to a king-sized bed, vanity desk, lounge area, walk-in closet, mini-bar and refrigerator, and bathroom with full-size bathtub, washbasin and toilet. Personalized stationery and complimentary dry cleaning are included, as are hot hors d'oeuvres and other goodies.

Verandah Suites: There are 100 of these Verandah Suites (actually they are cabins, not suites, and measure (284 sq. ft/26.3 sq. meters). Twin beds can convert to a queen-sized bed; there is also a lounge area, mini-bar and refrigerator, while the bathroom has a tub, washbasin and toilet. Floor to ceiling windows open onto a private balcony (verandah).

Outside-view Cabins: Standard outside cabins (197 sq. ft/18.3 sq. meters) have twin beds that can convert to a queen-size bed. There's a small sitting area, while the bathroom has a tub/ shower combination. The interior (no view) cabins are slightly smaller (182.9 sq. ft/ 17 sq. meters).

CUISINE. The 1,045-seat Vista (main) Dining Room is two decks high, with seating at tables for two, four, six or eight on both main and balcony levels – the galley is underneath the restaurant, accessed by port and starboard escalators – and is at the stern. It provides a traditional Holland America

Line dining experience, with friendly service from smiling Indonesian and Filipino stewards. Both open seating and fixed (assigned tables and times) seating are available, while breakfast and lunch are open-seating (you'll be seated by restaurant staff when you enter). The dining room is a non-smoking venue.

Holland America Line can provide Kosher meals, although these are prepared ashore, frozen, and brought to your table sealed in their original containers.

Alternative Dining Option: The 130-seat Pinnacle Grill is a slightly more upscale dining spot (with higher quality ingredients, and better presentation than in the larger main dining room). It is on Lower Promenade Deck, and fronts onto the second level of the atrium lobby. Pacific Northwest cuisine is featured (with items such as sesame-crusted halibut with ginger-miso, Peking duck breast with blackberry sauce, and an array of premium quality steaks). Fine table settings, china and silverware are featured, as are leather-bound menus. The wine bar offers mostly American wines. Reservations are required and there is a cover charge of $30 per person for service and gratuity.

Informal Eateries: For casual eating, there is an extensive Lido Cafe, an eatery that wraps around the funnel housing and extends aft; there are also some fine views over the ship's central multi-deck atrium. It includes a pizzeria/Italian specialties counter, a salad bar, Asian stir-fry counter, deli sandwiches, and a separate dessert buffet, although movement around the buffet area can be very slow.

There is an outdoor self-serve buffet (adjacent to the fantail pool), which serves fast-food items such as hamburgers and hot dogs, chicken and fries, as well as two smaller buffets adjacent to the midships swimming pool area, and a Windsurf Cafe in the atrium lobby (open 20 hours a day), for coffee, pastries, snack foods, deli sandwiches and liqueur coffees (evenings only) – all at extra cost.

ENTERTAINMENT. The 867-seat Vista Lounge is the ship's principal venue for Las Vegas-style revues and major cabaret shows. The main floor level has a bar in its starboard aft section. Spiral stairways at the back of the lounge connect all levels. Stage shows are best seen from the upper levels, from where the sightlines are quite good.

SPA/FITNESS. The Greenhouse Spa is a large, two-decks-high health spa, and is located directly above the navigation bridge. Facilities include a solarium, hydrotherapy pool, unisex thermal suite – a unisex area incorporating a Laconium (gentle sauna), Hammam (mild steam), and Camomile Grotto (small aromatic steam room). There is also a beauty parlor, 11 massage/therapy rooms (including one for couples), and a large gymnasium with floor-to-ceiling windows on three sides and forward-facing ocean views, and the latest high-tech muscle-toning equipment.

● **For more extensive general information on what a Holland America Line cruise is like, see pages 126–28.**

Oriana
★★★★

Large Resort Ship: ....69,153 tons	Total Crew: 760	Cabins (with private balcony): 118
Lifestyle: ....Standard	Passengers	Cabins (wheelchair accessible): 8
Cruise Line: ....P&O Cruises	(lower beds/all berths): 1,828/1,975	Cabin Current: ....110 and 220 volts
Former Names: ....none	Passenger Space Ratio	Elevators: 10
Builder: ....Meyer Werft (Germany)	(lower beds/all berths): 37.8/35.0	Casino (gaming tables): ....Yes
Original Cost: ....£200 million	Crew/Passenger Ratio	Slot Machines: ....Yes
Entered Service: ....Apr 1995	(lower beds/all berths): 2.4/2.5	Swimming Pools (outdoors): 3
Registry: ....Bermuda	Navigation Officers: ....British	Swimming Pools (indoors): 0
Length (ft/m): 853.0/260.0	Cabins (total): 914	Whirlpools: 5
Beam (ft/m): 105.6/32.2	Size Range (sq ft/m): 150.6–500.5/	Self-Service Launderette: ....Yes
Draft (ft/m): 25.9/7.9	14.0–46.5	Dedicated Cinema/Seats: Yes/189
Propulsion/Propellers: ....diesel	Cabins (outside view): 594	Library: ....Yes
(47,750 kW)/2	Cabins (interior/no view): 320	
Passenger Decks: 10	Cabins (for one person): 112	

OVERALL SCORE: 1,503 (OUT OF A POSSIBLE 2,000 POINTS)

OVERVIEW. This ship has a feeling of timeless elegance. It has a good amount of outdoor space, and enough sun-loungers for all passengers. The interiors are gentle, welcoming and restrained, and a 2006 revamp refreshed some of the interior spaces and cabins, and added more children's facilities. There is a splendid amount of open deck and sunbathing space – an important plus for its outdoors-loving British passengers. It has an extra-wide wrap-around promenade deck outdoors. The stern superstructure is nicely rounded and has several tiers that overlook the pool and children's outdoor facilities.

Inside, the well laid-out design provides good horizontal passenger flow, and wide passageways. Very noticeable are the fine, detailed ceiling treatments. As it is a ship for all types of people, specific areas have been designed to attract different age groups and lifestyles.

There is a four-deck-high atrium with a soft waterfall. It is elegant but not glitzy, and is topped by a dome of Tiffany glass. The many public rooms provide plenty of choice, with lots of nooks and crannies in which to sit and read.

The L-shaped Anderson's Lounge (named after the founder of the Peninsular Steam Navigation Company in the 1830s) contains an attractive series of 19th-century marine paintings, and is decorated in the manner of a fine British gentleman's club.

Atop the ship and forward is the Crow's Nest, a U-shaped room with one small wing that can be closed off for small groups. A long bar includes a ship model (former P&O ship *Ranpura*) in a glass case. Two small stages are set into the forward port and starboard sections, and there is a wooden dance floor. The lounge has smoking and non-smoking sections, although smoke lingers everywhere.

BERLITZ'S RATINGS		
	Possible	Achieved
Ship	500	417
Accommodation	200	157
Food	400	248
Service	400	309
Entertainment	100	82
Cruise	400	290

The library is a fine room, with a good range of hardback books (and a librarian), inlaid wood tables skillfully crafted by Lord Linley's company, and some comfortable chairs. On the second day of almost any cruise, however, the library will have been almost stripped of books by word-hungry passengers. Adjacent is Thackeray's, a writing room named after the novelist William Makepeace Thackeray, a P&O passenger in 1844. Lord's Tavern, now with more seating, is the most sporting place to pitch a beverage or two, or take part in a singalong – rather like group karaoke. It is decorated with cricket memorabilia. There's also a small casino, with table games and slot machines.

The carpeting throughout is of a high quality, much of it custom designed and made from 100% wool. There are some fine pieces of sculpture that add the feeling of a floating museum, and original artworks by all-British artists that include several tapestries and sculptures.

Children and teens have "Club Oriana", their own rooms (Peter Pan and Decibels), their own daily programming and activities, Play Station 2 units, and their own outdoor pool. Children can be entertained until 10pm, which gives parents time to have dinner and go dancing. The cabins also have a baby-listening device. A special night nursery for small children (ages 2–5) is available (6pm–midnight, no charge; from midnight to 2am there is a charge).

There is a wide variety of mainly British entertainment. There is also a program of theme cruises (antiques, art appreciation, classical music, comedy, cricket, gardening, jazz, motoring, popular fiction, Scottish dance).

Oriana provides a decent, well organized, "traditional" cruise experience. It's all about Britishness and will be comfortingly familiar for families with children who want to go abroad but take their British values and food preferences with them, and sail from a UK port. Most cabin stewards and dining room personnel are from India, and provide service with a well balanced smile and warmth that many other nationals find hard to equal. However, in the quest for increased onboard revenue, even birthday cakes are an extra cost, as are real espressos and cappuccinos (fake ones, made from instant coffee, are available in the dining rooms). Ice cream and bottled water also cost extra.

A British brass band send-off usually accompanies sailings from Southampton. Other touches include church bells sounded for the interdenominational Sunday church service. The onboard currency is the British pound. For gratuities (optional), you should allow £3 (around US$5) per person, per day.

Passenger gripes include ear-splitting announcements, poorly trained reception desk staff, and poor hospitality from many of the crew. Beware the many smokers.

SUITABLE FOR: *Oriana* is best for adults of all ages (although most cruises attract passengers over 50), and families with children of all ages who want a cruise that starts and ends in the UK, aboard a large ship with all the facilities of a small resort, with food and service that are acceptable, though not as good as aboard some other cruise ships.

ACCOMMODATION. The wide range of cabin configurations and categories (in 18 grades) includes family cabins with extra beds (110 cabins can accommodate up to four persons). In a 2006 make-over, all received new 8-inch Slumberland mattresses, duvets and high-quality bedlinen.

Standard interior (no view) cabins and outside-view cabins are well equipped, but compact. There is much use of rich, warm limed oak or cherry wood in all cabins, which makes even the least expensive four-berth cabin seem inviting. All cabins have good closet and drawer space, small refrigerator, full-length mirror, and blackout curtains (essential for North Cape cruises). Satellite television provided typically includes BBC World, although reception may not be good in all areas. Cabin soundproofing could be better.

A number of cabins are provided for passengers traveling singly. Singles who share a cabin should note that only one personal safe is provided in most twin-bedded cabins. Although the cabins for four persons (family cabins) do have four small personal safes, there are no privacy curtains.

The standard cabin bathrooms are modestly sized, and have mirror-fronted cabinets, although the lighting is quite soft; all have a wall-mounted hairdryer. High-quality personal toiletries are by Temple Spa; suite occupants get larger bottles and more of a choice.

There are eight suites, each measuring 500 sq. ft (46 sq. meters), with butler service. Features include a separate bedroom with two lower beds convertible to a queen-sized bed, walk-in dressing area, two double closets, plenty of drawer space. The lounge area has a sofa, armchairs and table, writing desk, binoculars, umbrella, trouser press, iron and ironing board, two TV sets, VCR, personal safe, hairdryer and refrigerator. The bathroom has a whirlpool bath, shower and

toilet, and there is also a guest bathroom. All in all, the suites, and particularly the bathrooms, are very disappointing when compared with similar sized suites in other ships. The private balcony has two sunloungers, tables and chairs. Suite occupants get priority embarkation, and their own lounge in the Southampton cruise terminal.

Other balcony cabins (called outside deluxe) measure 210 sq. ft (19 sq. meters). There is plenty of closet and drawer space. The bathrooms are somewhat disappointing, however, and have a very small, plain sin. One would expect marble or granite units in these grades.

CUISINE. There are two restaurants, both non-smoking and with two seatings: Peninsula (located amidships), and Oriental (located aft). The galley is located between the two restaurants. Both are moderately handsome (each has tables for two, four, six or eight).

The meals are mostly of the unmemorable "Middle-England" variety, and the presentation generally lacks creativity. Curries are heavily featured, particularly on luncheon menus. Afternoon tea is disappointing. Note that the typical menu cycle is 14 days; anyone on a long voyage may find it quite repetitive. The former Curzon Room is now a 96-seat Oriana Rhodes (a Gary Rhodes at sea) restaurant (revenue comes before classical concerts, but provides an additional dining choice – good for special occasions). The adjacent Tiffany's Bar serves as a pre-dinner ante-room.

The Conservatory is for casual self-serve breakfast and luncheon buffets, and 24-hour self-serve beverage stands (although the selection of teas is poor). On selected evenings, it becomes a reservation-only alternative restaurant, Le Bistro, with sit-down service, featuring French Bistro, Indian or Southeast Asian cuisine.

An Al Fresco Pizzeria serves pizza slices; these are bread-based and not made from pizza dough.

ENTERTAINMENT. The Theatre Royal is a well designed room, located at the forward end of Promenade Deck. It has a sloping floor, and good sightlines from most seats. There is a wide variety of mainly British entertainment, from production shows to top British "names" and lesser artists.

A second, smaller Pacific Lounge is a multi-function entertainment venue, for cabaret acts (including late-night comedy), and can also be used as a lecture room. However, pillars obstruct the stage view from a number of seats.

Ballroom dance fans will be pleased to make use of the four good-sized wooden dance floors. The ship always carries a professional dance couple as hosts and teachers.

SPA/FITNESS. The Oasis Spa is reasonably large, and provides the latest alternative treatment therapies. A gymnasium features high-tech muscle toning equipment. The unisex sauna is a large facility; there is also a steam room.

The spa is operated by Harding Brothers, a UK concession that provides the staff and beauty treatments.

● **For more extensive general information on the P&O Cruise experience, see pages 133–34.**

Orient Queen
★★★

Mid-Size Ship: . . . . .16,916 tons	Total Crew: 400	Cabins (with private balcony): 0
Lifestyle: . . . . .Standard	Passengers	Cabins (wheelchair accessible): 2
Cruise Line: . . . . . . .Louis Hellenic Cruises	(lower beds/all berths): 828/910	Cabin Current: . . . . .110/220 volts
Former Names: . . . .*Orient Queen, Bolero,*	Passenger Space Ratio	Elevators: 4
Starward	(lower beds/all berths): 26.3/18.5	Casino (gaming tables): . . . . .Yes
Builder: . . . . .A.G. Weser (Germany)	Crew/Passenger Ratio	Slot Machines: .Yes
Original Cost: .n/a	(lower beds/all berths): 2.4/2.9	Swimming Pools (outdoors): 2
Entered Service: . . . . .Dec 1968/Aug 2006	Navigation Officers: . . . . .Greek	Swimming Pools (indoors): 0
Registry: . . . . .Greece	Cabins (total): 414	Whirlpools: 0
Length (ft/m): 525.9/160.30	Size Range (sq ft/m): 111.9–324.0/	Self-Service Launderette: . . . . .No
Beam (ft/m): 74.9/22.84	10.4–30.1	Dedicated Cinema/Seats: Yes/210
Draft (ft/m): 22.5/6.86	Cabins (outside view): 192	Library: . . . . .Yes
Propulsion/Propellers: diesel (12,950kW)/2	Cabins (interior/no view): 200	
Passenger Decks: 7	Cabins (for one person): 0	

BERLITZ'S OVERALL SCORE: 1,103 (OUT OF A POSSIBLE 2,000 POINTS)

OVERVIEW. The open deck and sun-bathing space is very limited (some of the decks are of plain, painted steel), and cluttered with (wood) sunloungers and sun shade umbrellas on the aft decks. Just forward of the twin funnels is an enclosed sports facility while aft of the mast is a large solarium-style shielded housing, with multi-level lounge/bar/disco that is adjacent to one of the ship's small swimming pools.

There is a decent choice of public rooms, including six bars, all of which have clean, contemporary furnishings and upbeat, cheerful fabric colors and a mix of traditional and contemporary decor. The Greek staff is friendly and welcoming. The dress code is casual and the onboard currency is the euro.

The diesel engines are noisy and tend to "throb" in some parts of the vessel (particularly when the ship is going full speed), including in many cabins on the lower decks.

SUITABLE FOR: *Orient Queen* is best suited to adult couples and single travelers who want to visit the Greek Isles in some degree of comfort. The ship provides a good basic cruise experience in rather crowded, but moderately comfortable surroundings, at a modest price.

ACCOMMODATION. There are four Royal Suites, and 54 "suites." Otherwise the cabins are very compact units that are moderately comfortable, and are decorated in soft colors. They are, however, adequate for a short cruise experience, particularly as the ship is in port each day. While the closet space is very limited, there are plenty of drawers, although they are metal and tinny. The bathrooms are small and tight, and the towels are not large. The toilets are

BERLITZ'S RATINGS		
	Possible	Achieved
Ship	500	279
Accommodation	200	94
Food	400	221
Service	400	245
Entertainment	100	56
Cruise	400	208

of the "gentle flush" (non-vacuum) variety. Soundproofing between cabins is poor, and the air-conditioning is quite noisy.

The four Royal suites are of a decent size (for the size of the ship). There is ample floor space to walk in these suites, which have a king-sized bed, vanity desk, curtained-off closet, plenty of drawer and storage space for luggage, a lounge with a sofa that converts into an additional bed, drinks table and two chairs. A large pillar obstructs the room's flow. The bathroom has a small but deep Jacuzzi tub with integral hand-held shower. All suites/cabins have flat-screen televisions, refrigerator and telephone.

CUISINE. There are four eateries. The 444-seat Mermaid (main) Restaurant is cheerful, even almost charming, and has some prime tables that overlook the stern. Seating is at tables for four, six or eight. There are two seatings, and smoking is permitted at any table. The cuisine is Mediterranean, with some Greek specialties, while the wine list features mainly young wines. Breakfast and lunch buffets are provided indoors at the casual self-serve Horizon Café with seating provided outdoors at tables set around the aft swimming pool, but space is tight.

ENTERTAINMENT. The 420-seat El Cabaret showlounge, a single-level room, provides "low budget, low quality" entertainment. There's also a nightclub/discotheque. A casino operates during cruises from Beirut.

SPA/FITNESS. There is a beauty salon, and a massage/body treatment room – on two different decks.

Boutique Ship: . . . . .4,050 tons	Total Crew: 75	Cabins (for one person): 0
Lifestyle: . . . . .Premium	Passengers	Cabins (with private balcony): 9
Cruise Line: . . . . .Orion Expedition Cruises	(lower beds/all berths): 106/125	Cabins (wheelchair accessible): 0
Former Names: . . . . .none	Passenger Space Ratio	Cabin Current: . . . . .110/220 volts
Builder: . . . . . . .Cassens-Werft (Germany)	(lower beds/all berths): 38.2/32.4	Elevators: 1
Original Cost: . . . . .n/a	Crew/Passenger Ratio	Casino (gaming tables): . . . . .No
Entered Service: . . . . .Nov 2003/Mar 2006	(lower beds/all berths): 1.4/1.6	Slot Machines: .No
Registry: . . . . .The Bahamas	Navigation Officers: . . . . .European	Swimming Pools (outdoors): 0
Length (ft/m): 337.0/102.7	Cabins (total): 53	Swimming Pools (indoors): 0
Beam (ft/m): 46.0/14.00	Size Range (sq ft/m): 175.0–345.0/	Whirlpools: 1
Draft (ft/m): 12.6/3.8	16.3/32.1	Self-Service Launderette: . . . . .No
Propulsion/Propellers: diesel/1	Cabins (outside view): 53	Lecture/Film Room/Seats: Yes/98
Passenger Decks: 5	Cabins (interior/no view): 0	Library: . . . . .Yes (open 24 hours)

BERLITZ'S OVERALL SCORE: 1,612 (OUT OF A POSSIBLE 2,000 POINTS)

OVERVIEW. This small ship, an enlargement and refinement of two previous cruise ships built at the same shipyard, *Sun Bay* and *Sun Bay II*, is a beauty, and the latest in the quest to build the ideal expedition cruise ship. It has all the comforts of home, and then some – as well as specialist equipment for expedition cruising. Although a small ship, *Orion* has stabilizers, bow and stern thrusters for maximum maneuverability, and a fleet of 10 heavy-duty Zodiac inflatable landing craft and a fishing boat (named *BeeKay*).

There is also an aft marina platform for swimming off. Orion Expedition Cruises has a long-term charter of this fine boutique expedition vessel. There is no swimming pool, nor is one needed, but there is a hot tub, set amid an open deck, which also houses a bar, and a small rock garden/water feature. All outdoor tables, chairs, and steamer-style sunloungers are made of hardwood.

The interior decor is really warm and inviting, and provides a cozy, cosseting atmosphere that is far removed from the majority of (larger) expedition-style cruise ships today. Public rooms include an observation lounge (Galaxy Lounge), which opens onto a wrap-around open promenade deck; it also connects with the small Vega Health Spa.

Other public rooms include Leda Lounge (main lounge), a boutique, and a dedicated Cosmos Lecture Hall with surround sound system for lectures and movies. Typically, five expedition, culture, history and marine biology lecturers are carried on each expedition voyage.

The reception desk is open 24 hours a day, and there's also an internet-connect computer in the library (with its green leather seating); the cost is A$50 for two hours.

Some rooms are clustered around a glass-walled atrium and the ship's single elevator. A special "mud room" is pro-

BERLITZ'S RATINGS

	Possible	Achieved
Ship	500	422
Accommodation	200	163
Food	400	309
Service	400	300
Entertainment	n/a	n/a
Cruise	400	418

vided (complete with boot washing stations), and this is adjacent to a Zodiac/tender loading platform on the port side. The artwork features one theme, exploration, and myth associated with exploration – according to one myth, Neptune was Orion's father, for example, while Queen Eurayle of the Amazon was his mother.

This is about as far away from big cruise ships as you can get, with well-planned itineraries to some of the most remote regions of the southern hemisphere, including the islands of Papua New Guinea, the Kimberly region of Australia, "Wild" Tasmania, and Antarctica's McMurdo Sound and Ross Sea regions. If you want magic moments in soft adventure travel, wrapped in the comfort of fine surroundings and good food, then it would be hard to beat *Orion*.

But make sure you can walk well, because some of the expeditions are quite demanding. Talk about exclusive cruising – this is it. Actually, cruising is the wrong word for this type of eco-travel; it's more like having a magic carpet whisk you to destinations that most people have never heard of – particularly on the spectacular Papua New Guinea itineraries. Most yachting types tend to want to sell their own boats after being pampered aboard an *Orion* expedition voyage. Incidentally, all cabins display black and white photographs of yachts, by Beken of Cowes.

The onboard currency is the Australian dollar (A$). Note that when the ship operates in Australian waters (on Kimberly itineraries, for example), an Australian sales tax is added to all wine and beverage accounts. Bottled water is provided for all passengers at no charge.

SUITABLE FOR: *Orion* is best suited to mature couples and single travelers who like learning about nature and wildlife up close, who enjoy quietly exploring the world around them, and who would not dream of cruising in the mainstream sense aboard ships with large numbers of people and a big city environment around them. This ship is for those in search of life enrichment in high-class surroundings and the company of well-educated and well-traveled people.

ACCOMMODATION. There are four grades of suites, and two grades of cabins. No matter what grade of accommodation you book (the size and location will dictate the price you pay), the facilities are top rate. All suites/cabins feature twin beds that can be converted to a queen-sized bed, a TV set, a DVD/CD player, a mini-refrigerator, ample closet space, a small personal safe.

The marble-clad bathroom houses a small toiletries cabinet, single washbasin, and a large shower enclosure, with a retractable clothes line. Personal toiletry items (shampoo, conditioner, body lotion, shower gel, and two sizes of soap) are by Escada. All the cabinetry was custom-made, and the bathrooms were fitted individually, which is rare in today's modular-fit world.

There are 13 suites, nine of which have a small "French" balcony (meaning you can just about step out onto it), four owner's suites, six balcony suites, two Deluxe suites, and one rather odd-shaped but delightful Junior suite. These have more space, and some share a narrow communal balcony (meaning there is no partition between them), sofa, glass drinks table, and good-sized vanity desk. Only the four owners' suites have a bathtub; all other suites/cabins have large shower enclosures.

CUISINE. The Constellation Restaurant has ocean-view picture windows, artwork based on the astrological signs, and serves all passengers in one open seating. However, because of its low ceiling, it can be a rather noisy. The cuisine is extremely good and varied, and, in addition to an à la carte menu, each dinner features a four-course signature menu by one of Australia's new breed of high-profile chefs, Serge Dansereau of "The Bathers' Pavilion" in Sydney.

The portions are not large but they are colourful and creative. Expect to find Tasmanian oysters, crocodile, emu,

and kangaroo among the offerings. Place settings include Bauscher china and Hepp silverware.

The ship carries a decent range of mostly Australian wines, including outstanding reds such as Wolf Blass Black Label, and Yalumba's The Octavius Old Vine Shiraz; and whites such as Leeuwin Estate's Art Series Chardonnay, and Devil's Lair 5th Leg Chardonnay-Sauvignon. There are also some nice, less-pricey alternatives whites such as the Bunnamagoo Estate Chardonnay, and the Chain of Ponds Unwooded Chardonnay; and reds such as the Penfolds Bin 389, and the perfectly acceptable Bunnamagoo Merlot. If you want champagne, several French champagnes are available, such as the top of the range Krug Grande Cuvee, or the tasty Veuve Cliqout. Note that there is no sommelier on board, but the wines are well served by the waiters or maître d' hotel.

Delphinus Outdoor Café, an open deck aft of the Leda Lounge, serves as an al fresco dining spot for casual breakfasts, lunches, and occasional barbecue dinners.

Continental breakfast and afternoon tea are also served in the Galaxy Lounge, and espresso/cappuccinos are available (at no extra charge) in two lounges/bars and restaurant, but do watch out for the delicious brownies on the bar counter!

The service staff is Filipino; they are warm, and communicate well with passengers.

ENTERTAINMENT. There is no formal entertainment (although the ship typically carries an entertaining duo), while lecturers provide daily recaps and fascinating, in-depth talks on marine or plant biology each evening.

SPA/FITNESS. The Vega Health Spa consists of a fitness center, sauna, shower enclosure, and a private treatment room (for massages). A beauty salon is located two decks below. Spa treatments include deep tissue massage (at A$ 90 for 60 minutes); facial (A$ 60 for 30 minutes, A$90 for 60 minutes). Four top-to-toe massage experiences: each lasts 90 minutes and costs A$130); they are called Top End, Island and Reef, Tasmania, and Antarctica, and include an aromatherapy massages. The ship carries a range of personal beauty products used on board and also for sale; creams, oils and other ingredients are also mixed by the therapist and tailored to your own needs and requirements.

Pacific
★★ +

Mid-Size Ship:	20,636 tons	Total Crew:	.350	Cabins (for one person):	.0
Lifestyle:	Standard	Passengers		Cabins (with private balcony):	.0
Cruise Line:	CVC/Pullmantur Cruises	(lower beds/all berths):	.640/750	Cabins (wheelchair accessible):	.2
Former Names:	Pacific Princess, Sea Venture	Passenger Space Ratio		Cabin Current:	110 and 220 volts
Builder:	Rheinstahl Nordseewerke (Germany)	(lower beds/all berths):	32.2/27.5	Elevators:	.4
Original Cost:	$25 million	Crew/Passenger Ratio		Casino (gaming tables):	Yes
Entered Service:	Feb 1972/May 2005	(lower beds/all berths):	1.8/2.1	Slot Machines:	Yes
Registry:	The Bahamas	Navigation Officers:	European	Swimming Pools (outdoors):	.2
Length (ft/m):	553.6/168.74	Cabins (total):	.320	Swimming Pools (indoors):	.0
Beam (ft/m):	80.7/24.6	Size Range (sq ft/m):	125.9 – 441.3/	Whirlpools:	.0
Draft (ft/m):	80.8/24.64		11.7 – 41.0	Self-Service Launderette:	No
Propulsion/Propellers:	diesel (13,400 kW)/2	Cabins (outside view):	.250	Dedicated Cinema/Seats:	Yes/170
Passenger Decks:	.8	Cabins (interior/no view):	.70	Library:	Yes

OVERALL SCORE: 1,094 (OUT OF A POSSIBLE 2,000 POINTS)

OVERVIEW. As the former *Pacific Princess*, this mid-size ship was one of the pair of original "Love Boats" in the American TV series *The Love Boat*. It is quite handsome, with a relatively high superstructure and well-balanced lines, but it now needs better maintenance. There is a decent amount of open deck space and several sunbathing areas, but no walk-around promenade deck outdoors. One swimming pool has a moveable glass roof for use in inclement weather.

Inside, the public areas are quite spacious considering the size of the ship, and there are numerous public rooms, with reasonably wide passageways. These include a movie theater, and an aft lounge has a two-deck high glass wall overlooking the aft pool deck. A forward observation lounge also acts as an indoor buffet dining area. The casino and the Cova da Pirate karaoke bar are popular. There's a boutique, small library and internet-connect center.

The ship provides comfortable surroundings for the passenger who does not want to be part of larger, more impersonal ships. Concessions operate the dining, spa/beauty services, and shops. The ship is presently operated exclusively for the Brazilian market under CVC. The onboard currency is the Brazilian Real.

SUITABLE FOR: *Pacific* is best suited to Portuguese-speaking couples, singles, and families with children of all ages who want a first cruise experience in a traditional ship, with plenty of public rooms and a lively party atmosphere, food that is quantity rather than quality, at low cost.

ACCOMMODATION. There are eight price grades. The five suites are of quite a decent size, and well designed, with

BERLITZ'S RATINGS

	Possible	Achieved
Ship	500	265
Accommodation	200	111
Food	400	219
Service	400	229
Entertainment	100	54
Cruise	400	216

plenty of space to move around in (two are located forward, just under the navigation bridge, and command good views). Most other cabins have ample room, are quite well appointed, and there is plenty of closet and drawer space. The top category cabins (on Bridge Deck and Promenade Deck) have a full bathtub, while all others have a shower enclosure. None of the suites or cabins has a private balcony.

No matter what category of suites or cabin you choose, each has a TV set, telephone, personal safe and hairdryer. Some cabins have interconnecting doors, and some can accommodate a third/fourth person.

CUISINE. The Coral Restaurant is a reasonably comfortable room, and is operated in two seatings. The wine list is adequate, and prices are reasonable, although the selection is small and consists mostly of younger wines. Casual breakfasts and lunches can be taken in the observation lounge, with fine ocean views on three sides or outdoors on the Lido Deck, adjacent to the swimming pool.

ENTERTAINMENT. The "theater-in-the-round" Showlounge has banquette-style seating in several tiers, set around a "thrust" stage. The entertainment is low-key, which means only the occasional cabaret act is featured. There is live music throughout the ship for dancing.

SPA/FITNESS. The Health Spa is positioned aft on two of the uppermost decks (a stairway connects the two). A beauty salon is on the upper deck, while a gymnasium (with aft-facing ocean-view windows), three treatment rooms, and male and female saunas are on the lower level.

Pacific Dawn
★★★

Large Resort Ship: ....69,845 tons	Total Crew: 696	Cabins (for one person): 0
Lifestyle: ....Standard	Passengers	Cabins (with private balcony): 184
Cruise Line: ......P&O Cruises (Australia)	(lower beds/all berths): 1,590/1,910	Cabins (wheelchair accessible): 10
Former Names: ....*Regal Princess*	Passenger Space Ratio	Cabin Current: ....110 and 220 volts
Builder: ....Fincantieri Navali (Italy)	(lower beds/all berths): 43.9/36.5	Elevators: 9
Original Cost: ....$276.8 million	Crew/Passenger Ratio	Casino (gaming tables): ....Yes
Entered Service: .....Aug 1991/Nov 2007	(lower beds/all berths): 2.2/2.7	Slot Machines: ....Yes
Registry: ....Great Britain	Navigation Officers: ....European	Swimming Pools (outdoors): 2
Length (ft/m): 811.0/247.2	Cabins (total): 795	Swimming Pools (indoors): 0
Beam (ft/m): 105.6/32.2	Size Range (sq ft/m): 189.4–586.6/	Whirlpools: 4
Draft (ft/m): 25.5/7.8	17.6–54.5	Self-Service Launderette: ....Yes
Propulsion/Propellers: diesel (24,000kW)/2	Cabins (outside view): 624	Dedicated Cinema/Seats: Yes/169
Passenger Decks: 11	Cabins (interior/no view): 171	Library: ....Yes

BERLITZ'S OVERALL SCORE: 1,181 (OUT OF A POSSIBLE 2,000 POINTS)

OVERVIEW. In October 2007, *Regal Princess* was withdrawn from the Princess Cruises fleet and transferred to P&O Cruises (Australia) for cruises down under, as *Pacific Dawn*. As *Regal Princess*, this was the second ship in the 70,000-ton range for Princess Cruises, and as such foreshadowed the even larger ships this successful company went on to build.

The ship has rather a jumbo-jet look to it when viewed from the front, with a dolphin-like upper structure (made of lightweight aluminum alloy), and a large upright "dustbin-like" funnel (also made from aluminum alloy) placed aft. Inside, the contemporary styling of the period is mixed with traditional features and a spacious interior layout. The interior spaces are well designed, although the layout itself is quite disjointed. The understated decor of soft pastel shades is highlighted by some colorful artwork.

An observation dome, set high atop the ship like the head of a dolphin, houses a large casino, numerous rubber trees, a dance floor and live music. The ship has decent health and fitness facilities. A striking, elegant three-deck-high atrium has a grand staircase with fountain sculpture (real, stand-up cocktail parties are held here).

Characters Bar, located adjacent to the pizzeria on the open deck forward, has wonderful drink concoctions and some unusual glasses.

This ship provides a very pleasant cruise in elegant and comfortable surroundings, and an attentive staff will make you feel welcome. Princess Cruises provides white-gloved stewards to take you to your cabin when you embark, another nice touch. *Pacific Dawn* has undergone an extensive refit in order to make the ship Aussie-friendly.

However, the open deck space is extremely limited for

BERLITZ'S RATINGS

	Possible	Achieved
Ship	500	295
Accommodation	200	132
Food	400	213
Service	400	244
Entertainment	100	60
Cruise	400	237

the size of the ship and the number of passengers carried, and, sadly, there is no forward observation viewpoint outdoors. There is no wrap-around promenade deck outdoors (the only walking space being along the sides of the ship). In fact, there is little contact with the outdoors at all. The sunbathing space is really limited when the ship is full, although as many passengers are often over 50 years old, perhaps this is not quite so crucial. The interior layout is reasonable, but a little disjointed. Galley fumes seem to waft constantly over the aft open decks.

The automated telephone system is frustrating for many, and luggage delivery needs to be more efficient. Lines often form, particularly for the purser's office, and for open-seating breakfast and lunch in the dining room.

ACCOMMODATION. There are many different price grades; the price will depend on the location and size you choose. In general, the cabins are well designed and have large bathrooms as well as good soundproofing. Walk-in closets, refrigerator, personal safe, color television and an interactive video system are provided in all cabins, as are chocolates on your pillow each night.

Twin beds convert to queen-size beds in standard cabins. Bathrobes and personal toiletry amenities are provided. The outside-view cabins for disabled passengers have their views obstructed by lifeboats.

The 14 most expensive suites (each with a large private balcony) are very well equipped, with a practical design that positions most things in just the right place. They have the following names (in alphabetical order): Amalfi, Antibes, Cannes, Capri, Corfu, La Palma, Madeira, Majorca, Malaga, Marbella, Monaco, Portofino, St. Tropez, and Sorrento.

The bedroom is separated from the living room by a heavy wooden door, and there are television sets in both rooms. The closet and drawer space is very generous, and there is enough of it even for long cruises.

CUISINE. Like all dining rooms aboard Princess Cruises, the Palm Court Dining Room is a no-smoking room, and is large, although the galley divides it into a U-shape. However, there are no tables for two, although the line's marketing tag line states that this is "The Love Boat" line. Some of the most desirable tables overlook the stern. There are two seatings.

Despite the fact that the portions are generous, the food and its presentation are somewhat disappointing, and tastes bland. The quality of fish is poor (often disguised by crumb or batter coatings), the selection of fresh green vegetables is limited, and few garnishes are used. However, do remember that this is big-ship banquet catering, with all its attendant standardization and production cooking.

Meats are of a decent quality, although often disguised by gravy-based sauces. Pasta dishes are large, served by the section headwaiters. If you like desserts, order a sundae at dinner, as most other desserts are just so-so.

While ice cream ordered in the dining room is included in the price, if you order one anywhere else, you'll have to pay extra for it.

There is a good pizzeria for informal meals; this is particularly popular at lunchtime and in the afternoons. Themed late-night buffets are provided, but afternoon teas are poor. For sweet snacks during the day, a patisserie (items cost extra) is located in the spacious lobby.

ENTERTAINMENT. The International Showlounge spans two decks (with seating on both main and balcony levels). It is located at the forward most part of the ship, and accessed by the forward stairway and elevators. The lower level has seating clustered around the stage, which is called a "thrust" stage, like you would find in a true variety theatre ashore.

Princess Cruises always provides plenty of live music for the various bars and lounges, with a wide mix of light classical, jazz, and dance music, from solo entertaining pianists to large show bands, and volume is normally kept to an acceptable level.

SPA/FITNESS. The spa/fitness center is located low down in the ship (accessible by elevator and stairs), and contains a gymnasium, aerobics exercise room, steam room, sauna and changing areas, and Images, the beauty salon.

The spa is operated by Steiner, a specialist concession, whose young staff will try to sell you Steiner's own-brand Elemis beauty products.

Pacific Princess
★★★★

Mid-Size Ship: . . . . .30,277 tons	Passenger Decks: 9	Cabins (for one person): 0
Lifestyle: . . . . .Standard	Total Crew: 373	Cabins (with private balcony): 232
Cruise Line: . . . . . .P&O Cruises Australia/	Passengers	Cabins (wheelchair accessible): 3
Princess Cruises	(lower beds/all berths): 688/826	Cabin Current: . . . . . . .110 and 220 volts
Former Names: . . . . .R Three	Passenger Space Ratio	Elevators: 4
Builder: Chantiers de l'Atlantique (France)	(lower beds/all berths): 44.1/36.6	Casino (gaming tables): . . . . .Yes
Original Cost: . . . .$150 million	Crew/Passenger Ratio	Slot Machines: . . . . .Yes
Entered Service: . . . . .Aug 1999/Nov 2002	(lower beds/all berths): 1.8/2.2	Swimming Pools (outdoors): 1
Registry: . . . . .Gibraltar	Navigation Officers: . . . . .European	Swimming Pools (indoors): 0
Length (ft/m): 593.7/181.0	Cabins (total): .344	Whirlpools: . . . . . .2 (+ 1 thalassotherapy)
Beam (ft/m): 83.5/25.5	Size Range (sq ft/m): . . . . .145.3 – 968.7/	Self-Service Launderette: . . . . .Yes
Draft (ft/m): 19.5/6.0	13.5 – 90.0	Dedicated Cinema/Seats: . . . . .No
Propulsion/Propellers: . . . . .diesel-electric	Cabins (outside view): 317	Library: . . . . .Yes
(18,600kW)/2	Cabins (interior/no view): 27	

BERLITZ'S OVERALL SCORE: 1,487 (OUT OF A POSSIBLE 2,000 POINTS)

OVERVIEW. *Pacific Princess* was originally one of eight almost identical ships ordered and operated by the now defunct Renaissance Cruises. It sports an all-white hull (it was formerly a black hull with white superstructure), which makes the ship appear larger. It has a large, square-ish funnel. The vessel cruises for part of the year under the Princess Cruises banner in French Polynesia, and six months under the P&O Cruises brand name in Australia (cruising from Sydney).

A lido deck has a swimming pool, and good sunbathing space, while one of the aft decks has a thalassotherapy pool. A jogging track circles the swimming pool deck (but one deck above). The uppermost outdoors deck includes a golf driving net and shuffleboard court.

The interior decor is quite stunning and elegant, a throwback to ship decor of the ocean liners of the 1920s and '30s, executed in fine taste. This includes detailed ceiling cornices, both real and faux wrought-iron staircase railings, leather- and cherry wood-paneled walls, *trompe l'oeil* ceilings, and rich carpeting in hallways with an Oriental rug-look center section. The overall feel is of an old-world country club. The staircase in the main, two-deck-high foyer recalls the staircase in the 1997 movie *Titanic*.

The public rooms are spread over three decks. The reception hall (lobby) has a staircase with intricate wrought-iron railings. The Nightclub, with forward-facing views, sits high in the ship and has Polynesian-inspired decor and furniture.

There are plenty of bars – including one in the entrance to each restaurant. Perhaps the nicest of all bars and lounges are in the casino bar/lounge that is a beautiful room reminiscent of London's grand hotels and understated gaming

BERLITZ'S RATINGS

	Possible	Achieved
Ship	500	406
Accommodation	200	155
Food	400	265
Service	400	287
Entertainment	100	72
Cruise	400	302

clubs. It has an inviting marble fireplace (in fact, there are three such fireplaces aboard) and comfortable sofas and individual chairs. There is also a large Card Room, which incorporates an internet center with eight stations.

The Library is a beautiful, grand Regency-style room, with a fireplace, a high, indented, *trompe l'oeil* ceiling, and an excellent selection of books, as well as some very comfortable wing-back chairs with footstools, and sofas you could sleep on (it's the most relaxing room aboard).

Although there may not be marble bathroom fittings, or caviar and other expensive niceties, the value for money is extremely good, and you have the opportunity to cruise in comfort aboard a mid-sized ship with plenty of dining choices. There's very little entertainment, but it is certainly not needed in the cruise areas featured. *Pacific Princess* and sister ships *Royal Princess* and *Tahitian Princess* are much more about relaxation than the larger ships in the Princess Cruises fleet, and would make good child-free vessels.

In common with all ships in the Princess Cruises fleet, 15% is added to all bar and spa accounts (drink prices are moderate, while beer prices are high), and a standard gratuity (about $10 per person, per day) is automatically added to your onboard account (if you think this is too much and want to reduce the amount, you'll need to go to the reception desk to do so).

There is no walk-around promenade deck outdoors (there is, however, a small jogging track around the perimeter of the swimming pool, and port and starboard side decks), and no wooden decks outdoors (instead, they are covered by Bollidt, a sand-colored rubberized material). There is no sauna. The room service menu is extremely limited. Stairways, although carpeted, are tinny. In order to keep the prices low, often the air routing to get to/from your ship is not the most direct.

There is a charge (tokens must be obtained from the reception desk) for using the machines in the self-service launderette (a change machine in the launderette itself would be more user-friendly).

ACCOMMODATION. There is a variety of about eight different cabin types to choose from (the price will depend on the grade, location and size you choose).

All of the standard interior (no view) and outside-view cabins are extremely compact units, and extremely tight for two persons (particularly for cruises longer than seven days). Cabins have twin beds (or queen-size bed), with good under-bed storage areas, personal safe, vanity desk with large mirror, good closet and drawer space (in rich, dark woods), and bathrobe. Color TVs carry a major news channel (where obtainable), plus a sports channel and several round-the-clock movie channels. The bathrooms, which have tiled floors and plain walls, are compact, standard units, and include a shower enclosure with a removable, strong hand-held shower unit, hairdryer, 100% cotton towels, toiletries storage shelves and a retractable clothesline.

The suites/cabins that have private balconies (66 percent of all suites/cabins, or 73 percent of all outside view suites/cabins) have partial, and not full, balcony partitions, sliding glass doors, and, due to good design and layout, only 14 cabins on Deck 6 have lifeboat-obstructed views. The balcony floor is covered in thick plastic matting (teak would be nicer) and some awful plastic furniture.

Mini-Suites: The 52 accommodation units designated as mini-suites, are in reality simply larger cabins than the standard varieties, as the sleeping and lounge areas are not divided. While not overly large, the bathrooms have a good-sized bathtub and ample space for storing personal toiletry items. The living area has a refrigerated mini-bar, lounge area with breakfast table, and a balcony with two plastic chairs and a table.

Owner's Suites: The 10 Owner's Suites are the most spacious accommodation, and are fine, large living spaces located in the forward-most and aft-most sections of the accommodation decks (particularly nice are those that overlook the stern, on Deck 6, 7 and 8). They have more extensive balconies that really are private and cannot be overlooked by anyone from the decks above. There is an entrance foyer, living room, bedroom (the bed faces the sea, which can be seen through the floor-to-ceiling windows and sliding glass door), CD player, bathroom with Jacuzzi bathtub, as well as a small guest bathroom.

CUISINE. There are four different dining spots: three restaurants and one casual self-serve buffet:

● **The Club Restaurant** has 338 seats (all chairs have armrests), and includes a large raised central section. There are large ocean-view windows on three sides, and some prime tables that overlook the stern, as well as a small bandstand for occasional live dinner music. However, the noise level can be high, owing to the single-deck-height ceiling.

● **Sabatini's Trattoria** is an Italian restaurant, with 96 seats (all chairs have armrests), windows along two sides, and a set *bellissima* three-hour "degustation" menu. The cover charge is $15 per person.

● **The Sterling Steakhouse** is an "American steak house" which has a good selection of large, prime steaks and other meats. It has 98 comfortable seats (all chairs have armrests), windows along two sides, and a set menu (together with added daily chef's specials). The cover charge is $8 per person.

● **The Lido Cafe** has seating for 154 indoors and 186 outdoors (with white plastic patio furniture). It is open for breakfast, lunch and casual dinners. It is the ship's self-serve buffet restaurant (open 24 hours a day), and has a small pizzeria and grill.

All restaurants have open-seating dining, so you dine when you want, although reservations are necessary for Sabatini's Trattoria and Sterling Steakhouse, where there are mostly tables for four or six (there are few tables for two). In addition, there is a Poolside Grill and Bar for those fast-food items provided for on-deck munching.

ENTERTAINMENT. The 345-seat Cabaret Lounge, located in the forward part of the ship on Deck 5, is the main venue for entertainment events and some social functions. The single-level room has a stage, and circular hardwood dance floor with adjacent banquette and individual tub chair seating, and raised sections on port and starboard sides. It is not a large room, and not really designed for production shows, so cabaret acts and local entertainment form the main focus, with mini-revue style shows with colorful costumes, presented by a troupe of resident singer/dancers in a potted version of what you might experience aboard the large ships of Princess Cruises. Inevitably, art auctions and bingo are pushed almost daily.

The ship carries a band, small musical units, and solo entertaining pianists to provide live music for shows and dancing in the lounges and bars before and after dinner.

SPA/FITNESS. Facilities, which are located in the forward part of the ship on a high deck (Deck 9) consist of a gymnasium (with ocean view windows) with some high-tech muscle-toning equipment and treadmills, steam rooms (no sauna) and changing areas for men and women, and a beauty salon with ocean view windows.

The spa is operated by Steiner, a specialist concession whose retail products will be pushed. Some fitness classes are free (Stepexpress, Power Walk, Total Body Conditioning, Xpress Circuit are examples), while some, such as yoga and kick-boxing, cost extra. Massage (including exotic massages such as Aroma Stone massage, Chakra Balancing massage and other well-being massages), facials, pedicures, and beauty salon treatments are at extra cost (massage, for example, costs about $2 per minute, plus gratuity).

● **For more extensive general information about the Princess Cruises experience, see pages 134–37.**

Pacific Venus
★★★★

Mid-Size Ship: . . . . .26,518 tons	Passenger Decks: 7	Cabins (with private balcony): 20
Lifestyle: . . . . .Standard	Total Crew: 180	Cabins (wheelchair accessible): 1
Cruise Line: . . . . .Venus Cruise	Passengers	Cabin Current: . . . . .110 volts
Former Names: . . . . .none	(lower beds/all berths): 532/720	Elevators: 4
Builder: . . . . .Ishikawajima Heavy	Passenger Space Ratio	Casino (gaming tables): . . . . .Yes
Industries (Japan)	(lower beds/all berths): 49.8/36.8	Slot Machines: .No
Original Cost: . . . .$114 million	Crew/Passenger Ratio	Swimming Pools (outdoors): 1
(Yen13 billion)	(lower beds/all berths): 2.9/4.0	(+ 1 for children)
Entered Service: . . . . .Apr 1998	Navigation Officers: . . . . .Japanese	Swimming Pools (indoors): 0
Registry: . . . . .Japan	Cabins (total): 266	Whirlpools: 1
Length (ft/m): 601.7/183.4	Size Range (sq ft/m): 164.6–699.6/	Self-Service Launderette: . . . . .Yes (2)
Beam (ft/m): 82.0/25.0	15.3–65.0	Dedicated Cinema/Seats: Yes/94
Draft (ft/m): 21.3/6.5	Cabins (outside view): 250	Library: . . . . .Yes
Propulsion/Propellers: . . . . .diesel	Cabins (interior/no view): 16	
(13,636 kW)/2	Cabins (for one person): 0	

OVERALL SCORE: 1,542 (OUT OF A POSSIBLE 2,000 POINTS)

OVERVIEW. Venus Cruise is part of Japan Cruise Line, which is itself part of SHK Line Group, a joint venture between the Shin Nohonkai, Hankyu and Kanpu ferry companies (operating more than 20 ferries). There is a decent amount of open deck space aft of the funnel, which is good for deck sports, while protected sunbathing space is provided around the small swimming pool (all sunloungers have cushioned pads).

The base of the funnel itself is the site of a day/night lounge, which overlooks the swimming pool (it is slightly reminiscent of Royal Caribbean International's lounges). There is a walk-around (rubber-coated) promenade deck outdoors. Inside the ship, there is plenty of space per passenger. The decor is clean and fresh, with much use of pastel colors and blond woods, giving the interiors a feeling of warmth.

One deck (Deck 7) has a double-width indoor promenade off which the dining rooms are located. The atrium is three decks high and has a crystal chandelier as its focal point.

There are special rooms for meetings and conference organizers, for times when the ship is chartered. There is a piano salon with colorful low-back chairs, a large main hall (with a finely sculptured high ceiling and 720 moveable seats – production shows are performed here), a 350-seat main lounge for cabaret shows, a small theater, a library and card room, a casino, two private karaoke rooms, a Japanese chashitsu room for tea ceremonies (a tatami-matted room), and a beauty salon. There is a 24-hour vending machine corner (juice, beer, camera film and other items), self-service launderette (no charge), and several (credit card/coin) public telephone booths. Overall, this company

BERLITZ'S RATINGS

	Possible	Achieved
Ship	500	387
Accommodation	200	145
Food	400	309
Service	400	316
Entertainment	100	76
Cruise	400	309

provides a well-packaged cruise in a ship that presents a very comfortable, serene environment. The dress code is . relaxed and no tipping is allowed. The onboard currency is the Japanese yen.

There are few cabins with private balcony. The open walking promenade decks are rubber-coated steel – teak would be more desirable.

SUITABLE FOR: *Pacific Venus* is best suited to Japanese-speaking couples and single travelers of mature years who enjoy traveling in very comfortable surroundings, and who enjoy good food and service, all at a moderate cost.

ACCOMMODATION. There are six different types: royal suites, suites, deluxe cabins, state cabins (in four different price grades), and standard cabins, all located from the uppermost to lowermost decks, respectively.

The four Royal Suites are decorated in two different styles – one contemporary, one more traditional Japanese style. Each has a private balcony, with sliding door (teak table and two chairs), an expansive lounge area with large sofa and plush armchairs, coffee table, window-side chairs and drinks table, floor-to-ceiling windows, and a VCR. There is a separate bedroom, with twin- or queen-sized bed, vanity/writing desk, large walk-in closet with personal safe, and a large bathroom with a tiny Jacuzzi bathtub. The bathroom has ocean-view windows, separate shower and his/hers sinks.

Sixteen suites also have private balconies (with teak table and two chairs), a good-sized living area with vanity/writing desk, dining table, chair and curved sofa, separate sleeping area, and bathroom with deep bathtub slightly larger than the Royal suites, and single large sink. There is ample lighted closet and drawer space (two locking drawers instead of a personal safe), and a VCR.

The 20 Deluxe cabins have large picture windows fronted by a large, curtained arch, sleeping area with twin (or queen) beds, plus a daytime sofa that converts into a third bed.

The 210 state cabins, (172 of which have upper berths for third passengers), have decor that is best described as basic, with a reasonable closet, but little drawer space.

The 16 standard cabins are really plain, but accommodate three persons, although the drawer and storage space is a bit tight.

All cabin grades have a tea drinking set (with electric hot water kettle), color TV, telephone, stocked mini-bar/ refrigerator (all items included in the cruise price). Bathrooms have a hairdryer, and lots of Shiseido personal toiletry items (particularly in the suites, which include after-shave, hair liquid, hair tonic, skin lotion, body lotion, shampoo, rinse, razor, toothbrush, toothpaste, sewing kit, shower cap, hairbrush, clothes brush and shoe horn). All room service menu items cost extra (this is typical of all Japanese cruise ships). All passengers receive a yukata (Japanese-style light cotton robe); suite occupants also get a plush bathrobe.

CUISINE. The Primavera Dining Room is the ship's main dining spot; it is located aft, with ocean views on three sides. Passengers dine in one seating, and tables are for six, 10 or 12. The food consists of both Japanese and Western items; the menu is varied and the food is attractively presented.

A second, intimate, yet moderately stately 42-seat alternative restaurant, called Grand Siècle, offers an à la carte menu, which incurs an extra charge for everything; it is tastefully decorated in Regency-style, with much fine wood-paneling and a detailed, indented ceiling.

ENTERTAINMENT. Le Pacific Main Lounge is the venue for all shipboard entertainment (it also functions as a lecture and activities room during the day). It is a single-level room with seating clustered around a "thrust" stage so that entertainers are in the very midst of their audience.

On most cruises, special featured entertainers are brought on board from ashore (singers, instrumentalists, storytellers, dance champions, and others).

SPA/FITNESS. Spa facilities include male and female Grand Baths, which include bathing pool and health/cleansing facilities, ocean-view windows; a gymnasium, also with ocean-view windows; and a sauna. Japanese massage is available, as are hairdressing and barber services in the small salon (located on the lowest passenger-accessible deck of the ship).

QUOTABLE QUOTES

Overheard in Alaska:
"Are the glaciers always here?"

Overheard in the cigar smoking room: "I'm looking for a no-smoking seat"

Overheard in the dining room in the Caribbean:
"Is all the salmon smoked? I am a non-smoker"
"Waiter, this vichyssoise is cold."
"Was the fish caught this morning by the crew?"

Overheard on an Antarctic cruise:
"Where is the good shopping in Antarctica?"

Overheard on a cruise taking in the British Isles:
"Windsor Castle is terrific. But why did they build it so close to the airport?"

Overheard on an Athens tour:
"Why did the Greeks build so many ruins?"

Overheard in the dining room:
Passenger: "Waiter: What is caviar?"
Waiter: "Fish eggs, sir."
Passenger: "In that case, I'll have two, over-easy!"

Overheard on a QE2 round-Japan cruise, in Kagoshima, with Mount Suribaya in the background: "Can you tell me what time the volcano will erupt? I want to be sure to take a photograph."

Paul Gauguin
★★★★

Small Ship:	19,200 tons	Total Crew:	211	Cabins (with private balcony):	89

Small Ship: . . . . .19,200 tons
Lifestyle: . . . . .Premium
Cruise Line: . .Regent Seven Seas Cruises
Former Names: . . . . .none
Builder: Chantiers de l'Atlantique (France)
Original Cost: . . . .$150 million
Entered Service: . . . . .Jan 1998
Registry: . . . . .The Bahamas
Length (ft/m): 513.4/156.50
Beam (ft/m): 72.1/22.00
Draft (ft/m): 16.8/5.15
Propulsion/Propellers: . . . . .diesel-electric
(9,000 kW/2
Passenger Decks: 7

Total Crew: 211
Passengers
(lower beds/all berths): 330/330
Passenger Space Ratio
(lower beds/all berths): 58.1/58.1
Crew/Passenger Ratio
(lower beds/all berths): 1.5/1.5
Navigation Officers: . . . . .European
Cabins (total): 165
Size Range (sq ft/m): 200.0–534.0/
18.5–49.6
Cabins (outside view): 165
Cabins (interior/no view): 0
Cabins (for one person): 0

Cabins (with private balcony): 89
Cabins (wheelchair accessible): 1
Cabin Current: . . . . .110 volts
Elevators: 4
Casino (gaming tables): . . . . .Yes
Slot Machines: . . . . .Yes
Swimming Pools (outdoors): 1
Swimming Pools (indoors): 0
Whirlpools: 0
Self-Service Launderette: . . . . .No
Dedicated Cinema/Seats: . . . . .No
Library: . . . . .Yes

OVERALL SCORE: 1,547 (OUT OF A POSSIBLE 2,000 POINTS)

OVERVIEW. Built by a French company, owned by Grand Circle Travel but managed, staffed and operated until January 2010 by the US-based Regent Seven Seas Cruises, this spacious ship cruises in French Polynesia. While it could carry many more passengers, it is forbidden to do so by French law. The ship, which underwent a $6 million refurbishment in 2006, has a well-balanced look, all in gleaming white, and is topped by a single funnel.

This smart ship also has a retractable aft marina platform, and carries two water skiing boats and two inflatable craft for water sports. Windsurfers, kayaks, plus scuba and snorkeling gear are available for your use (all except scuba gear, are included in the cruise fare).

Inside, there is a pleasant array of public rooms, and both the artwork and the decor have a real French Polynesia look and feel. The interior colors are quite restful, although a trifle bland.

Expert lecturers on Tahiti and Gauguin accompany each cruise, and a Fare (pronounced *foray*) Tahiti Gallery offers books, videos, and other materials on the unique art, history, and culture of the islands. Three original Gauguin sketches are displayed under glass.

Le Casino is where the casino action runs high, the major attraction being the roulette and blackjack gaming tables. The library is pleasant enough, although it really could be larger. This ship presents Seven Seas Cruises with the opportunity to score very high marks with its passengers, as the company is known for its attention to detail and passenger care.

A no-tie policy means that the dress code is very relaxed – every day. The standard itinerary means that the ship

BERLITZ'S RATINGS	Possible	Achieved
Ship	500	397
Accommodation	200	169
Food	400	304
Service	400	320
Entertainment	100	71
Cruise	400	286

docks only in Papeete and shore tenders are used in all other ports. There is little entertainment, as the ship stays overnight in several ports (so little is needed). The ship's high crew-to-passenger ratio translates to highly personalized service.

The ship has become a favorite of travelers to these climes, and the quiet, refined atmosphere on board makes it sort of clubby, with passengers getting to know each other easily.

Where the ship really shines is in the provision of a lot of water sports equipment, and its shallow draft allows it to navigate and anchor in lovely little places that larger ships couldn't possibly get to. All in all, it's a delightful cruise and product, and all gratuities to staff are included. The euro is now the currency in Tahiti and its islands, as Tahiti is a French territory.

Islands, beaches and watersports are what this ship is good at. Perhaps the best island experience is in Bora Bora. *Paul Gauguin*'s shallow draft means there could be some movement, as the ship is a little high-sided for its size. The spa is very small, and the fitness room is windowless.

SUITABLE FOR: *Paul Gauguin* is best suited to couples and single travelers (typically over 50) who seek specialized itineraries, good food and service, with almost no entertainment, all wrapped up in a contemporary ship which can best be described as elegant and quiet in its appointments and comfort levels.

ACCOMMODATION. There are eight grades, priced according to grade, location and size. The outside-view cabins, half of which have private balconies, are nicely equipped, although they are strictly rectangular (and none have more interesting shapes). Most have large windows, except those on the lowest accommodation deck, which have portholes. Each has queen- or twin-sized beds (convertible to queen), and wood-accented cabinetry with rounded edges. A mini-bar/refrigerator (stocked with complimentary soft drinks) DVD player, personal safe, hairdryer and umbrellas are standard.

The marble-look bathrooms are large and pleasing and have a tub as well as a separate shower enclosure. All passengers are provided with 100% cotton bathrobes, and soft drinks and mineral water are included in the cruise price.

The two largest suites have a private balcony at the front and side of the vessel. Although there is a decent amount of in-cabin space, with a beautiful long vanity unit (and plenty of drawer space), the bathrooms are disappointingly small and plain, and too similar to all other standard cabin bathrooms.

Butler service is provided in all accommodation designated as Owners Suite, Grand Suites, Ocean-view "A" and "B" category suites.

CUISINE/DINING. L'Etoile is the name of the main dining room for lunch and dinner, while La Veranda, an alternative dining spot, is open for breakfast, lunch and dinner. Both dining rooms feature "open seating" which means that passengers can choose when they want to dine and with whom. This provides a good opportunity to meet new people for dinner each evening. The chairs have armrests, making it more comfortable for a leisurely mealtime. La Veranda provides dinner by reservation, with alternating French and Italian menus; the French menus are provided by Jean-Pierre Vigato, a two-star Michelin chef with his own restaurant ("Apicius") in Paris.

The dining operation is well orchestrated, with cuisine and service of a high standard. All non-alcoholic beverages, plus select wines and liquor, are included in the fare, while premium wines are available at extra cost.

An outdoor bistro provides informal cafe fare on deck aft of the pool, while the Connoisseur Club offers a luxurious retreat for cigars, cognacs, and wine tasting.

ENTERTAINMENT. Le Grand Salon is the venue for shows and cabaret acts. It is a single-level room, and seating is in banquette and individual tub chairs. Sightlines are quite good from most seats, although there are some obstructions. Don't expect lavish production shows (there aren't any), as the main entertainment consists of local Polynesian shows brought on board from ashore, plus the odd cabaret act. A new piano lounge was added in the 2006 refit.

SPA/FITNESS. Spa Carita, on Deck 6 in the centre of the ship, is the name of the spa/wellbeing space. It includes a fitness centre with some muscle-pumping and body toning equipment, a steam room, several treatment rooms, changing area (very small), and beauty salon. The Spa/beauty services are provided by Carita of Paris, who also provides the staff. There is no sauna, but use of the steam room is complimentary.

Body pampering treatments include various massages, aromatherapy facials, manicures, pedicures, and hairdressing services.

Pearl
NOT YET RATED

Small Ship:.............. 8,700 tons	Total Crew: 60	Cabins (for one person): 0
Lifestyle:................. Standard	Passengers	Cabins (with private balcony):...... 108
Cruise Line:........ Pearl Seas Cruises	(lower beds/all berths): 214/214	Cabins (wheelchair accessible):...... 4
Former Names:............... none	Passenger Space Ratio	Cabin Voltage:.............. 110 volts
Builder:..... Irving Shipyards (Canada)	(lower beds/all berths): 40.6/40.6	Elevators: 1
Original Cost:............ $50 million	Crew/Passenger Ratio	Casino (gaming tables): .... No
Entered Service:........... Jan 2009	(lower beds/all berths): 3.5/3.5	Slot Machines: .... No
Registry: .... Marshall Islands	Navigation Officers:........ American	Swimming Pools (outdoors):......... 0
Length (ft/m):........... 330.0/100.5	Cabins (total): 105	Swimming Pools (indoors):.......... 0
Beam (ft/m):............... 55.7/17.0	Size Range (sq ft/m):..... 302.0–580.0/	Whirlpools: 1
Draft (ft/m): 10.0/3.1	28.0– 53.8	Self-Service Launderette:......... No
Propulsion/Propellers: diesel (6,300hp)/2	Cabins (outside view):........... 108	Dedicated Cinema/Seats:.......... No
Passenger Decks:................ 6	Cabins (interior/no view): 0	Library: .... Yes

OVERALL SCORE: NYR (OUT OF A POSSIBLE 2,000 POINTS)

OVERVIEW. This is Pearl Seas Cruises' first ship (delivered late by Canada's Irving Shipyards), designed and built for international ocean-going cruises with an all-American style. Pearl Seas Cruises is an outgrowth of the all-American company, American Cruise Lines, based in Connecticut, and the onboard product is expected to be an extension of the ACL onboard product. But don't confuse the USA's Pearl Seas Cruises with Australia's Pearl Sea Cruises.

Pearl is designed to be a much more comfortable and upscale vessel than the ships belonging to sister company American Cruise Lines. It has greater speed, the latest navigational technology, and better onboard facilities and service. It is meant to appeal to passengers who enjoy discovering ports in the company of like-minded people, away from the hunting grounds of the large resort ships and their attendant crowds.

Public rooms include two principal lounges, the Pacific Lounge, and the Atlantic Lounge; one is above, and the other is below the navigation bridge.

Other public rooms include a small Coral Lounge located just behind the mast; a library, and two small midship lounges – one named Caribbean lounge. A single elevator goes to all decks, including the outdoor sun deck.

SUITABLE FOR: Pearl is best suited to couples and single

BERLITZ'S RATINGS

	Possible	Achieved
Ship	500	NYR
Accommodation	200	NYR
Food	400	NYR
Service	400	NYR
Entertainment	100	NYR
Cruise	400	NYR

travelers of mature years sharing a cabin and wishing to cruise in an all-American environment aboard a small ship where the destinations are a more important consideration than food, service, or entertainment.

ACCOMMODATION. There are seven cabin price grades, but all accommodation grades are outside view suites/cabins with private balcony, although the balcony is not exactly what you would call large. All feature twin beds that convert to a king-sized bed, with high quality bed linens; bathrooms have a walk-in shower. Some cabins can be interconnected, so a couple can have a bathroom each.

CUISINE. The single dining room, at the stern of the ship, accommodates all passengers in a single, open seating, so you can sit where and with whom you want. Complimentary cocktails and hors d'oeuvres are offered before dinner in the lounges.

ENTERTAINMENT. The Main Lounge is the venue for evening entertainment, lectures, and recaps. Any entertainment will be brought on board from ashore in the ports of call.

SPA/FITNESS. The small spa features a beauty salon. There is also one hot tub (Jacuzzi) on deck.

Pride of America
★★★ +

Large Resort Ship: ....81,000 tons	Passenger Decks:.................11	Cabins (for one person): 0
Lifestyle: ....Standard	Total Crew: 1,000	Cabins (with private balcony): 665
Cruise Line: ....NCL America	Passengers	Cabins (wheelchair accessible): 22
Former Names: ....none	(lower beds/all berths): 2,144/2,440	Cabin Current: ....110 volts
Builder: .....Ingalls Shipbuilding (USA)/	Passenger Space Ratio	Elevators: 10
Lloyd Werft (Germany)	(lower beds/all berths): 37.7/33.1	Casino (gaming tables): ....Yes
Original Cost: ....$450 million	Crew/Passenger Ratio	Slot Machines: ....Yes
Entered Service: ....July 2005	(lower beds/all berths): 2.1/2.4	Swimming Pools (outdoors): 2
Registry:........................USA	Navigation Officers: ....Norwegian	Swimming Pools (indoors): 0
Length (ft/m): 921.9/281.0	Cabins (total): 1,072	Whirlpools: ....n/a
Beam (ft/m): 106.6/32.2	Size Range (sq ft/m): 129.1–1,377.8/	Self-Service Launderette: ....No
Draft (ft/m): 26.25/8.0	12.0 –128.0	Dedicated Cinema/Seats: ....No
Propulsion/Propellers: ....diesel-electric/	Cabins (outside view): 843	Library: ....Yes
2 pods (17MW each)	Cabins (interior/no view): 229	

BERLITZ'S OVERALL SCORE: 1,390 (OUT OF A POSSIBLE 2,000 POINTS)

OVERVIEW. *Pride of America* sails on inter-island cruises, focusing on the islands of Hawaii. The 85,850 sq.-ft./ 7,975 sq.-meter open deck space includes a sunning/ pool deck inspired by Miami's South Beach (think Ocean Drive/Lincoln Mall) and Art Deco area.

The stunning interior design of the ship is modeled after a "Best of America" theme (all the public rooms are named after famous Americans). Facilities include the Capitol Atrium (a lobby spanning eight decks and said to be inspired by the Capitol Building and White House), a large casino, a conservatory complete with tropical landscaped garden and live exotic birds, Soho Art Gallery (holding art auctions), Washington Library, and Newbury Shopping Center. The Rascal's Kids Center and Kids' Pool is a supervised facility designed around a theme of America's native animals.

There are extensive meeting and conference facilities (US corporations qualify for tax-deductible meetings expenses as the ship sails under the US flag), with six dedicated meetings rooms ranging in size from boardrooms for 10 people to an auditorium for up to 250. The ship has a mainly Hawaiian crew, and you can expect lots of Americana. The on-board currency is the US dollar. A (non-changeable) service charge (this is not a gratuity) for staff is automatically added to your onboard account at $10 per person ($5 for children aged 3–12) per day; this is pooled for all crew and provides payment when they are on vacation. You will also be expected to also provide gratuities. In addition, a 15% gratuity, plus Hawaii sales tax (this is a US flag ship) is added to all bar and spa treatment accounts.

SUITABLE FOR: *Pride of America* is best suited to first-

BERLITZ'S RATINGS

	Possible	Achieved
Ship	500	406
Accommodation	200	149
Food	400	248
Service	400	233
Entertainment	100	78
Cruise	400	276

time young (and young at heart) couples, single passengers, children and teenagers who enjoy big city nightlife, who want contemporary, upbeat, color-rich surroundings, and the latest in facilities, plenty of entertainment lounges and bars and high-tech sophistication – all in one neat, highly programmed, well packaged cruise vacation, with plenty of music, constant activity and entertainment.

ACCOMMODATION. Of the 950 cabins, 77% have outside views, while 64% of these have private balconies, and there are also a large number of family-friendly interconnecting cabins. Many cabins have third/fourth upper berths, some family-special cabins can accommodate as many as six. Some suites have king-sized beds, while most cabins have twin beds that can be placed together to make a queen-sized bed. A number of cabins are wheelchair-accessible, while some cabins are equipped for the hearing-impaired.

Grand Suite: The largest accommodation is in the Grand Suite, with approximately 1,400 sq. ft./130 sq. meters of living space. The suite is located high atop the ship forward of the sun deck and offers sweeping views from its wrap-around outdoor terrace. It has a large living room with Bang & Olufsen entertainment center (television, DVD/CD player with library), computer internet-connect access, and wet bar, separate dining room with dining table and six chairs (butler included). The master bedroom includes a king-sized bed, large bathroom, with whirlpool tub and separate shower enclosure; dressing area with flat-screen TV, and walk-in closet. At the entrance to the suite is a guest powder room. There is a wrap-around verandah, and facilities include open-air dining and a hot tub), plus a private sunbathing and entertainment area.

Owner's Suite: There are five, each measuring approximately 870 sq.ft./80 sq. meters and named after indigenous flowers in Hawaii (Bird of Paradise, Gardenia, Orchid, Plumeria). Each has a bedroom with king-sized bed, walk-in closet, dressing area, separate living room with Bang & Olufsen entertainment center (television, DVD/CD player with library), and computer internet-connect access. The bathroom has a whirlpool tub and separate shower enclosure. There is also a large private balcony with hot tub, outdoor dining facilities and sun beds.

Deluxe Penthouse Suites: There are six units, each measuring approximately 735 sq.ft./68 sq. meters. They have a separate bedroom with king-size bed and walk-in closet; the bathroom has a whirlpool tub, separate shower enclosure, two washbasins, dressing area; living room with Bang & Olufsen entertainment center, wet bar, and private balcony.

Penthouse Suites: There are 28, each measuring 504–585 sq.ft/47–54.5 sq. meters. These have a separate bedroom with king-size bed and walk-in closet; the bathroom has a whirlpool tub, separate shower enclosure, two washbasins, dressing area; living room with Bang & Olufsen entertainment center, wet bar, and private balcony.

Family Suites: There are eight, each measuring approximately 360 sq.ft./33.5 sq. meters. Each has a main bedroom with two twin beds that can be converted to a queen-sized bed, a living room with double sofa bed and entertainment center, separate den with single sofa bed. Another four family "suites" have an interconnecting door between two cabins (thus there are two bathrooms). These four measure 330–380 sq.ft./30.5–35 sq. meters.

Standard Outside View and Interior (No View) Cabins: Outside view cabins have either a window or porthole, depending on location. All cabins have twin beds that can convert into a queen-sized bed, TV, satellite-dial telephone, and personal safe; the bathrooms have a built-in hairdryer.

Cuisine. NCL America's ships operate "Freestyle Cruising," which means that there are several restaurants and informal dining spots. You can choose from two main dining rooms, and six other à la carte, informal and casual spots, some of which incur a cover (or portion) charge ($12.50–$17.50 per person). Smoking is banned in all restaurants and food outlets.

Traditional Dining Rooms:
● The 628-seat Skyline Restaurant is the main restaurant, and the decor is inspired by the skyscrapers of the 1930s.
● The 496-seat Liberty Dining Room is the second main restaurant, with two seatings.

Alternative Dining Options:
● The Lone Star Steak House seats 106. This is a contemporary steak house with Texan decor (the artwork includes Houston Space Center, Texas Rangers and Dallas Cowboys).
● China Town is a Pacific Rim/Asian Fusion restaurant that has a sushi/sashimi bar and a Teppanyaki grill room with two tables (food is prepared in front of you with a bit of showmanship) that can accommodate up to 32.
● Jefferson's Bistro, which accommodates 104, is the ship's "signature" restaurant, and features an à la carte menu of classic and nouvelle French cuisine. The decor is inspired by that of Thomas Jefferson's home in Monticello (Thomas Jefferson was the US ambassador to France from 1785 to 1789 before becoming America's third president).
● Little Italy is a casual Italian eatery that serves pasta, pizza and other popular light Italian fare. It has 116 seats.
● Cadillac Diner accommodates 106 (70 indoors, 36 outdoors) and is open 24 hours a day. It has Cadillac seats and a video juke box. There's fast food galore, with hamburgers and hot dogs, fish and chips, potpies and wok dishes.
● Aloha Cafe/Kids Cafe is an indoor/outdoor self-serve buffet-style eatery with a Hawaii theme; there are 322 indoor and 310 outdoor seats. A special section for children has counter tops just the right height, as well as chairs and tables that have been shrunk from adult to a kid-friendly size.

Other indoor eateries and bars include the Napa Wine Bar (wines by the glass), Pink's Champagne and Cigar Bar (inspired by Hawaii's "Pink Palace" Hotel on Waikiki Beach), the Gold Rush pub (karaoke is practiced here; there's also a darts board and bar billiards), and the John Adams Coffee Bar; while outdoor eateries and drinking places include the Key West Bar and Grill, and the Waikiki Bar.

ENTERTAINMENT. The Hollywood Theater, the ship's principal showlounge, seats 840. Large-scale production shows will be featured, together with local Hawaiian shows. There is also a 590-seat cabaret lounge, named the Mardi Gras Lounge, which will typically feature cabaret entertainment (including late-night comedy).

SPA/FITNESS. The Santa Fe Spa and Fitness Center is decorated with artifacts from New Mexico and designed to be a tranquil center for mind and body. The spa is staffed and operated by Mandara Spa (originating in Bali, now headquartered in Hawaii, but owned by Steiner Leisure), and includes Ayurvedic-style treatments. While some fitness classes are free, some – such as yoga, and kick-boxing – typically cost $10 per class.

Massage (including exotic massages such as Hot Stone, Lomi Lomi, and other well-being massages), facials, pedicures, and beauty salon treatments cost extra (massage, for example, costs about $2 per minute, plus gratuity).

● **For more extensive general information on what an NCL cruise is like, see pages 131–33.**

Prince Albert II
★★★★ +

Boutique Ship:. . . . . 6,072 tons	Passenger Decks:. 5	Cabins (with private balcony):. 6
Lifestyle:. . . . . Premium	Total Crew:. 111	+ 14 French balconies
Cruise Line:. . . . . Silversea Cruises	Passengers:	Cabins (wheelchair accessible):. 0
Former Names: . . World Discoverer, Dream 21,	(lower beds/all berths):. 132/158	Cabin Current:. . . . . 110/220 volts
Baltic Clipper, Sally Clipper, Delfin Star, Delfin	Passenger Space Ratio	Elevators:. 2
Clipper, World Adventurer, Delfin Clipper	(lower beds/all berths):. 46.0/38.4	Casino (gaming tables):. . . . . No
Builder:. . . . . Rauma-Repola (Finland)	Crew/Passenger Ratio:	Slot Machines:. . . . . No
Original Cost:. . . . . $50 million	(lower beds/all berths):. 1.1/1.4	Swimming Pools (outdoors):. 0
Entered Service:. . . . . . . July 1989/June 2008	Navigation Officers:. . . . . European	Swimming Pools (indoors):. 0
Registry:. . . . . The Bahamas	Cabins (total):. 66	Whirlpools:. 2
Length (ft/m):. 354.9/108.20	Size Range (sq.ft./m.):. . 172.2–785.7/16.0–73.0	Self-Service Launderette:. . . . . No
Beam (ft/m):. 51.1/15.60	Cabins (outside view):. 66	Movie Theater/Seats:. . . . . No
Draft (ft/m):. 13.1/4.00	Cabins (interior/no view):. 0	Library:. . . . . No
Propulsion/Propellers:. . . . diesel (4,500kw)/2	Cabins (for one person):. 0	

BERLITZ'S OVERALL SCORE: 1,684 (OUT OF A POSSIBLE 2,000 POINTS)

OVERVIEW. Twin swept-back outboard funnels highlight the semi-smart exterior design of this small specialist 20-year-old expedition cruise ship. It has a dark ice-hardened hull, carries a fleet of eight Zodiac inflatable landing craft for shore landings and exploration, and has one boot washing station (called the "Mud Room," it has six bays).

Silversea Cruises bought the ship in 2007, towed it to Italy from Singapore, where it had been laid up for four years, and had it completely refitted it at the Mariotti shipyard in Genoa. The idea behind the conversion is to take Silversea Cruises passengers to more remote regions of the world, but in style.

The accommodation is located forward, with all public rooms aft, an arrangement that helps keep noise to a minimum in accommodation areas. The interior has many European design elements, including warm color combinations. Public rooms include an observation lounge, large lecture room/cinema with bar, and library/internet center.

This small expedition cruise vessel has many of the creature comforts of much larger vessels. It will provide a very comfortable expedition-style cruise experience in tasteful and elegant surroundings. All passengers receive a pre-cruise amenities package that typically includes a field guide, backpack, carry-on travel bag, and luggage tags.

The ship will specialize in Polar itineraries. An expedition leader, plus other lecturers provide specialized in-depth education about wildlife, geography and other interesting subjects that enrich the expedition cruise experience. The onboard currencies are both the US dollar and the euro.

There is no walk-around promenade deck outdoors (the ship is too small for one).

BERLITZ'S RATINGS

	Possible	Achieved
Ship	500	411
Accommodation	200	174
Food	400	334
Service	400	334
Entertainment	n/a	n/a
Cruise	500	431

SUITABLE FOR: *Prince Albert II* is best suited to adventurous couples and single travelers of mature years who enjoy nature and wildlife at close range.

ACCOMMODATION. There are six types of accommodation, and 11 price grades. The cabins – quite large for such a small ship – are fitted out to a fairly high standard, with ample closet and drawer space. All cabins have outside views and have twin beds that can convert to a queen-sized bed, TV/DVD unit, telephone, hairdryer, refrigerator, and lockable drawer for valuables.

Although only six suites have a large private balcony (they really are not needed in cold-weather regions), another 14 cabins have glass doors that open onto a few inches of space outdoors. The suites have whirlpool bathtubs. The owner's suite has two rooms, linked by an interconnecting door, to provide a separate lounge, bedroom, and two bathrooms.

The sizes are: Owners Suites (538 sq.ft./50 sq.meters); Medallion Suites (358 sq.ft./33.2 sq.meters); Grand Suites (650 sq.ft./60.3 sq.meters); Silver Suites (430.5 sq.ft./40 sq.meters); Veranda Suites (215 sq.ft./20 sq.meters); Explorer Class (190 sq.ft./27.5 sq.meters); Expedition Suites (430.5 sq.ft./40 sq.meters).

CUISINE. The spacious dining room has pastel-colored decor, and accommodates all passengers in one seating. Casual alfresco bites can be had at the outdoor grill.

ENTERTAINMENT. Daily recaps; after-dinner conversation.

SPA/FITNESS. Facilities include a small gymnasium, sauna, and treatment room (for massage).

Princess Danae
★★★

Mid-Size Ship: . . . . .16,531 tons	Propulsion/Propellers: . . . . .diesel	Cabins (interior/no view): 66
Lifestyle: . . . . .Standard	(9,850 kW)/2	Cabins (for one person): 6
Cruise Line: . . . . . . .Classic International	Passenger Decks: 7	Cabins (with private balcony): 6
Cruises	Total Crew: 240	Cabins (wheelchair accessible): 0
Former Names: *Baltica, Starlight Express,*	Passengers	Cabin Current: . . . . .220 volts
Danae, Therisos Express, Port Melbourne	(lower beds/all berths): 560/690	Elevators: 2
Builder: . . . . .Swan, Hunter (UK)	Passenger Space Ratio	Casino (gaming tables): . . . . .Yes
Original Cost: . . . . .n/a	(lower beds/all berths): 29.5/23.9	Slot Machines: . . . . .Yes
Entered Service: . . . . . . .July 1955/1996	Crew/Passenger Ratio	Swimming Pools (outdoors): 1
Registry: . . . . .Panama	(lower beds/all berths): 2.3/2.7	Swimming Pools (indoors): 0
Length (ft/m): 532.4/162.30	Navigation Officers: . . . . .European	Whirlpools: 2
Beam (ft/m): 70.0/21.34	Cabins (total): 283	Self-Service Launderette: . . . . .No
Draft (ft/m): 25.2/7.69	Size Range (sq ft/m): . . .183.0–270.0/17.25	Dedicated Cinema/Seats: Yes/130
	Cabins (outside view): 217	Library: . . . . .Yes

OVERALL SCORE: 1,105 (OUT OF A POSSIBLE 2,000 POINTS)

OVERVIEW. *Princess Danae* began as a cargo-passenger liner, and was turned into a full-time cruise ship in 1972. Costa Cruises operated it for many years before it was bought by its present operator, Classic International Cruises. Because it is well-built with a deep draught, it is a good sea ship, and quite stable in all sea conditions. There is a decent amount of open deck space for sunbathing.

This ship was refurbished in 2005–6, and some public rooms were revamped. The decks are named after the planets. The interior decor is pleasing, but quite traditional, in keeping with the character of the ship. *Princess Danae* will provide a moderately comfortable cruise experience in unpretentious surroundings.

The ship has a pleasing traditional ambiance, combining traditional and contemporary features. The limited number of public rooms include a cinema (unusual for a ship of this size), a shop, small casino, piano bar, and a club room/library (with bar).

The ship typically operates Caribbean cruises in winter, and Mediterranean cruises in summer. It is often chartered to tour operators (of various nationalities), and so its character changes, as does the level of food and service. Use the rating only as a guide, as the actual product can be inconsistent. The onboard currency is the US dollar.

Passenger niggles include the fact that there is no observation lounge with forward-facing views over the bows; much of the open deck area is covered with Astroturf; the white plastic sunloungers (wood or stainless would be better) look tacky.

ACCOMMODATION. There are 11 price grades. Most cabins are of good size, are quite comfortable, and have rather

BERLITZ'S RATINGS		
	Possible	Achieved
Ship	500	292
Accommodation	200	116
Food	400	234
Service	400	223
Entertainment	100	42
Cruise	400	198

heavy-duty furniture and fittings with a decent amount of closet and drawer space. The lower-grade cabins are really plain, but adequate, although the bathrooms are minimal and functional, but uninviting. While 210 cabin bathrooms have a bathtub and shower, 70 have only a shower.

Accommodation designated as suites (six suites have a private balcony) and junior suites also have a writing/vanity desk, minibar, hairdryer, and satellite-link telephone. The towels are small.

CUISINE. The 394-seat Mimosa Restaurant is decorated quite nicely and has a high ceiling. It has open seating, and tables are for four, six or eight (the chairs do not have armrests). The cuisine is Continental/European, with some regional specialties. Typically, a self-serve buffet table is set up in the center of the restaurant for breakfast items, salads and cheeses for lunch, dinner and late-night snacks.

Casual, self-serve buffet meals are available in the Lido Bar, with its indoor-outdoor bamboo seating. The ship's former disco has been turned into a charming little Garden Café (with bamboo furniture).

ENTERTAINMENT. The Main Lounge is a single-level room with a thrust stage best used for cabaret acts. The stage lighting is minimal, and could be better. The ship carries a main band, and several small musical units, and solo pianists to provide live music for dancing or listening.

SPA/FITNESS. There is a gymnasium and sauna, and a windowless beauty salon.

Prinsendam
★★★★ +

Mid-Size Ship:	.37,845 tons	Passenger Decks:	.9	Cabins (for one person): .0
Lifestyle:	.Premium	Total Crew:	.443	Cabins (with private balcony): .153
Cruise Line:	.Holland America Line	Passengers		Cabins (wheelchair accessible): . 4
Former Names:	.Seabourn Sun,	(lower beds/all berths):	.790/840	Cabin Current: .110 volts
	Royal Viking Sun	Passenger Space Ratio		Elevators: .4
Builder:	.Wartsila (Finland)	(lower beds/all berths):	.47.6/46.4	Casino (gaming tables): .Yes
Original Cost:	.$125 million	Crew/Passenger Ratio		Slot Machines: .Yes
Entered Service:	.Dec 1988/May 2002	(lower beds/all berths):	.1.7/1.8	Swimming Pools (outdoors): .2
Registry:	.The Netherlands	Navigation Officers:	.European	Swimming Pools (indoors): .0
Length (ft/m):	.674.2/205.5	Cabins (total):	.395	Whirlpools: .4
Beam (ft/m):	.91.8/28.0	Size Range (sq ft/m):	.137.7–723.3/	Self-Service Launderette: .Yes
Draft (ft/m):	.23.6/7.2		12.8–67.2	Dedicated Cinema/Seats: .Yes/101
Propulsion/Propellers:	.diesel	Cabins (outside view):	.371	Library: .Yes
	(21,120 kW)/2	Cabins (interior/no view):	.24	

OVERALL SCORE: 1,662 (OUT OF A POSSIBLE 2,000 POINTS)

OVERVIEW. *Prinsendam* is a contemporary, well-designed ship with sleek, flowing lines, a sharply raked bow, and a well-rounded profile, with lots of floor-to-ceiling glass. Originally ordered and operated by the long defunct Royal Viking Line as *Royal Viking Sun*, it was bought by Seabourn Cruise Line in 1998. Following an extensive refit and refurbishment programme (which didn't go far enough), the ship was renamed *Seabourn Sun* in 1999. In 2002, it was transferred to Holland America Line as *Prinsendam*, and the hull color was changed from all-white to a dark blue hull with white superstructure. The shore tenders are thoughtfully air-conditioned.

Wide teak wood decks provide excellent walking areas including a decent wrap-around promenade deck outdoors. The swimming pool (outdoors on Lido Deck) is not large, but it is quite adequate, while the deck above has a croquet court and golf driving range. The interior layout is very spacious (it is even more ideal when a maximum of 600 passengers are aboard). Impressive public rooms and tasteful decor now reign. Two handrails – one of wood, one of chrome – are provided on all stairways, a thoughtful touch.

The Crow's Nest, the ship's forward observation lounge, is one of the most elegant, but contemporary (at least in decor), lounges at sea. Pebble Beach is the name of the electronic golf simulator room, complete with wet bar, with play possible on 11 virtual courses. An Explorations Café was installed at the end of 2007 in a refit that also saw an expansion of the shopping arcade and surrounding areas.

The Erasmus Library (formerly the Ibsen Library) is well organized, although it is simply not large enough for long-distance cruising. The former Compass Rose room

BERLITZ'S RATINGS

	Possible	Achieved
Ship	500	423
Accommodation	200	174
Food	400	321
Service	400	326
Entertainment	100	82
Cruise	400	336

has now become the Explorer's Lounge.

The Oak Room is the ship's cigar/pipe smoker's lounge; it has a marble fireplace, which sadly cannot be used due to United States Coast Guard regulations. I have always thought it would make a fine library, although it is also excellent as a cigar smoking room

There is a computer-learning center, with several workstations. Male "dance hosts" act as partners for women traveling alone.

Whether by intention or not, the ship has a two-class feeling, with passengers in "upstairs" penthouse suites and "A" grade staterooms gravitating to the quieter Crow's Nest lounge (particularly at night), while other passengers (the participants) go to the main entertainment deck.

The ship's wide range of facilities includes a concierge, self-service launderettes (useful on long voyages), a varied guest lecture program, 24-hour information office, and true 24-hour cabin service, for the discriminating passenger who demands spacious personal surroundings, and good food and service, regardless of price. This ship operates mainly long-distance cruises in great comfort, and free shuttle buses are provided in almost all ports of call.

While *Prinsendam* isn't perfect, the few design flaws (for example: poorly designed bar service counters) are minor points. Even though the hardware is not ideal, the software (personnel and service) is generally sound. It is an extremely comfortable ship – smaller than other Holland America Line ships, and more refined. The elegant decorative features include Dutch artwork and memorabilia.

Added benefits include a fine health spa facility, spacious, wide teakwood decks and many teak sunloungers. However, the good points are marred by the bland quality of the dining room food and service, and the lack of understanding of what it takes to make a "luxury" cruise experience, despite what is stated in the company's brochures.

There are only four elevators, so anyone with walking disabilities may have to wait for some time during periods of peak usage (e.g. before meals). The cabin ceilings are plain. This spacious ship shows signs of wear and tear in some areas (particularly in the accommodation passageways), despite recent refurbishments. The library is far too small (particularly for some of the long cruises operated) and difficult to enter for anyone confined to a wheelchair.

SUITABLE FOR: *Prinsendam* is best suited to older adult couples and singles who like to mingle in a mid-size ship operating longer cruises, in an unhurried setting with fine quality surroundings, with some eclectic, antique artwork, good food and service from a smiling Indonesian and Filipino crew who like to serve but who lack finesse.

ACCOMMODATION. There are 15 grades, ranging from Penthouse Verandah Suites to standard interior (no view) cabins. All suites and cabins have undergone some degree of refurbishment since the ship was taken over by Holland America Line in 2002.

Penthouse Verandah Suite: The Penthouse Verandah Suite (723 sq. ft/67 sq. meters), is a most desirable living space, although not as large as other penthouse suites aboard some other ships. It is light and airy, and has two bathrooms, one of which has a large whirlpool bathtub with ocean views, and anodized gold bathroom fittings. The living room contains a large dining table and chairs, and large sofas. There is also a substantial private balcony, and butler service.

Deluxe Verandah Suites: There are 18 of these (8 on Sports Deck/10 on Lido Deck). Located in the forward section of the ship, they have large balconies, two sofas, large bar/ entertainment center, (mini-bar/refrigerator, color television, VCR and CD player; bathrooms have separate toilet, sink and toiletries cabinets, connecting sliding door into the bedroom, large mirror, two toiletries cabinets, plenty of storage space, full bathtub, and anodized gold fittings. Each evening the butler brings different goodies – hot and cold hors d'oeuvres and other niceties. If you do choose one of these suites, it might be best on the starboard side where they are located in a private hallway, while those on the port side (including the Penthouse Verandah Suite) are positioned along a public hallway. The 10 suites on Lido Deck are positioned along private port and starboard side hallways.

Passengers in Penthouse and Deluxe Verandah Suites are provided with a private concierge lounge, high tea served in the suite each afternoon, hors d'oeuvres before dinner each evening (on request), complimentary laundry pressing and dry cleaning, private cocktail parties with captain, priority disembarkation, and more.

Other Cabin Grades: Most of the other cabins (spread over six other decks) are of generous proportions and have just about everything you would need (including a VCR).

Many (about 38 percent) have a small, private balcony. All cabins have walk-in closets, lockable drawers, full-length mirrors, hairdryers, and ample cotton towels. A few cabins have third berths, while some have interconnecting doors (good for couples who want two bathrooms and more space or for families with children).

In all grades of accommodation, passengers receive a basket of fresh fruit, fluffy cotton bathrobes, evening turndown service, and a Holland America Line signature tote bag. Filipino and Indonesian cabin stewards and stewardesses provide unobtrusive personal service.

Four well-equipped, L-shaped cabins for the disabled are quite well designed, fairly large, and equipped with special wheel-in bathrooms with shower facilities and closets.

CUISINE. The La Fontaine Dining Room wraps around the aft end of Lower Promenade Deck and has extensive ocean-view windows; there's a second, smaller (quieter) section along the starboard side. There is plenty of space around tables. A good number of window-side tables are for two persons, although there are also tables for four, six or eight. Crystal glasses, and Rosenthal china and fine cutlery are provided.

There are two seatings for dinner, at assigned tables, and an open-seating arrangement for breakfast and lunch (you'll be seated by restaurant staff when you enter). The dining room is a non-smoking venue.

Alternative Dining Option: A small, quiet dining spot is the Pinnacle Dining Room, with 48 seats, wood-paneled decor that increases the feeling of intimacy and privacy, and great ocean views, is set on the port side. Table settings include Bulgari china, Reidel glassware, and Frette table linens. The venue specializes in fine steaks and seafood. Seating preference is given to suite occupants. Reservations are required, and there is a cover charge.

There is a well-chosen wine list, although there is a great deal of emphasis on California wines, the prices of which are quite high.

There is also an enlarged Lido Restaurant, for decent casual dining and self-serve buffet-style meals. This eatery has both indoor and outdoor seating.

ENTERTAINMENT. The Queens showlounge is an amphitheater-style layout, with a well tiered floor, and both banquette and individual seating. While Holland America Line isn't known for fine entertainment, what it does offer is a consistently good, tried and tested array of cabaret acts.

SPA/FITNESS. The extensive Greenhouse Health Spa includes six treatment rooms (with integral showers), a rasul chamber (for mud and gentle steam heat treatments, combined with gentle steam), a gymnasium with views over the stern, and separate sauna, steam room, and changing rooms for men and women. The spa is operated by Steiner.

● **For more extensive general information on what a Holland America Line cruise is like, see pages 126–28.**

Professor Molchanov ★★

Boutique Ship: ....1,753 tons	Passenger Decks: 3	Cabins (for one person): 6
Lifestyle: ....Standard	Total Crew: 20	Cabins (with private balcony): 0
Cruise Line: ......Oceanwide Expeditions	Passengers	Cabins (wheelchair accessible): 0
Former Names: ....none	(lower beds/all berths): 52/52	Cabin Current: ....220 volts
Builder: ....Wartsila (Finland)	Passenger Space Ratio	Elevators: 0
Original Cost: ....n/a	(lower beds/all berths): 33.7/33.7	Casino (gaming tables): ....No
Entered Service: 1983	Crew/Passenger Ratio	Slot Machines: ....No
Registry: ....Russia	(lower beds/all berths): 2.6/2.6	Swimming Pools (outdoors): 0
Length (ft/m): 213.2/65.0	Navigation Officers: ....Russian	Swimming Pools (indoors): 0
Beam (ft/m): 42/12.8	Cabins (total): 26	Whirlpools: 0
Draft (ft/m): 15.0/4.6	Size Range (sq ft/m): ....n/a	Self-Service Launderette: ....No
Propulsion/Propellers: ....diesel	Cabins (outside view): 29	Dedicated Cinema/Seats: ....No
(2,327 kW)/2	Cabins (interior/no view): 0	Library: ....Yes

OVERALL SCORE: 947 (OUT OF A POSSIBLE 2,000 POINTS)

OVERVIEW. *Professor Molchanov* is an all-white vessel originally specially constructed in Finland for the former Soviet Union's polar and oceanographic research program and should not be taken as a cruise ship, although it was converted in the early 1990s to carry passengers, and then fitted out specifically for expedition cruising when refurbished in 1996. Other ships in the same series are *Akademik Boris Petrov, Akademik Golitsyn, Akademik M.A. Laurentiev, Akademik Nikolaj Strakhov, Livonia, Akademik Shokalskiy, Professor Khromov* and *Professor Multanovskiy*. It has an ice-hardened, steel hull, which is good for cruising in both the Arctic and Antarctic regions, and strong Russian diesel engines.

All passengers have access to the navigation bridge. There are several inflatable Zodiac landing craft for close-in shore excursions and nature observation trips.

Inside, the limited public rooms consist of a library and lounge/bar. The dining rooms also serve as a lecture room. The medical facilities are good.

This is expedition-style cruising, in a very small ship with limited facilities. However, it provides a somewhat primitive, but genuine adventure experience, taking you "up-close and personal" to places others only dream about. The bigger ships cannot get this close to Antarctica or the Arctic, but this little vessel will sail you right to the face of the ice continent.

Oceanwide Expeditions charters this ship for the Antarctic (winter) season, and has its own staff and lecturers on board, as well as oversees the food, to make sure that everything is up to the company's usual high standard.

BERLITZ'S RATINGS

	Possible	Achieved
Ship	500	227
Accommodation	200	87
Food	400	203
Service	400	188
Entertainment	n/a	n/a
Cruise	500	242

SUITABLE FOR: *Professor Molchanov* is best suited to couples and single travelers who enjoy viewing nature and wildlife at close quarters, and who would not dream of cruising in the mainstream sense aboard ships with large numbers of people. This is for hardy, adventurous types who don't feel the need for onboard entertainment.

ACCOMMODATION. There are five grades (the price you pay depends on the grade and location you choose). With the exception of a single "suite," almost all other cabins are very small, Spartan, and rather clinical. There are two-berth cabins with shower and toilet, or there are two-bed cabins on the lowest deck, whose occupants must share a bathroom.

CUISINE. There are two dining rooms (the galley is located between them), each with a single seating. The meals are hearty international fare, with no frills. When the ship is operated under charter to Oceanwide Expeditions, the quality of meals and variety of food is much better.

ENTERTAINMENT. There is no formal entertainment, although dinner and after-dinner conversation with fellow passengers in the ship's lounge/bar really becomes the entertainment each evening. So, if you don't want to talk to your fellow passengers, you should take a good book, or go outside, where you'll find nature is nothing less than diverting.

SPA/FITNESS. There are no spa or fitness facilities, although there is a sauna.

Professor Multanovskiy
★★

Boutique Ship: . . . . .1,753 tons	Passenger Decks: 3	Cabins (for one person): 9
Lifestyle: . . . . .Standard	Total Crew: 25	Cabins (with private balcony): 0
Cruise Line: . . . . . .Oceanwide Expeditions	Passengers	Cabins (wheelchair accessible): 0
Former Names: . . . . .none	(lower beds/all berths): 49/49	Cabin Current: . . . . .220 volts
Builder: . . . . .Wartsila (Finland)	Passenger Space Ratio	Elevators: 0
Original Cost: . . . . .n/a	(lower beds/all berths): 35.7/35.7	Casino (gaming tables): . . . . .No
Entered Service: 1983	Crew/Passenger Ratio	Slot Machines: .No
Registry: .Russia	(lower beds/all berths): 1.9/1.9	Swimming Pools (outdoors): 0
Length (ft/m): 213.2/65.0	Navigation Officers: . . . . .Russian	Swimming Pools (indoors): 0
Beam (ft/m): 42/12.8	Cabins (total): 29	Whirlpools: 0
Draft (ft/m): 15.0/4.6	Size Range (sq ft/m): . . . . .n/a	Self-Service Launderette: . . . . .No
Propulsion/Propellers: . . . . .diesel	Cabins (outside view): 29	Dedicated Cinema/Seats: . . . . .No
(2,327 kW)/2	Cabins (interior/no view): 0	Library: . . . . .Yes

OVERALL SCORE: 947 (OUT OF A POSSIBLE 2,000 POINTS)

OVERVIEW. *Professor Multanovskiy*, which has a dark hull and white super-structure, was originally built in Finland for the former Soviet Union's polar and oceanographic research programme run by the Russian Academy of Science. It should not be taken as a cruise ship, although it was converted in the early 1990s to carry passengers, and then fitted out specifically for expedition cruising when refurbished in 1996. Other ships in the series are *Akademik Boris Petrov, Akademik Golitsyn, Akademik M.A. Laurentiev, Akademik Nikolaj Strakhov, Akademik Shokalskiy, Livonia, Professor Khromov* and *Professor Molchanov.*

This ship is typically operated under charter to various "expedition" cruise companies. It has an ice-hardened, steel hull, which is good for cruising in both the Arctic and Antarctic, and strong Russian diesel engines. All passengers have access to the navigation bridge. There are several inflatable Zodiac landing craft for close-in shore excursions and nature observation trips. Inside, the limited public rooms consist of a library and lounge/bar. The dining rooms are also used for lectures. Medical facilities are good.

This is expedition-style cruising, in a very small ship with limited facilities. However, it provides a somewhat primitive, but genuine adventure experience, taking you "up-close and personal" to places others only dream about. The bigger ships cannot get this close to Antarctica or the Arctic, but this little vessel will sail you right to the face of the ice continent.

Quark Expeditions charters this ship for the Antarctic (winter) season, and has its own staff and lecturers on board. It also oversees the food, to make sure that everything is up to its usual high (Quark) standard.

BERLITZ'S RATINGS

	Possible	Achieved
Ship	500	227
Accommodation	200	87
Food	400	203
Service	400	188
Entertainment	n/a	n/a
Cruise	500	242

SUITABLE FOR: *Professor Multanovskiy* is best suited to couples and single travelers who enjoy viewing nature and wildlife at close quarters, and who would not dream of cruising in the mainstream sense aboard ships with large numbers of people. This is for hardy, adventurous types who don't feel the need for onboard entertainment.

ACCOMMODATION. There are five grades (the price you pay depends on the grade and location you choose). With the exception of one "suite," almost all other cabins are very small, Spartan, and rather clinical. There are two-berth cabins with shower and toilet, or there are two-bed cabins on the lowest deck, whose occupants must share a bathroom.

CUISINE. There are two dining rooms (the ship's galley is actually located between them), and all passengers are accommodated in a single seating. The meals are hearty international fare, with no frills. When the ship is under charter to Quark Expeditions, Western rather than Russian chefs oversee the food operation, and the quality of meals and variety of foods is much better.

ENTERTAINMENT. There is no formal entertainment, although dinner and after-dinner conversation with fellow passengers in the ship's lounge/bar really becomes the entertainment each evening. So, if you don't want to talk to your fellow passengers, take a good book, or go outside, where you'll find nature is nothing less than diverting.

SPA/FITNESS. There are no spa or fitness facilities, although there is a sauna.

Queen Mary 2
★★★★★ to ★★★★

Large Ocean Liner: . . . . .148,528 tons	Total Crew: 1,254	Cabins (wheelchair accessible): 30
Lifestyle: . . . . .Luxury/Premium/Standard	Passengers	Cabin Current: . . . . . . .110 and 220 volts
Cruise Line: . . . . .Cunard Line	(lower beds/all berths): 2,620/3,090	Elevators: 22
Former Names: . . . . .none	Passenger Space Ratio	Casino (gaming tables): . . . . .Yes
Builder: Chantiers de l'Atlantique (France)	(lower beds/all berths): 56.6/48.0	Slot Machines: . . . . .Yes
Original Cost: . . . .$800 million	Crew/Passenger Ratio	Swimming Pools (outdoors): 3
Entered Service: . . . . .Jan 2004	(lower beds/all berths): 2.0/2.4	Swimming Pools (indoors): 2
Registry: . . . . .Great Britain	Navigation Officers: . . . . .British	Whirlpools: 8
Length (ft/m): 1,131.9/345.03	Cabins (total): 1,310	Fitness Center: . . . . .Yes
Beam (ft/m): 134.5/41.00	Size Range (sq ft/m): 194.0–2,249.7/	Sauna/Steam Room: . . . . .Yes/Yes
Draft (ft/m): 32.6/9.95	18.0–209	Massage: . . . . .Yes
Propulsion/Propellers: . . . . . . .gas turbine	Cabins (outside view): 1,017	Self-Service Launderette: . . . . .Yes
(103,000kW) and diesel-electric/4 pods	Cabins (interior/no view): 293	Dedicated Cinema/Seats: . . . . .Yes
(2 azimuthing, 2 fixed/21.5 MW each)	Cabins (for one person): 0	Library: . . . . .Yes
Passenger Decks: 12	Cabins (with private balcony): 953	

OVERALL SCORE: (OUT OF A POSSIBLE 2,000 POINTS): GRILL CLASS 1,709; BRITANNIA CLASS 1,546

OVERVIEW. RMS *Queen Mary 2*, designated a Royal Mail Ship by the British Post Office, offers the pleasures of crossing the North Atlantic comfortably on a regular schedule, with the latest high-tech facilities and conveniences.

A ship of superlatives, *Queen Mary 2* (nicknamed *Proud Mary 2* by this author) is the largest passenger ship ever built (in terms of gross tonnage, length, and beam, though not passengers carried) and is five times the length of Cunard Line's first ship, *Britannia*. Taller than the Empire State Building, it is the first new ship to be built for Cunard Line since 1969, when *QE2* first sailed from Southampton to New York. *QM2* operates regularly scheduled transatlantic crossings for much of the year, and an annual round-the-world cruise from 2007.

Queen Mary 2's exterior design strongly resembles that of the now retired *QE2*, and for good reason: it was designed by naval architect Stephen Payne, an ocean liner specialist. This is a superbly designed ship, able to weather any unkind conditions on the North Atlantic, or anywhere else – hence her long foredeck, extra-thick plating and hull, designed to maintain a high speed and battle against unkind sea conditions. It has a large, contemporary funnel and beautifully tiered stern, but it is too wide of beam to transit the Panama Canal.

The power and propulsion system comprises an environmentally friendly General Electric marine gas turbine and diesel-electric power plant developing 157,000 horsepower (117.2 MW) – enough to provide power to the 200,000 inhabitants of its home port, Southampton. The ship is propeled by the world's first four-pod propulsion system (Rolls-

BERLITZ'S RATINGS

Grill Class	Possible	Achieved
Ship	500	440
Accommodation	200	175
Food	400	330
Service	400	336
Entertainment	100	84
Cruise	400	344
Britannia Class		
Ship	500	408
Accommodation	200	147
Food	400	285
Service	400	295
Entertainment	100	83
Cruise	400	328

Royce), which can power through the waters of the North Atlantic at up to 30 knots (the contracted top speed is 29.3 knots, although the ship can easily exceed this). Each pod weighs 270 tons (more than an empty Boeing 747 jumbo jet), and are powered by a diesel-electric system. Indeed, this ship can go backwards faster than many cruise ships can go forwards.

QM2 was built at the Chantiers de l'Atlantique shipyard in France, in a dry dock measuring 1,360 by 207 ft (415 by 63 meters). The first steel was cut on January 16, 2002, while the keel laying took place on July 4, 2002 – 162 years to the day that the first Cunard steamship, *Britannia*, made its first crossing. The huge ship, constructed in 98 large blocks, each weighing up to 600 tons, was completed an incredibly short 24 months later (964 days, to be exact).

One of the many delightful features is the ship's Tyfon whistle: (there are two: one is new, and the other a copy of the whistle from the original *Queen Mary*, carried to Europe by *QE 2* prior to being fitted to *QM2* in the shipyard). Manufactured by Kockums in Sweden, the replica was inspected, cleaned and converted from steam power to air power. It is 7 ft long and 3 ft high (2.1 meters by 0.9 meters), and weighs 1,400 pounds (635 kg). Both whistles are tuned so that they do not disturb passengers on deck, yet they can be heard 10 miles away.

Almost everything about the liner is British in style (but with some American decor input and accents), and even the four tender stations have London names: Belgravia, Chelsea, Kensington and Knightsbridge. There is a wide wrap-around promenade deck outdoors (with the forward section under cover from the weather or wind). Three times around is 6,102 ft (1,860 meters), or 1.1 miles (1.6 km). Inside are several other walking promenades – good if the weather is poor (for instance, it's almost 300 steps, or three minutes, from fore to aft along Deck 9). A full line of teak "steamer" chairs are provided on the open walk-around promenade deck, but still leaves plenty of room for walkers to pass (however, plastic sunloungers are provided on some other open decks – particularly at the aft of the ship). An exterior, winged observation platform, directly under the navigation bridge, offers great sightlines along the ship's length, as well as forward.

Robert Tillberg, the interior designer, has produced designs that are, for the most part, stylish and elegant, with towering public spaces, sweeping staircases and grand public rooms that exude a feeling of timelessness. High ceilings (typically two decks of *QM2* are the equivalent of three decks in height of a regular cruise vessel) provide a great sense of space and grandeur. While many ships are designed inward with a central atrium, *QM2* is very different. You enter the public rooms from a central location and will always be looking out, with the sea in the background. What's good is the fact that just four staircases traverse all decks (unlike *QE2*, which has 10, having been built as a three-class ship, then changed before introduction to a two-class liner). Deck signage is good, and it's quite easy to find one's way around the ship for the most part, although more fore and aft signs would be useful.

There are a few ostentatious gold pillars and tacky decorative elements (including some awful "bas-reliefs" in the accommodation passageways – perhaps the "Miami Beach" view of what a transatlantic liner looks like). But, for the most part, the ship's interiors are quite stunning, and subtly so. The use of wood laminate paneling may abhor ship buffs (as did the plastic laminates when *QE2* debuted in 1968–69), but is the result of stringent SOLAS regulations.

The spacious atrium lobby, spanning six decks, has an elegant staircase and exclusive works of art. In the main elevator lobby attached to the central atrium, a wall mural of Samuel Cunard welcomes you aboard; it looks like an enlarged photograph, although it is made from almost 700 postage stamp-sized digital images of previous Cunard ships.

Here's a deck-by-deck look at the facilities and public rooms aboard what is undoubtedly the most superlative ocean liner ever (starting at the lowest deck and working our way upward, forward to aft):

● Deck 2 has Illuminations (with planetarium), and the Royal Court Theatre, the lower level of the six-deck high atrium lobby, the Purser's Desk, Video Arcade, Empire Casino, Golden Lion Pub, and the lower level of the two-deck high Britannia Restaurant.

● Deck 3 has the upper level of Illuminations and the Royal Court Theatre, the second level of the six-deck high atrium lobby, Mayfair Shops, Sir Samuel's, The Chart Room, Champagne Bar (Veuve Clicquot is the "house" champagne), the upper level of the Britannia Restaurant, the Queens Room, and the G32 Nightclub.

● Decks 4/Deck 5/Deck 6 have accommodation and the third, fourth and fifth levels of the six-deck high atrium

lobby; at the aft end of Deck 6 are the facilities for children, including an outdoor pool (Minnows Pool).

● Deck 7 has the Canyon Ranch Spa, the Winter Garden, the sixth and uppermost level of the six-deck high atrium lobby, expansive Kings Court Buffet, Queens Grill Lounge, Queens Grill and Princess Grill dining salons.

● Deck 8 (forward) has the upper level of the Canyon Ranch Spa, and the Library and Bookshop. The center section has accommodation. In the aft section are the alternative restaurant Todd English, Terrace Bar, and swimming pool outdoors.

● Deck 9 (forward) has the Commodore Club, Boardroom and the Cigar Club (Churchills). The rest of the deck has accommodation and a Concierge Club for suite occupants.

● Deck 10 has accommodation only.

● Deck 11 (forward) has an outdoors observation area. The rest of the deck has accommodation. The aft section outdoors has a whirlpool tub and sunbathing deck.

● Deck 12 (forward) has accommodation. The mid-section has an indoor/outdoor pool (with sliding glass roof), and golf areas (Fairways). The aft section has the Boardwalk Cafe, dog kennels, and shuffleboard courts.

● Deck 13 has the Sports Centre, Regatta Bar, a splash pool, and extensive outdoor sunbathing space.

There are 14 lounges, clubs and bars. An observation lounge, the delightful Commodore Club, has commanding views forward over the bows; light jazz is played in this bar, which is connected to the Boardroom, and Cigar Lounge. Other drinking places include a Golden Lion Pub, a wine bar (Sir Samuel's), a nautically-themed cocktail bar (The Chart Room), and Champagne/Coffee Bar. Bars outdoors include the Regatta Bar and Terrace Bar. The G32 nightclub, which has a main and mezzanine level, is located at the aft end of the ship, away from passenger cabins; it is named after the number designated to the ship by its French builder. The Empire Casino has a bar, as well as the latest high-tech slot machines, and traditional gaming tables.

The Queens Room is a grand ballroom, and, with the largest dance floor at sea, is a stunning, gloriously proportioned room, with a Hollywood-Bowl-style bandstand canopy. It has a dramatic high ceiling, two huge crystal chandeliers, highly comfortable armchairs, and is used for dancing, cocktail parties, and afternoon teas.

Illuminations, the first full-scale planetarium at sea, is a stunning multi-purpose show lounge space that also functions as a 473-seat grand cinema and even a broadcasting studio. As a planetarium, it has tiered seating rows, with 150 very comfortable (reclining) seats and plush fabrics, allowing you to sit in a special area under a dome, which is 38 ft/11.5 meters in diameter and almost 20 ft/6 meters deep that forms the setting for the night sky. Whatever you do, don't miss reserving a seat for at least one of the five outstanding 20-minute programs, when the dome is lowered, and suspended over you and 13 computers take you out of this world.

A Maritime Quest Exhibit provides a beautifully constructed Cunard history plus shipbuilding milestones throughout history, including John Brown's shipyard that built the original *Queen Mary* in the 1930s.

Just aft of the Canyon Ranch Spa is a colonial-style Winter Garden (reminiscent of London's Kew Gardens), where flowers bloom year-round (which means they are artificial – some are downright tacky). This peaceful garden setting is for relaxation; a string quartet could well be playing for afternoon tea (which is also served in the much larger, elegant Queen's Room).

There are five swimming pools, including one that can be enclosed under a retractable sliding glass roof; this is useful in bad weather. A large area (21,100 sq. ft/1,960 sq. meters) of open sunning space includes a sports bar at one end. Sports facilities include an electronic golf simulator, putting green, giant chess board and a paddle tennis court.

The ship's Library and Bookshop, a fine facility that is very popular on transatlantic crossings, is located forward; it has a superb display of 8,000 books (in several languages). Full-time librarians are present, and the area includes leather sofas and armchairs, six internet-connect computers, and a large selection of magazines. It is a delightful facility, but there are few chairs, and the adjacent bookshop is quite small.

ConneXions, an education center, includes seven sophisticated classrooms for Oxford University's "Oxford Discovery" programs. Classes in such things as computer learning, seamanship and navigation, art and wine appreciation, history, languages and photography are taught. Meanwhile, fast-access internet connectivity and a multitude of computer terminals can be found in the Internet Center (several connection packages are provided: from $13.50 for 50 minutes' use, to $47.95 for 120 minutes, up to $479 for 1,920 minutes). Full wi-fi service for your own laptop is available round the clock in the Chart Room, Commodore Club, Golden Lion Pub, Grand Lobby, Library, Queens Grill Lounge, Sir Samuels Wine Bar and the Winter Garden.

Children have their own space, with a dedicated play area, the Play Zone. English nannies supervise toddlers, while older children use The Zone.

You can take your dog with you on transatlantic crossings – but not on cruises – and 12 kennels are overseen by a kennel master. Dogs (and cats) receive a complimentary gift pack containing a QM2-logo coat, frisbee, name tag, food dish and scoop; a portrait with pet owners; a crossing certificate and personalized cruise card. Other pet perks include an assortment of toys, cat posts and scratchers, and a selection of top-brand premium pet foods. You can make kennel reservations when you book. The cost: $300–$500.

SOME COMMENTS: *Queen Mary 2* is a floating city, and, like any city, there are several parts of town (some elegant, some not so elegant, some slightly tacky). To the disappointment of many regular transatlantic passengers, there are no single cabins.

QM2, unlike *QE2*, has no dedicated cinema – a shame since the ship is specifically built for the North Atlantic crossings, when a cinema is much appreciated by frequent passengers (films are, however, shown daily in Illuminations or the Royal Theatre). The grill rooms are too large to be intimate, and are more akin to the kind of grill/steakhouses one finds in large North American cities.

The framed, animated cartoons on display (and for sale) in The Gallery don't quite go with the *QM2*'s ocean liner image; neither do art auctions or bazaar stalls selling gold chains, tee-shirts and other tacky items found aboard many cruise ships today. Gratuities are charged to your onboard account at $11–$13 per person, per day, according to the grade of accommodation chosen. A 15% gratuity is included in all beverage and wine orders. As for extra charges, drinks prices are quite reasonable, but a 10-inch by 8-inch embarkation photo will cost $27.50.

A crossing or voyage aboard *QM2* can be considered luxurious only if you travel in Queens Grill accommodation. Otherwise, the experience ranges from "standard" to "premium" in the other accommodation grades (and little different to regular cruise ships in these market segments). While there are a few delightful wooden sunloungers (with green padded cushions), the majority of sunloungers (particularly on the open decks aft) are plastic.

QM2 passengers are a mixed bunch. Most are well dressed, although numerous "tracksuiters'" inhabit the ship, particularly in the Kings Court. Overall, some may feel overwhelmed by the decor's understated look, or by the bold carpets, but, whatever you may think, the ship absorbs passengers well. While not as ornate as some would like, *QM2* is decidedly spacious and comforting, once you find your way around, although it'll take a week to discover all the out-of-the-way nooks and crannies.

TRANSATLANTIC CROSSINGS: The ship is supremely quiet in operation, with almost no vibration, even when traveling at top speed in poor weather. The large amount of personal luggage allowed is especially useful for anyone relocating, or for extended holidays. When you arrive in New York or Southampton, after six days of not having to lift a finger, it often proves to be a bittersweet anti-climax after the calming effects of *QM2* on one's inner being. I can think of little that is more pleasing to the soul or more civilized than a transatlantic crossing, of being cosseted in the finery of dining in any of the three grill restaurants with their fine cuisine and presentation (Grill Class accommodations only).

As a transatlantic ocean liner, this ship has no equal; it rides extremely well, and displays superb sea-keeping characteristics, with virtually no vibration from its pod propulsion system. If you can afford to travel in Grill Class accommodation, you will be cosseted in high comfort, and experience the very best service available in the grand transatlantic ocean liner traditions of today (including reserved open deck sunning space). If you travel in Britannia Class accommodation, the ship will provide you with a way to cross the North Atlantic, but with dining arrangements that are more akin to many of the large (resort) ships of today (although this equates to a dumbing down of food quality and presentation).

Note that if you travel in accommodation with a balcony and you want sunshine on the crossing from Southampton to New York (westbound), book a suite/cabin on the port side. Eastbound, book on the starboard side. Going westbound, the Statue of Liberty will normally be on the port side, and, on leaving New York, on the starboard side.

QM2 now berths not in Manhattan but at the Red Hook Pier 12 passenger terminal in Brooklyn. In Southampton, England, the ship docks at the Queen Elizabeth II Ocean Terminal. Four special transatlantic packages are named The Queens, The Princess, The Buckingham and The Windsor. Each provides a combination of a one-way crossing with hotels and flights of differing classes and standards, according to the fare paid. Tailor-made programs are also available.

A few niggling items dent the premium image. One example is wooden stirrers (instead of real spoons) in the Kings Court – an indication of the "Carnivalization" of Cunard Line, although, to be honest, without the Carnival Corporation, Cunard Line would not have survived in today's harsh economic climate. Another regret is the removal of a transatlantic favorite, mid-morning bouillon service on deck.

Cunard Line charters the Orient Express Boat Train between London's Waterloo Station and Southampton Docks; the train pulls up right alongside the Ocean Terminal to connect with the ship. This special train consists exclusively of Pullman carriages, richly paneled and fitted with individual deep-upholstery seats. Complimentary hot canapés and champagne are served. Passengers can complete all formalities and ship check-in procedures on the train, and simply walk directly on board *QM2* on arrival in Southampton. Baggage loaded onto the train's baggage carriage in Waterloo is delivered directly to your cabin.

THE CRUISE EXPERIENCE: *QM2* is a large ship (with an elite Grill-class section), and, where several tender ports are included in itineraries, spending time obtaining tender tickets to go ashore detracts from the overall experience (although itineraries have been planned to include as many "alongside" ports as possible). The passenger flow is generally sound, although there are difficulties in accessing some of the public rooms due to the rather disjointed interior design, and the ship absorbs passengers extremely well with no sense of crowding. Sadly, there is nowhere to have breakfast outdoors if you don't have a balcony cabin (and lunch at the outdoors Boardwalk Café consists mainly of fast-food items).

COMPARING QM2 AND QE2: Cunard Line's many repeat passengers who loved *QE2* will inevitably make comparisons between the two ships. *QM2* has two classes and only four staircases; *QE2* had three classes and 10 staircases. *QE2* had many cabins for single occupancy; *QM2* has none, and single-occupancy premiums are extremely high. *QE2* had a Baggage Master; *QM2* does not. *QE2*'s Queens Grill and Princess Grill restaurants were far more intimate, and had nicer decor than those of *QM2*. Aboard *QM2* there is no private lounge for Princess Grill passengers; but they do share the Queens Grill Lounge.

SUITABLE FOR: *Queen Mary 2* is best suited to a wide range of couples and single travelers who enjoy the cosmopolitan setting of a floating city at sea that has a maritime heritage and background unequaled by any other ship and

cruise line today, with its extensive array of facilities, public rooms, and dining rooms.

ACCOMMODATION. Although there are now four separate categories (Queens Grill, Princess Grill, Britannia Club, and Britannia), *QM2* really operates as a two-class ship (Grill Class and Britannia Class), and the restaurant you are assigned to depends on the accommodation grade you choose. There are 10 categories, in 25 different price grades. The price you pay will depend on grade, location and size. From standard outside-view cabins to the most opulent suites afloat, there is something for every taste and pocketbook – a choice unrivaled aboard any other cruise vessel.

Perhaps the most noticeable difference between this ship and *QE2* is the addition of a large number of cabins with private balconies (75 percent of all cabins have them, although they are really of little use when crossing the North Atlantic (when *QE2* debuted in 1969, there was not one single balcony cabin). However, the balconies have steel bulkheads that obscure ocean views when you are seated. Some 12 cabins look inwards to the atrium lobby, which spans six decks.

All grades have a 20-inch (or larger) color television with concealed interactive keyboard, internet connectivity (via a data port for your laptop). All beds have fluffy European duvets, mini-fridge, personal safe, hand-held hairdryer, and all bathrooms have toiletry amenities supplied by Canyon Ranch (the spa/fitness concession).

Other features include digital video on demand (English-, French- and German-language movies are available), music on demand (with 3,000 titles), audio books on demand, and email and digital photographs preview and purchase (the system can be blocked so that children cannot access it). One channel is devoted to the history of Cunard Line.

The interactive system also lets you make restaurant reservations, order wine, or items from the shops on board, book shore excursions, look at your onboard account, and biuographies of entertainers on board. Portable computers can be connected via a port in the cabin telephone.

A number of cabins can accommodate a third or fourth person, although they are so small as to be useful only for contortionists (they are, however, the most inexpensive way of experiencing this fine ship). Note that you get a different cabin breakfast menu depending on whether you travel in Grill Class or Britannia Class accommodation.

For the largest accommodation in the cruise industry, two combinations offer the equivalent of a large house at sea. At the front of the ship, you can combine the Queen Elizabeth and Queen Mary suites with the Queen Anne and Queen Victoria suites to produce one huge suite measuring 5,016 sq. ft (466 sq. meters). Even this can be eclipsed at the other end of the ship, by joining Grand Duplex apartments at the lower level to the adjacent penthouses to produce an unprecedented 8,288 sq. ft (770 sq. meters).

Balmoral/Sandringham Duplexes (Grade Q1): The largest stand-alone accommodation can be found in the

Balmoral and Sandringham Duplexes (2,249 sq. ft/209 sq. meters). These are located aft in prime real estate territory, with superb views along the entire length of the ship. Upstairs is a bedroom with wood-framed king-sized bed, and large (but not so private) balcony; downstairs is a living room with sofa, coffee table, dining table, and writing desk. There are two marble-clad bathrooms with whirlpool bath and separate shower enclosure, toilet and bidet, and two washbasins.

Queen Elizabeth/Queen Mary Suites (Grade Q2): The Queen Elizabeth Suite and Queen Mary Suite (1,194 sq. ft/111 sq. meters) are both located just under the navigation bridge, with good views over the ship's long bows. There are living and dining areas, with a large private balcony (but not as large as the Balmoral/ Sandringham duplex balconies). The master, marble-clad bathroom has a whirlpool bathtub and shower enclosure, and a second bathroom with a shower enclosure (no bathtub). Each suite has the convenience of private elevator access.

Queen Anne/Queen Victoria Suites (Grade Q3): These two suites (796.5 sq. ft/74 sq. meters) have the most commanding views over the ship's long bows. They consist of a bedroom with master, marble-clad bathroom with whirlpool bathtub and separate shower enclosure; separate living/dining area, and a second bathroom with a shower enclosure (no bathtub).

Duplex Apartments: There are three duplex apartments: Buckingham and Windsor (each 1,291 sq. ft/120 sq. meters), and Hollyrood (1,566 sq. ft/145 sq. meters). Each has a gymnasium, balcony, butler and concierge service, and superb views over the ship's stern.

Penthouse Suites (Grade Q4): There are six penthouse suites (758 sq. ft/70 sq. meters). These have a living and dining area, large private balcony, bedroom and dressing room with master, marble-clad bathroom with whirlpool bathtub and separate shower enclosure.

Suites (506 sq ft (Grade Q5/Q6): These 82 suites (506 sq. ft/47 sq. meters) have a large private balcony, living area, dressing room, marble-clad bathroom with whirlpool bathtub and separate shower enclosure. Beds can be arranged in a king-size or twin-bed configuration.

Junior Suites (Grade P1/P2): There are 76 Junior Suites (381 sq. ft/35 sq. meters). Each has a lounge area, large private balcony, and marble-clad bathroom with whirlpool bathtub and separate shower enclosure. Beds can be arranged in a king-sized or twin-bed configuration.

Deluxe/Premium Balcony Cabins: These 782 cabins (248 sq. ft/23 sq. meters) include a sitting area with sofa, and bathroom with shower enclosure. Beds can be arranged in a king-sized or twin-bed configuration.

Standard Outside-View/Interior (No View) Cabins: There are 62 outside-view cabins and 281 interior (no view) cabins measuring 194 sq. ft/18 sq. meters). Beds can be arranged in a king-sized or twin-bed configuration.

Atrium View Cabins: Each of these 12 interior cabins (194 sq. ft/18 sq. meters) has an unusual view – into the six-deck high atrium lobby. Beds can be arranged in a king-sized or twin-bed configuration. An en-suite bath-

room has a shower enclosure, washbasin, toilet, and toiletries cabinet.

Wheelchair Accessible Cabins: There are 30 suites and cabins (in various categories) specially designed for wheelchair users. All have pull-down closet hanging rails, above-bed emergency pull-cord, and large, well-equipped bathrooms with roll-in showers and handrails. Facilities for blind passengers include Braille signs and tactile room signs. Eight special wheelchair-accessible elevators are provided to service the dining areas. Additionally, some 36 cabins have been designated to accommodate deaf or hearing-impaired passengers. There are headsets in the Royal Theatre and Planetarium, and close captioned television.

CUISINE. Naturally, you should expect lavish dining, and accept nothing less. In all there are 14 bars, and 7 galleys serving 10 dining rooms and eateries. All dining rooms and eateries have ocean-view windows.

An fine selection of wines and champagnes is available (selections and recommendations were made by Michael Broadbent, one of the world's top wine experts), with per bottle prices varying between $20 and $315 (white wines), $20 and $2,650 (red wines), and $35 and $875 (champagne), all plus a 15% gratuity.

Britannia Restaurant: This main dining room seats 1,347, and spans the full beam of the ship. A lavish room almost three decks high, it has two grand sweeping staircases which enable you to make your entry in style. Above the staircase is a huge light well (reminiscent of the great oceanliners of yesteryear) and large, classic columns, while the centerpiece backdrop to the staircase is a huge tapestry of *QM2* against the New York skyline. Breakfast and lunch are now in an open-seating arrangement, while dinner is in two seatings, all with crisp linen and fine china, of course. Vegetarian options are provided on all lunch and dinner menus. One downside of open seating for breakfast or lunch is that you will probably have a different waiter each time, who will not know your preferences. Another is that if you are seated on the lower level underneath the balcony formed along the port and starboard sides of the upper level, you'll get the feeling of being enclosed in an inferior space. And that is exactly what it is – an inferior space (better to get a table in the central well or on the upper level).

In 2007, 46 staterooms were re-graded (category AA) and occupants of these cabins are now served somewhat upgraded cuisine in an exclusive private dining area within the Britannia Restaurant (Britannia Club Class). This single-seating club-like restaurant will offer the Britannia Restaurant menu, plus various à la carte options and table-side flambé service.

Queens Grill/Princess Grill: There are two Grill Rooms (Queens Grill and Princess Grill), which I call small dining salons. Which restaurant you dine in depends on your accommodation grade (and the price paid). Both the 200-seat Queens Grill and 178-seat Princess Grill are located aft and have, in theory, fine ocean-view windows (although walkers passing by on the exterior promenade deck can be disturbing in the daytime, so window blinds have to be kept down, which rather negates the outside view). They were modified and given a more intimate feel during a dry-dock in 2005, and both feature an ungainly black marble contemporary statue I have named the "Black Widow" in their entrances. Passengers in the most spacious and luxurious suites, therefore, may feel less special, being mixed, as they are, among all others in Grill Class accommodation. Canyon Ranch Spaclub recommendations are provided on all lunch and dinner menus, as are vegetarian options.

The Queens Grill is decorated in gold, and passengers who dine in this exclusive establishment have their own Queens Grill Bar and Terrace. Unfortunately, Cunard chose not to dispense with waiter stations, which can be noisy at times. The chairs are comfortable, and many have armrests (curiously those at tables for two do not – although you could always request them), and the dining table height is just right. An impressive à la carte menu is provided in addition to the regular menu (Queens Grill regulars also know they can order specials at any time). The dining experience in the Queen Grill is, in a word, excellent.

Todd English Restaurant: This alternative 216-seat reservations-only restaurant (cover charge: $20 for lunch and $30 for dinner) is named after Todd English, the chef whose restaurant in Boston (Olives) has become one of the best-known in high gastronomic circles in the US. It represents the American television chef's first venture at sea. The restaurant, with its Moorish decor, features his noted Mediterranean cuisine. The room has been designed with intimate detailing and architecture and overlooks the Pool Terrace, allowing for al fresco dining. Food presentation is excellent, although overly fussy at times, but the venue is disappointing.

Kings Court: This nondescript, informal eatery has 478 seats and obnoxious daytime lighting, and is reminiscent of such eateries found in land-based shopping malls. It offers self-serve breakfast and lunch. Breakfast is basically the same every day and includes British traditional standards: eggs, bacon, kippers and fried tomatoes. The lunch menu changes daily, and includes several Indian dishes (such as curried rice and chicken). Pizza, however, cannot be recommended (think cardboard with toppings).

At night, decorated screens transform Kings Court into four different dining venues: an Italian Trattoria (La Piazza), Asian cuisine (Lotus), a British eatery (The Carvery) for roast meats, and a Chef's Galley; all have full sit-down tablecloth service. The 36-seat Chef's Galley has a live demonstration of the meal preparation that you then enjoy – at no extra charge. Cooking demonstrations can be broadcast via close circuit TV onto a large screen. Colorful "street entertainment" is performed in the Kings Court on some evenings.

Fast Foodies can find comfort foods in the outdoors Boardwalk cafe (weather permitting), while pub lovers can find traditional British fare in the always-popular Golden Lion Pub (including steak & mushroom pie, bangers and mash, and fish and chips). If you are shy and

retiring and want complete privacy, or if you are recuperating from a busy working life, you can also order from the restaurant menus and have breakfast, lunch and dinner served in your own suite or cabin.

ENTERTAINMENT. The Royal Court Theatre has tiered seating for 1,094, though some sightlines are less than ideal, and is the main venue for evening entertainment, with lavish West End-style productions as well as featured headline entertainers and cabaret acts such as illusionists, comedians, comedy jugglers, acrobats, vocalists, and others. The Royal Academy of Dramatic Art (RADA) supplies a company of actors/actresses to perform and lead acting workshops in both the Royal Court Theatre and Illuminations (incorporating the Planetarium).

The ship carries a number of high-class bands, small musical units, duos and solo entertainers who provide live music in most of the 14 lounges and bars. Also, under a partnership with Oxford University, the ship's enrichment program features specialist lecturers such as authors, artists, historians, scientists and other celebrated intellectuals.

SPA/FITNESS. Health Spa and Beauty Services are provided in a 20,000 sq. ft (1,850 sq. meters) Canyon Ranch Spa Club arranged on two decks. Wellbeing treatments include many variations on the theme of massage and skin treatments, including Ayurvedic massage, aromatherapy and seaweed treatments, facials and masks, conditioning body scrubs and therapeutic body cocoons.

A thalassotherapy pool (with airbed recliner loungers, neck fountains, a deluge waterfall, airtub and body massage jet benches), whirlpool, and thermal suite (with saunas and aromatic steam rooms, and a Rasul treatment chamber) are part of the facilities of the extensive spa; there is a daily charge for using the facilities ($25 on sea days, $19 for port days), although this is waived if you purchase a treatment. In all, there are 24 wellbeing (body and skin-care) treatment rooms.

Treatment price examples: Standard Massage $119 for 50 minutes; Hot Stone Massage $189 for 80 minutes; Aromatherapy Massage $129 for 50 minutes, $189 for 80 minutes; Facial $129 for 50 minutes; Shampoo/Set/Dry $39–$59 depending on hair length; Manicure $39 for 30 minutes; Pedicure $69-$119 for 60–80 minutes. You could also have a "Euphoria" treatment, which is a bath, facial and scalp massage followed by a body massage, for "just" $239. Prices include a gratuity. Treatment prices are for sea days (prices slightly less on port days).

A gymnasium has the latest equipment, as well as free weights. In addition, a beauty salon offers a full menu of services for hair and skin, and Canyon Ranch's own range of natural skincare products (Living Essentials) is available for sale. As there are only six hairdressing chairs, appointments should be booked as early as possible. The spa is staffed by 51 Canyon Ranch employees and operated as a concession.

Queen Victoria
★★★★ + to ★★★★

Large Resort Ship: ....90,049 tons	Total Crew: 1,001	Cabins (with private balcony): 718
Lifestyle: ....Premium	Passengers	Cabins (wheelchair accessible): 20
Cruise Line: ....Cunard Line	(lower beds/all berths): 2,014/2,172	Cabin Current: ....110/220 volts
Former Names: ....none	Passenger Space Ratio	Elevators: 12
Builder: ....Fincantieri (Italy)	(lower beds/all berths): 44.7/41.4	Casino (gaming tables): ....Yes
Original Cost: ....$390 million	Crew/Passenger Ratio	Slot Machines: ....Yes
Entered Service: ....Dec 2007	(lower beds/all berths): 2.2/2.4	Swimming Pools (outdoors): 2
Registry: ....Great Britain	Navigation Officers: ....British	Swimming Pools (indoors): 0
Length (ft/m): 964.5/294.0	Cabins (total): 1,007	Whirlpools: 5
Beam (ft/m): 105.9/32.3	Size Range (sq ft/m): 143.0–2,131.3/	Self-Service Launderette: ....Yes
Draft (ft/m): 26.2/8.0	13.2–198.0	Dedicated Cinema/Seats: ....No
Propulsion/Propellers: .....diesel-electric	Cabins (outside view): 864	Library: ....Yes
(66,000kW)/pod propulsion (2)	Cabins (interior/no view): 143	
Passenger Decks: 12	Cabins (for one person): 0	

OVERALL SCORE: (OUT OF A POSSIBLE 2,000 POINTS): GRILL CLASS 1,692; BRITANNIA CLASS 1,496

OVERVIEW. *Queen Victoria* flies the British Red Ensign for the ship's UK registry, and is aimed at both the North American and British markets. Unlike *Queen Mary 2*, it can transit the Panama Canal (useful for long voyages).

Although basically the same platform and layout as the "Vista" series of ships (examples: *Arcadia, Carnival Legend, Costa Atlantica, Oosterdam*), the Cunard version has an additional passenger deck, a specially strengthened hull lengthened by 36 ft (11 meters), giving the ship more of an "ocean liner" feel – although it's more of a cruise ship – and a dramatically modified interior layout.

Outdoors facilities include a promenade deck you can almost walk around (the forward section is for crew only), with several deck lounge chairs with comfortable Cunard-logo cushioned pads (good place to read a book). One open deck has a life-sized chess board.

Queen Victoria also has a classy interior layout that takes the best and most favourite public rooms, bars and lounges aboard *QM2* and from the now retired *Queen Elizabeth 2* and sets them into a high-tech ship designed to offer both trans-Atlantic and trans-Pacific crossings (but with a maximum speed of 23.7 knots), as well as squeeze through the Panama Canal and offer a mix or cruises and long voyages.

The interior decor is best termed "traditional" in Cunard-speak, with many of the public rooms finely decorated in Edwardian/Victoria styles, with delightful wrought-iron balustrading on the staircases and in some of the bars. Most rooms have fine wood (veneer) paneling and decorative

BERLITZ'S RATINGS

Grill Class	Possible	Achieved
Ship	500	430
Accommodation	200	171
Food	400	331
Service	400	335
Entertainment	100	83
Cruise	400	342
Britannia Class		
Ship	500	397
Accommodation	200	125
Food	400	281
Service	400	298
Entertainment	100	83
Cruise	400	312

accents like wrought-iron horseshoe-shaped stairways, scrolled woodwork and etched glass panels.

Other features include a majestic three-deck high Grand Lobby with a sweeping staircase, sculpted balconies and other elegant decorative touches, and a Cunardia floating museum whose glass cabinets display models of former Cunard ships, old menus and daily programs. A shop sells memorabilia.

Several public rooms are two decks high; these include the gold-beige Queen's Room, with a large, proper wooden ballroom dance floor (it measures about 1,000 sq.ft/93 sq. meters); above are two huge ceiling-mounted chandeliers. The bandstand is fronted by a large proscenium arch, while cantilevered balconies line the room's sides. Traditional British afternoon tea is served in this art deco-style grand room.

The Royal Arcade is a cluster of seven shops, including Harrods, Royal Doulton and Wedgwood, set in an arcade-like environment. At the forward end is a horseshoe-shaped staircase, above which is a magnificent British-made chiming pillar clock made by Dent of London – the company that created Big Ben at the Houses of Parliament and the official clockmaker to Queen Victoria herself, since 1841.

Some other venues worth noting:

● The **Library** is a stunning two-deck-high wood panelled 6,000-book facility with two full-time librarians, and bookshop selling maritime-related books, maps and stationery – but there are few chairs to sit and read in. It's a great place to meet people, quietly.

● **Golden Lion Pub** – a must aboard a Cunarder. This one

lies along the starboard side, and is a good gathering place.

● The **Commodore Club** acts as an observation lounge, with its ocean views on three sides.

● The adjacent **Churchill's Cigar Lounge**, on the starboard side, is a haven for smokers.

● **Chart Room Bar**, a conservatory with central fountain, greenery, and pool with a retractable glass dome roof.

● **Hemispheres**, positioned aft of the mast, overlooking the wood-decked Pavilion Pool.

● There's also a large **casino**.

Art works worth more than $2 million, including original etchings by the liner's namesake and her husband Prince Albert, adorn various walls.

The layout is a little disjointed on the uppermost decks. Note that access between the aft deck and the pool area and winter gardens can be gained only by going through the bufffet area. This makes for congestion at the self-serve buffet as people are constantly passing through.

The onboard currency is the UK pound. A per person, per day gratuity is charged to your onboard account, and a 15% gratuity is added to all bar and wine accounts.

SUITABLE FOR: *Queen Victoria* is best suited to a couples and single travelers who enjoy the cosmopolitan setting of a ship that features traditional British ocean liner decor and world-wide cruise itineraries.

ACCOMMODATION. There are 31 different price grades (but just eight types of accommodation, which ranges from "ample" to opulent (note: balconies are included in measurements, which are approximate); 7 Queens Grill, 8 Princess Grill, and 20 Britannia grades.

Grand Suites (4, measuring 1,918–2,131 sq.ft). They are located aft, with great ocean views from their private wraparound balconies, which contain a complete wet bar. The suites have two bedrooms with walk-in closets; bathroom with bathtub and separate shower enclosure; lounge; dining room (with seating for six). In-suite dining from the Queens Grill menus is also available.

Master Suites (2, measuring 1,100 sq.ft.), both located in the center of the ship (Deck 7).

Penthouse Suites (25, measuring 520–707 sq.ft).

Queens Suites (35, measuring 508–771 sq.ft).

Princess Suites (61, measuring 342–513 sq.ft).

Balcony Cabins (581, measuring 242–472 sq.ft).

Outside-View Cabins (146, measuring 180–201 sq.ft).

Interior (no-view) Cabins (143, measuring 151–243 sq.ft).

All accommodation grades have both British three-pin (240 volt) sockets and American and European-style two-pin (110 volt) sockets. Gilchrist & Soames personal toiletries (bath/shampoo gel, shampoo, shower cap, cotton buds) are supplied to all passengers, and a hairdryer is stored in the vanity desk units.

The regular cabins (Grades C/D) are small, but functional. However, the cabinetry resembles that in an Ibis hotel – a bit austere and lacking in character. There is a distinct lack of drawer space in a cabin supposedly designed for two persons – it's very noticeable on long voyages. The premium mattresses are, however, excellent. The bathrooms, also, are fairly bland and similar to those found aboard the ships of Princess Cruises, with small washbasins, and little storage space for personal toiletries. The fixed-head shower doesn't permit the thorough wash that hand-held flexible hoses do. Overall, the standard cabins are disappointing – so, for more space and quality, consider booking something better.

CUISINE/DINING. The **Britannia Restaurant** (the name is taken from a former Cunard ocean liner of 1914–50), located in the ship's aft section, is two decks high, with seating on both main and balcony levels – spiral stairways link both levels. There are two seatings. Waterford Wedgwood china is provided.

Exclusive Dining (Queen Grill, Princess Grill)
In keeping with *QM2,* there are special Grill-Class only restaurants in a single seating arrangement, providing a much more intimate and exclusive dining experience than can be found in the two-seating main Britannia Restaurant. The 142-seat Queens Grill, with its single-seating dining, is for passengers in suites and top category accommodation grades, and provides the best cuisine and service aboard the ship. The famous Cunard Grill experience also includes alfresco dining in a courtyard terrace suitably protected from the wind, and exclusive access for Grill-class passengers to their own upper terrace deck (The Courtyard), with dedicated staff as well as the Grills' lounge and bar (the facility is on Decks 11 and 12).

A grand conservatory, complete with central fountain and retractable glass roof, has a moveable glass wall to an open-air swimming pool. Rattan furniture and ceiling fans help to conjure up the area's colonial theme.

The 132-seat **Princess Grill**, with single-seating dining, is for passengers in middle-class accommodation grades.

Alternative Dining Venue: The Todd English Restaurant has the look and feel of a classic English dining salon, with Mediterranean cuisine presented on creative china. The restaurant is on the second level of the three-deck high lobby. Reservations are required, and there is a cover charge.

Casual Eatery: The Lido Café (on Deck 11) has good panoramic views aft, indoor/outdoor seating and features a fairly standard multi-line self-serve buffet arrangement. For coffees and light bites, there's also Café Carinthia.

ENTERTAINMENT. The 830-seat, three-deck-high Royal Court Theatre is designed in the style of a classic opera house. It provides for Queens Grill passengers 20 private "royal boxes" in the tradition of a real London West End theatre, and there's a lounge for pre-show drinks. The "Victoriana" show is all about good old British tradition.

SPA/FITNESS. The Cunard Royal Health Club and Spa consists of a beauty salon, gymnasium with great ocean views, aerobics area, changing rooms, a Thermal Area with sauna and steam rooms (extra-cost day passes available if you don't book a treatment), several body treatment rooms, a rasul chamber (for private Hammam-style mud/steam bathing), and a relaxation area.

Radiance of the Seas
★★★★

Large Resort Ship: ....90,090 tons	Passenger Decks: 12	Cabins (for one person): 0
Lifestyle: ....Standard	Total Crew: 858	Cabins (with private balcony): 577
Cruise Line: ....Royal Caribbean	Passengers	Cabins (wheelchair accessible): 14
International	(lower beds/all berths): 2,112/2,500	(8 with private balcony)
Former Names: ....none	Passenger Space Ratio	Cabin Current: ....110/220 volts
Builder: ....Meyer Werft (Germany)	(lower beds/all berths): 42.6/36.0	Elevators: 9
Original Cost: ....$350 million	Crew/Passenger Ratio	Casino (gaming tables): ....Yes
Entered Service: ....Apr 2001	(lower beds/all berths): 2.4/2.9	Slot Machines: ....Yes
Registry: ....The Bahamas	Navigation Officers: ....Norwegian	Swimming Pools (outdoors): 2
Length (ft/m): 961.9/293.2	Cabins (total): 1,056	Swimming Pools (indoors): 0
Beam (ft/m): 105.6/32.2	Size Range (sq ft/m): 165.8–1,216.3/	Whirlpools: 3
Draft (ft/m): 27.8/8.5	15.4–113.0	Self-Service Launderette: ....No
Propulsion/Propellers: .....Gas turbine/2	Cabins (outside view): 813	Dedicated Cinema/Seats: Yes/40
azimuthing pods (20 MW each)	Cabins (interior/no view): 237	Library: ....Yes

OVERALL SCORE: 1,496 (OUT OF A POSSIBLE 2,000 POINTS)

OVERVIEW. *Radiance of the Seas* was the first Royal Caribbean International ship to use gas and steam turbine power instead of the more conventional diesel or diesel-electric combination. Pod propulsion is provided *(see page 174 for detailed explanation)*.

As aboard all RCI vessels, the navigation bridge is of the fully enclosed type (good for cruising in cold-weather areas such as Alaska). In the very front of the ship is a helipad, which also acts as a viewing platform for passengers.

Radiance of the Seas is a streamlined contemporary ship, and has a two-deck-high wrap-around structure in the forward section of the funnel. Along the ship's starboard side, a central glass wall protrudes, giving great views (cabins with balconies occupy the space directly opposite on the port side). The gently rounded stern has nicely tiered decks. One of two swimming pools can be covered by a large glass dome for use as an indoor/outdoor pool.

Inside, the decor is contemporary, yet elegant, bright and cheerful. A nine-deck high atrium lobby has glass-walled elevators (on the port side of the ship) that travel through 12 decks, face the sea and provide a link with nature and the ocean. The Centrum (as the atrium is called), has several public rooms connected to it: the guest relations (the contemporary term for purser's office) and shore excursions desks, a Lobby Bar, Champagne Bar, the Library, Royal Caribbean Online, the Concierge Club, and a Crown & Anchor Lounge. A great view can be had of the atrium by looking down through the flat glass dome high above it.

Other facilities include a delightful, but very small library. There's also a Champagne Bar, and a large Schooner Bar that houses maritime art in an integral art gallery. Gamblers

BERLITZ'S RATINGS

	Possible	Achieved
Ship	500	429
Accommodation	200	159
Food	400	242
Service	400	279
Entertainment	100	81
Cruise	400	306

should enjoy Casino Royale, with its French Art Nouveau decorative theme and 11 crystal chandeliers. There's also a small dedicated screening room for movies (with space for two wheelchairs), as well as a 194-seat conference center, and a business center.

The Viking Crown Lounge is a large structure set around the base of the ship's funnel. It functions as an observation lounge during the daytime (with views forward over the swimming pool). In the evening, the space features Starquest – a futuristic, high-energy dance club, and Hollywood Odyssey – a more intimate and relaxed entertainment venue for softer mood music and "black box" theater.

For those who wish to go online, Royal Caribbean Online is a dedicated computer center with 12 computers, located in a semi-private setting (in addition, data ports are provided in all cabins). Four more internet-access terminals are located in Books 'n' Coffee, a bookshop with coffee and pastries, located in an extensive area of shops.

Youth facilities include Adventure Ocean, an "edutainment" area with four separate age-appropriate sections for junior passengers: Aquanaut Center (for ages 3–5); Explorer Center (6–8); Voyager Center (9–12); and the Optix Teen Center (13–17). There is also Adventure Beach, which includes a splash pool complete with waterslide; Surfside, with computer lab stations with entertaining software; and Ocean Arcade, a video games hangout.

The artwork aboard this ship is really eclectic (so there should be something for all tastes), and provides a spectrum and a half of color works. It ranges from Jenny M. Hansen's *A Vulnerable Moment* glass sculpture to David Buckland's "Industrial and Russian Constructionism

1920s" in photographic images on glass and painted canvas, to a huge multi-deck high contemporary bicycle-cum-paddlewheel sculpture design suspended in the atrium.

Radiance of the Seas offers more space and more comfortable public areas (and several more intimate spaces), slightly larger cabins and more dining options – for the younger, active, hip and trendy set – than most RCI ships. The grand amount of glass provides more contact with the ocean around you. In the final analysis, however, while the ship is quite delightful in many ways, the onboard operation is less so, and suffers from a lack of trained service staff.

ACCOMMODATION. There is a wide range of suites and standard outside-view and interior (no view) cabins in 10 different categories and 19 different price groups.

Apart from the largest suites (six owner's suites), which have king-sized beds, almost all other cabins have twin beds that convert to a queen-sized bed (all sheets are of 100% Egyptian cotton, although the blankets are synthetic). All cabins have rich (but faux) wood cabinetry, including a vanity desk (with hairdryer), faux wood drawers that close silently (hooray), television, personal safe, and three-sided mirrors. Some cabins have ceiling recessed, pull-down berths for third and fourth persons, although closet and drawer space would be extremely tight for four persons (even if two of them are children), and some have interconnecting doors (so families with children can cruise together, in separate, but adjacent cabins. Audio channels are available through the TV set, whose picture cannot be turned off while listening to an audio channel.

Most bathrooms have tiled accenting a terrazzo-style tiled floor, and a small shower enclosure in a half-moon shape, 100% Egyptian cotton towels, a small cabinet for personal toiletries and a small shelf. In reality, there is little space to stow personal toiletries for two (or more).

The largest accommodation consists of a family suite with two bedrooms. One bedroom has twin beds (convertible to queen-sized bed), while a second has two lower beds and two upper Pullman berths, a combination that can sleep up to eight persons (this would be suitable for large families).

Occupants of accommodation designated as suites also get the use of a private Concierge Lounge (where priority dining room reservations, shore excursion bookings and beauty salon/spa appointments can be made). Many of the "private" balcony cabins are not very private, as they can be overlooked from various locations.

CUISINE. Cascades, the main dining room, spans two decks (the upper deck level has floor-to-ceiling windows, while the lower deck level has picture windows), and is a lovely, but noisy, dining hall – reminiscent of those aboard the transatlantic liners in their heyday (however, eight huge, thick pillars do obstruct the sight lines). It seats 1,104, and has cascading water themed decor. There are tables for two, four, six, eight or 10 in two seatings. Two small private dining rooms (Breakers, with 94 seats and Tides, with 30 seats) are located off the main dining room. No smoking is permitted in the dining venues.

Alternative dining options: Portofino, with 112 seats (and a magnificent "cloud" ceiling), has Italian cuisine (choices include: antipasti, soup, salad, pasta, main dish, dessert, cheese and coffee). Chops Grill Steakhouse, with 95 seats and an open (show) kitchen, serves premium meats in the form of veal chops and steaks (New York Striploin Steak, Filet Mignon, and Prime Rib of Beef). The food in these venues is of a much higher quality than in the main dining room, though the menus do not change during the cruise. There is an additional charge of $20 per person (this includes gratuities to staff), and reservations are required for both dining spots, which are generally open 6pm –11pm. The dress code is smart casual.

Casual meals can be taken for breakfast, lunch and dinner in the self-serve, buffet-style Windjammer Cafe, accessible directly from the pool deck. It has islands dedicated to specific foods, and indoors and outdoors seating.

Additionally, there is the Seaview Café, open for lunch and dinner. The self-serve buffet and the menu feature fast-food seafood items, plus hamburgers and hot dogs.

ENTERTAINMENT. The three-level Aurora Theater has 874 seats (including 24 stations for wheelchairs) and good sightlines from most seats. The Colony Club hosts casual cabaret shows, including late-night adult (blue) comedy, and provides live music for dancing.

The entertainment throughout is upbeat. There is even background music in all corridors and elevators, and constant music outdoors on the pool deck. If you want a quiet relaxing holiday, choose another ship.

SPA/FITNESS. The ShipShape Spa's health, fitness and spa facilities have themed decor, and include a 10,176 sq.-ft (945 sq.-meter) solarium with whirlpool and counter current swimming under a retractable magrodome roof, a gymnasium (with 44 cardiovascular machines), 50-person aerobics room, sauna and steam rooms, and therapy treatment rooms. All are located on two of the uppermost decks, forward of the mast, with access from the forward stairway.

A climate-controlled 10,176 sq. ft (945 sq. meter) indoor/outdoor Solarium (with sliding glass roof that can be closed in cool or inclement weather) provides facilities for relaxation. It has a fascinating African themed decor, and includes a whirlpool and counter current swimming.

For more sporting passengers, there is activity galore – including a rock-climbing wall that's 30 ft (9 meters) high, with five separate climbing tracks. It is located outdoors at the aft end of the funnel. There is also an exterior jogging track.

Other sports facilities include a 9-hole miniature golf course (with novel 17th-century decorative ornaments), and an indoor/outdoor country club with golf simulator, a jogging track, and basketball court. Want to play pool? Well, you can, thanks to two specially stabilized tables.

● **For more extensive general information about the Royal Caribbean experience, see pages 137–42.**

Regal Empress
★+

Mid-Size Ship: ....21,909 tons	Total Crew: 396	Cabins (with private balcony): 8
Lifestyle: ....Standard	Passengers	Cabins (wheelchair accessible): 1
Cruise Line: .Imperial Majesty Cruise Line	(lower beds/all berths): 905/1,068	Cabin Current: ....110 and 220 volts
Former Names: ....Caribe I, Olympia	Passenger Space Ratio	Elevators: 3
Builder: ....Alex Stephen & Son (UK)	(lower beds/all berths): 24.2/20.5	Casino (gaming tables): ....Yes
Original Cost: ....n/a	Crew/Passenger Ratio	Slot Machines: ....Yes
Entered Service: .....Oct 1953/May 1993	(lower beds/all berths): 2.2/2.6	Swimming Pools (outdoors): 1
Registry: ....The Bahamas	Navigation Officers: ....European	Swimming Pools (indoors): 0
Length (ft/m): 611.8/186.5	Cabins (total): 457	Whirlpools: 2
Beam (ft/m): 79.0/24.1	Size Range (sq ft/m): 104.4–296.0/	Self-Service Launderette: ....No
Draft (ft/m): 28.2/8.6	9.7–27.5	Dedicated Cinema/Seats: Yes/90
Propulsion/Propellers: ....diesel	Cabins (outside view): 230	Library: ....Yes
(10,742kW)/2	Cabins (interior/no view): 227	
Passenger Decks: 8	Cabins (for one person): 9	

OVERALL SCORE: 791 (OUT OF A POSSIBLE 2,000 POINTS)

OVERVIEW. *Regal Empress*, now over 55 years old – has a traditional ocean liner profile (for many years, it sailed as a two-class liner between Greece and the United States. There is a limited amount of open deck space for sun worshippers. Traditional features include polished teakwood decking and handrails. Although the ship is old, the company spends much time and effort to maintain it.

In May 2003 the ship was sold at auction (Regal Cruises ceased operations in 2003 following non-payment of outstanding bills) to Imperial Majesty Cruise Line. It operates short "getaway" cruises. There is an enclosed (air-conditioned) promenade deck, popular with strollers, and for those who like to sit and read.

There is much real wood, heavy brass and art deco detailing throughout many of the public rooms, with fine satin woods and brass featured on the ship's interior staircases. However, there are few public rooms other than a casino, a showlounge, a nightclub/disco, and a piano lounge.

There is also a fine, old-fashioned library with almost untouched, original wood paneling and wood beam ceiling; the book selection, however, is poor and out of date. There is also an internet cafe (it's actually a bar).

The ship does carry families with children, although the facilities for junior passengers really are minimal as the vessel simply wasn't built to cater to their needs. It has an awkward, disjointed layout, with many passageways that are dead ends, and public room ceilings are low.

Regal Empress provides a basic, no-frills cruise experience at low cost, in adequate but dated surroundings. The onboard currency is the US dollar.

This is a high-density vessel that feels very crowded and

BERLITZ'S RATINGS		
	Possible	Achieved
Ship	500	168
Accommodation	200	91
Food	400	162
Service	400	191
Entertainment	100	34
Cruise	400	145

makes it difficult to find any quiet places to relax. There are no cushioned pads for the sunloungers outside on the open decks. Expect lines for embarkation, self-serve buffet meals, and for disembarking.

SUITABLE FOR: *Regal Empress* is best suited to anyone seeking a party atmosphere in a vintage ship with lots of character, where cheap and cheerful is the motto.

ACCOMMODATION. There is a wide range of cabin sizes and configurations, in 12 suite/cabin price grades. The price you pay will depend on the accommodation grade, size and location you choose. Most cabins are small yet comfortable, with reasonable closet and drawer space, and heavy-duty fittings.

However, the decor is generally dark. Many cabins (some of which can accommodate five people) have additional upper berths.

The largest accommodation can be found in four Admiral Suites. These have views over the ship's bows (when you stand up inside them, that is, as the windows are of the half-height, and not the floor-to-ceiling type), and in eight suites with private (covered and enclosed) verandas that were added in 1999, as were TV sets in all cabins (although some are positioned at odd angles, and often do not work).

CUISINE. The old-world Caribbean Dining Room is a step back in time to a more gracious era, with its original oil paintings on burnished wood paneling, ornate lighting fixtures and etched glass panels, and original murals depicting New York and Rio. There are two seatings, and the whole dining room is non-smoking. Don't expect a table for two, as most tables are for groups of six or more, with a few tables for four.

The food is plentiful and of a reasonable standard for the price (although there is much use of rice instead of potatoes and other starch-rich alternatives), with the exception of the self-serve buffets, which are really very basic, under-creative, and totally forgettable.

Lunches are quite repetitive. While the freshly baked breads (and different flavored butters daily) are good (passengers like the garlic bread, and the donut machine), the selection of real cheeses and fresh fruits is not.

La Trattoria is the place for casual self-serve buffet breakfasts, lunches and dinners. This eatery features Italian and other European-style cuisines.

ENTERTAINMENT. The main lounge is the venue for almost all entertainment events and social functions. It is a single level room designed for cabaret acts and nothing more. The sightlines fromsome seats are obstructed by pillars. Remember that the low price you pay for your cruise will dictate the kind of entertainment you can expect to see (low budget, low on quality, high on volume and color).

SPA/FITNESS. There is a small fitness center, but that's all (on the other hand, for such a short cruise, nothing else is needed, as there is simply no time).

HOW SYSTEMS WORK

Radar
Radar is one of the most important discoveries ever made for the development of navigational aids, providing a picture of all solid objects in a range selected by the navigator, which is from a half-mile (800 meters) to a 72-mile (116-km) radius. Its greatest asset is as an aid to collision avoidance with other ships, although it is of value in finding a position at a distance when navigational marks or charted coastlines are within its range.

Engine Telegraph
These automatic signaling devices are used to communicate orders between the bridge and the engine room. There may be three, one on the bridge and one on each bridgewing.

Bow Thruster
This small two-way handle is used to control the bow thrusters, powerful engines in the bow that push the ship away from the dockside without tugs. Some new ships may also have thrusters positioned at the stern.

Rudder Angle Indicator
This device is normally positioned in front of, and above, the quartermaster. It provides both the commanding officer and the quartermaster with a constant readout of the degrees of rudder angle, either to port (left) or starboard (right).

VHF Radio
This is a radio receiver and transmitter, operating on VHF (Very High Frequency) with a "line-of-sight" range. It is used for communicating with other ships, pilots, port authorities, and so on.

Radio Direction Finder
This operates on radio waves, enabling its operator to take bearings of shore radio stations. By crossing two or more bearings, you find the ship's position.

Depth Indicator
This equipment (which is an echo-sounder) provides a ship with a constant digital monitor readout, together with a printed chart.

Course Recorder
This records and prints all courses followed by the ship at all times.

Clearview Screen
This device makes simple but effective use of centrifugal force, where instead of an automobile-type windshield wiper, a ship has circular screens that rotate at high speed to clear rain or sea spray away, providing those on the bridge with the best possible view in even the worst weather.

Engine Speed Indicators
These provide a reading of the number of revolutions per minute being generated by the engines. Each engine has a separate indicator, giving the speed in forward or reverse.

Facsimile Recorder
This special radio device is designed to receive meteorological and oceanographic maps, satellite pictures, and other pertinent weather information transmitted by maritime broadcast stations throughout the world.

Mid-Size Ship: . . . . .30,277 tons	Total Crew: 386	Cabins (with private balcony): 232
Lifestyle: . . . . .Premium	Passengers	Cabins (wheelchair accessible): 3
Cruise Line: . . . . .Oceania Cruises	(lower beds/all berths): 684/824	Cabin Current: . . . . .110 and 220 volts
Former Names: . . . . .R Two	Passenger Space Ratio	Elevators: 4
Builder: . . . . . . .Chantiers de l'Atlantique	(lower beds/all berths): 44.2/36.7	Casino (gaming tables): . . . . .Yes
Original Cost: . . . .£150 million	Crew/Passenger Ratio	Slot Machines: . . . . .Yes
Entered Service: Dec1998/Dec 2003	(lower beds/all berths): 1.7/2.1	Swimming Pools (outdoors): 1
Registry: . . . . .Marshall Islands	Navigation Officers: . . . . .European	Swimming Pools (indoors): 0
Length (ft/m): 593.7/181.0	Cabins (total): 342	Whirlpools: . . . . . . .2 (+1 thalassotherapy)
Beam (ft/m): 83.5/25.5	Size Range (sq ft/m): 145.3–968.7/	Self-Service Launderette: . . . . .Yes
Draft (ft/m): 19.5/6.0	13.5–90.0	Dedicated Cinema/Seats: . . . . .No
Propulsion/Propellers: . . . . .diesel	Cabins (outside view): 317	Library: . . . . .Yes
. . . .(18,600 kW)/2	Cabins (interior/no view): 25	
Passenger Decks: 9	Cabins (for one person): 0	

OVERALL SCORE: 1,572 (OUT OF A POSSIBLE 2,000 POINTS)

OVERVIEW. *Regatta* was formerly one of a series of eight almost identical ships, originally built for the now-defunct Renaissance Cruises, the cruise industry's first totally non-smoking cruise line. The ship's present owners (Cruiseinvest) have chartered the ship to new start-up company Oceania Cruises. The exterior design manages to balance the ship's high sides by painting the whole ship white (it previously had a dark blue hull), with a large, square white funnel. The addition of teak overlaid decking and teak lounge chairs have greatly improved what was formerly a bland pool deck outdoors. .

The interior decor is stunning and elegant, a throwback to ship decor of the ocean liners of the 1920s and '30s, with dark woods and warm colors, all carried out in fine taste (but a bit *faux* in places). This includes detailed ceiling cornices, both real and *faux* wrought-iron staircase railings, leather-paneled walls, *trompe l'oeil* ceilings, rich carpeting in hallways with an Oriental rug-look center section, and many other interesting (and expensive-looking) decorative touches. It feels like an old-world country club.

The public rooms are spread over three decks. The reception hall (lobby) has a staircase with intricate wrought-iron railings. A large observation lounge, called the Horizon Bar, is located high atop ship.

There are plenty of bars – including one in each of the restaurant entrances. Perhaps the nicest is the casino bar/lounge, a beautiful room reminiscent of London's grand hotels and includes a martini bar. It has an inviting marble fireplace, comfortable sofas and individual chairs.

The Library is a grand Regency-style room, with a fireplace, a high, indented, *trompe l'oeil* ceiling, and

BERLITZ'S RATINGS		
	Possible	Achieved
Ship	500	416
Accommodation	200	160
Food	400	312
Service	400	295
Entertainment	100	76
Cruise	400	313

excellent selection of books, plus very comfortable wingback chairs with footstools, and sofas you could sleep on. Oceania@Sea is the ship's internet connect center.

The dress code is "smart casual." The onboard currency is the US dollar. Gratuities are added at $10.50 per person, per day (accommodation designated as suites have an extra $3 per person charge for the butler). A 15% gratuity is added to bar and spa accounts.

There is no walk-around promenade deck outdoors (there is, however, a small jogging track around the perimeter of the swimming pool, and port and starboard side decks). Stairways, though carpeted, are tinny. Oceania Cruises is a young company with a refreshing vision and desire to provide a high level of food and service in an informal setting that is at once elegant yet comfortable, and that is exactly what it has achieved in a short space of time.

SUITABLE FOR: *Regatta* is best suited to couples who like good food and style, but want informality with no formal nights on board, and interesting itineraries, all at a very reasonable price well below what the luxury ships charge.

ACCOMMODATION. There are six cabin categories, and 10 price grades (3 suite price grades; 5 outside-view cabin grades; 2 interior (no view) cabin grades. All of the standard interior (no view) and outside-view cabins (the lowest four grades) are extremely compact units, and extremely tight for two persons (particularly for cruises longer than five days). They have twin beds (or queen-sized bed), with good under-bed storage areas, personal safe, vanity desk with large mirror, good closet and drawer space (in rich, dark woods), 100% cotton bathrobe and towels, slippers, clothes brush and shoe horn. Color TVs carry a major news channel (where obtainable), plus a sports channel and round-the-clock movie channels.

Certain cabin categories (about 100 of them) qualify as "Concierge Level" accommodation, and occupants get extra goodies such as enhanced bathroom amenities, complimentary shoeshine, tote bag, cashmere throw blanket, bottle of champagne on arrival, hand-held hairdryer, priority restaurant reservations, and priority embarkation.

Owner's Suites. The six Owner's Suites, measuring around 962 sq.ft/89.3 sq.meters, provide the most spacious accommodation. They are fine, large living spaces located aft overlooking the stern on Decks 6, 7, and 8 (they are, however, subject to more movement and some vibration). They have extensive teak-floor private balconies that really are private and cannot be overlooked from the decks above. Each has an entrance foyer, living room, separate bedroom (the bed faces the sea, which can be seen through the floor-to-ceiling windows and sliding glass door), CD player (with selection of audio discs), fully tiled bathroom with Jacuzzi bathtub, and a small guest bathroom.

Vista Suites. There are four, each measuring around 785.7 sq.ft/73 sq.meters, and located forward on Decks 5 and 6. They have extensive teak-floor private balconies that cannot be overlooked by anyone from the decks above. Each has an entrance foyer, living room, separate bedroom (the bed faces the sea, which can be seen through the floor-to-ceiling windows and sliding glass door), CD player (with selection of audio discs), and fully tiled bathroom with Jacuzzi bathtub.

Penthouse Suites. There are 52 of these (actually, they are not suites at all, but large cabins as the bedrooms aren't separate from the living areas). They do, however, measure around 322.9 sq.ft (30 sq. meters), and have a good-sized teak-floor balcony with sliding glass door (but with partial, and not full, balcony partitions) and teak deck furniture. The lounge area has a proper dining table and there is ample clothes storage space. The bathroom has a tub, shower enclosure, washbasin and toilet.

Cabins with Balcony. Cabins with private balconies (around 216 sq.ft/20 sq. meters), comprise about 66% of all cabins. They have partial, not full, balcony partitions, sliding glass doors, and only 14 cabins on Deck 6 have lifeboat-obstructed views. The living area has a refrigerated mini-bar, lounge area with breakfast table, and a balcony with teak floor, two teak chairs and a drinks table. The bathrooms, with tiled floors and plain walls, are compact, standard units, and include a shower stall with a strong, removable hand-held shower unit, hairdryer, toiletries storage shelves and retractable clothesline.

Outside View and Interior (No View) Cabins. These measure around 160–165 sq.ft (14.8–15.3 sq.meters), and have twin beds (convertible to a queen-sized bed), vanity desk, small sofa and coffee table, and bathroom with a shower enclosure with a strong, removable hand-held shower unit, hairdryer, toiletries storage shelves, retractable clothes-line, washbasin, and toilet. Although they are not large, they are quite comfortable, with a decent amount of storage space.

CUISINE. Flexibility and choice are what the dining facilities aboard the Oceania ships are all about. There are four different restaurants:

● The **Grand Dining Room** has around 340 seats, and a raised central section, but the problem is the noise level – because of the low ceiling height, it's atrocious when the dining room is full. Being located at the stern, there are large ocean-view windows on three sides (prime tables overlook the stern). The chairs are comfortable and have armrests. The menus change daily for lunch and dinner.

● The **Toscana Italian Restaurant** has 96 seats, windows along two sides, and a set menu (plus daily chef's specials).

● The cozy **Polo Grill** has 98 seats, windows along two sides and a set menu including prime steaks and seafood.

● The **Terrace Cafe** has seats for 154 indoors – not enough during cruises to cold-weather areas – and 186 outdoors. It is open for breakfast, lunch and casual dinners, when it has tapas (Tapas on the Terrace) and other Mediterranean food. As the ship's self-serve buffet restaurant, it incorporates a small pizzeria and grill. There are basic salads, a meat carving station, and a reasonable selection of cheeses.

All restaurants have open-seating dining, so you can dine when you want, with whom you wish. Reservations are needed in Toscana Restaurant and Polo Grill (but there's no extra charge), where there are mostly tables for four or six; there are few tables for two. There is a Poolside Grill Bar. All cappuccino and espresso coffees cost extra.

The food and service staff is provided by Apollo, a respected maritime catering company that also has an interest in Oceania Cruises. The consultant chef is Jacques Pepin (well-known as a TV chef in America). Oceania Cruises' brochure claims "Cuisine so extraordinary it's unrivalled at sea" is hogwash – it's good, but not that good..

ENTERTAINMENT. The Regatta Lounge has entertainment, lectures and some social events. There is little entertainment due to the intensive nature of the itineraries. However, there is live music in several bars and lounges.

SPA/FITNESS. A lido deck has a swimming pool, and good sunbathing space, plus a thalassotherapy tub. A jogging track circles the swimming pool deck (but one deck above). The uppermost outdoors deck includes a golf driving net and shuffleboard court. The Oceania Spa consists of a beauty salon, three treatment rooms, men's and women's changing rooms, and steam room (there is no sauna). Harding Brothers operates the spa and beauty salon, and provides the staff. Examples of pricing include: full body massage $99 (50 minutes); foot and ankle massage $39 (20 minutes); body contour wrap, $159 (75 minutes); botanical therapy facial, $99 (75 minutes); personal training session $75 (75 minutes); shampoo, style and dry $29 (short hair); manicure $29; pedicure $39. Note that 15% is added to your spa account, whether you like it or not.

Rhapsody of the Seas
★★★★

Large Resort Ship: ....78,491 tons	Total Crew: 765	Cabins (with private balcony): 229
Lifestyle: ....Standard	Passengers	Cabins (wheelchair accessible): 14
Cruise Line: Royal Caribbean International	(lower beds/all berths): 2,000/2,435	Cabin Current: ....110 and 220 volts
Former Names: ....none	Passenger Space Ratio	Elevators: 9
Builder: Chantiers de l'Atlantique (France)	(lower beds/all berths): 39.2/32.2	Casino (gaming tables): ....Yes
Original Cost: ....$275 million	Crew/Passenger Ratio	Slot Machines: ....Yes
Entered Service: ....May 1997	(lower beds/all berths): 2.6/3.1	Swimming Pools (outdoors): 1
Registry: ....The Bahamas	Navigation Officers: ....International	Swimming Pools (indoors): 1
Length (ft/m): 915.3/279.0	Cabins (total): 1,000	(inside/outside)
Beam (ft/m): 105.6/32.2	Size Range (sq ft/m): 135.0–1,270.1/	Whirlpools: 6
Draft (ft/m): 24.9/7.6	12.5–118.0	Self-Service Launderette: ....No
Propulsion/Propellers: .....diesel-electric	Cabins (outside view): 593	Dedicated Cinema/Seats: ....No
(50,400kW)/2	Cabins (interior/no view): 407	Library: ....Yes
Passenger Decks: 11	Cabins (for one person): 0	

OVERALL SCORE: 1,490 (OUT OF A POSSIBLE 2,000 POINTS)

OVERVIEW. This striking all-white ship (sister to *Vision of the Seas*) shares design features that make many (but not all) of the Royal Caribbean International ships identifiable, including a Viking Crown Lounge and a terrific multi-level nightspot (the music can be loud and overbearing, however).

The Viking Crown Lounge (which is also the ship's disco) aboard this sister ship is positioned just aft of the center of the ship, above the central atrium lobby. The funnel is well aft – a departure from all other RCI ships to date – which positions the Viking Crown lounge around the funnel or at its base. The ship's stern is beautifully rounded.

There is a reasonable amount of open-air walking space, although this tends to become cluttered with sun-loungers. There's also a wide range of interesting public rooms, lounges and bars, and the interiors have been cleverly designed to avoid congestion and aid passenger flow into revenue areas. Speaking of which, for those who enjoy gambling, the astrologically-themed casino is large and rather glitzy (although not as bold as aboard some of the company's other ships); a couple of pieces of "electrostatic" art in globe form provide fascinating relief.

The atrium lobby is the ship's interior focal point (this is always a good place to arrange to meet anyone), and this one has a large kinetic sculpture, called *Diadem*. It is a multi-material construction that spans six decks, and features an astrological theme, as do many of the decorative elements throughout the ship. The interior decor throughout is imaginative, and provides a connection between sea and stars.

There is, predictably, a large shopping area, although the

BERLITZ'S RATINGS

	Possible	Achieved
Ship	500	425
Accommodation	200	166
Food	400	240
Service	400	286
Entertainment	100	81
Cruise	400	292

merchandise is consistently tacky. The artwork throughout the ship is really upbeat and colorful, and has a musical theme: classical, jazz, popular and rock 'n' roll. Much improved over previous new ships in the fleet is the theater, with more entrances and fewer bottlenecks; there are still pillars obstructing sight-lines from many seats. Also improved are the facilities for children and teens.

Ship enthusiasts will like the chair fabric in the Shall We Dance lounge, with its large aft-facing windows, and the glass case-enclosed mechanical sculptures. What, in particular, makes this ship feel warm and cozy are the use of fine, light wood surfaces throughout its public rooms, as well as the large array of potted plants everywhere.

ACCOMMODATION. There are 18 grades, prices depending on grade, size and location. The standard interior (no view) and exterior view cabins are of an adequate size, and have just enough functional facilities to make them comfortable for a one-week cruise, but longer might prove confining. The decor is bright and cheerful, although the ceilings are plain; the soft furnishings make this home away from home look like the inside of a modern Scandinavian hotel – with minimalist tones, and splashes of color. Twin lower beds convert to queen-sized beds, and there is a reasonable amount of closet and drawer space, but there is little room to maneuver between the bed and desk/television unit.

The bathrooms are small but functional, although the shower units themselves are small, and there is no cabinet for one's personal toiletries. The towels should be larger and thicker. In the passageways, upbeat artwork depicts musical themes, from classical to jazz and popular.

Choose a "C" grade suite if you want spacious accommodation that includes a separate (curtained-off) sleeping area, a good-sized outside balcony (with part, not full, partition), lounge with sofa, two chairs and coffee table, three closets, plenty of drawer and storage space, television and VCR. The bathroom is large and has a full-size bathtub, integral shower, and two washbasins/two toiletries cabinets.

For the best accommodation aboard this ship, choose the Royal Suite, which resembles a Palm Beach apartment, and comes complete with a white baby grand (player) piano. It has a separate bedroom with king-size bed, living room with queen-sized sofa bed, refrigerator/mini-bar, dining table, entertainment center, and vanity dressing area. The decor is simple and elegant, with pastel colors, and wood-accented ceiling treatments. Located just under the starboard side navigation bridge wing, it has its own private balcony.

CUISINE. The two-level Edelweiss Dining Room is attractive and works well, although the noise level can be high. There are two seatings. The quality and serving of meals aboard Royal Caribbean International ships has become quite robotic over the past few years.

The Windjammer Cafe is the casual dining spot for self-serve buffets. The area is well designed, with contemporary decor and colors, but the food is basic fare and disappointing; the four-sided self-service buffet area is small for the number of passengers using it. More money needs to be spent for better ingredients and more variety. Each evening, the room offers an alternative to the more formal dining room. The evening buffets have a different theme, something this company has been doing for more than 25 years – perhaps the time has come for more creativity.

There is a hamburger/hot dog grill counter in the Solarium, but typically you don't get a choice of how well done or not so well done you get your hamburgers – everything appears to be well done. The company has introduced a drinks package (available at all bars, in the form of cards or stickers) that enables you to pre-pay for a selection of standard soft drinks and alcoholic drinks. The packages are not exactly easy to understand.

ENTERTAINMENT. The Broadway Melodies Theater is the ship's principal showlounge. It is a large, but well-designed room with main and balcony levels, and good sight lines from most of the banquette seats.

Other cabaret acts are featured in the Shall We Dance Lounge, located aft, and these include late-night adult (blue) comedy, as well as live music for dancing. A number of other bars and lounges have live music of differing types.

The entertainment throughout is upbeat. There is even background music in all passenger hallways and elevators, and constant music outdoors on the pool deck. If you want a quiet relaxing holiday, choose another ship.

SPA/FITNESS. There are good health spa facilities, set in a spacious environment on one of the uppermost decks. The decor has Egypt as its theme, with pharaohs lining the pool. The spa is operated by Steiner, a specialist concession

For the more sporting, there is activity galore – including a rock-climbing wall, with several separate climbing tracks. It is located outdoors at the aft end of the funnel.

● **For more extensive general information on what a Royal Caribbean cruise is like, see pages 137–42.**

QUOTABLE QUOTES

These are some of the questions I have been asked over the years by passengers taking a cruise for the first time:

"Will we have time to take the shore excursion?"

"If I don't buy a shore excursion, am I allowed off in port?"

"Are the entertainers paid?"

"Why don't we have a Late Night Comedy Spot in the afternoon?"

"Is the mail brought in by plane?"

"Why aren't the dancers fully dressed?"

"How do we know which photos are ours?"

"Will the ship wait for the tour buses to get back?"

"Will I get wet if I go snorkeling?"

"Do the Chinese do the laundry by hand?"

"Does the ship dock in the middle of town?"

"Is the doctor qualified?"

"Who's driving the ship if the captain is at the cocktail party?"

"Does the sun always rise on the left side of the ship?"

"Is trapshooting held outside?"

"I'm married, but can I come to the Singles Party?"

"Should I put my luggage outside the cabin before or after I go to sleep?"

"Does an outside cabin mean it's outside the ship?"

Rotterdam
★★★★

Mid-Size Ship: . . . . .59,652 tons	Total Crew: 593	Cabins (with private balcony): 160
Lifestyle: . . . . .Premium	Passengers	Cabins (wheelchair accessible): 20
Cruise Line: . . . . . . .Holland America Line	(lower beds/all berths): 1,320/1,668	Cabin Current: . . . . .110 and 220 volts
Former Names: . . . . .none	Passenger Space Ratio	Elevators: 12
Builder: . . . . .Fincantieri (Italy)	(lower beds/all berths): 45.1/35.7	Casino (gaming tables): . . . . .Yes
Original Cost: . . . .$250 million	Crew/Passenger Ratio	Slot Machines: . . . . .Yes
Entered Service: . . . . .Dec 1997	(lower beds/all berths): 2.2/2.8	Swimming Pools (outdoors): 1
Registry: . . . . .The Netherlands	Navigation Officers: . . . . .Dutch	Swimming Pools (indoors): 1
Length (ft/m): 777.5/237.00	Cabins (total): 660	(magrodome cover)
Beam (ft/m): 105.8/32.25	Size Range (sq ft/m): 184.0–1,124.8/	Whirlpools: 2
Draft (ft/m): 25.5/7.80	17.1–104.5	Self-Service Launderette: . . . . .Yes
Propulsion/Propellers: . . . . .diesel-electric	Cabins (outside view): 542	Dedicated Cinema/Seats: Yes/235
(37,500kW)/2	Cabins (interior/no view): 118	Library: . . . . .Yes
Passenger Decks: 12	Cabins (for one person): 0	

OVERALL SCORE: 1,539 (OUT OF A POSSIBLE 2,000 POINTS)

OVERVIEW. This latest *Rotterdam* has been constructed to look like a slightly larger (longer and beamier), but certainly a much sleeker version of the *"S"-class* ships, while retaining the graceful lines of the former *Rotterdam*, including a nicely raked bow and a more rounded exterior, as well as the familiar interior flow and design style. Also retained is the twin-funnel feature well recognized by former Holland America Line passengers, though it has been somewhat more streamlined. This *Rotterdam* (the sixth Holland America Line ship to bear the name) is capable of 25 knots (some call it the *Fastdam*), which is useful for longer itineraries.

Two decks (Promenade Deck and Upper Promenade Deck) house most of the public rooms, and these are sandwiched between several accommodation decks. The layout is quite easy to learn, and the signage is good.

The interior decor is best described as restrained, with much use of wood accenting. As a whole, the decor of this ship is extremely refined, with much of the traditional ocean liner detailing so loved by frequent Holland America Line passengers. The focal interior point is a three-deck high atrium, in an oval, instead of circular, shape. The atrium's focal point is a huge "one-of-a-kind" custom-made clock, which includes an astrolabe, an astrological clock and 14 other clocks in a structure that takes up three decks (the clock's design is based on an antique Flemish original).

One room has a glass ceiling similar to that aboard a former *Statendam*. The Ambassador's Lounge has an interesting brass dance floor, similar to the dance floor that adorned the Ritz-Carlton room aboard the previous *Rotterdam*.

Instead of just two staircases aboard the "S"-class ships,

BERLITZ'S RATINGS

	Possible	Achieved
Ship	500	428
Accommodation	200	165
Food	400	281
Service	400	279
Entertainment	100	76
Cruise	400	310

Rotterdam has three (better from the viewpoint of safety, passenger accessibility and evacuation). There is a magrodome-covered pool on the Lido Deck between the mast and the ship's twin funnels, as aboard the company's "S"-class ships, which have only one large, very square funnel.

The ship has allotted more space to children's and teens' play areas, although these really are token gestures by a company that traditionally does not cater well to children. However, grandparents do take their grandchildren with them (to the delight of parents, who get a well-deserved break). Enhanced children's programming is brought into play according to the number of children carried.

Popcorn is available at the Wajang Theatre for movie-goers, while adjacent is the popular Java Cafe. The casino, which is located in the middle of a major passenger flow, has blackjack, roulette, poker and dice tables alongside the requisite rows of slot machines.

Holland America Line has a long legacy in Dutch maritime history. The artwork aboard this ship (it cost $2 million) consists of a collection of 17th-century Dutch and Japanese artifacts together with contemporary works specially created for the ship, although there seems little linkage between some of the items.

Holland America Line's flagship replaced the former ship of the same name when it was retired in 1997 – just in time for the start of the company's 125th anniversary in 1998. It is a most contemporary ship for Holland America Line, with lighter, brighter decor. It is an extremely comfortable vessel in which to cruise, with some fine, elegant and luxurious decorative features. However, these are marred somewhat by the poor quality of dining room food and service and the lack of understanding of what it takes to make a "luxury" cruise experience, despite what is touted in the company's brochures.

With one whole deck of suites (and a dedicated, private concierge lounge, and preferential passenger treatment), the company has in effect created a two-class ship. The charge to use the washing machines and dryers in the self-service launderette is really petty and irritating, particularly for the occupants of suites, as they pay high prices for their cruises. Room service could be better. Non-smokers should avoid this ship, as smokers seem to be everywhere.

ACCOMMODATION. There are 17 categories, prices depending on grade, size and location. Accommodation is spread over five decks (some cabins have full or partially obstructed views). Interestingly, no cabin is more than 144 ft (44 meters) from a stairway, which makes it easier to get from cabins to public rooms. All cabin doors have a bird's-eye maple look, and hallways have framed fabric panels to make them less clinical. Cabin televisions carry CNN and TNT.

All standard inside and outside cabins are tastefully furnished, and have twin beds that convert to a queen-sized bed (space is tight for walking between beds and vanity unit). There is a decent amount of closet and drawer space, although this will prove tight for the longer voyages featured. The bathrooms, which are fully tiled, are disappointingly small (particularly for long cruises) and have small shower tubs, utilitarian personal toiletries cupboards, and exposed under-sink plumbing. There is no detailing to distinguish them from bathrooms aboard the "S"-class ships.

There are 36 full verandah suites (Navigation Deck), including four penthouse suites, which share a private Concierge Lounge with a concierge to handle such things as special dining arrangements, shore excursions and special requests – although strangely there are no butlers for these suites, as aboard ships with similar facilities. Each suite has a separate steward's entrance and separate bedroom, dressing and living areas. Suite passengers get personal stationery, complimentary laundry and ironing, cocktail-hour hors d'oeuvres and other goodies, as well as priority embarkation and disembarkation. The concierge lounge, with its latticework teak detailing and private library is accessible only by private key-card.

Disabled passengers have a choice of 20 cabins, including two of the large "penthouse" suites (which include concierge services). However, there are different cabin configurations, and it is wise to check with your booking agent.

CUISINE. The La Fontaine Dining Room seats 747, spans two decks, and has are tables for four, six or eight, but only nine tables for two. Both open seating and fixed (assigned tables and times) seating are available, while breakfast and lunch are open-seating (you'll be seated by restaurant staff when you enter). Fine Rosenthal china and good cutlery are provided. It is a non-smoking venue.

Alternative (Reservations Required) Dining Option: There is also an 88-seat Odyssey Italian alternative restaurant, decorated in the manner of an opulent 17th-century baroque Italian villa, and available to all passengers. The room, whose basic color is black with gold accenting, is divided into three sections. Cuisines from the Perugia, Tuscany and Umbria regions of Italy are featured.

ENTERTAINMENT. The 577-seat Queen's Lounge is the venue for all production shows, strong cabaret, and other entertainment features. It is two decks high (with main and balcony level seating). The decor includes umbrella-shaped gold ceiling lamps of Murano glass, and the stage features hydraulic lifts and three video screens, as well as closed-loop system for the hearing-impaired.

SPA/FITNESS. The Ocean Spa is located one deck above the navigation bridge at the very forward part of the ship. It includes a gymnasium (with all the latest muscle-pumping exercise machines, including an abundance of treadmills) with forward views over the ship's bows, an aerobics exercise area, large beauty salon with ocean-view windows to the port side, several treatment rooms, and men's and women's sauna, steam room and changing areas.

● **For more extensive general information on what a Holland America Line cruise is like, see pages 126–28.**

Small Ship: .5,061 tons	Main Propulsion: .42 sails	Cabins (outside view): .108
Lifestyle: Premium	Propulsion/Propellers: diesel (3,700kW)/1	Cabins (interior/no view): .6
Cruise Line: Star Clippers	Passenger Decks: .5	Cabins (for one person): .0
Former Names: .none	Total Crew: .100	Cabins (with private balcony): .14
Builder: .De Merwede (Holland)	Passengers	Cabins (wheelchair accessible): .0
Original Cost: .$75 million	(lower beds/all berths): .228/255	Cabin Current: .110 and 220 volts
Entered Service: .Oct 2000	Passenger Space Ratio	Elevators: .0
Registry: .Luxembourg	(lower beds/all berths): .22.1/19.8	Casino (gaming tables): .No
Length (ft/m): .439.6/134.0	Crew/Passenger Ratio	Slot Machines: .No
Beam (ft/m): .54.1/16.5	(lower beds/all berths): .2.2/2.5	Swimming Pools (outdoors): .3
Draft (ft/m): .18.5/5.6	Navigation Officers: .International	Whirlpools: .0
Type of Vessel: sail-cruise (square rigger)	Cabins (total): .114	Self-Service Launderette: .No
No. of Masts: .5	Size Range (sq ft/m): .100.0–320.0/	Library: .Yes
Sail Area (sq ft/m2): .56,000/5,204.5	9.3–29.7	

OVERALL SCORE: 1,540 (OUT OF A POSSIBLE 2,000 POINTS)

OVERVIEW. The culmination of an owner's childhood dream, *Royal Clipper* is a stunning sight under sail. Being marketed as the world's largest true fully rigged sailing ship, this is a logical addition to the company's two other, smaller, 4-masted tall ships (*Star Clipper* and *Star Flyer*). *Royal Clipper*'s 5-masted design is based on the only other 5-masted sailing ship to be built, the 1902-built German tall ship *Preussen*, and has approximately the same dimensions, albeit 46 ft (14 meters) shorter (it is much larger than the famous *Cutty Sark*, for example). It is almost 40 ft (12.1 meters) longer than the largest sailing ship presently in commission – the four-mast Russian barkentine *Sedov*. To keep things in perspective, *Royal Clipper* is the same length overall as *Wind Spirit* and *Wind Star* – the computer-controlled cruise-sail vessels of Windstar Cruises.

The construction time for this ship was remarkably short, owing to the fact that its hull had been almost completed (at Gdansk shipyard, Poland) for another owner (the ship was to be named *Gwarek*) but became available to Star Clippers for completion and fitting out. The ship is instantly recognizable due to its geometric blue and white hull markings. Power winches, as well as hand winches, are employed in deck fittings, as well as a mix of horizontal furling for the square sails and hydraulic power assist to roll the square sails along the yardarm. The sail handling system, which was designed by the ship's owner, Mikael Krafft, is such that it can be converted from a full rigger to a schooner in an incredibly short time.

Its masts reach as high as 197 ft (60 meters) above the waterline, and the top 19 ft (5.8 meters) can be hinged over 90° to clear bridges, cable lines and other port-based

BERLITZ'S RATINGS

	Possible	Achieved
Ship	500	406
Accommodation	200	157
Food	400	288
Service	400	296
Entertainment	n/a	n/a
Cruise	500	393

obstacles. Up to 42 sails can be used: 26 square sails (fore upper topgallant, fore lower topgallant, fore upper topsail, fore lower topsail, foresail, main royal, main upper topgallant, main lower topgallant, main upper topsail, main lower topsail, mainsail, middle royal, middle upper topgallant, middle lower topgallant, middle upper topsail, middle lower topsail, middle course, mizzen upper topgallant, mizzen lower topgallant, mizzen upper topsail, mizzen lower topsail, mizzen course, jigger topgallant, jigger upper topsail, jigger lower topsail, crossjack), 11 staysails (main royal staysail, main topgallant staysail, main topmast staysail, middle royal staysail, middle topgallant staysail, middle topmast staysail, mizzen royal staysail, mizzen topgallant staysail, mizzen topmast staysail, jigger topgallant staysail, jigger topmast staysail); 4 jibs (flying jib, outer jib, inner jib, fore topmast staysail) and 1 gaff-rigged spanker, it looks quite magnificent when under full sail – an area of some 54,360 sq. ft (5,050 sq. meters). Also, watching the sailors manipulate ropes, rigging and sails is like watching a ballet – the precision and cohesion of a group of men who make it all look so simple.

As a passenger, you are allowed to climb to special lookout points aloft – maybe even for a glass of champagne. Passengers are also allowed on the bridge at any time (but not in the galley or engine room).

There is a large amount of open deck space and sunning space aboard this ship – something most tall ships lack, although, naturally, this is laid with ropes for the rigging. A marina platform can be lowered at the stern of the vessel, from where you can use the surfboards, sailing dinghies, take a ride on the ship's own banana boat, or go water-skiing or swimming. Snorkeling gear is available free, but there is a charge for scuba diving gear. You will be asked to sign a waiver if you wish to use the water sports equipment.

Inside, a midships atrium three decks high sits under one of the ship's three swimming pools, and sunlight streams down through a piano lounge on the uppermost level inside the ship and down into the dining room, which is on the lower level. A forward observation lounge is a real plus, and this is connected to the piano lounge via a central corridor. An Edwardian library/card room is decorated with a *belle époque* fireplace. A lounge, the Captain Nemo Club, is where passengers can observe fish and sea life when the ship is at anchor, through thick glass portholes (floodlit from underneath at night to attract the fish).

This delightful, quite spectacular tall ship for tourists operates 7-night and 14-day cruises in the Grenadines and Lower Windward Islands of the Caribbean during the winter and 7-night and 14-night cruises in the Mediterranean during the summer. It is good to note that the officers navigate using both traditional (sextant) and contemporary methods (advanced electronic positioning system).

Being a tall ship with true sailing traditions, there is, naturally, a parrot (sometimes kept in a large, gilded cage, but often seen around the ship on someone's shoulder), which is part of the crew (as aboard all Star Clippers' ships). The general ambiance is extremely relaxed, friendly and casual – completely unpretentious. The passenger mix is international (often consisting of a good cross-section of yachting types) and the dress code is casual at all times (shorts and casual tops are the order of the day – yachting wear), with no ties needed at any time.

There is no doubt that *Royal Clipper* is a superb vessel for the actual experience of sailing – a tall ship probably without equal, as much more time is spent actually under sail than aboard almost any other tall ship (including the smaller *Sea Cloud* and *Sea Cloud II*). However, apart from the sailing experience, it is in the cuisine and service that the lack of professionalism and poor standards of delivery shows. The result is a score that could be higher if the cuisine and service were better.

The suites and cabins are larger than those aboard the tall ships of the Windjammer Barefoot Cruises fleet, while, in general, smaller than aboard *Sea Cloud* and *Sea Cloud II*. While the food and service are far superior to the Windjammers, both are well below the standard found aboard *Sea Cloud* and *Sea Cloud II*. I do not include the Windstar Cruises ships (*Wind Spirit, Wind Star, Wind Surf*), because they cannot, in any sense of the word, be considered tall ships. *Royal Clipper*, however, is exactly that – a real, working, wind-and-sails-in-your-face tall ship with a highly personable captain and crew that welcome you as if you were part of the team. What also gives the ship a little extra in the scoring department is the fact that many water sports are included in the price of your cruise.

This vessel is not for the physically impaired, or for children. The steps of the internal stairs are steep, as in most sailing vessels. The tipping system, where all tips are pooled (the suggested amount is around $8 per pas-

senger, per day), causes concern for many passengers. The onboard currency is the euro.

SUITABLE FOR: *Royal Clipper* is best suited to couples and singles who would probably never even consider a "normal" cruise ship, but who enjoy sailing and the thrill of ocean and wind, but want these things wrapped in a package that includes accommodation, food, like-minded companions, interesting destinations, and don't want the bother of owning or chartering their own yacht.

ACCOMMODATION. There are eight accommodation grades (the price you pay will depend on the grade, size and location you choose): Owner's Suite (2), Deluxe Suite (14), and Categories 1–6. No matter what grade you choose (price will depend on location and size), all have polished wood-trimmed cabinetry and wall-to-wall carpeting, personal safe, full-length mirror, small television with audio channels and 24-hour text-based news, and private bathroom. All feature twin beds (86 of which convert into a queen-sized bed, while 28 are fixed queen-sized beds that cannot be separated), hairdryer and satellite-linked telephone. The six interior (no view) cabins and a handful of other cabins have a permanently fixed double bed.

Most cabins have a privacy curtain, so that you cannot be seen from the hallway when the cabin attendant opens the door (useful if you are not wearing any clothes). In addition, 27 cabins sleep three.

The two owner's suites, located at the very aft of the ship, provide the most lavish accommodation, and have one queen-sized bed and one double bed, a separate living area with semi-circular sofa, large vanity desk, wet bar/refrigerator, marble-clad bathroom with whirlpool bathtub, plus one guest bathroom, and butler service. The two suites have an interconnecting door, so that the combined super-suite can sleep eight persons. However, there is no private balcony.

The 14 "Deck Suites" have interesting names: Ariel, Cutty Sark, Doriana, Eagle Wing, Flying Cloud, France, Golden Gate, Gloria, Great Republic, Passat, Pommern, Preussen, and Thermopylae. However, they are not actually suites, as the sleeping area cannot be separated from the lounge – they are simply larger cabins with a more luxurious interior, more storage space and a larger bathroom. Each has two lower beds convertible to a queen-sized, small lounge area, mini-bar/refrigerator, writing desk, small private balcony, and marble-clad bathroom with combination whirlpool tub/shower, washbasin and toilet, and butler service. The door to the balcony can be opened so that fresh air floods the room; note that there is a 12-inch (30-cm) threshold to step over.

There are no curtains, only roll-down shades for the windows and balcony door. The balcony itself typically has two white plastic chairs and drinks table; however, teak chairs and table would be more in keeping with the nature of the ship. The 14 balconies are not particularly private, and most have ship's tenders or zodiacs overhanging them, or some rigging obscuring the views.

Two other name cabins (Lord Nelson and Marco Polo – designated as Category 1 cabins) are located aft, but do not have private balconies, although the facilities are similar.

The interior (no view) cabins and the lowest grades of outside-view cabins are extremely small and tight, with very little room to move around the beds. Therefore, take only the minimum amount of clothing and luggage. When in cabins where beds are linked together to form a double bed, you will have to clamber up over the front of the bed, as both sides have built-in storm barriers (this applies in inclement weather conditions only).

There is a small room service menu (all items cost extra).

CUISINE. The Dining Room is constructed on several connecting levels (getting used to the steps is not easy), and seats all passengers at one seating under a three-deck-high atrium dome. You can sit with whom you wish at tables for four, six, eight or 10. However, it is a noisy dining room, due to the positioning of the many waiter stations, and the waiting staff are poorly trained, making mealtimes less enjoyable than one would wish. Some tables are badly positioned so that correct waiter service is impossible, and much reaching over has to be done in order to serve everyone.

One corner can be closed off for private parties. Breakfasts and lunches are self-serve buffets, while dinner is a sit-down affair with table service, although the ambiance is always friendly and lighthearted. The wine list consists of very young wines, and prices are quite high.

The cuisine is certainly nothing to write home about.

Although perfectly acceptable, it certainly cannot be considered in the same class as that found aboard ships such as *Sea Cloud* or *Sea Cloud II*.

ENTERTAINMENT. There are no entertainment shows, nor are any expected by passengers aboard a tall ship such as this, where sailing is the main purpose of a cruise. There is, however, live music, which is provided by a single lounge pianist/singer. Otherwise, dinner is the main evening event, as well as "Captain's Storytime", recaps of the day's interesting events, and conversation with fellow passengers in the lounge or on deck (under the stars) provides engaging entertainment.

During the daytime, when the ship is sailing, passengers can learn about the sails, and the captain or chief officer will give briefings as the sails are being furled and unfurled. The closest this tall ship comes to any kind of "show" is when, one evening towards the end of each cruise, a "sailor's choir", comprised of the ship's crew, presents a nautical performance of sea songs, sea shanties, and other light diversions.

SPA/FITNESS. The Royal Spa is located on the lowest passenger deck and, although not large, incorporates a beauty salon, Moroccan steam room (for which there is a charge), and a small gymnasium with porthole views, several muscle-pump machines body toning equipment, treadmills, rowing machines, and exercycles. Thai massage as well as traditional massage, aromatherapy facials, and other beauty treatments, are available.

Royal Iris
★★

Mid-Size Ship . . . . 14,717 tons	Total Crew: 350	Cabins (for one person): 2
Lifestyle: . . . . Standard	Passengers	Cabins (with private balcony): 0
Cruise Line: . . . . Mano Cruise	(lower beds/all berths): 720/850	Cabins (wheelchair accessible): 2
Former Names: . . .Azur, The Azur, Azur, Eagle	Passenger Space Ratio	Cabin Current: . . . . .220 volts
Builder: . . . . . .Dubigeon-Normandie (France)	(lower beds/all berths): 20.4/17.3	Elevators: 3
Original Cost: . . . . .n/a	Crew/Passenger Ratio	Casino (gaming tables): . . . . .Yes
Entered Service: . . . . . .May 1971/Jun 2005	(lower beds/all berths): 2.0/2.4	Slot Machines: . . . . .Yes
Registry: .Panama	Navigation Officers: . . . . .European	Swimming Pools (outdoors): 2
Length (ft/m): 465.8/142.00	Cabins (total): 361	Swimming Pools (indoors): 0
Beam (ft/m): 71.8/21.90	Size Range (sq ft/m): 94.7–212.0/	Whirlpools: 0
Draft (ft/m): 18.7/5.73	8.8–19.7	Self-Service Launderette: . . . . .No
Propulsion/Propellers: . .diesel (16,300kW)/2	Cabins (outside view): 148	Dedicated Cinema/Seats: Yes/175
Passenger Decks: 7	Cabins (interior/no view): 213	Library: . . . . .Yes

OVERALL SCORE: 927 (OUT OF A POSSIBLE 2,000 POINTS)

OVERVIEW. Originally constructed as a cruise-ferry, this is a rather stubby-looking ship with a short bow and twin tall funnels. There is a modest amount of open deck space for sunbathing, but this is really tight when the ship is full.

The interior layout is awkward to get used to at first, with many stairways that have short, steep steps. There is a reasonable selection of public rooms and several bars, with light, upbeat decor and many mirrored surfaces. The ship looks reasonably neat and tidy in most areas, but in others it looks unkempt and sloppy, the result of uneven refurbishments. Mano Cruise has done a good job of tailoring the product for Israeli passengers.

It is difficult to find quiet spaces, as music is playing constantly in public rooms and open spaces. Although there are three lifts, they are tiny and hold no more than three persons (or one large person).

SUITABLE FOR: *Royal Iris* is best suited to couples and singles looking for an inexpensive first cruise with destination-intensive itineraries being the most important factor.

ACCOMMODATION. Most of the cabins are small, and many also have upper berths, thus accommodating three or four persons. There are many interior (no view) cabins, which have a limited amount of storage space (the under-bed storage space is decent, however). Although the cabins are plain, they are furnished and decorated in soft earth tones accented by brightly colored soft furnishings. All have a private bathroom with tiled floor, shower, retractable clothes line, and decent storage space for personal toiletries.

Some deluxe cabins have a full bathtub/shower combi-

BERLITZ'S RATINGS

	Possible	Achieved
Ship	500	219
Accommodation	200	95
Food	400	195
Service	400	199
Entertainment	100	42
Cruise	400	177

nation, hairdryer, illuminated closets, mini-bar/refrigerator, and lots of closet, drawer and under-bed storage space.

There are two outside cabins for the physically challenged, but the ship really cannot be recommended for anyone in a wheelchair, as access to most of it is difficult at best, and, to some areas, absolutely impossible.

CUISINE. The dining room has a low ceiling. It is a non-smoking room, is reasonably charming and has large ocean-view windows on three sides, but the chairs are not comfortable, and the tables are incredibly cramped. There are two seatings (the first is extremely rushed). The food is reasonably good, and its presentation is attractive, as are the menus.

ENTERTAINMENT. The Lounge is a long, rectangular, single-level room with a low ceiling, and pillars that obstruct sight lines from several seats. There is also a bar in the aft third of the room, which connects to a discotheque. Although it may be good for group meetings and lectures, it is not, in any sense of the word, a showlounge. Sightlines can also be awkward in the cinema because seats are not staggered.

SPA/FITNESS. There is no spa as such, although there is a small fitness room, sauna and a massage room (note that the soundproofing is poor and it is very difficult to have a relaxing massage, due to an adjacent children's play area and basketball court). A hairdresser is located in a passageway leading to the restaurant (this is where you must make appointments for massages, facials or pedicures).

For recreation, there are two small swimming pools (located on different decks, one atop the ship, the other aft).

Royal Princess
★★★★

Mid-Size Ship: . . . . .30,277 tons	Total Crew: 300	Cabins (for one person): 0
Lifestyle: . . . . .Standard	Passengers	Cabins (with private balcony): 258
Cruise Line: . . . . .Princess Cruises	(lower beds/all berths): 710/838	Cabins (wheelchair accessible): 4
Former Names: . . . . .Minerva II, R8	Passenger Space Ratio	Cabin Current: . . . . .110 and 220 volts
Builder: .Chantiers de l'Atlantique (France)	(lower beds/all berths): 42.6/36.1	Elevators: 4
Original Cost: . . . .$150 million	Crew/Passenger Ratio	Casino (gaming tables): . . . . .Yes
Entered Service: . . . .Feb 2001/May 2007	(lower beds/all berths): 1.8/2.2	Slot Machines: . . . . .Yes
Registry: . . . . .Bermuda	Navigation Officers: . . . . .European	Swimming Pools (outdoors): 1
Length (ft/m): 592.0/180.45	Cabins (total): 355	Swimming Pools (indoors): 0
Beam (ft/m): 83.5/25.46	Size Range (sq ft/m): 145.3–968.7/	Whirlpools: . . . . .2 (+ 1 thalassaotherapy)
Draft (ft/m): 19.5/6.0	13.5–90.0	Self-Service Launderette: . . . . .Yes
Propulsion/Propellers: diesel (18,600 kW)/2	Cabins (outside view): 332	Dedicated Cinema/Seats: . . . . .No
Passenger Decks: 9	Cabins (interior/no view): 23	Library: . . . . .Yes

BERLITZ'S OVERALL SCORE: 1,480 (OUT OF A POSSIBLE 2,000 POINTS)

OVERVIEW. *Royal Princess*, formerly *Minerva II* and originally *R8*, is the last in a series of eight almost identical ships built for the defunct Renaissance Cruises fleet. The ship's square funnel has acquired a Princess Cruises logo to balance the all-white hull, white superstructure, and high sides. An outside lido deck has a swimming pool and good sunbathing space; one of the aft decks has a thalassaotherapy pool. A jogging track circles the swimming pool deck (but one deck above).

BERLITZ'S RATINGS		
	Possible	Achieved
Ship	500	406
Accommodation	200	151
Food	400	265
Service	400	287
Entertainment	100	71
Cruise	400	300

The interior decor is quite elegant, and is a throwback to the darker ship decor of the ocean liners of the 1920s and '30s. This includes detailed ceiling cornices, both real and faux wrought-iron staircase railings, leather paneled walls, *trompe l'oeil* ceilings, rich carpeting in hallways with an Oriental rug-look center section, and many other interesting (and expensive-looking) decorative touches. The overall feel is of an old-world country club.

The public rooms are basically spread over three decks. The reception hall (lobby) has a staircase with intricate, real wrought-iron railings, but painted on plasti-glass panels on the stairways on other decks – a copy of the staircase aboard SS *Titanic*. A large observation lounge is located high atop the ship, with great views from its floor-to-ceiling windows. The room has a long bar which faces forward (the barmen actually have the best view) and very comfortable seating. There is also a small central bandstand and wooden dance floor forward of the bar, while the aft section on the port side has six internet-connect computer terminals (although there's little privacy).

Other public rooms: The Cabaret Lounge is used principally for evening theatrical shows and musical performances. The delightful wood-paneled Casino has a fireplace, and a long bar. *Royal Princess* has several bars – including one in each of the restaurant entrances. The Library is a beautiful, grand, restful room (perhaps the nicest public room), designed in Regency style. It has a fireplace, a high, indented, *trompe l'oeil* ceiling, and a collection of about 4,000 books, plus some very comfortable wingback chairs with footstools, and sofas you could sleep on.

Princess Cruises provides good cruise and tour programs, geared specifically to North American and British passengers, at a price that's very hard to beat considering the destination-rich itineraries, pre- and post-cruise land stays at high-quality hotels, all transfers, and the expert lecturers aboard every cruise. You should experience a fine, hassle-free cruise vacation aboard this ship. There may not be marble bathroom fittings, or other expensive niceties, but the value for money is excellent.

The onboard currency is the US dollar, and gratuities are charged to your onboard account.

There is no walk-around promenade deck outdoors, but there is a small jogging track around the perimeter of the swimming pool, and open decks on the port and starboard sides. There are no wooden decks outdoors; they are instead covered by Bolidt, a sand-colored rubberized material. The stairways, although carpeted, sound tinny.

In 2007, a casino was re-instated during the conversion from *Minerva II* to *Royal Princess*.

ACCOMMODATION. There are six basic cabin size categories, but 20 price categories (14 for double occupancy and 6 for single occupancy). The cabin size categories include: Owner's Suites (6), Master Suites (4), Deluxe with balcony, Superior Plus with balcony, Superior with balcony, and Standard Outside View/Standard Interior (No View)

Cabins. The price you pay will depend on grade, size and allocation. Some cabins have interconnecting doors (good for families with children), while 18 cabins on Deck 6 have lifeboat obstructed views. There are two interior accommodation passageways.

Only the 10 suites have tea/coffee making facilities, but tea and coffee are available from room service, and in the Panorama Buffet throughout the day.

One thing really spoils the many balcony cabins is the patio-style white plastic furniture – it would be more in keeping with the "country house" style if this were changed to teak).

Standard Outside-View and Interior (no view) Cabins: All the standard interior (no view) and outside-view cabins (the lowest four grades) are compact units, and tight for two persons (particularly for cruises longer than five days). They have twin beds (or queen-sized bed), with good under-bed storage areas, personal safe, vanity desk with large mirror, good closet and drawer space (in rich, dark woods), and waffle-pattern bathrobe. TV sets carry a major news channel (where obtainable), plus sport and several movie channels, including Romance Channel movies.

Cabins with Private Balcony: Cabins with private balconies (about 66 percent of all cabins) have partial, and not full, balcony partitions, sliding glass doors, and, due to good design and layout, only 14 cabins on Deck 6 have lifeboat-obstructed views. The bathrooms, which have tiled floors and plain walls, are compact, standard units, and include a shower stall with a removable hand-held shower unit, wall-mounted hairdryer, 100% cotton towels, toiletries storage shelves, and retractable clothesline. Personal toiletries include soap, shampoo, body lotion, and shower cap.

Owner's Suites/Master Suites: The six Owner's Suites and four Master Suites provide the most spacious accommodation (in my view, well worth the extra cost). These are fine, large living spaces located in the forward-most and aft-most sections of the accommodation decks (particularly nice are those that overlook the stern, on Deck 6, 7 and 8). They have more extensive private balconies that really are private and cannot be overlooked by anyone on the decks above. There is an entrance foyer, living room, bedroom (the bed faces the sea, which can be seen through the floor-to-ceiling windows and sliding glass door), CD player (with selection of audio discs), bathroom with Jacuzzi bathtub, and a small guest bathroom.

CUISINE. There are four restaurants:
The Club Restaurant (the most formal) has 338 seats, a raised central section; it is located in the aft section of the ship. It has large ocean-view windows on three sides, several prime tables overlooking the stern, and a small bandstand for occasional live music. The menu changes daily for lunch and dinner. However, the noise level in this main dining room can be high, due to its single-deck-height ceiling, and noisy waiter stations. Immediately in front of the restaurant entrance is the Club Bar – a cosy, open lounge and bar, with a white fireplace.

Sterling Steakhouse, with ocean-view windows along two sides, serves steak and seafood dishes (a $20 cover charge applies, and reservations are necessary).

Sabatini's is an Italian extra-cost trattoria-style venue (reservations are needed, and there's a $15 cover charge).

All restaurants have open-seating dining, although reservations are necessary in Sabatini's and Sterling Steakhouse, both of which are L-shaped and have ocean-view windows along two sides and at the stern; tables are mostly for four or six. In addition, there is a Poolside Grill for casual fast food items.

The Panorama Buffet has both indoor and outdoor seating, and is the ship's casual dining spot, in a self-serve buffet style. It is open for breakfast, lunch and casual dinners (the dinner menu is the same as that in the formal Dining Room). The oversized cutlery is rather cumbersome, however.

ENTERTAINMENT. The Cabaret Lounge, forward on Deck 5, is the venue for all main entertainment events, and occasional some social functions. The entertainment consists mainly of production shows (with the accompaniment of pre-recorded tracks) and cabaret shows.

An observation lounge, called the Royal Lounge, sits atop the ship (with good forward views) and includes a dnace floor and live music.

SPA/FITNESS. The Lotus Spa has a gymnasium with some muscle-toning equipment, a thalassotherapy pool, steam rooms for men and women (there are no saunas), several treatment rooms, and a beauty salon. The spa is operated by Steiner Leisure, a concession that provides beauty and wellness treatments.

Out on deck, there is a small swimming pool, two hot tubs, a jogging track, golf practice net and shuffleboard courts.

● **For more extensive general information on what the Princess Cruises experience is like, see pages 134–37.**

Royal Star
★★

Small Ship: ....5,360 tons	Propulsion/Propellers: .diesel (4,817kW)/2	Cabins (interior/no view): 14
Lifestyle: ....Standard	Passenger Decks: 5	Cabins (for one person): 0
Cruise Line: .....African Safari Cruises/	Total Crew: 130	Cabins (with private balcony): 1
Star Line Cruises	Passengers	Cabins (wheelchair accessible): 0
Former Names: ....*Ocean Islander,*	(lower beds/all berths): 222/255	Cabin Current: ....110 and 220 volts
San Giorgio, City of Andros	Passenger Space Ratio	Elevators: 1
Builder: ....Cantieri Riuniti dell' Adriatico	(lower beds/all berths): 24.1/21.0	Casino (gaming tables): ....Yes
(Italy)	Crew/Passenger Ratio	Slot Machines: ....Yes
Original Cost: ....n/a	(lower beds/all berths): 1.7/1.9	Swimming Pools (outdoors): 1
Entered Service: 1956/Dec 1990	Navigation Officers: ....Greek	Swimming Pools (indoors): 0
Registry: ....The Bahamas	Cabins (total): 111	Whirlpools: 0
Length (ft/m): 367.4/112.00	Size Range (sq ft/m): 107.0–398.0/	Self-Service Launderette: ....No
Beam (ft/m): 51.0/15.55	10.0–37.0	Dedicated Cinema/Seats: ....No
Draft (ft/m): 18.2/5.56	Cabins (outside view): 97	Library: ....Yes

OVERALL SCORE: 938 (OUT OF A POSSIBLE 2,000 POINTS)

OVERVIEW. The African Safari Club, a Swiss hotel and tour operator which manages hotels in Kenya, has been operating this ship for several years (as African Safari Cruises and Star Line Cruises) in conjunction with these land-based safaris. It is a charming, though dated, little vessel, with a well-balanced profile. There is an open-bridge policy while the ship is at sea (weather permitting). The ship, which limits passenger numbers to 200, has reasonable open deck space for sunbathing (but do remember that, close to the equator, the sun is dangerously strong).

Royal Star, now more than 50 years old, is quite suited to cruising in sheltered areas. Moderately clean and tidy, it has a reasonably warm, friendly, relaxed and person-able ambience, although service finesse is lacking. The main reason for taking it is to get to your safari in the lands of the Masai Tribe. So the fact that the ship is old, small, and lacks first-class facilities, food, service and entertainment is not crucial. The official currency on board is the US dollar.

The African Safari Club has its own A310 aircraft to transport you from several British and European airports to Mombasa. It also has an internal airline (Skytrail) for travel to the high plains, and a fleet of four-wheel-drive vehicles. All port taxes and airport transfers are included in the cruise fare, which also includes a stay at African Safari Club's own Flamingo Beach Hotel (with private beach).

SUITABLE FOR: *Royal Star* is best suited to couples and single travelers of mature years who are seeking a traditional (old) ship and safari park combination holiday that includes air transportation, accommodation, food, and small ship facilities in one neat package, at a reasonable cost.

BERLITZ'S RATINGS

	Possible	Achieved
Ship	500	199
Accommodation	200	99
Food	400	200
Service	400	223
Entertainment	100	40
Cruise	400	177

ACCOMMODATION. There are eight price grades. Except for one President Suite, with private balcony terrace, the cabins are not large, although they are well furnished and there is reasonable closet and drawer space. The cabin bathrooms are tiny, although accommodation designated as Superior Suites has two bathrooms, with hairdryer. Some cabins have additional third- and fourth-person upper berths. Only about a half a dozen cabins have double beds while others have a twin- or L-shaped bed configuration.

CUISINE. The charming Belvedere Restaurant has large portholes with views of the sea. There are two seatings, and tables are for four, six, or eight. The cuisine is international, although standards are variable. The menu is more like a set table d'hôte menu, with little choice (though some regional dishes are featured). The selection of breads, bread rolls, international cheeses, and fruits is very limited, and the choice of teas is poor. The dining room service is provided by friendly Filipino and Indonesian waiters.

This ship would not meet the minimum standards in cleanliness and hygiene required by the Maritime Evaluations Group (particularly the galley, food preparation, handling and storage areas).

ENTERTAINMENT. Not much, but there is a small dance troupe, and occasional cabaret acts.

SPA/FITNESS. There is a tiny gymnasium and a sauna.

Ruby Princess
NOT YET RATED

Large Resort Ship: . . . . 113,000 tons	Total Crew: 1,200	Cabins (with private balcony): 881
Lifestyle: . . . . Standard	Passengers	Cabins (wheelchair accessible): 25
Cruise Line: . . . . Princess Cruises	(lower beds/all berths): 3,114/3,782	Cabin Current: . . . . 110 volts
Former Names: . . . . none	Passenger Space Ratio	Elevators: 14
Builder: . . . . Fincantieri (Italy)	(lower beds/all berths): 36.2/29.8	Casino (gaming tables): . . . . Yes
Original Cost: . . . . $500 million	Crew/Passenger Ratio	Slot Machines: . . . . Yes
Entered Service: . . . . Sept 2008	(lower beds/all berths): 2.5/3.1	Swimming Pools (outdoors): 4
Registry: . . . . Bermuda	Navigation Officers: . . . British/European	Swimming Pools (indoors): 0
Length (ft/m): 951.4/290.0	Cabins (total): 1,557	Whirlpools: 9
Beam (ft/m): 118.1/36.0	Size Range (sq ft/m): 163–1,279/	Self-Service Launderette: . . . . Yes
Draft (ft/m): 26.2/8.0	15.1–118.8	Dedicated Cinema/Seats: . . . . No
Propulsion/Propellers: gas turbine (25MW)/	Cabins (outside view): 1,105	Library: . . . . Yes
2 azimuthing pods (21,000 kW each)	Cabins (interior/no view): 452	
Passenger Decks: 15	Cabins (for one person): 0	

BERLITZ'S OVERALL SCORE: NYR (OUT OF A POSSIBLE 2,000 POINTS)

OVERVIEW. *Ruby Princess* has the same profile, interior layout and public rooms as sister ships *Crown Princess* (2006) and *Emerald Princess* (2007), and all these ships are similar to half-sisters, *Diamond Princess, Golden Princess, Grand Princess, Sapphire Princess* and *Star Princess.* Although the ship accommodates over 500 more passengers than the half-sisters, the outdoor deck space remains the same, as do the number of elevators – so waiting time could increase during peak usage. The Passenger Space Ratio is also considerably reduced.

The Sanctuary, an extra-cost adults-only retreat, is a feature worth paying extra for if you are cruising in a warm-weather area. It is located forward on the uppermost deck, it provides a "private" place to relax and unwind and includes attendants to provide chilled face towels and deliver light bites; there are also two outdoor cabanas for massages. While The Sanctuary takes space away from what was formerly a communal passenger area, the extra cost is definitely worth it.

There is a good sheltered teakwood promenade strolling deck, which almost wraps around the front and aft sections

BERLITZ'S RATINGS		
	Possible	Achieved
Ship	500	NYR
Accommodation	200	NYR
Food	400	NYR
Service	400	NYR
Entertainment	100	NYR
Cruise	400	NYR

of the ship; three times round is equal to one mile; and a walkway which goes to the enclosed, protected bows of the ship. The outdoor pools have various beach-like surroundings, and "Movies Under the Skies" and major sporting events are shown on a 300-sq-ft (28-sq-meter) movie screen located at the pool in front of the large funnel structure. Movies afloat in the open are a big hit with passengers – they remind many of drive-in movies, which have mostly disappeared from land-based venues.

With the interior layout and flow similar to that of the sister ships, the main public bars and lounges are located on one double-wide promenade deck. The main lobby houses a library, internet-connect center, a café with patisserie/deli, a separate wine corner, and an Asian seafood tasting bar.

At the time this book was completed, the names of the public rooms had not been announced.

● **For more extensive general information on what the Princess Cruises experience is like, see pages 134–37. For comparisons with *Ruby Princess*, see the entries for *Crown Princess* and *Emerald Princess.***

Ryndam
★★★★

Mid-Size Ship: . . . . .55,451 tons	Total Crew: 557	Cabins (with private balcony): 150
Lifestyle: . . . . .Premium	Passengers	Cabins (wheelchair accessible): 6
Cruise Line: . . . . . . .Holland America Line	(lower beds/all berths): 1,266/1,627	Cabin Current: . . . . .110 and 220 volts
Former Names: . . . . .none	Passenger Space Ratio	Elevators: 8
Builder: . . . . .Fincantieri (Italy)	(lower beds/all berths): 43.8/34.0	Casino (gaming tables): . . . . .Yes
Original Cost: . . . .$215 million	Crew/Passenger Ratio	Slot Machines: . . . . .Yes
Entered Service: . . . . .Nov 1994	(lower beds/all berths): 2.2/2.9	Swimming Pools (outdoors): 1
Registry: . . . . .The Netherlands	Navigation Officers: . . . . . .British/Dutch	Swimming Pools (indoors): 1
Length (ft/m): 719.3/219.3	Cabins (total): 633	(magrodome)
Beam (ft/m): 101.0/30.8	Size Range (sq ft/m): 186.2–1,124.8/	Whirlpools: 2
Draft (ft/m): 24.6/7.5	17.3–104.5	Self-Service Launderette: . . . . .Yes
Propulsion/Propellers: . . . . .diesel-electric	Cabins (outside view): 502	Dedicated Cinema/Seats: Yes/249
(34,560kW)/2	Cabins (interior/no view): 131	Library: . . . . .Yes
Passenger Decks: 10	Cabins (for one person): 0	

OVERALL SCORE: 1,420 (OUT OF A POSSIBLE 2,000 POINTS)

OVERVIEW. *Ryndam* is one of a series of four almost identical ships – the others being *Maasdam, Statendam,* and *Veendam.* The exterior styling is rather angular (some would say boxy), although it is softened and balanced by the black hull. There is a full wrap-around teakwood promenade deck outdoors – excellent for strolling, and, thankfully, no sign of synthetic turf. The sunloungers on the exterior promenade deck are wood, and come with comfortable cushioned pads, while those at the swimming pool on Lido Deck are of white plastic. Holland America Line keeps its ships clean and tidy, and there is good passenger flow throughout the public areas.

In the interiors of this "S" -class ship, an asymmetrical layout helps to reduce bottlenecks and congestion. Most of the public rooms are concentrated on two decks, Promenade Deck, and Upper Promenade Deck, which creates a spacious feel. In general, a restrained approach to interior styling is taken, using a mixture of contemporary materials combined with traditional woods and ceramics. There is, fortunately, little "glitz" anywhere.

What is outstanding is the array of artworks throughout the ship (costing about $2 million), assembled and nicely displayed to represent the fine Dutch heritage of Holland America Line. Also noticeable are the fine flower arrangements throughout the public areas and foyers – used to good effect to brighten up what some consider dull decor.

Atop the ship, with forward facing views that wrap around the sides is the Crow's Nest Lounge. By day it makes a fine observation lounge, with large ocean-view windows, while by night it turns into a nightclub with extremely variable lighting. The three-deck high atrium foyer is attractive, although its sculptured centerpiece makes

BERLITZ'S RATINGS		
	Possible	Achieved
Ship	500	372
Accommodation	200	150
Food	400	254
Service	400	287
Entertainment	100	72
Cruise	400	285

it look a little crowded, and leaves little room in front of the purser's office. A hydraulic glass roof covers the reasonably sized swimming pool/whirlpools and central Lido area (whose focal point is a large dolphin sculpture) so that this can be used in fine or inclement weather. There is a large and quite lovely and relaxing reference library.

Ryndam is a well-built ship, and has fairly decent interior fit and finish. Holland America Line constantly fine-tunes its performance as a cruise operator and its regular passengers (almost all of whom are North American) find the company's ships very comfortable and well-run, even though the present food and service components let down the rest of the cruise experience.

Perhaps the ship's best asset is its friendly and personable Filipino and Indonesian crew, although communication can prove frustrating at times. The onboard currency is the US dollar.

Holland America Line's many repeat passengers always seem to enjoy the fact that social dancing is on the menu. The company provides complimentary cappuccino and espresso coffees, and free ice cream during certain hours of the day aboard its ships, as well as hot hors d'oeuvres in all bars – something other major lines seem to have dropped, or charge extra for. However, the score for this ship ends up a tad under what it could be if the food and waiting staff were better (more professional training might help). This ship is now deployed year-round in the Caribbean, where its rather dark interior decor contrasts with the strong sunlight.

An escalator travels between two of the lower decks (one of which was originally planned to be the embarkation point), but it is almost pointless. The charge to use the washing machines and dryers in the self-service launderette is petty, particularly for suite occupants, as they pay steep prices for their cruises. The men's urinals in public restrooms are unusually high.

ACCOMMODATION. This ranges from small interior (no view) cabins to a large penthouse suite, in 17 price categories. All cabin televisions carry CNN and TNT.

The interior (no view) and outside (with a view) standard cabins have twin beds that convert to a queen-sized bed, and there is a separate living space with sofa and coffee table. However, although the drawer space is generally good, the closet space is actually very tight, particularly for long cruises (although more than adequate for a 7-night cruise). Bathrobes are also provided for all suites/cabins, as are hairdryers, and a small range of personal amenities. The bathrooms are quite well laid out, but the bathtubs are small units better described as shower tubs. Some cabins have interconnecting doors.

On Navigation Deck, 28 suites have accommodation for up to four. These suites also have in-suite dining as an alternative to the dining room, for private, reclusive meals. These are very spacious, tastefully decorated and well laid-out, and have a separate living room, bedroom with two lower beds (convertible to a king-sized bed), a good sized living area, dressing room, plenty of closet and drawer space, marble bathroom with Jacuzzi tub.

The largest accommodation of all is a penthouse suite. There is only one, located on the starboard side of Navigation Deck at the forward staircase. It has a king-sized bed, a TV set and video player, and a vanity desk, a large walk-in closet with superb drawer space, oversize whirlpool bath (it could seat four) and separate shower enclosure, and a separate washroom with toilet, bidet and washbasin. The living room has a writing desk, a large television and a full set of audio equipment. There's a dressing room, a large private balcony (with teak lounge chairs and drinks tables, dining table and four chairs), a pantry (with large refrigerator, toaster unit, and full coffee/tea making facilities and food prepareation area, and a separate entrance from the hallway), mini-bar/refrigerator, a guest toilet and floor to ceiling windows. Note that there is no bell push.

CUISINE. The Rotterdam Dining Room spans two decks. It is located at the stern, is quite dramatic, and has two grand staircases to connect the two levels, panoramic views on three sides, and a music balcony. Both open seating and fixed (assigned tables and times) seating are available, while breakfast and lunch are open-seating (you'll be seated by restaurant staff when you enter). There are tables for two, four, six or eight. The dining room is a non-smoking venue. The waiter stations in the dining room are very noisy for anyone seated adjacent to them. Fine Rosenthal china and cutlery are used (although there are no fish knives). Live music is provided for dinner each evening; once each cruise, a Dutch Dinner is featured (hats are provided), as is

an Indonesian Lunch. "Lighter option" meals are always available for the health-conscious.

Alternative Dining Option: An intimate restaurant, the Pinnacle Grill, was added in 2002. It is located just forward of the balcony level of the main dining room on the starboard side. The 66-seat dining spot (reservations are necessary, and a cover/service charge of $20 applies) features Pacific Northwest cuisine (fresh Alaskan salmon and halibut, and other regional specialties, plus a selection of premium steaks such as filet mignon from Black Angus beef). The Pinnacle Grill is a much better dining experience than the main dining room and enhances that special celebration.

For more casual evening eating, the Lido Buffet is open for dinners on all except the last night of each cruise, in an open-seating arrangement. Tables are set with crisp linens, flatware and stemware. The set menu includes a choice of four entrées. The dual-line, self-serve Lido Buffet (one side is for smokers, the other side for non-smokers) is also the place for casual breakfasts and lunches. Again there is much use of canned fruits and packeted items, although there are several commercial low-calorie salad dressings. The choice of cheeses (and accompanying crackers) is very poor. The beverage station is also a let-down, for it is no better than those found in the average family outlet ashore in the United States. In addition, a poolside grill provides basic American hamburgers and hot dogs.

Passengers will need to eat in the Lido Cafe on days when the dining room is closed for lunch (typically once or twice per cruise, depending on the ship's itinerary).

ENTERTAINMENT. The Vermeer Showlounge spans two decks, with banquette seating on both main and upper levels. It is basically a well designed room, but the ceiling is low and the sightlines from the balcony level are poor.

While Holland America Line is not known for its fine entertainment (the budgets aren't high enough) what the line does offer is a consistently good, tried and tested array of cabaret acts that constantly rove the cruise ship circuit. The production shows, however, while a good attempt, fall short on storyline, choreography and performance, with colorful costuming and lighting hiding the weak spots.

A number of bands, a string ensemble and solo musicians present live music in many lounges and bars. There's dancing in the Crow's Nest (by day an observation lounge), and serenading string music in the Explorer's Lounge and dining room.

SPA/FITNESS. The Greenhouse Spa is one deck below the navigation bridge at the very forward part of the ship. It includes a gymnasium with ocean views, an aerobics exercise area, large beauty salon with ocean-view windows to the port side, several treatment rooms, and men's and women's sauna, steam room and changing areas. The spa is operated by Steiner, a specialist concession.

● **For more extensive general information on what a Holland America Line cruise is like, see pages 126–28.**

Saga Rose
★★★★

Mid-Size Ship: . . . . .24,474 tons	Passenger Decks: 7	Cabins (for one person): 60
Lifestyle: . . . . .Premium	Total Crew: .350	Cabins (with private balcony): 26
Cruise Line: . . . . .Saga Cruises	Passengers	Cabins (wheelchair accessible): 8
Former Names: . . . .*Gripsholm, Sagafjord*	(lower beds/all berths): 584/620	Cabin Current: . . . . .110 volts
Builder: . . . . . . .Forges et Chantiers de la	Passenger Space Ratio	Elevators: 4
Mediteranee (France)	(lower beds/all berths): 40.8/39.4	Casino (gaming tables): . . . . .No
Original Cost: . . . .$30 million	Crew/Passenger Ratio	Slot Machines: . . . . .No
Entered Service: . . . . .Oct 1965/May 1997	(lower beds/all berths): 1.6/1.7	Swimming Pools (outdoors): 1
Registry: . . . . .The Bahamas	Navigation Officers: . . . . .British	Swimming Pools (indoors): 1
Length (Ft/m): 619.6/188.88	Cabins (total): 322	Whirlpools: 0
Beam (ft/m): 80.3/24.49	Size Range (sq ft/m): 96.8–468.0/	Self-Service Launderette: . . . . .Yes
Draft (ft/m): 27.0/8.25	9.0–43.5	Dedicated Cinema/Seats: Yes/181
Propulsion/Propellers: . . . . .diesel	Cabins (outside view): 290	Library: . . . . .Yes
(20,150kW)/2	Cabins (interior/no view): 32	

OVERALL SCORE: 1,412 (OUT OF A POSSIBLE 2,000 POINTS)

OVERVIEW. Despite the ship's age, *Saga Rose* is still a finely proportioned, traditional cruise ship, and presents a sweeping profile and line of sheer, with clean, delightfully rounded lines, a royal blue hull and a well-placed buff-colored funnel amidships. This ship has classic liner styling and profile, and really does look like a ship. Like an aging Bentley, it will hopefully not go out of style. In fine maritime tradition, the ship's bell and whistle are sounded at noon each day. There is a walk-around teakwood promenade deck outdoors, and thick pads for all sunloungers. The ship has expansive open deck and sunbathing areas, and lots of nooks and crannies for privacy.

This classic vessel, built in the mid-1960s for long-distance cruising, provides a traditional cruise experience for discriminating passengers over 50 (note that those younger than 50 are not accepted as passengers). Constructed to a high standard (the French shipyard that built it went bankrupt as a result of the losses incurred), this ship has been quite well maintained and is operated with pride by the present owners, who have spent considerable sums of money in restoring it to fine condition.

The interiors of *Saga Rose* are quite dark (restful) and somber in places (particularly the accommodation hallways). But they are spacious, with high-ceilinged public rooms and tasteful decor (although there are, perhaps, too many low-back chairs). There are fine quality furnishings and fittings, including hardwoods, brass and stainless steel. In fact, it is quite difficult to find any plastic in the interior fittings, except for the laminates used to line the walls of the accommodation areas. The elevator does not go down as far as the indoor pool deck ("C" Deck).

BERLITZ'S RATINGS

	Possible	Achieved
Ship	500	356
Accommodation	200	152
Food	400	280
Service	400	272
Entertainment	100	81
Cruise	400	271

Public room facilities include a real ballroom/main lounge – among the nicest afloat for proper cocktail parties (where you stand and mingle, rather than sit), with furniture that can be moved for almost any configuration, and a large wood dance floor.

Other facilities include an indoor swimming pool (and adjacent fitness center) as well as an outdoor pool, lots of recreational space and delightful little nooks and crannies outdoors. The Britannia Lounge (observation lounge) is a fine room for social activities (or a spot of quiet reading), while the adjacent North Cape Bar provides a good bar and hangout for the cocktail crowd. The ship also has a delightful card room (Shakespeare's), a real, large traditional cinema (good for lectures as well as films), a nightclub, computer-learning center (in what used to be the upper level of the nightclub), and a good library.

Saga Rose fits like an old shoe made from fine materials, and most passengers find it so comfortable that they don't want to discard it. A voyage aboard this ship should prove to be a most pleasurable travel experience.

This is classic cruising for its mainly British passengers (the ship is based at Dover and Southampton), under the banner of Saga Cruises. *Saga Rose* is a gracious old lady, now in her late thirties. Although the ship looks a little tired in places, it continues to offer passengers the chance to cruise in comfortable surroundings of high quality, with roaming worldwide itineraries, and service that is friendly and unobtrusive. Saga Cruises includes many things that other UK-based cruise operators charge extra for. Transfers to the ship, port taxes, insurance and all gratuities are included, shuttle buses are provided in ports of call (where possible), and newspapers are provided in the library in each port of call (subject to availability). If you pay for your onboard expenses with a Saga Visa Card you get a 5% discount. The onboard currency is the UK pound.

SUITABLE FOR: *Saga Rose* is best suited to couples and single travelers over 50 who seek a holiday afloat in a very traditional ship setting that is unpretentious, yet provides a decent standard of accommodation, food and friendly service, as well as interesting itineraries and destinations, with fellow passengers likely to be almost all English.

ACCOMMODATION. There are 22 different grades, the price depending on location, size and grade: 3 designated as suites, 10 outside-view grades and 2 interior (no view) cabins (7 grades are designated for single occupancy, including one with a private balcony). Several cabins have interconnecting doors (useful for couples who, for whatever reason, like to have more space, and a bathroom each), and some have views obstructed by lifeboats.

No matter what grade you choose, all cabins have been refurbished, and have fine quality fittings and appointments, and excellent insulation. There are also many single cabins (useful for passengers who enjoy the privacy of their own space without having to share with someone else). There is a generous amount of drawer, under-bed storage and illuminated closet space, and all cabins have European duvets, and a small personal lockbox. All bathrooms have a combination tub/shower. The service provided by the cabin stewards and stewardesses is good. Soft, 100% cotton bathrobes and towels are provided, as well as several personal toiletry items: shampoo/conditioner, body lotion, bath gel, shower cap and soap.

Those who choose a cabin with a private balcony will find a teak decked balcony, with see-through railings, enough space for two sunloungers and table, and an outside light. The cabin voltage is 110 volts, so do take an adapter if you have a 220-volt electrical appliance (such as a hairdryer). There are few balcony cabins. Access to some of the upper grade cabins is a little disjointed.

CUISINE. The dining room is superb in the classic sense. It has a central ceiling two decks high (with three beautiful, large crystal chandeliers), with large ocean-view picture windows on the port and starboard sides and a horseshoe-shaped grand staircase at the forward end. There is one-seating dining at assigned tables – this is refreshing, when so many of today's cruise ships have two seatings – with tables for two (there are lots of these), four, six, eight or 10. The chinaware is Royal Doulton, while the flatware is also of a good quality.

The cuisine is quite creative, with a good variety of menu choices, and good-quality ingredients (diabetic, gluten-free and vegetarian alternatives are always available). The entrées are generally well presented, pastries and dessert items are of a good standard, and there is a reasonable choice of cheeses and fruits. There is a fairly comprehensive wine list, and the prices are very modest. Generally, the service is good, in the style of a grand hotel, from thoughtful and attentive waiters.

For casual meals, the Lido Cafe is available as a serve-yourself venue for breakfast and luncheon, and the outdoors aft of the cafe is expansive and very useful for al fresco dining. Several special theme buffets are provided for each cruise. cruise. While there is some repetition of breakfast items, other meals offer a wide variety of hot and cold food items.

ENTERTAINMENT. The Ballroom is the venue for all production shows, major cabaret acts, social functions, and, yes, dancing. The room was not designed as a showlounge, but as a ballroom, and, as such, it has a large properly sprung hardwood dance floor.

During the past two years, the colorful and intelligent British production shows were very well received by passengers. Since January 2003, however, new shows have been introduced by a different (American) company. String quartets and other classical concerts are much appreciated by passengers (especially delicious are the themed afternoon tea concerts: Chocolate, English, and Viennese).

SPA/FITNESS. The Spa and fitness facilities are located towards the bottom of the ship, on "C" Deck, where there is also an indoor swimming pool (aquacise classes are held here), gymnasium with a good range of muscle-pumping and body toning equipment, treadmills and exercycles; and men's and women's sauna and changing rooms with showers, and treatment rooms. A beauty salon is located in another area, on Main Deck.

The spa treatments and beauty services are staffed and operated by Harding Brothers, a concession whose staff also run the fitness and aerobics classes. Spa treatments offered include several types of massage, aromatherapy facials, seaweed body wraps, and hair beautifying services.

Saga Ruby
★★★★

Mid-Size Ship:	.24,492 tons	Passenger Decks:	.9
Lifestyle:	.Premium	Total Crew:	.380
Cruise Line:	.Saga Cruises	Passengers	
Former Names:	.Caronia, Vistafjord	(lower beds/all berths):	.655/655
Builder:	.Swan, Hunter (UK)	Passenger Space Ratio	
Original Cost:	.$35 million	(lower beds/all berths):	.37.3/37..3
Entered Service:	.May 1973/	Crew/Passenger Ratio	
	March 2005	(lower beds/all berths):	.1.7/1.7
Registry:	.Great Britain	Navigation Officers:	.British
Length (ft/m):	.626.9/191.09	Cabins (total):	.376
Beam (ft/m):	.82.1/25.05	Size Range (sq ft/m):	.66.7–871.9/
Draft (ft/m):	.27.0/8.23		6.2–81.0
Propulsion/Propellers:	.diesel	Cabins (outside view):	.324
	(17,900kW)/2	Cabins (interior/no view):	.52

Cabins (for one person):	.70
Cabins (with private balcony):	.25
Cabins (wheelchair accessible):	.4
Cabin Current:	.110 volts
Elevators:	.6
Casino (gaming tables):	.No
Slot Machines:	.No
Swimming Pools (outdoors):	.1
Swimming Pools (indoors):	.1
Whirlpools:	.2
Self-Service Launderette:	.Yes
Dedicated Cinema/Seats:	.Yes/190
Library:	.Yes

OVERALL SCORE: 1,425 (OUT OF A POSSIBLE 2,000 POINTS)

OVERVIEW. *Saga Ruby* has classic liner styling and profile, and really does look like a traditional ship. It is finely proportioned, with delightful, rounded, flowing lines, a sleek profile with a good line of sheer. The royal blue hull shows off strong, balanced lines, while the profile is further enhanced by a buff-and-black colored funnel amidships. The ship was built with excellent quality materials, has been well maintained, is smooth and quiet in operation, and is a stable ship at sea (due to its deep draft). Each day, the ship's bell is sounded at noon in accordance with maritime tradition. As the former *Caronia,* the ship finished its service under Cunard Line, and was taken over by Saga Cruises in 2004. Following an extensive £17 million refit in 2004–5, it became *Saga Ruby*.

The open decks and sunbathing space are expansive. There is a teak walk-around promenade deck outdoors, and sunloungers have cushioned pads (ideal for resting, relaxation, and for reading a good book).

Inside, the spacious and elegant public rooms – mostly located on one deck (Veranda Deck) – have high ceilings and tasteful decor, and wide interior stairwells are subtly illuminated. The ship's interior decor and soft furnishings are of soft, earth-toned colors that provide a calm, soothing and non-threatening environment for the longer cruises that Saga passengers enjoy. The Britannia Lounge is at the front of this deck; behind it the Theater (dedicated cinema), Card Room, Ballroom (show lounge) and the Lido Cafe. There's also an expansive library, a computer learning center, and separate internet-connect center. Few ships of this size can match the relaxing ambience and gracious service from a well-organized, friendly and happy mix of European and Filipino ser-

BERLITZ'S RATINGS		
	Possible	Achieved
Ship	500	362
Accommodation	200	152
Food	400	282
Service	400	274
Entertainment	100	81
Cruise	400	274

vice staff. There are refreshingly few announcements and interruptions.

This ship provides a refined, user-friendly environment with a wide range of public rooms for adults (the ship is child-free). Male dance hosts are provided for the many single women who travel. Although not shiny and new, the ship has been well cared for, and provides an excellent setting for a pleasant, gracious and civilized travel experience.

Saga Cruises includes many things that other UK-based cruise operators charge extra for: transfers to the ship, all gratuities, shuttle buses in ports of call (where possible), and newspapers in the library in each port of call (subject to availability). The onboard currency is the British pound.

SUITABLE FOR: *Saga Ruby* is best suited to couples and single travelers over 50 who seek a holiday afloat in a very traditional ship setting that is unpretentious, yet provides a decent standard of accommodation, food and friendly service, as well as interesting itineraries and destinations, with fellow passengers likely to be almost all English, in a setting that doesn't try to compete with today's warehouse-sized new ships.

ACCOMMODATION. The brochure lists 21 cabin categories (7 of which are for single travelers wanting a cabin for themselves), from duplex penthouse suites with huge private balconies, to small interior (no view) cabins, in a wide range of different configurations. Overall, the cabins are smaller than those aboard sister ship *Saga Rose* but all are well appointed, with good-sized bathrooms Many cabins have a full-sized bathtub, while other have a shower enclosure only; hand-held shower hoses are standard (better and more hygienic than fixed showers).

The grandest living spaces are in two duplex apartments (Saga Suite and Vista Suite). They are superb living spaces and occupy two levels. The lower level has a large bedroom and marble-clad bathroom with Jacuzzi bathtub. The upper level has an expansive living room with floor-to-ceiling windows with unobstructed front and side views, a Bang & Olufsen sound system, treadmill, private bar, and a large bathroom (with Jacuzzi bathtub) and separate private sauna. There is a huge, private balcony outdoors on deck, complete with a two-person hot tub, a teak deck, and great views. A private internal stairway connects the upper and lower levels.

Most other cabins designated as suites (on Bridge Deck lower level, and Sun Deck) have private balconies, are nicely equipped, and have ample closet and drawer space (some also have a large walk-in closet), vanity desk, large beds, and bookshelves filled with suitable destination books or novels. The marble-clad bathrooms are large and have a full-sized Jacuzzi bathtub, two washbasins, toilet and bidet.

All other cabins are tastefully decorated, and all have a refrigerator, mini-bar, personal safe, European duvets (in two thicknesses), a range of Molton Brown personal toiletries, and thick 100% cotton bathrobes. The wooden cabinetry has nicely rounded edges. Bathrooms have a whisper-quiet (gentle, non-vacuum) toilet.

This ship has an excellent range of cabins for single travelers (unlike almost all new cruise ships). Some Sun Deck and Promenade Deck suites have obstructed views. All suites and cabins have a flat-screen TV with integral DVD player.

CUISINE. Although it lacks the grandeur, high ceiling or grand stairway of sister ship *Saga Rose*, the Saga Dining Room is elegant, and single-seating dining at assigned tables is featured (this is refreshing, when so many of today's cruise ships have two seatings). There are tables for two, four, six or eight (there are more tables for two than aboard many other cruise ships). Senior officers often host tables for dinner (always on formal nights). Single-waiter service is provided as in the European tradition. Some tables are a little close together, however, making it hard for waiters to serve properly in some areas.

A wide range of menu items is provided (including many British favorites), with a reasonably high standard of quality and variety. A cold table is set for such things as breads and cheeses at lunchtime, and passengers can help themselves or be served. Salad items, many salad dressings, juices, and a selection of international cheeses are always available. Plate service (where vegetables and entrées are set on the main course plate) is provided. Extra vegetables can be obtained on request. This is service in the classic seagoing tradition.

There is a good selection of cakes and pastry items (and scones, of course) for afternoon tea. Vegetarian items and diabetic desserts are always available and other special dietary items can be provided with sufficient notice. The wine list has a good selection, with prices that reflect excellent value for money.

Alternative (Reservations Required) Dining: View is a delightful à la carte restaurant (an alternative no-smoking dining spot located above the nightclub) that is elegant and very intimate (with only 12 tables), with excellent cuisine from a varied menu. It has the feel of a small, exclusive bistro. Reservations are required, but there is no extra charge.

Casual Eatery: The Lido Café, greatly expanded in the 2004–5 refit, is a well laid out casual dining area with a range of self-service buffets for breakfast, lunch and dinner. While there is some repetition of breakfast items, other meals offer a wide variety of hot and cold food items. A self-serve tea/coffee/beverage station is available 24 hours a day; a machine provides espresso and cappuccino at no extra cost (most ships now charge extra for these items).

Note that bar drinks (and wine) prices are extremely reasonable, and include gratuities.

ENTERTAINMENT. The Ballroom is the main venue for entertainment, revue shows, cabaret acts, lectures, and social functions such as the Captain's Cocktail Party. It is among the nicest such rooms afloat for proper cocktail parties (where you stand and mingle, rather than sit), with furniture that can be moved for almost any configuration, and a large real wood dance floor. The port and starboard side seating sections are raised, and sight lines are generally good from most seats. The ship has conservative, reasonably sophisticated, classically oriented entertainment. A resident troupe of singers and dancers presents mini-revue shows.

Most of the other entertainment consists of cabaret acts (such as vocalists, magicians, ventriloquists, comedy jugglers and others), and there is a large floor for social dancing, an important feature for many passengers. A number of bands and musical units provide ample live music for dancing or listening throughout the various lounges and bars. Each evening, the Preview Club, which overlooks the ship's outdoor swimming pool at the aft end of the ship, becomes the late-night spot.

SPA/FITNESS. These facilities are towards the bottom of the ship, on "C" Deck, where there is also a rather nice indoor pool, gymnasium, men's and women's sauna and changing rooms with adjacent shower enclosures, plus a unisex steam room. A gymnasium, with elevator access, is located high up on Bridge Deck; it has high-tech equipment and great port and starboard ocean views.

The spa treatments and beauty services are staffed and operated by Harding Brothers, a concession whose staff also run the fitness and aerobics classes. Spa treatments offered include several types of massage, aromatherapy facials, seaweed body wraps, and hair beautifying services.

Sapphire
★★ +

Small Ship: ....12,263 tons	Passenger Decks: 8	Cabins (for one person): 0
Lifestyle: ....Standard	Total Crew: 250	Cabins (with private balcony): 0
Cruise Line: ....Louis Cruise Lines	Passengers	Cabins (wheelchair accessible): 0
Former Names: ......*Princesa Oceanica,*	(lower beds/all berths): 576/650	Cabin Current: ....110 volts
Sea Prince V, Sea Prince, Ocean	Passenger Space Ratio	Elevators: 5
Princess, Princess Italia, Italia	(lower beds/all berths): 21.1/18.7	Casino (gaming tables): ....Yes
Builder: ...Cantieri Navale Felszegi (Italy)	Crew/Passenger Ratio	Slot Machines: ....Yes
Original Cost: ....n/a	(lower beds/all berths): 2.3/2.6	Swimming Pools (outdoors): 1
Entered Service: ....Aug 1967/Apr 1996	Navigation Officers: ....Greek	Swimming Pools (indoors): 0
Registry: ....Marshall Islands	Cabins (total): 288	Whirlpools: 0
Length (ft/m): 491.7/149.8	Size Range (sq ft/m): 75.3–226.0/	Self-Service Launderette: ....No
Beam (ft/m): 70.9/21.5	7.0–21.0	Dedicated Cinema/Seats: Yes/170
Draft (ft/m): 22.3/6.8	Cabins (outside view): 157	Library: ....Yes
Propulsion/Propellers: diesel (11,050kW)/2	Cabins (interior/no view): 131	

OVERALL SCORE: 1,028 (OUT OF A POSSIBLE 2,000 POINTS)

OVERVIEW. *Sapphire* has had many previous names and owners, and an interesting life. In 1993, the ship sank in the Amazon River before being bought by its present owners and refitted. It has long, low-slung, handsome lines and a swept-back aft-placed funnel – all of which combine to provide a very attractive profile for this small ship. Louis Cruise Lines purchased the ship in 1995 and, following an extensive refurbishment, placed it into service in 1996. Since it took over the ship, the company has lavished much care and attention in keeping it in good condition.

There is a good amount of open deck and sunbathing space, but the heated swimming pool is very small, and is really only a "dip" pool.

Inside, the contemporary interior decor is fairly smart. There is a mix of attractive colors, together with much use of mirrored surfaces, which help to give the public rooms a feeling of spaciousness and warmth. Most public rooms do have a low ceiling height, however. Harry's Bar is the most popular gathering place, although there are few seats (the gaming tables are adjacent). Other public rooms include the Marco Polo Lounge for evening shows, the Monte Carlo Casino, the Starlight Theater (a cinema with comfortable seating), and a card room and token library.

This ship will take you to some decent destinations (for most of the year it operates 7-day Greek Island and Egypt cruises from Cyprus) in reasonably contemporary surroundings, and in a relaxed, casual, yet comfortable style. The realistic, inexpensive price of this product is a bonus for first-time passengers seeking a cruise aboard a mid-sized ship that is still considered very much a "traditional" cruise ship rather than one of the floating mega-resorts

BERLITZ'S RATINGS

	Possible	Achieved
Ship	500	242
Accommodation	200	105
Food	400	204
Service	400	225
Entertainment	100	48
Cruise	400	204

operated by the major cruise lines. Your fellow travelers are likely to be English-speaking British and Cypriot passengers. Gratuities are added to your onboard account at the rate of £2 per person per day.

The ceilings are quite low throughout the ship, with the exception of a couple of the public rooms. Some cabins are subject to noise from the engines and generators.

SUITABLE FOR: *Sapphire* is best suited to couples and single travelers (not recommended for children) for a first cruise in a comfortable, clubby setting that provides a decent array of public rooms and facilities, and a destination-intensive cruise that provides decent value for money.

ACCOMMODATION. There are five price grades: Premier Outside (the largest), Superior Outside, Standard Outside, Superior Interior (no view), and Standard Interior (no view). The price you pay will depend on the grade, size and location you choose (generally, the higher the deck, the more expensive the accommodation).

The outside-view and interior (no view) cabins are of a reasonable size, and have pleasing, though plain, decor, soft furnishings, and fittings. In almost all cases, the cabin closet and drawer space is very limited. Some cabins (but not many) have a double bed, while most have two beds and many cabins have a third or third and fourth upper berth (good for families with young children).

All cabins have tiled bathrooms, with a shower enclosure, toilet and washbasin, but they are small, and there is little storage space for personal toiletries. There is a 24-hour cabin service menu, although there is only a limited choice of items (and these come at extra cost).

The Premier Outside cabins are the largest, and have two beds, plus a sofa bed, and the bathroom has either a shower or bathtub. Nine out of the 15 Premier Outside grade cabins have a lifeboat-obstructed view (as do two of the Super Outside grade cabins).

CUISINE. The 330-seat Four Seasons Restaurant is quite a charming room that has an art deco feel to it, a raised center ceiling, and glass dividers, although the noise level from the waiter stations can be high. There are two seatings. The cuisine is international, but do remember that this is a low-cost cruise, and so you shouldn't expect high-class cuisine. What is provided, however, is surprisingly decent fare that is tasty and well presented. The service from a willing, friendly staff is reasonably attentive. Low-cost vegetarian lunch boxes are available upon request for anyone going ashore on shore excursions. The price of drinks is extremely reasonable, as are wines (but don't expect good vintages, as almost all the wine stock is very young).

For casual breakfasts and luncheons, the Cafe de Paris (located indoors but looking out onto the pool deck) is the place (it also has a bar) to head for (the self-serve breakfast buffets are a little repetitive, however).

ENTERTAINMENT. The Marco Polo Lounge is the venue for all entertainment events and most social functions. It is a single-level room that was designed for cabaret acts rather than "production" shows. The sight lines are fair from the majority of seats, but best from the first few rows closest to the stage. The room also has a hardwood dance floor and social dancing typically takes place after any shows. A resident troupe of dancers provides "openers and closers" for the revue-style shows, where a cabaret act (such as a singer, magician, comedian, or musical specialist) is inserted into the middle "star" spot. This is, however, a small ship operating low-budget cruises, so you should not expect much in the way of quality entertainment.

The ship has a band and a couple of small musical units for live dancing and listening music.

SPA/FITNESS. There are no facilities, with the exception of a small beauty salon, where basic hairdressing and hair beautifying treatments are available.

Sapphire Princess
★★★★

Large Resort Ship:	.......115,875 tons	Passenger Decks:	13	Cabins (for one person):	0
Lifestyle:	..................Standard	Total Crew:	1,238	Cabins (with private balcony):	750
Cruise Line:	..........Princess Cruises	Passengers		Cabins (wheelchair accessible):	28
Former Names:	................none	(lower beds/all berths):	.....2,674/3,100		(18 outside/10 interior)
Builder:	.....Mitsubishi Heavy Industries	Passenger Space Ratio		Cabin Current:	...............110 volts
	(Japan)	(lower beds/all berths):	.......43.3/37.3	Elevators:	14
Original Cost:	.............$400 million	Crew/Passenger Ratio		Casino (gaming tables):	............Yes
Entered Service:	.............May 2004	(lower beds/all berths):	........2.1/2.5	Slot Machines:	....................Yes
Registry:	...................Bermuda	Navigation Officers:	....British/Italian	Swimming Pools (outdoors):	4
Length (ft/m):	.........951.4/290.00	Cabins (total):	1,337	Swimming Pools (indoors):	0
Beam (ft/m):	..............123.0/37.50	Size Range (sq ft/m):	......168–1,329.3/	Whirlpools:	9
Draft (ft/m):	.................26.4/8.05		15.6–123.5	Self-Service Launderette:	..........Yes
Propulsion/Propellers:	......gas turbine	Cabins (outside view):	1,000	Dedicated Cinema/Seats:	..........No
	(25 MW)/2	Cabins (interior/no view):	337	Library:	........................Yes

OVERALL SCORE: 1,544 (OUT OF A POSSIBLE 2,000 POINTS)

OVERVIEW. *Sapphire Princess* has an instantly recognizable funnel due to two jet engine-like pods that sit high up on its structure, but really are mainly for decoration. This is the second ship to be constructed by a Japanese shipyard for Princess Cruises (sister ship *Diamond Princess* debuted in 2004). The ship is similar in size and internal layout to *Golden Princess, Grand Princess* and *Star Princess* (although of a slightly greater beam). Unlike its half-sister ships, however, all of which had a "spoiler" (containing a discotheque) located aft of the funnel, this has thankfully been removed from both *Diamond Princess* and *Sapphire Princess*, and has been replaced by a more sensible (and less weighty) aft-facing nightclub/discotheque structure (Skywalkers Nightclub) set around the base of the adjoining the funnel structure. The view from the nightclub overlooks aft-facing cascading decks and children's pool.

In December 2002, while the ship was under construction in the shipyard (as *Diamond Princess*), a fire broke out on Deck 5 and did much damage. The ship's hull was switched with that of identical sister *Sapphire Princess*, which was being built in the same yard at the same time.

The actual hull form in *Sapphire Princess* (and sister *Diamond Princess*) is slightly different to that of other "Grand Class" ships, and is slightly wider. Electrical power is provided by a combination of four diesel and one gas turbine (CODAG) unit; the diesel engines are located in the engine room, while the gas turbine unit is located in the ship's funnel housing, on each side of which is a cosmetic pod that resembles a jet aircraft engine.

Four areas focus on swimming pools, one of which is two decks high and is covered by a magrodome (retractable

BERLITZ'S RATINGS		
	Possible	Achieved
Ship	500	431
Accommodation	200	168
Food	400	256
Service	400	293
Entertainment	100	82
Cruise	400	314

glass dome), itself an extension of the funnel housing.

The interiors of the ship are overseen and outfitted by the Okura Group, whose Okura Hotel is one of the best in Tokyo. Fit and finish quality is superior that of the Italian-built *Golden Princess, Grand Princess* and *Star Princess*. Unlike the outside decks, there is plenty of space inside the ship (but there are also plenty of passengers), and a wide array of public rooms to choose from, with many "intimate" (this being a relative word) spaces and places to enjoy. The passenger flow has been well thought out, and works with little congestion. The decor is attractive, with lots of earth tones (well suited to both American and European tastes). In fact, this ship is perhaps the culmination of the best of all that Princess Cruises has to offer from its many years of operating what is now a well-tuned, good-quality product. An extensive collection of art works has been chosen, and this complements the interior design and colors well.

This ship also has a Wedding Chapel. The ship's captain can legally marry (American) couples (a live web-cam can relay ceremonies via the internet), due to the ship's Bermuda registry and a special dispensation (which should be verified when in the planning stage, according to where you reside). Princess Cruises offers three wedding packages – Pearl, Emerald, Diamond. The "Hearts & Minds" chapel is also useful for "renewal of vows" ceremonies.

Gaming lovers should enjoy what is presently one of the largest casinos at sea (Grand Casino), with more than 260 slot machines; there are blackjack, craps and roulette tables, plus newer games such as Let It Ride Bonus, Spanish 21 and Caribbean Draw Progressive. But the highlight could well be the specially linked slot machines that provide a combined payout.

Other features include a library/CD-Rom computer room, and a separate card room. Ship lovers should enjoy the wood-paneled Wheelhouse Bar, finely decorated with memorabilia and ship models tracing part of parent company P&O's history. Aft of the International Dining Room is the Wake View Bar, with a spiral stairway that leads down to a great viewing spot for those who want to watch the ship's wake; it is reached from the back of Club Fusion, on Promenade Deck.

A high-tech hospital is provided, with live SeaMed telemedicine link-ups with specialists at the Cedars-Sinai Medical Center in Los Angeles available for emergency help.

For youngsters and teenagers there is a two-deck-high playroom, teen room, and a host of specially trained counselors. Children have their own pools, hot tubs, and open deck area at the stern of the ship (away from adult areas).

Sapphire Princess is a grand playground in which to roam and play when you are not ashore. Princess Cruises delivers a fine, well-packaged holiday product, with some sense of style, at an attractive, highly competitive price, and this ship will appeal to those that really enjoy big city life, with all the trimmings and lots of fellow passengers. The ship is full of revenue centers, however, which are designed to help you part with even more money than you paid for in the price of your cruise ticket (cruise lines have become increasingly shrewd). Expect to be subjected to a stream of flyers advertising daily art auctions, "designer" watches and the like, while "artworks" for auction are strewn throughout the ship.

Whether a cruise aboard this ship really can be considered a relaxing holiday is a moot point, but with so many choices and "small" rooms to enjoy, the ship has been extremely well designed, and the odds are that you'll have a fine cruise holiday, as long as you plan your movements and timing carefully.

The dress code is formal or smart casual (translated by many as jeans and trainers). Gratuities to staff are automatically added to your account, at $10 per person, per day (with gratuities for children charged at the same rate). If you want to pay less, you'll need to go to the reception desk to have these charges adjusted (that could mean lining up with many other passengers wanting to do the same). The onboard currency is the US dollar.

If you are not used to large ships, it will take you some time to find your way around this one, despite the company's claim that this vessel offers passengers a "small ship feel, big ship choice."

Lines form for many things aboard large ships, but particularly so for the purser's (information) office, and for open-seating breakfast and lunch in the four main dining rooms. Long lines for shore excursions and shore tenders are also a fact of life aboard such large ships, as is waiting for elevators at peak times, embarkation (an "express check-in" option is available by completing certain documentation 40 days before your cruise) and disembarkation.

You'll have to live with the many extra charge items

(such as for ice cream, freshly squeezed orange juice, and activities such as yoga, group exercise bicycling and kick boxing classes (at $10 per session), and $4 per hour for group babysitting services (at the time this book was completed). There's also a charge for using the washers and dryers in the self-service launderettes.

ACCOMMODATION. All passengers receive turndown service and chocolates on pillows each night, bathrobes (on request) and toiletry amenity kits (larger, naturally, for suite/mini-suite occupants) that typically include soap, shampoo, conditioner, and hand/body lotion. A hairdryer is provided in all cabins, sensibly located at the vanity desk unit in the living area. All bathrooms are tiled and have a decent amount of open shelf storage space for toiletries.

You should note that the majority of the outside cabins on Emerald Deck have views obstructed by the lifeboats. Sadly, there are no cabins for singles. Your name is typically placed outside your suite or cabin – making it simple for delivery service personnel but also eroding your privacy. There is 24-hour room service (some items on the room service menu are not, however, available during early morning hours). Most of the balcony suites and cabins can be overlooked both from the navigation bridge wing.

Cabins with balconies on Baja, Caribe, and Dolphin decks are also overlooked by passengers on balconies on the deck above; they are, therefore, not at all private. Cabin bath towels are small, and drawer space is limited. There are no butlers – even for the top grade suites (which are not really large in comparison to similar suites aboard some other ships). Cabin attendants have too many cabins to look after (typically 20), which does not translate to fine personal service.

CUISINE. There are several "personal choice" dining options, but all dining rooms are located on one of two decks in the ship's center. There are five principal dining rooms with themed decor and cuisine – smaller than the three dining rooms in the similarly sized *Golden Princess, Grand Princess* and *Star Princess* (actually two dining rooms were halved in size to become four). They are: Sterling Steakhouse (for steak and grilled meats), Vivaldi (Italian fare), Santa Fe (southwestern USA cuisine) and Pacific Moon (Asian cuisine) and International (the largest, located aft with two seatings and "traditional" cuisine). These offer a mix of two seatings (seating is assigned according to the location of your cabin) and "anytime dining" (where you choose when and with whom you want to eat).

All dining rooms are non-smoking and are split into sections in a non-symmetrical design that breaks what are quite large spaces into many smaller sections, for better ambience and less noise pollution.

Specially designed dinnerware and good quality linens and silverware are used: Dudson of England (dinnerware), Frette Egyptian cotton table linens, and silverware by Hepp of Germany. Note that 15% is added to all beverage bills, including wines.

Alternative Dining Option: Trattoria Sabatini is an informal eatery (reservations required; cover charge $20 per person). It offers an eight-course meal, including Italian-style pizzas and pastas, with a variety of sauces, as well as Italian-style entrées including tiger prawns and lobster tailThe cuisine in this eatery is potentially better than in all the other dining rooms (better quality ingredients and more attention to presentation and taste, all delivered with more flair).

A poolside hamburger grill and pizza bar (no additional charge) are additional dining spots for casual bites, while extra charges will apply if you order items to eat at either the coffee bar/patisserie, or the caviar/champagne bar. Other casual meals can be taken in the Horizon Court, which is open 24 hours a day, with large ocean-view on port and starboard sides and direct access to the two principal swimming pools and lido deck (there is no finesse in presentation, however, as plastic plates are provided).

ENTERTAINMENT. The Princess Theatre (show lounge) spans two decks and has comfortable seating on both main and balcony levels. It has $3 million in sound and light equipment, plus a 9-piece orchestra, and a scenery loading bay that connects directly from stage to a hull door for direct transfer to the dockside.

Princess Cruises prides itself on its glamorous all-American production shows, and the shows aboard this ship should not disappoint (there are typically two or three shows each 7-day cruise). The ship carries its own resident troupe of singers/dancers and audio-visual support staff.

There is also a second large entertainment lounge, Club Fusion. It features cabaret acts (magicians, comedy jugglers, ventriloquists and others) at night, and lectures, bingo and horse racing during the day. A third entertainment lounge can also host cabaret acts and dance bands. A host of other lounges and bars have live music, and Princess Cruises will have a number of male dance hosts as partners for women traveling alone.

SPA/FITNESS. The Lotus Spa is located forward on Sun Deck – one of the uppermost decks. Separate facilities for men and women include a sauna, steam room, and changing rooms; common facilities include a relaxation/waiting zone, body-pampering treatment rooms, and a gymnasium with packed with the latest high-tech muscle-pumping, cardio-vascular equipment, and great ocean views. Some fitness classes are free, while some incur an extra charge.

The Lotus Spa is operated by Steiner Leisure. You can make online reservations for any spa treatments before your cruise – so you can obtain the time you want, instead of all that frustration often encountered when aboard a ship.

● **For more extensive general information on what the Princess Cruises experience is like, see pages 134–37.**

Sea Bird
★★

Boutique Ship: . . . . .99.7 tons
Lifestyle: . . . . .Standard
Cruise Line: . . . . .Lindblad Expeditions
Former Names: . . . .*Majestic Explorer*
Builder: . . . . .Whidbey Island
(USA)
Original Cost: .n/a
Entered Service: 1981
Registry: . . . . .The Bahamas
Length (ft/m): 151.9/46.3
Beam (ft/m): 30.8/9.4
Draft (ft/m): 8.0/2.4
Propulsion/Propellers: diesel/2
Passenger Decks: 4

Total Crew: 22
Passengers
(lower beds/all berths): 70/70
Passenger Space Ratio
(lower beds/all berths): 1.4/1.4
Crew/Passenger Ratio
(lower beds/all berths): 3.1/3.1
Navigation Officers: . . . . . . .Scandinavian
Cabins (total): .36
Size Range (sq ft/m): 73.0–202.0/
6.7–18.7
Cabins (outside view): 36
Cabins (interior/no view): 0
Cabins (for one person): 2

Cabins (with private balcony): 0
Cabins (wheelchair accessible): 0
Cabin Current: . . . . .110 volts
Elevators: 0
Casino (gaming tables): . . . . .No
Slot Machines: . . . . .No
Swimming Pools (outdoors): 0
Swimming Pools (indoors): 0
Whirlpools: 0
Self-Service Launderette: . . . . .No
Dedicated Cinema/Seats: . . . . .No
Library: . . . . .No

BERLITZ'S OVERALL SCORE: 903 (OUT OF A POSSIBLE 2,000 POINTS)

OVERVIEW. *Sea Bird* carries a fleet of motorized Zodiac landing craft for use as shore tenders and for up-close shore exploration. A number of sea kayaks are also carried. An open-bridge policy means you can go to the navigation bridge at any time. The vessel is small enough to operate in ports and narrow inlets inaccessible to larger ships. Lecturers and recap sessions are held daily.

This small craft (and sister ship *Sea Lion*) is adequate for looking at nature and wildlife close-up, in modest but comfortable surroundings that provide an alternative to big-ship cruising. Cruises visit Alaska, Baja California and the Sea of Cortes. Tipping is suggested at about $7 per person per day. The onboard currency is the US dollar.

In the cabins, the mattresses are enclosed in a wood frame with sharp corners, which you bang into constantly.

SUITABLE FOR: *Sea Bird* is best suited to older couples and single travelers who enjoy learning about nature, geography, history and other life sciences in casual, non-dressy surroundings without a hint of pretension. They are likely to be hardy, outdoors types who don't need entertainment or silly parlor games.

ACCOMMODATION. All cabins have rudimentary furniture, but all have an outside view through picture windows, except for those on the lowest deck, which have portholes

BERLITZ'S RATINGS		
	Possible	Achieved
Ship	500	178
Accommodation	200	78
Food	400	191
Service	400	207
Entertainment	n/a	n/a
Cruise	500	249

but no view. Some cabins have double beds, some have twin beds (they can be pushed together to form a queen-sized bed), and some are for singles (at a surcharge of 150 percent). There is just enough room to stow your luggage.

All cabins have a private bathroom, although it really is tiny. There is no room service for food or beverages.

CUISINE. The dining room (non-smoking), which has ocean-view picture windows, is large enough to accommodate all passengers in a single seating. The tables are not assigned, and so you can sit with whom you like. The food is unpretentious, good and wholesome, although its presentation is very plain, with no frills, and features regional specialties. The wine list is very limited, and is comprised mostly of wines from California.

ENTERTAINMENT. There is no formal entertainment, although dinner and after-dinner conversation with fellow passengers in the ship's lounge/bar really becomes the entertainment. So, if you're not in the mood to talk to your fellow passengers, retire with a good book, or go outside, where you'll usually find that nature provides varied entertainment.

SPA/FITNESS. There are no spa or fitness facilities aboard this very small cruise vessel.

Sea Cloud
★★★★★

Boutique Ship: . . . . .2,532 tons	Sail Area (sq ft/m2): 32,292/3,000	Cabins (outside view): 34
Lifestyle: . . . . .Luxury	Main Propulsion: . . . . .sail power	Cabins (interior/no view): 0
Cruise Line: . . . . .Sea Cloud Cruises	Propulsion/Propellers: diesel (4,476kW)/2	Cabins (for one person): 0
Former Names: . . . . . .Sea Cloud of Grand	Passenger Decks: 3	Cabins (with private balcony): 0
Cayman, IX-99, Antama, Patria,	Total Crew: 60	Cabins (wheelchair accessible): 0
Angelita, Sea Cloud, Hussar	Passengers	Cabin Current: . . . . .220 volts
Builder: . . . . .Krupp Werft (Germany)	(lower beds/all berths): 68/69	Elevators: 0
Entered Service: . . . . .Aug 1931/1979	Passenger Space Ratio	Casino (gaming tables): . . . . .No
(restored)	(lower beds/all berths): 37.2/36.6	Slot Machines: . . . . .No
Registry: . . . . .Malta	Crew/Passenger Ratio	Swimming Pools (outdoors): 0
Length (ft/m): 359.2/109.5	(lower beds/all berths): 1.1/1.1	Whirlpools: 0
Beam (ft/m): 48.2814.9	Navigation Officers: . . . . .European	Self-Service Launderette: . . . . .No
Draft (ft/m): 16.8/5.13	Cabins (total): 34	Library: . . . . .Yes
Type of Vessel: . . . . .barque	Size Range (sq ft/m): 102.2–409.0/	
No. of Masts: . . . .4 (17.7 meters)/30 sails	9.5–38.0	

OVERALL SCORE: 1,704 (OUT OF A POSSIBLE 2,000 POINTS)

OVERVIEW. If you want the most romantic, exhilarating, inspiring, soul-refreshing time of your life, take a cruise aboard *Sea Cloud*, the oldest and most beautiful sailing ship in the world (its 75th birthday was celebrated in style in 2006). It is the largest private yacht ever built (three times the size of Captain Cook's *Endeavour*) and a stunningly beautiful ship when under sail.

Sea Cloud is a completely authentic 1930s barque whose three masts are almost as high as a 20-story building (the main mast is 178 ft/ 54 meters above the main deck). This was the largest private yacht ever built when completed in 1931 by E.F. Hutton for his wife, Marjorie Merriweather Post, the American cereal heiress. Originally constructed for $1 million as *Hussar* in the Krupp shipyard in Kiel, Germany, this steel-hulled yacht is immensely impressive when in port, but exhilarating when under full sail.

During World War II, the vessel saw action as a weather observation ship, under the code name *IX-99*. You can still see five chevrons on the bridge, one for each half-year of duty, serving as a reminder of those important years.

There is plenty of deck space, even under the vast expanse of white sail, and the promenade deck outdoors still has wonderful varnished sea chests. The decks themselves are made of mahogany and teak, and wooden "steamer"-style sunloungers are provided.

One of the most beautiful aspects of sailing aboard this ship is its "Blue Lagoon," which is located at the very stern of the vessel. Weather permitting, you can lie down on the thick blue padding and gaze up at the stars and night sky – it's one of the great pleasures – particu-

BERLITZ'S RATINGS		
	Possible	Achieved
Ship	500	423
Accommodation	200	173
Food	400	348
Service	400	335
Entertainment	n/a	n/a
Cruise	500	425

larly when the ship is under sail, with engines turned off.

The original engine room (with diesel engines) is still in operation for the rare occasions when sail power can't be used. An open-bridge policy is the norm (except during times of poor weather or navigational maneuvers).

In addition to its retained and refurbished original suites and cabins, some newer, smaller cabins were added in 1979 when a consortium of German yachtsmen and businessmen purchased the ship. The owners spent $7.5 million refurbishing it. The interiors exude warmth, and are finely hand crafted. There is much antique mahogany furniture, fine original oil paintings, gorgeous carved oak paneling, parquet flooring and burnished brass everywhere, as well as some finely detailed ceilings. There is no doubt that Marjorie Merryweather Post was accustomed only to the very finest things in life.

Sea Cloud is the most romantic sailing ship afloat. It operates under charter for much of the year, and sails in both the Caribbean and European/Mediterranean waters.

A cruise aboard *Sea Cloud* is, in summary, a really exhilarating experience. This is a ship like no other, for the discerning few to relish the uncompromising comfort and elegance of a bygone era. A kind of stately home afloat, *Sea Cloud* remains one of the finest and nicest travel experiences in the world. The activities are few, and so relaxation is the key, in a setting that provides fine service and style, but in an unpretentious way. Note that some staircases are steep, as they are aboard almost all sailing vessels.

The only "dress-up" night is the Captain's Welcome Aboard Dinner, but otherwise, smart casual clothing is all that is needed (no tuxedo). Note that mini-skirts would be impractical due to the steep staircases in some places – trousers are more practical. Also note that a big sailing vessel such as this can heel to one side occasionally (so take flat shoes rather than high heels).

The crew is of mixed nationality, and the sailors who climb the rigging and set the sails include females as well as males. On the last night of the cruise, the sailors' choir sings seafaring songs. Gratuities are suggested at $15 per person, per day, although these can be charged to your account. The US dollar is the onboard currency.

The German owner, Sea Cloud Cruises, also operates the rivercruise vessels *River Cloud* and *River Cloud II* for cruising along the rivers of Europe, and, in 2001 introduced a brand new companion sailing ship, *Sea Cloud II*.

Sea Cloud sails, for part of each year, under charter to Hapag-Lloyd Cruises. On those occasions, white and red wines and beer are included for lunch and dinner; soft drinks, espresso and cappuccino coffees are also included at any time; shore excursions are an optional extra, as are gratuities. Details may be different for other charter operators (such as Abercrombie & Kent).

Passengers are not permitted to climb the rigging, as may be possible aboard some other tall ships. This is because the mast rigging on this vintage sailing ship is of a very different type to the more modern sailing vessels (such as *Royal Clipper, Star Clipper, Star Flyer,* and *Sea Cloud II*). However, passengers may be able participate occasionally in the furling and unfurling of the sails.

Although just over a wonderful 75 years young, *Sea Cloud* is so lovingly maintained and operated that anyone who sails aboard it cannot fail to be impressed and totally absorbed by the character of this beautiful tall ship. If you seek entertainment, casinos, bingo, horse racing and flashy resort cruising, this is not the ship for you.

The food and service are good, as is the interaction between passengers and crew, many of whom have worked aboard the ship for many, many years. One bonus is the fact that the doctor on board is available at no charge for medical emergencies or seasickness medication.

In 2001, the ship suffered a fire while in Rijeka, which put it out of commission for many months. However, all necessary repairs have been painstakingly made and it is now in its beautiful original condition again.

Rigging: For the sailors among you, the sails are (in order, from fore to aft mast, top to bottom):

Fore Mast: flying jib, outer jib, inner jib, fore topmast staysail, fore royal, fore topgallant, fore upper-top sail, fore lower-top sail, foresail.

Main Mast: main royal staysail, main topgallant staysail, main topmast staysail, skysail, main royal, main topgallant, main upper topsail, main lower topsail, main sail.

Mizzen Mast: mizzen royal staysail, mizzen topgallant staysail, mizzen topmast staysail, mizzen royal topsail, mizzen topgallant, mizzen upper topsail, mizzen lower topsail, mizzen course.

Spanker Mast: spanker top mast staysail, spanker staysail, spanker-gaff topsail, spanker.

SUITABLE FOR: *Sea Cloud* is best suited to couples and singles (not children) who would probably never consider a "normal" cruise ship, but who enjoy sailing aboard a real tall ship but want the experience wrapped in a package that includes accommodation, good food, like-minded companions, interesting destinations, and don't want the bother of owning or chartering their own mega-yacht.

ACCOMMODATION. Because *Sea Cloud* was built as a private yacht, there is a wide variation in cabin sizes and configurations. Some cabins have double beds, while some have twin beds (side by side or in an L-shaped configuration) that are fixed and cannot be placed together. Many of the original cabins have a fireplace (now with an electric fire) and some of the fittings in some bathrooms remind me of those found in similar bathrooms in the lovely Hotel Abtei in Hamburg.

All the cabins are very comfortable, but those on Main Deck (Cabins 1–8) were part of the original accommodation aboard this ship. Of these, the two owner's suites (Cabins 1 and 2) are really opulent, and feature real, original Chippendale furniture, fine gilt detailing, a real fireplace, French canopy bed, and large Italian Carrara marble bathrooms with gold fittings.

Owner's Cabin Number 1 is decorated in white throughout, and has a French double bed, a marble fireplace and Louis Phillippe chairs; the bathroom is appointed in Carrara marble, with cut-glass mirrors, and faucets (taps) in the shape of swans. Owner's Cabin Number 2, completely paneled in rich woods, retains the mahogany secretary used 60 years ago by Edward F. Hutton (Marjorie's husband), its dark wood decor reminiscent of the 1930s.

Other cabins (both the original ones, and some newer additions) are beautifully furnished (all were refurbished in 1993) and are surprisingly large for the size of the ship. There is a good amount of closet and drawer space and all cabins have a personal safe and telephone. The cabin bathrooms, too, are quite luxurious, and equipped with everything you will need, including bathrobes and hairdryer, and an assortment of toiletries (there is a 110-volt AC shaver socket in each bathroom). The "new" cabins are rather small for two persons, so it's best to take minimal luggage.

There is no cabin food or beverage service. Also, if you occupy one of the original cabins on Main Deck you may be subjected to some noise when the motorized capstans are used to raise and lower or trim the sails. On one day each cruise, an "open-house" cocktail party is held on the Main Deck, with all cabins available for passengers to see.

CUISINE. The dining room, created from the original owner's living room/saloon, is located in the center of the vessel. It is exquisite and elegant in every detail (it also houses the ship's library) and has beautiful wood paneled walls and a wood beam ceiling. There is ample space at each table, so there is never a crowded feeling, and meals are taken in an open-seating arrangement. German chefs are in charge, and the cuisine is very international, with a good balance of nouvelle cuisine and regional dishes featured (depending on which region the ship is sailing in). High quality food and cuisine are featured throughout, although there is little choice, due to the size of the galley. Place settings for dinner (often by candlelight) are navy blue, white and gold Bauscher china.

There is always excellent seafood and fish (this is purchased fresh, locally, when available, as are most other ingredients). For breakfast and lunch, there are self-serve buffets. These are really good, and beautifully presented (usually indoors for breakfast and outdoors on the Promenade Deck for lunch). Meal times are announced by the ship's bell. European wines are provided for lunch and dinner (vintages tend to be young, however). Soft drinks and bottled water are included in the price, while alcoholic drinks cost extra. On the last day of each cruise, homemade ice cream is produced.

ENTERTAINMENT. There is a keyboard player/singer for the occasional soirée, but nothing else (nothing else needed – the thrill of sailing is the entertainment). Dinner and after-dinner conversation with fellow passengers really becomes the entertainment each evening. So, if you are feeling anti-social and don't want to talk to your fellow passengers, take a good book (or two).

SPA/FITNESS. There are no spa or fitness facilities. However, for recreation (particularly at night), there is the Blue Lagoon, an area of seating (with blue cushioned pads) at the very aft of the ship, where you can lie down and watch the heavens.

ENVIRONMENTAL ISSUES

There are three types of waste water: bilge water, black water (or sewage) and grey water.

Bilge water is oily engine run-off and condensation that collects in the bilge, a compartment at the bottom of a vessel's hull where water is collected and later pumped out. Grey water comes from showers and sinks. Black water, perhaps the most damaging to the environment, comes from the toilets and from the drains and sinks of the medical center. When water is treated to reduce its oil content below 15 parts of oil per million parts of water, international law allows it to be discharged virtually anywhere.

Few accidents have happened, and most cruise ships' environmental standards meet or surpass all international laws; the cruise industry represents only 0.2 percent of all ocean-going vessels worldwide.

Cruise ship owners are working towards stricter emission limits for particulate matter and sulfur oxides, and reducing nitrogen oxide levels (compared to existing emissions levels) that will probably be imposed within the next few years. Older engines (those built before January 1, 2000) will be required to achieve a 20% reduction in nitrogen oxides starting in 2010.

The latest generation of propulsion machinery (engines) is, however, much more fuel efficient than older ships. For example, RCI's *Freedom*-class ships are 10% more fuel efficient than the *Voyager*-class ships, and, when introduced in 2009, the *Genesis*-class ships will be 15% more fuel efficient than the *Freedom*-class ships.

In the past 10 years, cruise ships have spent huge sums of money in new technology; the result is that waste and garbage has been almost cut in half, while sustaining cruise capacity growth just approaching around eight percent annually. The latest hull coatings increase fuel efficiency; the coating, which reduces surface resistance in the water, is completely non-toxic. Many large resort ships now have environmental officers on board to oversee compliance with environmental regulations and requirements.

Cruise lines reduce the solid waste they generate by purchasing in bulk, encouraging suppliers to use more efficient packaging, reusing packaging when possible and packaging more environmentally friendly materials. Other examples:
● Advanced purification systems treat all onboard wastewater.
● Ships actively recycle glass, metals, wood, cardboard and paper.
● Excess heat generated in the ships' engine boilers is rerouted to power evaporators used in the process of turning sea water into potable water.
● Special high-tech compacters process garbage (the one aboard *Queen Mary 2*, for example, is four decks high).
● Dry cleaning machines now use non-hazardous detergents formulated with soy, banana and orange extracts.
● Materials printed on board can now be produced using soy-based inks.
● Some ships "plug in" to clean, local hydroelectric when they dock in ports cities such as Seattle and Juneau.
● The only solid waste discharged to sea is food waste, considered safe because, either animals consume it or natural elements break it down in the water. And some use only seafood farmed from sustainable sources. NCL and NCL America ships offload their used cooking oil for recycling to bio-diesel.

What you can do to help

Specially marked containers are scattered throughout each ship for you to use.

Sea Cloud II
★★★★★

Boutique Ship: . . . . .3,849 tons	
Lifestyle: .Luxury	
Cruise Line: . . . . .Sea Cloud Cruises	
Former Names: . . . . .none	
Builder: Astilleros Gondan, Figueras (Spain)	
Original Cost: . . . . .DM 50 million	
Entered Service: . . . . .Feb 2001	
Registry: . . . . .Malta	
Length (ft/m): 383.8/117.0	
Beam (ft/m): 52.9/16.15	
Draft (ft/m): 17.7/5.4	
Type of Vessel: . . . . .barque	
No. of Masts: . . . . .3 (24 sails)	
Sail Area (sq ft/m2): 32,292/3,000	

Main Propulsion: . . . . .sail power	
Propulsion/Propellers: diesel (2,500kW)/2	
Passenger Decks: 4	
Total Crew: 60	
Passengers	
(lower beds/all berths): 96/96	
Passenger Space Ratio	
(lower beds/all berths): 40.0/40.0	
Crew/Passenger Ratio	
(lower beds/all berths): 1.6/1.6	
Navigation Officers: . .American/European	
Cabins (total): 48	
Size Range (sq ft/m): 215.2–322.9/	
20.0–30.0	

Cabins (outside view): 48	
Cabins (interior/no view): 0	
Cabins (for one person): 0	
Cabins (with private balcony): 0	
Cabins (wheelchair accessible): 0	
Cabin Current: . . . . . . .110 and 220 volts	
Elevators: 0	
Swimming Pools (outdoors): 0	
Whirlpools: 0	
Self-Service Launderette: . . . . .No	
Library: . . . . .Yes	
Classification Society: . . . . .Germanischer	
Lloyd	

BERLITZ'S OVERALL SCORE: 1,703 (OUT OF A POSSIBLE 2,000 POINTS)

OVERVIEW. This new, three-mast tall ship is slightly longer (and beamier) than the original *Sea Cloud*, and has the look, ambience and feel of a 1930s sailing vessel, but with all the latest high-tech navigational aids. The ship complements the company's beautiful, original, 1931-built *Sea Cloud* in almost every way, including its external appearance – except for a very rounded stern in place of the counter stern of sister ship *Sea Cloud*.

BERLITZ'S RATINGS

	Possible	Achieved
Ship	500	435
Accommodation	200	173
Food	400	338
Service	400	333
Entertainment	n/a	n/a
Cruise	500	424

Despite some appallingly low standards in the original fitting out of its interiors and carpeting by a shipyard that needs to learn the meaning of the word "quality", Sea Cloud Cruises quickly acted to correct the irritating items, and can now satisfy those seeking the very best of luxurious comfort and surroundings inside a wonderful sailing vessel.

A small water sports platform is built into the aft quarter of the starboard side (with adjacent shower), and the ship carries four inflatable craft for close-in shore landings, as well as snorkeling equipment.

The interior designers have managed to continue the same beautiful traditional look and design as that of *Sea Cloud*. These design details and special decorative touches will make those who have been on the sister ship feel instantly at home. Whether the modern materials used will stand up to 70 years of use like those of the original *Sea Cloud* remains to be seen, although they are of a high quality. In any event, passengers who have sailed aboard the original ship will compare the original with the new.

The main lounge is truly elegant, with sofa and large individual tub chair seating around oval drinks tables. The ceiling is ornate, with an abundance of wood detailing, and an oval centerpiece is set around skylights to the open deck above. A bar is set into the aft port side of the room, which has audio-visual aids built in – for lectures and presentations.

A treasured aspect of sailing aboard this ship is its "Blue Lagoon", at the very stern of the vessel – part of the outdoor bar and casual dining area. Weather permitting, you can lie on thick blue padding and gaze up at the stars and warm night sky – it's a huge pleasure, particularly when the ship is under sail, with the engines turned off.

Overall, *Sea Cloud II* is one of the most luxurious true sailing ships in the world, although it is not the largest (that distinction goes to competitor Star Clippers' *Royal Clipper*). However, in terms of interior design, degree of luxury in appointments, the passenger flow, fabrics, food and service, the ceiling height of public rooms, larger cabins, great open deck space, better passenger space ratio and crew to passenger ratio, there is none better than *Sea Cloud II*. If you sail both vessels (as I have), I am absolutely certain you would agree with me, and that your overall sail-cruise experience will be a truly memorable one.

Your personal experience will depend on which company is operating the ship under charter when you sail, and exactly what is to be included in the package. This is, however, as exclusive as it gets – sailing in the lap of luxury. **Rigging:** This consists of up to 24 sails: flying jib, outer jib, inner jib; fore royal, fore topgallant, fore upper topsail, fore lower topsail, fore course; main royal staysail, main topgallant staysail, main topmast staysail; sky sail, main royal, main topgallant, main upper topsail, main lower topsail, main sail; mizzen topgallant staysail, mizzen topmast staysail; mizzen gaff topsail, mizzen upper gaff sail, mizzen lower gaff sail, middle gaff, upper gaff.

If you have sailed aboard the original *Sea Cloud*, you will probably be disappointed with the more limited space and decoration of the equivalent cabins aboard this ship.

SUITABLE FOR: *Sea Cloud II* is best suited to couples and singles (not children) who would probably never consider a "normal" cruise ship, but who enjoy sailing aboard a real tall ship and want this experience wrapped in a package that includes accommodation, good food, like-minded companions, interesting destinations, and don't want the bother of owning or chartering their own mega-yacht.

ACCOMMODATION. The decor in the cabins is very tasteful 1920s retro, with lots of bird's-eye maple wood paneling, brass accenting, and beautiful molded white ceilings. All cabins have a vanity desk, hairdryer, refrigerator (typically stocked with soft drinks and bottled water), and a combination TV/video player. All cabins have a private bathroom with shower enclosure (or bathtub/shower combination), and plenty of storage space for your personal toiletries. Note that the cabin electrical current is 220 volts, although all bathrooms also include a 110-volt socket for shavers.

There are two suites. Naturally, these have more space (but not as much space as the two owner's suites aboard *Sea Cloud*), and comprise a completely separate bedroom (with four-poster bed) and living room, while the marble-clad bathroom has a full-sized tub.

There are 16 junior suites. These provide a living area and sleeping area with twin beds that convert to a queen-sized bed. The marble-clad bathroom is quite opulent, and has a small tub/shower combination, with lots of little cubbyholes to store personal toiletry items.

CUISINE. The one-seating dining room operates an open-seating policy, so you can dine with whom you wish, when you wish. It is decorated in a light, modern maritime style, with wood and carpeted flooring, comfortable chairs with armrests, and circular light fixtures. The gold-rimmed plates used for the captain's dinner (typically a candlelit affair) have the ship's crest embedded in the white porcelain; they are extremely elegant (and highly collectible). The place settings for dinner (often by candlelight) are navy blue, white and gold Bauscher china.

There is always excellent seafood and fish (this is purchased fresh, locally, when available, as are most other ingredients). For breakfast and lunch, there are self-serve buffets. These are really good, and beautifully presented (usually indoors for breakfast and outdoors on the Promenade Deck for lunch). Meal times are announced by the ship's bell. European wines are typically provided for lunch and dinner (vintages tend to be young, however). Soft drinks and bottled water are included in the price, while alcoholic drinks cost extra. On the last day of each cruise, homemade ice cream is produced.

ENTERTAINMENT. There is a keyboard player/singer for the occasional soirée, but nothing else (nothing else needed – the thrill of sailing is the entertainment). Dinner and after-dinner conversation with fellow passengers really becomes the entertainment each evening. So, if you are feeling anti-social and don't want to talk to your fellow passengers, take a good book (or two).

SPA/FITNESS. There is a health/fitness area, with small gymnasium, sauna and steam room. Massage is available.

Sea Lion
★★

Boutique Ship: . . . . .99.7 tons	Total Crew: 22	Cabins (with private balcony): 0
Lifestyle: . . . . .Standard	Passengers	Cabins (wheelchair accessible): 0
Cruise Line: . . . . .Lindblad Expeditions	(lower beds/all berths): 72/76	Cabin Current: . . . . .110 volts
Former Names: . . . .*Great Rivers Explorer*	Passenger Space Ratio	Elevators: 0
Builder: . . . . .Whidbey Island	(lower beds/all berths): 1.3/1.3	Casino (gaming tables): . . . . .No
(USA)	Crew/Passenger Ratio	Slot Machines: .No
Original Cost: . . . . .n/a	(lower beds/all berths): 3.2/3.4	Swimming Pools (outdoors): 0
Entered Service: 1982	Navigation Officers: . . . . . .Scandinavian	Swimming Pools (indoors): 0
Registry: . . . . .The Bahamas	Cabins (total): 37	Whirlpools: 0
Length (ft/m): 151.9/46.3	Size Range (sq ft/m): 73.0–202.0/	Self-Service Launderette: . . . . .No
Beam (ft/m): 30.8/9.4	6.7–18.7	Dedicated Cinema/Seats: . . . . .No
Draft (ft/m): 8.0/2.4	Cabins (outside view): 37	Library: . . . . .No
Propulsion/Propellers: diesel/2	Cabins (interior/no view): 0	
Passenger Decks: 4	Cabins (for one person): 2	

OVERALL SCORE: 904 (OUT OF A POSSIBLE 2,000 POINTS)

OVERVIEW. *Sea Lion* carries a fleet of motorized Zodiac landing craft for use as shore tenders and for up-close shore exploration. A number of sea kayaks are also carried. An open-bridge policy means that you are allowed to go to the navigation bridge at any time.

This small craft is adequate for looking at nature and wildlife close up, in modest but comfortable surroundings that provide an alternative to big-ship cruising. It is small enough to operate in ports and narrow inlets inaccessible to larger ships. Lectures and recap sessions are held each day.

Cruises visit Alaska, Baja California and the Sea of Cortes. Tipping is suggested at about $7 per person per day. The onboard currency is the US dollar.

Note that in the cabins, the mattresses are enclosed in a wood frame with sharp corners, which you can all too easily bang into constantly.

SUITABLE FOR: *Sea Lion* is best suited to older couples and single travelers who enjoy learning about nature, geography, history and other life sciences, in casual, non-dressy surroundings without a hint of pretension. They are likely to be hardy, outdoors types who don't need entertainment or silly parlor games.

ACCOMMODATION. All the cabins aboard this little ship have an outside view through picture windows, except for those

BERLITZ'S RATINGS		
	Possible	Achieved
Ship	500	179
Accommodation	200	78
Food	400	191
Service	400	207
Entertainment	n/a	n/a
Cruise	500	249

on the lowest deck, which have portholes. Some cabins have double beds, some have twin beds (they can be pushed together to form a queen-sized bed), and some are for singles (at a surcharge). There is plenty of room to stow your luggage.

All cabins have a private bathroom, although it really is tiny. There is no room service for food or beverages.

CUISINE. The dining room (non-smoking), which has ocean-view picture windows, is large enough to accommodate all passengers in a single seating. The tables are not assigned, and so you can sit with whom you like. The food is unpretentious, good and wholesome, although its presentation is very plain, with no frills, and features regional specialties.

The wine list is very limited, and is comprised mostly of wines from California.

ENTERTAINMENT. There is no formal entertainment, although dinner and after-dinner conversation with fellow passengers in the ship's lounge/bar really becomes the entertainment each evening. So, if you don't want to talk to your fellow passengers, take a good book, or go outside, where you'll find nature provides the rest of the entertainment.

SPA/FITNESS. There are no spa or fitness facilities aboard this very small cruise vessel.

Sea Princess
★★★★

Large Resort Ship: ....77,690 tons	Total Crew: 850	Cabins (with private balcony): 411
Lifestyle: ....Standard	Passengers	Cabins (wheelchair accessible): 19
Cruise Line: ....Princess Cruises	(lower beds/all berths): 2,016/2,272	Cabin Current: ....110 and 220 volts
Former Names: ......*Adonia, Sea Princess*	Passenger Space Ratio	Elevators: 11
Builder: ....Fincantieri (Italy)	(lower beds/all berths): 39.3/34.1	Casino (gaming tables): ....Yes
Original Cost: ....$300 million	Crew/Passenger Ratio	Slot Machines: ....Yes
Entered Service: ......Dec 1998/Apr 2005	(lower beds/all berths): 2.2/2.5	Swimming Pools (outdoors): 4
Registry: ....Great Britain	Navigation Officers: ....British	Swimming Pools (indoors): 0
Length (ft/m): 857.2/261.3	Cabins (total): 1,008	Whirlpools: 5
Beam (ft/m): 105.6/32.2	Size Range (sq ft/m): 158.2–610.3/	Self-Service Launderette: ....Yes
Draft (ft/m): 26.5/8.1	14.7–56.7	Dedicated Cinema/Seats: ....No
Propulsion/Propellers: .....diesel-electric	Cabins (outside view): 603	Library: ....Yes
(46,080kW)/2	Cabins (interior/no view): 405	
Passenger Decks: 10	Cabins (for one person): 0	

OVERALL SCORE: 1,525 (OUT OF A POSSIBLE 2,000 POINTS)

OVERVIEW. This all-white ship (sister ships: *Dawn Princess, Sun Princess*) has a profile balanced by a large, swept-back funnel which contains a deck tennis/basketball/volleyball court in its sheltered aft base. There is a wide, teak wrap-around promenade deck outdoors, some real teak steamer-style deck chairs (with cushioned pads), and 93,000 sq. ft (8,640 sq. meters) of out-doors space. A large glazed area on the upper decks provides plenty of light and connection with the outside world.

Sea Princess absorbs passengers well and has a decent passenger space ratio for a large ship; some areas even have an intimate feel to them, which is what the interior designers intended. The interiors are attractive and welcoming with pastel colors and decor that includes countless wall murals and other artwork.

There is a wide range of public rooms to choose from (including 13 bars), with several intimate rooms and spaces so that you aren't overwhelmed by large spaces. A large, four-deck-high atrium lobby has winding, double stairways and two panoramic glass-walled elevators.

There is a library, a warm room that has large buttery leather chairs for listening to CDs and audio books, with ocean-view windows; a card room and reading room. The artwork collection is good, particularly on the stairways, and helps make the ship feel smaller than it is. The Grand Casino is slightly out of the main passenger flow and so it does not generate the "walk-through" factor found aboard so many ships. Internet connectivity can be found in Cyber-space, a lounge/internet connect room close to the pools on Riviera Deck.

Perhaps the most popular drinking venue is the Wheel-

BERLITZ'S RATINGS	Possible	Achieved
Ship	500	424
Accommodation	200	162
Food	400	264
Service	400	291
Entertainment	100	82
Cruise	400	302

house Bar, with decor that is a pleasing mix of traditional and modern (it's like a gentleman's club, with its wood panel-ing and comfortable seating), a band-stand and dance floor. For families with children, plenty of space is provided in The Fun Zone children's center, on the starboard side of the Riviera (pool) Deck.

One nice feature is the fact that the captain's cocktail party – normally held in the four-deck-high main atrium, so you can come and go as you please. However, note that in the quest for increased onboard revenue, even birthday cakes are now an extra-cost item, as are espressos and cappuccinos (fake ones, made from instant coffee, are available in the dining rooms). Also at extra cost are ice cream (except in the restaurant), and bottled water (these can add up to a considerable amount on a long cruise).

Sea Princess, transferred from the UK-based P&O Cruises to Princess Cruises in 2005 and now marketed to both British and North American passengers, operates cruises from the UK in summer and in the Caribbean in winter. The onboard currency is the US dollar.

Note that there are a number of dead ends in the interior layout, so it's not as user-friendly as it could be. The swim-ming pools are quite small considering the number of pas-sengers carried, and the pool deck is cluttered with plastic sunloungers. The digital voice announcing lift deck stops is annoying for many. At the end of the day – as is the case aboard most large ships – you will be well attended if you live in the top-grade cabins; if you do not, you will merely be one of a very large number of passengers.

ACCOMMODATION. There are 19 different cabin price grades, designated as: suites (with private balcony), mini-suites (with private balcony), outside-view twin-bedded cabins with balcony, outside-view twin-bedded cabins, and interior (no view) twin-bedded cabins. Although the standard outside-view and interior (no view) cabins are a little small, they are functional, and have earth tone colors accentuated by splashes of color from the bedspreads. Proportionately, there are quite a lot of interior (no view) cabins.

Many outside-view cabins have private balconies, and all seem to be quite well soundproofed, although the balcony partition is not of the floor to ceiling type, so you can hear your neighbors (or smell their smoke). The balconies are very narrow – just large enough for two small chairs – and there is no outdoor balcony light. Some cabins have third- and fourth-person upper bunk beds – good for families with children.

There is a reasonable amount of closet space and abundant drawer and other storage space in the cabins; although adequate for a 7-night cruise, it can prove challenging for longer cruises. Also provided are a color television, and refrigerator, and each night a chocolate will appear on your pillow. The cabin bathrooms are practical units, and come complete with all the facilities one needs, although again, they really are tight spaces. Fortunately, they have a shower enclosure of a decent size, a small amount of shelving for your toiletries, real glasses, and a hairdryer.

Suites: The largest cabins are six suites (two on each of three decks at the stern), each with its own large private balcony. These suites are well laid out, and the large bathrooms have two washbasins, a Jacuzzi tub and separate shower enclosure. The bedroom has generous amounts of wood accenting and detailing, indented ceilings, TV sets in the bedroom and lounge areas, and a dining table and four chairs.

Mini-Suites: These typically have two lower beds convertible into a queen-sized bed. There is a separate bedroom/sleeping area with vanity desk, and a lounge with sofa and coffee table, indented ceilings, generous amounts of wood accenting and detailing, walk-in closet; the bathroom has a Jacuzzi bathtub and separate shower enclosure.

Standard Outside-view/Interior (No View) Cabins: The cabin bathrooms are practical, but compact. They do, however, have a decent shower enclosure, a small amount of shelving for toiletries, real glasses, and a hairdryer.

The cabin numbering system is quite illogical, however, with numbers going through several hundred series on the same deck. The room service menu is very limited.

CUISINE. There are two main, asymmetrically designed dining rooms (each seating about 500), Rigoletto and Traviata, located adjacent to the two lower levels of the four-deck high atrium lobby. They are non-smoking, and the one you are assigned to depends on your cabin location. Each has its own galley and each is split into multi-tier sections, which help create a feeling of intimacy, although there is a lot of noise from the waiter stations. Breakfast and lunch are provided in an open seating arrangement; dinner is in two seatings. The wine list is quite reasonable; 15% is added to all beverage bills, including wines.

Horizon Court is the ship's 24-hour casual, self-serve buffet. At night, this large room, which resembles a food court, can be transformed into an informal bistro dinner setting with waiter service (reservations are necessary and there may be a cover charge).

Outdoors on deck, with a sheltered view over the Riviera Pool, the Terrace Grill features fast-food items for those who don't want to change from sunbathing attire. In the evening, the grill offers steaks, seafood, and a "white sisters" mixed grill (a cover charge applies for dining under the stars).

For informal eats, Verdi's (on the uppermost level of the atrium lobby) features steaks and seafood (at extra cost). In addition, there's a patisserie (for cappuccino/ espresso coffees and pastries) opposite the reception desk on the lowest deck of the atrium, and a wine/caviar bar called Rendezvous (on Promenade Deck). Note that coffee or tea from any of the ship's bars costs extra.

ENTERTAINMENT. There are two showlounges (Princess Theater, and the Vista Lounge), one forward, one aft. The Princess Theater, located forward, is a 550-seat, theater-style showlounge, where the main production shows and theater events are staged (movies can also be shown here), while the Vista Lounge is a 480-seat lounge and bar for cabaret entertainment, and lectures.

In addition, the ship has an array of cabaret acts. Although many are not what you would call headliners, they regularly travel the cruise ship circuit. Classical concerts are scheduled for many cruises throughout the year.

SPA/FITNESS. The Lotus Spa has facilities that are contained in a glass-walled complex located on Lido Deck – one of the highest decks, at the aft section of the ship. It includes a gymnasium with ocean views aft and to port, with all the associated high-tech muscle-pumping and body toning equipment, a combination aerobics/exercise room, sauna and steam room, and several well-being treatment rooms. Some fitness and exercise classes may cost extra.

Forming part of the outside area of the spa complex, one swimming pool is "suspended" aft between two decks (two other pools are located in another area in the center of the ship), although they are not large for the size of the ship. Sports facilities are located in an open-air sports deck positioned inside the ship's funnel and adaptable for basketball, volleyball, badminton, or paddle tennis. Joggers can exercise on the wrap-around open Promenade Deck. There's also an electronic golf simulator (no need to bring your own clubs).

● **For more extensive general information about the Princess Cruises experience, see pages 134–37.**

Seabourn Legend
★★★★★

Boutique Ship: . . . . .9,961 tons	Passenger Decks: 6	Cabins (for one person): 0
Lifestyle: .Luxury	Total Crew: 160	Cabins (with private balcony): 6
Cruise Line: . . . . . . .Seabourn Cruise Line	Passengers	Cabins (wheelchair accessible): 4
Former Names: . . . .*Queen Odyssey,*	(lower beds/all berths): 212/212	Cabin Current: . . . . . . .110 and 220 volts
Royal Viking Queen	Passenger Space Ratio	Elevators: 3
Builder: . . . . . . .Schichau Seebeckwerft	(lower beds/all berths): 46.9/46.9	Casino (gaming tables): . . . . .Yes
(Germany)	Crew/Passenger Ratio	Slot Machines: . . . . .Yes
Original Cost: . . . .$87 million	(lower beds/all berths): 1.3/1.3	Swimming Pools (outdoors): 1
Entered Service: . . . .Mar 1992/July 1996	Navigation Officers: . . . . .Norwegian	Swimming Pools (indoors): 0
Registry: . . . . .Bahamas	Cabins (total): .106	Whirlpools: 3
Length (ft/m): 442.9/135.0	Size Range (sq ft/m): 277.0–575.8/	Self-Service Launderette: . . . . .Yes
Beam (ft/m): 62.9/19.20	25.7–53.5	Dedicated Cinema/Seats: . . . . .No
Draft (ft/m): 16.4/5.0	Cabins (outside view): 106	Library: . . . . .Yes
Propulsion/Propellers: diesel (7,280kW)/2	Cabins (interior/no view): 0	

OVERALL SCORE: 1,779 (OUT OF A POSSIBLE 2,000 POINTS)

OVERVIEW. *Seabourn Legend* is a contemporary ship with a handsome profile, almost identical in looks and size to *Seabourn Pride* and *Seabourn Spirit*, but younger, and built to a much higher standard, with streamline "decorator" bars (made by Mercedes Benz) located along the side of the upper superstructure and a slightly different swept-over funnel design. The ship has two fine mahogany water taxis for use as shore tenders. There is also an aft water sports platform and marina, which can be used in suitably calm warm-water areas. Water sports facilities include a small, enclosed "dip" pool, sea kayaks, snorkel equipment, windsurfers, water ski boat, and Zodiac inflatable boats. An open-bridge policy exists, so you can visit the ship's navigation bridge at almost any time (except during bad weather or especially tricky maneuvers).

Inside, a wide central passageway divides port and starboard side accommodation. The finest quality interior fixtures, fittings, and fabrics have been combined in its sumptuous public areas to present an outstanding, elegant decor, with warm color combinations (there is no glitz anywhere) and some fine artwork. The dress code, relaxed by day, is more formal at night.

There have been many recent complaints about falling standards aboard the Seabourn ships, particularly in regard to maintenance (the ships are more than 10 years old). Food, presentation and service, passengers said, wasn't what it used to be. However, I am happy to report that the product delivered now is extremely good, and more consistent (particularly in food and service) than, say, the Silversea Cruises ships, which are larger and carry more passengers.

Seabourn Legend provides discerning passengers with

BERLITZ'S RATINGS

	Possible	Achieved
Ship	500	454
Accommodation	200	186
Food	400	347
Service	400	353
Entertainment	100	86
Cruise	400	353

an outstanding level of personal service and a very civilized cruise experience. For a grand, small-ship cruise experience in fine surroundings, with only just over 100 other couples as neighbors, this ship is difficult to beat. All drinks (except premium brands and connoisseur wines) are included, as are gratuities, fine aromatherapy Molton Brown bath products and large soaps by Bronnley, Chanel and Hermès, short massages (called "massage moments") on deck, open-seating dining, use of watersports equipment, one included Exclusively Seabourn shore excursion per cruise, and movies under the stars. *Seabourn Legend* can cruise to places where large cruise ships can't, thanks to its ocean-yacht size. DHL can provide luggage pick-up and delivery service. Port charges and insurance are not included. The onboard currency is the US dollar.

The three Seabourn ships provide an excellent product, and are superior to other upscale ships such as *Seven Seas Mariner* and *Seven Seas Voyager*, but still not up to the standard of *Europa*'s fine product delivery and hospitality.

The plastic chairs on the open decks really are unacceptable for this type of ship and should be changed to stainless steel or teak. There is no wrap-around promenade deck outdoors. The range of cigars offered is limited. The Club suffers from over-amplified music. Non-American passengers should note that almost all entertainment and activities are geared towards American tastes, despite the increasingly international passenger mix.

SUITABLE FOR: *Seabourn Legend* is best suited to sophisticated, well traveled couples (typically over 50, but possibly younger) who seek a small ship setting (they wouldn't be seen dead aboard today's huge standard resort cruise ships), with excellent food that approaches gourmet standards, and fine European-style service in chic surroundings that border on the elegant and luxurious.

ACCOMMODATION. This is spread over three decks, and there are nine price categories, the price depending on size, grade and location. All suites are comfortably large and very nicely equipped with everything one might need (they are, for example, larger than those aboard the smaller SeaDream I and SeaDream II, but then the ship is also larger, and carries almost twice as many passengers).

All suites have a sleeping area with European duvets and Frette linens (but there is a vanity mirror opposite the bed, which won't please *feng shui* practitioners) and separate lounge area with Bose wave radio/CD unit, DVD player and flat-screen TV, vanity desk (with hairdyer) and personalized stationery, world atlas, mini-bar and refrigerator (stocked with soft drinks, and two bottles of your favorite liquor at embarkation), a large walk-in closet (illuminated automatically when you open the door), digital personal safe, and wall-mounted clock and barometer. A full passenger list is also provided – a rarity today – as are a fresh fruit basket (replenished daily) and flowers..

Marble-clad bathrooms have one or two washbasins (depending on accommodation grade), a decent (but not full-sized) bathtub (four suites have a shower enclosure only – no bathtub), plenty of storage areas, 100% thick cotton towels, plush terrycloth bathrobe, designer soaps and Molton Brown toiletries. A selection of five aromatherapy bath preparations by Molton Brown can be ordered from your stewardess, who will prepare your bath for you.

Course-by-course in-cabin dining is available during dinner hours (the cocktail table raises to form a dining table); there is 24-hour room service. Also provided are: personalized stationery, and fancy ticket wallet (suitably boxed and nicely packaged before your cruise). Non-smoking cabins are available. Menus for each dinner are delivered to your suite during the day.

In 2001, Seabourn Cruise Line added 36 French balconies to suites on two out of three accommodation decks. These are not balconies in the true sense, but have two doors that open wide onto a tiny teakwood balcony that is just 27 cm (about 10.6 inches) wide. The balconies do allow you to have fresh sea air, however, together with some salt spray.

Four Owner's suites (Ibsen/Grieg, each measuring 530 sq. ft/49 sq. meters and Eriksson/Heyerdahl, each 575 sq. ft/53 sq. meters), and two Classic Suites (Queen Maud/ Queen Sonja, each 400 sq. ft/37 sq. meters) offer superb, private living spaces. Each has a walk-in closet, second closet, full bathroom plus a guest toilet with washbasin. There is a fully secluded forward- or side-facing balcony, with sun lounge chairs and wooden drinks table (Ibsen/ Grieg do not have balconies). The living area has ample bookshelf space (including a complete edition of *Encyclopaedia Britannica*), large refrigerator/drinks cabinet, television and DVD player (plus a second TV set in the bedroom). All windows, as well as the door to the balcony,

have manually operated blackout blinds, and a complete blackout is possible in both bedroom and living room.

CUISINE. The Restaurant is a part-marble, part-carpeted dining room that has portholes and elegant decor but it is not as warm and intimate as that found aboard the smaller SeaDream ships, with their wood paneling. The silverware (150 gram weight – the best available) is by Robbe & Berking. Open-seating dining means that you can dine when you want, with whom you wish. Course-by-course meals can also be served in your cabin.

Dining is memorable. The menus, overseen by celebrity chef Charlie Palmer, are creative and well-balanced, with a wide selection of foods, including regional dishes. Seabourn Cruise Line's cuisine is artfully presented, with many items cooked to order. Special orders are available, as is caviar (sevruga). Flambeaus and flaming desserts can be cooked at your table. The selection of exotic fruits and cheeses is good.

Each day, basic table wine is included for lunch and dinner, but all others (the decent ones) cost extra. The wine list is quite extensive, with prices ranging from moderate to high; many of the wines come from the smaller, more exclusive vineyards. The European dining room staff is hand picked and provides excellent, unhurried service.

Relaxed breakfasts (until 11am), lunch buffets and casual (themed) candlelight dinners (including a new "2" tasting menu) can be taken in the popular Veranda Cafe, adjacent to the swimming pool, instead of in the dining room. Additionally, the Sky Grill provides an above-poolside setting complete with candlelit dining and specializing in steaks and seafood. All dining venues are non-smoking.

ENTERTAINMENT. The King Olaf Lounge is the venue for all entertainment events, including shows, cabaret acts, lectures, and most social functions. It has a sloping floor that provides good sightlines from just about every seat. Because this is a small, upscale ship, the (typically four-person) "production" shows are of limited scope, as dinner is almost always the main event. You can, however, expect to see the occasional cabaret act. Singers also tend to do mini-cabaret performances in The Club (one deck above the showlounge), the gathering place for late-night drinkers.

SPA/FITNESS. A small but well equipped health spa/fitness center, called The Spa at Seabourn, is located just aft of the navigation bridge. The spa complex provides sauna and steam rooms (with separate facilities for men and women) and integral changing room; and a separate exercise room with video tapes for private, individual aerobics workouts; and a beauty salon.

The Spa at Seabourn is staffed and operated by concession Elemis by Steiner. Treatment prices are equal to those in an expensive land-based spa (examples: Elemis Aroma Stone Therapy $178 for 75 mins, Facial $111). The beauty salon offers hair beautifying treatments and conditioning, while in the gymnasium, personal training sessions, yoga classes, mat Pilates and body composition analysis are available (at extra cost).

Seabourn Odyssey
NOT YET RATED

Small Ship: . . . . 32,000 tons	Total Crew: 330	Cabins (for one person): 0
Lifestyle: . . . . Standard	Passengers	Cabins (with private balcony): 199
Cruise Line: . . . . . . Seabourn Cruise Line	(lower beds/all berths): 450/462	Cabins (wheelchair accessible): 7
Former Names: . . . . none	Passenger Space Ratio	Cabin Voltage: . . . . 110 volts
Builder: . . . . Mariotti (Italy)	(lower beds/all berths): 71.1/69.2	Lifts: 3
Original Cost: . . . . $250 million	Crew/Passenger Ratio	Casino (gaming tables): . . . . Yes
Entered Service: . . . . Jun 2009	(lower beds/all berths): 1.3/1.4	Slot Machines: . . . . Yes
Registry: . . . . Bahamas	Navigation Officers: . . . . . . Scandinavian	Swimming Pools (outdoors): 2
Length (ft/m): 649.6/198.0	Cabins (total): 225	Swimming Pools (indoors): 0
Beam (ft/m): 83.9/25.6	Size Range (sq ft/m): 295.0–,438.1/	Whirlpools: 6
Draft (ft/m): 21.3/6.5	27.5–133.6	Self-Service Launderette: . . . . Yes
Propulsion/Propellers: . . diesel-electric/2	Cabins (outside view): 225	Dedicated Cinema/Seats: . . . . No
Passenger Decks: 8	Cabins (interior/no view): 0	Library: . . . . Yes

BERLITZ'S OVERALL SCORE: NYR (OUT OF A POSSIBLE 2,000 POINTS)

OVERVIEW. This is the first of three new ships for Seabourn, looks like a ship-sized version of its three smaller "yachts" (*Seabourn Legend, Seabourn Pride, Seabourn Spirit*). However, *Seabourn Odyssey* does have the highest passenger space ratio in the cruise industry, so passengers should never feel crowded. All the accommodation areas are located forward, with public rooms located aft. The Marina, at the stern, has a staging area from which watersports are organized.

Seabourn Square, a "concierge lounge," has a relaxed, club-like ambiance designed to encourage sociability. The area includes a library, shops, an outdoor terrace and a coffee bar. Its "concierges" will provide in-port shopping tips, set up shore excursions, get dinner reservations in ports of call, etc. Wi-fi is available throughout the ship. The onboard currency is the US dollar, and drinks, wines with meals, and all gratuities are included.

Seabourn Odyssey will operate a 108-day around-the-world cruise in 2010 – Seabourn's first such cruise.

ACCOMMODATION. There are 13 different grades of suites in 18 price categories, although the smaller units are really large cabins. Fully 90 percent of cabins have a private balcony. Even the smallest cabin is a generous 269 sq.ft. All cabins have a separate bathtub and shower enclosure in a granite bathroom setting, twin beds convertible to a queen-sized bed, flat-screen TV plus CD and DVD, minibar , vanity desk (with hairdryer) world atlas, personalized stationery, and large walk-in closet with personal safe.

Some size examples (excluding balcony): Grand Suites (1,135 sq.ft), including two-bedrooms; Signature Suites (819 sq. ft); Wintergarden Suites (914 sq.ft). Rather neat suites within a glass-enclosed solarium, set in front of the funnel,

BERLITZ'S RATINGS

	Possible	Achieved
Ship	500	NYR
Accommodation	200	NYR
Food	400	NYR
Service	400	NYR
Entertainment	100	NYR
Cruise	400	NYR

with a side balcony; Owners Suites 611-675 sq.ft); Penthouse Suite 436-611 sq.ft); Veranda Suite (269-298 sq.ft); Seabourn Suite (295 sq.ft).

DINING. There's a choice of four dining venues:

● The Restaurant has open-seating dining at tables for two, four, six or eight, with menus designed by American celebrity chef Charlie Palmer.

● Restaurant 2, with around 50 seats, has regional, seasonal cuisine and tasting menus, perhaps for a mini-dégustation.

● The Colonnade has indoor/outdoor seating.

● The Patio Grill is in a casual poolside setting outdoors.

In addition, a 24-hour, in-suite menu offers the à la carte items served in the main dining room during dinner hours.

ENTERTAINMENT. The Grand Salon is the main entertainment venue, for cabaret performances, social dancing, and for use as a cinema. The Club is a nightclub/disco, located beneath the Grand salon. The room incorporates the casino.

SPA/FITNESS.

The Spa at Seabourn, operated by Elemis, occupies the aft section of two decks, and is the largest aboard any luxury ship, at 11,500 sq.ft (1,068 sq.meters). It offers full services in a very pleasant setting that includes a two-deck-high waterfall at the entrance and seven appealing indoor/outdoor treatment rooms, as well as a thalassotherapy pool and complete salon facilities, while a hot tub and relaxation area on the deck above is accessed by a spiral staircase. In the gymnasium, personal training sessions, yoga classes, mat Pilates and body composition analysis are available (at extra cost), but some basic exercise programs are free.

Seabourn Pride
★★★★★

Boutique Ship: . . . . .9,975 tons	Total Crew: 160	Cabins (with private balcony): 6
Lifestyle: .Luxury	Passengers	Cabins (wheelchair accessible): 4
Cruise Line: . . . . . .Seabourn Cruise Line	(lower beds/all berths): 212/212	Cabin Current: . . . . . . .110 and 220 volts
Former Names: . . . . .none	Passenger Space Ratio	Elevators: 3
Builder: . . . . . . .Seebeckwerft (Germany)	(lower beds/all berths): 47.09/47.09	Casino (gaming tables): . . . . .Yes
Original Cost: . . . .$50 million	Crew/Passenger Ratio	Slot Machines: . . . . .Yes
Entered Service: . . . . .Dec 1988	(lower beds/all berths): 1.3/1.3	Swimming Pools (outdoors): 1
Registry: . . . . .Bahamas	Navigation Officers: . . . . .Norwegian	(plus 1 aft marina-pool)
Length (ft/m): 439.9/134.10	Cabins (total): 106	Swimming Pools (indoors): 0
Beam (ft/m): 62.9/19.20	Size Range (sq ft/m): 277.0–575.0/	Whirlpools: 3
Draft (ft/m): 16.8/5.15	25.7–53.4	Self-Service Launderette: . . . . .Yes
Propulsion/Propellers: . . . . .diesel	Cabins (outside view): 106	Dedicated Cinema/Seats: . . . . .No
(5,355kW)/2	Cabins (interior/no view): 0	Library: . . . . .Yes
Passenger Decks: 6	Cabins (for one person): 0	

OVERALL SCORE: 1,769 (OUT OF A POSSIBLE 2,000 POINTS)

OVERVIEW. This pleasantly appointed cruise vessel has sleek exterior styling, handsome profile with swept-back, rounded lines, and is an identical sister vessel to *Seabourn Spirit*. It has two fine mahogany water taxis for use as shore tenders. An aft water sports platform and marina can be used in suitably calm warm-water areas. Water sports facilities include a small, enclosed "dip" pool, sea kayaks, snorkel equipment, windsurfers, water ski boat, and Zodiac inflatable boats. An open-bridge policy exists, so you can visit the ship's navigation bridge at almost any time (except during bad weather or especially tricky maneuvers).

A wide central passageway divides port and starboard side accommodation. Inviting, sumptuous public areas have warm colors. Fine quality interior fixtures, fittings, artwork and fabric combine to present an outstanding, elegant decor. For a small ship, there is wide range of public rooms. These include a main lounge (staging small cabaret shows), nightclub, an observation lounge with bar, large, deep armchairs, and a cigar smoking area complete with cabinet, cigar humidor and small selection of good cigars. There is a small business center, small meeting room, and a small casino with roulette and blackjack tables, plus a few slot machines tucked away.

Not for the budget-minded, this ship is for those desiring supremely elegant, stylish, small-ship surroundings, but is perhaps rather small for long voyages in open waters.

During the past two years, there have been many complaints about falling standards aboard the Seabourn ships, particularly with regard to maintenance (they are now over 10 years old), and that food, presentation and service had deteriorated. However, the company has now turned things

BERLITZ'S RATINGS		
	Possible	Achieved
Ship	500	452
Accommodation	200	186
Food	400	347
Service	400	348
Entertainment	100	86
Cruise	400	350

around, and the product delivered is extremely good.

Seabourn Pride provides discerning passengers with an outstanding level of personal service and an utterly civilized cruise experience. For a grand, small ship cruise experience in fine surroundings, with only just over 100 other couples as neighbors, this ship is difficult to beat. All drinks (except premium brands and connoisseur wines) are included, as are gratuities, fine aromatherapy bath selections from Molton Brown and large soaps by Bronnley, Chanel and Hermès, short massages on deck (called "massage moments"), open-seating dining, use of watersports equipment, one free Exclusively Seabourn shore excursion per cruise, and movies under the stars. *Seabourn Pride* is able to cruise to places where large cruise ships can't, due to its ocean-yacht size. DHL provides luggage pick-up and delivery service. Port charges and insurance are not included. The onboard currency is the US dollar.

In the final analysis, the three Seabourn ships provide an excellent product, and are superior to other upscale ships such as *Seven Seas Mariner* and *Seven Seas Voyager*, but still not up to the standard of *Europa*'s fine product delivery and hospitality.

The sunloungers are plastic (although light and easy to store, they are second-class, and should be made of wood or stainless steel). There is no walk-around promenade deck outdoors. There is only one dryer in the self-service launderette. Non-American passengers should note that almost all entertainment and activities are geared towards American tastes, despite the increasingly international passenger mix.

SUITABLE FOR: *Seabourn Pride* is best to sophisticated, well traveled couples (typically over 50, but possible younger) who seek a small ship setting with excellent food that approaches gourmet standards, and fine European-style service in surroundings that can best be described as bordering on the elegant and luxurious.

ACCOMMODATION. This is spread over three decks, and there are nine price categories, the price depending on size, grade and location you choose. The all-outside cabins (called suites in brochure-speak) are comfortably large and beautifully equipped with everything one could reasonably need. Electric blackout blinds are provided for the large windows in addition to curtains. All cabinetry is made of blond woods, with softly rounded edges, and cabin doors are neatly angled away from the passageway.

All the suites have a sleeping area (European duvets are standard, as are Frette linens) and separate lounge area with Bose Wave Radio/CD unit, DVD player and flat-screen TV, vanity desk (with hairdryer) and personalized stationery, world atlas, mini-bar and refrigerator (stocked with soft drinks, and two bottles of your favorite liquor when you embark), a large walk-in closet (illuminated automatically when you open the door) and wooden hangers, electronic personal safe, umbrella, and wall-mounted clock and barometer.

A full passenger list is also provided – a rarity these days – as are a fresh fruit basket (replenished daily) and flowers.

Marble-clad bathrooms have one or two washbasins (depending on the accommodation grade), a decent (but not full-sized) bathtub (four suites have a shower enclosure only – no tub), plenty of storage areas, 100% thick cotton towels, plush terrycloth bathrobe, designer soaps and Molton Brown personal amenity items. A selection of five Molton Brown aromatherapy bath preparations can be ordered from your stewardess, who will prepare your bath.

In 2001, Seabourn Cruise Line added 36 French balconies to suites on two out of three accommodation decks. These are not balconies in the true sense of the word, but they do have two doors that open wide, onto a tiny teakwood balcony that is just 27 cm (about 10.6 inches) wide. The balconies allow you to have fresh sea air, however, together with some salt spray.

Course-by-course in-cabin dining is available during dinner hours (the cocktail table can be raised to form a dining table); there is 24-hour room service. Also provided are: personalized stationery, and fancy ticket wallet. Non-smoking cabins are available. Menus for each dinner are delivered to your suite during the day.

Four Owner's suites (King Haakon/King Magnus, each measuring 530 sq. ft/49 sq. meters, and Amundsen/Nansen, each 575 sq. ft/53 sq. meters), and two Classic Suites (King Harald/King Olav, each 400 sq. ft/ 37 sq. meters) offer superb, private living spaces. Each has a walk-in closet, second closet, full bathroom plus a guest toilet with washbasin. There is a fully secluded forward- or side-facing balcony, with sunloungers and wooden drinks table. The living area has ample bookshelf space (including a complete edition of *Encyclopedia Britannica*), large refrigerator/drinks cabinet, television and DVD player (plus a second TV set in the bedroom). All windows, as well as the door to the balcony, have manually operated blackout blinds, and a complete blackout is possible in both bedroom and living room.

CUISINE. The Restaurant is a part-marble, part-carpeted dining room that has portholes and elegant decor. The silverware (150 gram weight – the best available) is by Robbe & Berking. Open-seating dining means that you can dine when you want, with whom you wish.

The menus, overseen by celebrity chef Charlie Palmer, are creative and well-balanced, with a wide selection of foods and regional cuisine. Seabourn Cruise Line's fine, creative cuisine is artfully presented, with many items cooked to order. Special orders are available, and caviar is always available on request. Tableside flambeaus and flaming desserts can be presented at your table. There is always a good selection of exotic fruits and cheeses.

Each day, basic table wine is included for lunch and dinner, but all others (the decent ones) cost extra. The wine list is quite extensive, with prices ranging from moderate to high; many of the wines come from the smaller, more exclusive vineyards. The hand-picked European dining room staff provide excellent, unhurried service.

In addition, relaxed breakfasts (available until 11am) and lunch buffets and casual (themed) candlelight dinners, including a new "2" tasting menu, can be taken in the popular Veranda Cafe adjacent to the swimming pool.

Additionally, the Sky Grill provides an above-poolside setting featuring candlelit dining and specializing in steaks and seafood. All dining venues are non-smoking.

ENTERTAINMENT. The Magellan Lounge is the venue for all entertainment events. It is a room with a sloping floor that provides good sight lines from just about every seat. "Production" shows are of limited scope, as dinner is usually the main event. You can, however, expect to see the occasional cabaret act. Singers also tend to do mini-cabaret performances in The Club (one deck above the show-lounge), the gathering place for late-night drinkers.

SPA/FITNESS. There's a small but well equipped health spa/fitness center, The Spa at Seabourn. It has sauna and steam rooms (separate facilities for men and women), an equipment-packed gymnasium (but the ceiling height is low), and a beauty salon.

The spa is staffed and operated by concession Elemis by Steiner. Treatment prices equal those in an expensive land-based spa (examples: Elemis Aroma Stone Therapy $178 for 75 mins; Reflexology $111 for 45 mins; Facial $111). The beauty salon has hair beautifying treatments and conditioning, while in the gymnasium, personal training sessions, yoga classes, mat Pilates and body composition analysis are available (at extra cost).

Seabourn Spirit
★★★★★

Boutique Ship: . . . . .9,975 tons	Total Crew: 160	Cabins (with private balcony): 6
Lifestyle: . . . . .Luxury	Passengers	Cabins (wheelchair accessible): 4
Cruise Line: . . . . . . .Seabourn Cruise Line	(lower beds/all berths): 212/212	Cabin Current: . . . . . . .110 and 220 volts
Former Names: . . . . .none	Passenger Space Ratio	Elevators: 3
Builder: . . . . . . .Seebeckwerft (Germany)	(lower beds/all berths): 47.0/47.0	Casino (gaming tables): . . . . .Yes
Original Cost: . . . .$50 million	Crew/Passenger Ratio	Slot Machines: . . . . .Yes
Entered Service: . . . . .Nov 1989	(lower beds/all berths): 1.3/1.3	Swimming Pools (outdoors): 1
Registry: . . . . .Bahamas	Navigation Officers: . . . . .Norwegian	(plus aft marina-pool)
Length (ft/m): 439.9/134.10	Cabins (total): 106	Swimming Pools (indoors): 0
Beam (ft/m): 62.9/19.20	Size Range (sq ft/m): 277.0–575.0/	Whirlpools: 3
Draft (ft/m): 16.8/5.15	25.7–53.4	Self-Service Launderette: . . . . .Yes
Propulsion/Propellers: . . . . .diesel	Cabins (outside view): 106	Dedicated Cinema/Seats: . . . . .No
(5,355kW)/2	Cabins (interior/no view): 0	Library: . . . . .Yes
Passenger Decks: 6	Cabins (for one person): 0	

OVERALL SCORE: 1,770 (OUT OF A POSSIBLE 2,000 POINTS)

OVERVIEW. This finely appointed cruise vessel has sleek exterior styling, handsome profile with swept-back, rounded lines, and is an identical sister vessel to *Seabourn Pride*. It has two fine mahogany water taxis for use as shore tenders. An aft water sports platform and marina can be used in suitably calm warm-water areas. Water sports facilities include a small, enclosed "dip" pool, sea kayaks, snorkel equipment, windsurfers, water ski boat, and Zodiac inflatable boats. An open-bridge policy exists, so you can visit the ship's navigation bridge at almost any time (except during bad weather or especially tricky maneuvers).

Inside, a wide central passageway divides port and starboard side accommodation. Inviting, sumptuous public areas have warm colors. Fine quality interior fixtures, fittings, fabric and artwork combine to present an outstanding, elegant (but minimalist) decor. For a small ship, there is wide range of public rooms. These include a main lounge (staging small cabaret shows), nightclub, an observation lounge with bar, large, deep armchairs, and a cigar smoking area with cabinet, cigar humidor and small selection of good cigars.

There is also a small business center, small meeting room, even a small casino with roulette and blackjack tables, with a few slot machines tucked away.

During the past two years, there have been many complaints about falling standards aboard the Seabourn ships, particularly in regard to maintenance (they are now over 10 years old). Food, presentation and service, passengers said, had deteriorated. However, the company has now turned things around, and the product is extremely good.

Seabourn Spirit provides discerning passengers with an

BERLITZ'S RATINGS

	Possible	Achieved
Ship	500	453
Accommodation	200	186
Food	400	347
Service	400	348
Entertainment	100	86
Cruise	400	350

outstanding level of service and an utterly civilized cruise. For a grand, small ship cruise experience in fine surroundings, with only just over 100 other couples as neighbors, this ship is hard to beat. All drinks (except for premium brands and connoisseur wines) are included, as are gratuities, Molton Brown aromatherapy bath products and large soaps by names such as Bijan, Chanel and Hermès, short massages on deck ("massage moments") , open-seating dining, use of watersports equipment, one free Exclusively Seabourn shore excursion per cruise, and movies under the stars. *Seabourn Spirit* is able to cruise to places where large cruise ships can't, due to its ocean-yacht size. Port charges and insurance are not included. The onboard currency is the US dollar.

The three Seabourn ships provide an excellent product, superior to other upscale ships such as *Seven Seas Mariner* and *Seven Seas Voyager*, but still not up to the standard of *Europa*'s fine product delivery and hospitality. DHL can provide luggage pick-up and delivery service.

The sunloungers are plastic (although light and easy to store, they are second-class, and should be made of wood or stainless steel). There is no walk-around promenade deck outdoors. There is only one dryer in the self-service launderette. Non-American passengers should note that almost all entertainment and activities are geared towards American tastes, despite the increasingly international passenger mix.

SUITABLE FOR: *Seabourn Spirit* best suits sophisticated couples (mostly over 50, but possibly younger) who seek a small-ship setting with excellent food approaching gourmet standards, and fine European-style service in surroundings best described as bordering on the elegant and luxurious.

ACCOMMODATION. This is spread over three decks, and there are nine price categories, the price depending on size, grade and location you choose. The all-outside cabins (called suites in brochure-speak) are comfortably large and beautifully equipped with everything one could reasonably need. Electric blackout blinds are provided for the large windows in addition to curtains. All cabinetry is made of blond woods, with softly rounded edges, and cabin doors are neatly angled away from the passageway.

The suites are larger than those aboard the smaller *Sea-Dream I* and *SeaDream II*, but then the ship is also larger, and carries almost twice as many passengers. All suites have a sleeping area (European duvets are standard, as are Frette linens) and separate lounge area with Bose Wave Radio/CD unit, DVD player and flat-screen TV, vanity desk (with hairdryer) and personalized stationery, world atlas, mini-bar and refrigerator (stocked with soft drinks, and two bottles of your favorite liquor when you embark), a large walk-in closet (illuminated automatically when you open the door) and wooden hangers, electronic personal safe, umbrella, and wall-mounted clock and barometer. A full passenger list is also provided – a rarity these days – as are a fresh fruit basket (replenished daily) and flowers.

Marble-clad bathrooms feature one or two washbasins (depending on the accommodation grade), a decent (but not full-sized) bathtub (four suites have a shower enclosure only – no tub), plenty of storage areas, 100% thick cotton towels, plush terrycloth bathrobe, designer soaps and Molton Brown personal amenity items. A selection of five special bath preparations by Molton Brown can be ordered from your stewardess, who will prepare your bath.

Course-by-course in-cabin dining is available during dinner hours (the cocktail table can be raised to form a dining table); there is 24-hour room service. Also provided are: personalized stationery, and fancy ticket wallet (suitably boxed and nicely packaged before your cruise). Non-smoking cabins are available. Menus for each dinner are delivered to your suite during the day.

In 2001, Seabourn Cruise Line added 36 French balconies to suites on two out of three accommodation decks. These are not balconies in the true sense of the word, but they do feature two doors that open wide, onto a tiny teakwood balcony that is just 27 cm (about 10.6 inches) wide. The balconies do allow you to have fresh sea air, however, together with some salt spray.

Four Owner's suites (Bergen/Oslo, each measuring 530 sq. ft/49 sq. meters and Copenhagen/Stockholm, each 575 sq. ft/53 sq. meters), and two Classic Suites (Helsinki/Reykjavik, each 400 sq. ft/37 sq. meters) offer superb, private living spaces. Each has a walk-in closet, second closet, full bathroom plus a guest toilet with washbasin. There is a fully secluded forward- or side-facing balcony, with sun lounge chairs and wooden drinks table. The living area has ample bookshelf space (including a complete edition of *Encyclopaedia Britannica*), large refrigerator/drinks cabinet, television and DVD player (plus a second TV set in the bedroom). All windows, as well as the door to the balcony, have manually operated blackout blinds, and a complete blackout is possible in both bedroom and living room.

CUISINE. The Restaurant is a part-marble, part-carpeted dining room that has portholes and elegant decor. The silverware (150 gram weight – the best available) is by Robbe & Berking. Open-seating dining means that you can dine when you want, with whom you wish.

The menus, overseen by celebrity chef Charlie Palmer, are nicely balanced, with a wide selection of foods and regional cuisine. Seabourn Cruise Line's fine, creative cuisine is artfully presented, with many items cooked to order. Special orders are available, and caviar is always available on request. Tableside flambeaus and flaming desserts are possible. There is a good selection of exotic fruits and cheeses.

Basic table wine is included for lunch and dinner, but all others (the decent ones) cost extra. The wine list is quite extensive, with prices ranging from moderate to high; many of the wines come from the smaller, more exclusive vineyards. The hand-picked European dining room staff provides excellent, unhurried service.

In addition, relaxed breakfasts (available until 11am), lunch buffets and casual (themed) candlelit dinners, including a new "2" tasting menu, can be taken in the popular Veranda Cafe adjacent to the swimming pool, instead of in the dining room.

Additionally, the Sky Grill provides an above-poolside setting featuring candlelit dining and specializing in steaks and seafood. All dining venues are non-smoking.

ENTERTAINMENT. The Amundsen Lounge is the venue for all entertainment events. It is a room with a sloping floor that provides good sightlines from just about every seat. "Production" shows are of limited scope, as dinner is usually the main event.

You can, however, expect to see the occasional cabaret act. Singers also tend to do mini-cabaret performances in The Club (one deck above the showlounge), the gathering place for late-night drinkers.

SPA/FITNESS. A small but well-equipped health spa/fitness center, called The Spa at Seabourn, has sauna and steam rooms (with separate facilities for men and women), and a separate exercise room, with video tapes for private, individual aerobics workouts, and a beauty salon.

The Spa at Seabourn is staffed and operated by concession Elemis by Steiner. Treatment prices are equal to those in an expensive land-based spa (examples: Elemis Aroma Stone Therapy $178 for 75 mins; Reflexology $111 for 45 mins; Facial $111). The beauty salon has hair beautifying treatments and conditioning, while in the gymnasium, personal training sessions, yoga classes, mat Pilates and body composition analysis are available (at extra cost).

SeaDream I
★★★★★

Boutique Ship:	4,253 tons
Lifestyle:	Exclusive
Cruise Line:	Seadream Yacht Club
Former Names:	*Seabourn Goddess I, Sea Goddess I*
Builder:	Wartsila (Finland)
Entered Service:	Apr 1984/May 2002
Registry:	The Bahamas
Length (ft/m):	343.8/104.81
Beam (ft/m):	47.9/14.60
Draft (ft/m):	13.6/4.17
Propulsion/Propellers:	diesel (3,540kW)/2
Passenger Decks:	5
Total Crew:	89
Passengers (lower beds/all berths):	108/108
Passenger Space Ratio (lower beds/all berths):	39.4/39.4
Crew/Passenger Ratio (lower beds/all berths):	1.2/1.2
Navigation Officers:	Norwegian/Scandinavian
Cabins (total):	54
Size Range (sq ft/m):	195.0–490.0/18.1–45.5
Cabins (outside view):	54
Cabins (interior/no view):	0
Cabins (for one person):	0
Cabins (with private balcony):	0
Cabins (wheelchair accessible):	0
Cabin Current:	110 and 220 volts
Elevators:	1
Casino (gaming tables):	Yes
Slot Machines:	Yes
Swimming Pools (outdoors):	1
Swimming Pools (indoors):	0
Whirlpools:	1
Self-Service Launderette:	No
Dedicated Cinema/Seats:	No
Library:	Yes

OVERALL SCORE: 1,786

BERLITZ'S RATINGS

	Possible	Achieved
Ship	500	439
Accommodation	200	173
Food	400	371
Service	400	370
Entertainment	n/a	n/a
Cruise	500	433

OVERVIEW. These small ships were originally built with money from about 800 investors, and operated under the Norske Cruise banner. It has an ultra-sleek profile, with deep blue hull and white superstructure, and the ambiance of a private club. After the ship was acquired by SeaDream Yacht Club in 2001, they were completely refurbished, with many changes to both public rooms and outdoor areas, and several new features added to create what are contemporary, chic, and desirable, if aging, vessels.

A "Top of the Yacht" bar, crafted in warm wood, was added to both ships in 2001. So were eight special alcoves set to the port and starboard sides of the funnel, equipped with two-person sun loungers with thick pads (and two equipped for one person); however, there is quite a bit of noise from the adjacent funnel. You are encouraged to sleep under the stars if you wish, and cotton sleep suits are provided.

At the front part of the deck there are more sun loungers and a couple of large hammocks, as well as a golf simulator (with a choice of 30 courses).

Inside, there is a feeling of unabashed but discreet sophistication. Elegant, chic public rooms have flowers and pot pourri everywhere. The main social gathering places are the lounge, a delightful library/living room with a selection of about 1,000 books, a piano bar (which can be more like a karaoke bar at times), and a small casino (two blackjack tables and five slot machines).

The two SeaDream ships really are the ultimate exclusive boutique vessels – like having your own private yacht in which hospitality, anticipation and personal recognition are art forms practiced to a high level. The staff is delightful and accommodating ("no" is not in their vocabulary). The dress code is resort casual. Fine-quality furnishings and fabrics are used throughout, with marble and blond wood accents.

So what type of persons will enjoy the SeaDream Yacht Club experience? This is for experienced, independent travelers who don't like regular cruise ships, large ships, glitzy lounges, a platoon of people and kids running around, or dressing up – no tuxedos or gowns are allowed, and ties are not needed. The *SeaDreams* provide the setting for personal indulgence and refined, unstructured and langorous private living at sea, in a casual, private setting akin to that on a mega-yacht. One delightful feature of each cruise in warm weather areas is a "caviar in the surf" beach barbecue.

Life could hardly be better at sea – so, as many regular SeaDream Yacht Club passengers say, why bother with ports of call at all? Embarkation never starts before 3pm, in case you are eager to get aboard.

All drinks (with the exception of premium brands and connoisseur wines), American farmed sevruga caviar, and gratuities are included, but port charges and insurance are not. The price of a cruise is just that: the price of a cruise. Air and/or other travel arrangements can be made on your own, or through your own travel agent, or you can use the excellent services of Total Travel Marine, whose offices in London and Miami specialize in first, business or coach air arrangements as partner to SeaDream Yacht Club, with 24-hour, 365-day service. The onboard currency is the US dollar.

These were the first of the mega-yacht-style ships when built, and none of the cabins has a private balcony – ships with private balconies made their debut just a couple of years later, and, anyway, yachts don't have balconies. One not so positive item is the fact that the reception desk is now called the Concierge, although it is doubtful whether the staff has the kind of in-depth knowledge that is expected of a concierge.

SeaDream II
★★★★★

Boutique Ship:	. . . . .4,333 tons
Lifestyle:	. . . . .Exclusive
Cruise Line:	. . . . . . .SeaDream Yacht Club
Former Names:	. . . .*Seabourn Goddess II,*
	Sea Goddess II
Builder:	. . . . .Wartsila (Finland)
Original Cost:	. . . .$34 million
Entered Service:	. . . .May 1985/Jan 2002
Registry:	. . . . .The Bahamas
Length (ft/m):	. . . . .343.8/104.81
Beam (ft/m):	. . . . .47.9/14.60
Draft (ft/m):	. . . . .13.6/4.17
Propulsion/Propellers:	diesel (3,540kW)/2
Passenger Decks:	5
Total Crew:	89
Passengers	
(lower beds/all berths):	. . . . .108/108
Passenger Space Ratio	
(lower beds/all berths):	. . . . . . .40.1/40.1
Crew/Passenger Ratio	
(lower beds/all berths):	. . . . .1.2/1.2
Navigation Officers:	. . . . .Norwegian/
	Scandinavian
Cabins (total):	54
Size Range (sq ft/m):	. . . . . .195.0–490.0/
	18.1–45.5
Cabins (outside view):	54
Cabins (interior/no view):	0
Cabins (for one person):	0
Cabins (with private balcony):	0
Cabins (wheelchair accessible):	0
Cabin Current:	. . . . .110 and 220 volts
Elevators:	1
Casino (gaming tables):	. . . . .Yes
Slot Machines:	. . . . .Yes
Swimming Pools (outdoors):	1
Swimming Pools (indoors):	0
Whirlpools:	1
Self-Service Launderette:	. . . . .No
Dedicated Cinema/Seats:	. . . . .No
Library:	. . . . .Yes

SUITABLE FOR: *The SeaDreams are* best suited to sophisticated, independent and well-traveled couples who are typically over 40, but possible younger - who seek a small ship setting (they wouldn't be seen dead aboard today's huge standard resort cruise ships), with excellent food that is approaching gourmet standards, and fine European-style service in surroundings that borders on the elegant and refined while remaining trendy.

ACCOMMODATION. There are three types, and five price categories (depending on location, size and grade): Yacht Club (standard) Cabin, Commodore Club Suite, and Owner's Suite.

Yacht Club Cabins: Incorrectly called "suites" in the brochure, the standard cabins are, more correctly, fully equipped "mini-suites" with an outside view through windows or portholes (depending on deck and price category). Each measures 195 sq. ft (18.1 sq. meters), which isn't large by today's cruise ship standards; however, it is large compared to cabins aboard many private motor yachts, and extremely large when compared to ocean-going racing yachts. The sleeping area has twin beds that can be put together to form a queen-sized configuration; beds are positioned next to the window (or porthole) so that you can entertain in the living area without going past the sleeping area, as you must aboard the slightly larger Seabourn or Silversea ships, for example; a curtain separates the sleeping and lounge areas. All cabinetry and furniture is of thick blond wood, with nicely rounded edges.

A long vanity desk in the sleeping area has a large mirror above it (however, there is no three-sided mirror for women to check the back of their hair) and two small drawers for cosmetic items; there is also a brass clock located on one wall. A mirror is placed opposite the bed, which won't please those who follow feng shui principles.

In the lounge area, a long desk has six drawers, plus a vertical cupboard unit that houses a sensible safe, refrigerator and drinks cabinet stocked with your choice of drinks. There is also a 20-inch (51.5-mm) flat-screen television, CD and DVD player, and an MP3 audio player with a choice of more than 100 selections. The beds have the finest linens, including thick cotton duvets, and non-allergenic pillows are also available. There's little room under the beds for luggage, although this can be taken away and stored.

One drawback is the fact that the insulation between cabins is not as good as it could be, although rarely does this present a problem, as most passengers aboard the SeaDreams are generally extremely quiet, considerate types who are allergic to noise. Incidentally, a sleep suit is supplied in case you want to sleep out on deck under the stars in one of the on-deck two-person beds – but more of those later.

When the ships became *SeaDreams I* and *II* all the bathrooms were totally refurbished. The old tiling was discarded and replaced by new cheerful decor that is more hip and trendy, with softer colors and larger (beige) marble tiles. The former tiny sit-in bathtubs have been taken out – these will be missed by many regular European passengers – and replaced by a multi-jet power glassed-in shower enclosure. A new washbasin set in a marble-look surround and two glass shelves make up the facilities, while an under-sink cupboard provides further space for larger personal toiletry items. Bulgari personal toiletries are provided. Gorgeously thick, plush, 100% cotton SeaDream-logo bathrobes and towels are also supplied.

However, the bathrooms really are small, particularly for those who are of

OVERALL SCORE: 1,788

BERLITZ'S RATINGS

	Possible	Achieved
Ship	500	440
Accommodation	200	173
Food	400	371
Service	400	370
Entertainment	n/a	n/a
Cruise	500	434

larger than average build, despite their having been completely rebuilt. Also, the doors still open inward, so space inside is at a premium. The toilet is located in a rather awkward position, and, unless you close the door, you can see yourself in the mirror facing of the closets, opposite the bathroom door.

Commodore Club Suites: For larger accommodation, choose one of 16 Commodore Club Suites. These consist of two standard cabins with an interconnecting door, thus providing you with a healthy 380 sq. ft (36 sq. meters) of living space. One cabin is made into a lounge and dining room, with table and up to four chairs, while the other becomes your sleeping area. The advantage is that you get two bathrooms (his and hers). One disadvantage is that the soundproofing between cabins could be better.

Owner's Suite: For the largest living space, go for the Owner's Suite. This measures a grand 490 sq. ft (45.5 sq. meters). It's the only accommodation with a bathroom that incorporates a real full-sized tub; there's also a separate shower enclosure and lots of space for personal toiletries.

No matter what grade of accommodation you choose, all passengers receive personalized stationery, a personal email address, a 100% cotton sleep suit, Bulgari personal toiletry amenities, 24-hour room service, and "sweet dreams" chocolates.

CUISINE. The dining salon (called The Restaurant) is elegant and inviting, and has bird's-eye maple wood paneled walls and alcoves showcasing beautiful hand-made glass creations. It is cozy, yet with plenty of space around each table for fine service, and the ship provides a floating culinary celebration in an open-seating arrangement, so you can dine whenever, and with whomever, you want. Course-by-course meals can also be served out on deck.

Tables can be configured for two, four, six, or eight. They are laid with a classic setting of a real glass base (show) plate, Porsgrund china, pristine white monogrammed table linen, and fresh flowers, while wall sconces house some superb glass ornaments.

Candlelit dinners are part of the inviting setting. There is even a box of spare spectacles for menu reading in case you forget your own. You get leather-bound menus, and supremely attentive, close to impeccable personalized European service.

The SeaDream Yacht Club experience really is all about dining. The ships will not disappoint, and culinary excellence prevails. Only the very freshest and finest quality ingredients are used in the best culinary artistry. Fine, unhurried European service is provided. Additionally, caviar (American farmed Hacklefish malossol caviar, sadly, and not Russian caviar, whose purchase and supply today is challenging) and good quality champagne are available whenever you want them. The ice cream is excellent, and it is carefully made on board.

The ships provide extremely creative cuisine, and everything is prepared individually to order. Special orders are possible, although the former popular flaming desserts have almost disappeared. You can also dine, course by course in your suite for any meal, at any time (you can also eat à la carte 24 hours a day if you wish). Thankfully, there's never a hint of baked Alaska.

Good-quality table wines are included in the cruise fare for lunch and dinner. Real wine connoisseurs, however, will appreciate the availability of an extra wine list, full of special vintages and premier crus at extra cost. If you want to do something different with a loved one, you can also arrange to dine one evening on the open (but covered) deck, overlooking the swimming pool and stern – it can be a magical and very romantic setting.

The Topside Restaurant is the informal open-air dining venue that was created from what used to be the outdoor cafe. Now it has glass sides and a glass ceiling. Informal dining is its theme, whether for breakfast, lunch or the occasional dinner. Teak tables and chairs add a touch of class.

ENTERTAINMENT. There is no evening entertainment as such, other than a duo or solo musician to provide music for listening and dancing in the lounge. Dinner is the main event, and videos are available to take to your cabin.

SPA/FITNESS. The holistic approach to wellbeing plays a big part in relaxation and body pampering aboard the *SeaDreams*. To this end, when you enter the Asian Spa/Wellness Centre you enter another world, housed together with a good sized gymnasium, and a small beauty salon. There are three massage rooms, a small sauna, and steam shower enclosure.

The spa, located in a private area forward on Deck 4, is staffed and operated as a concession, by Universal Maritime Services. SeaDream's Traditional Thai Massage ($115 for 50 minutes, or $145 for 75 minutes including herbal compresses). Massage on the beach is available when the ship operates its famous beach party.

Other types of massages offered include Shiatsu ($115 for 50 minutes), and Swedish Body Massage ($115 for 50 minutes). Body scrubs such as Body Glow, Javanese Lulur (Javanese body scrub, at $55 for 30 minutes). Papaya Body Mask ($70 for 30 minutes).

For the ultimate in "pampership", there's Perfect Bliss (3 hours 20 minutes of body pampering, for $320).

Meanwhile, golfers should enjoy the electronic golf simulator, with a choice of several golf courses to play. For more recreational facilities, note that at the stern is a small, retractable, water sports platform. Equipment carried for sporting types include a water-ski boat, sailboat, wave runners (jet skis), kayaks, wake boards, snorkeling equipment and two Zodiacs. The use of all this equipment is included in the price of a cruise.

The sea conditions have to be just right (minimal swell) for these items to be used, which, on average is once or twice during a typical 7-night cruise. You may also be allowed to swim off the stern platform if conditions permit. Ten mountain bikes are also carried, so you can pedal away when ashore.

Serenade of the Seas
★★★★

Large Resort Ship:	.........90,090 tons	Total Crew:	858
Lifestyle:	...................Standard	Passengers	
Cruise Line:	.Royal Caribbean Internttional	(lower beds/all berths):	.....2,100/2,500
Former Names:	................none	Passenger Space Ratio	
Builder:	........Meyer Werft (Germany)	(lower beds/all berths):	.......42.9/36.0
Original Cost:	............$350 million	Crew/Passenger Ratio	
Entered Service:	.........August 2003	(lower beds/all berths):	.........2.4/2.9
Registry:	...............The Bahamas	Navigation Officers:	.........Norwegian
Length (ft/m):	................961.9/293.2	Cabins (total):	1,050
Beam (ft/m):	...............105.6/32.2	Size Range (sq ft/m):	.....165.8–1,216.3/
Draft (ft/m):	.................27.8/8.5		15.4/113.0
Propulsion/Propellers:	.....gas turbine/2	Cabins (outside view):	813
azimuthing pods (20 MW each)		Cabins (interior/no view):	237
Passenger Decks:	12	Cabins (for one person):	0

Cabins (with private balcony): 577
Cabins (wheelchair accessible): 14
(8 with private balcony)
Cabin Current: ....110/220 volts
Elevators: 9
Casino (gaming tables): ....Yes
Slot Machines: ....Yes
Swimming Pools (outdoors): 2
Swimming Pools (indoors): 0
Whirlpools: 3
Self-Service Launderette: ....No
Dedicated Cinema/Seats: Yes/40
Library: ....Yes

OVERALL SCORE: 1,530 (OUT OF A POSSIBLE 2,000 POINTS)

OVERVIEW. This is the third Royal Caribbean International ship to use gas and steam turbine power (the others are sister ships *Brilliance of the Seas* and *Radiance of the Seas*) instead of the formerly conventional diesel or diesel-electric combination.

Podded propulsion power is also provided. Briefly, two pods, which resemble huge outboard motors, replace internal electric propulsion motors, shaft lines, rudders and their machinery, and are compact, self-contained units that typically weigh about 170 tons each. Although they are at the stern, pod units pull, rather than push, a ship through the water. As is common aboard all RCI vessels, the navigation bridge is of the fully enclosed type (good for cruising in cold-weather areas such as Alaska). In the very front of the ship is a helipad, which also acts as a viewing platform for passengers (good for up-close-and personal cruising in Alaska). One of two swimming pools can be covered by a large glass dome (a magrodome) for use as an indoor/outdoor pool.

Serenade of the Seas is a streamlined contemporary ship, and has a two-deck-high wrap-around structure in the forward section of the funnel. Along the starboard side, a central glass wall protrudes, giving great views (cabins with balconies occupy the space directly opposite on the port side). The gently rounded stern has nicely tiered decks, which gives the ship an extremely well-balanced look.

Inside the ship, the decor is contemporary, yet elegant, bright and cheerful, designed for young, active, hip and trendy types. The artwork is quite eclectic (so there should be something for all tastes), and provides a spectrum and a half of color works.

The interior focal point is a nine-deck high atrium lobby

BERLITZ'S RATINGS

	Possible	Achieved
Ship	500	431
Accommodation	200	158
Food	400	253
Service	400	298
Entertainment	100	81
Cruise	400	309

with glass-walled elevators (on the port side of the ship only) that travel through 12 decks, face the sea and provide a link with nature and the ocean. The Centrum (as the atrium is called), has several public rooms connected to it: the guest relations (the contemporary term for purser's office) and shore excursions desks, a Lobby Bar, Champagne Bar, the Library, Royal Caribbean Online (an internet-connect center), the Concierge Club, and a Crown & Anchor Lounge. A great view of the atrium can be had by looking down through the flat glass dome high above it.

Other facilities include a delightful, but very small library and, in the atrium lobby, a Coffee Shop that also sells pastries and cakes – it's rather like a small Seattle coffee house. There's a Champagne Bar, and a large Schooner Bar (a popular favorite aboard RCI ships, with nautical riggings, ship replicas, maritime art and other nautically-themed ephemera). Gambling devotees should enjoy the rather large, noisy and very colorful Casino Royale. There's also a small dedicated screening room for movies (with space for two wheelchairs), as well as a 194-seat conference center, and a business center.

This ship has a Viking Crown Lounge (a Royal Caribbean International trademark) is a large structure set around the base of the ship's funnel. It is an observation lounge during the daytime (with views forward over the swimming pool). In the evening, the space transforms itself into a futuristic, high-energy dance club, as well as a more intimate and relaxed entertainment venue for softer mood music and "black box" theater.

For those who wish to go online, Royal Caribbean Online, located in a semi-private setting, is a dedicated computer center with 12 stations providing high-speed internet access for sending and receiving email. Four more internet-access computer terminals are located in Books 'n' Coffee, a bookshop with coffee and pastries, located in an extensive area of shops.

Youth facilities include Adventure Ocean, an "edutainment" area with four separate age-appropriate sections for junior passengers: Aquanaut Center (for ages 3–5); Explorer Center (6–8); Voyager Center (9–12); and the Optix Teen Center (13–17). There is also Adventure Beach, which includes a splash pool complete with waterslide; Surfside, with computer lab stations with entertaining software; and Ocean Arcade, a video games hangout.

The onboard product delivery is more casual and unstructured than RCI has previously been delivering. *Serenade of the Seas* offers more space and more comfortable public areas (and several more intimate spaces), slightly larger cabins and more dining options than most of the larger ships in the RCI fleet.

There is also a grand amount of glass that provides more contact with the ocean around you; of course, more glass means more cleaning of glass. However, at the end of the day, the overall product is similar to that delivered aboard other ships in the fleet. In the final analysis, while the ship is quite delightful in many ways, the onboard operation is less spectacular, and suffers from a lack of service staff. The onboard currency is the US dollar, and 15% is added to all bar and spa bills.

Many of the "private" balcony cabins are not very private, as they can be overlooked by anyone standing in the port and starboard wings of the Solarium, and from other locations. There are no cushioned pads for the sunloungers, and the deck towels provided are quite thin and small. Spa treatments are extravagantly expensive (as they are aboard most ships today, in line with land-based spa prices in the USA). It is virtually impossible to escape background music anywhere aboard this ship. Standing in lines for embarkation, the reception desk, disembarkation, for port visits, shore tenders and for the self-serve buffet stations in the Windjammer Cafe is an inevitable aspect of cruising aboard this large ship.

ACCOMMODATION. There is a wide range of suites and standard outside-view and interior (no view) cabins to suit different tastes, requirements, and depth of wallet, in 10 different categories and 19 different price groups. The price will depend on the grade, size and location you choose.

Apart from the largest suites (six owner's suites), which have king-sized beds, almost all other cabins have twin beds that convert to a queen-sized bed (all sheets are of 100% Egyptian cotton, although blankets are of synthetic fabric). All cabins have rich (but faux) wood cabinetry, including a vanity desk (with hairdryer), faux wood drawers that close silently (hooray), television, personal safe, and three-sided mirrors. Some cabins have a recessed ceiling, pull-down berths for third and fourth persons, although closet and drawer space would be extremely tight for four persons (even if two of them are children), and some have interconnecting doors (so families with children can cruise together, in separate, but adjacent cabins).

Audio channels are available through the television; however, if you want to go to sleep with soft music playing in the background you'll need to put a towel over the television screen, as it is impossible to turn the picture off. Data ports are provided in all cabins.

Most cabin bathrooms have tiled accenting and a terrazzo-style tiled floor, and a shower enclosure in a half-moon shape (it is rather small, however), 100% Egyptian cotton towels, a small cabinet for personal toiletries and a small shelf. In reality, there is little space to stow personal toiletries for two (or more).

The largest accommodation consists of a family suite with two bedrooms. One bedroom has twin beds (convertible to queen-sized bed), while a second has two lower beds and two upper Pullman berths, a combination that can sleep up to eight persons (this would suit large families).

Occupants of accommodation designated as suites also get the use of a private Concierge Lounge (where priority dining room reservations, shore excursion bookings and beauty salon/spa appointments can be made).

CUISINE. "Reflections" is the name of the ship's principal dining room. It spans two decks; the upper deck level has floor-to-ceiling windows, while the lower deck level has picture windows. It is a lovely, but inevitably noisy dining hall – reminiscent of those aboard the transatlantic liners in their heyday (however, eight huge, thick pillars obstruct the sightlines – the dining room would be much nicer without them).

Reflections seats 1,104 hungry persons, and its decor features a cascading water theme. There are tables for two, four, six, eight or 10 in two seatings. Two small private dining rooms (Illusions with 94 seats and Mirage with 30 seats) are located off the main dining room. No smoking is permitted in the dining venues.

The cuisine is typical of mass banquet catering that offers standard fare comparable to that found in American family-style restaurants ashore. The menu descriptions make the food sound better than it is (the ship uses many mixes and pre-prepared items). However, a decent selection of light meals is provided, and a vegetarian menu is available. The selection of breads, rolls, fruit and cheese is quite poor, however, and could do with improvement. Caviar (once a standard menu item) now incurs a hefty extra charge. Menus typically include a "Welcome Aboard" Dinner, French Dinner, Italian Dinner, International Dinner, Captain's Gala Dinner.

One thing this company does once each cruise is to put on a "Galley Buffet" whereby passengers go through a section of the galley picking up food for a midnight buffet. There is an adequate wine list, moderately priced.

Alternative Restaurants. There are two: Portofino, with 112 seats, featuring Italian cuisine (choices include: antipasti, soup, salad, pasta, main dish, dessert, cheese and coffee); and Chops Grill Steakhouse, with 95 seats and an open "show" kitchen, serving premium meats in the form of veal chops and steaks (New York Striploin Steak, Filet Mignon, and Prime Rib of Beef).

Both alternative dining spots have food that is of a much higher quality than in the main dining room, with extremely good presentation and experienced service. The menus do not change throughout the cruise. There is an additional charge of $20 per person (this includes gratuities to staff), and reservations are required for both dining spots, which are typically open 6pm–11pm. Be prepared to eat a lot of food (do justice to the cover charge). The dress code in the alternative dining spots is smart casual.

Casual Eateries: Also, casual meals (for breakfast, lunch and dinner) can be taken in the self-serve, buffet-style Windjammer Cafe, which can be accessed directly from the pool deck. It has islands dedicated to specific foods, and indoors and outdoors seating. Additionally, there is the Seaview Cafe, open for lunch and dinner. Choose from the self-serve buffet, or from the menu for casual, fast-food seafood items including fish sandwiches, popcorn shrimp, fish 'n' chips, as well as non-seafood items such as hamburgers and hot dogs. The decor, naturally, is marine- and ocean related.

ENTERTAINMENT. Facilities include the three-level Tropical Theater, with 874 seats (including 24 stations for wheelchairs) and good sight lines from most seats. Strong cabaret acts are also featured in the main showlounge.

A second entertainment venue is the Safari Club. This is where more casual cabaret shows, including late-night adult (blue) comedy, and live music for dancing are featured.

All of the entertainment throughout this ship is upbeat (in fact, it is virtually impossible to get away from music and noise), but is typical of the kind of resort hotel found in Las Vegas. There is even background music in all corridors and elevators, and constant music on the pool deck. If you want a quiet holiday, choose another cruise line.

SPA/FITNESS. The ShipShape Spa's health, fitness and spa facilities have themed decor, and include a 10,176 sq.-ft (945 sq.-meter) solarium, a gymnasium (with 44 cardiovascular machines), 50-person aerobics room, sauna and steam rooms, and therapy treatment rooms. All are located on two of the uppermost decks of the ship, forward of the mast, with access from the forward stairway.

The climate-controlled 10,176 sq. ft (945 sq. meters) indoor/outdoor Solarium (with magrodome sliding glass roof that can be closed in cool or inclement weather conditions) provides facilities for relaxation. It has fascinating Balinese-themed decor, and includes a whirlpool and counter current swimming under a retractable magrodome roof. One neat feature is the Temple Gate Falls, a carved wooden gateway with water cascading down its sides.

For the more sporting passengers, there is activity galore – including a rock-climbing wall that's 30-ft (9 meters) high, with five separate climbing tracks. It is located outdoors at the aft end of the funnel.

Other sports facilities include a 9-hole miniature golf course, and an indoor/outdoor country club with golf simulator, a jogging track, and basketball court. Want to play pool? Well, you can, thanks to two special tables (called STables), whose technology adjusts to the movement of the ship automatically (you can find the tables in the Bombay Billiard Room, part of the Colony Club).

● **For more extensive general information about the Royal Caribbean experience, see pages 137–42.**

Seven Seas Mariner
★★★★ +

Mid-Size ship: . . . . .48,015 tons	Total Crew: 445	Cabins (with private balcony): 354
Lifestyle: . . . . .Luxury/Premium	Passengers	Cabins (wheelchair accessible): 6
Cruise Line: . .Regent Seven Seas Cruises	(lower beds/all berths): 708/752	Cabin Current: . . . . .110 volts
Former Names: . . . . .none	Passenger Space Ratio	Elevators: 6
Builder: Chantiers de l'Atlantique (France)	(lower beds/all berths): 67.8/63.8	Casino (gaming tables): . . . . .Yes
Original Cost: . . . .$240 million	Crew/Passenger Ratio	Slot Machines: . . . . .Yes
Entered Service: . . . . .Mar 2001	(lower beds/all berths): 1.6/1.7	Swimming Pools (outdoors): 1
Registry: . . . . .The Bahamas	Navigation Officers: . . . . .French	Swimming Pools (indoors): 0
Length (ft/m): 713/217.3	Cabins (total): 354	Whirlpools: 3
Beam (ft/m): 95.1/29.0	Size Range (sq ft/m): 301.3–2,002.0/	Self-Service Launderette: . . . . .Yes (3)
Draft (ft/m): 21.4/6.5	28.0–186.0	Dedicated Cinema/Seats: . . . . .No
Propulsion/Propellers: . . .diesel-electric/2	Cabins (outside view): 354	Library: . . . . .Yes
azimuthing pods (8.5 MW each)	Cabins (interior/no view): 0	
Passenger Decks: 9	Cabins (for one person): 0	

OVERALL SCORE: 1,695 (OUT OF A POSSIBLE 2,000 POINTS)

OVERVIEW. This is presently the largest ship in the Seven Seas Cruises fleet, and the first to receive a "pod" propulsion system, replacing the traditional shaft and rudder system (the pods have forward-facing propellers that can be turned through 360°). For the technically minded, the ship was built in 32 blocks, using the same hull design as for Festival Cruises' *Mistral*, although the interior design is totally different. In the fitting out stage, for example, many changes were made to accommodate Seven Seas Cruises' need for all-outside-view suites. Consequently, its passenger space ratio is now the highest in the cruise industry, at just a fraction above that for *Europa*.

Seven Seas Mariner is operated by Seven Seas Cruises, although the ship is actually owned by a joint venture company established with ship managers V-Ships.

There is a wide range of public rooms to play in, almost all of which are located under the accommodation decks. Three sets of stairways (forward, center, aft) mean it is easy to find your way around the vessel. An atrium lobby spans nine decks, with the lowest level opening directly onto the tender landing stage.

Facilities include a delightful observation lounge, a casino, a shopping concourse (conveniently located opposite the casino) – complete with open market area, a garden lounge/promenade arcade, a large library with internet-connect computers, business center, card room and a conference room, a cigar-smoking lounge (called the Connoisseur Club, for cigars, cognacs and other assorted niceties), and a photo gallery.

With the introduction of *Seven Seas Mariner*, Seven Seas Cruises moved into a new breed of larger ships that

BERLITZ'S RATINGS

	Possible	Achieved
Ship	500	443
Accommodation	200	177
Food	400	334
Service	400	324
Entertainment	100	83
Cruise	400	334

are more economical to operate, and provide more choices for passengers. However, the downside of a larger ship such as this is that there is a loss of the sense of intimacy that the company's smaller ships used to have. Thus, some of the former personal service of the smaller ships has been absorbed into a larger structure. Another downside is the fact that this ship is simply too large to enter the small harbors and berths that the company's smaller ships could access, and so loses some of the benefits of small upscale ship cruising.

So, it's swings and roundabouts when it comes to scoring the ship. At present, it scores very highly in terms of hardware and software, but operationally may lose a few points if it is deemed that it can enter only mid-size ship ports. By comparison, this ship is a more upscale version of the eight ships in the former Renaissance Cruises fleet – with better food, more choices, and a staff that are more hospitality-conscious and generally better trained. *Seven Seas Mariner* has ended up just a tad under the score base needed for it to join the "Berlitz Five Star" Club.

Basic gratuities are included, as are all alcoholic and non-alcoholic beverages and complimentary table wines for lunch and dinner (although premium and connoisseur selections are also available at extra cost). The onboard currency is the US dollar.

Service and hospitality are mostly very good. The same carpeting is used throughout the public areas – with no relief or change of color or pattern on the stairwells. The decor is a little glitzy in places. Much of the intimacy and close-knit ambience of the smaller vessels is missing, and, because of all those cabins with balconies, the feeling of privacy and relaxation can also translate into less passengers and ambience in public rooms and for entertainment events, depending on the passenger mix.

SUITABLE FOR: *Seven Seas Mariner* is best suited to well traveled couples and single travelers (typically over 50) who seek excellent itineraries, fine food and good service, with some entertainment, all wrapped up in a contemporary ship which can best be described as elegant and quiet in its appointments and comfort levels.

ACCOMMODATION. There are 13 categories of cabins. The price you pay will depend on the grade, location and size you choose. *Seven Seas Mariner* was the cruise industry's first "all-suite, all-balcony" ship (terminology that marketing departments enjoy, although it is not actually correct, as not all accommodation has sleeping areas completely separated from living areas).

All grades of accommodation have private, marble-clad bathrooms with bathtub, and all suite entrances are neatly recessed away from the passenger hallways, to provide an extra modicum of quietness. In comparison with *Seven Seas Navigator*, the bathrooms aboard this ship are not as large in the lower grade of accommodation.

Master Suite: The largest accommodation (1,580 sq. ft/147 sq. meters), in two Master Suites, has two separate bedrooms, living room with TV/VCR and CD player, walk-in closet, dining area, large, two marble-clad bathrooms with bathtub and separate shower enclosure, and two private teakwood-decked balconies. These suites are located on the deck under the ship's navigation bridge, one balcony providing delightful forward-facing views, while a second balcony provides port or starboard views. Butler service is provided, as is a Nespresso coffee machine. To keep things in perspective, these two Master Suites are nowhere near as large as the two Penthouse Suites aboard the much larger Celebrity Cruises ships *Constellation, Infinity, Millennium* and *Summit* (which measure 2,350 sq. ft/218 sq. meters).

Mariner Suite: Six Mariner Suites (739 sq. ft/69 sq. meters), located on port and starboard sides of the atrium on three separate decks, have a separate bedroom, living room with TV/VCR and CD player, walk-in closet, dining area, large, marble-clad bathroom with bathtub and separate shower enclosure, and a good sized private balcony with either port or starboard views. Butler service is provided, as is a Nespresso coffee machine.

Grand Suites: Two Grand Suites (707 sq. ft/66 sq. meters) are located one deck above the ship's navigation bridge, and have a separate bedroom, living room with TV/VCR and CD player, walk-in closet, dining area, two marble-clad bathrooms with bathtub and separate shower enclosure, and a good sized private balcony with port or starboard views. Butler service is provided, as is a Nespresso coffee machine.

Seven Seas Suites: Six spacious suites (697 sq. ft/65 sq. meters) overlook the ship's stern (two suites are located on each of four decks) and have very generous private balcony space and good wrap-around views over the ship's stern and to port or starboard. However, the balconies are only semi-private and can be partly overlooked by neighbors in Horizon Suites as well as from above. Another two Seven Seas Suites are located just aft of the ship's navigation bridge and measure a slightly smaller 600 sq ft (56 sq. meters) and have balconies with either port or starboard views. These suites have a separate bedroom, living room with TV/VCR and CD player, walk-in closet, dining area, large, and marble-clad bathroom with a combination bathtub/shower.

Horizon Suites: There are 12 Horizon Suites (522 sq. ft/48 sq. meters) overlooking the ship's stern (three suites are located on each of four decks, sandwiched between the Seven Seas Suites) and have a good-sized balcony (though not as large as the Seven Seas Suites) and good views. These suites have a separate bedroom, living room with TV/VCR, walk-in closet, dining area, large, marble-clad bathroom with a combination bathtub/shower.

All Other Cabins: All other cabins (Categories A–H in the brochure, listed as Deluxe Suites and Penthouse Suites) measure 300 sq. ft (28 sq. meters) and have twin beds that can convert to a queen-sized bed (European duvets are standard), small walk-in closet, marble-lined bathroom with combination bathtub/shower, 100% cotton Anichini bathrobe and towels, vanity desk, hairdryer, TV/VCR, refrigerator (stocked with soft drinks and bar set-up on embarkation), personal safe. In these suites, the sleeping area is separated from the living area only by partial room dividers, and therefore is a cabin (albeit a good-sized one), and not a suite.

Six wheelchair-accessible suites are located as close to an elevator as one could possibly get, and provide ample living space, together with a large roll-in shower and all bathroom fittings located at the correct height.

CUISINE. There are four different dining venues, all operated on an open-seating basis, so that you can sit with whom you want, when you wish. In reality, this means that dining aboard ship is like dining on land – you can go to a different dining spot each night. The downside of this is that waiters don't get to know and remember your preferences. Reservations are required in two of the four dining spots. In general, the cuisine is good to very good, with creative presentation and a wide variety of food choices.

The main dining room is the 570-seat Compass Rose Restaurant, located in the center of the ship. It has a light, fresh decor, and seating at tables for two, four, six or eight – although, with a majority of seating at tables for six or eight, it's not that intimate. A large pre-dinner drinks bar is conveniently located adjacent on the starboard side. For a mid-sized ship, the downside is that, with a single-deck height, the restaurant has a rather cramped feeling. Fine Dudson china is used.

The 80-seat Latitudes (located adjacent to the Compass Rose Restaurant) is the smallest of the specialty alternative dining spots. It features tableside preparation of dishes from its Indochine menu (the decor, too, is Oriental). It's the most intimate dining spot – though, again, the single-deck ceiling height makes it feel cramped. There is seating for two, four or six, and reservations are required.

A 120-seat "supper club", called Signatures, with its own dedicated galley, is located one deck above the main galley (for convenient vertical supply and staff access), and has ocean views along the room's port side. It is directed and staffed by chefs wearing the white toque and blue riband of Le Cordon Bleu, the world's most prestigious culinary society, and the cuisine is classic French. Doors open onto a covered area outdoors, complete with small stage and dance floor. Porsgrund china is used, as are silver show plates and the very finest silverware. Seating is at tables of two, four, or six, and reservations are required. However, the single-deck ceiling height robs the room of the feeling of grandeur that would better suit fine classic French cuisine.

For more casual meals, La Veranda is a large self-serve indoor/outdoor cafe with seats for 450 (the teakwood-decked outdoor seating is particularly pleasant), and the decor is fresh and light. This eatery has several food islands and substantial counter display space. There is also an outdoor grill, adjacent to the swimming pool.

As another variation on the dining theme, you can also choose to dine in your cabin (most passengers do so for breakfast, for example, and some do for dinner instead of "going out" to the "public" restaurants). There is a 24-hour room service menu, and, during regular dinner hours, the full dining room menu is available.

ENTERTAINMENT. The Constellation Theater is the ship's main showlounge. It spans two decks and is quite stunning, and the sight lines are very good from almost all seats on both main and balcony levels. The proscenium stage is large enough to provide space for scenery changes and includes a "thrust" stage that is good for presenting more intimate cabaret acts. Seven Seas Cruises has an eclectic entertainment program that is tailored to each individual ship. Aboard *Seven Seas Mariner*, both production shows and cabaret acts are featured. The ship carries its own production show troupe of eight singers/dancers who perform the colorful shows (the cast is, however, small for the size of the stage). Cabaret acts tend to feature vocalists, magicians and comedy jugglers, among others).

There is also Stars nightclub, with an oval-shaped dance floor, and a Horizon Lounge – both rooms could be used for intimate late-night cabaret. A number of bands and small musical units and solo pianist entertainers can be found providing live music in several lounges and bars.

SPA/FITNESS. Health and fitness facilities include an extensive health spa with gymnasium and aerobics room, beauty parlor, and separate changing, sauna and steam rooms for men and women. The spa is located not at the top of the ship, as is common with many other ships today, but just off the atrium in the center of the ship.

Carita of Paris operates the spa and beauty services as a concession, and provides the staff. Here are some sample prices for treatments: European aromatherapy massage, $120 (50 minutes); four hand massage, $220 (50 minutes); reflexology session, $60 (25 minutes); rejuvenation facial, $155 (60 minutes); mini facial, $70 (30 minutes); neck-to-toe seaweed body wrap, $75 (50 minutes); micro-sea body scrub, $40 (30 minutes). Carita also has a range of beauty products for the body and wellbeing books for sale.

Sports devotees can play in the paddle tennis court, golf driving and practice cages.

Seven Seas Navigator
★ ★ ★ ★ +

Small Ship: . . . . .28,550 tons	Total Crew: 325	Cabins (for one person): 0
Lifestyle: . . . . .Luxury/Premium	Passengers	Cabins (with private balcony): 196
Cruise Line: . .Regent Seven Seas Cruises	(lower beds/all berths): 490/530	Cabins (wheelchair accessible): 4
Former Names: . . . . .none	Passenger Space Ratio	Cabin Current: . . . . .110 and 220 volts
Builder: . . . . .T. Mariotti (Italy)	(lower beds/all berths): 58.2/53.8	Elevators: 5
Original Cost: . . . .$200 million	Crew/Passenger Ratio	Casino (gaming tables): . . . . .Yes
Entered Service: . . . . .Aug 1999	(lower beds/all berths): 1.5/1.6	Slot Machines: . . . . .Yes
Registry: . . . . .Bermuda	Navigation Officers: . . . . .European/	Swimming Pools (outdoors): 1
Length (ft/m): 559.7/170.6	International	Swimming Pools (indoors): 0
Beam (ft/m): 71.5/21.8	Cabins (total): 245	Whirlpools: 2
Draft (ft/m): 21.3.0/6.5	Size Range (sq ft/m): 301.3–1,173.3/	Self-Service Launderette: . . . . .Yes
Propulsion/Propellers: . . . . .diesel	28.0–109.0	Dedicated Cinema/Seats: . . . . .No
(13,000kW/2	Cabins (outside view): 245	Library: . . . . .Yes
Passenger Decks: 8	Cabins (interior/no view): 0	

OVERALL SCORE: 1,653 (OUT OF A POSSIBLE 2,000 POINTS)

OVERVIEW. *Seven Seas Navigator* was built using a hull that was already constructed in St. Petersburg, Russia, as the research vessel *Akademik Nikolay Pilyugin*. After launching the hull, the name *Blue Sea* was used for a short time. The superstructure was incorporated into the hull in an Italian shipyard – the result being that for all intents and purposes a new ship was delivered in record time. However, the result is less than handsome – particularly at the ship's stern. It is, however, large enough to be stable over long stretches of water, and there is an excellent amount of space per passenger.

The interiors have a mix of classical and contemporary Italian styling and decor throughout, with warm, soft colors and fine quality soft furnishings and fabrics. At the opposite end of the ship is Galileo's, a large piano lounge with good views over the stern.

A Navigator's Lounge has warm mahogany and cherry wood paneling and large, comfortable, mid-back tub chairs. Meanwhile, next door, cigars and cognac (and other niceties) can be taken in the delightful Connoisseur's Club – the first aboard a Regent Seven Seas Cruises vessel. The extensive library also has several computers with direct email/internet access (for a fee).

The ship is designed for worldwide cruise itineraries, and is one of the upscale ships in the diverse Regent Seven Seas Cruises fleet. As with all ships in the fleet, all gratuities are included. The onboard currency is the US dollar.

There is no wrap-around promenade deck outdoors, although there is a jogging track high atop the aft section of the ship around the funnel housing. Two of the upper, outer decks are laid with green Astroturf, which cheapens the look

BERLITZ'S RATINGS		
	Possible	Achieved
Ship	500	416
Accommodation	200	180
Food	400	332
Service	400	318
Entertainment	100	83
Cruise	400	324

of the ship – these decks would be better in teak. The ceilings in several public rooms (including the main restaurant) are quite low, which makes the ship feel smaller and more closed in than it is. The ship suffers from a considerable amount of vibration, which detracts from the comfort level when compared with other vessels of the same size.

Basic gratuities are included, as are all alcoholic and non-alcoholic beverages, starting in 2007, plus complimentary table wines for lunch and dinner.

SUITABLE FOR: *Seven Seas Navigator* is best suited to well-traveled couples and single travelers (typically over 50) who seek excellent itineraries, fine food and good service, with some entertainment, all wrapped up in a contemporary ship which can best be described as elegant and quiet in its appointments and comfort levels.

ACCOMMODATION. There are 11 price grades (priced by grade, location and size). The company markets this as an "all-suite" ship. Even the smallest suite is quite large, and all have outside views. Almost 90 percent of all suites have a private balcony, with floor-to-ceiling sliding glass doors, while 10 suites are interconnecting, and 38 suites have an extra bed for a third occupant. By comparison, even the smallest suite aboard this ship is more than twice the size of the smallest cabin aboard the world's largest cruise ships, Royal Caribbean International's Voyager-class ships.

All grades of accommodation have a walk-in closet, European king-sized bed or twin beds, wooden cabinetry with nicely rounded edges, plenty of drawer space, mini-bar/refrigerator (stocked with complimentary soft drinks and bar set-up on embarkation), TV/DVD, personal safe and other accoutrements of fine living at sea in the latest design format. The marble-appointed bathroom has a full-size bathtub, as well as a separate shower enclosure, 100% cotton bathrobe and towels, and hairdryer.

The largest living spaces can be found in four master suites, with forward-facing views (all have double-length side balconies). Each suite has a completely separate bedroom with dressing table; the living room has a full dining room table and chairs for up to six persons, wet bar, counter and bar stools, large 3-person sofa and six armchairs, and an audio-visual console/entertainment center, and a Nespresso coffee machine. Each suite has a large main, marble-clad, fully tiled bathroom with full-sized bathtub and separate shower enclosure, a separate room with bidet, toilet and washbasin, with plenty of shelf and other storage space for personal toiletries. There is a separate guest bathroom.

Next in size are the superb Navigator Suites, which have a completely separate bedroom, walk-in closet, large lounge with mini-bar/refrigerator (stocked with complimentary soft drinks and bar set-up on embarkation), personal safe, compact disc player, large TV/DVD player, and dining area with large table and four chairs. The marble-clad, fully tiled bathroom has a full-sized bathtub with hand-held shower, plus a separate shower enclosure (the door to which is only 18 inches/45 cm, however), large washbasin, toilet and bidet, and ample shelf space for personal toiletries.

It is unfortunate that the Navigator Suites are located in the center of the ship, as they are directly underneath the swimming pool deck. They are, thus, subject to noise attacks at 6am daily, when deck cleaning is carried out, and chairs are dragged across the deck directly over the suites. They are further subjected to noise attacks whenever pool deck stewards drag and drop sunloungers into place. Despite these disadvantages, the Navigator Suites are delightful living spaces.

Four suites for the physically challenged have private balconies, and are ideally located adjacent to the elevators (correcting a mistake made when the company's former *Radisson Diamond* was constructed, when they were located as far from any elevators as they possibly could be). However, while the suites are very practical, it is almost impossible to access the balcony, because of the "lip" or "threshold" at the bottom of the sliding glass door.

CUISINE. The Compass Rose Dining Room has large ocean-view picture windows and open-seating dining, which means that you may be seated when and with whom you wish. There are a few tables for two, but most are for four, six, or eight persons. Also, with a low ceiling height and noisy waiter stations, the overall feeling is cramped and unbecoming in terms of the lack of space and grace. Complimentary wines are served during dinner, although a connoisseur wine list is available for those who prefer to choose a vintage wine (at extra cost). The company also features "heart healthy" cuisine.

An alternative dining spot, Portofino Grill, has informal Italian dining for dinner (reservations are required). The Grill is part of a larger restaurant with indoor/outdoor seating. For fast-food items, there is also a small indoor/outdoor Grill, adjacent to the swimming pool.

You can also dine in your cabin. There is a 24-hour room service menu; also, during regular dinner hours, you can make your choice from the full dining room menu.

ENTERTAINMENT. The Seven Seas Lounge is a two-deck-high showlounge, with reasonable sightlines from most seats on both main and balcony levels (although several pillars obstruct the views from some of the side balcony seats). Seven Seas Cruises has an eclectic entertainment program tailored to each ship. *Seven Seas Navigator* features both production shows and cabaret acts.

Bands and small musical units and solo pianist entertainers provide live music in several lounges and bars.

SPA/FITNESS. The redesigned spa, fitness center and beauty salon are now located in the most forward part of the ship's top deck. Carita of Paris operates the spa and beauty services as a concession, and provides the staff. Here are some sample prices for treatments: European aromatherapy massage, $120 (50 minutes); four hand massage, $220 (50 minutes) and $310 (80 minutes); reflexology session, $60 (25 minutes); mini-facial, $70 (30 minutes); "anti-aging" facial, $185 (75 minutes). Carita also sells its own beauty products.

Seven Seas Voyager
★★★★+

Mid-Size Ship:	.41,827 tons	Total Crew:	.445
Lifestyle:	.Luxury/Premium	Passengers	
Cruise Line:	.Regent Seven Seas Cruises	(lower beds/all berths):	.708/752
Former Names:	.none	Passenger Space Ratio	
Builder:	.T. Mariotti (Italy)	(lower beds/all berths):	.59.0/55.6
Original Cost:	.$240 million	Crew/Passenger Ratio	
Entered Service:	.Mar 2003	(lower beds/all berths):	.1.65/1.6
Registry:	.The Bahamas	Navigation Officers:	.French
Length (ft/m):	.669.2/204.0	Cabins (total):	.354
Beam (ft/m):	.94.5/28.8	Size Range (sq ft/m):	.356.0/1,399.3/
Draft (ft/m):	.23.0/7.0		33.0–130.0
Propulsion/Propellers:	.diesel-electric/2	Cabins (outside view):	.354
	azimuthing pods (8.5MW each)	Cabins (interior/no view):	.0
Passenger Decks:	.9	Cabins (for one person):	.0

Cabins (with private balcony):	.354
Cabins (wheelchair accessible):	.4
Cabin Current:	.110 volts
Elevators:	.6
Casino (gaming tables):	.Yes
Slot Machines:	.Yes
Swimming Pools (outdoors):	.1
Swimming Pools (indoors):	.0
Whirlpools:	.3
Self-Service Launderette:	.Yes (3)
Dedicated Cinema/Seats:	.No
Library:	.Yes

OVERALL SCORE: 1,698 (OUT OF A POSSIBLE 2,000 POINTS)

OVERVIEW. Slightly narrower and smaller than *Seven Seas Mariner*, this one has a central corridor for accommodation designated as suites (sister ship *Seven Seas Mariner* has two corridors – port and starboard). This is presently the second ship in the Regent Seven Seas Cruises fleet to receive a "pod" propulsion system (the first being *Seven Seas Mariner*), replacing the traditional shaft and rudder system (the pods have forward-facing propellers that can be turned through 360°).

For the technically minded, the ship was built in 32 blocks (with the same basic hull design as *Seven Seas Mariner*), with a few modifications. The passenger space ratio is among the highest in the cruise industry, at about the same as the smaller, but better-built *Europa*. *Seven Seas Voyager* is operated by Regent Seven Seas Cruises, although the ship is actually owned by a joint-venture company established between RSSC and ship managers V-Ships.

There is a decent range of public rooms in which to play, almost all of which are located under the accommodation decks. Three sets of stairways (forward, center, aft) mean it is easy to find your way around the vessel. An atrium lobby spans nine decks, with the lowest level opening directly onto the tender landing stage.

Facilities include a showlounge that spans two decks, an observation lounge (it's the only place aboard this ship where you can see the bows, a casino, a shopping concourse (conveniently located opposite the casino) – complete with an open "market" area, a large library, internet-connect center and business center (Club.com, and Coffee.com), card room and a small conference room.

There is also a nightclub (Voyager) with an oval-shaped

BERLITZ'S RATINGS		
	Possible	Achieved
Ship	500	445
Accommodation	200	177
Food	400	334
Service	400	324
Entertainment	100	83
Cruise	400	335

dance floor, a cigar-smoking lounge (the Connoisseur Club, for cigars, cognacs and other assorted niceties), and the usual photo gallery.

Regent Seven Seas Cruises has clearly moved into a new breed of larger ships that are more economical to operate, provide better economies of scale, as well as more choices for passengers. However, the downside of a larger ship such as this is that there is a loss of the sense of intimacy that the company's smaller ships used to have. Thus, some of the former personal service of the smaller ships has been absorbed into a larger structure, although this does not always translate well.

Another downside is the fact that this ship is too large to enter the small harbors and berths that smaller ships can, and so loses some of the benefits of the smaller upscale ships such as those of the more stylish Hapag-Lloyd, SeaDream, Seabourn and Silversea. Also, much of the intimacy and close-knit ambiance of the smaller vessels is missing. So it's swings and roundabouts when it comes to scoring the ship.

At present, the ship scores well in terms of hardware (it's a combination of all the best of *Seven Seas Mariner* and *Seven Seas Navigator*) and software, but operationally may lose a few points if it is deemed that the ship can only enter mid-size ship ports. By comparison, this ship is a more upscale version of the eight ships in the former Renaissance Cruises fleet – with better food, more choices, and a staff that is more hospitality-conscious and generally better trained.

Basic gratuities are included, as are all drinks, including complimentary table wines for lunch and dinner (premium and connoisseur selections are available at extra cost). The onboard currency is the US dollar. *Seven Seas Voyager* has ended up just a tad under the score base needed for it to join the "Berlitz Five Star" Club.

Service and hospitality are good. The decor is a little glitzy in places, plain in others (beiges and browns are the prevailing colors). Passenger gripes: there is no walk-around outdoor promenade deck (and the promenade on Deck is only partially covered in teak), and no forward-viewing exterior deck with views over the ship's bows; the white plastic sunloungers should really be replaced by those made of teak, or stainless steel (plastic is not luxury).

SUITABLE FOR: *Seven Seas Voyager* is best suited to well-traveled couples and single travelers (typically over 50) who seek excellent itineraries, fine food and good service, with some entertainment, all wrapped up in a contemporary ship which can best be described as elegant and quiet in its appointments and comfort levels.

ACCOMMODATION. There are 12 accommodation price grades. The price you pay will depend on the grade, size and location you choose. As the ship was built with a central corridor design, this has allowed for larger suites (and much larger bathrooms) than aboard *Seven Seas Mariner*, with which many repeat passengers will no doubt compare it. This is Regent Seven Seas Cruises' second "all-suite all-balcony" ship (terminology that marketing departments thoroughly enjoy, although not actually correct, as not all accommodation has sleeping areas that are completely separated from living areas).

However, all grades of accommodation have private, marble-clad bathrooms with tub (although marble floors can be very cold on bare feet), walk-in closet with personal safe, and most suite entrances are neatly recessed away from passenger hallways (a central corridor), so as to provide an extra modicum of quietness. All have a "private" balcony, although all measure only 50 sq. ft (4.6 sq. meters) with the exception of those in the Master Suites and Grand Suites; however, they do have pleasing teak decking. All partitions are of the partial type, except for the Master Suites and Grand Suites, which have full floor-to-ceiling partitions, and are completely private.

Master Suites (1,162 sq. ft/108 sq. meters). The largest accommodation can be found in two Master Suites (1100 and 1001 each measure 1,403 sq. ft/130.3 sq. meters when added with one Grand Suite via an interconnecting door,) while (700 and 701 measure 1,335 sq. ft (124 sq. meters). Each has two separate bedrooms, living room with TV/DVD player, walk-in closet with personal safe, dining area, large, two marble-clad bathrooms with bathtub and separate shower enclosure, and private teakwood-decked balconies. These suites are located on the deck under the ship's navigation bridge, one balcony providing delightful forward-facing views, while a second balcony provides port or starboard views. Butler service is provided, as is a Nespresso coffee machine. To keep things in perspective, these two Master Suites are nowhere near as large as the two Penthouse Suites aboard the much larger Celebrity Cruises ships

Constellation, Infinity, Millennium and *Summit* (which measure 2,350 sq. ft/235 sq. meters). The bathrooms, which are open to the bedroom, feature a stand-alone tub with integral shower, separate shower enclosure, toilet, bidet and washbasin. The private balcony (the partitions are floor-to-ceiling, and, therefore, completely private) has teak decking and teak deck furniture (two chairs and drinks table).

Grand Suites (876 sq. ft/81.3 sq. meters). Two Grand Suites (1104, 1005) are located one deck above the ship's navigation bridge. They are very pleasant living spaces, and feature a separate bedroom, living room with TV/DVD player, walk-in closet, dining area, and two marble-clad bathing areas. One bathing area, which is open to the bedroom (a curtain can be used to close it off), has a large five-sided sit-in bathtub placed in a glass walled enclosure on the balcony (but with no access door to the balcony, which can only be accessed from the lounge/dining area). The second is a bathroom with separate shower enclosure, bidet, toilet and washbasin. The suites have a private balcony with port or starboard views. There is also an additional (guest) toilet. Butler service is provided, as is a Nespresso coffee machine. The private balcony (the partitions are floor-to-ceiling, and, therefore, completely private) has teak decking and teak deck furniture (two chairs and drinks table).

Voyager Suites (603 sq. ft/56 sq. meters). Eight Voyager Suites, located on port and starboard sides of the atrium on three separate decks, have a separate bedroom, living room with TV/DVD player, walk-in closet, dining area, large, marble-clad bathroom with bathtub and separate shower enclosure, and a good sized private balcony with either port or starboard views. Butler service is provided. The balcony has teakwood deck, part partitions, and white plastic deck furniture.

Seven Seas Suites (657 sq. ft/61 sq. meters) Aft. Six spacious suites overlook the ship's stern (two suites are located on each of four decks), and have a generous wrap-around balcony, and good views over the ship's stern and to port or starboard. However, the balconies are only semi-private and can be partly overlooked by neighbors in other suites as well as from above (they do have teak decking, but white plastic deck furniture). Butler service is provided.

Another four Seven Seas Suites are located amidships and measure a slightly smaller 545 sq. ft (50.6 sq. meters), and have small balconies with either port or starboard views. These suites have a separate bedroom, living room with TV/DVD player, walk-in closet, dining area, large, and marble-clad bathroom with a combination bathtub/shower. Butler service is provided.

Penthouse Suites (370 sq. ft/34.3 sq. meters). There are 32 Category "A" Penthouse Suites and 32 Category "B" Penthouse Suites (Category "A" Suites have the better location, but the size is the same). These have a sleeping area with dressing table and adjacent lounge area, walk-in closet, and bathroom with bathtub, washbasin, separate shower enclosure, and toilet. The balcony is accessed from the lounge. The balcony has teakwood deck, part partitions, and white plastic deck furniture. Butler service is provided.

Horizon Suites (522 sq. ft/48.4 sq. meters). There are

29 Horizon Suites overlooking the ship's stern (some are sandwiched between the larger Seven Seas Suites) and have a good-sized balcony (though not as large as those of the Seven Seas Suites) and delightful aft-facing views. These suites have a separate bedroom, living room with TV/DVD player, walk-in closet, dining area, large, marble-clad bathroom with a combination tub/shower. The balcony has teakwood deck, part partitions, and white plastic deck furniture.

All Other Cabins (356 sq. ft/33 sq. meters). All other cabins (Categories C–H in the brochure, listed as Deluxe Suites) are larger than those of the same grade aboard *Seven Seas Mariner*. They have twin beds that can convert to a queen-sized bed (European duvets are standard), small walk-in closet, marble-lined bathroom with combination tub/shower, 100% cotton bathrobe 100% cotton towels, vanity desk, hairdryer, TV/DVD player, refrigerator (stocked with soft drinks and bar set-up on embarkation), personal safe. In these suites, the sleeping area is separated from the living area only by partial room dividers, and therefore is a cabin (albeit a good-sized one), and not a suite.

Four wheelchair-accessible suites (761, 762, 859, and 860) are all located as close to an elevator as one could possibly get, and provide ample living space, together with a large roll-in shower and all bathroom fittings located at the correct height.

CUISINE. There are four different dining venues, all of which are operated on an open-seating basis, so that you can sit with whom you want, when you wish. In reality, this means that dining aboard ship is like dining on land – you can go to a different dining spot each night. The downside of this is that waiters do not get to know and remember your preferences.

Reservations are required in two of the four dining spots. In general, the cuisine is very good, with creative presentation and a wide variety of food choices.

The main dining room is the 570-seat Compass Rose Restaurant, which is located in the center of the ship, has a light, fresh decor, and seating at tables for two, four, six or eight (with more tables for two or four than *Seven Seas Mariner*). A large pre-dinner drinks bar (actually the Voyager Lounge) is conveniently located close by on the port side. Dudson china, from England, is used.

A 120-seat supper club, Signatures – which shares a galley with Latitudes – is located one deck above the Compass Rose Restaurant galley (for convenient vertical supply and staff access), and has ocean views along the room's port side. It is directed and staffed by chefs wearing the white toque and Blue Riband of Le Cordon Bleu in Paris, the most prestigious culinary authority in the world; hence the cuisine is classic French. Doors open onto a covered area outdoors, complete with stage and dance floor. Porsgrund china is used, as are custom-made silver show plates and the fine silverware. Seating is at tables of two, four, or six, and reservations are required.

For food entertainment, make a reservation in Latitudes. It has real show business flair and an open "show" kitchen (also used for Le Cordon Bleu cooking demos). Dinner is at a set time (typically 7.30pm) and consists of a set menu (the only choice being the main course, which is fish or meat). Seating is in alcoves or at open tables. This restaurant provides an entertaining meal.

For more casual meals, La Veranda is a large self-serve indoor/outdoor café with seats for 450 (the teakwood-decked outdoor seating is particularly pleasant), and the decor is fresh and light. This eatery has a substantial amount of counter display space. There is also an outdoor grill, adjacent to the swimming pool, for fast food items.

For another variation on the dining theme, you can also choose to dine in your cabin. There is a comprehensive 24-hour room service menu, and, during regular dinner hours, you can choose from the full (Compass Rose) dining room menu, and be served course by course.

ENTERTAINMENT. The Constellation Showlounge spans two decks and is quite a stunning room; the sightlines are very good from almost all seats in both main and balcony levels.

A troupe of 10 singers/dancers provides colorful mini-Las Vegas-style revues and production shows that are entertaining. Additionally, cabaret acts (vocalists, illusionists, ventriloquists, comedians, and others) provide stand-alone evening shows. The ship carries a main showband, and several small musical units and soloists (such as a singer/harpist and singer/pianist).

SPA/FITNESS. The Carita Cruise Spa include a reasonably extensive (though not quite as large as one might expect) health spa with gymnasium (plenty of cardiovascular equipment) and aerobics room, beauty salon, and separate changing, sauna and steam rooms (small) for men and women.

Specialist Carita provides the staff and spa and beauty services, which are located not at the top of the ship, as is common with many other ships today, but in the forward section of the ship, above the showlounge.

Here are some sample prices for treatments: European aromatherapy massage, $120 (50 minutes); four hand massage, $220 (50 minutes) and $310 (80 minutes); reflexology session, $60 (25 minutes); mini-facial, $70 (30 minutes); "anti-aging" facial, $185 (75 minutes). Carita (of Paris) also sells its own range of beauty products.

Sports devotees can play in the paddle tennis court, golf driving and practice cages.

Silver Cloud
★★★★+

Small Ship: ....16,927 tons	Total Crew: 210	Cabins (with private balcony): 110
Lifestyle: ....Luxury	Passengers	Cabins (wheelchair accessible): 2
Cruise Line: ....Silversea Cruises	(lower beds/all berths): 296/315	Cabin Current: ....110 and 220 volts
Former Names: ....none	Passenger Space Ratio	Elevators: 4
Builder: ....Visentini/Mariotti (Italy)	(lower beds/all berths): 57.1/53.7	Casino (gaming tables): ....Yes
Original Cost: ....$125 million	Crew/Passenger Ratio	Slot Machines: ....Yes
Entered Service: ....Apr 1994	(lower beds/all berths): 1.4/1.5	Swimming Pools (outdoors): 1
Registry: ....The Bahamas	Navigation Officers: ....European	Swimming Pools (indoors): 0
Length (ft/m): 514.4/155.8	Cabins (total): 148	Whirlpools: 2
Beam (ft/m): 70.62/21.4	Size Range (sq ft/m): 240.0–1,314.0/	Self-Service Launderette: ....Yes
Draft (ft/m): 17.3/5.3	22.2–122.0	Dedicated Cinema/Seats: Yes/306
Propulsion/Propellers: ....diesel	Cabins (outside view): 148	Library: ....Yes
(11,700kW)/2	Cabins (interior/no view): 0	
Passenger Decks: 6	Cabins (for one person): 0	

OVERALL SCORE: 1,664 (OUT OF A POSSIBLE 2,000 POINTS)

OVERVIEW. *Silver Cloud* has quite a handsome profile, with a sloping stern reminiscent of an "Airstream" trailer. The size is just about ideal for highly personalized cruising in an elegant environment. The vertical cake-layer stacking of public rooms aft and the location of accommodation units forward ensures quiet cabins. There is a synthetic turf-covered wrap-around promenade deck outdoors, and a spacious swimming pool deck with teak/aluminum deck furniture (little "Silversea" touches such as cold towels, water sprays and fresh fruit provide poolside pampering on hot days)..

The spacious interior is well planned, with elegant decor and fine quality soft furnishings throughout, accented by the gentle use of brass fittings (some of sub-standard quality and now showing blotchy patches in several places), fine woods and creative ceilings. Although the ship was given a multi-million dollar makeover in 2003, some parts show signs of aging (the spa and shore tenders need attention).

There is a useful business center as well as a CD-ROM and hardback book library, open 24 hours a day. There is an excellent amount of space per passenger and there is no hint of a line anywhere in this unhurried environment. Good documentation is provided before your cruise, all of which comes in a high-quality document wallet.

An elegant, announcement-free onboard ambience prevails, and there is no pressure, no hype, and an enthusiastic staff to pamper you, with a high ratio of Europeans. Insurance is now extra (it was included when Silversea Cruises first started). All drinks, gratuities and port taxes are included, and no further tipping anywhere on board is necessary (though it is not prohibited). This ship is perhaps ideal for those who enjoy spacious surroundings, excellent

BERLITZ'S RATINGS		
	Possible	Achieved
Ship	500	411
Accommodation	200	177
Food	400	333
Service	400	335
Entertainment	100	74
Cruise	400	334

food, and some entertainment. It would be difficult not to have a good cruise holiday aboard this ship, albeit at a fairly high price.

Silversea Cruises has come a long way since it began in 1994 and, after 10 years, has re-invented itself, with a more defined and refined product, and its Italian Heritage theme. The company's many international passengers react well to the ambience, food, service and the staff, most of whom will go out of their way to please.

Silversea Cruises has "all-inclusive" fares, including gratuities (they do not, however, include vintage wines, or massage, or other personal services), but they do include many things that cost extra aboard the ships of many other cruise lines. The passenger mix includes many nationalities, which makes for a more interesting experience, although the majority of passengers are North American (children are sometimes seen aboard, although they are not really welcomed by most passengers, who enjoy cruising without them). The onboard currency is the US dollar.

In 2002, Silversea Cruises introduced "Personalized Voyages" whereby you choose the port of embarkation and disembarkation and the length of cruise you want (minimum is five days). While this is a flexible feature, the onboard programming is already set, so you may be joining and leaving in the middle of a "normal" cruise.

Although the ship is showing signs of wear, it will undergo a big refurbishment in 2009. The actual onboard product delivered is very good, particularly with regard to the cuisine and its presentation. Shuttle buses are provided in most ports of call, and all the little extras that passengers receive aboard this ship makes it an extremely pleasant cruise experience, in surroundings that are very comfortable and contemporary without being extravagant, with open seating dining and drinks included, cold canapés and hot hors d'oeuvres served in the bars in the pre-dinner cocktail hour, a captain's welcome aboard and farewell cocktail party and other niceties.

Some vibration is evident when bow thrusters or the anchors are used, particularly in the forward-most cabins. Plastic sunloungers and drinks tables do not indicate a luxury product. The self-service launderette is poor and not large enough for longer cruises. Crew facilities are minimal, leading to a high crew turnover which undermines service.

SUITABLE FOR: *Silver Cloud* is best suited to discerning, well-traveled couples (typically over 50) who seek a small ship setting (they wouldn't be seen dead aboard today's huge standard resort cruise ships), with excellent food that is approaching gourmet standards, and fine European-style service in surroundings that can best be described as bordering on the elegant and luxurious.

ACCOMMODATION. There are seven price grades in this "all-suite" ship. The all-outside-view suites (75 percent of which have fine private teakwood balconies) have convertible queen-to-twin beds and are beautifully fitted out. They have huge floor-to-ceiling windows, large walk-in closets, dressing table, writing desk, stocked mini-bar/refrigerator (no charge), and fresh flowers. The marble floor bathrooms have a bathtub, fixed showerhead (this is not as hygienic as a hand-held unit), single washbasin, and plenty of high-quality towels. Personalized stationery, bathrobes, and a range of Acqua di Parma bathroom amenities are provided in all suites.

All suites have televisions and VCR or DVD players (top grade suites also have CD-players). However, the walk-in closets do not actually provide much hanging space (particularly for such items as full-length dresses), and it would be better for the door to open outward instead of inward. The drawers themselves are poorly positioned, but several other drawers and storage areas are provided in the living area. Although the cabin insulation above and below each cabin is good, the insulation between cabins is not (a privacy curtain installed between entry door and sleeping area would be most useful), and light from the passageway leaks into the cabin, making it hard to achieve a dark room.

The top-grade suites feature teak balcony furniture, while all other suites have white plastic deck furniture (but all balconies have teak floors) Suites with balconies on the lowest deck can suffer from sticky salt spray when the ship is moving, so the balconies require lots of cleaning. Each evening, the stewardesses bring plates of canapés to your suite – just right for a light bite with cocktails. Stay in the Grand, Royal, Rossellini or Owner's Suite and you get (unobtrusive) butler service (butlers are certified by the Guild of Professional Butlers, London).

CUISINE. The main dining room (called, simply, "The Restaurant") provides open-seating dining in elegant surroundings. It has an attractive arched gazebo center and a wavy ceiling design as its focal point, and is set with fine Eschenbach china and well-balanced Christofle silverware. Meals are served in an open seating, which means you can eat when you like (within the given dining room opening times), and with whom you like.

The dining is good throughout the ship, with a choice of three dining salons, and both the cuisine and its presentation have been improved substantially since the beginning of 2004. Standard table wines are included for lunch and dinner, but there is also a "connoisseur list" of premium wines at extra charge. All meals are prepared as à la carte items, with almost none of the pre-preparation that existed previously.)

An alternative, intimate 24-seat dining salon, La Saletta (adjacent to the main dining room) and degustation menus include dishes designed by Relais Châteaux Gourmands chefs for Silversea Cruises (the cuisine-oriented division of Relais & Châteaux) paired with selected wines. Reservations are required, and the per person extra cost is $30.

For more informal dining, there's La Terrazza for self-serve breakfast and lunch buffets and informal evening-dining with different regional Italian dishes nightly. Both indoor and outdoor seating is at teakwood tables and chairs.

The ship also provides 24-hour in-cabin dining service (full course-by-course dinners are available, although the balcony tables in the standard suites are rather low for dining outdoors).

ENTERTAINMENT. The Showlounge is the venue for all entertainment events and some social functions. The room spans two decks and has a sloping floor; both banquette and individual seating are provided, with good sightlines.

Although Silversea Cruises places more emphasis on food than entertainment, what is provided is quite tasteful and not overbearing, as aboard some larger ships. A decent array of cabaret acts does the Silversea circuit and small colorful production shows have been reintroduced.

Most of the cabaret acts provide intelligent entertainment that is generally appreciated by the ship's well-traveled international clientele. Also, more emphasis is now placed on classical music ensembles. There is also a band, as well as several small musical units for live music in the evenings in The Bar, and Panorama Lounge.

SPA/FITNESS. Although "The Spa at Silversea" facility is not large, it underwent a sea change in 2007, with redesigned, more welcoming decor, and an updated range of treatments and spa packages for both men and women. Massage and other body pampering treatments, facials, pedicures, and beauty salon treatments cost extra.

Facilities include a separate sauna for men and women, several treatment rooms, and a beauty salon. A separate gymnasium (formerly an observation lounge), located atop the ship, provides sea views.

Silver Shadow
★★★★★

Small Ship: . . . . .28,258 tons
Lifestyle: .Luxury
Cruise Line: . . . . .Silversea Cruises
Former Names: . . . . .none
Builder: . . . . .Visentini/Mariotti
(Italy)
Original Cost: . . . .$150 million
Entered Service: . . . . .Sept 2000
Registry: . . . . .The Bahamas
Length (ft/m): 610.2/186.0
Beam (ft/m): 81.8/24.8
Draft (ft/m): 19.6/6.0
Propulsion/Propellers: diesel/2
Passenger Decks: 7

Total Crew: 295
Passengers
(lower beds/all berths): 388/400
Passenger Space Ratio
(lower beds/all berths): 72.8/70.6
Crew/Passenger Ratio
(lower beds/all berths): 1.3/1.3
Navigation Officers: . . . . .Italian
Cabins (total): 194
Size Range (sq ft/m): 287.0–1,435.0/
26.6–133.3
Cabins (outside view): 194
Cabins (interior/no view): 0
Cabins (for one person): 0

Cabins (with private balcony): 157
Cabins (wheelchair accessible): 2
Cabin Current: . . . . . . .110 and 220 volts
Elevators: 5
Casino (gaming tables): . . . . .Yes
Slot Machines: . . . . .Yes
Swimming Pools (outdoors): 1
Swimming Pools (indoors): 0
Whirlpools: 2
Self-Service Launderette: . . . . .Yes
Dedicated Cinema/Seats: . . . . .No
Library: . . . . .Yes

OVERALL SCORE: 1,760 (OUT OF A POSSIBLE 2,000 POINTS)

OVERVIEW. *Silver Shadow* is one of the second generation of vessels in the four-ship Silversea Cruises fleet. It is slightly larger than the first two ships, *Silver Cloud* and *Silver Wind*, with a more streamlined forward profile and large, sleek single funnel. However, the stern section is not particularly handsome. There is a generous amount of open deck and sunbathing space, and aluminum/teak deck furniture is provided.

Silversea Cruises has come a long way since it began in 1994, and is re-inventing itself, with a more defined and refined product, and its Italian Heritage theme. The company's many international passengers react well to the ambience, food, service and the helpful staff. The cruise line has "all-inclusive" fares, including gratuities (they do not, however, include vintage wines, or massage, or other personal services), but they do include many things that are at extra cost compared aboard the ships of many other cruise lines. The passenger mix includes many nationalities, which makes for a more interesting experience although the majority of passengers are North American (children are sometimes seen aboard, although they are not really welcomed by most passengers, who enjoy cruising without them). The onboard currency is the US dollar.

Few ships make it to a five-star Berlitz rating, but Silversea Cruises has earned an enviable reputation for high quality, and, although the ship is showing signs of wear, the onboard product is very good, particularly the cuisine and its presentation. Shuttle buses are provided in most ports of call, and all the little extras that passengers receive make this an extremely pleasant cruise experience, in surroundings that are comfortable and contemporary without being extravagant, with open seating dining and drinks included,

BERLITZ'S RATINGS		
	Possible	Achieved
Ship	500	454
Accommodation	200	181
Food	400	341
Service	400	349
Entertainment	100	86
Cruise	400	349

cold canapés and hot hors d'oeuvres served in the bars in the pre-dinner cocktail hour, a captain's welcome aboard and farewell cocktail party. The swimming pool is surprisingly small, as is the fitness room, although it was expanded in 2007.

In 2002, Silversea Cruises introduced "Personalized Voyages" whereby you choose the port of embarkation and disembarkation and the length of cruise (minimum five days). While this is flexible, the onboard programming is already set, so you may be joining and leaving in the middle of a "normal" cruise.

"The Humidor, by Davidoff," the cigar smoking lounge; has 25 seats and the style of an English smoking club. Other additions include a champagne bar and a computer-learning center, with four computer terminals (wi-fi costs extra).

SUITABLE FOR: *Silver Shadow* is best suited to discerning, well-traveled couples (typically over 50) who seek a small ship setting, with excellent food that is approaching gourmet standards, and fine European-style service in surroundings bordering on the elegant and luxurious.

ACCOMMODATION. There are eight price grades in this all-suite ship. All suites have double vanities in the marble-floored bathrooms, which also have a bathtub and separate shower enclosure. Silversea-monogrammed Frette bed linen is provided in all grades, as are soft down pillows, 100% cotton bathrobes, a range of Acqua di Parma bathroom amenities, and personalized stationery. Stay in the Grand, Royal, Rossellini or Owner's Suite and you get unobtrusive butler service (butlers are certified by the Guild of Professional Butlers, London).

Vista Suites: These suites (287 sq. ft/27 sq. meters) do not have a private balcony. Instead there is a large window, twin beds that convert to a queen-sized bed, sitting area, television and VCR, refrigerator, writing desk, personal safe, cocktail cabinet, dressing table with hairdryer, and walk-in closet. The bathroom is marble-clad in gentle colors, and has two (his 'n' hers) washbasins, full-sized bathtub, separate shower enclosure, and toilet.

Veranda Suites: Each of the Veranda Suites (really a Vista Suite plus a veranda) measures 345 sq. ft (33 sq. meters) and have convertible twin-to-queen beds. They are well fitted out with just about everything you would need, including large floor-to-ceiling windows, large walk-in closet, dressing table, writing desk, stocked mini-bar/refrigerator (all drinks are included in the price of your cruise), and fresh flowers. The marble-clad bathrooms have two washbasins, full-sized tub, separate shower enclosure, and toilet.

Silver Suites: These measure 701 sq. ft (65 sq. meters). These are much wider than the Vista Suites or Veranda Suites and have a separate bedroom, an entertainment center with CD player, TV/VCR unit (in both bedroom and living room) and much more living space that includes a large dining area with table and four chairs. The marble-clad bathrooms have two washbasins, full sized tub, separate shower enclosure, and toilet.

Owner's Suites: The two Owner's Suites, each of which measures 1,208 sq. ft (112 sq. meters), are much larger units and includes an extra powder room/toilet for guests, as well as more living space. There is a 200 sq.-ft (18 sq.-meter) veranda, two bedrooms (with queen-sized beds), two walk-in closets, two living rooms, two sitting areas, separate dining area, an entertainment center with flat-screen plasma television in the living room and TV/VCR player in each bedroom, telephones, refrigerators, cocktail cabinet, writing desk, dressing tables with hairdryers. There are two marble-clad bathrooms, one with a full sized whirlpool bathtub and two washbasins, separate toilet, and separate shower, as well as a powder room for guests. Owner's Suites can be configured as one or two bedrooms.

Royal Suites: Stately accommodation can be found in two Royal Suites, which measure either 1,312 sq. ft (122 sq. meters) or 1,352 sq. ft (126 sq. meters). These are two-bedroom suites, with two teakwood verandas, two living rooms, sitting areas, dining area, queen-size beds, an entertainment center with flat-screen plasma television in the living room and TV/VCR player in each bedroom, telephones, refrigerators, cocktail cabinet, writing desk, two closets, dressing tables with hairdryers. There are two marble-clad bathrooms, one with a full-sized whirlpool bathtub and two washbasins, separate toilet, and separate shower, as well as a powder room for guests. Royal Suites can be either a one- or two-bedroom configuration.

Grand Suites: There are two of these, one measuring 1,286 sq. ft (119 sq. meters), and the other (including an adjoining suite with interconnecting door) 1,435 sq. ft (133 sq. meters). These have two bedrooms, two large walk-in closets, two living rooms, Bang & Olufsen entertainment centers, and large, forward-facing, private verandas that face forwards. These really are sumptuous apartments that have all the comforts of home, and then some.

Disabled Suites: There are two suites for the physically disabled (535 and 537), both adjacent to a lift and next to each other. Measuring a generous 398 sq. ft (37 sq. meters), they are well equipped with an accessible hanging rail, and roll-in bathroom with roll-in shower unit.

CUISINE. The main dining room, "The Restaurant," provides open-seating dining in elegant surroundings. Three grand chandeliers provide an upward focal point, while you can dine when you want, and with whom you wish. Meals can also be served, course-by-course, in your suite, although the balcony tables are rather low for dining outdoors. The cuisine is very good, with a choice of formal and informal areas. Standard table wines are included for lunch and dinner, with a "connoisseur list" of premium wines at extra cost. Once each cruise, there's a "Galley Brunch" when the galley is transformed into a large "chef's kitchen." There's dinner dancing with a live band on some nights.

As an alternative to the main restaurant, Le Champagne, at an extra cost of $30 per person, offers a more intimate, reservation-only dining spot that enables diners to dine from highly specialized dégustation menus that marries international cuisine together with vintage wines selection by Relais et Châteaux sommeliers (although the wines cost extra).

For more informal meals, La Terrazza is for self-serve breakfast and lunch buffets; outdoor seating is at teakwood tables and chairs. The buffet design and set-up presents flow problems during breakfast, however, and "active" stations for cooking eggs or pasta to order would help. In the evening, La Terrazza features regional Italian cuisine, and softer lighting to create a more intimate atmosphere and experience.

Adjacent to La Terazza is a wine bar and a cigar smoking room. A poolside grill provides a casual alternative daytime bistro-style eatery, for grilled and fast food items.

ENTERTAINMENT. The Showlounge is the venue for all entertainment events and some social functions. The room spans two decks and has a sloping floor; both banquette and individual seating are provided, with good sightlines from almost all seats.

Although Silversea Cruises places more emphasis on food than entertainment, what is provided is quite tasteful. A decent array of cabaret acts does the Silversea circuit, and small, colorful production shows have been reintroduced. More emphasis is now placed on classical music ensembles. There is a band, and several small musical units for live music in the evenings in The Bar, and the Panorama Lounge.

SPA/FITNESS. "The Spa at Silversea" health/fitness facility, just behind the Observation Lounge, high atop the ship. had a complete make-over in 2007. It includes a gymnasium, beauty salon, and separate saunas and steam rooms for men and women, plus several personal treatment rooms. A new range of body-pampering services was introduced for men and women (massage and other treatments, facials, pedicures, and beauty salon treatments cost extra).

Silver Whisper
★★★★★

Small Ship: . . . . .28,258 tons	Passengers	Cabins (wheelchair accessible): 2
Lifestyle: .Luxury	(lower beds/all berths): 388/400	Cabin Current: . . . . .110 and 220 volts
Cruise Line: . . . . .Silversea Cruises	Passenger Space Ratio	Elevators: 5
Former Names: . . . . .none	(lower beds/all berths): 72.8/70.6	Casino (gaming tables): . . . . .Yes
Builder: . . . . .Visentini/Mariotti(Italy)	Crew/Passenger Ratio	Slot Machines: . . . . .Yes
Original Cost: . . . .$150 million	(lower beds/all berths): 1.3/1.3	Swimming Pools (outdoors): 1
Entered Service: . . . . .July 2001	Navigation Officers: . . . . .Italian	Swimming Pools (indoors): 0
Registry: . . . . .The Bahamas	Cabins (total): 194	Whirlpools: 2
Length (ft/m): 610.2/186.0	Size Range (sq ft/m): 287.0–1,435.0/	Fitness Center: . . . . .Yes
Beam (ft/m): 81.8/24.8	26.6–133.3	Sauna/Steam Room: . . . . .Yes/Yes
Draft (ft/m): 19.6/6.0	Cabins (outside view): 194	Massage: . . . . .Yes
Propulsion/Propellers: diesel/2	Cabins (interior/no view): 0	Self-Service Launderette: . . . . .Yes
Passenger Decks: 7	Cabins (for one person): 0	Dedicated Cinema/Seats: . . . . .No
Total Crew: .295	Cabins (with private balcony): 157	Library: . . . . .Yes

OVERALL SCORE: 1,760 (OUT OF A POSSIBLE 2,000 POINTS)

OVERVIEW. *Silver Whisper*, which Russia's Vladimir Putin chartered in 2003 to host guests for the three-day celebrations of St. Petersburg's 300th anniversary, is the second generation of vessels in the Silversea Cruises fleet (its sister is *Silver Shadow*), and is slightly larger than the line's first two ships, *Silver Cloud* and *Silver Wind*, but with a more streamlined profile and large, sleek single funnel.

Silversea Cruises has come a long way since it began in 1994, and is re-inventing itself with a more defined and refined product, and its Italian Heritage theme. The company's many international passengers react well to the ambience, food, service and the staff, most of whom go out of their way to please. The cruise line has "all-inclusive" fares, including gratuities (although additional grauities are not expected, they are not prohibited). The fares do not include vintage wines, or massage, or other personal services, but they do include many things that are at extra cost compared aboard the ships of many other cruise lines. The passenger mix includes many nationalities, which makes for a more interesting experience, although the majority of passengers are North American (children are sometimes seen aboard, although they are not really welcomed by most passengers). The onboard currency is the US dollar.

Few ships make it to a five-star Berlitz rating today, but Silversea Cruises emphasis on quality has earned it an enviable reputation, particularly for cuisine, although the ship is showing signs of wear. Shuttle buses are provided in most ports of call, and all the little extras that passengers receive aboard this ship makes it an extremely pleasant cruise experience, in surroundings that are very comfortable and contemporary without being extravagant, with open seating

BERLITZ'S RATINGS

	Possible	Achieved
Ship	500	454
Accommodation	200	181
Food	400	341
Service	400	349
Entertainment	100	86
Cruise	400	349

dining and drinks included, cold canapés and hot hors d'oeuvres served in the bars in the pre-dinner cocktail hour, a captain's welcome aboard and farewell cocktail party and other niceties.

In 2002, Silversea Cruises introduced "Personalized Voyages" whereby you choose the port of embarkation and disembarkation and the length of cruise (minimum is five days). But the onboard programming is set, so you may be joining and leaving in the middle of a cruise.

Aluminum/teak deck furniture is provided around the ship's swimming pool (although the pool itself is quite small).

"The Humidor, by Davidoff," the 25-seat cigar smoking lounge, has been styled like an English smoking club. There's also a wine bar and computer learning center.

SUITABLE FOR: *Silver Whisper* is best suited to discerning, well-traveled couples (typically over 50) who are looking for a small-ship setting with excellent food approaching gourmet standards, and fine European-style service in surroundings bordering on the elegant and luxurious.

ACCOMMODATION. There are eight cabin price categories in this "all-suite" ship. All grades have double vanities in the marble-floored bathrooms, which also have a tub and separate shower enclosure. Silversea-monogrammed Frette bed linen is provided in all grades, as are soft down pillows, 100% cotton bathrobes, a fine array of Acqua di Parma bathroom amenities, and personalized stationery. Stay in the Grand, Royal, Rossellini or Owner's Suite and you get unobtrusive butler service (butlers are certified by the Guild of Professional Butlers, London).

Vista Suites: These suites measure 287 sq. ft (27 sq.

metes), and do not have a private balcony. Instead there is a large window, twin beds that convert to a queen-sized bed, sitting area, TV and VCR player, refrigerator, writing desk, personal safe, cocktail cabinet, dressing table with hairdryer, and walk-in closet. The bathroom is marble-clad in gentle colors, and has two (his 'n' hers) washbasins, full-sized tub, separate shower enclosure, and toilet.

Veranda Suites: Each of the Veranda Suites (really a Vista Suite plus a veranda) measures 345 sq. ft (32 sq. meters) and has convertible twin-to-queen beds. They are well fitted-out, and have large floor-to-ceiling windows, large walk-in closet, dressing table, writing desk, stocked mini-bar/refrigerator (drinks included in the cruise price), and fresh flowers. The marble-clad bathrooms have two washbasins, full-sized bathtub, separate shower enclosure, and toilet.

Silver Suites: The Silver Suites measure 701 sq. ft. (65 sq. meters). These are much wider than the Vista Suites or Veranda Suites and have a separate bedroom, an entertainment center with CD player, TV/VCR unit (in both bedroom and living room) and much more living space that includes a large dining area with table and four chairs. The marble-clad bathrooms have two washbasins, full-sized tub, separate shower enclosure, and toilet.

Owner's Suites: The two Owner's Suites, each 1,208 sq. ft (112 sq. meters), are much larger units and includes an extra bathroom for guests, as well as more living space. There is a 200 sq. ft (18 sq. meter) veranda, two bedrooms (with queen-sized beds), two walk-in closets, two living rooms, two sitting areas, separate dining area, an entertainment center with flat-screen plasma television in the living room and TV/VCR player in each bedroom, telephones, refrigerators, cocktail cabinet, writing desk, dressing tables with hairdryers. There are two marble-clad bathrooms, one with a full-sized whirlpool bathtub and two washbasins, separate toilet, and separate shower, plus a powder room for guests. Owner's Suites can be a one- or two-bedroom configuration.

Royal Suites: Stately accommodation can be found in two Royal Suites, which measure either 1,312 sq. ft (122 sq. meters) or 1,352 sq. ft (126 sq. meters). These are two-bedroom suites, with two teakwood verandas, two living rooms, sitting areas, dining area, queen-size beds, an entertainment center with flat-screen plasma television in the living room and TV/VCR player in each bedroom, telephones, refrigerators, cocktail cabinet, writing desk, two closets, dressing tables with hairdryers. There are two marble-clad bathrooms, one with a full-sized whirlpool bathtub and two washbasins, separate toilet, and separate shower, as well as a powder room for guests. Royal Suites can be either a one- or two-bedroom configuration.

Grand Suites: There are two Grand Suites, one 1,286 sq. ft (119 sq. meters), and the other (including an adjoining suite with interconnecting door) 1,435 sq. ft (133 sq. meters). These have two bedrooms, two large walk-in closets, two living rooms, Bang & Olufsen entertainment centers, and large, forward-facing, private verandas that face forwards. These really are sumptuous apartments that have all the comforts of home, and then some.

Disabled Suites: There are two suites for the physically disabled (535 and 537), both adjacent to an elevator, and next to each other. They measure a generous 398 sq. ft (37 sq. meters). The suites are well-equipped with an accessible hanging rail, and roll-in bathroom with roll-in shower unit.

CUISINE. The main dining room ("The Restaurant") provides open-seating dining in elegant surroundings. Three grand chandeliers provide an upward focal point, while you can dine when you want, and with whom you wish (within the given opening times). Meals can also be served, course-by-course, in your suite, although the balcony tables are rather low for dining outdoors. The dining is good throughout the ship, with a choice of formal and informal areas, although the cuisine and presentation doesn't quite match up to that of products such as the smaller Seabourn Cruise Line ships. Cristofle silverware is provided. Standard table wines are included for lunch and dinner, but there is also a "connoisseur list" of premium wines at extra charge.

Once each cruise, there's a "Galley Brunch" when the galley is transformed into a large "chef's kitchen."

As an alternative to the main restaurant, Le Champagne, at an extra-cost of $30 per person, offers a more intimate, reservation-only dining spot that enables diners to dine from highly specialized dégustation menus that marries international cuisine together with vintage wines selection by Relais et Châteaux sommeliers (and Reidel wine glasses).

La Terrazza has self-serve breakfast and lunch buffets. The buffet design and set-up presents flow problems during breakfast, however, and "active" stations for cooking eggs or pasta to order would help. In the evening this room La Terrazza serves regional Italian cuisine, and softer lighting to create a more intimate atmosphere and experience.

Adjacent to the café is a wine bar and a cigar smoking room. A poolside grill provides a casual alternative daytime dining spot.

ENTERTAINMENT. The Showlounge spans two decks and has a sloping floor; both banquette and individual seating are provided, with good sightlines from almost all seats.

A decent array of cabaret acts does the Silversea circuit, most of them providing intelligent entertainment, and colorful production shows have been reintroduced. More emphasis is now placed on classical music ensembles. There is a band, and small musical units for live music in the evenings in The Bar, and the Panorama Lounge.

SPA/FITNESS. "The Spa at Silversea" health/fitness facility, just behind the Observation Lounge, high atop the ship, had a complete make-over in 2007. It includes a gymnasium, beauty salon, and separate saunas and steam rooms for men and women, plus several personal treatment rooms. A new range of body-pampering services was introduced for men and women (massage and other treatments, facials, pedicures, and beauty salon treatments cost extra). Treatment examples: Deep Tissue Massage, $116 for 50 minutes; Hot Stones Massage, $210 for 75 minutes; In-Suite Couples Massage, $320 for 50 minutes, or $385 for 80 minutes; Elemis Aromapure Facial, $115 for 50 minutes.

Silver Wind
★★★★+

Small Ship:	...............16,927 tons	Total Crew:	197	Cabins (for one person):	0
Lifestyle:	.....................Luxury	Passengers		Cabins (with private balcony):	110
Cruise Line:	..........Silversea Cruises	(lower beds/all berths):	........296/315	Cabins (wheelchair accessible):	2
Former Names:	.................none	Passenger Space Ratio		Cabin Current:	.......110 and 220 volts
Builder:	........Visentini/Mariotti (Italy)	(lower beds/all berths):	........57.1/53.7	Elevators:	4
Original Cost:	.............$125 million	Crew/Passenger Ratio		Casino (gaming tables):	...........Yes
Entered Service:	.............Jan 1995	(lower beds/all berths):	..........1.5/1.5	Slot Machines:	...................Yes
Registry:	..........................Italy	Navigation Officers:	.............Italian	Swimming Pools (outdoors):	1
Length (ft/m):	.............514.4/155.8	Cabins (total):	148	Swimming Pools (indoors):	0
Beam (ft/m):	.................70.62/21.4	Size Range (sq ft/m):	.....240.0–1,314.0/	Whirlpools:	2
Draft (ft/m):	...................17.3/5.3		22.2–122.0	Self-Service Launderette:	...........Yes
Propulsion/Propellers: diesel (11,700kW)/2		Cabins (outside view):	148	Dedicated Cinema/Seats:	.......Yes/306
Passenger Decks:	6	Cabins (interior/no view):	0	Library:	..........................Yes

---

OVERALL SCORE: 1,669 (OUT OF A POSSIBLE 2,000 POINTS)

OVERVIEW. *Silver Wind* has a quite handsome profile, with a sloping stern reminiscent of an "Airstream" trailer. The size is just about ideal for personalized cruising in an elegant environment. The vertical cake-layer stacking of public rooms aft and the location of accommodation units forward ensures quiet cabins. There is a synthetic turf-covered walk-around promenade deck outdoors (this should be upgraded to teak or Bolidt), and a fairly spacious swimming pool and sunbathing deck, with teak/aluminum deck furniture (little "Silversea" touches such as cold towels, water sprays and fresh fruit provide poolside pampering on hot days).

Although the ship underwent a multi-million dollar makeover in 2003, another makeover is planned for 2009. Some parts show signs of ageing (the spa and shore tenders need replacing). The spacious interior is well-planned, with elegant decor and fine-quality soft furnishings throughout, accented by brass fittings (some of which is of sub-standard quality and shows blotchy patches in several places), fine woods and creative ceilings.

There is an excellent amount of space per passenger and there is no hint of a line anywhere in this unhurried environment. Before your cruise, good documentation is provided in a high-quality document wallet and presentation box. There is a useful internet center, a 24-hour library with hardback books, CD-ROMs and DVDs, and a cigar lounge.

An elegant, announcement-free onboard ambiance prevails, and there is no pressure, no hype, and an enthusiastic staff to pamper you, with a high ratio of Europeans. Insurance costs extra (it was included when Silversea Cruises first started). All drinks, gratuities and port taxes are included, and no further tipping anywhere on board is nec-

BERLITZ'S RATINGS

	Possible	Achieved
Ship	500	413
Accommodation	200	177
Food	400	333
Service	400	335
Entertainment	100	74
Cruise	400	337

essary (though it is not prohibited). This ship is ideal for those who enjoy spacious surroundings, excellent food, and some entertainment. It would be difficult not to have good cruise holiday aboard this ship, albeit at a fairly high price. The company's many international passengers like the ambiance, food, service and the staff, most of whom go out of their way to please.

Silversea Cruises has "all-inclusive" fares, including gratuities (they do not, however, include vintage wines, or massage, or other personal services), but they do include many things that are at extra cost compared aboard the ships of many other cruise lines. The passenger mix includes many nationalities, which makes for a more interesting experience, although most passengers are North American (children are sometimes seen aboard, although they are not really welcomed by most passengers). The onboard currency is the US dollar.

After 10 years, Silversea Cruises re-invented itself, with a more defined and refined product and an Italian Heritage theme. The past few years saw the delivery of a tarnished Silver(sea) service; however, I am pleased that this is now recognized and that Silversea Cruises is now polishing the silver again). Shuttle buses are provided in most ports of call, and all the little extras that passengers receive aboard this ship makes it an extremely pleasant cruise experience, in surroundings that are very comfortable and contemporary without being extravagant, with open seating dining and drinks included, cold canapés and hot hors d'oeuvres served in the bars in the pre-dinner cocktail hour, a captain's welcome aboard and farewell cocktail party and other niceties.

In 2002, Silversea Cruises introduced "Personalized Voyages" whereby you choose the port of embarkation and disembarkation and the length of cruise you want (minimum is five days). While this is a flexible feature, the onboard programming is already set, so you may be joining and leaving in the middle of a "normal" cruise.

Passenger niggles include the fact that some vibration is evident when bow thrusters or the anchors are used, particularly in the forward-most suites. The self-service launderette is poor and not large enough for longer cruises, when passengers like to wash their own small items.

Crew facilities are minimal, and so keeping consistency is difficult, because the crew turnover is quite high.

SUITABLE FOR: *Silver Wind* is best suited to discerning, well-traveled couples (typically over 50) who seek a small ship setting, with food approaching gourmet standards, and fine European-style service in surroundings that can best be described as bordering on the elegant and luxurious.

ACCOMMODATION. There are seven price grades. The all-outside suites (75 percent of which have fine private teak-wood-floor balconies) have convertible queen-to-twin beds and are nicely fitted out with just about everything one needs, including large floor-to-ceiling windows, large walk-in closets, dressing table, writing desk, stocked mini-bar/refrigerator (no charge), and fresh flowers. The marble floor bathrooms have a tub, fixed shower head (this is not as hygienic as a hand-held unit), single washbasin, and plenty of high-quality towels. Personalized stationery, bathrobes, and an array of Acqua di Parma bathroom amenities are provided in all suites. Stay in the Grand, Royal, Rossellini or Owner's Suite and you get unobtrusive butler service (butlers are certified by the Guild of Professional Butlers, London).

All suites have TV and VCR or DVD players (top-grade suites also have CD players). However, the walk-in closets don't actually provide much hanging space (particularly for such items as full-length dresses), and it would be better for the door to open outward instead of inward. The drawers themselves are poorly positioned, although several other drawers and storage areas are provided in the living area. Although the cabin insulation above and below each suite is good, the insulation between them is not (a privacy curtain installed between entry door and sleeping area would be useful), and light from the passageway leaks into the suite, making it hard to achieve a dark room.

The top grades of suites have teak balcony furniture, while all others have plastic furniture (but all balconies have teak floors). Suites with balconies on the lowest deck can suffer from sticky salt spray when the ship is moving, so the balconies need lots of cleaning. Each evening, the stewardesses bring plates of canapés to your suite – just right for a light bite with cocktails.

CUISINE. The main dining room (called, simply, "The Restaurant") provides open-seating dining in elegant sur-

roundings. It has an attractive arched gazebo center and a wavy ceiling design as its focal point, and is set with fine Limoges china and well-balanced Christofle silverware. Meals are served in an open seating, which means you can eat when you like (within the given dining room opening times), and with whom you like.

The cuisine/dining experience is good, with a choice of three dining salons. Standard table wines are included for lunch and dinner, but there is also a "connoisseur list" of premium wines at extra charge. All meals are now prepared as à la carte items, with almost none of the pre-preparation that existed previously (special orders are also possible).

An alternative dining salon, the intimate 24-seat La Saletta, adjacent to the main dining room, has dégustation menus that include dishes designed by Relais Châteaux Gourmands chefs for Silversea Cruises (the cuisine-oriented division of Relais & Châteaux) paired with selected wines. Reservations are required, and the per person extra cost is $30.

For more informal dining, there's La Terrazza for self-serve breakfast and lunch buffets. In the evening this room features Italian regional dishes and softer lighting, with both indoor and outdoors seating at teakwood tables and chairs.

There is a 24-hour in-cabin dining service; full course-by-course dinners are available, although the balcony tables in the standard suites are rather low for dining outdoors.

ENTERTAINMENT. The Showlounge is the venue for all entertainment events and some social functions. The room spans two decks and has a sloping floor; both banquette and individual seating are provided, with good sightlines from almost all seats.

Although Silversea Cruises places more emphasis on food than entertainment, what is provided is quite tasteful and not overbearing, as aboard some larger ships. A decent array of cabaret acts does the Silversea circuit, and small, colorful production shows have been reintroduced. Most of the cabaret acts provide intelligent entertainment.

Also, more emphasis is now placed on classical music ensembles. There is also a band, as well as several small musical units for live music in the evenings in The Bar, and the Panorama Lounge.

SPA/FITNESS. Although "The Spa at Silversea" facility is not large, it underwent a sea change in 2007, with redesigned, more welcoming decor, and an updated range of treatments and spa packages for both men and women. Massage and other body pampering treatments, facials, pedicures, and beauty salon treatments cost extra.

Facilities include a separate sauna for men and women, several treatment rooms, and a beauty salon. A separate gymnasium (formerly an observation lounge), located atop the ship, provides sea views.

Sky Wonder
★★★

Mid-Size Ship:	.46,392 tons	Passenger Decks:	.11
Lifestyle:	.Standard	Total Crew:	.550
Cruise Line:	.Pullmantur Cruises	Passengers	
Former Names:	.Pacific Sky,	(lower beds/all berths):	.1,200/1,550
	Sky Princess, Fairsky	Passenger Space Ratio	
Builder:	.C.N.I.M. (France)	(lower beds/all berths):	.38.6/34.3
Original Cost:	.$156 million	Crew/Passenger Ratio	
Entered Service:	.Mar 1984/Jun 2006	(lower beds/all berths):	.2.1/2.8
Registry:	.Spain	Navigation Officers:	.European
Length (ft/m):	.788.6/240.39	Cabins (total):	.600
Beam (ft/m):	.91.3/27.84	Size Range (sq ft/m):	.168.9–519.9/
Draft (ft/m):	.26.7/8.15		.15.7–48.3
Propulsion/Propellers:	.steam turbine	Cabins (outside view):	.385
	.(21,700 kW)/2	Cabins (interior/no view):	.215

Cabins (for one person):	.0
Cabins (with private balcony):	.10
Cabins (wheelchair accessible):	.10
Cabin Current:	.110 and 220 volts
Elevators:	.6
Casino (gaming tables):	.Yes
Slot Machines:	.Yes
Swimming Pools (outdoors):	.3
Swimming Pools (indoors):	.0
Whirlpools:	.1
Self-Service Launderette:	.Yes
Dedicated Cinema/Seats:	.Yes/283
Library:	.Yes

OVERALL SCORE: 1,246 (OUT OF A POSSIBLE 2,000 POINTS)

OVERVIEW. *Sky Wonder* is a well-designed vessel, with a large, swept-back funnel, although it has a sharply raked bow that is short. It is unusual in that it was the first cruise ship to have steam turbine machinery since Cunard Line's *Queen Elizabeth 2* debuted in 1969, which translates to very little vibration. The outdoors deck and sun-bathing space is not very good, but cushioned pads are at least provided for the sunloungers.

Inside the ship, the user-friendly layout makes it is easy to find your way around – good signage also helps. There is a decent enough array of public rooms, including some expansive shopping and duty-free outlets. There are nine bars/lounges, including a showlounge, sports bar, and an internet facility. An observation lounge, set atop the ship, is restful at night. The casino has a split configuration. Several lounges include a dance floor, live music, and for late-night cabaret acts. The ship also has its own dedicated cinema (something that few new ships seem to provide), complete with balcony level.

Families with children are well cared for; children also have their own area, which includes an outdoor splash pool, and a whole, brightly colored roomful of activities and fun things to play with. A team of children's counselors attends to the children and provides special activities daily.

This ship provides a reasonably well-balanced, pleasing cruise experience for the mature passenger, with plenty of space and little crowding. Spanish officers and an international dining staff help to create a friendly ambiance aboard this ship. The onboard currency is the euro.

All-inclusive (including all drinks) is what this ship is all about – so there's no signing for anything (unless it's an

BERLITZ'S RATINGS

	Possible	Achieved
Ship	500	331
Accommodation	200	139
Food	400	237
Service	400	230
Entertainment	100	62
Cruise	400	255

extra charge personal item such as a spa treatment). The outdoors promenade deck doesn't quite wrap around the front of the ship, but there is plenty of walking space nonetheless. Note that standing in line for embarkation, dis-embarkation, shore tenders and for self-serve buffet meals is an inevitable aspect of cruising aboard all large ships; this one is no exception.

SUITABLE FOR: *Sky Wonder* is best suited to young, and young-at-heart Spanish-speaking couples and singles seeking an all-inclusive cruise, and those who want a good basic getaway cruise aboard a ship that offers some good drinking places, lots of noise and good cheer, in fairly comfortable surroundings.

ACCOMMODATION. There are 11 grades (the price you pay will depend on the grade, location and size you choose): there are suites (including honeymoon suites), outside-view cabins and interior (no view) cabins.

Most of the cabins are quite spacious, comfortable, and well-appointed, with all the essentials and good-sized rectangular showers. There are, however, many interior (no view) cabins. The cabin walls and ceilings are plain and unappealing, and need some splashes of color.

The largest accommodation can be found in 10 suites on Lido Deck, all of which are named after famous resorts (Capri, Portofino, Estoril, Monaco, Malaga on the port side, and Antibes, Minorca, St. Tropez, San Remo, Amalfi on the starboard side). These are really fine living spaces, and provide extra comforts such as a mini-bar/refrigerator, walk-in closet, and a larger bathroom (with bathtub and shower), and a private (but narrow) balcony. All have a queen-sized bed, with the exception of Amalfi and Malaga, which have fixed twin beds.

There are 28 mini-suites, all of which have separate sleeping and living areas, with dressing table, sofa, coffee table and chairs, and mini-bar/refrigerator.

Many cabins have one or two additional upper berths, making them extremely cramped when occupied (storage of luggage can be a problem), but they are useful for families with children. All cabins suffer from inadequate sound-proofing, but all have a color television, and two lower beds. Note that cabins at the aft end of Aloha Deck may be subject to noise from the adjacent Children's Playroom.

CUISINE. There are two dining rooms, with the galley positioned between them, assigned according to the accommodation you choose. Both are non-smoking, brightly lit and have pleasant decor. There are two seatings (dinner is typically at 8pm or 10.15pm), and tables are for four, six or eight (there are no tables for two). The food is largely standard banquet fare, and a little repetitive; quality, flair and presentation could be better. The choice of salad items could be better, too, and the selection of desserts includes many canned items (cheap and cheerful). A "Buffet Magnifico" is featured once each cruise. The wine list includes a good variety of Spanish wines (but red wine glasses are small).

For casual daytime snacking, there is an al fresco self-serve buffet on deck. Other casual eateries include a Pizzeria, open 24 hours a day. There's also a café for fast food grilled items.

ENTERTAINMENT. Production shows and major cabaret acts are presented in the Showlounge, located at the forward end of Promenade Deck, with easy access from the forward stairway and lifts. Although it is a single-level room (most new cruise ships today have at least two levels for their showlounges), decent visibility can be had from most seats, following improvements that were made by the ship's previous owners, Princess Cruises.

SPA/FITNESS. The Spa is located on Sun Deck, and houses an L-shaped gymnasium (with starboard side ocean-view windows), and saunas, massage rooms (there aren't enough of them) and changing rooms for men and women. If you want to book spa treatments (massages, facials, pedicures, hair beautification), it is wise to do so as soon after you embark as possible, as the limited number of time slots do fill up quickly. There is a beauty salon, but it is located on a different deck. Outdoors on deck is a jogging track.

Spa/beauty treatments and fitness facilities are operated by a concession, and being aboard will give you an opportunity to try some body-pampering treatments. All treatments cost extra.

Spirit of '98
★★

Boutique Ship: . . . . .1,472 tons	Total Crew: 30	Cabins (with private balcony): 0
Lifestyle: . . . . .Standard	Passengers	Cabins (wheelchair accessible): 1
Cruise Line: . . . . .Cruise West	(lower beds/all berths): 96/96	Cabin Current: . . . . .110 volts
Former Names: . . . .*Pilgrim Belle,*	Passenger Space Ratio	Elevators: 1
Victorian Empress	(lower beds/all berths): 15.3/15.3	Casino (gaming tables): . . . . .No
Builder: . . . . . .Bender Shipbuilding (USA)	Crew/Passenger Ratio	Slot Machines: .No
Original Cost: .n/a	(lower beds/all berths): 3.2/3.2	Swimming Pools (outdoors): 0
Entered Service: 1984/1993	Navigation Officers: . . . . .American	Swimming Pools (indoors): 0
Registry: . . . . .USA	Cabins (total): 49	Whirlpools: 0
Length (ft/m): 192.0/58.2	Size Range (sq ft/m): 80.0–510.0/	Self-Service Launderette: . . . . .No
Beam (ft/m): 40.0/12.1	7.4–47.3	Dedicated Cinema/Seats: . . . . .No
Draft (ft/m): 9.3/2.8	Cabins (outside view): 49	Library: . . . . .Some bookshelves
Propulsion/Propellers: diesel/1	Cabins (interior/no view): 0	
Passenger Decks: 4	Cabins (for one person): 0	

OVERALL SCORE: 946 (OUT OF A POSSIBLE 2,000 POINTS)

OVERVIEW. *Spirit of '98* is a distinctive-looking vessel built to resemble a late 1800s coastal cruising vessel. It is particularly suited to in-depth glacier spotting, and for close-in cruising along the coastline of Alaska. There is only one public room – the Grand Salon, although it is large. You are much closer to nature aboard a small cruise vessel such as this. There are no lines, no loud rap and rock music, no shows, no casino. There is a viewing area outdoors right at the ship's bow. There is an "open bridge" policy, and the company is concerned about protecting the natural environment.

The dress code is absolutely casual (not even a jacket for men, and no ties, please). However, do take comfortable walking shoes, as well as photographic materials for wildlife spotting. Smoking is permitted only on the outside decks. All tips are pooled by all staff, using the amounts recommended in the cruise line's brochure of $10 per passenger, per day (this is high for the services offered). The cruising areas are Alaska, the Pacific Northwest, and California's wine country. The onboard currency is the US dollar.

This ship is very small. There is an almost constant throbbing from the diesel engines/generator. There is no doctor on board (except for cruises in the Sea of Cortes). There are no cushioned pads for the sunloungers.

SUITABLE FOR: *Spirit of '98* is best suited to couples and single travelers (mostly over 60) who enjoy nature and wildlife up close and personal. It would particularly suit those seeking an all-American crew and cruise experience, and those who don't need the kind of entertainment or vapid parlor games that some large ships provide.

BERLITZ'S RATINGS

	Possible	Achieved
Ship	500	196
Accommodation	200	118
Food	400	189
Service	400	212
Entertainment	n/a	n/a
Cruise	500	231

ACCOMMODATION. There are six grades of cabin. The Owner's Suite is the largest accommodation in the Cruise West fleet, and has large picture windows on three sides. It consists of two rooms; a lounge/living room with game table, TV/VCR, refrigerator and fully stocked complimentary bar. There is a separate bedroom with a king-sized bed, and large bathroom with Jacuzzi tub.

There are also four irregular-shaped deluxe cabins at the front of the vessel, with decent closet space, a queen-sized bed (or twin beds that convert to a double bed), and a bathroom with a separate shower enclosure. Two of the cabins also have an extra sofa bed. The other cabins are quite small, but are reasonably comfortable, and have a large picture window. While a few cabins have queen-sized or double beds, most have single beds that cannot be moved together. Each cabin has its own private bathroom, although these really are tiny, and have a wall-mounted shower. There is no room service for food or snack items.

CUISINE. The Klondyke Dining Room, decorated in the style of 100 years ago, is elegant. The cuisine is decidedly plain and simple (though tasty) American fare. Expect lots of seafood. The ingredients are mostly fresh, and local. Wine and full bar services are provided.

ENTERTAINMENT. There is no formal entertainment, although dinner and after-dinner conversation with fellow passengers in the ship's lounge/bar really constitutes the entertainment each evening.

SPA/FITNESS. There are no spa or fitness facilities.

Spirit of Adventure
★★★

Small Ship:	9,570 tons	Passenger Decks:	.8
Lifestyle:	Standard	Total Crew:	.168
Cruise Line:	Spirit of Adventure/	Passengers	
	Saga Cruises	(lower beds/all berths):	.352/352
Former Names:Berlin, Princess Mahsuri, Berlin		Passenger Space Ratio	
Builder:	Howaldtswerke Deutsche Werft	(lower beds/all berths):	.27.1/27.1
	(Germany)	Crew/Passenger Ratio	
Original Cost:	n/a	(lower beds/all berths):	.2.0/2.0
Entered Service:	June 1980/Mar 2006	Navigation Officers:	British
Registry:	The Bahamas	Cabins (total):	.206
Length (ft/m):	457.0/139.3	Size Range (sq ft/m):	.92.5–191.6/8.6–17.8
Beam (ft/m):	57.5/17.52	Cabins (outside view):	.174
Draft (ft/m):	15.7/4.8	Cabins (interior/no view):	.32
Propulsion/Propellers:	diesel (7,060kW)/2	Cabins (for one person):	.60

Cabins (with private balcony):	.0
Cabins (wheelchair accessible):	.1
Cabin Current:	.220 volts
Elevators:	.1
Casino (gaming tables):	.No
Slot Machines:	.No
Swimming Pools (outdoors):	.1
Swimming Pools (indoors):	.1
Whirlpools:	.0
Self-Service Launderette:	.Yes
Dedicated Cinema/Seats:	.No
Library:	.Yes

OVERALL SCORE: 1,249 (OUT OF A POSSIBLE 2,000 POINTS)

OVERVIEW. *Spirit of Adventure,* a somewhat angular ship, has an all-white hull (with blue line between hull and superstructure), a balanced profile with buff-colored funnel and black top, and an ice-strengthened hull. As *Berlin,* the ship was featured for many years in the long running German TV show *Traumschiff* (Dream Ship).

In 1986 the ship was "chopped and stretched" and a 20-meter mid-section was added. Saga Holidays purchased it in April 2005, refurbished it for warm-weather cruising, and assigned it to sister company, Spirit of Adventure. Despite its small size, it is a good sea ship and rides well.

The interiors are crisp, contemporary and well-appointed, with tasteful European decor and furnishings. The Library is a fine room, with a 3,000-book library/DVD collection (open 24 hours), plus internet access at four computer stations.

The swimming pool, located aft, is tiny (it's really just a "dip" pool). The surrounding open-deck and sunbathing space is cramped, because it's in the same area as the outdoor seating for The Verandah dining venue. However, a reasonable amount of open-deck sunbathing space can be found on the uppermost deck, forward of the mast.

This well-run (soft-adventure) ship provides a destination-intensive fly-cruise experience in a comfortable, well maintained, intimate ship for those who seek to explore and learn about less visited places, and who do not need constant entertainment. Itineraries include Europe, the Aegean Sea and Black Sea, Indian Ocean, Southeast Asia, and Antarctica.

The value for money is good. Insurance and staff gratuities are included in the cruise fare, as are scheduled or

BERLITZ'S RATINGS

	Possible	Achieved
Ship	500	275
Accommodation	200	109
Food	400	276
Service	400	251
Entertainment	n/a	n/a
Cruise	500	338

charter flights (plus all airport fees and taxes), visas (for full UK-resident British citizens), port taxes, luggage handling, some shore excursions (others are available at extra cost), and lectures. Additionally, mountain bikes are available for anyone wanting to explore independently (or on escorted rides). The onboard currency is the British pound.

While the ship is not the latest, and doesn't have any cabins with balconies, its attention to passenger care, and the company's meet-and-greet and transfer services are extremely good. Shuttle buses are also provided in many ports of call. Onboard wines and drinks prices are very low in comparison with almost all other cruise lines.

Note that there is only one elevator – it doesn't go to the two topmost decks or to the Spa Aquarius on the lowermost deck – and the passenger accommodation hallways are rather narrow. However, it's the Filippino hotel crew that makes this ship so popular with passengers. It's also the manner in which Saga's meet-and-greet and passenger handling systems work, supplying the kind of care and attention many cruisle lines seem to have forgotten about.

SUITABLE FOR: *Spirit of Adventure* is best suited to couples and single travelers over 21 who seek a holiday in a traditional ship setting that is unpretentious, yet provides a decent standard of accommodation, food and friendly service, as well as some interesting itineraries, destinations, and shore programs (many of which are included).

ACCOMMODATION. There are four types: Superior Suite, Junior Suite, Standard outside-view and interior (no view) cabins, in 20 price categories (12 for double occupancy and eight for single occupancy – a wide range). Most of the cabins are small by today's standards, but they are comfortable enough for short cruises. There are no balcony cabins. While most cabins have fixed twin beds that cannot be moved together (over 60 cabins do have a double bed), there are also many cabins for single occupancy (unlike most large ships today). The bathrooms have showers but no tubs, and storage space for toiletries is quite limited. All cabins have a refrigerator, TV/DVD player and a pair of binoculars. A range of Molton Brown personal toiletry items is provided for all accommodation grades. Note that cabins nearest the engine room do suffer from more noise, otherwise the cabins are quiet, although the insulation is actually rather poor.

The largest accommodation can be found in two Owner's Suites (Rhapsody and Sonata); both have a double bed, lounge area, more closet and drawer space, and larger bathroom.

Regardless of which accommodation is chosen, an extensive 24-hour room service menu is available.

The ships's 220-volt electricity system uses European-style two-pin round sockets, so UK passengers will need to bring converters.

CUISINE. The charming dining room has large, ocean-view picture windows and dark wood accents. There are tables for four, six, and dining is in an open seating arrangement. Regional specialties are featured, plus an international cuisine that includes many traditional British favorites. The chef often goes ashore in ports of call to buy fresh local fish and produce when possible.

Casual meals (breakfast, lunch and dinner) can be taken in The Verandah, a self-serve buffet-style venue with both indoor and outdoor seating areas; a self-help beverage station is open 24 hours a day. A good variety of well prepared and presented items is the norm. There's also 24-hour room service.

ENTERTAINMENT. The Sirocco Lounge is a single-level venue designed for cabaret performances, but used principally for musical concerts, destination and specialist subject lectures and guest speakers, and other social gatherings. The Yacht Club Lounge/Bar is the evening/late-night gathering place for pub-style entertainment and passenger participation events.

SPA/FITNESS. Spa Aquarius is an indoor health spa, including a shallow swimming pool, small fitness area, massage room, sauna and relaxation room – deep inside the ship on a lower deck (there is no elevator access). A beauty salon is in a separate location, adjacent to the Library. Some fitness classes are free, while others (such as Pilates/Yoga) incur a £5 charge. Sample treatment prices: Hot Stones Massage (£60 for 75 minutes); Combination Seaweed Wrap and Body Massage (£65 for 90 minutes); Well-Being Full Body Massage (£45 for 50 minutes); Facials (£42–£68)

Four of the ships operated by Cruise West (*Spirit of Alaska, Spirit of Columbia, Spirit of Discovery, Spirit of Endeavour*) all are similar in terms of size, facilities, and the onboard dining and cruise experience, and so we have combined our assessment.

Spirit of Alaska
★★

OVERVIEW. These little ships are all about eco-tourism, and can take you close to nature and wildlife for an up-close experience. Cruising aboard these ships is all about simple pleasures and being with nature, especially as they're not allowed out into the big seas and oceans of the world.

Public rooms consist of a lounge that is a multi-functional space for meetings (plus a couple of bookcases with books about nature and wildlife), and a dining room. There are no cruise directors; instead, naturalists and other specialists give talks and act as leaders on shore excursions.

The staff aboard these small ships have to be multi-flexible, doing a little of this and a little of that. The result is that, although service comes with a smile, it rarely comes with finesse or correctness. Small ship service can be compared to that provided by B&B establishments ashore – homely but not perect. The captains have the flexibility to deviate to take in particular areas of interest.

The dress code is absolutely casual (not even a jacket for men, and no ties, please). However, do take comfortable walking shoes, as well as photographic materials for wildlife spotting. Smoking is permitted only on the outside decks. All tips are pooled by all staff, using the amounts recommended in the cruise line's brochure of $10 per passenger, per day (this is high for the services offered). The cruising areas are Alaska, the Pacific Northwest, and California's wine country. The onboard currency is the US dollar.

Passenger gripes: Because the ships are small, there is an almost constant throbbing from the diesel engines/generator. There is no doctor on board (except for cruises in the Sea of Cortes), and there are no cushioned pads for the deck lounge chairs.

SUITABLE FOR: These small ships are best suited to couples and single travelers (mostly over 60) who enjoy nature and wildlife up close and personal. It would particularly suit those seeking an all-American crew and cruise experience, and those who don't need the kind of entertainment large ships provide.

DINING. All meals are taken in the dining room at a set time (except for Continental breakfast, which is typically provided in the lounge), which tends to be early, which means it's regimented and not at all flexible. Don't expect outstanding cuisine (the galley is small, and the range of food items very limited, except for fresh local fish and seafood, which is normally very good); it's really simple Americana fare. As for wines, well, the choice is extremely limited (as in family restaurants on land).

ACCOMMODATION. There are several cabin categories, depending on the ship. All are small when compared to most cruise ships, but they are basically comfortable, and each cabin has a large picture window (a few cabins have portholes) and a (very) small clothes closet. A few cabins have double beds, but most have single beds that cannot be moved together (a few cabins may also have upper/lower berths instead of beds). Each has its own little bathroom, with a wall-mounted shower. Each cabin also has a small washbasin. There is no room service for food or snack items.

Bulky clothing for the outdoors is necessary in Alaska, but there's almost no storage space for it in the tiny, utilitarian cabins aboard these small ships.

ENTERTAINMENT. Dinner and after-dinner conversation with fellow passengers in the ship's lounge/bar constitutes the entertainment each evening.

SPA/FITNESS. There are no spa or fitness facilities

Boutique Ship:	.97 tons
Lifestyle:	.Standard
Cruise Line:	.Cruise West
Former Names:	.Pacific Northwest Explorer
Builder:	.Blount Marine (USA)
Original Cost:	.n/a
Entered Service:	.1980/1991
Registry:	.USA
Length (ft/m):	.143.0/43.5
Beam (ft/m):	.28.5/8.6
Draft (ft/m):	.7.5/2.2
Propulsion/Propellers:	.diesel/1
Passenger Decks:	.4
Total Crew:	.20
Passengers (lower beds/all berths):	.78/78
Passenger Space Ratio (lower beds/all berths):	.6.7/6.7
Crew/Passenger Ratio (lower beds/all berths):	.3.9
Navigation Officers:	.American
Cabins (total):	.39
Size Range (sq ft/m):	.80–128/7.4–11.6
Cabins (outside view):	.27
Cabins (interior/no view):	.12
Cabins (for one person):	.0
Cabins (with private balcony):	.0
Cabins (wheelchair accessible):	.0
Cabin Current:	.110 volts
Elevators:	.0
Casino (gaming tables):	.No
Slot Machines:	.No
Swimming Pools (outdoors):	.0
Swimming Pools (indoors):	.0
Whirlpools:	.0
Self-Service Launderette:	.0
Dedicated Cinema/Seats:	.No
Library:	.Some bookshelves

OVERALL SCORE: 920

BERLITZ'S RATINGS		
	Possible	Achieved
Ship	500	173
Accommodation	200	83
Food	400	199
Service	400	210
Entertainment	n/a	n/a
Cruise	500	255

Spirit of Columbia
★★

Boutique Ship:	.514 tons
Lifestyle:	Standard
Cruise Line:	Cruise West
Former Names:	*New Shoreham II*
Builder:	Blount Marine (USA)
Original Cost:	n/a
Entered Service:	1979/1995
Registry:	USA
Length (ft/m):	143.0/43.5
Beam (ft/m):	28.0/8.5
Draft (ft/m):	6.5/1.9
Propulsion/Propellers:	diesel/1
Passenger Decks:	4
Total Crew:	20
Passengers	
(lower beds/all berths):	78/82
Passenger Space Ratio	
(lower beds/all berths):	6.5/6.5
Crew/Passenger Ratio	
(lower beds/all berths):	3.9/4.1
Navigation Officers:	American
Cabins (total):	39
Size Range (sq ft/m):	.80–121.0/7.4–11.2
Cabins (outside view):	27
Cabins (interior/no view):	12
Cabins (for one person):	0
Cabins (with private balcony):	0
Cabins (wheelchair accessible):	0
Cabin Current:	110 volts
Elevators:	0
Casino (gaming tables):	No
Slot Machines:	No
Swimming Pools (outdoors):	0
Swimming Pools (indoors):	0
Whirlpools:	0
Self-Service Launderette:	0
Dedicated Cinema/Seats:	No
Library:	Some bookshelves

OVERALL SCORE: 919

BERLITZ'S RATINGS

	Possible	Achieved
Ship	500	174
Accommodation	200	82
Food	400	199
Service	400	209
Entertainment	n/a	n/a
Cruise	500	255

Spirit of Discovery
★★

Boutique Ship:	.94 tons
Lifestyle:	Standard
Cruise Line:	Cruise West
Former Names:	*Independence, Columbia*
Builder:	Blount Marine (USA)
Original Cost:	n/a
Entered Service:	1982/1992
Registry:	USA
Length (ft/m):	166.0/50.5
Beam (ft/m):	37.0/11.2
Draft (ft/m):	7.5/2.2
Propulsion/Propellers:	diesel/1
Passenger Decks:	3
Total Crew:	20
Passengers	
(lower beds/all berths):	84/84
Passenger Space Ratio	
(lower beds/all berths):	10.8/10.8
Crew/Passenger Ratio	
(lower beds/all berths):	4.2/4.2
Navigation Officers:	American
Cabins (total):	43
Size Range (sq ft/m):	.64–126.0/5.9–11.7
Cabins (outside view):	43
Cabins (interior/no view):	0
Cabins (for one person):	2
Cabins (with private balcony):	0
Cabins (wheelchair accessible):	0
Cabin Current:	110 volts
Elevators:	0
Casino (gaming tables):	No
Slot Machines:	No
Swimming Pools (outdoors):	0
Swimming Pools (indoors):	0
Whirlpools:	0
Self-Service Launderette:	No
Dedicated Cinema/Seats:	No
Library:	Some bookshelves

OVERALL SCORE: 920

BERLITZ'S RATINGS

	Possible	Achieved
Ship	500	175
Accommodation	200	82
Food	400	199
Service	400	209
Entertainment	n/a	n/a
Cruise	500	255

Spirit of Endeavour
★★

Boutique Ship:	1,425 tons
Lifestyle:	Standard
Cruise Line:	Cruise West
Former Names:	*Pacific Northwest Explorer*
Builder:	Blount Marine (USA)
Original Cost:	n/a
Entered Service:	1980/1991
Registry:	USA
Length (ft/m):	143.0/43.5
Beam (ft/m):	28.5/8.6
Draft (ft/m):	7.5/2.2
Propulsion/Propellers:	diesel/1
Passenger Decks:	4
Total Crew:	20
Passengers	
(lower beds/all berths):	78/78
Passenger Space Ratio	
(lower beds/all berths):	18.2/18.2
Crew/Passenger Ratio	
(lower beds/all berths):	3.9
Navigation Officers:	American
Cabins (total):	39
Size Range (sq ft/m):	.80–128/7.4–11.6
Cabins (outside view):	27
Cabins (interior/no view):	12
Cabins (for one person):	0
Cabins (with private balcony):	0
Cabins (wheelchair accessible):	0
Cabin Current:	110 volts
Elevators:	0
Casino (gaming tables):	No
Slot Machines:	No
Swimming Pools (outdoors):	0
Swimming Pools (indoors):	0
Whirlpools:	0
Self-Service Launderette:	0
Dedicated Cinema/Seats:	No
Library:	Some bookshelves

OVERALL SCORE: 920

BERLITZ'S RATINGS

	Possible	Achieved
Ship	500	175
Accommodation	200	82
Food	400	199
Service	400	209
Entertainment	n/a	n/a
Cruise	500	255

Spirit of Glacier Bay
★★

Boutique Ship: ....1,471 tons	Total Crew: 32	Cabins (with private balcony): 0
Lifestyle: ....Standard	Passengers	Cabins (wheelchair accessible): 0
Cruise Line: ....Cruise West	(lower beds/all berths): 102/102	Cabin Current: ....110 volts
Former Names: ....*Spirit of Nantucket,*	Passenger Space Ratio	Elevators: 0
Nantucket Clipper	(lower beds/all berths): 14.4/14.4	Casino (gaming tables): ....No
Builder: ....Jeffboat (USA)	Crew/Passenger Ratio	Slot Machines: ....No
Original Cost: ....$9 million	(lower beds/all berths): 3.1/3.1	Swimming Pools (outdoors): 0
Entered Service: ....Dec 1984/May 2008	Navigation Officers: ....American	Swimming Pools (indoors): 0
Registry: ....USA	Cabins (total): 51	Whirlpools: 0
Length (ft/m): 207.0/63.00	Size Range (sq ft/m): 120.5–137.7/	Self-Service Launderette: ....No
Beam (ft/m): 37.0/11.20	11.2–12.8	Dedicated Cinema/Seats: ....No
Draft (ft/m): 8.0/2.40	Cabins (outside view): 51	Library: ....Yes
Propulsion/Propellers: ....diesel (700 kW)/2	Cabins (interior/no view): 0	
Passenger Decks: 4	Cabins (for one person): 0	

OVERALL SCORE: 948 (OUT OF A POSSIBLE 2,000 POINTS)

OVERVIEW. This small, shallow draft, American-registered ship, renamed in 2008, was built for coastal and inland cruises and is very maneuverable. It has been quite well maintained, although it is now showing signs of aging, and some serious attention is needed. There is a wrap-around teakwood walking deck outdoors.

The extremely high-density ship has only two public rooms: the dining room, and an observation lounge. Passengers can visit the bridge at any time. This ship is not recommended for night owls. Although passengers are typically over 60, there is no elevator.

The service is provided by young, friendly all-American college-age types. This is most definitely an "Americana" experience for those seeking particularly to learn more about the coastal ports around the USA, including Alaska. The ship has a casual, unstructured lifestyle, rather like a small (but certainly not luxurious) country club afloat. This should not be compared with big-ship ocean cruising.

Specialist lecturers are part of every cruise. These highlight the learning experience that is an essential part of cruising with Cruise West. As the ship is often in coastal destinations, a few bicycles would be a welcome addition for many passengers. There is a no-smoking policy for all interior areas. The onboard currency is the US dollar.

The engine noise level is high when the ship is underway. The per diem price is steep for what you get, and the air fare is extra.

SUITABLE FOR: *Spirit of Glacier Bay* is best suited to couples and single travelers who enjoy nature and wildlife up close and personal, and who would not dream of cruising in

BERLITZ'S RATINGS		
	Possible	Achieved
Ship	500	199
Accommodation	200	76
Food	400	209
Service	400	231
Entertainment	n/a	n/a
Cruise	500	233

the mainstream sense, aboard ships with large numbers of people. This is for outdoors types who don't need entertainment or mindless parlor games, but do want an all-American cruise experience.

ACCOMMODATION. There are four grades of all-outside cabins. All are extremely small and equipped in a very basic manner (think mobile home rather than cruise ships or hotels). They are fairly tastefully furnished, with wood-accented trim and good sound insulation. The windows are fixed and cannot be opened.

Honeymooners and lovers should note that beds are of the twin variety, and are bolted to the deck and wall.

Bathrooms are cramped and the shower head is fixed, but, thoughtfully, a night-light is provided. There's little space for personal toiletries. No cabins have personal balconies.

CUISINE. The dining room is warm and inviting, and has large picture windows. There is one seating, and you can sit with whomever you wish. There are no tables for two. The ship has simple and plain American cuisine that is quite tasty, although the menu choice is limited and the portions are small. The chefs are trained by the Culinary Institute of America, and all ingredients are fresh. The chocolate chip cookies are popular and are served at various times, typically in the lounge.

ENTERTAINMENT. The main entertainment is dinner and after-dinner conversation with fellow passengers.

SPA/FITNESS. No facilities aboard this very small vessel.

Spirit of Oceanus
★★★

Boutique Ship: . . . . .4,200 tons	Passenger Decks: 5	Cabins (for one person): 0
Lifestyle: . . . . .Standard	Total Crew: 55	Cabins (with private balcony): 12
Cruise Line: . . . . .Cruise West	Passengers	Cabins (wheelchair accessible): 0
Former Names: . . . .*MegaStar Sagittarius,*	(lower beds/all berths): 114/127	Cabin Current: . . . . .110 volts
Sun Viva, Renaissance Five	Passenger Space Ratio	Dining Rooms: .1
Builder: . . . . .Nuovi Cantieri Apuania	(lower beds/all berths): 37.5/33.0	Elevators: 1
(Italy)	Crew/Passenger Ratio	Casino (gaming tables): . . . . .No
Entered Service: 1991/2001	(lower beds/all berths): 2.0/4.7	Slot Machines: .No
Registry: . . . . .The Bahamas	Navigation Officers: . . . . .American	Swimming Pools (outdoors): 1
Length (ft/m): 294.5/89.7	Cabins (total): 57	Swimming Pools (indoors): 0
Beam (ft/m): 50.1/15.30	Size Range (sq ft/m): 215.0–353.0/	Whirlpools: 1
Draft (ft/m): 13.2/4.05	20.0–32.7	Self-Service Launderette: . . . . .No
Propulsion/Propellers: . . . . .diesel	Cabins (outside view): 57	Dedicated Cinema/Seats: . . . . .No
(5,000kW)/2	Cabins (interior/no view): 0	Library: . . . . .Yes

OVERALL SCORE: 1,218 (OUT OF A POSSIBLE 2,000 POINTS)

OVERVIEW. *Spirit of Oceanus* has a contemporary exterior, a private yacht-like look and handsome styling with twin, flared funnels. The navigation bridge is a well-rounded half-moon design. There is a teakwood promenade deck outdoors, and a reasonable amount of open deck and sunbathing space. The deck furniture is teak and the sunloungers have thick cushioned pads. There is a teakwood water sports platform at the stern of the ship (not used in Alaska), plus a number of Zodiac inflatable rubber landing craft. Snorkeling gear is provided (not used in Alaska).

The main lounge, the focal point for social activities, has six pillars that destroy sightlines to the small stage area. There is a very small book and video library.

The ship was acquired by Cruise West in 2001 and is the only ocean-going vessel in its fleet. It cruises Alaska and British Columbia in summer, and sails to Tahiti, the Fijian Islands and other Pacific Ocean itineraries in winter. The onboard currency is the US dollar.

SUITABLE FOR: *Spirit of Oceanus* is best suited to couples and single travelers who enjoy nature and wildlife up close in a contemporary small-ship setting, and who would not dream of cruising in the mainstream sense aboard ships with large numbers of people.

ACCOMMODATION. There are six price categories. Fine all-outside-view cabins (called "suites" in the brochure) combine highly polished imitation rosewood paneling with lots of mirrors, and fine, hand-crafted Italian furniture. All suites have twin beds that can convert to a queen-sized bed, a sit-

BERLITZ'S RATINGS		
	Possible	Achieved
Ship	500	339
Accommodation	200	150
Food	400	211
Service	400	237
Entertainment	n/a	n/a
Cruise	500	281

ting area with three-person sofa, one individual chair, coffee table, mini-bar/refrigerator (stocked with juices and bottled water), TV/VCR, direct-dial satellite telephone, and a bowl of fresh fruit on embarkation day. While closet space is good, space for stowing luggage is tight, and there is little drawer space. There are no music channels in the cabins, and there is no switch to turn off announcements in your cabin.

The marble bathrooms are compact units that have showers (no bathrooms have a tub) with fold-down (plastic) seat, real teakwood floor, marble vanity, large mirror, recessed towel rail , and built-in hairdryer. There is a high "lip" into the bathroom.

CUISINE. The Restaurant, which has an open-seating policy, is bright, elegant, welcoming, and non-smoking. It is on the lowest deck and has portholes rather than windows, due to international maritime construction and insurance regulations. There are tables for two, four, six, or eight. Dinners are normally sit-down affairs, although, depending on the itinerary and length of cruise, there could be an occasional buffet. Breakfast and lunch are typically self-serve buffets and can be taken at the poolside (weather permitting), in your cabin, or in the restaurant.

ENTERTAINMENT. There is no formal entertainment, so dinner and after-dinner conversation with fellow passengers in the ship's lounge/bar really constitutes the entertainment each evening.

SPA/FITNESS. Small fitness center. Massage is available.

Spirit of Yorktown
★★

Boutique Ship: . . . . .2,354 tons	Total Crew: 40	Cabins (for one person): 0
Lifestyle: . . . . .Standard	Passengers	Cabins (with private balcony): 0
Cruise Line: . . . . .Cruise West	(lower beds/all berths): 138/138	Cabins (wheelchair accessible): 0
Former Names: . . . .*Yorktown Clipper*	Passenger Space Ratio	Cabin Current: . . . . .110 volts
Builder: . . . .First Coast Shipbuilding (USA)	(lower beds/all berths): 17.0/17.0	Elevators: 0
Original Cost: . . . .$12 million	Crew/Passenger Ratio	Casino (gaming tables): . . . . .No
Entered Service: . . . . .Apr 1988	(lower beds/all berths): 3.4/3.4	Slot Machines: .No
Registry: . . . . .USA	Navigation Officers: . . . . .American	Swimming Pools (outdoors): 0
Length (ft/m): 257.0/78.30	Cabins (total): .69	Swimming Pools (indoors): 0
Beam (ft/m): 43.0/13.10	Size Range (sq ft/m): 121.0–138.0/	Whirlpools: 0
Draft (ft/m): 8.0/2.43	11.2–12.8	Self-Service Launderette: . . . . .No
Propulsion/Propellers: .diesel (1,044kW)/2	Cabins (outside view): 69	Dedicated Cinema/Seats: . . . . .No
Passenger Decks: 4	Cabins (interior/no view): 0	Library: . . . . .Yes

BERLITZ'S OVERALL SCORE: 949 (OUT OF A POSSIBLE 2,000 POINTS)

OVERVIEW. *Yorktown Clipper* was built specifically to operate coastal and inland waterway cruises. The draft is small, and the ship has good maneuverability, and has been quite well maintained since new, although it is showing signs of wear and tear. There is a teakwood outdoor sun deck. Inflatable rubber Zodiac craft are used for close-in shore excursions.

Inside, there is a glass-walled observation lounge (the ship's principal public room). This ship offers a decidedly American experience for those seeking to learn more about the coastal ports around the USA during the summer months, while Caribbean cruises are operated in winter.

The lifestyle is casual and unregimented – rather like a small, congenial country club. There are always one or two lecturers aboard, which enhances the learning experience. The price, however, is very high for what you get when compared to many other ships, and the air fare is extra. There is a no-smoking policy throughout all interior areas.

This is a high-density ship, with only two public rooms: a dining room and a lounge. The engine noise level is high when the ship is underway. Although there is a wrap-around teakwood walking deck outdoors, it is quite narrow. The per diem price is steep, and the air fare is extra. There is no elevator (which can be a disadvantage for older passengers).

SUITABLE FOR: The vessel is best suited to couples and single travelers who enjoy nature and wildlife at close range. This is for outdoors types who don't need constant entertainment, but do want an all-American cruise experience. The onboard currency is the US dollar.

BERLITZ'S RATINGS

	Possible	Achieved
Ship	500	200
Accommodation	200	76
Food	400	209
Service	400	231
Entertainment	n/a	n/a
Cruise	500	233

ACCOMMODATION. The all-outside cabins are all quite small (think mobile home, not cruise ship), but, with lots of wood-accented trim and restful colors, they are marginally comfortable and tastefully furnished. There are no cabins with private balconies, and the fixed windows cannot be opened. The bathrooms, too, are small, with little space for toiletries, but a night-light is provided, so you don't have to turn on bright lights in the middle of the night – a thoughtful touch. Fixed shower heads are provided (making it difficult to wash thoroughly). There is no room service for food and beverage items, as found aboard larger ships.

CUISINE. The dining room is warm and fairly inviting and has large picture windows, although there are no tables for two. There is one open seating, so you can dine with whom you wish. The service is provided by a young, all-American, mid-western team, whose friendly approach makes up for a lack of finesse.

The cuisine is generally of a good quality, made from locally purchased fresh ingredients. There is little menu choice, but the food provided is nicely presented. There is an adequate but very limited selection of breads and fruits, and the wine list is generally limited to American wines.

ENTERTAINMENT. There is no formal entertainment. Dinner and after-dinner conversation with fellow passengers in the ship's lounge/bar really constitute the main diversion each evening.

SPA/FITNESS. No facilities are provided.

Splendour of the Seas
★★★★

Large Resort Ship: ....69,130 tons	Passenger Decks:..................11	Cabins (for one person): 0
Lifestyle: ....Standard	Total Crew: 720	Cabins (with private balcony): 231
Cruise Line: ....Royal Caribbean	Passengers	Cabins (wheelchair accessible): 17
International	(lower beds/all berths): 1,804/2,064	Cabin Current: ....110 and 220 volts
Former Names: ....none	Passenger Space Ratio	Elevators: 11
Builder: ....Chantiers de l'Atlantique	(lower beds/all berths): 38.3/33.4	Casino (gaming tables): ....Yes
(France)	Crew/Passenger Ratio	Slot Machines: ....Yes
Original Cost: ....$325 million	(lower beds/all berths): 2.5/2.8	Swimming Pools (outdoors): 2
Entered Service: ....Mar 1996	Navigation Officers: ....Norwegian	(1 with sliding roof)
Registry: ....The Bahamas	Cabins (total): 902	Swimming Pools (indoors): 0
Length (ft/m): 867.0/264.2	Size Range (sq ft/m): 137.7–1,147.4/	Whirlpools: 4
Beam (ft/m): 105.0/32.0	12.8–106.6	Self-Service Launderette: ....No
Draft (ft/m): 24.5/7.3	Cabins (outside view): 575	Dedicated Cinema/Seats: ....No
Propulsion/Propellers: diesel(40,200kW)/2	Cabins (interior/no view): 327	Library: ....Yes

OVERALL SCORE: 1,499 (OUT OF A POSSIBLE 2,000 POINTS)

OVERVIEW. *Splendour of the Seas* (sister to *Legend of the Seas*) has a contemporary profile that looks somewhat unbalanced (although it grows on you), and does have a nicely tiered stern. The pool deck amidships overhangs the hull to provide an extremely wide deck, while still allowing the ship to navigate the Panama Canal. With engines placed amidships, there is little noise and no noticeable vibration, and the ship has an operating speed of up to 24 knots.

The interior decor is very colorful, but perhaps a little too glitzy for European tastes. The outside light is brought inside in many places, with an extensive amount of glass area that provides contact with sea and air (more than 2 acres/8,000 sq. meters of glass). There's an innovative single-level sliding glass roof (not a magrodome) over the more formal setting of one of two swimming pools, providing a large, multi-activity, all-weather indoor/outdoor area, called the Solarium. The glass roof provides shelter for the Roman-style pool and adjacent health and fitness facilities (which are superb) and slides aft to cover the miniature golf course when required (both cannot be covered at the same time, however).

Golfers might enjoy the 18-hole, 6,000 sq.-ft (557 sq.-meter) miniature golf course, with the topography of a real golf course, complete with trees, foliage, grass, bridges, water hazards, and lighting for play at night. The holes are 155–230 sq. ft. (14–21 sq. meters).

Inside, two full entertainment decks are sandwiched between five decks full of cabins. The tiered and balconied showlounge, which covers two decks, is expansive and has excellent sightlines, and very comfortable seats. Several large-scale production shows are provided here, and the orchestra

BERLITZ'S RATINGS

	Possible	Achieved
Ship	500	425
Accommodation	200	163
Food	400	242
Service	400	299
Entertainment	100	78
Cruise	400	292

pit can be raised or lowered as required. A multi-tiered seven-deck-high atrium lobby, complete with a huge stainless steel sculpture, connects with the impressive Viking Crown Lounge via glass-walled elevators. The casino is really expansive, overly glitzy and absolutely packed. The library, outside of which is a bust of Shakespeare, is a fine facility, and has more than 2,000 books.

The casino could be somewhat disorienting, with its mirrored walls and lights flashing everywhere, although it is no different to those found in Las Vegas gaming halls. There is, sadly, no separate cinema. As with any large ship, you can expect to find yourself standing in lines for embarkation, disembarkation, buffets and shore excursions, although the company does its best to minimize such lines.

ACCOMMODATION. There are 17 cabin price grades, which is far too many. The price you pay will depend on the grade, location and size you choose.

Royal Caribbean International has realized that small cabins do not please passengers. The company therefore set about designing a ship with much larger standard cabins than in any of the company's previous vessels – except for sister ship *Legend of the Seas*.

Some cabins on Deck 8 also have a larger door for wheelchair access in addition to the 17 cabins for the disabled, and the ship is very accessible, with ample ramped areas and sloping decks.

All cabins have a sitting area and beds that convert to double configuration, and there is ample closet and drawer space, although there is not much space around the bed (and the showers could have been better designed).

Cabins with balconies have glass railings rather than steel/wood to provide less intrusive sightlines.

The largest accommodation, the Royal Suite, is a superb living space for those who can afford the best. It is beautifully designed, finely decorated, and has a baby grand piano and whirlpool bathtub. Quiet sitting areas are located adjacent to the best cabins amidships. There are no cabins for singles.

CUISINE. The two-deck-high King and I dining room has dramatic two-deck-high glass side walls, so many passengers both upstairs and downstairs can see both the ocean and each other in reflection (it would, perhaps, have been even better located at the stern), but it is quite noisy when full (call it atmosphere). There are two seatings.

For casual meals, there are two informal options: a cavernous indoor-outdoor cafe, located towards the bow and above the bridge, and a good-sized snack area.

ENTERTAINMENT. The 42nd Street Theater seats 802 and is a single-level showlounge with tiered seating levels. The sightlines are generally good from almost all seats. Strong cabaret acts are also featured in the main show lounge.

Other cabaret acts are featured in the Top Hat Lounge, and these include late-night adult (blue) comedy, as well as live music for dancing. A number of other bars and lounges have live music of differing types.

SPA/FITNESS. The ShipShape Fitness Center has a gymnasium (it is located on the port side of the ship, aft of the funnel), and has a small selection of high-tech muscle-pumping equipment. There is also an aerobics studio (classes are offered in a variety of keep-fit regimes), a beauty salon, and a sauna, as well as rooms for such pampering treatments as massages, facials, etc. While the facilities are quite small when compared with those aboard the company's newer ships, they are adequate for the short cruises that this ship operates. The spa is operated by Steiner, a specialist concession.

For the more sporting, there is activity galore – including a rock-climbing wall, with several separate climbing tracks. It is outdoors at the aft end of the funnel.

● **For more extensive general information about the Royal Caribbean cruise experience, see pages 137–42.**

WHERE WELL-KNOWN TERMS CAME FROM

Brass monkeys

Ever wondered where the expression "Cold enough to freeze the balls off a brass monkey" came from? Well, maritime history tells us that in the days when war ships and most freighters carried cannons (and round cannon balls) made of iron. In order to keep a supply of supply of cannon balls near each cannon, a method of keeping them from rolling around had to be found.

The best storage device consisted of a square-based pyramid. One cannon ball rested on top of four others, which rested on top of nine other, which rested on a base of sixteen. Thus, a supply of 30 cannon balls could be stacked in a small area. There was, however, a small problem – how to prevent the bottom layer from rolling out from under the others on a moving ship. The solution was a metal plate called a "monkey." It had 16 round indentations – one for each of the 16 "base layer" of cannon balls.

If the "monkey" were made of iron, the cannon balls placed on it would rust to it; the solution was to make the "monkey" out of brass. However, brass contracts more than iron when it is chilled. Unfortunately, when the temperature dipped too far, the brass indentations would shrink so much that the iron cannon balls would come adrift from the "monkey." It was, thus, really case of being "cold enough to freeze the balls off a brass monkey."

He let the cat out of the bag

On board a square-rigger 150 years ago, this would have sent shudders through one's spine – for it meant that a sailor had committed an offense serious enough to have the "cat o' nine tails" extracted from its bag.

The "cat" was a whip made of nine lengths of cord, each being about 18 inches (45 cm) long with three knots at the end, all fixed to a rope handle. It could seriously injure, or even kill, the victim. It was finally outlawed by the US Congress in 1850, and then by Britain's Royal Navy in 1879.

Star Clipper
★★★★

Boutique Ship: . . . . .2,298 tons	Sail Area (sq ft/m2): 36,221/3,365/	Size Range (sq ft/m): .95.0–225.0/8.8–21.0
Lifestyle: . . . . .Standard	16 manually furled sails	Cabins (outside view): 79
Cruise Line: . . . . .Star Clippers	Main Propulsion: . . . . .sail power	Cabins (interior/no view): 6
Former Names: . . . . .none	Propulsion/Propellers: . . . . .diesel	Cabins (for one person): 0
Builder: . . . . .Scheepswerven van	(1,030kW)/1	Cabins (with private balcony): 0
Langerbrugge (Belgium)	Passenger Decks: 4	Cabins (wheelchair accessible): 0
Original Cost: . . . .$30 million	Total Crew: 72	Cabin Current: . . . . .110 volts
Entered Service: . . . . .May 1992	Passengers	Elevators: 0
Registry: . . . . .Luxembourg	(lower beds/all berths): 170/180	Casino (gaming tables): . . . . .No
Length (ft/m): 378.9/115.5	Passenger Space Ratio	Slot Machines: . . . . .No
Beam (ft/m): 49.2/15.0	(lower beds/all berths): 13.5/12.7	Swimming Pools (outdoors): 2
Draft (ft/m): 17.7/5.6	Crew/Passenger Ratio	Whirlpools: 0
Type of Vessel: . . . .barkentine schooner	(lower beds/all berths): 2.3/2.5	Self-Service Launderette: . . . . .No
No. of Masts: . . . . .4 (208 ft)	Navigation Officers: . . . . .European	Library: . . . . .Yes
	Cabins (total): .85	

OVERALL SCORE: 1,402 (OUT OF A POSSIBLE 2,000 POINTS)

OVERVIEW. *Star Clipper* is one of a pair of almost identical tall ships (its sister ship is *Star Flyer*, which was the first clipper sailing ship to be built for 140 years, became the first commercial sailing vessel to cross the North Atlantic in 90 years). It is, first and foremost a sailing vessel with cruise accommodation that evokes memories of the 19th-century clipper sailing ships. This is an accurate four-mast, barkentine-rigged vessel with graceful lines, a finely shaped hull and masts that are 206 ft (63 meters) tall.

Breathtaking when under full sail, the ship displays excellent sea manners (healing is kept to a very comfortable 6%). This working sailing ship relies on the wind about 80 percent of the time. For the nautically-minded, the sailing rig consists of 16 sails. These include: fore staysail, inner jib, outer jib, flying jib, fore course, lower topsail, upper topsail, lower topgallant, upper topgallant, main staysail, upper main staysail, mizzen staysail, main fisherman, jigger staysail, mizzen fisherman, and spanker. The square sails are furled electronically by custom-made winches.

During a typical cruise, you'll be able to climb the main mast (to a platform 75 ft/25 meters above the sea – this could be an unnerving experience if you're not used to heights, but it is an exhilarating experience when the ship is moving, under sail), and help with the ropes and sails. However, one of the nicest of chill-out pleasures is to lie in the netting at the front of the ship's bows, watching the bow wake as it streams along the ship's sides.

A diesel engine is used as the main propulsion engine when the ship is not under sail (in poor wind conditions), and two generators are provided for supplying electrical

BERLITZ'S RATINGS		
	Possible	Achieved
Ship	500	382
Accommodation	200	134
Food	400	249
Service	400	271
Entertainment	n/a	n/a
Cruise	500	366

power and for desalinating the approximately 40 tons of seawater each day for shipboard needs (engine room visits are offered). The crew performs almost every task, including hoisting, trimming, winching and repairing the sails (helped by electric winches). Water sports facilities include a water ski boat, sunfish, scuba and snorkel equipment, and eight Zodiac inflatable craft. Sports directors provide basic dive instruction (for a fee).

Some of the amenities of large modern cruise vessels are provided, such as air conditioning, cashless cruising, occasional live music, a small shop, and two pools to "dip" in. Inside the vessel, classic Edwardian nautical decor throughout is clean, warm, intimate, and inviting. The paneled library has a fireplace, and chairs that are comfortable. A cruise aboard it means no lines, no hassle, and "Sailing a Square Rigger" classes are a part of every cruise.

Each morning, passengers usually gather for "captain's story time" – normally held on an open deck area adjacent to the bar (which, incidentally, has a collection of single malt whiskies) or on the bridge. The captain explains sailing maneuvers when changing the rigging or directing the ship as it sails into port, and notes the important events of the day.

The vessel promotes total informality and provides a carefree sailing cruise experience in a totally unstructured setting at a modest price. Take minimal clothing: short sleeved shirts and shorts for the men, shorts and tops for the women are the order of the day (smart casual at night). No jackets, ties, high-heeled shoes, cocktail dresses, or formal wear are needed. In fact, you should take only casual clothes, and flat shoes (there are lots of ropes and sailing rig to negotiate on deck, not to mention the main high thresholds to climb over and steps to negotiate – this is, after all a tall ship, not a cruise ship). The deck crew consists of real sailors, brought up with yachts and tall ships – most wouldn't set foot aboard a "normal" cruise ship.

It is no exaggeration to say that to be sailing aboard either *Star Clipper* or *Star Flyer* is to seem to have died and gone to yachtsman's heaven, as there is plenty of sailing during the course of a typical one-week cruise. The whole experience evokes the feeling of sailing aboard some famous private yacht, and even the most jaded passenger should enjoy the feel of the wind and sea close at hand. Just don't expect fine food to go with what is decidedly a fine sailing experience – which is what Star Clipper is all about. Note that 12.5% is added to all beverage purchases. The onboard currency is the euro (wherever the ship operates). Tips are pooled (the suggested amount is 8 euros per passenger, per day).

Note that the steps of the internal stairways are short and steep, as in all sailing vessels, and so this ship cannot be recommended for anyone with walking disabilities. Also, there is no doctor on board (although there is a nurse)

SUITABLE FOR: *Star Clipper* is best suited to couples and singles who would probably never even consider a "normal" cruise ship, but who enjoy sailing and the thrill of ocean and wind, but want these things wrapped in a package that includes accommodation, food, like-minded companions, interesting destinations, an almost unstructured lifestyle, and for those who don't want the bother of owning or chartering their own yacht.

ACCOMMODATION. There are six cabin price grades (plus one owner's suite). The price will depend on grade, location and size (generally, the higher the deck, the more expensive a cabin). The cabins are quite well equipped and comfortable; they have rosewood-trimmed cabinetry and wall-to-wall carpeting, two-channel audio, color TV and individual DVD player, lockable personal safe and full-length mirrors. The bathrooms are very compact but practical units, and have gray marble tiling, glazed rosewood toiletries cabinet and paneling, some under-shelf storage space, washbasin, shower stall and toilet. There is no "lip" to prevent water from the shower from moving over the bathroom floor. Individual European 100% individual cotton duvets are provided. There is no cabin food or beverage service.

The deluxe cabins (called "deck cabins") are larger, and additional features include a full-sized Jacuzzi tub (or corner tub), flat-screen television and individual DVD player, and mini-bar/refrigerator (note, however, that these cabins are subject to noise pollution from the same-deck Tropical Bar's music at night (typically until midnight), from the electric winches during sail maneuvers, and from noisy walkabout exercisers in the early morning.

The cabins in the lowest price grade are interior cabins with upper and lower berths, and not two lower beds – so someone will need to be agile to climb up to the upper berth (a ladder is provided, of course). A handful of cabins have a third, upper Pullman-style berth (good for families with

children, but note that closet and drawer space will be at a premium with three persons in a cabin, so do take only the minimal amount of clothing). Luggage can be stored under the bed, where extra large drawers are also provided.

CUISINE. The dining room is quite attractive, and has lots of wood and brass accenting and nautical decor. There are self-serve buffet breakfasts and lunches, together with a mix of buffet and à la carte dinners (generally with a choice of three entrées) in a one (open) seating environment. The seating arrangement (mostly at tables of six, adjacent to a porthole or inboard) makes it difficult for waiters to serve properly (food is passed along the tables that occupy a porthole position). However, you can dine with whomever you wish, and this is supposed to be a casual experience, after all.

While cuisine aboard the Star Clippers ships is perhaps less than the advertised "gourmet" excellence (as far as presentation and choice are concerned), it is fairly creative (and there's plenty of it), and one has to take into account the small galley provided (changed to a better layout in a recent refurbishment). Passenger niggles include repetitious breakfasts and lunchtime salad items (lack of space prevents more choices), although most passengers are happy with the dinners, which tend to be good, although there is a lack of green vegetables.

Perhaps fewer passenger cabins and more room in the galley would have enabled the chefs to provide a better dining experience than the present arrangement. There is a good choice of bread rolls, pastry items, and fruit.

Tea and coffee is available 24 hours a day (mugs, tea cups and saucers are provided), in the lounge (in view of the fact that there is no cabin food service. Drinks prices include a service charge (presently 12.5%).

ENTERTAINMENT. There are no entertainment shows as such, nor are any expected by passengers aboard a tall ship such as this, where sailing is the main purpose of a cruise. There is, however, live music, which is typically provided by a solo lounge pianist/singer. Otherwise, dinner is the main evening event, as well as "captain's story-time" recapping the day's events, and conversation with fellow passengers in the lounge or on deck (under the stars) provides engaging entertainment (plus occasional crew events).

During the day, when the ship is sailing, passengers can learn about the sails, and the captain or chief officer will give briefings as the sails are being furled and unfurled. The closest this tall ship comes to any kind of "show" is when, one evening towards the end of each cruise, a "sailor's choir", comprised of the ship's crew, presents a nautical performance of sea songs, sea shanties, and other light diversions.

SPA/FITNESS. There are no fitness facilities, or beauty salon, although a masseuse provides several types of Oriental massage and body scrub treatments. However, for recreation, the ship does have a water sports program. Facilities include a water ski boat, sunfish, scuba and snorkel equipment, and eight Zodiac inflatable craft.

Star Flyer
★★★★

Boutique Ship: . . . . .2,298 tons	Sail Area (sq ft/m2): 36,221/3,365/	Size Range (sq ft/m): .95.0–225.9/8.8–21.0
Lifestyle: . . . . .Standard	16 manually furled sails	Cabins (outside view): 79
Cruise Line: . . . . .Star Clippers	Main Propulsion: . . . . .sail power	Cabins (interior/no view): 6
Former Names: . . . . .none	Propulsion/Propellers: . . . . .diesel	Cabins (for one person): 0
Builder: . . . . .Sheepswerven van	(1,030kW)/1	Cabins (with private balcony): 0
Langerbrugge (Belgium)	Passenger Decks: 4	Cabins (wheelchair accessible): 0
Original Cost: . . . .$25 million	Total Crew: 72	Cabin Current: . . . . .110 volts
Entered Service: . . . . .July 1991	Passengers	Elevators: 0
Registry: . . . . .Luxembourg	(lower beds/all berths): 170/180	Casino (gaming tables): . . . . .No
Length (ft/m): 378.9/115.5	Passenger Space Ratio	Slot Machines: . . . . .No
Beam (ft/m): 49.2/15.0	(lower beds/all berths): 13.5/12.7	Swimming Pools (outdoors): 2
Draft (ft/m): 17.7/5.6	Crew/Passenger Ratio	Whirlpools: 0
Type of Vessel: . . . .barkentine schooner	(lower beds/all berths): 2.3/2.5	Self-Service Launderette: . . . . .No
No. of Masts: . . . . .4 (208 ft)	Navigation Officers: . . . . .European	Library: . . . . .Yes
	Cabins (total): 85	

OVERALL SCORE: 1,402 (OUT OF A POSSIBLE 2,000 POINTS)

OVERVIEW. *Star Flyer* is one of a pair of almost identical tall ships (its sister ship is *Star Clipper*). It is, first and foremost, a sailing vessel with cruise accommodation that evokes memories of the 19th-century clipper sailing ships. This is an accurate four-mast, barkentine-rigged vessel with graceful lines, a finely shaped hull and masts that are 206 ft (63 meters) tall. The ship now sails year-round from Papeete, Tahiti.

Breathtaking when under full sail, the ship displays excellent sea manners. This working sailing ship relies on the wind about 80 percent of the time. A diesel engine is used as backup in emergencies, for generating electrical power and for desalinating the approximately 40 tons of seawater each day for shipboard needs. The crew performs almost every task, including hoisting, trimming, winching and repairing the sails (helped by electric winches).

The whole cruise experience evokes the feeling of sailing aboard some famous private yacht a century ago. *Star Flyer*, the first clipper sailing ship to be built for 140 years, became the first commercial sailing vessel to cross the North Atlantic in 90 years.

Some of the amenities of large modern cruise vessels are provided, such as air-conditioning, cashless cruising, occasional live music, a small shop, and two pools to "dip" in. Inside the vessel, classic Edwardian nautical decor throughout is clean, warm, intimate, and inviting. The paneled library has a fireplace, and chairs that are comfortable. A cruise aboard it means no lines, no hassle, and "Sailing a Square Rigger" classes are a part of every cruise.

Each morning, passengers typically gather for "captain's

BERLITZ'S RATINGS		
	Possible	Achieved
Ship	500	382
Accommodation	200	134
Food	400	249
Service	400	271
Entertainment	n/a	n/a
Cruise	500	366

story-time" – normally held on an open deck area adjacent to the bar – which, incidentally, has a fine collection of single malt whiskies. The captain also explains sailing maneuvers when changing the rigging or directing the ship as it sails into port, and notes the important events of the day. Passengers are encouraged to lend a hand, pulling on thick ropes to haul up the main sail. And they love it.

The vessel promotes total informality and provides a carefree sailing cruise experience in a totally unstructured setting at a modest price. Take minimal clothing: short-sleeved shirts and shorts for the men, shorts and tops for the women are the order of the day (and night). No jackets, ties, high-heeled shoes, cocktail dresses, or the slightest hint of formal wear is needed. The deck crew consists of real sailors, brought up with yachts and tall ships – and most would not set foot aboard a cruise ship.

It is no exaggeration to say that to be sailing aboard either *Star Clipper* or *Star Flyer* is to seem to have died and gone to yachtsman's heaven, as there is plenty of sailing during the course of a typical one-week cruise. Even the most jaded passenger should enjoy the feel of the wind and sea close at hand – just don't expect fine food to go with what is decidedly a fine sailing experience. The food, its quality, variety, presentation and service are sound, but there's room for improvement.

The steps of the internal stairs are steep, as in most sailing vessels.

Tips are pooled (the suggested amount is $8 per passenger, per day) and 12.5% is added to all beverage purchases. The onboard currency is the euro.

SUITABLE FOR: *Star Flyer* is best suited to couples and singles who would probably never even consider a "normal" cruise ship, but who enjoy sailing and the thrill of ocean and wind, but want these things wrapped in a package that includes accommodation, food, like-minded companions, interesting destinations, and don't want the bother of owning or chartering their own yacht.

ACCOMMODATION. There are six cabin price grades (plus one owner's suite). The price will depend on the grade, location and size chosen (generally, the higher the deck, the more expensive your cabin will be). The cabins are quite well equipped and comfortable; they have rosewood-trimmed cabinetry and wall-to-wall carpeting, two-channel audio, color TV and individual DVD player, lockable personal safe and full-length mirrors.

The bathrooms are very compact but practical units, and have gray marble tiling, glazed rosewood toiletries cabinet and paneling, some under-shelf storage space, washbasin, shower stall and toilet. There is no "lip" to prevent water from the shower from moving over the bathroom floor. Individual European 100% individual cotton duvets are provided. Note that there is no cabin food or beverage service.

The deluxe cabins (called "deck cabins") are larger, and additional features include a full-sized Jacuzzi tub (or corner tub), flat-screen television and individual DVD player, and mini-bar/refrigerator. But these cabins are subject to noise pollution from the same-deck Tropical Bar's music at night (typically until midnight), from the electric winches during sail maneuvers, and from noisy walkabout exercisers in the early morning.

The cabins in the lowest price grade are interior cabins with upper and lower berths, and not two lower beds – so someone will need to be agile to climb up to the upper berth (a ladder is provided, of course). A handful of cabins have a third, upper Pullman-style berth – good for families with children, but note that closet and drawer space will be at a premium with three persons in a cabin, so do take only the minimal amount of clothing. Luggage can be stored under the bed, where extra large drawers are also provided.

CUISINE. The dining room is quite attractive, and has lots of wood and brass accenting and nautical decor. There are self-serve buffet breakfasts and lunches, together with a mix of buffet and à la carte dinners (generally with a choice of two entrées). There is one (open) seating. The seating arrangement (mostly with tables of six, adjacent to a porthole) makes it difficult for waiters to serve properly. However, you can dine with whomever you wish, and this is supposed to be a casual experience. While cuisine aboard Star Clippers' ships is perhaps less than the advertised "gourmet" excellence (as far as presentation and choice are concerned), it is fairly creative, and one has to take into account the small galley provided (changed to a better layout in a recent refurbishment).

Perhaps fewer passenger cabins and more room in the galley would have enabled the chefs to provide a better dining experience than the present arrangement. There is a limited choice of bread rolls, pastry items, and fruit.

Tea and coffee should be, but is not, available 24 hours a day (now provided in china mugs), particularly in view of the fact that there is no cabin food service. Note that drinks prices include a service charge (presently 12.5%).

ENTERTAINMENT. There are no entertainment shows, nor are any expected by passengers aboard a tall ship such as this, where sailing is the main purpose of a cruise aboard *Star Flyer*. There is, however, live music, which is provided by a single lounge pianist/singer. Otherwise, dinner is the main evening event, as well as talks by the captain. Conversation with fellow passengers in the lounge or on deck (under the stars) provides engaging entertainment.

During the daytime, when the ship is sailing, passengers can learn about the sails, and the captain or chief officer will give briefings as the sails are being furled and unfurled. The closest this tall ship comes to any kind of "show" is when, one evening towards the end of each cruise, a "sailor's choir", comprised of the ship's crew, presents a nautical performance of sea songs, sea shanties, and other light diversions.

SPA/FITNESS. There are no fitness facilities, or beauty salon, or anything related to spa services aboard this tall ship. However, for recreation, the ship does have a water sports programme. Facilities include a water ski boat, sunfish, scuba and snorkel equipment, and eight Zodiac inflatable craft. Water sports directors provide basic dive instruction (for a fee).

Star Pisces
★★★

Mid-Size Ship:	.40,053 tons	Total Crew:	.750	Cabins (for one person):	.42
Lifestyle:	Standard	Passengers		Cabins (with private balcony):	.0
Cruise Line:	Star Cruises	(lower beds/all berths):	.1,394/1,900	Cabins (wheelchair accessible):	.6
Former Names:	*Kalypso*	Passenger Space Ratio		Cabin Current:	.220 volts
Entered Service:	.1990	(lower beds/all berths):	.28.7/21.0	Elevators:	.5
Builder:	Wartsila (Finland)	Crew/Passenger Ratio		Casino (gaming tables):	Yes
Original Cost:	SEK650 million	(lower beds/all berths):	.1.8/2.5	Slot Machines:	Yes
Registry:	Panama	Navigation Officers:	Scandinavian	Swimming Pools (outdoors):	.1
Length (ft/m):	.579.3/176.6	Cabins (total):	.776	Swimming Pools (indoors):	.1
Beam (ft/m):	.97.1/29.6	Size Range (sq ft/m):	.67.8–145.3/	Whirlpools:	.3
Draft (ft/m):	.20.3/6.2		6.3–13.5	Self-Service Launderette:	No
Propulsion/Propellers: diesel (23,760kW)/2		Cabins (outside view):	.303	Dedicated Cinema/Seats:	No
Passenger Decks:	.12	Cabins (interior/no view):	.415	Library:	Yes

OVERALL SCORE: 1,247 (OUT OF A POSSIBLE 2,000 POINTS)

OVERVIEW. This ship, formerly a Baltic car-passenger ferry, is wide and squat looking. Although the outdoor deck and sunbathing space is limited, it is little used by its Asian passengers. There is a helipad, a huge duty-free shopping center and a supermarket. The Regal Casino (essentially for VIPs) is large and has a high, detailed ceiling. There is a second casino for general use. There are many meeting rooms, conference auditoriums and a business center. The extensive facilities for children include computers and educational rooms, play areas and a huge video machine section. There is free ice cream for kids.

Skillfully converted into a cruise vessel for the Asian family market, *Star Pisces* is normally based on Hong Kong. The ship offers short cruises, with lots of good Asian hospitality, wide choice of dining, lots of karaoke and gambling, all in a modern ship with colorful surroundings. The initial ticket price is extremely low, but almost everything on board costs extra. All gratuities are included.

Many of the public rooms are always crowded. The cabins (and bathrooms) are very small – particularly when occupied by three or four persons. Standing in line for embarkation, disembarkation, shore tenders and for buffet meals is inevitable when cruising aboard all large ships.

SUITABLE FOR: *Star Pisces* is best suited to Mandarin- and English-speaking passengers wanting a cruise in a casual, yet comfortable environment with a range of foods and dining spots, as an introduction to cruising, at low cost.

ACCOMMODATION. There are six grades. Except for some large "imperial" suites, almost all cabins are extremely

BERLITZ'S RATINGS		
	Possible	Achieved
Ship	500	277
Accommodation	200	123
Food	400	275
Service	400	265
Entertainment	100	56
Cruise	400	251

small, with just the basic facilities, and very little closet and drawer space. Many cabins have third- and fourth-person upper berths – good for families who don't mind tight quarters. The cabin insulation is quite poor, and the bathrooms are really tiny. The largest suites are very spacious, and are decorated in luxurious, richly lacquered materials, have two bathrooms, butler service, a private club meeting room, private sun deck and spa.

CUISINE. There are seven restaurants. A Chinese restaurant has live fish tanks from which to select your seafood. A Japanese restaurant includes a sushi bar, waitresses in kimonos, and private tatami rooms. An Italian restaurant has candlelight dining. A Spice Island buffet restaurant has items such as laksa, satay and hawker delights. In addition, there are three other snack cafes. The cruise fare includes only the basic buffet restaurants.

ENTERTAINMENT. Because this ship operates short cruises for the local Southeast Asian market, the entertainment actually consists of the casino, and onboard shopping, with the occasional cabaret act taking center stage (particularly during special celebration, holiday or themed cruises). There is also live music for listening or dancing to, in several of the lounges and bars.

SPA/FITNESS. There's a decent health club for men (some "extra" services are available, even if they are not listed on the rate card). Facilities include a gymnasium with high-tech muscle-pumping equipment, sauna, steam room, and massage/treatment rooms.

Large Resort Ship: ....108,977 tons	Passenger Decks: 13	Cabins (for one person): 0
Lifestyle: ....Standard	Total Crew: 1,200	Cabins (with private balcony): 711
Cruise Line: ....Princess Cruises	Passengers	Cabins (wheelchair accessible): 28
Former Names: ....none	(lower beds/all berths): 2,602/3,102	(18 outside/10 interior)
Builder: ....Fincantieri	Passenger Space Ratio	Cabin Current: ....110 volts
(Italy)	(lower beds/all berths): 41.8/35.1	Elevators: 14
Original Cost: ....$460 million	Crew/Passenger Ratio	Casino (gaming tables): ....Yes
Entered Service: ....Feb 2002	(lower beds/all berths): 2.3/2.8	Slot Machines: ....Yes
Registry: ....Bermuda	Navigation Officers: .....British/European	Swimming Pools (outdoors): 4
Length (ft/m): 951.4/290.0	Cabins (total): 1,301	Swimming Pools (indoors): 0
Beam (ft/m): 118.1/36.0	Size Range (sq ft/m): 161.4–1,314.0/	Whirlpools: 9
Draft (ft/m): 26.2/8.0	15.0–122.0	Self-Service Launderette: ....Yes
Propulsion/Propellers: .....diesel-electric	Cabins (outside view): 935	Dedicated Cinema/Seats: ....No
(42,000kW)/2	Cabins (interior/no view): 366	Library: ....Yes

OVERALL SCORE: 1,542 (OUT OF A POSSIBLE 2,000 POINTS)

OVERVIEW. The design for this large cruise ship, whose sister ships are *Golden Princess* and *Grand Princess* (and slightly larger half-sister *Caribbean Princess*), presents a bold, forthright profile, with a racy "spoiler" effect at its galleon-like transom stern that I (and others) do not consider handsome (the "spoiler" acts as a stern observation lounge by day, and a stunning discotheque by night). *Star Princess* is quite a ship. With a beam of 118 ft/36 meters, including the navigation bridge wings and with many balcony cabins overhanging the ship's hull, it is too wide – by more than 13 ft/3.9 meters – to transit the Panama Canal. When the ship was delivered by the shipyard in Italy, *Star Princess* went through the Suez Canal (the largest passenger ship ever to do so), then sailed to Singapore for its maiden voyage, before going to Los Angeles; thus the ship did half an around-the-world sailing before commencing service on the US west coast.

A few changes (compared with *Golden Princess* and *Grand Princess*) have been incorporated, including a substantially enlarged and much improved children's area (the Fun Zone) at the stern of the vessel. Also different (and improved) is the layout of the Lotus Spa (particularly the placement of the saunas/changing rooms).

There is a good sheltered teakwood promenade deck, which almost wraps around (three times round is equal to one mile) and a walkway which goes right to the (enclosed, protected) bow of the ship. The outdoor pools have various beach-like surroundings. One lap pool has a pumped "current" to swim against.

Unlike the outside decks, there is plenty of space inside the ship (but there are also plenty of passengers), and a wide

BERLITZ'S RATINGS		
	Possible	Achieved
Ship	500	430
Accommodation	200	167
Food	400	256
Service	400	293
Entertainment	100	82
Cruise	400	314

array of public rooms to choose from, with many "intimate" (this being a relative word) spaces and places to play. The passenger flow has been well thought-out, and works with little congestion. The decor is attractive, with lots of earth tones (well suited to both American and European tastes). In fact, this is a culmination of the best of all that Princess Cruises has to offer from its many years of operating what is now a well-tuned, good-quality product.

Four areas center on swimming pools, one of which is two decks high and is covered by a magrodome, itself an extension of the funnel housing. High atop the stern of the ship is a ship-wide glass-walled disco pod. It looks like an aerodynamic "spoiler" and is positioned high above the water, with spectacular views from the extreme port and starboard side windows.

An extensive collection of art works complements the interior design and colors well. If you see something you like, you can buy it on board – it's almost all for sale.

Like its sisters *Golden Princess* and *Grand Princess*, *Star Princess* also has a Wedding Chapel (a live web-cam can relay ceremonies via the internet). The ship's captain can legally marry (American) couples, thanks to the ship's Bermuda registry and a special dispensation (which should be verified when in the planning stage, according to where you reside). Princess Cruises offers three wedding packages – Pearl, Emerald, Diamond. The fee includes registration and official marriage certificate. However, to get married and take your close family members and entourage with you on your honeymoon is going to cost a lot of money. The "Hearts & Minds" chapel is also useful for "renewal of vows" ceremonies.

For children, there is a two-deck-high playroom, teen room, and a host of specially trained counselors. Children have their own pools, hot tubs, and open deck area at the stern of the ship, thankfully away from adult areas. There are good netted-in areas; one section has a dip pool, while another has a mini-basketball court.

Gamers should enjoy the Grand Casino, with more than 260 slot machines; there are blackjack, craps and roulette tables, plus newer games such as Let It Ride Bonus, Spanish 21 and Caribbean Draw Progressive. But the highlight could well be the specially linked slot machines that provide a combined payout.

Other features include a decent library/CD-Rom computer room, and a separate card room. Ship lovers should enjoy the wood-paneled Wheelhouse Bar, finely decorated with memorabilia and ship models tracing part of parent company P&O's history; this ship highlights the 1950-built cargo ship *Ganges*. A sports bar, Shooters, has two billiard tables, as well as eight television screens.

A high-tech hospital is provided, with live SeaMed telemedicine link-ups with specialists at the Cedars-Sinai Medical Center in Los Angeles available for emergency help.

The ship is a stunning, grand resort playground in which to roam when you are not ashore. Princess Cruises delivers a consistently fine, well-packaged vacation product, with a good sense of style, at an attractive, highly competitive price, and this ship will appeal to those that really enjoy a big city to play in, with all the trimmings and lots of fellow passengers. The ship is full of revenue centers, however, designed to help part you from your money. As cruising aboard large ships such as this has become increasingly an onboard revenue-based product, you can expect to be subjected to a stream of flyers advertising daily art auctions, "designer" watches and other promotions, while "artworks" for auction are strewn throughout the ship.

The dress code has been simplified – reduced to formal or smart casual, which seems to be translated by many as jeans and trainers. Gratuities to staff are added to your account, at $10 per person, per day (gratuities for children are charged at the same rate). If you want to pay less, you'll need to go to the reception desk to have these charges adjusted; this could mean lining up with many other passengers wanting to do the same. The onboard currency is the US dollar.

Whether this really can be considered a relaxing holiday is a moot point, but with so many choices and "small" rooms to enjoy, the ship has been extremely well designed, and the odds are that you'll have a fine cruise vacation.

If you are not used to large ships, it will take you some time to find your way around, despite the company's claim that this vessel offers passengers a "small ship feel, big ship choice." The cabin bath towels are small, and drawer space is very limited. There are no butlers – even for the top-grade suites (which are not really large in comparison similar suites aboard some other ships). Cabin attendants have too many cabins to look after (typically 20), which does not translate to fine personal service.

The automated telephone system is frustrating, and luggage delivery is inefficient.

ACCOMMODATION. There are six principal types of cabins and configurations: (a) grand suite, (b) suite, (c) mini-suite, (d) outside-view double cabins with balcony, (e) outside-view double cabins, and (f) interior (no view) double cabins. These come in 35 different brochure price categories (the price you pay will depend on the grade, location and size chosen). The choice is quite bewildering for both travel agents and passengers; pricing will depend on two things, size and location.

(a) The largest, most lavish suite is the Grand Suite (B748, which is located at the ship's stern – a different position to the two Grand Suites aboard Grand Princess). It has a large bedroom with queen-sized bed, huge walk-in (illuminated) closets, two bathrooms, a lounge (with fireplace and sofa bed) with wet bar and refrigerator, and a large private balcony on the port side (with hot tub that can be accessed from both balcony and bedroom).

(b/c) Suites (with a semi-private balcony) have a separate living room with sofa bed and bedroom (with a television in each). The bathroom is quite large and has both a tub and shower stall. The mini-suites also have a private balcony, and a separate living and sleeping area (with a television in each). The differences between the suites and mini-suites are basically in the size and appointments, the suite being more of a square shape while mini-suites are more rectangular, and have few drawers. Both suites and mini-suites have plush bathrobes, and fully tiled bathrooms with ample open shelf storage space. Suite and mini-suite passengers receive greater attention, including priority embarkation and disembarkation privileges. What is not good is that the most expensive accommodation has only semi-private balconies that can be seen from above and so there is little privacy (Suites C401, 402, 409, 410, 414, 415, 420, 421, 422, 423, 424 and 425 on Caribe Deck in particular). Also, the suites D105 and D106 (Dolphin Deck), which are extremely large, have balconies that are overlooked from above.

(d/e/f) Both interior (no view) and outside-view (the outsides come either with or without private balcony) cabins are of a functional design, although almost no drawers are provided. They are quite attractive, with warm, pleasing decor and fine soft furnishing fabrics; 80 percent of the outside-view cabins have a private balcony. Interior (no view) cabins measure 160 sq. ft (14.4 sq. meters), while the standard outside-view cabins measure 228 sq. ft (21 sq. meters).

The 28 wheelchair-accessible cabins measure 250–385 sq. ft (23.2–35.7 sq. meters). Surprisingly, there is no mirror for dressing, and no full-length hanging space for long dresses (yes, some passengers in wheelchairs do also use mirrors and full-length clothing). Additionally, two family suites consist of two suites with an interconnecting door, plus a large balcony. These can sleep up to 10 (if at least four are children) or up to eight people (if all are adults).

All passengers receive turndown service and chocolates on pillows each night, bathrobes (on request), and toiletry amenity kits (larger for suite/mini-suite occupants). A hairdryer is provided in all cabins, sensibly located at the vanity desk unit in the living area. All bathrooms have tiled floors, and there is a decent amount of open shelf storage space for personal toiletries, although the plain beige decor is very basic and unappealing. Princess Cruises typically carries CNN, CNBC, ESPN and TNT on the in-cabin color television system (when available, depending on cruise area).

Most outside cabins on Emerald Deck have views obstructed by the lifeboats. There are no cabins for singles. Your name is placed outside your suite or cabin in a documents holder – making it simple for delivery service personnel but also making it intrusive as far as privacy is concerned. There is 24-hour room service (but some items on the room service menu are not available during early morning hours).

Some cabins can accommodate a third and fourth person in upper berths. However, in such cabins, the lower beds cannot then be pushed together to make queen-sized bed.

Almost all balcony suites and cabins can be overlooked both from the navigation bridge wing, as well as from the port and starboard sections of the ship's discotheque – located high above the ship at the stern. Cabins with balconies on Dolphin, Caribe and Baja decks are also overlooked by passengers on balconies on the deck above. They are, therefore, not at all private. However, perhaps the least desirable balcony cabins are eight balcony cabins located forward on Emerald Deck, as the balconies do not extend to the side of the ship and can be passed by walkers and gawkers on the adjacent Upper Promenade walkway, so occupants need to keep their curtains closed most of the time. Also, passengers occupying some the most expensive suites with balconies at the stern of the vessel may experience considerable vibration during certain ship maneuvers.

CUISINE. As befits the size of the ship, there is a variety of dining options. For formal meals there are three principal dining rooms (Amalfi, with 504 seats; Capri, with 486 seats; and Portofino, with 486 seats), and seating is assigned according to the location of your cabin. There are two seatings in one restaurant (Amalfi), while "anytime dining" (where you choose when and with whom you want to eat) is typically offered by the other two. All three are non-smoking and split into multi-tier sections in a non-symmetrical design that breaks what are quite large spaces into many smaller sections, for better ambiance. Each dining room has its own galley.

While four elevators go to Fiesta Deck where the amalfi and Portofino restaurants are located, only two elevators go to Plaza Deck 5 where the Capri Restaurant is located (this can cause long wait problems at peak times, particularly for anyone in a wheelchair).

Specially designed dinnerware and high-quality linens and silverware are used in the main dining rooms; by Dudson of England (dinnerware), Frette Egyptian cotton table linens, and silverware by Hepp of Germany. Note that 15% is added to all beverage bills, including wines.

Alternative (Extra Charge) Dining Options: There are two: Sabatini's Trattoria and Tequila's. Both are open for lunch and dinner on days at sea. Sabatini's is an Italian eatery, with colorful tiled Mediterranean-style decor; it is named after Trattoria Sabatini, the 200-year old institution in Florence (where there is no cover charge). It has Italian-style pizzas and pastas, with a variety of sauces, as well as Italian-style entrées (including tiger prawns and lobster tail – all provided with flair and entertainment from by the staff of waiters (by reservation only, with a cover charge of $15 per person, for lunch or dinner on sea days only).

Tequila's has "southwestern American" food; by reservation only, with a cover charge of $8 per person, for lunch or dinner on sea days only. However, do note that Tequila's is spread over the whole beam (width) of the ship, and two walkways intersect it, which means that it's a very open area, with people walking through it as you eat – not a very comfortable arrangement. The cuisine in both of these spots is decidedly better than in the three main dining rooms, with better quality ingredients and more attention to presentation and taste.

A poolside hamburger grill and pizza bar (no additional charge) are dining spots for casual bites, while extra charges will apply if you order items to eat at either the coffee bar/patisserie, or the caviar/champagne bar.

Other casual meals can be taken in the Horizon Court, which is open 24 hours a day. It has large ocean-view on port and starboard sides and direct access to the two principal swimming pools and lido deck. There is no real finesse in presentation, however, as plastic plates are provided.

ENTERTAINMENT. The Princess Theater (showlounge) is the main entertainment venue; it spans two decks and has comfortable seating on both main and balcony levels. It has $3 million in sound and light equipment, plus a 9-piece orchestra, and a scenery loading bay that connects directly from stage to a hull door for direct transfer to the dockside).

The Vista Lounge is a second entertainment lounge. It has cabaret acts (magicians, comedy jugglers, ventriloquists and others) at night, and lectures, bingo and horse racing during the day. Explorers, a third entertainment lounge, can also host cabaret acts and dance bands. A variety of other lounges and bars feature live music, and Princess Cruises has a number of male dance hosts as partners for women traveling alone.

SPA/FITNESS. The Lotus Spa has Japanese-style decor, and surrounds one of the swimming pools (you can have a massage or other spa treatment in an ocean-view treatment room). It is unfortunate, however (perhaps a lack of knowledge or respect on the part of the interior designer), that the Japanese symbol on the door of the steam inhalation rooms means insect – not a nice thing to call passengers. Note also that some of the spa (massage) treatment rooms are located directly underneath the jogging track.

● **For more extensive general information about the Princess Cruises experience, see pages 134–37.**

Statendam
★★★★

Mid-Size Ship: ....55,451 tons	Total Crew: 557	Cabins (with private balcony): 150
Lifestyle: ....Premium	Passengers	Cabins (wheelchair accessible): 6
Cruise Line: ....Holland America Line	(lower beds/all berths): 1,266/1,627	Cabin Current: ....110 and 220 volts
Former Names: ....none	Passenger Space Ratio	Elevators: 8
Builder: ....Fincantieri (Italy)	(lower beds/all berths): 43.8/34.0	Casino (gaming tables): ....Yes
Original Cost: ....$215 million	Crew/Passenger Ratio	Slot Machines: ....Yes
Entered Service: ....Jan 1993	(lower beds/all berths): 2.2/2.9	Swimming Pools (outdoors): 1
Registry: ....The Netherlands	Navigation Officers: ....Dutch	Swimming Pools (indoors): 1
Length (ft/m): 719.4/219.3	Cabins (total): 633	(magrodome)
Beam (ft/m): 101.0/30.8	Size Range (sq ft/m): 186.2–1,124.8/	Whirlpools: 2
Draft (ft/m): 24.6/7.5	17.3–104.5	Self-Service Launderette: ....Yes
Propulsion/Propellers: .....diesel-electric	Cabins (outside view): 502	Dedicated Cinema/Seats: Yes/249
(34,560kW)/2	Cabins (interior/no view): 131	Library: ....Yes
Passenger Decks: 10	Cabins (for one person): 0	

OVERALL SCORE: 1,415 (OUT OF A POSSIBLE 2,000 POINTS)

OVERVIEW. *Statendam* is the first of a series of four almost identical ships in the same series – the others being *Maasdam*, *Ryndam* and *Veendam*. The exterior styling is rather angular (some would say boxy – the funnel certainly is), although it is softened and balanced somewhat by the fact that the hull is painted black.

There is a full wrap-around teakwood promenade deck outdoors – excellent for strolling, and, thankfully, there's no sign of synthetic turf. The sunloungers on the exterior promenade deck are wood, and come with comfortable cushioned pads, while those at the swimming pool on Lido Deck are of white plastic. Holland America Line keeps its ships clean and tidy, and there is good passenger flow throughout the public areas.

In the interiors of this "S" -class ship, an asymmetrical layout helps to reduce bottlenecks and congestion. Most of the public rooms are concentrated on two decks, Promenade Deck, and Upper Promenade Deck, which creates a spacious feel to the ship's interiors. In general, a restrained approach to interior styling is taken, using a mixture of contemporary materials combined with traditional woods and ceramics. There is, fortunately, little "glitz" anywhere.

What is outstanding is the array of artworks throughout the ship (costing about $2 million), assembled and nicely displayed to represent the fine Dutch heritage of Holland America Line and to present a balance between standard itineraries and onboard creature comforts. Also noticeable are the fine flower arrangements throughout the public areas and foyers – used to good effect to brighten up what to some is dull decor.

Atop the ship, with forward facing views that wrap around the sides is the Crow's Nest Lounge. By day it makes a fine

BERLITZ'S RATINGS		
	Possible	Achieved
Ship	500	372
Accommodation	200	150
Food	400	254
Service	400	285
Entertainment	100	72
Cruise	400	282

observation lounge, with large ocean-view windows, while by night it turns into a nightclub with extremely variable lighting. The atrium foyer is three decks high, although its sculptured centerpiece (*Fountain of the Sirens*, a late 17th-century bronze piece by Willem de Groat) makes it look a little crowded, and leaves little room in front of the purser's office (called the Front Office). A hydraulic magrodome (glass) roof covers the reasonably sized swimming pool/whirlpools and central Lido area (whose focal point is a large dolphin sculpture) so that this can be used in either fine or inclement weather.

The ship has a large, relaxing library. There's also a cardroom, an Explorer's Lounge (good for relaxing in, for afternoon tea, and after-dinner coffees), a Crows Nest (the ship's observation lounge that doubles as a late-night spot and discotheque), an intimate Piano Bar, and, of course, a casino. Adorning stairway landings are several oil paintings by Stephen Card (an ex-captain) showing former Holland America Line ships that bore the name *Statendam*.

Statendam is a fairly well-built ship, and has reasonably decent interior fit and finish. Holland America Line is constantly fine-tuning its performance as a cruise operator and its regular passengers (almost all of whom are North American – there are few international passengers) find the company's ships very comfortable and well-run. The company continues its strong maritime traditions, although the present food and service components let down the rest of the cruise experience. Perhaps the ship's best asset is its friendly and personable Filipino and Indonesian crew, although communication can prove frustrating at times. The onboard currency is the US dollar.

An escalator travels between two of the lower decks (one of which was originally planned to be the embarkation point), but it is almost pointless. The charge to use the washing machines and dryers in the self-service launderette is petty, particularly for occupants of expensive suites. The men's urinals in public restrooms are unusually high.

ACCOMMODATION. There are 17 cabin price grades. The price you pay will depend on the grade, location and size you choose. Cabins range from small interior (no view) cabins to a large penthouse suite (with ocean views). All cabin televisions carry CNN and TNT.

The interior (no view) and outside-view standard cabins have twin beds that can be converted to a queen-sized bed, and there is a separate living space with sofa and coffee table. However, although the drawer space is generally good, the closet space is very tight, particularly for long cruises (although more than adequate for a 7-night cruise). The bathrooms are tiled, and compact but practical. Bathrobes are also provided for all suites/cabins, as are hairdryers, and a small range of personal amenities (soap, conditioning shampoo, body lotion, shower cap, vanity kit). The bathrooms are quite well laid out, but the bathtubs are small units better described as shower tubs.

On Navigation Deck, 28 suites have accommodation for up to four persons. These also have in-suite dining as an alternative to the dining room, for private, reclusive meals. These are very spacious, tastefully decorated and well laid-out, and have a separate living room, bedroom with two lower beds (convertible to a king-size bed), a good size living area, dressing room, plenty of closet and drawer space, marble bathroom with whirlpool bathtub.

The largest accommodation of all is a penthouse suite. There is only one, located on the starboard side of Navigation Deck at the forward staircase. It has a king-sized bed, television and video player, and vanity desk. A large walk-in closet has superb drawer space. There is an oversize whirlpool bath (it could seat four) and separate shower enclosure, and a separate washroom with toilet, bidet and washbasin. The living room has a writing desk, a large television and a full set of audio equipment. The dressing room has a large private balcony (with teak lounge chairs and drinks tables, dining table and four chairs). The pantry has a large refrigerator, toaster unit, and full coffee/tea making facilities and food prepareation area, and a separate entrance from the hallway. There's a mini-bar/refrigerator, a guest toilet and floor to ceiling windows. Note that there is no bell push.

Passengers in accommodation designated as suites and mini-suites have the use of a private concierge club called the Neptune Lounge, where light breakfast and snacks throughout the day can be taken.

CUISINE. The Rotterdam Dining Room, a no-smoking venue, spans two decks. It is located at the stern of the ship, is quite dramatic, and has two grand staircases to connect the two levels, panoramic views on three sides, and a music balcony. Both open seating and fixed (assigned tables and times) seating are available, while breakfast and lunch are open-seating – you'll be seated by restaurant staff when you enter. There are tables for two, four, six or eight note that the waiter stations in the dining room are very noisy for anyone seated adjacent to them. Fine Rosenthal china and cutlery are used.

Alternative Dining Option: A small restaurant was added in 2002. Called the Pinnacle Grill, it is located just forward of the balcony level of the main dining room on the starboard side. The 66-seat dining spot has Pacific Northwest cuisine (Alaska salmon, halibut and other regional specialities, plus a selection of premium steaks). The new venue (reservations are necessary, and a cover/service charge of $20 applies) was created out of the the former private dining wing of the main dining room, plus a slice of the Explorer's Lounge. A Bulgari show plate, Rosenthal china, Reidel wine glasses, and Frette table linen are used. The Pinnacle Grill is a much better dining experience than the main dining room, and worth it for that special celebration.

For more casual evening eating, the Lido Buffet is open for dinners on all except the last night of each cruise, in an open-seating arrangement. Tables are set with crisp linens, flatware and stemware. A set menu is featured, and this includes a choice of four entrées.

The dual-line, self-serve Lido Buffet (one side is for smokers, the other side for non-smokers) is also the place for casual breakfasts and lunches. Again there is much use of canned fruits (good for dentally challenged older passengers) and packeted items, although there are several commercial low-calorie salad dressings. The choice of cheeses and accompanying crackers is very poor. The beverage station also lets it down, for it is no better than those found in family outlets ashore in the United States. In addition, a poolside grill provides basic American hamburgers and hot dogs.

Passengers will need to eat in the Lido Cafe on any days when the dining room is closed for lunch (typically once or twice per cruise, depending on the ship's itinerary).

ENTERTAINMENT. The Van Gogh Showlounge, located at the forward part of the ship, spans two decks, with banquette seating on both main and upper levels. It is basically a well-designed room, but the ceiling is low and the sightlines from the balcony level are quite poor.

SPA/FITNESS. The Ocean Spa is located one deck below the navigation bridge at the very forward part of the ship. It includes a gymnasium (with all the latest muscle-pumping exercise machines, including an abundance of treadmills) with ocean views, an aerobics exercise area, large beauty salon with ocean-view windows to the port side, several treatment rooms, and men's and women's sauna, steam room and changing areas.

● **For more extensive general information on what a Holland America Line cruise is like, see pages 126–28.**

Sun Princess
★★★★

Large Resort Ship: ....77,499 tons	Total Crew: 900	Cabins (with private balcony): 410
Lifestyle: ....Standard	Passengers	Cabins (wheelchair accessible): 19
Cruise Line: ....Princess Cruises	(lower beds/all berths): 1,950/2,250	Cabin Current: ....110 and 220 volts
Former Names: ....none	Passenger Space Ratio	Elevators: 11
Builder: ....Fincantieri (Italy)	(lower beds/all berths): 39.7/34.4	Casino (gaming tables): ....Yes
Original Cost: ....$300 million	Crew/Passenger Ratio	Slot Machines: ....Yes
Entered Service: ....Dec 1995	(lower beds/all berths): 2.0/2.5	Swimming Pools (outdoors): 4
Registry: ....Great Britain	Navigation Officers: ....Italian	Swimming Pools (indoors): 0
Length (ft/m): 857.2/261.3	Cabins (total): 975	Whirlpools: 5
Beam (ft/m): 105.6/32.2	Size Range (sq ft/m): 134.5–753.4/	Self-Service Launderette: ....Yes
Draft (ft/m): 26.5/8.1	12.5–70.0	Dedicated Cinema/Seats: ....No
Propulsion/Propellers: .....diesel-electric	Cabins (outside view): 603	Library: ....Yes
(28,000kW)/2	Cabins (interior/no view): 372	
Passenger Decks: 10	Cabins (for one person): 0	

OVERALL SCORE: 1,496 (OUT OF A POSSIBLE 2,000 POINTS)

OVERVIEW. In November 2007, *Sun Princess* moved its permanent base to Australia, operating cruises from Sydney, Melbourne, and Freemantle. The onboard currency became the Australian dollar, the entertainment was geared to Australian tastes, and other aspects of the cruise operation modified accordingly. Note that, for long voyages (such as a Grand Circle Pacific cruise), the cabin closet space is extremely small.

Although large, this all-white ship has a good profile, and is well balanced by its large funnel, which contains a deck tennis/basketball/volleyball court in its sheltered aft base. There is a wide, teakwood wrap-around promenade deck outdoors, some real teak steamer-style deck chairs (complete with royal blue cushioned pads), and 93,000 sq. ft (8,600 sq. meters) of space outdoors. An extensive glass area on the upper decks provides plenty of light and connection with the outside world.

The ship, while large, absorbs passengers well, and has an almost intimate feel to it, which is what the designers intended. The interiors are very pretty and warm, with attractive colors and welcoming decor that includes some very attractive wall murals and other artwork. The signs around the ship could be improved, however. There is a wide range of public rooms, with several intimate rooms and spaces so that you don't get the feel of being overwhelmed by large spaces. The interior focal point is a huge four-deck-high atrium lobby with winding, double stairways, complete with two panoramic glass-walled elevators.

The main public entertainment rooms are located under three decks of cabins. There is plenty of space, the traffic flow is good, and the ship absorbs people well. There are two showlounges, one at each end of the ship; one is a

BERLITZ'S RATINGS		
	Possible	Achieved
Ship	500	421
Accommodation	200	162
Food	400	257
Service	400	278
Entertainment	100	81
Cruise	400	297

superb 550-seat, theater-style show-lounge (movies are also shown here) and the other is a 480-seat cabaret-style lounge, complete with bar.

The library is a very warm room with ocean-view windows, and has six large buttery leather chairs for listening to audio CDs. There is a conference center for up to 300, as well as a business center, with computers, photocopiers and fax machines. The collection of artwork is good, particularly on the stairways, and helps make the ship feel smaller than it is, although in places it doesn't always seem co-coordinated. The casino, while large, is not really in the main passenger flow and so it does not generate the "walk-through" factor found aboard so many ships.

The most traditional (many say the nicest) room aboard is the Wheelhouse Lounge/Bar, which is decorated in the style of a late 19th-century gentleman's club, complete with wood paneling and comfortable seating. Its focal point is a large ship model from the P&O archives.

At the end of the day, as is the case aboard most large ships today, if you live in the top suites, you will be well attended; if you do not, you will merely be one of a very large number of passengers. One nice feature is the captain's cocktail party; it is held in the four-deck-high main atrium so you can come and go as you please – and there's no standing in line to have your photograph taken with the captain if you don't want to.

There are a number of dead ends in the interior layout, so it's not as user-friendly as a ship this size should be. The cabin numbering system is extremely illogical, with numbers going through several hundred series on the same deck. The walls of the passenger accommodation decks are very plain (some artwork would be a distinct improvement).

The swimming pools are quite small for so many passengers, and the pool deck is cluttered with white, plastic sunloungers, which do not have cushioned pads.

ACCOMMODATION. There are 28 different cabin grades: 20 outside-view and 8 interior (no view) cabins. Although the standard outside-view and interior (no view) cabins are a little small, they are well designed and functional in layout, and have earth tone colors accentuated by splashes of color from the bedspreads. Proportionately, there are quite a lot of interior (no view) cabins. Many of the outside-view cabins have private balconies, and all seem to be quite well soundproofed, although the balcony partition is not floor to ceiling type, so you can hear your neighbors clearly (or smell their smoke). Note that the balconies are very narrow, only just large enough for two small chairs, and there is balcony light.

A reasonable amount of closet and abundant drawer and other storage space is provided in all cabins – adequate for a 7-night cruise, as are a television and refrigerator. Each night a chocolate will appear on your pillow. The cabin bathrooms are practical, and come complete with all the details one needs, although they really are tight spaces, best described as one person at-a-time units. They do, however, have a decent shower enclosure, a small amount of shelving for your personal toiletries, real glasses, a hairdryer and a bathrobe.

The largest accommodation can be found in six suites, two on each of three decks located at the stern of the ship, with large private balcony (536–754 sq. ft./49.8–21.3 sq. meters, including balcony). These are well laid-out, and have large bathrooms with two basins, a Jacuzzi bathtub, and a separate shower enclosure. The bedroom has generous amounts of wood accenting and detailing, TV sets in both bedroom and lounge areas. The suites also have a dining room table and four chairs.

The 32 mini-suites (374–536 sq. ft./34.7–49.7 sq. meters) typically have two lower beds that convert into a queen-sized bed. There is a separate bedroom/sleeping area with vanity desk, and a lounge with sofa and coffee table, indented ceilings with generous amounts of wood accenting and detailing, walk-in closet, and larger bathroom with Jacuzzi tub and separate shower enclosure.

There are 19 wheelchair-accessible cabins, which measure 213–305 sq. ft (19.7–28.2 sq. meters.), and are a mix of 7 outside-view and 12 interior (no view) cabins.

CUISINE. There are two main dining rooms of asymmetrical design: Marquis, and Regency. Both are non-smoking, as are all dining rooms aboard the ships of Princess Cruises. They are located adjacent to the two lower levels of the four-deck high atrium lobby. Each seats around 500, has its own galley, and is split into multi-tier sections, which help create a feeling of intimacy, although there is a lot of noise from the waiter stations adjacent to many tables. Breakfast and lunch are provided in an open-seating arrangement, while dinner is in two seatings.

On any given 7-day cruise, a typical menu cycle will include a Sailaway Dinner, Captain's Welcome Dinner, Chef's Dinner, Italian Dinner, French Dinner, Captain's Gala Dinner, and Landfall Dinner. The wine list is reasonable, but not good, and the company has, sadly, dispensed with wine waiters. Note that 15% is added to all beverage bills, including wines.

Alternative Dining (Extra Charge) Option: For some really good meat, however, consider the Sterling Steakhouse; it's for those that want to taste four different cuts of Angus beef from the popular "Sterling Silver" brand of USDA prime meats – Filet Mignon, New York Strip, Porterhouse, and Rib-Eye – all presented on a silver tray.

There is also a barbecue chicken option, plus the usual baked potato or French fries as accompaniments. This is available as an alternative to the dining rooms, between 6.30pm and 9.30pm only, at an additional charge of $8 per person. However, it is not, as you might expect, a separate, intimate dining room, but is located in a section of the Horizon Buffet, with its own portable bar and some decorative touches to set it apart from the regular Horizon Buffet.

The Horizon Buffet is open 24 hours a day, and, at night, has an informal dinner setting with sit-down waiter service; a small bistro menu is also available. The buffet displays are, for the most part, quite repetitious, but better than they have been in the past few years (there is no real finesse in presentation, however, as plastic plates are provided, instead of trays). The cabin service menu is very limited, and presentation of the food items featured is poor.

There is also a pâtisserie (for cappuccino/espresso coffees and pastries), a wine/caviar bar, and a pizzeria (complete with cobblestone floors and wrought-iron decorative features), and excellent pizzas (there are six to choose from).

ENTERTAINMENT. There are two showlounges (both theater and cabaret style). The principal showlounge, the Princess Theater, has a sloping floor, with aisle-style seating (as typically found in shore-side movie houses) that is well-tiered, and with good sightlines to the raised stage from most of the 500 seats.

The second showlounge (Vista Lounge), located at the aft end of the ship, has cabaret entertainment, and also acts as a lecture and presentation room. Princess Cruises has a good stable of regular cabaret acts to draw from, so there should be something for almost all tastes.

SPA/FITNESS. A glass-walled Lotus Spa complex is located high atop ship and includes a gymnasium with high-tech machines. One swimming pool is "suspended" aft between two decks (there are two other pools, although they are not large for the size of the ship).

Sports facilities are located in an open-air sports deck positioned inside the ship's funnel and adaptable for basketball, volleyball, badminton or paddle tennis. Joggers can exercise on the wrap-around open Promenade Deck.

● **For more extensive general information about the Princess Cruises experience, see pages 134–37.**

Superstar Aquarius
★★★

Mid-Size Ship: . . . . .50,760 tons	Passengers	Cabins (wheelchair accessible): 6
Lifestyle: . . . . .Standard	(lower beds/all berths): 1,530/2,156	(+ 30 for hearing impaired)
Cruise Line: . . . . .Star Cruises	Passenger Space Ratio	Cabin Current: . . . . .110 volts
Former Names: *Norwegian Wind, Windward*	(lower beds/all berths): 33.1/23.5	Elevators: 10
Builder: .Chantiers de l'Atlantique (France)	Crew/Passenger Ratio	Casino (gaming tables): . . . . .Yes
Original Cost: . . . .$240 million	(lower beds/all berths): 2.5/3.1	Slot Machines: . . . . .Yes
Entered Service: . . .June 1993/May 2007	Navigation Officers: . . . . .Norwegian	Swimming Pools (outdoors): 1
Registry: . . . . .The Bahamas	Cabins (total): 765	Swimming Pools (indoors): 0
Length (ft/m): 754.0/229.8	Size Range (sq ft/m): 139.9–349.8/	Whirlpools: 2
Beam (ft/m): 93.5/28.5	13.0–32.5	Self-Service Launderette: . . . . .No
Draft (ft/m): 22.3/6.8	Cabins (outside view): 696	Dedicated Cinema/Seats: . . . . .No
Propulsion/Propellers: diesel (18,480 kW)/2	Cabins (interior/no view): 179	Library: . . . . .Yes
Passenger Decks: 10	Cabins (for one person): 0	
Total Crew: .700	Cabins (with private balcony): 48	

BERLITZ'S OVERALL SCORE: 1,234 (OUT OF A POSSIBLE 2,000 POINTS)

OVERVIEW. The exterior design emphasizes a clever and extensive use of large windows that help create a sense of open spaces, but the interior design has many smaller public rooms (better for Asian passengers). There is no big atrium lobby, as one might expect, and the ceiling height is low. .

Public rooms include several bars and lounges, Skyline Karaoke (with five private karaoke rooms), mahjong/card room, childcare center, video arcade, Genting Club (for invited gaming guests), three small business meeting rooms, an internet-connect center/library, cigar lounge, and a small boutique. There is a blue rubber-covered wrap-around promenade deck outdoors.

This ship was transferred from Norwegian Cruise Line to the Star Cruises fleet in 2007 to operate overnight and short cruises from Hong Kong. The dress code is strictly casual. Some lounges were converted into a large Star Club, for casino gamers. The onboard currency is the Hong Kong dollar, and all gratuities for staff are included.

Outdoor stairways are numerous and confusing, while the carpeted steel interior stairwell steps are tinny. Standing in line for embarkation, disembarkation, and for buffet meals is inevitable aspect when cruising aboard large ships.

ACCOMMODATION. There are 16 cabin price grades, depending on grade, location and size). Most cabins have outside views and wood-trimmed cabinetry and warm decor, with multi-colored soft furnishings, but there is almost no drawer space (the closets have open shelves, however), so take minimal clothing. All cabins have a sitting area. The bathrooms are small but practical, although there is little space for storage of personal toiletry items.

BERLITZ'S RATINGS

	Possible	Achieved
Ship	500	331
Accommodation	200	124
Food	400	216
Service	400	251
Entertainment	100	64
Cruise	400	248

There are 18 suites (12 of which have a private entrance and a small, private balcony), each with separate living room and bedroom, and plenty of closet and drawer space. Occupants of suites receive "concierge" service.

In addition, 16 suites and 70 cabins have inter-connecting doors. Several cabins are specially equipped for the hearing-impaired.

CUISINE. Freestyle Dining venues include the 280-seat Dynasty Restaurant, for Chinese family-style food; Spices Restaurant, an Asian specialty buffet venue with 180 seats; Oceana Barbeque, an outdoor buffet venue; Blue Lagoon, a 24-hour bistro, with 80 seats; Mariner's Buffet, international self-service buffet.

The Dynasty Restaurant, the largest sit-down dining spot, has some prime tables at ocean-view window seats in a section that extends from the ship's port and starboard sides in half-moon shapes.

ENTERTAINMENT. The 700-seat Stardust Lounge is the ship's only venue for production shows and cabaret acts. It is two decks high (but the banquette and individual tub chair seating is only on the main level) and is located not in the forward part of the ship as is normal, but almost in the center.

High-volume razzle-dazzle shows are presented each cruise, to a recorded "click"-track (there is no live show-band), as well as special individual cabaret acts.

SPA/FITNESS. A gymnasium has high-tech muscle-toning equipment, reflexology lounge, and Oscar Hair and Beauty Salon. Therer's a ping pong table, basketball/volleyball court, golf driving range, and a jogging track.

SuperStar Libra
★★★ +

Mid-Size Ship:. . . . . 42,276 tons	Total Crew: .680	Cabins (with private balcony): 0
Lifestyle: . . . . .Standard	Passengers	Cabins (wheelchair accessible): 4
Cruise Line: . . . . .Star Cruises	(lower beds/all berths): 1,510/1,798	Cabin Current: . . . . .110 volts
Former Names: . . .Norwegian Sea, Seaward	Passenger Space Ratio	Elevators: 6
Builder: . . . . .Wartsila (Finland)	(lower beds/all berths): 28.0/23.5	Casino (gaming tables): . . . . .Yes
Original Cost: . . . .$120 million	Crew/Passenger Ratio	Slot Machines: . . . . .Yes
Entered Service: . . . . . .June 1988/Oct 2005	(lower beds/all berths): 2.3/2.8	Swimming Pools (outdoors): 2
Registry: . . . . .The Bahamas	Navigation Officers: . . . . . . .International	Swimming Pools (indoors): 0
Length (ft/m): 708.6/216.0	Cabins (total): 755	Whirlpools: 2
Beam (ft/m): 95.1/29.0	Size Range (sq ft/m): 109.7–269.1/	Self-Service Launderette: . . . . .No
Draft (ft/m): 22.9/7.0	10.2–25.0	Dedicated Cinema/Seats: . . . . .No
Propulsion/Propellers: . . . . .diesel	Cabins (outside view): 512	Library: . . . . .No
(21,120 kW)/2	Cabins (interior/no view): 243	
Passenger Decks: 9	Cabins (for one person): 0	

OVERALL SCORE: 1,286 (OUT OF A POSSIBLE 2,000 POINTS)

OVERVIEW. This is an angular yet reasonably attractive ship that has a contemporary European cruise-ferry profile with a sharply raked bow and sleek mast and funnel added. The ship (the first to be totally geared to passengers from India) is quite well designed, with generally sound passenger flow. The interior decor, stressing corals, blues and mauves, reminds you of sea and sky.

The lobby, two decks high, is pleasing without being overwhelming. There is a decent selection of public rooms, bars and lounges, including an inviting wood-paneled Admiral's Lounge and Star Club (casino), a discotheque (Boomer's), and The Bollywood (karaoke lounge). The onboard currency is the Indian rupee, and gratuities are included in the cruise fare.

The open decks are cluttered, and badly dented and scuffed panels in the accommodation hallways are unattractive. The steps on the stairways are quite tinny. The constant background music in the hallways is irritating. There is too much use of synthetic turf on the upper outdoors decks (this gets soggy when wet).

SUITABLE FOR: *SuperStar Libra* is suited specifically for passengers from the Indian continent seeking a short cruise experience in surroundings tailored for them.

ACCOMMODATION. There are 16 suite/cabin price categories. This ship was built before balcony cabins came into vogue – so there aren't any. The cabins are of average size (which translates to "a bit cramped for two") although they are tastefully appointed and comfortable, with warm, pastel colors, bright soft furnishings and a touch of art deco styling; however, the walls and ceilings are plain and sim-

BERLITZ'S RATINGS

	Possible	Achieved
Ship	500	327
Accommodation	200	124
Food	400	250
Service	400	260
Entertainment	100	62
Cruise	400	263

ple. Audio channels are available via the TV set, although the picture cannot be turned off. The bathrooms are efficient units that are well designed but basic; hairdryers (they are weak) are included.

If you book a suite or one of two upper-grade cabins, you'll get a little more space, a lounge area with table and sofa that converts into another bed (good for families), European duvets, and a refrigerator (top categories only). The bathrooms also have a bathtub, shower and retractable clothesline.

CUISINE. There are no assigned dining rooms, tables or seats, but some eateries incur an extra charge. All restaurants and eateries are non-smoking. They include: Four Seasons Restaurant (the principal dining room, serving Continental Cuisine); The Saffron (Indian vegetarian and Jain buffet, located aft with fine ocean views); Two Trees Restaurant (exclusive lounge/restaurant); Taj by the Bay (Indian family-style restaurant, with aft-facing ocean views); Blue Lagoon (24-hour casual refreshments and snacks); and Coconut Willy's (poolside refreshment center).

ENTERTAINMENT. The 770-seat Stardust Lounge is the venue for shows and major cabaret acts, although 12 thick pillars obstruct many sightlines. The Galaxy of the Stars Lounge, is located aft, and is for cabaret acts. A number of bands and solo entertaining musicians provide live music for listening and dancing in several lounges and bars.

SPA/FITNESS. There's a good gymnasium/fitness center, located around the mast and accessible only from the outside deck (not good when it rains).

SuperStar Virgo
★★★★

Large Resort Ship:	.........75,338 tons	Total Crew:	1,300
Lifestyle:	..................Standard	Passengers	
Cruise Line:	..............Star Cruises	(lower beds/all berths):	.....1,974/2,800
Former Names:	.................none	Passenger Space Ratio	
Builder:	........Meyer Werft (Germany)	(lower beds/all berths):	........38.1/26.9
Original Cost:	.............$350 million	Crew/Passenger Ratio	
Entered Service:	.............Aug 1999	(lower beds/all berths):	..........1.5/2.1
Registry:	.....................Panama	Navigation Officers:	......Scandinavian
Length (ft/m):	.............879.2/268.0	Cabins (total):	987
Beam (ft/m):	..............105.6/32.2	Size Range (sq ft/m):	......150.6–638.3/
Draft (ft/m):	..................25.9/7.9		14.0–59.3
Propulsion/Propellers: diesel (50,400kW)/2		Cabins (outside view):	608
Passenger Decks:	10	Cabins (interior/no view):	379

Cabins (for one person):	0
Cabins (with private balcony):	391
Cabins (wheelchair accessible):	4
Cabin Current:	..............240 volts
Elevators:	9
Casino (gaming tables):	...........Yes
Slot Machines:	....................Yes
Swimming Pools (outdoors):	2
Swimming Pools (indoors):	0
Whirlpools:	4
Self-Service Launderette:	..........No
Dedicated Cinema/Seats:	..........No
Library:	.........................Yes

OVERALL SCORE: 1,522 (OUT OF A POSSIBLE 2,000 POINTS)

OVERVIEW. *SuperStar Virgo* (sister to *SuperStar Leo,* now renamed *Norwegian Spirit*) was the second new ship ordered for the Asian market. The all-white ship has a distinctive red/blue funnel with gold star logo. There are three distinct classes of passengers. As you check-in, you will be issued with a different color boarding card: Admiral Class passengers get Yellow; Balcony Class passengers get red; World Cruisers class get Blue.

BERLITZ'S RATINGS

	Possible	Achieved
Ship	500	421
Accommodation	200	156
Food	400	293
Service	400	284
Entertainment	100	66
Cruise	400	302

There is a walk-aroun promenade deck outdoors, good for strolling. Inside, there are two boulevards, and a stunning, larger two-deck-high central atrium lobby, with three glass-walled elevators and ample space to peruse the shops and cafes that line its inner sanctum.

The casino complex is at the forward end of the atrium boulevard on Deck 7. This includes a large general-purpose, brightly lit casino, called Oasis, with gaming tables and slot machines. There's a smaller "members only" gaming club, as well as VIP gaming rooms, one of which has its own access to the upper level of the showlounge. The 450-seat Galaxy of the Stars Lounge is an observation lounge by day and a nightclub at night, with live music.

The interior decor has some distinctly European touches in its design, taste and color combinations, and the layout was modified and improved slightly from that of the sister ship (for a slightly different market). The lobby, for example, has become an Italian Piazza, with a stunning *trompe l'oeil* and multi-colored stained-glass ceiling. The decor mixes east and west, and public room names have been chosen to appeal to a mixture of Australian, European and Asian passengers. Three stairways are each carpeted in a different color, which helps new cruise passengers find their way around easily.

Other facilities include a business center (with six meet-

ing rooms), a large library and writing room, plus private mahjong and karaoke rooms, and a smoking room. A shopping concourse includes a wine shop.

Teens have their own huge video arcade, while younger children get to play in a wet 'n' wild aft pool (complete with pirate ship and caves) and two whirlpool tubs. Plus there's all the fun and facilities of Charlie's childcare center (open 24 hours a day), which includes a painting room, computer learning center, and small cinema. There's a room full of cots for toddlers to use for sleepovers, and even the toilets are at a special low height. About 15,000 sq. ft (1,400 sq. meters) is devoted to children's facilities.

Star Cruises has established a Southeast Asian regional cruise audience for its diverse fleet of ships. *SuperStar Virgo* is a good ship for the active local market, and is certainly the most comprehensive of any of the ships sailing year-round in this popular Southeast Asian region. The passenger mix is international, although the local (regional) market is now developed, so you can expect to find lots of families with children (who are allowed to roam around the ship uncontrolled – particularly on the weekend cruise).

Lots of choices, more dining options, and Asian hospitality all add up to a very attractive holiday package particularly suitable for families with children, in a very contemporary floating resort that operates from Hong Kong (Apr–Nov) and Singapore (Nov–Mar). The dress code is ultra-casual (no jacket and tie needed), and the ship operates under a "no-tipping" policy. While the initial cruise fare seems very reasonable, the extra costs and charges soon mount up if you want to indulge in more than the basics. Although service levels and finesse are inconsistent, hospitality is very good.

There are many extra cost items (in addition to the à la

carte dining spots), such as for morning tea, afternoon tea, most cabaret shows (except a crew show), and childcare. There are some inevitable entertainment and activity announcements (in English and Mandarin). Finding your way around the many areas blocked by portable "crowd containment" ribbon barriers can prove frustrating.

SUITABLE FOR: *SuperStar Virgo* is best suited to couples, singles, and families with children of all ages who want to cruise aboard a real contemporary floating resort with decent facilities and many dining spots that are really dedicated to Asians, at a very attractive price.

ACCOMMODATION. There are seven types of accommodation, in 15 price categories. Three entire decks of cabins feature private balconies, while two-thirds of all cabins have an outside view. Both the standard outside-view and interior (no view) cabins really are very small (particularly since all cabins have extra berths for a third/fourth person), so take only the very smallest amount of clothing you can (there's almost no storage space for luggage).

All cabins have a personal safe, 100% cotton towels and duvets or sheets. Bathrooms have a good-sized shower enclosure, and include personal toiletries such as Burberry soap, conditioning shampoo and body lotion.

For more space, choose one of 13 suites. Each suite has a separate lounge/dining room, bedroom, and bathroom, and an interconnecting door to an ocean-view cabin with private balcony (with light). All cabinetry features richly lacquered woods, large (stocked) wet bar with refrigerator, dining table (with a top that flips over to reveal a card table) and four chairs, sofa and drinks table, and trouser press.

The bedroom is small, completely filled by its queen-sized bed; there is a reasonable amount of drawer space (but the drawers are very small), and the closet space is rather tight (it contains two personal safes). A large en-suite bathroom is part of the bedroom and open to it – as is the trend in high-cost, interior architect-designed bathrooms ashore, and has a gorgeous mosaic tiled floor, kidney bean-shaped whirlpool bathtub, two basins, separate shower enclosure (with floor-to-ceiling ocean-view window) and separate toilet (with glass door). There are TV sets in the lounge, bedroom and bathroom.

For even more space, choose one of the six largest suites (Boracay, Nicobar, Langkawi, Majorca, Phuket, and Sentosa) and you'll have a generous amount of private living space, with a separate lounge, dining area, bedroom, large bathroom, and private balcony (with light). All cabinetry features richly lacquered woods, large (stocked) wet bar with refrigerator, dining table (with a top that flips over to reveal a card table) and four chairs, sofa and drinks table, and trouser press. The bedrooms and large en-suite bathrooms are similar to those in the suites already described. There are televisions in the lounge, bedroom and bathroom.

A small room service menu is available (with a 15% service charge plus a gratuity).

CUISINE. There is certainly plenty of choice, with eight venues (all non-smoking). You need to plan your venue in advance, or you may be disappointed. The following eateries are included in the cruise price:

● **Bella Vista** seats over 600 in an open-seating arrangement, although, in effect it operates two seatings. The aft section is two decks high, and huge cathedral-style windows are set in three sections overlooking the stern.

● **Mediterranean Buffet:** this is a large self-serve buffet restaurant with indoor/outdoor seating for 400.

● **The Pavilion Room:** has traditional Cantonese Chinese cuisine, including dim sum at lunchtime.

The following are à la carte (extra-cost) dining spots:

● **Noble House:** a Chinese Restaurant, with traditional Hong Kong-themed decor and items such as dim sum (there are also two small private dining rooms).

● **Palazzo:** a beautiful, if slightly ostentatious Italian restaurant. It has fine food, and a genuine Renoir painting (well protected by cameras and alarms).

● **Samurai:** a Japanese restaurant and sushi bar (for sashimi and sushi). There are two teppanyaki grills, each with 10 seats, where the chef cooks in front of you.

● **The Taj:** an Indian/Vegetarian dining spot that offers a range of food in a self-serve buffet setup.

● **Blue Lagoon:** a casual 24-hour street cafe with noodle dishes, fried rice and other Southeast Asian dishes.

● **Out of Africa:** a casual karaoke cafe and bar, where coffees, teas and pastries are available.

ENTERTAINMENT. The Lido showlounge, with 934 seats, is two decks high, with a main and balcony levels (the balcony level is reserved for "gaming club" members only). The room has almost no support columns to obstruct the sightlines, and a revolving stage for revues and other production shows (typically to recorded music – there is no live showband). "Kingdom of Kung-Fu," with a cast of 30, features the power and form of the Shaolin Masters in an action-packed martial arts show. The showlounge can also be used as a large-screen cinema, with superb surround sound.

In addition, local specialty cabaret acts are brought on board, as are revue-style shows (complete with topless dancers). Bands and small musical units provide plenty of live music for dancing and listening in the various lounges.

SPA/FITNESS. The Roman Spa and Fitness Center is located on one of the uppermost decks, just forward of the Tivoli Pool. It has a gymnasium full of high-tech muscle-toning equipment, and aerobics exercise room, hair and beauty salon, and saunas, steam rooms, and changing rooms for men and women, as well as several treatment rooms, and aqua-swim pools that provide counter-flow jets. There is an extra charge for use of the sauna and steam rooms.

Although there are several types of massages available, Thai massage is a specialty of the spa (you can have it in the spa, outdoors on deck, in your cabin or on your private balcony, space permitting). Sports facilities include a jogging track, golf driving range, basketball and tennis courts, and there are four levels of sunbathing decks.

The Calypso
★★★+

Small Ship: . . . . .11,162 tons	Passenger Decks: 8	Cabins (with private balcony): 0
Lifestyle: . . . . .Standard	Total Crew: 220	Cabins (wheelchair accessible): 2
Cruise Line: . . . . .Thomson Cruises/	Passengers	Cabin Current: . . . . .110 volts
Louis Cruise Lines	(lower beds/all berths): 486/740	Dining Rooms: 1
Former Names: . . . . . .*Regent Jewel, Sun*	Passenger Space Ratio	Elevators: 2
Fiesta, Ionian Harmony, Canguro Verde	(lower beds/all berths): 22.9/15.0	Casino (gaming tables): . . . . .Yes
Builder: . . . . .Fincantieri (Italy)	Crew/Passenger Ratio	Slot Machines: . . . . .Yes
Original Cost: .n/a	(lower beds/all berths): 2.2/3.3	Swimming Pools (outdoors): 1
Entered Service: 1968/July 2000	Navigation Officers: . . . . .European	Swimming Pools (indoors): 0
Registry: . . . . .Cyprus	Cabins (total): 243	Whirlpools: 0
Length (ft/m): 444.2/135.4	Size Range (sq ft/m): .135–244/12.5–22.6	Self-Service Launderette: . . . . .No
Beam (ft/m): 62.9/19.2	Cabins (outside view): 158	Dedicated Cinema/Seats: . . . . .No
Draft (ft/m): 20.6/6.3	Cabins (interior/no view): 85	Library: . . . . .Yes
Propulsion/Propellers: .diesel (9,000kW)/2	Cabins (for one person): 0	

OVERALL SCORE: 990 (OUT OF A POSSIBLE 2,000 POINTS)

OVERVIEW. *The Calypso*, a former Mediterranean ferry, was extensively reconstructed in 1999. Although its profile is a little bit unusual, one nice aspect is its enclosed wooden promenade deck (good for strolling, or just sitting and reading). There is a decent selection of public rooms, bars and lounges, considering the ship's size. The interior decor is very pleasant; there's a cozy and unpretentious ambiance, and the dress code is relaxed, with formal attire not required. The onboard currency is the UK pound.

This is a high-density ship, so it is very crowded when full, and there may be a large number of smokers. There are very steep, narrow stairways on the outer decks. The ship operates under charter to Thomson Cruises for adults-only cruises during the summer months of 2008 and 2009.

SUITABLE FOR: The ship is best suited to adult couples seeking a low-priced, but comfortable ship for a first short cruise experience, with unpretentious and unstuffy surroundings and acceptable food and service.

ACCOMMODATION. There are four suites, seven semi-deluxe, 147 outside-view cabins and 85 interior (no view) cabins. The price you pay depends on grade, size and location (cabins on higher decks command higher prices). No matter which cabin you choose, however, all have double or twin beds, television set, telephone, personal safe, and bathrooms have a shower enclosure, toilet and washbasin.

The cabins have warm pastel decor, although the artwork

BERLITZ'S RATINGS

	Possible	Achieved
Ship	500	195
Accommodation	200	95
Food	400	209
Service	400	241
Entertainment	100	55
Cruise	400	195

is minimal, and the fabrics and other soft furnishings could be of better quality. Some cabins have a third and fourth upper berth (there is only one personal safe), and drawer and storage space is very limited (in other words, take as little clothing as possible). Those designated as suites also have a refrigerator/minibar. There is a cabin service menu, although it is quite limited.

CUISINE. L'Orchidee dining room, in the aft section of the ship, is reasonably attractive and decorated, although its layout is somewhat awkward, as it is positioned on two slightly different levels. There are two seatings, and tables are for four, six or eight persons.

The menu choice is quite good (it includes a vegetarian option), and the food has plenty of taste. The service comes with a smile. Breakfast and lunch buffets are quite attractive, with plenty of variety. The wine list is very small, but prices are reasonable (don't expect vintage wines).

ENTERTAINMENT. The showlounge is a single-level room, and pillars obstruct sightlines from many seats. The entertainment is adequate, and consists mainly of cabaret acts (singers, comedians, magic acts) strung together to make shows that are sometimes overlong. Several bands and musical units provide live music for dancing and listening.

SPA/FITNESS. Apart from a small gymnasium and sauna, there is little else. Massage, however, is available (the massage room is tiny), as are beauty/hair treatments.

The Emerald
★★ +

Mid-Size Ship: . . . . .26,428 tons	Passenger Decks: 10	Cabins (for one person): 10
Lifestyle: . . . . .Standard	Total Crew: 412	Cabins (with private balcony): 0
Cruise Line: . . . . .Louis Cruise Lines	Passengers	Cabins (wheelchair accessible): 2
Former Names: . . . . . . .Regent Rainbow,	(lower beds/all berths): 990/1,198	Cabin Current: . . . . . . .110 and 220 volts
Diamond Island, Santa Rosa	Passenger Space Ratio	Elevators: 3
Builder: Newport News Shipbuilding (USA)	(lower beds/all berths): 26.6/22.0	Casino (gaming tables): . . . . .Yes
Original Cost: . . . .$25 million	Crew/Passenger Ratio	Slot Machines: . . . . .Yes
Entered Service: . . . .June 1958/Apr 1997	(lower beds/all berths): 2.4/2.9	Swimming Pools (outdoors): 1
Registry: .Cyprus	Navigation Officers: . . . . .Greek/European	Swimming Pools (indoors): 0
Length (ft/m): 599.0/182.57	Cabins (total): 500	Whirlpools: 2
Beam (ft/m): 84.0/25.60	Size Range (sq ft/m): 124.8–304.6/	Self-Service Launderette: . . . . .No
Draft (ft/m): 27.5/8.38	11.6–28.3	Dedicated Cinema/Seats: . . . . .No
Propulsion/Propellers: . . . . .steam turbine	Cabins (outside view): 338	Library: . . . . .Yes
(16,400kW)/2	Cabins (interior/no view): 162	

BERLITZ'S OVERALL SCORE: 1,061 (OUT OF A POSSIBLE 2,000 POINTS)

OVERVIEW. This solid, American-built, former ocean liner benefits from a strong, riveted hull, while all new ships are seam-welded. The open deck and sunbathing space is quite limited when the ship is full, although there are a good number of sunloungers. There is, however, a good wrap-around promenade deck outdoors, with plenty of chairs.

The ship's interiors are quite pleasant and surprisingly comfortable, and have a warm decor that is contemporary without being at all brash. Many of the public rooms have high ceilings, and the ship has a spacious ocean-liner feel. There are some fine wrought-iron railings on the stairways. The artwork, unfortunately, is low-budget stuff.

For short cruises, this ship provides a range of public spaces that, in turn, promote a good party ambiance and a number of bars for drinking in (five, actually). The casino is quite large, and has a high ceiling.

SUITABLE FOR: The Emerald is best suited to adult couples and singles who want a first cruise providing very good value-for-money vacation in unpretentious, old-style surroundings (typically 80 percent of passengers are over 45).

ACCOMMODATION. There are six main categories: Premier, Superior Outside Plus, Superior Outside, Superior Inside (no view), Standard Outside, and Standard Inside (no view).

Cabins are assigned at embarkation check-in unless you pay a supplement of £30 per cabin to pre-book (you can choose your preferred cabin from the deck plan. This method of assigning cabins means that those who book first, and those who arrive first at the embarkation port, probably will get the best cabins. It's better to pre-book.

BERLITZ'S RATINGS		
	Possible	Achieved
Ship	500	243
Accommodation	200	107
Food	400	208
Service	400	238
Entertainment	100	50
Cruise	400	215

Many of the original cabins are quite spacious, with good closet and drawer space, while newer ones are a little more compact, and have poor insulation. Continental breakfast in your cabin will cost about $7.50 (£4.50) extra per person (each time). There is also a 24-hour cabin service menu for snacks, all of which cost extra.

CUISINE. The Chanterelle Dining Room (non-smoking) is in the center of the ship. It has large ocean-view windows. A second restaurant, Le Bistro (non-smoking), is also in the center of the ship, but two decks above the Chanterelle.

While it won't win any awards, the food quality and its variety and presentation are actually quite decent considering the cost of a cruise. That there is always a vegetarian entrée for lunch and dinner (as well as vegetarian appetizers and soups). The service is friendly and quite attentive, but don't expect grand hotel-style service.

ENTERTAINMENT. The sight lines in the showlounge really are poor (particularly from port and starboard side seating areas, where there is obstruction from 12 thick pillars). The shows, although not of the top professional variety, are, nonetheless fun and entertaining for the whole family. In addition, there is plenty of music for dancing, both live and recorded.

SPA/FITNESS. There is a small, windowless fitness center, located low down in the ship. There's also a sauna, while the ship's beauty salon is located on another deck – again in an interior position (there is no natural light, which makes tinting and coloring difficult).

The Iris
★★

Small Ship: . . . . .12,688 tons	Passenger Decks: 7	Cabins (for one person): 3
Lifestyle: . . . . .Standard	Total Crew: 170	Cabins (with private balcony): 0
Cruise Line: . . . . .Mano Cruise	Passengers	Cabins (wheelchair accessible): 1
Former Names: . . . .*Francesca,*	(lower beds/all berths): 462/828	Cabin Current: . . . . .220 volts
Konstantin Simonov	Passenger Space Ratio	Elevators: 2
Builder: . . . . . .Szczesin Stocznia (Poland)	(lower beds/all berths): 27.4/15.3	Casino (gaming tables): . . . . .Yes
Original Cost: .n/a	Crew/Passenger Ratio	Slot Machines: . . . . .Yes
Entered Service: . . . . .Apr 1982/Mar 2001	(lower beds/all berths): 2.7/4.8	Swimming Pools (outdoors): 1
Registry: . . . . .Malta	Navigation Officers: . . . . .European	Swimming Pools (indoors): 0
Length (ft/m): 452.7/138.0	Cabins (total): .231	Whirlpools: 1
Beam (ft/m): 68.8/21.0	Size Range (sq ft/m): . . . . .n/a	Self-Service Launderette: . . . . .Yes
Draft (ft/m): 19.0/5.8	Cabins (outside view): 157	Dedicated Cinema/Seats: . . . . .No
Propulsion/Propellers: diesel (12,800kW)/2	Cabins (interior/no view): 74	Library: . . . . .No

OVERALL SCORE: 890 (OUT OF A POSSIBLE 2,000 POINTS)

OVERVIEW. *The Iris*, which was refurbished in 2001, has an angular profile with a boxy stern (complete with fold-down car ramps), stubby bow and a fat funnel placed amidships – otherwise it's a moderately handsome vessel. It has a fully enclosed bridge for all-weather operation. There is also a small helicopter landing deck, and the ship can also take about 20 private cars.

This vessel was placed under charter to Israel's Mano Cruise in 2001. Maintenance is generally sound, and the ship is clean and tidy. By international standards, though, its quality, facilities, fittings and fixtures only match ships of a low standard. It's the onboard product, however, and particularly the food, where Mano Cruise achieves some distinction.

Some cruises during Jewish holidays cost more. To the cost of your cruise, you need to add port charges, handling fees and administrative expenses.

Both interior and exterior staircases are quite steep, the ship having been originally built in Poland as a ro-ro/passenger ferry. There's a limited amount of open deck and sunning space (particularly if the ship is full) and a tiny swimming pool that is really a "dip" pool. Public rooms include the Galaxy Piano Bar, a casino (with tables and slot machines), a discotheque, main lounge, a large duty-free shop, and a small children's playroom.

SUITABLE FOR: *The Iris* is best suited to Hebrew-speaking passengers seeking a first taste of cruising aboard a ship of very modest facilities and features, but with good food.

ACCOMMODATION. There are eight price grades. These include 20 Presidential Suites, 4 Royal Suites, the other

BERLITZ'S RATINGS

	Possible	Achieved
Ship	500	207
Accommodation	200	90
Food	400	191
Service	400	194
Entertainment	100	41
Cruise	400	167

accommodation being a variety of outside-view and interior (no view) cabins. Except for the 13 large cabins classed as "suites," all are small and somewhat utilitarian in their fittings and furnishings. Cabin hallways are plain.

There is very little drawer space, the under-bed storage space for luggage is tight, and lighting is minimal. Some 33 cabins are fitted with upper two lower beds and two upper berths. All have a private bathroom, with shower, and a small cabinet for toiletry items (only soap is supplied).

The suites have a much larger bathroom, with bathtub and shower combination, and each has a television and video player. The two largest of the "luxe" cabins have a separate bedroom with plenty of closet and drawer space, and a large bathroom with bathtub and shower combination.

CUISINE. The Grand Restaurant and Topaz Restaurant have two seatings, and tables for four, six or eight. The food is surprisingly good, with lots of fresh salads and vegetables, as well as good meats and local fish. There is certainly plenty of variety. Kosher food can also be supplied for a surcharge of around $19 per passenger, per day.

ENTERTAINMENT. The shows in the L-shaped Palace Club are strictly geared to the Israeli cruise market, with visiting cabaret acts and a small troupe of resident dancers. There is live and recorded music for dancing and listening.

SPA/FITNESS. In 2004, a small spa/health club was created in a space previously part of the garage/storage area. The facilities include a small gym, sauna, and massage rooms.

Thomson Celebration
★★★ +

Mid-Size Ship: . . . . .33,930 tons	Passenger Decks: 10	Cabins (for one person): 0
Lifestyle: . . . . .Standard	Total Crew: .520	Cabins (with private balcony): 0
Cruise Line: . . . . .Thomson Cruises	Passengers	Cabins (wheelchair accessible): 4
Former Names: . . . .*Noordam*	(lower beds/all berths): 1,254/1,350	Cabin Current: . . . . .110 and 220 volts
Builder: . . . . . . .Chantiers de l'Atlantique	Passenger Space Ratio	Elevators: 7
(France)	(lower beds/all berths): 27.0/25.1	Casino (gaming tables): . . . . .Yes
Original Cost: . . . .$160 million	Crew/Passenger Ratio	Slot Machines: . . . . .Yes
Entered Service: . . . . .Apr 1984/May 2005	(lower beds/all berths): 2.4/2.6	Swimming Pools (outdoors): 2
Registry: . . . . .Dutch Antilles	Navigation Officers: . . . . .European	Swimming Pools (indoors): 0
Length (ft/m): 704.2/214.66	Cabins (total): .627	Whirlpools: 1
Beam (ft/m): 89.4/27.26	Size Range (sq ft/m): 150.6–296.0/	Self-Service Launderette: . . . . .Yes
Draft (ft/m): 24.2/7.40	14.0–27.5	Dedicated Cinema/Seats: Yes/230
Propulsion/Propellers: . . . . .diesel	Cabins (outside view): 413	Library: . . . . .Yes
(21,600 kW)/2	Cabins (interior/no view): 194	

OVERALL SCORE: 1,313 (OUT OF A POSSIBLE 2,000 POINTS)

OVERVIEW. *Thomson Celebration* (formerly Holland America Line's *Noordam*) and sister to *Thomson Spirit* (formerly Holland America Line's *Nieuw Amsterdam*), has a nicely raked bow and a contemporary transom stern, but overall the ship's angular exterior superstructure design makes it look rather squat. There is a good amount of open deck space, and the traditional teakwood decks outdoors include a wrap-around promenade deck. The ship, however, is now quite dated and occasionally suffers from some vibration. Perhaps its best asset is its friendly and personable international crew.

The ship has a spacious interior design and layout, with most public rooms located aft in a vertical arrangement, while accommodation is positioned in the forward section, which keeps noise away from the accommodation areas. The soothing color combinations do not jar the senses; although they are rather dark and somber, with some new color splashes added during the ship's refurbishment in 2005. There is much polished teakwood and rosewood paneling throughout the interiors. Horizon's observation lounge, atop the ship, is a pleasant retreat, with fine views forward. The main lounge, which has a small balcony level, is reminiscent of those found on former ocean liners, and is really more suited to cabaret entertainment, and not full production shows. While children are also catered to (with their own play areas and hosts), the majority of passengers are adults.

The ship is exclusively chartered by Thomson Cruises, so your fellow passengers are likely to be mostly British, and typically about 90 percent of passengers will be over 55. Refreshingly, all gratuities are included, and the onboard currency is the pound sterling. Thomson Celebration oper-

BERLITZ'S RATINGS

	Possible	Achieved
Ship	500	332
Accommodation	200	137
Food	400	241
Service	400	261
Entertainment	100	64
Cruise	400	278

ates a wide variety of cruises, and, for part of the year, is based in the UK.

Thomson Cruises' ships are non-smoking, although smoking areas are provided in most public rooms. Note that there are many interior (no view) cabins, and standing in line for embarkation, disembarkation, shore tenders and for self-serve buffet meals is an inevitable aspect of cruising aboard all large ships.

SUITABLE FOR: *Thomson Celebration* is best suited to adult couples and singles taking their first or second cruise, seeking a modern (but not glitzy) ship with a wide array of public lounges and bars, and a middle-of-the-road lifestyle, with food and entertainment that is quite acceptable rather than fancy.

ACCOMMODATION. There is one suite grade, four grades of outside-view cabins (one designated Deluxe), two grades of interior (no view) cabins. There are four cabins for the disabled (these are large, and have great forward-facing views). You can pre-book your preferred cabin for a per cabin fee of £30 (around US$50).

In general, most cabins have a reasonable amount of space, although they are small when compared with those of many other ships. In general, they are adequately appointed and practically laid out, with some wood furniture and fittings, wood paneling, good counter and storage space (although there is very little drawer space), a large mirror, and a private bathroom very modest in size.

The top three categories of cabins (which are only marginally larger and should not really be called suites or mini-suites) have bathtubs while all others have shower enclosures only. Several cabins have king- or queen-sized beds, although most have twin beds (some, but not all, can be pushed together). In many cabins, particularly those that are interior (no view), the bed configuration is L-shaped, and the beds cannot be pushed together.

A number of cabins also have additional upper berths for a third/fourth person. Room service is provided 24 hours a day. All cabin televisions receive live news via satellite. Note that the cabin insulation is really quite poor, and bathroom towels are small. In addition, some cabins on Boat and Navigation Decks have lifeboat-obstructed views.

CUISINE. The Meridian Restaurant, which sits in the center of the ship, is a reasonably large and attractive room, with warm decor, and ample space. Breakfast and lunch and dinner (6pm–10.30pm) are served in an open-seating arrangement, so you may get a different table and different waiters for each meal. Although there are a few tables for two, most are for four, six or eight. Dinners typically include a choice of four entrées; a vegetarian entrée is also available daily.

Children have their very own menu, with "home-from-home" dishes and small portions. Dessert and pastry items will typically be of good quality, and made specifically for British tastes, although there is much use of canned fruits and jellies.

A small à la carte restaurant is an alternative dining spot (reservations are required and a per-person cover charge applies). It seats up to 45 and has superior food and service as well as a quieter, more refined atmosphere. It is located adjacent to the Meridian Restaurant, but is best entered from the aft stairway.

Instead of the more formal dining room, there is also a Lido Restaurant for a more casual setting. This is open 24 hours a day in an open-seating arrangement. Tables are set with crisp linens, flatware and stemware for dinner, when a set menu includes a choice of four entrées. Each week a themed buffet (Chinese, Indian or Mexican, depending on the cruise itinerary) may be featured for dinner. On Lido Deck, the outdoor Terrace Grill provides fast-food grilled items and pizza during the day. Note that all dining venues are non-smoking.

ENTERTAINMENT. The 600-seat Broadway Showlounge, two decks high (with a main and balcony level), is the principal venue for production shows and cabaret entertainment. Note that there are many pillars in the show lounge, so sightlines are obstructed from some seats.

Thomson presents an array of production shows that are colorful, lively, and entertaining (aboard other Thomson charters, the young entertainment/cruise staff enthusiastically provide the shows), while cabaret acts provide entertainment on evenings when there are no production shows.

A second entertainment venue (Hemingway's) is a multifunctional room for quizzes, dancing, and for use as a latenight discotheque. A number of bands and musical units provide live music for dancing and listening in several lounges and bars.

SPA/FITNESS. Oceans Health Club is atop the ship at the aft end. It has good ocean views, and overlooks the aft pool. Facilities include an aerobics exercise room, a decent size gymnasium (there are plenty of treadmills, exercycles, and other body-toning and muscle-pumping equipment), sauna (there is no steam room), and four body treatment rooms. You can have massages, aromatherapy facials, body wraps, manicures, pedicures, and hair beautifying treatments.

Note that the beauty salon is located in a completely different area (close to the Reception Desk on the port side) to the health and fitness facilities.

Sample treatment prices: Swedish Classic Massage/ Indian Head Massage £30 (30 minutes) or £44 (45 minutes) or £52 (60 minutes); Cleansing Facial £36; Pedicure and Foot Massage £22; Exfoliating Body Polish £34.

Thomson Destiny
★★★ +

Mid-Size Ship: ....37,773 tons	Total Crew: 540	Cabins (for one person): 0
Lifestyle: ....Standard	Passengers	Cabins (with private balcony): 9
Cruise Line: ....Thomson Cruises	(lower beds/all berths): 1,450/1,611	Cabins (wheelchair accessible): 0
Former Names: *Sunbird, Song of America*	Passenger Space Ratio	Cabin Current: ....110 volts
Builder: ....Wartsila (Finland)	(lower beds/all berths): 26.0/23.4	Elevators: 7
Original Cost: ....$140 million	Crew/Passenger Ratio	Casino (gaming tables): ....Yes
Entered Service: ....Dec 1982/May 2005	(lower beds/all berths): 2.6/2.9	Slot Machines: ....Yes
Registry: ....The Bahamas	Navigation Officers: ....International	Swimming Pools (outdoors): 2
Length (ft/m): 705.0/214.88	Cabins (total): 725	Swimming Pools (indoors): 0
Beam (ft/m): 93.1/28.40	Size Range (sq ft/m): 118.4–425.1/	Whirlpools: 0
Draft (ft/m): 22.3/6.80	11.0–39.5	Self-Service Launderette: ....No
Propulsion/Propellers: diesel (16,480kW)/2	Cabins (outside view): 425	Dedicated Cinema/Seats: ....No
Passenger Decks: 11	Cabins (interior/no view): 300	Library: ....Yes

OVERALL SCORE: 1,303 (OUT OF A POSSIBLE 2,000 POINTS)

OVERVIEW. Originally built for Royal Caribbean International, the ship was sold in 1999 to My Travel/Sun Cruises, which pulled out of cruise vacations and ship ownership towards the end of 2004. It is now the largest ship in the Thomson Cruises fleet (on charter until 2011). The all-white ship, now refurbished, is smart-looking, with nicely rounded lines, sharply raked bow, and a single funnel with a cantilevered, wrap-around lounge called the Chart Room (a fine place from which to observe the world around and below you).

BERLITZ'S RATINGS		
	Possible	Achieved
Ship	500	340
Accommodation	200	125
Food	400	241
Service	400	261
Entertainment	100	66
Cruise	400	270

There is a decent amount of open deck and sunbathing space (but it will be crowded when the ship sails full, which is most of the time), and some nicely polished wooden decks and rails. There are two swimming pools – the aft pool designated for children, the forward pool for adults.

The interior decor is bright and breezy. There is a good array of public rooms, most of which have high ceilings, and are one deck above the dining room. These include the main show lounge, casino and nightclub. There is also a small conference center for meetings, as well as an internet café (with six computer terminals – but no café).

Thomson Cruises provides a consistent, well-tuned and well-packaged, fun product, in comfortable surroundings. As part of Thomson Holidays, it uses the Thomson-owned Britannia Airways and is therefore able to offer complete cruise-air-stay packages at such attractive rates. The company does a good job of getting you and your luggage from aircraft to ship without having to go through immigration (depending on itinerary) in foreign countries whenever possible – so your cruise holiday is relatively seamless. The company offers airlift from almost a score of UK airports via Britannia Airlines. You can pre-book a window seat for an extra £10 per adult (£5 for children), and a premium seat (more space than standard seats) for £20 per person, while pre-booked meals cost £10 per person (£5 per child).

The company's brochures tell it like it is – so you know before you go exactly what you will get for your money. Like other ships in the Thomson Cruises fleet, the space per passenger (particularly on the open decks) is very tight when the ships are full. There is little choice of tea and coffee. There are no cushioned pads for the sunloungers.

Standing in line for embarkation, disembarkation, shore tenders and for self-serve buffet meals is an inevitable aspect of cruising aboard all large ships.

Your fellow passengers are likely to be British (typically about 80 percent of passengers will be over 45). During the summer a lot of families with children go cruising, so you can expect to find them everywhere. Perhaps the best part of cruising aboard *Thomson Destiny* lies in the destinations, and not the ship (although it is perfectly comfortable). Hotel add-ons can extend a cruise vacation, and Thomson has a fine collection, depending on your needs, budget, and whether you are traveling with children (or grandchildren). The onboard currency is the British pound. All Thomson Cruises' ships are non-smoking, although smoking areas are provided in most public rooms.

SUITABLE FOR: *Thomson Destiny* is best suited to adult couples, singles, singles taking their first or second cruise, and families with children, all seeking a modern (but not glitzy) ship with a wide array of public lounges and bars, a middle-of-the-road lifestyle, with food and entertainment that is quite acceptable rather than fancy, and a British ambience. The company does not actively market or specialize in cruises for families with children because the children's and youth facilities are limited (there is also no evening babysitting service).

ACCOMMODATION. This is provided in five categories and nine price bands: Interior (no-view) Cabins (parallel or L-shaped bed arrangement), Outside View Cabins (parallel or L-shaped bed arrangement), Deluxe Cabins (with parallel twin beds that can be converted to a queen-sized bed), Suites and Grand Suites. You can now also book the exact cabin and location you want if you pay an extra charge of £30 per cabin (roughly US$55), which also lets you choose whether to dine at the early or late evening seating.

Most cabins are of a similar size (actually very small compared to today's newer ships) and the insulation between them is quite poor. The cabins also have mediocre closets and very little storage space, yet somehow everyone seems to manage. They are just about adequate for a one-week cruise, as you will need only a small selection of mainly casual clothes (you'll probably have to put your shoes – and luggage – under the bed).

Most bathrooms typically contain a washbasin, toilet, and shower, with very little space for your toiletry items. Although they are reasonably cheerful, the shower enclosure is small, and has a curtain that you will probably end up dancing with. Towels are 100% cotton.

In some cabins, twin beds are fixed in a parallel mode (some are moveable and can be made into a queen-sized bed), while others may be in an L-shape. Note that in almost all cabins there is a "lip" or threshold (of about 9 inches/23 cm) at the bathroom door step over.

You can get more space and a larger cabin if you book one of the 21 slightly more expensive deluxe-grade cabins on Promenade Deck. These have twin beds that convert to a queen-sized bed, set diagonally into a sleeping area adjacent to outside-view windows. There is more drawer space, more closet space, and the bathroom has a half-size tub and shower combination – bathrobes are also provided. The largest of these deluxe-grade cabins is Cabin 7000.

For even more exclusivity, you can book one of nine Suites. All are located in a private area, have fine wood paneling and trim, and come with additional space and better, more personalized service.

The additional space includes a lounge area with sofa (this converts to a double bed – making it ideal for families with children), coffee table and two chairs, a vanity desk, combination TV/VCR, an abundance of drawers, illuminated closets (with both hanging space and several shelves), excellent storage space, king-sized bed, and bathrobes. The bathroom is fully tiled, and has a full-sized enamel bathtub (rare in ships today) with shower, pink granite-look washbasin, and plenty of storage space for toiletry items. Suite occupants also get a semi-private balcony (the door of which is extremely heavy and difficult to open) with drinks table and two teak chairs. Book one of the two Grand Suites, and you'll get even more room – plus views over the ship's bows and a larger balcony (these can be overlooked

from the open deck above), more floor space, and a walk-in closet. Missing are a bedside telephone and a bathroom telephone.

The cabin voltage is 110 volts, so British passengers will need to take a US-style adapter for any electrical appliances such as a hairdryer. Note that the accommodation deck hallways are also very narrow on some decks.

CUISINE. The Seven Seas Restaurant, a large room, consists of a central main section and two long, narrow wings (the Magellan Room and Galileo Room) with large, ocean-view windows. The low ceiling creates a high level of ambient noise. There are two seatings, both no-smoking. There are tables for two (but only 14), four, six or eight (window tables are for two or six). The service is average.

The cuisine is basic, no-frills food. There is plenty of it, though; indeed, it is quantity, not quality, that prevails, but do remember that it is all provided at a low cost. Presentation is a weak point, and there are no fish knives. If you enjoy going out to eat, and enjoy being adventurous with your food and eating habits – then you could be disappointed. The menus are standard and deviation is difficult. Bottled water is offered, and costs extra; the ship's drinking water (for which there is no charge) is adequate.

There is an adequate, but limited, wine list, and the wines are almost all very young – typical of supermarket bottles. Wine prices are quite modest, as are the prices for most alcoholic beverages.

For casual, self-serve breakfasts and lunches, the Veranda Cafe is the alternative choice, although the tables and seats outdoors are of metal and plastic, and the buffets are basic and old-fashioned. The low cruise price dictates the use of plastic cups and plastic stirrers (teaspoons are unheard of). At night you can "dine" under the steel and canvas canopy, where the café becomes a pleasant, outdoors alternative to the dining room – and includes waiter service.

ENTERTAINMENT. The Can Can Lounge is the venue for all entertainment events and social functions, and has a stage and hardwood dance floor. It is a single-level room, designed more for cabaret acts than for large-scale production shows. The revue-style shows are typically of the end-of-pier variety type, with an energetic, well-meaning cast of young people who also double as cruise staff during the day, together with some professional cabaret acts.

Another, smaller room, the Oklahoma Lounge, has a stage and dance floor, and is often used to present late-night comedy and other acts.

SPA/FITNESS. Although the spa facilities are not exactly generous, there is a gymnasium, sauna (no steam room), changing rooms for men and women, and a beauty salon. Spa and beauty services are provided by Harding Brothers, who operate similar beauty services for a number of cruise lines. You can book a massage, an aromatherapy facial, manicure and pedicure, among other treatments.

Thomson Spirit
★★★ +

Large Resort Ship: ....33,930 tons	Passenger Decks: 10	Cabins (for one person): 0
Lifestyle: ....Standard	Total Crew: 520	Cabins (with private balcony): 0
Cruise Line: ....Thomson Cruises	Passengers	Cabins (wheelchair accessible): 4
Former Names: ......Nieuw Amsterdam,	(lower beds/all berths): 1,254/1,350	Cabin Current: ....110 and 220 volts
Patriot, Nieuw Amsterdam	Passenger Space Ratio	Elevators: 7
Builder: .Chantiers de l'Atlantique (France)	(lower beds/all berths): 27.0/25.1	Casino (gaming tables): ....Yes
Original Cost: ....$150 million	Crew/Passenger Ratio	Slot Machines: ....Yes
Entered Service: ....July 1983/May 2002	(lower beds/all berths): 2.4/2.6	Swimming Pools (outdoors): 2
Registry: ....The Bahamas	Navigation Officers: ....European	Swimming Pools (indoors): 0
Length (ft/m): 704.2/214.66	Cabins (total): 627	Whirlpools: 1
Beam (ft/m): 89.4/27.26	Size Range (sq ft/m): 150.6–296.0/	Self-Service Launderette: ....Yes (3)
Draft (ft/m): 24.6/7.52	14.0–27.5	Dedicated Cinema/Seats: Yes/230
Propulsion/Propellers:	Cabins (outside view): 413	Library: ....Yes
diesel (21,600 kW)/2	Cabins (interior/no view): 194	

OVERALL SCORE: 1,311 (OUT OF A POSSIBLE 2,000 POINTS)

OVERVIEW. *Thomson Spirit* was originally built for and operated by Holland America Line. It has a nicely raked bow and a contemporary transom stern, but overall the ship's angular exterior superstructure design makes it look squat and quite boxy. The ship's exterior has an all-white hull and superstructure. There is a good amount of open teakwood deck space (particularly at the aft section of the ship), and the traditional outdoors teakwood decks include a wrap-around promenade deck. Unfortunately, the ship has always suffered from poor build quality (it was built in a French shipyard) and excessive vibration, particularly at the stern, since new.

As *Patriot*, the ship had a disastrous, short-lived liaison with United States Lines, following its sale by Holland America Line to the publicly funded United States Lines in 2000. That venture was short-lived, and United States Lines collapsed in a sea of debt owed to US taxpayers in October 2001. Carnival Corporation (owners of Holland America Line) repurchased the ship for the amount outstanding ($79.8 million), and then chartered it to Louis Cruise Lines, who in turn has sub-chartered it to Thomson Cruises for a three-and-a-half year period. *Thomson Spirit* has a sister ship in the slightly newer, 1984-built *Thomson Celebration* (formerly Holland America Line's *Noordam*).

Thomson first operated cruises in the 1970s, then abandoned them, only to start cruises operations again in the mid-1990s (it has proved a highly successful venture, offering extremely good value for money, particularly for adult couples, and occasionally families with children), using chartered, rather than wholly-owned ships.

Thomson Spirit has quite a spacious interior design and

BERLITZ'S RATINGS		
	Possible	Achieved
Ship	500	330
Accommodation	200	137
Food	400	241
Service	400	261
Entertainment	100	64
Cruise	400	278

layout, with little crowding and almost no points of congestion, and most of the public rooms are located on a single deck. The color combinations do not jar the senses (most are pretty nondescript, although there are many splashes of color), and the decor was greatly changed and brightened during the change to its new owners. There is much polished teakwood and rosewood paneling throughout the interiors. For quieter moments, try the Horizon Lounge, atop the ship; it has a wooden dance floor. The main lounge, with a small balcony level, is reminiscent of the ocean liners of yesteryear.

Children are well catered to, with their own play areas at the aft of Bridge Deck. There are several children's clubs: Tots is for 3–5 year-olds, Team is for 6–8 year-olds, while Tribe is for 9–12 year-olds. The clubs operate five days a week (not on embarkation or disembarkation days), and are supervised by qualified "Children's Hosts."

It's good to see a tour operator like Thomson Cruises charter and operate this ship, especially since competition in the cruise industry is increasing. This ship is quite acceptable for passengers wanting pleasant surroundings and an all-British ambiance. However, many newer ships have more space, better facilities and more options, and these leave this ship losing a few points in relation to the increased competition in the international marketplace.

Perhaps the best part of cruising aboard *Thomson Spirit* lies in the destinations, and not the ship (although it is perfectly comfortable). Hotel add-ons can extend a cruise vacation, and Thomson has a fine collection, depending on your needs, budget, and whether you are traveling with children (or grandchildren). The ship is exclusive to Thomson

Cruises, so your fellow passengers are likely to be British (typically about 80 percent of passengers will be over 45).

In the UK market, Thomson goes head to head with the *Ocean Village* and Island Cruises' *Island Escape* cruise concept for the young at heart. However, Thomson, like Island Cruises, owns its own airline (Britannia Airlines), and has much experience in operating fly-cruises to the Mediterranean (the company offers airlift from almost a score of UK airports). With Thomson, you only pay for what you want. As far as Britannia aircraft seats go, you can pre-book a window seat for an extra £10 per adult (£5 for children), and a premium seat (more space than standard seats) for £25 per person, while pre-booked meals cost £10 per person (£5 per child).

All Thomson Cruises' ships are non-smoking, although smoking areas are provided in most public rooms. Standing in line for embarkation, disembarkation, shore tenders and for self-serve buffet meals is inevitable aboard all large ships.

SUITABLE FOR: *Thomson Spirit* is best suited to adult couples and singles taking their first or second cruise, families with children of all ages, all seeking a modern (but not glitzy) ship with a wide array of public lounges and bars, and a middle-of-the-road lifestyle, with food and entertainment that is quite acceptable rather than fancy.

ACCOMMODATION. There is one suite grade, four grades of outside-view cabins (one designated Deluxe), two grades of interior (no view) cabins. There are four cabins for the disabled (these are large, and have great forward-facing views). You can pre-book your preferred cabin for a per cabin fee of £30 (around US$50).

Most of the cabins are quite small (below the industry standard of 170 sq. ft/15.7 sq. meters). They are reasonably well appointed and practically laid out. Some have wood furniture, fittings, or accenting, good counter and storage space (but little drawer space), a large dressing mirror, and private bathrooms that are adequate, but no more. The top cabin categories (which are only marginally larger and should not really be called suites) have full-sized bathtubs while all others have showers. Several cabins have king- or queen-sized beds, although most have twin beds.

The largest accommodation is in the Presidential Suite (on Eagle Deck). Small by comparison to suites aboard many other ships, it measures 464 sq. ft (43.1 sq. meters) and is located on the uppermost accommodation deck. There is a king-sized bed, walk-in closet, wet bar, study and dining areas, television, VCR, and stereo system. The bathroom includes a whirlpool tub, double sink unit, and a separate powder room.

A number of cabins also have additional berths for a third/fourth person. Room service is provided 24 hours a day. All cabin TVs carry live news channels (when available). The cabin insulation is extremely poor, and the bathroom towels are small.

CUISINE. The Compass Rose Restaurant is reasonably large and attractive, with warm decor and ample space. Breakfast, lunch and dinner (6pm–10.30pm) are served in an open-seating arrangement (so you may get a different table and different waiters for each meal). Although there are a few tables for two, most are for four, six or eight. Dinners typically include a choice of four entrées; a vegetarian entrée is also available daily. Children have their own menu, with "home-from-home" dishes and small portions.

Dessert and pastry items will typically be of good quality, and made specifically for British tastes, although there is much use of canned fruits and jellies.

Sirocco's A La Carte Restaurant is the ship's alternative dining spot (reservations are required and a per-person cover charge applies). It seats only 45 and has superior food and service as well as a more refined, quieter atmosphere. It is located adjacent to the Compass Rose Restaurant, but is best entered from the aft stairway.

Instead of the more formal dining room, there is a more casual Lido Restaurant. This is open 24 hours a day, with open-seating. Tables are set with crisp linens, flatware and stemware for dinner, when the set menu includes a choice of four entrées. Each week a themed buffet (Chinese, Indian or Mexican, depending on the cruise itinerary) may be featured for dinner. On Lido Deck, the outdoor Terrace Grill provides fast-food grilled items and pizza during the day. All dining venues are non-smoking (except outdoor areas).

ENTERTAINMENT. The 600-seat Broadway Showlounge is two decks high (main and balcony levels) and is the ship's principal venue for production shows and cabaret entertainment. Although Thomson is not generally known for high-quality shows, they are, in fact, good fun, and are professionally produced (aboard other ships chartered by Thomson the young entertainment/cruise staff enthusiastically provide the shows), while cabaret acts provide entertainment on evenings when there is no production show.

A second entertainment venue, High Spirits, is a multifunctional room for quizzes, dancing, and late-night discotheque. A number of bands and musical units provide live music for dancing and listening in several lounges and bars.

SPA/FITNESS. Oceans Health Club is atop the ship at the aft end. It has good ocean views, and overlooks the aft pool and hot tub, on Bridge Deck. Facilities include an aerobics exercise room, a decent size gymnasium (there are plenty of treadmills, exercycles, and other body-toning and muscle-pumping equipment), sauna (there is no steam room), and several treatment rooms.

You can have massages, aromatherapy facials, body wraps, manicures, pedicures, and hair beautifying treatments. Note that the beauty salon is located in a completely different area (close to the Reception Desk on the port side) to the health and fitness facilities.

Sample prices: Swedish Classic Massage/Indian Head Massage £30 (30 minutes) or £44 (45 minutes) or £52 (60 minutes); Cleansing Facial £36; Pedicure and Foot Massage £22; Exfoliating Body Polish £34.

Veendam
★★★★

Mid-Size Ship: . . . . .55,451 tons	Total Crew: 561	Cabins (with private balcony): 150
Lifestyle: .Premium	Passengers	Cabins (wheelchair accessible): 6
Cruise Line: . . . . . . .Holland America Line	(lower beds/all berths): 1,266/1,627	Cabin Current: . . . . .110 and 220 volts
Former Names: . . . . .none	Passenger Space Ratio	Elevators: 8
Builder: . . . . .Fincantieri (Italy)	(lower beds/all berths): 43.8/34.0	Casino (gaming tables): . . . . .Yes
Original Cost: . . . .$215 million	Crew/Passenger Ratio	Slot Machines: . . . . .Yes
Entered Service: . . . . .May 1996	(lower beds/all berths): 2.2/2.9	Swimming Pools (outdoors): 1
Registry: . . . . .The Bahamas	Navigation Officers: . . . . . .British/Dutch	Swimming Pools (indoors): 1
Length (ft/m): 719.3/219.3	Cabins (total): 633	(magrodome)
Beam (ft/m): 101.0/30.8	Size Range (sq ft/m): 186.2–1,124.8/	Whirlpools: 2
Draft (ft/m): 24.6/7.5	17.3–104.5	Self-Service Launderette: . . . . .Yes
Propulsion/Propellers: . . . . .diesel-electric	Cabins (outside view): 502	Dedicated Cinema/Seats: Yes/249
(34,560kW)/2	Cabins (interior/no view): 131	Library: . . . . .Yes
Passenger Decks: 10	Cabins (for one person): 0	

OVERALL SCORE: 1,420 (OUT OF A POSSIBLE 2,000 POINTS)

OVERVIEW. *Veendam* is one of a series of four almost identical ships in the same series – the others being *Maasdam, Statendam,* and *Ryndam.* The exterior styling is rather angular (some would say boxy – the funnel certainly is), although it is softened and balanced somewhat by the fact that the hull is painted black. There is a full wrap-around teakwood promenade deck outdoors – excellent for strolling, and, thankfully, no sign of synthetic turf anywhere. The sunloungers one the exterior promenade deck are wood, and come with comfortable cushioned pads, while those at the swimming pool on Lido Deck are of white plastic.

In the interiors of this "S" -class ship, an asymmetrical layout helps to reduce bottlenecks and congestion. Most of the public rooms are concentrated on two decks, Promenade Deck, and Upper Promenade Deck, which creates a spacious feel to the ship's interiors. In general, a restrained approach to interior styling is taken, using a mixture of contemporary materials combined with traditional woods and ceramics. There is, fortunately, little "glitz" anywhere.

What is outstanding is the array of artworks throughout the ship (costing about $2 million), assembled and nicely displayed to represent the fine Dutch heritage of Holland America Line and to present a balance between standard itineraries and onboard creature comforts. Also noticeable are the fine flower arrangements throughout the public areas and foyers – used to good effect to brighten up what to some is rather dull decor.

Atop the ship, with forward-facing views that wrap around the sides is the Crow's Nest Lounge. By day it makes a fine observation lounge, with large ocean-view windows; by night it is a nightclub with extremely variable lighting.

BERLITZ'S RATINGS		
	Possible	Achieved
Ship	500	372
Accommodation	200	150
Food	400	254
Service	400	287
Entertainment	100	72
Cruise	400	285

A three-deck high atrium foyer is quite appealing, although its sculpted centerpiece makes it look a little crowded, and leaves little room in front of the purser's office. A hydraulic magrodome (glass) roof covers the reasonably sized swimming pool/whirlpools and central Lido area (whose focal point is a large dolphin sculpture) so that this can be used in good or bad weather.

There is a large reference library, quite lovely and relaxing. The company keeps its ships very clean and tidy, and there is good passenger flow throughout.

Veendam is well-built, with fairly decent interior fit and finish. Holland America Line is constantly fine-tuning its performance and its regular passengers, almost all of whom are North American, find the company's ships very comfortable and well-run. The company continues its strong maritime traditions, although the present food and service components still let the rest of the cruise experience down.

The service staff is Indonesian, and, although they are mostly quite charming, communication often proves frustrating, and service is spotty and inconsistent.

An escalator travels between two of the lower decks (one was originally planned to be the embarkation point), but it is almost pointless. The charge to use the washing machines and dryers in the self-service launderette is petty, particularly for suite occupants, who pay high prices for their cruises. The men's urinals in public restrooms are unusually high.

ACCOMMODATION. The accommodation ranges from small interior (no view) cabins to a large penthouse suite, in 17 price categories (the price will depend on the grade, location and size chosen). All cabin televisions normally carry CNN and TNT programming.

The interior (no view) and outside-view standard cabins have twin beds that convert to a queen-size bed, and there is a separate living space with sofa and coffee table. However, although the drawer space is generally good, the closet space is actually very tight, particularly for long cruises (although more than adequate for a 7-night cruise). The bathrooms are tiled, and compact but practical. Bathrobes are also provided, as are hairdryers.

Bathrobes are also provided for all suites/cabins, as are hairdryers, and a small range of personal amenities (soap, conditioning shampoo, body lotion, shower cap, vanity kit). The bathrooms are quite well laid out, but the bathtubs are small units better described as shower tubs. Some cabins have interconnecting doors.

On Navigation Deck, 28 suites have accommodation for up to four. These also have in-suite dining as an alternative to the dining room, for private, reclusive meals. These are very spacious, tastefully decorated and well laid-out, and feature a separate living room, bedroom with two lower beds (convertible to a king-sized bed), a good-sized living area, dressing room, plenty of closet and drawer space, marble bathroom with Jacuzzi tub.

The largest accommodation of all is a penthouse suite. There is only one, located on the starboard side of Navigation Deck at the forward staircase. It has a king-sized bed (TV and video player) and vanity desk; large walk-in closet with superb drawer space, oversize whirlpool bath (it could seat four) and separate shower enclosure, separate washroom with toilet, bidet and washbasin; living room with writing desk, large TV and full set of audio equipment); dressing room, large private balcony (with teak lounge chairs and drinks tables, dining table and four chairs), pantry (with large refrigerator, toaster unit, and full coffee/tea making facilities and food preparation area, and a separate entrance from the hallway), mini-bar/refrigerator, a guest toilet and floor-to-ceiling windows. There is no bell push.

CUISINE/DINING. The non-smoking Rotterdam Dining Room, with smoking and no-smoking sections, spans two decks. It is located at the stern of the ship, is quite dramatic, and has two grand staircases to connect the two levels, panoramic views on three sides, and a music balcony. Both open seating and fixed (assigned tables and times) seating are available, while breakfast and lunch are open-seating (you'll be seated by restaurant staff when you enter). There are tables for two, four, six or eight. The waiter stations in the dining room are very noisy for those seated near them. Fine Rosenthal china and good-quality cutlery are provided. **Alternative Dining Option:** The intimate Pinnacle Grill, added in 2002, is located just forward of the balcony level of the main dining room on the starboard side. The 66-seat

dining spot has Pacific Northwest cuisine (fresh Alaskan salmon and halibut, and other regional specialties, plus a selection of premium steaks such as filet mignon from Black Angus beef). The venue (reservations are necessary, and a cover/service charge of $20 applies for dinner, $10 for lunch) was created out of the former private dining wing of the main dining room, plus a slice of the Explorer's Lounge. A Bulgari show plate, Rosenthal china, Reidel wine glasses, and Frette table linen are featured. The Pinnacle Grill is a much better dining experience than the main dining room and worth it for that special celebration.

Instead of the more formal dining room or Pinnacle Grill, the Lido Buffet is open for casual dinners on all but the last night of a cruise, in an open-seating arrangement. Tables are set with crisp linens, flatware and stemware. A set menu includes a choice of four entrées.

For more casual evening eating, the Lido Buffet is open for casual dinners on all except the last night of each cruise, in an open-seating arrangement. Tables are set with crisp linens, flatware and stemware. A set menu is featured, and this includes a choice of four entrées.

The dual-line, self-serve Lido Buffet (one side is for smokers, the other side for non-smokers) is also the place for casual breakfasts and lunches. Again there is much use of canned fruits (good for dentally challenged older passengers) and packeted items, although there are several commercial low-calorie salad dressings. The choice of cheeses and accompanying crackers is very poor. The beverage station also lets it down, for it is no better than those found in family outlets ashore in the United States. In addition, a poolside grill provides basic American hamburgers and hot dogs.

Passengers will need to eat in the Lido Cafe on any days when the dining room is closed for lunch (typically once or twice per cruise, depending on the ship's itinerary).

ENTERTAINMENT. The Rubens Showlounge, located at the forward part of the ship, spans two decks, with banquette seating on both main and upper levels. It is basically a well designed room, but the ceiling is low and the sightlines from the balcony level are quite poor.

SPA/FITNESS. The Ocean Spa is located one deck below the navigation bridge at the very forward part of the ship. It includes a gymnasium (with all the latest muscle-pumping exercise machines, including an abundance of treadmills) with ocean views, an aerobics exercise area, large beauty salon with ocean-view windows to the port side, several treatment rooms, and men's and women's sauna, steam room and changing areas.

● **For more extensive general information on what a Holland America Line cruise is like, see pages 126–28.**

Ventura
★★★★

Large Resort Ship:	.116,000 tons	Total Crew:	.1,239	Cabins (with private balcony):	.880
Lifestyle:	.Standard	Passengers		Cabins (wheelchair accessible):	.25
Cruise Line:	.P&O Cruises	(lower beds/all berths):	.3,092/3,574	Cabin Voltage:	.220 volts
Former Names:	.none	Passenger Space Ratio		Lifts:	.12
Builder:	.Fincantieri (Italy)	(lower beds/all berths):	.37.5/32.4	Casino (gaming tables):	.Yes
Original Cost:	.€535 million	Crew/Passenger Ratio		Slot Machines:	.Yes
Entered Service:	.April 2008	(lower beds/all berths):	.2.4/2.8	Swimming Pools (outdoors):	.3
Registry:	.Bermuda	Navigation Officers:	.British	Swimming Pools (indoors):	.0
Length (ft/m):	.951.4/290.0	Cabins (total):	.1,546	Whirlpools:	.6
Beam (ft/m):	.118.1/36.0	Size Range (sq ft/m):	.134.5–534.0/	Self-Service Launderette:	.Yes
Draft (ft/m):	.27.8/8.5		12.5–49.6	Dedicated Cinema/Seats:	.No
Propulsion/Propellers:	.diesel-electric	Cabins (outside view):	.1,101	Library:	.Yes
	(42,000kW)/2	Cabins (interior/no view):	.445		
Passenger Decks:	.15	Cabins (for one person):	.0		

BERLITZ'S OVERALL SCORE: 1,543 (OUT OF A POSSIBLE 2,000 POINTS)

OVERVIEW. *Ventura*, named in South-ampton by actress Helen Mirren, is the P&O version of Princess Cruises' Grand-class ships, and the largest cruise ship yet built specifically for UK pas-sengers. With its flat stern, it looks a bit like a giant hatchback, but the ship's side profile is softer and more balanced. Promenade walking decks are to port and starboard sides, underneath the lifeboats (you can't walk completely around, however). There are three pools (two on the pool deck, one at the stern). The center pool can be covered by a glass-roofed skydome. If your cabin is towards the front of the ship, it's a long walk to get to the pool at the stern. Considering the number of passengers carried, there's not a lot of outdoor deck space.

Inside the ship, a three-deck atrium is the focal point. Designed on a gateway theme, central to which are four tow-ering black granite archways specially sourced from India, it's the place to see and be seen, and the best location to arrange to meet friends. The ship's upper-deck public room layout, however, is challenging because you can't go from one end of the ship to the other without first going down, along and up – so, not so good for those with mobility prob-lems. In other words, you'll need to plan your journey and use the most appropriate of three elevator banks.

Other public rooms include a surprisingly small, rather open-plan library (Chapter One) that is not at all intimate, a Cyb@center (for internet connections), an overly large Cruise Sales Centre, Fortunes Casino, and several bars, including The Exchange (an urban warehouse bar), and Metropolis (set high atop the ship with great aft views and views along the sides of the ship – over everyone's balcony), a Cuban bar, and a Spanish bar with tapas. All rather multi-

BERLITZ'S RATINGS

	Possible	Achieved
Ship	500	432
Accommodation	200	168
Food	400	255
Service	400	293
Entertainment	100	82
Cruise	400	313

cultural and not so British. But, do check out the train that runs around the upper part of the upper bar of The Exchange.

There are 7,000 pieces of art on board, sourced from 55 British artists; naturally, there's an art gallery so you can also buy "artwork."

Ventura is targeted at families and children. Indeed, children will be pleased to find that, for 2–4-year olds, Noddy is on board. There are children's clubs for the under-2s up to 17 years, plus a rock 'n' roll school. Youngsters can also enjoy Scalextric at sea with Grand Prix-style track, 3D cinema, and interactive art classes. Family shore programs feature aqua and "theme parks." There's a very useful Night Nursery for the under-5s.

Active types can take instruction and participate in Cirque Ventura's activities, including juggling, acro-balancing, tight-wire walking, stilt walking, and clowning. Also, the area has four bungee trampolines and a flying trapeze – all up high on Deck 19. If you tire of acrobatics, there are plenty of lounges and places to escape to.

It's possible to get married on board, with the captain offi-ciating. This can be arranged in the romantic Ivory Suite.

All in all, this is P&O Cruises' most advanced, facility-rich cruise ship to date, and has a good passenger space ratio. The onboard currency is the British pound. Gratu-ities are recommended at £3.75 per person, per day.

SUITABLE FOR: *Ventura* is best suited to families with children and adult couples who want to spend time together, and are seeking a big-ship environment with comfortable but unstuffy surroundings and lots of options.

ACCOMMODATION. There are 31 accommodation price grades,

according to size and location chosen, although there are really just five types of accommodation: suite with balcony; family suite with balcony; outside-view twin/queen with balcony; outside-view twin/queen; interior no-view cabin. Note that more than one-third of all cabins are of the interior no-view variety. Some cabins have extra third/fourth berths that fold down from the ceiling.

While the suites are quite spacious, they are quite small when compared to suites aboard some other cruise lines, such as Celebrity Cruises or Norwegian Cruise Line, whose top suites are four or five times the size. Most cabins are intelligently laid out, and manage to provide a feeling of space – well, sort of.

As aboard all P&O Cruises' ships, the following items are now standard in all cabins: bed runners, 10.5 tog duvets, Slumberland 8-inch sprung mattresses, Egyptian cotton towels and robes, extensive Nick Munro-designed stainless steel tea/coffee making facilities (including water kettle, coffee pot, proper teapot, milk jug, two glass mugs), all on a bespoke silver tray. The tea-making set-up is excellent, but getting fresh milk can sometimes be a problem.

Open closets are new for P&O Cruises, however (no doors – save money), and actually provide easier access. Balcony cabins have teak patio furniture, and an outside light. Decent-quality personal toiletries are by Temple Spa, an upgrade from what was previously provided aboard the ships of P&O Cruises (with larger bottles and more selection choice provided for suite occupants).

Wheelchair-accessible cabins have a shower enclosure, except one (R415) that has a bathtub with integral shower.

CUISINE/DINING. P&O's marketing blurb claims that there are 10 restaurants. There aren't. There are five genuine restaurants (Bay Tree, Cinnnamon, Saffron, The White Room, and East); the rest are eateries.

The three principal dining rooms, Bay Tree, Cinnamon, and Saffron, have standard à la carte menus. The Bay Tree offers fixed seating dining, with assigned tables (typical seating times: 6:30pm or 8:30pm). In the other two, you can dine when you want, with whom you want, at any time between 6pm and 10pm – P&O calls it "Freedom Dining."

If you eat in the Cinnamon or Saffron restaurants, a "gratuity charge" of £1.50 per person, per day is added to your account. Once or twice per cruise, additional special dinners will be served in the main dining rooms, one of which will be a Chaîne des Rôtisseurs culinary dining event.

Alternative dining venues include the following:
● *The White Room* is located high up on the ship, above the children's play area, with a quarter of the tables on deck. It serves modern European dishes by celebrity chef Marco Pierre White in an environment which is intimate and attentive but not stuffy and is particularly suitable for families.

Reservations are necessary, and the cost to dine here is about £15 per person.

● For complete privacy, private balcony dining, with selections from the Marco Pierre White menu, is also available as a rather pricey (but perhaps worthwhile) extra-cost option.
● *The Waterside* is a large, self-serve buffet "seaside chic" dining spot, with indoor-outdoor seating.
● On the same deck, adjacent to the forward pool, are *Frankie's Grill* and *Frankie's Pizzeria*.
● *Tazzine*, a coffee lounge by day, turns into a cocktail bar in the evening.
● *The Beach House* is a casual dining spot for families, open 24 hours. Marco's roof-side café serves gourmet pizzas, grills and original ice cream flavors, such as chocolate truffle and prune and Armagnac. Children's cutlery, bibs and beakers are available.
● *Ramblas* is a tapas and wine bar (some items at extra cost).
● *East* is an Asian fusion eatery, located on the main indoor promenade.

In addition, 24-hour room service is available in cabins.

ENTERTAINMENT. P&O claims the 785-seat Arena Theatre, located at the front of the ship and spanning two decks, is the largest showlounge aboard a UK-based cruise ship, but in fact the showlounge aboard *Queen Mary 2* is bigger, with 1,094 seats, as is the Showlounge aboard *Independence of the Seas*. Havana, the main nightclub and entertainment venue, is an activities room by day and a sultry Cuba-inspired club by night, but sightlines to the stage area are poor from many seats.

A video wall in the Cosmopolitan club lounge screens real-time footage of the world's seven most famous city skylines – Sydney, Paris, New York, Rio de Janeiro, Las Vegas, Hong Kong and London. It's neat.

SPA/FITNESS. The Oasis Spa is located forward, almost atop the ship. It includes a gymnasium, aerobics room, beauty salon, separate male and female sauna and steam rooms, and 11 treatment rooms. An internal stairway connects to the deck below, which contains an extra-charge Thermal Suite. Harding Brothers provide the spa staff and services.

Treatments include special packages for couples, and the SilverSpa Generation, as well as a whole range of individual treatments. Examples of prices: Swedish Massage is £66 for 60 minutes; a Hot Stones massage is £77 for 60 minutes; Couples massage is £220 for 100 minutes; Oriental Massage Ritual is £99 for 90 minutes; and a holistic facial is £45 for 75 minutes. A manicure is £22 for 30 minutes, while a pedicure is £28 for 30 minutes.

● **For more extensive general information on what a P&O cruise is like, see pages 133–34.**

Vision of the Seas
★★★★

Large Resort Ship:	........78,491 tons	Total Crew:	765	Cabins (with private balcony):	229

Large Resort Ship: ....78,491 tons
Lifestyle: ....Standard
Cruise Line: Royal Caribbean International
Former Names: ....none
Builder: Chantiers de l'Atlantique (France)
Original Cost: ....$275 million
Entered Service: ....May 1998
Registry: ....The Bahamas
Length (ft/m): 915.3/279.0
Beam (ft/m): 105.6/32.2
Draft (ft/m): 24.9/7.6
Propulsion/Propellers: .....diesel-electric
(50,400kW)2
Passenger Decks: 11

Total Crew: 765
Passengers
(lower beds/all berths): 2,000/2,435
Passenger Space Ratio
(lower beds/all berths): 39.2/32.2
Crew/Passenger Ratio
(lower beds/all berths): 3.0/3.6
Navigation Officers: ....International
Cabins (total): 1,000
Size Range (sq ft/m): 135.0–1,270.1/
12.5–118.0
Cabins (outside view): 593
Cabins (interior/no view): 407
Cabins (for one person): 0

Cabins (with private balcony): 229
Cabins (wheelchair accessible): 14
Cabin Current: ....110 and 220 volts
Elevators: 9
Casino (gaming tables): ....Yes
Slot Machines: ....Yes
Swimming Pools (outdoors): 1
Swimming Pools (indoors): 1
(inside/outside)
Whirlpools: 6
Self-Service Launderette: ....No
Dedicated Cinema/Seats: ....No
Library: ....Yes

OVERALL SCORE: 1,491 (OUT OF A POSSIBLE 2,000 POINTS)

OVERVIEW. This contemporary ship, sister to *Rhapsody of the Seas*, shares design features that make all Royal Caribbean International ships identifiable, including a Viking Crown Lounge (which is also the ship's disco). The Viking Crown Lounge is just aft of the center of the ship (above the central atrium lobby), with the funnel located well aft – a departure from all other RCI ships to date. The ship's stern is beautifully rounded. There is a reasonable amount of open-air walking space, although this can become cluttered with sunloungers (which, incidentally, do not have cushioned pads).

Inside, the ship provides RCI's interpretation of a floating contemporary hotel, and presents the nicest mix of colors and decor of any of the Vision-class ships, with lots of warm beige and pink tones (particularly in the expansive atrium).

The artwork (which cost $6 million) is plentiful, colorful and very creative, with more previously blank wall space covered with interesting artworks of differing shapes and sizes. Most noticeable is the extensive use of glass (two beautiful glass sculptures stand out – one in the atrium (at the entrance to a Champagne Bar), one on the upper level of the Viking Crown Lounge). There are plenty of public rooms, bars and lounges, as well as a large, well-lit casino.

The Viking Crown Lounge is a multi-level nightspot (the music can be loud and overbearing, however, and so can cigarette smoke around the bar – one of few places where smokers can light up). Perhaps the best atmosphere is in the nautical-theme Schooner Bar. The Library has an excellent array of hardbacks, and a neat wooden sculpture of some-

BERLITZ'S RATINGS

	Possible	Achieved
Ship	500	425
Accommodation	200	166
Food	400	240
Service	400	287
Entertainment	100	81
Cruise	400	292

thing that looks like the Tin Man from *The Wizard of Oz.*

ACCOMMODATION. There are 18 cabin categories, in 11 pricing units (the price you pay will depend on the grade, location and size chosen).

The standard interior (no view) and exterior view cabins are of an adequate size, and have just enough functional facilities to make them comfortable for a one-week cruise, but longer might prove confining. The decor is bright and cheerful, although the ceilings are plain; colorful soft furnishings make one's home away from home look like the inside of a modern Scandinavian hotel – minimalist, yet colorful. Twin lower beds convert to queen-sized beds, and there is a reasonable amount of closet and drawer space, but there is little room to maneuver between the bed and desk/television unit.

The bathrooms are small but functional, although the shower units are small, and there is no cabinet for personal toiletry items. The towels could be larger and thicker.

Choose a "C" grade suite if you want spacious accommodation that includes a separate (curtained-off) sleeping area, a good-sized outside balcony (with part, not full, partition), lounge with sofa, two chairs and coffee table, three closets, plenty of drawer and storage space, television and VCR. The bathroom is large and has a full-size tub, integral shower, and two washbasins/two toiletries cabinets.

For the ultimate accommodation aboard this ship, choose the Royal Suite, which resembles a Palm Beach apartment, and comes with a white baby grand player piano. It has a separate bedroom with king-sized bed, living room with queen-size sofa bed, refrigerator/mini-bar, dining table, entertainment center, and vanity dressing area. The decor is simple and elegant, with pastel colors, and wood accented ceiling treatments. Located just under the starboard side navigation bridge wing, it has its own private balcony.

CUISINE. The no-smoking Aquarius Dining Room is set on two levels with large ocean-view picture windows on two sides (rectangular windows on the upper level, large circular windows on the lower level) and a large connecting stairway. There are two seatings.

The Windjammer Cafe is the casual dining spot for self-serve buffets. The area is well-designed, with contemporary decor and colors, but the food is really basic fare and disappointing; the four-sided self-service buffet area is small for the number of passengers that use it. More money needs to be spent for better-quality ingredients and more variety is needed. Each evening, the room offers an alternative to the more dressy dining room. The evening buffets typically feature a different theme, something this company has been doing for more than 25 years – perhaps the time has come for more creativity.

A hamburger/hot dog grill counter in the Solarium, but typically you don't get a choice of how well done or not so well done you get your hamburgers – everything appears to be well done.

The company has introduced a drinks package (available at all bars, in the form of cards or stickers) that enables you to pre-pay for a selection of standard soft drinks and alcoholic drinks. The packages are not easy to understand.

ENTERTAINMENT. The Masquerade Theatre is the ship's principal showlounge, located in the forward section of the ship (accessed by the forward stairway/elevators), for production shows and other major cabaret shows. It is a large, but a well-designed room with main and balcony levels, and good sightlines from most of the banquette seats.

Other cabaret acts are featured in the Some Enchanted Evening Lounge, located aft, and these include late-night adult (blue) comedy, as well as live music for dancing. A number of other bars and lounges have live music of differing types.

The entertainment throughout is upbeat (in fact, it is difficult to get away from music and noise). There is even background music in all corridors and elevators, and constant music outdoors on the pool deck. If you want a quiet relaxing holiday, choose another ship.

SPA/FITNESS. The spa, with its solarium and indoor/outdoor dome-covered pool, Inca- and Mayan-theme decor, sauna/steam rooms and gymnasium, provides a haven for the health-conscious and fitness buff, although there is a pizza bar forward of the pool area. A lovely "Mayan Serpent" sculpture is featured in the solarium.

For more sporting passengers, there is activity galore – including a rock-climbing wall, with several separate climbing tracks. It is located outdoors at the aft end of the funnel.

● **For more extensive general information about the Royal Caribbean cruise experience, see pages 137–42.**

WATERTIGHT CONTRACTS

Cruise lines are masters of small print when it comes to contracts. A clause in the ticket typically reads: "The Carrier's legal responsibility for death, injury, illness, damage, delay, or other loss or detriment of person or property of whatever kind suffered by the Passenger will, in the first instance, be governed by the Athens Convention relating to the Carriage of Passengers and their Luggage by Sea, 1974, with protocols and amendments, together with the further provisions of the International Convention on Limitation of Liability for Maritime Claims, 1976, with revisions and amendments (hereinafter collectively referred to as the "Convention"). The Carrier shall not be liable for any such death, injury, illness, damage, delay, loss, or detriment caused by Act of God, war or warlike operations, civil commotions, labor trouble, interference by Authorities, perils of the sea, or any other cause beyond the control of the Carrier, fire, thefts or any other crime, errors in the navigation or management of the Vessel, or defect in, or unseaworthiness of hull, machinery, appurtenances, equipment, furnishings, or supplies of the Vessel, fault or neglect of pilot, tugs, agents, independent contractors, such as ship's Physician, Passengers or other persons on board not in the Carrier's employ or for any other cause of whatsoever nature except and unless it is proven that such death, injury, illness, damage, delay, loss resulting from Carrier's act or omission was committed with the intent to cause such loss or with knowledge that such loss would probably result therefrom and in that event the Carrier's liability therefore shall not exceed the specified limitations per Passenger in Special Drawing Rights (S.D.R.) as defined in the applicable conventions or in any further revision and/or amendment thereto as shall become applicable."

Vistamar
★★ +

Small Ship: ....7,478 tons	Passenger Decks: 6	Cabins (for one person): 5
Lifestyle: ....Standard	Total Crew: 110	Cabins (with private balcony): 11
Cruise Line: ....Plantours & Partners	Passengers	Cabins (wheelchair accessible): 0
Former Names: ...Santa Cruz de Tenerife	(lower beds/all berths): 299/320	Cabin Current: ....220 volts
Builder: ......Union Navale de Levante	Passenger Space Ratio	Elevators: 1
(Spain)	(lower beds/all berths): 25.3/23.3	Casino (gaming tables): ....No
Original Cost: ....$45 million	Crew/Passenger Ratio	Slot Machines: ....No
Entered Service: ....Sept 1989	(lower beds/all berths): 2.7/2.9	Swimming Pools (outdoors): 1
Registry: ....Italy	Navigation Officers: ....Spanish	Swimming Pools (indoors): 0
Length (ft/m): 396.9/121.00	Cabins (total): 152	Whirlpools: 0
Beam (ft/m): 55.1/16.82	Size Range (sq ft/m): 129.1–150.6/	Self-Service Launderette: ....No
Draft (ft/m): 14.9/4.55	12.0–14.0	Dedicated Cinema/Seats: ....No
Propulsion/Propellers: ....diesel	Cabins (outside view): 126	Library: ....Yes
(3,900kW)/2	Cabins (interior/no view): 26	

OVERALL SCORE: 1,061 (OUT OF A POSSIBLE 2,000 POINTS)

OVERVIEW. *Vistamar* has a moderately smart, reasonably contemporary, but rather squat small ship profile. The ship, which has an ice-hardened hull, also carries several inflatable rubber landing craft for close-up landings during certain itineraries that include the Arctic and Antarctic.

There is an "open bridge" policy, so you can join the captain and other navigation officers at almost any time (except during difficult maneuvers). There is a good open observation deck at the forward-most part of the ship – atop the navigation bridge, although the other open deck and sunbathing space is a little limited, particularly on the aft open deck around the small outdoor pool (it is really only a "dip" pool, although it has a large splash surround).

The interior layout has all the public rooms located aft, in a "cake-layer" stacking, with a single, central staircase that takes up most of the space in an atrium lobby that spans three decks (with a glass elevator shaped like half a cable car). Features include wood-trimmed interior decor, which is quite jazzy, attractive and warm, although the mirrored metallic ceilings are somewhat irritating.

A four-deck high atrium with a "sky dome" has a glass-walled elevator and a wrap-around staircase, and is the focal point of the ship's interior. The library has comfortable high wingback chairs, but there aren't many books. There is also a Card Room, and board games are available.

The ship's main lounge, Don Fernando, is named after Senor Don Fernando Abril Martorell, the president of the Union Navale de Levante shipyard that constructed *Vistamar* in 444 days (perhaps if more time had been taken, the ship would have been built better). Additionally, there is a

BERLITZ'S RATINGS

	Possible	Achieved
Ship	500	232
Accommodation	200	107
Food	400	210
Service	400	237
Entertainment	100	56
Cruise	400	219

rather jazzy nightclub/disco, with acres of glass, set around the base of the funnel, with a long bar, and dance floor, for the late-night set.

This ship has been under charter to Plantours & Partner, specifically for German-speaking passengers, since 1991, and the product is aimed at the inexpensive end of the market. The dress code is ultra-casual (no tuxedos, no ties). While the ship is not in the best condition, and maintenance is spotty (shoddy tenders, for example), there is a friendly ambiance, which attracts many repeat passengers. There is an abundance of greenery throughout the ship, which helps to make it feel warm, more comfortable and less clinical. The ship is quite small, and so passengers can enjoy interesting destination-intensive cruises, with many port calls that larger ships simply can't get into. Tipping is recommended at 5–6 euros (the onboard currency) per person, per day.

The tiny "dip" swimming pool is virtually useless. There is a distinct odor of diesel fuel at the upper level of the lobby, where there is also a complete lack of air-conditioning. The ship's hotel operation is rather sloppy and needs streamlining. There is no walking track or wrap-around promenade deck outdoors. The fit, finish and maintenance of this ship are all quite poor, and well below the standard expected. The sightlines in the single-level showlounge are very poor, and there is a lack of good stage lighting.

SUITABLE FOR: *Vistamar* is best suited to German-speaking couples and single travelers looking for a first cruise in the comfortable, contemporary, but not luxurious or pretentious surroundings of a small ship featuring interesting itineraries, and all at a low price.

ACCOMMODATION. The passenger accommodation areas are located forward, while the public rooms are positioned aft, which means there is a minimal amount of noise in the cabins – good if you're having an early night.

There are 11 cabin grades, but in just two different sizes: suites with private (covered) balcony and queen-sized bed; outside-view or interior (no view) cabins for two, three or four persons, all with fixed, wide single beds. All of the cabins are reasonably comfortable, although the bathrooms are extremely small and tight (there is a considerable "lip" to step over to access the bathroom), and both closet and drawer space is limited.

Cabins have twin beds with wooden headboard, small vanity/writing desk, color television, climate-control, telephone, and hairdryer. Most of the cabinetry is made with a wood finish.

There are 11 suites, each of which has a small, narrow, private, covered balcony outdoors. The suites are: Alboran, Algarve, Almeria, Armador, Cadiz, Cordoba, Granada, Huelva, Jaen, Malaga, Seville – all of which are regions of Andalucia. They also have a more spacious bathroom, with a large bathtub and integral shower. The living area s also larger, and comes with a sofa, coffee table, vanity/writing desk, and a larger color television. Note that Armador is the owner's suite, and comes with a circular bathtub with integral shower, set against large picture windows (wonderful for the Arctic and Antarctic cruises that this company typically operates in the appropriate season).

No matter what accommodation grade or location they choose, all passengers get personal amenities that include soap, shampoo, body lotion and bath/shower gel, and shoeshine mitt. Accommodation hallways are provided either in hospital green, powder blue, or hot pink.

CUISINE. The Andalucia Restaurant is quite warm and inviting, with contemporary colors and decor, and large picture windows, although the six pillars detract from the otherwise attractive room. The room's focal point is a model of a sailing vessel with an emerald green hull (about the same color as the fabrics on the dining room chairs.There is one seating for all passengers (so meals are leisurely), with assigned tables for four, six or eight (there are no tables for two). Window-side tables are for six, and all chairs have armrests.

The food is reasonably adequate, and quite sound, and dinners typically come with a choice of three entrées (plus a vegetarian selection). The selection of cooked green vegetables, breads, cheeses and fruits is limited, and the overall cuisine really is of quite a low standard (it could be said to be quite similar to that found aboard other ships operated for German-speaking passengers, such as *Albatros* and *Maxim Gorkiy*, which have two seatings for dinner). The service is adequate, no more, as is the wine list. Sekt (sweet sparkling wine) is provided for breakfast, while white and red table wines are provided for lunch and dinner.

ENTERTAINMENT. There is little entertainment apart from some cabaret acts and live music for dancing and listening.

SPA/FITNESS. There is no spa to speak of, although there is a fitness room, a sauna, a massage treatment room, and a small beauty salon.

Volendam
★★★★

Mid-Size Ship: . . . . .60,906 tons	Total Crew: 561	Cabins (with private balcony): 197
Lifestyle: . . . . .Premium	Passengers	Cabins (wheelchair accessible): 23
Cruise Line: . . . . . .Holland America Line	(lower beds/all berths): 1,440/1,850	Cabin Current: . . . . .110 volts
Former Names: . . . . .none	Passenger Space Ratio	Elevators: 12
Builder: . . . . .Fincantieri (Italy)	(lower beds/all berths): 42.2/32.9	Casino (gaming tables): . . . . .Yes
Original Cost: . . . .$300 million	Crew/Passenger Ratio	Slot Machines: . . . . .Yes
Entered Service: . . . . .Nov 1999	(lower beds/all berths): 2.5/2.5	Swimming Pools (outdoors): 2
Registry: . . . . .The Netherlands	Navigation Officers: . . . . .Dutch	Swimming Pools (indoors): 1
Length (ft/m): 781.0/238.00	Cabins (total): .720	(magrodome cover)
Beam (ft/m): 105.8/32.25	Size Range (sq ft/m): 113.0–1,126.0/	Whirlpools: 2
Draft (ft/m): 25.5/7.80	10.5–104.6	Self-Service Launderette: . . . . .Yes (2)
Propulsion/Propellers: . . . . .diesel-electric	Cabins (outside view): 581	Dedicated Cinema/Seats: Yes/205
(37,500kW)/2	Cabins (interior/no view): 139	Library: . . . . .Yes
Passenger Decks: 10	Cabins (for one person): 0	

OVERALL SCORE: 1,540 (OUT OF A POSSIBLE 2,000 POINTS)

OVERVIEW. The ship's name is derived from the fishing village of Volendam, located north of Amsterdam, Holland. The hull is dark blue, in keeping with all Holland America Line ships. Having been built to approximately the same size as the company's newest *Rotterdam*, the same layout and public rooms have been incorporated into the interiors. This carries on the same flow and comfortable feeling so that repeat passengers will quickly feel at home aboard almost any ship in the Holland America Line fleet.

Volendam has three main passenger stairways, which is so much better than two stairways, particularly the viewpoints of safety, accessibility and passenger flow. There is a magrodome-covered pool on the Lido Deck between the mast and the ship's funnel. The main interior design theme is flowers, from the 17th to the 21st centuries. The interior focal point is a huge crystal sculpture, *Caleido*, in the three-deck-high atrium, by one of Italy's leading contemporary glass artists, Luciano Vistosi. Health spa facilities include more treatment rooms (each has a shower and toilet).

In the casino bar (also known as the ship's sports bar), a cinematic theme presents visions of Hollywood, and includes a collection of costumes, props, photos and posters of movies and the actors who starred in them.

At the Lido Deck swimming pool, leaping dolphins are the focal point. The pool itself is also one deck higher than the Statendam-class ships, with the positive result being the fact that there is now direct access between the aft and midships pools (not so aboard the S-class ships).

There is a charge to use the washing machines and dryers in the self-service launderette, although it really should be included for the occupants of high priced suites. Although

BERLITZ'S RATINGS

	Possible	Achieved
Ship	500	429
Accommodation	200	165
Food	400	282
Service	400	276
Entertainment	100	77
Cruise	400	311

room service is adequate, it remains a weak point.

ACCOMMODATION. The range is similar to that found aboard the similarly sized *Rotterdam*, and comprises 17 different categories. The price you pay will depend on the grade, location and size you choose. There is one penthouse suite, and 28 suites, with the rest of the accommodation a mix of outside-view and interior (no view) cabins, and many more balcony cabins ("mini-suites") aboard this ship than aboard the slightly smaller *Statendam*-class ships.

All standard interior and outside cabins are tastefully furnished, and have twin beds that convert to a queen-sized bed, but space is tight for walking between beds and vanity unit. All cabin televisions carry CNN and TNT. The bathrooms (fully tiled) are disappointingly small (particularly for long cruises) and have small shower tubs, utilitarian personal toiletries cupboards, and exposed under-sink plumbing. Storage space is also small for long cruises.

There are 28 full Verandah Suites (Navigation Deck), and one Penthouse Suite. All suite occupants share a private Concierge Lounge (the concierge handles such things as special dining arrangements, shore excursions, private parties and special requests). Strangely, there are no butlers for these suites. Each Verandah Suite has a separate bedroom, dressing and living areas. Suite passengers get personal stationery, complimentary laundry and ironing, cocktail hour hors d'oeuvres and other goodies, as well as priority embarkation and disembarkation.

For the ultimate in accommodation and living space aboard this ship, choose the Penthouse Suite. It has a separate steward's entrance, a large bedroom with king-sized bed, separate living room (with baby grand piano) and a dining room, dressing room, walk-in closet, butler's pantry, and private balcony (though the balcony is no large than that of any other suite). Other facilities include an audio-visual center with television and VCR, wet bar with refrigerator, large bathroom with Jacuzzi bathtub, separate toilet with bidet, and a guest bathroom (with toilet and washbasin).

With the exception of the penthouse suite, located forward on the starboard side, the bathrooms in the other suites and "mini-suites" are a little disappointing – neither as spacious nor as opulent as one would expect. All outside-view suites and cabin bathrooms feature a bathtub/shower while interior (no view) cabins have a shower only. Also, note that the 23 cabins for the mobility-limited have a roll-in shower enclosure for wheelchair users (none have bathtubs, no matter what the category).

CUISINE. There is one main dining room, and one alternative dining spot (dinner only). The 747-seat Rotterdam Dining Room, a no-smoking venue, is a traditional, grand room, spread over two decks, with ocean views on three sides and an imposing staircase connecting upper and lower levels.

Both open seating and fixed (assigned tables and times) seating are available, while breakfast and lunch are open-seating (you'll be seated by restaurant staff when you enter). Fine Rosenthal china and good-quality cutlery are provided (but there are no fish knives). Tables are four two, four, six or eight.

Alternative Dining Option: The casual-dress Marco Polo Restaurant seats 88, and there is no charge, although reservations are required. It is created in the style of a California artists' bistro and provides Italian cuisine (this has a set menu together with nightly specials). Passengers thus have more choice and an occasional change of venue (anyone booking suite-grade accommodation get priority reservations).

The Lido Buffet is a self-serve cafe for casual breakfasts and luncheons. There is also an outdoor grill for those who enjoy hamburgers, hot dogs and other grilled fast-food items. The Lido Buffet is also open for casual dinners on each night except for the last one, in an open-seating arrangement. Tables are set with crisp linens, flatware and stemware. A set menu includes a choice of four entrées.

ENTERTAINMENT. The two-deck-high Frans Hals Show-lounge spans two decks, with banquette seating on both main and upper levels. It is basically a well-designed room, but the ceiling is low and the sight lines from the balcony level are poor.

SPA/FITNESS. The health spa facilities are quite extensive, and include a gymnasium (with good muscle-toning equipment), separate saunas and steam rooms for men and women, and more treatment rooms (each has a shower and toilet). Practice tennis courts can be fund outdoor, as well as the traditional shuffleboard courts, jogging track, and a full wrap-around teakwood promenade deck for strolling.

The Ocean Spa and onboard fitness classes are operated by Steiner, a specialist concession.

● **For more extensive general information on what a Holland America Line cruise is like, see pages 126–28.**

Voyager of the Seas
★★★★

Large Resort Ship:	........137,280 tons	
Lifestyle:	..................Standard	
Cruise Line:	Royal Caribbean International	
Former Names:	................none	
Builder:	...Kvaerner Masa-Yards (Finland)	
Original Cost:	............$500 million	
Entered Service:	............Nov 1999	
Registry:	...............The Bahamas	
Length (ft/m):	...........1,020.6/311.1	
Beam (ft/m):	...............155.5/47.4	
Draft (ft/m):	.................28.8/8.8	
Propulsion/Propellers:	.....diesel-electric	
	(42,000 kW)/3 pods (14 MW each)	
Passenger Decks:	14	

Total Crew: 1,176
Passengers
(lower beds/all berths): 3,114/3,838
Passenger Space Ratio
(lower beds/all berths): 44.0/35.7
Crew/Passenger Ratio
(lower beds/all berths): 2.6/3.2
Navigation Officers: ....Scandinavian
Cabins (total): 1,557
Size Range (sq ft/m): 151.0–1,358.0/
14.0–126.1
Cabins (outside view): 939
Cabins (interior/no view): 618
Cabins (for one person): 0

Cabins (with private balcony): 757
Cabins (wheelchair accessible): 26
Cabin Current: ....110 volts
Elevators: ....14 (6 glass-enclosed)
Casino (gaming tables): ....Yes
Slot Machines: ....Yes
Swimming Pools (outdoors): 3
Swimming Pools (indoors): 0
Whirlpools: 6
Self-Service Launderette: ....No
Dedicated Cinema/Seats: ....No
Library: ....Yes

OVERALL SCORE: 1,460 (OUT OF A POSSIBLE 2,000 POINTS)

OVERVIEW. The exterior design of *Voyager of the Seas* is not unlike an enlarged version of the Royal Caribbean International's Vision-class ships. Its propulsion is derived from three pod units, powered by electric motors: two azimuthing (rotating), and one fixed at the centerline, instead of conventional rudders and propellers, in the latest configuration of high-tech systems.

With its large proportions, it provides more facilities and options, yet manages to have a healthy passenger space ratio (the amount of space per passenger). It's too large to go through the Panama Canal, thus limiting itineraries almost exclusively to the Caribbean (where few islands have decent enough sized facilities to service it), or for use as a floating island resort. When you step aboard, spend the first few hours exploring all the many facilities and public spaces aboard this vessel; you'll find it to be time well spent.

Although *Voyager of the Seas* is large, the cabin hallways have an extremely warm and attractive feel to them, with artwork cabinets and wavy lines to lead you along and break up the monotony. In fact, there are plenty of colorful, even whimsical, decorative touches to help you avoid what would otherwise be a very clinical environment.

At certain times, passengers may be allowed to stand right at the bows of the ship on an observation platform, perhaps with arms spread in an "eagle-like" position, just like the stars in the film *Titanic*. What a photo opportunity! However, for the best ones, as in the film, you'll need to bring a helicopter. But looking up at the cake-layer stacking of the decks towards the bridge gives you an idea of the size of the ship.

Embarkation and disembarkation take place through two

BERLITZ'S RATINGS		
	Possible	Achieved
Ship	500	414
Accommodation	200	150
Food	400	237
Service	400	272
Entertainment	100	83
Cruise	400	304

stations/access points, designed to minimize the inevitable lines at the start and end of the cruise (that's more than 1,500 people for each access point). Once inside the ship, you'll need good walking shoes, particularly when you need to go from one end to the other – it really is quite a long way.

A four-decks-high Royal Promenade is the interior focal point of the ship, and is a good place to arrange to meet someone. It is 393.7 ft (120 meters) long – the length of two football fields (American football, that is), and has two internal lobbies (atria) that rise through 11 decks, one at each end. There are 16 elevators in four banks of four.

The entrance to one of three levels of the main restaurant, together with shops and entertainment locations are spun off from this "boulevard", while interior "interior promenade-view" cabins, with bay windows, look into it from above. It houses a traditional English "pub" (the "Pig 'n' Whistle, with draft beer and "street-front" seating), a Promenade Café (for continental breakfast, all-day pizzas, sandwiches and coffees), Ben & Jerry's Ice Cream (at extra cost), Sprinkles (for round-the-clock ice-cream and yoghurt), and Scoreboard (a sports bar).

Several shops complete the picture: a jewelry shop, gift shop, perfume shop, liquor shop and a logo souvenir shop. There's also a bright red telephone kiosk that houses an ATM cash machine. Altogether, it's a nice place to see and be seen, and street performers complete the scene. It really is a cross between a shopping arcade and an amusement park (Florida's Aventura meets New York's Coney Island). The chairman of Royal Caribbean International even donated his own beloved Morgan sports car to grace the

Royal Promenade, which is supposedly designed in the image of London's fashionable Burlington Arcade. Actually, by far the best view of the whole promenade is from one of the 138 premium-price cabins that look into it, or from a "captain's bridge" that crosses above it. At the forward end is the showlounge, and a Connoisseur's Club cigar lounge sited on the starboard side between the showlounge and the main section of the Royal Promenade.

Arched across the grand promenade is a captain's balcony, and in the center of the promenade a stairway connects you to the deck below, where you'll find the Schooner Bar (a piano lounge that is a feature of all RCI ships) and the colorful Casino Royale (large and full of flashing lights and noises). Gaming includes blackjack, Caribbean stud poker, roulette (including the world's largest interactive roulette wheel that is activated by a roulette ball tower four decks high), and craps, as well as 300 slot machines.

A second showlounge (Studio B, a regulation-size ice-skating rink that has real, not fake, ice) has arena seating for up to 900, and the latest in broadcast facilities. A number of slim pillars obstruct the clear-view arena stage sightlines, however. An Ice Follies show is presented by a professional ice-skating show team each cruise. If ice-skating in the Caribbean doesn't particularly appeal, you might like to visit the stunning two-deck library; it's the first aboard any cruise ship, and is open 24 hours a day. A total of $12 million was spent on permanent artwork.

Drinking places include a neat Aquarium Bar, with 50 tons of glass and water in four large aquariums (whose combined value is over $1 million), the small and intimate Champagne Bar, and the Connoisseur's Club – for cigars and cognacs. Lovers of jazz might appreciate High Notes, an intimate room for cool music atop the ship within the Viking Crown Lounge, or the Schooner Bar piano lounge. Golfers might enjoy the 19th Hole, a golf bar, as they play the Voyager Links.

There is a large TV studio, part of Studio "B", located adjacent to rooms that can be used for trade show exhibit space, with a 400-seat conference center and a 60-seat multimedia screening room. Meanwhile, many decks above, lovers can tie the knot in a 'wedding chapel in the sky,' the Skylight Chapel (it's located on the upper level of the Viking Crown Lounge, and even has wheelchair access via an electric stairway elevator). Outdoors, the pool and open deck areas (Deck 11) provide a resort-like environment.

Facilities for children and teenagers are quite extensive. "Aquanauts" is for 3–5-year-olds. "Explorers" is for 6–8-year-olds. "Voyagers" is for 9–12-year-olds. Optix is a dedicated area for teenagers, including a daytime club (with computers), soda bar, disk jockey and dance floor. Challenger's Arcade has an array of the latest video games. Virtual Submarine is a virtual reality underwater center for all ages. Computer Lab has 14 computer stations loaded with fun and games. Paint and Clay is an arts and crafts center for younger children. Adjacent to these indoor areas is Adventure Beach, an area for all the family: it includes swimming pools, a water slide and game areas outdoors. Royal Caribbean International has, since its inception,

always been an innovator in the cruise industry, and will probably remain so with this family-friendly vessel.

In terms of sheer size, this ship presently dwarfs many other ships in the cruise industry, but in terms of personal service, the reverse is the case, unless you happen to reside in one of the top suites. Royal Caribbean International does, however, try hard to provide a good standard of programmed service from its hotel staff. This is impersonal city life at sea, and a superb, well-designed alternative to a land-based resort, which is what the company wanted to build. Remember to take lots of extra pennies: you'll need them to pay for all the additional-cost items. The onboard currency is the US dollar.

Expect some standing in lines for the reception desk, and waiting for elevators (particularly at peak meal times), as well as for embarkation and disembarkation. If you arrange to meet someone, be very specific about the location – for this really is a large ship. My advice is to arrange to meet somewhere along the Royal Promenade.

The theme-park, banquet-style regimentation is well organized, but it's hard to find better value for money, particularly for families with children. You will, however, need to plan your time aboard, otherwise you'll miss out on some of the things that you might like to include in your vacation.

Because the cruise fares are so reasonable, you can expect a big push aboard the ship for extra revenue items, drinks packages, extra-cost dining options, etc. In the end, however, you should have a decent floating vacation. Note that the same comments apply to the other sister ships (*Adventure of the Seas, Explorer of the Seas, Mariner of the Seas*, and *Navigator of the Seas*); their layout and flow are the same, and, although there may be some slight differences, it's mainly in the decor and trimmings.

ACCOMMODATION. There is a wide range of 22 cabin price grades, in four major groupings: Premium ocean-view suites and cabins, interior (atrium-view) cabins, Ocean-view cabins, and Interior (no view) cabins. Note that many cabins are of a similar size (good for incentives and large groups), and 300 have interconnecting doors (good for families). Price depends on grade, location and size.

A total of 138 interior (no view) cabins have bay windows that look into an interior horizontal atrium – a cruise industry first when the ship debuted. Regardless of what cabin grade you choose, however, all except for the Royal Suite and Owner's Suite have twin beds that convert to a queen-sized unit, television, radio and telephone, personal safe, vanity unit, hairdryer and private bathroom. However, you'll need to keep the curtains closed in the bay windows if you wear little clothing, because you can be seen easily from adjacent bay windows (Bay Watch?).

Royal Suite (Deck 10): The Royal Suite (there's only one), which measuring approximately 1,146 sq. ft (106.5 sq. meters) is the ship's largest private living space, and is located almost at the top of the Centrum lobby on the port side. It is a nicely appointed penthouse suite (whose occupants, sadly, must share the rest of the ship with everyone else, except for access to their own exclusive concierge club).. It has a king-sized circular bed in a separate large bedroom that can be fully closed off; a living room with an additional queen-sized sofa bed, baby grand piano (pianist not included), refrigerator/wet bar, dining table and four chairs, expansive entertainment center, and a reasonably large bathroom.

Royal Family Suite: The four Royal Family suites (two aft on Deck 9, two aft on Deck 8, each measuring approximately 574 sq. ft/53 sq. meters), have two separate bedrooms – the main bedroom has a large vanity desk (the second, smaller bedroom also includes two beds and third/fourth upper Pullman berths). There's also a lounge with dining table and four chairs, wet bar, walk-in closet; and large bathroom with Jacuzzi bathtub, washbasin, and separate shower enclosure. The suites are located at the stern of the ship and have large balconies with views out over the ship's wash.

Owner's Suites: Ten slightly smaller but desirable Owner's Suites (approximately 468 sq. ft/43 sq. meters) are located in the center of the ship, on both port and starboard sides, adjacent to the Centrum lobby on Deck 10. Each features a bedroom with queen-sized bed) or twin beds); lounge with large sofa; wet bar; bathroom with Jacuzzi bathtub, washbasin and separate shower enclosure. There's also a private balcony, although it is not very large.

Standard Outside-View and Interior (no-view) Cabins: All cabins have a private bathroom, as well as interactive TV and pay-per-view movies, including an X-rated channel. Cabin bathrooms really are compact, but at least they have a proper shower enclosure instead of a shower curtain – so you won't have to dance with a curtain.

Some accommodation grades have a refrigerator/minibar, although there is no space left because it is crammed with "take-and-pay" items. If you take anything from the mini-bar/refrigerator on the day of embarkation in Miami, Florida sales tax will be added to your bill.

Cabins with "private balconies" are not so private. The balcony decking is made of Bolidt – a sort of rubberized sand – and not wood, while the balcony rail is of wood. If you have a cabin with a door that interconnecting door to another cabin, be aware that you'll probably be able to hear everything your next-door neighbors say and do. Note that bathroom toilets are explosively noisy, based on the vacuum system. Cabin bath towels are small and skimpy. Room service food menus are very basic.

CUISINE. The main dining room is extremely large and is set on three levels, each with an operatic name and theme: Carmen, La Boheme and Magic Flute. A dramatic staircase connects all three levels, and huge, fat support pillars obstruct the sight lines from many seats. All three have exactly the same menus and food. The dining room is totally non-smoking, there are two seatings, and tables are for four, six, eight 10 or 12.

Alternative Dining Options: Alternative dining options for casual and informal meals at all hours (according to company releases) include:
● *Promenade Café:* for continental breakfast, all-day

pizzas, sandwiches and coffees (provided in paper cups).
● *Windjammer Café:* for casual buffet-style breakfast, lunch and light dinner (except for the cruise's last night).
● *Island Grill* (this is actually a section inside the Windjammer Café): for casual dinner (no reservations necessary) featuring a grill and open kitchen.
● *Portofino:* this is the ship's "upscale" (non-smoking) Euro-Italian restaurant, open for dinner only. Reservations are required, and a $6 gratuity per person is charged. The food and its presentation are better than the food in the dining room, although the restaurant is not large enough for all passengers to try even once during a cruise. Choices include: antipasti, soup, salad, pasta, main dish, dessert, cheese and coffee.
● *Chop's Grille:* Aboard all other Voyager-class ships, but not *Voyager of the Seas*.
● *Johnny Rockets*, a retro 1950s all-day, all-night diner-style eatery that has hamburgers, malt shakes, and jukebox hits, with both indoor and outdoor seating (all indoor tables have a mini-jukebox; dimes are provided for you to make your selection of vintage records), and all-singing, all-dancing waitresses. There is a charge of $3.95 whether you eat in or take out.
● *Sprinkles:* for round-the-clock ice cream and free yoghurt, pastries and coffee.

ENTERTAINMENT. The 1,350-seat Showlounge is a really stunning space. It is located at the forward end of the ship and spans the height of five decks (with only a few slim pillars and almost no disruption of sightlines from any seat in the house). The room has a hydraulic orchestra pit and huge stage areas, together with sonic-boom loud sound, and some superb lighting equipment.

In addition, the ship has an array of cabaret acts. Although many are not what you would call headliners (the strongest cabaret acts are featured in the main showlounge, while others are presented in the Cleopatra's Needle Lounge, also the venue for late-night adults-only comedy), they regularly travel the cruise ship circuit. The best shows, however, are the Ice Spectaculars.

There is also a TV studio that can be used, for example, for trade show exhibit space (good for conventions at sea).

SPA/FITNESS. The ShipShape health spa is large, measuring 15,000 sq. ft (1,400 sq. meters). It includes a large aerobics room, fitness center (with the usual stairmasters, treadmills, stationary bikes, weight machines and free weights), treatment rooms, and men's and women's sauna/steam rooms. Another 10,000 sq. ft (930 sq. meters) is devoted to a Solarium (with magrodome sliding glass roof).

For the more sporting, there is activity galore – including a rock-climbing wall that's 32.8 ft high (10 meters), with five separate climbing tracks. Other sports facilities include a roller-blading track, a dive-and-snorkel shop, a full-size basketball court and 9-hole, par 26 golf course.

● **For more extensive general information about a Royal Caribbean cruise experience, see pages 137–42.**

Westerdam
★★★★

Large Resort Ship:	.81,811 tons	Total Crew:	.817	Cabins (with private balcony):	.641

Large Resort Ship: ....81,811 tons
Lifestyle: ....Premium
Cruise Line: ......Holland America Line
Former Names: ....none
Builder: ....Fincantieri (Italy)
Original Cost: ....$400 million
Entered Service: ....Apr 2004
Registry: ....The Netherlands
Length (ft/m): 935.0/285.0
Beam (ft/m): 105.6/32.2
Draft (ft/m): 25.5/7.80
Propulsion/Propellers ....diesel-electric
(34,000 kW)/2 pods, (17.6 MW each)
Passenger Decks: 11

Total Crew: 817
Passengers
(lower beds/all berths): 1,916/2,455
Passenger Space Ratio
(lower beds/all berths): 42.6/33.3
Crew/Passenger Ratio
(lower beds/all berths): 2.3/3.0
Navigation Officers: ....European
Cabins (total): 958
Size Range (sq ft/m): 170.0–1,318.6/
15.7–122.5
Cabins (outside view): 804
Cabins (interior/no view): 154
Cabins (for one person): 0

Cabins (with private balcony): 641
Cabins (wheelchair accessible): 28
Cabin Current: ....110 volts
Elevators: 14
Casino (gaming tables): ....Yes
Slot Machines: ....Yes
Swimming Pools (outdoors): 2
+1 children's pool
Swimming Pools (indoors): 1
(indoor/outdoor)
Whirlpools: 5
Self-Service Launderette: ....No
Dedicated Cinema/Seats Yes/170
Library: ....Yes

OVERALL SCORE: 1,522 (OUT OF A POSSIBLE 2,000 POINTS)

OVERVIEW. *Westerdam* is another in the latest generation of Vista-class ships (sister ships: *Eurodam, Oosterdam, Noordam* and *Zuiderdam*), designed to appeal to younger, active vacationers. Westerdam has two funnels, placed close together, one in front of the other, the result of the slightly unusual machinery configuration. The ship has, in effect, two engine rooms – one with three diesels, and one with two diesels and a gas turbine. Podded propulsion *(see page 174 for explanation)* is provided, powered by a diesel-electric system, plus a small gas turbine located in the funnel for the reduction of emissions.

There's a complete walk-around exterior teak promenade deck, and teak "steamer" style sunloungers are provided. A jogging track is located around the mast and the forward third of the ship. Exterior glass elevators, mounted midships on both port and starboard sides, provide ocean views. There are two centrally located swimming pools outdoors, and one can be used in inclement weather due to its retractable sliding glass roof. Two whirlpool tubs, adjacent to the swimming pools, are abridged by a bar. Another smaller pool is available for children; it incorporates a winding water slide that spans two decks in height. There is an additional whirlpool tub outdoors.

You enter the ship through an intimate lobby that spans three decks, and is topped by a beautiful, rotating, Waterford crystal globe of the world. The interior decor is interesting; the ceilings are particularly noticeable in the public rooms. In terms of overall decor, the colours are muted, warm. Maintaining its traditions, Holland America Line provides a large collection of artwork, including Dutch exploration, maritime history and art. The focal point of the ship is its soothing midnight blue atrium lobby (like a hotel

BERLITZ'S RATINGS

	Possible	Achieved
Ship	500	428
Accommodation	200	162
Food	400	269
Service	400	278
Entertainment	100	77
Cruise	400	308

lobby), containing a glass replica of a sailing ship.

There are two whole entertainment/public room decks. The most dramatic room is the showlounge, spanning four decks in the forward section.

Other facilities include a winding shopping street with several boutique stores and logo shops, an internet center, a fine library, card room, an art gallery, photo gallery, and several small meeting rooms. The casino is large (one has to walk through it to get from the restaurant to the show lounge on one of the entertainments decks), and has the usual gaming tables and slot machines.

There's a basketball court, volleyball court, and golf simulator. Club HAL's KidZone is dedicated to kids' facilities and extensive programming for different age groups (5–17), with one counselor for every 30 children. An Explorations Café was added to the Crow's Nest (a HAL trademark observation lounge atop ship) in a 2007 refit.

With this large resort ship, Holland America Line tries hard to be all things to all people, although this reviewer is not convinced that the formula works well for the many loyal repeat passengers used to the smaller ships. However, this vessel does offer a range of public rooms that have a reasonably intimate feel to them and the overall feel of the ship (relative to its size) and its eclectic decor is quite homely and comforting.

The information desk in the lobby is small and somewhat removed from the main passenger flow on the two decks above it. Many pillars obstruct the passenger flow and lines of sight throughout the ship.

There are no self-service launderettes (something families with children might miss – although special laundry packages *are* available).

ACCOMMODATION. There are 24 price categories (16 outside-view/eight interior (no view). Some cabins on the lowest accommodation deck (Main Deck) have views obstructed by lifeboats. Some cabins that can accommodate a third and fourth person have very little closet space, and only one personal safe. Some cabins have interconnecting doors – good for families with children.

Occupants of suites also get exclusive use of the Neptune Lounge and concierge service, priority embarkation and disembarkation, and other benefits (thus, in effect, making this a two-class ship). In many of the suites and cabins with private balconies the balconies are not really very private, as many can be overlooked from various public locations.

Penthouse Verandah Suites: These two suites have the largest accommodation (1,318 sq. ft/122.5 sq. meters, including balcony). These have a separate bedroom with a king-sized bed; there's also a walk-in closet, dressing room, living room, dining room, butler's pantry, mini-bar and refrigerator, and private balcony (verandah). The main bathroom has a large whirlpool bathtub, two washbasins, toilet, and plenty of storage space for personal toiletries. Personalized stationery and complimentary dry cleaning are included, as are hot hors d'oeuvres daily.

DeLuxe Verandah Suites: Next in size are 60 of these suites (563 sq. ft/52.3 sq. meters). These have twin beds that convert to a king-sized bed, vanity desk, lounge area, walk-in closet, mini-bar and refrigerator, and bathroom with full-size bathtub, washbasin and toilet. Personalized stationery and complimentary dry cleaning are included, as are hot hors d'oeuvres and other goodies.

Verandah Suites: There are 100 of these Verandah Suites (actually they are cabins, not suites, and measure (284 sq. ft/26.3 sq. meters). Twin beds convert to a queen-sized bed; there is also a lounge area, mini-bar and refrigerator, while the bathroom has a tub, washbasin and toilet. Floor to ceiling windows open onto a private balcony (verandah).

Outside-view Cabins: Standard outside cabins (197 sq. ft/18.3 sq. meters) have twin beds that convert to a queen-sized bed. There's also a small sitting area, while the bathroom has a bathtub/shower combination. The interior (no view) cabins are slightly smaller (182.9 sq. ft/17 sq. meters).

CUISINE. Dining options range from full-service meals in the main dining room and à la carte restaurant to casual, self-serve buffet-style meals and fast-food outlets.

The 1,045-seat Vista (main) Dining Room is two decks high, with seating provided on both main and balcony levels, and is located at the stern of the ship. It provides a traditional Holland America Line dining experience, with friendly service from smiling Indonesian and Filipino stewards. Both open seating and fixed (assigned tables and times) seating are available, while breakfast and lunch are open-seating (you'll be seated by restaurant staff when you enter).

There are tables for two, four, six or eight, and both smoking and no-smoking sections. The waiter stations can be noisy

for anyone seated adjacent to them. Fine Rosenthal china and decent cutlery are used (but there are no fish knives). Live music is provided for dinner each evening. Once each cruise, a Dutch Dinner is held (hats are provided), as is an Indonesian Lunch. "Lighter option" meals are available for the nutrition-conscious. Holland America Line can provide Kosher meals, although these are prepared ashore, frozen, and brought to the table sealed in their original containers.

Alternative Dining Option: The 130-seat Pinnacle Grill is a more upscale dining spot (with higher quality ingredients, and smarter presentation than in the larger main dining room). It is located on Lower Promenade Deck, and fronts onto the second level of the atrium lobby; a Pinnacle Bar was added in the 2007 refit. Pacific Northwest cuisine is featured (with items such as sesame-crusted halibut with ginger-miso, Peking duck breast with blackberry sauce, and an array of premium quality steaks from hand-selected cuts of beef – shown to you at tableside). Fine table settings, china and silverware are provided, as are leather-bound menus. The wine bar offers mostly American wines. Reservations are required and there is a cover charge of $30 per person for service and gratuity.

Informal Eateries: For casual eating, there is an extensive Lido Cafe, which wraps around the funnel housing and extends aft. It includes a pizzeria counter, a salad bar, Asian stir-fry counter, deli sandwiches, and a separate dessert buffet. Movement around the buffet area can be very slow.

Additionally, there is an outdoor self-serve buffet (adjacent to the fantail pool), which serves fast-food items such as hamburgers and hot dogs, chicken and fries, as well as two smaller buffets adjacent to the midships swimming pool area, and a Windsurf Cafe in the atrium lobby (open 20 hours a day), for coffee, pastries, snack foods, deli sandwiches and liqueur coffees (evenings only) – all at extra cost.

ENTERTAINMENT. The 867-seat Vista Lounge is the ship's principal venue for Las Vegas-style revue shows and major cabaret presentations. It spans three decks in the forward section of the ship. The main floor level has a bar in its starboard aft section, while the upper two levels. Spiral stairways at the back of the lounge connect all levels. The upper levels have better sightlines.

SPA/FITNESS. The Greenhouse Spa, a large, two-decks-high health spa, is directly above the navigation bridge. Facilities include a solarium, hydrotherapy pool, unisex thermal suite – a unisex area incorporating a Laconium (gentle sauna), Hammam (mild steam), and Camomile Grotto (small aromatic steam room). There is also a beauty parlor, 11 massage/therapy rooms (including one for couples), and a large gymnasium with floor-to-ceiling windows on three sides and forward-facing ocean views, and the latest high-tech muscle-toning equipment.

● **For more extensive general information on what a Holland America Line cruise is like, see pages 126–28.**

Wind Spirit
★★★ +

Boutique Ship: . . . . .5,350 tons	Sail Area (sq ft/m2): 21,489/1,996.4
Lifestyle: . . . . .Premium	Main Propulsion: . . . . . .a) engines/b) sails
Cruise Line: . . . . .Windstar Cruises	Propulsion/Propellers: . . . . .diesel-electric
Former Names: . . . . .none	(1,400kW)/1
Builder: . . . . .Ateliers et Chantiers	Passenger Decks: 5
du Havre (France)	Total Crew: 88
Original Cost: . . . .$34.2 million	Passengers
Entered Service: . . . . .Apr 1988	(lower beds/all berths): 148/159
Registry: . . . . .The Bahamas	Passenger Space Ratio
Length (ft/m): 439.6/134.0	(lower beds/all berths): 36.1/33.6
Beam (ft/m): 51.8/15.8	Crew/Passenger Ratio
Draft (ft/m): 13.4/4.1	(lower beds/all berths): 1.6/1.8
Type of Vessel: . . . . . .computer-controlled	Navigation Officers: . . . . .European
sail-cruiser	Cabins (total): 74
No. of Masts: . . . . . . .4/6 self-furling sails	

Size Range (sq ft/m): 185.0–220.0/
17.0–22.5
Cabins (outside view): 74
Cabins (interior/no view): 0
Cabins (for one person): 0
Cabins (with private balcony): 0
Cabins (wheelchair accessible): 0
Cabin Current: . . . . .110 volts
Casino (gaming tables): . . . . .Yes
Slot Machines: . . . . .Yes
Swimming Pools (outdoors): . .1 (dip pool)
Whirlpools: 1
Self-Service Launderette: . . . . .No
Library: . . . . .Yes

OVERALL SCORE: 1,394 (OUT OF A POSSIBLE 2,000 POINTS)

OVERVIEW. *Wind Spirit*, when built, was one of three identical vessels (a fourth, *Wind Saga*, was planned but never built). One of the original three sister ships, *Wind Song*, suffered a fire and was declared a constructive total loss in Tahiti in 2002.

Wind Spirit is a long, sleek-looking craft that is part-yacht, part-cruise ship, with four giant masts that tower 170 ft (52 meters) above the deck (they are actually 204 ft, or 62 meters) high, and fitted with computer-controlled sails; the masts, sails and rigging alone cost $5 million. The computer keeps the ship on an even keel (via the movement of a water hydraulic ballast system of 142,653 gallons/540,000 liters), so there is no heeling (rolling) over 6 degrees.

There is little open deck space when the ship is full, due to the amount of complex sail machinery. At the stern is a small water sports platform for those who enjoy all the goodies the ship offers (but only when at anchor and only in really calm sea conditions). Water sports facilities include a banana boat, kayaks, sunfish sailboats, windsurf boards, water ski boat, scuba and snorkel equipment, and four Zodiacs. You will be asked to sign a waiver if you wish to use the water sports equipment.

The ship has a finely crafted interior with pleasing, blond woods, together with soft, complementary colors and decor that is chic, even elegant, but a little cold. Note that the main lounge aboard this ship is of a slightly different design than sister ship *Wind Star*.

No scheduled activities help to make this a real relaxing, unregimented "get away from it all" vacation. The Windstar ships help you to cruise in very comfortable, contempo-

BERLITZ'S RATINGS		
	Possible	Achieved
Ship	500	361
Accommodation	200	160
Food	400	265
Service	400	270
Entertainment	n/a	n/a
Cruise	500	338

rary surroundings bordering on the luxurious, yet in an unstructured environment. They provide a very relaxing, virtually unstructured cruise experience just right for seven idyllic nights in sheltered areas (but can be disturbing when a Windstar vessel is in small ports alongside several gigantic cruise ships).

This ship is ideal for couples who do not like large ships. The dress code is casual (no jackets and ties), even for dinner – the brochure states casual elegance. There are no formal nights or theme nights.

You will probably be under sail for less than 40 percent of the time (conditions and cruise area winds permitting).

Gratuities are charged at $11 per person, per day, and 15% is added to bar and wine accounts. The onboard currency is the US dollar.

Note that the swimming pool is really only a tiny "dip" pool. Be prepared for the "whine" of the vessel's generators, which are needed to run the air-conditioning and lighting systems 24 hours a day. That means you will also hear it at night in your cabin (any cabin); it takes most passengers a day or two to get used to.

Beverage prices are high. The library is small, and needs more hardback fiction. The staff, though friendly, is casual and a little sloppy at times in the finer points of service.

SUITABLE FOR: *Wind Spirit* is best suited to young-minded couples and singles who want contemporary facilities and some watersports in a very relaxed but chic setting that is different to "normal" cruise ships, with good food and service, but with no entertainment, time-passing parlour games, structured activities, or ship's photographers.

ACCOMMODATION. Regardless of the category you choose, all cabins are nicely equipped, have crisp, inviting décor and a mini-bar/refrigerator (stocked when you embark, but all drinks are at extra cost), 24-hour room service, personal safe, television (with CNN, when available, for news) that rotates so that it is viewable from the bed and the bathroom, video player, compact disc player, plenty of storage space, and two portholes. The cabins all have two portholes with outside views, and deadlights (steel covers that provide a complete blackout at night and can be closed in inclement weather conditions). The decor is a pleasant mix of rich woods, natural fabrics and colorful soft furnishings, and hi-tech yacht-style amenities. However, note that some of the cabinetry is looking a little tired, and has that "I've been varnished many times" look. A basket of fruit is provided, and replenished daily.

The bathrooms are best described as compact units, designed in a figure of eight, with a teakwood floor in the central section. There is a good amount of storage space for personal toiletries in two cabinets, as well as under-sink cupboard space; a wall-mounted hairdryer is also provided. The shower enclosure (no cabins have bathtubs) is circular (like many of today's passengers), and has both a hand-held as well as a fixed shower (so you can wash your hair without getting the rest of your body wet). Personal bathroom amenities by L'Occitane are provided, as are a vanity kit and shower cap.

Note, however, that the lighting is not strong enough for women to apply make-up – this is better applied at the vanity desk in the cabin, which has stronger overhead (halogen) lighting. Bathrobes and towels are 100% cotton.

CUISINE. There is one rather chic and elegant dining room (The Restaurant), with ocean views from large, picture windows, a lovely wood ceiling and wood paneling on the walls. California-style nouvelle cuisine is served, with dishes that are attractively presented. Additionally, "signature" dishes, created by master chefs Joachim Splichal and Jeanne Jones, are offered daily. Open seating means you dine when you want and with whomever you wish to.

When the company first started, European waiters provided service with practiced European finesse. However, those waiters have been replaced by Indonesians and Filipinos, whose communication skills at times can prove inadequate, although their service is pleasant enough. The selection of breads, cheeses, and fruits could be better. There is a big push to sell wines, although the prices are extremely high, as they are for most alcoholic drinks (even bottled water is the highest in the industry, at $7 per liter bottle).

There is often casual dinner on the open deck under the stars, with grilled seafood and steaks. At the bars, hot and cold hors d'oeuvres appear at cocktail times.

Fancy something romantic? One nicety introduced in 2006 is a "Cuisine de l'Amour" romantic dinner for two (at no extra charge) served to you in your cabin, complete with candle. The menu, with seductive sounding selections, offers a choice of appetizer, a set soup, choice of salad, and two entrée options, and a set dessert to finish (ideal for that quiet romantic dinner you've always wanted).

ENTERTAINMENT. There is no showlounge, shows or cabaret. However, none are really needed, because a cruise aboard this high-tech sailing ship provides an opportunity to get away from all that noise and "entertainment". The main lounge (a corner of which is dedicated to a small casino) does have a small dance floor, and, typically, a trio is there to play for your dancing or listening pleasure.

The main lounge is also used for cocktail parties and other social functions. Otherwise, it's down to more personal entertainment, such as a video in your cabin late at night – or, much more romantic, after-dinner hours spent outside strolling or simply lounging on deck.

SPA/FITNESS. A gymnasium (with a modicum of muscle-toning equipment, treadmills and exercycles) and sauna are located at the aft of the ship, adjacent to the Watersports platform. Special spa packages can be pre-booked through your travel agent before you arrive at the ship. Well-being massages, aromatherapy facials, manicures, pedicures, and hair beautifying treatments are all at extra cost (massage, for example, costs about $2 per minute, plus gratuity). The spa is operated by Steiner Leisure, a specialist concession, whose young staff may try to sell you Steiner's own-brand Elemis beauty products (spa girls have sales targets).

Wind Star
★★★ +

Boutique Ship: . . . . .5,350 tons	Sail Area (sq ft/m2): 21,489/1,996.4	Size Range (sq ft/m): 185.0–220.0/
Lifestyle: . . . . .Premium	Main Propulsion: . . . . . .a) engines/b) sails	17.0–22.5
Cruise Line: . . . . .Windstar Cruises	Propulsion/Propellers: . . . . .diesel-electric	Cabins (outside view): 74
Former Names: . . . . .none	(1,400kW)/1	Cabins (interior/no view): 0
Builder: . . . . .Ateliers et Chantiers	Passenger Decks: 5	Cabins (for one person): 0
du Havre (France)	Total Crew: 88	Cabins (with private balcony): 0
Original Cost: . . . .$34.2 million	Passengers	Cabins (wheelchair accessible): 0
Entered Service: . . . . Dec 1986	(lower beds/all berths): 148/168	Cabin Current: . . . . .110 volts
Registry: . . . . .The Bahamas	Passenger Space Ratio	Casino (gaming tables): . . . . .Yes
Length (ft/m): 439.6/134.0	(lower beds/all berths): 36.1/33.6	Slot Machines: . . . . .Yes
Beam (ft/m): 51.8/15.8	Crew/Passenger Ratio	Swimming Pools (outdoors): . .1 (dip pool)
Draft (ft/m): 13.4/4.1	(lower beds/all berths): 1.6/1.8	Whirlpools: 1
Type of Vessel: . . . . . .computer-controlled	Navigation Officers: . . . . .European	Self-Service Launderette: . . . . .No
sail-cruiser	Cabins (total): 74	Library: . . . . .Yes
No. of Masts: . . . . . . .4/6 self-furling sails		

OVERALL SCORE: 1,393 (OUT OF A POSSIBLE 2,000 POINTS)

OVERVIEW. *Wind Star* is one of three identical vessels (a fourth, *Wind Saga*, was planned but never built). One of the original three sister ships, *Wind Song*, suffered a fire and was declared a constructive total loss in Tahiti in 2002. *Wind Star* is a sleek-looking craft that is part-yacht, part-cruise ship, with four giant masts that tower 170 ft (52 meters) above the deck (they are actually 204 ft, or 62 meters) high, and fitted with computer-controlled sails; the masts, sails and rigging alone cost $5 million. The computer keeps the ship on an even keel (via the movement of a water hydraulic ballast system of 142,650 gallons/540,000 litres), so there is no heeling (rolling) over 6 degrees. When the masts for Wind Star (first of the three original Windstar vessels) were lowered into position, a US silver dollar, dated 1889, was placed under mast number two (the main mast).

There is very little open deck space when the ship is full, due to the amount of complex sail machinery. There is a tiny dip pool. At the stern is a small water sports platform for those who enjoy all the goodies the ship offers (but only when at anchor, and only in really calm sea conditions). Water sports facilities include a banana boat kayaks, sunfish sailboats, windsurf boards, water ski boat, scuba and snorkel equipment, and four Zodiacs. You will be asked to sign a waiver if you wish to use the water sports equipment.

The ship has a finely crafted interior with pleasing, blond woods, together with soft, complementary colors and decor that is chic, even elegant, but a little cold. Note that the main lounge aboard Wind Star is of a different design than sister ship *Wind Spirit*.

No scheduled activities help to make this a real relaxing,

BERLITZ'S RATINGS

	Possible	Achieved
Ship	500	359
Accommodation	200	160
Food	400	265
Service	400	270
Entertainment	n/a	n/a
Cruise	500	339

unregimented "get away from it all" vacation. The Windstar ships will cruise you in extremely comfortable surroundings bordering on contemporary luxury, yet in an unstructured environment. They provide a very relaxing, virtually unstructured cruise experience just right for seven idyllic nights in sheltered areas (but can be disturbing when a Windstar vessel is in small ports alongside several huge cruise ships).

This ship is ideal for couples who do not like large ships. The dress code is casual (no jackets and ties required), even for dinner (the brochure states casual elegance). There are no formal nights or theme nights. You will probably be under sail for less than 40 percent of the time (conditions and cruise area winds permitting).

Gratuities are charged at $11 per person, per day, and 15% is added to bar and wine accounts. The onboard currency is the US dollar.

Note that the swimming pool is really only a tiny "dip" pool. Be prepared for the "whine" of the vessel's generators, which are needed to run the air-conditioning and lighting systems 24 hours a day. That means you will also hear it at night in your cabin (any cabin), and takes most passengers a day or two to get used to.

Beverage prices are high. The library is small, and needs more hardback fiction. The staff, though friendly, is casual and can be a little sloppy at times in the finer points of service.

SUITABLE FOR: *Wind Star* is best suited to young-minded couples and singles who want contemporary facilities and some watersports in a very relaxed but chic setting that is different to "normal" cruise ships, with good food and service, but with no entertainment, time-passing parlour games, structured activities or ship's photographers.

ACCOMMODATION. Regardless of the category you choose, all cabins are very nicely equipped, have crisp, inviting decor, and a mini-bar/refrigerator (stocked when you embark, but all drinks are at extra cost), 24-hour room service, personal safe, television (with CNN, when available, for news) that rotates so that it is viewable from the bed and the bathroom, video player, compact disc player, plenty of storage space, and two portholes.

The cabins all have two portholes with outside views, and deadlights (steel covers that provide a complete blackout at night and can be closed in inclement weather conditions). The decor is a pleasant mix of rich woods, natural fabrics and colorful soft furnishings, and hi-tech yacht-style amenities. However, note that some of the cabinetry is looking a little tired, and has that "I've been varnished many times" look. A basket of fruit is provided, and replenished daily.

The bathrooms are best described as very compact units, designed in a figure of eight, with a teakwood floor in the central section. There is a good amount of storage space for personal toiletries in two cabinets, as well as under-sink cupboard space; a wall-mounted hairdryer is also provided. The shower enclosure (no cabins have bathtubs) is circular (like many of today's passengers), and has both a handheld, as well as a fixed shower (so you can wash your hair without getting the rest of your body wet). Personal bathroom amenities by L'Occitane provided, as is a vanity kit and shower cap.

Note, however, that the lighting is not strong enough for women to apply make-up – this is better applied at the vanity desk in the cabin, which has stronger overhead (halogen) lighting. Bathrobes and towels are 100% cotton.

CUISINE. There is one rather chic and elegant dining room (The Restaurant), with ocean views from large, picture windows, a lovely wood ceiling and wood paneling on the walls. California-style nouvelle cuisine is served, with dishes that are attractively presented. Additionally, "signature" dishes, created by master chefs Joachim Splichal and Jeanne Jones, are offered daily.

Open seating means you dine when you want and with whomever you wish to. Both smoking and no-smoking sections are provided.

When the company made its debut, European waiters provided service with practiced European finesse; those waiters are now from Indonesia and the Philippines, who provide friendly service but with less finesse. The selection of breads, cheeses, and fruits could be better. There is a big push to sell wines, although the prices are extremely high, as they are for most alcoholic drinks (even bottled water is the highest in the industry, at $7 per liter bottle).

There is often casual dinner on the open deck under the stars, with grilled seafood and steaks. At the bars, hot and cold hors d'oeuvres appear at cocktail times.

A nice addition is a "Cuisine de l'Amour" romantic dinner for two (at no extra charge) served to you in your cabin, complete with candle. The menu (with seductive sounding selections) offers a choice of appetizer, a set soup, choice of salad, and two entrée options, and a set dessert to finish (ideal for that quiet romantic dinner you've always wanted).

ENTERTAINMENT. There is no showlounge, shows or cabaret. However, none are really needed, because a cruise aboard this high-tech sailing ship provides an opportunity to get away from all that noise and "entertainment". The main lounge (a corner of which is dedicated to a small casino) does have a small dance floor, and, typically, a trio is there to play for your dancing or listening pleasure. The main lounge is also used for cocktail parties and other social functions. Otherwise, it's down to more personal entertainment, such as a video in your cabin late at night – or, much more romantic, after-dinner hours spent outside strolling or simply lounging on deck.

SPA/FITNESS. A gymnasium (with a modicum of muscle-toning equipment, treadmills and exercycles) and sauna are located at the aft of the ship, adjacent to the Watersports platform. Special spa packages can be pre-booked through your travel agent before you arrive at the ship. Well-being massages, aromatherapy facials, manicures, pedicures, and hair beautifying treatments are all at extra cost (massage, for example, costs about $2 per minute, plus gratuity). The spa is operated by Steiner Leisure, a specialist concession, whose young staff may try to sell you Steiner's own-brand Elemis beauty products (spa girls have sales targets).

Wind Surf
★★★ +

Small Ship: ....14,745 tons	Sail Area (sq ft/m2): 26,910/2,500	Cabins (outside view): 156
Lifestyle: ....Premium	Main Propulsion: ......a) engines/b) sails	Cabins (interior/no view): 0
Cruise Line: ....Windstar Cruises	Propulsion/Propellers: diesel (9,120kW)/2	Cabins (for one person): 0
Former Names: ....*Club Med I*	Passenger Decks: 8	Cabins (with private balcony): 0
Builder: ....Ateliers et Chantiers	Total Crew: 163	Cabins (wheelchair accessible): 0
du Havre (France)	Passengers	Cabin Current: ....220 volts
Original Cost: ....$140 million	(lower beds/all berths): 312/347	Elevators: 2
Entered Service: ....Feb 1990/May 1998	Passenger Space Ratio	Casino (gaming tables): ....Yes
Registry: ....The Bahamas	(lower beds/all berths): 47.2/42.4	Slot Machines: ....Yes
Length (ft/m): 613.5/187.0	Crew/Passenger Ratio	Swimming Pools (outdoors): 2
Beam (ft/m): 65.6/20.0	(lower beds/all berths): 1.9/2.1	Whirlpools: 2
Draft (ft/m): 16.4/5.0	Navigation Officers: ....European	Self-Service Launderette: ....No
Type of Vessel: .....high-tech sail-cruiser	Cabins (total): 156	Library: ....Yes
No. of Masts: ....5/7 computer-controlled	Size Range (sq ft/m): 188.0–500.5/	
sails	17.5-46.5	

OVERALL SCORE: 1,396 (OUT OF A POSSIBLE 2,000 POINTS)

OVERVIEW. One of a pair of the world's largest sail-cruisers, *Wind Surf* is part-cruise ship, part-yacht (its sister ship operates as *Club Med II*). This is a larger, grander sister to the original three Windstar Cruises vessels. Five huge masts of 164 ft/50 meters (these actually rise 221 feet, or 67.5 meters above sea level) carry seven triangular, self-furling sails (made of Dacron) with a total surface area of 26,881 sq. ft (2,497 sq. meters). No human hands touch the sails, as everything is handled electronically by computer control from the bridge.

A computer keeps the ship on an even keel (via the movement of a water hydraulic ballast system of 266,800 gallons/1 million liters), so there is no heeling (rolling) over 6 degrees. When the ship is not using the sails, four diesel-electric motors propel it at up to approximately 12 knots.

There is a large, hydraulic water sports platform at the stern that hasn't functioned properly for over two years – it's time it was fixed. Swimming from it is not allowed, but extensive water sports facilities include 12 windsurfers, 3 sailboats, 2 water-ski boats, 20 single scuba tanks, snorkels, fins and masks, and 4 inflatable Zodiac motorized boats (for water-skiing, etc), and all at no extra charge (except for the scuba tanks). Note that you will be asked to sign a waiver if you wish to use the water sports equipment.

There are two (saltwater) swimming pools (really little more than dip pools); one is located amidships on the uppermost deck of the ship, while the other is located aft, together with two hot tubs, and an adjacent bar.

In 2000, the ship underwent further internal redesign, with enhancement of some features and the addition of

BERLITZ'S RATINGS		
	Possible	Achieved
Ship	500	361
Accommodation	200	160
Food	400	264
Service	400	271
Entertainment	n/a	n/a
Cruise	500	340

new ones. A new gangway was installed to improve embarkation and disembarkation. A business center incorporated a computer center (with 10 internet-access computer terminals, and a meeting room for between 30 and 60 people. In the casino/main lounge (with 4 blackjack and one roulette table, and 21 slot machines), which has an unusually high ceiling for the size of the ship, the dance floor has thankfully been relocated for better access and flow.

In the 2006 refit a Yacht Club replaced the library; it provides comfortable seating for socializing. An espresso bar offers gourmet coffee drinks; there are eight computers with internet access, and wi-fi access for laptops.

Wind Surf cruises from Barbados (November–March) and in the Mediterranean (May–October). However, the European itineraries are really port-intensive, which means you sail each night and are in port each day. With such itineraries, there seems little point to having the sails, as passengers don't get to experience them.

All gratuities and port taxes are included in the brochure price (no additional tips expected), which itself is considerably higher than those of the two smaller vessels in the fleet (*Wind Spirit, Wind Star*). The onboard currency is the US dollar. Gratuities are charged at $11 per person, per day, and 15% is added to bar and wine accounts.

There are no showers at either of the two swimming pools (they really are just dip pools for cooling off) – passengers get into pool or hot tubs, while covered in oil or lotion, an unhygienic arrangement. Don't buy a cigar from the onboard shop – because the air temperature in the shop is high, cigars will be dry and absolutely worthless (they should, of course, be sold from a properly kept humidor).

SUITABLE FOR: *Wind Surf* is a good choice for couples seeking the "California Casual" dress code (no jackets or ties required) and informality found aboard this vessel, yet don't want the inconvenience of the workings of a real tall ship. The quality of food and its presentation is a definite plus, as is the policy of no music in passenger hallways or elevators – in other words, it's a delightful, peaceful environment.

ACCOMMODATION. There are just three price categories, making your choice a simple one. Regardless of category, all cabins are very nicely equipped, have crisp, inviting decor, and a mini-bar/refrigerator (stocked when you embark, but all drinks are at extra cost), 24-hour room service, personal safe, a TV set (with CNN, when available) that rotates so that it is viewable from the bed and the bathroom, video player, compact disc player, plenty of storage space, and two portholes. Videos and compact discs are available from the library. There are six 4-person cabins; 35 doubles are fitted with an extra Pullman berth, and several cabins have an interconnecting door (good for families). Some of the cabinetry is looking a little tired.

The bathrooms are compact units, designed in a figure of eight, with a teakwood floor in the central section. There is a good amount of storage space for personal toiletries in two cabinets, as well as under-sink cupboard space, and a wall-mounted hairdryer. The shower enclosure (cabins, except two new suites, do not have bathtubs) is circular, and has both a hand-held and a fixed shower (so you can wash your hair without getting the rest of your body wet).

A range of L'Occitaine amenities is provided, as.is a vanity kit and shower cap. The lighting is not strong enough for women to apply make-up – this is better applied at the vanity desk in the cabin. Bathrobes and towels are 100% cotton, while bed linen is of a mix of 50% cotton/50% polyester (100% cotton sheets available on request).

In 1998, 31 new suites were added to Deck 3 during an extensive refit (one Owner's Suite plus 30 suites created by combining former standard cabins). All but one of these suites have two bathrooms, a separate living/dining area, sleeping area (this can be curtained off from the lounge), two writing desks (there is even enough room for you to have an in-suite massage), and four portholes instead of two. A further two new suites (approximately 500 sq.ft./46.4 sq.m) were added during a 2006 refit; it has a bedroom, separate living/dining room, and marble bathroom with Jacuzzi bathtub. In the 2006 refit all bathrooms were refurbished with granite countertops, open glass shelves, new cabinets, and magnifying mirror, making bathrooms more contemporary.

There are two TV sets (one in the lounge, on in the sleeping area), VCR and CD player, and BOSE SoundDock for ipods. However, note that movies cannot be watched from the bed – only from the sofa in the lounge area. Popcorn is available from room service.

CUISINE. The 272-seat Restaurant has tables for two, four or six, and open seating (with no pre-assigned tables), so you can sit with whom you wish, when you like. It is open only for dinner, which is typically between 7.30pm and 9.30pm. Both smoking and no-smoking sections are provided. California-style nouvelle cuisine is served, with dishes that are attractively presented. Additionally, "signature" dishes, created by master chefs Joachim Splichal and Jeanne Jones, are offered daily.

A 124-seat Degrees Bistro provides an alternative venue to the main restaurant (for dinner), with menus from around the world as well as Joachim Splichal-developed steakhouse cuisine. It is located high atop the ship (on Star Deck) and has picture windows on port and starboard sides, an open kitchen, and tables for two, four or six. This is a no-smoking dining spot. Reservations are required for dinner (although there is no extra charge), and passengers are restricted to two visits per 7-day cruise.

The Veranda, amidships (on Star Deck), has its own open terrace for informal, self-serve breakfast and lunch buffets. It really is very pleasant to be outside, eating an informal meal on a balmy night. Do try the bread pudding – the ship is famous for it (available after lunch each day). Additionally, a permanent barbecue is also set up aft of the Veranda, for fresh grilled items for breakfast and lunch.

The Compass Rose, an indoor/outdoor bar, provides snack items plus some pastries and coffee for breakfast.

Windstar Cruises food is generally very good, although highly geared toward American tastes. Europeans and other nationals should note that items such as bacon is fried to death, and the choice of cheeses and teas is poor. Note that the service in the dining room is also quite fast, geared towards those who have not yet learned to unwind.

A nice addition is a "Cuisine de l'Amour" romantic dinner for two (at no extra charge) served to you in your cabin, complete with candle. The menu (with its seductive sounding selections) offers a choice of appetizer, a set soup, choice of salad, and two entrée options, and a set dessert to finish.

ENTERTAINMENT. There is no showlounge, shows or cabaret. However, none are really needed, because a cruise aboard this high-tech sailing ship provides an opportunity to get away from all that noise and "entertainment". The main lounge (a corner of which is dedicated to a small casino) does have a small dance floor, and music typically provided by a trio. The main lounge is also used for cocktail parties and other social functions.

One disturbing trend, however, is use of the lounge for art auctions after dinner. How sad that an otherwise pleasant, casual cruise experience is ruined in this way. Better to retire to your cabin and take in a video, or spend it out on deck taking a stroll or lounging under the stars.

SPA/FITNESS. The Health Spa has a unisex sauna (bathing suits required), beauty salon, and several treatment rooms for massage, facials and body wraps; there is also a decent gymnasium (on a separate deck – with ocean views), and an aerobics workout room.

Unfortunately, the spa facilities are split on three separate decks, making them rather disjointed. Special spa packages can be pre-booked through your travel agent before you embark. The spa is operated by Steiner Leisure, the industry's leading concession.

Yamal
★★★

Boutique Ship: . . . . .23,445 tons	Passenger Decks: 4	Cabins (with private balcony): 0
Lifestyle: . . . . .Standard	Total Crew: 150	Cabins (wheelchair accessible): 0
Cruise Line: . . . . .Poseidon Arctic	Passengers	Cabin Current: . . . . .220 volts
Voyages	(lower beds/all berths): 100/100	Dining Rooms: .1
Former Names: . . . . .none	Passenger Space Ratio	Elevators: 0
Builder: . . . . .Baltic Shipyard &	(lower beds/all berths): 234.0/234.0	Casino (gaming tables): . . . . .No
Engineering (Russia)	Crew/Passenger Ratio	Slot Machines: .No
Original Cost: . . . .$150 million	(lower beds/all berths): 0.6/0.6	Swimming Pools (indoors): 1
Entered Service: . . . . .Nov 1992	Navigation Officers: . . .Russian/Ukrainian	Whirlpools: 0
Registry: . . . . .Russia	Cabins (total): .56	Self-Service Launderette: . . . . .Yes
Length (ft/m): 492.1/150.0	Size Range (sq ft/m): 130.0–300.0/	Lecture/Film Room: . . . . . .Yes (seats 100)
Beam (ft/m): 98.4/30.0	14.3–27.8	Library: . . . . .Yes
Draft (ft/m): 36.0/11.0	Cabins (outside view): 56	Zodiacs: 4
Propulsion/Propellers: . .nuclear-powered	Cabins (interior/no view): 0	Helicopter Pad: . . . . . . .2 helicopters for
turbo-electric (55,950kW)/3	Cabins (for one person): 3	passenger use

---

OVERALL SCORE: 1,247 (OUT OF A POSSIBLE 2,000 POINTS)

OVERVIEW. The ultimate in technology accompanies this special ship, one of a fleet of four Arktica-class vessesls (three are still operating) that comprise the world's most powerful icebreakers, with a 48mm-thick (about 3 inches) armored double hull. Propulsion power is provided by two nuclear-powered reactors (encased in 160 tons of steel), which provide the steam for propulsion via a pair of steam turbines. Each turbine operates three generators, and these in turn produce DC power for the electric propulsion motors that power the three powerful four-bladed propellers, each of which weighs about seven tons. The ship carries enough fuel for four years without refueling. Of the 150 crew, 50 are officers and engineers dedicated to the maintenance and operation of the highly specialized vessel.

Yamal is one of few surface ships ever to reach the North Pole, assisted by an air-bubbling system which delivers hot water through jets under the surface of the ice (rather like the feeling of being in a floating whirlpool bath). Two helicopters are carried for reconnaissance and passenger sightseeing use; their use is included in the expedition fare, and provide a bird's-eye view of the polar landscape. The ship carries a fleet of Zodiac inflatable landing craft.

Rugged yet surprisingly comfortable surroundings prevail inside. There are two lounges. A tiered lecture theater with stage is the setting for a team of biologists, scientists, geologists, and other lecturers. There is a heated indoor seawater pool. Light but warm parkas are provided for everyone.

Yamal is occasionally placed under charter to various operators (mostly the immensely experienced Quark Expeditions, based in Darien, USA). This is one of the most

BERLITZ'S RATINGS		
	Possible	Achieved
Ship	500	307
Accommodation	200	120
Food	400	244
Service	400	250
Entertainment	n/a	n/a
Cruise	500	331

exciting, seat-of-your-pants expedition cruise experiences available. The onboard currency is the US dollar.

SUITABLE FOR: This type of expedition cruising vessel is best suited to adventurous, hardy outdoors types who enjoy being with nature and wildlife in some of the most inhospitable places on earth and don't mind roughing it a little.

ACCOMMODATION. All cabins are generously sized (considering the type of specialized vessel this is), and all are outside, with private facilities, TV (for in-house viewing), VCR (suites only), refrigerator and desk. There is, however, a limited amount of closet and drawer space in most cabins.

The bathrooms are small and utilitarian, and you will need to take your own toiletry items.

CUISINE. The dining room is nicely appointed, and all passengers dine in one seating. The carbohydrate-rich food is hearty, with plenty of meat and potato dishes, but little fruit and cheese. When the ship is under charter to Western companies, Western rather than Russian chefs oversee the food operation, and the selection of foods is better.

ENTERTAINMENT. The expedition cruise itself, into inhospitable regions such as the Arctic and northern hemisphere, is really the main diversion. However, a recap of each day's events and experiences makes for a fascinating evening's conversation.

SPA/FITNESS. There is a small gymnasium, and a sauna.

Zaandam
★★★★

Mid-Size Ship: . . . . .60,906 tons
Lifestyle: . . . . .Premium
Cruise Line: . . . . . .Holland America Line
Former Names: . . . . .none
Builder: . . . . .Fincantieri (Italy)
Original Cost: . . . .$300 million
Entered Service: . . . . .May 2000
Registry: . . . . .The Netherlands
Length (ft/m): 777.5/237.00
Beam (ft/m): 105.8/32.25
Draft (ft/m): 25.5/7.80
Propulsion/Propellers: . . . . .diesel-electric
(37,500kW)/2
Passenger Decks: 10

Total Crew: 561
Passengers
(lower beds/all berths): 1,440/1,850
Passenger Space Ratio
(lower beds/all berths): 42.3/32.9
Crew/Passenger Ratio
(lower beds/all berths): 2.5/2.5
Navigation Officers: . . . . .Dutch
Cabins (total): 720
Size Range (sq ft/m): 113.0–1,126.3/
10.5–104.6
Cabins (outside view): 581
Cabins (interior/no view): 139
Cabins (for one person): 0

Cabins (with private balcony): 197
Cabins (wheelchair accessible): 23
Cabin Current: . . . . .110 volts
Elevators: 12
Casino (gaming tables): . . . . .Yes
Slot Machines: . . . . .Yes
Swimming Pools (outdoors): 2
Swimming Pools (indoors): 1
(magrodome cover)
Whirlpools: 2
Self-Service Launderette: . . . . .Yes
Dedicated Cinema/Seats: Yes/205
Library: . . . . .Yes

OVERALL SCORE: 1,541 (OUT OF A POSSIBLE 2,000 POINTS)

OVERVIEW. *Zaandam's* hull is dark blue, in keeping with all Holland America Line ships. Although similar in size to *Rotterdam*, this ship has a single funnel, and is a sister ship to *Volendam*.

Zaandam has three principal passenger stairways, which is so much better than two stairways, particularly from the viewpoints of safety, accessibility and passenger flow. There is a magrodome-covered pool on the Lido Deck between the mast and the ship's funnel.

The interior decor is restrained, with much traditional ocean liner detailing, wood accenting, and the design theme of music incorporated throughout. Music memorabilia is scattered throughout the ship, in fabrics, posters, and – believe it or not – real instruments. The musical instruments and other memorabilia were acquired from the "Pop and Guitars" auction at Christie's in London in 1997. They include a Fender Squire Telecaster guitar signed by Mick Jagger, Keith Richards, Charlie Watts, Ronnie Wood and Bill Wyman of the Rolling Stones; a Conn Saxophone signed on the mouthpiece by former US President Bill Clinton; an Ariana acoustic guitar signed by David Bowie and Iggy Pop; a Fender Stratocaster guitar signed in silver ink by the members of the rock band Queen; a Bently "Les Paul" style guitar signed by various artists, including Carlos Santana, Eric Clapton, B.B. King, Robert Cray, Keith Richards and Les Paul (perhaps the ship should be named *Rockerdam*).

New additions include The Oasis outdoor relaxation areas (aft of the funnel, including a waterfall and family gathering areas), Explorations (an excellent combination coffee/tea café, internet connection center, and library; and children's and teens' play areas. Popcorn is even provided at the Wajang

BERLITZ'S RATINGS		
	Possible	Achieved
Ship	500	430
Accommodation	200	165
Food	400	282
Service	400	276
Entertainment	100	77
Cruise	400	311

Theater for moviegoers (just like ashore), and this location now incorporates a fully equipped kitchen for HAL's "Culinary Arts" program, which involves visiting chefs and interactive cooking and tasting demonstrations.

The casino has blackjack, roulette, stud poker and dice tables alongside the requisite rows of slot machines. Adjacent is a sports bar.

The ship's focal point is a three-deck-high atrium, around which the ship's main offices can be found (reception desk, shore excursions desk, photo shop, and photo gallery). It also houses a real showpiece – a fancy 22-ft (6.7-meter) high pipe organ that comes complete with puppets that move in time with the music; it is one of the largest such Dutch band organs ever built (it was custom-built in Hilversum in the Netherlands especially for Holland America Line).

As in *Volendam*, the Lido Deck swimming pool is located one deck higher than the *Statendam*-class ships, so that you can now have direct access between the aft and midships pools aboard this ship (not so aboard the S-class ships). This provided more space on the Navigation Deck below for extra cabins to be accommodated.

With one whole deck of suites (and a dedicated, private concierge lounge), the company has in effect created a two-class ship. The charge to use the washing machines and dryers in the self-service launderette is petty and irritating, particularly for the occupants of suites, as they pay high prices for their cruises.

Holland America Line's "Signature of Excellence" program, now introduced fleetwide, provides passengers with more choice, and has given a boost to the cabin toiletry amenities provided. Communication (in English) with many of the staff, particularly in the dining room and buffet areas, can be frustrating. Room service is poor. Non-smokers should avoid this ship, as smokers are everywhere. Standing in line for embarkation, disembarkation, shore tenders and for self-serve buffet meals is inevitable aboard large ships.

ACCOMMODATION. The range is comparable to that found aboard the similarly sized *Rotterdam*, and comprises 17 different categories. The price will depend on the grade, location and size you choose. There is one penthouse suite, 28 suites, and 168 mini-suites, with the rest of the accommodation comprised of a mix of outside-view and interior (no view) cabins. However, there are many more balcony cabins (called "mini-suites") aboard this ship than aboard the slightly smaller *Statendam*-class ships (*Maasdam, Ryndam, Statendam,* and *Veendam*). All passenger hallways now include pleasing artwork.

All standard interior and outside cabins are tastefully furnished, and have twin beds that convert to a queen-sized bed (space is tight for walking between beds and vanity unit). There is a decent amount of closet and drawer space, although this will prove tight for the longer voyages featured. All cabin televisions carry CNN and TNT. The bathrooms, which are fully tiled, are disappointingly small (particularly for long cruises) and have small shower tubs, utilitarian personal toiletries cupboards, and exposed under-sink plumbing. There is no detailing to distinguish them from bathrooms aboard the *Statendam*-class ships.

There are 28 full Verandah Suites (Navigation Deck), and one penthouse suites. All suite occupants share a private concierge lounge, called the Neptune Lounge (the concierge handles such things as special dining arrangements, shore excursions and special requests). Strangely, there are no butlers for these suites, as aboard ships with similar facilities.

Each Verandah Suite has a separate bedroom, dressing and living areas. Suite passengers get personal stationery, complimentary laundry and ironing, cocktail hour hors d'oeuvres and other goodies, as well as priority embarkation and disembarkation. The concierge lounge, with its latticework teak detailing and private library, is accessible only by private key-card.

The ultimate in living space is the Penthouse Suite. It has a separate steward's entrance, and has a large bedroom with king-sized bed, separate living room (with baby grand piano) and a dining room, dressing room, walk-in closet, butler's pantry, private balcony (the balcony is no larger than the balcony of any of the other suites).

Other facilities include an audio-visual center with television and VCR, wet bar with refrigerator, large bathroom with Jacuzzi bathtub, separate toilet with bidet, and a guest bathroom (with toilet and washbasin).

With the exception of the penthouse suite, located forward on the starboard side, the bathrooms in the other suites and "mini-suites" are a little disappointing – not as spacious or opulent as one might expect. All outside-view suites and cabin bathrooms have a bathtub/shower while interior (no view) cabins have a shower only. Also, note that the 23 cabins for the mobility-limited are very spacious and have a large roll-in shower enclosure for wheelchair users (some also have a bathtub), and ramped access to the balcony.

CUISINE. The Rotterdam Dining Room is a grand, traditional room, and is spread over two decks, with ocean views on three sides with a grand staircase to connect the upper and lower levels. Both open seating and fixed (assigned tables and times) seating are available, while breakfast and lunch are open-seating (you'll be seated by restaurant staff when you enter).

There are tables for two, four, six or eight. The waiter stations are very noisy for anyone seated adjacent to them.

Live music is provided for dinner each evening; once each cruise, a Dutch Dinner is featured (hats are provided), as is an Indonesian Lunch. "Lighter option" meals are available for the nutrition- and weight-conscious. Fine Rosenthal china and cutlery are used (although there are no fish knives).

Alternative Dining Option: The Pinnacle Grill features Pacific Northwest cuisine and seats 88 (reservations are required, and anyone booking suite-grade accommodation qualifies for priority reservations).

In addition, the Lido Buffet is a casual, self-serve cafe for casual breakfasts and luncheons, and a poolside grill (Terrace Café) has hamburgers, hot dogs and other fast-food items. The Lido Buffet is also open for casual dinners on several nights each cruise (typically three nights on a 7-night cruise), in an open-seating arrangement. Tables are set with crisp linens, flatware and stemware. The set menu includes a choice of four entrées.

All dining venues are no-smoking areas.

ENTERTAINMENT. The Mondriaan Showlounge, located at the forward part of the ship, spans two decks, with banquette seating on both main and upper levels. It is basically a well-designed room, but the ceiling is low and the sightlines from the balcony level are quite poor.

SPA/FITNESS. The Greenhouse Spa facilities are quite extensive, and include a gymnasium (with good muscle-toning equipment), separate saunas and steam rooms for men and women, and several treatment rooms (each has a shower and toilet). Outdoor facilities include basketball and shuffleboard courts, a jogging track, and a full wrap-around teakwood promenade deck for strolling.

● **For more extensive general information on what a Holland America Line cruise is like, see pages 126–28.**

Zenith
★★★+

Mid-Size Ship: . . . . .47,255 tons	Total Crew: 670	Cabins (for one person): 0
Lifestyle: . . . . .Standard	Passengers	Cabins (with private balcony): 110
Cruise Line: . . . . .Pullmantur Cruises	(lower beds/all berths): 1,378/1,800	Cabins (wheelchair accessible): 4
Former Names: . . . . .none	Passenger Space Ratio	Cabin Current: . . . . .110/220 volts
Builder: . . . . .Meyer Werft (Germany)	(lower beds/all berths): . . . . . .34.2 /26.2	Elevators: 7
Original Cost: . . . .$210 million	Crew/Passenger Ratio	Casino (gaming tables): . . . . .Yes
Entered Service: . . . . .Apr 1992/Jun 2007	(lower beds/all berths): 2.0/2.6	Slot Machines: . . . . .Yes
Registry: . . . . .The Bahamas	Navigation Officers: . . . . .European	Swimming Pools (outdoors): 2
Length (ft/m): 681.0/207.59	Cabins (total): 720	Swimming Pools (indoors): 0
Beam (ft/m): 95.1/29.00	Size Range (sq ft/m): 172.2–500.5/	Whirlpools: 3
Draft (ft/m): 23.6/7.20	. . . . .16.0–46.50	Self-Service Launderette: . . . . .No
Propulsion/Propellers: diesel (19,960kW)/2	Cabins (outside view): 572	Dedicated Cinema/Seats: . . . . .No
Passenger Decks: 10	Cabins (interior/no view): 148	Library: . . . . .Yes

OVERALL SCORE: 1,343 (OUT OF A POSSIBLE 2,000 POINTS)

OVERVIEW. *Zenith*, formerly owned and operated by Celebrity Cruises (the sister ship is Island Cruises' *Island Star*, formerly *Horizon*), is now over 15 years old. However, the ship still has a contemporary, though rather sharp, angular profile that gives the impression of power and speed owing to its blue paint striping along the sides, separating the hull from the superstructure (the hull was designed by mega-yacht designer Jon Bannenberg). Pullmantur Cruises took over the ship in 2007, installed 220-volt (European) outlets in all cabins, and started operations in June.

Inside, there is a similar interior layout to its sister ship, *Island Star*, and elegant and restrained decor. The feeling is one of uncluttered surroundings, and the ship benefits from some interesting artwork. Soothing, pastel colors and high-quality soft furnishings are used throughout the interiors.

The ship's art deco-style hotel-like lobby (reminiscent of hotels in Miami Beach) has a two-deck-high ceiling and a spacious feel to it, and is the contact point for the reception desk, shore excursions, and onboard accounts.

The principal deck that houses many of the public entertainment rooms has a double-width indoor promenade. There is a good-sized library, relocated and enlarged in a 1999 refit. Other facilities include Harry's Bar – a cigar smoking lounge complete with fireplace and bookshelves containing leather-bound volumes), library and internet-connect center; a Plaza Café, for coffee and loud chat. A large, elegantly appointed casino has its own bar.

Pullmantur Cruises has made changes to some of the public rooms and open areas, and has added splashes of bright colors, motifs, and new signage. The hospitality and the range and variety of food have been tailored to its Span-

BERLITZ'S RATINGS		
	Possible	Achieved
Ship	500	371
Accommodation	200	147
Food	400	234
Service	400	263
Entertainment	100	63
Cruise	400	265

ish-speaking family clientele. Pullmantur Cruises also has a good programme for children and teenagers, with specially trained youth counsellors, and lots of activities. You will typically find a lot of smokers aboard.

Standing in line for embarkation, disembarkation, shore tenders and for self-serve buffet meals is inevitable cruising aboard large ships. Also, the doors to the public restrooms and the outdoor decks are rather heavy. The public restrooms are clinical and need some softer decor. There are no cushioned pads for poolside sunloungers.

SUITABLE FOR: *Zenith* is best suited to young (and young at heart) Spanish-speaking couples, singles, and families with children of all ages who want a first cruise experience in an elegant ship, with plenty of public rooms and a lively atmosphere, food that is quantity rather than quality, at low cost. The onboard currency is the euro, and gratuities are extra. However, all drinks are included, and that makes it easy for families with children.

ACCOMMODATION. There are 15 price grades, including outside-view suites and cabins, and interior (no view) cabins, but even the smallest cabin is a decent size. Note that many outside-view cabins on Fantasy Deck have lifeboat-obstructed views.

Standard Cabins: The outside-view and interior (no view) cabins have good-quality fittings with lots of wood accenting, are tastefully decorated and of an above-average size, with an excellent amount of closet and drawer space, and reasonable insulation between cabins. All have twin beds that convert to a queen-sized bed, and a good amount of closet and drawer space. The cabin soundproofing is quite good although this depends on location (some cabins are located opposite crew access doors, which can prove to be busy and noisy.

The bathrooms have a generous shower area, and a small range of toiletries is provided, although bathroom towels are a little small, as is storage space for toiletries. The lowest-grade outside-view cabins have a porthole, but all others have picture windows.

Royal Suites: The largest accommodation is in two Royal Suites midships on Atlantic Deck (Deck 10), and forward on Marina Deck. These have a large private balcony, and feature a separate bedroom and lounge, dining area with glass dining table (with CD player and VCR player in addition to the large television). The bathroom is also larger and has a whirlpool bathtub with integral shower.

Another 20 suites (also on Atlantic Deck) are very tastefully furnished, although they are really just larger cabins rather than suites. They do have a generous amount of drawer and other storage space, however, and a sleeping area (with European duvets on the beds instead of sheets and blankets) plus a lounge area. They also have good bathrooms. Butler service is standard.

All accommodation designated as suites does suffer from noise generated on the swimming pool deck directly above. No suites or cabins have private balconies (they weren't in vogue when this ship was built).

In early 2005, *Zenith* underwent a major refit and reconstruction program that moved the navigation bridge forward so that additional cabins could be added. Balconies were added to many cabins on Atlantic and Marina Decks, while the spa/fitness area was expanded, the observation lounge was expanded forwards; a new "alternative" restaurant was added, and public rooms and foyers were redecorated. All cabins were refurbished (new furniture was introduced), and bathrooms were renewed.

CUISINE. The Caravelle Dining Room, which has a raised section in its center, has several tables for two, as well as for four, six or eight (in banquettes), although the chairs do not have armrests. There are two seatings for dinner (open seating for breakfast and lunch), at tables for two, four, six, eight or 10. The cuisine, its presentation and service are more quantity rather than quality, and green vegetables are hard to come by.

For informal meals, the Windsurf Buffet (non-smoking) has a traditional single line self-service buffet for breakfast and luncheon, and includes a pasta station, rotisserie and pizza ovens. At peak times, however, the buffet is simply too small, too crowded, and very noisy. The Grill, located outdoors adjacent to (but aft of) the Windsurf Cafe, serves typical fast-food items such as pizzas.

ENTERTAINMENT. The two-level Celebrity Showlounge/theatre, with main and balcony levels, and good sightlines from almost all seats (however, the railing at the front of the balcony level does impede sight lines). It has a large stage for this size of ship, and decent lighting and sound equipment.

The shows consist of a troupe of showgirl dancers, whose routines are reminiscent of high-school shows. Cabaret acts are the main feature; these include singers, magicians, and comedians, among others, and very much geared to the family audience that this ship carries on most cruises. There is also plenty of live (loud) music for dancing to in various bars and lounges, plus the inevitable discotheque. Participation activities tend to be quite amateurish.

SPA/FITNESS. The Belleza Spa, the health and fitness center is high in the ship, aft of the funnel. It has a gymnasium with ocean-view windows and high-tech muscle-pump equipment, an exercise area, several therapy treatment rooms (including a rasul room), and men's/ women's saunas.

Zuiderdam
★★★★

Large Resort Ship:	.81,679 tons	Total Crew:	.800
Lifestyle:	.Premium	Passengers	
Cruise Line:	.Holland America Line	(lower beds/all berths):	.1,848/2,387
Former Names:	.none	Passenger Space Ratio	
Builder:	.Fincantieri (Italy)	(lower beds/all berths):	.43.6/34.2
Original Cost:	.$400 million	Crew/Passenger Ratio	
Entered Service:	.Dec 2002	(lower beds/all berths):	.2.3/2.9
Registry:	.The Netherlands	Navigation Officers:	.European
Length (ft/m):	.935.0/285.00	Cabins (total):	.924
Beam (ft/m):	.105.6/32.25	Size Range (sq ft/m):	.185.0–1,318.6/
Draft (ft/m):	.25.5/7.80		17.1–122.5
Propulsion/Propellers:	.diesel-electric	Cabins (outside view):	.788
	(34,000 kW)/2 azimuthing pods	Cabins (interior/no view):	.136
	(17.6 MW each)	Cabins (for one person):	.0
Passenger Decks:	.11	Cabins (with private balcony):	.623

Cabins (wheelchair accessible):	.28
Cabin Current:	.110 volts
Elevators:	.14
Casino (gaming tables):	.Yes
Slot Machines:	.Yes
Swimming Pools (outdoors):	.2+1 children's pool
Swimming Pools (indoors):	.1 (indoor/outdoor)
Whirlpools:	.5
Self-Service Launderette:	.Yes
Dedicated Cinema/Seats:	.Yes/170
Library:	.Yes

OVERALL SCORE: 1,517 (OUT OF A POSSIBLE 2,000 POINTS)

OVERVIEW. *Zuiderdam* (sister to *Euro-dam, Noordam, Oosterdam* and *Wester-dam*) shares a common platform and hull shape (*Zuiderdam* is pronounced Zider-dam), and is designed to appeal to younger, more vibrant, multi-genera-tional family-oriented passengers. There are two funnels, placed close together, one in front of the other, and not side by side as aboard the smaller *Amsterdam* and *Rotterdam*. This placement is the result of the slightly unusual machinery configuration. The ship has, in effect, two engine rooms – one with three diesels, and one with two diesels and a gas turbine. A pod propulsion *(see page 174 for definition)* is pro-vided, powered by a diesel-electric system, with a small gas turbine located in the funnel for the reduction of emissions.

A complete wrap-around exterior promenade deck is enjoyed by many. Exterior glass elevators, mounted mid-ships on both port and starboard sides, provide fine ocean views. There are two centrally located swimming pools out-doors, and one of the pools can be used in poor weather due to its retractable magrodome (glass dome) cover. Two whirlpool tubs, adjacent to the swimming pools, are abridged by a bar. Another smaller pool is provided for children.

When you first walk into the ship's interior, you'll be greeted by the small size of the lobby space that spans just three decks. It has a stairway, and its focal point is a large, 10-foot high transparent seahorse. In keeping with the tra-ditions of Holland America Line, there is a large collection of artwork. The decor is extremely bright for a Holland America Line ship, and an eclectic color and pattern mix that assails you from all directions.

There are two entertainment/public room decks, the

BERLITZ'S RATINGS

	Possible	Achieved
Ship	500	426
Accommodation	200	162
Food	400	269
Service	400	277
Entertainment	100	77
Cruise	400	306

upper of which has an exterior prome-nade deck – something new for this tra-ditional cruise line. Although it doesn't go around the whole ship, it's long enough to do some serious walking on. Additionally, there is also a jogging track outdoors, located around the mast and the forward third of the ship.

The most dramatic public room is the Vista Lounge, the ship's show-lounge; it spans three decks in the for-ward section of the ship. The main floor level has a bar in its starboard aft section. Other facilities include a winding shopping street with boutique stores and logo shops.

The casino is large (one has to walk through it to get from the restaurant to the showlounge), and this is equipped with all the gaming paraphernalia and array of slot machines you can think of – all designed, of course, to entertain you while you are relieved of your money.

Children have KidZone (an indoor/outdoor facility), and Cub Hal for ages 5–12 (sleepovers aren't allowed, though), with dedicated youth counselors. Teenagers get to use WaveRunner, which includes a dance floor, special lighting effects, and booming sound system. There's also a video game room, and big-screen television for movies.

The information desk in the lobby is small in comparison to the size of the lobby. Many of the private balconies are not so private, and can be overlooked from various public loca-tions. Many pillars obstruct the passenger flow and lines of sight throughout the ship.

Communication (in English) with many of the staff, par-ticularly in the dining room and buffet areas, can prove very frustrating. It may be difficult to escape from smokers, and people walking around in unsuitable clothing, clutching plastic sport drinks bottles.

ACCOMMODATION. There are 19 price grades. In keeping with industry trends, there are more cabins with private balconies than aboard any other Holland America Line ship. **Penthouse Verandah Suites:** The largest accommodation (1,318 sq. ft/122.5 sq. meters, including balcony) is in two Penthouse Verandah Suites. These have a separate bedroom with a king-sized bed; there's also a walk-in closet, dressing room, living room, dining room, butler's pantry, mini-bar and refrigerator, and private balcony (verandah). The main bathroom has a large whirlpool bathtub, two wash-basins, toilet, and plenty of storage space for personal toiletries. Personalized stationery and complimentary dry cleaning are included, as are hot hors d'oeuvres and other goodies daily.
DeLuxe Verandah Suites: Next in size are 60 DeLuxe Verandah Suites (563 sq. ft/52.3 sq. meters). These have twin beds that can convert to a king-sized bed, vanity desk, lounge area, walk-in closet, mini-bar and refrigerator, and bathroom with full-sized tub, washbasin and toilet. Personalized stationery and complimentary dry cleaning are included, as are hot hors d'oeuvres daily and other goodies.
Verandah Suites: There are 100 of these (actually they are cabins, not suites, and measure 284 sq. ft/26.3 sq. meters). Twin beds can convert to a queen-sized bed; there is also a lounge area, mini-bar and refrigerator, while the bathroom has a tub, washbasin and toilet. Floor-to-ceiling windows open onto a private balcony (verandah).
Outside-view Cabins: Standard outside cabins (197 sq. ft/18.3 sq. meters) have twin beds that convert to make a queen-sized bed. There's a small sitting area, while the bathroom has a bathtub/shower combination. The interior (no view) cabins are slightly smaller, at 182.9 sq ft/17 sq. meters.

A number of cabins on the lowest accommodation deck (Main Deck) have views obstructed by lifeboats. Some cabins that can accommodate a third and fourth person have very little closet space, and there's only one personal safe. There is no separate radio in each cabin – instead, audio channels are provided on the in-cabin TV system.

Each morning, an eight-page *New York Times* (Times Fax) is provided for each cabin. Fresh fruit is available on request, shoe shine service, and evening turndown service are also provided, as is a small range of bathroom toiletries including shampoo, bath and facial soaps, and body lotion.

CUISINE. The non-smoking 1,045-seat Vista (main) Dining Room, located at the stern, is two decks high, and is quite stunning. Both open seating and fixed (assigned tables and times) seating are available, while breakfast and lunch are open-seating (you'll be seated by restaurant staff when you enter). It is traditional Holland America Line in its operation, with friendly service from smiling Indonesian stewards, and has Rosenthal china (but no fish knives).

There are tables for two, four, six or eight. The waiter stations in the dining room can be noisy for anyone seated adjacent to them. Live music is provided for dinner each evening; once each cruise, a Dutch Dinner is featured (hats are provided), as is an Indonesian Lunch. "Lighter option" meals are always available for the nutrition-conscious and the weight-conscious.
Alternative Dining Option: The 130-seat Pinnacle Grill is a slightly more upscale dining spot (with higher-quality ingredients and better presentation than in the larger main dining room). Located on Lower Promenade Deck, it fronts onto the second level of the atrium lobby. The cuisine is Pacific Northwest (with items such as sesame-crusted halibut with ginger-miso, Peking duck breast with blackberry sauce, premium quality steaks from hand-selected cuts of beef). Fine table settings, china and silverware are provided, as are leather-bound menus. The wine bar offers mostly American wines. Reservations are needed and there is a cover charge of $30 per person for service and gratuity.
Informal Eateries: For casual eating, there is an extensive Lido Cafe, which form an eatery that wraps around the funnel housing and extends aft; there are also some fine views over the ship's central multi-deck atrium. It includes a pizzeria counter, a salad bar, Asian stir-fry counter, deli sandwiches, and a separate dessert buffet, although movement around the buffet area is very slow (particularly at peak times, such as in the mornings in port before shore excursions), and requires you to stand in line for everything.

Additionally, there is an outdoor self-serve buffet (adjacent to the fantail pool), which serves fast-food items such as hamburgers and hot dogs, chicken and fries. There are two smaller buffets adjacent to the midships swimming pool area, and a Windsurf Cafe in the atrium lobby (open 20 hours a day), for pastries, snack foods, deli sandwiches and liqueur coffees (evenings only).

ENTERTAINMENT. The 867-seat Vista Lounge is the principal venue for Las Vegas-style revue shows and major cabaret presentations. It spans three decks in the forward section of the ship. The main floor level has a bar in its starboard aft section. Spiral stairways at the back of the lounge connect all levels. Stage shows are best seen from the upper levels, from where the sightlines are quite good.

SPA/FITNESS. The Greenhouse Spa is a large, two-decks-high health spa, located directly above the navigation bridge. Facilities include a solarium, unisex thermal suite – a unisex area incorporating a Laconium (gentle sauna), Hammam (mild steam), and Camomile Grotto (small aromatic steam room). There's also a beauty parlor, 11 massage/therapy rooms (including one for couples), and a large gymnasium with floor-to-ceiling windows on three sides and forward-facing ocean views, and the latest high-tech muscle-toning equipment.

● **For more extensive general information on what a Holland America Line cruise is like, see pages 126–28.**

SHIPS RATED BY SCORE

Ship	Score	Rating	Ship	Score	Rating
LARGE (RESORT) SHIPS			Oriana	1,503	4
(over 1,600 passengers)			Oceana	1,502	4
			Brilliance of the Seas	1,501	4
Queen Mary 2 (Grill Class)	1,709	5	Splendour of the Seas	1,499	4
Queen Victoria (Grill Class)	1,692	4+	Legend of the Seas	1,497	4
Celebrity Millennium	1,666	4+	Queen Victoria (Britannia Class)	1,496	4
Celebrity Constellation	1,665	4+	Radiance of the Seas	1,496	4
Celebrity Infinity	1,663	4+	Sun Princess	1,496	4
Celebrity Summit	1,661	4+	AIDAbella	1,495	4
Celebrity Century	1,615	4+	Norwegian Spirit	1,495	4
Emerald Princess	1,546	4	AIDAdiva	1,494	4
Queen Mary 2 (Britannia Class)	1,546	4	Grandeur of the Seas	1,492	4
Crown Princess	1,545	4	Enchantment of the Seas	1,491	4
Celebrity Mercury	1,544	4	Vision of the Seas	1,491	4
Coral Princess	1,544	4	Arcadia	1,490	4
Diamond Princess	1,544	4	Rhapsody of the Seas	1,490	4
Sapphire Princess	1,544	4	Adventure of the Seas	1,477	4
Ventura	1,543	4	Explorer of the Seas	1,476	4
Celebrity Galaxy	1,542	4	Mariner of the Seas	1,472	4
Island Princess	1,542	4	Navigator of the Seas	1,471	4
Star Princess	1,542	4	MSC Poesia	1,467	4
Golden Princess	1,541	4	MSC Orchestra	1,465	4
Grand Princess	1,541	4	MSC Musica	1,462	4
Zaandam	1,541	4	Voyager of the Seas	1,460	4
Volendam	1,540	4	Costa Serena	1,452	4
Caribbean Princess	1,539	4	Costa Concordia	1,450	4
Rotterdam	1,539	4	Costa Magica	1,445	4
Amsterdam	1,537	4	Costa Fortuna	1,444	4
Dawn Princess	1,532	4	MSC Lirica	1,439	4
Independence of the Seas	1,532	4	MSC Opera	1,438	4
Liberty of the Seas	1,532	4	Costa Mediterranea	1,437	4
Freedom of the Seas	1,530	4	Costa Atlantica	1,436	4
Serenade of the Seas	1,530	4	MSC Sinfonia	1,435	4
Sea Princess	1,525	4	MSC Armonia	1,434	4
Jewel of the Seas	1,522	4	AIDAaura	1,403	4
SuperStar Virgo	1,522	4	AIDAvita	1,402	4
Westerdam	1,522	4	Carnival Splendor	1,393	3+
Norwegian Gem	1,521	4	Carnival Freedom	1,390	3+
Norwegian Dawn	1,520	4	Carnival Spirit	1,390	3+
Norwegian Pearl	1,520	4	Pride of America	1,390	3+
Norwegian Star	1,520	4	Carnival Legend	1,388	3+
Oosterdam	1,520	4	Carnival Miracle	1,387	3+
Noordam	1,519	4	Norwegian Sky	1,387	3+
Zuiderdam	1,517	4	Carnival Pride	1,386	3+
Norwegian Jewel	1,516	4	Carnival Conquest	1,385	3+
Norwegian Jade	1,514	4	Carnival Liberty	1,383	3+
Norwegian Sun	1,514	4	Costa Victoria	1,384	3+
Disney Wonder	1,509	4	Carnival Glory	1,380	3+
Disney Magic	1,508	4	Carnival Valor	1,380	3+
Aurora	1,507	4	Carnival Triumph	1,379	3+

Ship	Score	Rating	Ship	Score	Rating
Carnival Victory	1,369	3+	Regatta	1,572	4+
Ocean Village Two	1,365	3+	Pacific Venus	1,542	4
Carnival Destiny	1,361	3+	Ocean Princess	1,487	4
Ocean Village	1,351	3+	Pacific Princess	1,487	4
Island Star	1,328	3+	Royal Princess	1,480	4
Thomson Celebration	1,313	3+	Azamara Quest	1,466	4
Thomson Spirit	1,311	3+	Azamara Journey	1,465	4
Thomson Destiny	1,303	3+	Saga Ruby	1,425	4
Monarch of the Seas	1,248	3	Ryndam	1,420	4
Carnival Ecstasy	1,248	3	Veendam	1,420	4
Carnival Fantasy	1,247	3	Maasdam	1,418	4
Carnival Fascination	1,247	3	Statendam	1,415	4
Costa Romantica	1,247	3	Saga Rose	1,412	4
Empress	1,246	3	Bleu de France	1,402	4
Majesty of the Seas	1,246	3	AIDAcara	1,401	4
Sky Wonder	1,246	3	Balmoral	1,398	3+
Costa Classica	1,245	3	Artemis	1,385	3+
Carnival Sensation	1,244	3	Astor	1,370	3+
Costa Europa	1,244	3	Boudicca	1,357	3+
Norwegian Majesty	1,242	3	Zenith	1,343	3+
Carnival Imagination	1,226	3	Black Watch	1,339	3+
Carnival Elation	1,225	3	Minerva	1,324	3+
Carnival Inspiration	1,223	3	Grand Mistral	1,315	3+
Carnival Paradise	1,222	3	Grand Voyager	1,314	3+
Sovereign	1,219	3	Braemar	1,312	3+
Island Escape	1,193	3	Astoria	1,309	3+
Grand Celebration	1,182	3	SuperStar Libra	1,286	3+
Pacific Dawn	1,181	3	Albatros	1,269	3+
Holiday	1,134	3	MSC Melody	1,248	3
Pacific Sun	1,104	3	Star Pisces	1,247	3
AIDAluna	NYR	NYR	Discovery	1,245	3
Costa Luminosa	NYR	NYR	Delphin Voyager	1,243	3
Costa Pacifica	NYR	NYR	Cristal	1,236	3
Eurodam	NYR	NYR	SuperStar Aquarius	1,234	3
Grand Celebration	NYR	NYR	Marco Polo	1,222	3
MSC Fantasia	NYR	NYR	MSC Rhapsody	1,177	3
MSC Splendida	NYR	NYR	Ocean Dream	1,110	3
Ruby Princess	NYR	NYR	Princess Danae	1,105	3
			Orient Queen	1,103	3
			Princess Daphne	1,098	2+
MID-SIZE SHIPS			Pacific	1,094	2+
(600–1,600 passengers)			Costa Allegra	1,092	2+
			Costa Marina	1,090	2+
Crystal Serenity	1,702	5	Pacific Star	1,089	2+
Crystal Symphony	1,701	5	Aquamarine	1,084	2+
Seven Seas Voyager	1,698	4+	The Emerald	1,061	2+
Seven Seas Mariner	1,695	4+	Oceanic	1,047	2+
Asuka II	1,685	4+	Ocean Majesty	992	2+
Prinsendam	1,662	4+	Coral	944	2
Amadea	1,600	4+	Royal Iris	927	2
Nautica	1,575	4+	Aegean Pearl	918	2
Insignia	1,574	4+	Ivory	885	2

Ship	Score	Rating	Ship	Score	Rating
Regal Empress	791	1+	Sea Cloud	1,704	5
Deutschland	NYR	NYR	Sea Cloud II	1,703	5
			Hebridean Spirit	1,697	4+
			Prince Albert II	1,684	4+
SMALL SHIPS			Hebridean Princess	1,671	4+
(201–600 passengers)			Orion	1,612	4+
			Corinthian II	1,546	4
Europa	1,852	5+	Island Sky	1,540	4
Silver Shadow	1,760	5	Bremen	1,461	4
Silver Whisper	1,760	5	Le Levant	1,434	4
Silver Wind	1,669	4+	Celebrity Xpedition	1,404	4
Silver Cloud	1,664	4+	Clelia II	1,404	4
Seven Seas Navigator	1,653	4+	Star Clipper	1,402	4
Royal Clipper	1,540	4	Star Flyer	1,402	4
Club Med 2	1,477	4	Clipper Odyssey	1,396	3+
Paul Gauguin	1,547	4	Le Ponant	1,396	3+
C. Columbus	1,396	3+	Wind Spirit	1,394	3+
Wind Surf	1,396	3+	Wind Star	1,393	3+
Nippon Maru	1,390	3+	Le Diamant	1,340	3+
Spirit of Adventure	1,249	3	Yamal	1,247	3
Alexander von Humboldt	1,248	3	Galapagos Explorer II	1,244	3
Explorer II	1,229	3	Spirit of Oceanus	1,218	3
Fuji Maru	1,195	3	Kapitan Khlebnikov	1,164	3
Delphin	1,092	2+	Kapitan Dranitsyn	1,162	3
Vistamar	1,061	2+	Clipper Adventurer	1,098	2+
Funchal	1,045	2+	Kristina Regina	1,052	2+
Sapphire	1,028	2+	Spirit of Yorktown	949	2
Black Prince	1,014	2+	Spirit of Glacier Bay	948	2
The Calypso	990	2+	Professor Molchanov	947	2
Royal Star	938	2	Professor Multanovskiy	947	2
Blue Monarch	929	2	Spirit of '98	946	2
Arion	902	2	National Geographic Endeavour	945	2
The Iris	890	2	National Geographic Polaris	943	2
Ivory	885	2	Monet	941	2
Pearl	NYR	NYR	Andrea	927	2
Seabourn Odyssey	NYR	NYR	American Star	925	2
			American Spirit	922	2
			Spirit of Alaska	920	2
BOUTIQUE SHIPS			Spirit of Discovery	920	2
(50–200 passengers)			Spirit of Endeavour	920	2
			Spirit of Columbia	919	2
SeaDream II	1,788	5	Sea Lion	904	2
SeaDream I	1,786	5	Sea Bird	903	2
Seabourn Legend	1,779	5	American Glory	835	2
Seabourn Spirit	1,770	5	American Eagle	830	2
Seabourn Pride	1,769	5	Grande Mariner	747	1+
Hanseatic	1,740	5	Grande Caribe	744	1+

NYR = Not Yet Rated

BOOKING AND BUDGETING

Is it better to book a cruise directly with the operator or through a travel agent? And what hidden extras should you look for when calculating costs?

Booking direct

In the 1960s, about 90% of all cruises were booked by passengers directly with cruise lines and about 10% were booked by travel agents. Then along came some enterprising travel agents. They saw a golden opportunity and started to act on behalf of the cruise lines, who were happy to accept such bookings because they could then reduce staff and overheads in their sales offices.

Established companies such as American Express and Thomas Cook booked cruises, as did many others, and received a commission. During the 1970s, that percentage quickly reversed. Today, about 80% of all cruises are booked by travel agents, and about 20% are booked direct (including internet bookings).

With all the adverts in the newspapers for cruises, make sure you check what's included in any offers, particularly when huge discounts tend to catch your eye. For example, make sure that all port charges, government fees, and any additional fuel surcharges are included in the quote.

The internet

While the Internet may be a good *resource* tool, it is not the place to book your cruise, unless you know *exactly* what you want. You can't ask questions, and most of the information provided by the cruise companies is strictly marketing hype. Most sites providing cruise ship reviews have something to sell, and the sound-byte information can be misleading or outdated.

If you do book a cruise with an internet-based cruise agency or wholesaler, you should confirm with the actual cruise line that the booking has been made and that final payment has been received. Note that many internet booking agents are unlicensed and unregulated.

The internet vs travel agents

So, you've found a discounted rate for your cruise on the net. That's fine. But, if a cruise line suddenly offers special discounts for your sailing, or cabin upgrades, or things go wrong with your booking, your internet booking service may prove very unfriendly. Your travel agent, however, can probably work magic in making those special discounts work for *you* and perhaps even providing upgrades. It's called personal service.

Large travel agency groups and consortiums, such as American Express, often reserve huge blocks of cabins, and smaller independent agencies can access extensive discounts not available on the internet. Furthermore, the

cruise lines consider travel agents as their distribution system, and provide special discounts and value added amenities that are not provided over the internet.

Travel agents

Travel agents do not generally charge for their services, although they earn a commission from cruise lines. Consider a travel agent as your business advisor, not just a ticket agent. He/she will handle all matters relevant to your booking and should have the latest information on changes of itinerary, cruise fares, fuel surcharges, discounts, and any other related items, including insurance in case you have to cancel prior to sailing. Most travel agents are linked into cruise line computer systems and have access to most shipboard information.

Your travel agent should find exactly the right ship for your needs and lifestyle. Some sell only a limited number of cruises and are known as "preferred suppliers," because they receive special "overrides" on top of their normal commission (they probably know their limited number of ships well, however).

If *you* have chosen a ship and cruise, be firm and book exactly what you want, or change agencies. In the UK, look for a member of the Guild of Professional Cruise Agents. ACE (Association for Cruise Education), part of the UK's Passenger Shipping Association, provides in-depth agent training in the UK, as well as a full "bonding" scheme to protect passengers from failed cruise lines. In the US, look for a CLIA (Cruise Lines International Association) affiliated agency, or one belonging to the National Association of Cruise Oriented Agencies (NACOA), or the National Association of Commissioned Travel Agents (NACTA).

Questions to ask a travel agent

● Is air transportation included in the cabin rate quoted? If not, what will be the extra cost?

● What other extra costs will be involved? These can include port charges, insurance, gratuities, shore excursions, laundry, and drinks.

● What is the cruise line's cancellation policy?

● If I want to make changes to my flight, routing, dates, and so on, will the insurance policy cover everything in case of missed or canceled flights?

● Does your agency deal with only one, or several different insurance companies?

● Does the cruise line offer advance booking discounts or other incentives?

● Do you have preferred suppliers, or do you book any cruise on any cruise ship?

LEFT: the engine room aboard *Hebridean Princess*.

● Have you sailed aboard the ship I want to book or that you are recommending?
● Is your agency bonded and insured? If so, by whom?
● If you book the shore excursions offered by the cruise line, is insurance coverage provided?
● Can I occupy my cabin on the day of disembarkation until I am ready to disembark?

Reservations

Do plan ahead and book early. After choosing a ship, cruise, date, and cabin, you pay a deposit that is roughly 10 percent for long cruises, 20 percent for short cruises. The balance is normally payable 45 to 60 days before departure. For a late reservation, you pay in full when space is confirmed (when booking via the internet, for example). Cruise lines reserve the right to change prices in the event of tax increases, fluctuating exchange rates, fuel surcharges, or other costs beyond their control.

When you make your reservation, also make special dining requests known: seating preference, smoking or nonsmoking sections. It's useful to keep a note of them.

After the line has received full payment, your cruise ticket will be sent. Check all documents. Make sure the ship, date, and cruise details are correctly noted. Verify connecting flight times that seem suspiciously short.

Extra costs

Cruise brochures boldly proclaim that "almost everything's included," but in most cases you will find this is not strictly true. In fact, for some cruises "all-exclusive" would be a more appropriate term. In the aftermath of the September 11, 2001, terrorist attacks in the USA, many cruise lines cut their fares dramatically in order to attract business. At the same time, the cost of many onboard items went up. So allow for extra onboard costs.

Your fare covers the ship as transportation, your cabin, meals, entertainment, activities, and service on board; it typically does not include alcoholic beverages, laundry, dry cleaning or valet services, shore excursions, meals ashore, gratuities, port charges, cancellation insurance, optional onboard activities such as gambling.

Expect to spend about $25 a day per person on extras, plus another $10–$12 a day per person in gratuities. Genuine exceptions can be found in some small ships (those with fewer than 600 passengers) where just about everything is included.

Calculate the total cost of your cruise (not including any extra-cost services you might decide you want once on board) with the help of your travel agent. Here are the approximate prices per person for a typical seven-day cruise aboard a well-rated mid-size or large cruise ship, based on an outside-view two-bed cabin:

Cruise fare	*$1,200*
Port charges	*$100 (if not included)*
Gratuities	*$50*
Total per person	*$1,350*

This is less than $200 per person per day. For this price, you wouldn't get a decent hotel room, without meals, in London, Miami, New York, Tokyo, or Venice.

However, your 7-day cruise can become expensive when you start adding on a few extra touches. For example, add two flight-seeing excursions in Alaska (at about $250 each), two cappuccinos each a day ($25), a scotch and soda each a day ($35), a massage ($100), 7 mineral waters ($28), 30 minutes' access to the internet for emails ($15), three other assorted excursions $120), and gratuities $50). That's an extra $838 – without even one bottle of wine with dinner! So a couple will need to add an extra $1,576 for a 7-day cruise, plus the cruise fare, of course, and the cost of getting to and from your local airport, or ship port.

Discounts and incentives

Book ahead to get the best discounts (discounts decrease closer to the cruise date).

You may be able to reserve a cabin grade, but not a specific cabin — "tba" (to be assigned). Some lines will accept this arrangement and may even upgrade you. It is useful to know that the first cabins to be sold out are usually those at minimum and maximum rates. Note: Premium rates apply to Christmas/New Year cruises.

TYPICAL EXTRA-COST ITEMS	
"Alternative" dining (cover charge)	$15–$30 a person
Baby-sitting (per hour)	$5
Bottled water	$2.50–$7 (per bottle)
Cappuccino/espresso	$1.75–$3
Cartoon character bedtime "tuck-In" service	$20
Wash one shirt	$1.50–$3
Dry-clean dress	$3–$7.50
Dry-clean jacket	$4–$8
Golf simulator	$20 (30 minutes)
Group bicycling class	$10 per class
Hair wash/set	$25–$50
Haircut (men)	$20
Ice cream	$1–$3.75
In-cabin movies	$6.95–$12.95
Internet connection	$0.50 per minute
Kick-boxing class	$10 per class
Laundry soap	$1–$1.50
Massage	$2-plus a minute (plus tip)
Pottery class	$40
Satellite phone/fax	$4.95–$15 per minute
Send/receive e-mails	$0.75 per minute
Sodas (soft drinks)	$1–$2
Souvenir photograph (8" by 6")	$10–$12
Souvenir photograph (10" by 8")	$20–$27.50
Trapshooting (three or five shots)	$5, $8
Tuxedo rental (7-day cruise)	$85
Use of Aqua Spa (*Queen Mary 2*)	$25 per day
Video postcard	$4.95–$6.95
Wine/cheese tasting	$10–$15
Wine with dinner	$7–$500
Yoga class	$10 per class

Cancellations and refunds

Do take out full cancellation insurance (if it is not included), as cruises (and air transportation to/from them) must be paid in full before your tickets are issued. Otherwise, if you cancel at the last minute – even for medical reasons – you could lose the whole fare. Insurance coverage can be obtained from your travel agent or from an independent company, and paying by credit card makes sense (you'll probably get your money back if the agency goes bust) or through the internet.

Cruise lines usually accept cancellations more than 30 days before sailing, but all charge full fare if you don't turn up on sailing day. Other cancellation fees depend on the cruise and length of trip. Many lines do not return port taxes, which are not part of the cruise fare.

Medical insurance

Whether you intend to travel overseas or cruise down a local river, and your present medical insurance does not cover you, you should look into extra coverage for your cruise. A "passenger protection program" may be offered by the cruise line, the charge for which will appear on your final invoice, unless you decline. It is worth every penny, and it typically covers such things as evacuation by air ambulance, high-limit baggage, baggage transfers, personal liability, and missed departure.

Port taxes/Handling charges

These are assessed by individual port authorities and are usually shown in the brochure. Port charges form part of the final payment, although they can be changed right up to the day of embarkation.

Fuel surcharges

Cruise lines publish their brochures a year ahead. If oil and other fuel costs rise in the interim, a fuel surcharge may be imposed, in addition to the quoted fare.

Air/Sea packages

If your cruise fare includes air transportation (as in a one-way or round-trip air ticket), then airline arrangements usually cannot be changed without paying a premium, as cruise lines often book group space on aircraft to obtain the lowest rates.

If you do make changes, remember that, if the airline cancels your flight, the cruise line is under no obligation to help you or return your cruise fare if you don't reach the ship on time. If flying to a foreign country, allow extra time (particularly in winter) for flight delays and cancellations.

Airlines often use a "hub-and-spoke" system, which can prove frustrating. Because of changes to air schedules, cruise and air tickets may not be sent to passengers until a few days before the cruise.

In Europe, air/sea packages generally start at a major metropolitan airport; some include first-class rail travel from outlying districts. In the United States, many cruise lines include connecting flights from suburban airports

convenient to the traveler. Remember that, if you fly and want to lock your check-in baggage, make sure you do so with a TSA (Transportation Security Administration)-approved security lock.

Most cruise lines allow you to fly out to join a ship in one port and fly home from another. An advantage is that you only have to check your baggage once at the departure airport and the baggage transfer from plane to ship is handled for you. This does not include intercontinental fly/ cruises, where you must claim your baggage at the airport on arrival to clear it though customs.

Travel insurance

Note that cruise lines and travel agents routinely sell travel cover policies that, on close inspection, appear to wriggle out of payment due to a litany of exclusion clauses, most of which are never explained. Examples:
● "Pre-existing" medical conditions.
● "Valuables" left unattended on a tour bus, even though the tour guide says it is safe and that the driver will lock the door.

Getting the best travel insurance deal:

● Allow time to shop around and don't accept the first travel insurance policy you are offered.
● Read the contract carefully and make sure you know exactly what you are covered for.
● Beware of the "box ticking" approach to travel cover, which is often done quickly at the travel agent's office in lieu of providing expert advice. However, watch out for questions relating to "pre-existing medical conditions" as this little gem alone could cost you dearly. Insurers should not, in reality, be allowed to apply exclusions that have not been clearly pointed out to the policyholder.
● Ask for a detailed explanation of all exclusions, excesses, and limitations.
● Check out the procedure you need to follow if you are the victim of a crime, such as your wallet or camera being stolen while on a shore excursion. If anything does happen, *always* obtain a police report as soon as possible. Note that many insurance policies will reimburse you only for the secondhand value of any lost or stolen item, rather than the full cost of replacement, and you may be required to produce the original receipt for any such items claimed.
● Watch out for exclusions for "hazardous sports." These could include things typically offered as shore excursions aboard ships. Examples: horse riding (there goes that horse riding on the beach excursion in Jamaica) or cycling (mountain biking excursions in Alaska, Antigua or Rhodes, for example), jet skiing (most beaches), or ziplining (Hawaii).
● If you purchase travel cover over the internet, check the credentials of the company underwriting the scheme. It is best to deal with well-established names, and not to take what appears to be the cheapest deal offered. ❑

DON'T LEAVE HOME WITHOUT...

Cruise ships are well stocked for most people's everyday needs, but there are certain things you need to take with you

Baggage

There is generally no limit to the amount of personal baggage you can take on your cruise (most ships provide towels, soap, shampoo, and shower caps), but airlines do have weight limits. Do allow extra space for purchases on the cruise.

Tag all baggage with your name, ship, cabin number, sailing date, and port of embarkation (tags are provided with your tickets). Baggage transfers from airport to ship are generally smooth and problem-free when handled by the cruise line.

Liability for loss or damage to baggage is contained in the passenger contract (part of your ticket). Do take out insurance; the policy should extend from the date of departure until two or three days after your return home.

Some cruise lines offer fee-based luggage courier services that collect your luggage from your home and the next time you see your luggage, it will be in your cabin (and vice versa at the end of the cruise).

Clothing

Closet space aboard many ships is at a premium. So, unless you are on an extended cruise, keep your baggage to a minimum. It's a good idea to choose four or five interchangeable outfits to wear throughout the week, in two or three color groups and mix-and-match clothing that can be layered. Black is always a good neutral color to team with other colors.

For cruises to tropical areas, casual wear should include plenty of lightweight cottons and other natural fibers. Synthetic materials do not "breathe" as well and often retain heat. Clothes should be as opaque as possible to counteract the sun's ultraviolet rays. Take a lightweight cotton sweater or windbreaker for the evenings, when the ship's air-conditioning will seem even more powerful after a day in the sun. Pack sunglasses and a hat. Rainstorms in the tropics don't last long, but they can give you a good soaking, so take inexpensive, lightweight rainwear for excursions.

The same is true for cruises to the Mediterranean, Greek Isles, or North Africa, although there will be little or no humidity for most of the year. Certain areas may be dusty as well as dry. In these latitudes, the weather can be cool in the evenings from October to March, so take extra sweaters and a windbreaker.

For cruises to Alaska, the North Cape, or the Norwegian fjords, pack warm comfortable clothing layers, plus a raincoat or parka for the northernmost port calls. Cruises to Alaska and the Land of the Midnight Sun

are operated in summer, when temperatures are pleasant. Unless you are going to northern ports such as St. Petersburg in winter, you will not need thermal underwear. However, you will need thermal underwear, thick socks – and heavy sweaters – if you take an expedition cruise to the Antarctic Peninsula or through the Northwest Passage.

In destinations with a strong religious tradition, like Venezuela, Haiti, the Dominican Republic, Colombia, and countries in the Middle East and Far East, shorts or bare shoulders may cause offense, so cover up.

Aboard ship, dress rules are relaxed by day, but in the evening what you wear should be tasteful. Men should take a blazer or sports jacket and ties for the dining room and for any "informal" occasions. Transatlantic crossings are normally more elegant and require formal attire.

For formal nights (usually two out of seven), women can wear a long evening gown, elegant cocktail dress, or a smart pants suit. Gentlemen are expected to wear either a tuxedo or dark business suit and tie. These "rules" are less rigid on short and moderately priced cruises. If you are the athletic type, pack sportswear and gym shoes for the gymnasium or aerobics classes.

No matter where you are going, comfortable low- or flat-heeled shoes are a must for women, except for formal nights. Light, airy walking shoes are best for walking. If you are in the Caribbean or Pan-Pacific region and you are not used to heat and humidity, your ankles may swell, so tight shoes are not recommended. Rubber soles are best for walking on the open deck of a ship.
Formal: Tuxedo, dinner jacket or dark suit and tie for men; evening gown or other appropriate formal attire for women.
Informal: Jacket and tie for men; cocktail dress, dressy pantsuit, or the like for women.
Casual (Elegant/Smart): While this is an oxymoron, it generally means long trousers (no shorts or jeans), proper collared and sleeved shirt (gentlemen); skirt or slacks and top for women.
Casual (Relaxed): Slacks over sweater or open shirt (no tie) for men (no beach wear or muscle shirts); a blouse with skirt, slacks, or similar comfortable attire for women. Shoes are required.

Documents

A passport is the most practical proof of your citizenship and identification. Visas are required for some countries (allow time to obtain these). On most cruises, you will hand in your passport to the company at embarkation (it would be wise to keep a copy of the main pages with you). This helps the ship to clear customs and immigration inspection on arrival in ports of call. It will be returned before you reach the port of disembarkation.

Flying... and jet lag

Several cruise lines have "air deviation" desks that allow you to change your flights and connections, for a fee (typically $25–$50 per person).

Air travel today is fast and efficient. But even experienced travelers find that the stress of international travel can persist long after the flight is over (for long international flights, I recommend the flat beds in Club Class on British Airways or in Upper Class on Virgin Atlantic aircraft). Eastbound flights tend to cause more pronounced jet lag than westbound flights. Jet aircraft are generally pressurized to some 8,000 ft (2,400 meters) in altitude, causing discomfort in the ears and the stomach, and swollen feet.

A few precautions should reduce the less pleasant effects of flying around the world. Plan as far in advance of your cruise as possible. Take a daytime flight, so that you can arrive at, or close to, your normal bedtime. Try to be as quiet as possible before flying, and allow for another five hours of rest after any flight that crosses more than five time zones.

Medication

Take any medicine and other medical supplies that you need, plus spare eyeglasses or contact lenses. In many countries it may be difficult to find certain medicines. Others may be sold under different names. If you are taking a long cruise, ask your doctor for names of alternatives.

SIX FIRSTS

● In 1903 the British liner *Lucania* became the first ship to acquire wireless equipment, which enabled it to keep in touch with both sides of the Atlantic Ocean at the same time.

● The first ship-to-shore wireless telegraphy took place on the American passenger ship *St. Paul* in 1899.

● The first twin-screw passenger ship was the Compagnie Générale Transatlantique's 3,200-ton *Washington*, built in 1863 and converted in 1868.

● The first floating eclipse expedition was led by the US astronomer Ted Pedas in 1972, when 800 passengers sailed to a spectacular rendezvous with a total sun eclipse in the North Atlantic.

● The first passenger ship to exceed 80,000 tons was the Compagnie Générale Transatlantique's *Normandie*, which measured 82,799 tons in 1936.

● The first gravity lifeboats were installed aboard the Compagnie Générale Transatlantique's *Ile de France* in 1928.

The ship's pharmacy will stock certain standard remedies, but do not expect a supply of the more unusual medicines. Remember to take along a doctor's prescription for any medication (required if you join a cruise in Dubai).

Also, be advised that if you run out of your medication and you need to get a supply aboard ship, most ships will require that you see the doctor, even if you have a prescription. There is a charge for each visit, plus the cost of any medication.

Let spouses/companions carry a supply of your medicine and medical supplies. Do not pack medicine or medical information in luggage to be checked in when flying; take it in your carry-on.

Money matters

Most ships operate primarily in US dollars, euros or UK pounds, but a few use other currencies (check with your travel agent or supplier). Major credit cards and traveler's checks are accepted on board (few lines take personal checks). You sign for drinks and other services, as part of "cashless cruising." Some large resort ships have ATM cash machines, although a "transaction fee" is assessed.

Pets

Pets are not allowed aboard cruise ships, with one exception: the regular transatlantic crossings aboard Cunard Line's *Queen Mary 2* ocean liner, which has air-conditioned kennels, plus a genuine British lamp-post, New York fire hydrant, and cat containers.

Photography

Users of digital cameras should pack a spare memory card unless they are carrying a laptop onto which they can transfer pictures. Users of film should bring low-speed film for tropical areas such as the Caribbean or South Pacific – heat can damage high-speed film.

Sun protection

Take suncream/sunlotion with a minimum SPF 15 or higher protection factor. Keep reapplying it after you take a dip in the pool or hot tub, and allow for the fact that if you perspire, the suncream/sunlotion dissolves. If you wear a tee-shirt over your swimsuit, its SPF protection factor is between 7 (white tee-shirt), and 10 (dark tee-shirt).

While cotton tee-shirts allow more "breathing," unbleached cotton has special pigments that can actually absorb UV rays vs polyester/other synthetic or silk tee-shirts that reflect radiation.

Clothing designated as sun-protective - including swimwear - carries a UPF number. This is similar to the SPF factor, except that the UPT number shows how much UVA and UVB is blocked. Companies specializing in outdoor sports clothing and swimwear now make sun-protective clothing from special microfibers that have a very tight weave to block out the sun. ❑

WHAT TO EXPECT

Your first cruise? Here is what you need to know
about a typical initial embarkation process

Testing the waters by taking your first cruise? Make sure you have your passport and any visas required (in some countries – such as the People's Republic of China, or Russia – you might go ashore on organized excursions under a group visa). Pack any medication you may need (in original, labelled containers) in your carry-on hand luggage, and advise family members and friends where you are going.

You already have been sent your cruise tickets and documents by the cruise line or your travel agent. Increasingly, e-documents are provided. A typical document package might include:

● Air ticket (or e-ticket boarding pass or reference code)
● Cruise ticket and e-boarding pass (not all lines)
● Luggage tags
● Embarkation/Immigration card (to fill out before you get to the ship)
● Discount coupons for the shops on board
● Bon Voyage gift selection form
● Shore excursion brochure
● Onboard credit account form
● Guide to services on board (including e-mail)
● Ship's telephone and fax contact numbers
● Coupon for tuxedo rental

Assume that you've arrived at the airport closest to your ship's embarkation point, and retrieved your luggage. It is likely that there will be a representative from the cruise line waiting, holding aloft the company's name. You will be asked to place your luggage in a cluster together with those of other passengers. The next time you see your luggage should be aboard your ship, where it will be delivered to your cabin.

You'll find numerous desks will be set up in the passenger terminal. Go to the desk that displays the first letter of your surname, wait in line (having filled out all embarkation, registration, and immigration documents), and then check in. If your accommodation is designated as a "suite," there should be a separate check-in facility.

If you are cruising from a US port and you are a non-US citizen or "Resident Alien," you will go to a separate desk to check in (*Note*: Do not buy duty-free liquor to take on board – it will not be allowed by the cruise line and will be confiscated until the last day of the cruise). You will be asked for your passport, which you deposit with the check-in personnel. Be sure to ask for a receipt – it is, after all, a valuable document, and preferably have a photocopy of the main pages to keep with you. If you are cruising from any other port in the world that is not a US port, be advised that each country has its own check-in requirements, setups, and procedures.

You will then proceed through a security-screening device, for both your body and hand luggage, as at airports. Next, you'll walk a few paces towards the gangway. This may be a covered, airport-type gangway, or an open one (hopefully with a net underneath it in case you drop something over the side). The gangway could be flat, or you may have to walk up (or down) an incline, depending on the location of the gangway, the tide, or other local conditions.

As you approach the gangway you will probably be greeted by the ship's photographers, a snap-happy team ready to take your photograph, bedraggled as you may appear after having traveled for hours. If you do not want your photograph taken, say "no" firmly, and proceed.

At the ship end of the gangway, you will find a decorated (hopefully) entrance and the comfortable feel of air-conditioning if the weather is hot. The ship's cruise staff will welcome you aboard. Give them your cabin number, and a steward should appear to take your carry-on luggage from you and take you directly to your cabin.

Things to check

The door to your cabin should be open. If it is locked, ask the steward to obtain the key to open the door. Aboard the newest ships, you will probably be handed an electronically coded key card. Once inside the cabin, take a good look. Is it clean? Is it tidy? Are the beds properly made? Check under them to make sure the floor is clean. On one cruise I found a pair of red ladies' shoes, but, alas, no lady to go with them.

Make sure there is ice in the ice container. Check the bathroom, bathtub (if there is one), or shower. Make sure there are towels and soap. If all is clean and shipshape, fine.

If there are problems, bring them to the attention of your cabin steward immediately. Or call the purser's office (reception desk), and explain the problem, then quietly, but firmly request that someone in a supervisory position see you to resolve it. The housekeeping aboard cruise ships is generally very good, but sometimes when "turn-around" time is tight, when passengers disembark in the morning and new passengers embark in the afternoon, little things get overlooked – just as they sometimes do in a hotel on land.

One thing you also should do immediately is to remember the telephone number for the ship's hospital, doctor, or for medical emergencies, just so you know how to call for help should any medical emergency arise.

Your luggage probably will not have arrived yet (if it is a ship carrying more than 1,000 passengers) so don't sit in the cabin waiting for it. Put your hand luggage away somewhere, and, deck plan in hand, take a walk.

Familiarize yourself with the layout of the ship. Learn which way is forward, which way is aft, and how to reach your cabin from the main stairways. This is also a good time to learn how to get from your cabin to the outside decks in an emergency (these are rare, but they do happen).

Control that thirst

You're thirsty when you arrive in your cabin. You notice a bottle of water with a tab around its neck. You take off the tab, open the bottle and have a drink. Then you read the notice: "This bottle is provided for your convenience. If you open it, your account will be charged $4.50."

On deck, you are greeted by a smiling, happy waiter offering you a colorful, cool drink. But, put your fingers on the glass as he hands it to you and he'll also ask for your cruise card. Bang, you've just paid $6.95 for a drink worth 5 cents.

Be careful with the drinks. They soon add up. Note that aboard ships operated by Europe-based companies, mixers such as tonic for gin usually are charged separately.

The safety drill

Regulations dictate that a Passenger Lifeboat Drill must take place within 24 hours after the ship sails from the embarkation port, but typically takes place before the ship sails (you'll find your lifejacket in the cabin and directions to your assembly station will be posted on the back of the cabin door). After the drill, you can take off the lifejacket and relax. By now, your luggage probably will have arrived.

Time to unpack

Unpack, then go out on deck just before the ship sails. It's always a magical moment, and a good time to meet some new faces. You'll soon be ready for that first night's dinner. It is simply amazing how the sea air gives you an appetite. ❑

CRUISE LINES BY MARKET CLASSIFICATION

Although there are three fairly distinctive divisions of cruise lines and their ships, some blurring between these divisions has occurred as companies have responded to changing passenger tastes and to the market conditions created by the threat of international terrorism and a harsher economic climate.

LUXURY
Crystal Cruises *
Cunard Line *
Hapag-Lloyd Cruises **
Hebridean International
  Cruises ***
Sea Cloud Cruises
Seabourn Cruise Line
Regent Seven Seas Cruises *
SeaDream Yacht Club
Silversea Cruises

PREMIUM
Asuka Cruise (NYK)
Azamara Cruises
Celebrity Cruises
Holland America Line
Oceania Cruises
Orion Expedition Cruises
Peter Deilmann Cruises
Ponant Cruises (CIP)

Saga Cruises
Venus Cruise
Windstar Cruises

STANDARD
Abercrombie & Kent
AIDA Cruises
American Canadian
  Caribbean Line
American Cruise Lines
CDF Croisières de France
Canodros
Carnival Cruise Lines
Classic International Cruises
Club Mediterranée Cruises
Costa Cruises
Cruise West
Delphin Seereisen
Disney Cruise Line
easyCruise.com
Elegant Cruises & Tours

Fred Olsen Cruise Lines
Galapagos Cruises
Golden Star Cruises
Hansa Touristik
Hapag-Lloyd Cruises *
Hurtigruten
Iberocruceros
Imperial Majesty Cruise Line
Island Cruises
Kristina Cruises
Lindblad Expeditions
Louis Cruise Lines
Louis Hellenic Cruises
MSC Cruises
Mano Cruise
Mitsui OSK Passenger Line
Monarch Classic Cruises
NCL America
Noble Caledonia
Norwegian Cruise Line
Ocean Village

P&O Cruises
P&O Cruises (Australia)
Page & Moy Cruises
Phoenix Reisen
Plantours & Partner
Princess Cruises
Pullmantur Cruises
Quark Expeditions
Royal Caribbean
  International
Star Cruises
Star Clippers
Star Line Cruises
Swan Hellenic Cruises
Thomson Cruises
Transocean Tours
TUI Cruises
Vision Cruises
Voyages of Discovery
Zegrahm Expeditions

Notes: * This company operates ships that straddle
              the line between Luxury and Premium.

** Europa only
*** Hebridean Spirit only

WHAT TO DO IF...

Twenty practical tips for a good cruise experience

❶ Your luggage does not arrive at the ship.
If you are part of the cruise line's air/sea package, the airline is responsible for locating your luggage and delivering it to the next port. If you arranged your own air transportation it is wholly *your* problem. Always have easy-to-read name and address tags both *inside* as well as *outside* your luggage. Keep track of claim documents and give the airline a detailed itinerary and list of port agents (usually included with your documents).

❷ *You* miss the ship.
If you miss the ship's departure (due to late or non-performing flight connections, etc), and you are traveling on an air/sea package, the airline will arrange to get you to the ship. If you are traveling "cruise-only," however, and have arranged your own air transportation, then *you* are responsible for onward flights, hotel stays, and transfers. Many cruise lines now have "deviation" desks, where, for a fee, you can adjust airline flights and dates to suit personal preferences. If you arrive at the port just as your ship is pulling away, see the ship's port agent immediately.

❸ Your cabin is too small.
Almost all cruise ship cabins are too small (I am convinced that some are designed for packages rather than people). When you book a cruise, you pay for a certain category and type of cabin but have little or no control over which one you actually get. See the hotel manager as soon as possible and explain what is wrong with the cabin (noisy, too hot, etc). If the ship is full (most are nowadays), it will be difficult to change. However, the hotel manager will probably try to move you from known problem cabins, although they are not required to do so.

❹ Your cabin has no air-conditioning, it is noisy, or there are plumbing problems.
If there is anything wrong in your cabin, or if there is something wrong with the plumbing in your bathroom, bring it to the attention of your cabin steward immediately. If nothing gets better, complain to the hotel manager. Some cabins, for example, are located above the ship's laundry, generator, or galley (hot); others may be above the disco (noisy). If the ship is full, it may be difficult to change.

❺ You have noisy cabin neighbors.
First, politely tell your neighbors that you can hear them brushing their hair as the cabin walls are so thin, and would they please not bang the drawers shut at 2am! If that does not work, complain to the purser or hotel manager, and ask them to attend to the problem.

❻ You have small children and the brochure implied that the ship has special programs for them, but when on board you find out it is not an all-year-round program.
In this instance, either the brochure was misleading, or your travel agent did not know enough about the ship or did not bother to ask the right questions. If you have genuine cause for complaint, then see your travel agent when you get home. Most ships generally will try to accommodate your young ones (the large resort ships – those carrying more than 1,600 passengers – have more facilities), but may not be covered by their insurance for "looking after" them throughout the day, as the brochure seemed to promise. Again, check thoroughly with your travel agent *before* you book.

❼ You do not like your dining room seating.
Most "standard" market ships (particularly the large "resort" ships) operate two seatings for dinner (sometimes this applies to all meals). When you book your cruise, you are asked whether you want the first or second seating. The line will make every attempt to please you. But if you want second seating and are given first seating (perhaps a large group has taken over the entire second seating, or the ship is full), there may be little the restaurant manager can do.

❽ You want a table for two and are put at a table for eight.
Again, see the restaurant manager (maître d') and explain why you are not satisfied. A little gratuity should prove helpful.

❾ You cannot communicate with your dining room waiter.
Dining room waiters are probably of a nationality and tongue completely foreign to yours, and all they can do is smile. This could prove frustrating for a whole cruise, especially if you need something out of the ordinary. See the restaurant manager, and tell him you want a waiter with whom

you can communicate. If he does not solve the problem, see the hotel manager.

⑩ The food is definitely not "gourmet" cuisine as advertised in the brochure.

If the food is not as described (for example, whole lobster in the brochure, but only cold lobster salad once during the cruise, or the "fresh squeezed" orange juice on the breakfast menu is anything but), inform the maître d' of the problem.

⑪ A large group has taken over the ship.

Sometimes, large groups have blocked (pre-booked) several public rooms for meetings (seemingly every hour on the hour in the rooms you want to use). This means the individual passenger (that is you) becomes a second-class citizen. Make your displeasure known to the hotel manager immediately, tell your travel agent, and write a follow-up letter to the line when you return home.

⑫ A port of call is deleted from the itinerary.

If you only took the cruise because the ship goes to the place you have wanted to go for years, then read the fine print in the brochure *before* you book. A cruise line is under *no* obligation to perform the stated itinerary. For whatever reason (political unrest, weather, mechanical problems, no berth space, safety, etc.), the ship's captain has the ultimate say.

⑬ You are unwell aboard ship.

Do not worry. There will be a qualified doctor (who generally operates as a concession, and therefore charges) and medical facilities, including a small pharmacy. You will be well taken care of. Although there are charges for medical services rendered, almost all cruise lines offer insurance packages that include medical coverage for most eventualities. It is wise to take out this insurance when you book.

⑭ You have a problem with a crew member.

Go to the hotel manager or chief purser and explain the problem; for single women this could be a persistent cabin steward who has a master door key. No one will do anything unless you complain. Cruise ships try to hire decent staff, but, with so many crew, there are bound to be a few bad apples. Insist on a full written report of the incident, which must be entered into the ship's daily log by the staff captain (deputy captain).

⑮ You leave some personal belongings on a tour bus.

If you find you have left something on a tour bus, and you are back on board your ship, the first thing to do is advise the shore excursion manager or the purser's office. The tour operator ashore will then be contacted to ascertain whether any items have been handed in to their office.

⑯ The cruise line's air arrangements have you flying from Los Angeles via Timbuktu to get to your cruise ship.

Fine if your cruise ship is in Timbuktu (difficult, as it is inland). Most cruise lines that have low rates also use the cheapest air routing to get you to your ship. That could mean flights from a central hub. Be warned: you get what you pay for. Ask questions *before* you book.

⑰ You fly internationally to take a cruise.

If your cruise is a long distance away from your home, then it usually makes good sense to fly to your cruise embarkation point and stay for at least a day or two before the cruise. Why? Because you will be better rested and you will have time to adjust to any time changes. You will step aboard your ship already relaxed and ready for a real vacation. As a bonus, you will get to know the port of departure.

⑱ The ship's laundry ruins your clothes.

If any of your clothing is ruined or discolored by the ship's laundry, first tell your cabin steward(ess), and then follow up by going to the purser's office and getting it registered as a proper complaint. Take a copy of the complaint with you, so you can follow up when you get home. Unfortunately, you will probably find a disclaimer on the laundry list saying something to the effect that liability is limited to about $1 per item, which is not a lot. So, although the laundry and dry cleaning facilities generally work well, things can occasionally go wrong just like ashore.

⑲ You have extra charges on your bill.

Check your itemized bill carefully. Then talk to the purser's office and ask them to show you the charge slips. Finally, make sure you are given a copy of your bill, *after* any modifications have been made.

⑳ You're unhappy with your cruise experience.

You (or your travel agent) ultimately choose the ship and cruise. But if your ship does not meet your specific lifestyle and interests, or the ship performs less well than the brochure promises, then let your travel agent and the cruise line know as soon as possible. If your grievance is valid, many cruise lines will offer a credit, good towards a future cruise. But do be sure to read the fine print on the ticket. ❑

HOW SAFE ARE CRUISE SHIPS?

How likely is an accident at sea? What if there's a fire? Is lifeboat
training provided? How good are are medical facilities aboard?

You can't always stop passengers having too much
to drink and falling over balconies. But, as far as
maritime accidents are concerned, cruising can
claim the travel industry's best safety record, with
fewer than 20 passenger fatalities during the past 20
years. Eleven of those happened when the *Royal
Pacific* sank off Malaysia in 1992 after colliding with
a Taiwanese trawler.

International regulations require all crew to undergo
basic safety training *before* they are allowed to work
aboard any cruise ship. On-the-job training is no longer
enough. And safety regulations are getting more stringent all the time, governed by an international convention called SOLAS (Safety of Life at Sea).

Safety measures

All cruise ships built since July 1, 1986, must have
either totally enclosed or partially enclosed lifeboats
with diesel engines that will operate even if the lifeboat
is inverted.

Since October 1997, cruise ships have had:
● All stairways fully enclosed in self-contained fire
zones.
● Smoke detectors and smoke alarms fitted in all pas-
senger cabins and all public spaces.
● Low-level lighting showing routes of escape (such as
in corridors and stairways).
● All fire doors throughout the ship controllable from
the ship's navigation bridge.
● All fire doors that are held open by hinges capable of
release from a remote location.
● Emergency alarms audible in all cabins.

Since 2002, ocean-going cruise ships on international
voyages have had to carry voyage data recorders
(VDRs), similar to black boxes carries by aircraft).

In October 2010, SOLAS regulations will prohibit the
use of combustible materials in cruise ship construction.
This means that as many as 50 pre-1974 vessels will
either have to be withdrawn or be expensively upgraded.

Crew members attend frequent emergency drills, the
lifeboat equipment is regularly tested, and the fire-
detecting devices, and alarm and fire-fighting systems
are checked. Any passenger spotting fire or smoke is
encouraged to use the nearest fire alarm box, alert a
member of staff, or contact the bridge.

Lifeboat drill

Few recent incidents have required the evacuation of
passengers, although two cruise ships were lost following collisions (*Jupiter* in 1988, and *Royal Pacific* in
1992), one after striking an iceberg near Antarctica

(*Explorer* in 2007) and one after foundering on a reef off
the Greek island of Santorini (*Sea Diamond* in 2007).

A passenger lifeboat drill, announced publicly by the
captain, must be held within 24 hours of leaving the
embarkation port. Attendance is compulsory. Make sure
you know your boat station or assembly point and how
to get to it in the event of an emergency. If other passengers are lighthearted about the drill, don't be dis-
tracted. Note your exit and escape pathways and learn
how to put on your lifejacket correctly. The drill takes
no more than 15 minutes and is a good investment in
playing safe – the *Royal Pacific* took less than 20 minutes to sink after its collision.

Medical services

Except for ships registered in the UK or Norway, there
are no mandatory international maritime requirements
for cruise lines to carry a licensed physician or to have
hospital facilities aboard. However, in general, all ships
carrying over 50 passengers do have medical facilities
and at least one doctor.

The standard of medical practice and of the doctors
themselves may vary from line to line. Most shipboard
doctors are generalists; there are no cardiologists or neu-
rosurgeons. Doctors are typically employed as outside
contractors and will charge for use of their services,
including seasickness shots.

Regrettably, many cruise lines make medical services
a low priority. Most shipboard physicians are not certified
in trauma treatment or medical evacuation procedures,
for example. However, some medical organizations, such
as the American College of Emergency Physicians, have
a special division for cruise medicine. Most ships catering to North American passengers carry doctors licensed
in the United States, Canada, or Britain, but doctors
aboard many other ships come from a variety of countries
and disciplines.

Cunard Line's *QM2*, with 4,344 passengers and crew,
has a fully equipped hospital with one surgeon, one
doctor, a staff of six nurses, and two medical orderlies;
contrast this with *Carnival Sensation*, which carries up
to 3,514 passengers and crew, with just one doctor and
two nurses.

Any ship operating long-distance cruises, with several days at sea should have better medical facilities
than one engaged in a standard 7-day Caribbean cruise,
with a port of call almost every day.

Ideally, a ship's medical staff should be certified in
advanced cardiac life support. The equipment should
include an examination room, isolation ward/bed, X-
ray machine (to verify fractures), cardiac monitor

(EKG) and defibrillator, oxygen-saturation monitor, external pacemaker, oxygen, suction and ventilators, hematology analyzer, culture incubator, and a mobile trolley intensive care unit.

Any existing health problems requiring treatment on board must be reported when you book. Aboard some ships, you may be charged for filling a prescription as well as for the cost of prescribed drugs. There may also be a charge if, as a result of being unwell, you have to cancel a shore excursion and need a doctor's letter to prove that you are ill.

Shipboard injury

Slipping, tripping, and falling are the major sources of shipboard injury. There are things you can do to mini-mize the chance of injury.

● Aboard many pre-1980 ships, raised thresholds sep-arate a cabin's bathroom from its sleeping area. Don't hang anything from the fire sprinkler heads on the cabin ceilings.

● On older ships, it is wise to note how the door lock works. Some require a key on the inside in order to unlock the door. Leave the key in the lock, so that in the event of a real emergency, you don't have to hunt for the key.

● Aboard older ships, take care not to trip over raised thresholds in doorways leading to the open deck.

● Walk with caution when the outer decks are wet after being washed, or if they are wet after rain. This applies especially to solid steel decks – falling onto them is really painful.

● Do not throw a lighted cigarette or cigar butt, or knock out your pipe, over the ship's side. They can eas-ily be sucked into an opening in the ship's side or onto an aft open deck area, and cause a fire.

Legal action: If you do suffer from injury aboard ship,

feel it is the cruise line's fault, and want to take legal action against the company, you should be aware of the following, which applies to American passengers:

In the United States, Appendix 46, Section 183(b) of the US Civil Code requires that "the injured passenger notify the cruise line in writing within six months from the date of the injury to file a claim and suit must be filed within one year from the date of injury." So, if you file a claim after the one-year period, the cruise line will probably seek a summary judgment for dismissal.

First, however, read your ticket. The passenger ticket is a legal contract between passenger and cruise line. It will invariably state that you must file suit in the state (or country) designated in the ticket. Thus, if a resident of California buys a cruise, and the cruise line is based in Florida, then the lawsuit must be filed in Florida. If you reside in the US and you purchase a cruise in the Mediterranean and the ship's registry is Italy, then you would have to file suit in Italy. This is known as the Forum Clause.

Surviving a shipboard fire

Shipboard fires can generate an incredible amount of heat, smoke, and often panic. In the unlikely event that you are in one, try to remain calm and think logically and clearly.

When you board the ship and get to your cabin, check the way to the nearest emergency exits fore and aft. Count the number of cabin doorways and other dis-tinguishing features to the exits in case you have to escape without the benefit of lighting, or in case the passageway is filled with smoke. All ships use "low location" lighting systems.

Exit signs are normally located just above your head – this is virtually useless, as smoke and flames rise. Note the nearest fire alarm location and know how to use it in case of dense smoke. In future, it is likely that directional sound evacuation beacons will be mandated; these will direct passengers to exits, escape-ways and other safe areas and may be better than the present inad-equate visual aids.

If you are in your cabin and there is fire in the pas-sageway outside, put on your lifejacket. If the cabin's door handle is hot, soak a towel in water and use it to turn the handle. If a fire is raging in the passageway, cover yourself in wet towels and go through the flames.

Check the passageway. If there are no flames, or if everything looks clear, walk to the nearest emergency exit or stairway. If there is smoke in the passageway, crawl to the nearest exit. If the exit is blocked, go to an alternate one. It may take considerable effort to open a heavy fire door to the exit. Don't use the elevators: they may stop at a deck that's on fire, or they may stop working.

If there's a fire in your cabin or on the balcony, report it immediately by telephone. Then get out of your cabin, close the door behind you, sound the alarm, and alert your neighbors. ❑

Is Security Good Enough?

Cruise lines are subject to stringent international safety and security regulations. Passengers and crew can embark or disembark only by passing through a security checkpoint. Cruise ships maintain zero tolerance for onboard crime or offences against the person. Trained security professionals are employed aboard all cruise ships. In the case of the USA, where more than 60 percent of cruise passengers reside, you will be far more secure aboard a cruise ship than almost anywhere on land.

It is recommended that you keep your cabin locked at all times when you are not there. All new ships have encoded plastic key cards that operate a lock electronically; older ships have metal keys. Cruise lines do not accept respon-sibility for any money or valuables left in cabins and suggest that you store them in a safety deposit box at the purser's office, or, if one is provided, in your in-cabin personal safe.

You will be issued a personal boarding pass when you embark. This typically includes your photo, lifeboat station, restaurant seating, and other pertinent information, and serves as identification to be shown at the gangway each time you board. You may also be asked for a government-issued photo ID, such as a passport.

OCEAN SHIPS TO DEBUT: 2009–2012

CRUISE LINE	NAME OF SHIP	TONS	COST	LENGTH (feet)	LENGTH (meters)
2009 (13 Ships)					
AIDA Cruises	AIDAluna	68,500	€330 million	826.7	252.0
American Cruise Lines	Independence	3,000	$30 million	220.0	67.0
Carnival Cruise Lines	Carnival Dream	130,000	$668 million	1,092.5	330.0
Celebrity Cruises	Celebrity Equinox	122,000	$641 million	1,033.4	315.0
Costa Cruises	Costa Luminosa	92,700	$528 million	902.2	275.0
Costa Cruises	Costa Pacifica	114,500	$579 million	951.4	290.0
MSC Cruises	MSC Splendida	133,500	$550 million	1,092.5	330.0
Norwegian Cruise Line	to be announced	150,000	$940 million	1,066.2	325.0
Pearl Seas Cruises	Pearl	8,700	$64 million	324.8	99.0
Royal Caribbean International	Oasis of the Seas	220,000	$1.24 billion	1,181.1	360.0
Seabourn Cruise Line	Seabourn Odyssey	32,000	$275 million	650.0	198.0
Sea Cloud Cruises	Sea Cloud Hussar	4,200	€69 million	445.2	135.7
Silversea Cruises	Silver Spirit	36,000	$250 million	650.0	198.0
2010 (14 Ships)					
AIDA Cruises	to be announced	71,000	€350 million	826.7	252.0
CIP Cruises	to be announced	10,700	$100 million	459.3	140.0
CIP Cruises	to be announced	10,700	$100 million	459.3	140.0
Celebrity Cruises	Celebrity Eclipse	122,000	$641 million	1,033.4	315.0
Costa Cruises	to be announced	92,700	€548 million	902.2	275.0
Cunard Line	Queen Elizabeth	92,000	€500 million	967.8	295.0
Holland America Line	to be announced	86,000	€425 million	959.6	292.5
MSC Cruises	MSC Magnifica	90,000	$548 million	964.5	294.0
Norwegian Cruise Line	F3	150,000	$940 million	1,066.2	325.0
Oceania Cruises	to be announced	65,000	$500 million	823.4	251.0
P&O Cruises	to be announced	116,000	€535 million	951.4	290.0
Royal Caribbean International	to be announced	220,000	$1.4 billion	1,092.5	330.0
Seabourn Cruise Line	to be announced	32,000	$200 million	650.0	198.0
Star Clippers	to be announced	7,400		518.0	157.8
2011 (7 Ships)					
AIDA Cruises	to be announced	71,000	€380 million	826.7	252.0
Carnival Cruise Lines	Carnival Magic	130,000	$738 million	1,092.5	330.0
Celebrity Cruises	to be announced	122,000	$641 million	1,033.4	315.0
Costa Cruises	to be announced	114,200	$726 million	951.4	290.0
Disney Cruise Line	to be announced	124,000	$900 million	1,114.8	339.8
Oceania Cruises	to be announced	65,000	$530 million	823.4	251.0
Seabourn Cruise Line	to be announced	32,000	€200 million	650.0	198.0
2012 (5 Ships)					
AIDA Cruises	to be announced	71,000	€385 million	826.7	252.0
Celebrity Cruises	to be announced	122,000	$641 million	1,033.4	315.0
Costa Cruises	to be announced	114,200	$726 million	951.4	290.0
Disney Cruise Line	to be announced	124,000	$900 million	1,114.8	339.8
Oceania Cruises	to be announced	65,000	$530 million	823.4	251.0

This chart, alphabetically by cruise line, shows ships under firm contract. Delivery dates may change.

PASSENGERS (lower bed capacity)	BUILDER	MONTH
2,030	Meyer Werft (Germany)	April
104	Chesapeake Shipbuilding	August
3,652	Fincantieri (Italy)	October
2,850	Meyer Werft (Germany)	August
2,260	Fincantieri (Italy)	Spring
3,004	Fincantieri (Italy)	Summer
3,887	Aker Yards (France)	June
4,200	Aker Yards (France)	Fall
214	Irving Shipbuilding (Canada)	July
5,400	Aker Yards (Finland)	Fall
550	Mariotti (Italy)	Spring
138	Factoria de Naval Marin (Spain)	September
540	Fincantieri (Italy)	November
2,174	Meyer Werft (Germany)	Spring
264	Fincantieri (Italy)	March
264	Fincantieri (Italy)	June
2,850	Meyer Werft (Germany)	June
2,260	Fincantieri (Italy)	October
2,092	Fincantieri (Italy)	Fall
2,100	Fincantieri (Italy)	Spring
2,568	Aker Yards (France)	Spring
4,200	Aker Yards (France)	Spring
1,260	Fincantieri (Italy)	Fall
3,110	Fincantieri (Italy)	Spring
3,887	Aker Yards (Finland)	August
550	Mariotti (Italy)	Summer
296		
2,174	Meyer Werft (Germany)	April
3,652	Fincantieri (Italy)	June
2,850	Meyer Werft (Germany)	Fall
3,012	Fincantieri (Italy)	Fall
2,500	Meyer Werft (Germany)	Spring
1,260	Fincantieri (Italy)	Summer
550	Mariotti (Italy)	Fall
2,174	Meyer Werft (Germany)	Fall
2,850	Meyer Werft (Germany)	Fall
3,012	Fincantieri (Italy)	Spring
2,500	Meyer Werft (Germany)	Spring
1,260	Fincantieri (Italy)	Spring

A SHIP TAKES SHAPE

Modern techniques allow a giant liner such as Cunard Line's *Queen Mary 2* to be built in 18 months. Below we show how Chantiers de l'Atlantique did it in 2002–3.

1. The first preconstructed block is lowered into position in the dry dock at Saint-Nazaire, France.
2. Similar blocks are added as the vessel takes shape.
3. The bulbous bow is lowered into place.
4. The steel shell containing only machinery rooms is floated out of dry dock before its interiors are fitted.

Credits

Photography:

AIDA Cruises 62, 146, 171
Alamy 86
American Canadian Caribbean Line 85, 147B
American Safari Cruises 26, 83
Apa Publications 96B, 147T, 153, 162, 163T, 163B, 164
Carnival Cruise Lines 4–5, 10B, 14B, 23T, 58, 65T, 66, 69B, 70, 71B, 72, 74, 77, 100, 103, 107, 108, 113, 114T, 114B, 115, 116, 117
Celebrity Cruises 8, 8–9, 12, 64, 67, 79B, 80–1, 81, 101, 111T, 118, 119T, 119B, 120, 121, 148
Corbis 39T, 42B, 73, 97B, 99
Costa Cruises 25, 59T, 105, 122T, 122B, 123, 124, 156–7
Cruise People, The 89T, 89B
Cruise West 149T
Crystal Cruises 55T, 93T

Cunard Line 9, 10T, 17T, 20, 42–3, 46T, 48, 51B, 52, 73T, 90–1, 91B, 125, 167, 683
Disney Cruise Line 14T, 68, 149B
4Corners Images 94
Fred Olsen Cruise Line 106, 150B
Freighter World Cruises 88
Glyn Genin 145
Getty Images 41
Hapag Lloyd 21, 54B, 61B, 78, 104, 150–1, 161, 166, 168, 169
Hebridean International Cruises 159, 670
Holland America Line 1, 15, 17B, 36, 37, 38, 39B, 45, 61T, 126, 127T, 127B, 128, 172B
Hurtigruten 7, 79T, 82, 151B
iStockphoto cover
Bob Krist 71T
MSC Cruises 3, 11B, 16, 47, 54T, 55B, 62–3, 97T, 129, 130
Norwegian Cruise Line 57, 59B, 111B(2), 131, 132, 152
P&O Cruises 11T, 13T, 13B, 53B, 93B, 102, 133, 134

Plainpicture/Photolibrary 18
Princess Cruises 135BL, 135BR, 136, 165
Robert Harding Picture Library 98T
Royal Caribbean International 2, 6, 19, 22, 24, 27, 44, 48–9, 50, 51T, 53T, 65T, 69T, 111B(3), 137, 138–9, 140, 141, 142, 144B, 170, 172T, 176
Saga Cruises 154B
Seabourn Cruise Line 56, 95, 154–5
SeaDream Yacht Cruises 155B, 158
Silversea Cruises 111B(1), 156B
Star Cruises 60, 143, 144T
Topham Picturepoint 40
Douglas Ward 23B, 46B, 75, 87, 96T, 157B

Picture Research: Celia Sterne
Cover design: Ian Spick
Cartography Editor: Zoë Goodwin
Map Production Tyne Mapping
Maps © 2008 Apa Publications GmbH
& Co. Verlag KG (Singapore branch)

WHERE TO FIND THE CRUISE LINES ONLINE

Abercrombie & Kent
www.aandktours.com

African Safari Cruises
www.africansafariclub.com

AIDA Cruises
www.aida.de

American Canadian Caribbean Line
www.accl-smallships.com

American Cruise Lines
www.americancruiselines.com

American Safari Cruises
www.amsafari.com

Antarctic Shipping
www.antarctic.cl

CDF Croisières de France
www.cdfsroisieresdefrance.fr

Captain Cook Cruises
www.captcookcrus.com.au

Carnival Cruise Lines
www.carnival.com

Celebrity Cruises/ Azamara Cruises
www.celebrity-cruises.com

Classic International Cruises
www.cic-cruises.com

Club Med Cruises
www.clubmed.com

Coral Princess Cruises
www.cruisingaustralia.com

Costa Cruises
www.costacruises.com

Cruceros Australis
www.crucerosaustralis.com

Cruise West
www.cruisewest.com

Crystal Cruises
www.crystalcruises.com

Cunard Line
www.Cunard Line.com

Delphin Seereisen
www:delphin-cruises.com

Disney Cruise Line
www.disneycruise.com

easyCruise.com
www.easycruise.com

Elegant Cruises &Tours
www.elegantcruises.com

Fred Olsen Cruise Lines
www.fredolsencruises.com

Galapagos Cruises
www.galapagos-inc.com

Hansa Touristik
www.hansatourstik.com

Hapag-Lloyd Cruises
www.hlkf.com

Hebridean International Cruises
www.hebdrideanislandcruises.com

Holland America Line
www.hollandamerica.com

Hurtigruten
www.coastalvoyage.com

Iberocruceros
www.iberojet.es

Imperial Majesty Cruise Line
www.imperialmajesty.com

Indian Ocean Cruises
www.indianoceancruises.net

Island Cruises
www.islandcruises.com

Kristina Cruises
www.kristinacruises.com

Lindblad Expeditions
www.expeditions.com

Louis Cruise Lines
www.louiscruises.com

Majestic America Line
www.majesticamericaline.com

Mitsui OSK Passenger Line
www.mopas.co.jp.com

Monarch Classic Cruises
www.mccruises.gr

MSC Cruises
www.msccruises.com

MSC Cruises USA
www.msccruisesusa.com

NYK Line
www.asukacruise.co.jp

Noble Caledonia
www.noble-caledonia.co.uk

Norwegian Cruise Line/ NCL America
www.ncl.com

Oceania Cruises
www.oceaniacruises.com

Ocean Village
www.oceanvillageholidays.co.uk

Orion Expedition Cruises
www.orioncruises.com

P&O Cruises
www.pocruises.com

P&O Cruises (Australia)
www.pocruises.com.au

Pearl Seas Cruises
www.pearlseascruises.com

Peter Deilmann Cruises
www.deilmann-cruises.com

Phoenix Reisen
www.phoenixreisen.com

Plantours & Partner
www.plantours-partner.de

Ponant Cruises
www.ponant.com

Princess Cruises
www.princesscruises.com

Quark Expeditions
www.quark-expeditions.com

Regent Seven Seas Cruises
www.rssc.com

Royal Caribbean International
www.royalcaribbean.com

Saga Cruises
www.saga.co.uk

Sea Cloud Cruises
www.seacloud.com

Seabourn Cruise Line
www.seabourn.com

SeaDream Yacht Club
www.seadreamyachtclub.com

Silversea Cruises
www.silversea.com

Star Clippers
www.star-clippers.com

Star Cruises
www.starcruises.com.my

Swan Hellenic Cruises
www.swanhelleniccruises.com

Thomson Cruises
www.thomson-holidays.com

Transocean Tours
www.transocean.de

Travel Dynamics International
www.classicalcruises.com

Venus Cruise
www.venus-cruise.co.jp

Vision Cruises
www.visioncruises.com

Voyages of Discovery/ Swan Hellenic Cruises
www.voyagesofdiscovery.com

Windstar Cruises
www.windstarcruises.com

Zegrahm Expeditions
www.zeco.com

RESIDENTIAL SHIPS

Resident Sea
www.residensea.com

FREIGHTER CRUISE COMPANIES

Andrew Weir Shipping
www.aws.co.uk

Aranui Polynesienne
www.aranui.com

CMA-CGM
www.cma-cgm.com

Grimaldi Freighter Cruises
www.grimaldi-freightercruises.com

Hapag-Lloyd Container Line
www.hapag-lloyd.com

Horn Line Hamburg
www.hornlinie.com

Reederei F. Laeisz
www.laeiszline.de

Rickmers Reederei
www.rickmers.de

RMS St. Helena
www.RMS-St-Helena.com

Safmarine Container
www.safmarine.com

Senator Line
www.senatorlines.com

Transeste Schiffart
www.transeste.de

DEAR PASSENGER,

You are most welcome to send me your observations concerning any recent cruises taken. Please complete the following basic information when sending comments.

Although I cannot acknowledge receipt of this comment form, or any letters, because of my intensive travel schedule, I do thank you for your input, and for purchasing this book.

Cruise Date . . . .   Ship Name . . . .

Cruise Line . . . .   Suite/Cabin Number . . . .

Dining Room Seating (tick box):   ❑ Open   ❑ First   ❑ Second

Your Comments . . . .

. . . .

. . . .

. . . .

Your Pet Peeves

(1) . . . .

. . . .

(2) . . . .

. . . .

Your name . . . .

Address . . . .

. . . .

email address: . . . .

Please send to the address below:

Mr Douglas Ward
The Maritime Evaluations Group
Canada House, 1 Carrick Way
New Milton, Hampshire BH25 6UD
United Kingdom

Alternatively, please email these details to:

dw@berlitzcruising.com

Sign up now for free updates of this book...

As new ships are launched and cruise lines compete ever more fiercely, it's hard to keep up. Forewarned is forearmed, and you can learn of the latest changes by signing up for Douglas Ward's free quarterly newsletter, available through Berlitz's website. Based on his intensive schedule of ship visits, he will detail the facilities that have changed aboard ships reviewed in this book. He will also keep readers abreast of the latest industry news – cruise lines changing ownership, ships changing their names, new cruise terminals, and money-saving tips.

To sign up for this free service, available during the lifetime of the 2009 edition of this book, simply email your name and place of residence to **cruiseletter@berlitzpublishing.com**